MW00999999

HANDBOOK OF

CRITICAL AND INDIGENOUS METHODOLOGIES

HANDBOOK OF

CRITICAL AND INDIGENOUS METHODOLOGIES

EDITORS

NORMAN K. DENZIN

University of Illinois at Urbana-Champaign

YVONNA S. LINCOLN

Texas A&M University

LINDA TUHIWAI SMITH

University of Auckland, New Zealand

Los Angeles • London • New Delhi • Singapore

For information:

SAGE Publications, Inc.
2455 Teller Road
Thousand Oaks, California 91320
E-mail: order@sagepub.com

SAGE Publications Ltd.
1 Oliver's Yard
55 City Road
London EC1Y 1SP
United Kingdom

SAGE Publications India Pvt. Ltd.
B 1/I 1 Mohan Cooperative Industrial Area
Mathura Road, New Delhi 110 044
India

SAGE Publications Asia-Pacific Pte. Ltd.
33 Pekin Street #02-01
Far East Square
Singapore 048763
Printed in the United States of America

Library of Congress Cataloging-in-Publication Data

Handbook of critical and indigenous methodologies / editors, Norman K. Denzin, Yvonna S. Lincoln, Linda Tuhiwai Smith.
p. cm.
Includes bibliographical references and index.
ISBN 978-1-4129-1803-9 (cloth)
1. Ethnology—Methodology. 2. Ethnology—Research. 3. Social sciences—Research. 4. Critical theory.
I. Denzin, Norman K. II. Lincoln, Yvonna S. III. Smith, Linda Tuhiwai, 1950-

GN345.H364 2008
305.8001—dc22 2007047620

This book is printed on acid-free paper.

08 09 10 11 12 10 9 8 7 6 5 4 3 2 1

Acquisitions Editor: Vicki Knight
Associate Editor: Sean Connelly
Editorial Assistant: Lauren Habib
Production Editor: Astrid Virding
Copy Editor: Gillian Dickens
Typesetter: C & M Digitals (P) Ltd
Proofreader: Dennis Webb
Indexer: Kathy Paparchontis
Cover Designer: Bryan Fishman
Marketing Manager: Stephanie Adams

CONTENTS

PREFACE

Norman K. Denzin and Yvonna S. Lincoln

From the vantage point of the colonized . . . the word "research" . . . is probably one of the dirtiest words in the indigenous world's vocabulary.

—Smith (1999, p. 1)

One of the greatest failures of critical pedagogy . . . involves the inability to engage indigenous scholars.

—Kincheloe (2007, p. 11, paraphrase)

Despite its seeming import, indigenous scholars have been reluctant to engage critical [pedagogical] theory.

—Grande (2007, p. 316)

I used . . . social justice theatre . . . Augusto Boal's . . . Theatre of the Oppressed . . . to help my students make the connection between critical thinking and critical consciousness.

—Yellow Bird (2005, p. 13)

The Decade of the World's Indigenous Peoples (1994–2004; Henderson, 2000, p. 168) has ended. Nonindigenous scholars have yet to learn from it, to learn that it is time to dismantle, deconstruct, and decolonize Western epistemologies from within, to learn that research does not have to be a dirty word, to learn that research is always already moral and political. It is time to chart a new decade, the Decade of Critical, Indigenous Inquiry. This handbook is dedicated to this charge.

This Preface, written in the form of a manifesto, is an invitation to indigenous and nonindigenous qualitative researchers to think through the implications of connecting indigenous epistemologies (Rains, Archibald, & Deyhle, 2000, p. 338), as well as theories of decolonization[1] and the postcolonial[2] (Soto, 2004, p. ix; Swadener & Mutua, 2004, p. 255), with emancipatory discourses (Freire, 2001), with critical theory, and with critical pedagogy (McLaren & Kincheloe, 2007).

This is a call to work through a progressive politics of performative inquiry, with new ways of reading, writing, and performing global and local culture in the first decade of a new century (Kincheloe & McLaren, 2000, p. 285).[3] And in this new century, qualitative scholars face a crisis of global proportion: how to realize progressive dreams such as those of Freire in the wake of post-9/11 global atrocities, including hurricanes, wars, genocide, and human rights violations (Grande, 2007, p. 316).

▣ ▣ ▣

With Sandy Grande, Michael Yellow Bird, and Joe Kincheloe, we believe there is a great need for a dialogue between critical theorists and indigenous scholars and indigenous peoples.[4] We believe indigenous scholars can show critical theorists how to ground their methodologies at the local level. For present purposes, *indigenous methodology* "can be defined as research by and for Indigenous peoples, using techniques and methods drawn from the traditions and knowledges of those peoples" (Evans, Hole, Berg, Hutchinson, & Sookraj, in press).[5] Critical methodology embodies the emancipatory, empowering values of critical pedagogy, critical race, and poststructural feminism (Lather, 2007). *Critical methodology* may be defined as scholarship done for explicit political, utopian purposes, a discourse of critique and criticism, a politics of liberation, a reflexive discourse constantly in search of an open-ended, subversive, multivoiced, participatory epistemology (Lather, 2007, pp. x–xi).

Because of their liberatory, emancipatory commitments, we believe critical methodologists can, in concert with indigenous methodologists, speak to oppressed, colonized persons living in postcolonial situations of injustice: women, women of color, Third World women, African American women, Black women, Chicana and other minority group women, queer, lesbian, and transgendered, Aboriginal, First Nation, Native American, South African, Latin American, and Pacific and Asian Islander persons.

It is our hope that the readers of this handbook will gain a deeper appreciation of the depth of the discourse in this field, including these topics:

- the history of critical and indigenous theories;
- the ways in which critical, feminist, postcolonial, critical race, critical pedagogy, and indigenous theory have informed one another and have affected qualitative research;
- the particularities and common themes uniting indigenous Māori, Hawaiian, Red, borderland, endarkened, and Islamic pedagogies;
- critical pedagogy (and theory), critical indigenous interpretive pedagogies, and inquiry practices, including narrative, life story, autoethnography, poetics, and indigenous performance ethnography;
- the role of power, truth, ethics, truth tribunals, and discourses of social justice;
- the relations between indigenous inquiry and epistemologies, as well as the processes of decolonization in the academy;
- the development of critical constructs themselves, including race/diversity, gender representation (queer theory, feminism), culture, politics, and indigenous racial subjects;
- the use of critical and indigenous concepts within specific disciplines (critical psychology, critical communication/mass communication, media studies, cultural studies, political economy, education, sociology, anthropology, history, literature, nursing and health sciences, business);
- how critical qualitative scholars have deployed specific methods/techniques/data analysis, including autoethnography, narrative, oral/life history, and performance studies, among others;
- emerging definition(s) of emancipatory research and what critical qualitative research can do for social change and social justice, as well as the practices of democracy.

▣ ▣ ▣

The late 1980s is a starting place for one version of this project. The work of a new generation of primarily North American scholars, some represented in this volume (Fine, McLaren, Kincheloe, Giroux) and some not (Ellsworth, Minh-ha, Mohanty, Heshusius, Lather, Kellner), came into contact with critical pedagogy and the work of Paulo Freire. Freire's critical pedagogy took critical theory into the classroom. His *Pedagogy of the Oppressed* (2001) illuminated the "oppressive contradictions that existed in the social, political, and economic realities of Indigenous Peoples" (Yellow Bird, 2005, p. 13).

In Lather's *Getting Smart* (1991; see also Lather, 2007) poststructuralism clashed with critical theory and critical pedagogy. Some indigenous scholars at first rejected critical theory and critical pedagogy, contending it was suited only or primarily to local, indigenous concerns. As this was happening, a new generation of indigenous scholars, many in this volume, also started to appropriate and rework Western qualitative methodologies, epistemologies, and systems of ethics (Grande, 2004). Critical theorists were working over the same terrain, trying to answer questions raised by indigenous scholars.

An explosion occurred, and we want to capture at least some part of it! Postcolonial, subaltern, First Nation, and Red pedagogies; post-poststructuralism criticism; cultural critique; critical race feminism; critical White studies; Latino criticism/critical theories (LatCrit); critical pedagogy; pragmatic action theory; participatory action research (PAR); and critical race and queer theories erupted alongside this discourse. Critical theory and action theory interacted with one another, producing a variety of hybrid discourses:

PAR and community action research

Critical race theory, LatCrit, and Whiteness studies

Decolonizing theories and the global postcolonial

New developments in critical pedagogy

New developments in performance ethnography

Third World, postcolonial, marginalized, endarkened, and borderland feminisms

Emancipatory and pragmatic action research

Social constructivism

Narrative poetics

Poetics of ethnography and participatory inquiry

Ethnodrama and theaters of the oppressed.

▣ ▣ ▣

Out of this intersection of discourses, the crisscrossing of theories of performance, pedagogy, and interpretive practice, came a fourfold interest focused on performance, interpretive pedagogies, indigenous inquiry practices, and theories of power, truth, ethics, and social justice. Taking our lead from the performance turn in the human disciplines (Denzin, 2003), we argue that everything is always already performative. The performative, in addition, is always pedagogical, and the pedagogical is always political.

The outline of this handbook thus charts this confluence of interests. The nine chapters in Part I argue that decolonizing inquiry involves the performance of counterhegemonic theories that disrupt the colonial and the postcolonial. The five chapters in Part II examine particular indigenous interpretive pedagogies, those associated with Hawaiian, Native American, borderland-Mestizaje, endarkened, and Islamic epistemologies. The five chapters in Part III examine indigenous inquiry practices. The eight chapters in Part IV anchor indigenous interpretive pedagogies and practices in the discourses surrounding democracy, power, truth, ethics, and social justice.

To summarize, we believe that the performance-based human disciplines can contribute to radical social change, to economic justice, to a utopian cultural politics that extends localized critical (race) theory and the principles of a radical democracy to all aspects of decolonizing, indigenous societies (Swadener & Mutua, 2004, p. 257). We believe that nonindigenous interpretive scholars should be part of this project. How this endeavor is implemented in any specific indigenous context should be determined by indigenous peoples.

We also believe that this initiative should be part of a larger conversation—namely, the global decolonizing discourse connected to the works of anticolonialist scholars and artists, including First Nation, Native American, Alaskan, Australian Aboriginal, New Zealand Māori, and native Hawaiian peoples (see the chapters in Parts I, II, and III of this handbook).

▣ Constructing This Handbook

Our invitation letter to prospective authors described this handbook thusly:

> This is a formal letter asking you to contribute to the *Handbook of Critical and Indigenous Methodologies* (*HCIM*). We believe that critical qualitative research has come of age as a field, and needs to be taken seriously. Critical and indigenous methodology necessarily speaks to oppressed, colonized persons living in postcolonial situations of injustice.... We need to show how critical qualitative research can be used to address issues that matter to oppressed, colonized persons.... How do we move the current generation of critical, interpretive thought and inquiry beyond rage to progressive political action, to theory and method that connect politics, pedagogy and ethics to action in the world? We want *HCIM* to carry critical qualitative inquiry well into this new century. We want authors who can write chapters that will address practical, concrete issues of implementation while critiquing the field and mapping key current and emergent themes, debates and developments....
>
> We want *HCIM* to cover everything from the history of critical (and indigenous) theory and how it came to inform and impact qualitative research and indigenous peoples to the critical constructs themselves ... to critical concepts within specific disciplines....

We then reviewed the points raised above, concerning the history of this field since the late 1980s. We asked that each chapter consider the following questions and topics:

> Among the questions and topics which we would hope that chapter authors would consider in their chapters would be the following: the history of the area, the major interpretive paradigms that operate in it, exemplary texts, major epistemological issues, and approaches to such problems as decolonizing strategies, values, ethics, empowerment, voice, textual authority, and so on. We would hope that a reader of this chapter would come away with answers to the classic, contemporary and cutting-edge questions and issues that you and your students are bringing to bear on this area.

Many but not all of the authors named above agreed to write chapters that did this for us.

The chapters that follow think through the complex theoretical issues embedded in decolonizing inquiry (Part I). They offer interpretive views of a variety of differing indigenous pedagogies (Part II). They show how these pedagogies can be implemented in concrete research practices (Part III). They connect the conduct of research with ethics and social justice (Part IV).

Still, this is not a how-to-do-it handbook. It is only a road map and a bridge into a new decade of critical, indigenous inquiry.

Limitations

We were unable to locate persons who could write chapters on disability and indigenous studies, insider/indigenous inquiry, Philippine pedagogy, multiple versions of Red and Māori pedagogy, investigative poetics, arts-based methodologies, case studies and genealogies of truth, indigenous property rights, environmental justice, indigenous models of collaboration and self-determination, Third World queer studies, and indigenous performance studies. Some authors we wanted to write for us were unable to, because of prior commitments. Regrettably, there is a Latin American and Asian absence. Critical work by Spanish- and Portuguese-speaking scholars and by Japanese, Korean, and Chinese researchers that resonates with indigenous discourse is not represented (but see Netz, 2007).

These above absences are limitations, and there are surely others that we are not aware of at this time.

Audience

This handbook is for a new (and old) generation of qualitative researchers. We believe that over the past quarter century, a significant number of indigenous and nonindigenous scholars have moved into the spaces we attempt to chart in this handbook. These scholars are from a host of different nations and disciplines, from health care to business, organizational studies, advertising and consumer research, education, communications, social work, sociology, anthropology, psychology, performance studies, and drama. They are committed to using qualitative research methods for social justice purposes.[6] We believe this handbook can be used in advanced undergraduate and graduate research methodology courses. If one could take only one book on critical and indigenous methodologies to a desert island, this, we feel, would be that book.

Acknowledgments

This handbook would not be without its authors and the editorial board members who gave freely, often on very short notice, of their time, advice, and ever courteous suggestions. We acknowledge en masse the support of the authors, as well as the editorial board members, whose names are listed facing the title page. These individuals were able to offer both long-term, sustained commitments to the project and short-term emergency assistance.

There are other debts, intensely personal and closer to home. The handbook never would have been possible without the ever present help, support, wisdom, and encouragement of our editors and publishers at Sage: Alison Mudditt, Lisa Cuevas (who came to us with the original idea for this project), Vicki Knight, Chris Klein, and Sean Connelly. Their grasp of this field, its history and diversity, is extraordinary. Their conceptions of what this project should look like were extremely valuable. Their energy kept us moving forward. Furthermore, whenever we confronted a problem, Vicki, Sean, and Chris were there with their assistance and good-natured humor.

We would also like to thank the following individuals and institutions for their assistance, support, insights, and patience: our respective universities and departments, especially Yvonna's dean, Douglas Palmer; Associate Dean Ernest Goetz; and Department Heads Bryan R. Cole and James J. Scheurich, each of whom facilitated this work in some important way. In Urbana, James Salvo was the sine qua non. His good humor and grace kept our ever growing files in order and everyone on the same timetable. Without James, this project never would have been completed! Aisha Durham's extensive archival research on indigenous scholarship was invaluable.

In College Station, Elsa González y González, provided endless intellectual and technical support for this project.

Norman also gratefully acknowledges the moral, intellectual, and financial support given this project by the College of Communication, the Department of Advertising, and the Institute of Communication. The following individuals at Sage Publications helped move this project through production: Astrid Virding and Gillian Dickens. We are extremely grateful to them, as well as to Dennis Webb and Kathy Paparchontis for their excellent work during the proofreading and indexing phases of production. Himika Bhattacharya, Christina Ceisel, YiYe Liu, James Salvo, Li Xiong, and David Haskell provided outstanding proofreading services. Our spouses, Katherine Ryan and Egon Guba, helped keep us on track, listened to our complaints, and generally displayed extraordinary patience, forbearance, and support.

There is another group of individuals who gave unstintingly of their time and energy to provide us with their expertise and thoughtful reviews when we needed additional guidance. Without the help of these individuals, we would often have found ourselves with less than complete understandings of the various traditions, perspectives, and methods represented in this volume. We would also like to acknowledge the important contributions of the following individuals to this project: Bryant Alexander, Tim Begaye, Gloria Ladson-Billings, Russell Bishop, Gaile S. Cannella, Elizabeth Cook-Lynn, Michelle Fine, Sandy Grande, Joe L. Kincheloe, Luis Mirón, Radhika Parameswaran, Caroline Joan Kay Picart, Christopher Darius Stonebanks, Shirley R. Steinberg, and Keyan G. Tomaselli.

Finally, Norman and Yvonna must give a special word of thanks to their wonderful colleague Linda Tuhiwai Smith. As a coeditor in the formative stages of this project, Linda was invaluable. Her insights, understandings, and grasp of the field of indigenous scholarship, in its multiple discourses, are unparalleled. Unfortunately, her many commitments prohibited her from participating at the level she would have desired. Nonetheless, her presence is everywhere in the pages that follow. Her stamp on this field is monumental (1999, 2000, 2005, 2006). We have drawn heavily on her work in our introductory chapter. Her help in identifying potential contributors was enormous, and we remain deeply appreciative of her willingness to share her expertise with us.

Norman K. Denzin
University of Illinois at Urbana-Champaign

Yvonna S. Lincoln
Texas A&M University

Linda Tuhiwai Smith
University of Auckland

Notes

1. Decolonizing research is not necessarily postcolonial research. Decolonization is a process that critically engages, at all levels, imperialism, colonialism, and postcoloniality. Decolonizing research implements indigenous epistemologies and critical interpretive practices that are shaped by indigenous research agendas (Smith, 1999, p. 20).

2. With Swadener and Mutua (2004), we trouble the concept of *postcolonial*—with asking, where was the *colonial* ever *post?* The term *postcolonial* functions as a temporal marker implying linearity and chronology. With Swadener and Mutua, we prefer the term *postcolonial* to imply a constant, complex, intertwined, back-and-forth relationship between past and present. In this sense, there is no postcolonial, only endless variations on neocolonial formations (Soto, 2004, p. ix).

3. For Kincheloe and McLaren (2000), cultural pedagogy refers to the ways that cultural production functions as a form of education, as "it generates knowledge, shapes values and constructs identity . . . cultural pedagogy refers to the ways particular cultural agents produce . . . hegemonic ways of seeing" (p. 285). Critical pedagogy attempts to performatively disrupt and deconstruct these cultural practices in the name of a "more just, democratic and egalitarian society" (Kincheloe & McLaren, 2000).

4. According to Marie Battiste (Chapter 25, this volume), more than 5,000 distinct indigenous peoples live in 70 countries, with a world population of more than 300 million peoples.

5. Indigenous knowledge (and epistemology) embodies the cosmologies, values, cultural beliefs, and webs of relationship that exist within specific indigenous communities.

6. Many of them are members of the International Association Qualitative Inquiry and regularly participate in its annual International Congresses (see Denzin & Giardina, 2007).

References

Denzin, N. K. (2003). *Performance ethnography: Critical pedagogy and the politics of culture.* Thousand Oaks, CA: Sage.

Denzin, N. K., & Giardina, M. D. (Eds.). (2007). *Ethical futures in qualitative research: Decolonizing the politics of knowledge.* Walnut Creek. CA: Left Coast Press.

Evans, M., Hole, R., Berg, L. D., Hutchinson, P., & Sookraj, D. (in press). Common insights, differing methodologies: Toward a fusion of indigenous methodologies, participatory action research, and White studies in an Urbana aboriginal research agenda. *Qualitative Inquiry.*

Freire, P. (2001). *Pedagogy of the oppressed* (30th anniversary ed., with an introduction by Donaldo Macedo). New York: Continuum.

Grande, S. (2004). *Red pedagogy.* New York: Routledge.

Grande, S. (2007). Red Lake Woebegone, pedagogy, decolonization, and the critical project. In P. McLaren & J. L. Kincheloe (Eds.), *Critical pedagogy: Where are we now?* (pp. 315–336). New York: Peter Lang.

Henderson, J. (S.) Y. (2000). Postcolonial ledger drawing: Legal reform. In M. Battiste (Ed.), *Reclaiming indigenous voice and vision* (pp. 161–171). Vancouver: University of British Columbia Press.

Kincheloe, J. L. (2007). Critical pedagogy in the twenty-first century: Evolution for survival. In P. McLaren & J. L. Kincheloe (Eds.), *Critical pedagogy: Where are we now?* (pp. 9–42). New York: Peter Lang.

Kincheloe, J. L., & McLaren, P. (2000). Rethinking critical theory and qualitative research. In N. K. Denzin & Y. S. Lincoln (Eds.), *The SAGE handbook of qualitative research* (2nd ed., pp. 279–314). Thousand Oaks, CA: Sage.

Lather, P. (1991). *Getting smart: Feminist research and pedagogy within the postmodern.* New York: Routledge.

Lather, P. (2007). *Getting lost.* Albany: SUNY Press.

McLaren, P., & Kincheloe, J. L. (2007). *Critical pedagogy: Where are we now?* New York: Peter Lang.

Netz, S. R. (Trans.). (2007). *The landscape of qualitative research* (2nd ed.; N. K. Denzin & Y. S. Lincoln, Eds.). Thousand Oaks, CA: Sage.

Rains, F. V., Archibald, J. A., & Deyhle, D. (2000). Introduction: Through our eyes and in our own words—The voices of indigenous scholars. *International Journal of Qualitative Studies in Education, 13,* 337–342.

Smith, L. T. (1999). *Decolonizing methodologies: Research and indigenous peoples.* Dunedin, New Zealand: University of Otago Press.

Smith, L. T. (2000). Kaupapa Māori research. In M. Battiste (Ed.), *Reclaiming indigenous voice and vision* (pp. 225–247). Vancouver: UBC Press.

Smith, L. T. (2005). On tricky ground: Researching the native in the age of uncertainty. In N. K. Denzin & Y. S. Lincoln (Eds.), *The SAGE handbook of qualitative research* (3rd ed., pp. 85–107). Thousand Oaks, CA: Sage.

Smith, L. T. (2006). Choosing the margins: The role of research in indigenous struggles for social justice. In N. K. Denzin & M. D. Giardina (Eds.), *Qualitative inquiry and the conservative challenge: Confronting methodological fundamentalism* (pp. 151–174). Walnut Creek, CA: Left Coast Press.

Soto, L. D. (2004). Foreword: Decolonizing research in cross-cultural contexts: Issues of voice and power. In K. Mutua & B. B. Swadener (Eds.), *Decolonizing research in cross-cultural contexts: Critical personal narratives* (pp. ix–xi). Albany, NY: SUNY Press.

Swadener, B. B., & Mutua, K. (2004). Afterword. In K. Mutua & B. B. Swadener (Eds.), *Decolonizing research in cross-cultural contexts: Critical personal narratives* (pp. 255–260) Albany: SUNY Press.

Yellow Bird, M. (2005). Tribal critical thinking centers. In W. A. Wilson & M. Yellow Bird (Eds.), *For indigenous eyes only: A decolonization handbook* (pp. 9–30). Santa Fe, NM: School of American Research Handbook.

1

INTRODUCTION

Critical Methodologies and Indigenous Inquiry

Norman K. Denzin and Yvonna S. Lincoln

Despite the guarantees of the Treaty of Waitangi, the colonization of Aotearoa/New Zealand and the subsequent neocolonial dominance of majority interests in social and educational research have continued. The result has been the development of a tradition of research into Māori people's lives that addresses concerns and interests of the predominantly non-Māori researchers' own making, as defined and made accountable in terms of the researchers' own cultural worldview(s).

—Bishop (2005, p. 110)

The capitalist system, and globalization theory which speak of ethics, hide the fact that their ethics are those of the marketplace and not the universal ethics of the human person. It is for these matters that we ought to struggle courageously if we have, in truth, made a choice for a humanized world.

—Freire (1998, p. 114, paraphrase)

There is hope, however timid, on the street corners, a hope in each and everyone of us. . . . Hope is an ontological need.

—Freire (1992/1999, p. 8)

When I discovered the work of . . . Paulo Freire, my first introduction to critical pedagogy, I found a mentor and a guide.

—hooks (1994, p. 6)

We seek a productive dialogue between indigenous and critical scholars. This involves a re-visioning of critical pedagogy, a re-grounding of Paulo Freire's (2000) pedagogy of the oppressed in local, indigenous contexts. We call this merger of indigenous and critical methodologies *critical indigenous pedagogy* (CIP). It understands that all inquiry is both political and moral. It uses methods critically, for explicit social justice purposes. It values the transformative power of indigenous, subjugated knowledges. It values the pedagogical practices that produce these knowledges (Semali & Kincheloe, 1999, p. 15), and it seeks forms of praxis and inquiry that are emancipatory and empowering. It embraces the commitment by indigenous scholars to decolonize Western methodologies, to criticize and demystify the ways in which Western science and the modern academy have been part of the colonial apparatus. This revisioning of critical pedagogy understands with Paulo Freire and Antonio Faundez (1989, p. 46) that "indigenous knowledge is a rich social resource for any justice-related attempt to bring about social change" (Semali & Kincheloe, 1999, p. 15).

In this introduction, we will outline a methodology, a borderland epistemology, and a set of interpretive practices that we hope will move this dialogue forward. This will entail a critique of traditional research approaches to indigenous life—that is, those positivist and postpositivist approaches that address the concerns and interests of nonindigenous scholars (Bishop, 2005, p. 110; Semali & Kincheloe, 1999, p. 15).

Such inquiry should meet multiple criteria. It must be ethical, performative, healing, transformative, decolonizing, and participatory. It must be committed to dialogue, community, self-determination, and cultural autonomy. It must meet people's perceived needs. It must resist efforts to confine inquiry to a single paradigm or interpretive strategy. It must be unruly, disruptive, critical, and dedicated to the goals of justice and equity. Such a framework lays the foundation for the Decade of Critical Indigenous Inquiry.

At this level, *critical indigenous qualitative research* is always already political. The researcher must consider how his or her research benefits, as well as promotes, self-determination for research participants. According to Bishop (2005, p. 112), self-determination intersects with the locus of power in the research setting. It concerns issues of initiation, benefits, representation, legitimacy, and accountability. Critical indigenous inquiry begins with the concerns of indigenous people. It is assessed in terms of the benefits it creates for them. The work must represent indigenous persons honestly, without distortion or stereotype, and the research should honor indigenous knowledge, customs, and rituals. It should not be judged in terms of neocolonial paradigms. Finally, researchers should be accountable to indigenous persons. They, not Western scholars, should have first access to research findings and control over the distribution of knowledge.

▣ ▣ ▣

Our argument unfolds in several parts. We begin by locating qualitative research and the current move to indigenous inquiry within their historical moments. We then briefly discuss the obstacles that confront the nonindigenous critical theorist. We next take up a group of terms and arguments, including critical methodology, indigenous epistemology, pedagogy, discourses of resistance, politics as performance, and counternarratives, as critical inquiry. A variety of indigenous pedagogies are briefly discussed, as is indigenous research as localized critical theory. We elaborate variations within the personal narrative approach to decolonized inquiry, extending Richardson's (2000) model of creative analytic practices, or what she calls CAP ethnography (p. 929). A politics of resistance is next outlined. We conclude with a discussion of indigenous models of power, truth, ethics, and social justice.

▣ ▣ ▣

Sandoval (2000), Collins (1998), Mutua and Swadener (2004), Bishop (2005), and Lopez

(1998) observe that we are in the midst of "a large-scale social movement of anticolonialist discourse" (Lopez, 1998, p. 226). This movement is evident in the emergence and proliferation of indigenous epistemologies and methodologies (Sandoval, 2000), including the arguments of African American, Chicano, Latina/o, Native American, First Nation, Hawaiian, African, and Māori scholars, among others. These epistemologies are forms of critical pedagogy; that is, they embody a critical politics of representation that is embedded in the rituals of indigenous communities. Always already political, they are relentlessly critical of transnational capitalism and its destructive presence in the indigenous world (see Kincheloe & McLaren, 2000).

Qualitative research exists in a time of global uncertainty. Around the world, government agencies are attempting to regulate scientific inquiry by defining what counts as "good" science (for the case in Australia, see Cheek, 2006; for the case in the United Kingdom, see Torrance, 2006). Conservative regimes are enforcing evidence-based or scientifically based biomedical models of research (SBR). Yet, as in the case with such ill-conceived endeavors as, in the United States, the No Child Left Behind Act of 2002, this experimental quantitative model is ill suited to

> examining the complex and dynamic contexts of public education in its many forms, sites, and variations, especially considering the . . . subtle social difference produced by gender, race, ethnicity, linguistic status or class. Indeed, multiple kinds of knowledge, produced by multiple epistemologies and methodologies, are not only worth having but also demanded if policy, legislation and practice are to be sensitive to social needs. (Lincoln & Cannella, 2004a, p. 7; see also Lincoln & Cannella, 2004b)

Born out of a "methodological fundamentalism" that returns to a much-discredited model of empirical inquiry in which "only randomized experiments produce truth" (House, 2006, pp. 100–101), such regulatory activities raise fundamental philosophical, epistemological, political, and pedagogical issues for scholarship and freedom of speech in the decolonized academy.

In response to such challenges, a methodology of the heart (Pelias, 2004), a prophetic, feminist postpragmatism that embraces an ethics of truth grounded in love, care, hope, and forgiveness, is needed. Love, here, to borrow from Antonia Darder and Luis F. Mirón (2006),

> means to comprehend that the moral and the material are inextricably linked. And, as such, [we] must recognize love as an essential ingredient of a just society . . . love is a political principle through which we struggle to create mutually life-enhancing opportunities for all people. It is grounded in the mutuality and interdependence of our human existence—that which we share, as much as that which we do not. This is a love nurtured by the act of relationship itself. It cultivates relationships with the freedom to be at one's best without undue fear. Such an emancipatory love allows us to realize our nature in a way that allows others to do so as well. Inherent in such a love is the understanding that we are not at liberty to be violent, authoritarian, or self-seeking. (p. 150)

Indigenous scholars are leading the way on this front.[1] During the "Decade of the World's Indigenous Peoples" (1994–2004), a full-scale attack was launched on Western epistemologies and methodologies. Indigenous scholars asked that the academy decolonize its scientific practices (Battiste, 2006; Grande, 2004; L. T. Smith, 2006). At the same time, these scholars sought to disrupt traditional ways of knowing, while developing "methodologies and approaches to research that privileged indigenous knowledges, voices, and experiences" (L. T. Smith, 2005, p. 87). An alliance with the critical strands of qualitative inquiry and its practitioners seemed inevitable.

Today, nonindigenous scholars are building these connections, learning how to dismantle, deconstruct, and decolonize traditional ways of doing science, learning that research is always already both moral and political, learning how to let go. Ironically, as this letting go occurs, a backlash against critical qualitative research gains momentum. New "gold standards" for reliability and validity, as well as design, are being advanced (St. Pierre, 2004). So-called evidence-based research—including the Campbell and Cochrane[2] models and protocols—have become fashionable (Pring, 2004; Thomas, 2004) even while its proponents fail to recognize that the very act of labeling some research as "evidence based" implies that some research fails to mount evidence—a strongly political and decidedly nonobjective stance. The criticisms, it seems, are coming in from all sides.

The Historical Field

The term *research* is inextricably linked to European imperialism and colonialism (L. T. Smith, 1999, p. 1). L. T. Smith (1999) contends that "the word itself is probably one of the dirtiest words in the indigenous world's vocabulary. . . . It is implicated in the worst excesses of colonialism" (p. 1), with the ways in which "knowledge about indigenous peoples was collected, classified, and then represented back to the West" (p. 1). Sadly, qualitative research in many, if not all, of its forms (observation, participation, interviewing, ethnography) serves as a metaphor for colonial knowledge, for power, and for truth. The metaphor works this way: Research, quantitative and qualitative, is scientific. Research provides the foundation for reports about and representations of the other. In the colonial context, research becomes an objective way of representing the dark-skinned other to the White world. Colonizing nations relied on the human disciplines, especially sociology and anthropology, as well as their field note–taking journaling observers, to produce knowledge about strange and foreign worlds. This close involvement with the colonial project contributed, in significant ways, to qualitative research's long and anguished history, to its becoming a dirty word.

Anthropological and sociological observers went to a foreign setting to study the culture, customs, and habits of another human group. Often, this was a group that stood in the way of White settlers. Ethnographic reports of these groups were incorporated into colonizing strategies, ways of controlling the foreign, deviant, or troublesome other. Soon qualitative research would be employed in other social and behavioral science disciplines, including education (especially the work of Dewey), history, political science, business, medicine, nursing, social work, and communications.

By the 1960s, battle lines were drawn within the quantitative and qualitative camps. Quantitative scholars relegated qualitative research to a subordinate status in the scientific arena. In response, qualitative researchers extolled the humanistic virtues of their subjective, interpretive approach to human group life. In the meantime, indigenous peoples found themselves subjected to the indignities of both approaches, each methodology used in the name of a colonizing power (see Battiste, 2000b).

In North America, qualitative research operates in a complex historical field that crosscuts at least eight historical moments. These moments overlap and simultaneously operate in the present.[3] We define them as the *traditional* (1900–1950); the *modernist,* or golden, age (1950–1970); *blurred genres* (1970–1986); the *crisis of representation* (1986–1990); the *postmodern,* a period of experimental and new ethnographies (1990–1995); *postexperimental inquiry* (1995–2000); the *methodologically contested present* (2000–2008); and the *future* (2008–), which is now. The future, the eighth moment, confronts the methodological backlash associated with the evidence-based social movement. It is concerned with moral discourse, with the development of sacred textualities. The eighth moment asks that the social sciences and the humanities become sites for critical conversations about democracy, race, gender, class, nation-states, globalization, freedom, and community.[4] Successive waves of epistemological theorizing move across these eight moments. In the first decade of this new century, we struggle to connect qualitative research to the hopes, needs, goals, and promises of a free democratic society.

Many critical methodologists and indigenous scholars are in the eighth moment, performing culture as they write it, understanding that the dividing line between performativity (doing) and performance (done) has disappeared (Conquergood, 1998, p. 25). But even as this disappearance occurs, matters of racial injustice remain. The indigenous other is a racialized other.

Any discussion of critical, indigenous qualitative research must work within this complex historical field. Qualitative research means different things in each of these moments. Nonetheless, an initial, generic definition can be offered, understanding that there is no longer an objective, god's-eye view of reality. *Critical qualitative research* is a situated activity that locates the gendered observer in the world. It consists of a set of interpretive, material practices that make the world visible. These practices are forms of critical pedagogy. They transform the world.

Critical qualitative research embodies the emancipatory, empowering values of critical pedagogy. Like critical race theories and poststructural feminism (St. Pierre & Pillow, 2000), critical qualitative research represents inquiry done for explicit political, utopian purposes, a politics of liberation, a reflexive discourse constantly in search of an open-ended, subversive, multivoiced epistemology (Lather, 2007, pp. x–xi).

Interpretive research practices turn the world into a series of performances and representations, including case study documents, critical personal experience narratives, life stories, field notes, interviews, conversations, photographs, recordings, and memos to the self. These performances create the space for critical, collaborative, dialogical work. They bring researchers and their research participants into a shared, critical space, a space where the work of resistance, critique, and empowerment can occur.

As indicated in the Preface, we locate indigenous methodology in an intersection of discourses, the site where theories of performance, pedagogy, and interpretive practice come together. This produces a focus on performance, interpretive pedagogies, indigenous inquiry practices, and theories of power, truth, ethics, and social justice. Taking our lead from the performance turn in the human disciplines (Denzin, 2003), we assert that the performative is always pedagogical, and the pedagogical is always political. Critical personal narratives enact this view of the pedagogical. They can be turned into performance texts that function as performative interventions. Such work may queer autoethnography, by politicizing memory and reconfiguring storytelling and personal history, as counternarratives. Such work disrupts taken-for-granted epistemologies, by privileging indigenous interpretive pedagogies and inquiry practices.

▣ A Caveat

In proposing a conversation between indigenous and nonindigenous discourses, we are mindful of several difficulties. First, the legacy of the helping Western colonizing Other must be resisted. As Linda Smith observes (1999), "They came, They saw, They named, They Claimed" (p. 80). As agents of colonial power, Western scientists discovered, extracted, appropriated, commodified, and distributed knowledge about the indigenous other. Māoris, for example, contend that these practices place control over research in the hands of the Western scholar. This means, Bishop (2005) argues, that the Māori are excluded from discussions concerning who has control over the initiation, methodologies, evaluations, assessments, representations, and distribution of the newly defined knowledge. The decolonization project challenges these practices that perpetuate Western power by misrepresenting and essentializing indigenous persons, often denying them a voice or an identity (Bishop, 2005).

Second, however, critical, interpretive performance theory and critical race theory, without modification, will not work within indigenous settings. The criticisms of G. Smith (2000), L. T. Smith (1999, 2000), Bishop (1994, 1998), Battiste (2000a, 2000b), Churchill (1996), Cook-Lynn (1998), and others make this very clear. Critical theory's criteria for self-determination and empowerment perpetuate neocolonial sentiments while turning the indigenous person into an essentialized "other" who is spoken for (Bishop, 2005). The categories of race, gender, and racialized identities cannot be turned into frozen, essential terms, nor is racial identity a free-floating signifier (Grande, 2000, p. 348). Critical theory must be localized, grounded in the specific meanings, traditions, customs, and community relations that operate in each indigenous setting. Localized critical theory can work if the goals of critique, resistance, struggle, and emancipation are not treated as if they have "universal characteristics that are independent of history, context, and agency" (L. T. Smith, 2000, p. 229).

Third, there is a pressing need to decolonize and deconstruct those structures within the Western academy that privilege Western knowledge systems and their epistemologies (Mutua & Swadener, 2004, p. 10; Semali & Kincheloe, 1999). Indigenous knowledge systems are too frequently made into objects of study, treated as if they were instances of quaint folk theory held by the members of a primitive culture. The decolonizing project reverses this equation, making Western systems of knowledge the object of critique and inquiry.

Fourth, paraphrasing L. T. Smith (2005), the spaces between decolonizing research practices and indigenous communities must be carefully and cautiously articulated. They are fraught with uncertainty. Neoliberal and neoconservative political economies both act to turn knowledge about indigenous peoples into a marketable commodity. There are conflicts between competing epistemological and ethical frameworks, including (Western) institutional human subject research regulations. Research is regulated according to positivist epistemologies. Indigenous scholars and native intellectuals are pressed to produce technical knowledge that conforms to Western standards of truth and validity. Conflicts over who initiates and who benefits from such research are especially problematic (Bishop, 2005). Culturally responsive research practices must be developed. Such practices would locate power within the indigenous community. What is acceptable and not acceptable research is determined and defined from within the community. Such work encourages self-determination and empowerment (Bishop, 2005). In fact, in some indigenous communities, such practices are already codified (L. T. Smith, 1999); such codes, regulating the activities, roles, and powers of nonindigenous researchers, might serve as a preliminary model for other such communities.

Fifth, in arguing for a dialogue between critical and indigenous theories, Denzin and Lincoln recognize that they are outsiders to the indigenous colonized experience. We write as privileged Westerners. At the same time, we seek to be "allied others" (Kaomea, 2004, p. 32; Mutua & Swadener, 2004, p. 4), fellow travelers of sorts, antipositivists, friendly insiders who wish to deconstruct from within the Western academy and its positivist epistemologies. We endorse a critical epistemology that contests notions of objectivity and neutrality. We value autoethnographic, insider, participatory, collaborative methodologies (Fine et al., 2003). These are narrative, performative methodologies—research practices that are reflexively consequential, ethical, critical, respectful, and humble. These practices require that scholars live with the consequences of their research actions (L. T. Smith, 1999, pp. 137–139).

▣ ▣ ▣

In calling for a dialogue between indigenous and nonindigenous qualitative researchers, we are mindful of Terry Tempest Williams's cautious advice about borrowing stories and narratives from indigenous peoples. In her autoethnography, *Pieces of White Shell: A Journey to Navajoland* (1984, p. 3), she praises the wisdom of Navajo storytellers and the stories they tell (p. 4). But she warns the reader we cannot emulate Native peoples: "We are not Navajo . . . their traditional stories don't work for us. Their stories hold meaning for us only as examples. They can teach us what is possible. We must create our own stories" (p. 5).

As nonindigenous scholars seeking a dialogue with indigenous scholars, we (Denzin and Lincoln) must construct stories that are embedded in the landscapes through which we travel. These will be dialogical counternarratives, stories of resistance, of struggle, of hope, stories that create spaces for multicultural conversations, stories embedded in the critical democratic imagination.

Performance and Critical Pedagogy

Shaped by the sociological imagination (Mills, 1959), building on George Herbert Mead's (1938, p. 460) discursive, performative model of the act, critical qualitative research methodology imagines and explores the multiple ways in which performance can be understood, including as imitation, or *mimesis;* as *poiesis,* or construction; and as *kinesis,* movement, gendered bodies in motion (Conquergood, 1998, p. 31; Pollock, 1998, p. 43). The researcher-as-performer moves from a view of performance as imitation, or dramaturgical staging (Goffman, 1959), to an emphasis on performance as liminality, construction (McLaren, 1999), to a view of performance as embodied struggle, as an intervention, as breaking and remaking, and as kinesis, that is, a sociopolitical act (Conquergood, 1998, p. 32).

Viewed as struggles and interventions, performances and performance events become gendered, transgressive achievements, political accomplishments that break through "sedimented meanings and normative traditions" (Conquergood, 1998, p. 32). It is this performative model of emancipatory decolonized indigenous research that we endorse (see the Chapters 4, 9, 18, and 19, this volume).

The call to performance in the human disciplines requires a commitment to a progressive democratic politics, an ethics and aesthetics of performance (Pollock, 1998) that moves from critical race theory (Ladson-Billings & Donnor, 2005) to the radical pedagogical formulations of Paulo Freire (1998, 1992/1999, 2000), as his work is reformulated and reinvented by Antonia Darder (2002), Mirón (Chapter 28, this volume), Kincheloe and McLaren (2000, 2005), McLaren and Jaramillo (Chapter 10, this volume), Giroux and Giroux (Chapter 9, this volume), and others. This performance ethic borrows from and is grounded in the discourses of indigenous peoples (Mutua & Swadener, 2004).

Within this radical pedagogical space, the performative and the political intersect on the terrain of a praxis-based ethic. This is the space of postcolonial, indigenous participatory theater, a form of critical pedagogical theater that draws its inspirations from Boal's major works: *Theatre of the Oppressed* (1974/1979), *The Rainbow of Desire* (1995), and *Legislative Theatre* (1998). This theater performs pedagogies that resist oppression (Balme & Carstensen, 2001; Greenwood, 2001).[5] It enacts a politics of possibility (Madison, 1998) grounded in performative practices that embody love, hope, care, and compassion.

Consider the following:

> In *House Arrest and Piano,* Anna Deavere Smith (2003) offers "an epic view of slavery, sexual misconduct, and the American presidency." Twelve actors, some in blackface, "play across lines of race, age and gender to 'become' Bill Clinton, Thomas Jefferson, Sally Hemings . . . and a vast array of historical and contemporary figures" (Kondo, 2000, p. 81).

> In Native Canadian Bill Moses' play *Almighty Voice and His Wife* (1993) Native performers, wearing whiteface minstrel masks, mock such historical figures as Wild Bill Cody, Sitting Bull, and young Indian maidens called Sweet Sioux. (Gilbert, 2003, p. 692)

Contemporary indigenous playwrights and performers revisit and make a mockery of 19th-, 20th-, and 21st-century racist practices. They interrogate and turn the tables on blackface minstrelsy and the global colonial theater that reproduced racist politics through specific cross-race and cross-gender performances. These performances reflexively use historical restagings, masquerade, ventriloquism, and doubly inverted performances involving male and female impersonators to create a subversive theater that undermines colonial racial representations (see Gilbert, 2003; Kondo, 2000, p. 83). This theater takes up key diasporic concerns, including those of memory, cultural loss, disorientation, violence, and exploitation (Balme & Carstensen, 2001, p. 45).[6] This is a utopian theater that addresses issues of equity, healing, and social justice.[7]

A Glossary and a Genealogy

Pedagogy: To teach in a way that leads. Pedagogy is always ideological and political.

Cultural pedagogy: The ways that cultural production functions as a form of education, as "it generates knowledge, shapes values and constructs identity . . . cultural pedagogy refers to the ways particular cultural agents produce . . . hegemonic ways of seeing" (Kincheloe & McLaren, 2000, p. 285; McLaren, 1999, p. 441).

Critical pedagogy: To performatively disrupt and deconstruct these cultural practices in the name of a "more just, democratic and egalitarian society" (Kincheloe & McLaren, 2000, p. 285).

Democracy and Pedagogy

The "democratic character of critical pedagogy is defined largely through a set of basic assumptions" (Giroux & Giroux, 2005, p. 21). Educational and everyday realities "are constructed in and through people's linguistic, cultural, social and behavioral interactions which both shape and are shaped by social, political, economic and cultural forces" (Fishman & McLaren, 2005, p. 33). It is not enough to understand any given reality. There is a need to "transform it with the goal of radically democratizing educational sites and societies" (Fishman & McLaren, 2005, p. 33). Educators, as transformative intellectuals, actively shape and lead this project.

Through performances, critical pedagogy disrupts those hegemonic cultural and educational practices that reproduce the logics of neoliberal conservatism (Giroux & Giroux, 2005). Critical pedagogy subjects structures of power, knowledge, and practice to critical scrutiny, demanding that they be evaluated "in terms of how they might open up or close down democratic experiences" (Giroux & Giroux, 2005, p. 21). Critical pedagogy and critical pedagogical theater hold systems of authority accountable through the critical reading of texts, the creation of radical educational practices, and the promotion of critical literacy (Giroux & Giroux, 2005, p. 22). Critical pedagogy is "a transgressive discourse, a fluid way of seeing the world, a pedagogy of insubordination" (Steinberg, 2007, p. ix). In turn, critical pedagogy encourages resistance to the "discourses of privatization, consumerism, the methodologies of standardization and accountability, and the new disciplinary techniques of surveillance" (Giroux & Giroux, 2005, p. 23).

Critical pedagogy and its related critical methodologies can be summarized in terms of a small set of principles involving cultural politics, political economy, and critical theory. Critical pedagogy embraces a dialectical, relational view of knowledge. It conceives of the human agent in active terms. Following Gramsci, there is an emphasis on critiques of ideology and the development of counterhegemonic forms of discourse and praxis, as well as theories of resistance that presume the historicity of knowledge (Darder, Baltodano, & Torres, 2003, pp. 12–14). With the Frankfurt school, efforts are made to show how theory and praxis are intertwined. Truth claims are subject to the critiques of praxis as well as to critical pedagogy, to counterhegemonic discourses that embrace an emancipatory cultural politics, including principles of radical democracy.

New regimes of truth are sought. What is true must also be just and right. What is just is based on pedagogies of kindness, hope, and love (Darder, 2002, p. 32). Critical pedagogy and its methodologies honor the experiences of indigenous persons and build on these experiences to construct empowering cultures of compassion and care (Darder et al., 2003, p. 11).

The Critics

Critical pedagogy has not been without its critics (Darder et al., 2003, pp. 16, 21; Ellsworth, 1989; Grande, Chapter 12, this volume; Kincheloe, 2005, pp. 48–49; Lather, 1991, pp. 43–49, 1998; Luke & Gore, 1992; L. T. Smith, 1999, pp. 185–189). While committed to critical pedagogy's key values of critique, resistance, struggle, and emancipation, critics nonetheless take issue with how these values are implemented in practice. Indigenous scholars argue that some versions of critical pedagogy undertheorize and diminish the importance of indigenous concepts of identity, sovereignty, land, tradition, literacy, and language. Grande (Chapter 12, this volume) fears that some critical pedagogy theorists persist in imposing

Western, Enlightenment views of these terms on the indigenous experience.

Poststructural and postmodern feminists assert that critical pedagogy did not adequately engage the issues of biography, history, emotionality, sexual politics, gender, and patriarchy. Furthermore, they challenge the privileging of reason "as the ultimate sphere upon which knowledge is constructed" (Darder et al., 2003, p. 16). Critics contended that the rationalist premise silences the voices of repressed persons (Darder et al., 2003, p. 16).

Ellsworth (1989, p. 309) argued that the theory failed to interrogate the perspective of the White male theorist. She and others asserted that this failure compromises the emancipatory goals of the theory (Lather, 1991, p. 48; L. T. Smith, 1999, p. 186). Feminist scholars of color pointed to the failure of critical theory to take up "questions of subordinate cultures from the specific location of racialized populations themselves" (Darder et al., 2003, p. 17). Working-class educators criticized the theory because they felt its language was elitist and created a new form of oppression. Classroom educators and curriculum theorists contended that critical pedagogy was about politics and not education. Political economy critics argued that critical pedagogy theorists were obsessed with struggles surrounding culture and identity politics. This meant they were retreating from issues of class and capital, politics and the media.

Indigenous Research as Localized Critical Theory

Indigenous critics, including Bishop (1994, 2005) and L. T. Smith (1999, pp. 185–186), observe that critical theory failed to address how indigenous cultures and their epistemologies were sites of resistance and empowerment. This criticism, however, was muted by the commitment of indigenous scholars to the same values as critical theory—namely, to resistance and struggle at the local level.

Indeed, L. T. Smith (2000) connects her version of indigenous inquiry, Kaupapa Māori research, with critical theory, as well as cultural studies, suggesting, with G. Smith (2000), that Kaupapa Māori research is a "local theoretical position that is the modality through which the emancipatory goal of critical theory, in a specific historical, political and social context, is practised" (L. T. Smith, 2000, p. 229; see also Bishop, 2005). However, critical theory is fitted to the Māori worldview, which asserts that Māori are connected to the universe and their place in it through the principle of *Whakapapa.* This principle tells Māori that they are the seeds or direct descendants of the heavens. Whakapapa turns the universe into a moral space where all things great and small are interconnected, including science and research.

The "local" that localizes critical theory is always historically specific. The local is grounded in the politics, circumstances, and economies of a particular moment, a particular time and place, a particular set of problems, struggles, and desires. There is a politics of resistance and possibility (Madison, 1998; Pollock, 1998) embedded in the local. This is a politics that confronts and breaks through local structures of resistance and oppression. This is a politics that asks, "Who writes for whom? Who is representing indigenous peoples, how, for what purposes, for which audiences, who is doing science for whom?" (L. T. Smith, 1999, p. 37).

A critical politics of interpretation leads the indigenous scholar to ask eight questions about any research project, including those projects guided by critical theory:

1. What research do we want done?
2. Whom is it for?
3. What difference will it make?
4. Who will carry it out?
5. How do we want the research done?
6. How will we know it is worthwhile?
7. Who will own the research?
8. Who will benefit? (L. T. Smith, 2000, p. 239)

These questions are addressed to indigenous and nonindigenous researchers alike. They must be answered in the affirmative; that is, indigenous persons must conduct, own, and benefit from any research that is done on, for, or with them.

These eight questions serve to interpret critical theory through a moral lens, through key indigenous principles. They shape the moral space that aligns indigenous research with critical theory. Thus, both formations are situated within the antipositivist debate. They both rest on antifoundational epistemologies. Each privileges performative issues of gender, race, class, equity, and social justice. Each develops its own understandings of community, critique, resistance, struggle, and emancipation (L. T. Smith, 2000, p. 228). Each understands that the outcome of a struggle can never be predicted in advance, that struggle is always local and contingent; it is never final (L. T. Smith, 2000, p. 229).

By localizing discourses of resistance and by connecting these discourses to performance ethnography and critical pedagogy, indigenous research enacts what critical theory "actually offers to oppressed, marginalized and silenced groups . . . [that is] through emancipation groups such as the Māori would take greater control of their own lives and humanity" (L. T. Smith, 2000, p. 229). This requires that indigenous groups "take hold of the project of emancipation and attempt to make it a reality on their own terms" (L. T. Smith, 2000, p. 229). This means that inquiry is always grounded in principles centered on autonomy, home, family, and kinship. It presupposes a shared collective community vision. Under this framework, research is not a commodity or "purchased product . . . owned by the state" (L. T. Smith, 2000, p. 231).

Localized critical indigenous theory and critical indigenous pedagogy encourages indigenists, as well as nonindigenous scholars, to confront key challenges connected to the meanings of science, community, and democracy. G. Smith (2000, pp. 212–215) and L. T. Smith (2000) have outlined these challenges, asking that indigenists

1. be proactive; they should name the world for themselves—furthermore, "being Māori is an essential criterion for carrying out Kaupapa Māori research" (L. T. Smith, 2000, pp. 229–230);
2. craft their own version of science and empirical activity, including how science and scientific understandings will be used in their world;
3. develop a participatory model of democracy that goes beyond the "Westminister 'one person, one vote, majority rule'" (G. Smith, 2000, p. 212);
4. use theory proactively, as an agent of change, but act in ways that are accountable to the indigenous community and not just the academy;
5. resist new forms of colonization, such as the North American Free Trade Agreement (NAFTA), while contesting neocolonial efforts to commodify indigenous knowledge.

In proactively framing participatory views of science, empirical research, democracy, and community, indigenous peoples advance the project of decolonization.

Indigenous Voices, Critical Pedagogy, and Epistemologies of Resistance

Indigenous pedagogies are grounded in an oppositional consciousness that resists "neocolonizing postmodern global formations" (Sandoval, 2000, pp. 1–2). These pedagogies fold theory, epistemology, methodology, and praxis into strategies of resistance unique to each indigenous community. Thus, the oppositional consciousness of Kaupapa Māori research is like, but unlike, Black feminist epistemology (Collins, 1991, 1998), Chicano feminisms (Anzaldúa, 1987; Moraga, 1995), Red pedagogy (Grande, 2000; Harjo & Bird, 1997), and Hawaiian epistemology (Meyer, 2003). Still, there is a commitment to an indigenism, to an indigenist outlook, which, after Ward Churchill (1996), assigns the highest priority to the rights of indigenous peoples, to the traditions, bodies of knowledge, and values that have "evolved over many thousands of years by native peoples the world over" (p. 509).

Indigenist pedagogies are informed, in varying and contested ways, by decolonizing, revolutionary, and socialist feminisms. Such feminisms, in turn, address issues of social justice, equal rights, and nationalisms of "every racial, ethnic, gender, sex, class, religion or loyalist type" (Sandoval, 2000, p. 7). Underlying each indigenist formation is a commitment to moral praxis, to issues of self-determination, empowerment, healing, love, community solidarity, respect for the Earth, and respect for elders.

Indigenists resist the positivist and postpositivist methodologies of Western science because these formations are too frequently used to validate colonizing knowledge about indigenous peoples. Indigenists deploy, instead, interpretive strategies and skills fitted to the needs, language, and traditions of their respective indigenous community. These strategies emphasize personal performance narratives and *testimonios.*

A Māori Pedagogy

As an example, Māori scholar Russell Bishop (1994, 1998, 2005; see also Chapter 21, this volume) presents a collaborative, participatory epistemological model of Kaupapa Māori research. This model is characterized by the absence of a need to be in control, by a desire to be connected to and to be a part of a moral community where a primary goal is the compassionate understanding of another's moral position (Bishop, 1998, p. 203; Heshusius, 1994). The indigenist researcher wants to participate in a collaborative, altruistic relationship, where nothing "is desired for the self" (Bishop, 1998, p. 207), where research is evaluated by participant-driven criteria, by the cultural values and practices that circulate, for example, in Māori culture, including metaphors stressing self-determination, the sacredness of relationships, embodied understanding, and the priority of community over self. Researchers are led to develop new story lines and criteria of evaluation reflecting these understandings. These participant-driven criteria function as resources for resisting positivist and neoconservative desires to "establish and maintain control of the criteria for evaluating Māori experience" (Bishop, 1998, p. 212).

Extending Sandoval (2000), indigenists enact an ethically democratizing stance that is committed to "equalizing power differentials between humans" (Sandoval, 2000, p. 114). The goal "is to consolidate and extend . . . manifestos of liberation in order to better identify and specify a mode of emancipation that is effective within first world decolonizing global conditions during the twenty-first century" (Sandoval, 2000, p. 2).

Treaties as Political Pedagogy

These pedagogies confront and work through governmental treaties, ideological formations, historical documents, and broken promises that connect the indigenist group and its fate to the colonizing capitalist state. Thus, for example, during the "first 90-odd years of its existence the United States entered into and ratified more than 370 separate treaties . . . [and] has . . . defaulted on its responsibilities under every single treaty obligation it ever incurred with regard to Indians" (Churchill, 1996, pp. 516–517). First Nation tribes in Canada did not have aboriginal rights recognized in law until the Constitution Act of 1982 (Henderson, 2000, p. 165). In New Zealand, Māori debate the Treaty of Waitangi, which was signed between Māori chiefs and the British Crown in 1840. Pedagogically, these treaties inscribed and prescribed only one way of being indigenous—that is, as a person subservient to the colonial powers-to-be.

When Rigoberta Menchú accepted the Nobel Peace Prize on behalf of indigenes, she reminded her audience that "we indigenous Peoples attach a great importance to the Treaties, Agreements, and other constructive accords that have been reached between Indigenous Peoples and the former colonial powers or states. They should be fully respected in order to establish new and harmonious relationships based on mutual respect and cooperation" (Menchú, quoted in Cook-Lynn, 2001, p. 34). Thus, does Menchú announce an ethical tenet, a requirement that the agreements of the past be respected and honored, held as sacred truths (Cook-Lynn, 2001, p. 35)?

Decolonizing the Academy

As argued above, critical indigenist pedagogy contests the complicity of the modern university with neocolonial forces (Battiste, 2000a, p. xi). It encourages and empowers indigenous peoples to make colonizers confront and be accountable for the traumas of colonization. In rethinking and radically transforming the colonizing encounter, this pedagogy imagines a postcolonial society and academy that honor difference and promote healing. A decolonized academy is interdisciplinary and politically proactive. It respects indigenous epistemologies and encourages interpretive, first-person methodologies. It honors different versions of science and empirical activity, as well as values cultural criticism in the name of social justice. It seeks models of human subject research that are not constrained by biomedical, positivist assumptions. It turns the academy and its classrooms into sacred spaces, sites where indigenous and nonindigenous scholars interact, share experiences, take risks, explore alternative modes of interpretation, and participate in a shared agenda, coming together in a spirit of hope, love, and shared community.

This decolonizing project attempts to rebuild nations, communities, and their people through the use of restorative indigenous ecologies. These native ecologies celebrate survival, remembering, sharing, gendering, new forms of naming, networking, protecting, and democratizing daily life (Battiste, 2000b; L. T. Smith, 1999, pp. 142–162).

Theory, method, and epistemology are aligned in this project, anchored in the moral philosophies that are taken for granted in Māori and other indigenous cultures and language communities (L. T. Smith, 2000, p. 225). A pedagogy of emancipation and empowerment is endorsed, a pedagogy that encourages struggles for autonomy, cultural well-being, cooperation, and collective responsibility. This pedagogy demands that indigenous groups own the research process. It speaks the truth "to people about the reality of their lives" (Collins, 1998, p. 198). It equips them with the tools to resist oppression, and it moves them to struggle, to search for justice (Collins, 1998, pp. 198–199).

Pedagogies of Resistance

In response to the continuing pressures of neocolonialism and neocolonization, L. T. Smith (1999, pp. 142–162) outlines some 25 different indigenous projects, including those that create, name, democratize, reclaim, protect, remember, restore, and celebrate lost histories and cultural practices.[8] These indigenous projects embody a pedagogy of hope and freedom. They turn the pedagogies of oppression and colonization into pedagogies of liberation. They are not purely utopian, for they map concrete performances that can lead to positive social transformations. They embody ways of resisting the process of colonization. They encourage processes that mobilize and transform communities at the local level. They honor indigenous cultural practices and, in so doing, contribute to steps that heal the wounds of colonization. Thus are issues of cultural survival and collective self-determination addressed.

Critical Personal Narrative as Counternarrative

The move to the politics of performance has been accompanied by a shift in the meaning of ethnography and ethnographic writing. Richardson (2000) observes that the narrative genres connected to ethnographic writing have "been blurred, enlarged, altered to include poetry, [and] drama" (p. 929). She uses the term *creative analytic practice* (CAP) to describe these many different reflexive performance narrative forms.

These forms include not only performance autoethnography but also short stories; conversations; fiction; personal narratives; creative nonfiction; photographic essays; personal essays; personal narratives of the self; writing stories; self stories; fragmented, layered texts; critical autobiography; memoirs; personal histories; cultural criticism; co-constructed performance narratives; and performance writing that blurs the edges between text, representation, and criticism.

Critical personal narratives are counternarratives, testimonies, autoethnographies, performance texts, stories, and accounts that disrupt and disturb discourse by exposing the complexities and contradictions that exist under official history (Mutua & Swadener, 2004, p. 16). The critical personal narrative is a central genre of contemporary decolonizing writing. As a creative analytic practice, it is used to criticize "prevailing structures and relationships of power and inequity in a relational context" (Mutua & Swadener, 2004, p. 16).[9]

Counternarratives explore the "intersections of gender and voice, border crossing, dual consciousness, multiple identities, and selfhood in a . . . post-colonial and postmodern world" (Mutua & Swadener, 2004, p. 16). The *testimonio* is another form of counternarrative. Its purpose, in part, is to raise political consciousness. In it, the writer bears witness to social injustices experienced at the group level (Mutua & Swadener, 2004, p. 18). It is always an indigenous project, for it presumes that the subaltern can speak, and does, with power, conviction, and firsthand experience.

The testimonio has a central place in this project. Rigoberta Menchú (1984, p. 1) begins her testimonio with these words: "My name is Rigoberta Menchú, I am twenty-three years old, and this is my testimony." Critics contended that Menchú made up her story, that it was not truthful and could not be verified through scientific methodology (Cook-Lynn, 2001, p. 203). But as Cook-Lynn (2001) observes, respectfully remembering and honoring the past, not factual truthfulness, is how the testimonio should be read. Furthermore, Menchú was asking that the treaty agreements of the past be respected, so that new and harmonious relationships based on mutual respect and cooperation could be built (Cook-Lynn, 2001, p. 34). This ethical tenet and utopian impulse have been ignored by Menchú's critics (Cook-Lynn, 2001, p. 35). The struggle of colonized indigenous peoples to tell their own stories is at stake in these criticisms.

Performance, Pedagogy, and Politics

Clearly, the current historical moment requires morally informed performance and arts-based disciplines that will help indigenous and nonindigenous peoples recover meaning in the face of senseless, brutal violence, violence that produces voiceless screams of terror and insanity. Cynicism and despair reign on a global scale. Never have we had a greater need for a militant utopianism to help us imagine a world free of conflict, oppression, terror, and death. We need oppositional performance disciplines that will show us how to create radical utopian spaces within our public institutions.

The central tensions in the world today go beyond the crises in capitalism and neoliberalism's version of democracy. The central crisis, as defined by Native Canadian, Hawaiian, Māori, and American Indian pedagogy, is spiritual, "rooted in the increasingly virulent relationship between human beings and the rest of nature" (Grande, 2000, p. 354). Linda Tuhiwai Smith (1999) discusses the concept of spirituality within Māori discourse, giving added meaning to the crisis at hand:

> The essence of a person has a genealogy which could be traced back to an earth parent. . . . A human person does not stand alone, but shares with other animate . . . beings relationships based on a shared "essence" of life . . . [including] the significance of place, of land, of landscape, of other things in the universe. . . . Concepts of spirituality which Christianity attempted to destroy, and then to appropriate, and then to claim, are critical sites of resistance for indigenous peoples. The value, attitudes, concepts and language embedded in beliefs about spirituality represent . . . the clearest contrast and mark of difference between indigenous peoples and the West. It is one of the few parts of ourselves which the West cannot decipher, cannot understand and cannot control . . . yet. (p. 74)

A respectful performance pedagogy honors these views of spirituality. It works to construct a vision of the person, ecology, and environment that is compatible with these principles. This pedagogy demands a politics of hope, of loving, of caring nonviolence grounded in inclusive moral and spiritual terms.

Cultural Politics and an Indigenous Research Ethic

There is much to be learned from indigenous scholars about how radical democratic practices can be made to work. As indicated above, indigenous scholars are committed to a set of moral and pedagogical imperatives and "to acts of reclaiming, reformulating, and reconstituting indigenous cultures and languages . . . to the struggle to become self-determining" (L. T. Smith, 1999, p. 142). These acts lead to a research program devoted to the pursuit of social justice. In turn, a specific approach to inquiry is required. In his discussion of a Māori approach to creating knowledge, Bishop (1998) observes that researchers in Kaupapa Māori contexts are

> repositioned in such a way as to no longer need to seek to give voice to others, to empower others, to emancipate others, to refer to others as *subjugated* voices, but rather to listen and participate . . . in a process that facilitates the development in people as a sense of themselves as agentic and of having an authoritative voice. . . . An indigenous Kaupapa Māori approach to research . . . challenges colonial and neo-colonial discourses that inscribe "otherness." (Bishop, 1998, pp. 207–208)

This participatory mode of knowing privileges sharing, subjectivity, personal knowledge, and the specialized knowledges of oppressed groups. It uses concrete experience as a criterion for meaning and truth. It encourages a participatory mode of consciousness (Bishop, 1998, p. 205), asking that the researcher give the group a gift as a way of honoring the group's sacred spaces. If the group picks up the gift, then a shared reciprocal relationship can be created (Bishop, 1998, p. 207). The relationship that follows is built on understandings involving shared Māori beliefs and cultural practices.

In turn, research is evaluated by Māori-based criteria. Like Freire's revolutionary pedagogy, West's (1993) prophetic pragmatism, and Collins's (1991) Afrocentic feminist moral ethic, the Māori value dialogue as a method for assessing knowledge claims. The Māori moral position also privileges storytelling, listening, voice, and personal performance narratives (see also Collins, 1991, pp. 208–212). This moral pedagogy rests on an ethic of care and love and personal accountability that honors individual uniqueness and emotionality in dialogue (Collins, 1991, pp. 215–217). This is a performative, pedagogical ethic, grounded in the ritual, sacred spaces of family, community, and everyday moral life (Bishop, 1998, p. 203). It is not imposed by some external, bureaucratic agency. This view of knowing parallels the commitment within certain forms of Red pedagogy to the performative as a way of being, as a way of knowing, as a way of expressing moral and spiritual ties to the community (Grande, 2000, p. 356; Graveline, 2000, p. 361).

Moral Codes and the Performative as a Site of Resistance

Because it expresses and embodies moral ties to the community, the performative view of meaning serves to legitimate indigenous worldviews. Meaning and resistance are embodied in the act of performance itself. The performative is where the soul of the culture resides. In their sacred and secular performances, the members of the culture honor one another and the culture itself.

A new set of moral and ethical research protocols is required. Fitted to the indigenous (and nonindigenous) perspective, these are moral matters. They are shaped by the feminist, communitarian principles of sharing, reciprocity, relationality, community, and neighborliness (Lincoln, 1995, p. 287). They embody a dialogic ethic of love and faith grounded in compassion (Bracci & Christians, 2002, p. 13; West, 1993). Accordingly, the purpose of research is not the production of new knowledge per se. Rather, the purposes are pedagogical, political, moral, and ethical, involving the enhancement of moral agency, the production of moral discernment, a commitment to praxis, justice, an ethic of resistance, and a performative pedagogy that resists oppression (Christians, 2002, p. 409).

A code embodying these principles interrupts the practice of positivist research, resists the idea of research being something that White men do to indigenous peoples. Furthermore, unlike in the United States, where an institutional review board (IRB) model of inquiry is used that is not content driven, indigenous codes are anchored in a culture and its way of life. Unlike the IRB mode, it connects its moral model to a set of political and ethical actions that will increase well-being in indigenous culture. The code refuses to define indigenous peoples as subjects who have been turned into the natural objects of White inquiry. Indigenous codes reject the Western utilitarian model of the individual as someone who has rights distinct from the rights of the larger group, "for example the right of an individual to give his or her own knowledge, or the right to give informed consent . . . community and indigenous rights or views in this area are generally not . . . respected" (L. T. Smith, 1999, p. 118). Individual Māori do not have these rights.

Research ethics for Māori and other indigenous communities "extend far beyond issues of individual consent and confidentiality" (L. T. Smith, 2000, p. 241). These ethics are not "prescribed in codes of conduct for researchers but tend to be prescribed for Māori researchers in cultural terms" (L. T. Smith, 2000, p. 242). These terms ask that researchers show respect for the Māori by exhibiting a willingness to listen, to be humble, to be cautious, to increase knowledge, to not "trample over the *mana* of people" (L. T. Smith, 2000, p. 242).

Conclusion: Turning the Tables on the Colonizers

Here at the end, it is possible to imagine scenarios that turn the tables on the neocolonizer. It is possible to imagine, for example, human subject research practices that really do respect human rights, protocols of informed consent that inform and do not deceive, research projects that do not harm, and projects that in fact benefit human communities.

Indigenous ethical and moral models call into question the more generic, utilitarian, biomedical, Western model of ethical inquiry (see Bracci & Christians, 2002; Christians, 2000, 2002). They outline a radical ethical path for the future. They transcend IRB principles that focus almost exclusively on the problems associated with betrayal, deception, and harm. They call for a collaborative social science research model that makes the researcher responsible, not to a removed discipline (or institution) but rather to those studied. This model stresses personal accountability, caring, the value of individual expressiveness, the capacity for empathy, and the sharing of emotionality (Collins, 1991, p. 216). This model implements collaborative, participatory performative inquiry. It forcefully aligns the ethics of research with a politics of the oppressed, with a politics of resistance, hope, and freedom.

This model directs scholars to take up moral projects that respect and reclaim indigenous cultural practices. Such work produces spiritual, social, and psychological healing. Healing, in turn, leads to multiple forms of transformation at the personal and social levels. These transformations shape processes of mobilization and collective action. These actions help persons realize a radical performative politics of possibility. This politics enacts emancipatory discourses and critical pedagogies that honor human difference and draw for inspiration on the struggles of indigenous persons. In listening to the stories of indigenous storytellers, we learn new ways of being moral and political in the social world. We come together in a shared agenda, with a shared imagination and a new language, struggling together to find liberating ways of interpreting and performing in the world (L. T. Smith, 1999, p. 37). In this way, does *research* cease to be a dirty word?

Notes

1. The list of names is long. It is nearly impossible to be complete. In addition to the indigenous authors in this handbook, see Bishop (2005, p. 111), L. T. Smith (2005, pp. 103–107), Ladson-Billings and Donnor (Chapter 4, this volume), and Battiste (2000a, 200b).

2. For a concise overview of the Campbell and Cochrane models, see Mosteller and Boruch (2002).

3. Jameson (1991, pp. 3–4) reminds us that any periodization hypothesis is always suspect, even those that reject linear, stage-like models. It is never clear what reality a stage refers to. What divides one stage from another is always debatable. Our eight moments are meant to mark discernible shifts in style, genre, epistemology, ethics, politics, and aesthetics.

4. See Denzin and Lincoln (2005, pp. 2–3, 13–20, for an extended discussion of these moments). This model has been termed a "progress narrative" by Alasuutari (2004, pp. 599–600) and Seale, Gobo, Gubrium, and Silverman (2004, p. 2). The critics assert that we believe that the most recent moment is the most up-to-date, the avant-garde, the cutting edge (Alasuutari, 2004, p. 601). Naturally, we dispute this reading. Tashakkori and Teddlie (2003, pp. 5–8) have modified our historical periods to fit their historical analysis of the major moments in the emergence of mixed methods in the past century.

5. This theater often uses verbatim accounts of injustice and violence in daily life. See Mienczakowski (1995, p. 5; see also Chessman, 1971) for a history of "verbatim theater" and Mienczakowski's extensions of this approach, using oral history, participant observation, and the methods of ethnodrama. A contemporary use of verbatim theater is the play *Guantanamo: Honor Bound to Defend Freedom* (Riding, 2004). This anti-Iraq war play addresses the plight of British citizens imprisoned at Guantanamo. The "power of Guantanamo is that it is not really a play but a re-enactment of views expressed in interviews, letters, news conferences, and speeches by various players in the post-Sept 11 Iraq war drama, from British Muslim detainees, to lawyers, from U.S. Defense Secretary Donald H. Rumsfield, to Jack Straw, Britain's foreign secretary" (Riding, 2004, p. B2). Nicolas Kent, the play's director, says he believes "political theater works here because the British have an innate sense of justice. When we do stories about injustice . . . there is a groundswell of sympathy . . . people are furious that there isn't due process. With Islamophobia growing around the world I wanted to show that we, too, think there is an injustice" (Riding, 2004, p. B2).

6. W. E. B. Du Bois (1901/1978) reminds us that "the problem of the twenty-first century, on a global scale, will be the problem of the color line . . . modern democracy cannot succeed unless peoples of different races and religions are also integrated into the democratic whole" (pp. 281, 288). This democratic whole cannot be imposed by one culture or nation on another; it must come from within the culture itself.

7. At another level, indigenous participatory theater extends the project connected to Third World popular theater. This is political "theatre used by oppressed Third World people to achieve justice and development for themselves" (Etherton, 1988, p. 991). The International Popular Theatre Alliance, organized in the 1980s, uses existing forms of cultural expression to fashion improvised dramatic productions that analyze situations of poverty and oppression. This grassroots approach uses agit-prop and sloganizing theater (theater pieces devised to foment political action) to create collective awareness and collective action at the local level. This form of theater has been popular in Latin America, Africa, parts of Asia, India, and among Native populations in the Americas (Etherton, 1988, p. 992).

8. Other projects involve a focus on testimonies, new forms of storytelling, returning to, as well as reframing and regendering, key cultural debates.

9. Cast in this form, the critical personal narrative counters the criticisms that it is inherently conservative because it romanticizes marginality, ignores issues of political economy, and engages in simplistic, chauvinistic essentialisms (see Darder & Torres, 2004, pp. 103–104).

References

Alasuutari, P. (2004). The globalization of qualitative research. In C. Seale, G. Gobo, J. F. Gubrium, & D. Silverman (Eds.), *Qualitative research practice.* London: Sage.

Anzaldúa, G. (1987). *Borderlands/la frontera: The new mestiza.* San Francisco: Spinsters/Aunt Lute.

Balme, C., & Carstensen, A. (2001). Home fires: Creating a Pacific theatre in the diaspora. *Theatre Research International, 26*(1), 35–46.

Battiste, M. (2000a). Introduction: Unfolding lessons of colonization. In M. Battiste (Ed.), *Reclaiming indigenous voice and vision* (pp. xvi–xxx). Vancouver: UBC Press.

Battiste, M. (2000b). Maintaining aboriginal identity: Language and culture in modern society. In M. Battiste (Ed.), *Reclaiming indigenous voice and vision* (pp. 192–208). Vancouver: UBC Press.

Battiste, M. (2006, May 4). *The global challenge: Research ethics for protecting indigenous knowledge and heritage.* Keynote address presented at the Second

International Congress of Qualitative Inquiry, University of Illinois, Urbana-Champaign.

Bishop, R. (1994). Initiating empowering research. *New Zealand Journal of Educational Studies, 29*(1), 175–188.

Bishop, R. (1998). Freeing ourselves from neo-colonial domination in research: A Māori approach to creating knowledge. *International Journal of Qualitative Studies in Education, 11,* 199–219.

Bishop, R. (2005). Freeing ourselves from neo-colonial domination in research: A Kaupapa Māori approach to creating knowledge. In N. K. Denzin & Y. S. Lincoln (Eds.), *The SAGE handbook of qualitative research* (3rd ed., pp. 109–138). Thousand Oaks, CA: Sage.

Boal, A. (1979). *Theatre of the oppressed.* New York: Urizen Books. (Originally published in Spanish in 1974)

Boal, A. (1995). *The rainbow of desire: The Boal method of theatre and therapy.* London: Routledge.

Boal, A. (1998). *Legislative theatre.* London: Routledge.

Bracci, S. L., & Christians, C. G. (2002). Editors' introduction. In S. L. Bracci & C.G. Christians (Eds.), *Moral engagement in public life: Theorists for contemporary ethics* (pp. 1–15). New York: Peter Lang.

Cheek, J. (2006). The challenge of tailor-made research quality: The RQF in Australia. In N. K. Denzin & M. D. Giardina (Eds.), *Qualitative inquiry and the conservative challenge: Confronting methodological fundamentalism* (pp. 109–126). Walnut Creek, CA: Left Coast Press.

Christians, C. (2000). Ethics and politics in qualitative research. In N. K. Denzin & Y. S. Lincoln (Eds.), *The SAGE handbook of qualitative research* (2nd ed., pp. 133–155). Thousand Oaks, CA: Sage.

Christians, C. (2002). Introduction. *Qualitative Inquiry, 8,* 407–410.

Churchill, W. (1996). I am an indigenist: Notes on the ideology of the Fourth World. In W. Churchill (Ed.), *From a native son: Selected essays in indigenism, 1985–1995* (pp. 509–546). Boston: South End.

Collins, P. H. (1991). *Black feminist thought.* New York: Routledge.

Collins, P. H. (1998). *Fighting words: Black women and the search for justice.* Minneapolis: University of Minnesota Press.

Conquergood, D. (1998). Beyond the text: Toward a performative cultural politics. In S. J. Dailey (Ed.), *The future of performance studies: Visions and revisions* (pp. 25–36). Annadale, VA: National Communication Association.

Cook-Lynn, E. (1998). American Indian intellectualism and the new Indian story. In D. A. Mihesuah (Ed.), *Natives and academics: Researching and writing about American Indians* (pp. 111–138). Lincoln: University of Nebraska Press.

Cook-Lynn, E. (2001). *Anti-Indianism in modern America: A voice from Tatekeya's Earth.* Urbana: University of Illinois Press.

Darder, A. (2002). *Reinventing Paulo Freire: A pedagogy of love.* Boulder, CO: Westview.

Darder, A., Baltodano, M., & Torres, R. D. (Eds.). (2003). *The critical pedagogy reader.* New York: Routledge.

Darder, A., & Mirón, L. F. (2006). Critical pedagogy in a time of uncertainty: A call to action. In N. K. Denzin & M. D. Giardina (Eds.), *Contesting empire/globalizing dissent: Cultural studies after 9/11* (pp. 136–151). Boulder, CO: Paradigm.

Darder, A., & Torres, R. D. (2004). *After race: Racism after multiculturalism.* New York: New York University Press.

Denzin, N. K. (2003). *Performance ethnography: Critical pedagogy and the politics of culture.* Thousand Oaks, CA: Sage.

Denzin, N. K., & Lincoln, Y. S. (2005). Introduction: The discipline and practice of qualitative research. In N. K. Denzin & Y. S. Lincoln (Eds.), *The SAGE handbook of qualitative research* (3rd ed., pp. 1–32). Thousand Oaks, CA: Sage.

Du Bois, W. (1978). The problem of the twentieth century is the problem of the color line. In *On sociology and the Black community* (D. S. Green & E. Driver, Eds., pp. 281–289). Chicago: University of Chicago Press. (Original work published 1901)

Ellsworth, E. (1989). Why doesn't this feel empowering? Working through the repressive myths of critical methodology. *Harvard Education Review, 59*(4), 297–324.

Etherton, M. (1988). Third World popular theatre. In M. Banham (Ed.), *The Cambridge guide to theatre* (pp. 991–992). Cambridge, UK: Cambridge University Press.

Fine, M., Torre, M. E., Boudin, K., Bowen, I., Clark, J., Hylton, D., et al. (2003). Participatory action research: From within and beyond prison bars. In P. M. Camic, J. E. Rhodes, & L. Yardley (Eds.), *Qualitative research in psychology: Expanding perspectives in methodology and design* (pp. 173–198). Washington, DC: American Psychological Association.

Fishman, G. E., & McLaren, P. (2005). Rethinking critical pedagogy and the Gramscian legacy: From organic to committed intellectuals. *Cultural Studies <=> Critical Methodologies, 6*(1), 33–52.

Freire, P. (1998). *Pedagogy of freedom: Ethics, democracy, and civic courage* (P. Clarke, Trans.). Boulder, CO: Rowman & Littlefield.

Freire, P. (1999). *Pedagogy of hope.* New York: Continuum. (Original work published 1992)

Freire, P. (2000). *Pedagogy of the oppressed* (30th anniversary ed., with an introduction by Donaldo Macedo). New York: Continuum.

Freire, P., & Faundez, A. (1989). *Learning to question: A pedagogy of liberation.* New York: Continuum.

Gilbert, H. (2003). Black and white and re(a)d all over again: Indigenous minstrelsy in contemporary Canadian and Australian theatre. *Theatre Journal, 55,* 679–698.

Giroux, H., & Giroux, S. S. (2005). Challenging neoliberalism's new world order: The promise of critical pedagogy. *Cultural Studies <=> Critical Methodologies, 6*(1), 21–32.

Goffman, E. (1959). *The presentation of self in everyday life.* New York: Doubleday.

Grande, S. (2000). American Indian identity and intellectualism: The quest for a new Red pedagogy. *Qualitative Studies in Education, 13,* 343–360.

Grande, S. (2004). *Red pedagogy: Native American social and political thought.* Lanham, MD: Rowman & Littlefield.

Graveline, F. J. (2000). Circle as methodology: Enacting an aboriginal paradigm. *International Journal of Qualitative Studies in Education, 13,* 361–370.

Greenwood, J. (2001). Within a third space. *Research in Drama Education, 6,* 193–205.

Harjo, Joy, & Bird, G. (1997). Introduction. In J. Harjo & G. Bird (Eds.), *Reinventing the enemy's language: Contemporary Native women's writings of North America* (pp. 19–31). New York: W. W. Norton.

Henderson, J. Y. (2000). Postcolonial ledger drawing: Legal reform. In M. Battiste (Ed.), *Reclaiming indigenous voice and vision* (pp. 161–170). Vancouver: UBC Press.

Heshusius, L. (1994). Freeing ourselves from objectivity: Managing subjectivity or turning toward a participatory mode of consciousness. *Educational Researcher, 23*(3), 15–22.

hooks, b. (1994). *Teaching to transgress: Education as the practice of freedom.* New York: Routledge.

House, E. R. (2006). Methodological fundamentalism and the quest for control(s). In N. K. Denzin & M. D. Giardina (Eds.), *Qualitative inquiry and the conservative challenge: Confronting methodological fundamentalism* (pp. 93–108). Walnut Creek, CA: Left Coast Press.

Jameson, F. (1991). *Postmodernism; or, The cultural logic of late capitalism.* Durham, NC: Duke University Press.

Kaomea, J. (2004). Dilemmas of an indigenous academic: A Native Hawaiian story. In K. Mutua & B. B. Swadener (Eds.), *Decolonizing research in cross-cultural contexts: Critical personal narratives* (pp. 27–44). Albany, NY: SUNY Press.

Kincheloe, J. L. (2005). *Critical pedagogy primer.* New York: Peter Lang.

Kincheloe, J. L., & McLaren, P. (2000). Rethinking critical theory and qualitative research. In N. K. Denzin & Y. S. Lincoln (Eds.), *The SAGE handbook of qualitative research* (2nd ed., pp. 279–314). Thousand Oaks, CA: Sage.

Kincheloe, J. L., & McLaren, P. (2005). Rethinking critical theory and qualitative research. In N. K. Denzin & Y. S. Lincoln (Eds.), *The SAGE handbook of qualitative research* (3rd ed., pp. 303–342). Thousand Oaks, CA: Sage.

Kondo, D. (2000). (Re) visions of race: Contemporary race theory and the cultural politics of racial crossover in documentary theatre. *Theatre Journal, 52,* 81–107.

Ladson-Billings, G., & Donnor, J. (2005). The moral activist role of critical race theory scholarship. In N. K. Denzin & Y. S. Lincoln (Eds.), *The SAGE handbook of qualitative research* (3rd ed., pp. 279–302). Thousand Oaks, CA: Sage.

Lather, P. (1991). *Getting smart: Feminist research and pedagogy within the postmodern.* New York: Routledge.

Lather, P. (1998). Critical pedagogy and its complicities: A praxis of stuck places. *Educational Theory, 48,* 487–497.

Lather, P. (2007). *Getting lost: Feminist efforts toward a double (d) science.* Albany, NY: SUNY Press.

Lincoln, Y. S. (1995). Emerging criteria for quality in qualitative and interpretive inquiry. *Qualitative Inquiry, 1,* 275–289.

Lincoln, Y. S., & Cannella, G. S. (2004a). Dangerous discourses, methodological conservatism and governmental regimes of truth. *Qualitative Inquiry, 10*(1), 5–14.

Lincoln, Y. S., & Cannella, G. S. (2004b). Qualitative research, power, and the radical right. *Qualitative Inquiry, 10*(2), 175–201.

Lopez, G. R. (1998). Reflections on epistemology and standpoint theories: A response to "A Māori approach to creating knowledge." *International Journal of Qualitative Studies in Education, 11,* 225–231.

Luke, C., & Gore, J. (1992). Introduction. In C. Luke & J. Gore (Eds.), *Feminisms and critical pedagogy* (pp. 1–14). New York: Routledge.

Madison, D. S. (1998). Performances, personal narratives, and the politics of possibility. In S. J. Dailey (Ed.), *The future of performance studies: Visions and revisions* (pp. 276–286). Annadale, VA: National Communication Association.

McLaren, P. (1999). *Schooling as ritual performance* (3rd ed.). Lanham, MD: Rowman & Littlefield.

Mead, G. H. (1938). *The philosophy of the act.* Chicago: University of Chicago Press.

Menchú, R. (1984). *I, Rigoberta Menchú: An Indian woman in Guatemala* (A. Wright, Trans.). London: Verso.

Meyer, M. A. (2003). *Ho'oulu: Our time of becoming: Hawaiian epistemology and early writings.* Honolulu, HI: 'Ai Pohaku Press Native Books.

Mienczakowski, J. (1995). The theater of ethnography: The reconstruction of ethnography into theater with emancipatory potential. *Qualitative Inquiry, 1,* 360–375.

Mills, C. W. (1959). *The sociological imagination.* New York: Oxford University Press.

Moraga, C. (1995). *The last generation.* Boston: South End.

Mosteller, F., & Boruch, R. (Eds.). (2002). *Evidence matters: Randomized trials in education research.* Washington, DC: Brookings Institution.

Mutua, K., & Swadener, B. B. (2004). Introduction. In K. Mutua & B. B. Swadener (Eds.), *Decolonizing research in cross-cultural contexts: Critical personal narratives* (pp. 1–23). Albany, NY: SUNY Press.

Pelias, R. J. (2004). *A methodology of the heart.* Walnut Creek, CA: AltaMira Press.

Pollock, D. (1998). A response to Dwight Conquergood's essay: "Beyond the text: Towards a performative cultural politics." In S. J. Dailey (Ed.), *The future of performance studies: Visions and revisions* (pp. 37–46). Annadale, VA: National Communication Association.

Pring, R. (2004). Conclusion: Evidence-based policy and practice. In G. Thomas & R. Pring (Eds.), *Evidence-based practice in education* (pp. 201–212). Berkshire, England: Open University Press.

Richardson, L. (2000). Writing: A method of inquiry. In N. K. Denzin & Y. S. Lincoln (Eds.), *The SAGE handbook of qualitative research* (2nd ed., pp. 923–948). Thousand Oaks, CA: Sage.

Riding, A. (2004, June 15). On a London stage, a hearing for Guantanamo detainees. *New York Times,* p. B2.

Sandoval, C. (2000). *Methodology of the oppressed: Theory out of bounds.* Minneapolis: University of Minnesota Press.

Seale, C., Gobo, G., Gubrium, J. F., & Silverman, D. (Eds.). (2004). *Qualitative research practice.* London: Sage.

Semali, L. M., & Kincheloe, J. L. (1999). Introduction: What is indigenous knowledge and why should we study it? In L. M. Semali & J. L. Kincheloe (Eds.), *What is indigenous knowledge? Voices from the academy* (pp. 3–57). New York: Falmer.

Smith, A. D. (2003). *House arrest and piano.* New York: Anchor.

Smith, G. (2000). Protecting and respecting indigenous knowledge. In M. Battiste (Ed.), *Reclaiming indigenous voice and vision* (pp. 209–224). Vancouver: UBC Press.

Smith, L. T. (1999). *Decolonizing methodologies: Research and indigenous peoples.* Dunedin, New Zealand: University of Otago Press.

Smith, L. T. (2000). Kaupapa Māori research. In M. Battiste (Ed.), *Reclaiming indigenous voice and vision* (pp. 225–247). Vancouver: UBC Press.

Smith, L. T. (2005). On tricky ground: Researching the Native in the age of uncertainty. In N. K. Denzin & Y. S. Lincoln (Eds.), *The SAGE handbook of qualitative research* (3rd ed., pp. 85–108). Thousand Oaks, CA: Sage.

Smith, L. T. (2006). Choosing the margins: The role of research in indigenous struggles for social justice. In N. K. Denzin & M. D. Giardina (Eds.), *Qualitative inquiry and the conservative challenge: Confronting methodological fundamentalism* (pp. 151–174). Walnut Creek, CA: Left Coast Press.

St. Pierre, E. A. (2004). Refusing alternatives: A science of contestation. *Qualitative Inquiry, 10*(1), 130–139.

St. Pierre, E., & Pillow, W. (Eds.). (2000). *Working the ruins: Feminist poststructural practice and theory in education.* New York: Routledge.

Steinberg, S. (2007). Preface: Where are we now? In P. McClaren & J. L. Kincheloe (Eds.), *Critical pedagogy: Where are we now?* (pp. ix–x). New York: Peter Lang.

Tashakkori, A., & Teddlie, C. (Eds.). (2003). *Handbook of mixed methods in social and behavioral research.* Thousand Oaks, CA: Sage.

Thomas, G. (2004). Introduction: Evidence and practice. In G. Thomas & R. Pring (Eds.), *Evidence-based practice in education* (pp. 21–33). Berkshire, England: Open University Press.

Torrance, H. (2006). Research quality and research governance in the United Kingdom: From methodology to management. In N. K. Denzin & M. D. Giardina (Eds.), *Qualitative inquiry and the conservative challenge: Confronting methodological fundamentalism* (pp. 127–148). Walnut Creek, CA: Left Coast Press.

West, C. (1993). *Keeping the faith: Philosophy and race in America.* New York: Routledge.

Williams, T. T. (1984). *Pieces of white shell: A journey to Navajoland.* Albuquerque: University of New Mexico Press.

Part I

LOCATING THE FIELD

Performing Theories of Decolonizing Inquiry

- Chapter 2: Decolonizing Performances: Deconstructing the Global Postcolonial
- Chapter 3: Feminisms From Unthought Locations: Indigenous Worldviews, Marginalized Feminisms, and Revisioning an Anticolonial Social Science
- Chapter 4: Waiting for the Call: The Moral Activist Role of Critical Race Theory Scholarship
- Chapter 5: Critical Race Theory and Indigenous Methodologies
- Chapter 6: Queer(y)ing the Postcolonial Through the West(ern)
- Chapter 7: Indigenous Knowledges in Education: Complexities, Dangers, and Profound Benefits
- Chapter 8: Do You Believe in Geneva? Methods and Ethics at the Global-Local Nexus
- Chapter 9: Challenging Neoliberalism's New World Order: The Promise of Critical Pedagogy
- Chapter 10: Rethinking Critical Pedagogy: *Socialismo Nepantla* and the Specter of Che

Part I of the *Handbook* begins with the suggested reform and decolonization of the academy through critical research. The nine chapters in Part I take up multiple paradigmatic and theoretical formations, including those connected to postcolonial theory; feminist, critical race, and queer theory; participatory action research; and critical pedagogy. We choose to interpret these presentations of theory as if they were performances—disruptive, unruly attempts to decolonize and indigenize research in the academy. These decolonizing performances contest and challenge the complicity of many modern universities possessed of neoconservative, neocolonial belief systems.

These theoretical performances document the ways in which decolonization is a reaction to the dark side of neocolonialism. It is impossible to escape the colonial formations of the past. They are always with us—in social conservatism, as evidenced in postpositivist epistemologies; in cultural imperialism; in vestiges of patriarchy and racism; and in the demand for standardization and accountability in the educational arena.

The chapters in Part I (indeed, this entire handbook) are haunted by the neocolonial. Of course, as we noted in the Preface, there is no postcolonial, only endless variations on the present (and the past). All efforts at decolonization swim upstream against these ever present forces.

Decolonizing Performances

For Swadener and Mutua, decolonization is about the process, in both research and performance, of valuing, reclaiming, and foregrounding indigenous voices and epistemologies. Their emphasis on the performative and on critical personal narratives opens a space for cross-cultural partnerships between and among indigenous researchers and allied others. They explore and deconstruct related critical themes, including the notions of "insider" and "outsider,"[1] and native versus postcolonial intellectual. They borrow Linda Smith's distinction between methodology as a *theory of research* and a research method as a technique or way of gathering empirical materials. Indigenous methodology thus is defined as a theory of inquiry. Indigenous methods—including poetry, drama, storytelling, and critical personal narratives—are performative practices that represent and make indigenous life visible.

Elaborating these distinctions, we can argue that decolonizing (and postcolonial) theory represents one version of a critical theory paradigm.[2] All paradigms encompass four terms: ethics, epistemology, ontology, and methodology. *Decolonizing ethics* ask, "What does it mean to be a moral person in an indigenous, decolonized world?" *Decolonizing epistemology* asks, "How do we, in a decolonizing framework, know the world? What is the relationship between inquirer and the known?" Every epistemology implies an ethical, moral stance between the world and the self of the researcher. *Decolonizing ontology* raises basic questions about the nature of reality and the nature of the human being in the world. *Decolonizing methodology* focuses on the best means of acquiring and interpreting knowledge about the world.

Lincoln and Guba (2000; see also Guba & Lincoln, 2005) suggest that in the present moment, all paradigms must confront seven basic, critical issues. These issues involve axiology (ethics and values), accommodation and commensurability (whether paradigms can be fitted into one another), action (what the researcher does in the world), control (who initiates inquiry, who asks questions), foundations of truth (foundationalism vs. anti- and nonfoundationalism), validity (traditional positivist models vs. poststructural-constructionist criteria), voice, reflexivity, and postmodern representation (single vs. multivoiced).

Critical, indigenous, decolonizing theory articulates an ontology based on historical realism, an epistemology that is transactional and a methodology that is performative, dialogic, and dialectical. It values ethical systems embedded in indigenous values. It transfers control to the indigenous community. It uses spiritual models of truth and validity and values multivoiced, performative forms of textuality.

Swadener and Mutua elaborate further the decolonizing paradigm. In so doing, they reflect on their own research careers. This allows them to offer personal guidelines for decolonizing inquiry. Such work should be owned by, and done for, indigenous persons. It should be evaluated in terms of indigenous, not Western, epistemological and political criteria. It should avoid simplistic dichotomies and either/or binaries. It should foreground indigenous narratives and traditions. It should showcase the many ways in which indigenous and critical postcolonial scholars are part of a "cacophony of subaltern voices." So conceived, decolonizing methodologies embody "activist agendas working toward social justice, sovereignty, self-determination, and emancipatory goals."

▣ Feminisms From Unthought Locations

Cannella and Manuelito observe that critical, feminist qualitative research, at the dawn of this new century, is a highly diversified and contested site. Under the current conservative backlash, which is global, all forms of feminism—from critical to poststructural, postmodern, standpoint, borderland, Mestizaje, Chicana, Afro-feminist, White, Native, and womanist—have been marginalized. Already we see multiple articulations of gender and its enactment in post-9/11 spaces. Competing models of feminism on a global scale—indigenous, nonindigenous, First World, Third World—blur together. But beneath the fray and the debate, there is agreement that feminist inquiry, like critical theory, is committed to action in the world in the new millennium (Olesen, 2005, p. 235). Feminists insist that a social justice agenda should address the needs of men and women of color because gender, class, and race are intimately interconnected. Cannella and Manuelito's is an impassioned feminism. For them, as for Olesen (2005, p. 236), "Rage is not enough."

Writing from their own life spaces, Cannella and Manuelito seek to form an alliance of feminist, Native, and womanist worldviews. They seek a reinvisioning of native feminist worldviews, a reinvisioning that will challenge and unsettle the repressive structures of hypercapitalist patriarchy. Their anticolonial text intertwines the voices of a Euro-American mixed-race White feminist (Cannella) and a Diné (Navajo) female (Manuelito) who is a member of four clans. (Manuelito's voice and story are privileged.)

In 2005, Olesen identified three major strands of feminist inquiry (standpoint epistemology, empiricist, postmodernism-cultural studies). These strands continue to multiply. There are today separate feminisms associated with specific disciplines: the writings of women of color, women problematizing Whiteness, postcolonial discourse, decolonizing arguments of indigenous women, lesbian research and queer theory, disabled women, standpoint theory, and postmodern and deconstructive theory. This complexity has made the researcher-participant relationship more complicated. It has destablized the insider-outsider model of inquiry. Within indigenous spaces, it has produced a call for the decolonization of the academy. This is linked to a deconstruction of such traditional terms as *experience, difference,* and *gender.*

A feminist decolonizing discourse focuses on the concepts of ethics, voice, and empowerment. Cannella and Manuelito's masterful chapter rethinks the grounds for critical inquiry, unsettling traditional positivist notions of research goals, empirical materials, and the contexts of inquiry. They privilege the concept of Native transformative egalitarianism. Drawn from an indigenous feminism, this concept emphasizes Native epistemologies and Native spirituality, as well as ways of being with and caring for one another that are egalitarian and life affirming. They ground this concept in the Diné way of life and the relationship of Changing Woman to her children, a woman-oriented egalitarianism. This model of Native womanism is then extended to ecofeminism, a feminist-based environmentalism, an ecofeminist ethic of care, and social activism.

Cannella and Manuelitos rightfully note that in these ways Native epistemologies and marginalized feminisms can serve as foundational for the construction of an anticolonial, egalitarian social science. An anticolonial social science would no longer assume that humans have the right to judge other minds or cultures. It would challenge oppressive social institutions, support transformative systems of knowing, and engage in activist, participatory models of research.

Moral Activism and Critical Race Theory Scholarship

Gloria Ladson-Billings and Jamel Donnor move critical race theory directly into the fields of politics and indigenous inquiry. They advocate an activist, moral, and ethical epistemology committed to social justice and a revolutionary habitus. They focus their analysis on the meaning of the "call," those epiphanic moments when persons of color are reminded that they are locked into a hierarchical racial structure. The "N-word" can be invoked at any time to hail a person of color. Racialized others occupy the liminal space of alterity in White society; they are forced to play the role of alter ego to the ideal self prescribed by the dominant cultural model. Critical race theory (CRT) "seeks to decloak the seemingly race-neutral, and color-blind ways . . . of constructing and administering race-based appraisals . . . of the law, administrative policy, electoral politics . . . political discourse [and education] in the USA" (Parker, Deyhle, Villenas, & Nebeker, 1998, p. 5). Critical race theory uses multiple interpretive methodologies and representations—stories, plays, and performance, as well as more traditional empirical qualitative research. Critical race theory enacts an ethnic and ethical epistemology, arguing that ways of knowing and being are shaped by one's standpoint or position in the world. This standpoint undoes the cultural, ethical, and epistemological logic (and racism) of the Eurocentric, Enlightenment paradigm. At the same time, it contests positivism's hegemonic control over what is and what is not acceptable research. Thus, they also criticize the National Research Council's *Scientific Research in Education* report (National Research Council, 2002).

Drawing on recent work by African American, Asian Pacific Islander, Asian American, Latino, and Native American scholars, Ladson-Billings and Donnor introduce the concepts of multiple or doubled consciousness, *mestiza* consciousness, and tribal secrets. The analysis of these terms allows them to show how the dominant cultural paradigms have produced fractured, racialized identities and experiences of exclusion for minority scholars. American society, they observe, has been constructed as a nation of White people whose politics and culture are designed to serve the interests of Whites. Critical race theorists experiment with multiple interpretive strategies, including storytelling, autoethnography, case studies, textual and narrative analyses, traditional fieldwork, and, most important, collaborative, action-based inquiries and studies of race, gender, law, education, and racial oppression in daily life.

Using the construct of "political race," they call for street-level, cross-racial coalitions and alliances involving grassroots workers seeking to invigorate democracy. Connections with the hip-hop generation are central to this project. Political race enlarges the critical race project. It is not color blind. It proposes multitextured political strategies that go beyond traditional legal economic solutions to issues of racial justice. Ladson-Billings and Donnor show, drawing from Hill Collins, how "political" race embodies a nonviolent visionary pragmatism that is "actualized in the hearts and minds of ordinary people." For this to happen, the academy must change; it must embrace the principles of decolonization. A reconstructed university will become a home for racialized others, a place where indigenous, liberating empowering pedagogies have become commonplace. In such a place, Ladson-Billings and Donnor argue, a new version of *the* call will be answered to.

Critical Race Theory and Indigenous Methodologies

Drawing on his own experiences with racism in American society, Dunbar extends the above argument. His personal experience narratives show how race prejudice, hate, and de facto segregation continue to have a profound impact on indigenous research, including the belief that legitimate research on race matters should be done by White scholars. There is a mystique about Negro scholarship, just as there is about Negro spirituals—that is, only a person with a black skin can sing them. In turn, scholarship done by Blacks on or about Blacks is not scholarship but is folklore; it is not science, it is not objective, and it should not be taken seriously. This injunction, which this handbook rejects, has been applied across the board to indigenous and racialized scholarship.

Probing the underside of CRT and its criticisms from LatCrit theory, Dunbar insists that race cannot be moved from the center of analysis and replaced with considerations of class. Such a move fails to address the multiple injustices that have occurred daily in the lives of persons of color and indigenous people. With other indigenous scholars, Dunbar explores the need for alternative indigenous research methodologies. This means scholars of color have the freedom to design, define, organize, and evaluate indigenous research.

Dunbar and Ladson-Billings and Donnor clearly and persuasively establish the relevance of CRT for critical indigenous pedagogy and methodology. This suggests the need for greater dialogue between the proponents of these multiple discourses.

Queering the Postcolonial

Critical race theory brought race and the concept of a complex racial subject squarely into qualitative inquiry. It remained for queer theory to do the same—namely, to question and deconstruct the concept of a unified sexual (and racialized) subject. Bryant Keith Alexander, in Chapter 6 (and Adams and Jones in Chapter 18, this volume), takes queer theory in new directions. Alexander writes from his own biography, a gay Black man, a poet writing out of the postcolonial, queering the postcolonial, formulating a critical interpretive queer methodology. The postcolonial perspective and queer theory are both grounded in Whiteness. Each is committed to rescuing the silenced other, even as traces of homophobia linger in certain versions of postcolonial theory.

Indigenous theories must be located in and alongside, even as they critique theories of, the postcolonial, asking always what it means to ask, "Can the subaltern speak?" Who speaks for whom, how, and for whose benefit (Spivak, 1988)? Yet, too often, indigenous people speak on the fringes of postcolonial theory, understanding that the postcolonial is an imaginary space, for we are always in neocolonial discourses (see Cook-Lynn, Chapter 16, this volume). With the arrival of queer theory, so-called postcolonial theory enters a new space.

This is the age of neocolonial fragmentation, globalization, a time for new research styles, styles that take up the reflexive queer, polyphonic, narrative, ethical turn. Alexander's queer theory is radical. It is Black and transgressive; it deconstructs all conventional categories of sexuality and gender. It challenges the heterosexual-homosexual binary. His queer methodology takes the textual turn seriously and endorses subversive ethnographies, ethnographic performances, and queered case studies—for example, his extended interpretation of the 2005 film *Brokeback Mountain.* His reading of this so-called gay cowboy movie is not so much queer as it is an unmasking to the film. Alexander shows how an outwardly gay text is in fact propaganda for a heterosexual logic that perpetuates hatred and violence against gay men.

By troubling the place of the homosexual-heterosexual binary in everyday life, queer theory has created spaces for multiple discourses on gay, bisexual, transgendered, and lesbian subjects. This means researchers must examine how any social arena is structured, in part, by this homo-hetero dichotomy. They must ask how the epistemology of the closet is central to the sexual and material practices of everyday life. Queer theory challenges this epistemology, just as it deconstructs the notion of unified subjects. Queerness becomes a topic and a resource for investigating the way group boundaries are created, negotiated, and changed. Institutional and historical analyses are central to this project, for they shed light on how the self and its identities are embedded in institutional and cultural practices. Reading between the lines, a critical interpretive queer methodology moves always within and between those ideological, embodied spaces where bodies, desires, and sexualities intertwine.

▣ Indigenous Knowledges, Borderland Epistemologies

Kincheloe and Steinberg outline a critical theory, an evolving criticality for the new millennium, beginning with the assumption that the societies of the West are not unproblematically democratic and free. Their version of critical theory rejects economic determinism and focuses on the media, culture, language, power, desire, critical enlightenment, and critical emancipation. Critical theorists, as *bricoleurs,* seek to produce practical, pragmatic knowledge, a bricolage that is cultural and structural, judged by its degree of historical situatedness and its ability to produce praxis, or action.

In an effort to construct a critical standpoint epistemology, what they call *critical multilogicality,* Kincheloe and Steinberg explore the educational and epistemological value of indigenous knowledge. Humans need to encounter and learn to value multiple perspectives in all areas of their lives. A critical multilogicality values indigenous knowledge because indigenous knowledge has transformative power. It can be used to foster empowerment and social justice. It can be used to counter the destructive effects of Western science on the Earth. This appreciation of indigenous knowledge requires a reassessment of the traditional Western criteria for judging knowledge claims. An indigenous epistemology is antiessentialist, is contextual, and emphasizes self-determination, the sacred, the personal, community.

Critical indigenous pedagogy focuses attention on the ways knowledge is produced, legitimated, and taught. Critical pedagogy demands that the curriculum in our schools be grounded in and respectful of indigenous knowledge practices. Such curriculum works within the spaces of borderland epistemologies—different systems of knowing, knowledge production, and knowledge assessment. Kincheloe and Steinberg assert that these standpoint epistemologies and the knowledges they produce can be used to resist those oppressive structures that produce human suffering.

This chapter is a call to arms. Getting mad is no longer enough. We must learn how to act in the world in ways that allow us to expose the workings of an invisible empire that has given us yet another war and another economic agenda that leaves even more children behind.

Participatory Inquiry

Fine, Tuck, and Zeller-Berkman, in a wonderfully dialogic and self-reflexive chapter, invite a conversation at the global-local nexus. Their Global Rights project—Is There a Geneva?—implements multisited and place-based versions of participatory action research (PAR). In moving from youth chat groups in cyberspace to youth in local and global contexts, and back again, they caution nonindigenous scholars from attempting to appropriate the pain of oppressed persons. It is our pain, not yours, Marie Battiste reminds us. Still, a cartography of pain is required, with its markers of shame, destruction, abuse, self-doubt, drug and alcohol abuse, sexual violence, abuse in the kitchen, bruises on the soul.

Fine and her coauthors also remind us that colonization, in all its capitalist forms, is the primary relationship between the United States and oppressed persons. Their version of PAR travels over and around the territories of democracy and sovereignty. There can be no self-government, no democracy without sovereignty, no critical pedagogy without sovereignty. And of course the oppressors control sovereignty.

In the end, we are left with questions. Whose terms define the conversation, whose criteria? How do we move forward? What does it mean to move forward? What is meant by radical evidence? Who governs the work of proving what is truth? Whose ethics of care is embraced? Can we get beyond outrage? Can we understand how the notion of scientific generalizability functions as a form of domination?

The questions linger, and they are haunting. Are there only fading footprints in the snow? Is nothing certain? Where next? Whose footprints? Few answers. We must refuse closure. This is the road map we are offered by Fine, Tuck, and Zeller-Berkman. No guarantees, only hope.

The Promises of Critical Pedagogy

Giroux and Giroux locate the promise of critical pedagogy in neoliberalism's new world order. They believe that critical pedagogy faces a crisis of enormous proportions. It is a crisis grounded in the cultures of neoliberalism and globalization. These cultures, in the name of democracy, economic development, and social progress, perpetuate racism, sexism, inequality, and human suffering. Under a predatory crony-oriented capitalism, they implement conservative notions of social justice (Darder & Mirón, 2006, p. 16).

Elaborating and paraphrasing, Giroux and Giroux observe that this global crisis, which critical pedagogy must confront, is grounded in four commonsense beliefs. Education should be divorced from politics. Scientific research is objective and removed from politics. Politics should be removed from the demands of democracy, but the demands of neoliberal capitalism equal the demands of neoliberal democracy.

These understandings are myths that underpin the ideological foundations of neoliberalism. On this, critical pedagogy is clear. Teachers and researchers are cultural workers. They should be empowered to prepare students in emancipatory pedagogies. They should be shown how to engage in critical thought, including how to participate in democratic dialogue, understanding that it is criticism that is patriotic. They should be taught a faith in social amelioration, a belief that social justice is possible. They should be shown how to fight through these dark times that threaten to shut down democracy.

These views of critical pedagogy move directly into the spaces of indigenous peoples. Capitalism, under neoliberalism (with its executors, the International Monetary Fund and the World Bank), has reordered human societies on a global scale. Virtually no indigenous population is untouched. The increase in the efficiency of capitalist production and the accumulation of wealth has produced new forms of exploitation. The result has been "a new wave of massive immigration to the center of the empire. As a consequence, a revival of alarmist rhetoric and vicious attacks against immigrants has ensued, particularly against immigrants from Mexico, Latin America, and the Middle East" (Darder & Mirón, 2006, p. 15).

Giroux and Giroux model an emancipatory pedagogy. Cultural workers, researchers, and critical indigenous scholars believe that public education is a critical sphere for creating citizens equipped to exercise their freedoms and self-determination. These freedoms are grounded in indigenous cultural spaces and shaped by them. Critical indigenous scholars face the challenge of creating new discourses, new pedagogies, new ethics of love and care, new tools for liberation, tools of hope. Therein lies the promise of critical pedagogy in these new times.

Marxist Humanism

Marxist humanists Peter McLaren and Nathalia Jaramillo rethink critical pedagogy, also locating its discourses within this time of global crisis. They attend to the recent climate of anti-immigration and vigilante justice. Their critical pedagogy imagines a socialist society where class consciousness is replaced by a *napantla,* or borderland, indigenous pedagogy. In the 16th century, *las indigenas* in Mexico under Spanish conquest expressed their resistance to Christian beliefs through napantla. Napantla signified an intermediary space where the beliefs of the oppressor could be resisted, in overlapping and layered practices and spaces. For McLaren and Jaramillo, following Gloria Anzaldúa, the concept of nepantla refers to a space where students, teachers, and scholars can engage in resistance, critique, and a politics of negation.

With Che Guevara, McLaren and Jaramillo assert that you cannot build a more just socialist society without "at the same time creating a new human being." Of course, a new human being will require a new society. The practices of critical indigenous pedagogy help us imagine that society, but it must always be located in the sensuous, immediate world of indigenous persons.

Conclusion

As decolonizing interventions, the theoretical performances in Part I move in several directions at the same time, crisscrossing indigenous methodologies and worldviews, marginalized feminisms, moral activism, critical race, LatCrit, participatory action theory, critical pedagogy, and Marxist humanism. These variations on the critical paradigm embody specific ethical, epistemological, ontological, and methodological assumptions and practices. Fitted into an emerging decolonizing paradigm, they suggest that a Decade of Critical Indigenous Inquiry has arrived.

Notes

1. See also Chapter 23 by Jones and Jenkins, which rethinks the indigene-colonizer hyphen.

2. Elsewhere (Denzin & Lincoln, 2005), we have examined the major paradigms and perspectives that now structure and organize qualitative research. These paradigms and perspectives are positivism, postpositivism, constructivism, and participatory action frameworks. Alongside these paradigms are the perspectives of feminism (in its multiple forms), critical race theory, queer theory, and cultural studies. Each of these perspectives has developed its own criteria, assumptions, and methodological practices. These practices are then applied to disciplined inquiry within that framework.

References

Darder, A., & Mirón, L. F. (2006). Critical pedagogy in a time of uncertainty: A call to action. *Cultural Studies <=> Critical Methodologies, 6*(1), 5–20.

Denzin, N. K., & Lincoln, Y. S. (2005). Introduction: The discipline and practice of qualitative research. In N. K. Denzin & Y. S. Lincoln (Eds.), *The SAGE handbook of qualitative research* (3rd ed., pp. 1–32). Thousand Oaks, CA: Sage.

Guba, E., & Lincoln, Y. S. (2005). Paradigmatic controversies, contradictions, and emerging confluences. In N. K. Denzin & Y. S. Lincoln (Eds.),*The SAGE handbook of qualitative research* (2nd ed., pp. 163–188). Thousand Oaks, CA: Sage.

Lincoln, Y. S., & Guba, E. (2000). Paradigmatic controversies, contradictions, and emerging confluences. In N. K. Denzin & Y. S. Lincoln (Eds.), *The SAGE handbook of qualitative research* (3rd ed., pp. 191–216). Thousand Oaks, CA: Sage.

National Research Council. (2002). *Scientific research in education* (R. Shavelson & L. Towne, Eds.). Washington, DC: National Academies Press.

Olesen, V. (2005). Early millennial feminist qualitative research: Challenges and contours. In N. K. Denzin & Y. S. Lincoln (Eds.), *The SAGE handbook of qualitative research* (3rd ed., pp. 235–278). Thousand Oaks, CA: Sage.

Parker, L., Deyhle, D., Villenas, S., & Nebeker, K. C. (1998). Guest editors' introduction: Critical race theory and qualitative studies in education. *Qualitative Studies in Education, 11*, 5–6.

Spivak, G. C. (1988). Can the subaltern speak? In C. Nelson & L. Grossberg (Eds.), *Marxist interpretations of culture* (pp. 271–313). Urbana: University of Illinois Press.

2

DECOLONIZING PERFORMANCES

Deconstructing the Global Postcolonial

Beth Blue Swadener and Kagendo Mutua

Colonial leopards rarely change their spots. They just stalk their prey in different ways.

—Moana Jackson (Ngati Kahungunu, Ngati Porou), Māori lawyer and sovereignty advocate (as cited in Choudry, 2003)

The project of decolonization has been viewed and interpreted variously, but in this chapter, we highlight the ways in which decolonization is about the process in both research and performance of valuing, reclaiming, and foregrounding indigenous voices and epistemologies. Thus, we see decolonizing research resisting the lures and mires of postcolonial reason that position certain players within postcoloniality as more "valid" postcolonial researchers/scholars. Rather, within decolonizing projects, the possibilities of forging cross cultural partnerships with, between, and among indigenous researchers and "allied others" (Rogers & Swadener, 1999) and working collaboratively on common goals that reflect anticolonial sensibilities in action are important facets of decolonization. By bringing together critical personal narratives and postcolonial theory, we will demonstrate how decolonizing research uncovers the colonizing tendencies of language, specifically the English language, which threatens many indigenous languages with extinction; the centrality of the U.S. academy in the articulation of "valid" research questions and processes for investigating those questions; the cultural imperialism of research funding agencies, particularly in, but not limited to, "developing" regions of the world and their role in defining "valid" (read: positivist) research; and how such research produces discourses that inscribe and render Others powerless by producing a discourse that "author-ises certain people to speak and correspondingly silences others, or at least makes their voices less authoritative. A discourse [that] is, therefore, exclusionary" (Usher & Edwards, 1994, p. 90).

Furthermore, we explore the challenges posed to decolonizing performance in the current global neoconservative and "hyper"-positivist times.

In setting the context, we begin this chapter by describing what projects of decolonizing research might entail and the questions that decolonization engages. Not wishing to imply or inscribe any static forms in decolonization vis-à-vis research methods or methodologies, we share illustrations from our stories as players working to decolonize research as a way to demonstrate the fluidity of decolonizing research, while at the same time highlighting what we perceive to be some defining features of decolonizing performances. In so doing, we draw from critical personal narratives reflecting our collaborative work, beginning with highlights from our own discussions and deconstructions of our attempts to "decolonize" research, making reference to indigenous narratives and reflecting on the possibilities and limitations of performing decolonizing methodologies (Mutua & Swadener, 2004). Drawing on the work of Ngũgĩ wa Thiong'o (1986), Spivak (1999), McCarthy (1998), Bhabha (1994), and others, we explore several themes related to decolonization and briefly deconstruct notions of "insider" and "outsider," and with Linda Tuhiwai Smith (1999), Graham Hingangaroa Smith (2005), and others, we trouble overdetermined notions of the "native" or "postcolonial intellectual." Finally, we focus on performance theories in various research-focused decolonization projects and suggest future directions for these genres of research.

We also argue that particular culturally framed genres of research and methodology are necessary and should reflect indigenous epistemologies, languages, and expressive forms in relevant ways to the issues of interest. L. T. Smith (1999) states, "Methodology is important because it frames the questions being asked, determines the set of instruments and methods to be employed and shapes the analysis" (p. 143). Her distinction between methodology as a theory of how research does or should proceed and a method as a technique for or way of proceeding to gather evidence is one that is increasingly used in both indigenous and feminist research contexts (G. H. Smith, 2002). While this chapter draws heavily from the work of Māori scholars, particularly Linda Smith and Graham Smith, we recognize that much of their work focuses on issues specific to their geopolitical, national, and indigenous contexts. Recognizing the complexities of any anticolonial project and the need for specific, local enactments that often draw ideas from larger global struggles, we draw inspiration but not universal formulas from this powerful body of work.

We write as longtime colleagues, friends, and collaborative researchers, sharing a commitment to naming colonial and imperialist patterns in research and contexts of our work and daily lives. We struggle with understanding the subtle ways that colonization manifests in our respective (and shared) fields of early childhood education, special education, and policy studies and do not limit our analyses of colonization and so-called postcolonial issues to geopolitical contexts. We, with a growing number of researchers (e.g., Cannella & Viruru, 2004; Kaomea, 2003, 2005), recognize the colonization inherent in constructions of categories of people (e.g., children, persons with disabilities, English-language learners, indigenous scholars, etc.) and have worked to understand these often oppressive and typically limiting constructions to interrupt and reframe them in our work. We approach research, then, from an antioppressive and decolonizing stance while realizing the (im)possibilities and complexities of a truly decolonizing endeavor.

▣ Setting the Context

In this section, we attempt to articulate our most recent thinking about what may constitute decolonizing research. However, like several other scholars (see, e.g., Denzin, 2005; Lincoln & Cannella, 2004; Lather, 2004; Ryan & Hood, 2004), we recognize that within an era of growing neoconservatism in the United States, particularly as evidenced in the current forced adherence to neopositivism in educational research, increased demand in education for standardization, documentation of outcomes, and the deployment of other accountability measures, spaces for the articulation or performance of decolonization and the use of other interpretative methodologies are at best radically reduced or altogether dismantled. This reversal to positivist notions of research and the recentering of the scientific method threatens the progress made performatively and in research in terms of the articulation of the histories and experiences of indigenous/colonized groups whom traditional/positivist research has quite often denied agency. Traditionally, positivist research has prescribed a static and fixed subject that, according to Serres (1995), spawned static systems of knowing and histories of being, even though they claimed to describe a process of becoming. Viewed within this larger sociopolitical context, decolonizing performances that offer counterhegemonic accounts of the experiences of indigenous/colonized, racialized, and quite often non-Western groups that reflect and sustain indigenous epistemologies, in turn, have to fight for their own survival within and against the colonizing tendencies of this neopositivist impulse.

In an attempt to illustrate the elements that we think are central and unique to decolonizing research and performances/praxis, we describe in the remainder of this section what we perceive to be attributes of decolonizing research and share illustrative elements of our story as players working to decolonize research. In recent years, we have been asked by various readers of our work to tell them what decolonizing research is. Inherent in this question is an inquiry that simultaneously asks several questions: What makes decolonizing research decolonizing? Can I know it when I see it? Is it a set of methods and/or methodologies? If so, what are they? We have grappled with this question and the challenge that it poses to us to define decolonizing research, and in this section, we attempt to answer that question and all those that it subsumes while being cautious not to inscribe some sort of a litmus test for claims of decolonizing research.

Upon reviewing many publications that we consider to be exemplars of decolonizing research (Cary & Mutua, in press; Hamza, 2004; Jankie, 2004; Kaomea, 2004; G. H. Smith, 2005; L. T. Smith, 1999), as well as texts on research methods and methodology, it has become apparently clear that what makes decolonizing research decolonizing is not an adherence to a specific research method or methodology. Decolonizing research does not constitute a single agreed-upon set of guidelines or methods, although several indigenous scholars have offered lists of minimal criteria to be met (e.g., Linda Tuhiwai Smith and Graham Hingangaroa Smith). Furthermore, decolonizing research does not have a common definition. Indeed, having engaged with decolonizing research on a number of performative and theoretical levels as researchers, activists, and writers, we see the distinctive hallmarks of decolonizing research lying in the motives, concerns, and knowledge brought to the research process. We contend that decolonizing research is defined by certain themes and defining elements and concepts that arise when researchers engage in what they describe as decolonizing research versus research that studies coloniality or postcoloniality.

Furthermore, we would argue that decolonizing research is performative—it is enmeshed in activism. Graham Smith (e.g., 2004, 2005) has spoken and written in recent years critiquing the use of the construct *decolonizing,* arguing that it still foregrounds colonization, and other indigenous scholars have called for the use of *anticolonial* research as a more accurate descriptor of this endeavor. This example speaks to the issue of the performativity and continual interrogation of not only the process of research but also its outcomes/outputs. These recent moves in decolonizing illustrate ways in which scholars engaged in decolonizing research remain constantly mindful of the ways in which the process or outcomes of their research endeavors might reify hegemonic power structures, thereby creating marginality.

As an overarching schema, decolonizing research recognizes and works within the belief that non-Western knowledge forms are excluded from or marginalized in normative research paradigms, and therefore non-Western/indigenous voices and epistemologies are silenced and subjects lack agency within such representations. Furthermore, decolonizing research recognizes the role of colonization in the scripting and encrypting of a silent, inarticulate, and inconsequential indigenous subject and how such encryptions legitimize oppression. Finally, individually and collectively, decolonizing research as a performative act functions to highlight and advocate for the ending of both discursive and material oppression that is produced at the site of the encryption of the non-Western subject as a "governable body" (Foucault, 1977).

Main Concerns

Over the years at professional meetings (e.g., Swadener & Mutua, 2001), informally in spoken communications, and in our writing (e.g., Mutua & Swadener, 2004; Soto & Swadener, 2001, 2005), one role that our work has played has been to raise questions regarding the dynamics, complexities, and contradictory nature of "decolonizing research." Issues raised have included questioning of whose agenda it is to decolonize research; who holds the power to name and how such power reifies existing power relations; who and how "scholarship" is legitimized; ways educational research creates "data plantations"; tensions between "indigenous insiders" versus etic researchers; exclusivity of the availability of tools for decolonization only to indigenous researchers and whether this can be a shared process; reductive, binary categories (e.g., "developed" versus "developing," "First World" versus "Third World," "Western" versus "non-Western") and the dichotomization and polarization of discourses, thereby reinscribing patterns of exploitation and privilege; subtle dynamics of "Third World" intellectuals working within the "First World" academy; role of funders in the de/colonization of research and the articulation of "valid" research questions; and how the discourse on decolonizing research might be colonized or appropriated. Given the complexities of the questions we have raised over the years, we have become more aware of our changing subject positions (as "indigenous"/ "foreigner"/"insider"/ "outsider") and the issues those changing subject positions bring to bear on the research process. Linda Smith (1999) also analyzes the contested/resisted roles of "Native intellectuals" in postcolonial contexts.

> Currently, the role of the "Native" intellectual has been reformulated not in relation to nationalist or liberatory discourses but in relation to the "postcolonial" intellectual. Many intellectuals who position themselves as "postcolonial" move across the boundaries of indigenous and metropolitan, institution and community, politics and scholarship. Their place in the academy is still highly problematic (L. T. Smith, 1999, p. 71).

L. T. Smith's (1999) criticisms of the "postcolonial" intellectual are important in drawing a distinction between postcolonial research and research that is decolonizing. Writing about postcoloniality, Leela Gandhi (1998) states that postcolonial works do not represent a unified unit, but rather what she refers to as a "cacophony of subaltern voices." While indeed there is disparateness in postcolonial theorizing and postcolonial reason, there cannot be any denying that the temporal and lived experience of geopolitical colonialism is evidently filled with subaltern voices that are now allowing themselves and/or being allowed to speak. So it is not at all a bad thing that this is happening, because these voices bring to bear issues and perspectives that were not considered, much less valued, in colonial research. On the one hand, decolonizing research is at least in part about resisting colonization in terms of its affirmation of indigenous epistemologies and the reclamation and affirmation of indigenous languages, as well as observance in the research process of indigenous customs.

On the other hand, our work, which extends beyond research within indigenous contexts, recognizes that colonization in representation is more than a spatial-temporal experience, and by stating this, we are by no means minimizing the brutalities of that experience. With colonization as a way of representing, producing/inscribing, and consuming the Other through the silencing and denial of agency, the centrality and primacy of specific institutions in the validation of what constitutes research and knowledge extend beyond what are often constructed as the geospatial and historical epicenters of the experience of colonization. Hence our work recognizes the same mechanisms and colonizing ways in certain research that studies, produces, and silences specific groups (e.g., persons with disabilities) through the ways it constructs and consumes knowledge and experiences about such groups. Therefore, in our work, we recognize that decolonizing research extends to conducting research, not exclusively in contexts where the geopolitical experience of colonization happened, but indeed among groups where colonizing research approaches are deployed.

Our Journeys Into Decolonizing Research

In the remainder of this section, we each discuss our journeys as researchers and scholars and how we came to work with decolonizing discourse/collaborative methodologies. Our narratives highlight the way our experiences, while different, led us to a similar rethinking about the power of representation in texts that script, ascribe, and/or reify identities. Our narratives also highlight our theoretical and professional journeys within the U.S. academy from the standpoint of polarized identities as "insider/outsider," "indigenous/foreigner," "citizen/alien," and so on, as well as our struggles and resistance to those ascriptive identities. We use the narratives of our lived experiences to contextualize who we are or who we are constructed to be both in the U.S. academy and in contexts where we conduct our research, spaces that are not indeterminate or unsubscribed (Spivak, 1993). Furthermore, we hope to uncover the texts and discourses that have scripted our identities.

Beth: As a European American woman of lower middle-class background and benefiting from an array of unearned privileges, I have actively interrogated ways in which my work may be reproducing colonial, exploitive, or oppressive patterns and relationships. My commitment has been strengthened by my work in "unlearning oppression" and participation in multiracial alliances since the early 1980s, as well as by my activism in social justice movements from the early 1970s through the present. I have been doing research in sub-Saharan Africa since the mid-1980s and have worked in high-poverty, urban school, and preschool settings in the United States for the past 16 years.

Prior to using the language of decolonization, I spoke (and wrote) more about "authentic collaboration" or "partnership research" and attempted, in my collaborative work with classroom teachers and African colleagues, to foreground the voice and worldviews of such collaborators. I have also raised concerns about urban schools serving as "data plantations" that serve the researcher and exploit those in urban communities and schools, without sustained relationships being built or reciprocal possibilities explored.

Similarly, doing cross-cultural or cross-national work in neocolonial settings presents many ethical and methodological dilemmas, particularly when there is a conscious attempt to decolonize the research (Gandhi, 1998; L. T. Smith, 1999). I was never particularly fond of postcolonial theory, but I had been deeply influenced in the early 1990s by reading Harrison's (1991) *Decolonizing Anthropology.* When I first began to write about decolonizing research in the mid-1990s, I emphasized authentic collaboration in which colleagues in the setting of study are as fully involved as possible—a setting that is functional and desirable to them, framed in relationship to the still-centered "visiting researcher." At that time, Kenyan colleagues and I generated guidelines for decolonizing research involving "insider" and "outsider" partners, which we asserted involved (at minimum) the following (Swadener, Kabiru, & Njenga, 2000): collaboration on all phases of the study; sustained time in a culture; studying the language(s) and cultures to the degree possible and developing the ability to code-switch and understand indigenous "ways of knowing" and communicating; coauthorship of all papers and publications resulting from the collaborative work; compensation of local collaborators, translators, and research partners for their time; and making findings available in relevant ways to local shareholders, including finding funding to distribute publications in the home country of the local community. I have also emphasized the importance, for "outsiders," of participating in the community in ongoing (nonmissionary) ways, including supporting organizations and individuals doing "anticolonial" work, and, finally, interrogating privilege and the "myths of meritocracy" while strengthening alliances.

In more recent years, I have been interrogating and "troubling" my comfortable, rule-governed formulas for decolonizing research across differentiated power relationships, wherever they may be found. I have confronted the likelihood that decolonizing research is a messy, complex, and perhaps impossible endeavor—yet have affirmed that attempting to decolonize one's work is a project worth pursuing, in solidarity with local colleagues and movements. My sense is that decolonization transcends individual action and requires working with collectives or alliances that concern themselves with decolonizing projects. I will admit that in my most self-critical moments, I have considered focusing only on antiracist, social justice scholarship in my own community. This distancing from international projects has never lasted long. I return nearly every year to Kenya, and my visits are more about relationships and community volunteer projects than about my research agenda.

I have also been concerned with colonizing discourses and decolonizing possibilities in my primary disciplines of early childhood education and policy studies (Soto & Swadener, 2005) and have been influenced by the work of Kaomea (2003, 2005), who uses postcolonial and indigenous methodologies to complicate culturally based curriculum issues in early childhood contexts, and Cannella and Viruru (2004), who advocate the terminology of "younger human beings" in order to resist social constructions of childhood that reflect patterns of power and patriarchy that pervade our field. My examination, with Lourdes Diaz Soto, of issues of power and voice in research with children has included an in-depth analysis of ways in which early childhood theory, research, and practices with children embody colonizing patterns. Soto's work, as well as mine in recent years, has focused on issues navigated by bilingual children (e.g., Rolstad, Swadener, & Nakagawa, 2004; Soto, 2002) and counterhegemonic practices in an era of antibilingual education policies in the United States.

Kagendo: It took me a number of years studying and living in the United States to come to the realization that many of the experiences that I came to find objectionable in my everyday interactions with certain people who variously constructed me first and foremost as alien/foreigner/African and so on were directly linked to the notion that I was an already "known" abject subject (Erevelles, 2005): African, woman, Black. Early cultural anthropological studies, cultural exposés of Africa broadcast as television shows of the National Geographic Explorer and the Discovery Channel, and a number of other texts had encrypted my identity long before I learned to appreciate what it all meant, much less find ways to subversively resist its encryption in empowering and decolonizing ways. Up until the moment of my advent into the United States, I had not described myself or been described in so many heavily coded terms, and if those terms were used (and I know some of them were) during my growing up and school years in Kenya, I never really interrogated their nuanced meanings. Part of that may be due to the invisibility of their oppressive tendencies in Kenya, the other part may be due to the fact that they were not as heavily laden in oppressive nuances as they are in the United States, and yet another part may be my lack of political savvy. Therefore, it was a loss of naïveté that I experienced when I finally began to appreciate the depth of their nuanced sense as well as the historicized, racialized, and genderized oppression that they carried. As I have done elsewhere (Cary & Mutua, in press), I share snippets of my decolonizing journey to highlight the presence/disturbance of a number of discourses that have shaped my colonial and postcolonial lives (not that I can separate these political spaces—nor would I want to).

In this narrative, the scripting of my identity as the always already "known" alien, "residing in the United States at the exhaustible pleasure of the U.S. Bureau of Citizenship and Immigration (formerly Department of Immigration and Naturalization Service)" (see Cary & Mutua, in press), comes with unearned liberties and permissions granted certain people (quite often strangers) to ask all kinds of prying personal questions: "Do they have plumbing where you are from?" "How many brothers and sisters do you have/are you from a *really* big family?" (when I answer that I have four sisters and two brothers, I can see the inquirer put a checkmark on the list of "facts" already and always known about me!) "Has anyone else in your family gone to school/have a college education?" (and when I answer, yes, all have college degrees and traveled in many other parts of the world, I can see an asterisk against that disturbed "fact" that is creating some dissonance on the factual checklist!). Typically at this point, the inquirer might switch to a compliment: "You speak English very well!" and often add how much they just love to listen to my accent, which then accords them the liberty to ask me to speak for no reason at all, other than entertainment! The consistent inquiry/interrogation to which I am often subjected appears to be premised on nothing other than my alien/postcolonial status. As argued elsewhere, the often unstated yet expected demand to explain my presence (and intentions) in the United States is the question that stays in permanent default mode (Cary & Mutua, in press). I am required for no other reason other than being alien/postcolonial to explain what I am doing in the United States. I find that the hypocrisy engendered in the collective amnesia of non–Native Americans, who all have an immigrant history yet make the proximity of my advent into the United States to be of consequence, is morbidly interesting. I bring with me cultural differences that make difficult the lives of those who have to deal with me or the lives of those who arrived here before me. So, in the United States, the issue of cultural difference has been constructed as a problem of the alien; for instance, it is my problem that people cannot pronounce my name, so it behooves me to make it easier on everyone by taking on an American name or a nickname.

Furthermore, as a professional in special education, specifically severe disabilities, a field that is laden with labels, I began to notice and be troubled by the ways in which cognitive, physical, and sensory differences among people are coded and positions assigned to those people based on the ascriptive identities circumscribed by those labels, which are often negative, silencing, and disempowering. Using semiotics as a theoretical standpoint that allowed me to delve into the signs and symbols of disability and the meanings and relationships experienced as everyday life by persons with disabilities, I first began to grapple with how identities are created and what assumptions are made about people who bear certain ascriptive identities. Working with Beth, I became exposed to a different way of thinking about and engaging with these issues that lent new thinking about my own identity (real and/or ascribed) and that of the youth with disabilities with whom I worked. I started to see ways in which colonization and its products are more than a geopolitical historical experience that is limited in terms of both spatiality and temporality. Rather, I began to appreciate that the processes and outcomes of coloniality are manifest in multiple ways in which "knowledge" makes possible the production and consumption of the Other. Furthermore, in such knowledge production, certain hegemonic power arrangements ensure the silence of certain Others in the process of the knowledge production that encrypts Othering identities. My work, therefore, as a decolonizing scholar/researcher shaped by a colonial and postcolonial experience attempts to highlight the presence/disturbance of a number of discourses that produce ascriptive identities that are disabled, colonized, voiceless, powerless, nameless, and hence presumed known and therefore dismissible.

Foundational Matters and History

In laying a foundational history, we draw on the works of postcolonial scholars, including Eze (1997), Gandhi (1998), Mignolo (2000), Shohat (1992), Spivak (1993, 1999), and others, to describe ways in which decolonizing research draws from and is based on postcolonial theory and postcolonial studies. We argue that unlike postcolonial theory, decolonizing research goes beyond the mires/lure of defining *colonialism* solely in terms of spatial or temporal dimensions (see, e.g., McLeod, 2000; Mihesuah, 2003), often ignoring the brutality of the material consequences of coloniality.

Decolonizing research argues for materialist and discursive connection within postcoloniality and lays open the technologies of colonization, including language (English language) as the medium of research representation (Skutnabb-Kangas, 2000), deployment of Western epistemologies (often in diametric opposition to indigenous epistemologies), deployment of methodological imperialism (as defined within the Western academy versus indigenous modes of inquiry, representation, and ways of knowing) (L. T. Smith, 1999), and the determination of "valid" research questions (generated in the Western academy and "investigated" in indigenous contexts) (Mutua & Swadener, 2004). Our aim in this section is to intersect qualitative research and postcolonial theory in ways that make possible the production of new spaces for recasting research in liberatory ways that foreground indigenous epistemologies and ways of knowing in the field. In particular, we aim at destabilizing the "center" of research and academic ways of knowing by reframing "the field" (Rogers & Swadener, 1999).

In this chapter, decolonizing research emphasizes performativity. Decolonizing research is not only concerned with building a theoretical foundation for studies that claim to engage in decolonizing endeavors, but also many decolonizing researchers (e.g., Kaomea, 2001, 2005; G. H. Smith, 2004; L. T. Smith 1999; Warrior, 1995; Womack,1999) are actively engaged performatively in decolonizing acts framed variously as activism, advocacy, or cultural reclamation. In terms of critical developments in the broad and often divergent area of "decolonizing research" and critical postcolonial paradigms in educational research, our chapter highlights some examples of indigenous "reclaiming" projects and research collectives in various cultural, national, and geopolitical contexts foregrounding indigenous researchers' concerns and voices. Indeed, in step with this expanding scholarship, growing numbers of conferences on indigenous scholarship, journals, and other venues are creating more openings for this dialogue. Such avenues are creating decolonizing spaces for the representation of indigenous epistemologies that are performative in style and reflect indigenous expressions that go far beyond prevailing Western academic styles and venues for dissemination, including the centering of indigenous languages and modes of communication in song, oral storytelling, dance, poetry, and other cultural oral forms of expression.

Contemporary Issues

The spatiality of research, as well as attempts to "decolonize" it, has also been increasingly contested. Calling for a reframing of the "field," Rogers and Swadener (1999) reposition the field at the center for defining and initiating research agendas, as well as functioning in a dialectical relationship with the Western academy. Therefore, within the framework that Rogers and Swadener suggest in advocating a reframing of the field, researchers actively decenter the Western academy as the exclusive locus of authorizing power that defines research agenda. Working within this sort of reframed field, the research, whether foreign or indigenous, can never be permanently located at either the emic or etic pole. Such a deconstruction of the Western academy and the validity of its role in defining research and scholarship reconstitutes, redistributes, and reauthors the power of the margins (hooks, 1989; McCarthy, 1998). This redefined field is rife with new, possible researcher identities for both the indigenous and foreign researcher as the "allied other," a point that Rogers and Swadener (1999) describe, drawing in part from an antioppressive, feminist alliance model. Framed broadly, none of us carries only "one" colonized/colonizer subjectivity/identity.

Among the recent issues raised regarding the potential of decolonizing methodologies are concerns about the risks of such methodologies being appropriated, indeed recolonized, and at times reduced to slogans and superficial versions of the intended project. We will link some of these concerns to the impacts of neopositivism and an "identity politics" backlash on interpretive research and discuss the growing challenges to performing decolonizing or anticolonial research.

We share both the concerns and sense of possibility that Gandhi (1998) and others have articulated regarding the lack of a unified voice in postcolonial and critical research, which at times makes our work vulnerable to criticism due to divergent, even competing, voices. Hence, such methodologies can be more easily dismissed, which may lead to backlash for these genres, while at the same time having strength in number, diversity of approaches, and creativity. We argue that this phenomenon is reflected in many global movements, including the rise of global anticapitalism, which reflects a complex network of indigenous and localized movements. In other words, despite the lack of unity of message or approach that undergirds these methodologies, the voices are too numerous and strong to silence. In the words of Gandhi (1998), indigenous researchers and critical postcolonial scholars are part of a "cacophony of subaltern voices."

Furthermore, a growing number of Native American scholars have written powerfully about resistance to the Western academy and have called for indigenizing the academy (e.g., Mihesuah & Wilson, 2004) and "literary separatism" (e.g., Womack, 1999), foregrounding indigenous narratives and traditions. Others have focused on critiquing and reframing historical texts (e.g., Cook-Lynn, 1996; Erdich & Tohe, 2002; Miller, 2003) and contesting dominant religious, epistemological, and scientific theories (e.g., Deloria, 1995, 2003; Douglas & Armstrong, 1998). The divergent nature of the issues that are important to the decolonizing project further speaks to the diverse nature of the issues on which possibilities for decolonization hinge. Indeed, as we have stated elsewhere, it is the nature of the diversity of the issues that lends the decolonizing project its strength and staying power. As powerfully articulated in the opening quote of this chapter, colonization is colonization, though tactics may change—hence the diverse nature of the issues that are of concern to the decolonization project.

It should be noted that such "subaltern" voices speak hundreds of languages and communicate in song, oral storytelling, dance, poetry, and rituals. Such voices use performative styles, reflecting an array of indigenous epistemologies that go far beyond prevailing Western academic styles and venues for dissemination, resisting external definitions of what is of worth, and often reflecting relational versus individualistic constructions of human beings and other creatures. This came up recently at one of our campuses as we planned for our second Indigenous Issues and Voices in Educational Research conference. As we worked on the call for proposals, we realized that the meeting needed to emphasize more performative expressions versus traditional scholarly papers. For example, we needed to plan for song, relevant cultural dance, poetry, storytelling, and other alternative "forms" of expression related to education, assessment, and identity issues in education and educational research.

Increasingly, indigenous scholars are serving as their own gatekeepers (one example of recent critical literacy scholarship asserts that only indigenous authors should do a literary critique of indigenous text; e.g., Warrior, 1995). Decolonizing or anticolonial(ist) scholars also must grapple with the issue of which language(s) in which to publish their work (e.g., Hamza, 2004). Currently, one of the issues in a number of disciplines related to language policy (e.g., applied linguistics, bilingual education, English as a second language, language and literacy, etc.) concerns *heritage languages.* As discussed in a previous section of this chapter, linguicide has become a powerful force, with the hegemony of English and other "globalized" languages threatening indigenous languages and the language rights of those who speak such "endangered" languages or feel pressured to write in English when many indigenous concepts do not accurately translate—if they translate at all—into English or other European languages. A recent issue of *The Modern Language Journal,* for example, raises a number of questions about heritage languages and language policy, including the following: What counts as a heritage language, and what issues of heritage language are associated with policy, research foci, programs, curricula, and pedagogies (Byrnes, 2005, p. 583)?

Social Action Issues and the Future of Decolonizing Research

"Colonisation is colonisation, whatever new name we may like to give to it. Globalisation, free market, neoliberalism, profitability, capitalism, it is all fundamentally about colonisation. The privatization agenda in this country did not start with the 1984 Labour government or the MAI or the GATT" (Leonie Pihama [Te Atiawa, Ngati Mahanga], cited in Choudry, 2003).

Social action or praxis has a critical role in the performance of decolonizing methodologies. Indeed, critical, culturally framed praxis is at the heart of many enactments of decolonizing methodology. The example of Kenyan Nobel Laureate Wangari Maathai and the greenbelt movement reflects these larger movements and decolonizing discourses. Much of the international resistance to (corporate) globalization and "free trade" agreements (brokered by wealthy nations and multinational corporations) has arisen from grassroots indigenous movements that have used anticolonial research methods to document damage done to local economies and traditional lifestyles. This research and the social action it informs is being carried out in thousands of settings and is connected through broad alliances within the anticorporate globalization movement(s). Whether it is the Zapatista compasino resistance in Mexico or countless examples of rural parents advocating for free public education for their children, the spirit of grassroots movements and resistance exists in the face of increasing multinational corporate power and globalization. Many have also argued that globalization is just another form of colonization that threatens sovereignty of nations and first peoples while advantaging rich nations at the cost of culture and even survival in poor nations.

Some of the most powerful current examples of anticolonial research related to education and human services come from Māori scholars, as previously discussed. Both Linda Smith (1999) and Graham Smith (2002) have written about specific methodologies and "key expectations" used in their indigenous and activist research, and they have provided guidelines specific to the context of particular Māori projects. For example, G. H. Smith (2002) led a team of indigenous researchers in a study of the family court system in New Zealand. The project used a small number of *kanohi ki te kanohi* (face-to-face) interviews with *whanau* who have been involved in guardianship proceedings. It also included interviews with legal counsel and social service providers involved in the family courts. From these interviews, valuable insights are gained about the impact of the guardianship, custody, and access arrangements on Māori *whanau*. Smith described the overall study as follows:

> The project brief established some key expectations in terms of the methodology. Accordingly, this is a piece of research that is qualitative in nature, and based on a narrative enquiry or storytelling approach. The demographic profile of the areas in which the research was carried out was the means used to try and ensure that a diversity of *whanau* type and Māori experience was represented. As the case profiles show, this diversity of experience was evident. It should be noted that while clear themes emerge, we only have the stories of those who felt confident enough to take part in a research process. . . . The researchers who worked on the project are Māori, and have had considerable experience in working with *whanau* in social services and justice settings. Our values and beliefs as Māori researchers formed the basis of our analytical framework or methodology.

Reflecting these indigenous values, L. T. Smith (1999, p. 185) contends that *kaupapa* Māori research must (a) be related to being Māori; (b) be related to Māori values and principles; (c) take for granted the value and legitimacy of Māori, as well as the importance of Māori language and culture; and (d) be concerned with "the struggle for autonomy over our own culture and well-being."

The interview procedures that Graham Smith (2002) used in the family court study placed emphasis on several key issues that reframe and shift the participant-researcher relationship, language of the research, documentation of data during interviews, location/venue of interviews/data collection, mindfulness/awareness or knowledge of the participant's cultural norms and expectations, freedom of the participant to withdraw, and knowledge of systems of support should the participant need such support. A primary emphasis was placed on the use of a *korero mai* approach that allowed participants to tell their stories in their own way. It was the responsibility of the researchers to listen to the stories and link the stories back to the information needs (G. H. Smith, 2002).

G. H. Smith's (2002) suggestions raise several issues relevant and important to decolonization. Within this framework, there is a redefinition of the field and, furthermore, the centrality of the researcher in directing the research project insofar as determining how questions would be answered, as well as in what language answered, in having the participant adhere to the research "norms" rather than the research respecting the norms of communities where research is being conducted. To sum it up, Smith's suggestions require a relinquishing of the power and authority that has traditionally rested unquestionably on the researcher and the institutions that the researcher represents.

Questions we would raise about both social action projects and the future of decolonizing research include persistent concerns regarding how research benefits particular communities and subgroups/cultures in those communities, revisiting the persistent questions, Who benefits? Who may still be colonized, and how might "internalized colonization" be a factor? We also briefly discussed ways of resisting domination and performing counterhegemonic work while remaining viable (e.g., still being able to fund various research and community projects). We linked some of this work to antioppressive work (e.g., Kumashiro, 2004).

In anticipating various futures of decolonizing research, we anticipate the expanded use of alternative, performative genres including arts, music, drama, oral storytelling, narratives, and work with popular media ("zines," indymedia, and other use of Internet strategies to internationalize indigenous issues) as vehicles of growing resistance to Western, neoconservative, and positivist paradigms. We also anticipate more hybrid identities and border-crossers performing research in ways that resist "insider-outsider" dichotomies while continuing to authentically foreground indigenous issues and work—though not without complications and contestations.

▣ Summary

In this chapter, we have attempted to provide an overview of research that positions itself as working against colonization and reflecting indigenous or nondominant epistemologies and traditions. We have argued that, while there are no formulaic universals of "decolonizing" research methodologies, there are compelling examples of systematic approaches, including narrative and performative genres, most of which include activist agendas working toward social justice, sovereignty, self-determination, and emancipatory goals. Major contributions to this growing literature have come from Māori and indigenous North American scholars, as well as from all continents. We have also argued that decolonizing research goes beyond a postcolonial analysis to a more socially engaged, collaborative alliance model that reconstructs the very purposes of research and epistemologies that inform it. We have troubled binary categories such as "insider/outside" and argued that colonization occurs in a wide range of settings and contexts and is pervasive in educational research. In evoking a performative metaphor, we recognize the many forms of knowing, communication, and being in a complex and persistently oppressive world.

▣ References

Bhabha, H. K. (1994). *The location of culture.* London: Routledge.

Byrnes, H. (2005). Perspectives. *The Modern Language Journal, 89,* 582–616.

Cannella, G. S., & Viruru, R. (2004). *Childhood and postcolonization.* New York: Routledge Falmer.

Cary, L., & Mutua, K. (in press). Postcolonial curriculum narratives: Using a different lens on curriculum narratives. *Journal of Curriculum Theorizing.*

Choudry, A. (2003). *New wave/old wave: Aotearoa New Zealand's colonial continuum.* Retrieved from www.voiceoftheturtle.org/show_article.php?aid=328

Cook-Lynn, E. (1996). *Why I can't read Wallace Stegner and other essays: A tribal voice.* Madison: University of Wisconsin Press.

Deloria, V., Jr. (1995). *Red earth, white lies: Native Americans and the myth of scientific fact.* Golden, CO: Fulcrum.

Deloria, V., Jr. (2003). *God is red: A Native view of religions* (3rd ed.). Golden, CO: Fulcrum.

Denzin, N. K. (2005). First International Congress of Qualitative Inquiry. *Qualitative Social Work, 4*(1), 105-111.

Douglas, J. C., & Armstrong, J. C. (1998). *The Native creative process.* Penticton, British Columbia, Canada: Theytus Books.

Erdich, H. E., & Tohe, L. (2002). *Sister Nations: Native American women writers on community.* St. Paul: Minnesota Historical Society Press.

Erevelles, N. (2005) Reconceptualizing curriculum as "normalizing" text: Disability Studies meets curriculum theory. *Journal of Curriculum Studies, 37*(4), 421–439.

Eze, E. C. (Ed.). (1997). *Postcolonial African philosophy: A critical reader.* Oxford, UK: Blackwell.

Foucault, M. (1977). *Discipline and punish* (A. Sheridan, Trans.). New York: Vintage.

Gandhi, L. (1998). *Postcolonial theory: A critical introduction.* New York: Columbia University Press.

Hamza, H. M. (2004). Decolonizing research on gender disparity in education in Niger: Complexities of language, culture and homecoming. In K. Mutua & B. B. Swadener (Eds.), *Decolonizing research in cross-cultural contexts: Critical personal narratives* (pp. 123–134). Albany, NY: SUNY Press.

Harrison, F. V. (Ed.). (1991). *Decolonizing anthropology: Moving further toward an anthropology for liberation.* Washington, DC: Association for Black Anthropologists, American Anthropological Association.

hooks, b. (1989). *Talking back: thinking feminist, thinking black.* Boston: South End.

Jankie, D. (2004). "Tell me who you are?" Problematizing the construction and positionalities of "insider/outsider" of a "Native" ethnographer in a postcolonial context. In K. Mutua & B. B. Swadener (Eds.), *Decolonizing research in cross-cultural contexts: Critical personal narratives* (pp. 87–105). Albany, NY: SUNY Press.

Kaomea, J. (2001). Dilemmas of an indigenous academic: A Native Hawaiian story. *Contemporary Issues in Early Childhood, 2*(1), 67–82.

Kaomea, J. (2003). Reading erasures and making the familiar strange: Defamiliarizing methods for research in formerly colonized and historically oppressed communities. *Educational Researcher, 32*(2), 14–25.

Kaomea, J. (2005). Reflections on an "always already" failing Native Hawaiian mother: Deconstructing colonial discourses on indigenous childrearing and early childhood education. *Hulili: Multidisciplinary Research on Hawaiian Well-Being, 2*(1), 67–85.

Kumashiro, K. K. (2004). *Against common sense: Teaching and learning toward social justice.* New York: RoutledgeFalmer.

Lather, P. (2004). This is your father's paradigm: Government intrusion and the case of qualitative research in education. *Qualitative Inquiry, 10*(1), 15–34.

Lincoln, Y. S., & Cannella, G. S. (2004). Dangerous discourses, methodological conservatism and governmental regimes of truth. *Qualitative Inquiry, 10*(1), 5–14.

McCarthy, C. (1998). *The uses of culture: Education and the limits of ethnic affiliation.* New York: Routledge.

McLeod, J. (2000). *Beginning postcolonialism.* Manchester, UK: Manchester University Press.

Mignolo, W. D. (2000). *Local histories/global designs: Coloniality, subaltern knowledges, and border thinking.* Princeton, NJ: Princeton University Press.

Mihesuah, D. A. (Ed.). (2003). *American Indian women: Decolonization, empowerment, activism.* Lincoln: University of Nebraska Press.

Mihesuah, D. A., & Wilson, A. C. (2004). *Indigenizing the academy.* Lincoln: University of Nebraska Press.

Miller, S. A. (2003). *Coacoochee's bones: A Seminole saga.* Lawrence: University Press of Kansas.

Mutua, K., & Swadener, B. B. (Eds.). (2004). *Decolonizing research in cross-cultural contexts: Critical personal narratives.* Albany, NY: SUNY Press.

Ngũgĩ, wa Thiong'o. (1986). *Decolonizing the mind: The politics of language in African literature.* London: James Currey Ltd.

Rogers, L. J., & Swadener, B. B. (1999). Reflections on the future work on anthropology and education: Reframing the field. *Anthropology and Education Quarterly, 30,* 436–440.

Rolstad, K., Swadener, B. B., & Nakagawa, K. (2004, April). *"Verde—sometimes we call it green": Construal of language difference and power in a preschool dual immersion program.* Paper presented at the annual meeting of the Educational Research Association, San Diego.

Ryan, K. E., & Hood, L. K. (2004). Guarding the castle and opening the gates. *Qualitative Inquiry, 10*(1), 79–95.

Serres, M. (with Latour, B.). (1995). *Conversations on science, culture and time.* Ann Arbor: University of Michigan Press.

Shohat, E. (1992). Notes on the "post-colonial." *Social Text, 31/32,* 99–112.

Skutnabb-Kangas, T. (2000). *Linguistic genocide in education—or worldwide diversity and human rights?* Mahwah, NJ: Lawrence Erlbaum.

Smith, G. H. (Ed.). (2002). *Guardianship, custody and access: Māori perspectives and experiences.* Auckland, New Zealand: Ministry of Justice, Government Publications. Retrieved from www.justice.govt.n/pubs/custody-access-māori/chapter-4.html

Smith, G. H. (2004, April). *Keynote address.* Presented at the Distinguished Scholars Colloquia—Indigenous Perspectives on Educational Research and Schooling in Global Contexts, Tempe, AZ.

Smith, G. H. (2005). *Why the University of Auckland?* Retrieved from www.eo.auckland.ac.nz/māori/why_auckland

Smith, L. T. (1999). *Decolonizing methodologies: Research and indigenous peoples.* London: Zed Books.

Soto, L. D. (Ed.). (2002). *Making a difference in the lives of bilingual/bicultural children.* New York: Peter Lang.

Soto, L. D., & Swadener, B. B. (2001). Toward a liberatory early childhood theory, research and praxis: Decolonizing a field. *International Journal of Contemporary Issues in Early Childhood, 2*(1).

Soto, L. D., & Swadener, B. B. (Eds.). (2005). *Power and voice in research with children.* New York: Peter Lang.

Spivak, G. C. (1993). *Outside the teaching machine.* New York: Routledge.

Spivak, G. C. (1999). *A critique of postcolonial reason: Toward a history of the vanishing present.* Cambridge, MA: Harvard University Press.

Swadener, B., & Mutua, K. (2001, April). *Interactive symposium co-organizer: Problematizing "decolonizing research" in cross-cultural contexts: Complexities, contradictions and [im]possibilities.* Paper presented at the annual meeting of the American Educational Research Association, Seattle, WA.

Swadener, B. B., Kabiru, M., & Njenga, A. (2000). *Does the village still raise the child? A collaborative study of changing childrearing and early education in Kenya.* Albany, NY: SUNY Press.

Usher, R., & Edwards, R. (1994). *Postmodernism and education.* London: Routledge.

Warrior, R. A. (1995). *Tribal secrets: Recovering American Indian intellectual traditions.* Minneapolis: University of Minnesota Press.

Womack, S. C. (1999). *Red on red: Native American literary separatism.* Minneapolis: University of Minnesota Press.

3

FEMINISMS FROM UNTHOUGHT LOCATIONS

Indigenous Worldviews, Marginalized Feminisms, and Revisioning an Anticolonial Social Science

Gaile S. Cannella and Kathryn D. Manuelito

> *A transnational feminist practice depends on building feminist solidarities across the divisions of place, identity, class, work, belief. . . . In these very fragmented times it is both very difficult to build these alliances and also never more important to do so.*
>
> —Mohanty (2003, p. 250)

Feminist research epistemologies have played a major role in the conceptualization and reconceptualization of qualitative, and especially critical qualitative, research purposes and methods. In addition to equity and social justice for women, scholars and activists have even focused on and problematized constructions of gender. Theorists and researchers have used the various versions of feminism (whether or not consciously defined or labeled) to analyze, challenge, and counter dominant forms of knowledge, discourse, and institutional practices and to examine experiences in the everyday world (Olesen, 2005). The work of women of color has also forcefully implicated Western White feminisms in the creation of the "other" (Collins, 1986; Hurtado, 1989; Mohanty, 1988; Zevella, 1987; Zinn, 1982). Various critical and postmodern feminisms, like standpoint research, have replaced constructions of the universalized "woman" with the recognition of specifically situated "women" located within varying complex systems of power (Haraway, 1987, 1988; Harding, 1987; Hartsock, 1997; D. Smith, 1992). Furthermore, a range of feminisms from diverse locations has introduced issues of voice, representation, text, and ethics to the conceptualization and practice of qualitative research (Fine, 1992; Mauthner, Birch, Jessop, & Miller, 2002; Spivak, 1988).

Theories and languages generated by those concerned with gender and oppression have fostered understandings of qualitative research that are multivocal, fluid, and hybrid. These understandings challenge the conceptualization of women/gender while at the same time recognizing the material effects of oppression and attempting to facilitate a social justice agenda. Many of these research issues are illustrated in the model of transgressive validity posed by Lather (1993) that would require the researcher to attend to the problem of representation, embrace uncertainty, challenge authority through multiplicity, and practice reflexivity. Feminist scholars from dominant and marginalized locations have questioned the purposes of research, used methods such as autoethnography that relate the personal to larger social issues, and even engaged in performative forms of interpretation (Case & Abbitt, 2004; Ellis, 1995; Wheeler, 2003). Feminist research conceptualizations and practices are wide ranging and acknowledge the complexity and diversity of human beings.

However, female "identified" forms of thought remain in the margin of society generally and continue to be relegated to the periphery of social science research, whether the perspectives are more closely associated with White female privilege or the historical marginalizing of female experience as intersecting other forms of oppression (e.g., race, sexual orientation, the discrediting of indigenous peoples). As evidenced by antifeminist movements, even in the academy, patriarchy and misogyny are alive and well (Lincoln & Cannella, 2004). Conservative backlash against women, people of color, and anyone who would dissent places all of us in the margins. We are pushed to the periphery by a contemporary invasive hypercapitalism that is transnational and patriarchal. This contemporary hypercondition would discredit, erase, control, or market for personal gain across individual, group, and geographic borders (Cannella & Swadener, 2005). Furthermore, the condition multiplies and intensifies the power of intersecting oppressions (Collins, 2000). As Mohanty (2003) stresses, alliances across complex differences and power matrices are difficult but have never been more important than now.

The purpose of this chapter is to form an alliance of feminist, Native, and womanist worldviews that would provide a radical rethinking of the purposes, methods, and interpretations of research applicable to the construction of social justice in contemporary hypercapitalist patriarchy. We believe that native worldviews (especially those of women), traditionally marginalized feminisms, and womanist forms of female identification provide needed possibilities for activist reinvisionings of research as construct (and social science as disciplinary practice). This revisioning is especially necessary at a time when science (grounded in the linear notions of knowledge accumulation and progress that actually generate vulnerabilities to simplistic, dualistic thinking) is being attacked by those who would use vulnerabilities to reinscribe power over all of us. We recognize that "native" perspectives, the various feminisms, and activist, womanist forms of thought have been at odds with each other. These conflicts are understandable as people are embedded within different histories and various intersecting survival locations within patriarchy and colonialism. As authors, we struggle from our diverse locations to create a solidarity that bridges a Euro-American educated White feminist, mixed-race adoptive family orientation with a Diné (Navajo) female ancestry, mother-clan heritage orientation. We recognize that we share much (e.g., as females, friends, daughters, wives, mothers, and educators) but are entirely different in so many ways (also as females, friends, daughters, wives, mothers, and educators). Finally, we recognize that we all always run the risk of privileging particular perspectives and marginalizing, essentializing, or even erasing others, even as we attempt to join together reciprocally across differences. In sharing our hopes for a conceptualization of social science research that would increase social justice from within these differences, we attempt to create transformative solidarities that can generate unthought possibilities for us as human beings who care for each other.

Integrating Native worldviews with traditionally marginalized feminisms involves the intertwining of disposition, theory, and actions. The purposes, questions, and methods of research must be transformed. Our narrative is categorical and linear, so obviously uses traditional, colonialist, academic forms of presentation—because we believe that for contemporary academic usefulness, at least the structure of "the master's tools" (Lorde, 1984) must be employed. However, we attempt to ground our categorizations in Diné (Navajo) life heritage and epistemology (Manuelito, 2005) and expand from that point into the diversity of Indigenous perspectives, as well as the strengths and ways of being represented by the range of women of color. Infused with academic theoretical narrative and possibilities for transforming the practice of research, we move back and forth between life narrative and theory, hoping to explain while at the same time challenge and disrupt the dualisms created by our text and the theories chosen within it. We write together because our joining both symbolizes the diversity of women's lives and feminist perspectives and the urgency with which we must create solidarities in the contemporary world in which new forms of patriarchy and colonialism are taking hold.

We propose an anticolonialist social science that would generate visions of egalitarianism and social justice. This anticolonialist social science would recognize the intersection of new oppressive forms of power created even within attempts to decolonize. Furthermore, new imaginings, the unthought social science, and egalitarian activism would be absolute necessities. Although academic writing creates an illusion of authority, and there is much debate concerning who speaks and how regarding the topics that we discuss, we hope that the reader will respond to our ideas as attempts to communicate, not as authority or new false truth, but as human beings who (from within our differences) hope for egalitarian forms of social justice.

Seeing the Past in the Present: Visioning an Anticolonialist Social Science

Insidious Colonialism: Contemporary Patriarchal Hypercapitalism

> As Diné Diné we were colonized by the Spaniards first, the Mexicans, and the Americans. The Spanish and Mexican colonizers imposed their names upon us so that many if not most of our people today have Spanish surnames such as Manuelito, Alonzo, Garcia, and so on. Surnames of fathers in the Euro-Western tradition conflicted with our Diné (Navajo) identity as being recognized as our Mother's children. . . . I only heard and read denigrating commentaries about American Indians and Navajos in our books and from teachers in our school.
>
> As a Diné (Navajo) student from early childhood onward, I had not heard any references in school of our Diné (Navajo) history. During childhood, in the company of adults and elders at family gatherings or community meetings, I often saw them wiping their tears when Hweeldi (The Long Walk) was mentioned and discussed. I knew that Hweeldi (The Long Walk) was traumatic and a time marker in Diné (Navajo) history, denoting a time of great suffering for our ancestors. Instead I learned in school about the "heroic" Kit Carson, who I later learned was the evil military person who rounded up the Diné (Navajo) and was responsible for the horrific treatment of the Diné (Navajo) during Hweeldi (The Long Walk). . . . I learned about Manifest Destiny in high school and college. As a youngster, I felt the stinging unfairness toward American Indians as nonentities who had no right to live and had to make way or provide convenience for a dominant, hegemonic society whose god favored them.
>
> Federal policies have dictated who should be a leader in Diné (Navajo) society as in the 1934 Indian Reorganization Act when government men handpicked Diné (Navajo) men in each community. Women were not even considered, and most handpicked leaders were not considered as such in their own community (Iverson, 2002), yet they were selected to facilitate oil and gas agreements. Since the 1600s, mission boarding schools and, later in the 1800s, government boarding schools sought to

> strip Diné children of their language and culture (Szasz, 1977). "Specifically, reformists [including women] worked together with the BIA to enact a social reform program that identified the American Indian family as ground zero in the cold war against 'Indian savages.' In these efforts, reformists served as the principal agents in the reeducation of American Indian women" (Grande, 2004, p. 129). The resulting repercussions of government interference upon our Diné (Navajo) society, especially Diné women, continues generation after generation and is manifested in the high suicide rates, violent deaths, and even the low academic achievement scores of our precious youth.
>
> —Kathryn

The public, dominant history of American Indians has been formulated since colonization, not only with the assumption that (mostly) males of European descent had the "right" to represent (interpret and judge) the lives of "others" but through the construction and continued use of inaccuracies, misinterpretations, and misrepresentations. Labeling these inaccuracies the "Eurocentric error," Jaimes (1992) has demonstrated that even ethnographic, qualitative, and well-intended interpretations have distorted meanings in ways that constructed females as exotic and erotic, and peoples as tribal (read: "pack of wolves," "primitive or barbarous," or "inferior culture") and conforming (Jaimes, 2003, p. 4). Unconsciously, yet repeatedly committing this Eurocentric error, scholars have constructed and interpreted marginalized peoples as "artifacts," imposing characterizations such as "communal" in ways that distort prepatriarchal and precolonialist lifeways. Furthermore, mainstream feminism(s), even focusing on issues of individual civil rights (an important, but again Eurocentric concept), has not usually acknowledged "indigenism" (Jaimes Guerrero, 1997, p. 102). Human worldviews based on collective human rights, communal orientations, and constructions of sovereignty grounded in reciprocity rather than individual ownership have been treated as if nonexistent. The complex matrix of power generated by a patriarchal, colonialist Eurocentrism that attempted to eliminate all remnants of cultures that were matrifocal or egalitarian or that represented a challenge to European male power is not usually addressed.

Native women and a range of women of color who identify themselves as feminists have pointed to similar forms of unquestioned Eurocentric assumptions (distortions). Initially challenging Euro-American feminist constructions of universal female experience and White, privileged criticisms of patriarchy (Collins, 1998; Mohanty, Russo, & Torres, 1991), most recently, feminists of color, especially Black feminist scholars such as Patricia Hill Collins, have described new forms of racism that rework and reconstitute the intersection of race, gender, and the various institutionalized forms of oppressive power that are embedded within Eurocentric and dominant American error (Collins, 2005). She demonstrates how chattel slavery, labor exploitation, and racial segregation have left their mark even today in cities with de facto ghettos, exploitation of children and young adults in prostitution, and debt bondage imposed on illegal immigrants. In addition, Collins expresses the concern that the "door of opportunity" (p. 84) opened in the 1960s is closing.

We agree with Collins and many others who would refer to contemporary times as also exhibiting a new colonialism, reworking the past in ways that are more insidious, that interconnect the violence of racism, sexism, and oppression of the poor (as well as increasing their numbers), with a form of culture erasure that is so thorough that it rivals physical genocide. This new colonialism (with all its forms of oppression) is a patriarchal hypercapitalism (Cannella & Swadener, 2005; Cannella & Viruru, 2004) that imposes market domination (another form of Eurocentric and American error) over diverse epistemologies around the world as if a superior and therefore legitimate authority. Underlying this domination is a reconceptualized and institutionalized matrix of racism, sexism, and classism that has become invisible. A recent example is the struggle for intellectual property rights. Corporate claims to indigenous knowledge (whether cultural practices or knowledge of the biological environment) employ Western definitions of science and free trade to literally perform "intellectual piracy"

(Mohanty, 2003, p. 232; Shiva, 2000). Shiva (2000) has demonstrated how the epistemologies of poor, indigenous women in India make possible globalization and biopiracy (knowledge of seeds, plants, systems of medicine) by "reading up" the power hierarchy from the locations of peasant women to the practices of the World Trade Organization (WTO). The United States patented approximately 4,000 plant-based formulations in the year 2000 from plants originating in India alone. The country of India is therefore taking steps to create a digital library of 30 million pages of indigenous knowledge to safeguard a 5,000-year tradition (Das, 2006) of a collective "intellectual commons" (Mohanty, 2003, p. 233), to create a database of knowledge that cannot be patented and sold. One of the most disturbing forms of biopiracy is that associated with genetic racism, as illustrated in the Diversity Project that would patent DNA from 700 groups of indigenous people worldwide in the name of blood certification as objective science (Jaimes, 2003). Were we not already aware that the practice of research is problematic (L. T. Smith, 1999), the contemporary acceptance of intellectual piracy and biopiracy would certainly clarify that position.

Rethinking the Consciousness and Purposes of Research

Research as construct is so deeply embedded within Enlightenment/modernist thought that arguing for its continued practice is actually a reproduction of the Eurocentric and American error. However, we believe that the contemporary world will continue to use the research-as-power construct. Rejection of research as practice is also most likely not an option; therefore, reconceptualization is of great importance. The Eurocentric error that assumes that scientists have the "right" (and ability) to intellectually know, interpret, and represent others should, however, be eliminated (whether that so-called right is imposed on individual learner, child, woman, man, Indigenous person, or anyone or group constructed as the "other" through fields such as psychology, sociology, and anthropology, or even by engaging in experimental, ethnographic, or naturalistic research). As has been demonstrated from a range of research locations (Denzin, 2005), entirely different purposes and questions can be generated that would transform the disciplines and the conceptualization and practice of science in ways that would not assume the right to know, understand, or name "others." Describing the Māori principle of *whakapapa,* which locates Māori as connected morally to all things, L. T. Smith (2000) has clearly identified critical moral questions that should be asked regarding any form of research. These questions relate to the power inscribed through research as construct, whether traditionally designed or reconceptualized, and require the involvement of people in creating, conducting, owning, and judging research about themselves. Furthermore, Native and non-Native, Indigenous and non-Indigenous, must recognize that there is no singular voice, no prototype of Native or Indigenous peoples.

In addition, Cannella and Viruru (2004; Viruru & Cannella, 2006) have proposed that a decolonialist science would privilege research goals/purposes that no longer accept the Eurocentric assumption (error) that some human beings have the power to "know" others (whether cognitively or through personal stories) but would rather acknowledge and focus on the complexities of our contemporary sociopolitical condition(s). This decolonialist social science would (a) investigate ways that society(ies) produce(s) forms of exclusion and erasure; (b) examine new forms of domination, as well as reinscribe/reinforce codes of imperialism; and (c) facilitate community action research originating from traditionally marginalized people. Consistent with the long history of American Indian anticolonialist struggle, Rau (2005), a Māori educator, has insisted that this decolonialist perspective actually be referred to as anticolonial social science, a perspective that would challenge the illusion that decolonizing can eliminate the effects of oppression. The notion of anticolonialism then requires an orientation that is radically activist and does not support a false separation between academic research and transformative actions in the contemporary world.

Conceived from within hegemonic orientations, research cannot appropriately be practiced without questions of power always being addressed. Furthermore, research conceptualized as anticolonialist social science would acknowledge the intersections of various manifestations of oppressive power and the multidirectionality and complexity of that power contemporarily and contextually. We would propose that research as construct would then engage with public discourses and policy practices (ranging from notions of school readiness, to the purposes and practices of education, to constructions of mental illness, to views of sexual orientation and marriage and family) to determine the underlying and unexamined Eurocentric, dominant American assumptions, as well as who is privileged and credited, and who is marginalized and discredited. Research would take on a nonviolent revolutionary consciousness that would also transform the researcher (hooks, 2000). No longer would it be appropriate to label other human beings as "ready for school learning" or "exhibiting mental illness"; rather, the research focus would be on the underlying assumptions, the will to power, that creates such constructs in the first place. Even our current academic attempts to recognize, hear, understand, and celebrate (and, however unintended, essentialize) Indigenous or Native voices would be examined.

Research Interactions (Between People and With Data and Context)

Anticolonialist research interactions can be found in the range of postmodern, poststructural, Indigenous, and feminist techniques that have already deconstructed knowledge and engaged in various forms of discourse analyses in a variety of fields over the past several years (Cannella, 1997; de la Torre & Pesquera, 1993; Gandhi, 1998; Moraga, 1983). However, an "activist" anticolonialism would require that traditional and newly emergent methodologies be transformed into public conversations in ways that avoid the construction of dualist counternarratives that actually reinscribe modernist simplicities (Butler, 2004). Although sharing an affinity for coresearch with such practices as participatory action research (PAR), for example, anticolonialist social science would necessarily critique from within to avoid the reinscription of new (less overt, but insidious) forms of patriarchy and capitalism (for critiques of issues related to PAR, see Chambers, 1983; Escobar, 1992, 1995; Rocheleau, 1994). Furthermore, while agreeing with critical revolutionary pedagogy related to the "importance of contesting the unconstrained domination of capital that masquerades as freedom" (McLaren, 2005, p. 89) and the pressing need to counter capitalist reconstitution of institutions such as higher education, an anticolonialist social science would go beyond and outside of such perspectives. Anticolonialism would also avoid the reinscription of economic power that results when the dominant also becomes the method for the elimination of oppression/colonialism. Identification would be with the traditionally marginalized; for example, rather than privileging identification with males or Whites, anticolonialism would challenge the researcher to identify with females and people of color (hooks, 2000).

Anticolonialist research practices would be turned inside out to generate possibilities for continued dialogue with self and others regarding reconceptualization of even the techniques designed to counter colonialism and to generate unthought possibilities (see Viruru & Cannella, 2006, for an example as the authors place the ethnographic interview under the postcolonial lens). Anticolonialist research perspectives would, themselves, require continued examination as positions from which new forms of power could be emerging. Research interactions would be revised in ways that create transparent public conversations (not just academic dialogue) concerning philosophy, agenda, method, and results. Anticolonialism requires that no issue is off limits, yet all are treated with respect for complexity and influence on human beings, as well as positions that could unintentionally inscribe new imperialisms.

Black feminists and other feminists of color have called for and designed intersectional analyses of forms of erasure, domination, and exclusion since the 1980s (Crenshaw, 1991; Davis, 1981; Yuval-Davis, 1997), valuable methods that reject essentializing while at the same time revealing power hierarchal matrices that frame social institutions (e.g., interactions between racism, gender, heterosexism, socioeconomic positioning, nationality, and ageism). An example of this research methodology is illustrated in Collins's (1998) analysis of the ties between gender, race, and violence in the United States. She illustrates how elite groups define violence and use those definitions to maintain power relations (e.g., placing private violence against women and children under erasure, excluding verbal abuse, legitimating violence within social institutions such as police actions). Furthermore, she constructs a conceptual framework that can be used for analysis of dominant forms of power and as vocabulary that would construct action. This framework is referred to as a matrix of domination and includes structural domain, social institutions that organize oppression; disciplinary domain, systems for managing power; hegemonic domain, justifications for and fostering of one's own oppression; and interpersonal domain, seductive pressures that lead to acceptance of dominant power structures (Collins, 2000).

▣ Research as Egalitarian and Activist Life Force

Native Transformative Egalitarianism

> I am a Diné (Navajo) woman and a Diné (Navajo) researcher. My Western name is unimportant in the Diné (Navajo) society, but the identification of my four clans is of utmost importance. To not identify who I am through my clans is an affront to Diné (Navajo) protocol as well as a display of disrespect for myself. Unlike the Euro-Western tradition of having a given name, I am first and foremost a member of my four clans, which represent my female ancestry, my mother, and grandmother's heritage. I belong to my mother's mother's family for generations previous and time immemorial. In the end, as Diné (Navajo), we all belong to our Mother and have the intense Mother-Child bond that specifies our relations to others, both animate and inanimate, and our behavior is guided by who we are as members of our clan throughout our lifetime.
>
> We are children of Asdzaan Nadleehi (Changing Woman). She made the first four clans from her body. . . . Kinaalda was performed by the Diyiin Diné 'e (Holy People) when Changing Woman had her first period. . . . Colonization has manipulated and tried to crush the Diné (Navajo) identity. Yet, the Mother-Child bond in our society has remained. . . . It is evident in the ever-present Kinaalda, a girl's puberty ceremony, which is conducted widely throughout our Diné tah. It is evident when Diné (Navajo) men, women, and children all line up at the end of the Kinaalda, girl's puberty ceremony, to be touched and blessed by the Kinaalda, the girl representing and actually becoming Asdzaan Nadleehi, Changing Woman.
>
> —Kathryn

Discussing Black feminist politics in contemporary times, Collins (2005) recently wrote that "being in one's honest body becomes an essential part of the 'force of life'" (p. 289). This quote illustrates much of the belief in the interconnectedness of life forms and nature, spiritualized egalitarian respect for all, and the importance of transformative actions that are found (however differently expressed) in Native epistemologies and feminisms from often marginalized or purposely discredited locations. These epistemologies can provide new (and/or reconceptualized) knowledges and ways of speaking, unthought possibilities, and positive emotional-intellectual locations from which to generate being with, and caring for, each other that are egalitarian and life affirming. While an anticolonialist social science may at first appear negative by continually focusing on the challenge to matrices of power, these challenges are only one component and one kind of knowledge that is necessary (but not sufficient) for an anticolonial, egalitarian consciousness. Various forms of being, understanding, and interpreting offer unlimited positions from which to construct social science.

For Diné, this point of reference for the interpretation of research is the relationship of Changing Woman to her children. Jaimes Guerrero

(1997) refers to this relationship as the feminine organic archetype, sacred images present in most Native creation stories. Furthermore, this construction of feminine is not the European, male-dominated form but a women-oriented egalitarianism. As members of Indigenous societies, Native American women were respected and influential. Male council members and chiefs were chosen by clan mothers. Women played critical roles in government as communal structures were designed for balance. Fluid sexual and gender roles were practiced with acceptance by all until Christian Europeans imposed judgment and patriarchy (Jaimes Guerrero, 1997). The status of women and men were equal (Blackwood, 1984). Although most societies were matrilinear, even in those that were patrilinear, women were not placed in subordinate positions. Although devastated by patriarchal European colonialism that was certainly not egalitarian and continually controlled by individualist property-based forms of American capitalism, Native societies have survived with major components of philosophical systems in tact (Schwarz, 1997). As an example, for Diné, the image of Changing Woman represents the power of creation, transformation, equality, and life as bodily realm (an entirely different ontological and epistemological perspective than that demonstrated in the dualist notion of separation of mind/body, objectivity/subjectivity, male/female that dominants modernist Euro-American science). This organic feminine archetype represents an egalitarian position from which multiple, even contradictory, epistemologies can engage equitably and with caring support.

Although questioned by some Native scholars as to method and interpretation (Jaimes Guerrero, 1997), Paula Gunn Allen (1992), of Laguna Pueblo and Sioux heritage, traces the roots of modern feminism to Native mothers. She states,

> If American society judiciously modeled the traditions of the various Native Nations, the place of women in society would be central, the distribution of goods and power would be egalitarian, the elderly would be respected, honored, and protected as a primary social and cultural resource, the ideals of physical beauty would be considerably enlarged . . . the destruction of the biota, the life sphere, and the natural resources of the planet would be curtailed, and the spiritual nature of human and nonhuman life would become a primary organizing force of human society. (p. 211)

She proposes that the historical attitudes and actions of early Native women influenced visions for human liberation around the world, including American feminists, as well as early discussions of women's liberation that were included in socialist literature and egalitarian rejection of European notions of aristocracy in the Americas. Furthermore, identification with the power of the female body (as evidenced by Diné blessings given to others as they are touched by the Kinaaldah, who becomes Changing Woman in the puberty ceremony) is a notion that is supported in a range of feminist perspectives, from Lerner's (1986) proposal that women identify with women to Walker's (1999) Black feminist construction of womanism.

The feminine organic archetype does not separate mind and body. Chicana feminists, for example, have used the body as a medium from which to theorize and illuminate the notion of border bodies using deeply personal stories to combine spirituality, geography, history, and diverse languages as embodied and *mestiza* (biologically, physically, or culturally mixed) consciousness (Anzaldúa, 1987, 1990). *La mestiza* embodies the potential for blurring the boundaries of identity, space, and time. Trujillo (1998) centers *mestiza* women as not to be essentialized but as a collective of multiple and unlimited possibilities. Some have even proposed the creation of a "decolonial imaginary," as a space for construction and balance of bodies and lives living within colonial patriarchy (Perez, 1999). This imagining of the multiple addresses the postcolonial scholars' perspective that cautions against focusing on the body in a way that reconstitutes colonizer and colonized (Loomba, 1998; Spivak, 1996, 1999) as entirely absent from human agency represented in the creation of dichotomies. These dualisms can actually result in a power relation that constructs greater possibilities for oppression by creating an illusion that power is a simple, one-way process. *La mestiza* is the embodiment of challenges to dualistic ways of questioning, being, and interpreting.

Poststructuralists and feminists of color have illustrated transformational possibilities for the body by demonstrating multidirectionality within diverse practices and conceptualizations of maternity (Kristeva, 1987), the ways that women's bodies are spatially encoded as representing nation (Mohanram, 1999), and possibilities for unsettling bodies so that new ways for "bodies to matter" become possible (Butler, 1993, p. 30; 2004). Embracing, exploring, and privileging (without attempting to market) egalitarian, reproductive life force, and body knowledges from the margin would result in an entirely reconceptualized social science.

Collective Reciprocal Relations

> Land is a macro prototype of our Mother, Changing Woman. Both land and the Hogan are synonymous. Both are "mothers" to our people. Land known as Mother Earth is not a metaphor to Diné. Mother Earth is a being who is a source of life, gives birth to all living creatures, and sustains the life of her children by providing them with food and protection. Mother Earth, like our human mothers, is priceless and not a commodity that can be sold or bought as real estate. According to Diné (Navajo) philosophical teachings, land and the environment exist as sacred space. For Diné, life is a journey through sacred landscape. Land, like the Hogan, is a place of conception, birth, growth and development, and death. Thus, the highest desire for Diné (Navajo) is to maintain their land through the acknowledgment of their sovereignty from the United States government.... Our four sacred mountains in each direction define our land, our space. As Diné we have traversed four other worlds previous and have stories of each of these worlds....
>
> —Kathryn

Using Walker's (1999) notion of womanism, Jaimes (2003) proposes a native womanism in which the female principle that calls for women to identify with women serves to challenge patriarchal, colonialist, and capitalist oppression of both women and nature, forming a collective reciprocity that is relational and connected. This form of spirituality includes forms of indigenism and ecofeminism. For Native peoples, *indigenous* means living in reciprocal relations with one's place of birth. This relationship incorporates a native spirituality with a land ethic that celebrates biodiversity as the connection between the bioregion and human culture (Jaimes, 2003; Jaimes Guerrero, 2004) but does not accept the commodification of biodiversity.

Ecofeminism, a feminist-based environmentalism, offers unique epistemologies that assume interconnections between human and nonhuman, life and nonlife. Actually, these epistemologies avoid the construction of (and therefore challenge) such dualistic thinking (Plumwood, 1991). An ecofeminist ethic of care involves grassroots political actions (originating in the community) developed through the exploration of woman-nature connections, engaging in the theorizing and construction of knowledges that avoid dualistic, rational individualism (Plant, 1990; Warren, 1993). Examples include India's Chipko (tree-hugging) movement in which the traditional worship of tree goddesses and tree embracing were revived in attempts to save forests from erosion and cash cropping (Shiva, 1988), using an ancient paradigm that is actually similar to the emergent academic concept of agroforestry, and the Kenyan women's movement for the past 30 years to reverse desertification that has been produced by humans and to restore sustainable woodlands (Maathai, 1988).

Although ecofeminisms have emerged from a range of philosophical perspectives (with some views even generating causal epistemologies), the focus on the woman-nature connection (and the history of denigration) draws attention to new forms of conquest (of nature and ideas) in the contemporary world. The new forms are entrepreneurial, are market based, and even blur the boundaries of national sovereignty (Brown, 2002). The erosion (and/or genocide) of peoples, cultures, and environments is understood as inextricably linked by these new forms of conquest (Jaimes Guerrero,

2004). Corporate claims to both indigenous knowledge and biology, as discussed earlier in the form of intellectual piracy and biopiracy, are examples (Mohanty, 2003; Shiva, 2000). Liberal, cultural, social, and socialist feminists differ as to the ultimate focus for ecopolitical actions but are similar in emphasizing reproduction and the continuation of life on Earth (Merchant, 2005); ecofeminists would reverse priorities away from capitalist production toward sustainable reproduction and ecology. Furthermore, notions of sustainable development are critiqued as reinforcing dominance; people's oriented approaches that would eliminate poverty, as well as grant women control over their own bodies and resources, and the realization of basic health, employment, and security needs are emphasized (Braidotti, Charkiewics, Hausler, & Wieringa, 1994).

Neoliberal policies have supported market orientations that institutionalize a capitalist ideology of commodification (over nature, environment, culture, gender, ideas, and on and on). Globalization privileges privatization and the primacy of market rationality by facilitating competition and increased internationalization of business. Fleeing wage requirements, taxation, and regulation, corporations have expanded their operations transnationally. This extended influence over public and private spaces transcends national boundaries and has eroded the sovereignty of nation-states (an ironic condition considering that Native American, and various other Indigenous groups, have never been fully heard regarding notions of reciprocal sovereignty). Furthermore, economic decision making is replacing political (and potentially democratic) decision making (Brown, 2002). Combined with hypercapitalism, this decline in nation-state sovereignty undermines and even reconstructs the purposes of citizenship and the civil function of government. Poor women, children, traditionally marginalized people, the environment, ideas, the spiritual collective life force—everyone and everything is interpreted in relation to market investment and profitability. The conceptualization of citizen has been recast as consumer.

To illustrate, Mohanty (2003) discusses "privatization, labor, and the entrepreneurial university" (p. 177). Deregulation, cost cutting, and discourses of privatization and market economies have invaded all aspects of society, as well as universities (Slaughter & Leslie, 1997). Exhibiting "academic capitalism" (p. 178), universities are increasingly restructured to function based on market rationalism both financially and related to policy. The professoriate faces loss of autonomy, intense monitoring, and decreased power in decision making (Currie, 1998). Academic citizenship is being actively reconceptualized in the corporate university as feminist and antiracist scholars face organized attempts to disqualify and discredit their professional and personal ways of understanding and experiencing the world (Lincoln & Cannella, 2004). In the past 30 years, the percentage of female professors with tenure has not changed as almost 80% of full professors are male and mostly White. The gap between male and female salaries has actually widened (Chait & Trower, 2001). Students are defined as consumers as professors are constructed as the proleteriat who work for powerful corporate academic administrators. Discourses of investment, entrepreneurialism, and corporate partnership abound. The purpose of an education that would develop liberated citizens is reconceived as the development of consumer citizens (Reading, 1996).

Collectivist, reciprocal ways of being and living in respectful and honest relations are of utmost importance as we have increasingly denounced our connectedness, spiritualities, and possibilities in the name of competition, efficiency, individualism, measurement, and profitability. Social science discourses, knowledges, and ways of being that are caring, insightful, and that value our collective connections to each other (including all forms of life and "nonlife"), while fostering our diversities in ways that challenge commodification, may be the most needed contemporary emotional and intellectual acts.

Mestiza Warrior Activism(s)

> I am also a warrior person as specified by my Diné (Navajo) name. I am not a warrior "princess." Most female Diné (Navajo) names have -Ba' as a suffix in

their name, describing and denoting us as a warrior. My family history stories contain references to women who bravely fought, protected, and provided for family. Oral stories of Hweeldi/The Long Walk provide examples of Diné (Navajo) women who courageously led or supported their people to survival.

The tragedy of the Oklahoma City government building that was bombed in the 1990s was referred to as the first ever terror in the heartland. Yet, I knew that thousands, if not millions, of American Indians died in the heartland of America while defending their land.

—Kathryn

Just as Collins (2000, 2005) discusses the separation of Black feminist thought from Black women's community activism, so too has the separation of Navajo academic lives (locating them in Euro-American institutions) from the Diné community resulted in less transformative power for diverse knowledges, discourses, and ways of being. Collins describes the activist resistance methodologies of women in the African American community as historical analysis; motherwork that focused on the development of identities that could withstand racist assault (a notion similar to othermothering in Diné culture); reviving institutions of civil society; using "an oppressed person's most potent weapons: information, analysis and positive group identity" (Cleage, 1993, p. 31); and activist Black community work (Collins, 2000). Furthermore, she stresses that Black and Latina community activists have historically attempted to generate ways to transcend their differences.

A related form of activism is evident in the Diné womanist warrior archetype (Manuelito, in press). Creation stories are replete with warrior women who fight to protect and shelter their children. Including the suffix *-ba'* which means *war,* women's names describe forms of endurance during war. This image is contemporarily played out as mothers and grandmothers take the lead in marches against relocation. Warrior strengths, wisdom, and critical judgments of Diné women are credited with the survival of a people. To some extent, this womanist warrior archetype embodies *la mestiza* mixed consciousness, an activism that maintains a proud people while surviving within and confronting colonialist patriarchy.

At least some researchers in the social sciences have tended to consider their scholarly work to be activism, which in our academic communities may have been fairly accurate in the past. However, research that would reveal the will to power, challenge connections that create new forms of oppression, and construct an egalitarian essence requires new critical forms of activism. The traditional academic view of research activism that would collect human data yet remain intellectually separated from communities was never really egalitarian and is certainly no longer a viable option. Furthermore, even research conceptualizations (like qualitative participatory action research) that construct false illusions of equity or beliefs that the local is countering the global would require astute critical examination. Researchers can no longer be individuals who decide to interview others as if power were not an issue, fool themselves into thinking they are collaborating, or legitimate obtaining research funds from dominant sources with the false pretence that the money can also be used subversively (to counter dominant power). Political and academic activism has become much more complex. For those who would research and publish, academic colonialist powers that would further impose Euro-American errors (as if truths for everyone) have reinscribed old forms of review and exclusion, as well as generated new methods to discredit and silence (e.g., think tanks, conservative foundations, funding networks, attempts to discredit higher education; see Lincoln & Cannella, 2004). For those who believe that they should follow 1960s forms of social activism by marching and participating in nonviolent protests, locations of invisibility have been legislated that place those who disagree simply out of sight, with activism constructed as nonexistent (through media silence). The 1960s successes of special interest groups that attempted to address racism, sexism, and various other forms of injustice have been turned upside down as well-funded lobbyists representing transnational business agendas and conservative antidemocracy have become the leaders of special interests. Furthermore, hypercapitalist patriarchy now uses money, religious rhetoric, or whatever means necessary to create an illusion of public outcry, protest marches, and grassroots activism related to their own issues. Forms of activism are necessary that acknowledge intersecting oppressions within a contemporary hypercapitalist patriarchal context that is so invasive that those who choose to confront and challenge risk being destroyed.

This contemporary condition requires a *mestiza* warrior activism for the construction of an anticolonialist social science. This radical activism would question the appropriateness of collecting data from "Others" (and obviously decry the creation of others) but would also focus on the unthought, the blurring of the accepted, and the generation of new images of being. *Mestiza* warrior wisdom would consciously construct new spaces for multiplicity, border essences, and woman identification.

Research and Marginalization in Contemporary Times

Native epistemologies and marginalized feminisms can actually serve as foundational for the construction of an anticolonial, egalitarian social science. While by no means representing a "theory of the development of egalitarianism" (a form of rationalist thinking that we would try to avoid), topics generated by Diné narratives provide an emotional-intellectual consciousness from which to approach social science research. A transformative egalitarianism would insist that the purposes of research are to make visible, center, and privilege those knowledges that have been placed in the margins because they represented threats to power, while avoiding the creation of new power hierarchies or the objectification of those knowledges (or people associated with them).

Research interactions are needed that allow for the different epistemological spaces from which to collect and analyze data without imposing power on others. For example, we (as researchers, community members, women) may come to feel that we cannot collect data from "others" in ways that ultimately increase our authority as researchers (over the researched). The analysis of public and dominant discourses and the construction of new activist methodologies can involve research interactions that use public sources, so do not involve representing the "other." As we struggle together to form collectivist, relational ways of being and acting that are transformative, working together to determine our conceptualizations of knowledge, new methodologies should and will emerge. Because we must use research, and because new conceptualizations of research as construct are necessary, we must document our actions and possibilities.

This anticolonial social science would no longer accept the assumptions that human beings have the ability or "right" to define, know, or judge the minds, cultures, or ways of being of others. Rather, the focus of research in such a social science would be to (a) reveal and actively challenge social systems, discourses, and institutions that are oppressive and that perpetuate injustice (even if those systems are represented in disciplinary knowledge) and explore ways of making those systems obviously visible in society; (b) support knowledges that have been discredited by dominant power orientations in ways that are transformative (rather than simply revealing); and (c) construct activist conceptualizations of research that are critical and multiple in ways that are transparent, reflexive, and collaborative. Some of our research practices can be transformed and/or extended; many must be eliminated. Others will emerge as we struggle together to hear, respect, and support each other and the collective environment that surrounds us all.

References

Allen, P. G. (1992). *The sacred hoop: Recovering the feminine in American Indian traditions.* Boston: Beacon.

Anzaldúa, G. (1987). *Borderlands/La frontera.* San Francisco: Aunt Lute Books.

Anzaldúa, G. (Ed.). (1990). *Making face, making soul.* San Francisco: Aunt Lute Books.

Blackwood, E. (1984). Sexuality and gender in certain Native American tribes: The case of cross-gender females. *Signs, 10,* 27–42.

Braidotti, R., Charkiewics, E., Hausler, S., & Wieringa, S. (1994). *Women, the environment, and sustainable development.* London: Zed Books.

Brown, R. H. (2002). Global capitalism, national sovereignty, and the decline of democratic space. *Rhetoric & Public Affairs, 5,* 347–357.

Butler, J. (1993). *Bodies that matter: On the discursive limits of "sex."* New York: Routledge.

Butler, J. (2004). *Undoing gender.* New York: Routledge.

Cannella, G. S. (1997). *Deconstructing early childhood education: Social justice and revolution.* New York: Peter Lang.

Cannella, G. S., & Swadener, B. B. (2005, April). *Contemporary public policy influencing children and families: "Compassionate" social provision or the regulation of "Others."* Paper presented at the 2005 American Educational Research Association Conference, Montreal, Canada.

Cannella, G. S., & Viruru, R. (2004). *Childhood and postcolonization: Power, education, and contemporary practice.* New York: RouledgeFalmer.

Case, S. E., & Abbitt, E. W. (2004). Disidentifications, diaspora and desire: Questions on the future of the feminist critique of performance. *Signs, 29,* 925–938.

Chait, R., & Trower, C. (2001, September 11). Professors at the color line. *New York Times.*

Chambers, R. (1983). *Rural development: Putting the last first.* London: Longman.

Cleage, P. (1993). *Deals with the devil and other reasons to riot.* New York: Ballantine.

Collins, P. H. (1986). Learning from the outsider within: The sociological significance of Black feminist thought. *Social Problems, 33,* 514–532.

Collins, P. H. (1998). The tie that binds: Race, gender and US violence. *Ethnic and Racial Studies, 21,* 917–938.

Collins, P. H. (2000). *Black feminist thought: Knowledge, consciousness, and the politics of empowerment.* New York: Routledge.

Collins, P. H. (2005). *Black sexual politics: African Americans, gender, and the new racism.* New York: Routledge.

Crenshaw, K. W. (1991). Mapping the margins: Intersectionality, identity politics, and violence against women of color. *Stanford Law Review, 43,* 1241–1299.

Currie, J. (1998). Globalization practices and the professoriate in Anglo-Pacific and North American universities. *Comparative Education Review, 42*(1), 15–30.

Das, A. (2006, February 18). India tries to protect intellectual property: Nations begin documenting age-old wisdom. *The Arizona Republic,* p. A30.

Davis, A. (1981). *Women, race, and class.* New York: Random House.

de la Torre, A., & Pesquera, B. (1993). *Building with our hands: New directions in Chicana studies.* Berkeley: University of California Press.

Denzin, N. K. (2005). Emancipatory discourses and the ethics and politics of interpretation. In N. K. Denzin & Y. S. Lincoln (Eds.), *The SAGE handbook of qualitative research* (3rd ed., pp. 933–958). Thousand Oaks, CA: Sage.

Ellis, C. (1995). *Final negotiations: A story of love, loss, and chronic illness.* Philadelphia: Temple University Press.

Escobar, A. (1992). Culture, economics, and politics in Latin American social movements theory and research. In A. Escobar & S. Alvarez (Eds.), *The making of social movements in Latin America* (pp. 62–85). Boulder, CO: Westview.

Escobar, A. (1995). *Encountering development: The making and unmaking of the Third World.* Princeton, NJ: Princeton University Press.

Fine, M. (1992). Passions, politics and power: Feminist research possibilities. In M. Fine (Ed.), *Disruptive voices* (pp. 205–232). Ann Arbor: University of Michigan Press.

Gandhi, L. (1998). *Postcolonial theory: A critical introduction.* New York: Columbia University Press.

Grande, S. (2004). *Red pedagogy, Native American social and political thought.* New York: Rowman & Littlefield.

Haraway, D. J. (1987). A manifesto for cyborgs: Science, technology, and socialist feminism in the 1980's. *Australian Feminist Studies, 4,* 1–41.

Haraway, D. J. (1988). Situated knowledges: The science question in feminism and the privilege of partial perspectives. *Feminist Studies, 14,* 575–599.

Harding, S. (1987). Conclusion: Epistemological questions. In S. Harding (Ed.), *Feminism and methodology* (pp. 181–190). Bloomington: Indiana University Press.

Hartsock, N. (1997). Comment on Hekman's "Truth and method: Feminist standpoint theory revisited": Truth or justice? *Signs, 22,* 367–374.

hooks, b. (2000). *Feminism is for everybody: Passionate politics.* Cambridge, MA: South End.

Hurtado, A. (1989). Relating to privilege: Seduction and rejection in the subordination of white women and women of color. *Signs, 14,* 833–855.

Iverson, P. (2002). *Diné: A history of the Navajos* (M. Roessel, Illustrator). Albuquerque: University of New Mexico Press.

Jaimes, M. A. (1992). La raza and indigenism: Alternatives to autogenocide in North America. *Global Justice, 3*(2–3), 4–19.

Jaimes, M. A. (2003). "Patriarchal colonialism" and "indigenism": Implications for native feminist spirituality and native womanism. *Hypatia—A Journal of Feminist Philosophy, 18*(2). Retrieved February 4, 2006, from http://rdsweb1.rdsinc.com.ezproxy1.libasu.edu/texis/rds/suite2/+sceJjD6emxwwwwwFqz6

Jaimes Guerrero, M. A. (1997). Civil rights versus sovereignty: Native American women in life and land struggles. In M. J. Alexander & C. T. Mohanty (Eds.), *Feminist genealogies, colonial legacies, democratic futures* (pp. 101–121). New York: Routledge.

Jaimes Guerrero, M. A. (2004). Biocolonialism and isolates of historic interest. In M. Riley (Ed.), *Indigenous intellectual property rights: Legal obstacles and innovative solutions* (pp. 251–277). Walnut Creek, CA: AltaMira Press.

Kristeva, J. (1987). *In the beginning was love: Psychoanalysis and faith* (A. Goldhammer, Trans.). New York: Columbia University Press.

Lather, P. (1993). Fertile obsession: Validity after poststructuralism. *The Sociological Quarterly, 34,* 673–694.

Lerner, G. (1986). *The creation of patriarchy.* New York: Oxford University Press.

Lincoln, Y. S., & Cannella, G. S. (2004). Qualitative research, power, and the radical right. *Qualitative Inquiry, 10*(2), 175–201.

Loomba, A. (1998). *Colonialism/postcolonialism.* London: Routledge.

Lorde, A. (1984). *Sister outsider.* Trumansberg, NY: Crossing Press.

Maathai, W. (1988). *The green belt movement: Sharing the approach and the experience.* Nairobi, Kenya: Environment Liaison Centre International.

Manuelito, K. (2005). The role of education in American Indian self-determination: Lessons from the Ramah Navajo community school. *Anthropology and Education Quarterly, 36*(1), 73–87.

Manuelito, K. (in press). Womanism to indigenism: African American womanism and American Indian women's identity and experience. *Journal of Work and Days.*

Mauthner, M., Birch, M., Jessop, J., & Miller, T. (Eds.). (2002). *Ethics in qualitative research.* Thousand Oaks, CA: Sage.

McLaren, P. (2005). *Capitalists & conquerors: A critical pedagogy against empire.* Lanham, MD: Rowman & Littlefield.

Merchant, C. (2005). *Radical ecology: The search for a livable world.* New York: Routledge.

Mohanram, R. (1999). *Black body: Women, colonialism, and space.* Minneapolis: University of Minnesota Press.

Mohanty, C. T. (1988). Under Western eyes: Feminist scholarship and colonial discourses. *Feminist Review, 30,* 60–88.

Mohanty, C. T. (2003). *Feminism without borders: Decolonizing theory, practicing solidarity.* Durham, NC: Duke University Press.

Mohanty, C. T., Russo, A., & Torres, L. (Eds.). (1991). *Third World women and the politics of feminism.* Bloomington: Indiana University Press.

Moraga, C. (1983). *Loving in the war years: Lo que nunca paso por sus labios.* Cambridge, MA: South End.

Olesen, V. (2005). Early millennial feminist qualitative research. In N. K. Denzin & Y. S. Lincoln (Eds.), *The SAGE handbook of qualitative research* (3rd ed., pp. 235–278). Thousand Oaks, CA: Sage.

Perez, E. (1999). *The decolonial imaginary: Writing Chicanas into history.* Bloomington: Indiana University Press.

Plant, J. (1990). Searching for common ground: Ecofeminism and bioregionalism. In I. Diamond & G. F. Orenstein (Eds.), *Reweaving the world: The emergence of ecofeminism.* San Francisco: Sierra Club Books.

Plumwood, V. (1991). Nature, self, and gender: Feminism, environmental philosophy and the critique of rationalism. *Hypatia, 6*(1), 3–37.

Rau, C. (2005, October). *Indigenous metaphors of the heart: Transformative praxis in early childhood education in Aotearoa, privileging Māori women's educator's voices.* Paper presented at the 13th

International Conference on Reconceptualizing Early Childhood Research Theory and Practice, Madison, WI.

Reading, W. (1996). *The university in ruins.* Cambridge, MA: Harvard University Press.

Rocheleau, D. E. (1994). Participatory research and the race to save the planet: Questions, critique, and lessons from the field. *Agriculture and Human Values, 11*(2–3), 4–25.

Schwarz, M. T. (1997). *Molded in the image of Changing Woman: Navajo views on the human body and personhood.* Tucson: University of Arizona Press.

Shiva, V. (1988). *Staying alive: Women, ecology, and development.* London: Zed Books.

Shiva, V. (2000). *Betting on biodiversity: Why genetic engineering will not feed the hungry or save the planet.* New Delhi, India: Research Foundation for Science, Technology and Ecology.

Slaughter, S., & Leslie, L. (1997). *Academic capitalism: Politics, policies, and the entrepreneurial university.* Baltimore: Johns Hopkins University Press.

Smith, D. (1992). Sociology from women's experience: A reaffirmation. *Sociological Quarterly, 10,* 88–98.

Smith, L. T. (1999). *Decolonizing methodologies: Research and indigenous peoples.* London: Zed Books.

Smith, L. T. (2000). Kauppapa Māori research. In M. Battiste (Ed.), *Reclaiming indigenous voice and vision* (pp. 225–247). Vancouver: University of British Columbia Press.

Spivak, G. C. (1996). Poststructuralism, marginality, postcoloniality, and value. In P. Mongia (Ed.), *Contemporary postcolonial theory: A reader* (pp. 198–223). London: Arnold.

Spivak, G. C. (1988). Can the subaltern speak? In C. Nelson & L. Grossberg (Eds.), *Marxism and the interpretation of culture* (pp. 271–313). Urbana: University of Illinois Press.

Spivak, G. C. (1999). *A critique of postcolonial reason: Toward a history of the vanishing present.* Cambridge, MA: Harvard University Press.

Szasz, M. C. (1977). *Education and the American Indian: The road to self-determination.* Albuquerque: University of New Mexico Press.

Trujillo, C. (Ed.). (1998). *Living Chicana theory.* Berkeley, CA: Third Woman Press.

Viruru, R., & Cannella, G. S. (2006). A postcolonial critique of the ethnographic interview: Research analyzes research. In N. K. Denzin & M. D. Giardina (Eds.), *Qualitative inquiry and the conservative challenge: Confronting methodological fundamentalism* (pp. 175–191). Walnut Creek, CA: Left Coast Press.

Walker, A. (1999). *In search of our mothers' gardens: Womanist prose.* San Diego: Harvest.

Warren, K. J. (1993). Introduction. In M. E. Zimmerman, J. B. Callicott, G. Sessions, K. J. Warren, & J. Clark (Eds.), *Environmental philosophy: From animal rights to radical ecology.* Englewood Cliffs, NJ: Prentice Hall.

Wheeler, B. (2003). The institutionalization of an American avant-garde: Performance art as democratic culture, 1970–2000. *Sociological Perspectives, 46*(4), 491–512.

Yuval-Davis, N. (1997). *Gender and nation.* Thousand Oaks, CA: Sage.

Zevella, P. (1987). *Women's work and Chicano families: Cannery workers of the Santa Clara Valley.* Ithaca, NY: Cornell University Press.

Zinn, M. B. (1982). Mexican-American women in the social sciences. *Signs, 8,* 251–272.

4

WAITING FOR THE CALL

The Moral Activist Role of Critical Race Theory Scholarship

Gloria Ladson-Billings and Jamel K. Donnor

It doesn't matter who you are, or how high you rise. One day you will get your call. The question is how will you respond?

—African American university senior administrator

The epigraph that opens this chapter comes from a colleague and friend who serves as a top administrator at a major university. His use of the term *your call* is his reference to what in African American vernacular is known as an "N-word" call. Rather than focus on the controversy over the term and its appropriateness (see Kennedy, 2002), this chapter looks more specifically at the meaning of the "call" and the ways it should mobilize scholars of color[1] and others who share commitments to equity, social justice, and human liberation. This friend was referring to the way African Americans are almost never permitted to break out of the prism (and prison) of race that has been imposed by a racially coded and constraining society. Clearly, this same hierarchy and power dynamic operates for all people of color, women, the poor, and other "marginals."[2] The call is that moment where, regardless of one's stature and/or accomplishments, race (and other categories of otherness) is invoked to remind one that she or he still remains locked in the racial construction. Below we provide examples from popular culture and each of the authors to demonstrate how the "call" is mobilized to maintain the power dynamic and hierarchical racial structures of the society.

The first example comes from the 1995 murder trial of Orenthal James Simpson, more commonly known as O. J. Simpson. Simpson was an American hero. He was revered for his exploits on the football field at the University of Southern California, as

SOURCE: Ladson-Billings, G., & Donnor, J. (2005). The moral activist role of critical race theory scholarship. In N. K. Denzin & Y. S. Lincoln (Eds.), *The SAGE handbook of qualitative research* (3rd ed., pp. 279–302). Thousand Oaks, CA: Sage.

well as with the professional football franchises in Buffalo and San Francisco, coupled with his good looks and "articulateness."[3] The latter two qualities allowed Simpson to turn his postcompetition years into a successful sports broadcast career and a mediocre but profitable acting career. Simpson moved comfortably in the world of money and power—the White world. He was said to be someone who "transcended race" (Roediger, 2002), which is a code expression for those people of color who Whites claim they no longer think of as people of color. Michael Jordan and Colin Powell also are considered in this vein. They are, according to Dyson (1993), "symbolic figures who embodied social possibilities of success denied to other people of color" (p. 67).

Some might argue that Simpson did not get a "call"; he was a murderer who got the notoriety and degradation he deserved while also getting away with a heinous crime. Our point is not to argue Simpson's guilt or innocence (and from where we stand, he indeed looks guilty) but rather to describe his devolution from White to Black in the midst of the legal spectacle. Simpson learned quickly that the honorary White status accorded to him by the larger society was tentative and ephemeral. Some might argue that anyone charged with murder would receive the same treatment, but consider that Ray Carruth, a National Football League player who was convicted of a murder for hire of his pregnant girlfriend, was regarded as "just another Black hoodlum." His actions barely caused a collective raised eyebrow in the larger society. We argue that Simpson's crimes are not only the murder of Nicole Brown and Ron Goodman but also the perceived "betrayal" of White trust.

Simpson went from conceptually White to conceptually Black (King, 1995)—from a "Fresh Prince of Brentwood" to the "Pariah of Portrero Hill" (the San Francisco community in which he grew up). One of the weekly newsmagazines admits to "colorizing" Simpson's police mug shot on its cover, giving him a more sinister look. We read that editorial decision as a symbol of Simpson's "return to Black." He no longer transcended race. He was just another N-word who was dangerous, sinister, and unworthy of honorary White status. O. J. Simpson received his call.

Of course, the bizarre and circus-like circumstances of the Simpson trial make it an outlier example of receiving a call. Thus, we use more personal examples that better situate this argument in our everyday life experiences. Ladson-Billings (1998b) describes her experience where she was invited to a major university to be a speaker in the distinguished scholars lecture series. After the speech, she returned to her hotel and decided to unwind in the hotel's concierge floor lounge. Dressed in business attire and reading the newspaper, she noticed a White man who popped his head in the door. "What time are y'all serving?" he asked. As the only person in the lounge, it was clear that he was addressing Ladson-Billings. She politely, but firmly replied, "I don't know what time *they* are serving. I'm here as a guest." Red faced and clearly embarrassed, the man quietly left. One might argue that he made a simple mistake. Perhaps he would have asked the same question of anyone who was sitting in the lounge. But the moment reminded Ladson-Billings that no matter what her scholarly reputation, at any time she could be snapped back into the constraining racial paradigm, complete with all the limitations such designations carry.

Donnor asserts that one of his many calls came when he served as an instructor for a "diversity" class that enrolled all White, middle-class teachers. As a graduate course, Donnor expected the students to adhere to the rigors of a master's-level class. After assigning homework following the first class meeting, Donnor was challenged by one of the few male students about the amount of homework. When Donnor told the student that he expected the students to complete the assignment, the inquirer responded, "It ain't going to happen." At the next class meeting, the program's site coordinator, a White woman, arrived at the class, ostensibly to share some program information with the students. However, as she addressed the students, she began to talk to them about modifications in assignments and contacting her if they had issues and concerns regarding the course.

The issue with the student's complaint about the volume of work is a common one in a society that regularly rejects intellectual pursuits. However, graduate students typically exercise some level of courtesy and skill in negotiating the amount of work they are willing (or able) to do. The blatant remark that "it ain't going to happen" may reflect the certainty with which the student approached the racial power dynamic. As a White male approaching an African American male, this student understood that he could challenge Donnor's credentials and abilities. More pointedly, the experience with the site coordinator underscored the fact that although Donnor was hired to teach the course, authority flowed to the White woman. Students could essentially discount Donnor whenever he did anything they disagreed with. Both incidents serve as powerful reminders for Donnor that despite his academic credentials and experience, his racial identity always serves as a mitigating factor for determining his authority and legitimacy.

Receiving a call is a regular reminder of the liminal space of alterity (Wynter, 1992) that racialized others occupy. But it is important not to solely regard the liminal space as a place of degradation and disadvantage. Wynter (1992) assures us that this place of alterity offers a perspective advantage where those excluded from the center (of social, cultural, political, economic activity) experience "wide-angle" vision. This perspective advantage is not due to an inherent racial/cultural difference but is the result of the dialectical nature of constructed otherness that prescribes the liminal status of people of color as beyond the normative boundary of the conception of Self/Other (King, 1995).

In the previous iteration of this chapter, Ladson-Billings (2000)[4] cited King (1995), who argued that the epistemic project that scholars of color and their allies must undertake is more than simply adding on multiple perspectives or "pivoting" the center. Such scholars occupy a liminal position whose perspective is one of alterity. This liminal position or point of alterity that we inhabit attempts to transcend an "either/or" epistemology. Alterity is not a dualistic position in which there are multiple or equally partial standpoints that are either valid or inexorably ranked hierarchically. Recognizing the alterity perspective does not essentialize other perspectives such as Blackness, Indian-ness, Asian-ness, or Latino-ness as homogenizing reverse epistemics (West, 1990).

Ethiopian anthropologist Asmaron Legesse (1973) asserts that the liminal group is that which is forcibly constrained to play the role of alter ego to the ideal self prescribed by the dominant cultural model. This dominant model sets up prescriptive rules and canons for regulating thought and action in the society. Thus, the "issue is about the 'nature of human knowing' of the social reality, in a model of which the knower is already a socialized subject" (Wynter, 1990, p. 26).

> The system-conserving mainstream perspectives of each order (or well-established scholarship) therefore clash with the challenges made from the perspectives of alterity. . . . For, it is the task of established scholarship to rigorously maintain those prescriptions which are critical to the order's existence. (Wynter, 1990, p. 27)

This focus on the ways of the dominant order is important in helping us explore the ways such an order distorts the realities of the Other in an effort to maintain power relations that continue to disadvantage those who are excluded from that order. As Wynter (1990) so eloquently argues, this liminal perspective is the condition of the dominant order's self-definition that "can empower us to free ourselves from the 'categories and prescriptions' of our specific order and from its 'generalized horizon of understanding'" (p. 27).

In this iteration of the handbook, we move away from solely describing the epistemological terrain (both dominant and liminal) to advocating the kinds of moral and ethical responsibilities various epistemologies embody. We do this in hopes of mobilizing scholarship that will take a stance on behalf of human liberation. The subsequent sections of this chapter examine the position of intellectuals as constructors of ethical epistemologies, the discursive and material limits of liberal ideology, new templates for ethical action, moving from research to activism, reconstructing the intellect, and the search for a revolutionary habitus.

We admit at the outset that this is an ambitious project and that we are likely to fall short of our stated goals. However, because a task is hard does not imply that we should not undertake it. Similarly, Derrick Bell (1991) argued that even though racism was a permanent fixture of American life, we must still struggle against it. Our success will not necessarily come in the form of a tightly constructed scholarly treatise but rather in the form of scores of other community, student, and scholar activists who continue or take up this cause rather than merely waiting for "the call."

Intellectual Marginals as Constructors of Ethical Epistemologies

> The special function of the Negro intellectual is a cultural one. He should . . . assail the stultifying blight of the commercially depraved white middle-class who has poisoned the structural roots of the American ethos and transformed the American people into a nation of intellectual dolts.
>
> —Harold Cruse (1967/1984, p. 455)

We would be remiss if we did not acknowledge the incredible volume of work that scholars of color have produced that we regard as ethical epistemologies. Clearly, in a chapter of this length, it is impossible to do justice to all (or even most) of this work. Thus, we will attempt to make this "review of the literature" more a grand tour (Spradley, 1979) to outline the contours of the foundation on which we are building. We start our foundational work with a look at W. E. B. DuBois's (1903/1953) construct of "double consciousness," where he argues that the African American "ever feels his two-ness . . . two souls, two thoughts, two unreconciled strivings" (p. 5). David Levering Lewis (1993) addressed the importance of DuBois's conception, stating,

> It was a revolutionary concept. It was not just revolutionary; the concept of the divided self was profoundly mystical, for DuBois invested this double consciousness with a capacity to see incomparably farther and deeper. The African American . . . possessed the gift of "second sight in this American world," an intuitive faculty enabling him/her to see and say things about American society that possessed heightened moral validity. (p. 281)

Ladson-Billings (2000) argued previously that DuBois's work had an important synchronic aspect in that he raised the issues of double consciousness prior to the formation of the Frankfurt School, out of which critical theories emerged. Coincidentally, DuBois had studied at the University of Berlin in the late 1800s, yet his name is never mentioned in the same context as Max Horkheimer, Theodor Adorno, and Herbert Marcuse. DuBois remains a "Negro" intellectual concerned with the "Negro" problem, but it was in Germany that DuBois recognized the race problems in the Americas, Africa, and Asia, as well as the political development of Europe as one. This was the period of his life that united his studies of history, economics, and politics into a scientific approach of social research.

DuBois's notion of double consciousness applies not only to African Americans but also to all people who are constructed outside the dominant paradigm. Although DuBois refers to a double consciousness, we know that our sense of identity may evoke multiple consciousness, and it is important to read our discussion of multiple consciousness as a description of complex phenomena that do impose essentialized concepts of "blackness," "Latina/o-ness," "Asian American-ness," or "Native American-ness" onto specific individuals or groups.[5]

In addition to DuBois's conception of double consciousness, we rely on Anzaldúa's (1987) perspective that identities are fractured not only by gender, class, race, religion, and sexuality but also by geographic realities such as living along the U.S.-Mexico border, in urban spaces, or on government-created Indian reservations. Anzaldúa's work continues a long intellectual history of Chicanas/os (see Acuna, 1972; Almaguer,

1974; Balderrama, 1982; Gomez-Quinones, 1977; Mirande & Enriquez, 1979; Padilla, 1987; Paz, 1961) and extends what Delgado Bernal (1998) calls a Chicana feminist epistemology. This work includes writers such as Alarcon (1990), Castillo (1995), and de la Torre and Pesquera (1993) to illustrate the intersections of race, class, and gender.

Our reliance on these scholars is not to assume a unified Latino/a (or even Chicano/a) subject. Oboler (1995) challenges the amalgamation of Spanish speakers in the Western hemisphere under the rubric "Hispanic." The Hispanic label belies the problem inherent in attempts to create a unitary consciousness from one that is much more complex and multiple than imagined or constructed. According to Oboler,

> Insofar as the ethnic label Hispanic homogenizes the varied social and political experiences of 23 million people of different races, classes, languages, and national origins, genders, and religions, it is perhaps not so surprising that the meanings and uses of the term have become the subject of debate in the social sciences, government agencies, and much of society at large. (p. 3)

Oboler's (1995) argument is enacted in a scene in Rebecca Gilman's (2000) play, *Spinning Into Butter.* In one scene, a college student is told that he is eligible for a "minority" fellowship. When the student objects to the term *minority,* the dean informs him that he can designate himself as "Hispanic." He becomes more offended at that term, and when the dean asks him how he would like to identify himself, he says, "Newyorican." The dean then suggests that he list "Puerto Rican," but he explains to her that he is not Puerto Rican. "I have never been to Puerto Rico and I would be as lost as any American tourist there." They continue to argue over what label or category is appropriate. The dean cannot understand that a key feature of self-determination lies in the ability to name oneself. The failure of the dean to recognize Newyorican as an identity does not de-legitimate it, except in her mainstream world, which not insignificantly controls the resources that the student needs to be successful at the college.

American Indians grapple with these same questions of what it means to be Indian. Despite movements toward "pan-Indianism" (Hertzberg, 1971), the cultures of American Indians are both broad and diverse. While we warn against essentializing American Indians, we do not want to minimize the way the federal government's attempt to "civilize" and de-tribalize Indian children through boarding schools helped various groups of Indians realize that they shared a number of common problems and experiences (Snipp, 1995). Lomawaima (1995) stated that "since the federal government turned its attention to the 'problem' of the civilizing Indians, its overt goal has been to educate Indians to be non-Indians" (p. 332).

Much of the double consciousness Indians face revolves around issues of tribal sovereignty. A loss of sovereignty is amplified by four methods of disenfranchisement experienced by many American Indians (Lomawaima, 1995). Those four methods included relocation by colonial authorities (e.g., to missions or reservations), systematic eradication of the native language, religious conversion (to Christianity), and restructured economies toward sedentary agriculture, small-scale craft industry, and gendered labor.

Warrior (1995) asks whether an investigation of early American Indian writers can have a significant impact on the way contemporary Native intellectuals develop critical studies. He urges caution in understanding the scholarship of Fourth World formulations such as Ward Churchill and M. Annette Jaimes because it tends to be essentializing in its call for understanding American Indian culture as a part of a global consciousness shared by all indigenous people in all periods of history. Warrior's work is a call for "intellectual sovereignty" (p. 87)—a position free from the tyranny and oppression of the dominant discourse.

Despite the attempts to eradicate an Indian identity, the mainstream continues to embrace a "romantic" notion of the Indian. In Eyre's (1998) adaptation of Sherman Alexie's (1993) *The Lone Ranger and Tonto Fistfight in Heaven*, which became the film *Smoke Signals,* we see an excellent example of this. The character Victor tells his traveling companion Thomas that he is not Indian enough. Playing on the prevailing stereotypes that Whites have about Indians, Victor instructs Thomas to be "more stoic," to allow his hair to flow freely, and to get rid of his buttoned-down look. We see the humor in this scene because we recognize the ways we want Indians to appear to satisfy our preconceived notions of "Indian-ness."

Among Asian Pacific Islanders, there are notions of multiple consciousness. Lowe (1996) expresses this in terms of "heterogeneity, hybridity, and multiplicity" (p. 60). She points out that

> the articulation of an "Asian American identity" as an organizing tool has provided unity that enables diverse Asian groups to understand unequal circumstances and histories as being related. The building of "Asian American culture" is crucial to this effort, for it articulates and empowers the diverse Asian-origin community vis-à-vis the institutions and apparatuses that exclude and marginalize it. Yet to the extent that Asian American culture fixes Asian American identity and suppresses differences—of national origin, generation, gender, sexuality, class—it risks particular dangers: not only does it underestimate the differences and hybridities among Asians, but it may inadvertently support the racist discourse that constructs Asians as a homogenous group. (pp. 70–71)

Espiritu (1992) also reminds us that "Asian American" as an identity category came into being within the past 30 years. Prior to that time, most members of the Asian-descent immigrant population "considered themselves culturally and politically distinct" (p. 19). Indeed, the historical enmity that existed between and among various Asian groups made it difficult for groups to transcend their national allegiances to see themselves as one unified group. In addition, the growing anti-Asian sentiments with which the various Asian immigrant groups were faced in the United States caused specific groups to "disassociate themselves from the targeted group so as not to be mistaken for members of it and suffer any possible negative consequences" (p. 20).

Trin Minh-ha (1989) and Mohanty (1991) offer postmodern analyses of Asian American-ness that challenge any unitary definitions of Asian American. Rather than construct a mythical solidarity, their work examines the ways that Asianness is represented in the dominant imagination. One of the most vivid examples of the distorted, imagined Asian shows up in the work of David Henry Hwang, whose play, *M. Butterfly,* demonstrated how a constellation of characteristics—size, temperament, submissiveness—allowed a French armed services officer to intimately mistake a man for a woman.

Lowe (1996) reminds us that "the grouping 'Asian American' is not a natural or static category; it is a socially constructed unity, a situationally specific position assumed for political reasons" (p. 82). But it coexists with a "dynamic fluctuation and heterogeneity of Asian American culture" (p. 68).

What each of these groups (i.e., African Americans, Native Americans, Latinos, and Asian Americans) has in common is the experience of a racialized identity. Each group is constituted of a myriad of other national and ancestral origins, but the dominant ideology of the Euro-American epistemology has forced them into an essentialized and totalized unit that is perceived to have little or no internal variation. However, at the same moment, members of these groups have used these unitary racialized labels for political and cultural purposes. Identification with the racialized labels means an acknowledgment of some of the common experiences group members have had as outsiders and others.

In addition to this notion of double consciousness that we argue pervades the experience of racialized identities, we believe it is imperative to include another theoretical axis—that of postcolonialism. For while double consciousness speaks to the struggle for identities, postcolonialism speaks to the collective project of the modern world that was in no way prepared for the decolonized to talk back and "act up." As West (1990) asserts, decolonization took on both "impetuous ferocity and moral outrage" (p. 25). Frantz Fanon (1968) best describes this movement:

> Decolonization, which sets out to change the order of the world, is obviously a program of complete disorder. . . . Decolonization is the meeting of two

forces, opposed to each other by their very nature, which in fact owe their originality to that sort of substantification which results from and is nourished by the situation in the colonies.

In decolonization, there is therefore the need of a complete calling in question of the colonial situation. (p. 35)

Fanon (1994) helped us understand the dynamics of colonialism and why decolonization had to be the major project of the oppressed:

> Colonial domination, because it is total and tends to over-simplify, very soon manages to disrupt in spectacular fashion the cultural life of a conquered people. This cultural obliteration is made possible by the negation of national reality, by new legal relations introduced by the occupying power, by the banishment of the natives and their customs to outlying districts by colonial society, by expropriation, and by the systematic enslaving of men and women. (p. 45)

Postcolonial theory serves as a corrective to our penchant for casting these issues into a strictly U.S. context. It helps us see the worldwide oppression against the "other" and the ability of dominant groups to define the terms of being and nonbeing, of civilized and uncivilized, of developed and undeveloped, of human and nonhuman. But even as we attempt to incorporate the term *postcolonial* in our understanding of critical race theory, we are reminded of the limits of such terminology to fully explain conditions of hierarchy, hegemony, racism, sexism, and unequal power relations. As McClintock (1994) asserts, "'Post-colonialism' (like postmodernism) is unevenly developed globally. . . . Can most of the world's countries be said, in any meaningful or theoretically rigorous sense, to share a single 'common past,' or single common 'condition,' called 'the post-colonial condition,' or 'post-coloniality'" (p. 294)? Indeed, McClintock reminds us that "the term 'post-colonialism' is, in many cases, prematurely celebratory. Ireland may, at a pinch, be 'post-colonial,' but for the inhabitants of British-occupied Northern Ireland, not to mention the Palestinian inhabitants of the Israeli Occupied Territories and the West Bank, there may be nothing 'post' about colonialism at all" (p. 294). As Linda Tuhiwai Smith (1998) queries, "Post . . . have they left yet?"

"Is-ness" Versus "Us-ness": The Discursive and Material Limits of Liberal Ideology

> To the extent that we interpret our experience from within the master narrative, we reinforce our own subordination. Whether [people of color] can counter racism may depend, finally, on our ability to claim identities outside the master narrative.
>
> —Lisa Ikemoto (1995, pp. 312–313)

In the previous section, we addressed axes of moral and ethical epistemology on which much of the work of scholars of color rests (i.e., double consciousness, sovereignty, hybridity, heterogeneity, postcolonialism). In this section, we point toward the problems of dichotomy that current political and social rhetoric provokes.

After the September 11, 2001, terrorist attacks on the World Trade Center, the Pentagon, and a plane that crashed in Pennsylvania, George W. Bush addressed the nation (and ostensibly the world), letting the audience know that there were but two choices—to be with "us" or with the "terrorists." Those dichotomous choices were not nearly as simple as Bush suggested. For one thing, who is the "us?" Is the "us" the United States, regardless of the situation and circumstance? Is the "us" the United States, even when it oppresses you? Is the "us" the supporters of the U.S. Patriot Acts I and II? Second, who are the terrorists? Clearly, we are not confused about Al-Qaeda or the Taliban, but does objecting to U.S. foreign policy place us in league with them? If we stand in solidarity with the Palestinian people, are with "with the terrorists"? If we acknowledge the legitimacy of the claims of the Northern Ireland Catholics, have we lost our claim on being a part of "us"? In the face of this sharp dividing line, many liberals chose George W. Bush's "us."

Choosing this unified "us" is not unlike Lipsitz's (1998) argument that the United States has been constructed as a nation of White people whose public policy, politics, and culture are designed to serve the interests of Whites. Such a construction serves to maintain White privilege and justify the subordination of anyone outside this racial designation. Thus, even in the reporting of war casualties, we list the number of Americans (read: White, even if this is not the actual case) killed while ignoring the number of "the enemy" who are killed. What is important here is that Whiteness is not attached to phenotype, but rather a social construction of who is worthy of inclusion in the circle of Whiteness. The enemy is never White. His identity is subsumed in a nationality or ideology that can be defined as antithetical to Whiteness (e.g., Nazis, fascists, communists, Muslims).

In one of her classes, Ladson-Billings used to show students a videotape of the Rodney King beating and, following the viewing, distributed copies of blind editorials about the beating. She then asked the students to determine the political perspective of the writers. Without benefit of newspaper mastheads or authors' names, many of the students struggled to locate the writers' ideological views. Predictably, the students divided the editorials into "liberal" and "conservative." No students identified moderate, radical, or reactionary perspectives. Their failure to see a broader ideological continuum is indicative of the polarization and dichotomization of our discourses.

We make a specific assumption about where the discursive battles must be fought. We do not engage the conservative ideology because we take for granted its antagonism toward the issues we raise. We understand that conservative rhetoric has no space for discussions of ethical epistemologies, double consciousness, hybridity, or postcolonialism. Our battle is with liberals who presume the moral high ground and have situated themselves as "saviors" of the oppressed while simultaneously maintaining their White skin privilege (McIntosh, 1988).

A wonderful literary example of the moral vacuum in current liberal discourse appears in a novel by Bebe Moore Campbell (1995), *Your Blues Ain't Like Mine.* The novel is a fictionalized account of the horrible Emmitt Till murder of the 1950s. Instead of focusing solely on the victim's family and perspective, the author gives us multiple perspectives on the book, including that of the perpetrators, the various families, and the townspeople. One character, Clayton, is a classic White liberal. He is from a privileged family and is afraid to truly relinquish his access to that privilege. So, although Clayton tries to "help" various Black characters, at the end of the novel, when Clayton discovers he is related to one of the Black characters, he adamantly refuses to share his inheritance with her. Clayton's behavior is a metaphor for White liberalism. It is prepared to only go so far.

A real-life example of this moral vacuum was exemplified in the Clinton presidency. We are not referring to his personal transgressions and sexual exploits but rather his retreat from the political left. He packaged himself as a "New Democrat," which can only be described as an "Old Moderate Republican"—think Nelson Rockefeller, George Romney, or Lowell Weicker. The actual Clinton presidency record indicates, according to columnist Steve Perry (1996), "that [he] . . . co-opted the great middle while leaving liberals with no place to go" (p. 2). And Randall Kennedy (2001) suggests,

> For all Clinton's much-expressed concern about social justice in general and racial justice in particular, his programs, policies, and gestures have done painfully little to help those whom Professor William Julius Wilson calls "the truly disadvantaged"—impoverished people, disproportionately colored, who are locked away in pestilent and crime-ridden inner cities or forgotten rural or small-town wastelands, people who are bereft of money, training, skills or education needed to escape their plight. True, Clinton had to contend with a reactionary, Republican-led Congress for much of his presidency. But, even before the Gingrichian deluge of 1994 he had made it plain that his sympathies lay predominantly with "the middle class." For those below it, he offered chastising lectures that legitimated the essentially conservative notions that the predicament of

> the poor results primarily from their conduct and not from the deformative deprivations imposed on them by a grievously unfair social order that is in large part a class hierarchy and in smaller part a pigmentocracy. (p. 51)

Progressive columnist Malik Miah (1999) argues that Clinton's ease and fellow feeling with African Americans should not be interpreted as solidarity with the cause of African Americans or other people suffering oppression:

> While it is true Clinton plays the sax and is right at home visiting a Black church, his real policies have done more damage to the Black community than any president since the victory of civil rights movement in the 1960s.
>
> . . . On the issue of families and welfare he's ended programs that, while inadequate, provided some relief for the poorest sections of the population. Ironically, Nixon, Reagan and Bush—who all promised to end welfare—couldn't get it done. Clinton not only did it but claimed it as a great accomplishment of his first term in office.
>
> . . . He pushed through Congress a crime bill that restricts civil liberties and makes it easier to impose the death penalty.
>
> . . . The strong support [of African Americans] for Clinton is thus seen as "using common sense" and doing what's best for the future of our children, much more than having big illusions in Clinton and the "new" Democrats. The new middle-class layers in these communities also provide new potential voters and supporters for the two main parties of the rich. (p. 3)

Like Campbell's (1995) fictional character, Clayton, Bill Clinton was only prepared to go so far in his support of people of color. His liberal credentials relied on superficial and symbolic acts (i.e., associating with Blacks, attending Black churches, playing the saxophone); thus, at those places where people of color were most hurting (e.g., health, education, welfare), he was unwilling to spend political capital. Such a retreat from liberal ideals represented a more severe moral failing than afternoon trysts with a White House intern.

With the George W. Bush administration, people of color and poor people are faced with a more pressing concern—the legitimacy of their being. Rather than argue over whether they are "with us" or "with the terrorists," we must constantly assert that we *are* rather than reflect a solidarity with an overarching "us" that actively oppresses. At the time of this writing, there was a movement in California to prohibit the state from collecting data that identify people by racial categories (California Proposition 54). Passage of this proposition would have allowed the state not to report on the disparities that exist in school achievement, incarceration, income levels, health concerns, and other social and civic concerns between Whites and people of color. This so-called color-blind measure would have effectively erased the race and simultaneously maintain the social, political, economic, and cultural status quo. The significance of this proposition was lost in the media circus of the California gubernatorial recall of Gray Davis and cast of characters seeking to be governor of the most populous (and one of the most diverse) states in the nation.

At the same moment that the society seeks to erase and ignore the Other, it maintains a curious desire to consume and co-opt it. The appropriation of cultural forms from communities of color is not really flattery. It is a twisted embrace that simultaneously repels the Other. The complexity of this relationship allows White people, as performance artist Roger Guenveur Smith (Tate, 2003, p. 5) suggests, to love Black music and hate Black people. The mainstream community despises rap music for its violence, misogyny, and racial epithets but spends millions of dollars to produce and consume it. The mainstream decries illegal immigration from Mexico and Central America while refusing to acknowledge its own complicity in maintaining their presence through its demand for artificially depressed produce, domestic service, and the myriad of jobs that "Americans" refuse to do. The mainstream fights what it sees as the "overrepresentation" of Asian-descent people in certain industries or high-status universities but cultivates fetishes over "Oriental" artifacts—martial arts, feng shui, sushi, and "docile," "petite" women. The mainstream remained silent while the indigenous population was massacred and displaced onto reservations but now runs eagerly to participate in sweat lodges and powwows. Such fascination does nothing to liberate and enrich the Other. Instead, they remain on the margins and are conveniently exploited for the political, economic, social, and cultural benefit of the dominant group. We are not a part of the "us" or "the terrorists." We are the struggling to exist—to just "be."

New Templates for Ethical Action

> The past history of biology has shown that progress is equally inhibited by an anti-intellectual holism and a purely atomistic reductionism.
>
> —Ernst Mayr (1976, p. 290)

In his book, *Ethical Ambition,* legal scholar Derrick Bell (2002) addresses the question that plagues many scholars of color: "How can I succeed without selling my soul?" He argues that the qualities of passion, risk, courage, inspiration, faith, humility, and love are the keys to success that maintain one's integrity and dignity. He contends that scholars must consider these as standards of behavior in both scholarship and relationships. Clearly, this is a different set of standards than those the academy typically applies to research and scholarship. But how well have the usual standards served communities of color?

> From 1932 to 1972, 399 poor black sharecroppers in Macon County, Alabama were denied treatment for syphilis and deceived by physicians of the United States Public Health Service. As part of the Tuskegee Syphilis Study, designed to document the natural history of the disease, these men were told that they were being treated for "bad blood." In fact, government officials went to extreme lengths to insure that they received no therapy from any source. As reported by the *New York Times* on 26 July 1972, the Tuskegee Syphilis Study was revealed as "the longest nontherapeutic experiment on human beings in medical history." (Tuskegee Syphilis Study Legacy Committee, 1996, p. 1)

The Health News Network (2000) details a long list of unethical and egregious acts in the name of science. For example, in 1940, four hundred prisoners in Chicago were infected with malaria to study the effects of new and experimental drugs to combat the disease. In 1945, Project Paperclip was initiated by the U.S. State Department, Army Intelligence, and the CIA to recruit Nazi scientists and offer them immunity and secret identities in exchange for work on top-secret government projects in the United States. In 1947, the CIA began a study of LSD as a potential weapon for use by U.S. intelligence. Human subjects (both civilian and military) were used with and without their knowledge. In 1950, the U.S. Navy sprayed a cloud of bacteria over San Francisco to determine how susceptible a U.S. city would be to biological attack. In 1955, the CIA released bacteria over Tampa Bay, Florida, that had been withdrawn from the Army's biological warfare arsenal to determine its ability to infect human populations with biological agents. In 1958, the Army Chemical Welfare Laboratories tested LSD on 95 volunteers to determine its effect on intelligence. In 1965, prisoners at the Holmesburg State Prison in Philadelphia were subjected to dioxin, the highly toxic chemical compound of Agent Orange used in Viet Nam. In 1990, more than 1,500 six-month-old Black and Latino babies in Los Angeles were given an "experimental" measles vaccine that had never been licensed for use in the United States. The Centers for Disease Control and Prevention later admitted that the parents were never informed that their babies were receiving an experimental vaccine.

While these examples in the life sciences are extreme, it is important to recognize that social sciences have almost always tried to mimic the so-called hard sciences. We have accepted their paradigms and elevated their ways of knowing, even when they themselves challenge them (Kuhn, 1962). The standards that require research to be "objective," precise, accurate, generalizable, and replicable do not simultaneously produce moral and ethical research and scholarship. The current calls for "scientifically based" and "evidence-based" research in education from the U.S. Department of Education have provoked an interesting response from the education research community (Shavelson & Towne, 2003).

The National Research Council (NRC) report, *Scientific Research in Education* (Shavelson & Towne, 2003), outlines what it terms a "set of fundamental principles" for "a healthy community of researchers" (p. 2). These principles include the following:

1. Pose significant questions that can be investigated empirically.
2. Link research to relevant theory.
3. Use methods that permit direct investigation of the question.
4. Provide a coherent and explicit chain of reasoning.
5. Replicate and generalize across studies.
6. Disclose research to encourage professional scrutiny and critique. (pp. 3–5)

On their face, these seem to be "reasonable" principles around which the "scientific" community can coalesce. And, while it is beyond the scope of this chapter to do a thorough review of the NRC report, we do want to point out some of the problems such thinking provokes, particularly in the realm of ethics and moral activism. The first principle suggests that we "pose significant questions that can be investigated empirically." We cannot recall the last time a researcher asserted that she or he was investigating something "insignificant." Scholars research that which interests them, and no one would suggest that they are interested in insignificant things. More important, this principle assumes the supremacy of empirical work. Without taking our discussion too far into the philosophical, we assert that what constitutes the empirical is culturally coded. For example, many years ago, a researcher from a prestigious university was collecting data in an urban classroom. The researcher reported on the apparent chaos and disorder of the classroom and described her observation of some students openly snorting drugs in the back of the classroom. Later, a graduate student who knew the school and the community talked with some of the students and learned that the students knew that the researchers expected them to be "dangerous," "uncontrollable," and "frightening." Determined to meet the researcher's expectations, the students gathered up the chalk dust from the blackboard ledge and began treating it like a powdered drug. What the researcher actually saw were students who decided to fool a researcher. This may have been empirical work, but clearly it was wrong.

In a less extreme example, an anthropology of education professor regularly displayed a set of photographic slides to his class, requiring them to describe the contents of each slide. In one slide, a photo of a farmhouse in a small German village, there is a huge pile of manure (at least one full story high) in front of the house. Not one student out of a lecture section of about 100 noted the manure pile. Even if one might argue that it was difficult to determine what it was in the slide, not one student noted that there was a "pile of something" sitting in front of the farmhouse. Our point here is that our ability to access the empirical is culturally determined and always shaped by moral and political concerns.

Popkewitz (2003) argues that the NRC report rests on a number of assumptions that expose the writers' misunderstanding of scientific inquiry. These assumptions include the following:

> (1) There is a unity of foundational assumptions that cross all the natural and social sciences. This unity involves: (2) the importance of rigorous methods and design models; (3) the cumulative, sequential development of knowledge; (4) science is based on inferential reasoning; (5) the empirical testing and development of knowledge. Finally, the assumptions provide the expertise of what government needs—showing what works. This last point is important as the Report has a dual function. It is to outline a science of education and to propose how government can intervene in the development of a science that serves policy reforms. (pp. 2–3)

Popkewitz (2003) is elegant in his rebuttal of the NRC report, and we are limited in our ability to expend space to offer additional critique. However, our task is to point out that with all of the emphasis on "scientific principles," the NRC report fails to include the moral and ethical action that scholars must engage. Is it enough to follow human subjects protocols? That sets a very minimalist standard that is likely to continue the same moral and ethical abuses. For example, in a recent National Public Radio broadcast of *All Things Considered* (Mann, 2003), titled "New York Weighs Lead-Paint Laws," the reporter indicated that researchers were testing children for the levels of lead in their blood. While there was consensus that many of the children had elevated levels of lead, the researchers rejected the recommendation that the levels of lead in the building be tested. This second, more efficient method would allow for class action on the part of the building residents. But the researchers chose to persist in examining individuals. Rather than raise the moral bar by insisting that it is unsafe to live in buildings with lead paint and to test the buildings for lead paint, individuals (many who are poor and disenfranchised) are responsible for coming forth to be tested. One might argue that the researchers are abiding by the standards of scientific inquiry, but these standards are not inclusive of the moral and ethical action that must be taken.

In addition to Bell's (2002) call for ethical behavior in the academy, Guinier and Torres (2002) have argued that it is important to move past the current racial discourses because such discourses invariably keep us locked in race-power hierarchies that depend on a winner-take-all conclusion. Instead, Guinier and Torres give birth to a new construct—"political race"—that relies on building cross-racial coalitions and alliances that involve grassroots workers who strive to remake the terms of participation and invigorate democracy. Their work points to the coalition of African Americans and Latinos who devised the 10% decision to address inequity in Texas higher education. We would also point to the work of the modern civil rights movement of the 1960s and the antiapartheid work in South Africa. In both instances, we saw broad coalitions of people working for human liberation and justice. The aim of such work is not merely to remedy past racial injustice but rather to enlarge the democratic project to include many more participants. In the case of the United States, the civil rights movement became a template for addressing a number of undemocratic practices against women, immigrants, gays and lesbians, the disabled, and second-language speakers. The point of moral and ethical activism is not to secure privileges for one's own group. It is to make democracy a reality for increasing numbers of groups and individuals. Such work permits us to look at multiple axes of difference and take these intersections seriously.

In *Miner's Canary,* Guinier and Torres (2002) point out that our typical response to inequity is to feel sorry for the individuals but ignore the structure that produces such inequity. We would prefer to prepare the dispossessed and disenfranchised to better fit in a corrupt system rather than rethink the whole system. Instead of ignoring racial differences as the color-blind approach suggests, political race urges us to understand the way race and power intertwine at every level of the society, and only through cross-racial coalitions can we expose the embedded hierarchies of privilege and destroy them (www.minerscanary.org/about.shtml, retrieved December 1, 2003). Guinier and Torres call this notion of enlisting race to resist power *political race.* It requires diagnosing systemic injustice and organizing to resist it.

Political race challenges the social and economic consequences of race in a "third way" (www.minerscanary.org/about.shtml, retrieved December 1, 2003) that proposes a multitextured political strategy rather than the traditional legal solutions to the issues of racial justice. The authors argue that "political race dramatically transforms the use of race from a signifier of individual culpability and prejudice to an early warning sign of larger injustices" (www.minerscanary.org/about.shtml, retrieved December 1, 2003). When they speak of political, they are not referring to conventional electoral politics. Rather, their notion of political race challenges social activists and critical scholars to rethink what winning means and if winning in a corrupt system can ever be good enough. Instead, their focus is on the power of change through collective action and how such action can change (and challenge) us all to work in new ways.

We seek a methodology and a theory that, as Gayatri Spivak (1990) argues, seeks not merely reversal of roles in a hierarchy but rather displacement of taken-for-granted norms around unequal binaries (e.g., male-female, public-private, White–non-White, able-disabled, native-foreign). We see such possibility in critical race theory (CRT), and we point out that CRT is not limited to the old notions of race. Rather, CRT is a new analytic rubric for considering difference and inequity using multiple methodologies—story, voice, metaphor, analogy, critical social science, feminism, postmodernism. So visceral is our reaction to the word *race* that many scholars and consumers of scholarly literature cannot see beyond the word to appreciate the value of CRT for making sense of our current social condition. We would argue that scholars such as Trin-T Minh-ha, Robert Allen Warrior, Gloria Anzalduá, Ian Haney-Lopez, Richard Delgado, Lisa Lowe, David Palumbo-Liu, Gayatri Spivak, Chandra Mohanty, and Patricia Hill Collins all produce a kind of CRT. They are not bogged down with labels or dogmatic constraints. Rather, they are creatively and passionately engaging new visions of scholarship to do work that will ultimately serve people and lead to human liberation.

Thus, we argue that the work of critical scholars (from any variety of perspectives) is not merely to try to replicate the work of previous scholars in a cookie-cutter fashion but rather to break new epistemological, methodological, social activist, and moral ground. We do not need Derrick Bell, Lani Guinier, or Gerald Torres clones. We need scholars to take up their causes (along with causes they identify for themselves) and creatively engage them. We look to them because of their departure from the scholarly mainstream, not to make them idols.

Moving From Research to Activism—Street-Level Research in Ivory Towers

> Conflict—the real-world kind, I mean—can be bloody, misguided, and wholly tragic. It behooves us always to try to understand how and why bloodshed breaks out as it does. But the very narratives and stories we tell ourselves and each other afterwards, in an effort to explain, understand, excuse, and assign responsibility for conflict, may also be, in a sense, the source of the very violence we abhor.
>
> —Lisa Ikemoto (1995, p. 313)

Earlier in this chapter, we referenced Harold Cruse and *The Crisis of the Negro Intellectual* (1967/1984), and indeed we recognize the crisis that Cruse identifies is a crisis for all intellectuals of color. Cruse's point that "while Negro intellectuals are busy trying to interpret the nature of the black world and its aspirations to the whites, they should, in fact, be defining their own roles as intellectuals within both worlds" (p. 455) is applicable to all scholars of color. Novelists such as Toni Morrison, (1987), Shawn Wong (1995), Ana Castillo (1994), Sherman Alexie (1993), and Jhumpa Lahiri (1999) deftly accomplish what Cruse asks. They sit comfortably within the walls of the academy and on the street corners, barrios, and reservations of the people. They are "cultural brokers" who understand the need to be "in" the academy (or mainstream) but not "of" the academy.

In the foreword of Cruse's book, Allen and Wilson (1984) summarize the central tasks that this book outlines for "would-be intellectuals":

1. To familiarize themselves with their own intellectual antecedents and with previous political and cultural movements;

2. To analyze critically the bases for the pendulum swings between the two poles of integration and [Black] nationalism, and try to synthesize them into a single and consistent analysis;

3. To identify clearly the political, economic, and cultural requisites for black advancement in order to meld them into a single politics of progressive black culture. This process requires greater attention both to Afro-American popular culture and to the macroeconomic, structural context of modern capitalism in which group culture either flourishes or atrophies;

4. To recognize the uniqueness of American conditions and to insist that one incorporate this uniqueness when studying numbers 1 through 3 above. (p. v)

Despite Cruse's (1967/1984) focus on African Americans and their experiences in the United States, it is clear to us that such work is important for any marginalized group. All scholars of color must know the intellectual antecedents of their cultural, ethnic, or racial group. This is important for combating the persistent ideology of White supremacy that denigrates the intellectual contributions of others. All scholars of color must look to the epistemological underpinnings and legitimacy of their cultures and cultural ways of knowing. They must face the tensions that emerge in their communities between assimilation into the U.S. mainstream and the creation of separate and distinct cultural locations. For example, the construction of Asian Americans as articulated previously by Lowe (1996) and Espiritu (1992) is a powerful example of the synthesis Cruse speaks of. All scholars of color need to acknowledge the salience of popular culture in shaping our research and scholarly agendas, for it is in the popular that our theories and methodologies become living, breathing entities.

Martin Luther King, Jr., had a theory about "nonviolence" that came from his study of Gandhi and Dietrich Bonhoeffer, but the theory was actualized in the hearts and minds of ordinary people—Fannie Lou Hamer, Esau Jenkins, Septima Clark, and many others. So great is the desire for survival and liberation that it transcends geopolitical boundaries, languages, and cultures. The modern civil rights movement in the United States was replayed in China's Tiananmen Square, in the cities and townships of South Africa, and in liberation struggles the world over. In each instance, the power of the popular brings the music, art, and energy to the struggle. Ordinary people become the "street-level bureaucrats" (Lipsky, 1983) who translate theory into practice. However, we want to be clear that we are not suggesting that such "street-level bureaucrats" begin to behave as functionaries of the state where they become the new powerbrokers. Rather, we are suggesting a new vision of Lipsky's (1983) concept where people from the community represent a new form of leadership that is unafraid of shared power and real democracy.

But scholars who take on the challenge of moral and ethical activist work cannot rely solely on others to make sense of their work and translate it into usable form. Patricia Hill Collins (1998) speaks of a "visionary pragmatism" (p. 188) that may be helpful in the development of more politically and socially engaged scholarship. She uses this term to characterize the perspective of the working-class women of her childhood:

> The Black women on my block possessed a "visionary pragmatism" that emphasized the necessity of linking caring, theoretical vision with informed, practical struggle. A creative tension links visionary thinking and practical action. Any social theory that becomes too out of touch with everyday people and their lives, especially oppressed people, is of little use to them. The functionality and not just the logical consistency of visionary thinking determines its worth. At the same time, being too practical, looking only to the here and now—especially if present conditions seemingly offer little hope—can be debilitating. (p. 188)

Scholars must also engage new forms of scholarship that make translations of their work more seamless. Guinier and Torres (2002) speak to us of "political race" as a new conception we can embrace. Castillo (1994) offers magical realism as a rubric for Chicano coalescence. Lowe (1996) has taken up notions of hybridity, heterogeneity, and multiplicity to name the material contradictions that characterize immigrant groups—particularly Asian-descent immigrants—who are routinely lumped together and homogenized into a unitary and bounded category. Espiritu (2003) helps us link the study of race and ethnicity to the study of imperialism so that we can better understand transnational and diasporic lives. Similarly, Ong (1999) warns of the growing threat of global capital that destabilizes notions of cultural unity and/or allegiance. Instead, the overwhelming power of multinational corporations creates economic cleavages that force people, regardless of their racial, cultural, and ethnic locations, to chase jobs and compete against each other to subsist.

Promising scholarship that may disrupt the fixed categories that Whiteness has instantiated appears in work by Prashad (2002), who examines the cross-racial and interracial connections that reflect the reality of our histories and current conditions. Prashad argues that instead of the polarized notions of either "color blindness" or a primordial "multiculturalism," what we seek is a "polyculturalism," a term he borrows from Robin D. G. Kelley (1999), who argues that "so-called 'mixed-race' children are not the only ones with a claim to multiple heritages. All of us, and I mean ALL of us, are the inheritors of European, African, Native-American, and even Asian pasts, even if we can't exactly trace our bloodlines to all of these continents" (p. 6). Kelley further argues that our various cultures "have never been easily identifiable, secure in their boundaries, or clear to all people who live in or outside our skin. We were multi-ethnic and polycultural from the get-go" (p. 6). This challenge to notions of ethnic purity moves us away from the futile chase for "authenticity" and troubles the reification of ethnic and racial categories. We begin to understand as political activist Rev. Al Sharpton has said that "all my skin folks, ain't my kin folks." Just because people look like us by no means implies that they have our best interests at heart.

At the street level, we must acknowledge the power of hip-hop culture. It is important that we distinguish our acknowledgment from the negatives that the corporate interests promulgate—violence, racism, misogyny, and crass consumerism—from hip-hop as a vehicle for cross-racial, cross-cultural, and international coalitions. Organizations such as El Puente Academy for Peace and Justice in the Williamsburg section of Brooklyn, New York, and the Urban Think Tank Institute (www.UrbanThinkTank.org) provide a more democratic and politically progressive discourse. The Urban Think Tank Institute argues that the hip-hop generation "has become more politically sophisticated . . . [and needs] a space whereby grassroots thinkers, activists, and artists can come together, discuss relevant issues, devise strategies, and then articulate their analysis to the public and to policy makers" (see Yvonne Bynoe on the Urban Think Tank Web site). Such organizations have corollaries in the earlier work of Myles Horton (Horton, 1990; Horton & Freire, 1990), Paulo Freire (1970), Septima Clark (Brown, 1990), Marcus Garvey's Universal Negro Improvement Association (Prashad, 2002), and the Boggs Center (Boggs, 1971). It also resembles the worldwide liberation movements we have seen in India, South Africa, China, Brazil, Zimbabwe, and most everywhere in the world where people have organized to resist oppression and domination.

The hip-hop movement reminds us of the stirrings of the youth and young adults in the modern civil rights movement. When it became clear that the older, more conservative leadership was unwilling to make a space for young people in the movement, we began to see a new form of liberation work. Instead of attempting to assimilate and assert our rights as Americans, young people began to assert their rights to a distinct identity in which being an American may have been constitutive of this identity, but it was not the all-encompassing identity. Hip-hop's wide appeal, across geopolitical and ethnic boundaries (we found hip-hop Web sites in Latvia, Russia, Italy, and Japan), makes it a potent force for mobilizing young people worldwide. Unfortunately, most scholars (and, for that matter, most adults) have narrow views of hip-hop.[6] They see it merely as rap music and "gangsta" culture. However, the power of hip-hop is in its diffuseness. It encompasses art, music, dance, and self-presentation. Although much of the media attention has focused on notorious personalities such as Biggie Smalls, Snoop Dogg, P. Diddy, 50-Cent, Nelly, and others, there is a core group of hip-hop artists whose major purpose was to provide social commentary and awaken a somnambulant generation of young people from their drug, alcohol, and materialistic addictions. Some of these artists sought to contextualize the present conditions of the African American and other marginalized communities of color and call for action by making historical links to ideas (e.g., Black Power), social movements (e.g., cultural nationalism), and political figures (e.g., Malcolm X, Che Guevara). The need for this kind of work is not unlike the call of Ngũgĩ wa Thiongo (1991), who argued, in speaking of the emerging independent African nations, that we needed a radically democratic proposal for the production of art, literature, and culture based on our political praxis. Looking at the U.S. scene, Dyson (1993) argues

> Besides being the most powerful form of Black musical expression today, rap music projects a style of self into the world that generates forms of cultural resistance and transforms the ugly terrain of ghetto existence into a searing portrait of life as it must be lived by millions of voiceless people. For that reason alone, rap deserves attention and should be taken seriously. (p. 15)

Counted among these visionary hip-hop leaders[7] are Grandmaster Flash, Public Enemy, Run-DMC, The Fugees, Lauryn Hill, KRS-1, Diggable Planets, Arrested Development, the Roots, Mos Def, Common, Erykah Badu, the whole host of Nuyorican poets, and the organic intellectuals that produce *YO Magazine* in the San Francisco Bay Area. These are the people who have the ears (and hearts and minds) of the young people. It is among this group that new forms of scholarship that takes up moral and ethical positions will be forged. Scholars who choose to ignore the trenchant pleas of the hip-hop generation will find themselves increasingly out of touch and irrelevant to the everyday lives of people engaged in the cause of social justice.

A number of scholars have made connections with the hip-hop generation: Miguel Algarin, with his ties to both the academy and the Nuyorican Poet's Café; Cornel West and Michael Eric Dyson, with their face-to-face conversations with the hip-hop generation; and bell hooks, with her revolutionary Black feminism. The late poet June Jordan, Toni Morrison, Pablo Neruda, Carlos Bulosan, John Okada, Diego Rivera, Leslie Marmon Silko, Sherman Alexie, and others have deployed their art to speak across the generations.

Social scientists must similarly situate themselves to play a more active and progressive role in the fight for equity and social justice. Their work has to transcend narrow disciplinary boundaries if they are to have any impact on people who reside in subaltern sites, or even policy makers. Unfortunately, far too many academics spend their time talking to each other in the netherworld of the academy. We write in obscure journals and publish books in languages that do not translate to the lives and experiences of real people. We argue not for the seeming "simplicity" of the political right but the relevancy and the power of the popular.

Reconstruction of the Work of the Intellect

> Don't push me, cause I'm close to the edge
>
> I'm trying not to lose my head.
>
> It's like a jungle sometimes, it makes me wonder
>
> How I keep from going under
>
> —From *The Message,*
> Grandmaster Flash

It is typical for institutional recommendations to call for a "transformation" of some kind. In this case, were we to suggest that the academy needed to be transformed, we imagine that many would agree. However, transformation implies a change that emanates from an existing base. Clark Kent transformed himself into Superman, but underneath the blue tights he was still Clark Kent. Britt Reid transformed himself into the Green Hornet, but underneath the mask he was still Britt Reid.

Captain John Reid's brother Dan transformed himself into the Lone Ranger, but under that powder-blue, skin-tight outfit and mask he was still Dan Reid. What we are urging is the equivalent of having Jimmy Olsen, Kato, and Tonto assume the leadership and implement the plan.

Reconstruction comes after the destruction of what was. The Union Army did not attempt to massage the South into a new economy after the U.S. Civil War. The Cuban Revolution was not

Fidel Castro's attempt to adapt the Battista regime. The new South Africa is not trying to organize a new form of apartheid with Black dominance. Rather, these are instances where we see the entire destruction of the old in an attempt to make something new. So it may have to be with the academy in order for it to be responsive to the needs of everyday people.

The student movement at San Francisco State College (Prashad, 2002) revolutionized not only that local campus but also campuses across the country. It formed the basis for the development of what Wynter (1992) called "new studies" in Black, Latino, Asian, and Native American studies. It provided a template for women's studies, gay and lesbian studies, and disability studies. It reconfigured knowledge from static, fixed disciplines with the perception of cumulative information, to a realization of the dynamic and overlapping nature of knowledge and a more fluid sense of epistemology and methodology. But even with the strides made by these new studies, they still represent a very small crack in the solid, almost frozen traditions of the university. Indeed, the more careerist interests have made a more indelible imprint on the colleges and universities in the United States. Instead of seeing colleges and universities as the site of liberal education and free thinking, increasing numbers of young people (and their parents) see the university as a job training facility. Courses and programs of study in hotel and restaurant management, criminal justice, and sports management,[8] while representing legitimate job and career choices, are less likely to promote overall university goals of educating people to engage with knowledge and critical thinking across a wide variety of disciplines and traditions.

A reconstructed university would displace much of the credentialing function of the current system and organize itself around principles of intellectual enrichment, social justice, social betterment, and equity. Students would see the university as a vehicle for public service, not merely personal advancement. Students would study various courses and programs of study in an attempt to improve both their minds and the condition of life in the community, society, and the world. Such a program has little or no chance of success in our current sociopolitical atmosphere. Although colleges and universities are legitimately categorized as nonprofit entities, they do have fiscal responsibilities. Currently, those fiscal responsibilities are directed to continued employment of elites, supplying a well-prepared labor force, and increasing endowments. In a reconstructed university, the fiscal responsibility would be directed toward community development and improving the socioeconomic infrastructure.

A reconstructed university would have a different kind of reward system where teaching and service were true equals to research and scholarship. Perhaps these components would be more seamlessly wedded and more tightly related. Excellence would be judged by quality efforts in all areas. Admission to such a university would also mean that more complex standards would be applied to evaluating potential students. Instead of strict grade point averages, class rankings, standardized test scores, and inflated resumes,[9] colleges and universities could begin to select students for their ability to contribute to the body politic that will be formed on a particular campus.

Democracy is a complicated system of government, and it requires an educated citizenry to participate actively in it. By educated, we are not merely referring to holding degrees and credentials but knowing enough, as Freire (1970) insists, "to read the word and the world." We recognize the need for "organic intellectuals"[10] to help us as credentialed intellectuals do the reconstructive work. We find interesting (and paradoxical) that education at the two ends of the continuum (precollegiate and adult education) seems to be more progressive and proactive (at least from the point of view of the literature they produce and respond to). Colleges and universities seem to function as incubators for the soon-to-be (or wanna-be) guardians of the status quo. Too many of our college and university students want to assume a place in the current society without using their collegiate years as an opportunity to consider how the society could be different, how it could be more just.

Among precollegiate educators, Grace Boggs (1971) has developed a "new system of education" that makes a radical break from the current system that is designed to "prepare the great majority [of citizens] for labor and to advance a few out of their ranks to join the elite in governing" (p. 32). Boggs's vision is for a "new system of education that will have as its means and its ends the development of the great masses of people *to govern over themselves and to administer over things*" (p. 32). Boggs's system of education calls for an education that must

- be based on a philosophy of history—in order to realize his or her highest potential as a human being, every young person must be given a profound and continuing sense (a) of his or her own life as an integral part of the continuing evolution of the human species and (b) of the unique capacity of human beings to shape and create reality in accordance with conscious purposes and plans;

- include productive activity—productive activity, in which individuals choose a task and participate in its execution from beginning to end, remains the most effective and rapid means to internalize the relationship between cause and effect, between effort and result, between purposes (ends) and programs (means), an internalization that is necessary to rational behavior, creative thinking, and responsible activity;

- include living struggles—every young person must be given expanding opportunities to solve the problems of his physical and social environment, thereby developing the political and technical skills that are urgently needed to transform the social institutions as well as the physical environments of our communities and cities;

- include a wide variety of resources and environments—in our complex world, education must be consciously organized to take place not only in schools and not only using teachers and technology but also a multiplicity of physical and social environments (e.g., the countryside, the city, the sea, factories, offices, other countries, other cultures);

- include development in bodily self-knowledge and well-being—increased scientific and technological knowledge necessitates more active participation by laypeople and a greater focus on preventative medicine. Students must learn how to live healthy lives and work to reverse the devastating health conditions in poor and working-class communities;

- include clearly defined goals—education must move away from achieving more material goods and/or fitting people into the existing unequal structure. Education's primary purpose must be governing (pp. 33–36).

Early scholars in adult education (Freire, 1970; M. Horton, 1990; M. Horton & Freire, 1990) understood the need to develop education imbued with social purpose and grounded in grassroots, popular organizing movements. While there are a number of such examples, because of space limitations, we will focus on the Highlander Folk School. Aimee Horton (1989) documents the school's history and points out that its relationship with social movements is the key to understanding both the strength and limitations of its adult education program. The two—social movement and adult education—form a symbiotic relationship. As Myles Horton (1990) himself suggests,

> It is only in a movement that an idea is often made simple enough and direct enough that it can spread rapidly. . . . We cannot create movements, so if we want to be a part of a movement when it comes, we have to get ourselves into a position—by working with organizations that deal with structural change—to be on the inside of that movement when it comes, instead of on the outside trying to get accepted. (p. 114)

Highlander always saw itself as part of the larger goals of social movements while simultaneously "maintaining a critical and challenging voice within" (Heaney, 1992). Highlander based its work on two major components—an education grounded in the "real and realizable struggles of people for democratic control over their lives" (Heaney, 1992) and the need to challenge people to consider the present and the future simultaneously as they move toward social change.

One of Highlander's programs, the Citizenship Schools (which functioned between 1953 and 1961), was designed to help African American citizens of the deep South to become literate *and* protest for their rights. According to M. Horton (1990), "You can't read and write yourself into freedom. You [have] to fight for that and you [have] to do it as part of a group, not as an individual" (p. 104). The Citizenship Schools are a far cry from current adult literacy and vocational programs that have no political commitment and encourage individual and simple solutions to major social problems (Heaney, 1992).

We are skeptical of the academy's ability to reconstruct itself because of the complicity of its intellectuals with the current social order. Thus, we agree with Foucault (1977), who insists that

> intellectuals are no longer needed by the masses to gain knowledge: the masses know perfectly well, without illusion; they know far better than the intellectual and they are certainly capable of expressing themselves. But there exists a system of power which blocks, prohibits, and invalidates this discourse and this knowledge, a power not only found in manifest authority of censorship, but one that profoundly and subtly penetrates an entire societal network. Intellectuals are themselves agents of this system of power—the idea of their responsibility for "consciousness" and discourse forms part of the system. (p. 207)

Concluding Thoughts: In Search of Revolutionary Habitus

> As soon as possible he [the White man] will tell me that it is not enough to try to be white, but that a white totality must be achieved.
>
> —Frantz Fanon (1986, p. 112)

Our previous section suggests an almost nihilistic despair about the role of the intellectual in leading us toward more just and equitable societies. Actually, we point to the limits of the academy and suggest that committed intellectuals must move into spaces beyond the academy to participate in real change. Indeed, such a move may mean that academics take on less prominent roles in order to listen and learn from people actively engaged in social change. Thus, we speak to an audience who is willing to search for a revolutionary habitus.

Bourdieu (1990) brought us the concept of habitus that he vaguely defines as a system of

> durable, transposable dispositions, structured structures predisposed to function as structuring structures, that is, as principles which generate and organize practices and representations that can be objectively adapted to their outcomes without presupposing a conscious aiming at ends or an express mastery of the operations necessary in order to attain them. Objectively "regulated" and "regular" without being in any way the product of obedience to the rules, they can be collectively orchestrated without being the product of the organizing action of a conductor. (p. 53)

Thus, according to Palumbo-Liu (1993), "Individuals are inclined to act in certain ways given their implicit understanding of, their 'feel for,' the field" (p. 6). The habitus "expresses first the result of an organizing action with a meaning close to that of words such as structure: it also designates a way of being, a habitual state (especially of the body) and, in particular, a disposition, a tendency, propensity, or inclination" (Bourdieu, 1977, p. 214). This work provides us with both "the flexibility of what might otherwise be thought of as a strictly determinative structure (the field) and the ambiguity of a predisposed but not mandated agency (habitus) [and] signal Bourdieu's desire to go beyond the usual binary categories of external/internal, conscious/unconscious, determinism/free agency" (Palumbo-Liu, 1993, p. 7).

Our call for a revolutionary habitus recognizes that the "field" (Bourdieu, 1990) in which academics currently function constrains the social (and intellectual) agency that might move us toward social justice and human liberation. As Palumbo-Liu (1993) points out, a field is

> a particular grid of relations that governs specific areas of social life (economics, culture, education, politics, etc.): individuals do not act freely to achieve

> their goals and the creation of dispositions must be understood within historically specific formations of fields; each field has its own rules and protocols that open specific social positions for different agents. Yet this is not a static model: the field in turn is modified according to the manner in which those positions are occupied and mobilized. (p. 6)

Thus, despite notions of academic freedom and tenure, professors work within a field that may delimit and confine political activity and views unpopular with university administrators, state and national legislators, and policy makers. Subtle and not so subtle sanctions have the power to shape how an individual's habituses conform to the field. We must imagine new fields and new habituses that constitute a new vision of what it means to do academic work. According to Palumbo-Liu (1993), "The habitus we might imagine for social agents has not yet become habituated to postmodern globalized culture that continues to be reshaped as we speak. The field of culture must now be understood to accommodate both dominant and emergent social groups who differently and significantly inflect the consumption and production of an increasingly global and hybrid culture" (p. 8).

Perhaps our notion of a revolutionary habitus might better be realized through Espiritu's (2003) powerful conceptualization of "home" in which there is a keen awareness of the way racialized immigrants "from previously colonized nations are not exclusively formed as racial minorities within the United States but also as colonized nationals while in their 'homeland'—one that is deeply affected by U.S. influences and modes of social organization" (p. 1). Espiritu points out that the notion of home is not merely a physical place but is also "a concept and desire—a place that immigrants visit through the imagination" (p. 10). We assert that even those long-term racialized residents of the United States (e.g., African Americans, American Indians, Latinos) have experienced (and continue to experience) colonial oppression (Ladson-Billings, 1998a).

What Espiritu (2003) offers is a way to think about the permeable nature of concepts such as race, culture, ethnicity, gender, and ability. Rather than become fixated on who is included and who is excluded, we need to consider the way that we are all border dwellers who negotiate and renegotiate multiple places and spaces. According to Mahmud (1997), "Immigrants call into question implicit assumptions about 'fixed' identities, unproblematic nationhood, invisible sovereignty, ethnic homogeneity, and exclusive citizenship" (p. 633).

Thus, the challenge of those of us in the academy is not how to make those outside of the academy more like us but rather to recognize the "outside-the-academy" identities that we must recruit for ourselves in order to be more effective researchers on behalf of people who can make use of our skills and abilities. We must learn to be "at home" on the street corners, barrios, churches, mosques, kitchens, porches, and stoops of people and communities so that our work more accurately reflects their concerns and interests. Our challenge is to renounce our paternalistic tendencies and sympathetic leanings to move toward an empathic, ethical, and moral scholarship that propels us to a place where we are prepared to forcefully and courageously answer "the call."

▣ Notes

1. We are using the term *of color* to refer to all people who are raced and outside the construction of Whiteness (Haney Lopez, 1998).
2. Paulo Freire (1970) insists "that the oppressed are not 'marginals,' are not men living 'outside' society. They have always been 'inside'—inside the structure that made them 'beings' for others" (p. 27).
3. *Articulate* is a term seemingly reserved for African Americans and is seen by African Americans as a way to suggest that one speaks better than would be expected of "your kind."
4. We are restating at length portions of Ladson-Billings's (2000) discussion on alterity and liminality that appeared in Volume 2 of the handbook.
5. We remind the reader that we are aware of the dilemma of using racialized categories and that the boundaries between and among various racial, ethnic, and cultural groups are more permeable and more complex than the categories imply.

6. MacArthur fellow and civil rights leader Bernice Johnson Reagon asserts that no one has the right to tell the next generation what their freedom songs should be (Moyers, 1991).

7. We are aware that we are not acknowledging all of the artists in this tradition.

8. We want to be clear that we do not disparage these career choices. However, we question whether they represent what is meant by "liberal arts."

9. Increasingly, students seeking admission to selective colleges and universities participate in extracurricular activities (e.g., sports, clubs, the arts) and volunteer efforts not because of interests and commitments but rather because such participation may give them an advantage over other applicants.

10. We use this term to describe those grassroots people whose intellectual power convicts and persuades the masses of people to investigate and explore new ideas for human liberation. The late John Henrik Clark (New York), Clarence Kailin (Madison, WI), and the late James Boggs and his wife Grace Lee Boggs (Detroit) are examples of organic intellectuals.

References

Acuna, R. (1972). *Occupied America: The Chicano struggle toward liberation.* New York: Canfield Press.

Alarcon, N. (1990). Chicana feminism: In the tracks of "the" native woman. *Cultural Studies, 4,* 248–256.

Alexie, S. (1993). *The Lone Ranger and Tonto fistfight in heaven.* New York: Atlantic Monthly Press.

Allen, B., & Wilson, E. J. (1984). Foreword. In H. Cruse, *The crisis of the Negro intellectual.* New York: Quill.

Almaguer, T. (1974). Historical notes on Chicano oppression: The dialectics of racial and class domination in North America. *Aztlan, 5*(1–2), 27–56.

Anzaldúa, G. (1987). *Borderlands/la frontera: The new mestiza.* San Francisco: Spinsters/Aunt Lute.

Balderrama, F. E. (1982). *In defense of La Raza: The Los Angeles Mexican consulate and the Mexican community, 1929–1936.* Tucson: University of Arizona Press.

Bell, D. (1991). Racism is here to stay: Now what? *Howard Law Journal, 35*(79), 79–93.

Bell, D. (2002). *Ethical ambition.* New York: Bloomsbury.

Boggs, G. L. (1971). *Education to govern* [Pamphlet]. Detroit, MI: All-African People's Union.

Bourdieu, P. (1977). *Outline of a theory of practice.* Cambridge, UK: Cambridge University Press.

Bourdieu, P. (1990). *The logic of practice* (R. Nicc, Trans.). Stanford, CA: Stanford University Press.

Brown, C. S. (Ed.). (1990). *Ready from within: A first person narrative: Septima Clark and the civil rights movement.* Trenton, NJ: Africa World Press.

Campbell, B. M. (1995). *Your blues ain't like mine.* New York: Ballantine.

Castillo, A. (1994). *So far from God.* New York: Plume.

Castillo, A. (1995). *Massacre of the dreamers: Essays on Xicanisima.* New York: Plume.

Collins, P. H. (1998). *Fighting words: Black women and the search for justice.* Minneapolis: University of Minnesota Press.

Cruse, H. (1984). *The crisis of the Negro intellectual.* New York: Quill. (Original work published 1967)

de la Torre, A., & Pesquera, B. (Eds.). (1993). *Building with our hands: New directions in Chicano studies.* Berkeley: University of California Press.

Delgado Bernal, D. (1998). Using a Chicana feminist epistemology in educational research. *Harvard Educational Review, 68,* 555–582.

DuBois, W. E. B. (1953). *The souls of Black folk.* New York: Fawcett. (Original work published 1903)

Dyson, M. E. (1993). *Reflecting Black: African American cultural criticism.* Minneapolis: University of Minnesota Press.

Espiritu, Y. L. (1992). *Asian American panethnicity: Bridging institutions and identities.* Philadelphia: Temple University Press.

Espiritu, Y. L. (2003). *Homebound: Filipino Americans lives across cultures, communities, and countries.* Berkeley: University of California Press.

Eyre, C. (Director). (1998). *Smoke signals* [Film]. Los Angeles: Miramax.

Fanon, F. (1968). *The wretched of the earth.* New York: Grove.

Fanon, F. (1986). *Black skin, white masks.* London: Pluto.

Fanon, F. (1994). On national culture. In P. Williams & L. Chrisman (Eds.), *Colonial discourse and post-colonial theory* (pp. 36–52). New York: Columbia University Press.

Foucault, M. (1977). *Language, counter-memory, practice.* Ithaca, NY: Cornell University Press.

Freire, P. (1970). *Pedagogy of the oppressed.* New York: Continuum.

Gilman, R. (2000). *Spinning into butter: A play.* New York: Faber & Faber.

Gomez-Quinones, J. (1977). On culture. *Revista Chicano-Riquena, 5*(2), 35–53.

Guinier, L., & Torres, G. (2002). *Miner's canary: Enlisting race, resisting power, transforming democracy.* Cambridge, MA: Harvard University Press.

Haney Lopez, I. (1998). *White by law: The legal construction of race.* New York: New York University Press.

Health News Network. (2000). *A history of secret human experimentation.* Retrieved from www.healthnewsnet.com/humanexperiments.html

Heaney, T. (1992). When adult education stood for democracy. *Adult Education Quarterly, 43,* 51–59.

Hertzberg, H. W. (1971). *The search for an American Indian identity.* Syracuse, NY: Syracuse University Press.

Horton, A. (1989). *The Highlander Folk School: A history of its major programs, 1932–1961.* Brooklyn, NY: Carlson Publishing, Inc.

Horton, M. (with Kohl, H., & Kohl, J.). (1990). *The long haul: An autobiography.* New York: Doubleday.

Horton, M., & Freire, P. (1990). *We make the road by walking: Conversations on education and social change.* Philadelphia: Temple University Press.

Ikemoto, L. (1995). Traces of the master narrative in the story of African American/Korean American conflict: How we constructed "Los Angeles." In R. Delgado (Ed.), *Critical race theory: The cutting edge* (pp. 305–315). Philadelphia: Temple University Press.

Kelley, R. D. G. (1999). People in me. *Colorlines, 1*(3), 5–7.

Kennedy, R. (2001, February). The triumph of robust tokenism. *The Atlantic.* Retrieved from http://www.theatlantic.com/issues/2001/02/kennedy.htm

Kennedy, R. (2002). *Nigger: The strange career of a troublesome word.* New York: Pantheon.

King, J. E. (1995). Culture centered knowledge: Black studies, curriculum transformation, and social action. In J. A. Banks & C. M. Banks (Eds.), *Handbook of research on multicultural education* (pp. 265–290). New York: Macmillan.

Kuhn, T. (1962). *The structure of scientific revolutions.* Chicago: University of Chicago Press.

Ladson-Billings, G. (1998a). From Soweto to the South Bronx: African Americans and colonial education in the United States. In C. A. Torres & T. Mitchell (Eds.), *Sociology of education: Emerging perspectives* (pp. 247–264). Albany, NY: SUNY Press.

Ladson-Billings, G. (1998b). Just what is critical race theory and what is it doing in a "nice" field like education? *International Journal of Qualitative Studies in Education, 11,* 7–24.

Ladson-Billings, G. (2000). Racialized discourses and ethnic epistemologies. In N. K. Denzin & Y. S. Lincoln (Eds.), *The SAGE handbook of qualitative research* (2nd ed., pp. 257–277). Thousand Oaks, CA: Sage.

Lahiri, J. (1999). *Interpreter of maladies.* Boston: Houghton Mifflin.

Legesse, A. (1973). *Gada: Three approaches to the study of an African society.* New York: Free Press.

Lewis, D. L. (1993). *W. E. B. Du Bois: Biography of a race: 1868–1919.* New York: Holt.

Lipsitz, G. (1998). *The possessive investment in whiteness: How White people profit from identity politics.* Philadelphia: Temple University Press.

Lipsky, M. (1983). *Street-level bureaucrats.* New York: Russell Sage Foundation.

Lomawaima, K. T. (1995). Educating Native Americans. In J. A. Banks & C. M. Banks (Eds.), *Handbook of research on multicultural education* (pp. 331–347). New York: Macmillan.

Lowe, L. (1996). *Immigrant acts: On Asian-American cultural politics.* Durham, NC: Duke University Press.

Mahmud, T. (1997). Migration, identity, and the colonial encounter. *Oregon Law Review, 76,* 633–690.

Mann, B. (2003, October 6). New York weighs lead-paint laws. *All Things Considered* [Radio broadcast]. Washington, DC: National Public Radio.

Mayr, E. (1976). *Evolution and the diversity of life.* Cambridge, MA: Belknap.

McClintock, A. (1994). The angel of progress: Pitfalls of the term "post-colonialism." In P. Williams & L. Chrisman (Eds.), *Colonial discourse and post-colonial theory* (pp. 291–304). New York: Columbia University Press.

McIntosh, P. (1988). *White privilege and male privilege: A personal account of coming to see correspondences through work in women's studies* (Working Paper 189). Wellesley, MA: Wellesley College Center for Research on Women.

Miah, M. (1999). Race and politics: Black voters and "brother" Clinton. *Against the Current.* Retrieved from http://solidarity.us.org/atc/78Miah.html

Minh-ha, T. (1989). *Women, narrative, other: Writing postcoloniality and feminism.* Bloomington: Indiana University Press.

Mirande, A., & Enriquez, E. (1979). *La Chicana: The Mexican American woman.* Chicago: University of Chicago Press.

Mohanty, C. T. (1991). Under Western eyes: Feminist scholarship and colonial discourses. In C. T. Mohanty, A. Russo, & L. Torres (Eds.), *Third*

World women and the politics of feminism (pp. 50–80). Bloomington: Indiana University Press.

Morrison, T. (1987). *Beloved.* New York: Vintage.

Moyers, B. (1991, February). *The songs are free: Interview with Bernice Johnson Reagon* [Video recording]. Washington, DC: Public Broadcast Corporation.

Oboler, S. (1995). *Ethnic lives, ethnic labels.* Minneapolis: University of Minnesota Press.

Ong, A. (1999). *Flexible citizenship: The cultural logics of transnationality.* Raleigh, NC: Duke University Press.

Padilla, F. (1987). *Latino ethnic consciousness.* Notre Dame, IN: Notre Dame University Press.

Palumbo-Liu, D. (1993). Introduction: Unhabituated habituses. In D. Palumbo-Liu & H. U. Gumbrecht (Eds.), *Streams of cultural capital: Transnational cultural studies* (pp. 1–21) Stanford, CA: Stanford University Press.

Paz, O. (1961). *The labyrinth of solitude: Life and thought in Mexico.* New York: Random House.

Perry, S. (1996, May 29). *Bill Clinton's politics of meaning.* Retrieved from www.citypages.com/databank/17/808/article2724.asp

Popkewitz, T. (2003). Is the National Research Council Committee's Report on scientific research in education, scientific? On trusting the manifesto. *Qualitative Inquiry, 10,* 62–78.

Prashad, V. (2002). *Everybody was Kung-fu fighting: Afro-Asian connections and the myth of cultural purity.* New York: Beacon.

Roediger, D. (2002). *Colored White: Transcending the racial past.* Berkeley: University of California Press.

Shavelson, R., & Towne, L. (Eds.). (2003). *Scientific research in education.* Washington, DC: National Academies Press.

Smith, L. T. (1998). *Decolonising methodologies: Research and indigenous peoples.* London: Zed Books.

Snipp, C. M. (1995). American Indian studies. In J. A. Banks & C. M. Banks (Eds.), *Handbook of research on multicultural education* (pp. 245–258). New York: Macmillan.

Spivak, G. C. (1990). Explanation and culture: Marginalia. In R. Ferguson, M. Gever, & T. Minh-ha (Eds.), *Out there: Marginalization and contemporary cultures* (pp. 377–393). Cambridge: MIT Press.

Spradley, J. (1979). *The ethnographic interview.* New York: Holt, Rinehart & Winston.

Tate, G. (2003). Introduction: Nigs R Us, or how Blackfolks became fetish objects. In G. Tate (Ed.), *Everything but the burden: What White people are taking from Black culture* (pp. 1–14). New York: Broadway Books.

Tuskegee Syphilis Study Legacy Committee. (1996, May 26). *Final report.* Washington, DC: Author.

wa Thiongo, N. (1991). *Decolonising the mind.* Nairobi: Heinemann Kenya.

Warrior, R. A. (1995). *Tribal secrets: Recovering American Indian intellectual traditions.* Minneapolis: University of Minnesota Press.

West, C. (1990). The new cultural politics of difference. In R. Ferguson, M. Gever, & T. Minh-ha (Eds.), *Out there: Marginalization and contemporary cultures* (pp. 19–36). Cambridge: MIT Press.

Wong, S. (1995). *American knees.* New York: Simon & Schuster.

Wynter, S. (1990). *Do not call us "negros": How "multicultural" textbooks perpetuate racism.* San Francisco: Aspire Books.

5

CRITICAL RACE THEORY AND INDIGENOUS METHODOLOGIES

Christopher Dunbar Jr.

Carter G. Woodson (1933/2000) posed the query, "What different method of approach or what sort of appeal would one make to the Negro that cannot be made just as well by a white teacher?" "To be honest," he said, "There is no particular body of facts that Negro teachers can impart to children of their own race that may not be just as easily presented by persons of another race if they have the same attitude as Negro teachers; but in most cases, tradition, race hate, segregation and terrorism make such a thing impossible" (pp. 27–28).

John Hope Franklin (1963) pointed out that many White scholars had begun to concede, "Negroes had peculiar talents that fitted them to study themselves and their problems. To the extent that this concession was made, defeated a basic principle of scholarship—namely that given the materials and techniques of scholarship and given the mental capacity any person could engage in the study of any particular field" (p. 69). In other words, scholarship could be conducted regardless of mitigating circumstances that may shroud the conditions under which the study is conducted, which ultimately influence how one perceives a situation. However, Woodson (1933/2000) would argue that shared life experiences between researcher and the researched lend themselves to greater understanding of life's conditions and circumstances, therefore rendering the "Negro's" seeming propensity to conduct research and scholarship about like kind more accurate and necessary.

There was a downside to this concession, however. Negro scholarship "had become victim to the view that there was some 'mystique' about Negro studies similar to the view that there was some mystique about Negro spirituals, which requires that a person possess a black skin in order to sing them" (p. 69). This was not scholarship; it was folklore, it was voodoo. Ladson-Billings (2000) raised the same concern when she states, "Some works are called literature whereas other works are termed folklore. Not surprisingly, the literature of people of color is more likely to fall into the folklore category" (p. 258). This notion fed the belief that Negroes did not have the intellectual capacity to conduct valued research.

While Franklin (1963) viewed this interpretation (by Whites) of research conducted by Negroes as "tragic," stating, "Negro scholarship had foundered on the rocks of racism" (p. 69), other scholars of color positioned themselves differently, embracing a position that everything about race is subjective, hence challenging the notion of objectivity and the perception that given the same materials and resources, anyone could conduct research and arrive at the same findings—that is, the belief that life experiences and/or power relationships have no impact on research outcomes.

▣ Dominant Cultural Model

Ladson-Billings and Donnor (2005), however, suggest that power relationships (in fact) influence how research is collected and interpreted. That is, the sociocultural, political, and economic position of the researcher and the researched plays an acute role in how research is presented and therefore interpreted. In this instance, the researched is positioned or excluded from the mainstream or dominant culture. The researched is the object/other/subject whose existence is described/prescribed by members of the dominant culture model of knowing. They occupy a "liminal status/space" as people of color (Wynter, 1992, as cited in Ladson-Billings & Donnor, 2005). That is, there exists one "center" composed of those whose way of knowing determines how those outside the center are viewed. Therefore, what there is to know revolves around the center's interpretation of that which is perceived as outside the center. Thus, there are those who comprise the center and those who work their way around it, suggesting a dualistic position. The relationship between the knower and the object is regulated by the rules established by those in the center; consequently, the dominant cultural model became the standard by which all research is assessed. This dominant model sets up prescriptive rules and canons for regulating thought and action in society. Thus, the issue is about the "nature of human knowing of the social reality utilizing a model in which the knower is already a socialized subject" (Wynter, 1992, as cited by Ladson-Billings & Donnor, 2005).

Ladson-Billings and Donnor (2005) are careful to note that this liminal positioning is not necessarily a "place of degradation and disadvantage." On the contrary, Wynter (1992, as cited in Ladson-Billings & Donnor, 2005) suggests that this place of alterity provides a "wide angle advantage." The advantage is a result of the "dialectical nature of constructed otherness that prescribes the liminal status of people of color as beyond the normative boundary of the conception of Self/Other" (King, 1995, as cited in Ladson-Billings & Donnor, 2005). The advantage to scholars of color results from the opportunity/obligation to transcend the either/or way of knowing. Scholars included in this chapter argue against dualistic positioning. They provide multiple positions/lenses that challenge the dominant cultural model that they contend distorts their realities and has served only to sustain power relations that continue to place them at a disadvantage. This dichotomy is the focus of this chapter.

I began this chapter with quotes from Woodson (1933/2000) and Franklin (1963) because they speak in a profound way to issues concerned with critical race theory and Indigenous inquiries and methodologies. I contend that Woodson's insights lend support for the need and the strength of Indigenous methodologies. I concur with Woodson's belief that race (hate), de facto segregation, and terrorism continue to have a profound impact on one's way of knowing (epistemology) and one's relationship to what there is to know (ontology). Ladson-Billings (2000) suggests that epistemology is more than a way of knowing. She describes it as a "system of knowing that has both an internal logic and external validity" (p. 257). In this instance, a distinction is made between a way of knowing and a system of knowing. In the former, every individual has a relationship to what there is to know (and obviously, the relationships differ), while in the latter case, some ways of knowing are valued and validated while others are not dependent on one's position to the center. What there is to know is inextricably linked to an individual's past, present, and future. It is shaped by historical, social, political, and economic experiences. "I am my past, present and future" (Minh-ha, 1989). My reality suggests that race matters. Franklin's analysis of traditional research methods questioned the notion that legitimate research had to be conducted by White scholars.

This chapter is divided into two sections. The first section presents an overview/critique of critical race theory. The second section explores the imperative of both Indigenous scholars and scholars of color to provide alternative modes of inquiry that accurately represent/reflect and critique their experiences.

Understanding Critical Race: No Balcony Seats

The construction of racism from the "perpetrator perspective," according to Alan Freeman (1995), "restrictively conceived racism as an intentional, irrational deviation by a conscious wrongdoer from otherwise neutral rational and just ways of distributing jobs, power, prestige, and wealth. The adoption of this perspective allowed a broad cultural mainstream both explicitly to acknowledge the fact of racism and to simultaneously insist on its irregular occurrence and limited significance" (p. xiv). Freeman concludes that liberal race reform thus served to legitimize the basic myths of American meritocracy.

According to Freeman (1995), "Critical race theory (CRT) embraces a movement of left scholars, mostly scholars of color situated in law schools, whose works challenged the ways in which race and racial power are constructed and represented in America legal culture and more generally in American Society as a whole" (p. xiii). Two common interests unify critical race scholarship. The first is to understand how a regime of White supremacy and its subordination of people of color have been created and maintained in America, and the second is a particular examination of the relationship between that social structure and professed ideas such as the rule of law and "equal protection" (Freeman, 1995, p. xiii).

Critical race theory is an outgrowth of and is often allied with critical legal studies (CLS). The critical legal studies group, of whom the most prominent associates are Patricia Williams, Richard Delgado, Kimberlé Crenshaw, and Derrick Bell, is marked by their utilization of developments in postmodern poststructural scholarship, especially the focus on "liminal" or "marginalized" communities and the use of alternative methodology in the expression of theoretical work. Most notable is their use of "narratives" and other literary techniques. They reject the prevailing orthodoxy that scholarship could or should be "neutral" and "objective" (Crenshaw, Gotanda, Peller, & Thomas, 1995). These scholars believe that scholarship about race in America could never be written distanced from or with an attitude of objectivity. There is no scholarly perch outside the social dynamics of racial power from which to merely observe and analyze (Crenshaw et al., 1995). The formal selection process, collection, analyses, and organization of what is called knowledge are inevitably political (Crenshaw et al., 1995).

"Critical race theory aims to reexamine the terms by which race and racism have been negotiated in American consciousness and to recover the radical tradition of race consciousness among African Americans and other people of color" (Freeman, 1995, p. xiv). This race consciousness tradition was abandoned when integration, assimilation, and the idea of color blindness became the official norms of racial enlightenment.

Eleanor Marie Brown (1995) writes that CRT's reliance on narrative is explicitly pragmatic. "First, critical race theorists use narrative in a self-conscious effort to include the voices of people of color who have traditionally been excluded from conventionally 'appropriate' legal scholarship. Second, the use of narrative challenges the traditional meritocratic paradigm of the academy by attempting to subvert what are viewed as pretenses of 'objectivity,' 'neutrality,' 'meritocracy,' and 'color-blindness'" (Brown, cited in Shuford, 2001). To the extent that one writes in the conventional mode, one glorifies these traditional meritocratic standards that were conceptualized in a "raced" world.

Racelessness/Consciousness

John Shuford (2001) provides an analysis of W. E. B. DuBois's contributions to critical race theory through an essay penned *The DuBoisian Legacy to Critical Race Theory: The Impossibility of Racelessness and Whiteness as an Ontological Condition of Moral Indebtness?* In his essay, Shuford writes,

> Du Bois provided complex insights into racialization and racial identity formation as he simultaneously described the impossibility of racelessness, the inevitability of race-consciousness, and the worth of races toward liberatory culture-making. From all stages of his theorizing, Du Bois emphasized the ongoing relevance of racialization of certain morphological traits and genealogies (and how these were used as a basis for subordination or allocation of privilege; the social and cognitive freedoms and constraints individuals and groups face within racial identity formation; and how racialization practices could be put to greater liberatory use by and for racially oppressed people than could practices of racelessness).

▣ Rejection of Race Concept

While DuBois argued that the concept of racelessness is impossible, others such as Kwame A. Appiah and Naomi Zack argue that race is scientifically meaningless. That is, it is a socially constructed concept. "Antirace" and so-called mixed-race theorists have encouraged African Americans, Black Africans, multiracial people, and Whites alike to reject all race concepts on strategic, scientific, conceptual, sociohistorical, and existential grounds (Shuford, 2001). Proponents of this philosophy encourage all people to embrace racelessness toward the goals of individual and group inclusion, deconstruction of racial oppression and racial privilege, more holistic identity formation, and critical empowerment within massive scientific, social, and discursive shifts (Shuford, 2001).

Zack (2001), a philosopher and of mixed-race heritage, postulates,

> The main problem with "race" in common sense is a failure to recognize that there is no biological basis for racial categories. But, since such common sense illusions about race exist (that is, race is a social fact, socially constructed and practiced and subsequently normalized), it is important to note that they have been accompanied by a general denial of official recognition of mixed-race identity. This denial has supported ungrounded notions of racial purity. If race is (falsely) believed to be real, then mixed race ought to enjoy the same social status. Therefore, so long as beliefs in pure races persist in society, there would seem to be a need for a theoretical foundation that could be used for political and policy arguments that allow for the recognition of mixed-race identities.

Divergent Views

Brown (1995), author of "The Tower of Babel," argues, "Whether or not we realize we are raced necessarily implicates the extent to which we are raced. Some of us are raced, others of us are de-raced, and there is a continuum in between" (cited in Shuford, 2001). In recent years, Brown has postulated that "antirace" and so-called mixed-race race theorists have been at the forefront of discursive shifts to problematize, transform, or even obliterate practices of racialization. Their methods toward "antirace" or "mixed-race" ontologies and identities have included development of autobiographically based multiracial and "borderline" identity theories, refutations of biological essentialism, and identification of historical and conceptual underpinnings of White racism (cited in Shuford, 2001).

Luscious Outlaw (1996) provides a different perspective. He suggests,

> Lest we move too fast on this [on moving beyond racism in a pluralistic democracy] there is still to be explored the "other side" of "race": namely, the lived experiences of those within racial groups (e.g., blacks for whom Black nationalism, in many ways, is fundamental). That "race" is without a scientific basis in biological terms does not mean, thereby, that it is without any social value, racism notwithstanding. The exploration of "race" from this "other side" is required before we will have an adequate critical theory, one that truly contributes

to enlightenment and emancipation, in part by appreciating the integrity of those who see themselves through the prism of "race." We must not err yet again in thinking that "race thinking" must be completely eliminated on the way to emancipated society.

Living in a "Raced" Society

Issues of race have been the backdrop in all my lived experiences. That includes occasions when I was acutely aware that my race was an issue and instances when it was not so obvious. However, the question of race was/is always something I consider/ed, if not immediately, certainly soon after I left a situation. Race is a constant in my life. It may be the only constant. I am outside "the center" that Ladson-Billings (2000; Ladson-Billings & Donnor, 2005) posits and therefore have been positioned as a scholar of color and trained/directed to embrace the "dominant cultural model" of conducting research. Beginning with my academic training, I always wanted to begin with the story. As Bryant Alexander (2006) aptly posits, "There is always a story that frames the nature of research" (p. 34). Hence, my research inclination or my way of knowing was directly/indirectly related to my position in the story. "What's the story in there?" are words my father would ask upon hearing my siblings and me quibbling in an adjacent room. It was the launching of an investigation. There was no notion of objectivity except my response, "I didn't do it!"

However, in my academic training, I was often discouraged because this modality did not fit in the model of research that was imposed. The notion of objectivity when I describe the plight of people who look like me was never my first thought. Fact is, the requirement for me to remove my experience as a "raced" object from my work as an academic scholar was undesirable. For as long as I can remember, my race has been my "center." Acknowledgment of this positionality has dictated my behavior/research in this "raced society." Indeed, "I am my past, present and future" (Minh-ha, 1989).

I have framed much of my research in story form because I, too, agree that a story frames my research. For example, when I approached a young student attending an alternative school to introduce myself, he immediately responded, "Are you the 'poleecc?'" (Dunbar, 2001). His "lived experience" concerned with people asking questions about his life told him to be suspicious of anyone making such inquiries. It did not matter that I was a person who looked like him. The fact that (I said) I was a student researcher at the university did not prompt him to ask about the university or even why (because of my age) I was a still in school. *Researcher,* for this young African American man, was synonymous with *interrogator* or *investigator.* Hence, it was quite logical for him to pose this question. He had taken an appropriate cultural stance. To some, his cultural performance would have been anticipated and deemed authentic. Posing this question in front of his classmates rendered him an endeared and legitimate member of his peers.

Perhaps his response was predicated on the fact that most of the children interviewed were ordered by a judge not to be on the university campus unless they were accompanied by an adult. You see, most of the students in the study had previous encounters with the law (see Dunbar, 2001). Indeed, there existed borders and boundaries for these children (that were not imagined), and I had crossed the line. For me, it was necessary to share my apprehensiveness about police and my understanding of the necessity to build a border between those whom I suspected did not have my best interests in mind. My success was predicated on my capacity to understand and to convey that I, too, had similar lived experiences.

Significance of "Lived Experiences"

Woodson (1933/2000) argued that there is a distinct body of facts that one can only impart as a result of having shared experiences. He posits that particular insights provide entrance into a situation that might be otherwise misunderstood, viewed as insignificant or completely missed about the "lived experiences" of oppressed/colonized people. Woodson is explicit when he states that White teachers (and I would also argue researchers) may be able to do some work "better than the Negro and there is no objection to such service" (p. 28). However, there exist other intangibles/nuances that are best transmitted and understood when shared experiences, epistemologies, and the relationship to both are evident between the observer and the observed—that is, when the subject and the object have shared struggles not unlike experiences shared (stories) among recovering alcoholics. In both situations, there is a common experience/understanding between those who ask and those who are being asked. The subjects and the audience are not disconnected. They have similar lived experiences. Similar insights provide a window with which to share views without speaking, where a sound, seemingly inaudible to the unprepared ear, speaks volumes to a knowing listener, where the expression on one's face tells the whole story or a simple nod says, "I know where you're coming from."

Woodson (1933/2000) adds, "That if the Negro is to be forced to live in the ghetto, he can more easily develop out of it under his own leadership than under that which is super-imposed. The Negro will never be able to show his originality as long as his efforts are directed from without by those who socially proscribe him" (p. 28). That is, Woodson contends that the Negro will never be able to progress as long as the tools used for such progress serve more to condemn him than to uplift him. Similarly stated by Black feminist Audre Lorde (1984), "The master's tools will never dismantle the master's house." Hence the need for scholars of color to adopt critical methodologies toward the transformation and liberation of oppressed people. DuBois indicated that leadership of such a movement must come from the ranks of the "talented tenth" of the Negro population.

Talented Tenth

DuBois (1903/2003) espoused that a talented tenth of the African American population must take responsibility to lead. He posed the following question:

> Can the masses of the Negro people be in any possible way more quickly raised than by the effort and example of this aristocracy of talent and character? Was there ever a nation on God's fair earth civilized from the bottom upward? Never, it is, ever was and ever will be from the top downward that culture filters. This is the history of human progress. (p. 45)

DuBois (1903/2003) further explains how the most capable youth must be trained to take on this responsibility:

> The best and most capable of their youth must be schooled in the colleges and universities of the land. We will not quarrel as to just what the university of the Negro should teach or how it should teach it—I willingly admit that each soul and each race-soul needs its own peculiar curriculum. But this is true: A university is a human invention for the transmission of knowledge and culture from generation to generation, through the training of quick minds and pure hearts, and for this work no other human invention will suffice, not even trade and industrial schools. (p. 45)

DuBois (1903/2003) suggests, "Each soul and each race-soul needs its own peculiar curriculum." That is, each race-soul has needs that are particular to its set of experiences. In the case of the Negro, the set of experiences is peculiarly different from that of Euro-Americans. These experiences affect their relationship to what there is to know. Therefore, a curriculum that takes into account this unique set of experiences "is required before we will have an adequate critical theory, one that truly contributes to enlightenment and emancipation, in part by appreciating the integrity of those who see themselves through the prism of 'race'" (cited in Shuford, 2001).

Taking DuBois's assessment a step further, I would argue that the peculiar set of experiences of African Americans necessitates a methodological approach of inquiry that also differs from a Euro/Western approach to uncover and discover the lived experiences of disenfranchised, colonized, and Indigenous people. That is, there are (and need to be) multiple ways of inquiry/knowing.

Stories From an Indigenous Perspective

Stories provide data that have a focus on ways in which cultural and social constraints act upon individuals. They are a powerful tool for reflection. The language used is an act of epistemology. Bruner (1990) suggests that storytellers take meaning from the historical circumstances that gave shape to the culture of which they are an expression.

Impact of Colonialism on Knowing: First Nations' Viewpoint

Battiste and Youngblood Henderson (in Bennett & Blackstock, 2002) argue that the creation of knowledge is based on what they refer to as Eurocentricism. They explain that Eurocentricism supports the belief in the superiority of European people over non-European (Indigenous) peoples and extends to the lack of recognition (or ignorance) of Indigenous knowledge systems, ways of knowing and doing. Other Indigenous scholars postulate that to understand the impact of colonialism on research methods, one only has to look at the way First Nations are indoctrinated by Canadian universities (Cajete, 2000; Hampton, 1995). They explain that they are not from homogeneous cultures and backgrounds, yet in Western universities, they are expected to fit into "one-size-fits-all" institutions (Bailey, 2000).

"The unwritten rule of the dominant society requires that we all speak English, write research papers and exams assessed on specific criteria outside of our Indigenous worldviews, and learn what others decide we need to know. Nor does what we learn in these institutions assist us in reaffirming and legitimizing our own ways of knowing and doing. Further, the language in which knowledge is imparted is not ours by birth" (Bailey, 2000; see also Cajete, 2000; Hampton, 1995; Martin, 2001).

Battiste and Youngblood Henderson (2000) indicate that these kinds of activities establish the dominant group's knowledge, experience, culture, and language as the universal norm. In addition, this educational experience of Aboriginal people exemplifies the continued colonization where the dominant culture (university educators) expects students to conform to their expectations. Members of the dominant society control the structure, content, processes, and staff within these institutions, and they consciously or unconsciously reinforce the marginalization of Indigenous knowledge systems.

Martin (2001) asserts that too often, research about Aboriginals (Canada) has been done by outsiders who have dissected, labeled, and dehumanized Indigenous people, acting as helpers in the colonial disposition of Indigenous land and cultural heritage. Volumes of research have been generated about Aboriginals, but there is little research that Aboriginal people have been able to define for themselves. Bennett and Blackstock (2002) cite the daunting task of decolonizing the research process to legitimize their own way of generating Indigenous knowledge that is controlled, owned, and protected by First Nations peoples collectively. They further assert that they have an ethical responsibility to support initiatives that create opportunities for First Nations people to conduct research that is congruent with Indigenous values and priorities.

"Every Time Research Is Done a Piece of My Culture Is Erased . . ."

Aboriginals shared this perspective during an Indigenous Research Forum held at the University of Newcastle, Australia (2004). Participants addressed a variety of concerns that surround research methods that include ethics, feedback, interpretations, and outcomes. The prevailing consensus reported that research is conducted to benefit the researcher, interpretations are often incorrect, there is little feedback after the research is completed, and outcomes often create more harm than good for those studied. "We've been studied to death. . . . If you want something dead . . . research it" (see http://www.newcastle.edu.au/school/aborig-studies/index.html).

Umulliko: To Create, To Make, To Do in the Language of the Awabakai People

The Umulliko Indigenous Higher Education Research Center at the University of Newcastle takes on the challenges of increasing Indigenous control of research practice and outcome through the development of high-quality Indigenous student research education and practice. They espouse a holistic and culturally appropriate approach to research and education. The preeminent need of the Indigenous research agenda is for research that is conducted according to the concept of Indigenous worldview (IWV). This will usually be from Australian Indigenous perspectives, but on occasions of research with an international focus, the worldview has to be that of the Indigenous community in the country and community in question. The Indigenous worldview places Indigenous peoples at the center of the research environment and is cognizant of Indigenous values, beliefs, paradigms, social practices, ethical protocols, and pedagogies. The IWV identifies both Indigenous and non-Indigenous research voices and perspectives, but these will be filtered and framed by Indigenous worldview. The knowledge framework will be one that is holistic and integrated, and this will further inform the view of research and research training and its impact on peoples and cultures (see http://www.newcastle.edu.au/school/aborig-studies/index.html).

Consensus: Need for Alternative/ Indigenous Research Methodologies

More academics of color have questioned the Eurocentric or Western methodological approach to conducting research, particularly research on people of color. As Woodson (1933/2000) points out (in his example of teaching "Negro" children), there exists a difference in conducting research on people who do not share like lived experiences. There is a difference when the researcher is viewed as the colonizer/perpetrator and the subject is the colonized or the object of subjugation. The purpose of the research is often different in goals and sometimes its outcome. Dr. Howard Fuller (2000), chair of the Black Alliance of Educational Options (BAEO), once told an audience of educators that "some folk do research for the sake of doing research while black folk do research to save the lives of black children." Indigenous researchers such as Smith (2005) assert that Indigenous research is about changing and improving conditions. They are driven by a purposeful dream and not a prescription. Their subjects are not merely objects to be studied objectively (allegedly); rather, the desired outcome is that which challenges the worldview of Indigenous people based on a Eurocentric perspective.

▣ Narratives and Storytelling: "Otherwise It's Western Work Done by Aboriginals and the Disenfranchised"

Daddy, Tell Me It Ain't So

My five-year-old son awakened us in his fashioned way

yellin' to the top of his lungs "Time to wake-up!"

In one motion, I covered my vitals (as he leapt onto our bed), rolled over,

grabbed the remote, and invited the *Today Show* into our room—

I must admit, this scene is a constant in my morning ritual.

Matt Lauer began the morning news with a story about a Black woman stopped by the police on her way to the hospital believing she was having a miscarriage.

Despite her plea to be taken to the hospital she was taken into custody.

She was released the next morning and taken to the hospital.

Baby was delivered six months premature, lived one minute and died.

Hearing moans of discuss and despair from Mom and Dad over this story

Son asked, "What's the matter?" Now silenced, Mom and Dad respond, "Let's get ready for school."

The Ideal Black Man Jumps Off the Page of Biden's Storybook Into the Public Eye. And, He Can Talk, Too!

U.S. Senator Joe Biden declares that Barack Obama is *the first "mainstream African American [candidate] who is articulate and bright and clean and a nice-looking guy. I mean, that's a storybook, man."* Ole' Joe is just being himself, a news story read—you know, like the time he *managed* to offend Asian Indians by saying you must have an *Indian accent to patronize a 7-Eleven or Dunkin' Donuts.* I can hear him now attempting to *mimic* an accent. Biden authored this script as well. When you author a script, often more about you is revealed than is revealed about the person(s) about whom it is written. Taking a page from America's storybook reflects the quintessential fabric of Western culture. It reveals that "race" is at the center and, depending on what side of the "page" you're situated, determines how the story is told. Will someone turn the page? This script is old yet still lives!

I tell this story because in the words of Ladson-Billings (1994), "It diminishes the primacy of objectivity." In this instance, I write about my story that both challenges and reduces the dominance of the Western scholarly tradition. In addition, it provides a critique of the positionality of race in this dominant culture. It is an integration of my culture and my lived experiences. It is an effort to provide the reader lessons from my experiences with the intention to provide insights from the experiences of "others." They provide an illustration of continued subjugation of people of color in Western civilization.

Storytelling and Critiques of the Dominant Social Order

Laurence Parker (1998) suggests that CRT legitimates and promotes the voices of people of color by using storytelling to integrate the experiential knowledge drawn from history of the "other" into critiques of the dominant social order. He further states, "The critical centering of race (together with race, gender, sexual orientation, and other areas of difference) at the location where the research is conducted and discussions are held can serve as a major link between fully understanding the historical vestiges of discrimination and the present day manifestation of that discrimination" (p. 46).

Solorzano and Yosso (2002) suggest that storytelling from marginalized people of color provides powerful counterstories challenging the majoritarian stories that make White privilege appear natural. Bernal (2002) states that CRT is about learning to listen to other people's stories and finding ways to make them matter within the education system and within education research. Struthers and Peden-McAlpine (2005) suggest that "narratives assist Indigenous people in reproducing through narrative communication features of the past, present, future. The narrative process elicits significant implicit meaning of indigenous culture." A product of narrative storytelling is the capacity to reflect on change that will enhance in a holistic and culturally manner. The goal is social justice.

Brown (1995) writes, "Poor people write stories. I hear their stories daily. I have heard them in the words of a cousin who came dangerously close to losing a daughter in gang warfare. I have heard them in the words of an inmate as he explained just how a black man from the projects had ended up on death row" (p. 513).

I have also heard stories from poor children who had been displaced from public school. Bobby exclaimed how difficult it was to be a Black man. "You got to fight to get an education, you got to fight to have freedom, you got to fight to stay out of jail. For a white man you don't got to do nothing" (Dunbar, 2001, p. 39). The realities of race and its manifestations left an indelible impression on this 14-year-old adolescent. Bobby was critically aware that race mattered.

Brown (1995) further writes, "Disenfranchised black people also write poetry too. I have heard poems in the words of the aspiring rap artists who frequent my hairdresser's parlor. I have heard poetry in the Negro spirituals that my grandmother sings as she braided my hair" (p. 513).

"He may float like a butterfly and sting like a bee but I'm still gonna' call him Cassius. That's what his

Mama called him." Just one of a million stories (I heard as a child) bantered about on Saturday mornings at Coley's Barbershop. Stories are often accompanied with pain, tension, or fear. Stories are riddled with political and social implications. Often the messages are so clear they can be heard above the roar. "You can call me colored, you can call me Negro, you can call me pecan tan. Just don't call me black," said the preacher from the pulpit, struggling with what the dominant society deemed appropriate to refer to him as—and thinking he had made a conscious choice. The dominant society and its damming depiction of disenfranchised and Indigenous people—some of whom were/are so ensconced in their "place" in life—has resulted in confusion and disdain (about what we are to be called) from those whose very existence and dignity are at stake. This story is an effort to right/rewrite a narrative about a disenfranchised people desiring to make sense of the world we live in!

To write personal narratives involves the work of reflection and telling. This work produces visible, often painful moments. It is both a historical and political process that places people of color in control of their story. Stories often trace the path/history of the person telling the story.

Understanding From the Bottom

Brown (1995) challenges the exclusion of voices from the bottom. The use of narratives provides a "venue that privileges the experiential knowledge of people of color and our communities of origin." Maria Matsuda (1993) writes, "From the namelessness of the slave, from the broken treaties of the indigenous Americans, the desire to know history from the bottom has forced scholars to sources often ignored: poems, oral histories, and stories from their own experiences" (p. 19).

Challenges to Critical Race Theory

Latino critical race theory (LatCrit) has emerged as a field of study that is grounded in the belief that "much of the national dialogue on race relations takes place in the context of education" (Roithmayr, 1991, cited in Darder & Torres, 2004, p. 98). African American scholars and Latino scholars such as Parker (1998), Ladson-Billings (1994, 2000), and Solorzano and Bernal (2001) began to infuse their arguments in educational policy and critical race theory. These scholars argue that "racial liberation was the most important objective of any emancipatory vision of education and the larger society" (Darder & Torres, 2004, p. 98).

However, a recent shift from the view that race should be the center of any emancipatory vision of change for Indigenous people and people of color has emerged. That is, Latino critical race theorists challenge the use of race as the central unit of analysis. They argue that the use of race as the focus of analysis lends itself to the underdevelopment and a systematic analysis of class and subsequently ignores a substantive critique of capitalism. Darder and Torres (2004) indicate, "Much of critical race theory is informed by 'ambiguous ideas of' institutional racism or structural racism." These scholars find this notion problematic because of the potential of "conceptual inflation" (p. 99). Hence, the use of social theorist language and ideas on race is problematic. Race as the central unit of analysis in the absence of a clearly theorized conception renders little to the emancipation of colonized people (Darder & Torres, 2004).

In addition, Latino critical race theorists argue that critical race theory has provided little understanding of the political economy of racism and racialization. Darder and Torres (2004, p. 100) argue that the process of racialization is at work in all relations in a capitalist society. Consequently, LatCrit scholars begin their analysis of racism in contemporary society with the capitalist mode of production, classes, and class struggle. They argue that race was birthed by racism and subsequently has been used as a tool to justify the way jobs, power, prestige, and wealth are distributed.

LatCrit and Storytelling

Latino critical race theory scholars provide a critical view of the use of narratives and storytelling, positing that this method, though useful in its own respect, tends to essentialize the plight of a disenfranchised people. More specifically, they argue that the narrative approach often "fails to challenge the underlying socioeconomic, political and cultural structures that have excluded these groups to begin with and have sustained the illusion of choice" (Watts, cited in Darder & Torres, 2004, p. 102). In problematizing the use of storytelling, these scholars point to three additional concerns. The first concern is a perceived tendency to romanticize the experiences of marginalized groups based on their experiences of oppression. The second is (again) a perception that there is a tendency to "overhomogenize" both White and people of color respecting questions of voice and political representation. The third issue is the perceived inevitable "exaggerations, excesses and ideological trends for which the only possible name is chauvinism" (Lemme, cited in Darder & Torres, 2004, pp.104–105).

Exclusionary Forces and Not Race

LatCrit theorists argue that exclusionary forces rather than race sustain inequality (Darder & Torres, 2004, p. 32). They espouse a reconceptualization of race to racism. To do so will necessarily provide an "ideological context to engage the structures of inequalities in a capitalist society" (Darder & Torres, 2004, p. 32). They acknowledge the utility of storytelling and narratives. However, the effort toward the liberation of disenfranchised people requires moving race from the center of emancipatory efforts and placing the capitalist economy paradigm as the focus toward social and economic equality.

The Utility of Voices From the Bottom

Matsuda (1995) posits, "Those who experienced discrimination speak with a special voice to which we should listen" (p. 63). She further espouses "looking to the bottom—adopting the perspective of those who have seen and thought the falsity of the liberal promise can assist critical scholars in the task of fathoming the phenomenology of law and defining the elements of justice" (p. 63). One cannot create the experience of life on the bottom (p. 63). Matsuda refers to what Gramsci calls the "organic intellectual" or grassroots philosopher (p. 63). Matsuda suggests that to imagine being poor and Black is less effective than actually learning from those who have experienced these realities. When seeking to understand "notions of right and wrong, justice and injustice from groups who have suffered throughout history, moral relativism recedes and identifiable normative priorities emerge" (p. 63). Matsuda postulates a new epistemological source for critical scholars: the actual experience, history, and cultural and intellectual tradition of people of color in America (p. 63).

Freedom to Design, Organize, and Define Indigenous Research

New Zealand Māori scholars such as Linda T. Smith (2005) employ the term *Kaupapa Māori* or *Māori research* as opposed to *Indigenous research.* Naming their research method was purposeful. Their struggle, as Smith expounds, is viewed as a conflict over "Māori language and the ability by Māori as Māori to name the world, to theorize the world and to research back to power" (p. 90). The Māori approach to research employs a set of arguments, principles, and frameworks that relate to the purpose, ethics, analyses, and outcomes of research. Its purpose is to serve as a model of social change and transformation that privileges Māori knowledge and ways of being. More specifically, Māori research is an approach that actively seeks to build capacity and a research infrastructure that supports community aspirations and development (Smith, 2005).

Conclusion

Reflecting on what I have written over these several pages has served to solidify my belief that an understanding and utilization of critical race theory as a method of inquiry is essential to understanding the impact of racism and the ongoing struggle of Indigenous and people of color not only in the United States but in other countries around the world. Critical race theorists and Indigenous methodologists speak to the necessity of writing their own script. They note that storytelling is a sacred act shared from the heart that relives/recounts their history and culture. It is their story—stories that bring back life.

Ladson-Billings (1994) discusses the significance of storytelling as culturally relevant pedagogy. She explains how she reflected on how her schooling experiences and the memory of it allowed her to persevere and prevail. Her recounting helped her to understand current classroom practices. She points to culturally relevant stories as being critical to the creation of appropriate strategies and techniques for current classrooms composed of African American children, stories of how she "got over."

Indigenous scholars suggest that stories illustrate ways to reconnect and identify with the past, which has its own script to record history. These scholars acknowledge the difficulty in applying Western theories or assumptions about their stories, but there is not any particular desire to do so. The stories are a source of cultural history that connects cultural traditions, worldviews, and ideas about a people.

Benham (2007) suggests that the focus of Native/Indigenous scholars is "to relate the narratives of indigenous people and communities that describe the social, cultural, political organizational patterns that reveal ontological and epistemological dilemmas through authentic indigenous perspectives" (p. 518). Aluli-Meyers (cited in Benham, 2007) "asserts that transforming the root of (indigenous) work challenges the way indigenous scholars think and do narrative inquiry with respect to the description of cultural and social phenomena" (p. 518). Aluli-Meyers argues that the relationships among/between Indigenous people are relevant, sophisticated, and radically context specific. Benham asserts that "it moves us to the telling of stories in the field as opposed to telling Van Maanen's (1988) stories of the field" (p. 518).

Indigenous people have been scripted by colonists, imperialists, and voyeurs, whose vision is tainted by their sense of superiority and their belief that they are the creators of knowledge. Their anointed position as inventors, discoverers, and researchers places them at the center of what there is to know and situates their (former) captives and Indigenous people somewhere outside the focal point, to be scripted based on a dominant culture model that suggests there is one truth and that truth positions them in the center.

Indigenous scholars and critical race theorists reject the notion of one truth. They argue that there are multiple ways of knowing, depending on whose lens is used. The notion of objectivity as evidence of truth is deemed invalid. They challenge the immorality of subjugation and the concept that a "racelessness" society can exist. They contend that where there is a void in morality, justice cannot exist. The dominant culture framework that espouses truth and objectivity is at the center of untruth and subjectivity. Indigenous scholars argue they have their "own way of doing things"—their own set of what constitutes knowledge. They argue that the dominant cultural model continues to marginalize the Indigenous knowledge systems model.

Stories From the Field

My stories of the field (see Dunbar, 2001) tell of the plight of too many African American male adolescents who had become disconnected from traditional public schools and, as a result, had been placed in alternative school environments. To the broader society, these students were disposable. And the students sensed this. They had come to know and understand the system under which they were subjugated. They had been rejected by the traditional public schools system and placed in an environment meant to contain their rage. I recognized it because the same rage ran through my veins.

These males were not unlike many that I had faced while a classroom teacher. Many had been incarcerated, placed in foster care, and/or grew up in abject poverty. The world simply did not appear a place accepting of "kids" like them. A problem for the majority of them was, "I speak but no one listens."

In telling the stories of these students, a venue was provided for which to say anything they wanted to say. Despite the fact that I "looked like them," they were indeed guarded when I first approached them. They were guarded for good reason. Few had shown an interest in their lives beyond taking whatever they could and in turn used what they learned against them. In presenting their stories, I carefully considered the context—in this case, an alternative school, a juvenile detention center, and a courthouse. In these entire instances, the message to these students was clear . . . you are disposable! I presented their stories the way I heard them; so sometimes there was a subject-verb disagreement, words were spelled as I heard them, and accent for the significance of their point was indicated.

Some readers (of the work) suggested that perhaps I should have spelled their words correctly instead of the phonetic form in which I had heard them—that I had (in some way) depicted/represented them as (dumb) students. If those readers had listened to the message rather than focus on the spelling of what I heard, their stories would have been heard. Perhaps this interpretation is a result of the Western way of knowing, that is, correct spelling and enunciation. These stories are about students who have struggled in traditional public schools narrowly and more about their positionality in society in a broader sense. It is not so much predicated on what these students should know academically but rather their story of their circumstances. Their stories are about their being misunderstood, their confusion about their plight, or rather their sense of reality governing their situation. These students were making sense of their reality!

My Own Sense Making

I have experienced this struggle growing up in the sixties as I cheered on rebellious "Negroes" as they ran past our house with goods taken from a store on the corner of the street where I was raised. I experienced the struggle while being spat upon as I absorbed a battery of racial epithets in an effort to desegregate a predominantly White high school.

I have been made to read text that depicted African Americans as slaves rather than captured Africans who were treated as "slaves" and told that this was the reason for my existence. I remember playing "cowboys and Indians" as an adolescent, never wanting to be an Indian. Racism has been the bane of my existence. I remember the assassination of President Kennedy while in the fourth grade, and the class was instructed to put our heads on the desk in a moment of silence. In my moment of silence, I remember experiencing a sense of despair because I had come to believe that President Kennedy was our only chance of being treated equal. I also remember running home after hearing about the assassination of Dr. King (some 5 years later) as I ran into the house, crying to my mother, "They're going to kill us all." As early as 9 years old, notions of race and racism have been as much a part of my existence as opening my eyes each morning.

My stories are systematically pulled from my memory; I dare say that these notions/acts of racism continue to permeate my life today—hence the necessity to shield my son (to some extent) but to also share stories like these when the time is write/right!

LatCrit Scholars

LatCrit scholars propose moving race from the center of analysis and replacing it with a better understanding of exclusionary practices that give rise to structural inequalities (i.e., capitalism). Other scholars point to their "indigenousness" as the centerpiece for their scholarship. This proposal—though interesting—does not address the multiple injustices that have occurred in history and continue to occur daily in the lives of people of color and Indigenous people. To move race from the center would mean the dominant cultural model would have to surrender its positionality and hence power and domination. I know of no instances where power was willingly surrendered. To suggest that people of color remove race from their center would mean to ignore the injustices that have occurred throughout history. It would mean ignoring the truth and exposing social inequities that give rise to continued social injustice. Race gives rise to exclusionary practices and not the other way around. I see your face and hear your voice long before I see your bank account! Mary Weems (2003, p. 111) writes,

> Race is so personal
> If it was a carcass
> The stench would block
> The nose of the world
> And everybody would die
>
> (Reprinted with the permission of Peter Lang Publishers.)

Parker (1998) articulates a sentiment I share when he posits that "the critical centering of race (together with race, gender, sexual orientation, and other areas of difference) at the location where the research is conducted and discussions are held can serve as a major link between fully understanding the historical vestiges of discrimination and the present day manifestation of that discrimination" (p. 46). Matsuda (1995) suggests that it is less effective to imagine being poor and Black than it is to ask someone to tell what he experienced.

It is critical that Indigenous scholars and scholars of color take the lead in framing their stories. Benham (2007) reveals that the telling of memory can be both difficult and painful. She further argues that it takes work to access and release these stories. In addition, scholars must honor the process of telling these stories. The story is important because it has the capacity to tell the truth about history.

Indigenous scholars, in challenging traditional research methods, have adopted methods of their own. Their methods consider the whole person, that is, the religion, culture, language, nuances, spirituality, and other values shared by their people. It is Indigenous research practices for and conducted by Indigenous scholars. It is an effort to accurately depict, portray, and, most important, understand the lives (stories) of a culture of people whose story has been misrepresented, misunderstood, and, in some instances, vilified in an effort to provide justification and rationalization for the injustices acted on them. The methods have a primary purpose to liberate and transform the lives of colonized/oppressed people. These scholars have to undo the dehumanizing practices of colonization. They do so using their own language instead of "killing" it off. The research is intended to revive their people as opposed to researching them to "death."

References

Alexander, B. A. (2006). *Performing Black masculinity: Race, culture, and queer identity.* Walnut Creek, CA: AltaMira Press.

Bailey, B. (2000). A white paper on aboriginal education. *University Canadian Ethnic Studies, 32*(1), 126–135.

Battiste, M., & Youngblood Henderson, J. (2000). *Protecting indigenous knowledge and heritage: A global challenge.* Saskatoon, SK: Purich Publishing Ltd.

Benham, M. (2007). Mo'olelo on culturally relevant story making from an indigenous perspective. In J. D. Clandinin (Ed.), *Handbook of narrative: Mapping a methodology* (pp. 512–533). Thousand Oaks, CA: Sage.

Bennett, M., & Blackstock, C. (2002). *First Nations child and family services and indigenous knowledge as a framework for research policy and practice.* Retrieved from www.cecw-cepb.cal/DocEng/FNPresWaterloo

Bernal, D. (2002). Critical race theory, Latino critical theory and critical raced gendered epistemologies: Recognizing students of color as holders and creators of knowledge. *Qualitative Inquiry, 8*(1), 105–126.

Brown, E. M. (1995). The Tower of Babel: Bridging the divide between critical race theory and "mainstream" civil rights scholarship. *Yale Law Journal, 105,* 513–547.

Bruner, J. S. (1990). *Acts of meaning.* Cambridge, MA: Harvard University Press.

Cajete, G. (2000). *Native science: Natural laws of interdependence.* Santa Fe, NM: Clear Light Publishers.

Crenshaw, K., Gotanda, N., Peller, G., & Thomas, K. (Eds.). (1995). *Critical race theory: The key writings that formed the movement.* New York: New Press.

Darder, A., & Torres, R. (2004). *After race: Racism after multiculturalism.* New York: New York University Press.

DuBois, W. E. B. (2003). *The Negro problem* (Centennial ed.). Amherst, NY: Humanity Books. (Original work published 1903)

Dunbar, C. (2001). *Alternative schooling for African American youth: Does anyone know we're here?* New York: Peter Lang.

Franklin, J. H. (1963). The dilemma of the American Negro scholar. In H. Hill (Ed.), *Soon one morning: New writing by American Negroes* (pp. 62–76). New York: Knopf.

Freeman, A. (1995). Introduction. In K. Crenshaw, N. Gotanda, G. Peller, & K. Thomas (Eds.), *Critical race theory: The key writings that formed the movement.* New York: New Press.

Fuller, H. (2000). *Keynote address.* Presented at Michigan State University.

Hampton, E. (1995). Towards redefining Indian education in Canada. In M. Battiste & J. Barmen (Eds.), *The circle unfolds* (pp. 4–46). Vancouver: University of British Columbia Press.

Ladson-Billings, G. (1994). *The dream keepers: Successful teachers of African American children.* San Francisco: Jossey-Bass.

Ladson-Billings, G. (2000). Racialized discourses and ethnic epistemologies. In N. K. Denzin & Y. S. Lincoln (Eds.), *The SAGE handbook of qualitative research* (2nd ed., pp. 257–278). Thousand Oaks, CA: Sage.

Ladson-Billings, G., & Donnor, J. (2005). The moral activist role. In N. K. Denzin & Y. S. Lincoln (Eds.), *The SAGE handbook of qualitative research* (3rd ed., pp. 85–107). Thousand Oaks, CA: Sage.

Lorde, A. (1984). *Sister outsider: Essays and speeches.* New York: Crossing.

Martin, K. (2001). *Ways of knowing, ways of being, ways of doing: Developing a theoretical framework and methods for indigenous and indigenist research.* Retrieved from www.aiatsis.gov.au/rsrch/conf2001

Matsuda, M. (1993). Public response to racist speech: Considering the victims' story. In M. J. Matsuda, C. R. Lawrence III, R. Delgado, & K. W. Crenshaw (Eds.), *Words that wound: Critical race theory, assaultive speech, and the First Amendment.* Boulder, CO: Westview.

Matsuda, M. (1995). Looking to the bottom: Critical legal studies and reparations. In K. Crenshaw, N. Gotanda, G. Peller, & K. Thomas (Eds.), *Critical race theory: The key writings that formed the movement.* New York: New Press.

Minh-ha, T. (1989). *Woman Native Other.* Bloomington: Indiana University Press.

Outlaw, L. (1996). "Conserve" races? In B. Bell, E. Grosholz, & J. Steward (Eds.), *WEB DuBois on race and culture* (pp. 15–38). New York: Routledge.

Parker, L. (1998). Race is . . . race ain't: An exploration of the utility of critical race theory in qualitative research in education. *International Journal of Qualitative Studies in Education, 11,* 45–55.

Shuford, J. (2001, March). *The DuBoisian legacy to critical race theory: The impossibility of racelessness and Whiteness as an ontological condition of moral indebtedness?* Paper presented at the Society for Advancement of American Philosophy, Las Vegas, NV.

Smith, L. T. (2005). On tricky ground: Researching the Native in the age of uncertainty. In N. K. Denzin & Y. S. Lincoln (Eds.), *The SAGE handbook of qualitative research* (3rd ed., pp. 85–107). Thousand Oaks, CA: Sage.

Soloranzo, D., & Bernal, D. (2001). Examining transformational resistance through cultural race and LatCrit theory framework: Chicano and Chicana students in an urban context. *Urban Education, 36,* 308–346.

Soloranzo, D., & Yosso, T. (2002). Critical race methodologies: Counter storytelling as an analytical framework. *Qualitative Inquiry, 8*(1), 23–24.

Struthers, R., & Peden-McAlpine, C. (2005). Phenomenological research among Canadian and United States indigenous populations: Oral tradition and quintessence of time. *Qualitative Health Research, 15,* 1264–1276.

Weems, M. E. (2003). *Public education and the imagination-intellect: I speak from the wound in my mouth.* New York: Peter Lang.

Woodson, C. G. (2000). *The mis-education of the Negro.* Chicago: African American Images. (Original work published 1933)

Zack, N. (2001, Spring). American mixed race: The U.S. 2000 census and related issues. *Harvard Blackletter Law Journal, 17.*

6

QUEER(Y)ING THE POSTCOLONIAL THROUGH THE WEST(ERN)

Bryant Keith Alexander

Prologue

A Black Man Writing

I always wanted to write a poem about writing a poem.

No, I really wanted to write a poem about a Black gay man writing a poem.

The seeming incongruity—

For those in the Black community who resist the duality of Blackness and gayness,[1] like those who buy into the colonial marketing of Black virile bodies and penises designed for the mass reproduction of enslaved minds, bodies, delimited possibilities, and displaced desire.

And for those historical legacies perpetuated through contemporary social relations penetrating and infusing a double consciousness of social life, not just for Black folk, but that duality of presumed difference that creates hierarchies of worth in the performative exteriority of daily life, which circulates like conceit in the interiority of bodily experience and culture for both marked and unmarked others—which of course, is all of us.

The seamless congruity—

For those who say—You can't be a Black man and write. Like those who buy into the statistics of Black male genocide, crime, violence, and self-destruction as both character trait and genetic predisposition barred from the social and historical conditions of the past and our current predicament. Like the anthropological gaze that projected delimited possibilities of indigenous others filtered through the tyranny of colonialism and the need for dominance, hence the social construction of otherness that penetrates the visualicity of skin color as infestation; racism as a colonial legacy.

Where is that place from which poetry (and other intellectual and engaged scholarship like the postcolonial project and Queer theory) spawn?

Is it a space of tension & tensiveness?

Desire & Disdain,

joy & pain,

suffering & rejoicing,

reclaiming & avenging,

searching and defining,

including and marginalizing, at the same time.

Black gay men certainly know that space for it is one partially cleared by our hands, built on our backs, and excavated from our dreams. Yet we are often absented in the narrating of those particular histories, positionalities, and conversations of social import.

From whence comes the impulse to put thought into words?

The lyrical and the prosaic,

the intellectual and autobiographical,

finding a commonplace of conversation,

building a grounded theory of doing and thinking,

of knowing and living, at the same time.

Words hitting the page like tears.

pain striking verse like oppression.

Twisting words and turning phrases like lives denied.

Like the bumper sticker mentalities articulating public thought:

GET AIDS and DIE!! or GOD HATES FAGGOTS!

AMERICA, LOVE IT OR LEAVE IT!

NIGGER GO HOME! (Where is home?)

I know you've seen them.

Does the impulse come from seeing bodies crippled, dragged on pavement, or

sacrificed like a scarecrow in a field,

because being Black and Gay means double jeopardy?

Does the impulse come from the irony of voices silenced,

yet still singing songs of survival,

like Negro spirituals encoded with messages of transcendence and salvation

or other forms of escape and possibility?

Black gay men were born doing that—sometimes it was the blues linked to the poetic spirit. Sometimes it was dancing to house music at the Pink Flamingo Lounge. Sometimes it was *suicide when the rainbow wasn't enough* (you know that girl?). Sometimes it was poetry—semantic transconfigurations—turning feelings into sounds,

sounds into words,

words into worlds,

worlds of lived experiences,

harnessing hope and channeling desire.

The narratives of our lives are written on our flesh,

literally and figuratively transposed onto skin/paper,

telling stories trapped between worlds.

Our bodies bridge the middle passages of our travels,

charting directions for future adventure;

but not adventure like a westward folly for expansion and domination,

but a trip to discover untapped resources in our own possibility,

detangling the overgrowth on the paths of our destiny;

(re)claiming place, space, time, and voice;

teasing out our hair, so we can think

or locking it into place,

as claim on/to identity.

If in fact postcolonialism is often about renarrating and *reexamining the history and legacy of colonialism and incorporating the perspectives of the colonized* (Brydon, 2000, vol. 1, p. 1),[2] then as a Black/gay/man/teacher/performer/scholar—I speak/write from a place of both bondage and freedom, held in place by the tensive ties of history's legacy that depicts me as exotic other, a transplanted aborigine negotiating diaspora in a land that both recognizes and disowns. Not diaspora simply as the disruption of dispersion and longing for an unknown homeland in the bifurcated identity of being African American, but a *queer diaspora* that Gayati Gopinath (2005) describes, one that "mobilizes questions of the past, memory, and nostalgia for radically different purposes. Rather than evoking an imaginary homeland frozen in an idyllic moment outside history, what is remembered through queer diasporic desire and the queer diasporic body is a past time and place riven with contradictions and the violence of multiple uprootings, displacements, and exiles" (p. 4).

Diaspora not as a political or geosocial location, but as a critical lens in which I am always and already looking for the resonant traces of colonial occlusions, those moments when the concerted efforts of the exclusion of my racialized and sexualized self are marked as evident and ongoing stratagems of racial domination serving as an obstacle to my full actualization. In this sense, diaspora becomes key to how Homi Bhabha (1994) describes the postcolonial project as "never a quiet act of introspection or retrospection. It is a painful re-membering, a putting together of the dismembered past to make sense of the trauma of the present" (p. 63), reinforcing Paul Gilroy's (1995) theory of diaspora, which "accentuates *becoming* rather than *being* and identity conceived disaporically, along these lines, resists reification" (p. 24).

So in this space, fixed, social, and critical, I try to read myself between the lines of the multiple narrations of postcolonial and queer theory—lifelines written between the texts of other stories, practicing voice, telling my own stories. And within postcolonialism, I locate myself—within the logics of race and place, time and governance, or situated invasions of geographical and political territories signifying dominance and defeat, deployment and diaspora, captivity and freedom. In "Teaching for the Times," Gayatri Spivak (1997) makes an argument for the situatedness of the African American in the postcolonial:

> In its own context, postcoloniality is the achievement of an independence that removes the legal subject status of a people as the result of struggle, armed or otherwise. In terms of internal colonization, Emancipation, Reconstruction, civil rights is just such an achievement. Furthermore, postcoloniality is no guarantee of prosperity for all, but rather a signal for the consolidation of recolonizations. In that respect as well, the condition of the African-American fits the general picture of postcoloniality much more accurately than the unearned claims of the Eurocentric well-placed migrant. Paradoxically, the rising racist backlash is an acknowledgement of this. In the so-called postcolonial countries, postcoloniality is not a signal for an end to struggle, but rather a shifting of the struggle to the persistent register of decolonization . . . I am claiming postcoloniality for the African-American, then not because I want to interfere with her self-representation, but because I want to correct the self-representation of the new immigrant academic as postcolonial, indeed as the source of postcolonial theory. (p. 189)

I quote Spivak at length because she helps me to situate myself in the postcolonial: a Black academic with both an assigned and achieved independence, but still betwixt and between—cultural accomplishment and social construction; involved in a continual struggle in the shifting *persistent register of decolonization;* being both *native and settler,* trying to make room in an expansion of ideas and expressions that allows space to stretch paradigms of being, explore the predicament of identity and representation, riding the wave of *flexible foundations* in postcolonial thought (Duncan, 2002).

I claim a tensive comfort in postcolonialism and queer theory, knowing that I am both placed and displaced in both, yet I move forth boldly voicing experience, engaged in "the production of identity" by renarrating the past and resisting the treachery of invisibility and exclusion that each promotes (Hall, 1994, p. 393). As well as navigating that potentially transitory space in queer theory that "cuts across every locus of agency and subjectivity, but without homogenizing" (Sedgwick, 1990, p. xii). And the "I" of personal involvement and accountability becomes the central point of entry in discussion. So as the subaltern,

> I think
>
> I feel,
>
> I want,
>
> I know,
>
> I re-member.
>
> I resist,
>
> I speak.[3]
>
> I write.

The particular focus on writing here serves as sine qua non for voice and the postcolonial and queer projects of claiming space, as well as a stylistic approach to address identity politics through performative acts of self-expression, a kind of *queer poetics,* an aesthetic that Mary E. Galvin (1999) suggests "comes out of necessity. In a culture structured significantly by heterosexism [and Whiteness], the mind that can imagine other sexualities and gender [raced] identities must also imagine other ways of speaking, new forms to articulate our visions of difference. In a cultural setting that sees us unthinkable, we've had to imagine our own existence" (p. xii). But I want to also, in a later example of film analysis, look at the ways in which queers are represented through aesthetic texts and thus reduced in the tropological and rhetorical space between the theoretical and the social constructions of the performative.

The method that I engage here is a *critical interpretive queer methodology* that engages a particular focus on critique but uses a highly personalized reflective and refractive method of revealing the invested self-implication of the author in the telling of the told, in a form that both signals and subverts traditional forms of scholarly discourse, contributing to both the field of knowing and the field of expressing the known. And while I will spend time outlining the directions and potentials of such a methodology, dear reader, I am already in the mode of doing, building a kind of grounded theory, of doing and describing at the same time.[4]

The content and form of this chapter are queer because to some degree, it resists the all-encompassing strictures of traditional forms of scholarly discourse, while working the political line between what is assumed to be only an aesthetic form without substantive worth and a critical excavation of thought that often sanitizes the *dense particularity* of the writer, which often receives false accolades as objectivity in scholarship (Mohanty, 1989). Thus I seek to both illuminate and at the same time subvert that paradoxical trap of postcolonial studies in which it "focuses on an object that [it] is committed to dismantling even while necessarily analytically fixated with [in] it" (Goldberg & Quayson, 2002, p. xiii), a fixation that manifests itself in traditional scholarly forms that "generate a particular kind of knowledge" that is sometimes as sanitizing as the excavation process that it seeks to rescue (p. xvii).[5] And while through the necessary fixation on citationality—the form does open up space for alternative methods of expression so that I am not completely erased in the Whiteness of the scholarly mandate of academic performance to which I more than partially subscribe. Hence I echo Joseph Boone (2001), "In tracing the trajectories outlined above, my own narrative aims to traverse and unsettle, even as it provisionally inscribes, a number of the imposed boundaries" that I seek to bleed and blend (p. 46).

So my voice is still present; look for it in its changing forms, tones, and languages—seeking to foreground not their, but my, intention.

▣ Overlapping and Overarching Critiques of Postcolonial Studies and Queer Theory

I wish to further this discussion with a series of basic premises about the contact points, both caressing and strained intimacies, between what is loosely being referred to as *postcolonial thought* and *queer theory.* To me, each is engaged in a project of excavation and *rescue of the alienated and silenced other.* Each is engaged in acts of *subverting regimes of the normal* and *systematic deconstructions of colonial legacies,* to create spaces for the variable performative identities of racialized and gendered minorities to *practice voice.* Each is involved in *a rhetoric of critique* and *a rhetoric of possibility* that liberates alternate ways of knowing, constructing, and engaging the world through *the dense particularity of being.* Each *moves toward illuminating and dismantling systems of oppression* by engaging critical analysis of those systems and their attending manifestations in social, cultural, and political practice (Hawley, 2001a, 2001b).

The postcolonial perspective and queer theory are both grounded in Whiteness: one a resistance to Whiteness as in European territorial conquests and its consequences, the other a blanching of racialized sexual differences that do not necessarily foreground Whiteness as its intent but as its effect; an erasure of racialized difference within the quest of universalizing larger notions of queer identity. Each foreground what Leela Gandhi (1998) refers to as "a theoretical resistance to the mystifying amnesia aftermath" while simultaneously performing the same type of amnesia of diversity within particular communities, either communities "of color" or those distinguished by sex/sexuality/gender performance both in the United States and non-Western societies (p. 4).

Querying Postcolonial Perspectives

In the introduction to *Relocating Postcolonialism,* David Theo Goldberg and Ato Quayson (2002) write, "There are now many recognizable genealogies for postcolonial studies. They are regularly rehearsed in books and articles undertaking to map the field. Starting with comments on the significance of Said's *Orientalism* (1978), they veer through Ashcroft, Griffiths, and Tiffin's *The Empire Writes Back* (1989), and then expand into examinations of the relevance of postcolonialism for discussions of image, culture, representation, studies of imperial and colonial history, anthropology, cultural studies, multiculturalism, and diaspora, among assorted other areas" (p. xii). But as expansive as that overarching description is, I prefer Homi K. Bhabha's (2000) construction of the emergence of postcolonial perspectives. He writes, "Postcolonial perspectives emerge from the colonial testimony of Third World countries and the discourses of 'minorities' within the geopolitical divisions of east and west, north and south. They intervene in those ideological discourses of modernity that attempt to give hegemonic 'normality' to uneven development and the differential, often disadvantaged, histories of nations, races, communities and people" (p. 105). Such a construction identifies both a point of origin, as well as the expanse of possibility within an approach to criticism that has, as concerted effort, to crack the code of history's conceit and open spaces that question not only the master('s) narrative, but gives voice to untold stories cloistered in the margins of minority populations and lived experience; a space to both *talk back* and celebrate cultural identities, but also a space of contestation against colonialists discourses, not just contestation from the perspective of oppressed citizens of Third World countries once ruled by colonialism, but a broad construction of contestation of hegemonic discourses, power structures, or social hierarchies by those who suffer exclusion and occlusion because of minoritized identities.[6]

Goldberg and Quayson (2002) suggest that there are "at least three significant clusters of attitudes and ideas . . . [that] might be taken as constitutive of generative ambiguities in the field" of postcolonial studies: "The first cluster clearly concerns the desire to speak to the Western paradigm of knowledge in the voice of otherness. . . . In the case of the second, Postcolonial Studies is afflicted by the fact that it has to claim an object for academic study which it is obliged simultaneously to disavow. . . . The third set of themes in Postcolonial Studies is prompted by the fact that postcolonial theory thus seems to locate itself everywhere and nowhere" (pp. xii, xiii, xvi). For me, postcolonial theory pivots on the following logics. There is *a shift in voice*—who gets to speak—with and for whom, opening the categories of diversity in race, genders, and sexualities (see Spivak 1988a); *a shift in context*—from larger social and political systems to the specific contexts of private/public lives and the ways in which place and space become meaningful terrain of practiced lives, hence minority selves in relation to society and alternative selves in relation to constructions of normalcy (see Gandhi, 1998; Goldie, 1999; Hawley, 2001a, 2001b). There is *a shift in theory*—from modernity to postmodernity to critical postcoloniality, from abstracted generalizations to emergent constructions grounded in the articulation and actualization of experience (Hall, 1994; Parry, 2002).

Issues of voice, power, context, and theory are contingencies of human social relations that dictate the known and the knowing, histories and futures, and the quality of human existence that makes new histories and emergent identities possible. As Homi Bhabha (2000) writes,

> These contingencies are often the grounds of historical necessity for elaborating empowering strategies of emancipation, staging other social antagonisms. For to reconstitute the discourse of cultural difference demands not simply a change of cultural contents and symbols; a replacement within the same time frame of representation is never adequate. It requires a radical revision of the social temporality in which emergent histories may be written, the rearticulation of the "sign" in which cultural identities may be inscribed. (p. 105)

Hence for me, this is core logic for the transformative potential in critical postcolonial studies, one that takes as its project the *radical revisioning of social temporality,* one that reinserts the missing voices, which thereby reshapes and helps to revision the progenitors of human accomplishment, in a manner that is inclusive of the more collective contingencies of actual experience in the dynamism of human social relations.

Allow me to offer two purposeful and very idiosyncratic critiques of postcolonial studies that are specific to my larger project within this chapter. Each pivots on the narrowness of scope in a project dedicated to expanding a critique of social and cultural domination. First, in his essay "Broadening Postcolonial Studies/Decolonizing Queer Studies," William J. Spurlin (2001) writes, "Postcolonial inquiry has not sufficiently interrogated same-sex desire as a viable way of being positioned in the world. In its analysis of marginalization and subalteran experience, its emphasis on national identities and borders, and its attention to race, gender, and class, postcolonial studies have seriously neglected the ways in which heterosexism and homophobia have also shaped the world of hegemonic power" (p. 185, emphasis added). The result is a project of liberation and resistance that reifies its borders with a focus on the dominating qualities of heterosexual identities, their regenerative abilities to sustain domination over sexual minorities, and their contributions to the spectrum of intellectual, artistic, and practical human innovation.

For example, Frantz Fanon is noted as a key figure in postcolonial studies, and his particular brand of homophobia theorized in the germinal text *Black Skin, White Masks* (1967) establishes a pernicious homophobia in postcolonial studies that for him depicts homosexuality as a sign of psychological distress, a pathology, exclusive to Western peoples and in particular Whites/Caucasians. In other realms of postcolonial studies, the issue of homophobia and homosexuality goes unaddressed in significant ways, as to leave Fanon a space of authority in defining the terms of its justified absence in the larger course of postcolonial interest. In his theorizing of "negrophobia," Fanon engages in a complex attraction/repulsion dynamic between White (women and men) and Black men. This is complicated with his racializing of homosexuality as a White contagion that verges on narcissism. Thus he builds a restrictive matrix that links White racism and homosexuality—that nearly obliterates the subjective reality of Black women in general and the possibility of Black gay men altogether.

Second, and maybe clearly linked, *postcolonial studies is built around the concept of otherness*—as both a point of departure and critique; "a systematic reflection on center-periphery relations" (McCarthy, 2007, p. 284) that has the potential of opening spaces of critical discussion about how we construct self and other (*metropolis to colony*) and the resulting devastations of such differentiation. But we see also how such mechanisms can also reify difference and serve as a place of entrapment, whether through the germinal discussions in colonialism making distinctions between the West and the Orient (Said, 1978)—one being ordered, rational, masculine, and good; the other irrational, feminine, and bad—the binaries are established that pits difference against presumed normalcy, or at least dominant over subjugated—because issues of colonial rule were never about majority over minority; and the reference of racialized minority identities is more about marking difference than it is about statistical populations. The resurgence and foregrounding of "minority" voices in postcolonial studies always makes relative otherness, in terms of the reified minority voices talking back in resistance (from the margins to the center), at the same time always reifying their presumed subjugated positionality.

In a germinal sense, the construction of otherness in postcolonialism is linked with the relationship of origins—colonizer to colonized—but the relationship can also be distinguished by points of destination and departure—which leads to a particular resistance of indigenous people to feel that postcolonial theory has failed them. In his essay "Indigenousness and Indigeneity," Jace Weaver (2000) establishes an argument for the situatedness of indigenous people on the outskirts of the liberating potentials of postcolonial theory. In particular, a distinction is made between "internal colonialism" and traditional constructions of colonialisms. Weaver writes,

> *Internal colonialism* differs from classic colonialism ... in that in colonialism's classic form a small group of colonists occupy a land far from the colonial metropolis (*métropole*) and remain a minority, exercising control over a larger indigenous population. By contrast, in internal colonialism, the native population is swamped by a large mass of colonial settlers who, after generations, no longer have a *métropole* to which to return. *Métropole* and colony thus become geographically coexistent. (p. 223)

The resulting effect is sustained colonial domination of indigenous people in their native lands even in light of presumed civil yet never equal negotiations of cohabitation and conciliation. Hence calling into the question of *post* in postcolonial theory for indigenous people in a situation of sustained internal colonialism. Weaver (2000) later goes on to cite Elizabeth Cook-Lynn (1997), who, in her essay "Who Stole Native American Studies," offers a powerful epigram to the position of indigenous scholars.

> For American Indians ... and for the indigenes everywhere in the world, postcolonial studies has little to do with independence, nor does it have much to do with the actual deconstruction of oppressive colonial systems. It is not like the end of slavery in 1865, for example, when owning other human beings for economic reasons became illegal and a new status for African Americans as free citizens could become the focus of the discourse. Postcolonial thought in indigenous history, as a result of the prevailing definitions, has emerged as a subversion rather than a revolution. This fact has been a huge disappointment to those scholars whose interest has been in native-nation status and independence. (Cook-Lynn, 1997, p. 14)[7]

What is particularly telling for me in this revelation is the manner in which any disciplinary formation that "commits itself to a complex project of historical and psychological 'recovery' can easily fall short in the full embrasure of all minority identities and the specificity of their lived conditions" (Gandhi, 1998, p. 8). That failure, I suggest, is not just of reach, but of desire in the sense of maintaining structures of domination in the sustainability of particular hierarchies of worth and value, which often circulate around issues of race and otherness within presumed populations of equality. This argument will be made more salient in my discussion of queer theory. What I also appreciate in this construction is the manner in which Cook-Lynn (1997) echoes a previously presented sentiment of Spivak (1997) in situating African Americans in the postcolonial, though in this sense, Spivak's reference to postcoloniality as an *achievement of an independence that removes the legal subject status of a people as the result of struggle, armed or otherwise.* And the manner in which she includes the achievements of *internal colonization, Emancipation, Reconstruction, civil rights* within the vein of the postcolonial benefits my own positionality but falls short of Cook-Lynn's argument for indigenous people relegated as second-class citizens in a home place of their own desire.[8]

Queering Queer Theory[9]

Queer theory is a collective of intellectual speculations and challenges to the social and political constructions of sexualized and gender identity. Using the divisions of labor in William B. Turner's (2000) *A Genealogy of Queer Theory,* queer theory is engaged in an active process of contesting scholarship and politics, contesting categories, contesting identity, contesting liberalism, contesting truth, contesting history, and contesting subjectivity (pp. 1–35). In its most idealistic and liberatory impulse, queer theory pivots on the following logics. Queer is used not only as a gendered identity location but as resistance to orthodoxy—expounding, elaborating, and promoting alternative ways of being, knowing, and narrating experience—through scholarship, through embodied being, through social and political interventions in *regimes of the normal.* Yet queer theory is not presented as alternative, as the opposite of normal or standard of sexual performative identities, but as the reality of alterity that penetrates the suppressed and supplanted presence of difference that always and already exists in daily operations—both political and practical, as well academic and everyday. Hence queer is antifoundationalist work that focuses on the opposition to fixed identities.

> The preference of "queer" represents . . . an aggressive impulse of generalization; it rejects a minoritizing logic of toleration or simple political interest-representations in favor of a more thorough resistance to regimes of the normal. . . . The insistence on "queer"—a term initially generated in the context of text—has the effect of pointing out a wide field of normalization, rather than simple intolerance (Warner, 1993, p. xxvi). Queer theory offers "another discursive horizon, another way of thinking the sexual" (de Lauretis, 1991, p. iv) that debunks the stability of identity categories by focusing on the historical, social, and cultural constructions of desire and sexuality intersecting with other identity markers, such as race, class, and gender, among others. (Yep, Lovaas, & Elia, 2003, p. 2)

Queer theory is interested in remapping the terrain of gender, identity, and cultural studies. In engaging the proliferation of queer theory, gays, lesbians, and those aware of the entangled implications of these issues are negotiating the construction of queer identity within heterosexual spheres. More specifically, queer theory becomes a form of academic activism. In her essay "Queering the State," Lisa Duggan (1998) states, "Queer studies scholars are engaged in denaturalizing categories of sexual identity and mobilizing various critiques of the political practices referred to under the rubric 'identity politics'" (p. 566). Likewise, Janice M. Irvine (1998) states,

> Queer theory builds on social constructionism to further dismantle sexual identities and categories. Drawing on postmodern critiques, the new theoretical deployment of queerness recognizes the instabilities of traditional oppositions such as lesbian/gay and heterosexual. Queerness is often used as an inclusive signifier for lesbian, gay, bisexual, transgender, drag, straights who pass as gay . . . and any permutation of sex/gender dissent. (p. 582)

Most will agree that queer theory is grounded in feminist theory, constructionist history, and poststructuralism. Arlene Stein and Ken Plummer (1994) delineate the major theoretical departures of queer theory and the paradigmatic grounds of this specified locus. For them, queer theory is interested in exploring sexual identity and broad constructions of sexual politics:

> Queer as "sexual power embodied in different levels of social life, expressed discursively and enforced through boundaries and binary divides."
>
> Queer as "the problematization of sexual and gender categories and identities in general."

> Queer as "a rejection of civil rights strategies in favor of a politics of carnival, transgression, and parody which leads to deconstruction, decentering, revisionist readings and an antiassimilationalist politics."
>
> Queer as "a willingness to interrogate areas which normally would not be seen as the terrain of sexuality, and to conduct queer 'readings' of ostensibly heterosexual or nonsexualized texts." (p. 182)[10]

The boundaries of queer theory are articulated less in the realm of civil rights "in favor of a politics of carnival, transgression, and parody, which leads to deconstruction, decentering, revisionist readings, and an antiassimilationist politics" (Stein & Plummer, 1994, pp. 181–182). Queer theory in this construction seeks to broaden and de-ghettoize the homosexual/gay sphere. In "Tracking the Vampire," Sue-Ellen Case (1997) states, "Queer Theory, unlike lesbian theory or gay male theory, is not gender specific." She believes that "both gay and lesbian theory reinscribe sexual difference, to some extent, in their gender-specific constructions." She calls for a queer theory that "works not at the site of gender, but at the site of ontology"—the nature of beings and existents (p. 382). Yet, Eve Sedgwick (1993) argues for the centrality of "*samesexness* in the construction of *queerness.*" She states, "Given the historical and contemporary force of the prohibitions against *every* same-sex expression, for anyone to disavow those meanings, or to displace them from the term's definitional center, would be to dematerialize any possibility of queerness itself" (p. 8). And in *Fear of a Queer Planet,* Michael Warner (1993) states, "The preference for 'queer' represents, among other things, an aggressive impulse of generalization; it rejects a minoritizing logic of toleration or simple political interest representation in favor of a more thorough resistance to regimes of the normal" (p. xxvi).

The preceding definitional approaches to articulating queer theory were chosen specifically to point out some key and repetitive features, as well as the tensiveness embodied in queer theory, or in those who theorize under the rubric of queer theory. I pose the following queries: If queer theory is interested in "remapping the terrain of gender, identity, and cultural studies" by "denaturalizing categories of sexual identity and mobilizing various critiques of the political practices referred to under the rubric 'identity politics,'" and if queer theory is interested in "exploring sexual identity, sexual politics and sexual power in different levels of social life, expressed discursively and enforced through boundaries and binary divides," how does the occlusion of people of color become counterintuitive to the project and the very nature of cultural studies? Lawrence Grossberg (1994) states that "the 'main lesson of cultural studies' is that in order to understand ourselves, the discourse of the Other—of all the others—is that which we most urgently need to know" (p. 67).

If queer theory seeks to "dismantle sexual identities and categories" while "recogniz[ing] the instabilities of traditional oppositions such as lesbian/gay and heterosexual," making queer an "inclusive signifier," then what about any discussion that links perception, practices, performances, and politics of sexual identity to race, ethnicity, culture, time, place, and the discourses produced within these disparate locations? José Esteban Muñoz (1999) states,

> Most of the cornerstones of Queer Theory that are taught, cited and canonized in gay and lesbian classrooms, publications, and conferences are decidedly directed toward analyzing white lesbian and gay men. The lack of inclusion is most certainly not the main problem with the treatment of race. A soft multicultural *inclusion* of race and ethnicity does not, on its own, lead to a progressive identity discourse. Yvonne Yarbro-Bejarano has made the valuable point that "[t]he lack of attention to race in the work of leading lesbian theorists reaffirms the beliefs that it is possible to talk about sexuality without talking about race, which in turn reaffirms the beliefs that it is necessary to talk about race and sexuality only when discussing people of color and their text." (p. 10)

Are the specific experiences and concerns of queer folks of color erased in the dominant discourse of queer theory? And if queer theory is "grounded in feminist theory," then doesn't the collectivizing of experience prove unfaithful to the listening, debunking the singularity of voice, and the articulation of lived experience that undergirds feminism? In response, Alexander Doty (1995) succinctly says, "Queer is not an 'instead of.' I'd never want to lose the terms that specifically identify me" (p. 72).

If queer theory is interested in "an aggressive impulse of generalization [in which] it rejects a minoritizing logic of toleration or simple political interest representation in favor of a more thorough resistance to regimes of the normal," to what degree does it collectivize a struggle that is already grounded in *(in)*difference? This indifference exists within the unjustified generalization of common concerns and experiences within an imagined community in which there is contestation over the very terms *gay* and *queer.* Consequently, while queer studies grounds itself as an academic manifestation, it risks engaging and codifying the representational politics of alternative communities that it seeks to intervene in and thus becomes fraught with the danger of imperialism, colonialism, academic puffery, and racism.

Eve Sedgwick (1993) states that "queer" involves "the open mesh of possibilities, gaps, overlaps, dissonances and resonances, lapses and excesses of meaning [that occur] when constituent elements of anyone's gender, of anyone's sexuality aren't made (or *can't be* made) to signify monolithically" (p. 8). Yet within the employment of the notion of queer studies, the gaps have been large enough to cause considerable slippage, if not a complete occlusion of the experiences of queer colored folk. Lisa Duggan (1998) offers two critiques of queer studies that I find most compelling:

> [First,] The production of a politics from a fixed identity position privileges those for whom that position is the primary or only marked identity. . . . Every production of "identity" creates exclusions that reappear at the margins like ghosts to haunt identity-based politics. [Second,] Identity politics only replaces closets with ghettos. The closet as a cultural space has been defined and enforced by the existence of the ghetto. In coming out of the closet, identity politics offers us another bounded, fixed space of humiliation and another kind of social isolation. (p. 566)

And while Duggan's second critique may be read through the politics of visibility, I read the comment to be a specific critique on the manner in which words, language, and theoretical constructs such as "queer" limit its grasp. And like a metaphorical hug, it both includes and excludes at the same time. The question then becomes, what and why does it exclude? And the response to that question cannot be relegated to the impossibility or improbability of hugging everyone—for intentionality has a way of articulating the specificity of desire by marking difference.

Queer theory uses a false notion of building community in order to dissuade arguments of exclusion. In "Producing (Queer) Communities," Eric Freedman (1998) says, "On a fundamental level, do I define myself by race, gender, sexual preference, class, or nationality? . . . Indeed, are the borders of these communities mutually exclusive or even clearly defined? I want to explore the notion of community, and challenge any presupposition of an inherent unity. 'Community' is a term under which we can speak of collective involvement, or even unified resistance, while at the same time respect (and expect) difference" (p. 251). This is coupled with Kirk Fuoss's (1993) notion that communities like "all performances are essentially contestatory" (p. 347). Community only exists between the tensiveness of difference, the negotiation of worth, and the performance of civility.

Joshua Gamson (1998) offers what he calls the *queer dilemma:* "By constructing gays and lesbians as a single community (united by fixed erotic fates), [the term also] simplif[ies] complex internal differences and complex sexualities." He states that in using the term and promoting activism under this collective thought, we may also "avoid challenging the system of meaning that underlies the political oppression: the division of the world into man/woman and gay/straight" and some homogeneous collective entity. "On the contrary, [such actions] ratify and reinforce these categories. They therefore build distorted and incomplete political challenges, neglecting the political challenges, neglecting the political impact of cultural meanings, and do not do justice to the subversive and liberating aspects of loosened collective boundaries" (p. 597).

Gloria Anzaldúa (1987) explicitly argues, "Queer is used as a false unifying umbrella which all 'queers' of all races, ethnicities and classes are shored under. [Yet] even when we seek shelter under it, we must not forget that it homogenizes, and erases our difference," which is always and already meaningful to our lived existence and oddly serves as both buffer and magnet in interracial constructions of desire and the colonization of queer bodies of color (p. 250). And in this way, Cathy Cohen (1999) echoes this notion when she says, "Queer theorizing that calls for the elimination of fixed categories seems to ignore the ways in which some traditional identities and communal ties can, in fact, be important to one's survival" (p. 450). These communal ties cross borders of sexuality but are established through histories of experience, struggle, location, and displacement at the margin of nation and state, gender and sexuality, race and culture, and the promotion of particular ideologies in each, which promote and fuel identity politics around notions of queerness. These logics are particularly central in the work of Gaytri Gopinath (2005) as she writes, "When queer subjects register their refusal to abide by the demands placed on bodies to conform to sexual (as well as gendered racial) norms, they contest the logic and dominance of these regimes" (p. 28).

In making a reference to how analogies are drawn comparing racism and sexism, Trina Grillo and Stephanie M. Wildman (1995) make a keen observation. I apply this to the construction of queer theory (later this will play out in my queer analysis of *Brokeback Mountain*). Queer theory "perpetuate[s] patterns of racial domination by marginalizing and obscuring the different roles that race plays in the lives of people of color and of whites" (p. 566). And while race is a contested term that "may be a whole cluster of strands including color, culture, [nation,] identification and experience," it does offer points of unity and can become foundational elements in building community (Wildman & Davis, 1995, p. 578). These are not "imagined communities" in the sense of how Benedict Anderson (1991) articulates the desire for community "only in the minds" of those who seek it (p. 6). These are realized communities that offer support, familiarity, and strategies for living.

In his keynote address at the Black Queer in the Millennium Conference, Phillip Brian Harper makes an insightful critique that queer theory bridges what is often a racial divide of inclusion and exclusion in the discussion of sex and sexuality.

> Queer Studies is unacceptably Euro-American in orientation, its purview effectively determined by the practically invisible, because putatively nonexistent—bounds of racial whiteness. It encompasses as well, to continue for a moment with the topic of whiteness, the abiding failure of most supposedly queer critics to subject whiteness itself to sustained interrogation and thus to delineate its import in sexual terms, whether conceived in normative or non-normative modes. (Alexander, 2002b, p. 1288)

All of these constructions link the concerted exclusion of race, as an elemental criterion that articulates the experience of queers of color, to what appears as either an intentional or unintentional act of racism in a *project that has as its goals the notion of broad inclusivity.*

It is easy to point out those moments in which queer theory excludes the experience of queers of color. But is it problematic—if not dangerous—to engage a singular or delimited discussion of when it includes queers of colors—or begin to define those spaces, communities, and political manifestations in which queers of color begin to define themselves—as being included within specific communities or discourses? This is less a problem in finding the arguments, or defining the spaces, for there are clear and compelling examples (Cohen, 1999; Ferguson, 2004; Harper, 1998; Johnson & Henderson, 2005; Muñoz, 1999; Stockton, 2006). The risk is in defining and reifying the borders and frames that might also delimit the spaces that others inhabit, while also risking the impression of engaging a separate conversation—when the design is, in actuality, to critique and extend an already initiated discourse into new realms of knowing.

In her introduction to *Borders, Boundaries, and Frames: Cultural Criticism and Cultural Studies,* Mae Henderson (1995) begins to define the nature of my dilemma. She says, "Forever on the periphery of the possible, the border, the boundary, and the frame are always at issue—and their location and status inevitably raise the problematic of inside and outside and how to distinguish one from the other" (p. 2). She further uses Jacques Derrida's (1987) logic in *The Truth in Painting* (*La Vérité en Peinture*) that "'disconcerts any opposition' between 'the outside and the inside, between the external and the internal edge-line, the framer and the framed' in his attempt to deconstruct the self-presence of the visual image" (pp. 1–2). In using her frame, I suggest that the difficulty lies in the moment of my inhabitation of this scholarly instance and the space that these words occupy. For within the sameness of this instance, I am engaging a critique of queer theory while engaged in a process of a queer reading of queer theory and its relationship to the postcolonial project.

Alexander Doty (1993) states, "Queer reception doesn't stand outside personal and cultural histories; it is a part of the articulation of these histories. This is why, politically, queer reception (and production) practices can include everything from the reactionary to the radical to the indeterminate" (pp. 15–16). And with this logic, queer reception does not stand outside critiques of things that are queer but also uses the reception space of queer theory to engage a meta-critique of homonormative paradigms, or use of the strategies of mainstream culture in minoritian populations with the same results: exclusion and domination. In this way, while I may claim a certain border existence within the rhetoric of queer theory, I do not willingly renounce my citizenship in the location that seeks to articulate the lived experiences of queers (gays, lesbians, transsexuals, bisexuals, twin-spirits, same-gender loving, and the multiple and varying ways in which people articulate their sexed, sexual, and gendered selves in the influence of race, nation, and state).

And so maybe my particular construction and critique of queer theory in fact erases the divide that separates colonial and postcolonial theory. If queer theory seemingly promotes mostly White constructions of gay sexual identity, it most certainly is (inadvertently) complicit in racial domination in the service of sexual specificity; a study of White queers at the exclusionary expense of all others. But herein may lie both the limits and possibilities of queer epistemology—especially when pushed by a *queer of color critique* (Ferguson, 2004), a critically applied method of *disidentification* (Muñoz, 1999), and a burgeoning *quare studies* (Johnson, 2001), each demanding a culture-specific and text-specific analysis of racial and sexual deference, each examining the text and subtext of same-sex desire and the strategic rhetorics that both patronize and pathologize queer identity, and each examining the rhetorical strategies of exclusion and occlusion of racial sexual minorities that establish the motivating and guiding impulse in queer theory. Whether as a particular backlash to queer theory or as a culturally conscious/community-conscious critique for social transformation and empowerment—maybe a *queer of color critique* and the emergent interpretive queer methodology that I am espousing in this project—embody in more salient ways, the postcolonial move that should be at the core of queer theory, focusing on the complicated construals of queer identity across variables of race, class, and geography—with the particular focus on articulating experience and voice.

But this critique on the state of queer theory is not just an idiosyncratic bias. In *What's Queer About Queer Studies Now?* editors David L. Eng, Judith Halberstam, and José Esteban Muñoz (2005) call for *a renewed queers studies* with a *broadened consideration.* In there they state, "It is crucial to insist yet again on the capacity of queer studies to mobilize a broad social critique of race, gender, class, nationality, and religion, as well as sexuality. Such a theoretical project demands that queer epistemologies not only rethink the relationship between intersectionality and normalization from multiple points of view but also, and equally important, consider how gay and lesbian rights are being reconstituted as a type of reactionary (identity) politics of national and global consequences" (p. 4).[11]

So my approach to doing a queer reading in this project pivots off of these logics to foreground not just the obviously queer but the multiple logics in which queer is being promoted as a restrictive and delimited possibility within a larger heteronormative promotion of the ideal. But I want also to acknowledge the moments in which queers of color are excluded or constructed in ways that further marginalize that identity construct, in the service of promoting heteronormative constructions of White masculinity—even in the presumed context of foregrounding queer identity.

Moving Further Toward a Critically Interpretive Queer Methodology

Allow me the luxury of directing my focus to offer you, the reader, an alternative method of doing a *critically interpretive queer reading* that is an extension of the queer methodology that structures this text. This is a critical interpretive queer methodology that is closer to what Muñoz (1999) refers to as *disidentification,* or a "recycling and rethinking [of] encoded meanings . . . that both exposes the encoded message's universalizing and exclusionary machinations and recircuits its workings to account for, include, and empower minority identities and identifications" (p. 31). In my application, disidentification is a practiced positionality and a method that seeks to subvert mainstream constructions of queer identities in presumably liberal social texts. So in this particular case, the minority identities that I seek to empower are not just "queers of color," though of course I am a *Black queer* (in the ways in which that reference is both *reductive* to the materiality of my body and desire and *productive* as a political disposition), but actually the method that I am moving from places all queers within a minoritized position, by both collectivizing sexuality and minimizing difference.

Maybe I am moving closer to what Roderick A. Ferguson (2004) calls a *queer of color critique* that "approaches culture as one site that compels identification with and antagonisms to the normative ideals promoted by state and capital" (p. 3). Hence, I am moving toward a method of queer resistance that contests hegemonic colonial models of sexuality and queering through a critical method that has a "culture-specific positionality" that reveals my biases and investments without promoting yet another exclusionary method with a singular focus on raced identities, but one that promotes a critical awareness of exclusion and not self-promotion (Johnson, 2001, p. 2).[12]

In this approach, the act of *queering* a social text is not only a methodological offshoot of queer theory seeking to unmask sexual erotics, same-sex desire, or sexual deviancy in any particular text to denaturalize assumed natural social processes (Sullivan, 2003). This is an approach that always results in celebrating some assumed collective queer investment but still leaves queer lives written between the lines or in the margins of the social text and consciousness to which it critiques. Nor is it just a rearticulation of the postcolonial project, an analysis that shows how cultural, intellectual, economic, and political processes work together both to perpetuate and to dismantle colonialism. The method to which I am moving is a paradigmatic approach to reading social, cultural, and political texts that covertly seek to perpetuate violence against queer lives while maintaining human social relations that create hierarchies of race, class, and sexual identity.

And maybe more important in this approach, it is also a method that foregrounds the critical—as a systematic focus on content and intent with commentary and direction—and the ways in which particular queer identified texts are imbued with residual effects not only of heteronormative dominative values but a particular emphasis on Whiteness that is counterintuitive and often disparaging to the lives of racialized sexual minorities (Jakobsen, 2002).

What I am moving toward is the emergence of a critical interpretive queer methodology that addresses the concerns of both a nihilistic postcolonial perspective and homogenizing queer studies, thus suturing the pains and possibilities of each. This is a method that works toward elaborating social action issues without simply replacing ills with additional harms but introducing new spaces of inquiry, which I believe to be one of the most bracing qualities and intentions of postcolonial perspectives, in the caution and care of replacing an essentialist Eurocentrism and reestablishing what Edward Said (1990) might reference, as building a "culture of resistance as a cultural enterprise" (p. 73). Maybe this is a method like *quare studies,* which "would not only critique the concept of 'race' as historically contingent and socially and culturally constructed/performed, it would also address the material effects in a white supremacist society," crossing or bleeding the borders of identity construction, which affects the material practices of culture, gender/sexuality, and the socially delimited constructions of possibility (p. 73). Partially *quare studies,* as advocated by E. Patrick Johnson (2001), "moves beyond simply theorizing subjectivity and agency as discursively mediated to theorizing how that mediation may propel material bodies into action" (p. 9).

I am moving toward a method that acknowledges and taps into *indigenous knowledge.* Indigenous knowledge is understood both as the commonsense ideas and cultural knowledge of local peoples, concerning the everyday realities of living, but also *theories of the flesh,* which fuse the specificities of lived and embodied experiences to *create a politic born out of necessity* (Moraga & Anzaldúa, 1981).[13] Indigenous knowledge serves as the foundation and buffer for cultural critiques as a form of defense against false or circuitously deceptive representations of queer cultural lives. It is knowledge that can be extended to the most sincere acts of humanity and the rules that govern and guide social and cultural life.

Knowledges, as plural ways of knowing, serve as venue and method of resistance, advocacy, and transformation (Dei, Hall, & Rosenberg, 2000). Indigenous knowledge is not restricted to Third World constructions of the other, or romanticized notions of the noble savage, or even the wilds of some place other than the local, which I often find as a countereffect in postcolonial work and the colonial effects in ethnography, but a global perspective of indigenous knowledge from colonized people that also includes those particular spaces like prisons, ghettos, and underdeveloped nations within the backyards of developed countries (Semali & Kincheloe, 1999). Indigenous knowledge is the innate sense of understanding one's positionality in relation to the social and political constructs that strive, in both radical and subtle ways, to erase the significance of lived experience and bodily being to perform resistance, an indigenous and queer resistance that opens up a breathing space to know self in relation to hegemonic notions of racial and sexual identity as that particularly relates to the socially constructed marked other—which most often is the indigenous native withering under the colonial gaze.

A critical interpretive queer methodology is one that analyzes a social text to reveal how the cloistered gay lives in the text, living in a presumed democratic society, and is both celebrated—as a part of the commercial mainstreaming of queerness—yet penalized as sexual deviancy within the larger dominating construction of heteronormativity. And like the broad construction of *queer diasporas,* a method that contributes to "providing new ways of contesting traditional family and kinship structures—or reorganizing national and transnational communities based not in origin, filiation, and genetics but on destination, affiliation, and the assumption of a common set of social practices or political commitments" that extend outside of the specifics of queer communities and embrace the larger democratic ideals of queer theory that are uniquely American (Eng, 2003, p. 4).

It is a method that moves back and forth between social text and actual experience to reveal how the two are always and already co-constructed and codependent yet often placed in a hierarchical position of worth. In terms of hetero-homo dichotomies, this is most often revealed in the self-monitoring as well as the comparative relational and psychological realities of their coexistence in which sexual desire, romantic affiliation, and relational commitment are constructed as the same and not the same. Whether internalized by the players, which is the key effect of social enculturation, or as the point of view of the larger narrator, who crafts the telling of the tale to foreground tensions in the mind of the cultural consumer of these social texts, which often fixates on a presumed element of self-loathing that is socially inserted in the public construction of queer desire, as a heteronormative default setting, signaling pathology and a longing for (*hetero*) normalcy.

I am moving toward a method that moves between human rights and queer cosmopolitanism to develop what should be a grounded sense of common investments in human social relations—bleeding the borders of difference by foregrounding those very instances in which difference is marked and reified. This is from the perspective and articulated voice of one whose absented presence is only signaled in the text, but never actualized; one whose racialized possibility is presented as a counternarrative to the dominance of Whiteness—hence relegated as the other—both alternative for Whiteness and alterity to Whiteness.

This is a method that necessarily moves between queer racialized identity categories and neoliberal and posthuman models of citizenship to enact a critical and public pedagogy of social humanism, one that splays bare the issues that both unite and separate toward building a practice of democracy that is inclusive, while still showing the subtle variant dynamics of human social relations without creating sexual and racialized hierarchies of worth and value. Hence I am talking about a method that contributes to revisioning "a renewed queer studies [and postcolonial studies] ever vigilant to the fact that sexuality is intersectional, not extraneous to other modes of difference, and calibrated to a firm understanding of queer as a political metaphor without a fixed referent" (Eng et al., 2005, p. 1).

I am moving toward a method that deconstructs a social text for the tripartite and competing issues of foregrounding same-sex desire, while concomitantly promoting overt homophobic skcpticism, within the particularity of also foregrounding racial specificity that competes against notions of a multicultural community building: community both in the larger human social system and a presumed common political concerns. Such a method blends and bleeds the borders of postcolonial and queer studies—in what might be a form of *postcolonial queer analysis.* The film *Brokeback Mountain* serves as a good cultural text to demonstrate this burgeoning methodology.

Queering the West(ern): *Brokeback Mountain* as Subverted Queer Text

In their pithy anthology, *Queer Globalizations: Citizenships and the Afterlife of Colonialism,* editors Arnoldo Cruz-Malavé and Martin F. Manalansan IV (2002) cull together 13 critical essays from the 1998 conference of the same name, sponsored by the Center for Lesbian and Gay Studies of the City University of New York's Graduate Center. The essays included in the text offer bracing analyses of the global marketing of queer identities. For the purposes of this project, I want to outline a series of *counterhegemonic rhetorical strategies deployed by some of the queer critics in this collection*[14] and apply them as emergent tenets, if not pivot points, in doing a brief, critically interpretive queer analysis of the 2005 Academy Award–winning film *Brokeback Mountain,* directed by Ang Lee.

In using *Brokeback Mountain,* I am approaching the film through a frame of what John C. Hawley (2001b), editor of *Postcolonial, Queer: Theoretical Intersections,* might call *postcolonialities.* Postcolonial texts—and, more important in this case, social positions—presumably seek to open up spaces of liberation and possibility through "the revision of imposed histories and the proclamation of affiliation and identity declaration" (p. 3). And in this sense, I am also using the film as synecdoche for the culture machine of the film industry in the production of hegemonic notions of social propriety. In the introduction to *Out Takes: Essays on Queer Theory and Film,* editor Ellis Hanson (1999) writes that "the study of film is especially important to questions of desire, identification, fantasy, representation, spectatorship, cultural appropriation, performativity, and mass consumption, all of which have become important issues in queer theory" and are core to discussions on/of postcolonialism (p. 3). The film *Brokeback Mountain* becomes both a mechanism to out long-suppressed depictions of same-sex desire, through a presumed *proclamation of affiliation* (or at least support) and *identity declaration* (as presumed sexual alternative), but it also fulfills the critical possibility of the medium to question and *questions of desire.*

For the purposes of this analysis, I use a very selective interpretation and application of only three theoretical offerings from the Cruz-Malavé and Manalansan (2002) volume: (a) the appropriation of liberal stances for political purpose; (b) the reinforced contingency between sexuality, religion, and normalcy as a means of disciplining desire; and (c) normalization of indifference through analogy. In offering this brief sketch, I beg the indulgence of the authors in the reinterpretation and application of their arguments to what I truly believe are liberatory and democratic ends. I beg the reader to insert these elements as kernel logics to building a method of a critically interpretive queer analysis. I introduce the pivot point of my analysis and then apply them to specific scenes in *Brokeback Mountain.* These scenes are not contiguous in the film, but what I want to foreground is how the points of analysis work in relation to each other in developing the grounds for this particular approach to queer analysis. Also by displacing the scenes for analysis, I intentionally call the reader/viewer to see the scenes as particular building blocks, strategically constructed arguments in the larger rhetorical messaging of the film that creates a dispositive perspective of gay lives and how the reading of the text opens up new spaces for conversation and activism against the subtle social sanctioning of violence against queer bodies.

Appropriation of Liberal Stances for Political Purposes. In her essay "Stealth Bombers of Desire: The Globalization of 'Alterity' in Emerging Democracies," Cindy Patton (2002) outlines the Taiwan case of young men in the early 1990s waiting to be psychiatrically declared homosexual, as a means of avoiding mandatory military service. She frames this analysis as evidence of "emerging democracies that adopt apparently liberal stances on social issues as a means of demonstrating their modernness, or at least their distance from barbaric practices" (p. 195). Yet she states that the shifting policies were "far from making the state more democratic . . . put queerness at a further remove from emergent librationist politics" (p. 196). This small yet pivotal identification in Patton's analysis serves as the core of my particular critique of *Brokeback Mountain.*

The film contributes to the growing number of global texts both popularizing and penalizing the politics of queer identity as negotiated through heterosexual and uniquely White male sensibilities. In this particular case, the archetype of the American cowboy as the quintessential performance of masculinity (read: heterosexual and normal)[15] and the western motif as the unadulterated terrain of all that is natural (read: queers as abnormal) are used in order to foreground queer politics as both partisan and plural, bias and base, with intentions and outcomes that are both promotional and predictive, in ways that the film *outs* long-suppressed homosociality and homoeroticism in the American western genre. The film strategically uses the occasion and actualization of gay male desire, in a culturally masculinized (read: straight) genre—as a mechanism to uphold the virtues of (performing) White male heterosexuality, as a mechanism to perpetuate a pernicious homophobia,[16] as well as social and religious constructions of "family values" that further instantiate the specificity of gender roles.[17]

Thus, these are translated into social acts of public maintenance and enculturation. Such mechanisms are played out in the film and the social terrain of public life, as both external pressures for normalcy (read: straightness) by the overt acts and comments of others, while the seeds of such enculturation manifest as the to-be-assumed-natural, as necessary performances of self-constraint and self-hatred for the potency of same-sex desire portrayed by the main character (played by the late Heath Ledger). This as an internal, yet culturally inseminated, mechanism to control the lures of libidinal gay desire—which are never completely held at bay but later held in disguise behind the portrait of the ultimate sign of heteronormativity—male/female marriage.

In their quest to maintain a sense of normalcy, or at least the socially expected, each of the male characters marked as queer marries and has children, but they meet periodically through the years for what is constructed as the love story, but what one character, Jack Twist[18] (played by Jake Gyllenhaal), mournfully calls it, for "a high-altitude fuck." And though Gyllenhaal's character is the one most open to a domestic same-sex living/loving relationship, the scripting of the text also invalidates love between men and reduces it to the social construction of carnal desire and the act of sex and not the commitment to love or making love. Hence, *Brokeback Mountain* not only queers the archetype of the western cowboy, but it also queers a particular construction of heterosexual marriage that, at its best, is always a tensive negotiation of competing intentions and desires (or so I am told).[19] The film also offers a disparaging, if not dispositive, view of women (the particular women who marry these men). Following the logics of Eve Sedgwick (1985), the role of the wives of these two queer men is to provide the men the social legitimacy while enhancing the eroticism of their male/male contact in relation to their sexual encounters with their women. The film is very particular in showing both men in what appears to be sincere yet hurried sexual encounters with their wives—juxtaposed against more tender and passionate encounters with each other.[20] And like Diana Fuss's (2000) analysis of Frantz Fanon, the film does not move "beyond the presuppositions of colonial discourse to examine how colonial domination itself works partially through the social institutionalization of misogyny and homophobia" (p. 1120), both of which the film upholds—in its object lesson about the queer lives and the unrequited subjectivity of the women that these men marry.

In using the film text of *Brokeback Mountain,* I am not doing a queer reading in that traditional sense of trying to unveil the gay undertones of what is already assumed as an outwardly gay text, but in fact, the queerness of this reading is to reveal how what presumes to be a markedly gay text is, in actuality, a propaganda for the always and already present heteronormative logic that perpetuates hatred of and violence against "queer" populations, particularly in the case of gay men. Hence, what is queer in this film is not the main characters (who of course are queer) but the rhetorical strategy of the text that lulls the viewer into the assumption of an alternative love story with a "happy ending" (either in the tradition of the filmic western motif or the fairytale genre), but with an altogether traditional moral of applied heteronormativity that trumps queerness in the most vile and violent ways—ways that are always and altogether known. Thereby it reinforces the notion that homosexuality is not a socially sanctioned "way of life" and queers do not have happy endings. With these logics, *Brokeback Mountain* becomes what Mae G. Henderson (1995) might call a *coy text.*

Coy texts or *textual coyness,* whether in literary texts, which is Henderson's medium, or film (as I am applying it here), divert or avert the reader's attention from one site or locus of meaning potentially risky or dangerous to what appears to be a more comfortable and secure space but in fact becomes a place of entrapment.[21] While the notion of textual coyness might suggest pretense or an annoying reluctance to write or say something into being, it is that very quality in the coy text that creates the openness that allows the listener/reader to enter. For example, the public marketing of *Brokeback Mountain* did not overtly suggest a queer theme, though from the onset, the social imaginary clearly reads the text as "a gay cowboy story." A promotional description of the film that appears on the DVD cover offers a coy text as a lure that can be used as proxy for the entire marketing campaign.

> *Brokeback Mountain* is a sweeping epic that explores the lives of two young men, a ranch hand and a rodeo cowboy, who meet in the summer of 1963 and unexpectedly forge a life-long connection. The complications, joys and heartbreak they experience provide a testament to the endurance and power of love.

In such a carefully constructed and strategically innocuous description, the marketers of this film lure multiple audiences to the film—those who are interested in a western motif focusing on ranch hands, rodeo cowboys, and sheepherding; those interested in a sweeping epic story of male bonding; and those who clearly read the text as same-sex desire or a queer inspired story—and to the theaters. Their lure, like a worm at the end of a hook (which is made literal by the queers in this film, who use the metaphorical reference of "going fishing" or "fishing buddies" as a secret code for escaped same-sex/sexual encounters on *Brokeback Mountain*[22]), traps the audience as an element of the rhetorical construction in order to promote particular consequences about same-sex desire and resistance. And it is in this sense that what I am referring to as a critical queer and globalizing analysis of the film finds its importance. I believe that a part of the intent or, maybe more important, the effect of the film is to make (in a rather coy way) sweeping commentaries on queer lives in ways that breach the specific borders of time, place, and genre of the film, to effect the larger constructions and perception of queer realities. And in this sense, the west(ern)—both as a specific genre of film and also the gross assumptions about the West as a unadulterated geographical, political, and ideological terrain—does in fact become adulterous by the sinful carnal desires of gays—and the act of gay bashing and murder are in fact used in the film as an act of purifying the west(tern) through the enforcement of normative standards of gender performance.

A queer reading as a form of *disidentification* asks the reader to, in fact, reread the encoded message of this particular cultural text (the film) in a fashion that exposes the encoded message, which in fact universalizes a particular construction of queer lives toward particular heterosexual, if not mainstream, constructions of normalcy and the consequences of presumed-to-be deviant behavior. The exclusion of minority identities in this film is apparent (read this in alignment with my critique of queer theory) as to go almost unnecessarily critiqued in this coverage. The film is (reductively speaking) about two White queers. The only reference and allusion to *queers of color* pinpoints Mexican queers, presumable prostitutes, who become literally shadow figures in a darkened alley across the border, suggestively secondary and expedient choices of sexual fulfillment when Jack Twist (played by Jake Gyllenhaal) feels lonely and rejected from his ideal White male lover, played by Heath Ledger.[23]

The film offers complicated construals or what Patton and Sánchez-Eppler (2000) describe as "complex erotics of patronage across colonial borders" of sex and sexuality—as related to two queer guys marrying women and having children. Yet the film only offers a suggestion of the sexuality of the Mexican men in this particular scene. And in and of itself, the sexual exchange in what is constructed as prostitution does not exclusively signal sexuality as much as commerce and the fluidity of sex as a practiced activity as *a by-product of colonialism.* In her essay "Interior Colonies," Diana Fuss (2000) uses a similar construction to address issues of Black male prostitution as economic necessity "forced into homosexual prostitution in the metropole in order to survive economically" (p. 1117).[24] Yet the liminal construction of these sexed identities is actually more reductive in that it restricts desire in the service of commerce, reducing the Mexican queer only to a commodity and not an agent of choice, and not a specified focus of desire but expediency.

In the film, the character played by Gyllenhaal literally crosses the border to gain access to colored bodies to fulfill his sexual desire. But not just desirous colored bodies, but bodies knowingly situated in an economic dilemma in which prostitution is expedient financial gain, hence becoming portal, promotion, and possibility for the sexual desires of others. In this case, the border is a geographical divide only mediated by the particularity of class and White desire for the other in the presence of expendable capital.[25] The colonial encounter is staged[26] in the film and maybe described in terms of what Hema Chari (2001) phrases as *colonial fantasies and postcolonial identities—interracial desire of same-sex and of homoerotic colonial fantasy* come true, deregulated by economic power and made manifest as acceptable within the larger frame of the film that promotes, if not rehistorizes, such convenient colonial relations that *realign identity, politics, and desire.*[27] In a moment of dramatic pause, Jack Twist is depicted standing between nation and state, and between location and space—as he stands in the light before entering a dimly lit alley of prostitution to engage his brown sex partner. Standing in the light while his potential sex partner is in the dark signifies Jack's choice and power in the situation. Their locked visual gazes signify both a homoerotic recognition (often reductively referenced as the *gaydar*) and the cost of economically driven desire outside the social constructions of building interpersonal relations. It is a momentary standoff before the confirmation and nonverbally cost-based negotiation of sex that leads the two men down the dimly lit alley into the realm of otherness.[28]

In reducing people of color to commodities, people to be purchased or engaged as second alternatives, the film reinforces not so subtle aspects of racism and sexism and what Gayatri Gopinath (2005), in *Impossible Desires: Queer Diasporas and South Asian Public Cultures,* might describe as the "historical availability of brown bodies to a white imperial gaze" or more specific to issues of desire and sexual utility (p. 2). And with the presumed marketing of brown flesh and the exchange of money for sex that is suggested in the scene, the brown bodies in question become what Roderick A. Ferguson (2004) in *Toward a Queer of Color Critique: Aberrations in Black,* would call "fixture(s) of urban capitalism," financially negotiated objects for White desire (p. 1). This overall pivot point for analysis, a*ppropriation of liberal stances for political purposes,* is linked with the second theme of invoking the conservative links between sexuality, religion, and normalcy as a means of establishing standards of social conduct.

Sexuality, Religion, and Normalcy. In her essay "Can Homosexuals End Western Civilization as We Know It? Family Values in a Global Economy," Janet R. Jakobsen (2002) poses the question that "connects religion, values, conversatism, and sexual regulation [as] connected to another chain in a story of Americanness: America must have values and the site of values is religion" (pp. 49–50). Specifically, she "argues that 'family values' mediates between the economy and the 'American' nation under contemporary market conditions by offering a discourse that can mediate between exploitation and domination. In other words 'family' (rather than the state) mediates between economy and nation, and 'values' mediates between exploitation and domination" (p. 50). While Jakobsen does her "particular incitements" through the work of Gayatri Spivak (1988b), who explicitly addresses the relationship between exploitation and domination as complicity rather than analogy, linking cultural values with economic interests, I am reading notions of exploitation and domination in doing a queer analysis of *Brokeback Mountain* as a very literal exploitation of the popularity of all things queer (e.g., U.S. television programming such as *Will & Grace; Queer Eye for the Straight Guy; Noah's Arc; Logo TV; Gay, Straight, or Taken?;* and the inclusion of at least one gay character in most reality-based programs, etc.).[29] Yet for me, there is another level of pernicious violence that is perpetuated by this film as cultural value.

I believe that *Brokeback Mountain* works in opposition to particular movie dramas that foreground the nexus of gay-life-tragedy—stories such as the *Matthew Shepard Story,* the 21-year-old gay man killed in a gay bashing in Laramie, Wyoming, and others that have as their intent to politicize alterity and promote tolerance. I believe that *Brokeback Mountain* establishes a fictive location of critique that becomes a site of real domination; the object of critique becomes the abject gay bodies bashed, beaten, and narrated in the film as historical object lessons for heteronormativity. Though beautiful in its cinematic scope and attractive to queer viewers, the film *Brokeback Mountain* actually becomes another mechanism of disciplining gays. In not so subtle ways, it draws the viewer from the realistic depiction of tragic stories of battered gay lives, like Matthew Shepard and the onslaught of demonstrations around the country that served as public outrage and response against hate crimes, and resituates gay bashing in the realm of fiction and maybe even fantasy. The film almost uses the act of violence against gays as a promotion or performative act of *compulsory heterosexuality* in a manner that goes uncritiqued and without social consequences (Butler, 1990). I will discuss this issue further under the theme of the *recognition of a complicity in the construction of the categories* to which the film promotes. Yet in her analysis of *The Laramie Project*, a performative response to the Matthew Shepard incident,[30] Jill Dolan (2005) writes that "theatre can be a secular template of social and spiritual union not with a mystified, mythologized higher power, but with the more prosaic, earthbound, yearnings, ethical subjects who are citizens of the world community, who need places to connect with one another and with the fragile, necessary wish for a better future" (p. 137). While Dolan is speaking of staged performances, the theatrical film project of *Brokeback Mountain* has the potential but falls short of this social justice and community-building goal.

Within the context of the film, there is a not so subtle commentary on religion linked with issues of desire and the consequences of sinning, which establishes a backdrop for religious dictates on the social propriety of sexuality and, more specifically, homosexual activity. In Scene 5 of the film, Jake belts out a verse of an old Pentecostal spiritual: "I know I will meet you on that fine old day . . . walking Jesus come take me away." When queried by Ennis about what Pentecostal is, and mentioning his own Methodist background, Jake responds by saying, "Pentecostal . . . I don't know what Pentecostal is . . . momma never explained it to me . . . I guess it is when the world ends and fellas like you and me go marching off to hell." Ennis retorts, "Speak for yourself. You may be a sinner, but I haven't had the opportunity."

The retort reads as both a defense and a curiosity. Immediately after this utterance, Jake offers a bottle of liquor to Ennis, almost as an invitation to sin—liquid courage to sin. Ennis takes it. The following scene is a drunken Ennis beckoning Jake to take the tent alone while he sleeps outdoors. The scene plays somewhat as an avoidance of the presumed potential and evitable intimacy of the two men sharing a tent. In the late night, as the temperature gets colder, Jake demands that Ennis enter the tent out of necessity. What follows is their first sexual contact, presumed *sin*.

This particular scene is prefaced by Ennis mentioning that he was saving up for a house, and when he returned from the mountain, he was going to marry Alma. The scene as a whole is complex and illuminates Ennis's conflicted feelings between his sexual desire for Jack, his commitment to marriage, and religion—all of which illuminates Jakobsen's (2002) equation that links *religion, values, conservatism, and sexual regulation to a particular performance of storied Americanness* through or within the archetype of the American cowboy. And in this sense, the viewer of the film begins to see a particular struggle and denial, not between the two men, but a struggle within the character played by Heath Ledger (Ennis) that foregrounds a classically promoted image of psychological, if not diseased, confusion in queer identities linked with Fanon's (1967) terms related to the subject of homosexuality—"fault, guilt, refusal of guilt, paranoia"(p. 183). So in order to be a real man (specifically in the genre of the western), in order to be a good God-fearing citizen, in order to be socially acceptable, the character of Ennis must resist libidinal gay sexual desire—or at least must not give completely into his desires as some recalcitrant religious ethic; an ecclesiastical dictate of self-denial in a struggle toward perfection or purification that "marks a different economy of desire that escapes legibility" or legitimation in either heterosexual or queer spheres (Gopinath, 2005, p. 13).[31] Hence, the choice made by the character leaves him in an altogether unsatisfied state throughout the film, and maybe this is the suggestive state of all who stray from normative standards of sexual practice or desire. In Mary E. Galvin's (1999) analysis of the heterosexual order as fetish, she states that the "fetishizing practices of heterosexist thinking condemn the possibility of diversity, variety, or multiplicity as 'deviance': inversion, perversion, corruption, or illness is made to reside within the politics transgressor's inner being, a constitutional flaw, rather than a conscious choice to resist the social of heterosexist thinking" (p. 2).

The character Ennis Del Mar also blames his state of same-sex desire for Jack—for "making me this way." And while the naïve reader of this social text might interpret this utterance as some romantic variation of "you made me love," the queer reading that I am engaging must acknowledge how this is suggestive within a larger context. Ennis's persistent resistance, as well as his lack of fulfillment in marital relations, suggests in a larger sense that Jack made him gay. This works in that larger and more problematic social accusation of gays recruiting members and ultimately luring, if not turning "perfectly normal" boys and men gay. Ledger's character channels the anxiety of a larger heteronormative culture as he both gives into and resists his own desires (DeCecco & Elia, 1993).

Upon their impending return from Brokeback Mountain (which now becomes its own metaphorical reference to clandestine gay sexual encounters, if not a White reconstruction and appropriation of *living on the down low*),[32] the two men, Ennis and Jack, engage in a tensively masculine good-bye. First, playful roughhousing (the often only socially acceptable way in which men can touch and show affection toward each other) turns into violent fighting (which is its own performance of masculinity that Ennis turns toward often throughout the film). Ennis is somehow struggling with his own demons, resisting his desire for this man, and seemingly rehearsing himself for the more traditional performances of masculinity that he must engage when he returns to town. Second, upon arrival in town, Ennis engages that public performance of masculinity that avoids sentimentality and affection toward other men, the manly handshake. When alone, Ennis breaks down and cries for what is assumed to be both the departure of the man he loves, a particular way of being, and curiously maybe even the anticipated dread of his impending marriage to a woman.

The next scene is Ennis and Alma's marriage. The particularity of the scene is the narration of the Lord's Prayer, which states, "Lead us not into temptation, but deliver us from sin." The marriage is depicted as ritual baptismal, a washing away of sin, and the viewer is to make the specific link to his sinful gay exploits on Brokeback Mountain. In the following scenes, there is a series of oddly iconic and romanticized moments that attempt to rewrite (read: *make right*) his gay encounters, in contradistinction to his heterosexual marriage: scenes of Ennis and Alma rolling in the snow are seemingly meant to counteract scenes of Ennis and Jack rolling in the grass (same and not the same)—though each image makes literal a ritual performance of/if not bathing in purity. Each scene is a relentless search for a purity that is both Whiteness and a sense of the *hetero*normal, against the constructed backdrop of forbidden and resistant desire that is not about discovery but erasure.[33]

Despite the juxtaposing value judgment of normalcy linked between homo- and heterosexualities—the conflicted nature of the Heath Ledger (Ennis) character, who is copresent in each scene, makes purity suspect. An intimate scene between Ennis and a pregnant Alma at a drive-in theater when she directs his hand to feel the baby kicking is further meant (for me) to counteract the scenes of intimacy with Jack and to project the particular and natural effects of proper sexual insemination (same and not the same). These scenes play as presumptions of the natural—until and maybe inclusive of a lovemaking scene when Ennis (reminiscent of his first depicted sexual encounter with Jack) aggressively turns Alma on her stomach and suggestively penetrates her from behind. The scene is suggestive of his continued desire for what is presumed to be exclusively "gay sex," but within the context of the marital bed, it also queers the very notion of normalcy in sexual practices among heterosexuals. Each scene from the film depicts suggestive moments of penetration—Ennis with Jack and Ennis with Alma—same and not the same and, from the expression on the face of the receiving partner, presumed pleasure versus presumed humiliation.

I briefly juxtapose this scene against a later scene when the two of them, Ennis and Alma, are having sex, this after her knowledge of his intimate relationship with Jack. While in the missionary position, with what is assumed to be full vaginal penetration, Alma speaks of the need to begin taking "precautions." This is immediately directed to issues of birth control, child support, and maybe a commitment to their marriage.

Ennis: "If you don't want any more of my babies just say so."

Alma: "I will have them if you support them."

Yet, it could easily, with her suspicion of his sexual relationship with Jack (his penchant for rear entry and the dramatic irony/knowledge of the audience who knows the extent of his relationship with Jack), be a particular allusion to *practicing safe sex*—as a precaution against the transmittal of disease that is reductively associated particularly with gay sex—which is always characterized as more disease prone than "heterosexually marked" practices. (This scene is noted as taking place in 1975.) Upon this social exchange and negotiation, Ennis withdraws and the couple retreats, each to either side of the bed. The scene that immediately follows is Ennis and Alma in divorce court. Once again, this is a scene that seems to parallel the marriage ceremony, both socialized and legal institutional mechanisms that attempt to dictate particular human social relations. Both are promoted within the film as social sanctions—normalization and its presumed opposite.

Normalization of Indifference Through Analogy.[34] Referencing the work of Jakobsen in the same volume, Miranda Joseph (2002) states, "Analogy can function as powerful political tool by which . . . the articulation of equivalence among social struggles makes those struggles recognizable on the mainstream political landscape, and potentially allies for each other. However, Jakobsen argues [*in her* analogy between Jews and queers], analogy also separates such movements and elides their connection with each other "*to a recognition of a complicity in the construction of the categories* (p. 80)."[35] Within the film, as a further justification of why the two men could not live together, Ennis, the character played by Heath Ledger, offers a childhood experience as evidence.

Ennis: There was these two old guys ranched together down home, Earl and Rich—Dad would pass a remark when he seen them. They was a joke even though they was pretty tough old birds. I was what, nine years old and they found Earl dead in a irrigation ditch. They'd took a tire iron to him, spurred him up, drug him around by his dick until it pulled off, just bloody pulp. What the tire iron done looked like pieces of burned tomatoes all over him, nose tore down from skiddin on gravel.

Jack: You seen that?

Ennis: Dad made sure I seen it. Took me to see it. Me and K.E. Dad laughed about it. Hell, for all I know he done the job. If he was alive and was to put his head in that door right now you bet he'd go get his tire iron. Two guys livin together? No. All I can see is we get together once in a while way the hell out in the back a nowhere—[36]

As he tells the story of Earl and Rich, there is a staged flashback scene. In the flashback, their father is leading the image of an almost 9-year-old Ennis and his slightly older brother to the location of the dead body. The father takes the boys to view the dead body as an object lesson, to enforce heteronormativity and the socially sanctioned consequences of its opposite. The literalness of this restaging as filmic technique reinforces a particular bent of the film. So like the impulse of the father bringing his sons to view the results of gay bashing, the film promotes a normalization of indifference through actual example. This becomes the grounding logics for the analogy used to justify and reinforce the social hysteria around homosexuality that Ennis perpetuates, nay promotes in his telling—to forestall any possibility in the social acceptability of two men living together. The analogy serves as both comparative template and prophecy.[37]

Years later, when Ennis receives the news of Jack's death, in a telephone call he asks Jack's wife how he died. The wife, Lureen (played by Anne Hathaway), systematically retells a constructed narrative about Jack's dying after an accident while changing a tire on a desolate stretch of road. While she is retelling the story, the actuality of a vicious gay bashing is visualized in a flashback scene, almost like a dream sequence, almost as evidence or fantasy of the social imaginary. It is not clear if Ennis is projecting or if Jack's wife is staving off the reality of the happening in relation to the tale she is telling. The duality of the scene—the social construction of the telling and the actuality of the happening—illuminates the *recognition of a complicity in the construction of the categories*—the telling and the told, the imagined and the actualized—of both the characters and the film itself, sutured together by the politeness of the telling and the viciousness of the reality; how the wife constructs the death and how the moral ethic of the film is altogether brought home in the flashback scene. The message: This is the projected and inevitable end for all queers, and from his own experience with Earl and Rich, Ennis knows it.[38]

The tale the wife tells borders between a performance of social propriety (in not telling the real story as a eulogistic act of care)[39] and personal shame (both for the fate that befalls queers and the manner in which her own sexual identity is reductively tied up in her husband's performance of masculinity/sexuality). This is of course also played out in rather coarse ways with Alma, the wife of Ennis, who sees her husband in a passionate kiss with Jack and who later, after the divorce, violently/vilely confronts him with her knowledge of his "fishing trips."

Ennis, as both a character in the film and a projective social agent, is complicit in the social outcome of Jack's murder—by his queerness and his particular phobias and inhibitions, but also more literally that in the telling of "the Earl and Rich story," the tropological fields within the analogy become conflated and defined as actuality—as projective fate of queerness to which he has invested and helped call into being. In the envisioned scene of Jack's death, he too, like Earl, is beaten with a tire iron, and his genitals are targeted as the offending parts in some skewed biblical application of justice. The sequence is staged as a reality that plays in the mind of both the teller and the told, the wife and the lover; who are the same and not the same—though each mourns for potentially the same reasons. Queers in the viewing audience must also mourn this projective fate of gay lives.

In offering these three pivot points toward doing a critically interpretive queer analysis of *Brokeback Mountain,* I want the reader to see an attempt at not revealing the queer undertones in the text already marked as "queer," but in a Muñozian sense of *disidentification,* an attempt to recycle and rethink encoded meanings in a cultural text that is presumably liberal but in fact perpetuates very conservative notions of social priority that can easily (and not so easily) go undetected within the political processes of promoting the particularity of dominative values. "Dominative values, those values that structure heterosexism among other dominations, may work with and for capitalism, but they also make capitalism work in a way that it does, thus making dominative values co-originary with the imperative to produce value under capitalism" (Jakobsen, 2002, p. 59).

I want the reader to see that this is done, as Johnson (2001) and Ferguson (2004) suggest, from a culture-specific positionality that might be referred to as a *queer of color critique* that identifies investments that are both specific to race and culture but does not fixate in those disparate territories while addressing issues most pertinent to a renewed queer theory interested in transforming the politics of representation that restrict and diminish all of our lives.

While the film *Brokeback Mountain* is presumed to be about homosexual desire, it is always and already a heteronormatively constructed and hegemonically dominating text that seeks to *set straight* issues of desire, happiness, and socially sanctioned happy endings in the west*(ern).* The film is a capitalist venture, with its success being measured both by box office receipts and the number of awards garnered, which is also about the marketability of actors, directors, producers,

DVD sales, and the promotion of particular narratives. The film, while read as "a gay cowboy story," is always and already directed by the dominative values of heterosexuality, which serves as the template and backdrop on which the story is told; heterosexuality, if not the attending values attributed to that sexual-social positionality, trumps homosexuality (queerness) in the film. Hence, there can be no *dismissal of the politics and economics* of the film because any such *omissions reflect the scandal* both of the film and the lack of reflectivity of the viewing public, who do not read the meaningful implications of it as a promotional social text of gay bashing packaged as a love story.[40]

At the end of the film, while some queers are left with the warmth of seeing an aspect of our lives depicted (what is the sincere love/desire and negotiations between two men), such *identification* must also be closely linked with an act of *mourning* the despair of particular gay lives of which the film also narrates and perpetuates.[41] The project of queer lives is only understood within the larger context of the film. The film encourages the continuation of cloistered lives within the shadows of the dominative value of heteronormativity. The contributing social variable of the plotline clearly (for me) forestalls and subjugates the queers in the text and in fact exploits queerness as a practiced identity location that must be kept privatized. As in Cindy Patton's (2002) analysis, the film initiates itself as a liberal stance on social issues but in fact sustains, if not sanctions, the same barbaric practices toward queers. The fact that the overt acts of violence are suggestive and appear in dream-like sequences only serves to further embed these values into social consciousness. In furthering her analysis of Spivak, Janet Jakobsen (2002) states that such "exploitation is never itself 'value-free,' because it is *both* dependent on *and* structured by the values carried by [and] . . . normatively inscribed, [upon] the dominated, body" (p. 58).

▣ ▣ ▣

Thus, within the brevity of my critically interpretive queer analysis of *Brokeback Mountain,* I seek to unveil the value of specific aspects of the film that are far from celebratory of queer lives, but in fact serve as a continued critique and projected despair of/on queer lives. And unlike the sometime critique of postcolonial theory that "centers mainly on the degree to which textual analysis seems to take the place of engagement with real life struggles" (Goldberg & Quayson, 2002, p. xxi),[42] my critique is an act of resistance against the presumed-to-be-normal outcome of gay lives, the perpetuation of heteronormative domination, and the particular representation in the film that has actual consequences on queer lives; truly this is a site of real struggle. And like Johnson's (2001) impetus in introducing the notion of *quare theory,* maybe my move toward a critically interpretive queer methodology works in alignment with his to "move beyond simply theorizing subjectivity and agency as discursively mediated to theorizing how that mediation may propel material bodies into action" (p. 9).

> Action, as continued critical readings of socially constructed texts about queer lives.
>
> Action, as resistance to nostalgic romanticized depictions of queer lives with all too predictable tragic endings.
>
> Action, as resistance to being happy with unsavory representations and promotions of cloistered gay lives.
>
> Action, as the resistance of *queers of color* to being reduced to shadow figures and secondary choices of white lovers.
>
> Action, as the continued construction of essays written from a *queer of color* analytical perspective.
>
> Action, as resistance against the form of institutional and ideological domination that such films as *Brokeback Mountain* subtly promote, resembling forms of disaffection and dissent always expressed under colonial rule. (Parry, 1994, p. 173)
>
> Action, as critiquing the everyday cultural practices of home and community that establish the

> foundations of our deepest insecurities and pains about sex and sexuality; that homeplace where the seeds of ignorance, hate, and reduced self-worth are most often deeply sown; that homeplace where issues of religion and sexual identity become both seductive and reductive—instilling a kind of social myopia about sexually transmitted diseases and HIV/AIDS that ravish minds and communities of color while maintaining religiously informed notions of the socially acceptable.[43]

Such actions need to bleed the borders of the academy into the streets and the places that we call home—to manifest themselves not just in the mechanisms of scholarly discourse, but made manifest in the doing of social transformation; in the changing of cultural practices, in the voicing of dissent even within the communities in which we claim as home.

> Action, like the keen acknowledgment that the young Taiwanese men in Cindy Patton's (2002) reference, who stood in line waiting to be declared homosexual as a means of avoiding mandatory military service and who were in fact performing a radical subversion; using the legalistically confirmed paranoia of gay sexuality to politically oppose the power of the colonizing state; *an appropriations of liberal stance,* not as compromise and conciliation, but for political purposes working from within the system to subvert and foreground a queer performativity in which politics, identity, and desire are turned on their heads as queer resistance to *regimes of the normal.*
>
> *Or* action like in the edited volume *Infamous Desire: Male Homosexuality in Colonial Latin America,* in which Pete Sigal (2003) points to the complexity of homosexual desire; representations of masculinity, femininity, and power; and the more important understanding of the sometimes integrated practices of race, power, and sexuality as key components of cultural practice.
>
> Action, not only in how indigenous queers subvert opposing forces in the specificity of their home place in the context of presumed Third World countries, but also like in the work of Patton and Sánchez-Eppler (2000), *Queer Diasporas,* in which *tactical queerness* is used as *therapeutics for any thinking that occludes bodies and places.* It is like the case of *transmigrant* Filipino queers in New York who re-create and subvert a queer version of The Santacruzan Filipino religious ritual, as an act of subversion to restrictive cultural mandates on homosexuality in their homeland, moving towards conversion and renewal, thereby building an emergent and resistant spirituality within a queer Filipino community in diaspora.
>
> Or as in the groundbreaking work of David Román (1998), *Acts of Intervention: Performance, Gay Culture, and AIDS,* featuring U.S.-based performance traditions with particular features on *Pomo Afro Homos* (postmodern, African American homosexuals), a performance troupe, and *Teatre Vitro,* a Latino performance troupe addressing the politics of AIDS in Los Angeles—each offering subversive strategies of illuminating and critiquing queer life from within the private and public confines of culture, race, and sexuality.

At the end of *Brokeback Mountain,* like the characters themselves, I am left battered and bereft. In writing this queer reading of the text, I know that I am not complicit in the construction of these categories and the retelling of these particular tales that further my own marginalization. Like other *queers of color,* I know that my queer reading is both *an act* and *a call* for disidentification from the particular perspective that "disidentification is the hermeneutical performance of decoding mass, high, or any other cultural fields from the perspective of a minority subject who is disempowered in such a representational hierarchy" (Muñoz, 1999, p. 25).

This reading also foregrounds a particular location in which "queer desires, bodies and subjectivities become dense sites of meaning in the production and reproduction of notions of 'culture,' 'tradition,' and communal" constructions of the acceptable normal (Gopinath, 2005, p. 2). In this sense, I seek to use the raw materials of this decoded text as a means of representing the disempowered politics of queer lives that the film perpetuates through a particular brand of hegemony and heteronormativity promoted within the text, and in fact empower the queer lives that the film very strategically patronizes and pathologizes. Such acts might in fact be the core logics of any project that seeks to queer postcolonialism, an act that at once focuses and distinguishes the radical possibilities of being and sounds out voice from the marginalized spaces of nation and state from which such social and political texts promote their particular rhetorics.

Maybe in some sense, I am engaging in what Homi Bhabha calls a "vernacular cosmopolitanism ... one that translates between cultures and across them in order to survive, not in order to assert the sovereignty of a civilized class, or the spiritual autonomy of a reversed ideal ... [but] one that that find[s] [its] ethical and creative direction in learning that hard lesson of ambivalence and forbearance" (Bhabha & Comaroff, 2002, p. 24) to which Blacks and queers have historically been forced to engage, but have done so in a radical resistance of difference. Such a resistance in the context of this reading of the film *Brokeback Mountain* might signal still other ways of claiming our voices in the often-thought silenced margins, voices only made amplified by the walls of indifference, arching their way above the center toward actualization.

Epilogue

The generalized context for this chapter situates postcolonial theory and queer studies on/in a terrain of embodied struggle in/of/for difference and against indifference. And if postcolonial theory arose from the dissatisfaction with imperial accounts of colonial peoples (Brydon, 2000), and if, as Gayatri Spivak (1997) suggests, the African American fits the general picture of postcoloniality much more accurately than the unearned claims of the Eurocentric well-placed migrant, then I claim this space to practice voice at the intersection of a nihilistic postcolonial perspective and a homogenizing queer studies (p. 189).

In the beginning was the word and the word was made flesh.

Flesh into words,

words into flesh.

Writing as scarification—marking difference—

and legislating desire.

The results—a poem, a novel, a manifesto, a theoretical perspective,

a cultural critique;

a film critique;

an articulation of lived experience isolated from the projection of the known.

Storing storied histories in condensed spaces, oral traditions made manifest in meter and rhyme or prose and other scholarly forms.

The rhythmicity of our soul force dancing on the page,

in the borders and boundaries of social life,

in the margins of larger social texts,

stepping out of the shadows and into the light of choice.

Words making manly love between the spaces;

not violently attacking,

but gently loving.

Sharing and rejoicing jointly.

Writing as performance, recreating ourselves—in verse

making not faking.[44]

R*E*A*L as we are in the world, our prideful bold (black and brown) gay selves wanting to be acknowledged in our fullness, in our beauty, in our humanity, in our gentle spirits (twin or otherwise) in our potential and possibility.

Not always victimized in acts of violence (through exclusion or occlusion),

Not R*E*E*L as we are depicted on the screen—as flaming faggots,

bitch prostitutes in the shadow lands of our own existence,

or with attitudes, snapping in a Z formation,

secondary choices living cloistered lives,

living on the down low,

stealing *high-altitude fucks.*

So I am writing a poem.

So I am writing about a Black gay man writing a poem,

which is really not unusual.

All Black men enact poetry: articulated expressions with thought to form.

The slide into home base—that you celebrate.

The leap at the goal line—that you are in awe of.

The grace of that touchdown pass—that takes your breath away.

Poetry—can you see it?

The gay Black man fashion designer,

the gay Black man directing the church choir.

the gay Black man teaching—-the poetic spirit in action.

The felt expression of desire & disdain articulated into words, or thoughts, or actions.

Writing is form.

Poetry is motion.

Brothers are moving—ever changing.

Like the poem I want to be read with an eye for detail.

Not *read*—as in put in my place.

I want you to see me in my simplistic complexity.

I want you to see the care for detail and fluidity of form.

Yes I want you to see my form—not necessarily iambic, pentametrian, or some free form.

And not those quintessential markers of Black masculinity—which have historically been

signifiers for social praise and marketing, another site of entrapment.

But Blackness, and understand that rich history that is narrated in this dark flesh long before I begin to tell my story.

And when you see me, I want you to see my dick, not as some limp phallus that cannot

penetrate a vagina—as if that is the measure of a man (been there, done that!).

But a dick with a mind of its own, like that room that some feminists talk about as some

liberatory space of identification and self-determination.

But then I also want you to read between the lines to do a critically queer reading, and see me as a Black gay man, and see that I have fully engaged that as the choice to follow an internal impulse, not clearly dictated like my Black body or my male body, or the social investments in either—but the divine, divining, and dividing impulse to charter my own destiny.

Yes, I want you to read my body like you would read a poem,

for you will anyway

A poem that is highly politicized,

sexualized,

racialized,

genderized, and

culturalized.

But these things are not written

under the surface for only the skilled eye to read.

Not encoded in non-sense language waiting for a Nazi spy of an English professor to break the code, like breaking the silence of thoughts, feelings

and interpretations of lived experiences,

to dictate the TRUTH of THE WORD (or author intent) in some mockery of pedagogy.

I want you to read openly for face value—

a message spliced open like an autopsy for all to see.

Words like organs serving their function in a system of thought,

a sentence like a vein trailing desire.

The impulse of my thoughts beating;

the heart of a poem,

the meaning of my message.

You know what I mean.

NOTES

1. Here I am making a particular allusion to the work of Frantz Fanon (1967), for whom homosexuality is a particularly White contagion and his references to no (Black) homosexuality in the Antilles (*Black Skin, White Masks*).

2. Brydon (2000) edits five volumes of *Postcolonalism: Critical Concepts.*

3. Here, of course, I am making an allusion to Gayatri Spivak's (1988a) "Can the Subaltern Speak?"

4. See Kathy Charmaz's (2005) discussion of "Grounded Theory in the 21st Century."

5. Russell Jacoby (1995) writes, "While post-colonial studies claims to be subversive and profound, the politics tends to be banal; the language jargonized; the radical one-upmanship infantile; the self-obsession tiresome; and the theory bloated" (p. 37).

6. See Gilbert and Tompkins (1996).

7. Weaver (2000, p. 232) includes the Cook-Lynn (1997) quote in the conclusion of his essay.

8. See also the section on "Internal Colonialisms and Subaltern Studies" in Brydon (2000, vol. 4).

9. This section is drawn heavily from Alexander (2002a).

10. Stein and Plummer (1994) are drawing from these categorical descriptors for queer theory through the works of Butler (1990), Sedgwick (1990), Warner (1991), and Fuss (1991).

11. I particularly like Katie King's (2000) project "Global Gay Formations and Local Homosexualities," in which she addresses the productive instability of the term *queer.*

12. See the important essay by Diana Fuss (2000), in which she engages a project that I want to describe as queering Frantz Fanon while doing a survey of sexuality studies.

13. Moraga and Anzaldúa (1981): A theory in the flesh means one where the physical realities of our lives—our skin color, the land or concrete we grew up on, our sexual longings—all fuse to create a politic born out of necessity.

14. The editors, Cruz-Malavé and Manalansan (2002), use this description in the introduction to the book.

15. Read Nikki Sullivan's (2003) chapter on "Queering 'Straight' Sex" as a further analysis that plays out in *Brokeback Mountain* as both men are depicted as intermittently involved in both heterosexual and homosexual sexual acts.

16. In "Colonial Fantasies and Postcolonial Identities," Hema Chari (2001) correlates the primary themes of her analysis to the *homosocial, homoerotic, and homophobic strains* in the novel *The Moor's Last Sigh* by Salman Rushdie.

17. In this context, I am using the reference to *performance* as expected cultural behavior, the embodiment of gender norms, although Victor Turner's (1982) defense of performance as "making not faking" becomes apparently evident in the shifting social enactments of the two male lovers in this film, as they move from the routinized mechanisms of their marital lives (with their wives) to the emotional intimacies of their same-sex relationship.

18. I suspect that the name Jack Twist is a reductive reference to sexual positionality, both in the ways in which a performative homotrope of gay identity is a suggestive "twist" when walking, to suggest the opposite of straight, and also because the character played by Jake Gyllenhaal is constructed as being more comfortable with his queer identity (though both characters clearly state that they are not queer in the film); he is also the character that is reductively constructed as "the bottom" in the sexual relationship.

19. The film ends with a scene of Ennis living alone in a trailer. Before sanctioning and agreeing to attend the marriage of his daughter, he asks her if her intended loves her. His question is both a desire for her happiness and is a reflection on the altogether real negotiations and compromises of heterosexual marriage and his love for Jack.

20. I am indebted to Hema Chari—signaling me to this particular element in the work of Sedgwick (1985, p. 298, n7). In particular, Sedgwick (1985) makes such allusions to the role that women play in regulating men that may lead to homoerotic desire in *Between Men.* The role that women play in bringing men together is also depicted in the dance scene where Jack Twist and his wife double date with another couple. The character played by Anne Hathaway also says during the dance, "Husbands never seem to want to dance with their wives." She directs this as a query to her husband, Jack Twist, who, as a form of diversion from the specificity of the question and an allusion to his queer identity, invites the other woman at the table—while her husband smiles. There is a building of desire between the two men, leading toward a later invitation to share private time at a cabin, while the two women are powdering their noses.

21. These are excerpted and transcribed comments from a paper presented by Mae G. Henderson at the Black Queer Studies in the Millennium Conference. These excerpts are documented in the review essay of that conference (Alexander, 2002b, p. 1297).

22. In fact, the name Brokeback Mountain has unfortunate resonances to the reference of unprotected anal sex, *barebacking,* which is also seemingly promoted in the film—by the clear absence of condoms.

23. The only other image of a person of color is in the role of a trail drive merchant, a Mexican or Hispanic man who brings food supplies and provisions to White herdsmen. His thick Spanish accent marks him as other, as his role is clearly to serve the needs of the White men who are doing the real work. In such case, this character is also feminized in a manner that makes him secondary—in the way in which the film is really about the dominance of a particular performance of White masculinity—even in the face of being about same-sex desire.

24. Fuss's (2000) commentary serves as both critique and support of Frantz Fanon's (1967) assertions and denials about the presence of homosexuality in the Antilles.

25. In the introduction to *Queer Diasporas,* Patton and Sánchez-Eppler (2000) write, "When a practitioner of 'homosexual acts,' or a body that carries any of many queering marks moves between officially designated spaces—nation, region, metropole, neighborhood, or even culture, gender, religion, disease—intricate realignments of identity, politics, and desire take place" (p. 3).

26. Fuss (2000, p. 1120) uses this construction in her critique of Frantz Fanon.

27. The title of Chari's (2001) essay is "Colonial Fantasies and Postcolonial Identities." In the essay, she states, "The powerful dynamics of interracial desires of same-sex and of homoerotic colonial fantasies continue to be elusive and contradictory in most commentaries on colonial narratives including the works of Alloula and Said" (p. 280).

28. The original draft of this essay contained images that could not be printed in this copy. I still would like to offer special thanks to Matthew Gatlin for his efforts in image retrieval of the six comparative images from *Brokeback Mountain,* which were scheduled to appear in this chapter.

29. In the introduction to *Queer Globalizations,* Cruz-Malavé and Manalansan (2002) extend this logic in stating, "Representations of queer lives and desires in such mainstream Hollywood films as *Philadelphia, To Wong Foo,* and *Go Fish,* and in the more artsy international productions, the British *The Crying Game,* the Cuban *Strawberry and Chocolate,* and the Indian *Fire,* it is true, are selling increasingly well as a global commodities to 'general audiences'" (p. 1). *Gay, Straight, or Taken?* is a new game show-type reality show on the Lifetime network that pits a heterosexual woman in a dating game to determine which of three men is gay, straight, or married.

30. Jill Dolan (2005) does a wonderful job of describing *The Laramie Project,* a performative response to the Matthew Shepard story. She describes the project as such: "The Tectonic Theatre Project traveled to Laramie to create a performance based on the events; their motivating question, according to director Moisés Kaufman, was, 'How is Laramie different from the rest of the county and how is it similar?'" (p. 113).

31. Please note that in this construction ("heterosexual or queer spheres"), I am not placing these as a specific binary—opposites to the other—as much as I am suggesting these as a range of possibilities—from the delimited construction of heterosexuality to the range of possibilities not to, but within, the construct of queerness.

32. In referencing "the down low," I am of course making allusion to the construction that speaks to "straight" Black men who sleep with men—as popularized in J. L. King's (2004) book, *Life on the Down Low,*

and the later rebuttal, *Beyond the Down Low,* written by Black queer activist and writer Keith Boykin (2005).

33. In *Cities of the Dead,* Joseph Roach (1996) uses the construction "the relentless search for the purity of origins is a voyage not of discovery but of erasure" (p. 6).

34. In their chapter overviews, Cruz-Malavé and Manalansan (2002) use the construction "normalization of difference through analogy." I am strategically inserting *in* to suggest indifference as an elemental component of my analysis.

35. Joseph (2002, p. 95, n11) offers an explication of Jakobsen's (2002) intent. I have inserted an aspect of that note in the text for purposes of clarity for the argument that I am building.

36. I am drawing this text directly from the short story "Brokeback Mountain," written by Annie Proulx (1999).

37. For you see, in the western genre, the hero of the text (some highly masculinized type like John Wayne, Clint Eastwood, or Audie Murphy) completes some noble task—saving a village, a successful battle, or a socially validated revenge (as Clint Eastwood does in *Unforgiven* (1992)—he takes revenge on a town and a group of marauders for cutting up a woman and later torturing and killing his partner/colleague [played by Morgan Freeman]). Eastwood's action is both an act of performative masculinity that is about protecting its opposite (femininity) and the homosocial honor between men. *Unforgiven* is also a complex text in that it also invokes a particular violence on the Black male body—in that Morgan Freeman is beaten by White men (Gene Hackman and others) in a manner that is reminiscent of the fate of a runaway or petulant slave or the Jim Crow South. While Clint Eastwood inflicts his own revenge, the Black male body is still made a pawn in the social negotiations of White masculinity.

38. In the short story that inspired the film, upon hearing Lureen's telling of the death, it is written, "No, he thought, they got him with the tire iron."

39. I explore the qualities and accountabilities of doing eulogies in Alexander (2006, chap. 6).

40. I am borrowing and reframing Benita Parry's (2002) closing line in her essay, "Directions and Dead Ends in Postcolonial Studies." In particular, Parry's argument is thus: "Predictably those committed to postmodern analytic paradigms are hostile in the movements of sublation, or preservation/cancellation/transcendence in liberation theory, where the anticipation of egalitarian postcolonial conditions subsumes the retention and supersession of the technical advances inadvertently effected by capitalism-as-colonialism. In scorning liberatory expectations as naïve, the purpose of critics has been to render nugatory the joining of intelligible and still viable indigenous resources and age-old tradition of colonial resistance with the ethical horizons and utopian reach of socialism. The sanctioned occlusions in postcolonial criticism are a debilitating loss to thinking about colonialism and late imperialism. The dismissal of politics and economics which these omissions reflect is a scandal" (p. 78).

41. See how Sigmund Freud discusses the relationship between identification, mourning, and melancholia in "Mourning and Melancholia" (Freud, 1953–1974, p. 243).

42. In offering this commentary, the authors cite Ahmad (1992), Dirlik (1994), Kennedy (1996), and San Juan (1998).

43. My respected friend and colleague E. Patrick Johnson (2001, p. 18) offers a similarly intentioned call at the end of his essay introducing *quare studies.*

44. See Note 16.

▣ References

Ahmad, A. (1992). *In theory: Classes, nations, literatures.* London: Verso.

Alexander, B. K. (2002a). The outsider (or *Invisible Man* all over again): Contesting the absented Black gay body in queer theory (with apologies to Ralph Ellison). In W. Wright & S. Kaplan (Eds.), *The image of the outsider: Proceedings of the 2002 Society for the Interdisciplinary Study of Social Imagery Conference* (pp. 308–315). Pueblo: University of Southern Colorado.

Alexander, B. K. (2002b). Reflections, riffs and remembrances: The Black queer studies in the millennium conference. *Callaloo, 23,* 1285–1302.

Alexander, B. K. (2006). *Performing black masculinity: Race, culture and queer identity.* Lanham, MD: AltaMira Press.

Anderson, B. (1991). *Imagined communities: Reflections on the origin and spread of nationalism.* New York: Verso.

Anzaldúa, G. (1987). *Borderlands/la frontera: The new mestiza.* San Francisco: Spinsters/Aunt Lute.

Bhabha, H. K. (1994). *The location of culture.* New York: Routledge.

Bhabha, H. K. (2000). Postcolonial criticism. In D. Brydon (Ed.), *Postcolonialism: Critical concepts* (Vol.1, pp. 105–132). New York: Routledge.

Bhabha, H. K., & Comaroff, J. (2002). Speaking of postcoloniality, in the continuous present: A conversation. In D. T. Goldberg & A. Quayson (Eds.), *Relocating postcolonialism* (pp. 15–46). Malden, MA: Blackwell.

Boone, J. (2001). Vacation cruises; or, the homoerotics of orientalism. In J. C. Hawley (Ed.), *Post-colonial queer: Theoretical intersections* (pp. 43–78). Albany, NY: SUNY Press.

Boykin, K. (2005). *Beyond the down low: Sex, lies and denial in Black America.* New York: Carroll & Graf.

Brydon, D. (Ed.). (2000). *Postcolonalism: Critical concepts* (5 vols.). New York: Routledge.

Butler, J. (1990). *Gender trouble: Feminism and the subversion of identity.* New York: Routledge.

Butler, J. (1990). Performative acts and gender constitution: An essay in phenomenology and feminist theory. In S. E. Case (Ed.), *Performing feminisms: Feminist critical theory and theatre.* Baltimore: Johns Hopkins University Press.

Case, S. E. (1997). Tracking the vampire. In K. Conboy, N. Medina, & S. Stanbury (Eds.), *Writing on the body: Female embodiment and feminist theory* (pp. 380–400). New York: Columbia University Press.

Chari, H. (2001). Colonial fantasies and postcolonial identities: Elaboration of postcolonial masculinity and homoerotic desire. In J. C. Hawley (Ed.), *Post-colonial queer: Theoretical intersections* (pp. 227–304). Albany, NY: SUNY Press.

Charmaz, K. (2005). Grounded theory in the 21st century: Applications for advancing socially just studies. In N. K. Denzin & Y. S. Lincoln (Eds.), *The SAGE handbook of qualitative research* (3rd ed., pp. 507–535). Thousand Oaks, CA: Sage.

Cohen, C. (1999). *The boundaries of blackness: AIDS and the breakdown of Black politics.* Chicago: University of Chicago Press.

Cook-Lynn, E. (1997, Spring). Who stole Native American studies? *Wicazo Sa Review.*

Cruz-Malavé, A., & Manalansan, M. F., IV. (2002). Introduction: Dissident sexualities/alternative globalisms. In A. Cruz-Malavé & M. F. Manalansan IV (Eds.), *Queer globalizations: Citizenships and the afterlife of colonialism* (pp. 1–10). New York: New York University Press.

DeCecco, J. P., & Elia, J. P. (Eds.). (1993). *If you seduce a straight person can you make them gay? Issues in biological essentialism versus social constructionism in gay and lesbian identities.* New York: Harrington Park Press.

Dei, G. J. S., Hall, B. L., & Rosenberg, D. G. (2000). *Indigenous knowledges in global contexts: Multiple readings of our world.* Toronto: University of Toronto Press.

Derrida, J. (1987). *La Vérité en peinture* [Truth in painting] (G. Bennington & I. McLeod, Trans.). Chicago: University of Chicago Press.

Dirlik, A. (1994). *Asia/Pacific as space of cultural production.* Durham, NC: Duke University Press.

Dolan, J. (2005). The Laramie Project: Rehearsing for the example. In *Utopia in performance: Finding hope at the theatre* (pp. 113–138). Ann Arbor: University of Michigan Press.

Doty, A. (1993). *Making things perfectly queer: Interpreting mass culture.* Minneapolis: University of Minnesota Press.

Doty, A. (1995). There is something queer here. In C. K. Creekmur & A. Doty (Eds.), *Out in culture: Gay, lesbian and queer essays on popular culture* (pp. 71–90). Durham, NC: Duke University Press.

Duncan, P. (2002). A flexible foundation: Constructing a postcolonial dialogue. In D. T. Goldberg & A. Quayson (Eds.), *Relocating postcolonialism* (pp. 320–333). Malden, MA: Blackwell.

Duggan, L. (1998). Queering the state. In P. M. Nardi & B. E. Schneider (Eds.), *Social perspective in lesbian and gay studies* (pp. 564–572). New York: Routledge.

Eastwood, C. (Director). (1992). *Unforgiven* [Motion picture]. United States: Malpaso Productions.

Eng, D. L. (2003). Transnational adoption and queer diasporas. *Social Text, 21*(3), 1–37.

Eng, D. L., Halberstam, J., & Muñoz, J. E. (Eds.). (2005). *What's queer about queer studies now?* Durham, NC: Duke University Press.

Esteban, J. (1999). *Disidentitfication: Queers of color and the performance of politics.* Minneapolis: University of Minnesota Press.

Fanon, F. (1967). *Black skin, white masks* (C. L. Markmann, Trans.). New York: Grove.

Ferguson, R. A. (2004). *Toward a queer of color critique: Aberrations in black.* Minneapolis: University of Minnesota Press.

Freedman, E. (1998). Producing (queer) communities: Public access cable TV in the USA. In C. Geraghty & D. Lusted (Eds.),*The television studies book.* New York: St. Martin's.

Freud, S. (1953–1974). Mourning and melancholia. In J. Strachery (Ed. & Trans.), *The standard edition of the completed psychological works of Sigmund Freud* (24 vols.). London: Hogarth.

Fuoss, K. W. (1993). Performance as contestation: An agonisitic perspective on the insurgent assembly. *Text and Performance Quarterly, 13,* 331–349.

Fuss, D. (1991). *Inside/out: Lesbian theories, gay theories.* New York: Routledge.

Fuss, D. (2000). Interior colonies: Frantz Fanon and the politics of identification. In D. Brydon (Ed.), *Postcolonalism: Critical concepts* (Vol. III, pp. 1103–1131). New York: Routledge.

Galvin, M. E. (1999). *Queer poetics: Five modernist women writers.* Westport, CT: Praeger.

Gamson, J. (1998). Must identity movements self-destruct? A queer dilemma. In P. M. Nardi & B. E. Schneider (Eds.), *Social perspective in lesbian and gay studies* (pp. 589–604). New York: Routledge.

Gandhi, L. (1998). *Postcolonial theory: A critical introduction.* New York: Columbia University Press.

Gilbert, H., & Tompkins, J. (1996). *Post-colonial drama: Theory, practice, politics.* New York: Routledge.

Gilroy, P. (1995). "to be real": The dissident forms of Black expressive culture. In C. Ugwu (Ed.), *Let's get it on: The politics of Black performance* (pp. 12–33). Seattle, WA: Bay.

Goldberg, D. T., & Quayson, A. (Eds.). (2002). *Relocating postcolonialism.* Malden, MA: Blackwell.

Goldie, T. (1999). Queerly postcolonial: Social issues on postcolonial and queer theory and praxis. *ARIEL, 30*(2), 9–26.

Gopinath, G. (2005). *Impossible desires: Queer diasporas and South Asian public cultures.* Durham, NC: Duke University Press.

Grillo, T., & Wildman, S. M. (1995). Obscuring the importance of race: The implication of making comparisons between racism and sexism (or other-isms). In R. Delgado (Ed.), *Critical race theory: The cutting edge* (pp. 564–572). Philadelphia: Temple University Press.

Grossberg, L. (1994). Introduction. In H. A. Giroux & P. McLaren (Eds.), *Between borders: Pedagogy and the politics of cultural studies* (pp. 1–25). New York: Routledge.

Hall, S. (1994). Cultural identity and diaspora. In P. Williams & L. Chrisman (Eds.), *Colonial discourse and post-colonial theory: A reader* (pp. 392–402). New York: Columbia University Press.

Hanson, E. (1999). *Out takes: Essays on queer theory and film.* Durham, NC: Duke University Press.

Harper, P. B. (1998). *Are we not men: Masculine anxiety and the problem of African American identity.* Oxford, UK: Oxford University Press.

Hawley, J. C. (Ed.). (2001a). *Postcolonial and queer theories: Intersections and essays.* Westport, CT: Greenwood.

Hawley, J. C. (Ed.). (2001b). *Postcolonial, queer: Theoretical intersections.* Albany, NY: SUNY Press.

Henderson, M. G. (Ed.). (1995). *Borders, boundaries, and frames: Cultural criticism and cultural studies.* New York: Routledge.

Irvine, J. M. (1998). A place in the rainbow: Theorizing lesbian and gay culture. In P. M. Nardi & B. E. Schneider (Eds.), *Social perspectives in lesbian and gay studies* (pp. 573–588). New York: Routledge.

Jacoby, R. (1995, September–October). Marginal returns: The trouble with post-colonial theory. *Lingua Franca,* pp. 30–37.

Jakobsen, J. R. (2002). Can homosexuals end Western civilization as we know it? Family values in a global economy. In A. Cruz-Malavé & M. F. Manalansan IV (Eds.), *Queer globalizations: Citizenships and the afterlife of colonialism* (pp. 49–70). New York: New York University Press.

Johnson, E. P. (2001). Quare studies, or (almost) everything I know about queer studies I learned from my grandmother. *Text and Performance Quarterly, 21*(1), 1–25.

Johnson, E. P., & Henderson, M. G. (Eds.). (2005). *Black queer studies: A critical anthology.* Durham, NC: Duke University Press.

Joseph, M. (2002). The discourse of global/localization. In A. Cruz-Malavé & M. F. Manalansan IV (Eds.), *Queer globalizations: Citizenships and the afterlife of colonialism* (pp. 71–99). New York: New York University Press.

Kennedy, D. (1996). Imperial history and postcolonial theory. *Journal of Imperial and Commonwealth History, 24,* 345–363.

King, J. L. (2004). *Life on the down low: A journey into the lives of "straight" Black men who sleep with men.* New York: Harlem Moon.

King, K. (2000). Global gay formations and local homosexualities. In H. Schwartz & S. Ray (Eds.), *A companion to postcolonial studies* (pp. 508–519). Malden, MA: Blackwell.

McCarthy, C. R. (2007). Coda: After 9/11 thinking about the global, thinking about empathy, thinking about the postcolonial. In N. K. Denzin & M. D. Giardina (Eds.), *Contesting empire, globalizing dissent: Cultural studies after 9/11* (pp. 280–289). Boulder, CO: Paradigm.

Mohanty, S. P. (1989). Us and them: On the philosophical bases of political criticism. *Yale Journal of Criticism, 2*(2), 1–31.

Moraga, C., & Anzaldúa, G. (1981). *This bridge called my back: Writings by radical women of color.* New York: Kitchen Table, Women of Color Press.

Muñoz, J. E. (1999). *Disidentification: Queers of color and the performance of politics.* Minneapolis: University of Minnesota Press.

Parry, B. (1994). Resistance theory/theorizing resistance or two cheers for nativism. In F. Barker, P. Hulme, & M. Iversen (Eds.), *Colonial discourse/postcolonial theory* (pp. 172–196). Manchester, UK: Manchester University Press.

Parry, B. (2002). Directions and dead ends in postcolonial studies. In D. T. Goldberg & A. Quayson (Eds.), *Relocating postcolonialism* (pp. 66–81). Malden, MA: Blackwell.

Patton, C. (2002). Stealth bombers of desire: The globalization of "alterity" in emerging democracies. In A. Cruz-Malavé & M. P. Manalanson (Eds.), *Queer globalizations: Citizenship and the afterlife of colonialism* (pp. 195–218). New York: New York University Press.

Patton, C., & Sánchez-Eppler, B. (Eds.). (2000). *Queer diasporas.* Durham, NC: Duke University Press.

Proulx, A. (1999). Brokeback Mountain. In *Close range: Wyoming stories* (pp. 253–283). New York: Scribner's.

Roach, J. (1996). *Cities of the dead: Circum-Atlantic performance.* New York: Columbia University Press.

Román, D. (1998). *Acts of intervention: Performance, gay culture, and AIDS.* Bloomington: Indiana University Press.

Said, E. (1978). *Orientalism.* New York: Pantheon.

Said, E. (1990). Yeats and decolonization. In T. Eagleton, F. Jameson, & E. W. Said (Eds.), *Nationalism, colonialism, and literature* (pp. 69–95). Minneapolis: University of Minnesota Press.

San Juan, E., Jr. (1998). *Beyond postcolonial theory.* London: Palgrave.

Sedgwick, E. K. (1985). *Between men: English literature and male homosocial desire.* New York: Columbia University Press.

Sedgwick, E. K. (1990). *Epistemology of the closet.* Berkeley: University of California Press.

Sedgwick, E. K. (1993). *Tendencies.* Durham, NC: Duke University Press.

Semali, L. M., & Kincheloe, J. L. (1999). *What is indigenous knowledge: Voices from the academy.* New York: Falmer.

Sigal, P. (2003). *Infamous desire: Male homosexuality in colonial Latin America.* Chicago: University of Chicago Press.

Spivak, G. C. (1988a). Can the subaltern speak? In C. Nelson & L. Grossberg (Eds.), *Marxist interpretations of culture* (pp. 271–313). Basingstoke, UK: Macmillan Education.

Spivak, G. C. (1988b). Scattered speculation on the question of value. In *Other worlds: Essays in cultural politics* (pp. 154–175). New York: Methuen.

Spivak, G. C. (1997). Teaching for the times. In J. N. Pieterse & B. Parekh (Eds.), *The decolonization of imagination: Culture, knowledge and power* (pp. 177–202). Calcutta, India: Oxford University Press.

Spurlin, W. J. (2001). Broadening postcolonial studies/decolonizing queer studies: Emerging "queer" identities and culture in southern Africa. In J. C. Hawley (Ed.), *Postcolonial queer: Theoretical intersections* (pp. 185–206). Albany, NY: SUNY Press.

Stein, A., & Plummer, K. (1994). "I can't even think straight": Queer theory and the missing sexual revolution in sociology. *Sociological Theory, 12,* 178–187.

Stockton, K. B. (2006). *Beautiful bottom, beautiful shame: Where "black" meets "queer."* Durham, NC: Duke University Press.

Sullivan, N. (2003). Queering "straight" sex. In *A critical introduction to queer theory* (pp. 119–135). New York: New York University Press.

Turner, V. (1982). *From ritual to theatre.* New York: PAJ.

Turner, W. B. (2000). *A genealogy of queer theory.* Philadelphia: Temple University Press.

Warner, M. (1991). Fear of a queer planet. *Social Text,* 9(14), 3–17.

Warner, M. (1993). *Fear of a queer planet: Queer politics and social theory.* Minneapolis: University of Minnesota Press.

Weaver, J. (2000). Indigenousness and indigeneity. In H. Schwarz & S. Ray (Eds.), *A companion to postcolonial studies* (pp. 221–235). Malden, MA: Blackwell.

Wildman, S. M., & Davis, A. D. (1995). Language and silence: Making systems of privilege visible. In R. Delgado (Ed.), *Critical race theory: The cutting edge* (pp. 573–579). Philadelphia: Temple University Press.

Yep, G. A., Lovass, K. E., & Elia, J. P. (2003). Introduction: Queering communication: Starting the conversation. In G. A. Yep, K. E. Lovass, & J. P. Elia (Eds.), *Queer theory and communication: From disciplining queers to queering the discipline(s).* New York: Harrington Park Press.

7

INDIGENOUS KNOWLEDGES IN EDUCATION

Complexities, Dangers, and Profound Benefits

Joe L. Kincheloe and Shirley R. Steinberg

Since the time that I (Joe Kincheloe) published *What Is Indigenous Knowledge? Voices From the Academy* (Semali & Kincheloe, 1999), I have had an opportunity to speak to a variety of audiences about the topic around North America and the world. Of course, many individuals from diverse backgrounds are profoundly informed about the topic and have provided me with a wide variety of insights to my efforts to better understand and engage the issue of indigenous knowledge in the academy. At the same time, numerous individuals engaged in research and education—especially from dominant cultural backgrounds—continue to dismiss the importance of indigenous knowledge in academic work and pedagogy. In the last half of the first decade of the 21st century, in an era of an expanding U.S. empire replete with mutating forms of political, economic, military, educational, and epistemological colonialism, indigenous knowledge comes to be viewed by the agents of empire as a threat to Euro/Americentrism and/or as a commodity to be exploited.

This chapter explores the educational and epistemological value of indigenous knowledge in the larger effort to expand a form of critical multilogicality—an effort to act educationally and politically on the calls for diversity and justice that have echoed through the halls of academia over the past several decades. Such an effort seeks an intercultural/interracial effort to question the hegemonic and oppressive aspects of Western education and to work for justice and self-direction for indigenous peoples around the world. In this critical multilogical context, the purpose of indigenous education and the production of indigenous knowledge does not involve "saving" indigenous people but helping construct conditions that allow for indigenous self-sufficiency while learning from the vast storehouse of indigenous knowledges that provide compelling insights into all domains of human endeavor.

By the term *indigenous knowledge*, we are referring to a multidimensional body of understandings that have—especially since the beginnings of the European scientific revolution of the 17th and 18th centuries—been viewed by Euroculture as inferior and primitive. For the vast numbers of indigenous peoples from North America, South America, Australia, New Zealand, Africa, Asia, Oceania, and parts of Europe, indigenous knowledge is a lived-world form of reason that informs and sustains people who make their homes in a local area. In such a context, such peoples have produced knowledges, epistemologies, ontologies, and cosmologies that construct ways of being and seeing in relationship to their physical surroundings. Such knowledges involve insights into plant and animal life, cultural dynamics, and historical information used to provide acumen in dealing with the challenges of contemporary existence.

Our use of this definition of indigenous knowledge accounts for the many complexities that surround the term and the issues it raises. We are aware of our privileged positionalities as Western scholars analyzing cultural, political, and epistemological dynamics as power inscribed as indigeneity and indigenous knowledge. In this complex context, we are aware that many problematize the term *indigenous* itself, as it appears to conflate numerous, separate groups of people whose histories and cultures may be profoundly divergent. Obviously, in this chapter, it is not our intent to essentialize or conflate diverse indigenous groups. It is important also to note that our definition of indigeneity and indigenous knowledge always takes into account the colonial/power dimensions of the political/epistemological relationship between the indigenous cosmos and the Western world. A critical dimension of the study of indigenous knowledge involves the insight indigenous peoples bring to the study of epistemology and research as colonized peoples (Dei & Kempf, 2006; Mutua & Swadener, 2004; G. H. Smith, 2000; L. T. Smith, 1999). In this context, the standpoint of colonized peoples on a geopolitics built on hierarchies, hegemony, and privilege is an invaluable resource in the larger effort to transform an unjust world.

The Unique Power of Indigenous Knowledge: Transformational Possibilities

We believe in the transformative power of indigenous knowledge, the ways that such knowledge can be used to foster empowerment and justice in a variety of cultural contexts. A key aspect of this transformative power involves the exploration of human consciousness, the nature of its production, and the process of its engagement with cultural difference. As Paulo Freire and Antonio Faundez (1989) argue, indigenous knowledge is a rich social resource for any justice-related attempt to bring about social change. In this context, indigenous ways of knowing become a central resource for the work of academics, whether they are professors in the universities, teachers in elementary and secondary schools, social workers, media analysts, and so on. Intellectuals, Freire and Faundez conclude, should "soak themselves in this knowledge . . . assimilate the feelings, the sensitivity" (p. 46) of epistemologies that move in ways unimagined by most Western academic impulses.

We find it pedagogically tragic that various indigenous knowledges of how action affects reality in particular locales have been dismissed from academic curricula. Such ways of knowing and acting could contribute so much to the educational experiences of all students, but because of the rules of evidence and the dominant epistemologies of Western knowledge production, such understandings are deemed irrelevant by the academic gatekeepers. Our intention is to challenge the academy and its "normal science" with the questions indigenous knowledges raise about the nature of our existence, our consciousness, our knowledge production, and the "globalized," imperial future that faces all peoples of the planet at this historical juncture.

Some indigenous educators and philosophers put it succinctly: We want to use indigenous knowledge to counter Western science's destruction of the Earth. Indigenous knowledge can facilitate this ambitious 21st-century project because of its tendency to focus on relationships of human beings to both one another and to their ecosystem. Such an emphasis on relationships has been notoriously absent in the knowledge produced in Western science over the past four centuries (Dei, 1994; Keith & Keith, 1993; Simonelli, 1994).

The stakes are high, as scholars the world over attempt to bring indigenous knowledge to the academy. Linking it to an educational reform that is part of a larger sociopolitical struggle, advocates for indigenous knowledge delineate the inseparability of academic reform, the reconceptualization of science, and struggles for justice and environmental protection. Ann Parrish (1999) maintains, for example, that an understanding of indigenous agricultural knowledge may be necessary to any successful contemporary effort to feed the world. The work that has taken place in the field of Native American and First Nations (Canadian) studies over the past couple of decades grants other advocates of indigenous knowledge a lesson in how such academic operations can be directly linked to political action. Indigenous/Aboriginal scholars use their indigenous analyses to inform a variety of Native American legal and political organizations, including the Indian Law Resource Center, the National Indian Youth Council, the World Council of Indigenous Peoples, and the United Nations Working Group on Indigenous Populations, to mention only a few.

In indigenous studies, such as the Native American academic programs, emerging new political awarenesses have been expressed in terms of the existence of a global Fourth World indigeneity. Proponents of such a view claim that Fourth World peoples share the commonality of domination and are constituted by indigenous groups as diverse as the native peoples of the Americas, the Innuit and Sammis of the Arctic north, the Māori of New Zealand, the Koori of Australia, the Karens and Katchins of Burma, the Kurds of Persia, the Bedouins of the African/Middle Eastern desert, many African tribal peoples, and even the Basques and Gaels of contemporary Europe. In this context, it is important to avoid the essentialist tendency to lump together all indigenous cultures as one, yet at the same time maintain an understanding of the nearly worldwide oppression of indigenous peoples and the destruction of indigenous languages and knowledges. We will address this complex dynamic throughout this chapter, pointing to the constant need for awareness of the ambiguous theme in all academic and political work involving indigenous peoples and their knowledges (Hess, 1995; Jaimes, 1987).

As complex as the question of indigeneity may be, we believe that the best interests of indigenous and nonindigenous peoples are served by the study of indigenous knowledges and epistemologies. An appreciation of indigenous epistemology, for example, provides Western peoples with another view of knowledge production in diverse cultural sites. Such a perspective holds transformative possibilities, as people from dominant cultures come to understand the overtly cultural processes by which information is legitimated and delimited. An awareness of the ways epistemological "truth production" operates in the lived world may shake the Western scientific faith in the Cartesian-Newtonian epistemological foundation as well as the certainty and ethnocentrism that often accompany it. Indeed, in such a meta-epistemological context, Westerners of diverse belief structures and vocational backgrounds may experience a fundamental transformation of both outlook and identity, resulting in a much more reflective and progressive consciousness. Such a consciousness would encounter the possibility that the de/legitimation of knowledge is more a sociopolitical process than an exercise of a universal form of disinterested abstract reason.

In this context, the Western analyst confronts the need to reassess the criteria for judging knowledge claims in light of the problems inherent in calling upon a transcultural, universal faculty of reason. Questioning and even rejecting absolute and transcendent Western reason does not mean that we are mired forever in a hell of relativism. One of the concepts Western analysts have learned in their encounters with non-Western knowledge systems is that Western certainty cannot survive, that the confrontation with difference out of necessity demands some degree of epistemological contingency. Universality cannot escape unscathed in its encounter with sociocultural, epistemological particularity, just as Newtonian physics could not survive the Einsteinian understanding of the power of different frames of reference. In these antifoundational (a rejection of a transcultural referent for truth such as the Western scientific method) dynamics, the hell of relativism is avoided by an understanding of culturally specific discursive practices.

For example, the indigenous knowledge produced by the Chagga people in Tanzania can be both true and just in relation to the discursive practices of the Chagga culture (Mosha, 2000). The Chagga criteria for truth make no claim for universality and would not feign to determine truth claims for various other cultural groups around the world. Thus, Chagga truth as a contingent, local epistemology would not claim power via its ability to negate or validate knowledge produced in non-Chagga cultures. Such an epistemological issue holds profound social and political implications, for it helps determine the power relations between diverse cultural groups. Culture A certainly gains an element of domination over Cultures B and C, if it can represent its knowledge as transcendent truth and Cultures B's and C's knowledge as a "superstition." This is, of course, an example of the epistemological colonialism referenced above.

In this reconceptualized, antifoundational epistemological context, analysts must consider the process of knowledge production and truth claims in relation to the historical setting, cultural situatedness, and moral needs of the reality they confront. Such understandings do not negate our ability to act as political agents, but they do force us to consider our political and pedagogical actions in a more tentative and culturally informed manner. In this new reconfigured context, we no longer possess the privilege of simply turning to the authority of "civilization" for validation of the "unqualified methods of truth production." Such a position removes some simplistic certainty but at the same time provides great possibility for Western and indigenous people to enter into a profound transformative negotiation around the complexity of these issues and concepts—a negotiation that demands no final, end-of-history resolution.

▣ Indigenous Knowledge in Critical Multilogical Contexts: The Benefits to Individuals From Dominant Euro/Americentric Cultures

Our point here is on one level quite simple—humans need to encounter multiple perspectives in all dimensions of their lives. This concept of multilogicality is central to our understanding of indigenous knowledges. I (Joe Kincheloe) have expanded these notions in my extension of Denzin and Lincoln's (2000) description of the research bricolage. A complex science is grounded on this multilogicality. One of the reasons we use the term *complex* is that the more we understand about the world, the more complex it appears to be. In this recognition of complexity, we begin to see multiple causations and the possibility of differing vantage points from which to view a phenomenon. It is extremely important to note that the context from which one observes an entity shapes what he or she sees—the concept of standpoint epistemology delineated by Sandra Harding (1998) and many other feminist theorists. Here the assumptions or the system of meaning making the observer consciously or unconsciously employs shape the observation.

This assertion is not some esoteric, academic point—it shapes social analysis, political perspectives, knowledge production, and action in the world. Acting upon this understanding, we understand that scholarly observations hold more within them to be analyzed than first impressions sometimes reveal. In this sense, different frames of reference produce multiple interpretations and multiple realities. The mundane, the everyday, the social, cultural, and psychological dimensions of human life are multiplex and continuously unfolding—while this is taking place, human interpretation is simultaneously constructing and reconstructing the meaning of what we observe. A multilogical epistemology and ontology promotes a spatial distancing from reality that allows an observer diverse frames of reference.

The distancing may range from the extremely distant, like astronauts looking at the Earth from the moon, to the extremely close, like Georgia O'Keeffe viewing a flower. At the same time, a multilogical scholar values the intimacy of an emotional connectedness that allows empathetic passion to draw knower and known together. In the multiplex, complex, and critical view of reality, Western linearity often gives way to simultaneity, as texts become a kaleidoscope of images filled with signs, symbols, and signifiers to be decoded and interpreted. William Carlos Williams illustrated an understanding of such complexity in the early 20th century as he depicted multiple, simultaneous images and frames of reference in his poetry. Williams attempted to poetically interpret Marcel Duchamp's "Nude Descending a Staircase," with its simultaneous, overlapping representations serving as a model for what postformalists call a cubist cognition.

Teachers and scholars informed by this critical multilogicality understand these concepts. Such educators and researchers work to extend their students' cognitive abilities, as they create situations where students come to view the world and disciplinary knowledge from as many frames of reference as possible. In a sense, the single photograph of Cartesian thinking is replaced by the multiple angles of the holographic photograph. Energized by this cubist cognition, educators come to understand that the models of teaching they have been taught, the definitions of inquiry with which they have been supplied, the angle from which they have been instructed to view intelligence, and the modes of learning that shape what they perceive to be sophisticated thinking all reflect a particular vantage point in the web of reality. They seek more than one perspective—they seek multilogical insights. Of course, in such a context, one can discern the value of indigenous knowledges to such pedagogues.

Like reality itself, schools and classrooms are complex matrices of interactions, codes, and signifiers in which both students and teachers are interlaced. Just as a complex and critical pedagogy asserts that there is no single, privileged way to see the world, there is no one way of representing the world artistically, no one way of teaching science, no one way of writing history. Once teachers escape the entrapment of the positivist guardians of Western tradition and their monocultural, one-truth way of seeing, they come to value and thus pursue new frames of reference in regard to their students, classrooms, and workplaces. In this cognitivist cubist spirit, critical multilogical teachers begin to look at lessons from the perspectives of individuals from different race, class, gender, and sexual orientations. They study the perspectives their indigenous, African American, Latino, White, poor, and wealthy students bring to their classrooms. They are dedicated to the search for new perspectives.

Drawing on this critical multilogicality in this pedagogical pursuit, these educators, like liberation theologians in Latin America, make no apology for seeking the viewpoints, insights, and sensitivities of the marginalized. The way to see from a perspective differing from that of the positivist guardians involves exploring an institution such as Western education from the vantage point of those who have been marginalized by it. In such a process, subjugated and indigenous knowledges once again emerge allowing teachers to gain the cognitive power of empathy—a power that enables them to take pictures of reality from different vantage points. The intersection of these diverse vantage points allows for a form of analysis that moves beyond the isolated, decontextualized, and fragmented analysis of positivist reductionism.

Cognitively empowered by these multiplex perspectives, complexity-sensitive, multilogical educators seek a multicultural dialogue between Eastern cultures and Western cultures, a conversation between the relatively wealthy Northern cultures and the impoverished Southern cultures, and an intracultural interchange among a variety of subcultures. In this way, forms of knowing, representing, and making meaning that have been excluded by the positivist West move us to new vantage points and unexplored planetary perspectives. Understandings derived from the perspective of the excluded or the "culturally different" allow for an appreciation of the nature of justice, the invisibility of the process of oppression, the power of difference, and the insight to be gained from a recognition of divergent cultural uses of long hidden knowledges that highlight both our social construction as individuals and the limitations of monocultural ways of meaning making.

Taking advantage of these complex ways of seeing, a whole new world is opened to educators and scholars. As cognitive cubists, teachers, students, psychologists, and cultural analysts all come to understand that there are always multiple perspectives; no conversation is over, no discipline totally complete. The domain of art and aesthetics helps us appreciate this concept, as it exposes new dimensions of meaning, new forms of logic unrecognized by the sleepwalking dominant culture. As a cognitive wake-up call, art can challenge what Herbert Marcuse (1955), in *Eros and Civilization,* called "the prevailing principle of reason" (p. 185). In this context, we come to realize that art and other aesthetic productions provide an alternate epistemology, a way of knowing that moves beyond declarative forms of knowledge. Here we see clearly the power of multilogicality and the bricolage: Educational psychologists gain new insights into the traditional concerns of their academic domain by looking outside the frameworks of one discipline. It could be quantum physics, it could be history, or, as in this case, it could be art and aesthetics.

▣ The Study of Indigenous Knowledge for Social Change: Making Sure the Interests of Indigenous People Are Served

The transformation of Western consciousness via its encounter with multilogicality vis-à-vis indigenous knowledges takes on much of its importance in relation to a more humble and empathetic Western perspective toward indigenous peoples and their understandings of the world. Such a new perspective will manifest itself in a greater awareness of neocolonialism and other Western social practices that harm indigenous peoples. It will be the responsibility of social and political activists all over the world to translate these awarenesses into concrete political actions that benefit indigenous people. While in no way advocating that Western peoples speak and act for indigenous peoples, it is important for indigenous peoples to have informed allies outside their local communities. Such allies can play an important role in helping indigenous peoples deal with the cultural, psychological, and environmental devastation of traditional colonialism and neocolonialism.

In the Republic of Congo (formerly Zaire), for example, before the advent of Western colonialism, local peoples lived in what has been described as a "cereal civilization." In this agricultural society, individuals sowed grain in a land that could easily support good harvests. When the European colonists arrived, however, they destroyed the land to the point that it could no longer sustain the cereal way of life (Freire & Faundez, 1989). With their land and their civilization in shambles, what were the indigenous peoples to do? In this case and many others, Westerners cannot simply say, "Let the Congolese tribesmen reclaim and redeploy their indigenous agricultural and social practices and solve their problems in their own way." Traditional knowledge has been lost and worldviews have been shattered. Questions of cultural renewal and indigenous knowledge are not as easy as some represent them to be.

In these (yet again) complex circumstances, we examine the ways the indigenous knowledge studies advocated here can facilitate indigenous people's struggle against the ravages of colonialism, especially its neocolonialist articulation in the domains of the political, economic, and pedagogical. Scholars conversant with the transformative dynamics of the multilogical epistemological insights emerging from the critical confrontation with indigenous ways of seeing will be far less likely to formulate, for example, anthropological studies of indigeneity in traditional unreflective ways. One of the criteria for anthropological studies in a reconceptualized Western social science would involve the relevance and benefits of the work for the indigenous group studied. In this reconceived anthropology, research methodologies could be adjusted to account for the interests of indigenous subjects.

An important aspect of such a transformed social science would involve the pedagogical task of affirming indigenous perspectives, in the process reversing the disaffirmations of the traditional Western, social scientific project. Operating in this manner, social scientists could make use of a variety of previously excluded local knowledges (Sponsel, 1992). Such knowledges could be deployed to rethink the meaning of development in numerous locales where various marginalized peoples reside. Using such knowledges, indigenous peoples—with the help of outside political allies to facilitate their fight against further neocolonial encroachments—could move closer to the possibility of solving their problems in their own ways. The possibility of some magical return to an uncontaminated precolonial past, however, does not exist. Thus, the use of indigenous knowledge as the basis of local problem-solving strategies will always have to deal with the reality of colonization, not to mention the effects of the economic globalization that will continue to challenge indigenous peoples. Resistance to such powerful neocolonial movements will need all the transformative knowledges and political allies it can get.

▣ The Road of Good Intentions: Western Scholars and Their Efforts to Help Indigenous Peoples

Western scholars and cultural workers concerned with the plight of indigenous peoples and their knowledges are faced with a set of dilemmas. Not only must they avoid essentialism and its accompanying romanticization of the indigene, but they must also sidestep the traps that transform their attempts at facilitation into further marginalization. Walking the well-intentioned road to hell, Western scholars dedicated to the best interests of indigenous peoples often unwittingly participate in the Western hegemonic process. The question, "How can the agency, the self-direction of indigenous peoples be enhanced?" must constantly be asked by Western allies. What is the difference between a celebration of indigenous knowledge and an appropriation? Too often, Western allies, for example, do not simply want to work with indigenous peoples—they want to transform their identities and become indigenous persons themselves. As a teacher and researcher on the Rosebud Sioux Reservation in South Dakota, I (Joe) watched this "wannabe" phenomenon play out on numerous occasions. As White allies worked out their identity crises in the indigenous cultural context, they appropriated not only the cultural styles of the Sioux but many times claimed their "oppression capital"—the "status" of marginality among proponents of social justice. Ironically, the counter-hegemonic label of an "FBI" (full-blooded Indian) was a clever double-consciousness description that not only pointed to federal interference but to the non-Indian Whites who attempted to claim Indian status. This phenomenon plays itself out continually within the wigger tradition as non-Blacks appropriate the discourse, dress, and cultural manner of African Americans, even going so far as to claim the disenfranchisement of Blacks.

Such a vampirism sucked the blood of indigenous suffering out of the veins of the Native Americans/Canadians, in the process contributing little to the larger cause of social justice. The only struggle in which many of these vampires engaged was a personal quest for a new identity. Sioux leaders recognized this tendency and in our conversations referred to it as "playing Indian." Such an activity was viewed by tribal members with contempt and condescension. The Sioux, like other indigenous peoples, understood the dangers of Western "help." In this context, the following question must be asked: Is the study of indigenous peoples and their knowledges in itself a process of Europeanization? In some ways, of course, it is, as Western intellectuals conceptualize indigenous knowledge in contexts far removed from its production. In other ways, however, Western intellectuals have little choice; if they are to operate as agents of justice, they must understand the dynamics at work in the world of indigenous people. To refuse to operate out of fear of Europeanization reflects a view of indigenous culture as an authentic, uncontaminated artifact that must be hermetically preserved regardless of the needs of living indigenous people (Ashcroft, Griffiths, & Tiffin, 1995; Howard, 1995).

The process of Europeanization, with its colonialist perspectives toward indigenous knowledge, continues to operate despite both insightful and misguided attempts to thwart it. In this context, ethnocentric Western science claims a value for indigenous ways of seeing as an "ethnoscience." Western scientists maintain that much can be learned from a number of ethnosciences, including ethnobotany, ethnopharmacology, ethnomedicine, ethnocosmology, and ethnoastronomy. The concept discursively situates indigenous knowledge systems as ways of knowing that are culturally grounded, simultaneously representing Western science as "not culturally grounded" or transcultural and universal. Thus, in the process of ascribing worth to indigenous knowledge, such analysis implicitly relegates it to a lower order of knowledge production. Also, to speak of indigenous knowledge systems in Western terms such as botany, pharmacology, medicine, and so on is to inadvertently fragment knowledge systems in ways that subvert the holism of indigenous ways of understanding the world (Hess, 1995).

In this Western gaze, indigenous knowledge is tacitly decontextualized, severed of the cultural connections that grant it meaning to its indigenous producers, archived and classified in Western databases, and eventually used in scientific projects that may operate against the interests of indigenous peoples. All of this takes place in the name of Western scientific concessions to the importance of the information generated by local peoples. Arun Agrawal (1995) labels this archival project as *ex situ* conservation—a process that removes it from people's lives. Such indigenous knowledge is always changing in relation to the changing needs of its producers; ex situ conservation destroys the dynamic quality of such information. Despite their overt valorization of indigenous knowledge, these Western scientific archivists refuse to accept the worthiness of "raw" indigenous knowledge—upon collection, Western scientists insist on testing its validity via Western scientific testing. As Marcel Viergever (1999) maintains, this archival project and the scientific validation that accompanies it illustrate the Western disregard of the need to protect and perpetuate the cultural systems that produce dynamic indigenous knowledge. In this context, the Western proclamations of valorization ring hollow.

The Burden of Essentialism in the Study of Indigenous Knowledge

We continue to struggle with the problems inherent in the study of indigenous knowledge. How do we deal with the understandable tendency within indigenous studies to lapse into essentialism? Before answering that question, a brief discussion of essentialism is in order. Essentialism is a complex concept that is commonly understood as the belief that a set of unchanging properties (essences) delineates the construction of a particular category—for example, indigenous people, African Americans, White people, women, and so on. Addressing the problem of essentialism is a complex but necessary step in the study of indigenous knowledge. While there is no problem examining indigenous people/knowledge *as a discrete category,* we must always be careful to avoid racial or ethnic designations that fail to discern the differences between people included in a specific category. Cultural anthropology in its traditional effort to name and categorize indigeneity has produced a notion of essentialist authenticity that is now difficult to question.

In an indigenous context, this essentialist authenticity involves a semiotic of the prehistoric. Such a signification inscribes indigeneity as a historical artifact far removed from contemporary life. Activities or identities thus that fall outside of this narrow backward-looking classification are deemed unauthentic, impure, or phony. Indigenous knowledge in this essentialist configuration is caught in the prehistoric, stationary, and unchanging web that is ever separate from nonindigenous information. Indigeneity in this context becomes romanticized to the point of helpless innocence. Paulo Freire and Antonio Faundez (1989) warn us that our appreciation of indigenous peoples and their knowledges must avoid the tendency for romanticization. When advocates for indigenous peoples buy into such romanticization, they often attempt to censor "alien" presences and restore the indigene to a pure precolonial cosmos. Such a return is impossible, as all cultures (especially colonized ones) are perpetually in a state of change. The Aborigines of Australia, for example, were profoundly influenced by Indonesian peoples and vice versa. The premise that indigenous peoples were isolated from the rest of the world until European conquest and colonization is a myth that must be buried along with other manifestations of essentialist purity (Agrawal, 1995; Ashcroft et al., 1995; Goldie, 1995; Hall, 1995; Mudrooroo, 1995; Pieterse & Parekh, 1995).

Without such a burial, indigenous cultures are discouraged from shifting and adapting, and indigenous knowledges are viewed simply as sacred relics fixed in a decontextualized netherland. Any study of indigenous knowledge in the academy must allow for its evolution and ever changing relationship to Eurocentric scientific and educational practice. The essentialized approach undermines this relational dynamic, as it encodes indigeneity as freedom/nature and European culture as culture/reason—here, no room for dialogue exists. Our examination of indigenous knowledge attempts to enlarge the space for such dialogue, denying the assertion of many analysts that European and indigenous ways of seeing are totally antithetical to one another. These cultural and epistemological issues are complex, and our concern is to avoid essentialist solutions by invoking simplistic binary oppositions between indigeneity and colonialism. Once the binary opposition is embraced, we have to choose one and dismiss the other—not only indigeneity and colonialism but also local knowledge or academic knowledge. In this dichotomous mode, either everything academic is of no worth or, from the other way of seeing, everything indigenous is primitive.

The either-or approach leaves little room for dialogue, little space to operate. Counteressentialist views of indigenous knowledge understand the circulation of culture, the reality of "contamination." In a more complex, anticolonialist anthropology, for example, cultures are no longer seen as self-contained social organisms but as interrelated networks of localities. In such an anthropology, the cultural position of the observer helps construct the description of such cultural dynamics. The focus of the ethnographies produced in this context moves away from finite cultural systems operating in equilibrium to networks shaped and reshaped by boundary transgressions. If the emphasis is on transgressions, then no one is culturally pure. Western knowledge, for example, reaches indigenous peoples in a variety of ways from mass communications to developmental projects. In this increasingly globalized world, transnational population movements, refugee diasporas, and multinational capital infusions disrupt traditional cultural systems.

Another aspect of the essentialist demarcations concerning indigeneity involves the assertion of a fixed and stable indigenous identity. In our multilogical understanding of indigenous knowledge, we maintain that all identities are historically constructed, always in process, constantly dealing with intersections involving categories of status, religion, race, class, and gender. Such a position is conceptually unsettling, we admit, with its denial of the possibility of some final freedom from the cultural ambiguities that shape consciousness and subjectivity. If all of this were not enough, we question the essentialist assertion that there is a natural category of "indigenous persons." Indeed, there is great diversity within the label *indigenous people*. The indigenous cultural experience is not the same for everybody; indigenous knowledge is not a monolithic epistemological concept. In this context, the uncomfortable problem of cultural hybridity emerges. We will discuss this dynamic in more detail later, but suffice it to say here, many advocates of indigenous knowledge resent the use of the term *hybridity* and find it inappropriate in indigenous studies.

Concerned with the use of indigenous knowledge in education, we use our counteressentialist understandings to argue that there is no unitary indigenous curriculum to be factually delivered to students in various locations. Not everyone who identifies with a particular indigenous culture produces knowledge the same way, nor do different indigenous cultures produce the same knowledges. Even after delineating counteressentialist arguments, however, we still believe that the study of indigenous knowledge is valuable and that there may be some common threads running through many indigenous knowledge systems. A central feature of our work with indigenous knowledge in the academy involves exploring the political and curricular implications of the ways many indigenous cultures (a) relate to their habitat in ways that are harmonious, (b) have been conquered by a colonialist nation-state, and (c) provide a perspective on human experience that differs from Western empirical science (Apffel-Marglin, 1995; Appiah, 1995; Dei, 1994; Hall, 1995; Hess, 1995; Jaimes, 1987).

These features tell us that indigenous knowledge deserves analysis on a global level with particular attention directed to the epistemological patterns that emerge in a variety of cultural contexts. Such studies, we believe, are often so powerful that new understandings of the world appear and reinterpretations of "the way things are" materialize. Similarities between African, Native American/Canadian, Chinese, and even feminist views of the relationship between self and world provide us with fascinating new ways of making sense of realities and compelling topics for intercultural conversations (Kloppenberg, 1991). Our counteressentialist imperatives must always be understood within the framework of our valuing the diverse perspectives of indigenous peoples and our understanding of the continuing marginalization of their cultures and their perspectives. Indigenous studies may be problematic and complex, but educators will be well served to examine its provocative themes in light of the Western Enlightenment project, Euro/American colonialism, and its epistemological and pedagogical expressions.

Having made this antiessentialist argument, it is still important to note that within indigenous communities, the concept of essentialism is sometimes employed in ways significantly different than in the anti/postcolonial critical discourses of transgressive academics around the globe. Finding themselves in disempowered positions where they have to worry about basic human rights and survival, many indigenous peoples have claimed essential cultural characteristics for not only strategic purposes but also in relation to spiritual dynamics involved with one's genealogical connection to the Earth and its animate and (in Western ontologies) inanimate entities. Here the importance of geographical place in the construction of indigeneity is manifested in ways the land, flora and fauna, natural resources, and numerous other dynamics are integrated into indigenous identity. No discussion of essentialism vis-à-vis indigeneity should fail to account for these unique dimensions of indigenous life (G. H. Smith, 2000; L. T. Smith, 1999).

▣ Insurrections: Indigenous Knowledge as a Subjugated Knowledge

While operating at a far more subtle and sanitized manner in the contemporary era, epistemological tyranny still functions in the academy to undermine efforts to include other ways of knowing and knowledge production in the curriculum—it subverts multilogicality. The power issues here are naked and visible to all who want to look through the epistemological glory hole: The power struggle involves who is allowed to proclaim truth and to establish the procedures by which truth is to be established; it also involves who holds the power to determine what knowledge is of most worth and should be included in academic curricula. In this context, the notion of indigenous knowledge as a "subjugated knowledge" emerges to describe its marginalized relationship to Western epistemological and curricular power. The use of the term *subjugated knowledge* asserts the centrality of power in any study of indigenous knowledge and any effort to include it in the academy. Despite all the debates about what constitutes indigenous knowledge and separates it from scientific knowledge, one constant emerges: All indigenous knowledge is subjugated by Western science and its episteme (its rules for determining truth).

Irregardless of what area in the world it is found, indigenous knowledge has been produced by peoples facing diseases brought by European cultures, attempts at genocide, cultural assimilation, land appropriation, required emigration, and education as a colonial tool. Because of such oppressive processes, indigenous knowledge has, not surprisingly, often been hidden from history. It is our desire to become researchers of such repressed knowledges, to search out what Western and Western-influenced academics have previously neglected, to recover materials that may often work to change our consciousness in profound ways. When Western epistemologies are viewed in light of indigenous perspectives, Western ways of seeing, Western education, cannot remain the same. Analyzing these power dynamics surrounding indigenous knowledge, Gelsa Knijnik (1999) warns of their complexity and the need for the student of indigenous knowledge to explore the many ways power operates in the interactions of indigeneity, science, and epistemology.

In the reconceptualized academic curriculum that we imagine, indigenous/subjugated knowledge is not passed along as a new canon but becomes a living body of knowledge open to multiple interpretations. Viewed in its relationship to the traditional curriculum, subjugated knowledge is employed as a constellation of concepts that challenge the invisible cultural assumptions embedded in all aspects of schooling and knowledge production. Such subjugated knowledge contests dominant cultural views of reality, as it informs individuals from the White, middle/upper-middle-class mainstream that there are different ways of viewing the world. Indeed, individuals from such backgrounds begin to realize that their textbooks and curriculum have discarded data produced by indigenous peoples. The White dominant cultural power blocs that dominate contemporary Western societies reject the need to listen to marginalized people and take their knowledge seriously. Western/American power wielders are not good at listening to information that does not seem to contribute to hegemony, their ability to win the consent of the subjugated to their governance. Knowledge that emerges from and serves the purposes of the subjugated is often erased by dominant power wielders, as they make it appear dangerous and pathological to other citizens (Dion-Buffalo & Mohawk, 1993).

Many scholars, Graham Hingangaroa Smith (2000) in particular, have written about the labeling of indigenous peoples and indigenous knowledges. While is it vital that we understand the nature of oppression of indigenous peoples and the subjugation of their knowledges, it is also crucial that students of indigeneity and indigenous knowledge not see them only through the lens of subjugation. African American literary and aesthetic scholar Albert Murray (1996) agrees with Smith's point, maintaining that viewing an oppressed culture only in terms of its oppression unwittingly tends to reproduce and exacerbate the dynamics of disempowerment. Taking his cue from the African American blues aesthetic, Murray writes of the ability to acknowledge the pain of oppression at the same time we celebrate the genius of our cultural productions. Indigenous peoples with whom I have worked possess their own version of Murray's blues aesthetic.

In the years I (Joe Kincheloe) have worked with the peoples of the Rosebud Sioux Reservation in South Dakota, I have often observed the irreverent humor of tribal members making fun of the oppression they have faced. I find their ability to celebrate those dimensions of their culture that bring them great joy in the midst of tragedy to be profoundly informative to academics working in the area. Because of the gravitas surrounding the study of the oppression of indigenous peoples, the idea of celebration or laughter in a context where subjugation has occurred is viewed very negatively in many academic situations. Here is a space where we begin to understand the profound importance of Smith's and Murray's call to not simply view and name indigenous peoples as "the oppressed."

No doubt the dance connecting the celebration of the affirmative dimensions of indigenous cultures, engaging in humor in the midst of pain, and fighting against mutating forms of colonial oppression is a delicate and nuanced art form—but it is one worth learning. In this complex space, we begin to understand the value of understanding and developing multiple ways of viewing the power and agency of indigenous peoples and the brilliant knowledges they produce. Those of us who do not come from indigenous backgrounds learn to listen quietly in such contexts, in the process learning much about the indigene, the tacit privileges that accrue from coming from the world of the colonizers and the cosmos in general.

Thus, critical multilogical educators devoted to the value of subjugated knowledges uncover those dangerous memories that are involved in reconstructing the process through which the consciousness of various groups and individuals has come to be constructed. Such awareness frees teachers, students, and other individuals to claim an identity apart from the one forced upon them. Indeed, identity is constructed when submerged memories are aroused—in other words, confrontation with dangerous memory changes our perceptions of the forces that shape us, which in turn moves us to redefine our worldviews, our ways of seeing. The oppressive forces that shape us have formed the identities of both the powerful and the exploited. Without an analysis of this process, we will never understand why students succeed or fail in school; we will be forever blind to the tacit ideological forces that construct student perceptions of school and the impact such perceptions have on their school experiences. Such blindness restricts our view of our own and other people's perceptions of their place in history, in the web of reality. When history is erased and decontextualized, teachers, students, and other citizens are rendered vulnerable to the myths employed to perpetuate social domination.

In this multilogical context informed by indigenous knowledge, historians and other educational researchers enter a new domain of understanding and practice. In this zone of critical multilogicality, such scholars, if they are operating in North America, work in solidarity with Asians, Africans, Latin Americans, indigenous peoples, and subcultures within their own societies. In their "interracialism" and "interculturalism," they understand that there is far more to history than the socially constructed notion that civilization began in ancient Greece, migrated to Europe, and reached its zenith in the contemporary United States. In histories and other scholarly work that emerge in various fields, this assumption exists in an influential and unchallenged state. Critical multilogical scholars informed by indigenous knowledge challenge this monological Eurocentrism and search for the ways it insidiously inscribes knowledge production. At this point, researchers look for various forms of subjugated indigenous knowledge both as a focus for historical research and for their epistemological and ontological insights. Not only do we learn about such knowledges and the cultures that produced them, but we also use their ways of seeing and being to challenge Western monological perspectives. Here critical multilogical researchers use indigenous perspectives to question reductionist notions of epistemological objectivity and superficially validated "facts" that have for centuries been used to oppress indigenous peoples and degrade the value of their knowledges.

Historiographical multilogicality (Villaverde, Kincheloe, & Helyar, 2006) is a break from the class elitist, White-centered, colonial, patriarchal histories that have dominated Western historiography for too long. While many successful efforts have been made to get beyond elite, White, male history and other forms of knowledge, critical historians sensitive to the value of indigenous knowledge want to go farther—they want to understand the colonial impulses that work to exclude important insights into the social, cultural, historical, political, philosophical, psychological, and educational domains provided by indigenous peoples. Learning from previously dishonored indigenous knowledges, African, Islamic, Asian, and Latin American philosophies of history, critical historians, for example, learn new ways of practicing their craft. Those peoples who have suffered under existing political economic and social arrangements are central to the project of critical historiography. Because those who have suffered the most may not have left written records—the bread and butter of traditional historiographical source material—critical historians employ oral history and other research methods that grant voice to indigenous peoples while learning from and validating indigenous insights lost to traditional history.

Linda Tuhiwai Smith (1999) provides valuable insights into these issues of subjugated knowledges vis-à-vis historiography and other research methods. A central dimension of self-determination for indigenous peoples, she contends, has entailed questions related to indigenous histories and an analysis of how otherized indigenous peoples have been represented in traditional Western historiography. Indigenous historiography informs a critical multilogical view of the past because all indigenous history is, as Smith argues, "a *re*writing and *re*righting [of] our position in history" (p. 28). As indigenous peoples tell their stories and rethink their histories, it is the duty of critical multilogical historians to listen carefully and respectfully. In this process, historians from around the world can become not only better allies in the indigenous struggle against colonial subjugation, for social justice, and for self-determination. In the process, they also become better historians. Smith makes her point in a compelling manner:

> It is not simply about giving an oral account or a genealogical naming of the land and the events which raged over it, but a very powerful need to give testimony to and restore a spirit, to bring back into existence a world fragmented and dying. The sense of history conveyed by these approaches is not the same thing as the discipline of history, and so our accounts collide, crash into each other. (p. 28)

Indigenous Knowledge and Academic Transformation

In light of these insights, the following is an outline of the educational benefits to be gained from an analysis of academic practices vis-à-vis indigenous/subjugated knowledges. Keeping in mind both old and new ways Western researchers have appropriated indigenous knowledges for their own enrichment, the promoters of the educational benefits of indigenous knowledges are ever aware of the possibility of exploitation. To avoid such exploitive appropriation of indigenous wisdom, critical researchers should adhere to a strict set of ethics devoted to the self-determination of indigenous peoples; an awareness of the complex, ever evolving ways that colonialism oppresses them; the intercultural nature of all research and analysis of indigenous knowledge; and the dedication to use indigenous knowledge in ways that lead to political, epistemological, and ontological changes that support the expressed goals of the indigene. With these caveats in mind, the research and curricular use of such knowledges:

1. *Promotes rethinking our purposes as educators.* An understanding of indigenous ways of seeing as a subjugated knowledge alerts us to the fact that multilogicality exists—there are multiple perspectives of human and physical phenomena. With this understanding in mind, it becomes apparent that school and university curricula privilege particular views of the world. Those who hold Western views of the world and value them over all others are often deemed "intelligent" by positivist methods of measuring intellectual capabilities. According to mainstream Western educational psychology and cognitive science, the way of knowing ascribed to "rational man" constitutes the highest level of human thought. This rationality or logic is best exemplified in symbolic logic, mathematics, and scientific reasoning. With the birth of modernity (the Age of Reason) and its scientific method in the 17th and 18th centuries, scientific knowledge became the only game in the academic town. In this context, individuals can be represented in a dramatic new form—as abstracted entities standing outside the forces of history and culture. This abstract individualism eclipsed the Western understanding of how men and women are shaped by larger social forces that affect individuals from different social locations in different ways.

Western society was caught in a mode of perception that limited thinking to concepts that stay within White, Western, logocentric boundaries, far away from the "No Trespassing" signs of indigeneity. As academics begin to uncover these hidden values embedded in both prevailing definitions of intelligence and our scientific instruments that measure it, they embark on a journey into the excitement of a pedagogy that takes indigenous knowledges seriously. As they begin to search for forms of intelligence that fall outside traditional notions of abstract reasoning, they come to appreciate the multiple forms of intelligence that different individuals possess. In this context, academic analysts become detectives of intelligence, searching the world for valuable ways of making sense of the world. Operating this way, educational purpose cannot remain static, as academics explore the relationship between differing epistemologies and the knowledges they support. The purpose of schools no longer simply involves the transmission of validated Western information from teacher to student. Instead, a more compelling form of analysis is initiated with teachers engaging students in the interpretation of various knowledges and modes of knowledge production.

2. *Focuses attention on the ways knowledge is produced and legitimated.* As we have maintained throughout this chapter, the study of indigenous knowledges that we advocate is concerned with the process of knowledge production. Such an awareness is too often absent in Western education. In mainstream pedagogies, we are taught to believe that the knowledge we consider official and valid has been produced in a neutral, noble, and altruistic manner. Such a view dismisses the cultural and power-related dimensions of knowledge production. Knowledge of any form will always confront other knowledge forms. When this happens, a power struggle ensues; the decisions made in struggles between, for example, indigenous and Eurocentric views of colonialism exert dramatic but often unseen consequences in schools and the political domain. For example, the role of the academic as a neutral transmitter of prearranged facts is not understood as a politicized role accompanying knowledge production.

If schools are to become places that promote teacher and student empowerment, then the notion of what constitutes politicization will have to be reconceptualized. Battle with texts as a form of research, Ira Shor and Paulo Freire (1987) exhort educators. Resist the demand of the official curriculum for deference to texts, they argue in line with their larger, critically grounded political vision. Can it be argued that capitulation to textual authority constitutes political neutrality?

In this indigenously informed curriculum, educators and their students come to appreciate the need to analyze what they know, how they come to know it, why they believe or reject it, and how they evaluate the credibility of the evidence. Starting at this point, they begin to understand the social construction of knowledge and truth. In school, for example, they recognize that the taken-for-granted knowledges that are taught do not find justification as universal truth. Instead, they appreciate the fact that the purveyors of such information have won a long series of historical and political struggles over whose knowledge and ways of producing knowledge are the best. Thus, educators are able to uncover the socially created hierarchies that travel incognito as truth. Though everyone knows their nature, these hierarchies mask their "shady" backgrounds of political conflict. As truth, they are employed as rationales for cultural dominance and unequal power relations.

3. *Encourages the construction of just and inclusive academic spheres.* Indigenous/subjugated knowledges are not seen here as mere curricular add-ons that provide diversity and spice to Western academic institutions. Curricular reforms based on our analysis of indigenous knowledge require that educators become hermeneuts (scholars and teachers who structure their work and teaching around an effort to help students and other individuals to make sense of the world around them) and epistemologists (scholars and teachers who seek to expose how accepted knowledge came to be validated). Such educators bring a new dimension to the academy, as they use subjugated

knowledges to reconceptualize the practices of the academy, to uncover the etymology (origin) of its inclusions and exclusions, notions of superiority and inferiority, racism, and ethnocentrism. This historical dynamic is extremely important in the context of subjugated knowledge. Antonio Gramsci (1988) noted that philosophy cannot be understood apart from the history of philosophy; nor can culture and education be grasped outside the history of culture. Our conception of self, world, and education, therefore, can only become critical when we appreciate the historical nature of its formulation. We are never independent of the social and historical forces that surround us—we are all caught at a particular point in the web of reality. One of the most important aspects of subjugated knowledge is that it is a way of seeing that helps us to expose the fingerprints of power in existing academic knowledge. Subjugated knowledge, by its mere existence, proves to us that there are alternatives to knowledge produced within the boundaries of Western science.

4. *Produces new levels of insight.* Keeping in mind the dangers of essentialist readings of indigenous knowledge, we see such perspectives as subjugated knowledges that are local, life experience based, and non-Western science produced. Such knowledge is transmitted over time by individuals from a particular geographical or cultural locality. Indigenous ways of knowing help people to cope with their sociological and agricultural environments and are passed down from generation to generation. A curriculum that values subjugated knowledge in general realizes that indigenous knowledge is important not only for the culture that produced it but also for people from different cultures. Only now in the first decade of the 21st century are European peoples beginning to appreciate the value of indigenous knowledge about health, medicine, agriculture, philosophy, ecology, and education. Traditionally, these were the very types of knowledge European education tried to discredit and eradicate. Of course, unfortunately, the Western valuing of such knowledges emerges from a recognition of its monetary value in global markets.

A critical multilogical education sees a variety of purposes for the inclusion of indigenous knowledges in the school and university curriculum. Since indigenous knowledges do not correspond to Western notions of discrete bodies or practices of data, they must be approached with an understanding of their ambiguity and contextual embeddedness. Thus, any effort to understand or use such knowledges cannot be separated from the worldviews and epistemologies embraced by their producers. The confrontation with such non-Western ways of seeing moves the power of difference to a new level of utility, as it exposes the hidden worldviews and epistemologies of Westerners unaccustomed to viewing culture—their own and other cultural forms—at this level. In this context, the critical multicultural encounter with indigenous knowledge raises epistemological questions relating to the production and consumption of knowledge, the subtle connections between culture and what is defined as successful learning, the contestation of all forms of knowledge production, and the definition of education itself. An awareness of the intersection between subjugated ways of knowing and indigenous knowledge opens a conversation between the "north" and the "south," that is, between so-called developed and developing societies. Critical educators seek to use their awareness of this valuable intersection to produce new forms of global consciousness and intercultural solidarity.

5. *Demands that educators at all academic levels become researchers.* Contrary to the pronouncement of reactionary protectors of the Western academic status quo, a subjugated/indigenous knowledge-informed curriculum pushes education to achieve more rigor and higher pedagogical expectations. In the schools we envision, teachers and students understand multiple epistemologies, possess secondary and primary research skills, and can interpret the meaning of information from a variety of perspectives. In positivist Eurocentric education, teachers learned to say, "Give me the truth and I will pass it along to students in the most efficient manner possible."

In the indigenously informed schools we advocate, teachers are encouraged to understand a variety of subjugated knowledges, to support themselves, to assert their freedom from Eurocentric all-knowing experts. Such teachers might say, "Please support me as I explore multiple ways of seeing and making sense of the world." In this context, such teachers are intimately familiar with the Western canon but refuse to accept without question its status as universal, as the only body of cultural knowledge worth knowing. Of course, in light of No Child Left Behind legislation with its standardized curriculum, ideological cleansing, and scripts for teachers, these calls take on a new urgency. Thus, as scholars of Western knowledge, non-Western knowledge, and subjugated and indigenous knowledges, such teachers are not content to operate in socioeducational frameworks often taken for granted. Such culturally and epistemologically informed educators seek to rethink and recontextualize questions that have been traditionally asked about schooling and knowledge production in general.

▣ Diverse Constructions of the World: Indigeneity and Epistemology

On one level, the critical multilogical analysis of indigenous knowledge is an examination of how different peoples construct the world. Of course, such an epistemological study cannot be conducted in isolation, for any analysis of indigenous knowledge brings up profound political, cultural, pedagogical, and ethical questions that interact with and help shape the epistemological domain. This is why the questions—what is indigenous knowledge, and why should we study it?—do not lend themselves to easy and concise answers. With our concern with essentialism in mind, we attempt to answer these complex questions. When we focus on the first question—what is indigenous knowledge?—several descriptors quickly come to mind. We explore such characterizations from a meta-analytical perspective, maintaining throughout a tentativeness and contingency that comes from our appreciation of diversity within the category of indigeneity.

June George (1999) posits that *indigenous knowledge* is a term that can be used to designate knowledges produced in a specific social context and employed by laypeople in their everyday lives. It is typically not generated, she argues, by a set of prespecified procedures or rules and is orally passed down from one generation to the next. Mahia Maurial (1999) emphasizes this everyday use of indigenous knowledge, pointing out that it lives in indigenous people's cultures—not in archives or laboratories. While George's and Maurial's assertions are not meant to deny the cultural locality of Western scientific knowledge, they do induce us to provide a definition for who qualifies as an indigenous person. The World Council of Indigenous Peoples maintains that such individuals occupied lands prior to populations who now share or claim such territories and possess a distinct language and culture. With only a few exceptional cases, dominant ethnic groups control nation-states in which the indigene live. As a result, indigenous peoples are relatively excluded from power and occupy the lowest rungs of the social ladder. We understand that sociocultural interaction between dominant groups and the indigene is inexorably increasing, and any test of cultural purity for classification as indigenous is misguided and in opposition to the best interests of indigenous peoples.

Though the boundaries are blurring, indigenous peoples produce forms of knowledge that are inseparable from larger worldviews. Although similarities exist between indigenous and Western scientific knowledges—for example, their mutual status as locally produced ethnoknowledges—Consuelo Quiroz (1999) argues that modernist knowledges are situated in written texts, legal codes, and academic canons. Thus, a profound difference between the different knowledges involves mainstream societies' perception and qualitative evaluation of them as much as anything else. This concept of perception is becoming more and more important in the analysis and classification of different knowledge forms as indigenous studies matures as a field.

All knowledges are related to specific contexts and peoples. The questions become, what context, and what peoples? Though locality is implicated in any form of knowledge production, the worldview of the cultures that inhabit different locales may be profoundly different.

With these dynamics in mind, it appears that Cartesian-Newtonian-Baconian epistemologies and many indigenous knowledge systems differ in the very way they define life—moving, thus, from the epistemological to the ontological realm. As we have maintained in our indigenously informed work in postformalism (Kincheloe & Steinberg, 1993; Kincheloe, Steinberg, & Hinchey, 1999), the characteristics that scientific modernism defined as basic to life are found both in what the Western scientific tradition has labeled "living" and "nonliving." Many indigenous peoples have traditionally seen all life on the planet as so multidimensionally entwined that they have not been so quick to distinguish the living from the nonliving. The positivist use of the term *environment* for example, implies a separation between human and environment. At what point, it may be asked, do oxygen, water, and food become part of the human organism, and at what point are they separate? In this context, for example, the Andean peasants' and other indigenous people's belief that the rivers, mountains, land, soil, lakes, rocks, and animals are sentient may not be as preposterous as Westerners first perceived it.

From the indigenous Andean perspective, all these sentient entities nurture human beings, and it is our role as humans to nurture them. In this belief, the Andeans are expressing both an epistemological and ontological dynamic—a way of knowing and being that is *relational.* Indeed, the Western scientific epistemological concept of "knowing" may not fit the Andean context; the Andeans' connection with the world around them is not as much an expression of knowing as much as it is one of relating. Such relating is undoubtedly a spiritual process, as Andean peoples speak of their relations or kinship system as including human beings as well as animals, the elements and creations of nature, and deities of their "place." In Andean culture, these life forms relate to one another and work together to regenerate life. Thus, in Andean knowledge and many other indigenous knowledges, all aspects of the universe are interrelated; knowledge is in this context holistic, relational, and even spiritual. The rhetoric of conversation with the world is a more accurate descriptor of the process than the discourse of knowing in this context, for the Andeans do not conceptualize a knower and known. The point of the conversation is not the gaining of knowledge; it is to nurture and regenerate the world of which the individual is a part.

In such indigenous knowledge systems, the Eurocentric epistemology of studying, knowing (mastering), and then dominating the world seems frighteningly out of place, as it upsets the sacred kinship between humans and other creations of nature. From the perspective of many indigenous peoples, therefore, Cartesian-Newtonian-Baconian science is grounded on a violent epistemology that seeks to possess the Earth like a master owns a slave. In this context, the master seeks a certainty about the nature of his slave that allows complete control (Apffel-Marglin, 1995; Aronowitz, 1996; Dei, 1994). A less-than-certain knowledge is not good enough for the master and his goal of domination—for example, Sir Francis Bacon's attempt to "bind" nature and put it to work in service of human needs. The indigenous epistemologies referenced here are not uncomfortable with a lack of certainty about the social world and the world of nature, for many indigenous peoples have no need to solve all mysteries about the world they operate *with* and in.

The Power of Indigenous Knowledge to Reshape Western Science: Rigor in Multilogicality

The past 30 years have witnessed sharp criticisms of the Western scientific establishment by scholars engaged in cultural studies of science, sociologists of scientific knowledge, multiculturalists who uncover the gender and race inscriptions on the scientific method, and philosophers exposing science's bogus claims to objectivity. The purposes of such studies do not involve some effort to critique the truth-value of Western scientific knowledge, which is the correspondence of a scientific pronouncement to a reality existing in isolation to the knower. Rather, such critiques of science point out that Western science has created a self-validating frame of reference that provides authority to particular Western androcentric and culturally specific ways of seeing the world. Contemporary science studies apply the same forms of analysis to both physical and social sciences, asking in both domains how knowledge is produced and how do implicit worldviews shape the knowledge construction process.

Such questions, unfortunately, tend not to come from within the scientific establishment but from outsiders such as students of indigenous knowledge. From the voices and the knowledge of the indigene, Westerners may be induced to take a new look at positivism's decontextualized rationality and the harm it can cause in people's lives around the planet. Indigenous knowledge provides a provocative vantage point from which to view Eurocentric discourses, a starting place for a new conversation about the world and human beings' role in it. In some ways, the epistemological critique initiated by indigenous knowledge is more radical than other sociopolitical critiques of the West, for the indigenous critique questions the very foundations of Western ways of knowing and being (Aronowitz, 1996; Harding, 1996; Kloppenberg, 1991; Ross, 1996; L. T. Smith, 1999).

Thus, our intention here is to make the argument that a scholarly encounter with indigenous knowledge can enrich the ways we engage in research and conceptualize education while promoting the dignity, self-determination, and survival of indigenous people. It is, of course, extremely important to consider the types of questions we ask about the relationship between indigenous knowledge and these matters. As Marcel Viergever (1999) points out, what we know is contingent on the types of questions we ask and the manner in which we interpret the answers. Along with Viergever, we believe that familiarity with indigenous knowledge will help academics both see previously unseen problems and develop unique solutions to them.

Again, we simultaneously heed the warning that the emerging Western academic interest in indigenous knowledge may not be a positive movement if such knowledge is viewed as merely another resource to be exploited for the economic benefit of the West. Understanding this admonition, we frame indigenous knowledge not as a resource to be exploited but as a perspective that can help change the consciousness of Western academics and their students while enhancing the ability of such individuals to become valuable allies in the indigenous struggle for justice and self-determination. In the contemporary context where some Western academics are reassessing their science, their epistemology, their research methods, and their educational goals, the questions raised by indigenous knowledge hold a potential revolutionary effect. What a radical change this could initiate—Western researchers and educators learning from indigenous peoples in a respectful, nonexploitive manner.

The goal of such a learning process is to produce a transformative science, an approach to knowledge production that synthesizes ways of knowing expressed by the metonymies of hand, brain, and heart. Keeping in mind the omnipresent danger of the Western exploitation of indigenous knowledge, it may be possible to examine the relationship between Western science and indigenous ways of knowing in a manner that highlights their differences and complementarities. The purpose here is not simply to deconstruct Western methods of knowledge production or to engage Western scientists in a process of self-reflection. While deconstruction and self-reflection are important, we are more concerned with initiating a conversation resulting in a critique of Western science that leads to a reconceptualization of the Western scientific project and Western ways of being-in-the-world around issues of multiple ways of seeing, justice, power, and community. Our notion of an indigenously informed transformative science is not one that simply admits more peoples—"red and yellow, black and white"—into the country club of science but challenges the epistemological foundations of the ethnoknowledge known simply as science.

A transformative scientist understands that any science is a social construction, produced in a particular culture in a specific historical era—Sandra Harding (1998) turns positivism on itself, calling such a process a stronger form of objectivity (i.e., better science). Via a study of indigenous knowledge, Western scientists come to understand their work in unprecedented clarity. As they gain a critical distance from their scholarship, they also gain new insights into the culturally inscribed Eurocentrism of the academy and the politics of knowledge in general. Such informed scientists could begin to point out the similarities that connect indigenous perspectives with certain schools of feminism, agroecology, critical theory, and multilogical critiques. While obviously these perspectives are different and come from diverse contexts, there are points around issues of knowledge production where they all intersect. Important and strategic alliances can be constructed around these intersections. Operating in solidarity, individuals from these different backgrounds can ask new questions about what it means "to know," about the role of love and empathy in the epistemological process, and about the purposes of a critical multilogical education.

Transformative researchers do not see themselves as saviors. An offshoot of colonialism is the notion by the researcher (many times White, European) that the research or pedagogy he or she is introducing to the community is somehow a way to *benefit* his or her "subjects." Using Western tools of research and observation, the researcher acquires an elevated positionality within the venue of the research. I (Shirley) recall vividly situations on the Blood Reserve in Stand-Off, Alberta, in which the university researchers entered schools with the intent of enlightenment via the research they were pursuing. Instead of genuinely observing students in literacy classes and reading acquisition, the researchers attempted to implant reading curricula in what they already saw as a deficit-laden reading curriculum. By doing this, they made clear their expectation that what they introduced was superior. The cooperating teachers from the reserve felt compelled to make sure that the new reading curriculum *worked.* Interviews with the teachers were overwhelmingly positive about the introduced curriculum; there were no protestations or disagreements about the appropriateness of the new work. The experimental curriculum consisted of comic books depicting the literary "classics." Not only was the use of comic books pejorative in nature, but there was no connection to indigeneity or acknowledgment as to the definition of a classic as Western in origin. This example exhibits most of the research and pedagogy that is conducted on reserves and reservations in North America today. The residents are still the manifestation of the *White man's burden,* the same philosophy that was popularized by the Carlisle Indian School: *Kill the Indian, save the man.*

Multilogical Epistemologies: Producing Dialogical Systems of Knowledge Production

Once individuals come to believe that Western science is not the only legitimate knowledge producer, then maybe a conversation can be opened about how different forms of research and knowledge production take issues of locality, cultural values, and social justice seriously. Our goal as educators and researchers operating in Western academia is to conceptualize an indigenously informed science that is dedicated to the social needs of communities and is driven by humane concerns rather than the economic needs of corporate managers, government, and the military. Much too often, Western science is a key player in the continuation of Euro-expansion projects that reify the status quo and further the interests of those in power. In this context, we are not attempting to produce a grand synthesis that eventuates in one final epistemological/knowledge production system. Instead, we hope that we all can learn from difference, from the profound insights and the limitations of various ways of seeing the world and the humans who inhabit it.

Thus, different ways of seeing can coexist, many of them in what might be labeled confederations of solidarity, around a compact to encourage and engage in dialogue about the ethical, political, and pedagogical consequences of various forms of knowledge production. Caution is necessary here, for the types of dialogue that have taken place about these matters to date have too often been condescendingly Eurocentric. Indigenous knowledge producers have been positioned as exotic inferiors who must be introduced to the advanced world of Western science (Airhihenbuwa, 1995; Kloppenberg, 1991). With these ideas in mind, the term *hybridity* has been injected into the conversation about the dialogue between Western and indigenous knowledges. Such a term consciously references the effort to transcend essentialism with its understanding that cultural interaction is a historical inevitability. Frederique Apffel-Marglin (1995) is uncomfortable with the use of *hybridity* in this context, arguing that the concept renders the creative work and ingenuity of indigenous peoples invisible. Apffel-Marglin is writing in this case from the perspective of indigenous culture making use of Western knowledge; the point is still important to consider, even though in the context of this chapter, we are focusing on the role of indigenous knowledge in the Western education and knowledge production.

How are different cultural perspectives incorporated into other ways of seeing and systems of knowledge production? Can the indigenous confrontation with the Western paradigm help bring about a deep modification of Western perspectives? As previously asserted, our essentialism detector tells us that no cultures exist in a pristine, uncontaminated state and that some form of cultural interaction is always taking place. Yet, how does such interaction relate to the concept of cultural continuity and regeneration in light of the reality of the perseverance of long-lasting distinctive cultural traditions? Western students of indigenous knowledge and advocates of incorporating such knowledge into the Western curriculum must address these issues in their scholarship and pedagogy to protect themselves from simplistic applications of indigeneity to the Western context. Again, the purpose here is not to produce "the end of epistemological history," a final articulation of the best way to produce knowledge. Sandra Harding (1996), writing about a transformed science, uses the term *borderlands epistemology* to signify the valuing of different understandings of the world that diverse cultures produce.

Harding's (1996) concept of borderlands epistemology works well for our concerns. Western scholars in this context would be able to draw upon different systems of knowledge and knowledge production given the various situations they encounter. In this framework, we would not seek the final representation of the world or some infallible mapping of social and physical reality—the grand resolution of epistemological debate. While social, psychological, pedagogical, and physical scholars would modify their sciences in light of indigenous understandings, they would not work to merely copy non-Western ways of seeing. This is the type of dialogue we seek in indigenously informed knowledge production and curriculum development in Western societies. Thus, scientific boundaries would be redrawn and opened to new negotiations. Such a process not only will provide Western analysts with new physical and social scientific insights but will also open their eyes to the political and cultural forces at work in all scientific labor. Informed in this manner, Western scientists traditionally chained to their decontextualized "laboratories" will peer outside to study the effects of their isolated inquiries on living people in naturalistic environments. Indeed, neglected questions of sustainability and local contexts will enter the vocabularies of analysts who previously dismissed such concepts from the purview of their protocols (Kloppenberg, 1991; Ross, 1996).

A Modest Proposal: Generating an Intercultural, Synergistic Dialogue

What we are proposing here is a synergistic dialogue that pedagogically works to create conditions where both intra- and intercultural knowledge traditions can inform one another. Mahia Maurial (1999) well understands this concept as she imagines a dialogical educational future. These encounters reduce the ugly expression of epistemological xenophobia and the essentialism it spawns—whatever its source. In Australia's Center for Aboriginal Studies, Jill Abdullah and Ernie Stringer (1999) report, this synergistic dialogue is encouraged by the assumption of the intrinsic worth of various frames of reference. Different ways of seeing can illuminate problems in unique ways and should be understood in this manner—a central tenet of multilogicality.

Questions about the nature of indigenous knowledge and its academic uses are obviously complex but central to the future of education—a just, critical, practical, anticolonial, and transformative education in particular. No one said it would be easy—we know it won't. It is our hope that work such as ours and the other authors in this handbook will help educators and researchers from diverse backgrounds appreciate this complexity and give one another space and respect as they struggle to address the various issues raised here. An intercultural, synergistic, and unresolved conversation among a wide variety of players is central to our task. While open-ended, such a conversation would be marked by a recognition on the part of non-indigenous researchers of the ways that their cultural orientations and values (L. T. Smith, 1999) and the processes through which such dynamics inscribe their epistemologies, ontologies, and research methods can do great harm to indigenous peoples. All of these aspects of research involve power and its ability to construct oppressive structures and knowledges that produce/inflict human suffering.

▣ References

Abdullah, J., & Stringer, E. (1999). Indigenous knowledge, indigenous learning, indigenous research. In L. Semali & J. Kincheloe (Eds.), *What is indigenous knowledge? Voices from the academy* (pp. 143–156). Bristol, PA: Falmer.

Agrawal, A. (1995). Indigenous and scientific knowledge: Some critical comments. *Indigenous Knowledge and Development Monitor, 3*(3), 3–6.

Airhihenbuwa, C. (1995). *Health and culture: Beyond the Western paradigm.* Thousand Oaks, CA: Sage.

Apffel-Marglin, F. (1995). Development or decolonialization in the Andes? *Interculture: International Journal of Intercultural and Transdisciplinary Research, 28*(1), 3–17.

Appiah, K. (1995). The postcolonial and the postmodern. In. B. Ashcroft, G. Griffiths, & H. Tiffin (Eds.), *The post-colonial studies reader* (pp. 119–124). New York: Routledge.

Aronowitz, S. (1996). The politics of science wars. In A. Ross (Ed.), *Science wars* (pp. 202–225). Durham, NC: Duke University Press.

Ashcroft, B., Griffiths, G., & Tiffin, H. (Eds.). (1995). *The post-colonial studies reader.* New York: Routledge.

Dei, G. (1994, March). *Creating reality and understanding: The relevance of indigenous African world views.* Paper presented to the Comparative and International Education Society, San Diego, California.

Dei, G., & Kempf, A. (2006). *Anti-colonialism and education: The politics of resistance.* Rotterdam: Sense Publishers.

Denzin, N. K., & Lincoln, Y. S. (2000). *The SAGE handbook of qualitative research* (2nd ed.). Thousand Oaks, CA: Sage.

Dion-Buffalo, Y., & Mohawk, J. (1993). Thoughts from an autochthonous center: Postmodern and cultural studies. *Akweikon Journal, 9*(4), 16–21.

Freire, P., & Faundez, A. (1989). *Learning to question: A pedagogy of liberation.* New York: Continuum.

George, J. (1999). Indigenous knowledge as a component of the school curriculum. In L. Semali & J. Kincheloe (Eds.), *What is indigenous knowledge? Voices from the academy* (pp. 79–94). New York: Falmer.

Goldie, T. (1995). The representation of the indigene. In B. Ashcroft, G. Griffiths, & H. Tiffin (Eds.), *The post-colonial studies reader* (pp. 232–236). New York: Routledge.

Gramsci, A. (1988). *An Antonio Gramsci reader* (D. Sorgacs, Ed.). New York: Schocken Books.

Hall, S. (1995). New ethnicities. In B. Ashcroft, G. Griffiths, & H. Tiffin (Eds.), *The post-colonial studies reader* (pp. 223–227). New York: Routledge.

Harding, S. (1996). Science is "good to think with." In A. Ross (Ed.), *Science wars* (pp. 16–28). Durham, NC: Duke University Press.

Harding, S. (1998). *Is science multicultural? Postcolonialisms, feminisms, and epistemologies.* Bloomington: Indiana University Press.

Hess, D. (1995). *Science and technology in a multicultural world: The cultural politics of facts and artifacts.* New York: Columbia University Press.

Howard, G. (1995). Unraveling racism: Reflections on the role of nonindigenous people supporting indigenous education. *Australian Journal of Adult and Community Education, 35*(3), 229–237.

Jaimes, M. (1987). American Indian studies: Toward an indigenous model. *American Indian Culture and Research Journal, 11*(3), 1–16.

Keith, N., & Keith, N. (1993, November). *Education development and the rebuilding of urban community.* Paper presented at the Annual Conference of the Association for the Advancement of Research, Policy, and Development in the Third World, Cairo, Egypt.

Kincheloe, J., & Steinberg, S. (1993). A tentative description of post-formal thinking: The critical confrontation with cognitive theory. *Harvard Educational Review, 63,* 296–320.

Kincheloe, J., Steinberg, S., & Hinchey, P. (Eds.). (1999). *The postformal reader: Cognition and education.* New York: Falmer.

Kloppenberg, J. (1991). Social theory and the de/reconstruction of agricultural science: Local knowledge for an alternative agriculture. *Rural Sociology, 56,* 519–548.

Knijnik, G. (1999). Indigenous knowledge and ethnomathematics approach in the Brazilian landless people education. In L. Semali & J. Kincheloe (Eds.), *What is indigenous knowledge? Voices from the academy* (pp. 179–208). New York: Falmer.

Marcuse, H. (1955). *Eros and civilization.* Boston: Beacon.

Maurial, M. (1999). Indigenous knowledge and schooling: A continuum between conflict and dialogue. In L. Semali & J. Kincheloe (Eds.), *What is indigenous knowledge? Voices from the academy* (pp. 59–78). New York: Falmer.

Mosha, R. (2000). *The heartbeat of indigenous Africa: A study of the Chagga educational system.* New York: Garland.

Mudrooroo. (1995). White forms, Aboriginal content. In B. Ashcroft, G. Griffiths, & H. Tiffin (Eds.), *The post-colonial studies reader* (pp. 228–231). New York: Routledge.

Murray, A. (1996). *The blue devils of Nada: A contemporary American approach to aesthetic statement.* New York: Vintage.

Mutua, K., & Swadener, B. (2004). *Decolonizing research in cross-cultural contexts: Critical personal narratives.* Albany, NY: SUNY Press.

Parrish, A. (1999). Agricultural extension education and the transfer of knowledge in an Egyptian oasis. In L. Semali & J. Kincheloe (Eds.), *What is indigenous knowledge? Voices from the academy* (pp. 269–284). New York: Falmer.

Pieterse, J., & Parekh, B. (1995). Shifting imaginaries: Decolonization, internal decolonization, and postcoloniality. In J. Pieterse & B. Parekh (Eds.), *The decolonialization of imagination: Culture, knowledge, and power* (pp. 1–15). Atlantic Highlands, NJ: Zed.

Quiroz, C. (1999). Local knowledge systems and vocational education in developing countries. In L. Semali & J. Kincheloe (Eds.), *What is indigenous knowledge? Voices from the academy* (pp. 305–316). New York: Falmer.

Ross, A. (1996). Introduction. In A. Ross (Ed.), *Science wars* (pp. 1–15). Durham, NC: Duke University Press.

Semali, L., & Kincheloe, J. (Eds.). (1999). *What is indigenous knowledge? Voices from the academy.* New York: Falmer.

Shor, I., & Freire, P. (1987). *A pedagogy for liberation: Dialogues on transforming education.* South Hadley, MA: Bergin & Garvey.

Simonelli, R. (1994). Traditional knowledge leads to a Ph.D. *Winds of Change, 9,* 43–48.

Smith, G. H. (2000). Protecting and respecting indigenous knowledge. In M. Battiste (Ed.), *Reclaiming indigenous voice and vision* (pp. 209–224). Vancouver: University of British Columbia Press.

Smith, L. T. (1999). *Decolonizing methodologies: Research and indigenous peoples.* New York: Zed.

Sponsel, L. (1992). Information asymmetry and the democratization of anthropology. *Human Organization, 51,* 299–301.

Viergever, M. (1999). Indigenous knowledge: An interpretation of views from indigenous peoples. In L. Semali & J. Kincheloe (Eds.), *What is indigenous knowledge? Voices from the academy* (pp. 333–360). New York: Falmer.

Villaverde, L., Kincheloe, J., & Helyar, F. (2006). Historical research in education. In K. Tobin & J. Kincheloe (Eds.), *Doing educational research* (pp. 311–46). Rotterdam: Sense Publishers.

8

DO YOU BELIEVE IN GENEVA?

Methods and Ethics at the Global-Local Nexus

Michelle Fine, Eve Tuck, and Sarah Zeller-Berkman

The real justification for including Aboriginal knowledge in the modern curriculum is not so that Aboriginal students can compete with non-Aboriginal students in an imagined world. It is, rather, that immigrant society [all non-Aboriginal peoples] is sorely in need of what Aboriginal knowledge has to offer.

—Battiste (2000, p. 201)

Over the past 15 years, we have designed participatory action research (PAR) projects with differently situated young people in prisons, schools, and communities. Some projects have been planted firmly in the *politics of place:* the South Bronx, suburban privilege, a prison. Others have been designed to gather *material about domination and resistance across places,* what George Marcus (1995) might call a multisited ethnography. Most recently, we have begun to work with youth activists from around the globe in a human rights campaign designed to unmask the policies, practices, and patterns of injustice and reveal the flashpoints of collective resistance. At this global-local nexus, youth PAR excites and grows tangled—a clear window for witnessing and kneading the complex relation of critical and indigenous methods. Taking up the challenge offered by Marie Battiste, in this chapter, we cast a critical eye on our participatory research methods with youth, through the lens of Indigenous knowledge.

AUTHORS' NOTE: This chapter is being reprinted with permission from Fine, M., Tuck, E., & Zeller-Berkman, S. (2007). Do you believe in Geneva? In C. McCarthy, A. Durham, L. Engel, A. Filmer, M. Giardina, & M. Malagreca (Eds.), *Globalizing cultural studies* (pp. 493–525). New York: Peter Lang. The authors acknowledge Ryma Fares, Rodrigo de Paula, Tano Bechev, Leonard Habimana, Linda Kayseas, Aliou Sali, Elvia Duque, Ivrance Martine, Varshaa Ayyar, Mina Susana Setra, Bhaba Bahadur Thami, Sandra Rojas Hooker, Dabesaki Mac-Ikemeojima, James A. Baay, Randa Powell, Pinky Vincent, Tiffany McKinney, Neema Mgana, Diya Nijhowne, Jennifer Rasmussen, Perry Gilmore, Maria Elena Torre, Jennifer Ayala, Caitlin Cahill Carlos, Alza Barco, Renee Louis, and Sandy Grande.

We invite a conversation about participatory methods, oscillating at the global-local pivot, by commuting between three kinds of texts: participatory and Indigenous writings on method, online exchanges of an international discussion group of participatory researchers we convened, and collaborative work we have undertaken with the Global Rights coalition of youth activists. Across texts, we interrogate the dialectics of method that erupt as critical youth work digs deep into local places and travels cautiously across the globe (Chawla et al., 2005; Gilmore, Smith, & Kairaiuak, 2004; Hart, 1997). We end with suggestive thoughts for activist scholars inquiring with youth *in* a place, *across* places and then those who dare to trace *global footprints* of domination and resistance. To ground our thoughts, we enter the Global Rights training with youth activists from across the world.

▣ ▣ ▣

Surrounded by young activists, drawn from all corners of the globe, we gathered for Day 2 of our participatory action research training. Global Rights: Partners for Justice sponsored the Amplifying Youth Voices Participatory Action Research Project on rights, poverty, and discrimination program to mobilize young people from marginalized ethnic communities to improve their educational opportunities and amplify their decision making related to poverty reduction and development. As part of this program, the activists were to undertake participatory action research projects in which they would gather local evidence of educational discrimination and use this evidence to fashion an advocacy document that they would use to lobby for reform at the United Nations (UN) Commission on Human Rights in Geneva in 2006. The project is seeded in the international human rights agreement articulated in the Dakar Framework for Action on achieving the Education for All (EFA) goals, particularly Goal 2: *ensuring that by 2015, all children, particularly girls, children in difficult circumstances, and those belonging to ethnic minorities have access to complete, free, and compulsory primary education of good quality.* The project was organized to develop a radical, global participatory action research coalition, documenting local forms of educational discrimination in home countries as well as the global redlining of educational opportunity.

The training session was designed to generate a bottom-up survey that could travel respectfully across these very different communities to determine levels of discrimination in terms of denial of *access* (e.g., transportation, or local practices that disallow certain castes, colors, tribes) to *free* (e.g., fees for school, books, uniforms, travel), *complete* (e.g., how many years), and *quality* (e.g., adequate books; supports; desks; bathrooms; qualified educators; culturally sensitive and responsive curriculum; meaningful assessments, not just tests that punish) education. In each community, focus groups would be conducted to gather local stories of blocked and denied educational opportunities and stories of privilege. Global Rights would collect the material from across meridians, and some of the young people would speak back, in policy, scholarship, and outrage, to the UN Commission on Human Rights in Geneva 2006.

Our task was to help create, collaboratively, a survey that would speak to and migrate across territories, to assess what we were calling the global blades of educational discrimination that deny young people—girls and those who are of low caste, live in poverty, have dark skin, or belong to the wrong tribe—access to free, complete, quality education; then each of these young activists would return to his or her homes and create a participatory research team there, to conduct the work locally. As we tried to construct an instrument that could travel the globe, marking and tracking the international latitudes and local scratches of social oppression, we confronted key challenges of method that haunt any design, particularly one that yearns to stretch globally and yet put down roots locally.

The most palpable tension could be felt in the distinct goals of global and local work. A collective desire to be heard and to affect public policy saturated the room: This is really important for young people to gather together, across continents, and build a movement for educational justice, bolstered by statistics and testimonies about the global blades of domination. At the same time, the air thickened in an unspoken dialect, fuming in each of us: How will this help my people, my community, my family? Tensions of North and South; Indigenous, undocumented, and immigrant; and the imperial presence and terror exported by the United States and Great Britain seasoned the air, unspoken, as we sat together, with bagels and cream cheese, under the Manhattan Bridge in Brooklyn, New York.

Warning: Language and Land Have Been Stolen

As we prepared for this chapter, trying to write together as three differently positioned women, reading across literatures on Indigenous, participatory, and critical knowledges, we ran into the problem of language. The language of possibility, democracy, hope, and culture had already been coopted, distorted, stripped, and overdetermined by neoliberalism, colonialism, and the new scientism (Lather, 2005). Although we have published on the democratic commitments of PAR work with youth (Fine et al., 2004; Zeller-Berkman, 2007), we were stunned and compelled by Sandy Grande's (2004) work on the illusion of democracy without sovereignty. So, too, we had to reconsider the long-assumed PAR aim of youth "speaking back to power" (Cammarota & Ginwright, 2002; Fine & Torre, 2005; Lykes & Coquillon, 2006). Speaking back, like inviting "contact" between differently positioned groups, may be an opportunity for radical inclusion but more often degenerates into a contentious scene of exclusion and soul murder (Painter, 1995).

The more we wrote, the more we came to see that Michelle's desire to reclaim the research standard of generalizability as the radical linking of social resistance across sites of injustice has already been compromised by the hegemonic use of *generalizability* as universality and sameness, deployed to deny and smother difference. The more we read, the more infuriated we became, as we witnessed words such as *decolonization* and *Indigenous* swept into critical discourse as metaphors, decoupled from long histories of persecution and struggle.

One of our methods for writing this chapter has been to pay close attention to what, in our quilted discourse, can serve as a metaphor and what cannot. Rather than lines drawn in the sand, these are instead reminders of the slippery surface of language, the seductive pull of solidarity, and the terrific sloppiness with which we make names and claims under imperialism.

Both those who are served by domination and those who are committed to social justice, seeking solidarity among oppressed peoples, engage in the too common practice of taking on the charged, contextualized, experienced words of brilliant communities and stretching them to fit inside their own mouths and own communities. On one hand, we recognize the assimilationist, exploitive tradition that is at work behind this practice and recognize that there are some who always feel entitled to scoop out the most on-point language and plant it in their work. Marie Battiste highlights a keystone component of post-colonial indigenous thought as being based on "our pain and experiences and it refuses to allow others to appropriate this pain or these experiences" (Battiste, 2000, p. xix). We urge our readers and remind ourselves to resist the appropriation of pain and language of Indigenous peoples and other oppressed peoples.

On the other hand, there are some ideas that speak so poignantly to issues of maldistributed power that our work across space, across time, across disciplines is deepened, thickened, by being compelled by them into practice. Colonization and sovereignty, as a prerequisite to democracy, as we discuss later in this chapter, are examples of those ideas.

Being Indigenous are not metaphors. Those of us who are Indigenous have experienced the everyday realities of continued colonization, which has shaped the ways in which we think of ourselves, one another, and the "whitestream" (Grande, 2004) and the ways in which we write, speak, and come to research. Those of us who are not Indigenous have been profoundly shaped by our witnessing of colonization, by our roles as accomplices, abettors, exploiters, romanticizers, pacifiers, assimilators, includers, forgetters, and democratizers. Indigenous knowledge and experiences are markedly different from local knowledge.

While colonization and continued colonization are not metaphors, colonization, because it is the primary relationship between the United States and oppressed peoples, can be a lens through which to understand not only the rez but also the ghetto, the windswept island, the desert, the suburbs, the gated communities, and the country club. "When the United States takes control of Iraqi oil after the war, will it do a better job of holding 'in trust' that country's oil for its people than it did for Native Americans . . . and exactly who will handle the job, the BIA (Bureau of Iraqi Affairs)?" (Snell, 2003). Understanding colonization as the primary relationship between the United States and oppressed peoples makes us know that decolonization involves not only bodies but also structures, laws, codes, souls, and histories (L. T. Smith, 2005). This understanding affords us the reminder that it is not the Indigenous who need humanizing, it is the worldview of the whitestream that needs to be humanized.

Geneva, like Native America, "is not only a place but also a social, political, cultural, and economic space" (Grande, 2004). As places, Geneva and Indigenous communities and local communities represent two poles in a local to global hierarchy. Considering them as spaces, we resist this hierarchy, instead framing this relationship as the global-local nexus. Space is not a metaphor.

Despite the appropriation of language, as well as geographic and politically distinct biographies, we move forward in this chapter, stumbling across words that have been colonized, trying to sculpt research projects that span across sites and dig deeply into the local, drawing inspiration from Patti Lather's (2005) project of "using and troubling a category simultaneously" (p. 2). We work to carve out moments of conversation between participatory action research and Indigenous writings while refusing to paper over the tough differences. We aim toward research with youth that respects culture and place while it resists stultifying and suffocating presumptions of culture as static. We struggle toward research born in collectives that refuse the easy slide toward consensus and solidarity but leap cautiously to connect across movements of social resistance (e.g., see Correa & Petchesky, 1994, on international reproductive rights; Davis, 2003, on international solidarity for the abolition of prisons).

▣ Participatory Youth Inquiry

With long roots in Africa, Asia, and Central and South America, PAR was born in the soil of discontent, understanding critical inquiry to be a tool for social change (Brydon-Miller & Tolman, 2001; Lykes & Coquillon, 2006; Martín-Baró, 1994; Rahman, 2008). PAR is, at once, social movement, social science, and a radical challenge to the traditions of science. As Anisur Rahman (2008) has written, "The distinctive viewpoint of PAR [recognizes that the] domination of masses by elites is rooted not only in the polarization of control over the means of material production but also over the means of knowledge production, including . . . the social power to determine what is valid or useful knowledge."

Interested in social inquiry that documents (in)justice broadly, in terms of economics, land, cultural and personal integrity, bodily autonomy, educational opportunity, and knowledge production, our work with youth seeks to reveal the contours of injustice and resistance while we challenge the very bases on which social science sits. Enervated by the political urgency of the times, we work toward methods for a youth-based inquiry of contestation. At the same time, we worry about what can be done globally and locally when surveillance and fear surrounding the walls between rich and poor have thickened, and the "war on terror" and the war on knowledge production contaminate everyday life (see also Lather, 2005; Lewin, 1946; Payton, 1984; N. Smith, 1987).

Participatory methods respond to these crises in politics by deliberately inverting who constructs research questions, designs, methods, interpretations, and products, as well as who engages in surveillance. Researchers from the bottom of social hierarchies, the traditional objects of research, reposition as the subjects and architects of critical inquiry, contesting hierarchy and the distribution of resources, opportunities, and the right to produce knowledge (see also Lather, 2005).

In varied settings, our collectives have focused on the history and accumulation of privilege and oppression, the policies and practices of reproduction, the intimate relations that sustain inequity, the psychodynamic effects on the soul, and the vibrant forms of resistance enacted by individuals and collectives (we draw from and contribute to Anand, Fine, Perkins, & Surrey, 2000; Brydon-Miller & Tolman, 2001; Cahill, 2004; Cammarota & Ginwright, 2002; Chawla et al., 2005; Fals-Borda, 1985; Fine et al., 2003, 2004, 2005; Fine & Torre, 2005; Freire, 1982; Guhathakurta, 2008; Hart, 1997; Ormond, 2004; Rahman, 2008; L. T. Smith, 2005). We have built democratic spaces with youth and "elders" (teachers, ancestors, civil rights activists, "older" prisoners) to change the questions asked, challenge the assumptions (even our own), disagree, radically inquire, and challenge policy and practice.

While all PAR projects are constructed to speak critical truths to those in power—to change structures, not squeeze youth into them (Appadurai, 2002; Cabannes, 2005; Cahill, 2004; Chawla et al., 2005; Rahman, 2008)—some commit to writing academic scholarship, whereas others spawn organizing brochures, speak-outs, poetry, videos, popular youth writings, spoken word performances, theater of resistance, or maybe just a safe space free from toxic representations.

Many of our projects have been *place based,* dug into the soil of vibrant, if historically oppressed, ZIP codes, prisons, and schools. But many of our projects have also been multisited to "examine the circulation of cultural meanings, objects and identities in diffuse time-space" (Marcus, 1995, p. 96). We have worked with youth *across* elite and underfinanced schools, with women in prison and those now released, and with suburban and urban students. Youth have visited and surveyed each others' schools, crossing borders of politics, real estate, and emotion, inquiring across place to make visible the spikes of injustice that pierce specific sites and to document the patterned distributions of resources, opportunities, and respect that naturalize inequity across public schools in the United States. We have written about these youth PAR projects in varied venues and refer readers to those chapters for details of the theorizing and practice of participatory method (see Cammarota & Ginwright, 2002; see Chawla et al., 2005, on the Growing Up in Cities [GUIC] project for a rich description of a rich international work of support for the GUIC, and see also Cabannes, 2005, on that volume; Fine et al., 2003; Torre & Fine, 2005).

We write as three women who have been immersed in youth organizing, prison reform, social justice work, and feminist and antiracist campaigns; three women who believe in the possibilities of youth movements organized across time, space, and lines of power, with youth inquiry as a tool of political struggle. But we know that "fallen" power lines can kill. We believe deeply in the significance of working doggedly, *in a place,* with local history, context, and struggle under your fingernails, and we believe that *across places,* youth inquiry and resistance can be fueled by global connections and contentions. And finally and fundamentally, we assert that some knowledge carried in oppressed and indigenous communities should not be reported or documented; it is not to be known by those outside of the local community—that sacred local knowledges can be defiled and that research has, for too long, been the "neutral" handmaiden of knowledge commodification.

We return now to the Global Rights training—a place where the air of global possibility and colonial danger filled the room.

▣ ▣ ▣

Global Rights was onto a most significant human rights campaign. The cross-nation mapping of oppression, narrated by youth, swept through the room with winds of outrage, despair, and hope. The young people embodied incredibly rich, complex, and diverse histories, contexts, and contemporary relations to global capital and the new imperialism. The idea that we could come up with a common framework for measuring educational discrimination seemed, at once, enormously vital and nuts.

The more we talked, the more we realized that the concept of "discrimination" had its greatest clarity in the abstract, north of the grounds in which people live. Once we heard about life as lived in *real* towns, barrios, fields, cities, communities, or kitchens, we recognized that the ripples of globalized oppression take varied forms—alcoholism, domestic violence, hopelessness, economic indigency—none easily reduced to a simple descriptor of discrimination. We had to shovel down into the sands of local places, dotting the earth, to understand how discrimination is lived.

By Day 3, Michelle was "modeling" a focus group, the kind these young people might facilitate with youth back home in order to generate a map of deeply contextualized, situated stories of discrimination, denial of access, obstacles encountered, and resiliencies displayed by youth in their communities. We would put together a Global Advocacy Document and local advocacy documents, stuffed with numbers from "across" sites and within, seasoned with rich stories of living life locally, to facilitate testimonials and social change in home communities and, of course, Geneva.

It was in the focus group that some of the key issues we seek to discuss in this chapter were voiced. Michelle asked five participants (from Nepal, Tanzania, India, Cameroon, and Algeria) to first draw maps of their biographical travels from childhood to present, through schooling, and to draw through place, emotion, and struggle the obstacles they encountered, the people and movements that supported them. One chair was left empty for anyone in the "outer circle" to join us. The problematics of globalizing hope through research poured into the group like lava. The pain of everyday life inside long histories of colonialism, abuse, and injustice could no longer be denied. The existential question of "proof"—will they ever listen?—whispered in all of our ears.

There is, of course, an important project under way—to work deep and wide, to insist that Geneva listen. And yet throughout the room, like waves of hope and despair, you could read faces asking, "Will this matter back home?" "Do self doubts count as the last drop of oppression and discrimination?" "How are the fists and the slaps of a father accounted for in a human rights campaign for education?" "Should we consult the elders in our community about the work?" and "If we consult the elders, will they shut down the conversations of the young people?"

At the very exhausting and exhilarating end of our 3 days together, Aliou from Cameroon spoke, "You know, this isn't a criticism of the last few days, but I want to say that we might never get to Geneva. Even if we do, I don't think they believe in us. But I have grown so much, learned so much, being with all of you these last few days, listening to stories of young people fighting for justice in their own communities. Our relationships, our skills, that's what I'll take back to my community. But Geneva, I don't know that I believe in Geneva."

Aliou gave voice as others nodded; some whispered over cigarettes. Bold in his recognition that perhaps he does not believe in Geneva . . . and perhaps they do not believe in him, Aliou refused to be a trophy in a human rights race. He was soon joined by others who argued that the work would be hollow if it did not speak back to their home communities, if it was not organized for local audiences, if it did not provoke local change.

▣ ▣ ▣

Breathing in the power of possibility, our eyes stung, as well, at the treacherous contradictions that lay at the global-local intersection. Since then, we have been thinking hard about the dialectics of method tucked into the folds of global-local work. We take up four of these dialectics, to provoke imagination for method, to spark a conversation, to invite participatory inquiry that privileges the local while stretching thoughtfully toward the global.

The four dialectics examined here seem pivotal to us but may in fact be idiosyncratic or random. For a provisional moment, however, they seem worth speaking aloud: preserving the right to "difference" in human rights campaigns devoted to universal access, documenting the history and geography of privilege as well as pain, nesting research inside grounded struggles for sovereignty that must be addressed before claims of democracy can be voiced, and articulating the obligations to local audience and local use when "jumping scale" toward global analysis.

"Difference" and Access

Our eyes first stung when we realized that the discourse of human rights' struggles for universal "access" to education can silence or homogenize local demands for "difference."

Tano, a Roma student from Bulgaria, complained that Roma children "only have Roma educators and other Roma in their schools." Others were insistent on education with and for peers who "come from my community." While some want to be prepared to attend "elite" secondary and higher education, others—particularly Indigenous activists—are engaged in the fight for language schools, cultural respect, and challenges to colonizers' histories. Some want to be educated "with all kinds of students and teachers," while others want local, culturally sensitive, and immersed education. Some struggle for access to English as liberatory; others view it as imperialism. Some have no schools for miles; some have only seasonal teachers; some are segregated and want to be with "others"; some are "integrated" and yearn for a space of their own. Some trust contact with dominant groups, and many do not.

As the stories filled the room, many began to whisper, "Access to what?" Did we all want the same thing? Do all groups really seek access to a Western—"free, complete, quality"—education? A provocative essay by Michael Marker (2006), a Native scholar from British Columbia, helps us think through this dialectic of access and difference: "While other minoritized groups demand revisionist histories and increased access to power within educational institutions, Indigenous people present a more direct challenge to the core assumptions about life's goals and purposes. Urban African Americans and Latinos mobilize around equity and access discourses but Indigenous cultures posit a social stance outside of assertions of pluralism; rather claims to moral and epistemic preeminence based on ancient and sustained relationships to land" (p. 4).

When state institutions (or private ones) "allow" access to those who have historically been denied, too often, buried in the victory, lies an insistence on sameness in the name of inclusion. Access then doubles as vulnerability and sometimes degradation. Institutional racism gets a second life, unfettered (see Fine et al., 2005; Gilmore et al., 2004). Difference is the price of admission; failure, shame, and disappearance follow for most.

To this point, Sandy Grande (2004) "reject[s] the whitestream logic that 'we are all the same'; arguing that it not only denies the 'difference' of indigenous cultures and belief systems, but also tacitly reduces Indigenous peoples to the status of whites-without-technology" (p. 64). She continues, "American Indians are not like other subjugated groups struggling to define their place within the larger democratic project. Specifically, they do not seek greater 'inclusion'; rather, they are engaged in a perpetual struggle to have their legal and moral claims to sovereignty recognized" (p. 107).

If some groups reject dominant goals and purposes and do not seek access to the very institutions that sit at the belly of dominant goals or do not seek to "sit next to our oppressors" (personal communication, Jones, New Zealand, 2001), questions arise about how discrimination is enacted and corrected—how "difference" can be built into remedy. This question of "difference" looms large and clumsy, often silenced, in conversations for universal access to education, health care, housing, work, or even marriage rights, especially as researchers seek to document exclusion and policy makers/advocates seek remedy for all. It is not easy to hold the notion of "difference" in your head while trying to measure or "correct" injustice systematically. This is why civil rights lawyers often rely on extremely problematic standardized test scores to "prove" persistent inequity, even though they know well the racial and class biases of these tests. At the Global Rights workshop, we were situated squarely at the center of this dynamic.

The task of the workshop was to interrogate educational opportunity as (mal)distributed across and within nations. National and international statistics on literacy, the ratio of students to teachers, the rates of qualified teachers, and the percentage of boys and girls attending school, dropping out, and graduating offer metrics of access applicable across nations and communities. These statistics provide "firm" grounds for comparison and judgments of (in)equity but dangerous grounds for thinking through remedies (see Chawla et al., 2005, on the complexities of inquiring deeply across sites to public authorities).

To create a survey to be implemented in each participant's home community on issues of injustice in education, our large group split into three groups, each tackling a set of issues. The small groups had a hard task in front of them because time was limited and because the larger group had decided to keep the survey to just a few pages, there was space for only five or so survey items for each small group, and group members wanted to be sure that each of their questions gathered as much information as possible.

Eve met with the group that was working on creating survey questions that got at the things that kept students from completing school. The group began by listing the reasons that, from their own lives or siblings' or friends' lives, students might not finish their studies. They quite easily arrived at consensus on issues of access and generated this list: It wasn't safe for students to attend or travel to school, family issues and home issues prevented students from attending, there was no reason or benefit or incentive for students to complete their schooling, economic issues kept students working rather than attending school, the school language was different from the student's home language, the student or her or his family had health or mental health issues, the student's culture clashed with the school culture, religious issues prevented students from attending, and the schools did not meet the students' needs (including needs having to do with language, gender, age, and ability).

However, the group had generated too many reasons to ask individual questions about and needed to figure out a way to ask questions that had breadth, speaking to the wide variety of reasons students did not complete their schooling, but also depth, speaking to the intimacy of politics of injustice. Linda Kayseas, a Saulteaux woman from Fishing Lake First Nation, suggested that we go around and rate the top three issues for each of us, so that we might know better around which issues to dig deep and which to merely skim the surface.

Each person took a moment to prioritize the issues for his or her home communities, and this is where difference emerged. As each person listed his or her top three, Eve ticked a 1, 2, or 3 by each issue. There were no issues not in someone's top three, several issues were 3s for many participants, several were 2s for many participants, and several were a 1 for only one or two participants. The group laughed together at the tricky knot we had just created: Should we focus on the issues that received the most ticks? On the issues that had the most 1s? All the issues had at least one 1. A lively, educative discussion ensued, and it was here that the complexities of designing a global survey that was meaningful both across the globe and in the local communities were felt.

In the end, still needing to complete their task of creating a portion of the global survey, yet wanting to honor both the rich discussion and the differences that emerged through trying to prioritize, group members decided to pose the questions on the survey so that the ones being surveyed had the opportunity to prioritize the issues that kept them from completion.

Given the distinct histories, politics, and desires of each community, conversations about "difference" deserve to be aired, not suffocated, at the global-local nexus. Demands for "access" cannot mute noisy, contentious, sometimes divisive discussions of "difference." Damage is done when remedies to injustice are universalized. Oppression is fortified when the knowledge for solutions is homogenized. Commitments to access must always be welded to equally strong commitments to difference. Participatory cross-site work must always hold a "space" open for difference and rely on local knowledge to fill in.

Mapping Privilege and Pain

Everyone in the training knew that oppression lives in the systems and bodies and cells of deprivation and abundance. Most had traveled, attended university with elite students, and sat with nongovernmental organization (NGO) representatives of privilege. They recognized that the effects of global oppression are grossly uneven, but the system thrives across settings. This is why we wanted to study privilege as well as those who have been denied. Unless the very classed, gendered, ethnic, and racialized formations of accumulated capital are documented—not just the "damage" of those who pay the dearest price for globalized injustice—social analyses run the risk of obscuring the architecture and mechanisms of social oppression; we collude in the presumption that "merit" and privilege are trouble free. And, so we asked, how do we map the geography and distribution of pain and privilege—who has it? What does it look like? How is it reproduced? Where is it hidden? Whose sacred knowledge deserves to be protected, and whose deserves to be exposed?

In the framework of global human rights, the design and these questions made perfect sense. Each young person would travel back home, with a translated survey instrument to be administered to 50 males and females from the "dominant" group and 50 from the "marginalized." But on the ground, the constructs of *privileged* and *marginalized* (like *discrimination*) splintered:

We asked, "What does privilege look like in the Dominican Republic?"

> Ivrance Martinez, born in Haiti, now living in the Dominican Republic: "They think they are white in their minds."
>
> Varshaa Ayyar: "But I'm having trouble with the other side of this idea—how do we identify who is marginalized in India? There are so many layers?"
>
> Tano added, "Are the Turkish immigrants in Bulgaria part of the dominant . . . since they too discriminate against us, the Roma?"
>
> Sandra Carolina Rojas Hooker, a lawyer from Nicaragua, a Creole of African descent, acknowledged what so many in the room were thinking: "But really, so many of us are mixed, no?"
>
> Elvia Duque, an Afro-Colombia lawyer and president of the Regional Coalition in Health for African Descendants in the Americas, insisted that we think about how we ask people about race/ethnicity because so many deny their African heritage in "self-reports."

And then someone whispered, loud enough for us to hear but not notice who spoke, "What about those among us who are collaborators; are they dominants or marginalized?"

The young women from the United States and Canada asked that we extend the "age range" we are looking at in the survey, because access to rigorous (e.g., advanced placement [AP]) courses in high school and access to financial aid for college are a problem in the United States and Canada. So true, and yet it was so hard for that concern to sit next to communities in Indonesia where there are no schools or teachers to be found.

We eventually (unfortunately) walked away from trying to survey youth of privilege to track the institutional and personal accumulation and embodiment of capital. Most of the young people believed that privileged people would not stay in the room long enough to have a conversation about the geography of wealth, privilege, entitlement, and the false construction of merit (Burns, 2004). And as you can see, we had a hard time "operationalizing" privilege.

And yet we agree fervently with Susan George (2005) that "those who genuinely want to help the movement should study the rich and the powerful, not the 'poor and the powerless' because the 'poor and powerless already know what is wrong with their lives' and we need analyses of the transnational forces that marginalize particular populations in the West and non-West" (p. 8).

Social scientists do not have easy methods for documenting the material, social, and psychological circuits of privilege—policies and practices of hidden/denied/outsourced ownership, accumulation, exploitation, embodiment, and reproduction of privilege (see Burns, 2004; Low, 2003). To gather up this evidence about privilege requires far more than simple self-report: digging deep, investigating behind, and lifting the skirts of privilege to view beneath and under dominants' coattails, families, bank accounts, stock portfolios, sexual liaisons, pornographic Web sites, drug use, and "cleaned" police records (for excellent examples of research that reveals the material, social, and psychological elements of privilege, see April Burns's [2004] work on privileged youth theorizing structures of injustice, Neil Smith's [1987] work on gentrification, Setha Low's [2003] writings on gated communities, Bernard Lefkowitz's [1997] book on wealthy boys and rape, Melvin Oliver and Thomas Shapiro's [1997] writings on Black wealth/White wealth, Peter Cookson and Caroline Hodges Persell's [1985] work on elite boarding schools, and James Scott's [1990] writings on hidden transcripts of power and resistance).

Documenting the geography of pain, the shameful twin of privilege, may appear to be a somewhat easier task, but here we bump into issues of personal and community ethics and vulnerability. While the global human rights documents from which we launched our work were extremely articulate about what discrimination looks like from a legal, transnational view, the local indicia may curdle into self-doubt, drug and alcohol abuse, violence in the kitchen, and bruises on the soul.

Bhaba Bahadur Thami, born in a highly marginalized indigenous community in Nepal, spoke about the alienation of attending an elite university in Kathmandu. "Marginalized, indigenous students, in order to feel like they fit in, they hung with the Royal Family crowd. I didn't. Fortunately I was a nerd? Geek? Good at computers and kept to myself. But those who stayed with the Royal Family, many of them got into drugs and alcohol and had to return home."

Many, in their maps and stories, mentioned casually incidents of family illness, death of a sibling or a father, or a parent needing an operation. Health tragedies were spray painted all over the biographic journeys of poor youth trying to get educated. They detailed their inevitable return home, for a bit, to nurse a family—the world—back to health. Michelle commented on the emotion in the room, how many lives, cultures, communities, and responsibilities they were carrying in their hearts and souls, in their backpacks, as they traveled off to college, how heavy a burden, how joyous the support, they transported in their bellies.

These young people, in their lives and their work, carry the ashes of global capitalism, racism, sexism, and colonialism and now are imbued with the responsibility to carry hope.

Varshaa spoke up, again. She, more than anyone, had, for two days, carried and voiced the pain in the room, in the world, in the micropolitics of everyday life: "Please, I am not in the circle but I would like to present my map; I think it will tell you much about my community." Her map tells the story of family violence within her Dalit community.

Her map illuminated how the slow, toxic drip feed of discrimination seeps into homes, families, peer relations, and bodies and transforms. This is how reproduction works—through bodies, families, communities, networks, and relations. There is not always an empirical lineage to "discrimination" (Marston, 2000). And yet the young people would say, "Does this count as discrimination?"

The global policies and structures that lie at the source are camouflaged and twisted, with only split lips and bruised mother-bodies visible. And yet the work of critical scholars (see Fine & Weis, 2003) is precisely to document the classed, raced, gendered, and sexualized turns that local oppression can take, to make visible the strings that connect global imperialism, racism, political economy, and patriarchy to everyday life (see Anyon, 2005; Appelbaum & Robinson, 2005; Bhavnani, Foran, & Talcott, 2005; Ormond, 2004).

This knowledge task, in documenting the pain of oppression, is, however, "tricky" (L. T. Smith, 2005). It may be (relatively) easy for researchers to document the quantitative indicators of raw deprivation—in illness and mortality rates; access to hospitals, medical personnel, and insurance; number of teachers; schools; books; and literacy rates. But questions of *intimate subjectivities of deprivation* and the *collateral damage of psychic violence* are harder and more consequential to capture and, in some audiences, more likely to be resisted, too painful to hear, too costly to speak.

Youth engaged in social inquiry can help us think about if/how/when to track the sinews of oppression in intimate and private lives, how injustice metastasizes into a rusting of the soul, local warfare, and resilience. Even as young people of poverty and their communities are resilient and organizing, living under the thumb of global domination may invite a twitch, a stutter, clogged arteries of self-worth, more violence than we wish to announce. These are the sharp fingertips on the long arm of historic and contemporary global domination. Some young people may wish to stay clear of such discussions (Ormond, 2004). Others are literally dying to tell. What constitutes "sacred knowledge" or sovereignty in one community, or by some members of one community, may indeed be the primary purpose for the research in another.

In participatory work, some of the "trickiest" (L. T. Smith, 2005) conversations circled around pain, vulnerability, and damage, asking who gets to have a private life and whose troubles are public. What can be included in the net of "evidence" of social oppression? What will be used against my community, as we document histories of colonization? Do we ever get to reveal the pathology of the rich, their drug abuse, violence against women, and corporate and environmental violence enacted by elites? These are indeed hard calls and not ones that participatory researchers should make alone. The power of global analysis is, perhaps, to be able to speak the unspeakable without vulnerability. This is yet another rub at the intersection of privilege, pain, and outrage, at the global-local nexus, where a set of important conversations with youth are waiting to be hatched.

Sovereignty as Prerequisite to Democracy

The Global Rights workshop included a number of Indigenous people, whose experiences spoke to the complexity of a human rights–based campaign for the end of educational discrimination at the hands of governments that do not respect Indigenous sovereignty.

Mina Susana Setra, a member of the Pompakng peoples and who lives on the island of Borneo, told us that in 1979, Indonesia issued a law that established a uniform system of government at all levels, including the village level. This has paralyzed the Indigenous people's own government system. Local structures have been destroyed, and community leaders no longer have the power to determine local regulations. As time has gone by, community leaders have been replaced by people selected by the government. Slowly, the community has lost the right to make its own choices.

Leonard Habimana, from the Batwa (Pygmy) community of Burundi, a journalist and student at the University of Burundi, explains that since 85% of the Batwa do not have access to land, they face many different forms of poverty. Land in Burundi is the source of economic production. People with large tracts of land bring Batwa to their homes and work them like slaves, without any payments. Because the Batwa do not have money, they cannot pay for health services, education, or other basic services.

On Day 2, as we entered the room, someone whispered to Eve that the Indigenous participants often clustered together. As one who often was a clusterer and who is with Aleut ancestry herself, she was drawn to this group, interested to understand the concerns and experiences of the Indigenous people in the room. It had something to do with the urgency with which the Indigenous participants saw the unfolding plan as being severely mitigated by long histories of colonization and assumptions of equal opportunities and immunities to the dangers of transgression. Soon this group grew to include not only Indigenous participants but many others who were low caste, low positioned in global and local social hierarchies.

Then after the training, the three of us began to discuss our dis-ease with the ways in which democracy is being commodified as the rationale for war and invasion. Actually, there was an uneasy conversation among us about the relation of PAR and democracy. While Michelle and Sarah were well worn in their use of democratic practice to describe PAR, Eve was more skeptical. Serendipity allowed for Eve to meet Sandy Grande, who put words to the disconnect between critical pedagogy and red pedagogy: "Critical pedagogy situates this glorified democracy as the central struggle on the way to freedom. But, there cannot be democracy without sovereignty" (S. Grande, personal communication).

While writing this, we kept asking each other and ourselves, who has been allowed sovereignty? Does sovereignty have something to do with the right to not be occupied? So together we dug in, allowed ourselves the writing and talking through flipping stomachs and nerves, allowing ourselves to steep in the hard disharmonies between Indigenous thought and PAR, and arrived, steel bellied, grateful, and intact, with this section.

There is a struggle being waged for terms such as *democracy* and *participation.* It is being contested around the world in countries including, but not limited to, Venezuela, Iraq, South Africa, and the United States. Some would like to release the concepts without looking back, believing that they are too tainted to be of use. Others have refused to let go and work to deepen (Appadurai, 2002) and/or thicken (Gandin & Apple, 2002) their meanings. Here, we would like to explore how respectfully learning from (not appropriating, not absorbing) Indigenous thinkers and the ways in which critical participatory research with youth can contribute to wide and deep definitions of the terms *participation* and *democracy.*

Land and language are, and historically have been, stolen and occupied so fast in the United States that it almost stops the tongue. The struggle for sovereignty is a real, experienced struggle for tribal and detribalized people in the United States. The very existence of the struggle could be perceived as a threat to the fantasies we are taught to have of ourselves: sovereignty and the self-determined political, cultural, social status that Indigenous peoples all over the world demand from the governments that have otherwise attempted to absorb or destroy them, through a coarse eye that reads as separatism. Grande (2004, p. 32) maintains that it is not only this struggle but the tribes themselves that are viewed as an "inherent threat to the nation, poised to expose the great lies of U.S. democracy: that we are a nation of laws and not random power, that we are guided by reason and not faith, that we are governed by representation and not executive order, and, finally, that we stand as a self-determined citizenry and not a kingdom of blood or aristocracy."

At the opening of this chapter, we listed some terms that have been, troublingly, expanded to mean something beyond their intended meaning. It is with humility and respect for the Indigenous experience of the struggle for sovereignty that we take Sandy Grande's (2004, p. 32) assertion that sovereignty is democracy's only lifeline, seriously, allowing it to ripple fiercely into the ways that we perceive our own work. We take on sovereignty as a mentor, not metaphor.

In his memoir, Michael J. Fox (2002) describes the rush of feelings he experienced as he completed his first interview in which he, 7 years after first being diagnosed, went public with having young-onset Parkinson's disease. "*Oh my god, what have I done?* I hadn't *shared* my story, *I had given it away.* It was no longer *mine.*" In Julia Alvarez's (1997) novel, *Yo!,* the maid's daughter, Sarita, describes reading the report about her written by Yolanda Garcia, the daughter of the family her mother worked for. "I don't know what I can compare it to. Everything was set down more or less straight, for once. But still I felt as if someone had stolen something from me." Research, interviewing, and storytelling often require those of us with less power to give up more than we planned.

In Eve's experiences as a doctoral student with Aleut ancestry, there have been many times when she has been pressed by colleagues to serve up her grandmother's stories, sacred stories, secret stories, stories of humiliation, stories that would betray her grandmother, in order to placate her colleagues' desires to know her Aleut history. In a visit to a course taught by Joel Spring in the fall of 2005, Sandy Grande echoed this experience. For those imbibed in privilege, to know someone is to expect them to reveal themselves, to tell themselves, to give up their sovereignty, while at the same time, shielded by their privilege, never having to show their own bloodstains, track marks, piling bills, or mismatched socks.

As researchers of people's lives, there are often secrets, silences that, if revealed, make the lives of those vulnerable to institutions and governments more vulnerable. Jennifer Ayala, Latina scholar and participatory researcher, says it well in an online discussion forum we convened around the complexities of doing participatory research: "Knowing/having this is one thing; the choice how/to act on this insider knowledge is a different story altogether. For me, less energy was spent establishing trust, but more is spent with the weight of the responsibility associated with that trust. Here come the fears. Fear of the consequences of critique, fear of betraying those on whom you depend for daily functioning, fear of not asking or looking where you know you should, to avoid conflict."

Sifting through our collective, online chatting reveals a wealth of knowledge as activists/researchers struggle with the "sacred." To respect those secrets, to respect those humming silences, those smells in the hallway, those intimacies and even abuses behind closed doors, those illegal cable boxes, the sacred stories of our ancestors, is to respect the sovereignty that is necessary for democracy. (For a discussion on the teaching of sacred materials, see Allen, 1998.)

Sovereignty, complicated yet crucial to democracy in practice, is at the heart of how we as researchers and storytellers attend to our data.

Michelle: Remember, when you are engaged in participatory work, some knowledge is sacred. Stories of lives and relations are not sitting there like low-hanging fruit, ready for the picking. You have to work with community to determine what is sacred, what will not be documented, reported, defiled. In some communities, you will have to consult with elders, in others you may want to create an advisory group to help you identify where to find evidence of injustice, and what should remain within the group—not reported widely.

Participant: Can you give an example?

Michelle: In some communities, people prefer that instances of domestic violence not be documented because the group is already under siege and surveillance, and the information will only be used against the group.

Participant: But what if that's the reason we want to do the research? To expose how we mistreat each other in my community? How men mistreat women?

As we were reminded in the Global Rights workshop, that which is sacred cannot be relegated to the taboo or homogenized across communities. It is complicated, not to be assumed, and worth a populated discussion. Some researchers go to community elders to determine what is shared through the academy; others seek permission from key community leaders.

At the heart of participatory research lies a desire to resuscitate democracy as a whole, and yet this is an important historic moment to (re)consider democracy. Democracy has been and is being waged on our bodies, in our names, as an occupying force. It has been exposed by Indigenous thinkers as an ideology that thwarts Indigenous interests and maintains the privilege of the power elite (Grande, 2004; G. H. Smith, 2000, p. 211). The practice of democratizing has been a practice of desecration, of burning down, of forgetting, of washing home-language speakers' mouths with soap, of forced removal, of denial, of deprivation, of depletion. In the United States, in schools inculcated by hegemonic democracy, we are taught that democracy is our finest gift to ourselves and the world and our most valuable possession. It is dangerous to say that this emperor has no clothes.

Thus, the work of those involved in participatory research with youth to reclaim and reframe democracy is a vulnerable yet pivotal endeavor. What, then, does it mean for us involved in this endeavor to take sovereignty seriously as a prerequisite to democracy?

For now, for us, it means that each participant in our research has sovereign rights.

Sovereignty as a prerequisite to democracy involves the cease-and-desist of Eurocentric, colonizing power formations. This includes the rights to

> resist or reject Eurocentric theory (Battiste, 2000; Henderson, 2000),
>
> resist or reject versions of themselves that are fantasies of the power elite (Mihesuah, 1998),
>
> resist or reject cognitive imperialism (Battiste, 2000),
>
> explore epistemological differences (Marker, 2006),
>
> reclaim that which has been stolen from them (Marker, 2006),
>
> question democratic models of one person, one vote, and majority rule, or the Westminster model of democracy, which reifies the goals of dominant groups and squashes the rights of those in numeric minority (G. H. Smith, 2000).

Sovereignty as a prerequisite to democracy also calls for us to mind what is sacred. This includes the rights to

> keep what is sacred sacred and to make/mark new spaces and knowledges as sacred,
>
> choose what is and what is not on the table for documentation,
>
> seek the blessings or permission of their own communities of peers and elders to reveal significant information.

Finally, sovereignty as a prerequisite to democracy involves what Avery Gordon (1997) has called the right to complex personhood. Grande (2004) highlights that sovereignty is not a separatist discourse. On the contrary, it is a restorative process. As Warrior suggests, Indigenous peoples must learn to "withdraw without becoming separatists"; we must be "willing to reach out for the contradictions within our experience and open ourselves to the pain and the joy of others" (Warrior, 1995, p. 124, as quoted by Grande, 2004, p. 57). Gordon has called this willingness to reach for contradiction *complex personhood.* Gordon says,

> It has always baffled me why those most interested in understanding and changing the barbaric domination that characterizes our modernity often not always withhold from the very people they are most concerned with the right to complex personhood. . . . Complex personhood means that all people (albeit in specific forms whose specificity is sometimes everything) remember and forget, are beset by contradiction, and recognize and misrecognize themselves and others. At the very least, complex personhood is about conferring the respect on others that comes from presuming that life and people's lives are simultaneously straightforward and full of enormously subtle meaning. (p. 4)

The rights to complex personhood include the rights to

> work and learn and exist in wholeness and to thrive in their relations with other peoples (Grande, 2004, p. 171);
>
> be the sources of their own healing and renewal (Daes, 2000, p. 5);
>
> work and learn and exist in ways that are proactive, not only reactive;
>
> resist or reject propaganda carefully aimed at convincing them that they are backward, ignorant, weak, or insignificant (Daes, 2000, p. 7);
>
> make together a research community that, as Grande (2004, p. 54) cites as the key components of meaningfully sovereign governments, provides stable institutions and policies, fair and effective processes of dispute resolution, effective separation of politics from business management, a competent bureaucracy, and cultural match.

Marker (2006, pp. 3, 5), in his discussion of the Makeh whale hunt as an effort to reclaim stolen cultural space and autonomy in the shadow of colonial and corporate hegemony and the political backlash of local White people on Makeh people, contends that the expression of local Indigenous culture becomes contentious whenever claims on land and resources from tribal representatives are constituted from claims about historic cultural identity. The Makeh people's very rights to complex personhood are being undermined by revisionary history and whitestream Eurocentric culture, which, with law and reason on its side, makes the colonizer capable of sleeping at night or reaching across the dinner or communion table without recoiling from the sense of the blood of the other on his or her hands (Findlay, 2000, p. x). Sovereignty with a commitment to the rights of complex personhood does not defy democracy; it is a requirement.

Obligations and Opportunities of Jumping Scale

A bit deeper into the training, ethical questions about participatory research and indebtedness, loyalty, and betrayal began to fester, under the table, outside in the hallways, in quiet voices. We all understand that participatory work is tethered to political obligation. That is, PAR is undertaken with and for local community to incite protest, to insist on change. PAR with youth self-consciously challenges existing power relations in a place, an institution, for a group of marginalized youth, through a social movement, toward change. Messy audiences, confrontations with power, and tensions across boardroom tables are the stuff of PAR in local soil. This was easy to imagine in the Dominican Republic, Thailand, Colombia, Los Angeles, India....

When we shifted our focus to Geneva, however, asking the youth researchers to "jump scale" (Marston, 2000) to document global circuits of hegemony and resistance, the question of obligation to whom, accountability for what, and being grounded where grew more diffuse. As local projects coagulated toward a vague sense of the global, images of audience and purpose blurred. To whom, for what, with whom, and toward what end do we create materials, products, scholarly documents, performances, exhibitions, and/or protests for global analysis? And so we launched a conversation about the obligations to the ground when jumping scale in participatory work.

The distinct aims of work designed *in/for* place and work designed *across* places occupied the core of this dilemma. Vine Deloria (1994) writes that "most Americans raised in a society in which history is all encompassing . . . have very little idea of how radically their values would shift if they took the idea of place, both sacred and secular, seriously" (pp. 76–77). Sandy Grande (2004) extends the point when she argues that "the centrality of place in the indigenous thought-world is explicitly conveyed through tradition and language and implicitly through the relationship between human beings and the rest of nature" (p. 172). Many of the young people were committed to changes at home. Geneva was a distant romance.

And yet, as much as *place* is central to PAR, we were equally compelled by the idea of youth inquiry as cross-site *movement* of youth resistance, a challenge to the mainstream as Marker (2006) suggests when he writes, "Research on indigenous education is often framed as a glance into an ethnic community rather than a *deep challenge to the mainstream* values and goals of schooling. Indigenous knowledge and approaches to the natural world should become centerpieces for a much broader and substantive discussion rather than simply studying the Other" (p. 22).

While some have argued that human rights discourses have been misused by countries such as the United States as a guise for preemptive wars and/or economic leverage, and therefore are not useful tools for social justice (Chow, 2002), others engaged in transnational politics maintain that "whatever its theoretical weaknesses the polemical power of the rights language as an expression of aspirations for justice across widely different cultures and political-economic conditions cannot easily be dismissed" (Correa & Petchesky, 2003). We sat firmly (and squeamishly) in the latter camp.

Thus, in this section, we pencil in some thoughts about what we are calling the obligations of scale. We even have the audacity to try to tie these notions to the stuffy idea of generalizability, reinvigorating the concept with the radical potential to connect these waves of resistance and scars of oppression that dot the earth, on the heels of colonialism.

First and foremost, we caution that it is necessary that those of us who desire to leap between local participatory and global analyses build, self-consciously and transparently, mechanisms of participation so that our work remains situated, even if multisituated, and accountable to place. Global or cross-site work must remain nonhierarchical and have integrity with home spaces. Global research must remember, always, that the local is its mother.

Perhaps those doing deep local work would not be bound by a reciprocal obligation to think globally. Not clear. But the strings of participation should grow taut, not severed, when social analyses bungee across terrain. Work riding on the heights of global topographies cannot upstage but instead must move sovereign struggles forward in ways that are clear and palpable to those experiencing oppression on the ground.

The need to guard the sovereign demands for one's home struggle and the desire to create a unified coalition were ever present among the young people at Global Rights: Partners for Justice. The young people worked diligently at the nexus of global-local struggles, finding themselves negotiating between "the political quest for sovereignty and the socioeconomic urgency to build transnational coalitions" (Grande, 2004, p. 118).

As facilitators creating research in the service of transnational coalition building, we need to be listening for the whispers over coffee breaks, in informal spaces, that speak to the fear that local demands are being passed over for concepts far more grandiose and unclear. And, at the same time, we appreciate Saskia Sassen's (2005) distinction between global work that enables "transboundary political practices" (p. 163) and global work that is self-consciously about appeals to global actors, treaties, or conventions. These two projects are related, but perhaps important to distinguish. Participatory work ground in local settings may engage in cross-site coalition *and* may organize for/against global entities, but the obligation of accountability sits, we suggest, in the relation between these projects.

A second obligation of jumping scale concerns the tempting and treacherous slide toward homogenization, in the name of solidarity. For those who choose to engage PAR at the local-global juncture, beware the seduction of the universal, the slide toward "the same." Sandy Grande (2004) probes us to think that working across nations, like "multiculturalism," may operate in a homogenizing way. Cindi Katz (2001) contends that "homogenization is not the script of globalization so much as differentiation and even fragmentation" (p. 1215). As we anticipate that local struggles around issues that affect young people are simultaneously becoming more intertwined and more contradictory (Katz, 2001), we have an obligation to guard against silencing dissent/difference as we work to raise social issues in the service of transnational action.

A third obligation suggested by critical geographer Cindi Katz (2003), in her book *Growing Up Global,* and Parameswaran (Chapter 20, this volume) is to focus analytic energies on the *interrelations of youth struggles* in very different places. To this point, Katz's writing on topographies, countertopographies, and contour lines that map situated struggles and histories is useful. Katz encourages analysts to "recognize [that one site] . . . is connected analytically to other places along contour lines that represent not elevation but particular relations to a process (e.g., globalizing capitalist relations of production). This offers a multifaceted way of theorizing the connectedness of vastly different places made artifactually discrete by virtue of history and geography but which also reproduce themselves differently amidst the common political-economic and socio-cultural processes they experience" (p. 1229).

Theorizing the interrelations across place allows us to reveal the ways in which deprivation and privilege are codependent, where racism and global capital join, how patriarchy and homophobia slap each other on the back, how nationalism and colonialism feed each other, how youth bodies are exploited or discarded in the circuits of global power, and/or how resistance movements speak across continents (Winant, 2005).

Our last obligation of scale surfaced in an online discussion group constructed by the authors to push our thinking about participatory action research with young people even further via input from researchers across the globe. In this small corner of cyberspace, we were able to listen to and interact with people deeply embedded in facilitating youth research/activism in places such as Peru, Hawaii, and New Jersey. Although each person's work focused around issues of local importance, a fourth basket of obligations surfaced concerning the delicate ethics and responsibilities of PAR researchers—having access to and responsibility for local knowledge and action. Jennifer Ayala, Latina scholar and participatory researcher, speaks her biography and her research praxis:

> I learned the codes appropriate to each group and could slip and slide between them if/when I chose to. But I wonder. . . .
>
> Am I like
> fading footprints in the snow
> that melt and transform
> to a still water
> who changes shape
> according to what holds me,
> what surrounds me?
>
> I also discovered thin lines of intersection, spaces where bridges could be forged between the worlds I kept separate (Anzaldúa, 1987). Sometimes I danced around that thin line, sometimes I felt I was that thin line between. (Ayala, 2006, p. 5; reprinted with the permission of Jennifer Ayala)

Ayala's reflection on her position "between" and responsibilities with and for knowledge and action is echoed in the online conversation. We invite you to eavesdrop on dialogue that represents a small portion of the learning that was exchanged in this brief coming together:

Carlos Alza Barco (Peru): I work incorporating participatory methodologies in young people in Peru. We are not having a vertical approach of a learning process, but an active and participatory one. They identify their own "participatory practices," thinking about what they do in their participation process. But . . . once you have all the information given, I usually ask myself, *who is called to make the interpretation* of the given experiences?

Caitlin Cahill (NYC): Carlos, your question about who is called to make an interpretation of a given experience raises for me a related dilemma, "how to write about participatory work?" . . . *Representation comes with responsibility.* When I decided that my primary responsibility as a writer/academic researcher in a PAR process should be to the values and concerns of the research team (the collective), I think it made it easier for me to proceed in my own writing. In this regard, I think the PAR project provided for me a blueprint for me as an academic researcher to orient my work. . . . And, while I take seriously my particular contribution as a researcher to develop the analysis, to make connections to wider social and political processes and situate the project in the critical social science literature, I ground my project in collectively produced knowledge.

Renee Louis (Hawai'i): My question revolves around personal experiences. I am Hawaiian working with Hawaiians from another part of the island. At first

> I thought this would provide me more opportunity to view my research from an insider's perspective, and though it has for the most part, it has also provided me with an even larger responsibility.
>
> In relating with the community participants, or "partners in theorizing," I've learned there are subtle tests of character and skill. Once passed, in-depth knowledge is shared but cannot be corroborated because the learning/sharing process is one-on-one. I've been told not to tape anything, to remember everything, and share little to nothing with others.
>
> What I thought would be my opportunity to garner benign information has become a research puzzle as I can only share the tip of the iceberg . . . all the while knowing the information being shared with me is but the tip of another greater iceberg.
>
> Has anyone else ever dealt with such community confidence and responsibility? How do you reconcile that with academic or research imperatives?

As a research collective, we not only struggle with questions of *obligation* that were thrown and returned in our cyberspace volley, but we also thrill nervously at the *opportunities* of scale:

- How can each of us, in our home communities, use the spatialization of global networks and resistance to our advantage (Marston, 2000)?
- How can we deploy information technologies as a strategic opening in transnational space to further youth resistance . . . and still respect local elders and not further an imperialistic erosion of local leadership, community and culture? (Sassen, 2005).
- Can critical youth research form a counter-hegemonic shield against neo-liberal governmentality by "developing and enhancing the capacity of citizens to share power and hence, collaboratively govern themselves?" (Tuhiwai Smith, 2005).
- To what extent can critical youth PAR projects join, across sites and nations, to produce work that can "slow the apparent 'juggernaut of globalization' in favor of visions of development, planned social transformation and redistribution?" (Bhavnani et al., 2005, p. 323)

So, with a desire to contribute to societal transformation, influenced by Grande, Katz, and PAR activists from around the globe, we approach the question of how/what may be "generalized" from the local to global. Traditional notions of generalizability are deliberately troubled in our work—as they should be. But they are not discarded. The question of generalizability is perhaps one of the most vexing and difficult questions in critical inquiry. In common use, generalizability sanctions the application of findings from one study to other settings. Social scientists have been, at once, overly concerned with the technical specificity of empirical generalizability and profoundly underconcerned with generalizability of theory of domination and movements of resistance.

In our work at the global-local hinge, we aim for what we are provisionally calling an *intersectional generalizability*—work that digs deep and respectfully with community to record the particulars of historically oppressed and colonized peoples/communities and their social movements of resistance, as well as work that tracks patterns across nations, communities, homes, and bodies to theorize the arteries of oppression and colonialism. As Battiste suggests in the opening quote, researchers should not study native communities simply to document the "other" but to understand the very constructions of nation, democracy, privilege, and what is considered the nonnative world.

Inquiry that seeks to reveal the historic and contextual specificities of place and identity can shed light on the worldly effects of domination and resistance. For instance, sovereignty struggles came of age in real places, within fierce, place-based struggles for language, dignity, autonomy, and lands under siege. The notion of sovereignty represents the sacrifices and demands of so many peoples and places unearthed by the track marks of colonization. While the details of sovereignty demands differ greatly depending on history, place, and local politics, the broad-based struggle for sovereignty as a "personal" and "collective right" (G. H. Smith, 2000) travels well as an Indigenous demand and, in this text, swells to an obligation of method across oppressed groups. As our work spans between global and local, then, we can hold this exemplar in our head as we articulate methods that begin at home, kneading the local as the foundational base for building toward a global framework.

Justice in Open Air—Or Finding Home Far-There-Away From Geneva

Winona LaDuke (1999) tells us, "We have seen the great trees felled, the wolves taken for bounty, and the fish stacked rotting like cordwood. Those memories compel us, and the return of the descendants of these predators provoke us to stand again, stronger and hopefully with more allies. We are the ones who stand up to the land eaters, the tree eaters, the destroyers and culture eaters" (p. 3).

Linda T. Smith (1999) writes,

> In the first instance indigenous communities share with other marginalized and vulnerable communities a collective and historically sustained experience of research as the Object. They share too the use of research as expert representation of who they are. It is an experience indigenous communities associate with colonialism and racism, with inequality and injustice. More importantly indigenous communities hold an alternative way of knowing about themselves and the environment that has managed to survive the assaults of colonization and its impacts. This alternative way of knowing may be different from what was known several years ago by a community but it is still a way of knowing that provides a different epistemology, an alternative vision of society, an alternative ethics for human conduct. It is not therefore a question of whether the knowledge is "pure" and authentic but whether it has been the means through which people have made sense of their lives and circumstances, that has sustained them and their cultural practices over time, that forms the basis for their understanding of human conduct, that enriches their creative spirit and fuels their determination to be free. (p. 27)

French theorist Erika Apfelbaum (2001) writes, "The imperative to tell—the vital urge not to forget— . . . contains an injunction to the 'awakening of others.' . . . While the imperative to speak is necessary in order for survivors to re-enter a humane society, stubborn deafness may be equally necessary for the inhabitants of that society as they try to keep their ethical values stable and unchallenged" (p. 31).

We like to imagine LaDuke, Smith, and Apfelbaum sharing a park bench dedicated to urgency, outrage, a long struggle, an insistence that those in power listen to those who have been denied. We join them and respectfully ask that youth be invited to the bench, knee deep in social justice inquiry, participating fully, developed rigorously, held tightly, invited to fly.

And now, as we engage PAR collectives, in and beyond the United States, we know we must create participatory research spaces furnished well to comfort young people and elders as they dialogue through the messy dialectics we have surfaced in this chapter. We recognize that for each of these dialectical relations—access/difference, privilege/pain, democracy/sovereignty, global/local—there is an ideological valence, a gendering, racializing, and classing, attached to the split elements. Each prior element—access, privilege, democracy, and global—signals "modern." Each latter element—difference, pain, sovereignty, and local—embodies "backward" or conservative.

Democracy, access, privilege, and globalization are big ideas, associated with men, Whiteness, and progress. Calls for sovereignty, difference, pain, and the local weigh down people and movements. They are carried in the bodies of women, people of color, poor people who are viewed as holding back, resistant or ignorant of what is in their best interest.

We argue in this chapter that participatory work with youth must not only refuse these binaries and the associated valences but also must aggressively trouble the splitting as a form of political (and methodological) dissociation. The dialectics can be engaged through a process of what Meghna Guhathakurta (2008) calls the "incessant social process of problem identifying dialogues." At the heart of participatory design lies a recognition that when the stubborn particulars of local context, what Patti Lather (2005) calls a "sense of acute situatedness" and struggle, are disregarded, globalized justice research becomes another act of colonization. When difference, local, sovereignty, and pain are dissociated from global movements, justice campaigns simply fly above embodied lives and burning communities. But smoldering in these dialectical relations lies the possibility for radical work to be opened up, reconceived, unleashed, or—sometimes—placed away for sacred keeping. This is where critical and indigenous work joins, even as they tip toward very different sensibilities in praxis.

Finally, a word on proof or evidence. The Global Rights project was an exercise in the critical production of radical evidence. But whether we engage with Indigenous or urban youth and elders, women in prison or mothers struggling for quality schools in the Bronx, students working on a GED or first generation in college, or teens with mothers in prison or no mothers at all, a cloud of cynicism hovers—who will listen? As Linda Smith (1999) has written,

> One of the perspectives that indigenous research brings to an understanding of this moment in the history of globalization is that it is simply another historical moment (one of the many that indigenous communities have survived) that reinscribes imperialism with new versions of old colonialism. This is not as cynical as it may sound but rather it comes from the wisdom of survival on the margins. This moment can be analyzed, understood and disrupted by holding onto and rearticulating an alternative vision of life and society. It is also not the only defining moment as other changes have occurred that make communities somewhat more prepared to act or resist. (p. 18)

The work of *proving*, long colonized to mean the work of men, of progress, of the whitestream, the work of scientists, the work of the academy, is reclaimed through participatory research. Participatory research, mentored by Indigenous concepts of "researching back," infused by a call for knowingness, analysis, and recovery (L. T. Smith, 1999), means the proof is under our fingernails, in our melting footprints, on our park benches, in our clusters, in our flights, on our backs, on our chapped lips, in our stories and the grandmothers who told them. Proof is far-there-away from Geneva.

Struggle is ongoing; global provocation is powerful, but home is where we live. Changes in the kitchen are tithed to changes in the UN. And we know, as Aliou and many others have warned, that "proof"—in numbers and stories, in performances, in cost-benefit analyses and in white papers, in the body, the ghosts, the dreams, and the nightmares—constitutes only one resource that must be brought to bear in a long, participatory march toward social justice.

▣ Epilogue

In March 2006, we learned that the young activists of Global Rights would not attend the Human Rights Commission in Geneva but are eager to reconvene under the Manhattan Bridge, to share stories of youth organizing and research globally. Due to the reform process at the UN, the youth did not attend the UN Commission on Human Rights but will meet with representatives of the international financial institutions (World Bank, Inter-American Development Bank) and the donor community in Washington, D.C., to ensure that when loans are provided to implement poverty reduction strategies to achieve the Millennium Development Goals, the unique circumstances of members of minority communities are considered and strategies are designed to affect them positively and not detrimentally.

Back home, the young people have initiated an array of impressive and deeply rooted social change projects with young people in their villages and communities. So, for instance, Neema Mgana was negotiating with Architects for

Humanity to build a medical center in Singida, her community in Tanzania, and, since the Global Partners session, has effectively advocated that they also build a new school in the community. Rodrigo de Paula has selected eight research team members from a college-entry preparation course he leads for mainly Afro-descendant youth living in the *favelas,* and two additional research team members were selected from the dominant or Caucasian community. Together, they are organizing a workshop titled "Discrimination in Your Education," conducting the survey with 120 youth in different schools as well as at summer camps, football fields, the beach, malls, and capoeira classes and developing a Web site and a radio program called *Voices for Education* in conjunction with a community radio station.

James Baay from the Philippines has gathered youth leaders from different Indigenous and marginalized communities to come together to attend a focus group discussion on barriers to education and to discuss their experiences in administering the surveys in their communities.

Elvia Duque is working with Asociacion de Grupos Juveniles Libertad in Colombia and Movimiento Cultural Saya Afroboliviano in Bolivia—two organizations focused on the rights of Afro-descendants—to implement the research project, creating a particularly good opportunity to raise awareness about rights abuses against the Afro-descendant population in that country.

Linda Kayseas is conducting research on the Saulteaux Indigenous peoples from Fishing Lake First Nation in Canada (the marginalized group) and non-Aboriginal or Anglo-Canadians (the dominant group). With permission to conduct the research in the school on the Fishing Lake First Nation reserve, the research team consists of four students and two team leaders: The first leader is from the dominant group, who will lead the research in the school that is off the reserve, and the other leader is a member of the Saulteaux First Nation, who will lead the research in the school on the reserve.

And of course, new problems arise as the work takes on real meaning in real communities. As Mina Setra from Indonesia tells us,

> We decide that if we really want to picture the real story, then we have to do the research in places where the problems really are. And cities are not the place where we can get pure information, since (in our opinion) it has been a bias of social life and opportunities which could influence our resource persons (or even the result of the research itself) in a "place" between "yes or no problems" in education. Got what I mean?
>
> So, to get the better view, better information and better resource persons, peoples who really experience the origin of education problems, we have to conduct the research in villages and subdistricts. Those are places where we can really find and see how the barriers of education affect people's lives, especially when we are talking about Indigenous peoples.
>
> The problems are, we can't conduct this research with a very small budget. . . . It is not about salary or per diem or anything like that, because my team has agreed to do this without those. But, in West Kalimantan, if you want to go to a village or subdistrict, first, you will have to spend a lot of money for the transportation, since transportation facilities here are also still a problem, especially when we decide to divide the team to different villages and subdistricts. Second, with this situation, we can't come and go in one day. The team has to stay for few days, even weeks, to gather the information from peoples.

And so the struggle continues, as the work seeds itself in local places and webs across the globe. We remain privileged to play a small role in a global movement, trying to fight the undertow of global capital and launch a youth-based process for development and social justice.

Appendix

Youth involved came from many countries and communities, including Haitians living in the Dominican Republic; people of Afro-Caribbean descent in Colombia; people in Tanzania; Roma in Bulgaria; people in Brazil; Dalit in India; Pompakng peoples, who live on the island of Borneo; peoples of Injaw descent, from Nigeria; the Batwa (Pygmy) community of Burundi; the

Dibabawon peoples, an indigenous community in the Philippines; and from varied Indigenous and marginalized communities in the United States and Canada.

References

Allen, P. G. (1998). Special problems in teaching Leslie Marmon Silko's *Ceremony.* In D. A. Mihesuah (Ed.), *Natives and academics: Researching and writing about American Indians.* Lincoln: University of Nebraska Press.

Alvarez, J. (1997). *¡Yo!* Madrid: Alfaguara.

Anand, B., Fine, M., Perkins, T., & Surrey, D. (2000). *Keeping the struggle alive: Studying desegregation in our town.* New York: Teachers College Press.

Anyon, J. (2005). *Radical possibilities.* New York: Routledge.

Anzaldúa, G. (1987). *Borderlands/la frontera: The new mestiza.* San Francisco: Spinsters/Aunt Lute.

Apfelbaum, E. (2001). The dread: An essay on communication across cultural boundaries. *International Journal of Critical Psychology, 4,* 19–34.

Appadurai, A. (2002). Deep democracy: Urban governmentality and the horizon of politics. *Public Culture, 14*(1), 21–47.

Appelbaum, R., & Robinson, W. (Eds.). (2005). *Critical globalization studies.* New York: Routledge.

Ayala, J. (2006, April). *Voices in dialogue: What is our work in the academy?* Paper presented at the AERA Annual Meetings, San Francisco.

Battiste, M. (Ed.). (2000). *Reclaiming indigenous voices and vision.* Vancouver: University of British Columbia Press.

Bhavnani, K., Foran, J., & Talcott, M. (2005). The red, the green, the black and the purple: Reclaiming development, resisting globalization. In R. Appelbaum & W. Robinson (Eds.), *Critical globalization studies* (pp. 323–332). London: Routledge.

Brydon-Miller, M., & Tolman, D. (2001). *From subjects to subjectivities: A handbook of interpretive and participatory methods.* New York: New York University Press.

Burns, A. (2004). The racing of capability and culpability in desegregated schools: Discourses of merit and responsibility. In M. Fine, L. Weis, L. P. Pruitt, & A. Burns (Eds.), *Off white: Readings on power, privilege and resistance* (2nd ed., pp. 373–394). New York: Routledge.

Cabannes, Y. (2005). Children and young people build participatory democracy in Latin American cities. *Children, Youth and Environments, 15*(2), 185–210.

Cahill, C. (2004). Defying gravity? Raising consciousness through collective research. *Children's Geographies, 2*(2), 273–286.

Cammarota, J., & Ginwright, S. (2002). New terrain in youth development: The promise of a social justice approach. *Social Justice, 29*(4), 82–96.

Chawla, L., Blanchet-Cohen, N., Cosco, N., Driskell, D., Kruger, J., Malone, K., et al. (2005). Don't just listen—do something! Lessons learned about governance from the Growing Up in Cities Project. *Children, Youth and Environments, 15*(2), 54–88.

Chow, R. (2002). *The Protestant ethnic and the spirit of capitalism.* New York: Columbia University Press.

Cookson, P., & Persell, C. (1985). *Preparing for power.* New York: Basic Books.

Correa, S., & Petchesky, R. (1994). Reproductive and sexual rights: A feminist perspective. In G. Sen, A. Germain, & L. C. Chen (Eds.), *Population policies reconsidered: Health, empowerment, and rights.* Boston: Harvard University Press.

Correa, S., & Petchesky, R. (2003). Reproductive and sexual rights: A feminist perspective. In C. McCann & S. Kim (Eds.), *Feminist theory reader* (pp. 88–102). New York: Routledge.

Daes, E. I. (2000). The experience of colonization around the world. In M. Battiste (Ed.), *Reclaiming indigenous voices and vision* (pp. 3–8). Vancouver: University of British Columbia Press.

Davis, A. (2003). *Are prisons obsolete?* New York: Seven Stories Press.

Deloria, V., Jr. (1994). *God is red: A native view of religion.* Golden, CO: North American Press.

Fals-Borda, O. (Ed.). (1985). *The challenge of social change.* Beverly Hills, CA: Sage.

Findlay, L. M. (2000). Foreword. In M. Battiste (Ed.), *Reclaiming indigenous voices and vision* (pp. ix–xiii). Vancouver: University of British Columbia Press.

Fine, M. (2005). Contesting research: Rearticulation and "thick democracy" as political projects of method. In G. Dimitriadis, C. McCarthy, & L. Weis (Eds.), *Ideology, curriculum, and the new sociology of education: Revisiting the work of Michael Apple* (pp. 146–166). New York: Routledge.

Fine, M., Bloom, J., Burns, A., Chajet, L., Guishard, M., Payne, Y., et al. (2005). Dear Zora: A letter to Zora Neale Hurston fifty years after Brown. *Teachers College Record, 107,* 496–528.

Fine, M., Freudenberg, N., Payne, Y., Perkins, T., Smith, K., & Wanzer, K. (2003). "Anything can happen with police around": Urban youth evaluate strategies of surveillance in public places. *Journal of Social Issues, 59,* 141–158.

Fine, M., Roberts, R., Torre, M., Bloom, J., Chajet, L., Guishard, M., et al. (2004). *Echoes of* Brown: *Youth documenting and performing the legacy of* Brown v. Board of Education. New York: Teachers College Press.

Fine, M., & Torre, M. (2005). Resisting and researching: Youth participatory action research. In S. Ginwright, J. Cammarota, & P. Noguera (Eds.), *Social justice, youth and their communities* (pp. 269–285). New York: Routledge.

Fine, M., & Weis, L. (2003). *Silenced voices and extraordinary conversations: Re-imagining schools.* New York: Teachers College Press.

Fox, M. J. (2002). *Lucky man.* New York: Hyperion.

Freire, P. (1982). Creating alternative research methods: Learning to do it by doing it. In B. Hall, A. Gillette, & R. Tandon (Eds.), *Creating knowledge: A monopoly* (pp. xii–xx). New Delhi, India: Society for Participatory Research in Asia.

Gandin, L. A., & Apple, M. W. (2002). Thin versus thick Democracy in Education: Porto Alegre and the creation of alternatives to neo-liberalism. *International Studies in the Sociology of Education 12*(2), 99–115.

Gandin, L., Amando, A., & Michael, W. (2002). Can education challenge neo-liberalism? The citizen school and the struggle for democracy in Porto Alegre, Brazil. *Social Justice, 29*(4), 26–41.

George, S. (2005). If you want to be relevant: Advice to the academic from a scholar-activist. In R. Applebaum & W. Robinson (Eds.), *Critical globalization studies* (pp. 3–10). New York: Taylor & Francis.

Gilmore, P., Smith, D., & Kairaiuak, A. L. (2004). Resisting diversity: An Alaskan case of institutional struggle. In M. Fine, L. Weis, L. Pruitt, & A. Burns (Eds.), *Off white* (pp. 273–283). New York: Routledge.

Gordon, A. (1997). *Ghostly matters: Haunting and the sociological imagination.* Minneapolis: University of Minnesota Press.

Grande, S. (2004). *Red pedagogy: Native American social and political thought.* Lanham, MD: Rowman & Littlefield.

Guhathakurta, M. (2008). Theatre in participatory action research: Experiences from Bangladesh. In P. Reason & H. Bradbury (Eds.), *The SAGE handbook of action research: Participative inquiry and practice* (2nd ed., pp. 510–521). London: Sage.

Hart, R. (1997). *Children's participation: The theory and practice of involving young citizens in community and environmental care.* London: Earthscan Publications Ltd.

Henderson, J. Y. (2000). Postcolonial ghost dancing: Diagnosing European colonialism. In M. Battiste (Ed.), *Reclaiming indigenous voices and vision.* Vancouver: University of British Columbia Press.

Katz, C. (2001). On the grounds of globalization: A topography for feminist political engagement. *Signs: Journal of Women in Culture & Society, 26*(4), 1213–1234.

Katz, C. (2003). *Growing up global.* Minneapolis: University of Minnesota Press.

LaDuke, W. (1999). *All our relations: Native struggles for land and life.* Cambridge, MA: South End.

Lather, P. (2005, April). *Scientism and scientificity in the rage for accountability: A feminist deconstruction.* Paper presented at the AERA convention, Montreal, Canada.

Lefkowitz, B. (1997). *Our guys: The Glen Ridge rape and the secret life of the perfect suburb.* Berkeley: University of California Press.

Lewin, K. (1946). Action research and minority problems. *Journal of Social Issues, 2*(4), 34–46.

Low, S. (2003). *Behind the gates: Life, security, and the pursuit of happiness in fortress America.* New York: Routledge.

Lykes, M. B., & Coquillon, E. (2006). Participatory and action research and feminisms: Towards transformative praxis. In S. Hesse-Biber (Ed.), *Handbook of feminist research* (pp. 297–326). Thousand Oaks, CA: Sage.

Marcus, G. (1995). Ethnography in/of the world system: The emergency of multi-sited ethnography. *Annual Review of Anthropology, 24,* 95–117.

Marker, M. (2006). After the Makah whalehunt: Indigenous knowledge and limits to multicultural discourse. *Urban Education, 41,* 1–24.

Marston, S. (2000). The social construction of scale. *Progress in Human Geography, 24*(2), 219–242.

Martín-Baró, I. (1994). *Writings for a liberation psychology.* Cambridge, MA: Harvard University Press.

Mihesuah, D. (Ed.). (1998). *Natives and academics: Researching and writing about American Indians.* Lincoln: University of Nebraska Press.

Oliver, M., & Shapiro, T. (1997). *Black wealth/White wealth: A new perspective on racial inequality.* New York: Routledge.

Ormond, A. (2004). *The voices and silences of young Māori people: A world of (im)possibility.* Unpublished doctoral thesis, University of Auckland, New Zealand.

Painter, N. (1995). Soul murder and slavery: Toward a fully-loaded cost accounting. In L. K. Kerber, A. Kessler-Harris, & K. K. Sklar (Eds.), *U.S. history as women's history: New feminist essays* (pp. 125–146). Chapel Hill: University of North Carolina Press.

Payton, C. (1984). Who must do the hard things? *American Psychologist, 39,* 391–397.

Rahman, A. (2008). Some trends in the praxis of PAR. In P. Reason & H. Bradbury (Eds.), *The SAGE handbook of action research: Participative inquiry and practice* (2nd ed., pp. 49–62). London: Sage.

Sassen, S. (2005). The many scales of the global: Implications for theory and politics. In R. Applebaum & W. Robinson (Eds.), *Critical globalization studies* (pp. 155–166). New York: Taylor & Francis.

Scott, J. (1990). *Domination and the arts of resistance: Hidden transcripts.* New Haven, CT: Yale University Press.

Smith, G. H. (2000). Protecting and respecting indigenous knowledge. In M. Battiste (Ed.), *Reclaiming indigenous voices and vision* (pp. 209–224). Vancouver: University of British Columbia Press.

Smith, L. T. (1999). *Decolonizing methodologies: Research and indigenous peoples.* London: Zed.

Smith, L. T. (2005). On tricky ground: Researching the native in an age of uncertainty. In N. K. Denzin & Y. S. Lincoln (Eds.), *The SAGE handbook of qualitative research* (3rd ed., pp. 85–108). Thousand Oaks, CA: Sage.

Smith, N. (1987). Gentrification and the rent gap. *Annals of the Association of American Geographers, 77,* 462–465.

Snell, T. (2003). *BIA: Bureau of Iraqi Affairs?* Retrieved from http://thenativepress.com/rants2.html

Torre, M. E., & Fine, M. (with Alexander, N., & Genao, E.). (2005). "Don't die with your work balled up in your fists": Young urban women resisting the passive revolution. In N. Way & B. Leadbetter (Eds.), *Urban girls* (pp. 221–242). New York: New York University Press.

Winant, H. (2005). Globalization and racism: At home and abroad. In R. Applebaum & W. Robinson (Eds.), *Critical globalization studies* (pp. 121–130). New York: Taylor & Francis.

Zeller-Berkman, S. (2007). Peering in: A look into reflective practices in youth participatory action research. *Community, Youth, and Environments.*

9

CHALLENGING NEOLIBERALISM'S NEW WORLD ORDER

The Promise of Critical Pedagogy

Henry A. Giroux and Susan Searls Giroux

I

Although critical pedagogy has a long and diverse tradition in the United States, its innumerable variations reflect both a shared belief in education as a moral and political practice and a recognition that its value should be judged in terms of how it prepares students to engage in a common struggle for deepening the possibilities of autonomy, critical thought, and a substantive democracy. We believe that critical pedagogy at the current historical moment faces a crisis of enormous proportions. It is a crisis grounded in the now commonsense belief that education should be divorced from politics and that politics should be removed from the imperatives of democracy. At the center of this crisis is a tension between democratic values and market values, between dialogic engagement and an unbridled fundamentalism.

Faith in social amelioration and a sustainable future appears to be in short supply as neoliberal capitalism performs the dual task of using education to train workers for service sector jobs and produce lifelong consumers. At the same time, neoliberalism feeds a growing authoritarianism steeped in religious fundamentalism and jingoistic patriotism, encouraging intolerance and hate as it punishes critical thought, especially if it is at odds with the reactionary religious and political agenda pushed by the Bush administration. Increasingly, education appears useful to those who hold power, and issues concerning how public and higher education might contribute to the quality of democratic public life are either ignored or dismissed. Moral outrage and creative energy seem utterly limited in the political sphere, just as any collective struggle to preserve education as a basis for creating critical citizens is

SOURCE: *Cultural Studies <=> Critical Methodologies*, Volume 6, No. 1, February 2006. © 2006 Sage Publications.

rendered defunct within the corporate drive for efficiency, a logic that has inspired bankrupt reform initiatives such as standardization, high-stakes testing, rigid accountability schemes, and privatization.

Cornel West (2004) has argued that we need to analyze those dark forces shutting down democracy, but "we also need to be very clear about the vision that lures us toward hope and the sources of that vision" (p. 18). In what follows, we want to recapture the vital role that critical pedagogy might play as a language of both critique and possibility by addressing the growing threat of free market fundamentalism and rigid authoritarianism. At the same time, we want to explore what role critical pedagogy can take on in opposing these escalating antidemocratic tendencies and what it might mean to once again connect critical pedagogy to the more prophetic visions of a radical democracy.

Neoliberalism has become one of the most pervasive and dangerous ideologies of the 21st century. Its pervasiveness is evident not only by its unparalleled influence on the global economy but also by its power to redefine the very nature of politics and sociality. Free market fundamentalism rather than democratic idealism is now the driving force of economics and politics in most of the world. Its logic, moreover, has insinuated itself into every social relationship, such that the specificity of relations between parents and children, doctors and patients, teachers and students has been reduced to that of supplier and customer. It is a market ideology driven not just by profits but also by an ability to reproduce itself with such success that, to paraphrase Fred Jameson, it is easier to imagine the end of the world than the end of neoliberal capitalism. Wedded to the belief that the market should be the organizing principle for all political, social, and economic decisions, neoliberalism wages an incessant attack on democracy, public goods, the welfare state, and noncommodified values. Under neoliberalism, everything either is for sale or is plundered for profit: Public lands are looted by logging companies and corporate ranchers; politicians willingly hand the public's airwaves over to powerful broadcasters and large corporate interests without a dime going into the public trust; the environment is polluted and despoiled in the name of profit making just as the government passes legislation to make it easier for corporations to do so; what public services have survived the Reagan-Bush era are gutted to lower the taxes of major corporations (or line their pockets through no-bid contracts, as in the infamous case of Halliburton); schools more closely resemble either jails or high-end shopping malls, depending on their clientele, and teachers are forced to get revenue for their school by hawking everything from hamburgers to pizza parties.

Under neoliberalism, the state now makes a grim alignment with corporate capital and transnational corporations. Gone are the days when the social state "assumed responsibility for a range of social needs" and provisions (Steinmetz, 2003, p. 337). Instead, agencies of government now pursue a wide range of "'deregulations,' privatizations, and abdications of responsibility to the market and private philanthropy" (p. 337). Deregulation, in turn, promotes "widespread, systematic disinvestment in the nation's basic productive capacity" (Bluestone & Harrison, 1982, p. 6). As the search for ever greater profits leads to outsourcing, which accentuates the flight of capital and jobs abroad, flexible production encourages wage slavery for many formerly of the middle class and mass incarceration for those now viewed as disposable populations (i.e., neither good producers nor consumers) at home. Even among the traditionally prounion, proenvironment, prowelfare state Democratic Party, few seem moved to challenge the prevailing neoliberal economic doctrine that, according to Stanley Aronowitz (2003), proclaims "the superiority of free markets over public ownership, or even public regulation of private economic activities, [and] has become the conventional wisdom, not only among conservatives but among social progressives" (p. 21).

Tragically, the ideology and power of neoliberalism is not confined to U.S. borders. Throughout the globe (with the exception of some countries in Latin America), the forces of neoliberalism are on the march, dismantling the historically guaranteed social provisions provided by the welfare state, defining profit making as the essence of democracy, and equating freedom with the unrestricted ability of markets to "govern economic relations free of government regulation" (Aronowitz, 2003, p. 101). Transnational in scope, neoliberalism now imposes its economic regime and market values on developing weaker nations through structural adjustment policies enforced by powerful financial institutions such as the World Bank, the International Monetary Fund (IMF), and the World Trade Organization (WTO). The effect on schools in postcolonial nations is particularly bleak, as policy reforms financially starve institutions of higher learning as they standardize—with the usual emphasis on skills and drills over critical thinking or critical content—the curricula of primary schools.

Secure in its dystopian vision that there are no alternatives, as England's former Prime Minister Margaret Thatcher once put it, neoliberalism obviates issues of contingency, struggle, and social agency by celebrating the inevitability of economic laws in which the ethical ideal of intervening in the world in order to deepen and expand democratic values and relations gives way to the idea that we "have no choice but to adapt both our hopes and our abilities to the new global market" (Aronowitz, 1998, p. 7). Situated within a culture of fear, market freedoms seem securely grounded in a defense of national security, capital, and property rights. When coupled with a media-driven culture of panic and the everyday reality of insecurity, surviving public spaces have become increasingly monitored and militarized. Recently, events in New York, New Jersey, and Washington, D.C., provide an interesting case in point. When the media alerted the nation's citizenry to new terrorist threats specific to these areas, CNN ran a lead story on its effect on tourism—specifically on the enthusiastic clamor over a new kind of souvenir as families scrambled to get their pictures taken among U.S. paramilitary units now lining city streets, fully flanked with their imposing tanks and massive machine guns. The accoutrements of a police state now vie with high-end shopping and museum visits for the public's attention, all amid a thunderous absence of protest. But the investment in surveillance and containment is hardly new. Since the early 1990s, state governments have invested more in prison construction than in education; prison guards and security personnel in public schools are two of the fastest growing professions. Such revolutionary changes in the global body politic demand that we ask what citizens are learning from this not so hidden curriculum organized around markets and militarization. As that syllabus is written, we must ponder the social costs of breakneck corporatization bolstered by an authoritarianism that links dissent with abetting terrorism.

In its capacity to dehistoricize and naturalize such sweeping social change, as well as in its aggressive attempts to destroy all of the public spheres necessary for the defense of a genuine democracy, neoliberalism reproduces the conditions for unleashing the most brutalizing forces of capitalism. Social Darwinism has risen like a phoenix from the ashes of the 19th century and can now be seen in full display on most reality TV programs and in the unfettered self-interest that now drives popular culture. As social bonds are replaced by unadulterated materialism and narcissism, public concerns are now understood and experienced as utterly private miseries, except when offered up on *Jerry Springer* as fodder for entertainment. Where public space—or its mass-mediated simulacrum—does exist, it is mainly used as a highly orchestrated and sensational confessional for private woes, a cutthroat game of winner-take-all replacing more traditional forms of courtship, as in *Who Wants to Marry a Millionaire,* or as advertisement for crass consumerism, like MTV's *Cribs.*

As neoliberal policies dominate politics and social life, the breathless rhetoric of the global victory of free market rationality is invoked to cut public expenditures and undermine those noncommodified public spheres that serve as the repository for critical education, language, and public intervention. Spewed forth by the mass media, right-wing intellectuals, religious fanatics, and politicians, neoliberal ideology, with its merciless emphasis on deregulation and privatization, has found its material expression in an all-out attack on democratic values and social relations—particularly those spheres where such values are learned and take root. Public services such as health care, child care, public assistance, education, and transportation are now subject to the rules of the market. Forsaking the public good for the private good and representing the needs of the corporate and private sector as the only source of sound investment, neoliberal ideology produces, legitimates, and exacerbates the existence of persistent poverty, inadequate health care, racial apartheid in the inner cities, and the growing inequalities between the rich and the poor (Henwood, 2003; Krugman, 2003; Phillips, 2003).

As Stanley Aronowitz (2003) points out, the Bush administration has made neoliberal ideology the cornerstone of its program and has been in the forefront in actively supporting and implementing the following policies:

> deregulation of business at all levels of enterprises and trade; tax reduction for wealthy individuals and corporations; the revival of the near-dormant nuclear energy industry; limitations and abrogation of labor's right to organize and bargain collectively; a land policy favoring commercial and industrial development at the expense of conservation and other proenvironment policies; elimination of income support to the chronically unemployed; reduced federal aid to education and health; privatization of the main federal pension programs, Social Security; limitation on the right of aggrieved individuals to sue employers and corporations who provide services; in addition, as social programs are reduced, [Republicans] are joined by the Democrats in favoring increases in the repressive functions of the state, expressed in the dubious drug wars in the name of fighting crime, more funds for surveillance of ordinary citizens, and the expansion of the federal and local police forces. (p. 102)

Central to neoliberal ideology and its implementation by the Bush administration is the ongoing attempt by right-wing politicians to view government as the enemy of freedom (except when it aids big business) and discount it as a guardian of the public interest (Giroux, 2007). The call to eliminate big government is neoliberalism's grand unifying idea and has broad popular appeal in the United States because it is a principle deeply embedded in the country's history and tangled up with its notion of political freedom—not to mention the endless appeal of its clarion call to cut taxes. And yet, the right-wing appropriation of this tradition is racked with contradictions, as Republicans outspend their Democratic rivals, drive up deficits, and expand—not shrink—the largely repressive arm of big government's counterterrorism-military-surveillance-intelligence complex (Giroux, 2006).

Indeed, neoliberals have attacked what they call big government when it has provided crucial safety nets for the poor and dispossessed, but they have no qualms about using the government to bail out the airline industry after the economic nosedive that followed the 2000 election of George W. Bush and the events of 9/11. Nor are there any expressions of outrage from free market cheerleaders when the state engages in promoting various forms of corporate welfare by providing billions of dollars in direct and indirect subsidies to multinational corporations. In short, the current government responds not to citizens, but to citizens with money, bearing no obligation for the swelling ranks of the poor or for the collective future of young people.

The liberal democratic lexicon of rights, entitlements, social provisions, community, social responsibility, living wage, job security, equality, and justice seems oddly out of place in a country where the promise of democracy—and the institutions necessary for its survival over generations—has been gutted, replaced by casino capitalism, a winner-take-all philosophy suited to lotto players and day traders alike. As corporate culture extends even deeper into the basic institutions of civil and political society, buttressed daily by a culture industry in the hands of a few media giants, free market ideology is reinforced even further by the pervasive fear and insecurity of the public, who have little accessibility to countervailing ideas and believe that the future holds nothing beyond a watered-down version of the present. As the prevailing discourse of neoliberalism seizes the public imagination, there is no vocabulary for progressive social change, democratically inspired visions, critical notions of social agency, or the kinds of institutions that expand the meaning and purpose of democratic public life. In the vacuum left by diminishing democracy, a new kind of authoritarianism steeped in religious zealotry, cultural chauvinism, xenophobia, and racism has become the dominant trope of neoconservatives and other extremist groups eager to take advantage of the growing insecurity, fear, and anxiety that result from increased joblessness, the war on terror, and the unraveling of communities.

As a result of the consolidated corporate attack on public life, the maintenance of democratic public spheres from which to launch a moral vision or to engage in a viable struggle over institutions and political vision loses all credibility—as well as monetary support. As the alleged wisdom and commonsense of neoliberal ideology remains largely unchallenged within dominant pseudo public spheres, individual critique and collective political struggles become more difficult.[1] Dominated by extremists, the Bush administration is driven by an arrogance of power and inflated sense of moral righteousness mediated largely by a false sense of certitude and never-ending posture of triumphalism. As George Soros (2004) points out, this rigid ideology and inflexible sense of mission allows the Bush administration to believe that "because we are stronger than others, we must know better and we must have right on our side. This is where religious fundamentalism comes together with market fundamentalism to form the ideology of American supremacy" (p. 1).

II

As public space is increasingly commodified and the state becomes more closely aligned with capital, politics is defined largely by its policing functions rather than as an agency for peace and social reform. As the state abandons its social investments in health, education, and the public welfare, it increasingly takes on the functions of an enhanced security or police state, the signs of which are most visible in the increasing use of the state apparatus to spy on and arrest its subjects, the incarceration of individuals considered disposable (primarily people of color), and the ongoing criminalization of social policies. Nowhere is this more visible than in the nation's schools. Part of the reason for the continuing crisis in American public schooling is due to federal cuts in education ongoing since the Reagan administration. The stated rationale for such a shift in national priorities is that American public schools are bureaucratic, wasteful, and altogether ineffectual—the result of a "big government" monopoly on education. As a result of such inefficiency, the public school system poses a threat to national security and U.S. economic dominance in the world market. To be sure, some public schools are really ailing, but the reasons for this, according to David Berliner and Bruce Biddle (1996), authors of *The Manufactured Crisis,* have to do with the grossly unequal funding of public education, residential segregation, the astonishingly high poverty rates of U.S. schoolchildren relative to most other industrialized nations, coupled with inadequate health care and social services. Preferring the former diagnosis of general ineptitude, the current administration insists that throwing money at schools will not cure public school ills and will no longer be tolerated.

Rather than address the complexity of educational inequalities disproportionately affecting poor and minority students, the George W. Bush administration sought solutions to troubled public schools in the much touted No Child Left Behind (NCLB) legislation, which afforded certain key advantages to constituencies in favor of privatization, all the while appearing sympathetic to the plight of poor and minority youth. Not only do they maintain the advantages accorded White students who perform better on average than Black and Latino students on standardized tests, the proposed school reforms are also very business friendly. Renamed "No Child Left Untested" by critics, the reform places high priority on accountability, tying what little federal monies schools receive to improved test performance. For additional financial support, public schools are left no other meaningful option than engaging in public/private partnerships, like the highly publicized deals cut with soft drink giants that provide schools with needed revenue in exchange for soda machines in cafeterias. And it is clear that media giants who own the major publishing houses will benefit from the 52 million-strong market of public school students now required to take tests every year from the third grade on.

The effect of NCLB also proved highly televisable, with visibility now a key factor in the art of persuading a public weaned from political debate in favor of the spectacle. Thus, the media provide routine reportage of school districts' grade cards, public—often monetary—rewards given to those schools that score high marks on achievement tests, liquidation of those that don't. Media preoccupation with school safety issues, moreover, ensures highly publicized expulsion, sometimes felony incarceration, of troublemakers, typically students of color. In short, accountability for teachers and administrators and zero tolerance for students who commit even the most minor infractions are the new educational imperatives, all of which demonstrate that the federal government is "doing something" to assuage public fears about the nation's schools that it largely created through financial deprivation and policies favoring resegregation. As a result, financially strapped schools spend precious resources on testing and prep materials as well as new safety measures, such as metal detectors, armed guards, security cameras, and fencing, in accordance with NCLB. In addition to draining public schools financially, both high-stakes testing and zero-tolerance policies have served to push out or kick out Black and Latino youth in disproportionate numbers, as has been extensively documented by Henry Giroux (2003) in *The Abandoned Generation;* Ayers, Ayers, and Dohrn (2001) in *Zero Tolerance;* and Gary Orfield and Mindy Kornhaber (2001) in *Raising Standards or Raising Barriers?* As democracy becomes a burden under the reign of neoliberalism, civic discourse disappears or is subsumed by a growing authoritarianism in which politics is translated into unquestioning allegiance to authority and secular education is disdained as a violation of God's law.

Market fundamentalism increasingly appears at odds with any viable notion of critical education and appears even more ominous as it aligns itself with the ideologies of militarism and religious fundamentalism. The democratic character of critical pedagogy is defined largely through a set of basic assumptions, which holds that knowledge, power, values, and institutions must be made available to critical scrutiny, be understood as a product of human labor (as opposed to God-given), and evaluated in terms of how they might open up or close down democratic practices and experiences. Yet, critical pedagogy is about more than simply holding authority accountable through the close reading of texts, the creation of radical classroom practices, or the promotion of critical literacy. It is also about linking learning to social change, education to democracy, and knowledge to acts of intervention in public life. Critical pedagogy encourages students to learn to perceive the tolerable as intolerable, as well as to take risks in creating the conditions for forms of individual and social agency that are conducive to a substantive democracy. Part of the challenge of any critical pedagogy is making schools and other sites of pedagogy safe from the baneful influence of corporate power—ranging from the discourses of privatization and consumerism, the methodologies of standardization and accountability, to new disciplinary techniques of surveillance, expulsion, and incarceration aimed at the throwaways of global capital, principally poor youth and youth of color.

Resisting such a radical challenge to democratic principles and practices means that educators need to rethink the important presupposition that public education cannot be separated from the imperatives of a nonrepressive and inclusive democratic order and that the crisis of public education must be understood as part of the wider crisis of politics, power, and culture. Recognizing the inextricable link between education and democracy is central to reclaiming the sanctity of public education as a democratic public sphere, necessarily free of the slick come-ons of corporate advertisers or, for that matter, Junior Reserve Officers' Training Corps (JROTC). Central, too, is the recognition that the politics of persuasion cannot be separated from the pedagogical force of culture. Pedagogy should provide the theoretical tools and resources necessary for understanding how culture works as an educational force, how public education connects to other sites of pedagogy, and how identity, citizenship, and agency are organized through pedagogical relations and practices. Rather than viewed as an a priori method, pedagogy must be understood as a moral and political practice that always presupposes particular renditions of what represents legitimate knowledge, values, citizenship, modes of understanding, and views of the future.

Moreover, pedagogy as a critical practice should provide the classroom conditions that provide the knowledge, skills, and culture of questioning necessary for students to engage in critical dialogue with the past, question authority and its effects, struggle with ongoing relations of power, and prepare themselves for what it means to be critical, active citizens in the interrelated local, national, and global public spheres. Of course, acknowledging that pedagogy is political because it is always tangled up with power, ideologies, and the acquisition of agency does not mean that it is, by default, propagandistic, closed, dogmatic, or uncritical of its own authority. Most important, any viable notion of critical pedagogy must demonstrate that there is a difference between critical pedagogical practices and propagandizing, and demagoguery. Such a pedagogy should be open and discerning, fused with a spirit of inquiry that fosters rather than mandates critical modes of individual and social agency.

We believe that if public education is a crucial sphere for creating citizens equipped to exercise their freedoms and competent to question the basic assumptions that govern democratic political life, teachers in both public schools and higher education will have to assume their responsibility as citizen-scholars by taking critical positions; relating their work to larger social issues; offering students knowledge, debate, and dialogue about pressing social problems; and providing the conditions for students to have hope and believe that civic life matters, that they can make a difference in shaping it so as to expand its democratic possibilities for all groups. It means taking positions and engaging practices currently at odds with both religious fundamentalism and neoliberal ideology. Educators now face the daunting challenge of creating new discourses, pedagogies, and collective strategies that will offer students the hope and tools necessary to revive the culture of politics as an ethical response to the demise of democratic public life. Such a challenge suggests struggling to keep alive those institutional spaces, forums, and public spheres that support and defend critical education, helping students come to terms with their own power as individual and social agents, exercising civic courage, and engaging in community projects and research that are socially responsible, while refusing to surrender knowledge and skills to the highest bidder. In part, this requires pedagogical practices that connect the space of language, culture, and identity to its deployment in larger physical and social spaces. Such a pedagogy is based on the presupposition that it is not enough to teach students to break with accepted ideas. They must also learn to directly confront the threat from fundamentalisms of all varieties that seek to turn democracy into a mall, a sectarian church, or a wing of the coming punishing state, a set of options that must be understood as an assault on democracy.

There are those critics who in tough economic times insist that providing students with anything other than work skills threatens their future viability on the job market. Although we believe that public education should equip students with skills to enter the workplace, it should also educate them to contest workplace inequalities, imagine democratically organized forms of work, and identify and challenge those injustices that contradict and undercut the most fundamental principles of freedom, equality, and respect for all people who make up the global public sphere. Public education is about more than job preparation or even critical consciousness raising; it is also about imagining different futures and politics as a form of intervention into public life. In contrast to the cynicism and political withdrawal that media culture fosters, a critical education demands that its citizens be able to translate the interface of private considerations and public issues; be able to recognize those antidemocratic forces that deny social, economic, and political justice; and be willing to give some thought to their experiences as a matter of anticipating and struggling for a better world. In short, democratic rather than commercial values should be the primary concerns of both public education and the university.

If right-wing reforms in public education continue unchallenged, the consequences will reflect a society in which a highly trained, largely White elite will command the techno-information revolution while a vast, low-skilled majority of poor and minority workers will be relegated to filling the McJobs proliferating in the service sector. In contrast to this vision, we strongly believe that genuine, critical education cannot be confused with job training. If educators and others are to prevent this distinction from becoming blurred, it is crucial to challenge the ongoing corporatization of public schools while upholding the promise of the modern social contract in which all youth, guaranteed the necessary protections and opportunities, are a primary source of economic and moral investment, symbolizing the hope for a democratic future. In short, we need to recapture our commitment to future generations by taking seriously the Protestant theologian Dietrich Bonhoeffer's belief that the ultimate test of morality for any democratic society resides in the condition of its children. If public education is to honor this ethical commitment, it will have to not only reestablish its obligation to young people but also reclaim its role as a democratic public sphere.

Our insistence on the promise of critical pedagogy is not a call for any one ideology on the political spectrum to determine the shape of the future direction of public and university education. But at the same time, it reflects a particular vision of the purpose and meaning of public and higher education and their crucial role in educating students to participate in an inclusive democracy. Critical pedagogy is an ethical referent and a call to action for educators, parents, students, and others to reclaim public education as a democratic public sphere, a place where teaching is not reduced to learning how either to master tests or to acquire low-level job skills, but a safe space where reason, understanding, dialogue, and critical engagement are available to all faculty and students. Public education, in this reading, becomes a site of ongoing struggle to preserve and extend the conditions in which autonomy of judgment and freedom of action are informed by the democratic imperatives of equality, liberty, and justice. Public education has always, although within damaged traditions and burdened forms, served as a symbolic and concrete reminder that the struggle for democracy is, in part, an attempt to liberate humanity from the blind obedience to authority and that individual and social agency gain meaning primarily through the freedoms guaranteed by the public sphere, where the autonomy of individuals only becomes meaningful under those conditions that guarantee the workings of an autonomous society. Critical pedagogy is a reminder that the educational conditions that make democratic identities, values, and politics possible and effective have to be fought for more urgently at a time when democratic public spheres, public goods, and public spaces are under attack by market and other ideological fundamentalists who believe either that corporations in top competitive form can solve all human affliction or that dissent is comparable to aiding terrorists—positions that share the common denominator of disabling a substantive notion of ethics, politics, and democracy.

We live in very dark times, yet as educators, parents, activists, and workers, we can address the current assault on democracy by building local and global alliances and engaging in struggles that acknowledge and transcend national boundaries, while demonstrating how these intersect with people's everyday lives. Democratic struggles cannot underemphasize the special responsibility of intellectuals to shatter the conventional wisdom and myths of neoliberalism with its stunted definition of freedom and its depoliticized and dehistoricized definition of its own alleged inevitability. As the late Pierre Bourdieu (1998) argued, any viable politics that challenges neoliberalism must refigure the role of the state in limiting the excesses of capital and providing important social provisions. In particular, social movements must address the crucial issue of education as it develops both formally and informally throughout the cultural sphere because the "power of the dominant order is not just economic, but intellectual—lying in the realm of beliefs" (Bourdieu & Grass, 2003, p. 66), and it is precisely within the domain of ideas that a sense of utopian possibility can be restored to the public realm. Pedagogy in this instance is not simply about critical thinking but also about social engagement, a crucial element of not just learning but politics itself.

Most specifically, democracy necessitates forms of education and critical pedagogical practices that provide a new ethic of freedom and a reassertion of collective identity as central preoccupations of a vibrant democratic culture and society. Such a task, in part, suggests that intellectuals, artists, unions, and other progressive individuals and movements create teach-ins all over the country in order to name, critique, and connect the forces of market fundamentalism to the war at home and abroad, the shameful tax cuts for the rich, the dismantling of the welfare state, the attack on unions, the erosion of civil liberties, the incarceration of a generation of young black and brown men and women, the attack on public schools, and the growing militarization of public life. As Bush's credibility crisis grows, the time has come to link the matters of economics with the crisis of political culture and to connect the latter to the crisis of democracy itself. We need a new language for politics, for analyzing where it can take place, and what it means to mobilize various alliances to reclaim, as Cornel West (2004) has aptly put it, hope in dark times.

Note

1. Of course, there is widespread resistance to neoliberalism and its institutional enforcers such as the WTO and IMF among many intellectuals, students, and global justice movements, but this resistance rarely gets aired in the dominant media and, if it does, it is often dismissed as irrelevant or tainted by Marxist ideology.

References

Aronowitz, S. (1998). Introduction. In P. Freire (Ed.), *Pedagogy of freedom* (pp. 1–19). Lanham, MD: Rowman & Littlefield.

Aronowitz, S. (2003). *How class works.* New Haven, CT: Yale University Press.

Ayers, R., Ayers, W., & Dohrn, B. (Eds.). (2001). *Zero tolerance: Resisting the drive for punishment.* New York: The New Press.

Berliner, D., & Biddle, B. (1996). *The manufactured crisis.* New York: Addison-Wesley.

Bluestone, B., & Harrison, B. (1982). *The deindustrialization of America: Plant closings, community abandonment and the dismantling of basic industry.* New York: Basic Books.

Bourdieu, P. (1998). *Acts of resistance: Against the tyranny of the market.* New York: The New Press.

Bourdieu, P., & Grass, G. (2003, March–April). The "progressive" restoration: A Franco-German dialogue. *New Left Review, 14,* 63–77.

Giroux, H. (2003). *The abandoned generation.* New York: Palgrave McMillan.

Giroux, H. (2006). *The university in chains: Confronting the military/industrial/academic complex.* Boulder, CO: Paradigm.

Giroux, H. (2007). *Against the terror of neoliberalism: Beyond the politics of greed.* Boulder, CO: Paradigm.

Henwood, D. (2003). *After the new economy.* New York: The New Press.

Krugman, P. (2003). *The great unraveling: Losing our way in the new century.* New York: W. W. Norton.

Orfield, G., & Kornhaber, M. (2000). *Raising standards or raising barriers?* New York: Century Foundation Press.

Phillips, K. (2003). *Wealth and democracy: A political history of the American rich.* New York: Broadway.

Soros, G. (2004, January 26). The US is now in the hands of a group of extremists. *The Guardian/UK.* Retrieved from www.commondreams.org/views04/0126-01.htm.

Steinmetz, G. (2003). The state of emergency and the revival of American imperialism: Toward an authoritarian post-Fordism. *Public Culture, 15*(2), 323–346.

West, C. (2004). Finding hope in dark times. *Tikkun, 19*(4), 18–20.

10

RETHINKING CRITICAL PEDAGOGY

Socialismo Nepantla *and the Specter of Che*

Nathalia Jaramillo and Peter McLaren

It is difficult to imagine a more ominous time to be addressing the importance of indigenous knowledges and the struggle against imperialism, neoliberal capitalism, and what Peruvian scholar Aníbal Quijano (1998) describes as the "coloniality of power." We are challenged into believing that we live in anything but a racist state when anti-immigration zealots are sporting "Kill a Mexican Today?" shirts; when talk show hosts are calling for citizens to arm themselves in a defense of the border with Mexico (one Arizona talk show host, Brian James, even urged listeners to commit murder when he advocated that they converge on the border one day a week with high-powered weapons [he described what ammunition to use so that the shots were sure to be fatal] and shoot to kill those who dared cross the line); when members of Jim Gilchrist's neofascist The Minuteman Project are organizing for-profit human safaris where U.S. citizens can join them in capturing undocumented Mexicans who have managed to cross illegally into the United States; when a family-owned Mexican restaurant near San Diego is firebombed and the words "Fuck Mex" spray-painted on the walls (Ross, 2006); when vigilante ranchers such as Roger Barnett are accused of terrorizing the children of undocumented workers with a loaded AR-15 automatic rifle; when there is a sickening boost in popularity for the Internet video game *Border Patrol,* a Flash-based game (complete with splattered blood) that lets players shoot at undocumented Mexican immigrants as they try to cross the border into the United States; when the quiet Pennsylvania town of Hazleton, infamous for its "Illegal Immigrant Relief Act" that imposes penalties on businesses and landlords to deter them from hiring or renting rooms to undocumented immigrants, declares that as part of a citizen-organized public awareness program to

AUTHORS' NOTE: Our treatment of Che's work has been adapted from Peter McLaren, The Future of the Past: Foreword to the *Marxism of Che Guevara* by Michael Lowy (pp. vii–xxiv). Lanhanm, MD: Rowman and Littlefield, 2007.

demonstrate the town's "zero-tolerance" policy toward undocumented immigrants, it is banning Santa Claus this Christmas; and when more than 30 other towns are considering similar laws to the Illegal Immigrant Relief Act to drive out undocumented workers. These are more than malapropos, foot-in-the-mouth actions fired off in the heat of the moment; they are egregious hate-filled racist acts.

Immigration agents are sweeping through towns across the United States and, without warrants, seizing Latina/os from homes and factories. A recent roundup of undocumented workers in New Bedford, Massachusetts, by Immigration and Customs Enforcement (ICE) agents saw 361 workers from Guatemala, Honduras, El Salvador, Brazil, Cape Verde, and Portugal taken to Fort Devins in the Boston area and then shipped to prisons in Texas and Albuquerque, New Mexico. Nursing infants were separated from their mothers, and children were left in schools and day care centers while their parents were being detained. The ICE even tried to pressure the New Bedford Division of Social Services to put these motherless and/or fatherless children into foster homes. These actions bring to mind Herbert Hoover's Mexican Reparation campaign during the Great Depression that oversaw the deportation of two million Mexicans and Mexican Americans (60% of whom were children born in the United States while the rest were mostly U.S. citizens), the deportation of Chinese immigrants from more than two hundred towns at the turn of the century, and the creation of the "anti-Coolie" League and vigilante committees such as the "601"—six feet under, zero trial, one bullet. Recently, the Ku Klux Klan and the American Nazi Party announced in front of a burning cross to ABC *Evening News* that since they began assaulting, torching, and "bleaching" Latinos, their membership has grown by 40% (Pfaelzer, 2007).

With undocumented maids and housekeepers taking care of their children for the evening, couples of New York's ruling elite can kick up their magniloquent heels at the Algonquin Hotel, where they can purchase a $10,000 "martini on a rock" (that comes with a diamond at the bottom of the glass) or attend many of the fancy eateries of Manhattan that serve up $50 hamburgers, thousand dollar omelets, or Bling mineral water at $90 a bottle (Roberts, 2007).

Such unvarnished decadence means very little to those who bring beeswax candles to the graveyard shrine of Juan Soldado at Tijuana's Panteon No. 1, a green stucco shack filled with candles, urns, Mexican flags, chipped ceramic sculptures, and handwritten testimonios to this popular saint of border crossers. For them, miracles sometimes happen, and their trek to *las entranas de la bestia* in Gringolandia might prove fatefully important, if not for them, then for the future well-being of their children. Drinking a bottle of Bling would be much less satisfying for these stalwart souls than witnessing Soldado's corpse rising from his adjacent turquoise tomb, walking through the frayed Astroturf portal that frames it, and leading a sacred march north to the sound of *corridos* for all those past and present generations of Mexicans who have been humbled and humiliated by centuries of U.S. imperialism, both economic and military.

Those of us who work in the field of critical pedagogy are acutely aware of how the recent climate of anti-immigration and vigilante justice constrains the development of an informed, critical citizenry and instead enables further the naturalization of racialized capitalist social relations. Anti-immigrant fever is but a symptom of a much larger crisis of capitalism and the racialized social antagonisms that follow in its wake. Our concern over recent years has been to take critical pedagogy in a direction where it is able to address globalized capitalist relations by learning from anti-imperialist struggles in various sites worldwide, Venezuela being one example. Our own approach to this challenge has been to rethink critical pedagogy from a Marxist humanist perspective.

Critical pedagogy is best understood in relation to that from which it departs: mainstream-oriented pedagogy that seeks accommodation with the interest group political system that populates the dark chambers of corporate capital. While critical educators are indeed hospitable to efforts at progressive educational reform, even those incremental reforms that are fought for tooth and nail from the ground up in local educational wards, not all of them are committed to a project that seeks to transform the very system of capital from which they attempt to wrest their reforms. While all critical educators can, to a large extent, agree with making education a theme-driven, student-centered, humanizing experience by ridding pedagogical practices of their necromania (authoritarian teaching methods and "banking" practices where knowledge is deposited into what is perceived to be the empty heads of the students), not all of these same educators agree about the kind of society that critical pedagogy would like to take part in creating. To seek to create a postcapitalist society is, for many critical educators as well as mainstream educators, to mistake for reality a pipedream conjured from the rusted hookahs of *professeurs radicaux.* It is to join the chorus of the often raised and constantly repeated objections to socialism as an enemy of democracy that would create a society of idlers and parasites, recumbent figures inhabiting the streets, the taverns, and the billiard halls, utopian navel-gazers, and heartless bureaucrats seeking to maintain a hollow coexistence—an intoxicating numbness—among its listless masses. Finding such objections untenable, we have named the society that we seek to create with the help of critical pedagogy a socialist one, and our work draws widely on the socialist tradition. We seek to do more than gingerly take capitalism to task for its unfriendly shortcomings but to deracinate the very social relations spawned by capitalism's law of value. Because socialism is not an endpoint but an unfinished process that demands criticism in order to develop, we prefer to see it as a form of perpetual pedagogy.

As educators interested in an analysis of subjective formation and our self-constitution as social agents within the totality of capitalist social relations, we have followed the work of those scholars who have begun to explore the intersection of nationalism, imperialism, and subjective formation as these have been affected by contemporary geopolitics and the struggle among the oppressed for liberation. The work of these scholars has made important contributions to our understanding of the intersection between human agency and social, cultural, and institutional relations. What we have discovered is that ideas not only seek to be made into reality (through *hechos* or concrete actions) but reality itself reaches out to be made into an idea. Without such a reaching out, we are left only with empty gestures or disconnected, circular lucubrations. When these two processes occur simultaneously (we could even say dialectically), we call this praxis, and when praxis occurs in the context of class struggle, we call this a revolution. In this respect, reality does not need to accommodate or adjust itself to socialism; rather, socialism is reality coming into existence through the efforts of those who wish to expand the conditions of possibility for social justice and human freedom.

Capitalist social relations of production and accumulation have generated and continue to ignite global crises of overproduction and overaccumulation. On the horizon loom more potential wars and devastation more terrible than have ever been imagined by our most prescient science fiction writers. The U.S. military's pernicious geopolitical struggle for strategic advantage in regions throughout the world that contain scarce resources such as oil, natural gas, and water; the by-any-means-necessary strategy that the transnational capitalist class is ready to exercise on its own behalf in the face of U.S. and world economic stagnation; and the frenetic forward momentum of the U.S. war machine since the demise of the Soviet Union have all set the stage for what John Bellamy Foster (2005) calls "naked imperialism"—the vicious imperialistic pursuit of U.S. global hegemony. Against this brute panorama expanding its toxic reach across the planet and its inhabitants, we bring into focus the seldom cited domains of class and class consciousness in rethinking critical pedagogy toward a socialist future.

From Class Consciousness to *Nepantlismo*

One of the key areas of inquiry in our attempt to understand the formation of subjectivity and human agency has been that of class consciousness. Our application of the term *class consciousness* proceeds from the larger social formation of capitalism in reference to the dialectical relations that both constrain and broaden the conditions for classed societies to enact processes for social change. Contrary to orthodox conceptions of class as a set of individual or collective economic expressions (e.g., I, we reproduce capital) or the Weberian-derived formulations of class as a contingent effect of culture and market forces on lifestyle and consumption habits, status, or social prestige, we discuss class in relationship to ownership of the means of production and whether individuals and groups are dependent on wage labor to survive; we also discuss class consciousness in terms of a collective topography reflective of the means that shape ontological existence. Following Bertell Ollman (1993), our understanding of class is derived from a sense of place within the capitalist social structure. Composed of real people who cohere around the qualities of individuals that constitute a particular group formation, class underscores "the relation to the group, qua group, to a central organizing function of the system." On this point, Bertell Ollman is particularly insightful:

> It is not enough to treat people as embodiments of social-economic functions. As much as this helps us understand their conditions, the pressures they are under, and their options and opportunities, the people involved must still respond to these influences in ways that make what is possible actual. Here, class is a quality that is attached to people, who possess other qualities—such as nationality, race, or sex, for example—that reduce and may even nullify the influence on thinking and action that comes from their membership in the class. Conceived as a complex social relation, in line with Marx's dialectical outlook on the world, class invites analysis as both a function and a group, that is to say, from different sides of this relation. (p. 153)

In Ollman's (1993) terms, class consciousness refers both to one's objective condition (function/place) and subjective formation (social relations). More specifically, Ollman notes that class consciousness "refers to how, when, from and towards what a whole class of people are changing their minds." Ollman emphasizes class consciousness in relation to a group in his effort to denote the collective and interactive processes of coming to know and act upon the world. The way in which people organize often takes place across various dimensions—ethnicity, gender, and nationality—but as Ollman notes, the objective interests of people return to the organizing function of class membership in a capitalist society. In other words, while social movements and group formations are grounded in multiple orientations, they maintain an operational movement within, against, or in transcendence of capitalism.

Class underscores a person's relation to the material world. The liberal/postmodern tendency to reduce class to a "mode of social differentiation" along with race, gender, and sexuality neutralizes the perennial effects of the capitalist system and distills cultural differences into their "proper niches" without highlighting the common object of theorization that emerges from their condition (San Juan, 2004). Critical pedagogy intervenes in this encounter in its attempt to establish the pedagogical conditions whereby the authentic specificity of realities lived and histories known can be used to recuperate a vision of the world outside of the capital-labor relation. As Ollman (1993) notes, a look into class consciousness as an evolving process is not a facile form of utopian thinking. On the contrary, an analysis of class consciousness as an act that leads to transformative action requires an understanding of "becoming" as a form "assumed by the future within the present, and as such affects how we understand the present, how we should study it, and what we can do to help change it" (p. 160). The study of class consciousness is simultaneously a look into capitalist society, into "how it works and where it is tending, viewed from the perspective of that moment when the mass of workers have acquired the understanding that is necessary for engaging in revolutionary activity" (p. 161).

The study of class consciousness is not an abstract exercise; it is a rigorous and purposeful analysis of the living material conditions that shape the collective thinking and organization of classes while simultaneously addressing the potential of the working class to defeat the capitalist class. This brings our attention to the importance of understanding the different modalities in which consciousness emerges, from the real and lived expressions of human agents to an analysis of the social structures that supply the "breathing matter" through which people make sense of the social world. A study of class consciousness without a due consideration of the various vectors that mark our daily living conditions fails to adequately grasp the explanatory power of class consciousness and its radical potential for enacting change. Class consciousness allows us to investigate and analyze multiple identity formations within and against the global backdrop of capitalist society. It is in the dialectical interchange "betwixt and between" agency and structure that a global consciousness can surface in our collective push toward creating the conditions in which we freely choose to construct, express, and enact knowledge.

Our work builds on that of Ollman (1993), who details workers' class consciousness as the site of revolutionary activity. We extend his analysis of class consciousness to those sites embedded within and in opposition to the broader capitalist social order. We recognize the importance of studying class consciousness from the standpoint of workers in the forms in which it exists, but we also contend that it is necessary to understand class consciousness from the very sites in which subjectivities are formed and contested, in the formal and informal educational spaces of social struggle. Our goal in all of this is to develop critical pedagogies that connect the language of everyday experiences to the larger struggle for emancipation and social justice carried out by various groups and agents. The emphasis here is on the creative capacity of all individuals to develop democratic social formations able to address local needs by means of political transformation. The questions that guide such a pursuit can be framed as follows: How do we find relevance and meaning in a social universe that denies our capacity to develop our humanity? How do we challenge a culture that nourishes a shameless politics of the lowest common denominator, a politics that has gutted democracy of any foundation for human decency, a foundation that has abandoned even a spineless and feckless official opposition whose purpose appears more soporific than subversive? How do we transform a social universe that gives us the capacity for community, solidarity, and freely associated labor but that denies us the social relations that make this a real possibility and that fails to pose the following question: How does society shape me in ways that enable me to develop a consciousness of social justice but that socially constrain me from contributing to a more humane world? How do we create an alternative to capitalist society—a postcapitalist society?

Finding answers to these questions requires that we undergo a systematic and profound process of coming to know the social world and the ways in which we are implicated in it. This is not a simple task; it requires that we simultaneously step within and outside the immediacy of the local environment that serves as the proximate architecture of our subjectivities. From within, we can identify that which brings an uncanny sense of comfort and awareness in what we come to know as focalist approaches to knowledge, or the "local experience." By ferreting out the instability within existing concepts of identity, we can locate and name its more tangible elements, but doing so will only give us a narrow view or different nook from which to examine the totality of that experience. Once we step outside local frames of references, we can call into question the deeper antagonisms of political consensus, exclusion, and alliance building. In rethinking critical pedagogy, we must be able to recognize and respond to those antagonisms that prevent the self and the collective "we" from perceiving an interconnectedness to the larger horizon against which culture is contested and struggles for justice are pursued.

Toward a *Nepantla* Pedagogy

Elsewhere, we (McLaren & Jaramillo, 2006, 2007) have discussed the importance of historical materialism in offering the means for "understanding the complex categories of identity based on race, ethnicity, sexuality and gender, not as autonomous formations but as interconnected processes within the larger dynamics of social relations" so that we are able to recognize "the particularity and relative autonomy of race without jettisoning the causal character of class relations" (Gonzalez, 2004, pp. 180–181). From such a perspective, reality is perceived not as an absolute truth but as "a set of processes" (p. 181). The purpose of historical materialist critique is not to "correct faulty ideas" (p. 182) analytically but "to negate them" and demystify them (as ideological correlates of real social contradictions) and, in doing so, "to transform them qualitatively" (p. 182). Historical materialism attempts to reinstate the importance of foregrounding the role of relations of production in a field of multiculturalism that has, regrettably in our view, overemphasized contingency and the reversibility of cultural practices at the level of the individual at the expense of challenging the structural determinations and productive forces of capital, its laws of motion, and its value form of labor—a move that we believe has replaced an undialectical theory of economic determination with a poststructuralist theory of cultural determination, one that underestimates the ways in which the so-called autonomy of cultural acts is already rooted in the coercive relationships of the realm of necessity. Indeed, questions of whose voice is heard and what knowledge is valued are important, but they cannot ultimately obfuscate the underlying sources of oppression (Grande, 2004).

On the question of voice, we recognize the ongoing need for developing languages of critique and resistance that help us to understand how the self—as racialized, indigenous, gendered, and alienated—is historically and contingently configured with respect to the totality of capitalist social relations. These languages of critique and resistance progress from the cognitive schemas of how we see and subsequently live in the world. For us, this means boundaries must be breached from the outside to the inside, while retaining a sense of "within" that organically constitutes the self. In advancing a historical materialist position, we are compelled to reflect on dimensions of social life that bring into central focus the liminal or border zones of identity, voice, agency, and resistance that can also recuperate the spiritual, temporal, and physical realms that have been forcibly erased through an ethnocentric colonialist perspective. We are aware that, just as we are located as subjects of enunciation with the global division of labor, we are also organized racially and geopolitically. As Ramon Grosfoguel (in press) notes,

> By hiding the location of the subject of enunciation, European/Euro-American colonial expansion and domination was able to construct a hierarchy of superior and inferior knowledge and, thus, of superior and inferior people around the world. We went from the 16th century characterization of "people without writing" to the 18th and 19th century characterization of "people without history," to the 20th century characterization of "people without development" and more recently, to the early 21st century of "people without democracy." We went from the 16th century "rights of people" (Sepulveda versus de las Casas debate in the school of Salamanca in the mid-sixteenth century), to the 18th century "rights of man" (Enlightenment philosophers), and to the late 20th century "human rights."
>
> All of these are part of global designs articulated to the simultaneous production and reproduction of an international division of labor of core/periphery that overlaps with the global racial/ethnic hierarchy of Europeans/non-Europeans.

Grosfoguel's important insights give strategic centrality both to the global division of labor under neoliberal capitalism and to how the global labor force is articulated within a racist and patriarchal logic of core/periphery that weighs heavily with colonial history. Grosfoguel (in press) notes that

> the racial/ethnic hierarchy of the European/non-European divide transversally reconfigures all of the other global power structures. What is new in the "coloniality of power" perspective is how the idea of race and racism becomes the organizing principle that structures all of the multiple hierarchies of the world-system.... The different forms of labor that are articulated to capitalist accumulation at a world-scale are assigned according to this racial hierarchy; coercive (or cheap) labor is done by non-European people in the periphery and "free wage labor" in the core. The global gender hierarchy is also affected by race: contrary to pre-European patriarchies where all women were inferior to all men, in the new colonial power matrix some

women (of European origin) have a higher status and access to resources than some men (of non-European origin). The idea of race organizes the world's population into a hierarchical order of superior and inferior people that becomes an organizing principle of the international division of labor and of the global patriarchal system. Contrary to the Eurocentric perspective, race, gender, sexuality, spirituality, and epistemology are not additive elements to the economic and political structures of the capitalist world-system, but an integral, entangled and constitutive part of the broad entangled "package" called the European modern/colonial capitalist/patriarchal world-system.

Grosfoguel (in press; see also Grosfoguel, 2005) draws a great deal on the important work of Aníbal Quijano (1991, 1993, 1998, 2000; Quijano & Wallerstein, 1992). Quijano's (1993) concept of "structural heterogeneity" is especially salient for our purposes, in that it "implies the construction of a global racial/ethnic hierarchy that was simultaneous, coeval in time and space, to the constitution of an international division of labor with core-periphery relationships at a world-scale" (Grosfoguel, in press). The accumulation of capital needs to be seen as constituted by and entangled with racist, homophobic, and sexist global ideologies that were part and parcel of European colonial expansion. Quijano's notion of the "coloniality of power" postulates "that there is no overarching capitalist accumulation logic that can instrumentalize ethnic/racial divisions and that precedes the formation of a global colonial, eurocentric culture" (Grosfoguel, in press). Quijano's notion that racism is constitutive and entangled with the international division of labor and capitalist accumulation at a world-scale suggests that multiple forms of labor coexist within a single historical process and that "free" forms of labor were assigned to the core or European origin populations and "coerced" forms of labor assigned to the periphery or non-European populations according to the racist Eurocentric rationality of the "coloniality of power." Arguing that there exists no linear teleology between the different forms of capitalist accumulation (primitive, absolute, and relative, in this order, according to some forms of Marxist Eurocentric analysis), Quijano asserts that multiple forms of accumulation also coexist simultaneously and are coeval in time. Seen as a long-term trend, the "violent" (called "primitive" accumulation in Eurocentric Marxism) and "absolute" forms of accumulation are predominant in the non-European periphery while the "relative" forms of accumulation predominate in the "free" labor zones of the European core (Grosfoguel, in press).

While clearly the core/periphery binarism of world-systems theory has serious shortcomings such as gross oversimplification, these insights of Grosfoguel bring us into direct contact in our work with indigenous, feminist, and anticolonial articulations of the self and the social as we uncover the boundaries in which difference is expressed (Jaramillo, 2007). To illustrate this point, we bring into discussion the work of the late Gloria Anzaldúa on the theory of *nepantla.*

At the beginning of the 16th century, *las indigenas* in Mexico under Spanish conquest and *la conquista spiritual* (see Leon-Portilla, 1974) expressed their resistance to Christian beliefs through nepantla. Nepantla signified an intermediary space *sin rumbo* (a "borderland" of "betwixt-and-between"), as las indigenas shifted their cultural and spiritual practices to accommodate the Christian doctrines being imposed upon them. The *teoria del nepantlismo cultural* surfaced from direct Spanish-Christian conquest and force, a temporary refuge from the terminal effects of absolute refusal (physical death) and complete assimilation (spiritual death). In nepantla, las indigenas began to undo the trauma of colonization. Remaining faithful to their hearts and in honor of their spirits, they acquired the determination and ability to resist the religious practices and rituals not of their own making (Leon-Portilla, 1974). Centuries later, Anzaldúa (2002) drew on *la teoria del nepantlismo* to "represent psychic/spiritual/material points of potential transformation" (Keating, 2006, p. 8). Nepantla was Anzaldúa's attempt to "theorize unarticulated dimensions of the experience of *mestizas* living in between overlapping and layered spaces of different cultures and social and geographic locations, of events and realities—psychological, sociological, political, spiritual, historical, creative, imagined" (Anzaldúa, 2000, p. 176). For Anzaldúa, nepantla represented the "zone between changes where you struggle to find equilibrium between the outer expression of change and your inner relationship to it" (pp. 548–549). And through nepantla, *nepantleras* emerged, *los sabios de la comunidad,* visionary cultural workers who risk self-isolation and shame to "see through restrictive cultural and personal scripts," as they move beyond "what is" to "what could be." We have expanded on the concept of nepantla as a space where students and teachers can engage in a dialectics of negation, as nepantla opens up possibilities for potentially new and transformative social practices to emerge. Through an individual and collective refusal of dominative social and cultural practices, a politics of renewal is born where nepantleras can create the material-spiritual-psychic conditions for direct participation in a social world of their own making (Anzaldúa, 2002).

For us, Anzaldúa's (2002) nepantla creates a context that enables teachers and students to mediate the schism between theory and practice as they move into less secure pedagogical processes. We extend Anzaldúa's concept of nepantla while building upon previous observations of the classroom as the site of liminality (McLaren, 1999) in which both student and teacher become objects of study in relation to the conditions of their immediate environment and of the larger social totality. Nepantla brings into focus the contradictions embedded within cultural forms, as each individual experience is understood to be further mediated by overlapping spheres of identity. In nepantla, the silent among the voiceless can be heard, as no fragmented marker of identity goes unnoticed. Women contest the social forms that constitute their consciousness within the colonized group politic, the body exposes its racial and sexual configuration, and culture is released from its embeddedness in logocentrism. In turn, a much more fluid acumen circulates between social actors with the understanding that no single or unitary individual can separate herself from the vestiges of her past, the remnants of her present, or from the objects yet unrealized that call her from an unknown future. Inquiring into the silences and subjugated knowledges of the students, nepantla pedagogy is guided by a shared (yet necessarily partial) understanding of the global relations that shape the self and the collective "we." Freeing the subject from constraints that limit one's critical activity gives rise to questions about the self in relation to various social, cultural, and institutional arrangements. We begin to recognize that while we appear to live in a world of singular persons who alternatively occupy the position of speakers and listeners, we share a responsibility to each other. We also recognize that we forget our reciprocal accountabilities to each other because we too often confuse subjective, autonomous self-identity with critical agency. Autonomous self-identity is what is historically and socially produced out of social contradictions and is presented as natural. The pursuit of autonomous self-identity is the opposite of the struggle for liberation. The space of nepantla enables students to recognize what they normally misrecognize: that capitalist-patriarchal-imperialist relations are historically produced and serve to repress the empirically given: the "not yet" or "what could be" of revolutionary hope. For us, formal and informational education sites are transgressions toward nepantla, where theory interfaces with practice in a process of delinking the self from the material architecture of oppression. *La teoria del nepantlismo* expands on the conceptual terrain where subjects begin to mediate their social roles and practices through critical reflection and political antiracist, anticapitalist, antisexist, and anti-imperialist struggle. In other words, they strive toward critical agency in a larger struggle that we would call *socialismo nepantlismo.*

The notion of the unified self is a tautology that denies the reality of historical contingency. Nepantla pedagogy occasions its learners into knowing the way of historical contingency, a way of thinking about self and other and the relations between them through an analysis of the systems of mediation that sustain and reproduce them. Here our approach is similar to Baldacchino's (2005) notion of finding pedagogical hope in groundlessness, that is, in a hope contained in the knowledge of the contingency of historical production (and the promise that the social can be reproduced anew in different social arrangements) and in the creation of a language able to rearticulate critical thinking beyond its current enmeshment in Cartesian rationality and Eurocentric arrogance. In this instance, nepantla pedagogy helps to develop a historical-contingency consciousness that rejects the epistemic closure of Enlightenment reasoning and that supersedes the dialectical tension between subject and object. In other words, we as nepantleras are intent on denaturalizing the language of truth and certainty insofar as we evoke paradox and liminality and challenge the unitary cohesiveness of the self (i.e., the notion of a metaphysical self that exists prior to its enmeshment in the world of social relations). Nepantla pedagogy rejects a unitary ground (via the self-conceits of certainty) for enacting civic agency.

Civic agency does not sever the subject from historical continuity, with the attempt to create a society predicated on the "new." The way we envision civic agency builds on Marx's attempt to create a society that is not premised on capital's value form and class hierarchy (Fritsch, 2005). Critical civic agency requires a movement outward to both analyze and undermine the material relations and structural edifices that condition our subjectivity a priori. In our work, this movement is directly connected to the development of class consciousness and class struggle. One challenge that we face (largely because we understand that structure and agency are mutually constitutive) is to ensure that nepantla pedagogy does not fall into a poststructuralist preoccupation with the primacy of discourse and a displacement of those social structures that invariably constrain and enable discourse. Nepantla pedagogy recognizes how social structures depend on being reproduced by agency (via political passivity, the production of intransitive consciousness and by means of ideological hegemony) but also stresses how those very structures can be transformed by means of protagonistic class struggle. It is in this context that nepantla pedagogy recognizes the positive relation inherent in the negative as in the supersession of alienation "through the supersession of the objective world in its estranged mode of being" (Marx, 1973, p. 341) and primarily with respect to the alienated labor that characterizes the capitalist mode of production. Marx uses the metaphor of religion to articulate this concept of positive humanism: "atheism is humanism mediated with itself through the supersession of religion whilst communism is humanism mediated with itself through the supersession of private property. Only through the supersession of this mediation—which is itself, however, a necessary premise—does positively self-deriving humanism, positive humanism, come into being" (Marx, 1973, pp. 341–342). In *Capital*, Volume 3, Marx stated, "The realm of freedom really begins only where labor determined by necessity and external expediency ends; it lies by its very nature beyond the sphere of material production proper.... The true realm of freedom, the development of human powers as an end in itself, begins beyond it, though it can only flourish with this realm of necessity at its basis. The reduction of the working day is the basic prerequisite" (Marx, 1992, pp. 958, 959).

The principles that guide our development of critical civic agency are those that the Bolivarian revolution in Venezuela have taught us: a commitment to struggle against racial, sexual, gender, and economic exploitation; a principled and practical opposition to imperialism (both economic and military); a celebration of the rich diversity of global human struggle for a socialism for the 21st century, a struggle that will involve democratically organized mass movements dedicated to self-emancipation, direct participatory democracy, and the pursuit of the expansion of human development for the purpose of creating a culture of freedom; and a commitment to communal ownership of social-economic resources and environment-friendly technologies that will respect and protect the integrity of ecosystems and the biocultural lifeworld (McNally, 2006). These principles are all conjointly animated by Marx's theory of social revolution: the self-emancipation of the working class through its own praxis.

In our ongoing work in Venezuela, we have been greatly impressed by the Bolivarian missions and their emphasis on human development and the creative capacity of all individuals to create democratic social formations able to address local needs in the context of a larger project of human emancipation by means of political transformation. These missions consist of antipoverty and social welfare programs. We were able to visit one of them in particular, Mission Ribas, a 2-year secondary school program (that teaches Spanish, mathematics, world geography, Venezuelan economics, world history, Venezuelan history, English, physics, chemistry, biology, and computer science), that targets five million Venezuelan dropouts. This program has a community and social labor component, where groups use their personal experience and their learning to develop practical proposals to address the needs of their communities and nation. We were fortunate enough to join in a group discussion of this component of the program in Barrio La Vega, on September 11, 2006. The facilitator of the class began by asking participants to relate their memories about the significance of September 11 in their regional histories. Participants began to recollect the Chilean coup led by Augusto Pinochet backed by the United States in establishing a military dictatorship that lasted 17 years. The discussion focused on the murdered and tortured victims under Pinochet's rule, leading to what participants described as one of the bloodiest coups in Latin American history. From this discussion point, people began to recollect their own resistance to the failed coup d'état that marked Venezuelan history in the year 2002. Many of those seated in the open-aired classroom chronicled the day in which thousands marched down from the shantytowns hovering over the presidential palace to defy the presumed natural order of history and to reinstate their democratically elected president. Their narratives collided against the dominant tropes of history and experience that, since 2001, locate terror and oppression within a Western Eurocentric topology. The point for the Bolivarian educators was not to privilege one form of terror over another but to recuperate their social struggle in relation to an unfolding epoch where terror is presumed to exist outside the chronology of their historical memory. The Bolivarian project assumes multiple forms. Whereas the educational missions seek to provide the disenfranchised with the necessary skills to build a society of their own making, they are also committed to decolonizing the self from a historical legacy of oppression.

▣ Critical Pedagogy for a Better Society

If, within the social universe of capital, we are inevitably lashed to the very conditions we as critical educators hope to abolish, then there is no sense in trying to strike a delicate equipoise between capital and labor. The time has come to look beyond the value form of labor and seek alternatives to capitalism. Those of us who work in the field of education cannot afford to sit on the sidelines and watch this debate over the future of education as passive spectators. We need to take direct action, creating the conditions for students to become critical agents of social transformation. This means subjecting social relations of everyday life to a different social logic—transforming them in terms of criteria that are not already seeped in the logic of commodification. Students can—and should—become resolute and intransigent adversaries of the values that lie at the heart of commodity capitalism. This implies a new social culture, control of work by the associated producers, and also the very transformation of the nature of work itself.

Critical educators need to move beyond the struggle for a redistribution of value because such a position ignores the social form of value and assumes, a priori, the vampire-like inevitability of the market. We need to transcend value, not redistribute it, since we cannot build a socialist society on the principle of selling one's labor for a wage. Nor will it suffice to substitute collective capital for private capital. We are in a struggle to negate the value form of mediation, not produce it in different degrees, scales, or registers. We need freedom, not to revert to some pristine substance or abstract essence prior to the point of production but the freedom to learn how to appropriate the many social developments formed on the basis of alienated activity; the freedom to realize our human capacities to be free, to be a self-directed subject and not merely an instrument of capital for the self-expansion of value; and the freedom to be a conscious and purposeful human being with the freedom to determine the basis of our relationships. Here, subjectivity would not be locked into the requirements of capital's valorization process.

Revolutionary critical pedagogy operates from an understanding that the basis of education is political and that spaces need to be created where students can imagine a different world outside of capitalism's law of value (i.e., social form of labor), where alternatives to capitalism and capitalist institutions can be discussed and debated, and where dialogue can occur about why so many revolutions in past history turned into their opposite. It looks to create a world where social labor is no longer an indirect part of the total social labor but a direct part it; where a new mode of distribution can prevail not based on socially necessary labor time but on actual labor time; where alienated human relations are subsumed by authentically transparent ones; where freely associated individuals can successfully work toward a permanent revolution; where the division between mental and manual labor can be abolished; where patriarchal relations and other privileging hierarchies of oppression and exploitation can be ended; where we can truly exercise the principle "from each according to his or her ability and to each according to his or her need"; where we can traverse the terrain of universal rights unburdened by necessity, moving sensuously and fluidly within that ontological space where subjectivity is exercised as a form of capacity-building and creative self-activity within and as a part of the social totality—a space where labor is no longer exploited and becomes a striving that will benefit all human beings; where labor refuses to be instrumentalized and commodified and ceases to be a compulsory activity; and where the full development of human capacity is encouraged. It also builds on forms of self-organization that are part of the history of liberation struggles worldwide, such as the 1871 Paris Commune or Cuba's Consejos Populares formed in 1989, or those that developed during the civil rights, feminist, and worker movements and those organizations of today that emphasize participatory democracy.

While our work has been greatly guided by the work of Marxist humanist critique, we stress that Marx's work is not in any way to be held as sacrosanct in defiance of its disputed legacy after the fall of the Soviet Union. Many contemporary educators, especially those involved in critical race theory and multicultural education, all too readily dismiss Marxist thought as being unaware of its own Eurocentrist assumptions and viewpoints, not to mention linked to a modernity that has long since faded after the demise of industrial society. While we do not have space to defend Marxist humanist critique, we would like to underscore that it is not necessary to remonstrate with or dismiss the works of prominent Western thinkers such as Marx *tout court* because we now would find their views on non-Western peoples to be essentializing and Eurocentric and perhaps even startlingly irrelevant. In our view, much of Marx's work can be seen as proleptic, as embodying "latencies" or implied developments that anticipated much of the stubborn intransigence of capitalism. His views continue to illuminate the present and instigate creative ideas even though his work might be viewed by some as politically incorrect. Remarks by Edward Said (2003) prove instructive:

> I have often been interpreted as retrospectively attacking great writers and thinkers like Jane Austen and Karl Marx because some of their ideas seem politically incorrect by the standards of our time. That is a stupid notion which, I just have to say categorically, is not true of anything I have either written or said. On the contrary, I am always trying to understand figures from the past whom I admire, even as I point out how bound they were by the perspectives of their own cultural moment as far as their views of other cultures and peoples were concerned. The special point I then try to make is that it is imperative to read them as intrinsically worthwhile for today's non-European or non-Western reader, who is often either happy to dismiss them altogether as dehumanizing or insufficiently aware of the colonized people . . . or reads

> them, in a way, "above" the historical circumstances of which the were so much a part. My approach tries to see them in their context as accurately as possible, but then—because they are extraordinary writers and thinkers whose work has enabled other, alternative work and reading based on developments of which they could not have been aware—I see them contrapuntally, that is, as figures whose writing travels across temporal, cultural and ideological boundaries in unforeseen ways to emerge as part of a new ensemble *along with* later history and subsequent art. (pp. 23–24)

For those who have ears, you can listen to the groans of Marx in his grave; he stubbornly refuses to die because his mission is not yet completed. The more his adversaries pronounce him dead, the more he bangs his fist against his crypt, reminding us that capitalism never sleeps, and neither should we until our job as its gravediggers is complete. For critical educators, Marx is no longer the backdrop on the shallow stage of history or a portent of failed worker states; nor is he heralded as the unsung savor of humankind, fulsomely celebrated by those who possess the correct interpretation of his texts. Rather, his work offers to educators a way to move forward in the struggle to make classrooms and other cultural sites spaces of social critique and social transformation where teachers and students alike can exercise a dialectical pedagogy of critique and hope, grounded in an exploration of what it means to labor and to educate one's labor power for the future purpose of selling it for a wage and understanding this process from the perspective of the larger totality of capitalist social relations. And, furthermore, to cultivate the necessary political agency to move from understanding the world to changing it. And while they might occasionally slip in the puddles of spittle hurled at them from neoconservative and Christian dominionist educators who equate anything Marxist with the gulags of Stalin, it is important that Marxist educators keep class struggle at the forefront of educational transformation.

But isn't Marxist humanist pedagogy ideologically partisan? We live in the academic world of Derridean indeterminacy, after all, where there is never a secure answer to any question and never an answer that does not eventually disappear into itself. Isn't discourse interminably complex? Shouldn't we aspire to be more objective? In our view, progressive educators make a mistake when they attempt to locate objectivity in the discourses of thought, not in the objective material conditions that produce the foundations for the development of knowledge (Zavarzadeh, 2003). Being "objective" does not reside in the processes of reasoning. If we look for it there, we will have to agree with the postmodernists that all knowledges are undecidable and the effects of the playfulness of signifiers. Postmodernists purge epistemology of its material conditions by grasping these conditions as only "ideas" and not objective structures. Acting ethically as revolutionary agents of social transformation means acting in order to resolve the contradictions of our objective location in relations of exploitation. It does not involve a Transcendent Self exhorting us to act according to abstract reasoning or set of rules (or according to a Magic 8 Ball), but rather by embodying an ethics that is related to our nexus of self-organization—to our "embodied" way of understanding and engaging everyday life in a world in which capitalism is so ominously monolithic and unmitigated (Varela, Thompson, & Rosch, 1991). We follow an approach to "mindfulness" articulated by Varela et al. (1991) insofar as we strive for a politics of transformation that is grounded in nonegocentric compassion—that is, for a politics of transformation that is not confused with the need to satisfy one's own cravings for recognition and self-evaluation. This means developing a spontaneous and self-sustaining ethical praxis that rejects rationalistic injunctions, dogmatic assertions, or obsessive ideals administered by some über-agent (or what Lacanians would call a "big other") in favor of releasing the mind from depending on such injunctions and ideals. Instead, the collective proscription of society would be challenged by the act of creating more sustainable, life-enhancing social and cultural practices that will abolish scarcity. This is consistent with our development of a nepantla pedagogy and nepantla socialismo. Here we admit to an epistemic relativity, recognizing that we have no guaranteed access to truth, that knowledge is socially and historically constructed, and that there is no direct correspondence between knowledge and its object. Yet we oppose judgmental relativism since, as socialists working within a Marxist humanist orientation, we do not believe all theories and explanations are equally valid. Human action and social structures exist in a dialectical relationship, and we adhere to those explanations with the greatest explanatory adequacy and that are guided by the elimination of capitalist exploitation and needless human suffering (see Joseph, 2006). We prefer to view "truth" not as an epistemological issue but an ontological one, centered on how we are conditioned (including how we are conditioned as scholars and activists) by the way we produce as a society our means of subsistence, our material means of life, and how we produce the goods and services that we need to survive and develop our humanity.

Making ethical decisions does not require an irascible homunculus sage squatting in our brainpans, barking messages into our mind with a magic megaphone. Rather, it involves an acquisition of certain habits of revolutionary praxis in which compassion and class struggle become spontaneous and self-sustaining. We reach for freedom yet too often remain ambivalent, not about our reaching but about freedom itself. Freedom is not simply an idea but also a practice. We try therefore to construct agency in our lives but not just in any free-floating fashion. We seek, instead, a form of "lived" civic agency aimed at ameliorating exploitation and oppression. Such agency—an open fissure in the process of capitalist social formation—constitutes a break in the paralysis of everyday capitalist social relations. This approach opens the way to a critical approach to the problem of individual agency.

At the forefront of our critical pedagogy is the realization that historical conditions up to the present time have not enabled the individual to become an independent, sovereign subject, exercising agency in the realm of social life outside of a relationship to others. Within capitalist society, agency, cogito, and self-consciousness relatively coincide, mediated by social relations of production, cultural and institutional formations, and social structures. We remain mindful of the fact that as long as our being, our "ergo sum," is conjoined to the ontology of our European imperial self-consciousness, to the sacrimonious mien of colonial intelligibility, to our "I think, therefore I am" of Descartes's "cogito," where ideas partake of sacerdotal status, we relegate those who do not share these ideas (since we have been conditioned to think of the European as the center of thinking, the center of history), who do not participate in our rationality, to the land of the unclean and the dead (Dussel, 1985). It is clear that the "other" is internal to the European system as an inert idea, a cogitatium, a "that which is thought." According to Enrique Dussel (1985), a liberation theologian highly critical of both Tridentine and existential theology, the European colonialist experience formed the substructure of the "ego cogito" ("I think"), and the colonialist "I" first experiences itself as "I conquer"—such as the "I conquer" of Cortes or of Columbus. Ramon Grosfoguel (in press) expands on this theme:

> René Descartes, the founder of Modern Western Philosophy, inaugurates a new moment in the history of Western thought. He replaces God, as the foundation of knowledge in the Theo-politics of knowledge of the European Middle Ages, with (Western) Man as the foundation of knowledge in European Modern times. All the attributes of God are now extrapolated to (Western) Man. Universal Truth beyond time and space, privilege access to the laws of the Universe, and the capacity to produce scientific knowledge and theory is now placed in the mind of Western Man. The Cartesian "ego-cogito" ("I think, therefore I am") is the foundation of modern Western sciences. By producing a dualism between mind and body and between mind and nature, Descartes was able to claim non-situated, universal, God-eyed view knowledge. This is what the Colombian philosopher Santiago Castro-Gomez called the "point zero" perspective of Eurocentric philosophies (Castro-Gomez 2003). The "point zero" is the point of view that hides and conceals itself as being beyond a particular point of view, that is, the point of view that represents itself as being without a point of view. It is this "god-eye view" that always hides its local and particular

> perspective under an abstract universalism. Western philosophy privileges "ego politics of knowledge" over the "geopolitics of knowledge" and the "body-politics of knowledge." Historically, this has allowed Western man (the gendered term is intentionally used here) to represent his knowledge as the only one capable of achieving a universal consciousness, and to dismiss non-Western knowledge as particularistic and, thus, unable to achieve universality.

This "othering" resulting from the "point zero" of the universality of Western rationality can be seen in the figure of the prisoner at Abu Ghraib in Iraq, perched on a box, covered in a pointed black hood, electrical wires dangling from the fingers of outstretched, crucified arms and leading to intimate parts of his body. Bill Blum (2007) has updated this image of the effects of "othering" by the American imperial regime with another iconic image, this time geopolitically situated not in some external colony or occupied territories but the internal colonies of the city slums throughout the United States. Here we find those indigent victims of the war waged by the U.S. capitalist class against its poor and dispossessed, victims created whenever the profligate ways of capitalism are mistaken for being anything other than barbaric, when human relations are reduced to market relations (Rivage-Seul & Rivage-Seul, 1995)—in this case, when the cost of saving lives (calculated as earning power over a normal life span) becomes greater than the anticipated benefit (in terms of opportunities to make a profit):

> Now we have, if a photo were available, what could be an iconic image of the US war against the people of America, or at least against their health care—a paraplegic man, no wheelchair or walker, somehow propelling himself along a street in Los Angeles, a broken colostomy bag dangling from his piteous body, clothed in a soiled hospital gown, dragging a bag of his belongings in his clenched teeth.... This human being had been taken by Hollywood Presbyterian Medical Center to a homeless mission, which refused to accept him; the man then hurled himself from the hospital van to the street. Witnesses said that the van driver ignored their cries for help and instead applied makeup and perfume before speeding off. This is one of several cases in the recent past of "homeless dumping" in Los Angeles. It's all very understandable, from a bookkeeping point of view. The homeless missions have only so many beds, the hospitals have a budget and the debits and the credits have to balance. It's what happens when a free market in a free society guarantees access to Coca Cola but not to health care. (Qtd. in Blum, 2007)

We do not yearn for total social revolution to appear after a sudden irruption into history of some sword-wielding anticapitalist messiah. History will not grant us such an unexpected gift. The way we try to engage history—to point it in the direction of socialism—is to join its most crucial aspect, that of class struggle. Class is an objective structure—a material contradiction—and, to emphasize what we have said earlier (see page 202), when we think of the concept of "objectivity," we think of class as the means by which human beings produce their material life through their labor, which in capitalist societies involves the exchange of labor power for a wage and extraction from workers of surplus labor. Objectivity as the objective social relations of production means that we must, as revolutionary critical educators, work to resolve these material conditions such that human beings are no longer exploited and oppressed. And this means struggling both locally and transnationally for a social universe outside of capital's social form, that is, outside of wage labor and property relations. To be objective, then, does not mean to be politically neutral. Here, objectivity is not a form of epistemology. Objectivity cannot be relegated to the realm of the discursive, to the domain of ideas. Rather, objectivity means grasping the world conceptually so that you are able to change it, to transform it (see Zavarzadeh, 2003) in the interests of a more humane and creative society (to which we give the name socialism). Rather than see objectivity as pertaining to the world of ideas (i.e., as statements about the objective, which is to slide into idealism), we prefer to see objectivity as an ontological intervention in and on the world (Zavarzadeh, 2003) that initially requires a conceptual grasp of the world capable of demythologizing its oppressive dimensions. These historically conditional structures that create the objective world are not visible without the help of concepts (as opposed to ideas). Unlike epistemological debates carried out in the realm of discourse, objectivity (which we see as having its roots in the savage ontology of capitalists' social life) has its "truth," which is the truth of social life, the truth of the exploitation of human beings by means of wage labor. For us, striving for objectivity is a form of ontological praxis, of making an intervention in the world by acknowledging and understanding the truth of capitalism as a means of exploitation. And, of course, by working to transform the structures of the social relations of production in the interests of creating a socialist society.

Revolutionary critical pedagogy as we have been developing it is a socialist pedagogy but one that does not seek a predetermined form or blueprint of socialist society. Neither does it endorse the idea of the spontaneous self-organization of the multitude. It has a dialectical and open-ended dimension. Its praxiological reaching out is similar to what Michael Steinberg (2005) refers to as a "negative politics." Steinberg writes,

> A negative politics . . . is grounded in the fact that our mutual self-constitution continues regardless of the ways in which we construe our experience. It opposes certainties and assurances of knowledge, but not in the name of either a different certainty or of a human characteristic that is presumed to lie beneath the social. It has hopes, not of a world that it already knows how to think about, but one that will not claim to be the culmination of time and that will not hold to ideas, ideals, or even values that seek to arrest the endless transformation of our lives together. It looks not to the perfection of detached knowledge but to an expanding attentiveness to embodied understanding. It is a path not to the future but to a deeper experience of the present. (p. 180)

A deeper experience of the present also requires a detour via the past. This sentiment is embodied in the work of what Michael Löwy and Robert Sayre (2001) refer to as revolutionary or utopian romanticism (as distinct from other forms of reactionary and reformist romanticism). They are worth quoting at length:

> Revolutionary romantics do not seek to restore the premodern past but to institute a new future, in which humanity would rediscover a portion of the qualities and values that it has lost with modernity: community, gratuitousness, gift giving, harmony with nature, work as art, the enchantment of life. But this implies a radical challenge to an economic system that is based on exchange value, profit, and the blind mechanism of the market: capitalism (or its alter ego that is in the process of dislocation, industrial despotism, bureaucratic dictatorship over needs). It is thus not a matter of finding solutions to certain problems but of aiming at an overall alternative to the existing state of affairs, a new civilization, a different mode of life, which would not be the abstract negation of modernity but its "sublation" or absorption (*Aufhebung*), its insistent negation, the conservation of its best gains, and its transcendence toward a higher form of culture—a form that would restore to society certain human qualities destroyed by bourgeois industrial civilization. That does not mean a return to the past but a detour via the past, toward a new future, a detour that allows the human spirit to become aware of all the cultural richness and all the social vitality that have been sacrificed by the historical process launched by the Industrial Revolution, and to seek ways of bringing them back to life. It is thus a question not of wanting to abolish machinery and technology but of subjecting them to a different social logic—that is, of transforming them, restructuring them, and planning them in terms of criteria that are not those of the circulation of merchandise. The self-governing socialist reflection on economic democracy and that of the ecologists on the new alternative technologies—such as geothermal or solar energy—are first steps in this direction. But these are objectives that require a revolutionary transformation of the entire set of current socioeconomic and political-military structures. (pp. 253–254)

How formidable this task appears today, especially as religious faiths seem locked in an eternal battle over the souls of humankind. Are we not experiencing in these times the aftershocks of colonialism? And perhaps some new tremors? Ignoring the legacy of colonialism only worsens its effects. Pope Benedict XVI, who as Cardinal Joseph Ratzinger headed the Congregation for the Doctrine of the Faith (organized much the same way as when it was known as the Holy Inquisition), was a founding board member with "Neilsy" Bush of the Foundation for Interreligious and Intercultural Research and Dialogue that was created in Geneva, Switzerland, in 1999. Ratzinger, we might recall, made a famous intervention into George Bush's 2004 election, condemning any Catholic who voted for Kerry to having formally cooperated in evil because Kerry supports a woman's right to choose to have an abortion. Now this same Ratzinger, as Pope Benedict XVI, has condemned Marxism and unbridled capitalism for the problems facing Latin America. Recently, in Aperecida, Brazil, he again attacked grassroots Catholic activists who were still influenced by liberation theology, a theology he tried to crush when he was a cardinal. While in Brazil, he made the outrageous claim that indigenous populations had welcomed the European priests who had arrived with the conquistadores, claiming that they had been "silently longing" for Christianity. He also said that colonial-era evangelization involving the proclaiming of Jesus and his Gospel "did not at any point involve an alienation of the pre-Columbus cultures, nor was it the imposition of a foreign culture." President Hugo Chavez of Venezuela has joined indigenous groups in condemning the Pope's remarks, claiming that Benedict XVI has ignored the enslavement and genocide of indigenous peoples in Latin America and the destruction of their native cultures, and has also ignored what in some cases amounts to the complicity of the Catholic Church in such violence and destruction. President Chavez proclaimed that "the bones of the indigenous martyrs of these lands are still burning." Clearly, the legacy of colonial violence lives on, not only in Latin America, but in North America as well. We see its offspring today.

We seek not to establish the fantasy of an opposite to capitalism but rather ground our vision of the future securely in the present and the possibility of change within the present, keeping in mind that socialism for the 21st century and our postrevolutionary future outside the value form of labor is still a product of the dialectic and can never be completely severed from the past in its search for its uniqueness and newness. The seeds of the future are in the present, and we need to recognize this at the same time as we fight to rid ourselves of what Marx and Engels (1932/1998) called "all the muck of ages." Of course, in our quest to universalize the struggle for socialism, we adopt a pluriversal approach. According to Grosfoguel (in press), "A truly universal decolonial perspective cannot be based on an abstract universal (one particular that raises itself as universal global design), but would have to be the result of the critical dialogue between diverse critical epistemic/ethical/political projects towards a pluriversal as oppose to a universal world." Furthermore, writes Grosfoguel, "decolonization of knowledge would require to take seriously the epistemic perspective/cosmologies/insights of critical thinkers from the Global South thinking from and with subalternized racial/ethnic/sexual spaces and bodies."

The concept of interculturality that we are using (see Walsh, in press) articulates a respect for ethnic/racial and cultural diversity and views the social, cultural, and political fields as structurally imbricated and tightly woven. It is driven by the primacy of participatory democracy as part of the struggle for social justice within a plurinational state and guided by the principles and practices of socialism. Furthermore, it operates within a larger political optic that is anticolonialist, anticapitalist, antiracist, and antisexist. In this model, human rights are conjoined with economic rights in an attempt to challenge the configuration of individual autonomy spawned by neoliberal capitalism. It is fundamentally a social logic or system of intelligibility that is both constitutive of and a social, political, and epistemic response to the brutal and anguished history of colonization/modernity from an indigenous place and space of enunciation. This enunciation exists in relation to and through lived experiences of subalternization and works toward the creation of a new political subjectivity and structure of social power from below, leading to horizontal rather than vertical relations of power. Using local knowledges (more specifically, border knowledges produced by processes of interculturation) that exist at the interstices of various social logics and intersubjective encounters within, outside, and alongside dominant Western ways of thinking, new constructions of the state and state formations can be considered along with alternative forms of education and governance that challenge the coloniality of power, knowledge, and being (see Walsh, in press). It moves beyond a monotopism and Eurocentrism to geopolitical spaces of enunciation and critical agency animated by a socialist imaginary and revolutionary praxis. Part of developing a critical agency based on interculturality requires what Walsh calls a critical border positioning. Walsh writes that a critical border positioning recognizes "the capacity of social-ethnic movements to enter in/to work within and between the social, political, and epistemological spaces previously denied them and to reconceptualize these spaces in ways that contest the persistent re-coloniality of power, knowledge, and being and look towards the creation of an alternative civilization, a kind of strategical confrontation with the subalternizing conditions established by coloniality itself."

For us, however, it is important that in our attempts to create a project of decolonization that will be able to contest the coloniality of power of modern imperial nation-states, we do not lose sight of the struggle for a socialist alternative to capitalism.

▣ The Specter of Che

While we remain mindful of the importance of sublating the categories of the old society in the struggle for the new society (a fundamental premise of nepantla pedagogy), we work toward a self-consciousness of how we exist as a union, as a group united in solidarity against capital and joined together by our common interests. Here we stress what Marx identified as "the coincidence of the changing of circumstances and human activity or self-change" (cited in Lebowitz, 2006, p. 70). Here, now, we need to build a society of associated producers that will permit the development of our creative powers (in Marx's spirit of forging "an association, in which the free development of each is the condition for the free development of all"), and such a struggle will require, in Lebowitz's (2006) terms, "the simultaneous changing of circumstances and self-change" (pp. 65, 206). We build new human beings while we build the new society. Lebowitz writes,

> Democratic, participatory, and protagonistic production both draws upon our hidden human resources and develops our capacities. But without that combination of head and hand, people *remain* the fragmented, crippled human beings that capitalism produces: the division between those who *think* and those who *do* continues—as does the pattern that Marx described in which "the development of the human capacities on the one side is based on the restriction of development on the other side." (p. 65)

We are constantly reminded of Che's storied admonition that you cannot build a socialist society without at the same time creating a new human being. Che sought the abolition of the economic vestiges of capitalism not as the automatic result of the development of the productive forces (he rejected unconditionally the evolutionist strain of capitalist-industrial progress) but through the intervention of social planning (in contrast to the centralized planning practiced under Stalin). Furthermore, Che recognized the specific autonomy of social, political, and ideological transformation that comprised the social whole, and he valued the importance of political–moral motivation and the need for multiform action to change the consciousness of the masses in order to bring about the ideological hegemony of communist values.

Such a struggle and change of consciousness is necessary for the revolutionary struggle worldwide. As Che notes, "Socialism cannot exist without a change in consciousness that will bring about a more brotherly disposition toward humanity, both at the individual level in those nations where socialism was being, or had been, built—and at the world level, with all the nations that are victims of imperialistic oppression" (qtd. in Löwy, 1997).

Today, it is the informal sector that is keeping Latin America from sinking into a deeper abyss of poverty created by the politics of neoliberalism.

Lands are being despoiled by international mining operations, water and forests have been destroyed by logging and toxic waste, air is clogged with lead and particulate matter, and health care, education, housing, and sanitation are in shambles. The conditions that spurred Che Guevara to take up arms are still there; they have, in fact, worsened.

Civil society has increasingly become the stage on which revolutions are now fought, with the state having been abandoned by many groups that feel that those who focus on seizing control of the state find themselves upholding the very relations of capital they originally fought to abolish. But it seems clear that we need more than just efforts to catalyze the self-organizing action of civil society against the state; we need to transform the very foundations of the state. Che's teachings can push us forward in our belief that smashing the old state and creating a new one is still a possibility, even today, while at the same time he helps us to recognize that there is no certainty to our struggle for socialism because in many ways, certainty is the enemy of revolutionary struggle.

What was remarkable about Che was the way he went against the traditional left of his day in the pursuit of new, more egalitarian and humane roads to this worthy goal, roads that he felt were more consistent with what he understood were the ethical principles of communism. Che rejected the Eastern European models of socialism that claimed to "conquer capitalism with its own fetishes." In his March 1965 essay, "Socialism and Man in Cuba," he wrote, "The pipe dream that socialism can be achieved with the help of the dull instruments bequeathed to us by capitalism (the commodity as the economic cell, profitability, individual material interest as a lever and so on) can lead into a blind alley. . . . To build communism it is necessary, simultaneous with the new material foundations, to build the new man" (qtd. in Löwy, 1997). By conjugating contingency with necessity, Che was not only rejecting the layers of technocracy and bureaucracy that such a model would bring to Cuba but also challenging the economistic view of socialism (which viewed the economic sphere as an autonomous system governed by its own laws of value or the market) with a more political view of socialism, in which issues concerning prices and production are made on the basis of social, ethical, and political criteria (Löwy, 2001). It is important to underscore that Che's Marxism has an essentially undogmatic character. As Löwy (1973) puts it,

> For Che, Marx was not a Pope endowed by the Holy Ghost with the gift of infallibility; nor were his writings Tables of the Law graciously handed down on Mount Sinai . . . Che stresses that Marx, although an intellectual giant, had committed mistakes which could and should be criticized. (p. 13)

Che's antidogmatism in the realm of theory (Che viewed Marxism as a guide to action, a philosophy of praxis, a theory of revolutionary action) was not unrelated to his pedagogical practice, as he rejected outright the Stalinist cult of authority (which he often referred to as scholasticism) and claimed it was impossible to educate the people from above. Echoing the question raised by Marx in his *Theses to Feuerbach* ("who will educate the educators"?), Che wrote in a speech in 1960, "The first recipe for educating the people is to bring them into the revolution. Never assume that by educating the people they will learn, by education alone, with a despotic government on their backs, how to conquer their rights. Teach them, first and foremost, to conquer their rights and when they are represented in government they will effortlessly learn whatever is taught to them and much more" (qtd. in Löwy, 2001).

The perspicacity of leftist critique, while historically devastating at times, is hardly indisputable and much less invincible, and insight alone (as Che made clear) will not carry us past the grand designs of the imperialist and subimperialist states, the subservient comprador classes, and obscurantist reactionary forces aligned against us. The burning actuality of global resistance to capital has not unleashed the sound and fury of previous international revolutionary struggles, but it is passionately fueled by indignation and an unconditional rejection of injustice and oppression and moving forward at a breakneck speed to every corner of the planet. It is the molten lava of a grand social eruption, sparked by the crushing internal contradictions within capital's deadly logic. It is as much the heir of the Zapatistas and Chavistas, of the Movimento dos Trabalhadores Rurais Sem Terra (MST) and the Abahlali base Mjondolo (Shack Dwellers) Movement in Durban, South Africa, as it is the revolutionary progeny of Carlos Mariategui, Che Guevara, Malcolm X, Camillo Torres, Jose Marti, Simon Bolivar, Emiliano Zapata, Rosa Luxemburg, Emma Goldman, Gramsci, Lenin, Trotsky, and Marx. It is an anti-neoliberal capitalist struggle whose collective intercontinental network is expanding into the avenues of the mind as well as the hearts and hands of all those who refuse to be ruled by a global logic and practice of oppression.

Following in the spirit of such a struggle, we seek not a grand narrative of historical necessity but a praxis of being that can animate the inert material reality of everyday life, recognizing that innovations are often a synthesis of the already known and new discoveries. Our praxis of being, our nepantlismo, is developed so that we can find new collective and systematic ways of re-creating the state from the bottom up, of building capacities that will help us administer everyday life in ways hitherto uncharted, such that these efforts can match—and eventually overwhelm—the forbidding scale of danger that we face in today's specter of neoliberalism and its accompanying coloniality of power.

La Revolucion Socialista presente!

References

Anzaldúa, G. (2000). *Interviews/Entrevistas* (A. Keating, Ed.). New York: Routledge.

Anzaldúa, G. (2002). Now let us shift . . . the path of conocimiento . . . inner work, public acts. In G. Anzaldúa & A. Keating (Eds.), *This bridge we call home* (pp. 540–578). New York: Routledge.

Baldacchino, J. (2005). Hope in groundlessness: Art's denial as pedagogy. *Journal of Maltese Education Research, 3*(1), 1–13.

Blum, B. (2007, March 5). *The anti-empire report.* Retrieved from http://www.scoop.co.nz/stories/HL0703/S00087.htm

Dussel, E. (1985). *Philosophy of liberation.* New York: Orbis.

Foster, J. B. (2005). Naked imperialism. *Monthly Review, 57*(4). Retrieved from http://www.monthlyreview.org/0905jbf.htm

Fritsch, M. (2005). *The promise of memory.* Albany, NY: SUNY Press.

Gonzalez, M. (2004). Postmodernism, historical materialism and Chicana/o cultural studies. *Science and Society, 68*(2), 161–186.

Grande, S. (2004). *Red pedagogy.* Lanham, MD: Rowman & Littlefield.

Grosfoguel, R. (2005). The implications of subaltern epistemologies for global capitalism: Transmodernity, border thinking, and global coloniality. In R. P. Applebaum & W. I. Robinson (Eds.), *Critical globalization studies* (pp. 283–292). London: Routledge.

Grosfoguel, R. (in press). Decolonizing political economy and post-colonial studies: Transmodernity, border thinking, and global community. In R. Grosfoguel, J. D. Saldivar, & N. Maldonado (Eds.), *Unsettling postcoloniality: Coloniality, transmodernity and border thinking.* Durham, NC: Duke University Press.

Jaramillo, N. (2007). *Las Madres, urban schools and nepantla pedagogy.* Unpublished dissertation, University of California Los Angeles.

Joseph, J. (2006). *Marxism and social theory.* New York: Palgrave Macmillan.

Keating, A. (2006, Summer). From borderlands and new *mestizas* to nepantla and nepantleras: Anzaldúan theories for social change. *Human Architecture,* pp. 5–16.

Lebowitz, M. A. (2006). *Build it now: Socialism for the twenty-first century.* New York: Monthly Review Press.

Leon-Portilla, M. (1974). Testimonios nahuas sobre la conquista spiritual [Nahuatl testimony on the spiritual conquest]. *Estudios de Cultura Náhuat, 11,* 11–36.

Löwy, M. (1973). *The Marxism of Che Guevara: Philosophy, economics, revolutionary warfare.* New York: Monthly Review Press.

Löwy, M. (1997). Che's revolutionary humanism: Ideals of Ernesto 'Che' Guevara. *Monthly Review, 49*(5), 1–7. Retrieved from http://www.findarticles.com/p/articles/mi_m1132/is_n5_v49/ai_20039201

Löwy, M. (2001, February). "Neither imitation nor copy": Che Guevara: In search of a new socialism. *Europe Solidaire Sans Frontieres.* Retrieved from http://www.europe-solidaire.org/spip.php?article5489

Löwy, M., & Sayre, R. (2001). *Romanticism against the tide of modernity* (C. Porter, Trans.). Durham, NC: Duke University Press.

Marx, K. (1973). *The collected works of Karl Marx and Friedrich Engels, 1843–44* (Vol. 3). New York: International Publishers.

Marx, K. (1992). *Capital: A critique of political economy* (Vol. 3; D. Fernbach, Trans.). New York: Penguin Classics.

Marx, K., & Engels, F. (1998). *The German ideology.* Retrieved from http://www.marxists.org/archive/marx/works/1845/german-ideology/ch01d.htm. (Original work published 1932)

McLaren, P. (1999). *Schooling as a ritual performance* (3rd ed.). Boulder, CO: Rowman & Littlefield.

McLaren, P., & Jaramillo, N. (2006). Juntos en la Lucha [Guest editorial]. *Ethnicities, 6*(3).

McLaren, P., & Jaramillo, N. (2007). *Pedagogy and praxis in the age of empire: Towards a new humanism.* Rotterdam: Sense Publishers.

McNally, D. (2006). *Another world is possible: Globalization and anti-capitalism* (Rev. ed.). Winnipeg: Arbeiter Ring.

Ollman, B. (1993). A model of activist research: How to study class consciousness . . . and why we should. In B. Ollman (Ed.), *Dialectical investigations* (pp. 147–179). London: Routledge.

Pfaelzer, J. (2007). What's scary about the anti-immigration debate. History News Network. Retrieved from http://hnn.us/articles/40316.html

Quijano, A. (1991). Colonialidad y Modernidad/Racionalidad [Coloniality and modernity/rationality]. *Perú Indígena, 29,* 11–21.

Quijano, A. (1993). "Raza," "Etnia" y "Nación" en Mariátegui: Cuestiones Abiertas [Race, ethnicity and nation in Mariategui: Open questions]. In R. Forgues (Ed.), *José Carlos Mariátgui y Europa: El Otro Aspecto del Descubrimiento* (pp. 167–187). Lima, Perú: Empresa Editora Amauta S.A.

Quijano, A. (1998). La colonialidad del poder y la experiencia cultural latinoamericana [The coloniality of power and the Latin America cultural experience]. In R. Briceño-León & H. R. Sonntag (Eds.), *Pueblo, época y desarrollo: la sociología de América Latina* (pp. 139–155). Caracas: Nueva Sociedad.

Quijano, A. (2000). Coloniality of power, ethnocentrism, and Latin America. *NEPANTLA, 1,* 533–580.

Quijano, A., & Wallerstein, I. (1992). Americanity as a concept, or the Americas in the modern world-system. *International Journal of Social Sciences, 134,* 583–591.

Rivage-Seul, D. M., & Rivage-Seul, M. (1995). *A kinder and gentler tyranny.* Westport, CT: Praeger.

Roberts, P. D. (2007). The return of the Robber Barons. Counterpunch. Retrieved from http://www.counterpunch.org/roberts08022007.html.

Ross, J. (2006, April 17). A real day without Mexican? *Counterpunch.* Retrieved from http://www.counterpunch.org/ross04172006.html

Said, E. (2003). *Freud and the non-European.* London: Verso.

San Juan, E. (2004). Post-9/11 reflections on multiculturalism and racism. *Axis of Logic.* Retrieved from http://www.axisoflogic.com/artman/publish/article_13554.shtml

Steinberg, M. (2005). *The fiction of a thinkable world: Body, meaning and the culture of capitalism.* New York: Monthly Review Press.

Varela, F., Thompson, E., & Rosch, E. (1991). *The embodied mind: Cognitive science and human experience.* Cambridge: MIT Press.

Walsh, C. (in press). Interculturality and the coloniality of power: An 'other' thinking and positioning from the colonial difference. In R. Grosfoguel, J. D. Saldivar, & N. Maldonado (Eds.), *Unsettling postcoloniality: Coloniality, transmodernity and border thinking.* Durham, NC: Duke University Press.

Zavarzadeh, M. (2003). The pedagogy of totality. *Journal of Advanced Composition, 23*(1), 1–52.

Part II

CRITICAL AND INDIGENOUS PEDAGOGIES

In the five chapters in Part II, indigenous scholars describe Hawaiian, Native American, Mestizaje, endarkened, and Islamic pedagogies. These pedagogies exist in in-between, border, marginal, and liminal spaces, the crossroads where colonializing and decolonializing frameworks intersect and come into conflict with one another. They are responsive to multiple versions of the paradigm associated with critical theory, including Marxism, critical pedagogy, and critical race, queer, and postcolonial theory, although each indigenous pedagogy has its own ethics, epistemology, ontology, and methodology. Each pedagogy represents a particular indigenous worldview. Each rests on special cultural and spiritual understandings. Each world is located within and shaped by a particular set of colonial and neocolonial experiences, including broken treaties, enforced systems of schooling, and ugly relations with Western positivist researchers, many of whom have turned *research* into a dirty word.

Hawaiian Epistemology and Pedagogy

Manulani Aluli Meyer outlines an indigenous Native Hawaiian epistemology. A Hawaiian pedagogy resists colonial systems of knowing and educating (Meyer, 2003, p. 192). It fights for an authentic Hawaiian identity (Meyer, 2003, p. 192).

It defines epistemology culturally; that is, there are specific Hawaiian ways of knowing and being in the world (Meyer, 2003, p. 187). Seven themes, organized around spirituality, physical space, the cultural nature of the senses, relational knowing, practical knowing, language as being, and the unity of mind and body, shape this epistemology (Meyer, 2003, p. 193).

This framework stresses the central place of morality in knowledge production. It regards culture as sacred, as the site of the spiritual. Knowledge and spirituality are experienced and expressed in sensuous terms, in stories and critical personal narratives that are performed (Meyer, 2003, p. 185). The self knows itself through the other. The person is embedded in a relational context. In this context, harmony, balance, generousity, responsibility, and kindness are valued.

Within this paradigm, knowledge is relational, embodied, spiritual, subjective, grounded in sense experiences, and shaped by language. The triangulation of meaning is central to this process. Meaningful experience exists at that point where the mind, the body, and the spirit interconnect. Meaning works outward from the Hawaiian body, through the mind and subjective consciousness to the spiritual realm. Spirituality connects Hawaiians to a spiritual essence—that is, to the sacred meanings given in the land, in oceans, in language, rituals, and family.

▣ Red Pedagogy

Native American indigenous scholars thicken the argument by articulating a spoken, indigenous epistemology "developed over *thousands* of years of *sustained* living on this Land" (Rains, Archibald, & Deyhle, 2000, p. 337). An American Indian Red pedagogy (Grande, 2007, 2004, 2000; see also Chapter 12, this volume) criticizes simplistic readings of race, ethnicity, and identity. It privileges personal identity performance narratives. These are stories and poetry that emphasize self-determination and indigenous theory (Brayboy, 2000).

For Grande, an indigenous perspective (and methodology) refers to a critical consciousness and approach to knowledge shaped by her experiences as an indigenous person (Quechua). Her Red pedagogy is not a methodology, per se. It is rather a space of engagement, an intellectual borderland where indigenous and nonindigenous scholars engage one another, in ways that will "redefine, and reverse the devastation of the original colonialist 'encounter.'"

Indianismo describes a distinctly indigenous space that is central to the quest for indigenous sovereignty. This space is shaped by a matrix of legacy, power, ceremony, and tradition, a space anchored in the histories of indigenous peoples. Indigenous struggles for self-determination and sovereignty occur in these spaces. In her chapter, Grande argues, "while Indigenous peoples resist the kind of essentialism that recognizes only one way of being, they also work to retain a vast constellation of distinct traditions that serve as the defining characteristics of tribal life." She contends that this allegiance to traditional knowledge "has protected American Indians from annihilation and absorption into the democratic mainstream."

Her Red pedagogy builds on Peter McLaren's revolutionary critical theory. It has seven characteristics. Pedagogically, it is a complex political, cultural, spiritual, and intellectual project. It is fundamentally rooted in indigenous knowledge and praxis. It is informed by critical theories of education. It promotes an education for decolonization. It interrogates both democracy and indigenous sovereignty. It cultivates actions that create spaces free from colonialist exploitation. It is grounded in hope.

Borderland-Mestizaje Feminism

Saavedra and Nymark dedicate their chapter to Gloria Evangelina Anzaldúa and her legacy of a borderland-Mestizaje feminism (BFM), a feminism that inspires a global solidarity that unites all oppressed women of color in a new tribalism. Extending the arguments of Cannella and Manuelito, Saavedra and Nymark resist attempts to marginalize BFM by critical and other theorists.

Work within the BFM framework centers on the everyday lives and bodies of oppressed persons. It relentlessly criticizes the methodologies of mainstream positivism. It welcomes hybrid forms of knowledge. And functions as a tool, methodology, and epistemology. As a tool, it helps persons survive in a racist, sexist culture. As a methodology, it offers guidelines for critically representing and analyzing the social world. It uses varied and creative methodologies, such as life histories, testimonials, interviews, personal narratives, *corridos,* and art. Epistemologically, it endorses an antifoundationalism grounded in the voices, sexualities, and subjective experiences of brown bodies.

The histories of BFM bear the scars of struggles with first-, second-, and third-wave feminisms, of battles between Chicano studies and White feminisms, as well as Gringa theory. The new tribalism is about how women of color build more inclusive feminisms, the bonds of new bridges, new alliances. In their nuanced and poignant endnotes, Saavedra and Nymark reflexively illustrate how this new BMF is embedded in their everyday lives as *mujeres,* minorities, and researchers.

Endarkened Feminist Epistemology

Cynthia B. Dillard (Nana Mansa II of Mpeasem) introduces spirituality and its place in the research process. In the social sciences, we are beyond a crisis in representation. We confront a crisis of spirituality, a failure of the sacred. We have neglected the ways in which our methodologies, epistemologies, and pedagogies affect spiritual well-being. We have neglected those epistemologies that locate spirituality at the center of thought and discourse. Dillard's chapter corrects this neglect. Working from an African and African feminist epistemological space, she honors an endarkened epistemology that examines the nature of Black women's knowing. She also examines the ways in which this epistemology of the spirit is a healing methodology, one that produces transformations of the self and the person, and that opens ways of healing the soul and its pains.

An African cosmology is central to her project. This cosmology stresses spirituality and the sacred, the notion of community-as-belonging, and praxis as action on behalf of freedom. Her endarkened feminist epistemology makes research a moral act, a responsibility "answerable and obligated to the very persons and communities being engaged in the inquiry." This epistemology is a call to resistance, a demand that the researcher confront, interrogate, and work to transform situations of oppression.

She offers a personal experience narrative based on her work in a West African village in Ghana's coastal Central Region. This narrative is a tale of how a healing methodology worked in her life. In her telling, she shows how she became a healing soul who made the pilgrimage to Ghana, where she discovered her spiritual ancestors. She was transformed into an American citizen with an African heritage. She is now an African living outside Africa, a part of the African diaspora. She is this flesh, bone, and blood, and mind, soul, and spirit.

Her healing methodology involves action, praxis, a letting go of old methodologies, and a focus on love, care, compassion, unconditional giving, ritual, and gratitude. These are the basic elements in methodologies of the spirit. Those who practice these methodologies may experience a wholeness, the sense of coming full circle. In coming full circle, the researcher recovers a sense of purpose. Thus, this involves learning how to experience the sacred. This extends to learning how to live a life helping others. Such a life is dedicated to teaching, to healing, to service, to helping persons of color "create an academic life that resonates with spirit" and love, and care, and compassion.

Dillard ends on this note: "If my purpose is to help others to experience the healing wisdom of Africa, Black Feminist praxis, and spirituality, the academic life I've known will not be the academic life that I am moving toward."

Who will want to be in the academy after it has been decolonized?

▣ Islamic Epistemology

Christopher Darius Stonebanks articulates an Islamic perspective on knowledge, knowing, and methodology. He writes against prevailing U.S. misconceptions concerning Muslims and their beliefs. He offers a counternarrative that is based on his experiences of being born of Iranian and European parents, raised in the Muslim culture, but living in North America and painfully aware of the West's negative views of Iran and Muslims. His narrative illuminates the many ways in which Muslim ways of knowing are connected and guided by Islam. His chapter creates a space for a conversation, a humanizing dialogue between Muslims and non-Muslims, between indigenous and nonindigenous persons. As a critical educator, he connects Freire's pedagogies of the oppressed to Muslim beliefs. Muslim religion direct scholars to produce ethical, empowering, caring work that is beneficial to the global Muslim community.

The Islamic paradigm de-Westernizes dominant Enlightenment beliefs concerning impartiality, objectivity, and the White man's burden to civilize backward people, including Muslims living in the Middle East. It encourages dialogue, tolerance, and respect for the other. It understands that theory and method are value laden. It asks, "What has Western research done to improve the lives of those being researched?" It explores how critical research can contribute to ways of knowing that are humanizing and liberating. It empowers Muslim scholars and educators, urging them to work against those stereotypes that dehumanize, marginalize and oppress non-Western persons, including Muslims.

▣ Conclusion

Indigenous pedagogies enact politics of liberation. They empower marginalized persons of color. They work the seams of borderland epistemologies. These are liminal, in-between spaces (*napantla, mestizaje, Indianismo*) where indigenous and nonindigenous persons engage one another. Indeed, indigenous pedagogies are all about creating these in-between, safe, sacred spaces. In them, endarkened, feminist, spiritual epistemologies can be enacted, and bruised, damaged souls can be healed. Whether Islamic or non-Islamic, African, Native American, Māori, Hawaiian, or Mestizaje, this move toward the spiritual unites all indigenous pedagogies.

Western, Enlightenment methodologies relegated the spiritual to the religious and theological realm, far from the rationality of science and the linearity of scientific method. There was little room for the sacred in Western science. The perspectives discussed in this section of the handbook challenge that position and render it no longer tenable.

References

Brayboy, B. M. (2000). The Indian and the researcher: Tales from the field. *International Journal of Qualitative Studies in Education, 13,* 415–426.

Grande, S. (2000). American Indian identity and intellectualism: The quest for a new red pedagogy. *Qualitative Studies in Education, 13,* 343–360.

Grande, S. (2004). *Red pedagogy: Native American social and political thought.* Lanham, MD: Rowman & Littlefield.

Grande, S. (2007). Red Lake Woebegone, pedagogy, decolonization, and the critical project. In P. McLaren & J. L. Kincheloe (Eds.), *Critical pedagogy: Where are we now?* (pp. 315–336). New York: Peter Lang.

Meyer, M. A. (2003). *Ho'oulu: Our time of becoming: Hawaiian epistemology and early writings.* Honolulu, HI: 'Ai Pohaku Press Native Books.

Rains, F. V., Archibald, J. A., & Deyhle, D. (2000). Introduction: Through our eyes and in our own words—The voices of indigenous scholars. *International Journal of Qualitative Studies in Education, 13,* 337–342.

11

INDIGENOUS AND AUTHENTIC

Hawaiian Epistemology and the Triangulation of Meaning

Manulani Aluli Meyer

Whether or not you can observe a thing depends on the theory you use. It is the theory that decides what can be observed.

—Albert Einstein

Indigenous and Authentic. We must develop new theories from ancient agency so we can accurately respond to what is right before our very eyes. It was Che Guevera, revolutionist extraordinaire, who believed the shackles of ignorance could be snapped via ideas that were indigenous *and* authentic, old *and* new, cycled *and* creative, ancient *and* developed-this-moment. So too with research. Can the idea, then, of duality combine itself into wholeness needed for this time? Dual to nondual, research to renewal, fragment to whole—yes this is the goal.

This chapter introduces you to indigenous epistemology as viewed by Native Hawaiian mentors, friends, and family so that you will understand that *specificity leads to universality.*[1] This is a spiritual principle within ancient streams of knowing. It nests itself within a wider and wider space I now experience as wonderment and truth in deeper and deeper dimensions. This chapter closes with a discussion of the Triangulation of Meaning, an authentic leap into new ways of viewing reality that will challenge current research paradigms based on Newtonian assumptions of space, time, and knowing. Indigenous and Authentic. Timeless and Timely. So, put on the tea. Here we go.

Hawaiian Epistemology: The Specifics of Universality

> But will it also be thought strange that education and knowledge of the world have enabled us to perceive that as a race we have some special mental and physical requirements not shared by the other races which have come among us?
>
> —Queen Lili'uokalani, 1898

All peoples have their own distinct beliefs of what knowledge is and what knowing entails. This idea is an example of epistemology[2] specific to place and people. Applying hermeneutics to politics, education, health, and all modern institutions details why such a simple epistemological truth is often denied.[3] Power, hegemony, colonialization, racism, and oppression are the labels on such acts of denial. I now see these as *unawareness.*

How I experience the world is different from how you experience the world, and both our interpretations matter. *This is an important point* as it links inevitably to transformative policies, awareness, and pathways to liberation via our own articulated epistemology. It expands the idea of what knowledge is supposed to be and in truth is—vast, limitless, and *completely* subjective. As ocean people in a warm climate, you bet we have a different way of knowing and thus being. Regardless of the fracas of modernity within our shorelines, we as the first peoples of Hawaiinuiakea have our own uniqueness for how we have approached knowledge/knowing for thousands of years. Our epistemology *still* differs from those who occupy our shores, and as we awaken, a revolution of remembering will bring us back to what is valuable about life and living, knowledge and knowing.

The following seven categories help to organize systems of consciousness that are needed to enliven what knowing means in today's rampage called modernity. They are doorways into a space without walls. They are notes in a song my people are singing to you. Do not be put off by its specificity, simple notions, and odd languaging. It is merely one group of people finding their way back into meaning—a space we all can share together. Remember, bear witness to your own thoughts now as you delve into these categories of knowing. How will you respond to the "exotic other"? Will you see the role of its vitality in your own capacity to see and hear? How will it inform your *own* ideas of research, knowing, and being of service to a worldwide awakening? Be open. Be ready. We have work to do.

1. Spirituality and Knowing: The Cultural Context of Knowledge

> The question is, Who is the self? You're not just who you are now. You're aligned with people who have gone through it lots and lots of times.
>
> —Calvin Hoe, Hakipuu

Knowledge that endures is spirit driven. It is a life force connected to all other life forces. It is more an extension than it is a thing to accumulate. When the Hawaiians I listened to[4] spoke of spirituality with regard to intelligence, they were not talking about religion. *These are two completely different ideas.* What was discovered in the thoughts of others and within my own reflection was the intentionality of process, the value and purpose of meaning, and the practice of mindfulness. These ideas, accessed via deep and enduring respect for our *kupuna,* our lands, our oceans, our language, rituals, and families, became the foundation of a Hawaiian essence. These are *spiritual principles* that, if played out as epistemology, help us enter spaces of wonderment, discernment, right viewing, and mature discourse. It is an old idea that does not clock answers or place you in special education classrooms because you cannot read at grade level. It is a rich and mature response to life's diversity and brilliance.

The spirituality of knowledge got entangled within the bureaucracy of its form and has been pulled back further and further away from the light of fundamental empirical knowing. It is now often confused with religion and relegated to backroom lectures and dismissed by mainstream science. Spirit as knowing is a *real idea* that allows us to ritualize ways to collect medicine, read a text, prepare a meal, or communicate with family. It allows knowing to be an act of consciousness that reaches beyond the mundane into connection and alignment with an essence that finds its renewal throughout the generations. This higher reach of knowing collapsed under the weight of homogeneity and assimilation—around the world. It must right itself through our engagement to secure our survival.

How does the interpretation of knowledge as spirit affect your research? It doesn't. *You do.* It merely points to a frequency that if heard will synergize with your courage when you write without fear after asking questions that search for deeper meaning to an act, an idea, a moment. An epistemology of spirit encourages us all to be of service, to not get drawn into the ego nurtured in academia, and to keep diving into the wellspring of our own awe. In that way, our research is bound in meaning and inspired by service to others or to our natural environment. That's an epistemology based on what we refer to as *ea* or animating principles. *Ea* is also our Hawaiian word for sovereignty. And as I believe more in the Nation-Within idea, let it inspire you to develop your own mind within the context of the needs of your own community. Do you see how it can assist you as you begin to formulate the why and what of your work? See your work as a *taonga* (sacred object) for your family, your community, your people—*because it is.*

2. That Which Feeds: Physical Place and Knowing

I am shaped by my geography.

—Hannah Kihalani Springer, Kukuiohiwai

Indigenous people are all about place. Land/*aina,* defined as "that which feeds," is the everything to our sense of love, joy, and nourishment. Land is our mother. *This is not a metaphor.* For the Native Hawaiians speaking of knowledge, land was the central theme that drew forth all others. You came from a place. You grew in a place and you had a relationship with that place. *This is an epistemological idea.* Because of the high mobility of Americans and billboards as childhood scenery, many find this idea difficult to comprehend. Land/ocean shapes my thinking, my way of being, and my priorities of what is of value. Remember, if knowledge is imbued with spirit, how much more is the land where we are inspired in this knowledge making? One does not simply learn about land, we learn best *from* land.[5] This knowing makes you *intelligent* to my people. How you are on land or in the ocean tells us something about you. *Absolutely.* It opens doors to the specificity of what it means to exist in a space and how that existing extends into how best to interact in it. This includes cities, rooms, suburbs, and all the many configurations we have found ourselves in.

Land is more than a physical place. It is an idea that engages knowledge and contextualizes knowing. It is the key that turns the doors inward to reflect on how space shapes us. Space as fullness, as interaction, as thoughts planted. It is not about emptiness but about *consciousness.* It is an epistemological idea because it conceptualizes those things of value to embed them in a *context.* Land is more than just a physical locale; it is a mental one that becomes water on the rock of our being. Consideration of our place, our mother, is the point here. And she is more than beautiful, or not. *She is your mother.*

How will this inspire your research? Well, to begin with, check your breathing. Is it deep and aware or are you troubled and in a hurry? Land as an epistemological cornerstone to our ways of rethinking is all about relating in ways that are sustaining, nourishing, receptive, wise. Knowing with land should help you find out more about your own self, and when that process begins as a researcher, you start to open your own phenomenological inquiry into *your* origins of space. Was it lined with books or were you in the lap of dandelions? One does not judge here. It's all about *recognizing* and finding how space influenced your thinking. Because it has. It does now. And what you bring to your knowing influences all that you do, write, and offer to the world. This epistemological category helps us all recover from our childhood traumatic belief that place is never recoverable. With regard to research, our early spaces help create the topic you choose, the questions you formulate, and the way you respond to data. It is all shaped by space. Not time. Conscious-shaping space. Space-shaped consciousness. An epistemological priority.

▣ 3. The Cultural Nature of the Senses: Expanding Our Ideas of Empiricism

> I don't think I was taught that! I was hearing it.
>
> —Irmgard Farden Aluli, Kailua

I surf. My ways of knowing a swell, where to line up for a wave, and why Kona winds were perfect for diving (not surfing) in my home waters off Kailua made me a beach rat. It has helped me know my place in the world. It is distinct and based on experiences of place and passion. It differs from yours. You have your own brilliance and priority of knowing. We are uniquely experienced, and my sensual history brings my current understanding into a fluid context that extends a modern Hawaiian worldview. I am empirically configured by my past, and my senses and body were the tools and recording devices through which I retrieved and stored all data. *Our senses are culturally shaped.* This is an epistemological idea. It is not a bad or good thing. It is a fact that for some reason has been misunderstood and developed as a polemic point in most matters of philosophy and basically ignored in research.

Differences at these fundamental levels begin to expand all points of epistemology that will open your mind and keep it open to alternative interpretations of how one hears a song or sees an event. They are the ABCs of how and why we engage with others and why we sometimes scratch our head with their renditions of reality. Remember, what we have in common is our difference. It begins first with this, and it is the leaping-off point to the beauty of specificity that will bring us to a common knowing. This contextualizes the once static notion of empiricism that believes you and I see the same cornfield. It's the maturing of objectivity into subjectivity. It is experience that tells the farmer his cornfield is in need of calcium and water as I, the beach rat from Kailua, notice nothing.

Every Native Hawaiian I listened to spoke in terms of her own epistemology, her own empirical understanding of the world. The aroma of a *lei pakalana,* sunrise pinks splashed in the heavens as Hiiaka, the touch of *kalo* in cool running waters, the thrill of sound in harmony. All these are aspects of a culture evolving in place, and they all shape the building blocks of knowing—our sensual organs that are culturally configured.

This fundamental idea that our senses are culturally shaped seems almost obvious, but it must be understood deeply if you are to proceed into what many may not understand. What this entails for your research is that you will need to slow down what it means to see something, hear something, or experience something. There is a wealth of diversity and knowledge in smells! An entire universe is found in how one catches a glance. It all shapes how you will gather data, think through findings, and report out.

Knowing that you are unique at this basic level will bring a keen understanding of the nuance of your own subjectivity. Begin to name it at this stage and write sharply about its impact in how you know and experience the world. Operating at this level may be challenging to current policies, philosophies, and faculty in most universities. Keep going! Your relationship to your research topic is your own. It springs from a lifetime of distinctness and uniqueness only you have history with. Be encouraged by this! Do not doubt your own capacity to scaffold complex and cultural ways in which to describe the world. It is time to be clear at this very fundamental level.

▣ 4. Relationship and Knowledge: Self Through Other

> How can you be happy in your experiences when others are unhappy?
>
> —Gladys Brandt, Honolulu

Here is an epistemological category that deepens all other categories. Existing in relationship triggers *everything:* with people, with ideas, with the natural world. It was a cornerstone inspiration to the people I listened to. It marked a consciousness of the dialectic, a reckoning with what one brought to other. Relationship gave mentors opportunities to practice generosity with others, harmony with land, and ways to develop their own pathway to an idea. *These are epistemological points.* One was in constant interdependence with others and with natural surroundings. Even in modern Hawai'i, family spoke of awareness of connection and being in right relation with all. Of course, this was the ideal that sometimes fell short in reality, but it was a priority most mentors lived out in their lives.

Knowledge was the by-product of slow and deliberate dialogue with an idea, with others' knowing, or with one's own experience with the world. Knowing was in relationship with knowledge, a nested idea that deepened information (knowledge) through direct experience (knowing). The focus is with connection and our capacity to be changed with the exchange. Thus the idea of self *through* other. I believe this is an idea more shaped by our practice of aloha, the intelligence of compassion, empathy, and care. It is an ancient idea to heal with all relations, and this included land and ocean. Aloha was a level of consciousness that defined our intelligence.[6] Vivid interconnection was valued, a lived dialectic. After all, did we not bring the endless joy of riding waves to the world?

How does this inspire research? It reminds us that knowledge does not exist in a vacuum. Intelligence is challenged, extended, and enriched when viewed in dyad awareness or group consciousness. Of course, this opens doors to the richness of hermeneutics and its inevitable worldwide focus, but first we segue with epistemology. It is the notion that intentions must harmonize with ideas, and ideas form the libretto of our transformational drama. It is all fundamentally done with awareness of other and, consequently, oneself. Will your research bring forth solutions that strengthen relationships with others or will it damage future collaborations? How will your own relationship with self inspire truth and courage to do what will be needed when predictable roadblocks enter your view? A knowledge that includes true awareness of other will radically alter research protocols, questions, and processes.

5. Utility and Knowledge: Ideas of Wealth and Usefulness

> Going to the beach for her (mother) was a place where you would go and gather and not a place for recreation.
>
> —Pua Kanahele, Panaewa

Function is the higher vibration of an idea, not the lower. How one defines function is first discovered in its meaning and then its interpretation. Here it is! Here is where the cosmological clashing began, not with the word but with its *meaning.*[7] This is why we go to epistemology and then, inevitably, to hermeneutics. This is where Descartes's error comes to light. *Cogito ergo sum*—I think therefore I am—does not divide us from our embodied selves; it can unite us in a wisdom that is embedded in usefulness, awareness, and function. This is edging into a universal epistemology. It's all about function. And as aloha is my intelligence, well, I guess this means you can use my board.

Hoa'e ka 'ike he'enalu i ka hokua o ka 'ale—show your knowledge of surfing on the back of a wave. Thus one knows. It's not about how well you can quote theory; it's whether those ideas affect how you *act.* Here is the focus of this entire book: How will you feel encouraged to go forth into the world to alter its frequency? How will you bring robustness to this flat land knowing literacy keeps undimensioned? How will you actualize these principles of being to expand what knowledge is at its core?

Make your work useful by your meaning and truth. I know it sounds somehow ethereal, but this is the point: Knowledge that does not heal, bring together, challenge, surprise, encourage, or expand our awareness is not part of the consciousness this world needs now. This is the function we as indigenous people posit. And the great clarity that I have been waiting to express through the beautiful mind of our beloved kupuna healer Halemakua: *We are all indigenous.*[8]

▣ 6. Words and Knowledge: Causality in Language

> Okay, you give an assignment to a family. Maybe to that family you'd say: You cook the long rice and chicken. Come that night it starts to bubble, then you would know they grumbled. They didn't put their heart and soul in making this so you can find out who grumbled, I mean, by the taste.
>
> —Florence Kumukahi, Kaipalaoa

Here is an epistemological category better reflected in Hawaiian literature and historic textual discussions than the mentors interviewed. It is a subtle category that was clearly repetitive throughout our Hawaiian written history but somehow silent in modern oral descriptions of intelligence. I believe this absence signals where precisely we must lend our awareness.

Hawaiians at one time believed in the causative agency of intention.[9] *Thought creates.* This is why it was seen as negative to even *think* of hitting a child. Negative thoughts then had negative consequences. This whole cycle of reciprocation turns on the integrity and life force of a thought expressed as action. The point here is that effect begins with intention. This is an epistemological idea that helps us mature into a deeper relationship with what action and reality is at its core: *thought.*

The idea that thought creates and intention shapes the observable world may seem far-fetched to some, but it is now recognized and discussed in depth by indigenous scholars, quantum physicists, mothers, and social scientists and summarized in groundbreaking works.[10] Specific to human problems in society, effective research stems from deeply looking into the *conditions* of what may be the cause of specific phenomena. And these conditions are inevitably found in *consciousness.* David Hawkins (2002) summarizes it thus: "There are no *causes* within the observable world . . . *the observable world is a world of effects.*"[11] Our thoughts create reality. This is where authentic dovetails with indigenous. This is where standardized tests miss the boat. This is where research comes in.

What this means is that poverty does not cause drug addiction but rather our *response* to poverty does. My *thoughts* about the effects of poverty affect how I respond to it. All bets are off, however, if my brain cells are not operable. It highlights the idea that postcolonialism for Hawai'i is not first a physical place but a *mental one.* It by *no means* dismisses the physical burden that poverty, oppression, and other acts of abuse put on the body, mind, and spirit; it simply names what is at the inevitable *core* of anything tangible: *thought.* It also helps us develop a different discourse for solution making that snaps us out of the level of consciousness it was created in.[12]

The question now may be, What is your intention in doing research? What are your thoughts about your topic? What do you bring to the phenomenon of a moment shared with other? How will you think through the process and product of data collection, or how will you respond to experiences and ideas that will be completely new to you? This is not a distant discussion of your bias or of your deductive or inductive realities. It is the pulse of your character that you must name. Understanding causation in intention and language helps us critically self-reflect. It can bring a vibrancy of purpose and truth to your findings and style of writing.

This is not objectivity we are discussing; it is fully conscious *subjectivity,* and it holds the promise of being effective in a radically different way if you understand its meaning and prioritize it at all levels of your research. It is called meta-consciousness. To be more than a woman of my word. To be a woman of my *intention.* Write about it. Put your thoughts in a prologue or in an appendix. It can be done.

7. THE BODY/MIND QUESTION: THE ILLUSION OF SEPARATION

Without heart we don't have sense.

—Keola Lake, Kahala

Here is the capstone of Hawaiian epistemology and its sharpest sword in this duel with mainstream expectations of what it means to know something. The separation of mind from body is not found in a Hawaiian worldview. It was not apparent in any interview, in any body of literature, in any dreams that arrived in service to this unfolding reflection. Indeed, intelligence and knowledge were embedded at the core of our bodies—the stomach or *na'au.* The na'au for Native Hawaiians is the site for both feeling and thinking. Wisdom, *na'auao,* also translates as heart, emotion, and intelligence. Modern Hawaiians are trained to dismiss these tuggings of one's embodied knowing for the objective, unfeeling one. Clearly, if one succeeds in this way, culture erodes and wisdom becomes a flimsy caricature of its potential.

Body is the *central* space in which knowing is embedded. It was not merely a passing idea but basic to all interviews. Our body holds truth, our body invigorates knowing, our body helps us become who we are. This was not simply a metaphoric discussion of union with sensation and conceptualization. Our thinking body is not separated from our feeling mind. *Our mind is our body. Our body is our mind.* And both connect to the spiritual act of knowledge acquisition. It is part of what we will discuss further as an integral space in the triangulation of meaning.

> Liver is where you digest the powers of perception. Digestion is not purely physical. I have "fed" on knowledge. It is an internal digestion. If I have digested a book, I have eaten it, digested it. This is where we separate epistemologies—in digestion and vital organs.
>
> —Rubellite Kawena Johnson, Scholar/Educator

> But that's what *na'auao* is. It's a cosmic center point. It has to do with your ancestors coming together with you. It has to do with your spiritual being coming together. It has to do with our physical being.
>
> —Pua Kanahele, Kumu Hula/Educator

Knowing there is intelligence in feeling and feeling in intelligence begins the long turnaround from an isolated thinking self void of the potential messiness of subjective realities found in all versions of the world. It brings us back into ancient sensibilities that recognize the strength found in conscious subjectivity and clearly stated origins of thought found in empirical, objective recognition. Objectivity is not the evil here. It does not serve a more awakened future to argue one is better than the other. In our evolving future, both are needed, both are useful, both will find their way to harmony. It is the bullying found in unconscious worldviews that would deny that subjectivity is actually a maturing of objectivity, not a dumbing down. Here is where indigeneity and authentic synergize.

HAWAIIAN EPISTEMOLOGY: IMPLICATIONS FOR RESEARCH

Aloha is the intelligence with which we meet life.

—Olana Kaipo Ai

True intelligence is not described by an SAT score. Here is the point to all this detail on what it means to be intelligent to my people. What are the implications of these seven categories of knowledge making and knowing on *your* research mind? Did you feel a *remembering* with these ideas? It has become clear to me that the specificity of these Hawaiian epistemological categories is indeed endemic to islands in the middle of the Pacific. But they also offer a way to organize universal truths you may wish to consider:

1. Finding knowledge that endures is a *spiritual* act that animates and educates.

2. We *are* earth, and our awareness of how to exist with it extends from this idea.
3. *Our senses are culturally shaped,* offering us distinct pathways to reality.
4. Knowing something is bound to how we develop a *relationship* with it.
5. *Function* is vital with regard to knowing something.
6. *Intention* shapes our language and *creates our reality.*
7. *Knowing is embodied* and in union with cognition.

I arrived at this view-plain through the specificity of knowing my ancient self—spaces we all can recognize because we all have them. True intelligence *is* self knowledge.[13] Self-inquiry helped shape my own understanding of knowing and put in the light bulbs on a path leading to wider application. It ends my feelings of inferiority and disconnection. It helps discern the glaring difference between uniformity and universality. It is best summarized by Nobel laureate Rabindranath Tagore (2004): *Man's individuality is not his highest truth, there is that in him which is universal.*

So, if specificity leads us into universal truths, how does *that* help us right what is so clearly wrong with our systems and thought patterns? How do we begin to effectively debate entrenched practices that do not recognize a more enduring way to engage in knowledge or a more enlivened way to live in harmony with all things? Why can't we approach research, scientific inquiry, and policy making with integral beliefs that honor and develop fractal approaches to intention?[14] Why do we not engage dialectically with those who oppose us? How are we to develop tools of self-reflection so that we become more capable agents of change and transformation? Here are questions that an expanding epistemology challenges us to think through. Perhaps as we enter the Triangulation of Meaning, we are heading into parts of how they will be answered. Indigenous and Authentic, remember? Yes, yes. Let's continue on. We've still got lots to do.

▣ The Triangulation of Meaning: Body, Mind, and Spirit

> Triangulation, three intimations of one idea, should be noted as a guide to edifying coherence among associations.
>
> —Zach Shatz (1998)

Here we go! Here is the authentic part of this chapter. It is a set of ideas that may bring you back to *remembering.* It extends indigenous epistemology into a context of world awakening. It is daringly simple, but then again, words only point to the truth. *Genuine knowledge must be experienced directly.*[15] It is meant to help you organize your research mind and give you the courage to do so with the rigor found in facts, logic, *and* metaphor. It is offered now because it organized my own thoughts and oiled the tools needed to dismantle the master's house found in perfect order *in my own mind.*[16] We as researchers can now become architects of meaning, shaping spaces as yet unseen. Here is the challenge. Here is a floor plan.

Let's begin with the idea of *triangulation.* Wilderness education teaches that if you wish to find your place on a topographical map, you need only locate two geographical distinctions on land, and with the use of a compass and pencil, the third and final spot—your location—can then be found. The use of three points to discover one's location in both two and three dimensions is the art and science of "triangulation," and I have always thrilled in its use and implication. Thus the metaphor of *triangulating our way to meaning* with the use of *three* points. These three points? Body, mind, and spirit.

Using body, mind, and spirit as a template in which to organize meaningful research asks us to extend through our objective/empirical knowing (body) into wider spaces of reflection offered through conscious subjectivity (mind) and, finally, via recognition and engagement with deeper realities (spirit). Finally, we are defining places science can follow into but not lead or illuminate. Other ways of knowing something *must* be introduced if we are to evolve into a more enlightened society. It will not occur with scientific or objective knowledge only. Nobel laureate Werner Heisenberg puts it more succinctly: *Physics can make statements about strictly limited relations that are only valid within the framework of those limitations* (Wilber, 2001).

So, before we begin this discussion, please understand that your schooled mind has been shaped by mostly one point in the triangulation—body. *Body* is a synonym for external, objective, literal, sensual, empirical. Change agents, indigenous researchers, cultural leaders, and transformational scholars are now working together to help this idea grow up. So, take a breath. Keep your mind open.

To begin, mahalo to Ken Wilber for his capacity to see patterns in philosophy and research that brought this idea to the world.[17] I have simply extended his preliminary list into trilogies that make sense to me and the needs of our focus. It was my wilderness education experiences that brought forth the idea of "triangulation" as I have experienced the beauty of its practice and utility. We are poised to use three points in our experiencing of life and research to find our way home. Not two. Not one. Three.

The Number Three

> The Tao gives birth to One.
>
> One gives birth to Two.
>
> Two gives birth to Three.
>
> Three gives birth to all things.
>
> —Tao Te Ching, Chapter 42

It is more like Bucky Fuller's tetrahedron.[18] It's about the structural integrity formed when *three* points meet in dimensioned space. The tetrahedron is also the sacred geometry of infinity, energy, and the perfect balance of equilibrium found in postquantum physics. It is the doorway into wholeness. We at first thought it was about opposites, about duality, about bridging polarity and painting our theories of gender, science, and life under this light. Black and white comparisons kept us busy for hundreds of years. It has shaped the polemic universe we now take for granted. True or false. Body or mind. Oppressor or oppressed. Cognition or feeling. Real or imagined.

The world is indeed perceived in binary systems. It has caused untold horror and helped create a rigid epistemology we now assume cannot evolve. We have options, however. Why not experience duality like the Yin and Yang, Ku and Hina of our ancient selves?[19] Life *is* found in dual forms, but as we gather evidence from all sectors of world scholars, mystics, and practitioners, we are discovering that life moves within a *context of dynamic consciousness* that synergizes with Aristotle's highest intellectual virtue he referred to as phronesis. This is not simply a discussion of moral relativity or the third point in duality; it is a piercing into different planes of epistemology to discuss what inevitably shifts into nonduality because of its inherent wholeness. It has helped me step from entrenched patterns of thinking to include older ways and more experienced expressions of what intelligence *really* is and how it can be expressed. It's about time, don't you think?

Reaching for Wholeness

> Relative and absolute, these two truths are declared to be. The absolute is not within the reach of the intellect, for intellect is grounded in the relative.
>
> —Shantidevi

The world is more than dual. It is whole. We have looked at parts so long we perhaps believe the gestalt of our knowing is not possible. With regard to research, we *still* believe statistics is synonymous with truth. It is a dangerous road to travel when we pack only empirical ways of being into our research backpack. Here is the point of doing research at this juncture of history: Empiricism is just one point in our triangulation of meaning, and although it may begin the process of research, it by *no means* is the final way in which to engage, experience, or summarize it.[20] Research and life are more in line with three simple categories that have been lost in theory and rhetoric: body, mind, *and* spirit. Thus begins the discussion of a triangulation of meaning. *Ho'omakaukau?* Let us begin.

Body: The Gross and Physical Knowing of Life—First Point in the Triangulation of Meaning

> I believe we carry our values in our bodies. We carry our culture in our bodies.
>
> —Peesee Pitsiulak, Inuit

We're not talking gross as in yucky. Gross starts this triangulation of meaning because it describes what is outside, what is external, what is seen, what is empirical. It is the *form* that consciousness has shaped. It is one way to begin this discussion of research for meaning because it is what we are familiar with. It is science in all its splendor. It is the part of your research that may be counted, sorted, and emphasized because of statistical analysis. It is what you see, not the way in which you interpret what you see or hear. It is the ABC of experience you may jot down in memo form so you don't forget specifics. This is the description of what was in the room, the time of day, what was said, or the written ideas on butcher paper informants shared. It is the information phase of gathering ideas. It is vital. It is the objective pathway we mistook for destination.

The body idea in the triangulation of meaning is what science has cornered. It is expressed through sensation via objective measurement and evaluation. It is a valuable and rigorous part in the triangulation of meaning and the center of most research processes. The gross/external part of the triangulation is the nitty-gritty of experience, the atomic process of physical movement, the force that moves objects. It is vital to not underestimate the beauty of research found at this level. The problem was that we assumed all the world could be described this way. In one sense, all the world can be described in this way. We are simply acknowledging the world to be fuller, richer, and lived deeply also in the internal processes that empiricism only points to. Thus, the world *can* be described via objectivity alone. It just would not be enough. *Is* not enough.

Table 11.1 draws out why detailing this portion of the triangulation is vital and yet only one third of the whole. It will give you a clearer picture of what we are talking about. Table 11.1 gives us a glance at the future of rigor. Gross/external/body knowing becomes part of a wholeness forming when combined with mind and spirit. Mature self-reflection finds objectivity moving in space/time toward a subjective reality that finally realizes the strength and beauty of its limitation and potential.

Study Table 11.1. Do you sense the simplicity here? The list is explained now so we can be on the same page when we discuss the other two parts of the triangulation. This body-centered aspect in the triangulation is absolutely vital if we are to evolve. It is not the "bad guy" of research but a critical link to help us expand what it is we are engaged in. Valuing an empirical relationship with the world *begins* the discussion we may have with aspects of an idea, event, or issue. It is simply not the end.

The body/external knowing of the triangulation is what we all can relate to because it is the template in which society and our institutions of higher learning operate from. It has been the bread and butter of research and science and the main assumption found in the notion of rigor. It is objective, tangible, and measurable. Now, don't you think it's time to evolve? After all, one does not live on bread alone.

Mind: The Subtle and Subjective Knowing of Life—Second Point in the Triangulation of Meaning

> The great consciousness exists in my mind.
>
> —Oscar Kawagley, Yupiaq

Finally! Truth that objectivity is a subjective idea that cannot possibly describe the all of our experience. To believe that science or objective and empirical-based research could describe all of life reduces it to its smallest part. Ken Wilber (2001) states it clearly: Physics is simply the study of the realm of least-Being. Claiming that all things are made of subatomic particles is the

Table 11.1 The Triangulation of Meaning in Its Many Forms

Body	*Mind*	*Spirit*	*(Source)*
Objective	Subjective	Cultural	Karl Popper
Facts	Logic	Metaphor	M. McCloskey
Perception	Conceptualization	Remembering	Yoga Sutra
Empiricism	Rationalism	Mysticism	Ken Wilber
Information	Knowledge	Understanding	Manu Aluli
Sensation	Reason	Contemplation	Ken Wilber
Instinct	Intelligence	Intuition	Halemakua
Emotion	Feeling	Awareness	Spinoza
Force	Power	Liberation	David Hawkins
Its	I	We	Buddhist inspired
Life	Mind	Joy	Upanishads
External	Internal	Transpatial	Ken Wilber
Knowledge	Knowing	Enlightenment	Māori inspired
True	Good	Beautiful	Plato
Gross	Subtle	Causal	Ken Wilber
Tinana	Hinengaro	Wairua	Māori
‘Ike (to see)	‘Ike (to know)	‘Ike (revelations)	Hawaiian
Hearing	Thought	Meditation	Buddhist
Duality	Nonduality	Wholeness	Ken Wilber
Biology	Psychology	Spirituality	Manu Aluli
Seeing	Thinking	Being	Ken Wilber
Word	Meaning	Perception	Patanjali
Monologue	Dialogue	Presence	Ken Wilber
Empiricism	Epistemology	Hermeneutics	Manu Aluli
Dot	Circle	Sphere	Mel Cheung
Eye of the Flesh	Eye of the Mind	Eye of Contemplation	Ken Wilber
Ways of Knowing	Ways of Being	Ways of Doing	Aboriginal
Decolonization	Transformation	Mobilization	Poka Laenui

NOTE: Unless noted specifically in the reference section at the end of this chapter, all descriptors in this list have been collected during a lifetime of experiences and kept as journal entries without citation. Students have also given me their renditions, and I have begun that list. The list itself is as self-evident as truth.

most reductionistic stance imaginable! Science and the belief in objectivity as the highest expression of our intellect works only in "restricted fields of experience" and is effective only within those fields (Wilber, 2001). What a revelation! Let me repeat that for the benefit of those in the back: *Objectivity is its own limitation.*

Enter mind, subjectivity, thought. Courage is needed to articulate these ideas with a robustness that will signal a leap in consciousness within our society. Even though insults will be hurled by mobs who have an investment in status quo thinking, be prepared with ideas that scaffold what has become obvious: Our rational minds, our inside thoughts, our subjective knowing are *vital* to how we experience and understand our world. The question remains: How will the internal process of thought-made-conscious affect the process and product of your work?

Return to Table 11.1 and look again at synonyms found in the mind category of the triangulation of meaning. They are not the EKG lines found on graph paper; they are the *thoughts* those lines represent. Thought is an inside and subtle experience inspired by a richness or poverty only you can imagine. Because thought shapes form, do you see how vital it is to develop our minds consciously and not get stuck on form? This is where we are heading as a planet—to become more mindful of what it is we must do, how we must heal, where we must go to invigorate our own process not fully encouraged within our institutions of learning.

The following four quotations are from my heroes. They are given here as an extension of what my own people have portrayed in their own reading of their world. As we begin to formulate authentic ideas within ancient streams of knowing, let the dialogue expand our connection to world-doers who have articulated the beauty found in their own knowing:

Māori Marsden *(Māori):*	*Abstract rational thought and empirical methods cannot grasp what is the concrete act of existing which is fragmentary, paradoxical and incomplete. The only way lies through a passionate, inward subjective approach.*
David Hawkins *(Psychiatrist):*	*To merely state that objectivity exists is already a subjective statement. All information, knowledge and the totality of all experience is the product of subjectivity, which is an absolute requirement intrinsic to life, awareness, existence and thought.*
Leroy Little Bear *(Blackfoot):*	*Subjectivity is your starting point to reality.*
Greg Cajete *(Tewa):*	*Native Science reflects the understanding that objectivity is founded on subjectivity.*

Subjective, thought, inside, logic, rationality, intelligence, conceptualization—these are some of the inside processes mind brings forward. They are the snapshots from our trip to meaning, heightened purpose, and useful inquiry that will aid in healing ourselves and our world. The mind part of this triangulation harnesses what is seen, counted, and expressed into a meta-consciousness that explains, contextualizes, or *challenges.* It gives us the green light to engage in creative exploration needed to unburden ourselves from the shriveled promise objectivity has offered the world. We are being asked to *think* now, to develop truth in our bias, to speak our common sense, to deepen what intelligence *really* means.

This will change your research process and structure. Knowing the relevance and maturation of conscious subjectivity will sharpen your rationality, help you speak through your gender so that you may lend what is beautiful about being alive, unique, and one of a kind. No kidding! Knowing mind, your mind, and how it has helped shape your thoughts, will make you honest and help you write truthfully as an incest survivor, or a Pacific Island scholar facing untold obstacles, or a recovering addict working in prisons. Whatever it is. Whoever you are. It is all distinct, all shaped in mind patterns that, if recognized, will bring forth greater intelligence, not less. Self-reflection of one's thoughts and actions helps you understand that who you are, how you were raised, what you eat . . . all act as agents for your mindfulness or mindlessness. And all affect how you see and experience the world.

Mind, as the second point in our triangulation of meaning, helps us recover from the bullying and uniformity of "power-over" epistemology. It gives us breathing space to self-reflect in meaningful ways and engage with a rigor perhaps not captured in academic citations. Remember this! You will have to expand your repertoire of writers and thinkers if you wish to explore beyond the limitations of predictable research methodologies. It will be your mind that recognizes and describes new patterns needed for rationality, logic, and the true rigor found in knowing something in depth. Follow mindfulness to its own intelligence and seek inevitably what most scholars refuse to admit exists: *spirit.* Yes, let us enter this grove with care and quietude.

Spirit: The Causative and Mystical Knowing of Life—Third Point in the Triangulation of Meaning

> At this point, the rational, conceptual aspect of the mind must let go, allowing a break-through into direct, intuitive experience.
>
> —Francesca Fremantle (2001)

Here it is, the third point in a spiral. It is what people misconstrue for religion and dogma. *It is not that.* To expand on ideas previously suggested earlier in this chapter, the spirit category in our triangulation of meaning is no less valuable, no more valuable. It is part of the whole, period. It is data moving toward usefulness, moving toward meaning and beauty. It is the contemplation part of your work that brings you to insight, steadiness, and interconnection. It is the joy or truthful insights of your lessons and the rigor found in your discipline and focus that is not so much written about but expressed nonetheless.

Spirit as a point in this triangulation is all about seeing what is significant and having the courage to discuss it. It is what Trungpa Rinpoche describes as "an innate intelligence that sees the clarity of things just as they are" (Fremantle, 2001, p. 59). This category that pulls facts into logic and finally into metaphor recognizes that one will eventually see more than what is presented. *You are being offered an opportunity to evolve.* Here is where the mystical aspects of this category encourage, inspire, calm. To know we are more than simply body and thought is to acknowledge how those ideas expand into wider realms of knowing and being. This is a spirit-centered truth that is older than time. Again, do not confuse the category of spirit with religion.

Look again at Table 11.1. What do you learn from the spirit category? Are these not the products and process of a conscious life? Is there any wonder billions of people wish to capture these values and ideas in ritual? The spirit part of triangulating ourselves back to meaning is all about the purpose and reason of our lives. It will help you think of your research as something of value and keep you at the edge of your wonder with how it will shape who you are becoming. This third category encompasses the first two. It is an advancement of earlier ideas and gives a structure of rigor that positivism ultimately is shaped by.

Spirit in the triangulation of meaning is as it says: whole, contemplative, intuitive, metaphoric, joyful, liberating. Within research, it is answers you will *remember* in your dreams. It is questions you will frame differently after eye contact with a child. It is understanding an unexpected experience that will heighten the clarity of your findings. It is the "Aha!" that came from stirring oatmeal after a night of transcription. Developing a respect for the qualities of awareness, joy, and beauty will actually develop how you *think* and thus *see* the world. Do you see how all categories are really just one?

The spiritual category in this triangulation of meaning holds more than the extension of the first two categories. It is the frequency by which *all* connect. It is not simply a linear sequence. All three categories occur *simultaneously.* It is an idea whose time has come as it helps subjectivity mature into the fullness of its potential. Do not fear what is inevitable—that we are all part of the birthing of a new culture. Why not do it with a consciousness courageous in its purpose and quiet in its consistency?

Here is the point: research or renewal; mundane or inspiring; fragmented or whole. Do you see why Sir Karl Popper called the advancing of objectivity toward subjectivity into the inevitability of *culture* something we need to recognize? Culture is defined as best practices of a group of people.[21] Here is the metaphor of this discussion: *that we change the culture of research.* We do this simply by engaging all *three* categories.

Ha'ina mai ka puana: Thus Ends My Story

> If knowledge is power then understanding is liberation.
>
> —Manu Aluli-Meyer (2003)

I believe it is time to think indigenous and act authentic even at the price of rejection. To disagree with mainstream expectations is to wake up, to understand what is happening, to be of service to a larger whole. You may even begin to work on behalf of our lands, water, and air. This is why we are heading into the field of hermeneutics—interpretation—via epistemology. We must first detail what we value about intelligence to even *see* there are other interpretations of life, brilliance, and knowing. The idea that the SAT or other measurable tools of "intelligence" are just *tiny* facets of intelligence is now timely. *Your* rendition of your own experience is now the point. Who are you then? What do you have to offer the world? Here is where hermeneutics enters with a bouquet of daisies. To realize that *all* ideas, *all* histories, *all* laws, *all* facts, and *all* theories are simply *interpretations* helps us see where to go from here. To understand this one idea has brought me to this point of liberation.

When ancient renditions of the world are offered for debate within a context of real-life knowing, there is a robustness that I find invigorating and breathtaking. Here is where interpretations matter and because indigenous folk are peopling places we were never found before, do you see why things are changing? We simply posit difference—a difference that knows place and encourages a harmony within that place. Of course, we are far from perfect, but we do bring something unique to the table. We bring dreams, food, elders, courage and the clarity of speech and purpose. After all, there is no time to waste.

We are shaping long boards for a winter swell that is coming. It's time to learn new skills with our ancient minds. Time to deploy common sense back into our consciousness. Time to triangulate our way back to meaning. Time to laugh more and bear witness to the deeper truth of why we do what we're doing. Time to see how we can connect and help others. Time to work on behalf of our lands, water, and air. Do you see how we are *all* on the path of sovereignty, and ultimately, of freedom?

It's funny how the depth and practice of cultural specificity helps me be interested in the collective again. The wider collective. As if the path to wholeness first begins with fragmentation. It's my own body, mind, and spiritual walk toward knowing that I have worked out in this chapter. And for this I'm grateful. Mahalo for sharing the space and making the time. May you find your own secret (Nityananda, 1996). May your bibliography be easy to gather. May you know your own brilliance. May it lead to collective joy.

Amama ua noa.

NOTES

1. Universality in this ideal is not to be confused with uniformity—America's answer to diversity. Universality is a fundamental spiritual truth exemplified in harmony, peace, and awareness. This can only occur through respect and honoring of distinctness, thus the idea that "specificity leads to universality." It is best described in *Sadhana,* by Nobel laureate Rabindranath Tagore (2004) of India. It was also the one big idea that surfaced from my MA-level class on Ethnicity and Education, held at UH Hilo's Education Department in 2003.

2. Epistemology is the philosophy of knowledge. It asks questions we have long taken for granted: "What is knowledge? What is intelligence? What is the difference between information, knowledge, and understanding?" It is *vital* to debate the issue of knowledge/intelligence because of the needs of our time.

3. Hermeneutics is the philosophy of interpretation. It helps us pause to ask, "Who is talking and what interpretation do they bring and not bring to the discussion, idea, or issue?" Hermeneutics makes the clear case that all ideas, all theories, all facts, all laws, or all histories are ultimately only *interpretations.* It is where philosophy is heading. The point here is that different ideas or priorities of knowledge (epistemology) are often dismissed given the nature of who is in control politically or ideologically.

4. Twenty-five Native Hawaiian educators, leaders, and cultural practitioners were interviewed on their views of Hawaiian intelligence and on their philosophy of knowledge. It culminated in my EdD thesis, *Native Hawaiian Epistemology: Contemporary Narratives* (Aluli-Meyer, 1998).

5. This idea that we must learn from land and not simply about land was first learned through the writings of Greg Cajete (2000). It has validated and informed our place-based pedagogy movement in Hawai'i.

6. Aloha as the origin of our intelligence was first shared by hula teacher Olana Kaipo Ai.

7. The Yoga Sutra (Patanjali) cautions us to understand the difference between "word, meaning and perception" in order to get to the bottom of the world's problems and thus their solutions (Hartranft, 2003).

8. "We are all indigenous" came from the mind and writings of a beloved elder, Halemakua (2004), a leader and teacher for our Hawaiian people and for many people around the world. I believe he meant that at one time we all came from a place familiar with our evolution and storied with our experiences. At one time, we all had a rhythmic understanding of time and potent experiences of harmony in space. He believed we can tap into this knowing to engender, again, acts of care, compassion, and the right relationship with land, sky, water, and ocean—vital for these modern times. To take this universal idea into race politics strips it of its truth.

9. For a discussion of this idea, please refer to Aluli-Meyer (2003).

10. Books that bring out the causative agency of thought: *Quantum Questions* (Wilber, 2001), *$E = Mc^2$* (Bodanis, 2000), *The Self-Aware Universe* (Goswami, 1993), *Spirit and Reason* (Deloria, 1999), *The Woven Universe* (Marsden, 2003), *The Yoga Sutra of Patanjali* (Hartranft, 2003), *The Holographic Universe* (Talbot, 1991), and so on.

11. The idea that "there are no causes within the observable world . . . the observable world is a world of effects" is detailed by Hawkins (2002).

12. Jean Houston (2004) in *Jump Time* summarized Einstein's famous idea that a new/different consciousness is needed to solve our current problems. Useful ideas were going to come from unknown places and differently trained individuals. She concurred that today, the consciousness that solves a problem can no longer be the same consciousness that developed it.

13. True intelligence as self-knowledge was put forth by Plato.

14. Fractals are basic expanding and contracting patterns in nature. They were first described via coherence theory (chaos theory) as smaller and smaller elements of a larger and larger whole. A vein is a fractal of a leaf, a leaf is a fractal of a stem, a stem is a fractal of a branch, and a branch is a fractal of a tree. It can then reverse itself back into the molecular level and then out into the forest, countryside, and world level. They represent a coherent whole we are not fully aware of. It is used here to infer that thoughts are also fractals in the world—change is directly linked to whether we think it possible. It begins first with an idea.

15. The idea that "words only point to truth, genuine knowledge must be experienced directly" came from Fremantle (2001).

16. Audre Lorde (1984) inspired this dilemma found in postcolonial theory classes: Can you dismantle the master's house (i.e., imperialism, colonialism, etc.) with the master's tools? Answer: *yes and no.* All outward realities are first inward expressions and thought patterns. A new consciousness must be forged to approach old issues. False dualities of master/slave must also be reconfigured.

17. Ken Wilber, integral philosopher, was the first to introduce me to three points in philosophy and research. I discovered this in his epic work, *Sex, Ecology, Spirituality* (Wilber, 2000).

18. I have always enjoyed the image of the tetrahedron learned from a lecture Buckminster Fuller gave in Honolulu before he died in the 1980s. He described the tetrahedron as "structural integrity" itself.

19. Yin/Yang is a Chinese way to organize female and male principles. Ku and Hina is a Hawaiian way. It gives us a way to recognize balance and to cultivate both aspects in our own character.

20. Empiricism is the belief that our five senses are the only modality in which to experience knowledge.

21. Kumu Hula, Keola Lake said this during an interview for Aluli-Meyer (1998).

References

Aluli-Meyer, M. (1998). *Native Hawaiian epistemology: Contemporary narratives.* EdD thesis, Harvard Graduate School of Education.

Aluli-Meyer, M. (2003). *Ho'oulu: Our time of becoming: Hawaiian epistemology and early writings.* Honolulu, HI: Ai Pohaku Press.

Bodanis, D. (2000). *$E = mc^2$: A biography of the world's most famous equation.* New York: Berkley Books.

Cajete, G. (2000). *Native science: Natural laws of interdependence.* Santa Fe, NM: Clear Light Publishers.

Deloria, V. (1999). *Spirit and reason: The Vine Deloria Jr. reader.* Golden, CO: Fulcrum Publishing.

Fremantle, F. (2001). *Luminous emptiness: Understanding the Tibetan book of the dead.* Boston: Shambhala.

Goswami, A. (1993). *The self-aware universe: How consciousness creates the material world.* New York: Putnam.

Halemakua. (2004). *Unpublished writings of Halemakua.* Hawaii Island.

Hartranft, C. (2003). *The Yoga Sutra of Patanjali.* Boston: Shambhala.

Hawkins, D. (2002). *Power vs. force: The hidden determinants of human behavior.* Carlsbad, CA: Hay House.

Houston, J. (2004). *Jump time: Shaping your future in a world of radical change.* Boulder, CO: Sentient Publications.

Lorde, A. (1984). *Sister outsider: Essays and speeches.* Berkeley, CA: The Crossing Press.

Marsden, M. (2003). *The woven universe.* Aotearoa, New Zealand: Te Wananga O Raukawa.

Nityananda. (1996). *The sky of the heart.* Portland, OR: Rudra Press.

Shatz, Z. (1998). *Prisms and mind: Unifying psychology, physics, and theology.* Berkeley, CA: Prismind.

Tagore, R. (2004). *Sadhana: The classic of Indian spirituality.* New York: Three Leaves Press.

Talbot, M. (1991). *The holographic universe.* New York: Harper Perennial.

Wilber, K. (2000). *Sex, ecology, spirituality: The spirit of evolution.* Boston: Shambhala.

Wilber, K. (2001). *Quantum questions: Mystical writings of the world's great physicists.* Boston: Shambhala.

12

RED PEDAGOGY

The Un-Methodology

Sandy Grande

Ever since I received the invitation to write this chapter, I've been thinking (read: obsessing) about methodology, asking everyone I know how they define it and trying to determine whether I do it or not. Ironically, through these discussions, I discovered that the social engagement of ideas is my method. Specifically, I learned that my research is about ideas in motion. That is, ideas as they come alive within and through people(s), communities, events, texts, practices, policies, institutions, artistic expression, ceremonies, and rituals. I engage them "in motion" through a process of active and close observation wherein I live with, try on, and wrestle with ideas in a manner akin to Geertz's (1998) notion of "deep hanging out" but without the distinction between participant/observer. Instead, the gaze is always shifting inward, outward, and throughout the spaces-in-between, with the idea itself holding ground as the independent variable. As I engage this process, I survey viewpoints on the genealogy of ideas, their representation and potential power to speak across boundaries, borders, and margins, and filter the gathered data through an indigenous perspective. When I say "indigenous perspective," what I mean is my perspective as an indigenous scholar. And when I say "my perspective," I mean from a consciousness shaped not only by my own experiences but also those of my peoples and ancestors. It is through this process that Red pedagogy—my indigenous methodology—emerged.

Introduction

When I think of indigenous methodologies, I think of Linda Tuhiwai Smith's (1999) classic text *Decolonizing Methodologies: Research and Indigenous Peoples.* This landmark publication defined the field of indigenous methodology, charting the path for those still navigating the deeply troubled waters of academic research. The historically turbulent relationship stems from centuries of use and abuse at the hands of Whitestream[1] prospectors (read: academics), mining the dark bodies of indigenous peoples—either out of self-interest or self-hatred. Smith

AUTHORS' NOTE: Portions of this chapter come from my text, *Red Pedagogy: Native American Social and Political Thought* (Grande, 2004).

names the animosity directly, writing, "The ways in which scientific research is implicated in the worst excesses of colonialism remains a powerful remembered history for many of the world's colonized peoples. It is a history that offends the deepest sense of our humanity" (p. 1).

This history of dehumanization raises significant questions for the indigenous scholar—presenting a kind of "Sophie's Choice" moment where one feels compelled to choose between retaining his or her integrity (identity) as a Native person or doing research. What does it mean for indigenous scholars to claim the space of educational research? Does it signify a final submission to the siren's song, seducing us into the colonialist abyss with promises of empowerment? Or is it the necessary first step in reclaiming and decolonizing an intellectual space—an inquiry room—of our own? Such questions provoke beyond the bounds of academic exercise, suggesting instead the need for an academic exorcism.

In this case, the demon to be purged is the specter of colonialism. As indigenous scholars, we live within, against, and outside of its constant company, witnessing its various manifestations as it shape-shifts its way into everything from research and public policy to textbooks and classrooms. In other words, the colonial tax of Native scholars not only requires a renegotiation of personal identity but also an analysis of how whole nations get trans- or (dis)figured when articulated through Western frames of knowing. As Edward Said (1978) observes, "Institutions, vocabulary, scholarship, imagery, doctrines, even colonial bureaucracies and colonial styles" support the "Western discourse" (p. 2). Such an observation begs the question: Is it possible to engage the grammar of empire without replicating its effects?

At the same time indigenous scholars entertain these ruminations, Native communities continue to be affected and transformed by the forces of colonization, rendering the "choice" of whether to employ Western research methods in the process of defining indigenous methodologies essentially moot. By virtue of living in the Whitestream world, indigenous scholars have no choice but to negotiate the forces of colonialism, to learn, understand, and converse in the grammar of empire as well as develop the skills to contest it.

Such is the premise and promise of *Red pedagogy.* It is an indigenous pedagogy that operates at the crossroads of Western theory—specifically critical pedagogy—and indigenous knowledge. By bridging these epistemological worlds, Red pedagogy abandons what Robert Allen Warrior (1995) refers to as "the death dance of dependence," that is, the vacillation between the wholesale adoption of Anglo-Western theories and stance that indigenous scholars need nothing outside of themselves or their communities to understand the world or their place within it. Specifically, Red pedagogy asks that as we examine our own communities, policies, and practices, that we take seriously the notion that knowing ourselves as revolutionary agents is more than an act of understanding who we are. It is an act of reinventing ourselves, of validating our overlapping cultural identifications and relating them to the materiality of social life and power relations (McLaren, 1997). To allow for the process of reinvention, it is important to understand that Red pedagogy is not a method or technique to be memorized, implemented, applied, or prescribed. Rather, it is space of engagement. It is the liminal and intellectual borderlands where indigenous and nonindigenous scholars encounter one another, working to remember, redefine, and reverse the devastation of the original colonialist "encounter."

What follows is a framework for thinking about indigenous knowledge as it encounters critical pedagogy or Red pedagogy. It begins with a "statement of the problem" or a tracing of the historical disconnect between indigenous education and Western theory. This discussion is followed by an articulation of the basic principles of critical theory, specifically revolutionary critical theory and the possibilities it holds for indigenous theories of decolonization. While it is evident that revolutionary critical theory holds great promise, because it also retains core Western assumptions, it also stands in tension with those central to indigenous pedagogies. Specifically, the radical notion of "democratization" does not theorize the difference of indigenous sovereignty;

revolutionary constructs of subjectivity remain tied to Western notions of citizenship, and insofar as the discourse of revolutionary critical pedagogy is informed by Marxist theory, it retains a measure of anthropocentrism that belies indigenous views of land and "nature." Each of these tensions will be examined more fully. Distilled from this analysis are seven precepts of Red pedagogy that are intended to serve as a point of departure for further discussion.

Statement of the Problem: The Historical Roots of Red Pedagogy

The miseducation of American Indians precedes the "birth" of this nation. Indeed, long before the first shots of the Revolutionary War were fired, American education was being conceived as a foundational weapon in the arsenal of American imperialism. By the mid-18th century, Harvard University (1654), the College of William and Mary (1693), and Dartmouth College (1769) had all been established with the express purpose of "civilizing" and "Christianizing" Indians. Perhaps the most critical insight to siphon from this history is that the colonialist project was never simply about the desire to "civilize" or even deculturalize indigenous peoples. Rather, it was deliberately designed to colonize Indian minds as a means of gaining access to indigenous resources. Thus, despite the tired characterization of the relationship between the United States and Indian tribes as one of cultural domination, the predominant relationship has been one of material exploitation: the forced extraction of labor and natural resources in the interest of capital gains.

Consider, for example, the Indian Removal Act (1830),[2] Dawes Allotment (1887),[3] and Termination Acts (1953)[4]—all typically viewed as legislated attempts to destroy Indian culture, but in the end, each policy provided the federal government greater access to Indian lands and resources, proffering a healthy windfall in capital gains. Similarly, while manual labor and boarding schools attempted to extinguish Indian-ness by imposing culturally imperialistic practices, they also profited from child labor and the unwritten policy to establish a permanent Indian proletariat.

While it is important to recognize the progress that has been made since colonial times, it is also evident that the legacy of colonization persists. As a group, American Indian students are still the most disproportionately affected by poverty, low educational attainment, and limited access to educational opportunities (Beaulieu, 2000, p. 33). Moreover, Native students are among the students most often to be categorized and treated as remedial students, subjected to racial slurs, and hindered by low teacher expectations—all of which lead to extreme alienation (Butterfield, 1994; Deyhle & Swisher, 1997). As a result, Native students exhibit the highest dropout rates, lowest academic performance rates, and lowest college admission and retention rates in the nation (American Council on Education, 2002).

In recognition of the seeming sociocultural nature of "the problem," some educators have advocated *multicultural education*[5] for American Indian students (Butterfield, 1994; Charleston & King, 1991; Reyhner, 1992; St. Germaine, 1995a, 1995b; Wilson, 1991). In particular, Native educators have stressed the role of culture and language, arguing that American Indian students "thrive at school when instruction is congruent with their culture, connected to their history, and consistent with their community's worldview" (Sherman, 2003). Among the principal advocates of a culturally based education (CBE) is indigenous educator William Demmert, who, along with John Towner, has defined the following six elements of CBE:

1. Recognition and use of Native languages
2. Pedagogy that stresses traditional cultural characteristics and adult-child interactions
3. Pedagogy in which teaching strategies are congruent with the traditional culture and ways of knowing and learning
4. Curriculum that is based on traditional culture and that recognizes the importance of Native spirituality

5. Strong Native community participation in educating children and in the planning and operation of school activities
6. Knowledge and use of the social and political mores of the community

While virtually no one would dispute the relevance of the above elements as being critical to the academic success of Native students, I maintain that unless educational reform also happens concurrently with an analysis of colonialism, it is bound to suffocate from the tentacles of imperialism. Moreover, in a time when 90% of American Indian students attend non-Indian schools (Gallagher, 2000), it is not only imperative for Native educators to insist on the incorporation of indigenous knowledge and praxis in school curricula but also to transform the institutional structures of schools themselves. In other words, indigenous educators need to theorize the ways in which power and domination inform the processes and procedures of schooling and develop pedagogies that disrupt their effects. Put simply, insofar as the project for colonialist education has been imbricated with the social, economic, and political policies of U.S. imperialism, an education for decolonization must also make no claim to political neutrality. Specifically, it must engage a method of analysis and social inquiry that troubles the capitalist, imperialist aims of unfettered competition, accumulation, and exploitation.

Historically, such systems of analysis have been the domain of critical theorists. Specifically, critical educators extend critiques of the social, economic, and political barriers to social justice as well as advocate for the transformation of schools along the imperatives of democracy. In so doing, they position schools as "sites of struggle" where the broader relations of power, domination, and authority are played out. In addition to their analyses of schools, critical educators theorize the intersections of race, class, gender, and sexuality as the fault lines of inequality. Within these analyses, they include the naming and examination of "Whiteness" as a significant marker of racial, class, and gender privilege. Finally, and perhaps most relevant to the concerns of indigenous education, proponents of "revolutionary" forms of critical pedagogy center their project in the transformation of capitalist social relations, recognizing that the attainment of real equity is impossible within the current imperialist system of economic exploitation. They take seriously the claims and struggles of colonized peoples by recognizing that movements against imperialism must begin with dismantling the "Eurocentric system of cultural valuation that rationalizes globalization as 'development' and 'progress'" (Rizvi, 2002).

Despite its seeming relevance, indigenous scholars have had limited engagement with critical theories of education. For the most part, they have concentrated on the social and political urgencies of their own communities. Against such immediate needs, engagement in abstract theory seems indulgent (a luxury and privilege of the academic elite), Eurocentric and thereby inherently contradictory to the aims of indigenous education.

Though this impulse is entirely rational, the lack of engagement with critical theory has ultimately limited possibilities for indigenous scholars to build broad-based coalitions and political solidarities. Particularly at a time when indigenous communities are under siege from the forces of global encroachment, such a limitation has serious implications. Communities either unable or unwilling to extend borders of coalition and enact *transcendent* theories of decolonization will only compound their vulnerability to the whims and demands of the "new global order."

These realities indicate that the time is ripe for indigenous scholars to engage in critique-al[6] studies. Native students and educators deserve a pedagogy that cultivates a sense of collective agency as well as a praxis that targets the dismantling of colonialism, helping them navigate the excesses of dominant power and revitalization of indigenous communities. While there is nothing inherently healing, liberatory, or revolutionary about theory, it is one of our primary responsibilities as educators to link the lived experience of theorizing to the processes of self-recovery and social transformation. That being said, this is not a call for indigenous scholars to simply join the conversation of critical theorists. Rather, Red pedagogy aims to initiate an indigenous conversation that can, in turn, engage in dialogical contestation with critical and revolutionary theories. The discussion that follows is intended to initiate this conversation, examining points of tension and intersection between Red pedagogy and critical theory: articulating possibilities for coalition.

At the Crossroads of Revolutionary Critical Theory and Red Pedagogy

Typically envisioned as leftist or *beyond* multicultural education, the "theoretical genesis" of North American critical pedagogy can be traced back to the work of Paulo Freire, John Dewey, and other social reconstructionists writing in the post-Depression years (McLaren, 2003a, 2003b). According to Peter McLaren (2003a), leading exponents have always "cross-fertilized critical pedagogy with just about every transdisciplinary tradition imaginable, including theoretical forays into the Frankfurt School . . . the work of Richard Rorty, Jacques Lacan, Jacques Derrida, and Michael Foucault" (p. 66). With such transdisciplinary beginnings, it is not surprising that critical pedagogy has emerged in more recent years as a kind of umbrella for a variety of educators and scholars working toward social justice and greater equity (Lather, 1998). As such, postmodern, poststructuralist, feminist, postcolonial, Marxist, and critical race theorists have all developed their own forms of critical pedagogy. While each school of critical pedagogy has made important contributions to the field, Marxist and other radical scholars are highly suspicious of the overall abandonment of emancipatory agendas within the field. As a corrective, they advocate a form of critical pedagogy with a strong anticapitalist and emancipatory agenda or a "revolutionary critical pedagogy" (Allman, 2001).[7]

The core theoretical commitments of revolutionary critical pedagogy are (a) recognize that capitalism, despite its power, is a "historically produced social relation that can be challenged (most forcefully by those exploited by it)" (McLaren & Farahmandpur, 2001, p. 272); (b) foreground historical materialist analysis, providing a theory of the material basis of social life rooted in historical social relations that uncover the structures of class conflict and the effects produced by the social division of labor;[8] (c) reimagine Marxist theory in the interests of the critical educational project; and (d) understand that Marxist revolutionary theory "must be flexible enough to reinvent itself" and not operate as "a universal truth but rather as a weapon of interpretation" (McLaren & Farahmandpur, 2001, pp. 301–302). Beyond these commitments, McLaren and Farahmandpur (2001) have also defined the following foundational principles of revolutionary critical praxis:[9]

1. A revolutionary critical pedagogy must be a *collective process,* one that involves using a Freirian dialogical learning approach.

2. A revolutionary critical pedagogy must be *critical;* that is, it works to locate the underlying causes of class exploitation and economic oppression within the social, political, and economic infrastructure of capitalist social relations of production.

3. A revolutionary critical pedagogy is profoundly *systematic* in the sense that it is guided by Marx's dialectical method of inquiry, which begins with the "real concrete" circumstances of the oppressed masses and moves toward a classification, conceptualization, analysis, and breaking down of the concrete social world into units of abstractions to get at the essence of social phenomena. It then reconstructs and makes the social world intelligible by transforming and translating theory into concrete social and political action.

4. A revolutionary critical pedagogy is *participatory,* involving building coalitions among community members, grassroots movements, church organizations, and labor unions.

5. A revolutionary critical pedagogy is a *creative process,* incorporating elements of popular culture (i.e., drama, music, oral history, narratives) as educational tools to politicize and revolutionize working-class consciousness.

Such principles are clearly relevant to Native students and educators in dire need of pedagogies of disruption, intervention, collectivity, hope, and possibility. The foregrounding of capitalist relations as the axis of exploitation helps reveal the history of indigenous peoples as one of dispossession and not simply oppression. Moreover, the trenchant critique of postmodernism reframes the "problem" of identity as a smokescreen that obfuscates the imperatives of indigenous sovereignty and self-determination.

That being said, it is important to recognize that revolutionary critical pedagogy remains rooted in the Western paradigm and therefore in tension with indigenous knowledge and praxis. In particular, the root constructs of democratization, subjectivity, and property are all defined through Western frames of reference that presume the individual as the primary subject of "rights" and social status. The myriad implications of these basic failures serve as the jumping-off point for Red pedagogy, raising three central questions:

1. Do critical/revolutionary pedagogies articulate constructions of subjectivity that can theorize the multiple and intersecting layers of indigenous identity as well as root them in the historical material realities of indigenous life?

2. Do critical/revolutionary pedagogies articulate a geopolitical landscape any more receptive to the notion of indigenous sovereignty than other critical pedagogies rooted in liberal conceptions of democracy?

3. Do critical/revolutionary pedagogies articulate a view of land and natural resources that is less anthropocentric than other Western discourses?

While these questions help formulate the Red critique of revolutionary critical pedagogy, the perceived aporias are not theorized as deficiencies. Rather, they are viewed as points of tension, helping to define the spaces-in-between the Western and indigenous thought-worlds. Revolutionary scholars themselves acknowledge that "no theory can fully anticipate or account for the consequences of its application but remains a living aperture through which specific histories are made visible and intelligible" (McLaren & Farahmandpur, 2001, p. 301). Therefore, while revolutionary critical theory can serve as a vital tool for indigenous students and educators, the basis of Red pedagogy remains distinctive, rooted in traditional indigenous knowledge and praxis. The implications of this difference are articulated below as filtered through each of the defining questions of Red pedagogy. The hope is to map a common ground of struggle with revolutionary critical pedagogy that may in turn serve as the foundation for eventual solidarities.

1. *Do critical/revolutionary pedagogies articulate constructions of subjectivity that can theorize the multiple and intersecting layers of indigenous identity as well as root them in the historical material realities of indigenous life?*

In a postmodern world, where "everything is everything," revolutionary critical scholars critique the liberal postmodern practice of framing questions of identity and difference exclusively in terms of the cultural and discursive (e.g., language, signs, tropes), cutting them off from the structural causes and material relations that create "difference." They also contest the overblurring of boundaries and emphasis of local over grand narratives, contending that such postmodern tactics serve to obfuscate, if not deny, the hierarchies of power. According to McLaren (1998), postmodernists ultimately promote "an ontological agnosticism" that not only relinquishes the primacy of social transformation but also encourages a kind of "epistemological relativism."

In response, revolutionary scholars advocate the postcolonial notion of *mestizaje*[10] as a more effectual model of multisubjectivity (Darder, Torres, & Gutierrez, 1997; Kincheloe & Steinberg, 1997; McLaren & Sleeter, 1995; Valle & Torres, 1995). The counterdiscourse of mestizaje is historically rooted in the Latin American subjectivity of the *mestízo/a*—literally, a person of mixed ancestry, especially of American Indian, European, and African backgrounds (Delgado Bernal, 1998). Chicana scholar Gloria Anzaldúa's (1987) seminal text *Borderlands/la Frontera: The New Mestíza* articulates, "The new mestíza copes by developing a tolerance for contradictions, a tolerance for ambiguity. She learns to be an Indian in Mexican culture (and) to be Mexican from an Anglo point of view" (p. 79).

Revolutionary scholars have embraced the spirit of the Chicana mestíza, viewing it as the postcolonial antidote to imperialist notions of racial purity (di Leonardo, 1998). The emergent discourse of mestizaje embodies the mestíza's demonstrated refusal to prefer one language, one national heritage, or one culture at the expense of others. McLaren (1997) articulates mestizaje as "the embodiment of a transcultural, transnational subject, a self-reflexive entity capable of rupturing the facile legitimization of 'authentic' national identities through (the) articulation of a subject who is conjunctural, who is a relational part of an ongoing negotiated connection to the larger society, and who is interpolated by multiple subject positionings" (p. 12). In so doing, unlike liberal notions of subjectivity, it also roots identity in the discourse of power. Ultimately, the critical notion of mestizaje is itself multifunctional. It not only signifies the decline of the imperial West but also decenters Whiteness and undermines the myth of a democratic nation-state based on borders and exclusions (Valle & Torres, 1995).

Insofar as the notion of mestizaje disrupts the jingoistic discourse of nationalism, it is indeed crucial to the emancipatory project. As McLaren (1997) notes, "Educators would do well to consider Gloria Anzaldúa's (1987) project of creating *mestizaje* theories that create new categories of identity for those left out or pushed out of existing ones" (p. 537). In so doing, however, he cautions that "care must be taken not to equate hybridity with equality" (p. 46).[11] Coco Fusco (1995) similarly notes, "The postcolonial celebration of hybridity has (too often) been interpreted as the sign that no further concern about the politics of representation and cultural exchange is needed. With ease, we lapse back into the integrationist rhetoric of the 1960's" (qtd. in McLaren, 1997, p. 46). In the wake of transgressing borders and building postnational coalitions, these words caution us against losing sight of the unique challenges of particular groups and their distinctive struggles for social justice. In taking this admonition seriously, it is important to consider the ways in which transgressive subjectivity—mestizaje—both furthers and impedes indigenous imperatives of self-determination and sovereignty.

Though the postcolonial construct of mestizaje (rooted in the discourses of power) differs from "free-floating" postmodern constructions of identity, an undercurrent of fluidity and displacedness continues to permeate, if not define, mestizaje. As such, it remains problematic for indigenous formations of subjectivity and the expressed need to forge and maintain integral connections to both land and place. Consider, for example, the following statement on the nature of critical subjectivity by Peter McLaren (1997):

> The struggle for critical subjectivity is the struggle to occupy a space of hope—a liminal space, an intimation of the anti-structure, of what lives in the in-between zone of undecidedability—in which one can work toward a praxis of redemption.... A sense of atopy has always been with me, a resplendent placelessness, a feeling of living in germinal formlessness ... I cannot find words to express what this border identity means to me. All I have are what Georges Bastille (1988) calls mots glissants (slippery words). (pp. 13–14)

Though McLaren speaks passionately about the need for a "praxis of redemption," the very possibility of redemption is situated within our willingness to not only accept but also flourish in the "liminal spaces," border identities, and postcolonial hybridities inherent to postmodern life. In fact, McLaren perceives the fostering of a "resplendent placelessness" itself as the gateway to a more just and democratic society. In so doing, he reveals the degree to which the radical mestizaje retains the same core assumption of other Western pedagogies. That is, in a democratic society, *the articulation of human subjectivity is rooted in the intangible notion of rights as opposed to the tangible reality of land.*

While indigenous scholars embrace the anticolonial aspects of mestizaje, the historical-material realities of their communities require a construct that is also geographically rooted and historically placed. Consider, for example, the following commentary by Deloria (1994) on the centrality of place and land in the construction of American Indian subjectivity:

> Recognizing the sacredness of lands on which previous generations have lived and died is the foundation of all other sentiment. Instead of denying this dimension of our emotional lives, we should be setting aside additional places that have transcendent meaning. Sacred sites that higher spiritual powers have chosen for manifestation enable us to focus our concerns on the specific form of our lives . . . Sacred places are the foundation of all other beliefs and practices because they represent the presence of the sacred in our lives. They properly inform us that we are not larger than nature and that we have responsibility to the rest of the natural world that transcend our own personal desires and wishes. This lesson must be learned by each generation. (pp. 278, 281)

Gross misunderstanding of this connection between American Indian subjectivity and place and, more important, between sovereignty and land has been the source of myriad ethnocentric policies and injustices in Indian Country.

Consider, for example, the impact of the Indian Religious Freedom Act (IRFA) of 1978. Government officials never anticipated that passage of this act would set up a virtually intractable conflict between property rights and religious freedom. But American Indians viewed the act as an invitation to return to their sacred sites. Since several sites were on government lands and being damaged by commercial use, numerous tribes filed lawsuits under the IRFA, alleging mismanagement and destruction of their "religious" sites. At the same time, Whitestream corporations, tourists, and even rock climbers filed their own lawsuits accusing federal land managers of illegally restricting access to Indian sacred sites. They argued that since such restrictions were placed on "public sites," the IRFA violated the constitutional separation of church and state. This history alone points to the central difference of American Indian and Whitestream subjectivity, whether articulated through the theoretical frames of essentialism, postmodernism, or postcolonialism.

To be clear, indigenous and critical scholars share some common ground. Namely, they envision an anti-imperialist theory of subjectivity, one free of the compulsions of global capitalism and the racism, classism, sexism, and xenophobia it engenders. But where revolutionary scholars ground their vision in Western conceptions of democracy and justice that presume a "liberated" self, indigenous scholars ground their vision in conceptions of sovereignty that presume a profound connection to place and land. Thus, to a large degree, the seemingly liberatory constructs of fluidity, mobility, and transgression are perceived not only as the language of critical subjectivity but also as part of the fundamental lexicon of Western imperialism. Deloria (1999) writes,

> Although the loss of land must be seen as a political and economic disaster of the first magnitude, the real exile of the tribes occurred with the destruction of ceremonial life (associated with the loss of land) and the failure or inability of white society to offer a sensible and cohesive alternative to the traditions, which Indians remembered. People became disoriented with respect to the world in which they lived. They could not practice their old ways, and the new ways which they were expected to learn were in a constant state of change because they were not part of a cohesive view of the world but simply adjustments which whites were making to the technology they invented. (p. 247)

Thus, insofar as American Indian identities continue to be defined and shaped in interdependence with place, the transgressive mestizaje functions as a potentially homogenizing force that presumes the continued exile of tribal peoples and their enduring absorption into the American "democratic" Whitestream. While critical scholars clearly aim to construct a very different kind of democratic solidarity that disrupts the sociopolitical and economic hegemony of the dominant culture around a transformed notion of mestizaje (one committed to the destabilization of the isolationist narratives of nationalism and cultural chauvinism), I argue that any liberatory project that does not begin with a clear understanding of the difference of indigenous sovereignty will, in the end, work to undermine tribal life.

The above analysis points to the need for an indigenous theory of subjectivity that addresses the political quest for sovereignty and the socioeconomic urgency to build transnational coalitions. In these efforts, it is critical that American Indians work to maintain their distinctiveness as tribal peoples of sovereign nations (construct effective means of border patrolling) while at the same time move toward building inter- and intratribal solidarity and political coalition (construct effective means of border crossing). Such a Red pedagogy would transform the struggle over identity to evolve, not apart from, but in relationship with, struggles over tribal land, resources, treaty rights, and intellectual property. A Red pedagogy also aims to construct a self-determined space for American Indian intellectualism, recognizing that survival depends on the ability not only to navigate the terrain of Western knowledge but also to theorize and negotiate a racist, sexist marketplace that aims to exploit the labor of signified "others" for capital gain. Finally, a Red pedagogy is committed to providing American Indian students the social and intellectual space to reimagine what it means to be Indian in contemporary U.S. society, arming them with a critical analysis of the intersecting systems of domination and the tools to navigate them.

Insofar as strong communities necessitate earnest and inspired leaders, the search for "comfortable modern identities" remains integral to the quest for sovereignty. The proposed *Red* construct of *Indianismo*[12] is intended to guide the search for a theory of subjectivity in a direction that embraces the location of Native peoples in the "constitutive outside." Specifically, it claims a distinctively indigenous space shaped by and through a matrix of *legacy, power, and ceremony.* In so doing, the notion of Indianismo stands outside the polarizing debates of essentialism and postmodernism, recognizing that both the timeless and temporal are essential for theorizing the complexity of indigenous realities (Dirlik, 1999).

While the constructs of revolutionary and postcolonial theories provide for a common ground of understanding, the Red notion of Indianismo remains grounded in the intellectual histories of indigenous peoples. As informed by this tradition, it is a subjectivity of shape more than temporality. As Deloria (1994) notes, "Most Americans raised in a society in which history is all encompassing, have very little idea of how radically their values would shift if they took the idea of place, both sacred and secular, seriously" (pp. 76–77). The centrality of place in the indigenous thought-world is explicitly conveyed through tradition and language and implicitly through the relationship between human beings and the rest of nature.

What distinguishes the indigenous struggle for self-determination from others is their collective effort to protect the rights of their peoples to live in accordance with traditional ways. It is the struggle to effectively negotiate the line between fetishizing such identities and recognizing their importance to the continuance of Indians as tribal peoples. Regardless of how any individual indigenous person chooses to live his or her life, he or she is responsible for protecting the right to live according to ancestral ways. As such, while indigenous peoples resist the kind of essentialism that recognizes only one way of being, they also work to retain a vast constellation of distinct traditions that serve as the defining characteristics of tribal life. As Deloria and Lytle (1983) note, this allegiance to traditional knowledge that has protected American Indians from annihilation and absorption into the democratic mainstream.

To this end, traditional tribal languages must play a crucial role in maintaining the fabric of Indianismo. Indigenous languages are replete with metaphors of existence that implicitly convey notions of multiplicity, hybridity, dialectics, contingency, and a sense of the "imaginary." For example, in Quéchua, the word for *being, person,* and *Andean person* is all the same—*Runa.* As such, this root term has the potential to incorporate the many subcategories of beingness while retaining the same basic reference group as in the words *llaqtaruna* (inhabitants of the village) and *qualaruna* (foreigner, literally naked, peeled).

In addition, the root can be used passively as in *yuyay runa* (one who is knowing or understanding), actively as in *runayachikk* (that which cultivates a person), or reflexively as in *runaman tukuy* (to complete oneself). In other words, runa is a virtually limitless category, one open to the sense of being as well as becoming. Thus, the "revolutionary" ideas of hybridity, relationality, and dialectics are neither new nor revolutionary to this indigenous community but rather have been an integral part of the Quéchua way of life for more than five hundred years.

2. *Do critical/revolutionary pedagogies articulate a geopolitical landscape any more receptive to the notion of indigenous sovereignty than other critical pedagogies rooted in liberal conceptions of democracy?*

From the vantage point of the federal government, the very notion of tribes as internal sovereigns or "domestic dependent nations" is destabilizing to democracy, defying the principle of America as one people, one nation. Yet, from the perspective of American Indians, "democracy" has been wielded with impunity, as the first and most virulent weapon of mass destruction. Resisting the tides of history, Red pedagogy operates on the assumption that indigenous sovereignty does not oppose democracy. On the contrary, it views sovereignty as democracy's only lifeline asking, Is it possible for democracy to grow from the seeds of tyranny? Can the "good life" be built upon the deaths of thousands?

The playing field for this discussion is the terrain of American education where "the production of democracy, the practice of education, and the constitution of the nation-state" have been interminably bound together (Mitchell, 2001). Historically, liberal educators have championed the notion of cultural pluralism as the pathway to democracy, imbricating the constructs of national unity, multicultural harmony, and inclusion as the guiding principles of American education. Within this rhetoric, schools were to become an extension of the public sphere, a place where citizens could participate in the democratic project by coming together and transcending their racial, class, and gendered differences to engage in "rational discourse." Though an improvement on "traditional" models of schooling, progressive education still functioned as an assimilationist pedagogy, designed to absorb cultural difference by "including" marginalized groups in the universality of the nation-state, advocating a kind of multicultural nationalism. As Mitchell (2001) notes, in the postwar years, "the philosophy of American pluralism was framed as an extension of equality of opportunity to all members of the national body, particularly those disenfranchised by racism" (p. 55). This ideology informed educational theory and practice from the Progressive education movement in the 1930s and 1940s to the intergroup education movement of the 1950s, the multicultural education movement from the 1960s onward, and liberal forms of critical pedagogy from the 1980s to the present.

Contemporary revolutionary scholars critique liberal forms of critical pedagogy, naming their "politics of inclusion" as an accomplice to the broader project of neoliberalism. Specifically, they argue that such models ignore the historic, economic, and material conditions of "difference," conspicuously averting attention away from issues of power. Critical scholars therefore maintain that while liberal theorists may invest in the "theoretical idealism" of democracy, they remain "amnesiatic toward the continued lived realities of democratically induced oppression" (Richardson & Villenas, 2000, p. 260). In contrast to liberal conceptions of democratic education, revolutionary scholars call attention to the "democratically induced" oppression experienced by colonized peoples. In response, they work to reenvision democratic education as a project "rooted in a radical and liberatory politics," replacing liberal (procapitalist) conceptions of democracy with Marxist formulations of a *socialist* democracy (Richardson & Villenas, 2000, p. 261). In so doing, they reconstitute democracy as a perpetually unfinished process, explicitly recentering democratic education around issues of power, dominance, subordination, and stratification.

Within this context, "democratic pedagogies" are defined as those that motivate teachers, students, schools, and communities to make choices with "the overarching purpose of contributing to increased social justice, equality, and improvement in the quality of life for all constituencies within the larger society" (Fischman & McLaren, 2000, p. 168). Giroux (2001) maintains that such pedagogies contest the dominant views of democracy propagated by "neoliberal gurus"—where profit making and material accumulation are defined as the essence of the good life. With these directives in mind, McLaren and Farahmandpur (2001) articulate two fundamental principles of a revolutionary critical pedagogy: (a) to recognize the "class character" of education in capitalist schooling and (b) to advocate a "socialist reorganization of capitalist society" (Krupskaya, 1985). Ultimately, they argue that education can never be "free" or "equal" as long as social classes exist (McLaren & Farahmandpur, 2001, p. 298).

While revolutionary theorists help articulate a more genuine democracy than neoliberal forms, they still theorize within a Western, linear political framework. For this reason, indigenous scholar José Barreiro (1995) notes that "in the context of jurisdiction and political autonomy, traditional Indigenous political processes are characterized by the struggle to stay independent of both left and right wing ideologies, political parties and their often sanguine hostilities."[13] Indeed, one would be hard-pressed to convince the Miskitus, Sumus, Ramas, Quéchua, and Aymara Indians of Central and South America that leftist or specifically Marxist-inspired regimes held any more promise for indigenous peoples than other Western formations of governance (Richardson & Villenas, 2000).

Thus, while the Marxist, leftist, socialist politics of revolutionary theorists expose important linkages between colonialist forces and capitalist greed, they do not, in and of themselves, represent an emancipatory politics for indigenous people. In particular, while revolutionary scholars may have successfully troubled dominant definitions of democracy, pluralism, and the nation-state by infusing the discourse with a cogent critique of global capitalism, it is not clear that they give any greater consideration to the pedagogical imperatives of indigenous sovereignty. Therein lies the central tension between revolutionary visions of a socialist democratic education and the indigenous project of education for sovereignty and self-determination. Specifically, while it is possible that the core construct of democracy can be sufficiently troubled and divested from its Western capitalist desires, a Red pedagogy requires that it be decentered as the primary struggle concept. This repositioning distinguishes the aim of indigenous education—sovereignty—from that of revolutionary critical pedagogy—liberation through socialist democracy. One of the most significant ways this difference plays out is the quest for indigenous sovereignty tied to issues of *land*, Western constructions of democracy are tied to issues of *property*.[14] This important distinction necessitates an unpacking of critical assumptions regarding the relationship between labor, property, citizenship, and nationhood, what Richardson and Villenas (2000, p. 268) identify as a critique of "assumed democracy." Moreover, given the inexorable ties between land and sovereignty, sovereignty and citizenship, and citizenship and the nation-state, one of the most glaring questions for indigenous scholars is how a revolutionary socialist politics can imagine a "new" social order unfolding upon (still) occupied land.

In other words, while revolutionary theorists advocate a "socialist commitment to [the] egalitarian distribution of economic power and exchange" (McLaren & Farahmandpur, 2001, p. 306), my question is this: *How does the "egalitarian distribution" of colonized lands constitute greater justice for indigenous peoples?* If the emancipatory project is built upon the spoils of conquest, how is that liberatory for Native peoples? While revolutionary scholars rightly challenge the inherent inequalities of capitalist society, they retain the metaphors of power and exchange as defined through the Western notion of property. This failure to problematize the issue of (colonized) land is perhaps the major deficiency of Marxist and other Western-centric politics.

Moreover, though the precepts of a revolutionary critical pedagogy and Red pedagogy agree on the enduring relevance of the nation-state and its role as an agent of capital, they diverge in their ideas of how these relations should reconceptualize democracy. Revolutionary theorists insist that the only way to manage diversity is through the practice of "genuine democracy," which is only possible in a socialist economy (McLaren & Farahmandpur, 2001, p. 295). *But, contrary to the assertions of revolutionary theorists, capitalist (exploitative) modes of production are not predicated on the exploitation of free (slave) labor but rather, first and foremost, premised on the colonization of indigenous land.* The privileging and distinguishing of "class struggle" and concomitant assertion of capitalism as *the* totality underestimates the overarching nature of *decolonization:* a totality that places capitalism, patriarchy, White supremacy, and Western Christianity in radical contingency. This tension alone necessitates an indigenous reinvisioning of the precepts of revolutionary theory, bringing them into alignment with the realities of indigenous struggle. The task ahead is to detach and *dethink* the notion of sovereignty from its connection to Western understandings of power and base it on indigenous notions of relationship.[15]

However the question of indigenous sovereignty is resolved politically, there will be significant implications on the intellectual lives of indigenous peoples, particularly in terms of education. Lyons (2000) views the history of colonization, in part, as the manifestation of "rhetorical imperialism," that is, "the ability of dominant powers to assert control of others by setting the terms of debate" (Lyons, 2000, p. 452). Indeed, throughout the history of federal Indian law, terms and definitions have continually changed over time. Indians have gone from "sovereigns" to "wards" and from "nations" to "tribes," while the practice of "treaty making" has given way to one of agreements (Lyons, 2000). As each change served the needs of the nation-state, Lyons argues that "the erosion of Indian national sovereignty can be credited in part to a rhetorically imperialist use of language by white powers" (Lyons, 2000, p. 453).

Thus, just as language was central to the colonialist project, it must be central to the project of decolonization. Indigenous scholar Haunani-Kay Trask (1993) writes, "Thinking in one's own cultural referents leads to conceptualizing in one's own world view which, in turn, leads to disagreement with and eventual opposition to the dominant ideology" (p. 54). Thus, where a revolutionary critical pedagogy compels students and educators to question how "knowledge is related historically, culturally and institutionally to the processes of production and consumption," a Red pedagogy compels students to question how knowledge is related to the processes of colonization. It furthermore asks how traditional indigenous knowledges can inform the project of decolonization. In short, this implies a threefold process for education. Specifically, a Red pedagogy necessitates (a) the subjection of the processes of Whitestream schooling to critical pedagogical analyses; (b) the decoupling and dethinking of education from its Western, colonialist contexts, including revolutionary critical pedagogy; and (c) the conceptualization of indigenous efforts to reground students and educators in traditional knowledge and teachings. In short, a Red pedagogy aims to create awareness of what Trask terms "disagreements," helping to foster discontent about the "inconsistencies between the world as it is and as it should be" (Alfred, 1999, p. 132).

Though this process might state the obvious, it is important to recognize the value and significance of each separate component. I wish to underscore that the project of decolonization not only demands students to acquire the knowledge of "the oppressor" but also the skills to negotiate and dismantle the implications of such knowledge. Concurrently, traditional perspectives on power, justice, and relationships are essential, both to defend against further co-optation and to build intellectual solidarity—a collectivity of indigenous knowledge. In short, "the time has come for people who are from someplace Indian to take back the discourse on Indians" (Alfred, 1999, p. 143).

Finally, it needs to be understood that sovereignty is not a separatist discourse. On the contrary, *it is a restorative process.* As Warrior (1995) suggests, indigenous peoples must learn to "withdraw without becoming separatists," and we must be "willing to reach out for the contradictions within our experience" and open ourselves to "the pain and the joy of others" (p. 124). This sentiment renders sovereignty a profoundly spiritual project involving questions about who we are as a people. Indeed, Deloria and Lytle (1984) suggest that indigenous sovereignty will not be possible until "Indians resolve for themselves a comfortable modern identity" (p. 266).

This "resolution" will require indigenous peoples to engage in the difficult process of self-definition, to come to consensus on a set of criteria that defines what behaviors and beliefs constitute acceptable expressions of their tribal heritage (Deloria & Lytle, 1984, p. 254). While this process is necessarily deliberative, it is not (as in revolutionary pedagogies) limited to the processes of *conscienctizacao.*[16] Rather, it remains an inward- and outward-looking process, a process of reenchantment, of ensoulment, that is both deeply spiritual and sincerely mindful. The guiding force in this process must be the tribe, the people, the community; the perseverance of these entities and their connection to indigenous lands and sacred places is what inherits "spirituality" and, in turn, the "sovereignty" of Native peoples. As Lyons notes, "rather than representing an enclave, sovereignty . . . is the ability to assert oneself renewed—in the presence of others. It is a people's right to rebuild its demand to exist and present its gifts to the world . . . an adamant refusal to dissociate culture, identity, and power from the *land*" (Lyons, 2000, p. 457). In other words, the vision of tribal and community stability rests in the desire and ability of indigenous peoples to listen to not only each other but also the land. The question remains, though, whether the ability to exercise spiritual sovereignty will continue to be fettered if not usurped by the desires of a capitalist state intent on devouring the land.

3. *Do critical/revolutionary pedagogies articulate a view of land and natural resources that is less anthropocentric than other Western discourses?*

While the tools of revolutionary critical pedagogy elicit a powerful critique of capitalism and other hegemonic forces that undermine tribal sovereignty, the question remains whether the Western, particularly Marxist, roots of revolutionary critical pedagogy preclude it from disrupting the deep structures of a colonialist discourse dependent on the "continued robbing of nature." As Bowers (2003) notes, though Marx was a critic of capitalism, he shared many of its deep cultural assumptions. Specifically, he argues that Marx shared

> the need to think in universal terms, the disdain for peasant and indigenous cultures as backward and thus in need of being brought into the industrial age, a linear view of progress that also assumed the West's leading role in establishing the new revolutionary consciousness that would replace the backward traditions of other cultures—and in supplying the elite vanguard of theorists, an anthropocentric way of thinking that reduced Nature to an exploitable resource (in the interests of the masses rather than for profit).

As such, Bowers is among the chief critics of revolutionary critical pedagogy and its lack of attention to the ecological crisis. He particularly indicts the following "core cultural assumptions" of revolutionary critical pedagogy as Eurocentric, rendering it indistinguishable from other Western pedagogies. According to Bowers (2003):

1. Critical pedagogy assumes that critical reflection, or what Freire (1998) calls "conscientization," is the only approach to "nonoppressive knowledge and cultural practices" (Bowers, 2003, p. 13). And that the imposition of "Enlightenment ways of thinking with all its culturally specific baggage, is no different from universalizing the Western industrialized approach to food production and consumption, forms of entertainment, and consumer-based subjectivity" (Bowers, 2003, p. 14). Moreover, the emphasis on critical reflection undermines the "mythopoetic narratives" that serve as "the basis of a culture's moral system, way of thinking about relationships, and its silences."

2. Critical pedagogy presumes that change is "a progressive force that requires the constant

overturning of traditions." The directives to "rename" and "transform" are equivalent to injunctions to replace "local traditions of self-sufficiency with a worldview that represents change and individual autonomy as expressions of progress." Moreover, the "emphasis on change, transformation, liberatory praxis, and the continual construction of experience" has led critical theorists to ignore what needs to be conserved and the value of "intergenerational knowledge" (aka tradition).

3. Critical pedagogy is "based on an anthropocentric view of human/nature relationships" that "contributes to the widely held view that humans can impose their will on the environment and that when the environment breaks down experts using an instrumentally based critical reflection will engineer a synthetic replacement" (Bowers, 2003, p. 15).

4. Critical pedagogy presumes a "Western approach to literacy" that "reinforces patterns of social relationships not found in oral-based cultures." In "oral-based cultures, participation is the central feature of life rather than the analytical and decontextualized judgment that fixed texts make possible" (Bowers, 2003).

While Bowers (2003) is right to caution against the unconscious and unilateral imposition of "enlightenment ways of thinking," the frameworks of revolutionary critical pedagogy are malleable by design, rendering the overall tone of his critique somewhat unwarranted. Indeed, McLaren (1991) himself (Bowers's chief target) concedes, "I am certainly aware of the implications of a creeping Eurocentrism slipping through the textual fissure of any theoretical discourse . . . and that the conceptual space of any work . . . is open to many forms of colonization" (p. 463). In addition to overgeneralizing the intentions of critical theorists, Bowers underestimates the capacities of indigenous teachers and scholars, basing much his critique on the assumption that they share his own expectations for critical pedagogy, namely, that it functions as a one-size-fit-all pedagogical elixir. Despite these shortcomings, Bowers raises some incisive and important points that compel closer examination.

First, while revolutionary theorists undoubtedly place a premium on critical reflection, any close reading of their pedagogies reveals that the primary emphasis is on *meaning*. This emphasis renders Bowers's (2003) claim that such theorists advocate critical reflection as *the only* viable approach to nonoppressive knowledge and cultural practices unfounded. Revolutionary theorists are quite clear that their pedagogies (including the adherence to Marxism) are intended to serve as guides to action, not as "a set of metaphysical dogmas" (McLaren, 2003b, p. 29). According to McLaren (2003b), revolutionary critical theory requires that "symbolic formations" be analyzed "in their spatio-temporal settings, within certain fields of interaction, and in the context of social institutions and structures so that teachers have a greater sense of how meanings are inscribed, encoded, decoded, transmitted, deployed, circulated and received in the arena of everyday social relations" (McLaren, 2003b, p. 29). The emphasis on "symbolic formations" (as opposed to the more limited category of text) conceivably includes expressions of meaning that are nontextually based (e.g., dance, ceremony, song), ones that Bowers identifies as the definitive features of "mythopoetic cultures."

Bowers's (2003) second claim, that critical pedagogy presumes change as a progressive force requiring "the constant overturning of traditions," is perhaps more warranted. Indeed, the discourse is littered with references to social and self-transformation. Specifically, revolutionary theorists posit an action-oriented pedagogy with the objective of encouraging students and teachers to use "critical knowledge that is *transformative* as opposed to *reproductive,* [and] *empowering* as opposed to *oppressing,*" asking, "what is the relationship between our classrooms and our effort to build a better society?" (McLaren, 2003b, pp. xv, xxxiv). The end goal is to encourage "students beyond the world they already know (and) to expand their range of human possibilities" (Giroux, 2001, p. 24).

While any pedagogy with a root metaphor of "change as progress" presents specific challenges to indigenous cultures rooted in tradition and intergenerational knowledge, revolutionary theorists do not categorically advocate change as *inherently* progressive. Rather, they are very definitive in their distinction between change that emancipates and change that merely furthers the dictates of market imperatives. McLaren (2003b), in particular, is candid in his advocacy of change as defined by Marxist imperatives to act against imperialism and exploitation. He writes, "Millions from aggrieved populations worldwide stand witness to the law governed process of exploitation known as capital accumulation, to the ravages of uneven development known as 'progress,' and to the practice of imperialism in new guises called 'globalization'" (McLaren, 2003b, p. 13). McLaren, moreover, agrees with Fromm's positioning of "revolutionary humanism" at the center of Marx's philosophy, quoting, "Marx's aim was that of the spiritual emancipation of man, of his liberation from the claims of economic determination, of restituting him in his human wholeness, of enabling him to find unity and harmony with his fellow man and with Nature" (qtd. in McLaren, 2003b, p. 13). While such sentiments reveal a pedagogy that is clearly concerned with change and social transformation, it is not unconcerned (as Bowers contends) with the interconnection between economic oppression and environmental destruction.

A more pertinent question is to what degree the acts of interrogation and transformation themselves encode the same sociotemporal markers of a colonialist consciousness intent on extinguishing "traditional" (sacred) ways of knowing with ostensibly more "progressive" (secular) understandings of the world. In other words, while revolutionary theorists challenge the moral imperatives of modern consciousness, they may inadvertently maintain its epistemic codes, reinforcing the bias toward "reflexively organized knowledge"—the same means by which "tradition" is undermined. Consider, for example, the following commentary on the role of tradition as expressed by McLaren (1991):

> [While] I do not object to tradition itself. What I do object to is the concealment of cultural uncertainties in the way that tradition gets ideologically produced . . . [and] while I agree that there are ecologically, morally, politically, enabling aspects to mythic, religious, and familial traditions, and that such traditions can be empowering to the extent that they locate subjectivity in a reciprocal relationship to the larger environment, critical pedagogy concentrates on the process of demythologization. That is I am concerned with uncovering the social contradictions that are ideologically resolved or harmonized to preserve existing relations of power—relations which have debilitating effects on certain groups. (p. 469)

And he goes on to ask,

> Why shouldn't all aspects of culture be problematized? To problematize culture does not guarantee that everything 'traditional' will be condemned or rejected . . . what it does mean is that we can recover from such traditional cultural texts and practices those aspects which empower and discard or transform those which don't. (p. 469)

Thus (contrary to Bowers's reading), while McLaren does consider the effect of revolutionary pedagogies on traditional knowledge, he may be too dismissive of the cultural codes embedded in the act of social transformation. It is, for instance, highly unlikely that the "pedagogical negativism" required of such emancipatory pedagogies can be wielded with the degree of surgical precision revolutionary theorists confidently express—teaching students to doubt everything but also believe in and take seriously the truth claims of their own traditions. In other words, the process of interrogation itself may encode the same sociotemporal markers of a colonialist consciousness that incites movement away from "sacred" ways of knowing toward increased secularization. In response to McLaren, rather than ask, "Why shouldn't all aspects of culture be problematized?" indigenous scholars should ask how the processes of problematizing itself may serve as a homogenizing force, muting and domesticating the distinctiveness of traditional ways of knowing.

That does not, however, preclude such processes of interrogation from being an integral part of Red pedagogy, particularly as indigenous communities remain threatened and deeply compromised by colonialist forces. Bowers's (2003) dismissal of the need for social transformation within indigenous communities is not only shortsighted but also patronizing. For example, while he admires with romantic fascination "how the Quéchua people have resisted European colonization," he does not specify which Quéchua peoples he is referring to—those in Paramus, New Jersey; Hartford, Connecticut; Ayacucho, Peru; or Quito, Ecuador? Like other indigenous nations, "the Quéchua" are profoundly diverse, and while most continue to resist the forces of colonization, such a stance is by no means universal. Moreover, while indigenous cultures have, for centuries, managed to retain their traditions in the face of imperialism—resisting and selectively employing facets of Western culture as they see fit—they can only resist what they fully know. When engaged with "caution and restraint," I believe the tools of revolutionary pedagogy can prove invaluable, particularly in revealing the inner sanctums of power and hidden structures of domination.

Bowers's (2003) third claim, that revolutionary critical pedagogy is "based on an anthropocentric view of human/nature relationships," is perhaps the most accurate. Consider, for example, the (anthropocentric) questions that revolutionary theorist Ramin Farahmandpur (see McLaren & Farahmandpur, 2001) positions at the center of the discourse: What does it mean to be human? How can we live humanely? What actions or steps must be taken to be able to live humanely? While such questions could be answered in a manner that decenters human beings (i.e., to be "human" means living in a way that accounts for the deep interconnection between all living entities), McLaren and Farahmandpur (2001) choose to reassert the primacy of Marxist theory in their responses. Specifically, they confirm and concur with Marx's radical assertion of a profoundly human-centered world, quoting the following from Volume 1 of *Capital:* "A spider conducts operations which resemble those of a weaver and a bee would put many a human architect to shame by the construction of its honeycomb cells. But what distinguishes the worst architect from the best of bees is that the architect builds the cell in his mind before he constructs it in wax" (Marx, 1977, p. 284).

McLaren and Farahmandpur (2001) respond, "In other words, the fundamental distinction between humans and other species is that humans are endowed with a social imagination, one that operates as a tool for transforming their social conditions," underscoring the primacy of consciousness as "a powerful mediating force in transforming the existing the social and economic structures that constrain it" (p. 307). Thus, following Marx, they insist that the "question of what it means to be human" is "conditioned by the specificity of the socio-historical conditions and circumstances of *human* society," believing that "the purpose of education is linked to men and women realizing their powers and capacities" (McLaren & Farahmandpur, 2001, p. 305, emphasis added).

Such expressions of profound anthropocentrism are not only unnecessary to the imperatives of the critical project but also weaken its validity. McLaren and Farahmandpur's (2001) maintenance of the hierarchy between human beings and nature not only prohibits us from learning from "all our relations" but also reinscribes the colonialist logic that conscripts "nature" to the service of human society. Indeed, McLaren (2003b) seconds Kovel's (2002) notion that "the transition to socialism will require the creation of a usufructuary of the earth" (p. 31). While he contends that a "usufructuary" implies "restoring ecosystemic integrity" so that "ecocentric modes of production" are made accessible to all, the model exists for the sole purposes of transferring assets "to the direct producers" (i.e., worker ownership and control). The value of the Earth itself is therefore only derived in terms of its ability to serve as a distinctly human resource, carrying no inherent worth or subjectivity.

While Bowers's (2003) final claim, that critical pedagogy presumes a "Western approach to literacy" and reinforces a "pattern of social relationships not found in oral-based cultures," is rather self-evident, it is unclear what kind of pedagogy (a Western construct) would not presume literacy as its basis. Moreover, indigenous cultures engaged in institutionalized forms of schooling are just as concerned with students' literacy as other cultures. Indeed, the value of revolutionary pedagogies is that the concept of "literacy" is reformed to take on meaning beyond a simple depoliticized notion of reading and writing. Specifically, it takes on a *politics* of literacy that recognizes it as being "socially constructed within political contexts: that is, within contexts where access to economic, cultural, political, and institutional power is structured unequally" (Lankshear & McLaren, 1993, p. xviii). In *Critical Literacy: Politics, Praxis, and the Postmodern,* Lankshear and McLaren (1993) further comment on the notion of critical literacy, writing,

> In short, literacies are ideological. They reflect the differential structured power available to human agents through which to secure the promotion and serving of their interests, including the power to shape literacy in ways consonant with those interests. Consequently, the conceptions people have of what literacy involves, of what *counts* as being literate, what they see as "real" or "appropriate" uses of reading and writing skills, and the way people actually read and write in the course of their daily lives—these all reflect and promote values, beliefs, assumptions, and practices which shape the way life is lived within a given social milieu and, in turn, influence which interests are promoted or undermined as a result of how life is lived there. Thus, literacies are indicies of the dynamics of power. (p. xviii)

Such a definition neither limits "literacy" to purely Western conceptions nor advocates an unconscious approach that merely "enables producers to get their message to individual consumers," as Bowers (2003) contends. On the contrary, critical theorists aim to disrupt the unconscious processes of "language" acquisition and communication. While the question regarding the homogenizing affects of critical literacy reemerges, indigenous cultures have been navigating the impact of such forces since the time of contact. Furthermore, knowledge of the oppressor and the oppressor's language is essential to the processes of resistance, particularly in a context where the vast majority of indigenous students are schooled in Whitestream institutions.

In summary, Bowers's (2003) critique of critical theory identifies significant points of tension but it is limited both by its inaccurate reading of such theories and its essentializing of indigenous cultures. In perhaps the final irony, Bowers's own outline for an eco-conscious education employs the same precepts of critical pedagogy that he discounts. Specifically, he calls for a pedagogy that helps students (a) understand the causes, extent, and political strategies necessary for addressing environmental racism; (b) clarify the nature of the ideological and economic forces that are perpetuating the domination of the South by the North; (c) revitalize noncommodified forms of knowledge, skills, and activities within the communities represented by the students in the classroom; and (d) recognize the many ecologically informed changes in individual lifestyles and uses of technology that will help ensure that future generations will not inherit a degraded environment. Such precepts clearly presume some of the cultural assumptions of critical pedagogy—namely, the importance of critical reflection, an orientation toward (emancipatory) change, and a mastery of critical forms of literacy that enable such reflection and change.

Revolutionary pedagogies have the potential to provide such a structure as they have the analytical robustness and ideological inclination needed to sort through the underlying power manipulations of colonialist forces. Yet, as noted by Bowers (2003) and other critics, critical pedagogy is born of a Western tradition that has many components in conflict with indigenous knowledge, including a view of time and progress that is linear and an anthropocentric view that puts humans at the center of the universe. Nevertheless, if revolutionary critical pedagogy is able to sustain the same kind of penetrating analysis it unleashes on capitalism, it may evolve into an invaluable tool for indigenous peoples and their allies, fighting to protect and extend indigenous sovereignty over tribal land and resources.

▣ Red Pedagogy: Implications for Education

From the standpoint of Red pedagogy, the primary lesson in all of this is pedagogical. In other words, as we are poised to raise yet another generation in a nation at war and at risk, we must consider how emerging conceptions of citizenship, sovereignty, and democracy will affect the (re)formation of our national identity, particularly among young people in schools. As Mitchell (2001) notes, "The production of democracy, the practice of education, and the constitution of the nation-state" have always been interminably bound together. The imperative before us as citizens is to engage a process of unthinking our colonial roots and rethinking democracy. For teachers and students, this means that we must be willing to act as agents of transgression, posing critical questions and engaging dangerous discourse. Such is the basis of Red pedagogy. In particular, Red pedagogy offers the following seven precepts as a way of thinking our way around and through the challenges facing American education in the 21st century and our mutual need to define decolonizing pedagogies:

1. *Red pedagogy is primarily a pedagogical project.* In this context, pedagogy is understood as being inherently political, cultural, spiritual, and intellectual.

2. *Red pedagogy is fundamentally rooted in indigenous knowledge and praxis.* It is particularly interested in knowledge that furthers understanding and analysis of the forces of colonization.

3. *Red pedagogy is informed by critical theories of education.* A Red pedagogy searches for ways it can both deepen and be deepened by engagement with critical and revolutionary theories and praxis.

4. *Red pedagogy promotes an education for decolonization.* Within Red pedagogy, the root metaphors of decolonization are articulated as equity, emancipation, sovereignty, and balance. In this sense, an education for decolonization makes no claim to political neutrality but rather engages a method of analysis and social inquiry that troubles the capitalist-imperialist aims of unfettered competition, accumulation, and exploitation.

5. *Red pedagogy is a project that interrogates both democracy and indigenous sovereignty.* In this context, sovereignty is broadly defined as "a people's right to rebuild its demand to exist and present its gifts to the world . . . an adamant refusal to dissociate culture, identity, and power from the land" (Lyons, 2000).

6. *Red pedagogy actively cultivates praxis of collective agency.* That is, Red pedagogy aims to build transcultural and transnational solidarities among indigenous peoples and others committed to reimagining a sovereign space free of imperialist, colonialist, and capitalist exploitation.

7. *Red pedagogy is grounded in hope.* This is, however, not the future-centered hope of the Western imagination but rather a hope that lives in contingency with the past—one that trusts the beliefs and understandings of our ancestors, the power of traditional knowledge, and the possibilities of new understandings.

In the end, a Red pedagogy is about engaging the development of "community-based power" in the interest of "a responsible political, economic, and spiritual society." That is, the power to live out "active presences and *survivances* rather than an illusionary democracy." Vizenor's (1993) notion of survivance signifies a state of being beyond "survival, endurance, or a mere response to colonization" and of moving toward "an active presence . . . and active repudiation of dominance, tragedy and victimry." In these post-Katrina times, I find the notion of survivance—particularly as it relates to colonized peoples—to be poignant and powerful. It speaks to our collective need to decolonize, to push back against empire, and to reclaim what it means to be a people of sovereign mind and body. The peoples of the Ninth Ward in New Orleans serve as a reminder to all of us that just as the specter of colonialism continues to haunt the collective soul of America, so too does the more hopeful spirit of indigeneity.

▣ NOTES

1. Adapting from the feminist notion of "malestream," Claude Denis (1997) defines "Whitestream" as the idea that while American society is not "White" in sociodemographic terms, it remains principally and

fundamentally structured on the basis of the Anglo-European "White" experience.

2. The Indian Removal Act (ch. 48, 4, Stat. 411) provided for "an exchange of lands with any of the Indians residing in any of the states and territories, and for their removal west of the river Mississippi." Passage of this act set in motion mass forced relocations of the Creek, Cherokee, Choctaw, Chickasaw, and Seminole among other Eastern nations. In the words of Churchill and Morris (1992), "The idea was to clear the native population from the entire region east of the Mississippi, opening it up for the exclusive use and occupancy of Euroamericans and their Black slaves."

3. The General Allotment Act, sponsored by Senator Henry Dawes, was passed in 1887. This act authorized the president, at his discretion, to survey and break up the communal landholdings of tribes into individual allotments. As a result of the Dawes Act, the Indian land base was reduced from approximately 138 million to 48 million acres or by nearly two thirds. In addition, tribes were divested of their right to determine their own membership, specious identification procedures were enacted, and the trust doctrine was severely violated.

4. The Termination policy was embodied in House Concurrent Resolution (HCR) No. 108, passed August 1, 1953. It reads as follows: "Whereas it is the policy of the Congress, as rapidly as possible, to make Indians within the territorial limits of the United States subject to the same laws and entitled to the same privileges and responsibilities as are applicable to other citizens of the United States, and to grant them all of the rights and prerogatives pertaining to American citizenship; and Whereas the Indian within the territorial limits of the United States should assume their full responsibilities as American citizens; Now, therefore, be it Resolved by the House of Representatives (the Senate concurring), That it is declared to be the sense of the Congress that, at the earliest possible time, all of the Indian tribes and individual members thereof located within the States of California, Florida, New York and Texas, and all of the following named Indian tribes and individual members thereof, should be freed from Federal supervision and control from all disabilities and limitations specially applicable to Indians."

5. According to Nieto (1995), multicultural education can be defined as "a process of comprehensive school reform and basic education for all students. It challenges and rejects racism and other forms of discrimination in schools and society and accepts and affirms the pluralism (ethnic, racial, linguistic, religious, and gender, among others) that students, their communities, and teachers represent. Multicultural education permeates the curriculum and instructional strategies used in schools, as well as the interactions among teachers, students, and parents, and the very way that schools conceptualize the nature of teaching and learning."

6. Marxist-feminist scholar Teresa Ebert (1991) distinguishes critical from critique-al studies as a means of recentering the importance of critique as opposed to criticism in discourse.

7. Leading advocates of revolutionary critical pedagogy include Paula Allman (who penned the term) and Peter McLaren, as well as Mike Cole, Terry Eagleton, Ramin Farahmandpur, Dave Hill, Jane Kenway, Helen Raduntz, Glen Rikowski, and Valerie Scatamburlo–D'Annibale. Others whose work has greatly influenced the formation of revolutionary critical pedagogy include Teresa Ebert, Paulo Friere, Martha Gimenez, Antonio Gramsci, Henry Giroux, Rosemary Hennessy, Chrys Ingraham, Karl Marx, and Ellen Meskins Wood.

8. Unlike other contemporary narratives that focus on one form of oppression or another, Scatamburlo–D'Annibale and McLaren (2003) note that the power of historical materialism resides in "its ability to reveal (a) how forms of oppression based on categories of difference do not possess relative autonomy from class relations but rather constitute the ways in which oppression is lived/experienced within a class based system and (b) how all forms of social oppression function within an overlapping capitalist system" (p. 149).

9. These principles are articulated by Farahmandpur in the foreword of McLaren's (2003b, p. xvii) seminal text *Life in Schools.*

10. The notion of *mestizaje* as absorption is particularly problematic for indigenous peoples of Central and South America, where the myth of the mestizaje (belief that the continent's original cultures and inhabitants no longer exist) has been used for centuries to force the integration of indigenous communities into the national mestizo model (Van Cott, 1994). According to Roldolfo Stavenhagen (1992), the myth of mestizaje has provided the ideological pretext for numerous South American governmental laws and policies expressly designed to strengthen the nation-state through the incorporation of all "nonnational" (read: indigenous) elements into the mainstream. Thus, what Valle and Torres (1995) describe as "the continents unfinished business of cultural hybridization" (p. 141),

indigenous peoples view as the continents' long and bloody battle to absorb their existence into the master narrative of the mestízo.

11. Critical scholars Cameron McCarthy (1988, 1995), John Ogbu (1978), Chandra Mohanty (1991), and Henry Giroux (1992) similarly caution against equating hybridity with equality.

12. The term *Indianismo* was coined by Alexander Ewen as a counterterm to *indigenismo* or *mestizaje,* which have served as assimilationist constructs with regard to indigenous sovereignty. Ewen defines *Indianismo* as "the Indian way," or from an indigenous perspective.

13. He cites the recent massacres of indigenous peoples in Brazil and Peru (by right- and left-wing elements, respectively) as evidence for the ongoing relevance of this struggle.

14. The indigenous conception of land is defined as "the inalienable foundation for the processes of kinship," distinguishing it from "property" which is defined by relations of alienability.

15. Indigenous notions of power are defined as being rooted in concepts of respect, balance, reciprocity, and peaceful coexistence.

16. *Conscientazcao* is a Frerian term that refers to the development of critical social consciousness, wherein dialogue and analysis serve as the foundation for reflection and action.

▣ References

Alfred, T. (1999). *Peace, power, righteousness: An indigenous manifesto.* Oxford, UK: Oxford University Press.

Allman, P. (2001). *Critical education against global capital: Karl Marx and revolutionary critical education.* Westport, CT: Bergin & Garvey.

American Council on Education. (2002). *Nineteenth annual report on the status of minorities in higher education.* Washington, DC: American Council on Education.

Anzaldúa, G. (1987). *Borderlands/la frontera: The new mestiza.* San Francisco: Spinsters/Aunt Lute.

Barreiro, J. (1995). *Indigenous peoples and development in the Americas: Lessons from a consultation.* Retrieved July, 2003, from http://www.brocku.ca/epi/casid/barriero.html

Beaulieu, D. (2000). Comprehensive reform and American Indian education. *Journal of American Indian Education, 39*(2), 29–38.

Bowers, C. A. (2003). Can critical pedagogy be greened? *Educational Studies, 34*(1), 11–21.

Bowers, C. A. (2004). Ecojustice and education. *Educational Studies, 36*(1).

Butterfield, R. (1994). *Blueprints for Indian education: Improving mainstream schooling.* Charleston, WV: ERIC Clearinghouse on Rural Education and Small Schools. (ERIC Documents Reproduction Service No. ED 372 898)

Charleston, G. M., & King, G. L. (1991). *Indian nations at risk task force: Listen to the people.* Washington, DC: U.S. Department of Education, Indian Nations At Risk Task Force.

Churchill, W., & Morris, G. T. (1992). Table key Indian cases. In M. A. Jaimes (Ed.), *State of Native America: Genocide, colonization and resistance.* Boston: South End.

Darder, A., Torres, R., & Gutierrez, H. (Eds.). (1997). *Latinos and education: A critical reader.* New York: Routledge.

Delgado Bernal, D. (1998). Using a Chicana feminist epistemology in educational research. *Harvard Educational Review, 68*(4), 55–82.

Deloria, V., Jr. (1994). *God is Red: A Native view of religion.* Golden, CO: Fulcrum.

Deloria, V., Jr. (1999). *For this land: Writings on religion in America.* New York: Routledge.

Deloria, V., Jr., & Lytle, C. M. (1983). *American Indians, American justice.* Austin: University of Texas Press.

Deloria, V., Jr., & Lytle, C. M. (1984). *The nations within: The past and future of American Indian sovereignty.* Austin: University of Texas Press.

Denis, C. (1997). *We are not you.* Toronto: Broadview.

Deyhle, D., & Swisher, K. (1997). Research in American Indian and Alaska Native education: From assimilation to self-determination. In M. Apple (Ed.), *Review of research in education* (pp. 113–194). Washington, DC: American Educational Research Association.

di Leonardo, M. (1998). *Exotics at home: Anthropologies, others and American modernity.* Chicago: University of Chicago Press.

Dirlik, A. (1999). The past as legacy and project: Postcolonial criticism in the perspective of indigenous historicism. In T. Johnson (Ed.), *Contemporary Native American political issues* (pp. 73–97). Walnut Creek, CA: AltaMira Press.

Ebert, T. (1991). *Ludic feminism and after: Postmodernism, desire, and labor in late capitalism.* Ann Arbor: University of Michigan Press.

Fischman, G., & McLaren, P. (2000). Schooling for democracy: Toward a critical utopianism. *Contemporary Schooling, 29*(1), 168–179.

Friere, P. (1998). *Pedagogy of freedom: Ethics, democracy and civic courage.* Lanham, MD: Rowman & Littlefield.

Gallagher, B. T. (2000, June 5). Tribes face an uphill battle to blend culture with traditional coursework: Teaching (Native) America. *The Nation,* p. 36.

Geertz, C. (1998). Deep hanging out. *New York Review of Books, 45*(16).

Giroux, H. (1992). *Border crossings: Cultural workers and the politics of education.* New York: Routledge.

Giroux, H. (2001). Pedagogy of the depressed: Beyond the new politics of cynicism. *College Literature, 28*(3), 1–32.

Grande, S. (2004). *Red pedagogy: Native American social and political thought.* Lanham, MD: Rowman & Littlefield.

Kincheloe, J., & Steinberg, S. (1997). *Changing multiculturalism.* Bristol, PA: Open University Press.

Kovel, J. (2002). *The enemy of nature: The end of capitalism or the end of the world?* Nova Scotia: Fernwood.

Krupskaya, N. (1985). *On labour-oriented education and instruction.* Moscow: Progressive Publishers.

Lankshear, C., & McLaren, P. (Eds.). (1993). *Critical literacy: Politics, praxis, and the postmodern.* Albany, NY: SUNY Press.

Lather, P. (1998). Critical pedagogy and its complicities: A praxis of stuck places. *Educational Theory, 48,* 431–462.

Lyons, S. R. (2000). Rhetorical sovereignty: What do American Indians want from writing? *College, Composition and Communication, 51,* 447–468.

Marx, K. (1977). *Capital: A critique of political economy: Vol. 1* (B. Fowkes, Trans.). New York: Vintage.

McCarthy, C. (1995). The problem with origins: Race and the contrapuntal nature of the educational experience. In P. McLaren & C. Sleeter (Eds.), *Multicultural education, critical pedagogy and the politics of difference* (pp. 245–268). Albany, NY: SUNY Press.

McLaren, P. (1991). The emptiness of nothingness: Criticism as imperial anti-politics. *Curriculum Inquiry, 21,* 459–487.

McLaren, P. (1997). *Revolutionary multiculturalism: Pedagogies of dissent for the new millennium.* Boulder, CO: Westview.

McLaren, P. (1998). Revolutionary pedagogy in post-revolutionary times: Rethinking the political economy of critical education. *Educational Theory, 48,* 431–462.

McLaren, P. (2003a). Critical pedagogy in the age of neoliberal globalization: Notes from history's underside. *Democracy and Nature, 9,* 65–90.

McLaren, P. (2003b). *Life in schools: An introduction to critical pedagogy in the foundations of education* (4th ed.). Boston: Allyn & Bacon.

McLaren, P., & Farahmandpur, R. (2001). The globalization of capitalism and the new imperialism: Notes toward a revolutionary pedagogy. *The Review of Education, Pedagogy, Cultural Studies, 23,* 271–315.

McLaren, P., & Sleeter, C. (Eds.). (1995). *Multicultural education, critical pedagogy and the politics of difference.* Albany, NY: SUNY Press.

Mitchell, K. (2001). Education for democratic citizenship: Transnationalism, multiculturalism, and the limits of liberalism. *Harvard Educational Review, 71*(1), 51–78.

Mohanty, C. T. (1991). Under Western eyes: Feminist scholarship and colonial discourses. In C. T. Mohanty, A. Russo, & L. Torres (Eds.), *Third World women and the politics of feminism.* Indianapolis: Indiana University Press.

Nieto, S. (1995). *Affirming diversity: The sociopolitical context of multicultural education* (2nd ed.). New York: Longman.

Ogbu, J. U. (1978). *Minority education and caste: The American system in cross-cultural perspective.* New York: Academic Press.

Reyhner, J. (Ed.). (1992). *Teaching American Indian students.* Norman: University of Oklahoma Press.

Richardson, T., & Villenas, S. (2000). "Other" encounters: Dances with Whiteness in multicultural education. *Educational Theory, 50,* 255–273.

Rizvi, M. (2002, August). Educating for social justice and liberation: An interview with Peter McLaren. *Znet: A Community of People Committed to Social Change.*

Said, E. (1978). *Orientalism.* New York: Random House.

Scatamburlo-D'Annibale, V., & McLaren, P. (2003). The strategic centrality of class in the politics of "race" and "difference." *Cultural Studies <=> Critical Methodologies, 3*(2), 148–175.

Sherman, L. (2003, March/April). Culture and language in Native America. *Northwest Regional Educational Laboratory Report (NWREL).*

Smith, L. T. (1999). *Decolonizing methodologies: Research and indigenous peoples.* London: Zed.

St. Germaine, R. (1995a). Bureau schools adopt goals 2000. *Journal of American Indian Education, 35*(1), 39–43.

St. Germaine, R. (1995b). *Drop out rates among American Indian and Alaska Native students: Beyond cultural discontinuity.* Charleston, WV: ERIC Clearinghouse on Rural Education and Small Schools.

Stavenhagen, R. (1992). Challenging the nation-state in Latin America. *Journal of International Affairs, 34,* 423.

Trask, H. K. (1993). *From a Native daughter: Colonialism and sovereignty in Hawaii.* Monroe, ME: Common Courage Press.

Valle, V., & Torres, R. D. (1995). The idea of the mestizaje and the "race" problematic: Racialized media discourse in a post-Fordist landscape. In A. Darder (Ed.), *Culture and difference: Critical perspectives on the bi-cultural experience in the United States.* Westport, CT: Bergin & Garvey.

Van Cott, D. L. (1994). *Indigenous peoples and democracy in Latin America.* New York: St. Martin's.

Vizenor, G. (1993). The ruins of representation. *American Indian Quarterly, 17,* 1–7.

Warrior, R. A. (1995). *Tribal secrets: Recovering American Indian intellectual traditions.* Minneapolis: University of Minnesota Press.

Wilson, P. (1991). Trauma of Sioux Indian high school students. *Anthropology & Education Quarterly, 22,* 367–383.

13

BORDERLAND-*MESTIZAJE* FEMINISM

The New Tribalism

Cinthya M. Saavedra and Ellen D. Nymark

> *A massive uprooting of dualistic thinking in the individual and collective consciousness is the beginning of a long struggle, but one that could, in our best hopes, bring us to the end of rape, of violence, of war.*
>
> —Anzaldúa (1987, p. 80)

In this chapter, we wish to introduce and invite educational researchers to step out of their Western frame of reference and into a hybrid and multidimensional mode of thinking—borderland-*mestizaje* feminism (BMF). Borderland-mestizaje feminism emerges out of the important work of scholars who center Chicana *feminista* perspectives and cultural practices in their inquiries, examinations, and analyses. Beginning in the mid to late eighties, BMF continues to challenge and decolonize Western mode of research and investigations (Elenes, 2005). This chapter addresses how research is being embodied by Chicana(o)s and Latina(o)s feminista scholars who find it necessary to decolonize educational research and practice. Using multiple methods and epistemologies, Chicana feminists focus and analyze the gender, class, and race "blank spots" left (intentionally or not) by dominant ideology and discourse (Anzaldúa, 1990) in order to expose ways to maneuver through theory (making, living, and rebuilding) and create *neuvas teorías*—teorías that reflect our understanding of the world and how to critically transform it. "We are articulating new positions in these 'in-between,' Borderland worlds of ethnic communities and academies, feminist and job worlds" (Anzaldúa, 1990, p. xxvi).

What follows is our perspective of BMF and how it can make a significant contribution to the field of educational research and practice. The first part of the chapter situates and defines borderland-mestizaje feminism. In the second part, we attempt to unbraid the aspects of BMF that have decolonial possibility.

Defining and Situating Borderland-Mestizaje Feminism

In the provocative and influential book, *Borderlands/La Frontera,* Gloria Anzaldúa (1987) crystallized, through autobiography, history, culture, poetics, and language, a hybrid mode of consciousness and meaning making that placed her Chicana feminist lesbian subjectivity, body, and material condition at the forefront of her scholarship. In this important piece, Anzaldúa envisioned and birthed *la conciencia de la mestiza*—a mestizaje *metodología* that attempts to uproot dualistic thinking, welcoming ambiguity and engendering an oppositional consciousness (Saldivar-Hull, 2000; Sandoval, 1991, 2000) as necessary engagements in the struggle against patriarchal, cultural, and imperialist domination. Thus, borderlands conceptualization comes from the experiences and lives of Chicanas/os or those living in the interstices of the geographical and metaphorical spaces of *la fronteras*/borderlands (but not limited to the United States/Mexico). As such, we use C. Alejandra Elenes's (2005) definition of the borderlands; she articulates, the "border in its literal meaning refers to the historical and contemporary context under which Mexican American communities have been formed in the U.S." (p. 1). In addition, she also argues that the "border refers to the symbolic barriers that divide communities along race, class, gender and sexual orientation lines, academic disciplines, political ideologies, and organizational structures" (p. 1).

Resisting these symbolic barriers gives way to borderland-mestizaje theorizing that further involves a constant struggle against and resistance to the histories of colonialism and the interrogations of dominant cultural politics (Córdova, 1999; Mignolo, 2000; Villenas & Foley, 2002). Borderland theorizing seeks social transformation not only for Chicana(o) people but for all whose voices have been silenced—*la(o)s deslenguada(o)s* (Anzaldúa, 1987; Chabram-Dernersesian, 1999a; Demas & Saavedra, 2004; Kaplan, Alarcón, & Moallem, 1999) and for those whose bodies have been policed, regulated, and medicalized (Cruz, 2001) through Western lenses and ultimately produced colonized *mentes y cuerpos.*

Borderland-mestizaje "feminism," then, is an evolution, extension, or perhaps a mutation *que nace* from the bodies of Chicana feminists (Sandoval, 1998) who recognized the androcentric, nationalistic, and homophobic tendency of Chican"o" border theory and cultural studies (Anzaldúa, 1987, 1990; Córdova, 1999; Trujillo, 1998). Moreover, it is a critical observation of how the "praxis of feminists of color is often not recognized or sanctioned in the academy" (Arredondo, Hurtado, Klahn, Najera-Ramirez, & Zavella, 2003, p. 1). What makes BMF necessary and important is the in(corp)oration of the critical pedagogies found in the mundane (Delgado Bernal, 2001; Elenes, 1997; Elenes, Gonzalez, Delgado Bernal, & Villenas, 2001; Rosaldo, 1989; Trinidad Galván, 2001; Villenas & Moreno, 2001). The definition of *pedagogy* is reworked by problematizing dominant perspectives and attitudes toward established ideas of pedagogical spaces (Trinidad Galván, 2001). Moreover, critical pedagogy is expanded, stretched, and problematized through a BMF lens by engaging in further discussions of what Elenes (1997) argues critical pedagogues have unintentionally marginalized—questions of difference and erasure. Those working within a critical pedagogy framework, according to Elenes, need to rethink and problematize the "usual suspects" (White America, men, and/or capitalism), move the critical dialogue beyond these visible enemies, and rearticulate the conversation to the invisible ideological and discursive regimes that privilege White maleness.

Furthermore, working within a BMF framework entails centering and listening to *el cuerpo* y *experiencias en nuestro analisis* (Anzaldúa, 1987; Cruz, 2001; Cruz & McLaren, 2002; Hurtado, 1998; Moraga, 1983; Saavedra, 2005; Trujillo, 1998; Yarbro-Bejarano, 1999). The realization that theorizing must come from the everyday lives and bodies of people and not from abstract and detached perspectives makes BMF a decolonizing method and tool that "de-academize[s] theory and [connects] the community to the academy" (Anzaldúa, 1990, p. xxvi). *Nuestros cuerpos* and experiences can be powerful sources and sites of knowledge and identity negotiation and production (Cruz, 2001). BMF constitutes and constructs knowledge from the bottom (Elenes, 1997) and from the body (Anzaldúa, 1987; Cruz, 2001; Moraga & Anzaldúa, 2002; Trujillo, 1998).

As a method, BMF allows epistemological mutations *que crean* critical tools *para usar contra* dominant ideologies and methods. We take what works for our survival and for our communities. Where a theory or method is not sufficient enough, we expand, perhaps fragment, the theoretical and methodological boundaries to fit our specific circumstance. In learning how to stretch dominant theories or methods, we also learn when and how to shift and maneuver through "currents of power" (Sandoval, 1991, p. 14) for our survival and coping strategies. Hence, working within this critical framework entails grappling with multiple epistemologies and rejecting binary, simplistic, and deterministic ways of theorizing and researching (Elenes, 1997; Sandoval, 1998) and instead forging intellectual dexterity (Arredondo et al., 2003). Likewise, Norma Gonzalez (2001) argues for a borderlands perspective and vision that should "accommodate contradiction and ambiguity" (p. 14). Although BMF may take a momentary stance (albeit ambiguous and fleeting), essentialist understandings and meaning making are not options. As Alarcón, Kaplan, and Moallem (1999) explain, "Our tasks as critics must revolve around a constant critique of the construction of all methods and disciplines" (p. 5), including our own.

Furthermore, BMF research and inquiry might lead us to illuminate the ways in which marginalized people are *already* living, struggling, and resisting multiple hegemonic forms of identity, patriarchy, and capitalist and sexual discourses (Elenes et al., 2001; Trinidad Galván, 2001).

As Chela Sandoval (1998) captures borderlands feminism,

> This "borderlands" feminism, many argue, calls up a syncretic form of consciousness made up of transversions and crossings; its recognition makes possible another kind of critical apparatus and political operation in which *mestiza* feminism comes to function as a working chiasmus (a mobile crossing) between races, genders, sexes, cultures, languages and nations. (p. 352)

BMF is, as Rosa Linda Fregoso (1993) asserts, "a paradigm of transcultural experience" (p. 65) that invites and welcomes hybrid forms of knowledge (de)construction, meaning, and maneuvering. BMF is also a way of living and existing for bodies caught between the intimate clash of two, three, or multiple discourses, cultures, languages, and sexual identities (Anzaldúa, 1987).

Borderlands-mestizaje feminism, then, is a tool, a methodology, and an epistemology. BMF is a tool insofar as it is used to travel and exist in our past and current sociopolitical borders and (multiple) *realidades*—the everyday lives we homegirls embody, the way we sway back and forth from strategic essentialism and dominant ideologies in the barrio, at school, at work *para sobrevivir.* As a methodology, BMF include the varied ways we rearticulate and reappropriate the hegemonic forms of knowledge, whether it is feminism, postmodernism, and so on in our theorizing, research, and writing. A BMF epistemology is the knowledge we embody that stems from our *cuerpos* and *vidas* as Third World feminists, outsiders, and insiders and guides our variegated understanding of knowledge and power. In our research endeavors, we are hesitant about standard and normal definitions of methodology. Our methodological approach tends to be interdisciplinary, subjective, and connected to our vidas and cuerpos. For example, Cinthya M. Saavedra (2006) uses multiple epistemologies of the body (Foucauldian, queer, feminist(s), and Chicana) to examine the (his)torical body of the teacher. Her methodology includes maneuvering through deconstruction and genealogical analysis as well as producing a new methodology that arose from her body and *experiencias* as she connected with the discourse of the history of the feminization of teaching—carnal methodologies.

Thus, we use what we need in order to be heard and better understand our endeavors.

Buscando/Searching for *Teorías Hasta en la Cocina*

In order to develop BMF, we sought theories in places that normally are not found under the category of "high" theory. We searched in nontraditional places. As Sonia Saldivar-Hull (2000) urges,

> Because our work has been ignored by the men and women in charge of the modes of cultural production, we must be innovative in our search. . . . As a consequence, we have to look in non-traditional places for our theories: in the prefaces to anthologies, in the interstices of autobiographies, in our cultural artifacts (the cuentos), and, if we are fortunate enough to have access to a good library, in the essays published in marginalized journals not widely distributed by the dominant institutions. (p. 46)

Therefore, this chapter attempts to find and highlight theory and theorizing in spaces perhaps not deemed "theoretical" from a Western academic perspective. Exciting borderlands-mestizaje feminist research is being implemented and constructed in educational circles (a field that is normally depoliticized). And because we (the authors) are educators, we want to present and introduce the important and critical borderland-mestizaje feminist work and theorizing that is taking place in educational spaces. From conversations, *entrevistas,* testimonials, and "discussions *en la cocina*" (Elenes et al., 2001, p. 595), *vive la teoría y los momentos de pedagogía.*

Las critical *lecciones de todos los días* are important especially as they pertain to our reconceptualization of critical pedagogy, knowledge creation, and identity production (Trinidad Galván, 2001). Moreover, critical pedagogical lessons can be learned even in places where dominant ideologies seem to reign. Great examples are the works of Ruth Trinidad Galván (2001) and Sofia Villenas and Melissa Moreno (2001). The research of these Chicana feminists challenges and expands traditional modes of understanding and examining theorizing spaces. Trinidad Galván problematizes pedagogical spaces by emphasizing *la vida cotidiana y la convivencia* that transpires among rural *mujers.* Villenas and Moreno explore *madres e hijas* in traditional Latino homes and negotiate and navigate through race, capitalism, and patriarchy.

What we can learn from their research is how we can theorize from the bottom and in places and spaces not deemed theoretical. Theory, then, is *cotidiano,* mundane, and ordinary. These are "powerful sites for learning and teaching" (Trinidad Galván, 2001, p. 605). But it is in and through our search for theory in nontraditional places that allows us to explore and experience *lo cotidiano* as powerful learning and teaching sites. We must (un)learn and have the mental and bodily flexibility to stretch and challenge ideas and concepts that are rigid and unbending.

◘ *Parto y (His)Tory*

Parto

We attempt in this section to show the varied and complex moments that scholars have identified as the emergence of borderlands feminist theorizing. We contend that the search for origins is subjective at best.

For Hector Calderón and José David Saldívar (1991), borderlands epistemology began to be widely used as a tool to describe and research the cross-cultural, intellectual, sexual, and territorial (physically and symbolically) mobility of hybrid bodies in the mid-19th century. According to Calderón and Saldívar, the mid-19th century is when Chicanos, Mexicanos, and/or *la mestiza* began to deconstruct the deficient mestiza(o) and critically reconstruct and name their bilingual and bicultural experiences "as a resistive measure against Anglo-American economic domination and ideological hegemony" (p. 4). Sandoval (1998) maps the emergence of Third World feminism, "later transformed into U.S. third world feminism, mestizaje feminism, and now 'borderlands' theory and 'diaspora' studies, by the end of the [20th] century's end" (p. 354). By the 1980s,

U.S. Third World feminism had become an intellectual and bodily discourse that would influence the work, practice, and theorizing of Chicana feminism, borderlands epistemology, and the merging/mutation of all into borderlands-mestizaje feminism. Norma Alarcón (1999) argues that the Chicano political (sub)conscious awakening, although dominated by men, has always had Chicana feminists' interventions and interruptions since the beginning of the Chicano movement. The erasure and exclusion of their work in the 1960s and 1970s is indicative of the lack of importance given to women of color in the cultural and political economy (Alarcón, 1999).

Gloria Anzaldúa (1987) and Naomi Quiñonez (2003), in tracing their mestiza feminist consciousness, reject the Western search for traditional literate subjects who fit neatly in reference sections and instead, without apology, place the body of *la india* and *La Malinche* at the forefront as evidence and testimony of their resistive roots—perhaps an anticolonial tactic. Knowledge in the Western sense is cumulative. *Tenemos que* back up anything we say or write because somehow we are rendered incapable of producing and constructing knowledge. This is a way to privilege literate societies and those who have and had access to produce and construct knowledge. Anzaldúa (1987) and Quiñonez (2003) are good examples of what happens when we search for marginalized knowledges.

As a way to de-academize the search for origins, Gloria Anzaldúa poses a different way to trace origins. Anzaldúa (1987) traces her identity of struggle and resistance back to the body of *la mujer india.* She contends that the Aztec females' "rites of mourning were rites of defiance protesting the cultural changes which disrupted the equality of and balance between female and male, and protesting their demotion to a lesser status, their denigration. Like *la Llorona,* the Indian woman's only means of protest was wailing" (p. 21). Furthermore, Anzaldúa writes la india was "silenced, gagged, caged . . . bludgeoned for 300 years, sterilized and castrated in the twentieth century . . . a light shone through her veil of silence . . . [and] she continues to tend the flame" (pp. 22–23). If this flame and light continues to shine after centuries of atrocities committed against her and yet she still *existe,* then struggle and resistance and renegotiation have been a part of her, if not her total, being and existence of la mujer india.

Like Anzaldúa, Naomi Quiñonez (2003) traces contemporary Chicana feminism or what she calls the "postcolonial first wave" of Chicana writers to *La Malinche,* the first interpreter to Hernán Cortés. According to Quiñonez, La Malinche embodied the survival skills that are relevant and prevalent to Chicana feminist writers. "*La Malinche* embodies those personal characteristics—such as intelligence, initiative, adaptability, and leadership" (Candelaria, 1980, quoted in Quiñonez, 2003, p. 138). Important also is how the myth of La Malinche, "*la Chingada,*" whore and traitor, has been transformed by Chicana feminist writers. El *mexicano y* Chicano have used La Malinche to denote their tragic self-perception as *hijos de la chingada* and blame La Malinche for selling out their people. But as Anzaldúa (1987) reminds us

> The worst kind of betrayal lies in making us believe that the Indian woman in us is the betrayer. We *indias y mestizas,* police the Indian in us, brutalize and condemn her. Male culture has done a good job on us. *Son las custumbres que traicionan. La india en mi es la sombra: La Chingada, Tlazolteotl, Coatlicue. Son ellas que oyemos lamentando a sus hijas perdidas.* (p. 22)

However, denied knowledge about ourselves is not the only quest. Naomi Quiñonez (2003) argues that, once she learned the history of her people, she was compelled to ask about the *mujeres* in that history—a much deeper examination of history. The postcolonial first-wave Chicana writers, *mujeres y hombres,* "participate in cultural resistance by utilizing their cultural production to reclaim buried histories. They also resist dominant discourses by appropriating, reconfiguring, and transforming it as part of their own" (Quiñonez, 2003, p. 141). In this way, Quiñonez explains, a politics of difference is engendered and "'writing back to the empire' not only involves resistance as a postcolonial subject but resolution as an empowered force" (p. 141).

Contesting and writing back to empire is an important aspect of BMF and has influenced how BMF scholars conceptualize and perform research.

Pedagogical Scars From Chicano Studies and White Feminism

Regardless of its ontology or what we think the exact time and origin of borderlands-mestizaje feminism, it emerges from contestations of colonialism and dominant cultural politics that have denied not only our *experiencias* but our *existencia* as, and *his*tory of, producers of culture. Teresa Córdova (1999), following Albert Memmi, argues that "colonialism has imbedded its memory in our spirits. After stripping us of our institutions, our resources, and our history, the colonizer asserts his superiority and declares us deficient and deserving of our own fate" (p. 11). Furthermore, due to our specific forced assignment in the symbolic geopolitical landscape of the United States and, like other groups who have been historically oppressed, borderlands-mestizaje feminism engenders the sensibility or the "cultural intuition" (Delgado Bernal, 1998) to see, feel, and experience counteroppressive patriarchal, racist, and sexist practices and politics. Our sensibility stems not from a utopian space we occupy that renders us some place above looking down with our mestiza "expert" gaze. But because we are immersed *hasta el copete* in the hegemonic Chicano, White feminist, and colonialist/imperialist projects, we have learned counterdiscourses in order to justify our existence. Dolores Delgado Bernal argues (1998) that Chicanas and Latinas lead lives with considerably different opportunity structures and conditions than men, including Chicano males, and White women. And perhaps that is an advantage, as Delgado Bernal reminds us of the strength found in Chicanas, Latinas, and other marginalized bodies that live and experience the literal and metaphorical space called borderlands.

But it has not been easy to find, trace, and hear the voices of *las mujeres.* The Latino and Chicano engaged in silencing the voices and bodies as well as denying *las experiencias* y *contribuciones de las mujeres.* Saldivar-Hull (2000) reflects on how the *o* in *Chicano* subsumed her body, and her search in White feminist theory was futile. Neither feminism nor Chicano nationalism quenched her search for a way or method to "discern the complex interconnections between race or ethnicity, class, gender, and sexuality" (p. 25). As a response, Cherrie Moraga and Gloria Anzaldúa (2002), in their groundbreaking anthology *This Bridge Called My Back: Writings by Radical Women of Color,* eloquently describe the need to create and speak out, be heard with our own voices. Their notion of a "theory in the flesh" describes the ways in which the physical realities of *las mujeres* shape their understandings of the world and are enacted as an embodied politics of resistance. Their "flesh and blood," cultural/racial experiences bridge theory and practice and accept the body as a source of knowledge. They critique imperial feminism and make visible the ways race, class, gender, sexuality, language, and culture are integrated.

> A theory in the flesh means one where the physical realities of our lives—our skin, the land or concrete we grew up on, our sexual longings—all fuse to create a politic born out of necessity. Here, we attempt to bridge the contradictions in our experience:
>
> We are the colored in a white feminist movement.
>
> We are the feminist among the people of our culture.
>
> We are often the lesbians among the straight.
>
> We do this bridging by naming our selves and by telling our stories in our own words. (Moraga & Anzaldúa, 2002, p. 21)

El Macho Academic

Feminism in the borderlands/fronteras stems from the recognition that our own culture (whether Mexican, Puerto Rican, or Nicaragüense), *nos traiciona,* betrays us (Anzaldúa, 1987). Although Chicano and other Latino scholars in the 1960s and 1970s from various disciplines and fields made remarkable contributions to outline, explore, and recover the lost voices and bodies of Chicana(o)s in history, politics, and literary representations, the voices and bodies of the *mujer Chicana* were too often ignored and more often in the footnote sections. As Saldivar-Hull (2000) argues, "If feminist scholars, activists, and writers—who have lived under the *o* in *Chicano*—had to rely on the historical record written by men and male-identified women, Chicanas' roles in history would remain obscured" (p. 27). Even though Chicanas struggled and resisted against *la cara palida del gringo* alongside the Chicano, the Chicano activist and scholar mimed the same patriarchal and sexist pedagogical practices toward and against *la mujer chicana.* Her place had been defined by *machista* understanding of women compiled with the patriarchal ideology of the Catholic Church that only reinforced the role of la mujer as servant to man (López, 1977).

Gringa Theory

White feminism was/is a theory that left women of color *vacia* and often times excluded and denied women of color theorizing spaces (Anzaldúa, 1990; Saldivar-Hull, 2000). During the 1970s and 1980s, European and American feminists marginalized not only Chicana feminism but also feminisms expressed by U.S. women of color (Saldivar-Hull, 2000). Even when White Anglo feminists were willing to provide opportunities for woman of color, Lynet Uttal (1990) argues that White feminist research did not acknowledge or learn anything from voices and concerns of women of color. A Euro-American-centric notion of class and gender emerged as well as hegemonic forms of feminist theorizing that excluded instead of invited multiple ways of theorizing.

Saldivar-Hull (2000) acknowledges the political doors opened by U.S. White feminists in academia. However, Saldivar-Hull examines how Euro-American feminists' works inadvertently espouse a monolithic view of women's experiences. For example, her scrutiny of Catharine MacKinnon's work on feminism and Marxism highlights the negation and often times the erasure of the multiple experiences of mujeres. In Saldivar-Hull's analysis, MacKinnon's work addresses only the plight of Black women to refer to all marginalized women. Euro-American feminist erasure of the different locations of women of color is problematic. All marginalized voices are lumped together. Thus, the feminist/Marxist debates on gender and class are not the only pressing concerns confronted by Chicanas and Latinas. In only addressing politics of gender and class, middle-class Anglo-American feminists wipe out and deny the varied subject positions of feminists of color and ignore the complexity of the politics and the interstitial space where class, race, gender, ethnicity, sexuality, and language (for those who straddle two or more languages) collide and hybrid consciousness on multiple levels exists.

Sandoval (1991) has examined how hegemonic feminist theory scholars constructed the histories of feminist consciousness. According to Sandoval, these are represented and manifested in four different typologies or systematic categorization of "*all possible forms of feminist praxis*" (p. 5, emphasis added). Sandoval argues how these feminist typologies (liberal, Marxists, radical/cultural, and socialist) have encapsulated *y han limitado,* "how the history of feminist activity can be conceptualized, while obstructing what can be perceived or even imagined by agents thinking within its constraints" (p. 10). *No hay lugar* for constructing different spaces. Hegemonic feminist scholars act like the *migra* of feminist praxis, building *parades* to keep the *ilegales* and illegitimate out.

Chicana feminists therefore have "created alternative avenues, 'safe spaces' to develop intellectually and continue the trajectory of political dissent," resulting in the development of "new categories of analysis that reshape and expand established intellectual boundaries" (Pasquera & de la Torre, 1993, p. 4) by reappropriating and renegotiating Euro-American feminist(s) and cultural theories (Pérez, 1998, 1999b; Sandoval, 2000). Thus, borderland-mestizaje feminism is traversing not among multiple epistemologies, theories, and methodologies but *in between* them. It is in this *in-between* space we inhabit where we "can negotiate an empowering racial, gendered, working-class, political terrain we also call mestizaje" (Saldivar-Hull, 2000, pp. 44–45). Mestizaje then becomes a methodology we can use to renegotiate and reconcile multiple ways of existing and researching. Furthermore, mestizaje becomes the bridge we often cross back and forth, a space from where we can theorize that attempts to engage rather than disengage with dominant and discursive ideologies.

▣ Mestizaje as Metodologia

The critical and important work that is being embodied within a borderland-mestizaje feminist framework is varied and interdisciplinary. Multiple epistemologies inform and influence the work, perspectives, and inquiries. We use, embody, and borrow from queer, feminist, postmodern, postcolonial, and poststructuralist scholarship and epistemologies. We take and use and discard from dominant ideologies "to ensure that ethical commitment to egalitarian social relations enters into everyday, political sphere of culture" (Sandoval, 1998, p. 360). Perhaps the inclusive nature of borderland-mestizaje feminism stems in part from the exclusionary practices aimed at silencing, gagging, and eradicating marginalized *voces y cuerpos.* But struggle and resistance give way to theorizing, and in some ways, *nos abre a incluir en vez de excluir.* Not only do we include but we renegotiate, reappropriate to our needs, goals, and experiencias. We are not bound to any particular way of thinking but instead welcome multiple perspectives and epistemologies, allowing for mutations and transgressions to occur. Borderland-mestizaje feminist methodologies are important in order to move away from reconstructing new discursive ideologies that seem liberatory but are indeed colonizing and regurgitating the same hierarchical, patriarchal, homophobic, and capitalist relations that we so wish to *eliminar* and eradicate from our *mentes y cuerpos,* even when it is our own discourses.

Perhaps that is why literary and cultural critic Norma Alarcón (2003) questions the epistemologies that continue to marginalize women of color and therefore uses Anzaldúa's (1987) work as a deconstructive methodology to unbraid the colonizing potential that Western theories reinscribe in our subjectivities and work. By centering Anzaldúa's *Borderlands/La Frontera,* Alarcón unleashes a borderlands-mestizaje feminist maneuvering that engages and reimagines new possibilities for the Western-based theories of Lacan, Derrida, Kristeva, and Butler. Furthermore, she provides alternate conceptualizations for Chicanas that reinvent the patriarchal, ethnonational Chicano appropriations. Influenced by Anzaldúa's use of a multifaceted feminine (Shadow Beast, Snake Woman, La Llorona, and many other figurations), Alarcón is able to use Anzaldúa's methodology to open up spaces for reworking both feminist theories and Chican*o* cultural studies.

Moreover, a borderland-mestizaje feminist methodology has the potential to highlight the complex nature of "doing" and experiencing research as academics and scholars of color (Bejarano, 2005; Delgado Bernal, 1998; Elenes et al., 2001; Saavedra, 2005; Villenas, 1996). Furthermore, articulations and examinations of race, class, gender, and privilege are central concerns at the interstices of queries for feminist mestizaje theorizing (Anzaldúa, 1990). Working within a borderland-mestizaje feminist framework places us in a position to question research practices and methodologies that ultimately serve to construct the "other" even within our own people and communities (Demas, 2004; Demas & Saavedra, 2004; Villenas, 1996). Illuminating and articulating the tensions surrounding the complicated space we occupy as researchers of color, privileged on one hand and marginalized on the other, is an important task and methodology that must be confronted and disrupted in educational research (Villenas, 1996).

Our research endeavors must at every step attempt to decenter Western modes of thinking, theorizing, and living, beginning with perhaps one of the major tenets of Western thinking—the bifurcation of the mind and body. We must center and sew together mind and body. As a methodology, BMF entails not forgetting the geography and history of the body (Pérez, 1999a). The Chicana feminist voice, in order to be heard, must first listen to her body (Anzaldúa, 1990). It is this carnal voice that can be used as a methodology of her own that dialogues with mainstream (educational) research and says "*y no se te olvide esto también*" (Saavedra, 2005) or perhaps as an invitation to Western modes of research to rethink, deconstruct, and reconstruct new and hybrid ways to know, be, and become. *Esperamos que,* this does not translate into invoking a new truth to research but only a different perspective to contemplate, thereby opening up multiple possibilities for educational research. BMF methodology revolves around the *constante crítica* of mainstream methodologies but also extends further to critique and challenge our own.

We contend that borderland-mestizaje feminism has important implications to consider in our (re)search. For example, we must acknowledge how research is potentially a colonizing tool (Cannella & Viruru 2004; Demas, 2004; Smith, 1999). Western research reifies the *nos/otros* (we/them) dichotomy. BMF also can create and construct moments of decolonial theorizing where critical resistance and social transformation are foregrounded and explored. And last, BMF provides possibilities for decolonizing research through the very act of illuminating and centering the body, sexuality, and subjectivities (Córdova, 1999; Cruz, 2001; Saavedra, 2005, 2006).

Research as Colonization: Reinscribing Nos/Otras

Elenes (2001) contends that integral to borderland discourse is the rejection of "dualistic, essentialists, and oversimplified thinking" (p. 691). However, the "us/them" dichotomies are inherent in the subject positions we embody as scholars, researchers, and pedagogues. But as Elenes reminds us, we must ourselves "constantly engage in a process where first [we] must continuously be self-reflective of [our] participation in dualistic thinking" (p. 693). Rethinking and being reflexive of *nuestro* research and pedagogy might potentially allow us to question our research intentions and our complicity in dominant ideologies.

And that is why we must be reflective. As bell hooks (1989) observes, "When we write about the experiences of a group to which we do not belong, we should think about the ethics of our action, considering whether or not our work will be used to reinforce or perpetuate domination" (p. 43). We must therefore contemplate and acknowledge the possibility that even critical research conceived, constructed, and performed through Western lenses and frameworks has a colonizing potential. Research, concerned with generating and legitimizing knowledge, is crucial to the colonization process as it creates power and privilege for some over others (e.g., situated superiority of Western knowledge, "expert" researcher, and objectification of the Other; Demas, 2004; Smith, 1999). *Despues de todo,* it was through establishing a "positional superiority" that the West was able to colonize knowledges around *el mundo.* It is important to understand how we create the "subject" as Other and how our research legitimizes colonial practices such as surveillance, observations, policing, and xenophobic policies that can result in the Othering of people's cultures, languages, knowledges, and bodies (Demas, 2004).

Borderland-mestizaje feminist framework has critical implications to consider with regards to the subject/object duality that is inherent in Western modes of research. Chicana/o and Latina/os working under this frame of thinking foreground and interweave the personal, political, historical, and cultural into a messy text where the subject of our gaze may have started out as the participant but then ricochets back to the researcher, history, culture, and the political. For example, Delgado Bernal (1998), Telléz (2005), Villenas (1996), and Pérez (1999a) illustrate how working within a borderland-mestizaje feminist epistemology attempts to reject simplistic and dualistic research endeavors in order to complicate the research process, possibly providing decolonial moments and "moving beyond binaries and toward intersectionality and hybridity" (Arredondo et al., 2003, p. 2).

Delgado Bernal (1998) uses this complex mestizaje interweaving as a methodological tool she calls "cultural intuition." By articulating the complicated and messy texts, Delgado Bernal's research avoids the "researcher as expert" position that ultimately perpetuates and reinscribes the us/them duality. For example, she included her participants in the analytical process, and equally shared that endeavor with her participants. She allowed her participants to really speak and interpret their own voices. The participants became "speaking subjects who [took] part in producing and validating knowledge" (Delgado Bernal, 1998, p. 15).

Michelle Téllez (2005) examines the tensions that Chicana feminists confront between activism/ scholarship, community/academia, and subject/researcher. Western social scientific methods inadvertently produce and prescribe a dichotomy between the latter. Her ethnographic research embodies a mestizaje lens that enables her to engage in complex issues of power, methods, and knowledges. For example, she challenges critical hermeneutic interpretation as potentially privileging literate participants who have access to formal education and are able to discuss interpretations with her. Also important in Telléz's work is the in(corp)oration of her experiencias as a border crosser. Sharing this aspect in her research contextualizes the whole process of research as "research of the particular" and avoids overgeneralization and essentialist understandings of the communities in which we work and research.

Sofia Villenas (1996) investigates how research projects are tenuous at best and at any one moment can be turned upside down and fragmented. Villenas's research project was funded for the purpose of examining the "apparent" educational and child-rearing practices that *impide* Latina/os from achieving educational success. However, through a critical ethnography, she complicated the space she occupied as a researcher of color. She highlights her positionality as both colonizer and colonized. Villenas realized that she needed to renegotiate her role as researcher/ethnographer to one that embodies her racial and gendered memory and in her researcher gaze. Neutrality and detachment in the field were not options.

Pérez's (1999a), inquiry illuminate the complexity of the entrapment of occupying the in-between moments and spaces that categorize our subjectivities and our search for our own knowledge and histories. Pérez contends that our project is to negotiate between the colonized/ colonizer subjectivities that we inevitably embody and to seek out the disturbing distance where the "political project is to decolonize otherness" (p. 6). Pérez argues that seeking the tension between colonize/colonizer spaces and bodies creates a third space where the "decolonial imaginary" is possible. We must venture into the uncomfortable, perhaps disturbing *espacios y cuerpos* to engender decolonial possibilities.

Ultimately, Delgado Bernal, Telléz, Villenas, and Pérez, in using a BMF methodology, are moving beyond the goals and scope of qualitative research. That is, all four Chicana scholars are engaging personally with their research by inviting emotion and personal experiences as well as resisting the *dis*embodied nature of research. Furthermore, they attempt to fragment the dichotomous lines that are inherent in qualitative research such as researcher/ subject, academia/community, activism/scholarship, and colonized/colonizer.

Theorizing *Desde Abajo:* Critical Resistance/Social Transformations

Nuestro research should be subversive acts. *Nuestras metodologías* and inquiries are not just to advance the literature and to be self-indulgent (Córdova, 1999) but to change and transform our local and global communities. We are but a microcosm of a broader hybrid transnational, multicolored, transformative feminist(s) pedagogies (Elenes, 2002; Kaplan, Alarcón, & Moallen, 1999; Sandoval, 2000). A Western framework of research alone will not accomplish our multiple transnational, transformative feminist(s) goals (Chabram-Dernersesian, 1999b). As Elenes et al. (2001) have articulated, "What we are concerned with is activist insurgent educators who interrogate social and educational theory and reproduction to create political and cultural projects to transform existing social inequalities and injustices" (p. 595). It is in seeking and acknowledging this activist insurgent, who constructs critical spaces, that we can illuminate and transform oppressive or colonizing forms of existing. Critical resistance, then, is about interrogating dominant ideology *and* nuestros reactions to that ideology. We must also learn to self-critique.

Rosaldo (1989) argues that boundaries need to be distorted when engaging in social analysis. That is, the lines between social science and art are fragmented and zigzagged. According to Elenes (1997), borderlands theories use multiple, varied, and creative methodologies such as "life histories, testimonials, and interviews, along with other forms of cultural productions such as narratives, *corridos,* and visual arts" (p. 366). She contends that this translates into a borderlands theorizing that constructs knowledge from the bottom—a very important tactic that deacademizes theorizing and provides resistance and counterdiscourses found in the mundane. *En la vida cotidiana,* we can excavate multiple enactments of the "pedagogical forms" that exist and are not found in traditional academic definitions (Trinidad Galván, 2001). Sites, knowledges, and resistance as we have come to know them through our academic training are problematized and extended. Nuestro research should include and examine multiple ways in which everyday people have embodied, negotiated, and reinvented resistance.

For example, Chicana feminists, working within (or in between) a borderland-mestizaje epistemology, problematize the sanctity of theorizing spaces (Hernandez, 1997) that occur and are dreamed up *en las "cabezas" de los academicos* (and we stress heads, *por que se olvidan que tienen cuerpos*). In a special issue of *Qualitative Studies in Education,* Elenes et al. (2001) set in motion such critique and possibility in educational research. By centering self-reflection, *el hogar, las madres e hijas y el cuerpo,* the authors of this special issue further expand male and Western definitions of praxis, critical pedagogies, and knowledge production. In a way, Elenes et al. have provided a fragile and fluid skeletal body that impels us to add more flesh to that body and advance the scholarship and *conocimientos de nuestras comunidades.*

In this special issue, Villenas and Moreno (2001) examine through oral life histories how mother-daughter pedagogies are spaces filled with tensions and contradictions but, at the same time, rip open a space for decolonial possibilities. Important is how traditional notions of *madres e hijas* are disrupted and reinvented when Villenas and Moreno are able to excavate how mother-daughter pedagogies in a *comunidad Latina* also serve as counterspaces for possibility. Moreover, Delgado Bernal (2001) centers *el hogar* as a space where critical pedagogies are engendered from cultural, historical, and political understandings found in the homes of Chicana college students. The critical lessons taught at home and through their communities via *corridos,* storytelling, and behavior provide Chicanas the *herramientas* to maneuver and resist multiple forms of domination. Delgado Bernal's study is an example of rethinking the deficit model that has been engrained in our memory and being. Latinas/Chicanas are not as deficient as we have been made out to be. Theory, resistance, and transformation stems from the everyday lives and not only in your *cabezas!*

In(corp)orating the Body/Sexuality as Intellectual Counterdiscourse

> To completely understand the complexities of the Chicana and Chicano subjectivity in the greater borderlands of the United States, discussions of gender and sexuality are central in our oppositional and liberatory projects. (Saldivar-Hull, 2000, p. 33)

> . . . pervasive homophobia constructs sociosexual power relations in society and pervasive homophobia in our Chicana/o community limits the potential for liberation and revolution. (Pérez, 1991, p. 163)

> For me, writing is a spiritual activity just as it's a political activity and a bodily act. (Anzaldúa, 2000, p. 252)

Chicana and Latina feminist writers have contributed to the field of cultural studies (including but not limited to history, sociology, education, and philosophy), the speaking body, and sexuality. Teresa Córdova (1999) asserts that by reclaiming self and space in their writing—and, we would like to add, the body—Chicana feminist writers *obsequian* anticolonial third space moments. For example, Córdova asserts that Chicanas' struggle for recovery and survival from the symbolic and literal rape by those who have silenced and maimed them has enabled *la Chicana* to unearth *una voz y cuerpo,*

> to rename herself in her own image, to recover mythic and historical female symbols that reconnect her to her past, and to celebrate and learn to love herself . . . to liberate [her] from the oppression of the colonialist construct whose only purpose is to debase her in order to control her. (p. 12)

Cultural and Chicana/o studies have benefited from such anticolonial tactics as they serve as subversive *herramientas* to deconstruct patriarchal and colonial projects, especially the works of Chicana lesbians. For example, the work of Gloria Anzaldúa, Cherrie Moraga, Emma Pérez, Carla Trujillo, Yvonne Yarbro-Bejarano, and many others has disturbed the clinical and the *de eso no se habla* mentality of Western theorizing. For example, personal experience, connections to our participants, emotions, *el cuerpo, lo sexual,* and critical self-reflection in quantitative research are taboos *y por eso el tema ni si toca;* we suppress them.

Córdova (1999) believes the lesbian voice has contributed significantly to the contestation of patriarchal and colonial conquest. Deena Gonzalez (1998) terms this *speaking secrets.* That is, giving voice to the experiences and conditions that negate the sexual and bodily existence. Speaking secrets is an uncomfortable, yet perhaps necessary, tactic needed to rip open spaces where critical dialogues and conversations can occur and where homophobia and misogyny can be, at the very least, unveiled in Chicana/o cultural studies. This also speaks to how, even in Chicana/o studies, we have subsumed the us/them dichotomy that prevents us from uniting without reservation and including all voices, gay and lesbian, in Chicana/o studies.

That is why, in order to achieve, advance, and construct a transnational feminist imperative, *debemos de incorporar* carnal methods (Saavedra, 2006) as decolonizing discourses that confront the Western need to bifurcate the mind and body. Centering *el cuerpo,* sexuality, and carnal knowing further disrupts the Western's simplistic and dualistic tendencies of theory, research, and practice. Perhaps two of the most subversive and anticolonial contributions that borderland-mestizaje feminism potentially offers are the body and sexuality as mediums and tools to theorize (Córdova, 1999; Cruz, 2001; Trujillo, 1998; Yarbro-Bejarano, 1999). Even though the legacy of colonialism has scarred and split the body, it has, however, painfully forged possibilities for Chicana and Latina feminists from various disciplines to begin to include their own experiencias, spaces, and bodies in their work in order to reclaim self/space and body/mind—an anticolonial strategy (Córdova, 1999). Voice comes in a variety of ways. For some Chicana feminists, it is about listening to and voicing the body and desire (Pérez, 1999a). If unleashed, the body can speak through our work, writing, and practices, possibly even engendering new counter carnal discourses.

For Chicana feminist scholars, the body and sexuality are not only theorized and centered but are theorizing mediums as well. *Al escuchar y centrar el cuerpo,* in their analysis, counter, even decolonial, discourses can emerge. Following Anzaldúa (1987), Saavedra (2005, 2006), and Cindy Cruz (2001) have argued that we must listen and center our bodies in our research endeavors. Carnal metodologías (Saavedra, 2006) can unleash ways to know that are radically and inherently different from sanctioned mind-oriented inquiries and methodologies. Similarly, Yvonne Yarbro-Bejarano (1999) *nos suplica* that we must place sexuality at the forefront of Chicana/o cultural studies rather than just interject it as an afterthought. She contends that this would allow for deeper examinations and move us away from reproducing hegemonic scripts and more toward sites of critical contestation.

Engendering an epistemology of the brown body, Cruz (2001) contends that recovery "is not only a strategy to make visible Chicana voices and histories, but it is also the struggle to develop critical practices that can propel the brown body from a neocolonial past and into the embodiments of radical subjectivities" (p. 658). In other words, the work of borderland-mestizaje feminism is not just to engender critical practices but also to decolonize the brown body. And as Cruz asserts, "Nothing provokes the custodians of normality and objectivity more than the excessiveness of a body" (p. 659). Thus, highlighting and using the body and sexuality decenters the Western clinical sterilized approach to theory, research, and practice. *El* messy *cuerpo,* is a taboo best kept behind closed doors and out of theory. For this reason, the canon is suspicious of scholars who use carnal metodologías (Saavedra, 2006), as they serve as blasphemous tools against the sanctity of academia.

For example, Anzaldúa (1990) (em)bodies theory and allows the carnal to surface. Carnality is felt by all senses through her writings. She reunites mind and body, defying the Cartesian mind and body split that reigns in modernist and Enlightenment minds. In *Making Face, Making Soul,* she conjures up an image of theory made of flesh. For Anzaldúa, to theorize is to make face, *caras.* She explains:

> For me, haciendo *caras* has the added connotation of making *gestos subversivos,* political subversive gestures, the piercing look that questions and challenges. . . . "Face" is the surface of the body that is most noticeably inscribed by social structures, marked with instructions on how to be *mujer,* macho, working class, Chicana. As *mestizas*—biologically and/or culturally mixed—we have different surfaces for each aspect of identity, each inscribed by a particular subculture. We are "written" all over, or should I say, carved and tattooed with the sharp needle of experience. (p. xv)

The *cara* and *cuerpo* have been carved on through/with discourses but ultimately enables her to produce theory. The power of dominant discourses interacts with the Chicana cuerpo, producing various forms of counterresistance, identities, and subjectivities. The potential to resist imposed borders, while at the same time allowing them to be fluid and fragmented, is *posible* through the body of the mestiza. The mestiza body becomes a metaphorical landscape where dominant discourses are constantly challenged (Saavedra, 2006).

Cherie Moraga (1983), in *Loving in the War Years: Lo Que Nunca Paso por Sus Labios,* discusses how the body and pain are associated to her theory building. According to Paula Moya (1997), Moraga's "'theory in the flesh' is derived from, although not uniformly determined by, the 'physical realities' of her life, her 'social location'" (p. 150). In certain ways, the body manifests itself in Moraga's work. For example, of her chronic back pain, she writes,

> Sometimes I feel my back will break from the pressure I feel to speak for others. A friend of mine told me once how no wonder I had called the first book I co-edited (with Gloria Anzaldúa), "This Bridge Called My Back." *You have chronic back trouble,* she says. Funny I had never considered this most obvious connection, all along my back giving me constant pain. And the spot that hurts the most is the muscle that controls the movement of my fingers and hands while typing. I feel it now straining at my desk. (Moraga, 1983, p. v)

Reevaluating the works of Anzaldúa and Moraga, Cruz (2001) welcomes the brown body as source and medium of deeper critical educational examination. She contends that because the brown body is at the interstices of multiple, often oppositional, sociopolitical locations, it has the potential to create new ways to know, examine, and create theorizing spaces. Further influenced by Michel Foucault and Bryan Turner, Cruz examines how the regulation of the brown body in Latina/o lesbian and gay youth can be rearticulated as an issue of the containment of the body. Subsequently, it allows us to contemplate and ask different questions with regards to the construction of pedagogy, identity, and bodies. And as Cruz justly states, "Understanding the brown body and the regulation of its movements is fundamental in reclaiming narrative and developing radical projects of transformation" (p. 664) otherwise denied in mind-oriented projects.

Following Anzaldúa, Saavedra (2005, 2006) has allowed her carnal *voz* (Anzaldúa, 1987) to infiltrate her own work as teacher and researcher. Her research questions *vienen de* her carnal experiences and feelings. For example, Saavedra (2006) grapples with the intricacies of listening to her carnal voice as a methodological *herramienta.* She contends that, if allowed, the carnal voice pierces through as a constant reminder that the body can theorize. Analyzing data and engaging in research are not just mind activities but bodily endeavors as well. However, Saavedra confronts not so much the problem of listening to the body but the problem of translating the carnal into a language that expresses and voices *el cuerpo.* As language is inextricably tied to Western positivistic rationalist thinking, it can sometimes become an obstacle and a nuisance, thereby contributing to the body's impossibility to speak. "Language is a male discourse," wrote Anzaldúa (1987, p. 54).

The body and sexuality are potential decolonizing tools that rupture and fragment the Western inorganic approach to theory. Listening and voicing el cuerpo and sexuality are important avenues that must be incorporated in order to forge new ways to increase our likelihood to build new *puentes* that connects as opposed to divides us. Important to mention is the groundbreaking work being produced on the body and performance *que nos puede ayudar* to examine multiple ways that our cuerpos perform dominant discursive ideologies. For example, Soyini Madison and Judith Hamera (2006) have compiled works of scholars who explore and examine performance and performativity through history, politics, pedagogy, literature, ethnography, and theory. Performance studies *abre otra avenida* "of comprehending how human beings fundamentally make culture, affect power and reinvent ways of being in the world" (Madison & Hamera, 2006, p. xii). Performance studies may contribute to a borderlands feminist framework different ways to a approach research, perhaps even creating the type of puente where dominant discourses can dialogue with marginalized discourses in order to forge new mutated discourses of resistance.

The New Tribalism: Mestizaje as Bridge

> In this millennium we are called to renew and birth a more inclusive feminism, one committed to basic human rights, equality, respect for all people and creatures, and for the earth. As keepers of the fire of transformation we invite awareness of soul into our daily acts, call richness and beauty into our lives; bid spirit to stir our blood, dissolve the rigid walls between us, and gather us in. May our voices proclaim the bonds of bridges. (Anzaldúa, 2002a, p. xxxix)

The title in this portion of our chapter is inspired by the visions and aspiration of the late Gloria Anzaldúa (2000, pp. 214–215). For us, her work has always been about stretching our *mentes y cuerpos* in order to connect in transnational, transborder fashion. For Anzaldúa, the "New Tribalism" was not about engendering a politic based solely on a Latina Chicana prerogative but also about the omnipresences of the nos/otras concept. Anzaldúa explains,

> Want to hear my rationale for my use of "New Tribalism"? I use the word nos/otras to illustrate how we're in each other's world, how we're each affected by the other, and how we're all dependent on the other. (p. 215)

The "New Tribalism," then, is about how we/you/they can witness how we are all in each other. Although the concept of tribalism might seem like the ghettotization of ideas and concepts, on the contrary, it is about all of us (you, us, they) in the tribe. Therefore, the New Tribalism avoids essentialist notions of who we/they/us are and constantly challenges who we are, critiquing others as a way to also reevaluate ourselves. *Por eso nuestros proyectos* should not only be "community" self-serving but also form alliances with those who are also feeling and living the historical and contemporary effects of Western hegemonic policies, juridical discourses, and economic disenfranchisement.

In forming alliances, we must at the same time do as Alarcón (1998) believes: "locate the point of theoretical and political consensus with other feminists (and 'feminist' men), and on the other, continue with projects that position [us] in paradoxical binds" (p. 380). In a similar fashion, Angie Chabram-Dernersesian (1999b) urges us to continue to rethink, rework, and maneuver Chicana/o, Latina/o cultural studies in order to forge transnational alliances. She argues that we must not only celebrate the *nosotras* but also facilitate a space for the engagement of critical dialogues between and among the various multiple Chicana/os, Latina/os subjectivities and indigenous realities that are embodied, lived, and experienced. Chabram-Dernersesian argues that

> [a] critical transnationalism of this sort must entertain other types of geopolitical and linguistic complexities, complexities that arise from making strategic connections with other people of colour in the Americas (here and there) and from engaging racial, class, sexual and gender dynamics that are often erased when referring to so-called "Spanish-speaking" groups. (p. 183)

For Chela Sandoval (2000), alliance building emerges from the reworking and rebuilding of the works of critical and cultural theorists who share an affinity for revolutionary resistance and critical liberation, even if they stem from the canon. Her (re)visioning of the works of Fredric Jameson, Donna Haraway, Michel Foucault, Hayden White, Jacques Derrida, Franz Fanon, Gloria Anzaldúa, Audre Lorde, Paula Gunn Allen, and Roland Barthes allows her to seek out that which inspires them and draws from global feminist and ethnic scholars in order to illuminate "the lines of force and affinity such writing shares that link them with the theories, hopes, desires, and aims of decolonizing sex, gender, race, ethnic, and identity liberationists" (Sandoval, 2000, p. 5). Sandoval believes that Western theory also communicates a vision for a postcolonial 21st century. As Western theory has been influenced by U.S. Third World feminist criticism, a puente has opened that allows cultural and critical theory to usurp their decolonial voices that drive anti- and postcolonial yearning and possibility. What Sandoval does so well is to bridge multiple theories and methodologies through a method of differential consciousness in order to forge a coalitional consciousness of possibility and of postmodern love. Sandoval's work is an example of mestizaje as bridge and method and the type of "new tribalism" that Anzaldúa (2002b) envisioned and engendered:

> To bridge means loosening our borders, not closing off borders, not closing off to others. Bridging is the work of opening the gate to the stranger, within and without. To step across the threshold is to be stripped of the illusion of safety because it moves us into unfamiliar territory and does not grant safe passage. To bridge is to attempt community, and for that we must risk being open to personal, political, and spiritual intimacy, to risk being wounded. Effective bridging comes from knowing when to close ranks to those outside our home, group, community, nation—and when to keep the gates open. (p. 3)

Conclusions: *Nuevas Posibilidades*

As a tool, methodology, epistemology, and a way of existing, borderland-mestizaje feminism embodies a hybrid mode of consciousness that challenges researchers to rethink new ways to know and to be. Emerging from the lives and experiences of Chicanas/os living in the *in-between* geographical and metaphorical spaces of the borderlands, borderland-mestizaje theorizing is intimately concerned with unweaving the legacies of colonialism and rebuilding transformative *nuevas teorías.* By implicating Western research in the continued colonization of peoples, BMF offers possibilities for reconceptualizing research toward decolonial practice.

In the struggle to decolonize educational research, BMF invites researchers to reconstruct their research practices and to subvert the boundaries of social science. We are urged to critique dominant discourses and ideologies, deconstruct unidimensional notions of identity, problematize "white-washed" representations, and interrogate Western modes of inquiry. Central to Chicana feminist oppositional projects are self-reflection, collaboration, their own subjectivities, sexuality, and theorizing with the body. These insurgent researchers tear open new spaces from which to theorize—spaces from where they can destabilize imperialist assumptions and contest Western narratives of domination. Our purpose in this chapter is not to present borderland-mestizaje feminism as a new truth but rather to offer a different approach that supports decolonial research agendas and emancipatory social transformation—that offers *nuevas posibilidades* for research and for being.

▣ *Platicas y Conversaciones:* The New End Notes

This is what we call the new end notes where we bounce off, converse, *platicamos* about and reflect on our own unabridged understanding of borderland-mestizaje feminism. What follows is our attempt at understanding how borderland-mestizaje feminism is embedded in our everyday lives as *mujeres,* minorities, and researchers. Our *conversaciones* are examples of the struggles and complexities we recognize and acknowledge as we endeavor to make sense of our lives and work, not to mention borderland-mestizaje feminism itself. Our conversations may show ambiguity and contradictions, but we contend that they demonstrate that our intention is not to make BMF a new "truth" or a static and unbending critical framework. To the contrary, we hope they highlight its continuity and discontinuity as well as its malleability.

CS: *Lo que estamos haciendo no es una nueva teoría.* I don't want *la gente* to think that we have come up with some new theory. In fact, *yo veo esto como un* plea to rethink educational research with the work that incorporates borderland-mestizaje feminism as well as to think it a valid option for thinking about our research.

ED: I agree and I hope that readers/researchers understand that we are not trying to offer a static, "true" notion of BMF. My concern is that, by trying to describe BMF in one chapter, we run the risk of essentializing it. Rather, *espero que,* we illustrate its complexity and inspire qualitative researchers to want to learn more and to read the primary works of those BM feminists we cite, as well as others.

CS: Excellent point! I want *la gente* to get a "feel" for this type of critical work and not the "methodological steps" to BMF. I was even scared to use words in the title such as "the new tribalism" for risk of researchers dismissing it as too ethnically driven. But I hope that the opposite is true. Gloria Anzaldúa's work was once labeled as "the new tribalism" because it was seen like too Chicana, too focused on issues that only pertain to Chicanas. However, Anzaldúa reappropriated that term to mean *we(us/they) are all* in the tribe, so in a way is a new type of tribalism.

ED: I get what you're saying, but what do you mean when you say that you want people to "get a 'feel' for this type of critical work?"

CS: Maybe I'm trying to challenge myself and others to feel and learn with the body and to embark on a bodily engagement with intellectual constructs and discourses, whether it be BMF, postmodern, postcolonial, or whatever criticalist framework. *Por eso,* when we were creating the outline for this chapter, I wanted a section on the body since it is a subtext in most Chicana feminist work. And sometimes we just have to think differently, and for me, then, it requires that I use my body and *feel* that difference. *Ay,* does this make sense?

ED: It makes sense to me, but I worry that some researchers will be resistant to explore this type of work. Part of that has to do with our training. That is, many of us have internalized the idea that research is something of the mind, not the body. It is a very different (and maybe uncomfortable) way for some of us to approach research. I think feeling uncomfortable is a good thing. Of course, we have to be careful not to assume that using our body automatically frees us from dominant and colonial research practices. I don't think it's entirely liberating or controlling, but rather a site of struggle. The fact is, I have a white body. As a white body, I really struggle with trying to (un)do research. You know that I grapple with the fact that I am a White woman engaged with BMF. I constantly ask myself how I may inadvertently trivialize BMF theory—imposing Whiteness and diluting BMF into something "nice" and "safe" for mainstream researchers. Yet, I am so drawn to it.

CS: You know it's interesting how you feel like you have a white body. I have always seen you as a woman of color. Maybe it's because you and I in many ways "see" how inappropriate research can be with children and women of color. You have what Dolores Delgado Bernal terms a cultural intuition in your pedagogy and in your research endeavors, at least with those that you have engaged with me. Having said that, I also feel like I have embodied some Whiteness and it's probably inescapable. That is why Gloria's concept of nos/otras would be so relevant in this conversation. We are never just us (*nos*) but also part of the other (*otras*). The word *nosotras* in English literally translates into "usthem," which means we or us. And no matter how much I can deconstruct White ways of being and existing, I have come to realize that I am that which I deconstruct constantly—body and mind. And you are right, the mind/body is a site of constant struggle; otherwise, our projects are just as colonizing as (post) positivist research and Euro-American male-dominated criticalist research.

ED: Yes! You know, only recently have I felt like I had a white body. My whole life I never felt "White" *porque soy morena.* However, as I became more engaged with BMF, I felt a need to disclose my "Whiteness." Maybe so people wouldn't think that I was claiming to be something I wasn't (with a Spanish-sounding surname and all)? I guess I think of myself as an ally—much like Sandoval discusses. My affinity for BMF is perhaps my way of reworking and reconceptualizing my research practices. It is my bridge to forming alliances.

CS: The first time I presented with a panel of Chicana feminists, I had to disclose the fact that I was not of Mexican descent. Actually soy *Nicaragüense!* But I have lived in Texas since I was eight years old. I absorbed the tex-mex *cultura.* And the same thing goes for me: BMF is my way of rethinking my research and pedagogical practices. You know I was told once that I had the ability to shift between and among identities. Important in BMF is the strategic essentialism or knowing when and how to move between/among identities. Sometimes I have to argue from a Latina feminist perspective but also know that sometimes that standpoint can limit possibilities instead of expanding them.

ED: I feel that this is part of my struggle to resist the "us/them" dichotomies and the identity imposed on me (and by me), which serves only to limit my possibilities. I try to continually critique the ways in which I engage in this dualistic thinking. It's not something that I will simply overcome, but rather have to continually reflect on and resist. Similarly, I try to continually critique my research and question what, how, and why I do it.

CS: A perfect example of this continuous reflection is one of the projects I am engaged in now. The purpose of the project is to identify the "needs" of immigrant mothers with regards to child care. Finding these "needs" will help us identify existing high-quality care programs and/or create new ones for immigrant mothers. I have real problems finding "needs" when "needs" are already embedded in the focus group questions. Here is where I think: Why are we doing this? Who will really benefit? Are we really going to address their needs or *our* need to get children under 5 "ready" for school? I think *otra vez,* colonizing hearts/minds/bodies with the rhetoric of finding needs. This all goes back to the value of engendering decolonizing methods, such as the ones presented in this chapter. Maybe, as we have discussed, research in and of itself *is* problematic perhaps even more now with our current political context, funding for research is not geared toward working with/for communities but more like for working on them to "fix" our perceived notions of their problems.

ED: I agree that we need to consider the possibility that research as construct is problematic. We must resist this legacy of Western modes of research—to "fix" Others. The project you mentioned is one among numerous examples of how seemingly benign research, in the name of "helping others," may serve to perpetuate hegemonic discourses and agendas. That's why we need to continually critique the ways in which our work may create privilege for some over others. So, considering your objections to this project, do you know how you might negotiate or resist this potentially colonizing agenda?

CS: One of the ways I have decided to include "subversive" acts of resistance was to bring up the fact that the initial focus group questions to me didn't seem to make sense from a Latina perspective. I use that strategic essentialism to make a point about the Euro-American-centric nature of the questions. The purpose of the project is to identify cultural practices of immigrants that could be incorporated to create high-quality early childhood programs, yet the questions are all about *early English literacy!* The questions were constructed specifically to answer the importance of early English literacy in immigrant homes. How in the world would that get at identifying cultural practices? Needless to say, after our first meeting, people (nonacademics) who are part of the steering committee in this project and work with the different immigrant populations in the area began to bring up other issues with the questions. What was so interesting was that several people began to say, "Let's just ask one broad question like—how is taking care of children different here than from your country?—and you'll see the flood gates open." Then others chimed in and said that health care was a major issue more so than English literacy. A woman who works with the Latino population suggested that the questions should be as broad as possible. What I have learned so far is that academia is disconnected from the community. Gloria Anzaldúa asks us in *Making Face, Making Soul* to de-academize theory and to connect the community to the academy. Supporting the steering committee nonacademics in this project is my way to connect the community to the academy.

ED: Did you face much resistance from the "academics" in the steering committee? It can be difficult for some folks to give up their role as the "expert" and open up to other ways of doing research. It is amazing how the ideas and questions raised by you and the nonacademics changed the entire project.

It's funny you say that about using strategic essentialism because I've been doing that lately in working with both faculty and students. I mentioned before that I've come to see myself as a "white body," so

I've tried to use that to my/our advantage. I've "played up" my Whiteness because it seems that people are less threatened by and more open to these ideas when it comes from someone they see as "like them." I wish that wasn't the case, but that's what I have experienced. These days, I feel like I have to try anything and everything to support critical work such as BMF or any social justice issue. I'm not sure if you are aware of what's happening here in Arizona, but a bill has been proposed that would ban K–12 teachers and professors in Arizona public colleges and universities from supporting or condoning any social, political, or cultural issue while teaching. Basically, banning any advocacy and all opinions, experience. All education, teaching, and knowledge must be "neutral." The bill would impose penalties (fines, firings, lawsuits) on faculty that discuss political and controversial subjects in higher education. If it passes, then how would we teach students about BMF? How would we teach students about qualitative and criticalist research? How would we teach anything? This is a disturbing, dangerous bill and one of many recent moves from the political right to eliminate any opposing views. That's why I think it is so important that we form these alliances to actively combat the push to narrow what is considered legitimate knowledge/research.

CS: To answer your first questions, no, there was not much resistance from the PI [principal investigator] because in some ways, she was aware that she knew very little about the populations. But I often wonder about the PIs that go on their sole hunch without a sounding board. And I believe that is why we currently have so much research on the deficit skills of young English as a second/third language children and such a focus on teaching parents how to interact with their children. It's a total colonization of the mind, heart, and soul. ¡*Hasta me duele!* (it hurts me).

And with regards to Arizona, I have a feeling that's where the country is going. Arizona is just the white head on the pimple. And it is scary! But this is why you are right *necesitamos,* critical research and multiple ways to push the boundaries. I think one way is to try to make our research connect with the community in all aspects but done very critically. You know, attending critical qualitative conferences was inspiring; there are many great kinds of critical research being conducted all over the U.S. and internationally from many disciplines. I have to believe *que hay esperanza.* There is hope. We just have to find resistance in small spaces, unexpected places, and in different types of locations. ¡*Que siga la lucha!*

And on a last note, *mil gracias* to C. Alejandra Elenes for her critical feedback on this chapter and her inspiring work that keeps us on our toes and pushes us to move beyond essentialist claims to/of anything!

We also thank Norman K. Denzin for his insightful feedback that helped us tremendously.

We thank all the *Chicana/Latina* scholars whose work has not only inspired us but has made our work possible.

Last, we dedicate this chapter to the late Gloria Evangelina Anzaldúa. We are forever indebted to her for her intellectual, spiritual, and carnal contributions to the field!

◘ References

Alarcón, N. (1998). Chicana feminism: In the tracks of "the" native woman. In C. Trujillo (Ed.), *Living Chicana theory* (pp. 371–382). Berkeley, CA: Third Woman Press.

Alarcón, N. (1999). Chicana feminism: In the tracks of "the" native woman. In C. Kaplan, N. Alarcón, &

M. Moallem (Eds.), *Between woman and nation: Nationalisms, transnational feminisms, and the state* (pp. 63–71). Durham, NC: Duke University Press.

Alarcón, N. (2003). Anzaldua's frontera: Inscribing gynetics. In G. F. Arredondo, A. Hurtado, N. Klahn, O. Najera-Ramirez, & P. Zavella (Eds.), *Chicana feminism: A critical reader* (p. 354–369). Durham, NC: Duke University Press.

Alarcón, N., Kaplan, C., & Moallem, M. (1999). Introduction. In C. Kaplan, N. Alarcón, & M. Moallem (Eds.), *Between women and nation: Nationalisms, transnational feminisms, and the state* (pp. 1–18). Durham, NC: Duke University Press.

Anzaldúa, G. (1987). *Borderlands/la frontera: The new mestiza.* San Francisco: Spinsters/Aunt Lute.

Anzaldúa, G. (Ed.). (1990). *Making face, making soul, hacienda caras: Creative and critical perspectives by women of color.* San Francisco: Aunt Lute Foundation Books.

Anzaldúa, G. (2000). Doing gigs. In A. Keating (Ed.), *Gloria Anzaldúa: Interviews/entrevistas* (pp. 211–234). New York: Routledge.

Anzaldúa, G. (2002a). Foreword. In C. Moraga & G. Anzaldúa (Eds.), *This bridge called my back: Writings by radical women of color* (3rd ed., pp. xxxv–xxxix). Berkeley, CA: Third Woman Press.

Anzaldúa, G. (2002b). (Un)natural bridges, (un)safe spaces. In G. Anzaldua & A. Keating (Eds.), *This bridge we call home: Radical visions for transformation* (pp. 1–5). New York: Routledge.

Arredondo, G. F., Hurtado, A., Klahn, N., Najera-Ramirez, O., & Zavella, P. (2003). Introduction. In G. F. Arredondo, A. Hurtado, N. Klahn, O. Najera-Ramirez, & P. Zavella (Eds.), *Chicana feminism: A critical reader* (pp. 1–18). Durham, NC: Duke University Press.

Bejarano, C. (2005, April). *Border theorizing methodologies to produce change "sabor" pedagogy.* Paper presented at AERA annual meeting, Montreal, Canada.

Calderón, H., & Saldívar, J. D. (Eds.). (1991).*Criticism in the borderlands.* Durham, NC: Duke University Press.

Cannella, G. S., & Viruru, R. (2004). *Childhood and (post)colonization: Power, education and contemporary practice.* New York: Routledge.

Chabram-Dernersesian, A. (1999a). Chicana! Rican! No, Chicana Riqueña! Refashioning the transnational connection. In C. Kaplan, N. Alarcón, & M. Moallem (Eds.), *Between woman and nation: Nationalisms, transnational feminisms, and the state* (pp. 264–295). Durham, NC: Duke University Press.

Chabram-Dernersesian, A. (1999b). Introduction section. *Cultural Studies, 13*(2), 173–194.

Córdova, T. (1999). Anti-colonial Chicana feminism. In R. D. Torres & G. Katsiaficas (Eds.), *Latino social movements: Historical and theoretical perspectives* (pp. 11–42). New York: Routledge.

Cruz, C. (2001). Towards an epistemology of the brown body. *Qualitative Studies in Education, 14,* 657–669.

Cruz, C., & McLaren, P. (2002). Queer bodies and configurations: Towards a critical pedagogy of the body. In S. B Shapiro & S. Shapiro (Eds.), *Body movements: Pedagogy, politics and social change* (pp. 187–207). Creskill, NJ: Hampton.

Delgado Bernal, D. (1998). Using a Chicana feminist epistemology in educational research. *Harvard Educational Review, 68,* 555–582.

Delgado Bernal, D. (2001). Learning and living pedagogies of the home: The mestiza consciousness of Chicana students. *Qualitative Studies in Education, 14,* 623–639.

Demas, E. (2004, April). *Decolonizing research: A postcolonial framework.* Paper presented at the AERA annual meeting, San Diego.

Demas, E., & Saavedra, C. M. (2004). (Re)conceptualizing language advocacy: Weaving a postmodern *mestizaje* image of language. In K. Mutua & B. B. Swadener (Eds.), *Decolonizing research in cross-cultural contexts: Critical personal narratives* (pp. 215–233). Albany, NY: SUNY Press.

Elenes, C. A. (1997). Reclaiming the borderlands: Chicana/o identity, difference, and critical pedagogy. *Educational Theory, 47,* 375.

Elenes, C. A. (2001). Transformando fronteras: Chicana feminist transformative pedagogies. *Qualitatives Studies in Education, 14,* 698–702.

Elenes, C. A. (2002). Border/transformative pedagogies at the end of the millennium: Chicana/o cultural studies and education. In A. Aladama & N. Quiñonez (Eds.), *Decolonial voices: Chicana and Chicano cultural studies in the 21st century* (pp. 245–261). Bloomington: Indiana University Press.

Elenes, C. A. (2005, April). *Decolonizing educational research and practice: Chicana feminism, border theory, and cultural practices.* Paper presented at the AERA annual meeting Montreal, Canada.

Elenes, C. A., Gonzalez, F. E., Delagado Bernal, D., & Villenas, S. (2001). Introduction: Chicana/Mexicana feminist pedagogies: Consejos, respeto, y educación in everyday life. *Qualitative Studies in Education, 14,* 595–602.

Fregoso, R. L. (1993). *The bronze screen: Chicana and Chicano film culture.* Minneapolis: University of Minnesota Press.

Gonzalez, D. (1998). Speaking secrets: Living Chicana theory. In C. Trujillo (Ed.), *Living Chicana theory* (pp. 46–77). Berkeley, CA: Third Woman Press.

Gonzalez, N. (2001). *I am my language: Discourse of women and children in the borderlands.* Tucson: University of Arizona Press.

Hernandez, A. (1997). *Pedagogy, democracy, and feminism: Rethinking the public sphere.* Albany, NY: SUNY Press.

hooks, b. (1989). *Talking back: Thinking feminist, thinking black.* Boston: South End.

Hurtado, A. (1998). The politics of sexuality in the gender subordination of Chicanas. In C. Trujillo (Ed.), *Living Chicana theory* (pp. 383–428). Berkeley, CA: Third Woman Press.

Kaplan, C., Alarcón, N., & Moallem, M. (1999). *Between woman and nation: Nationalisms, transnational feminisms, and the state.* Durham, NC: Duke University Press.

López, S. (1977). The role of the Chicana within the student movement. In R. Sanchez & R. Marinez (Eds.), *Essays on la mujer.* Los Angeles: Chicano Studies Research Center Publications, University of California.

Madison, S. D., & Hamera, J. (2006). Introduction: Performance studies at the intersections. In S. D. Madison & J. Hamera (Eds.), *The Sage handbook of performance studies* (pp. xi–xxiii). Thousand Oaks, CA: Sage.

Mignolo, W. D. (2000). *Local histories/global designs: Coloniality, subaltern knowledges, and border thinking.* Princeton, NJ: Princeton University Press.

Moraga, C. (1983). *Loving in the war years: Lo que nunca paso por sus labios.* Boston: South End.

Moraga, C., & Anzaldúa, G. (Eds.). (2002). *This bridge called my back: Writings by radical women of color* (3rd ed.). Berkeley, CA: Third Woman Press.

Moya, P. M. (1997). Postmodernism, "realism," and the politics of identity: Cherrie Moraga and Chicana feminism. In M. J. Alexander & C. T. Mohanty (Eds.), *Feminist genealogies, colonial legacies and democratic futures.* New York: Routledge.

Pasquera, B. M., & de la Torre, A. (1993). Introduction. In A. de la Torre & B. M. Pasquera (Eds.), *Building with our hands: New directions in Chicana studies* (pp. 1–14). Berkeley: University of California Press.

Pérez, E. (1991). Sexuality and discourse: Notes from a Chicana survivor. In C. Trujillo (Ed.), *Chicana Lesbians: The girls our mothers warned us about* (pp. 159–184). Berkeley, CA: Third Woman Press.

Pérez, E. (1998). Irigaray's female symbolic in the making of Chicana lesbians sitios y lenguas (sites and discourses). In C. Trujillo (Ed.), *Living Chicana theory.* Berkeley, CA: Third Woman Press.

Pérez, E. (1999a). *The decolonial imaginary, writing Chicanas into history.* Bloomington: Indiana University Press.

Pérez, E. (1999b). Feminism-in-nationalism: The gendered subaltern at the Yucatan feminist congress of 1916. In C. Kaplan, N. Alarcón, & M. Moallem (Eds.), *Between woman and nation: Nationalisms, transnational feminisms, and the state* (pp. 219–242). Durham, NC: Duke University Press.

Quiñonez, N. H. (2003). Re(writing) the Chicana postcolonial: From traitor to 21st century interpreter. In A. Aldama & N. Quiñonez (Eds.), *Decolonial voices: Chicana and Chicano cultural studies in the 21st century* (pp. 129–151). Bloomington: Indiana University Press.

Rosaldo, R. (1989). *Culture and truth: The remaking of social analysis.* Boston: Beacon.

Saavedra, C. M. (2005, April). *The body and educational research: Thoughts from Chicana feminist scholarship.* Paper presented at the AERA annual meeting, Montreal, Canada.

Saavedra, C. M. (2006). *The teacher's body: Discourse, power and discipline in the history of the feminization of teaching.* Unpublished doctoral dissertation, Texas A&M University, College Station, Texas.

Saldivar-Hull, S. (2000). *Feminism on the border: Chicana gender, politics and literature.* Berkeley, CA: University of California Press.

Sandoval, C. (1991). U.S. third world feminism: The theory and method of oppositional consciousness in the postmodern world. *Genders, 10,* 1–24.

Sandoval, C. (1998). Mestizaje as method: Feminists-of-color challenge the canon. In C. Trujillo (Ed.), *Living Chicana theory* (pp. 352–370). Berkeley, CA: Third Woman Press.

Sandoval, C. (2000). *Methodology of the oppressed.* Minneapolis: University of Minnesota Press.

Smith, L. (1999). *Decolonizing methodologies: Research and indigenous peoples.* London: Zed.

Telléz, M. (2005). Doing research at the borderlands: Notes from a Chicana feminist ethnographer. *Chicana/Latina Studies, 4*(2), 46–70.

Trinidad Galván, R. (2001). Portraits of *mujeres desjuiciadas:* Womanist pedagogies of the everyday, the mundane and the ordinary. *Qualitative Studies in Education, 14*, 603–621.

Trujillo, C. (Ed.). (1998). *Living Chicana theory.* Berkeley, CA: Third Woman Press.

Uttal, L. (1990). Inclusion without influence: The continuing tokenism of women of color. In G. Anzaldúa (Ed.) *Making face, making soul: Haciendo caras* (pp. 42-45). San Francisco: Aunt Lute.

Villenas, S. (1996). The colonizer/colonized Chicana ethnographer: Identity, marginalization, and co-optation in the field. *Harvard Educational Review, 66,* 711–731.

Villenas, S., & Foley, D. E. (2002). Chicano/Latino critical ethnography of education: Cultural production from *la frontera.* In R. R. Valencia (Ed.), *Chicano school failure and success: Past, present, and future* (2nd ed., pp. 195–226). London: RoutledgeFalmer.

Villenas, S., & Moreno, M. (2001). To valerse por si misma between race, capitalism and patriarchy: Latina mother-daughter pedagogies in North Carolina. *Qualitative Studies in Education, 14,* 671–687.

Yarbro-Bejarano, Y. (1999). Sexuality and Chicana/o studies: Toward a theoretical paradigm for the twenty-first century. *Cultural Studies, 13,* 335–345.

14

WHEN THE GROUND IS BLACK, THE GROUND IS FERTILE

Exploring Endarkened Feminist Epistemology and Healing Methodologies in the Spirit

Cynthia B. Dillard (Nana Mansa II
of Mpeasem, Ghana, West Africa)

> *In the midst of the familiar trappings of education—competition, intellectual combat, obsession with a narrow range of facts, credits, and credentials—what we seek is a way of working illumined by spirit and infused with soul.*
>
> —hooks (2003, p. 179)

> *An important component of African indigenous pedagogy is the vision of the teacher [and researcher] as a selfless healer intent on inspiring, transforming, and propelling students to a higher spiritual level.*
>
> —Hilliard (1995, pp. 69–70)

This chapter seeks to further our understanding of spirituality as it takes its place as a legitimate form of struggle in the production of knowledge and practices of qualitative research. There can be no doubt that introducing spirituality as a real and important topic in the research process invites us to reconsider deeply our positionalities in the research endeavor, to take into account new possibilities in our work, to remember intuition, and to pay special attention to what indigenous cultures can offer in terms of concrete ways to read/re-read our current situations in the world—and write them as well (Dillard, Tyson, & Abdur-Rashid, 2000). In the introduction to *The Landscape of Qualitative Research: Theories and Issues,* Denzin and Lincoln (2003) suggest that the field of qualitative research is in a "7th moment," one that typifies a crisis of representation. Furthermore, they speak of the ways that both our methods and texts "simultaneously create and enact moral meaning" (p. 7)—that is, are complexly personal, political, local, global, historical, and cultural all at the same time. However, many African ascendant[1] scholars (Asante, 1988; Cruse, 1967; Hilliard, 1995; hooks & West, 1991; King, 2005a) know that even as we recognize the messiness in interpretive practices and representations of qualitative research, there is another very fundamental crisis that goes far beyond the biographical situatedness of the researcher and the research project for us. The crisis we speak of here includes the hegemonic structures that have traditionally and historically negated and impeded the intellectual, social, and cultural contributions of African (and African feminist) knowledge. These are structures that have also negated the *spiritual* contributions of African ascendant people.

Thus, this chapter situates the crisis in qualitative research in an African and African feminist epistemological space that places spirituality at the center of the thought and discourse. I will first reflect on and discuss the concept of an endarkened feminist epistemology (Dillard, 2000) and the ways spirituality and epistemology "have tangible effects on our souls, on the material and spiritual well-being of our people and humanity" (Baba Ishangi, quoted in King, 2005a, p. 6). Honoring a long theoretical tradition of Black feminist thought (particularly in Collins, 1990), an endarkened epistemology attempts to examine the nature of Black women's knowing and the patterns of epistemology that undergird it. The second section of this chapter will examine the ways that an endarkened feminist epistemology is healing methodology and research practice when indigenous African knowledge, wisdom, and experience (in this case, from Ghana, West Africa) is the ground from which it emerges and is engaged by *both* researchers and participants as the split between them is a false one from African cosmology and perspectives. The final section of the chapter outlines what I call methodologies in the spirit. These indigenous methodologies acknowledge and affirm the shared cultural and spiritual being of African people and recognize that our collective survival depends on the methods and teachings we consciously (or unconsciously) embrace and engage. These practices/pedagogies arise from and are informed by traditional indigenous practices from both sides of the water, in Ghana, West Africa, and the United States, where I live and work. They offer counter-practices/pedagogies in qualitative research and humanizing practices/pedagogies that move us beyond thinking of research as solely academic practice, but as practice that serves humanity through the power and authority that rests within indigenous and African people.

▣ African Cosmology and Endarkened Feminist Epistemology

In my research and thinking, I have leaned on three key concepts of an African-based cosmology that are crucial to understanding the roots of an endarkened feminist epistemological stance. They are spirituality, community, and praxis (thought and action).[2]

According to Richards (1980), *spirituality* is not a rationalistic concept that can be measured, explained, or reduced to neat conceptual categories. Instead, as Vanzant (1996) suggests, it is "the truth of who we are at the core of our being . . . the consciously active means by which we can recognize, activate, and live the impartial, nonjudgmental, consistent truth of who we are" (p. xxiii). Spirituality, in African-centered thought is the very essence of African people, regardless of where we are in the world. It is a kind of cosmological spirituality that holds central the notion that all life is sacred and the moral virtue of individuals and that of the community is the same

(Paris, 1995). Martin Luther King Jr.'s enactment of nonviolence and the centrality of service to community are examples of an African spirituality, particularly in his work in the civil rights movement in the United States and its worldwide reverberations.

The second concept is *community.* Joy James (1993) argues for the theoretical and the pragmatic usefulness of pan-African experiences in her analysis of the concepts of community and praxis. According to James, a community is not bound by temporal or physical limits: Africans belong to the African community, even when not residing in a predominantly African community:

> Belonging is not determined by physical proximity. . . . You may move out of the state or the old neighborhood to "escape" your family or people, but you carry that family, the neighborhood, inside yourself. They remain your family. . . . You determine not whether you belong but the nature of the relationship and the meaning of the belonging. (p. 32)

Using this African understanding of community, there is a common theme of our ongoing need to connect the unfamiliar (whether language, traditions, or other cultural ways of knowing) to our "home" communities, communities that continue to be more expansive and generative given research connections made within the African world and beyond.

Thus, within traditional African cosmology, research and educational practice are not viewed as the luxury of a few or as alienated activity: They are *central* to the community and provide a way to realize the ideals of the community. In her groundbreaking edited volume, *Black Education: A Transformative Research and Action Agenda for the New Century* (commissioned by the American Educational Research Association and published in 2005), Joyce King poignantly illustrates the functions and challenges of African researchers and other researchers of conscience by asking a fundamental question to all who are engaged in the research endeavor: "How can educational research become one of the forms of struggle for Black education?" (King, 2005a, p. xxiv).

Activist praxis responds to King's question above, mandating research and educational practice that are concrete physical actions in service to community and beyond solely researcher theorizing. In this way, research as service on behalf of the community is indispensable to philosophizing and theorizing from an African epistemological standpoint—and activist praxis becomes essential:

> [Activist praxis] is a necessity, for it embodies active service for the good of the community and individuals within that community. . . . Theory is done from the standpoint of the individual—in relationship to community. Where you stand when you philosophize and theorize determines who benefits from your thinking. (James, 1993, pp. 33–34)

Thus, activist praxis on behalf of freedom, and with particular regard for education and research, is not a luxury from an African worldview: It is *essential.* Furthermore, I believe there is inherent goodness in the way that we, as African American women particularly, order our thoughts and actions within and through an endarkened feminist epistemology.

In articulating an endarkened feminist epistemology, I deliberately sought language that attempts to unmask traditionally held political and cultural constructions/constrictions, language that more accurately organizes, resists, and transforms oppressive descriptions of sociocultural phenomena and relationships. And language has historically served and continues to serve as a powerful tool in the mental, spiritual, and intellectual colonization of African and other marginalized peoples. According to Asante (1988), language itself is *epistemic:* It provides a way for persons to understand their reality. Thus, in order to transform that reality, the very language we use to define and describe phenomena must possess instrumentality: It must be able *to do something* toward transforming particular ways of knowing and producing knowledge.

Therefore, in contrast to the common use of the term *enlightened* as a way of expressing the having of new and important feminist insights (arising historically from the canon of White feminist thought), I use the term *endarkened feminist epistemology* to articulate how reality is known when based in the historical roots of Black feminist thought, embodying a distinguishable difference in cultural standpoint, located in the intersection/overlap of the culturally constructed socializations of race, gender, and other identities and the historical and contemporary contexts of oppressions and resistance for African ascendant women.[3] It is important for the reader to understand the relationship between Collins's (1990, 2000) notion of Black feminist thought and that of an endarkened feminist epistemology that I am putting forth. A brief description follows.

While intimately connected in our struggle to open up spaces from/through which Black women's realities are recognized as a coherent standpoint from which to address and transform inequities and social injustice, Black feminist thought and endarkened feminist epistemology arise from a coherent common ground. However, Collins's first edition of *Black Feminist Thought* (1990) did not address, in an explicit way, the more global role and nature of Black feminist thought (that is across nation-state, cultural groups, etc.). While in the second edition, Collins (2000) does attend more explicitly to the patterns of epistemology of pan-African/diasporic Black feminist thought, the goal of an endarkened feminist epistemology was to situate Black feminist thought in its diasporic milieu from its inception. In other words, through articulating the nature of truth as "endarkened," what is the nature of Black feminist thought (that is the ground from which it emerges) when placed in a global Black feminist public? That is the question that an endarkened feminist epistemology sought to address—and, given Collins's rather radical revisions in the second edition of *Black Feminist Thought,* is a current question on her mind as well.

From an endarkened feminist epistemological stance, research is defined as a *responsibility,* answerable and obligated to the very persons and communities being engaged in the inquiry. Six assumptions are inherent in an endarkened feminist epistemology:

1. Self-definition forms one's participation and responsibility to one's community.
2. Research is both an intellectual and a spiritual pursuit, a pursuit of purpose.
3. Only within the context of community does the individual appear (Palmer, 1983) and, through dialogue, continue to become.
4. Concrete experiences within everyday life form the criterion of meaning, the "matrix of meaning making" (Ephirim-Donkor, 1997, p. 8).
5. Knowing and research are both historical (extending backwards in time) and present, reaching outward into the world: To approach them otherwise is to diminish their cultural and empirical meaningfulness.
6. Power relations, manifest as racism, sexism, homophobia, and so on, structure gender, race, and other identity relations within research.[4]

In the Spirit of Her(story): Living Black Voices

Thus, an endarkened feminist epistemology has as its "project" the vigilant and consistent desire to dig up the nexus of racial/ethnic, gendered, and other identity realities, to understand how Black women particularly and Black people more globally experience the world. For feminist research to truly embrace such an epistemological stance, situated biographical accounts of Black people (what some have disparagingly referred to as personal experiences versus actual research texts), texts that explicate meanings within unequal access and/or power asymmetries (Harding, 1987), are positioned at the center of the research project. At the same time, an endarkened feminism seeks to resist and transform these social arrangements as well, seeking political and social change on behalf of the communities we represent as the purpose for our research versus solely the development of universal laws or theories for human behavior.

Articulating an endarkened feminist epistemology is clearly an act of resistance, a talking back to the oppressive and alienating conditions of Western conceptions of knowledge and the marginalization of indigenous, feminist ways of knowing and being. But what can happen when Black feminist epistemology and research are experienced in ways that explicitly make conscious the interrelationship between the spiritual and the intellectual and make the "project" that of liberation and affirmation? The outcome of such research is a humanizing and healing process that counters historical marginalization of African ascendant people's ways of knowing and being, particularly Black feminist knowledge.

At the level of representation, I now offer an impressionist tale (Van Maanan, 1988) as a way for the reader to envision what healing methodology looks like when enacted through an endarkened feminist epistemology (for other exemplars, see Hull, 2001; King, 2005a). Deeply situated in the assumptions of an endarkened feminist epistemology and arising from ongoing research and my own subjectivity as an African American feminist scholar, this tale explores how healing methodology can open the way for profound relationships with spirit in the research endeavor. Engaging a healing methodology from this stance means to embrace a research space that is both intimately meditative (that listens and heeds the wisdom of the ancestors and the Creator) and faith filled (prayerfully attentive and grateful to the spiritual world and the Creator). This tale is an example of the creation and engagement of such a spiritual space.

Contextually, the ground of this tale rests within a group of educators who made a sacred pilgrimage to Ghana, West Africa. A sacred pilgrimage is commonly viewed in religious terms: One travels to a holy land to celebrate and deepen one's personal and communal religious understanding and affiliation, a sort of grand tithing to a higher power. While these journeys most often occur in religious settings, they too can occur in educational and secular settings. And one such pilgrimage that is at once sacred, secular, *and* spiritual is in the return of African ascendant persons to the continent of Africa. I arranged this pilgrimage for a group of educators and educational professionals from across the United States who participated in a traditional African ritual ceremony of sacred inclusion: my enstoolment as Queen Mother of Mpeasem, a West African village in Ghana's coastal Central Region. Remember: From an endarkened feminist epistemological framework, research is seen as a reciprocal process. Thus, I am interested in the transformative nature and meanings of this work not only in my life as a researcher and teacher but in the lives of others (see Dillard & Dixson, 2006). More specifically, I seek in work on "both sides of the water" to open a way for relevant cultural connections and reciprocal possibilities for African people to address the very nature of domination and oppression of Black feminist and African-centered thought and indigenous cultural ways of knowing and being, through engaging indigenous and healing methodologies.

While a collective dialogue over time, this tale foregrounds Maya's voice as a participant in the research study. While it is the case that I am the teller of Maya's tale, it is a common tale of Black womanhood and spirituality, what Wade-Gayles (1995) describes as "witnessing" that Black women have engaged since time immemorial, a way of healing that we had to engage in order to "make it over." But it is through our collective and connected experience in Ghana that *both* Maya and I enacted healing methodologies—through love, reciprocity, ritual, compassion, and gratitude—that we could gain a deeper understanding of the worldwide struggle of domination for African people and heal our bodies, minds, and spirits in order to liberate ourselves, as African ascendant people. As an advocate for a revision of research practices that honor African heritage knowledge and ways of being in community with one another, I offer this endarkened story of what is possible when we center in an African homeplace, in African ritual practice, and in African thought: The outcome is one of transformation and healing of our humanity.

Cynthia and Maya's Tale of Healing Methodology

> I will cast mine eyes upon the ocean from whence cometh my help. My help cometh from [Ghana], which is heaven and earth. (Ladd, 1996, p. 8)

"Her spirit just lights up a room." "You can tell she is deeply spiritual." "That's just Maya," my students say, some with a concurrent rolling of the eyes in disbelief. "She's off reading tarot cards, doing astrology, seeing a spiritualist, or walking the labyrinth in her bare feet!" These are just a few of the many ways that Maya is described by others in the Ghana Retreat group. I have known Maya for more than 10 years, the first eight of which was as my doctoral student but all as a very dear friend. We shared a love of all things spiritual—with candles and incense, to red wine and vegetarian (often garden-grown) meals—we shared long talks about the role of spirit in our lives. We often gave gifts to one another of books and writings that inspired us: from Tolstoy to Zukav, DuBois to Thich Nhat Hanh, bell hooks to Ayi Kwei Armah. Mostly, though, we shared a love of all things African, captured in our ongoing wonderings about the deeper meanings and connections between our continental African brothers and sisters and our own relative economically privileged, deeply raced, and gendered lives as African American women, summarized by the question DuBois (1986) put forward decades before: "As I face Africa, I ask myself: What is it between us that constitutes a tie that I can feel better than I can explain?" (p. 639).

In one of our many afternoon conversations, Maya shared the origins of her desire to know this place called Africa. We sat in my house at the dining room table, surrounded by shelves of books and African art collected from time spent in Ghana.

"Oh yes, I know that longing," she says, her memory bringing a slight grimace of pain to her face:

> When I was a child, I wanted to know where my people came from and I always got answers like "from the jungle," "from slavery in the South," "from the darkest Africa." Even then, I knew that something was wrong with that.

She continues, straightening a bit in her chair, her voice more indignant.

> Other students came from Greece, London, Spain. They knew who they were, even if they didn't like it or have any connection to it. But I knew there was something wrong with the teachers' description of my homeland. I knew it.

Maya's voice sort of drifts off, a layer of pain on top, a deeper layer of confidence underneath. "I really *know* it, now." She is referring to our recent retreat to Ghana.

> When I first heard talk about the Full Circle Retreat to Ghana for your enstoolment, I was very excited and very determined to participate. I knew that it would be a tour, but it would have a more intimate and sensitive character. It would consider what I might need as an African American woman with a strong connection to that which is African in me as well as that which makes me an American. Like DuBois said: I live with these two selves and I frankly have no interest in killing off either of them! I felt this retreat would put these two selves on the path to merger because you and the Ghanaian people we'd meet have established your work together and in friendship. This was an insider's project that would allow me to have experiences in Ghana that tourists don't get to have. It was *authentic.*

Maya's desire to have both an intimate and authentic connection or relationship to the culture, rituals, peoples, and place of Ghana was clear in the descriptions of her hopes and deep desires for this pilgrimage to Ghana. I was accustomed to hearing the word *authentic* from Maya: It was a sort of mantra that seemed to guide her decisions about the level of engagement she would exercise in many areas of her life. But today I wanted to know: What made this trip to Ghana something *authentic* for her, given that she'd not even gone yet?

> You know, CBD (Cynthia). I really don't know much about African enstoolment. I know a few women who have been designated Queen Mothers of villages, but I know very little about the process, the commitment, the political structure. I just thought it was a traditional ceremony being used as a gimmick, in some cases, to get tourists' money. I never heard of what a Queen Mother did or anything. It's like too often we [African Americans] want a true experience of African culture. But on these trips to Africa, we get a watered-down experience just for tourists. That does not feed you. And I knew I didn't want to go to Disneyland!

Her reference to Disneyland as a metaphor for the sacred experiences of enstoolment of a Queen

Mother felt incongruent to me: How did she know she would not have a Disneyland enstoolment on this trip as well?

> Because *you* couldn't have a Disneyland enstoolment. Why do I know that? Because you have intimate relationships with Ghana and your village. You have spent a lot of time there. You have interacted with the people. Your relationship is built on mutual relation, reciprocity. You know at Disneyland, you give money and get a ride. It's a hollow exchange. But in Ghana, you too may use money, but the exchange is not hollow 'cuz it's like what the *Course in Miracles* says: "All that I give, I give to myself." That's why you couldn't have a Disneyland enstoolment.

Not only were intimacy and authenticity important to her encounters in Ghana, but so was *reciprocity:* the desire to share who she was at her essence with those she would encounter on the Ghanaian shores, those she considered brothers and sisters, even as she had not met them before in this life.

In terms of identity, Maya described herself this way prior to the trip:

> I am an American citizen with an African heritage, the result of the American melting pot, all colors rolled into one. Some of it is self-chosen, some of it is a forced identification with Africa and slavery.

As an African American woman myself, the heaviness of her description weighed on me too, as I prepared the way for this group of people to travel to Ghana (a place I've come to call home), but to an event that I was more ignorant about than I wanted to be: My own enstoolment as Queen Mother. I had no idea of the manner or nature of the ceremony and what I was about to subject myself to, and that made it difficult and even a little scary to fully explain the event to others. This was indeed a time when we would all have to have a little faith, to trust the evidence of things unseen.

An amazing storyteller, Maya's recollections of her experiences of the enstoolment are as vivid and colorful as the hundreds of photographs and videos that she took of the ceremony. In one of our many conversations immediately after the trip, I asked her to tell me about her most powerful remembrance of the enstoolment. Maya's enthusiasm just jumped through the phone lines:

> There were so many! The whole trip! But there's one that really captures the feeling I had while I was in Ghana and at the enstoolment. Lindsey [another participant] and I arrived early on the day of your enstoolment. You'd already been taken off to be dressed or something. Because we were there before the ceremony happened, we got to see life in the village. We saw people interacting with each other and with kids, with people passing by, as they prepared for this day. And it was not staged! *We* were a part of the environment, *we* were a part of the village. Before we knew it, we were surrounded by children. Beautiful smiling faces and reaching hands. My heart was so full of love, and a longing to respond to these children, just as it is when I interact with eager and curious African American children in the States. We took pictures of the children and let them see the digital results. They laughed with pleasure as they viewed their images and posed with us for more photos. We then saw some people gathering at the entrance of the village. When we got there, we saw that it was for the pouring of libations. I had attended many of these libations ceremonies in the States, as African Americans often begin important meetings and programs acknowledging the ancestors in pouring libations. But this was Ghana, West Africa, and I was here participating in this practice! What a powerful connection I felt to actually be in Africa taking part in this traditional act of honoring our ancestors. OUR ancestors. On my way back to the school/community center and venue for the enstoolment, three little girls took my hand and stayed with me for the rest of the day. I was not on the fringes of the ceremony: I was a part of it. People were laughing with you, dancing with you, inviting you to be a part of how things are done in this village. It was like somebody said, "Come on in to *your* neighborhood." I'd take a picture, then somebody else would take my camera and take a picture of me with the children or with some of the sisters! I was there to celebrate this merger of African and African American in this traditional ceremony, the enstoolment, where an individual dedicates herself to working for the welfare of the people in the village and the people celebrate and honor that commitment. It was not staged: *It was real.* And I had those experiences without somebody orchestrating them.

Maya's deep sense of connection in that moment was palatable in the reverent silences and pauses as she shared the story. Her voice seemed to carry a feeling of affirmation and an understanding of something being distinctly different in her experiences in the village of Mpeasem on that particular day, something she had not ever experienced in the United States in her 51 years of life. She seemed to struggle a bit with what she would say next, her voice quiet and pensive:

> You know, Cynthia, Ghanaians do not carry a spirit of rejection as many of us African Americans do. They don't know what it means to be seen as "the problem." People in Ghana certainly have problems they deal with everyday, but they are not *defined* as the problem based on their race or complexion. That is not to say that there are not . . . ethnic differences and power struggles [among different tribal groups and individuals]. But their very humanity is not seen as the problem. On the other hand, many Ghanaians were inclined to see me as Obruni[5] or as foreign and objectified me in their urgent need to make some cedis [Ghanaian currency]. I understood that and did not let it get in the way of pushing past that and developing deeper relationships and friendships with some folks and interacting on a more real level.

I was very interested in Maya's idea of "pushing past" the ways she felt objectified as an African American by some Ghanaians but found her description of the objectification to be rather contradictory with the feelings of reciprocity she had put forth earlier. How did she reconcile the desire for reciprocity with the sting of objectification?

> Do you know the movie *Chariots of Fire?* It's a film about running. There's a scene where this guy is in a grueling run. The pain and agony was just all over his face. And somebody asks: What is it that gives the man the will to finish the race? It is in the tension of what is happening that he is learning what it means to run. And he knows that the learning will deepen on the other side. That's what I mean by needing to push past and look deeper into the relationships I had and have with folks in Ghana. I understand that we are more alike than different: My spiritual understandings tell me so. We are whole, a whole people. So the other person is also changing, pushing past what he or she knows when they are interacting with me. You both have the sense that there is more to the person than you know right now. In the example I gave, pushing past means that I need to know why they call me Obruni, and what meaning that has for them. Different things have different meanings for all people. You have to push past what you initially see. Learning this has really made a tremendous impact on me. There are so many different ways to understanding a thing.

One lesson of reciprocity was particularly poignant for Maya. She had used the metaphor of lightness as a way to describe her being in Ghana and its meanings for her:

> In Ghana, in that space, I was more myself than I've ever been. That's what new experiences can do for you: Call into being aspects of yourself that no other experience can call. I don't know why I felt the way I did in Ghana. But while I was there, things were *light.* Maybe it was the burden of color that was removed. Maybe it was being away. Maybe it was seeing other ways of being. Maybe it was being in the sun. But in Ghana, I could see how people walk "lighter," how they don't carry the burdens of race and slavery. Even the way women carry stuff on their head. That stuff is heavy, but they carry it light. And I felt lighter there too. Now, I realize that, over time, that "lightness" might change, as one settles into what is not an easy life. I'm sure you feel that as you settle into a life here [in Ghana]. But as an African American woman who has grown up with all the racial images of not being pretty enough, or skinny enough or whatever, I just felt lighter there. And it was a wonderful feeling.

Time passed before Maya and I spoke again. She'd moved to West Virginia, to live and be with her mom and to prepare for one of her post-Ghana dreams: to go into the Peace Corps in Africa. Given our distance from one another (and instead of our usual lunch or dinner celebration and gift sharing together), her 55th birthday passed with me sending a box of Ghanaian food supplies that she had requested. But how I had missed deeply the sister conversations—the ongoing "re-search"—that had characterized the last 10 years of our lives. So when I called Maya for our interview (and having spent a sabbatical year in Ghana since we last talked), the first hour was about just catching up on our lives, dreams, and our work. As we finally settled into the questions, we focused on the meanings of the enstoolment trip to her current teaching and learning.

> As you know, when I was in the PhD program, I was involved in building relationships between institutions of higher education and urban public schools. Here in West Virginia, I am currently involved in administration and teaching in a child care facility. But I'm still waiting for the Peace Corps to evaluate my health status and hopefully by June, they'll assign me.

Today, I cannot read the tenor of Maya's voice as she speaks to me from West Virginia, having been there now for 8 months. There was a certain sadness, maybe touched by memories of the PhD uncompleted or by the dragging on of the requirements that continue to delay her dream of the Peace Corps. In another way, her voice seems at peace with the life that is presenting itself right now. While much simpler than the busyness of pursuing a doctoral degree and the full social schedule that was her life in Columbus, there is a contentment I cannot name. When I ask about it, she says it has something to do with the trip to Ghana and the enstoolment.

> That trip has played a significant role in helping me to understand how important it is to be *present* in my life: to see what is there, what is happening, who or what is important. We are socialized to focus on the past and future in the U.S. What is happening right now is never important enough to command our full attention. Look at people on cell phones: They are with somebody, but talking to someone else on the phone! Where we are is not where we want to be, and who we are is not who we want to be. I think it's really simple but we've made it complex . . . because living at that level of acceptance takes effort and courage and a submission to one's life. In Ghana, like I said, I felt more myself than I had ever allowed myself to be. I felt complete and whole there. I could feel it in the way I moved, hear it in my speech, observe it in my interaction with others. I was less fearful of being in my own space.
>
> One time in the market, an old man was trying to sell something and everyone around ignored him. Then he approached me. He was smelly and dirty, but I saw something beautiful in him. He unwrapped a small carving of a hand holding an egg and handed it to me. I gave him the cedis that I had left, which were not much to me, but a small fortune to him. I learned that the carving is symbolic of the delicate balance required of power and leadership. If the egg is held too firmly, it will be crushed. If it is held too loosely, it will fall to the ground and break.
>
> As teachers and in learning for ourselves and for our students, we must seek that balance. That's how this trip influenced me deeply. A teacher can only give what she knows, consciously or subconsciously, to her students. She can only give who she *is* to her students. And if she doesn't know who she is, some of what she gives will be nothing but garbage in the lives of her students. That is why life in the present moment—now—is where the important work of the teacher is done. In my work with the Urban School Initiative, my work was to develop relationships between higher education and public schools that benefited both. But I learned that those at the university have no problem getting what they need, but had a real problem in considering what others need. I made it my business to keep the focus on what K–12 teachers need to do their work with kids. That egg gave me a symbol of balance, a way to articulate that balance.
>
> In Ghana, I guess I felt that presence. As an African American, one who has had the experience of studying slavery, history, and all that—and then to stand in those places where those things happened, that's *basic.* What I mean is that it's reduced to what is crucial and critical. It makes it tangible, somehow more real. But having been in that physical space, I continue to this day to have a very spiritual experience with it.
>
> It's all about reciprocity. It requires us to listen. I now work with these little toddlers. When you listen to them, you know *when* you need to pay attention. When you see this or do this, the kids learn and smile. There's this little girl named Pinkett. She has learned that I listen to her, that I want to know what she says and means. Now she makes more of an attempt to speak, to talk more because she knows I will listen.

We can talk about the meanings of this trip to my teaching, but it is really a feeling. A knowing that goes beyond words to a level of truth. But once you know it, you are conscious of it. And you can look around and see evidence of it everywhere. I am a soul who made the pilgrimage to Ghana and I am healing from the realization and recognition of my relationship to the ancestors both there and here. But I am an American citizen (my country) with an African heritage. I am an African living outside of Africa, a part of the African diaspora. I am this flesh and bone and blood and mind and soul and spirit. I am this and so are we all. Connected. Whole. One.

Endarkened Feminist Epistemology as Methodologies in the Spirit: Guiding Principles

> Being aware of . . . spiritual experience, gathering the oral statements and written texts through which it is narrated, listening to its silences: These become the primordial duties of [research]. (Gutierrez, 2003, p. xx)

This tale of endarkened feminist epistemology points to important considerations relative to healing methodologies that truly engage the cultural knowledge, historical and traditional wisdom, and ever present spirit of Africa and her diaspora. At the 2005 Qualitative Inquiry Congress, I attended a presentation by Dr. Joyce King called "Liberating Methodology: Activist Research in the Spirit of Jemima" (King, 2005b). The session focused on the need for African ascendant scholars to recuperate identity, transform consciousness, and liberate methodologies from an African cultural and spiritual perspective. I was very much influenced and inspired by her ideas. At the conference, I'd also been reading Gustavo Gutierrez's (2003) insightful book on liberation theology, titled *We Drink From Our Own Wells: The Spiritual Journey of a People*. In this book, Gutierrez says these words: "Our methodology is our spirituality" (p. xvii). And I realized a fundamental truth about healing methodology. *Healing methodology* is both a verb and a noun: Healing *is* as healing *does*. As a noun, *healing methodology* are the indigenous practices/pedagogies that explicitly engage and enact the cultural knowledge, historical and traditional wisdom, politics, and ever present spiritualities of Africa and her diaspora. It is a "dynamic spirituality that does not allow for fixed or definitive theory that can be applied at all times and in all places" (Gutierrez, 2003, p. xiii) but is a form of struggle against domination and is "consistent with the profound indigenous pedagogical tradition of excellence in the history of African people" (King, 2005a, p. 15). Healing methodology as spirituality, then, is deeply rooted in the lived experiences of the Creator's presence within history and within the lives of African ascendant people.

However, if healing methodology is as it does, then, as a verb, it must also engage and change that which it encounters: *It must involve action*. To heal, methodology is to re-claim, re-vision, and re-cognize (that is to think again or anew with) African ascendant knowledge and experience as the epistemological and methodological frameworks and practices used in our inquiry. We must fundamentally transform what research is and whose knowledge and methodologies we privilege and engage. Healing methodology as an action is the manifestation of activist praxis from African cosmology, the act of centering our work in cultural practices that honor and respect what we know and are as African people generally and as Black feminist scholars more particularly.

In this spirit, there must be a "letting go" of knowledge, beliefs, and practices that dishonor the indigenous spiritual understandings that are present in African ascendant scholars, given our preparation and training in predominately Western, male, patriarchal, capitalist knowledge spaces and the manner in which our spiritual understandings are negated, marginalized, and degraded. Such a path has led me to attempt an articulation of what and how methodologies in the spirit would look and be, mindful of Gutierrez's (2003) words: "It is important to 'drink from our own wells,' from our own experience not only as individuals but also as members of a people" (p. xix). How, then, do we create or "be" healing methodologies that are both meditative (that is, that listen and heed the wisdom of our cultural knowledge, our ancestors, and the Creator) and faith filled (that is, prayerfully attentive and grateful to the spirits and the Creator)?

Healing methodologies, as responses to these questions, are situated: Such work can happen in multiple spaces and places where African ascendants find ourselves. And from the narrative tale above, we can see that for me—and for those I was engaged with—healing methodologies from an endarkened feminist framework involve several engagements. First of all, *one must be drawn into and present in a spiritual homeland,* in this case, in Ghana, West Africa. Second, *one must be engaged with/in the rituals, people, and places (of Ghana) in intimate and authentic ways.* Finally, regardless of positionality, *one must be open to being transformed by all that is encountered and recognize those encounters as purposeful and expansive,* as healing methodologies.

However, there are some larger principles at work in and with the processes of healing methodologies. Freire and Faundez (2000) define a method as "a series of principles which must be constantly reformulated, in that different, constantly changing situations demand that the principles be interpreted in a different way" (pp. 216–217). In other words, the challenge to us as researchers—and to our work—is to translate the fundamental principles of our method *as the situation demands,* in ways that are ultimately and intimately more responsive and responsible to multiple and diverse situations. If spirituality and transformation are central to healing methodologies, then explicit centering of methods *in the spirit,* including unconditional love, compassion, reciprocity, ritual, and gratitude, might be a response to the overwhelming negation of African ascendant and endarkened feminist epistemological knowings, through abusive hegemonic structures often masquerading as objectivity, and other forms of domination, patriarchy, and inequity that have characterized the methodologies and practice of research in the Western academy. Thus, I put forth five principles of methodologies in the spirit that have been especially powerful in helping me to, as Appiah (1992) suggests, read more productively my own subjectivities as a researcher and the spiritual world that is alive in research work in African contexts. In the spirit of Freire and Faundez's (2000) voices above, these principles are not given as the prescriptive list for all research projects: They are shared as a way to think about the spiritual nature of our projects and of healing methodologies both as a way to honor indigenous African cultural and knowledge production and as activist practice designed to acknowledge and embrace spirituality in the process of all of us becoming more fully human in and through the process of research (Dillard, 2006).

The first principle of methodologies in the spirit is *love.* According to Peck (1978), love is "the will to extend oneself for the purpose of nurturing one's own or another's spiritual growth." He continues, "Love is an act of will—namely, both an intention and an action. Will also implies choice. We do not have to love. We *choose* to love" (p. 4, emphasis added). hooks (2000) goes further, suggesting that the missing element (in research, in teaching, in life itself) is the need to engage love as the experience that creates more reciprocal (and thus more just) sites of inquiry. This includes developing the practice as a researcher of looking and listening deeply, not just for the often self-gratifying rewards of the research project, but so that we know what to do and what not to do in order to serve others in the process of research. It involves what Maya described as the deep listening that she engaged with the children in the preschool so as to invite transformative dialogue. It includes the struggles that one engages with one's identity locations, one's place in the world, one's work, one's community as we read in the struggles of identity that we heard in Maya's voice. Unconditional love also includes carefully seeking understanding of "the needs, aspiration, and suffering of the ones you love" (Hanh, 1998, p. 4). Understanding deeply the humanity of those with whom we engage in the research endeavor—whether ourselves, our participants, our students, whomever—is a necessary prerequisite for qualitative work in the spirit. And for African ascendant peoples, embracing a love ethic involves a deep understanding of the global community of

African people and our worldwide economic, cultural, social, political, and intellectual conditions and traditions, in order to transform these conditions and traditions both within and outside the academy. If we continue to offer to African ascendant communities knowledge, cultural products, engagements, and relationships that we don't need or readings and representations where we cannot recognize ourselves or see ourselves more clearly, we are not being as researchers in love with others or ourselves: From an African worldview, as Maya articulated so clearly, we are *one*. To honor love as a methodology in the spirit, we must also embrace the intimate nature of research, which ultimately forces us to surrender our sense of separateness, to see our selves in the lives of another.

Embracing compassion is the second principle of a methodology in the spirit. Compassion can be understood as the intention and capacity to relieve and transform suffering through our research work, a form of struggle against dehumanizing contexts and conditions. While in varying degrees, struggles against degradation have been a long and bitter historical reality for African ascendant people worldwide (Ani, 1994). No Black person has escaped the negation of our humanity, whether in the academy, the boardroom, on the farm, or in the streets. However, compassion as a methodology in the spirit is not a principle that suggests that we must each suffer the same to remove suffering from others. Just as doctors or nurses can help to relieve a patient's suffering without experiencing the same disease, compassion as a methodology suggests that researchers can also help to relieve communities of their suffering through the process of activist research without being crushed by the weight of suffering and being rendered unable to respond in any way. Again, as we look at the tale told earlier, the very context of my enstoolment, as an African ascendant in the United States, and our work and experiences in Ghana were filled with moments of compassion—for ourselves, for our brothers and sisters in Mpeasem, for Ghana herself in the very act of returning to Ghana for purposes of healing work. Compassionate outcomes included the celebration of the enstoolment (and all that we all learned within the experience), the supplies and equipment we brought to continue the ongoing work of the preschool in the village, even Maya's exchange with the old man at the market, to name a few. Embracing compassion in research methodologies means that one necessarily has *deep* and abiding concern for the community and the desire to bring joy to those in the community through the work that we do. As researchers, we must be culturally and historically knowledgeable about and aware of suffering, but retain our clarity, calmness, our voices and our strength so that we can, through our practice, help to transform the situation and ourselves.

The third principle to consider in methodologies in the spirit is to *seek reciprocity*. Seeking reciprocity is the intention and capacity to see human beings as equal, shedding all discrimination and prejudice and removing the boundaries between ourselves and others. As long as we continue to see ourselves as "researchers" and the other as the "researched," or as long as we continue to value an academic agenda for research as more important than the needs and desires of the community, we cannot be in loving, compassionate, or reciprocal relationships with others. As African ascendants, our collective heritage is clear: We must now engage in the dialogues and collective work of re-membering the African family, a family that was and continues to be systematically torn apart by degradation and domination. Seeing one's self as an African and all of us as spiritual beings having an earthly experience is the only way to narrow the chasm of "differences" between us that are too often the topics of our academic discussions and work—and that dishonor African cultural traditions, knowledge, and ways of being.

Fourth, *ritual* as methodology in the spirit can be understood as the intention and capacity to transcend the boundaries of ordinary space and time and the practice of unifying the human and the divine. While rituals may include the things one does as a discipline or with regularity to honor the continuous nature of those "boundaries" (for example, praying before engaging a task, lighting a candle, or regular meditation practice), I am referring here to the process and desire to recognize, in the everyday work of research, the "eternal moment" that is also present (Richards, 1980). As researchers, whether conscious or not, we are always one with spiritual reality, not removed from it, as has been the ethos of Western research traditions. And from an African worldview, when we engage in the practice of ritual in our work—in continuously and consistently re-membering (that is, putting back together) the spirit of those Africans physically deceased and who guide us from the spiritual realm, those here in the physical realm, and those yet to be born—we honor the transcendental nature and experience of research that provides the renewal of energy and wisdom necessary to be researchers who engage our craft as the intellectual *and* spiritual work that it is.

Finally, there is *gratitude,* the need to be thankful for the work of research as spiritual methodology, as a healing process for ourselves and others. Gratitude here means the quality or feeling of being grateful, of being aware and present to the deep and abiding love of Spirit, whether called God, Goddess, Allah, Buddha, or Divine Energy. It is the acknowledgment of service to "something bigger" that guides the very purposes of our research. It is recognizing, particularly from endarkened perspectives, the need to pray and bear witness to that inner power and its outward manifestations through us, as researchers who are also healers and teachers. In body, mind, and spirit, African ascendant people, then as now, bear witness and thanksgiving for the influence of Spirit in our lives. While difficult to define, we hear ourselves speaking and singing and testifying because we *must:* We are moved to do so. Engaging methodologies in the spirit of gratitude responds to our need to re-member, to put back together the pieces and fragments of cultural knowledge of Africa and her diaspora in ways that give thanks for all who have witnessed and worked on behalf of the humanity of Black people and the inclusion of our wisdom in the world's grand narrative. It is honoring the legacy of African people through the conscious connections and pilgrimage to the Motherland, not simply as takers but as givers, too. It is the ethos that guides the manner of doing and being that is embodied in the relationship between Maya, myself, Ghana, and the United States—and the possibilities for honoring African heritage and traditions of excellence as the very knowledge and wisdom that is required in the academy and beyond.

Love, compassion, reciprocity, ritual, and gratitude as methodologies in the spirit allow us to more clearly recognize humans in our various ways of being. In this way, more principled relationships can be realized—and love, compassion, reciprocity, ritual, and gratitude can be enacted in ways meaningful to African people and to others who struggle under various forms of domination and oppression. Such methodologies in the spirit also seek to honor and reconnect the African family in ways that better ensure our collective survival and contributions to the world. Endarkened feminist methodologies and methodologies in the spirit move African ascendant people—and thus *all* people—closer to the "way" that Ayi Kwei Armah (1973), our celebrated Ghanaian author, articulated in *Two Thousand Seasons:*

> Our way, the way, is not a random path. Our way begins from coherent understanding. It is a way that aims at preserving knowledge of who we are, knowledge of the best way we have found to relate each to each, each to all, ourselves to other peoples, all to our surroundings. If our individual lives have a worthwhile aim, that aim should be a purpose inseparable from the way.... Our way is reciprocity. The way is wholeness. (p. 39)

Resonances: A Postlude....[6]

A response to Armah's (1973) call for wholeness for African ascendant peoples is also a call to journey full circle. While writing this chapter, I also awaited the release of my first book, *On Spiritual Strivings: Transforming an African American Woman's Academic Life* (Dillard, 2006). And the resonances between/among its pages and this discussion of healing methodologies of the spirit were profound. At the center of the resonance was the way that revisioning one's methodologies as spiritual practice leads to a fundamental shift in the way one enacts the whole of an academic life: It is not an innocent or easy change that a person can make and continue "life as usual." Healing methodologies are also about healing one's spirit. So here, I will share a portion of the final chapter of *On Spiritual Strivings* that speaks to the nature of that transformation for me—and that may be illustrative of the depth of transformation that can come as a result of healing our methodologies.

> The phrase "coming full circle" is a very sacred phrase and is a way to express the uncovering of the very purposes and possibilities of my life generally and an academic life more specifically, having traversed the places and spaces of research, teaching and service work in Ghana, West Africa. Here, I want to explore, in a very intimate way, the meanings of these uncoverings in shaping an academic life and career. What is clear and important is to try to articulate this rather intimate understanding of full circle "as primarily a practice ordered by spirit, or authorized by spirit and executed by someone who recognizes that she cannot, by herself, make happen what she has been invited towards" (Some, 1997, p. viii). This includes a recognition that, as people of African ascent throughout the diaspora, we can only really live into our greatness when we *re-member* (that is, put back together) and respect the spirit within, our own brilliance, as human beings, and the grace inherent in the Creator's gift of breath.
>
> The idea of coming full circle came to me one day in Ghana, West Africa as I was walking through the Elmina slave dungeon with my Mom and my Aunt. In the reception area of the dungeons, there was an oil painting in very bright colors depicting a brutal scene of Africans captured and in shackles on the "final" journey through the "door of no return." (18) And a thought came into my mind that would change my life forever, and it is this: *When any person of African ascent chooses to return to the knowledge and motherland of Africa, we have in that brave act, come "full circle."* How powerful it was on that day to recognize that even those little doors of no return could not keep African people away from the place of our original breath!
>
> DuBois (1940, reprinted in 2005) asks: "What between Africa and America and my soul constitutes a tie that I can feel better than I can explain?" (p. 116). And coming full circle became a mantra, a metaphor, and a response to this question. And it is a description of the transformation that has so slowly and gracefully occurred in my academic life—and in the academic lives of many intellectuals of African ascent as we begin to make conscious and committed connections to Africa. The soul work that happens in experiences like that above in the slave dungeons—and illustrated throughout the pages of this chapter—helps me to see the way that every experience in our lives is sacred and the coming together of all of life's experiences is but preparation for what ever happens next in our lives. That is full circle work.
>
> My first trip to Ghana was with a group of educators. One of the benefits of going on an organized tour that focused on schools and educational settings was that I could see and extend my own experiences of the meanings and environments for learning, as they manifest in sites all over the country. And, as an educator, I was comfortable interacting and being primarily in primary schools and universities: While recognizably located in the cultural milieu of Ghana, they were somehow familiar, similar and known to me. And like many schools that I've visited all over the world, these sites mirrored my work in the United States as a faculty member in multicultural teacher education, preparing teachers for diverse populations of students in early childhood settings and elementary schools. But it was when I stepped outside of teaching courses at the University of Cape Coast or being with children in primary schools in Ghana and began to really *see* the country, to really talk and interact with people of various communities, I began to open to spirit, began to recognize the powerful role of Ghana and her people in my own healing (and re-search) process. Most profoundly, as I've traveled to Ghana over the years, I can better see that when one uncovers the wisdom and lessons of their ancestors and is able to make deep and personal connections with the "earth of their birth," the lessons can be transformative. Grounded in such knowledge, one can walk, teach and be in peace with self and others in more spiritual and ultimately more human ways.
>
> Because the purpose of my journey here on earth is to teach, and because I believe "guides" and opportunities for uncovering one's purpose are often found in educational pursuits, I built the preschool

in Mpeasem, Ghana that was discussed earlier. This was the beginning of work that continues to build bridges across continents, people, and traditions, to put it all back together in my life as an African American woman. However, even building the preschool, I was still within the familiar as an educator; I was still in the comfort of schools and schooling, in many ways similar to what I already know.

Coming full circle. I began to dream about the concept, about what it meant to live a life that really embraced the idea that everything was preparation for the next thing, that every mistake, challenge, joy, and life experience was preparation for what would come next. Mostly, I thought about coming full circle in terms that resonate with the academic life of research, teaching and service that I have so enjoyed. But at some level, as I look at my resume and reflect on my academic life, I have spent most of my time trying to change the academy, to create a fit between it and my understandings and realities as an African American woman. And throughout my career, I have seen this as a common pursuit amongst many colleagues of color. Whether in publication, in classes that we teach, in the everyday work in the academy, like many African ascendants, my academic life has focused on channeling my energies towards creating spaces and places and ways for people of color and others of conscious to create an academic life that resonates with spirit, with the intimate and personal understandings of how the world works (or doesn't) for African American women....

And that brings us full circle to the very purpose of teaching, research and service when spirit and African cultural knowledge and experience are at the center. For me, I've realize that if my purpose is to help others to experience the healing wisdom of Africa, Black feminist praxis, and spirituality, the academic life that I've known will not be the academic life that I am moving toward. In fact, my conscious embrace of spirit in my work as an African American feminist and critical multicultural educator may be slowly (but gracefully) moving me away from an academic life in university contexts and towards the overwhelming joy and vision of alternative contexts that bridge both the continent of Africa and her diaspora. And this transformation is bringing what a friend calls a "living sense of the alternative": The more I live and engage it, the more I know that coming full circle is the only work for us all to do.

Notes

1. In the spirit of the epistemic nature and power of language discussed by Asante (1988), Kohain Hahlevi, a Hebrew Israelite rabbi, uses the term *African ascendant* to describe people of African heritage. In contrast to the commonly used term *descendent*, he argues that *African ascendant* more accurately describes the upward and forward moving nature of African people throughout the diaspora as well as on the African continent herself. I subscribe to this notion.

2. This discussion of African cosmology is drawn largely from Dillard and Dixson (2006).

3. With early roots in the work of Barbara Smith, Akasha Hull, Audrey Lorde, and, more recently, Patricia Bell-Scott, Katie Cannon, Joy James, Ruth Farmer, Barbara Omolade, and Patricia Hill Collins, Black feminist voices argue that the very presence and positionality of Black women scholars and researchers gives us a coherent and distinctive cultural, analytical, and ideological location through which a coherent epistemology can be articulated.

4. For an in-depth discussion of an endarkened feminist epistemology, see Dillard (2000).

5. *Obruni* is a term used by many Ghanaians to refer to foreigners. The word literally translates from Twi as "white person" but is used to refer to all foreigners, regardless of skin color. Fair-skinned Ghanaians are often also referred to as Obruni, as either a way of teasing or a term of endearment.

6. The postlude is excerpted from the final chapter of Dillard (2006, pp. 109–118).

References

Ani, M. (1994). *Yurugu: An African-centered critique of European cultural thought and behavior.* Trenton, NJ: Africa World Press.

Appiah, K. A. (1992). *In my father's house: Africa in the philosophy of culture.* New York: Oxford University Press.

Armah, A. K. (1973). *Two thousand seasons.* Chicago: Third World Press.

Asante, M. K. (1988). *Afrocentricity.* Trenton, NJ: Africa World Press.

Collins, P. H. (1990). *Black feminist thought: Knowledge, consciousness, and the politics of empowerment.* New York: Routledge.

Collins, P. H. (2000). *Black feminist thought: Knowledge, consciousness, and the politics of empowerment* (2nd ed.). New York: Routledge.

Cruse, H. (1967). *The crisis of the Negro intellectual.* New York: Quill.

Denzin, N., & Lincoln, Y. (Eds.). (2003). *The landscape of qualitative research: Theories and issues.* Thousand Oaks, CA: Sage.

Dillard, C. B. (2000). The substance of things hoped for, the evidence of things not seen: Examining an endarkened feminist epistemology in educational research and leadership. *International Journal of Qualitative Studies in Education, 13,* 661–681.

Dillard, C. B. (2006). *On spiritual strivings: Transforming an African American woman's academic life.* Albany, NY: SUNY Press.

Dillard, C. B., & Dixson, A. D. (2006). Affirming the will and the way of the ancestors: Black feminist consciousness and the search for "good"[ness] in qualitative science. In N. Denzin (Ed.), *Qualitative inquiry and the conservative challenge: Confronting methodological fundamentalism* (pp. 227–254). Walnut Creek, CA: Left Coast Press.

Dillard, C. B., Tyson, C. A., & Abdur-Rashid, D. (2000). My soul is a witness: Affirming pedagogies of the spirit. *International Journal of Qualitative Studies in Education, 13,* 447–462.

DuBois, W. E. B. (1986). *Dusk of dawn.* New York: Library of America.

Ephirim-Donkor, A. (1997). *African spirituality: On becoming ancestors.* Trenton, NJ: Africa World Press.

Freire, P., & Faundez, A. (2000). Learning to question. In A. Freire & D. Macedo (Eds.), *The Paulo Freire reader* (pp. 186–230). New York: Continuum.

Gutierrez, G. (2003). *We drink from our own wells: The spiritual journey of a people.* Maryknoll, NY: Orbis.

Hanh, T. N. (1998). *Teachings on love.* Berkeley, CA: Parallax Press.

Harding, S. (1987). *Feminism and methodology: Social science issues.* Bloomington: Indiana University Press.

Hilliard, A. G. (1995). *The maroon within us: Selected essays on African American community socialization.* Baltimore: Black Classic Press.

hooks, b. (2000). *All about love: New visions.* New York: Morrow.

hooks, b. (2003). *Teaching community: A pedagogy of hope.* New York: Routledge.

hooks, b., & West, C. (1991). *Breaking bread: Insurgent Black intellectual life.* Boston: South End.

Hull, A. G. (2001). *Soul talk: The new spirituality of African American women.* Rochester, VT: Inner Traditions.

James, J. (1993). African philosophy, theory, and living thinkers. In J. James & R. Farmer (Eds.), *Spirit, space, and survival: African American women in (White) academe* (pp. 31–46). New York: Routledge.

King, J. E. (2005a). *Black education: A transformative research and action agenda for the new century.* Mahwah, NJ: Lawrence Erlbaum.

King, J. E. (2005b, May 3). *Liberating methodology: Activist research in the spirit of Jemima.* Paper presented at the First Qualitative Inquiry Congress, Urbana-Champaign, IL.

Ladd, F. (1996). *Sarah's psalm.* New York: Simon & Schuster.

Palmer, P. (1983). *To know as we are known: Education as a spiritual journey.* San Francisco: Harper.

Paris, P. J. (1995). *The spirituality of African peoples: The search for a common moral discourse.* Minneapolis, MN: Fortress Press.

Peck, M. S. (1978). *The road less traveled: A new psychology of love, traditional values and spiritual growth.* New York: Touchstone.

Richards, D. M. (1980). *Let the circle be unbroken: The implications of African spirituality in the diaspora.* Lawrenceville, NJ: The Red Sea Press.

Van Maanen, J. (1988). *Tales of the field: On writing ethnography.* Chicago: University of Chicago Press.

Vanzant, I. (1996). *The spirit of a man.* New York: HarperCollins.

Wade-Gayles, G. (Ed.). (1995). *My soul is a witness: African American women's spirituality.* Boston: Beacon.

15

AN ISLAMIC PERSPECTIVE ON KNOWLEDGE, KNOWING, AND METHODOLOGY

Christopher Darius Stonebanks

For many who are the children of immigrants or immigrants themselves to North America, the setting of parents espousing the intellectual and cultural contributions of their motherland to their adopted society is commonplace. For example, we have seen it represented by Canadian television and film artists such as Mike Myers and Nia Vardalos, each comically recounting (within an American context) their childhood experiences of endlessly being reminded by their respective Scottish and Greek "cinema parents" that everything of value came from their "home country." Much was the same in my household, where my mother's fairly constant observations that *everything* originates from Iran came to a zenith when she declared over dinner that bagpipes were invented in Persia and brought to Scotland by the Romans. This announcement was met with explosive laughter and followed by a humbling referral to sources she carefully laid out and an open-ended corroboration from our home encyclopedia; a publication that we often joked, from her interpretation, must have been a "Persian edition." Although my mother had partial support of the leather-bound tome, there was a strange disconnect between what my mother knew about the contributions of her people to the current knowledge base of North America and the kind of information that was being disseminated to us within formal and nonformal places of education. In the Middle Eastern immigrant experience, most of us have heard, to some extent, the names of Averoes, Avicenna, and/or Khayyam, some with greater connection to Islam than others, which are usually put forward to educate children of the contributions of their heritage to their new home. Most of the references we hear are set in the past, like in the opening of Tariq Ali's (1997) *Shadows of the Pomegranate Tree,* foreshadowing the silencing of a diverse civilization and narrating the destruction of centuries of learning and experiences within the Muslim culture. What remains from the past is a current silencing of Muslim knowledge or, more pertinent to this chapter, ways of knowing and the humanizing voices that derive from them.

Like many other pieces on the subject of Islam or Muslims, for instance, 5 minutes into the PBS (Kikim Media and Unity Productions Fdnt, 2002) biography on the Prophet Muhammad or five paragraphs into Armstrong's (2001) biography of the Prophet Muhammad, it takes little time until the direction sways to mention the politics and history that surround the atrocious act of 9/11, and it has taken me just under 400 words until I am obligated to do the same. For many in the "West," the effects of 9/11 have been a tragedy that has been often referred to as having "forever changed the world." For many Muslims, it was not only a tragedy but a signal of continued misunderstanding of their faith, ways of knowing, and indeed their very humanity (Kincheloe & Steinberg, 2004). These are methodological, ontological, and epistemological concerns that go beyond the Hollywood/mass media academic/ivory-tower stereotypes of the navel-gazing graduate students pondering "what exists, do I exist?" questions; rather, there is an urgency to this chapter as it is framed not only in the concerns of Freire and Said of dehumanizing the other but in the current and escalating global crisis between "East and West" as well. What's more, some readers may be put off at the connection that this chapter makes between education, Muslim ways of knowing, qualitative research, and politics, with the last item being disturbing for those teachers who believe schools to be free of political leaning. In brief, I am of the Freirian belief that "education is politics" (Shor & Pari, 1999), and for those who doubt this, North American examples can be found from Native residential schooling to the increase of science and math in the classrooms after the 1957 launch of *Sputnik*. Educators must increasingly ask themselves, "What and whose politics am I teaching in my class and to what end?"

For the sake of clarity in an era of "axis of evil"–like statements, let me elucidate on some terminology used within this chapter that discusses Muslim ways of knowing and voice. Although I will be using concepts such as "East" and "West," I do so only for the sake of simplifying the already challenging discussion. However, I still maintain that the idea of an Eastern World, Western World, Muslim World, or "an 'Arab World,' perhaps floating around somewhere between Venus and Jupiter" (Stonebanks, 2004) is divisive language that creates a "not of this world" or, perhaps better, "not of *our* world" mind-set and unwittingly or not plays into the dominant American political neoconservative-Straussian ideology of Western society building through the self-affirmation of "us" versus "them" (Drury, 1999; Norton, 2004), as well as some Islamic fundamentalists who forward the belief of "Westoxification." Similarly, the repeated message that "Allah" is the Arabic word for God or "The only God" is often lost in North America as "Allah" is often used with the intent of creating a division between Christianity, Judaism, and Islam. As my primary language of communication is English, I will use the word *God*. There is also the variance of using "Qur'an" or "Koran"; I will use "Qur'an" as it "reflects the correct Arabic transliteration and pronunciation of the word" (Abdul-Haleem, 2004, pp. xxvi–xxvii). Finally, as Hasan (2005) judiciously writes, "After invoking the name of God or the Prophet Mohammad, Muslims usually say a blessing. For God, Muslims say '*Subhanahu wa ta'ala,*' which means 'Praise the Lord.' For Muhammad, Muslims say, '*Sall-Allahu alayhi wa sallam,*' which means 'Peace be upon him.' I have left these blessings out in the text of this book in order to prevent the non-Muslim reader from becoming confused." She then continues by writing, "I encourage Muslim readers to say these blessings to themselves as they read along" (p. vii), and I encourage you, before you continue reading, and if it is your belief, to do the same.

In this chapter, I will briefly investigate the dilemma of identity and voice construction of Muslim people, within the mind of the West, from the past to the present, which continues to be profoundly influenced and projected through the master narrative of misconceptions, misrepresentations, and dehumanization. Lindemann Nelson (2001) advocates the use of "counterstory" narratives when working with groups who are dealing with damaged identities, noting that identity is "understood as a complicated interaction of one's sense of self and others understanding of who one is" (p. xi). In this framework, the counternarrative is used to empower and repair group and individual damaged identities that have derived from the dominant group constructs of identities of certain people through their socially shared narratives or master narratives. To repair the damaging narratives, Lindemann Nelson calls for oppressed groups to confront the master narratives by developing their own, thereby becoming "narrative acts of insubordination" (p. 8). Considering this, if the desire is to truly develop counternarratives that are authentic to the richness, oneness, and diversity of Islam, before examining this quandary that faces our classrooms, theory and methodology must be considered in relation to the Muslim experience and knowledge—specifically carrying out research that is ethically just and following the way of the Prophet Muhammad, beneficial to the Ummah (as a global Muslim community and collective consciousness, including those Muslims living in diaspora). This is a perspective on theory and methodology development that advocates against the popular perception of Muslim ways of knowing as being set within a backward-looking reaction to a Western concept of modernism and enlightenment that is monolithic, antimodern, premodern, and/or irrational, rather insisting that Muslim "ways of knowing" are both complex and diverse. Much of our formal and nonformal sources of education in the West promote the position that an achievable knowledge that is both universal and unbiased is fundamentally a product of the European mind, whereas Indigenous knowledge is mired in such descriptors as backward, one-dimensional, quaint, and ultimately inferior (Semali & Kincheloe, 1999). In this environment, Muslim perspectives are reduced in many forums to that of the irrational monolith as opposed to intellectual contributions that should be weighed on individual merit and balanced with the Muslim collective experience.

With the understanding of the variation and connections between Islam, the religion; Muslims, the followers of Islam; the cultural association of being born of and/or within the context of a family and/or community belonging to that which is associated with the Islamic faith and/or Muslim culture and the many variations of individuals and/or groups that are self-described or defined by others as Muslim, I connect Muslim ways of knowing to Indigenous ways of knowing primarily through the shared relationship with the ongoing experiences of colonialism and imperialism. It is important to note that, as Choudry (2006) writes, we must "frame Indigenous Peoples' struggles in an understanding of rights to self-determination in the context of ongoing colonialism, rather than viewing colonialism as a historical event" (p. 1). The history and current unequal relationship that has developed and continues to arise through colonialism and imperialism does indeed frame the Indigenous experience and is a current circumstance (Smith, 1999). This is a shared experience between many peoples that has not stopped at physical, ethnic, cultural, or religious borders, as can be made evident from many Indigenous people's use of Said's (1978) concept of "Other," for instance, examining the past and present Aboriginal experiences within North America compared to one's own Middle Eastern Indigenous understandings.

With this in mind, I contend that although I recognize that Muslim ways of knowing are both deeply connected and guided by Islam, within the divergences of Muslim voices, they cannot be understood apart from historical analysis, contextual perspectives, and, notwithstanding its diversity, a continually changing and emergent collective consciousness, much of which has stemmed from the experience of colonialism and imperialism. In this chapter, I invite the educator, Muslim or non-Muslim, Indigenous or non-Indigenous, who is interested in the use of exploring critical research to become a part of the dialogue in creating methodologies that can reflect Muslim ways of knowing and develop desperately needed humanizing voices in order to build a transformative classroom for social justice. In effect, I suggest that all educators endeavor to be teacher-researchers (Kincheloe, 2003).

Teacher as Researcher

As educators and qualitative researchers, we have a moral obligation to provide an avenue to allow the legitimate and free narrative of Muslim people (a significant population not only in a global sense but within North America), to be understood and heard within our society and provide a path to the diversity that exists while acknowledging the presence of the growing, diversely ethnic Muslim collective consciousness and knowledge. This obligation is forwarded with the intention of promoting Freire's transformative classroom, in which recognition of Muslim ways of knowing in our schools will lead to a critical consciousness that moves away from dehumanizing. My hope is to build upon Semali and Kincheloe's (1999) "belief in the transformative power of Indigenous knowledge" and examine "the ways that such knowledge can be used to foster empowerment and justice in a variety of cultural contexts" (p. 15). Teachers are in a unique position in our society to be at the forefront of such transformation and have the ability through their own classrooms to be actively conscious of social injustices, carry out research, and, with their students, work toward positive change (Kincheloe, 2003). The possibilities are present, and it is up to the individual educator to decide to what degree he or she wishes to be an agent of reproduction (realizing, of course, there are many positive elements of our society we *do* want to reproduce) or transformation (realizing, of course, there are many negative elements of our society we *do not* want to reproduce). In regard to the subject matter of this chapter, the first step toward creating the transformative classroom is to identify the negative imagery that silences Muslim perspectives and diminishes their presence and ways of knowing in schools.

I write this chapter with the hope of inspiring the teacher, in the spirit of Freire and the "teacher-researcher" (Kincheloe, 2003), who places importance on discovering the educational path her or his class should take despite and/or because of the dehumanization and miseducation that is prevalent in regards to Islam, as religion, culture, and people. My interests lie in perspective, voice, identity, and how they connect to ways of knowing. Especially as they relate to the educational context of the relationship between the student and schools, including the hidden and explicit aspects of curriculum (Apple, 2004) that place greater and lesser importance on differing sets of knowledge, the development and implementation of value-laden policies (Taylor, Rizvi, Lingard, & Henry, 1997), and the conscious, unconscious, and/or dysconscious miseducation (Kincheloe & Steinberg, 2004; King, 1991) that occurs in both our formal and nonformal locations of North American "learning." All of these issues have an impact on the identity of the minority student and his or her ability to comfortably and safely forward his or her narrative and ways of knowing within these settings.

Within the current global context, these areas of investigation have taken greater meaning for Muslim youth, especially those in the already significant and growing diaspora, as they struggle to define meaning in self, their religion, way of life, community, and knowledge all the while being bombarded with a multitude of multimedia entertainment images (Shaheen, 1984, 1991, 2001), a news media (Fairness & Accuracy in Reporting [FAIR], 2001), and an education system (Kincheloe & Steinberg, 2004) that consistently controls and dictates the portrayal of Islamic faith and Muslim culture and people in a negative manner. I write this chapter because all of which I have written has been a part of my own experience as well as the experience of many Muslim children I have observed attending schools in North America. In effect, like many others who write about Indigenous and/or epistemological issues, I acknowledge my own voice within the text.

"Value-free research is impossible" (Denzin, 1989, p. 23) was the motto during my graduate studies at Concordia University's Department of Education in the early and mid-1990s. Many of my professors at the time encouraged the principles of Denzin (1989) and Eisner (1990) and the idea that acknowledging one's values and subjectivity within one's research allowed greater understanding to the reader. The idea that all researchers, whether they be professional or student, bring their preconceived notions, prior knowledge, culture, and/or theoretical leanings on the subject to be studied with them has become understood, and researchers are acknowledging this by revealing their background to their readers so that the textual experience will be that much richer, of course, being mindful of not falling into the trap "of simply saying, 'But enough about you, let me tell you about me'" (Apple, 1996, p. xiv). In past writing, I have welcomed the reader to an insight of who I, as the author of the text, am (Stonebanks, 2004, 2008), and the forthcoming narrative, I hope, also adds to this disclosure within my research.

In many ways, stemming from my own experiences, this piece of writing is my exploration to encourage that methodology respects Islam and the variety of Muslim people's perspectives on knowledge and knowing. In presenting his own relationship with Islam, Said (2002) explained, "True, I was born in the Muslim world, and culturally my Christian Arab Palestinian parents grew up steeped, as every Arab was, in Muslim culture" (p. 69). Said connects culture with religion, and in my own life experience, growing up with relatives who were, in their multiplicities of approaches and commitments, Muslim also steeped me in this culture. This is as inescapable as being exposed to Christian culture in the West; one becomes "steeped" in the culture and the people with and/or without conscious effort. In this spirit, then, it should also be noted that despite my own education and teaching regarding or relating to religion, in light of those who truly dedicate their lives to the specific studies of Islam, I am by no means part of the very elite group that are experts on the Qur'an.

> He created man from a clinging form. (96:2, The Qur'an, translated by Abdul-Haleem, 2004)

Human embryology, botany, and astronomy are some of the many revelations renowned to be found within the Qur'an, and the depth and breadth of Islamic scholarship dedicated to pursuing this knowledge is far too vast to do it justice within the brief scope of this chapter and beyond my comprehension of the Qur'an. Reading the Qur'an leaves me baffled by its wealth, appreciative of its teachings, and, above all, when appropriate time permits, encouraged to return to it. Often, when I reach a point of contemplation or confusion while reading the Qur'an, I turn to biographical accounts of the life of the Prophet Muhammad and, in reading about his life, the context of his living and his actions; I gain greater appreciation of the Qur'an. Like many others in search of possible truths and meanings, I am a neophyte. I am also, among many other things, an educator, a qualitative researcher, and a person born of Iranian and European parents, raised in North America and painfully aware of the West's profoundly negative comprehension of Islam, Muslims, Iran, the Middle East, and their cultures. With an understanding of the presence of subjectivity in any research, I acknowledge that the experiences of being "half and half" (O'Hearn, 1998) place the perspectives of this writing firmly within this context. Much of this chapter stems from living in these two cultures and recognizing that the voices we (both Muslim and non-Muslim), in the West, hear in regard to Islam are, for the most part, harmful. For Muslim narratives to begin to enter the collective consciousness of the West, we must develop methodologies that value the knowledge of Muslims for the research to be truthful, ethical, and, in the way of the Prophet Muhammad, beneficial to the Ummah (again, as a global Muslim community and collective consciousness, including those Muslims living in diaspora). Having said this, perhaps in the current contexts of allegations of "axis of evil," "evil doers," and "holy wars," more people should partake on the journey of discovery instead of living in the vacuum of extremes that has led to unethical representations and actions. With this in mind, I forward my own narrative of my experience with Islam as an example of developing ethical counternarrative voices that benefit our communities.

Narrative: *Mamanjoon*

My most vivid early childhood memories of summer take place in Iran. More specifically, in a district of Tehran called Niavaran, which, at the time in the early to mid-1970s, can be described as a dichotomy between affluent homes, containing lush gardens and opulent pools surrounded by high walls, and the modest two- or three-storied apartment complexes and empty fields that filled the expanses between the prosperous residences. It is hard to explain the sharp contrasts to your senses as you step from outside the high gates, the flowers, the tall fruit trees, the freshly sprayed stoned walkways, the splashes of jumping goldfish, the gentle chiming of metal spoons against tea-filled glass, the familiar and soothing but mostly incomprehensible song of adults speaking Farsi into the dry streets, the humble homes, the sandy fields, and, if you were lucky, the passing children, their recognizable laughter and chatter, who shared your features and part of your heritage but were separated from you by language and a long-established social status you knew nothing about. Outside the walls, a longing, excitement, uncertainty, and wonder; inside the walls, a sense of belonging, boredom, family, security, and love. My mother took my siblings and me to Iran on a regular basis, and the central focus of that trip was our *mamanjoon,* our grandmother.

Memories of mamanjoon were also filled with sensations; warm touches, gentle smiles, and, of course, comforting smells associated with cooking. We were separated by language but that did not stop her from talking to me. An aged frame moving from task to task, she would maintain a continuous private conversation with me, periodically interjecting laughter after the recognizable linguistic pattern took the form of questioning or statement making. Already in her eighties when I became cognizant, she was a central role model in my life as I'm sure she was to all of my immediate family. She would project a feeling of absolute love for you despite the cultural and language differences, and, for my part, nothing symbolized this more than when I would watch her pray.

Although the schedule of her prayer customs was lost on me at the time, in retrospect I can remember her being quite diligent about quietly slipping away from the family to prepare herself to commit her faith to God. Of course, for a child raised in the northern climate of Canada, afternoons were not a time of prayer, reflection, or rest—rather, a time to play before the impending setting sun set off your parents' instincts for the routine of bedtime preparation. In the hot sun of Tehran, I would resist my mother's and aunt's insistence for naptime and would myself sneak away to continue trying to find something to amuse myself within the solitude of those walls, and in that pursuit I would often and consistently find mamanjoon in prayer.

Some of the images have been clouded over time, most significantly the meticulously noted step-by-step movements and process of prayer as spoken in the Qur'an were, I'm certain, faithfully adhered to in her ritual. Even the recital of her prayers was lost to me, as I unfortunately did and do not speak Arabic, nor was the importance of her words ever translated for me. For my part, I cannot authentically reproduce in the written word what mamanjoon achieved every day as testament to faith, based on her years of practice, experience, and learning. What I can speak about are the memories that have endured and the relationship we had while she prayed. It is difficult to describe the dignity and serenity of watching your grandmother pray. As a child who was not accustomed to the practice, save the occasions I saw my aunt pray, it seemed an event solely devised between her and God. Growing up in a Christian community and school system, but not as a Christian, I knew enough to understand she was communicating with God, but the tradition itself did not have the greater societal connection to me than, let's say, the neighborhood showing up for the annual elementary school Christmas concert (where I would habitually be cast in the role of cowering shepherd dressed in my bathrobe). For some reason, I don't remember seeking out my grandmother; however, it would seem that, at least once a day, I would always turn a corner and find her in prayer. Kneeling on her small Persian carpet and quietly reciting, she would be wrapped in the traditional Iranian chador that would frame her face, emphasizing her beauty, devotion, and age. Even with her eyes closed, she knew I was there, but she would not break from the ritual. I would watch passively for a short time, watch her hands go up and then down, then stand up and kneel back down and, from the kneeling position, bow her head and touch her forehead to her praying stone, or what I recently found out from my mother is called a *mohr.* I would lie down on my stomach directly in front of the mohr and quietly watch her, trying to be respectful, but too restless to understand what could possibly be more important than her grandchild. Most of the time, I would try and make eye contact with her, keeping pace with her movements and noticing how she would keep her eyes closed. Invariably, the mohr itself would grab my attention and I would start pushing it around the carpet, patting it back and forth and sliding it between my hands like a cartoon kitten playing with a ball of yarn.

In the kneeling position, she would continue her soft recitation, now aware that I had probably picked up the mohr and was examining it more closely, perhaps imagining what it was made of or what function it could personally serve. The prayer and movements would continue; the once relaxed eyes were now kept closed with concentration, and the crease lines became more pronounced. Her recitation became more well defined, and at the corner of her mouth curved a slight smile and one eye slightly opened to see where her mohr had now been placed by her unknowing grandchild. Again in the kneeling position, her hand would gently come out and try and locate the mohr, touching the carpet in hopes it had been returned to proper proximity. The words would continue, her eyes more open as she would see the mohr in my hand and try and time her prayers to reach out to take back her praying stone and return it to its rightful place. More often than not, with her concentration broken, you would find her kneeling on the carpet with her hands on her knees, laughing while simultaneously chastising me in a language I could not fully understand for once again disturbing her prayer. Always gently and tenderly, the mohr would be taken from my hand, and the immediacy, but not the loving tone, of her voice would signal that it was time for me to leave her to her prayers.

For many years, this was the face and spirit of Muslims in my mind; a caring and loving grandmother in prayer who would patiently endure the distraction of her half-Iranian, half-European grandson. Years later, when I would fondly recall these episodes with my mother, she would reveal that the encounters had even greater significance given the importance the Shiites place on undisturbed prayer. Patience, love, and a word that has escaped the Canadian debate on multiculturalism that stands higher than "tolerance" describe this woman of the Islamic faith. Despite the Western portrayal of Muslims during and after the Iranian Revolution, the most recent Intifada, the Reagan-era conflicts with the Middle East, Gulf War I, and many more, mamanjoon was the personal narrative I would share that described Islam. Given the opportunity to write about Indigenous knowledge, this is where I would have wanted to take the dialogue on voice, narrative, and ways of knowing. If she were in front of me, I'd ask her for her story, I'd ask her why did she demonstrate such love for this grandchild, who was half European, was not being brought up as Muslim, did not speak Farsi, did not share many of her customs, had no understanding of her history, and did not even know how inappropriate it was to interrupt her daily prayers. What created such affection and tolerance in her? Was it learned from her own family? Was it the teaching that was provided to her from God through the Prophet Muhammad? This is the voice I would want to know more about, to share; however, in the current context, I do not think I am at liberty to let a narrative like this stand on its own. In the flurry of negative responses and sentiments toward those who were perceived as being Muslim, Arab, Middle Eastern, or the wide categories and descriptors that were associated with being part of that Other (Said, 1985) belonging to those who committed 9/11, my response, for a time, was to describe my grandmother. Without even being able to communicate with me, as far as I was concerned, she was the picture of Muslims and the reflection of living life as taught by the Prophet Muhammad. Some would listen, but in a time when even the most educated and well meaning still refer to Muslims as "Muhammadans," many would have nothing to do with a gentle, tolerant, and loving descriptor of the religion, its people, and the culture. In effect, what I *knew,* what I *lived* about Islam, its people, its history, was and still is not acceptable dialogue or way of knowing in the post-9/11 climate where the distortion of the Other and consequently the Muslim sense of self continues to worsen in both formal and nonformal locations of education.

▣ Distortion of Humanity

> I maintain that if pedagogy involves issues of knowledge production and transmission, the shaping of values, and construction of subjectivity, then popular culture is the most powerful pedagogical force in contemporary America. (Steinberg, 2004, p. 173)

Steinberg (2004) writes of Muslims being Hollywood's enduring "desert minstrels," relegated to film characters that are ignorant, scheming, violent, or silent, and notes the profound influence that media have on shaping perspective and consciousness. Teachers, television, movies, comic books, parents, peers, and more all play an important part of ascribing and/or confirming how one sees oneself and how one should view others. As a minority student, it was painfully obvious that this relationship was unequal, especially considering the 1970s, 1980s, and 1990s had virtually no popular media that tackled issues of "Middle Eastern," South, or West Asian racism and oppression. The only representations we saw of ourselves were predominantly negative (Shaheen, 1984, 1991, 2001). The Canadian Islamic Congress (CIC) published a report in 2005 summarizing the Canadian media portrayal of Muslims in 2003. Using the term *image distortion disorder,* coined by physician LeNoir, to explain how "most of the images that one ethnic group has of another are developed by the media" (Lenoir, as cited in Solomon, 2002), the CIC examined the negative effects this has on our society, particularly our Muslim youth.

> The distorted perception that Islam condones and encourages violence is largely created by the media and it leads to societal anxiety among Canadians. This is called "image distortion disorder." Image distortion disorder is particularly dangerous in Canada, with its substantial multi-ethnic, multi-faith, and multi-cultural populations. Among most Canadians who have not knowingly ever met a Muslim in person, there is high likelihood that their perception of Muslim Canadians will be distorted. . . . Young Muslim Canadians of dark complexion, especially women with hijabs (traditional head coverings), or males with full beards, are particularly vulnerable to anxiety, fear and discrimination because of society's perception that their religion is violent, backward, restrictive, fundamentalist, and intolerant of opposing or alternative viewpoints. (CIC, 2005)

From disparaging accusations from North America's popular punditry and leaders regarding the Prophet Muhammad to the political and media-frenzied prelude to Gulf War II, Muslims have struggled to have their voices and perspectives heard or reflected within the public setting and popular mediums. The media shape our view of Islam and the Muslim people (Kincheloe & Steinberg, 2004), and whatever little doubt of their power and the scope of their message they could sell to the West that should have left us after the first Gulf War was put on the market through the provocative image conjuring—false narratives of Arab soldiers killing babies brought to us with the help of the public relations firm Hill and Knowlton (MacArthur, 2004). Regan's (2002) account of his brother's reaction to this "news" echoes the many responses I witnessed from peers when, at the time of Gulf War I, I was completing my undergraduate degree.

> More than 10 years later, I can still recall my brother Sean's face. It was bright red. Furious. Not one given to fits of temper, Sean was in an uproar. He was a father, and he had just heard that Iraqi soldiers had taken scores of babies out of incubators in Kuwait City and left them to die. The Iraqis had shipped the incubators back to Baghdad. A pacifist by nature, my brother was not in a peaceful mood that day. "We've got to go and get Saddam Hussein. Now," he said passionately. (Regan, 2002)

Absent from the postwar dialogue and counternarrative, at least in the larger collective consciousness of the West, was that these incidents never occurred and were fabricated to play upon not only the sympathies of the West but their bigotries as well. Yes, as MacArthur (2004) notes, there were some dissenting voices that pierced the cacophony of outrage, but they usually appeared buried "on page 13" (p. 67). I too remember pointing to newspaper pieces refuting or correcting the initial claims of Iraqi soldiers killing babies that appeared in the back pages, tightly worded documents with little of the value-filled descriptors and inflammatory language that existed in the original news pieces that drove us to war, but it had little impact on the twenty-something age group, non-Muslim, non–Middle Eastern friends I showed them to. The usual reaction was, "what's done is done" or "Well, Saddam was a bad man." From an Eastern perspective, the sense of confusion and anger over this page in history is augmented given that, as MacArthur points out, "This is not to say that babies did not perish by removal from their incubators during the Gulf War" (p. 76). MacArthur quotes an article from the *New York Times* where a Dr. Qasm Ismail, director of Bagdhad's Saddam Pediatric Hospital, recounts the first night of the allied bombardment. The doctor describes "the panic that ensued from the explosions and loss of electricity" (p. 76).

> Mothers grabbed their children out of incubators, took intravenous tubes out of their arms. . . . Others were removed from oxygen tents, and they ran to the basement, where there was no heat. I lost more than 40 prematures in the first 12 hours of the bombing. (MacArthur, 2004, p. 76)

Many of us with roots in the East wondered, "Where is the outrage, and when exactly is it all right to kill babies?" MacArthur's (2004) book, *Second Front,* chronicles the buildup to both Gulf Wars and the complicity of the media to repeat what their government (in the case of Gulf War I, Canada should be included) provided to them. The fact that this occurs within our Western societies should not be a shock to anyone who has even paid the slightest of attention to Chomsky and Herman's (1988) *Manufacturing Consent,* in that public approval and information are manufactured through a continuous and repetitive barrage of images and facts that are controlled by the agreement and approval of the privileged. What is perhaps more concerning is that much of this plays off the racism that exists in the Western collective consciousness against Muslims. The Program on International Policy Attitudes' (2003) study on *Misperceptions, the Media and the Iraq War* revealed that misperceptions derived through the news media contributed significantly to the American public's positive support for the war. Respondents to the research were taken from a randomly selected U.S. nationwide poll, and we can assume that people who work in education would also be part of this survey. Teachers, like any other member of our North American community, are not exempt from these powers of persuasion, and they, in return, reflect what they have consumed to their classroom. In Canada, knowing the extensive access to American news media, we are not free from this power of perception making, and being aware of the influence is essential in a democracy given the possible outcomes. As I write this chapter, more than 2,700 American soldiers have died (*The Washington Post,* October 2006), the minimum amount of Iraqi civilian deaths are numbered conservatively at 43,850 (Iraqibodycount.com, October 2006) to the staggering number of 655,000 (Burnham, Lafta, Doocy, & Roberts, 2006), we have no idea how many Iraqi soldiers have died, and the number of innocent civilian Afghanis that have been killed is difficult to access and confirm given the prevailing North American government stance on the subject.

> Gen. Tommy Franks, the top officer in the U.S. Central Command for the wars in Iraq and Afghanistan, summed up the American military's attitude when he told reporters during the Afghan campaign, "We don't do body counts." (Canadian Broadcasting Corporation News Online, 2005)

Given these lost lives, it seems imperative that as educators, we not contribute to perpetuating miseducation; rather, we should create solutions that create dialogue and understanding of the East, as well as provide an atmosphere where the Middle Eastern/Muslim/American/Canadian student is safely allowed to promote his or her perspectives and promote a curriculum that values or, at the very least, makes room for their Indigenous knowledge. The challenge is not an easy one, as the current conditions in the West make this difficult to promote. However, the danger in not addressing these dilemmas is admitting complacency in some of the worst aspects of social reproduction, contributing to stereotypes, prejudice, and the silencing of counterperspectives.

▣ Researcher's Preconception

The challenge to develop legitimate Muslim counternarratives in the West is even more daunting considering Vakily (2001) notes that methodological approaches to the study of Islam have been problematic due to the lack of objectivity on the part of the researchers, most of whom come from a Christian background. I take the use of "Christian background" in the sense that the researcher does not have to be a practicing Christian, per se, but raised and educated in an environment where Christianity is the unquestioned norm. In this atmosphere, the researcher is not only exposed to an experience that validates his or her own religious affiliations but, if not overtly taught against, can develop misconceptions over others. It is an ongoing process that Steinberg (2004) asserts prepares the Western collective consciousness for a distortion of the "Middle Eastern" or Muslim into the "bogeyman" (Abukhattala, 2004) and is persuasive enough to affect the researcher. Armstrong (2001) observes in the first paragraph in her book, *Muhammad, a Biography of the Prophet,* "For some time, I had been disturbed by the prejudice against Islam that I so frequently encountered, even in the most liberal and tolerant circles" (p. 11). Rogerson's (2003) biography of the Prophet Muhammad weaves a narrative that is both humanizing and inspiring of the Prophet's life. Although Rogerson's respectful admiration of the Prophet Muhammad stems from, what he calls "a good story" (p. 3) (and it should be noted that Rogerson does mean story in the narrative sense and not in the fictional manner), he acknowledges that it is a narrative that is vilified in the West:

> Try drawing a picture of a man wrapped in a cloak and lost in thought and introducing it to a classroom of schoolchildren or at a pub quiz night. Ask who it is meant to be, and what do you get? Dracula, Darth Vader or a Dark Rider from *The Lord of the Rings.* If you add a turban, the picture will most probably be taken for that of a wicked vizier or a Barbary pirate. Within Islam, however, he represents almost everything of human value. (p. 3)

The distorted image of the Prophet Muhammad, the very one often referred to by Muslims as "the perfect man," goes hand in hand with the West's distorted perspectives of the way he led his life as well. In September 2002, the politically influential Pat Robertson on Fox news said the following about the Prophet Muhammad: "This man was an absolute wild-eyed fanatic. He was a robber and a brigand. And to say that these terrorists distort Islam, they're carrying out Islam." If, as Bloom's (2005) writing so convincingly states, the American construct of (the Prophet or the Christians' the Lord) Jesus represents, among other things, someone who is "known intimately, as friend and comforter" (p. 25), then the West's creation of the Prophet Muhammad is the polar opposite. The September 2005 Danish *Jyllands-Posten* publication of the cartoon of the Prophet Muhammad is a current example of the double standard of representation as the newspaper in 2003 refused to publish cartoons lampooning the resurrection of Jesus Christ, responding to the artist who submitted the work, "I don't think *Jyllands-Posten*'s readers will enjoy the drawings. As a matter of fact, I think that they will provoke an outcry. Therefore, I will not use them" (Fouché, 2006). Incidents such as this occurred frequently during the buildup to both Gulf wars and the war in Afghanistan (often forgotten is the civilian death toll in Afghanistan that has superseded the tragedy of 9/11), with media and pundits misrepresenting Islam, its people, and its history while manufacturing consent for great suffering of Muslim people and denying their voice. Said (1998) observes that since the eras of European (and North American) colonialism and imperialism, when tensions grew between the West and *their* Islam, social and humanistic sciences, with their "objectivity" and "scientific impartiality," were used to cover their "deep-seated" prejudices about Islam and Muslim people: "In such a context both science and direct violence end up by being forms of aggression against Islam" (p. 7).

This is not to suggest that the dilemma of engaging in research reflecting Muslim ways of knowing is problematic only to the Western non-Muslim. Al-Attas (2002) states that through the process of colonization, the Western worldview dominated over the Muslims intellectually. Lamenting this effect, Al-Attas writes, "The dissemination of the basic essentials of the Western world view and its surreptitious consolidation in the Muslim mind was gradually accomplished through the educational system based upon a concept of knowledge and its principles that would ultimately bring about the deislamization of the Muslim mind" (p. 114). In response to this dilemma came Al-Attas's call in the late 1970s for the de-Westernization of knowledge.

Considering Theory and Methodology in Relation to the Muslim Knowledge

> I venture to maintain that the greatest challenge that has surreptitiously arisen in our age is the challenge of knowledge, indeed, not as against ignorance; but knowledge as conceived and disseminated throughout the world by Western civilization; knowledge whose nature has become problematic because it has lost its true purpose due to being unjustly conceived, and has brought about chaos in man's life instead of, and rather than peace and justice. (Al-Attas, 2002, p. 146)

Concentrating on the idea of "objectivity" and "scientific impartiality," the question asked is what has Western research, the researcher himself or herself, done to improve the lives of those being researched. Smith (1999) asks of the researcher, "Is her spirit clear? Does he have a good heart? What other baggage are they carrying? Are they useful to us? Can they fix the generator? Can they actually do anything?" (p. 10). Smith acknowledges that many of the researchers who have worked in Native communities have been well liked but is quick to add that despite the massive amount of research that has been carried out among Indigenous people, few positive results have been seen within the communities, and much is the same in the Muslim communities as well. Drawing upon Said's (1978) concept of an "Othered" representation of the researched, Smith candidly questions the right and motives of non-Indigenous researchers and the relevance of their Euro-centered research methods, in effect questioning the continued use of the "Orientalist" perspective. Recently, Said (2002) wrote on this subject "that Orientalist learning itself was premised on the silence of the Native . . . presenting that unfortunate creature as an undeveloped, deficient, and uncivilized being who couldn't represent himself" (p. 71). Although Said observes that some forms of representation regarding certain ethnic/racial groups from Occidental researchers are now considered politically incorrect—for instance, "it has now become inappropriate to speak on behalf of 'Negroes'" (p. 71)—and even though Said calls for the same respect for those who are still considered Others, it has yet to happen. If the hope is for research to benefit the community, then given the current tragedies relating to the Muslim communities, there has been a failing in representation that allows this to continue with very little concerns of humanity.

To develop counternarratives that are going to bring humanity to a people and religion that have been dehumanized, the researchers have to make a paramount step and ask themselves if they can account for their spirit and heart, ask themselves if their research is ethical, ask themselves if it pays its due respect to the beliefs relating to Islam, ask themselves whether it accounts for the context of the Muslim experience, and, finally, ask themselves if it is beneficial to the Ummah. This approach does not necessitate that researchers be experts in theology; rather, it requests that they venture into the counternarrative free of their own possible miseducation and be open to another way of knowing. Central to Freire's humanization through liberatory dialogue is the concept of humility; Freire (2005) writes, "How can I dialogue if I always project ignorance onto others and never perceive my own?" (p. 90). Continuing on this idea, Freire clarifies that upon a dialogue, neither are "utter ignoramuses nor perfect sages; there are only people who are attempting together, to learn more than they now know" (p. 90). Akin to Freire's sentiments, within Abdul-Haleem's (2004) "Introduction" of his translation of the Qur'an, he discusses the many misinterpretations the West has had of Islam and turns to the Qur'an for the basis of interfaith dialogue:

> The Qur'an forbids arguing with the people of the Book, except in the best ways and urges Muslims to say: "We believe in what was revealed to us and in what was revealed to you; our God and your God are one [and the same]" (29: 46). God addresses Muslims, Jews, and Christians with the following: "We have assigned a law and a path to each of you. If God had so willed, He would have made you one community, but he wanted to test you through that which He has given you, so race to do good: you will all return to God and He will make clear to you the matters you differed about" (5: 48). . . . These are explicit statements which Muslims involved in interfaith dialogue must rely on. (p. xxxv)

From Abdul-Haleem's interpretation, the Qur'an requires the approach one takes to dialogue with non-Muslims to be open, tolerant, ethical, and respectful. For the Muslim and non-Mulsim researcher alike, if humanizing voices of Islam are going to pierce the predominant collective consciousness of the West, then we must enter the dialogue showing humility to the experience and faith of the counternarrative rather than imposing knowledge. Nor is the answer, within this particular ethical context, to attempt to mold the Qu'ran to fit particular theoretical leanings. In fact, as a scholar on Islam, Al-Attas (2002) warns against the haphazard use of quoting the Qur'an as a means of justifying theory: "They futilely attempt to 'rationalize' Verses of the Holy Qur'an they find convenient to their purposes in line with the theories and findings of modern science. Their habit, however, is to remain silent on many of the Verses which in fact cannot be so fathomed and which prove their thinking to be inadequate and confused" (p. 131).

In my mind, the ultimate goal of the de-Westernization of knowledge is not to denounce theories and methodologies that have been initiated or reinitiated within a Western context; rather, it is to acknowledge "that knowledge is not neutral" (Al-Attas, 2002, p. 146). For some, like Al-Attas, the advancement of theory is encouraged, but along an Islamic framework. For others, the dilemma is easily rationalized that all knowledge is derived from God, so all knowledge is Islamic. Armstrong (2002) notes that "in India the poet philosopher Muhammad Iqbal (1876–1938) insisted that Islam was just as rational as any Western system. Indeed it was the most rational and advanced of all the confessional faiths. Its strict monotheism had liberated humanity from mythology, and the Quran had urged Muslims to observe nature closely, reflect upon their observations and subject their actions to constant scrutiny. Thus the empirical spirit that had given birth to modernity had in fact originated in Islam" (p. 154). And for the Islamic modernist that Al-Attas warns against, there is (thankfully, in my opinion) "liberal" interpretation of scripture combining theories such as feminism with Islam. Ultimately, in the end, researchers must ask themselves, How do any of these interpretations toward theories or methodologies help the Muslim people? As I negotiate the use of theory and methodology to address this dilemma of dehumanization and counternarratives, I consider both in judgment of my own and other lived experiences.

Theories aside for a moment, for the past 15 years of working in Canadian schools, I have always known that students' identities are profoundly influenced by significant others in their lives. As a student myself, I knew the authority that adults in schools had on children's sense of self and their relationship and place within society. In my attempts to make sense of the Indigenous and minority experience in school, both personal and other, I have found many socio/cultural and qualitative theories that have answered many questions but leave room for many more. As a result, I choose to take Wolcott's (1992) path when it comes to theory and methodology, as he prefers to work "on a gentle theoretical 'plain' where distinguishing features are not so prominent, watersheds not so sharply divided" (p. 10), and in the spirit of Smith's (1999) call to realize that methodologies must be scrutinized in juxtaposition to Indigenous experience and knowledge. With this in mind, and asking myself if, in the end, the theories answer my questions for alleviating the dilemmas that surround the dehumanization and identity construction of Muslims, I have found that a multiple theory approach to both theory and methodologies, all the while contrasting them with respect to indigenous experiences of research, has been revealing.

At the individual level, I have always admired the interactionist theory, which is an interpretative theory that concerns itself primarily with the role of the individual within society. "The social construction of meaning in social interactions" (DeMarrais & LeCompte, 1999, p. 19) is central to the interactionist perspective. George Herbert Mead and Charles Horton Cooley theorized that the genesis of the self is accomplished through the gradually developing ability of a person to take on the role of others and to then visualize his or her own performance from the point of view of others. Briefly, it was the belief of Mead (1934) that the human concept of "self" was derived through these social acts within a society. This means that we draw much of our identity through the ways others perceive us, just as others are influenced by how we perceive them. One's sense of self is intertwined with society, and the self arises simultaneously with the act of socialization. We can only develop a sense of identity when we understand who others are, so that we can then compare our differences. Cooley (1964) states, "There is no sense of 'I' . . . without its correlative sense of you, or he, or they" (p. 182) and maintains that there can be no isolates. One's consciousness of self is a reflection of the ideas about himself or herself that he or she attributes to other minds and perceptions. This action is called the "reflected self" or the "looking glass self" (Congalton & Daniel, 1976, p. 136). The reflected self implies that we are all a reflection of how others see us. One's identity is, therefore, foremost derived from others' perception of that individual, just as that of the others is somewhat molded from that first individual's perception of them. What I always felt the interactionist theory fell short on was explaining how one's group ascriptions affected one's sense of self.

At the group level, Fredrick Barth (1999) contends that cultural identity is not only formulated within one's own cultural collection but is also influenced through the defining of perceived differences that are ascribed by those outside of one's group's cultural boundaries. Within the anthropological publication, *Ethnic Groups and Boundaries,* Barth postulates that ethnicity evolves from the union of socially ascribed designation and group self-identification. According to Barth, ethnic identity is decided from both the group's view of itself as well as from how those outside the group view it. Barth states that "ethnic identity is a matter of self-ascription and ascription by others in interaction, not the analyst's construct on the basis of his or her construction of a group's 'culture'" (p. 6). Barth's perspectives are founded in the notion that the boundaries that separate ethnicities are created by cultural differences that are recognized by at least two groups. This means that an ethnic group's cultural identity is formed by the others' perspectives of the group as well. Initially, this then creates an awareness of variation between one's own group and the other, and among groups of equal power, the effects of defining each other based on their perspectives may confirm a group's own perceived identity; however, when the relationship is unbalanced, as is the case with Indigenous groups who have experienced oppression, it may be and usually is stigmatizing.

With the balance and checks of equal power, group identification can be a combination of self and other ascribed identifiers, but in the absence of an equal relationship, the dominant group has a powerful influence on forming and imposing perception. For Indigenous people, group and self-definition changes in the presence of imperialism and colonialism. Many who have researched the subject of Indigenous cultural identity have used

Edward Said's concept of "Other" to clarify their perspective. Within Said's (1978, 1994) *Orientalism,* he asserts that the creation of the Other helped define Europe's self-image, thereby having a continued impact on the manner in which the Other—in this case, the Indigenous people of the Middle East—were perceived. As Said proposes the Other, as constructed through the Orientalist gaze, "has less to do with the Orient than it does with 'our' world . . ." (p. 12). The formation of identity throughout history and within every society, Said maintains, involves creating opposites and Others. This occurs because "the development and maintenance of every culture require the existence of another different and competing *alter ego*" (pp. 331–332). This is a formation of cultural identity that is developed by one group's perception of identity over another, which, in this case of a dominant group constructing and defining the picture of a subordinate group, inevitably leads to the positive self-image of one group and the stereotyped negative images of another.

> One can only suspect that, in the face of racial prejudice and historic oppression, the ability and desire to find one's authentic selfhood are severely affected by negative images of that self as a racial Other. (Vickers, 1998, p. 10)

In regard to similar groups that have experienced colonialism, this becomes an oppression of cultural, religious, and self-identity that Vickers (1998) views as "a guiding mythos of the colonial cultures of white Euramerica . . . to destroy the historical identities of Indian cultures and individuals" (Vickers, 1998, p. 2). However, imperialist cultural oppression goes far beyond the denial of the Indigenous culture. The rejection of being perceived as "human" has its history as well, and its impact also leaves a heavy scar on cultural identity. In the introduction of *Pedagogy of the Oppressed: 30th Anniversary,* Macedo (2005) writes in response to Freire's mainstream academics accusing him of using jargon-laden language and mused why such criticism was rarely aimed at language, such as "ethnic cleansing," "smart bombs," and "theatre of operations," used by those of privilege and power. The result of which leads to passivity of Western consciousness, and such things as "the mass killing of women, children, and the elderly and the rape of women and girls as young as five years old take on the positive attribute of 'cleansing,' which leads us to conjure a reality of 'purification' of the ethnic 'filth' ascribed to Bosnian Muslims, in particular, and to Muslims the world over, in general" (p. 21). We can now add reality-changing terms such as *shock and awe* to the lexicon. Smith (1999) writes, "The struggle to assert and claim humanity has been a consistent thread of anti-colonial discourses on colonialism and oppression" (p. 26). North American news media demonstrate this fact every night, as they pay rightful homage to American/Canadian/British soldiers who die in their "war on terror" but ignore the far, far larger number of Iraqi and Afghani innocent civilian dead. Knowing this, it is far too intrusive and powerful an experience not to leave an impression on one's sense of cultural and religious identity.

All of these theories of identity construction take on greater meaning given the so-called neo-Straussian/conservative influence on Western politics and their need to create and manipulate national unity through a religious shared set of truths and maintenance of that unity through lies, if need be, and exploitation of the fear of the Other (Drury, 1999; Norton, 2004). The followers of Strauss, like Wolfowitz, believe "that politics is first and foremost about the distinction between WE and THEY. Strauss thinks that a political order can be stable only if it is united by an external threat . . . [and] he maintains that if no external threat exists, then one has to be manufactured" (Drury, 1999, p. 23). In the absence of the Soviet threat, 9/11 provided the vehicle to create a threat against an entire Muslim people, as opposed to 19 homicidal hijackers and their monetary accomplices. For the neo-Straussians, it would seem, the new THEY would play not only upon old fears of the West but their own prejudices as well.

> From the time I first came to Chicago to the present day, I have seen Arabs and Muslims made the targets of unrestrained persecution, especially among the Straussians. At School, Straussian students told me that Arabs were dirty, they were animals, they were

> vermin. Now I read in Straussian books and articles, in editorials and postings on websites that Arabs are violent, they are barbarous, they are enemies of civilization, they are Nazis. (Norton, 2004, pp. 210–211)

The current political climate of the West and its perception of the East has, in part, created the condition of either removing or limiting Muslims' knowledge and perceptions from the public forum; the only voice we do hear tends to be the ones that play into the image of the Other. It is within this condition of oppression that the ways of knowing and the sense of self of the Muslim and/or Middle Eastern identity are being reconstructed. What can be done in the West is to resist the historic tendency to create and impose the culture, values, identity, and knowledge on Muslims and listen to what is actually being said. Perhaps by beginning to hear the significant number of Muslim voices in the West, we will establish the condition to listen to the many voices of the Muslim East. This, of course, works against the prominent narrative of Islam that suggests a fanatic, radical fundamentalist irrationalism on THEIR side and a rational, detached modern scientific perspective from OUR side. What is lost is the diversity of Muslim perspectives toward the West's own concepts of self because it does not fit with the West's construction of the Other. This is an important consideration if the desire is to move away from the simplicity of dehumanizing through stereotyping, to humanizing through individualizing counternarratives.

Multiple Responses to Western Concepts of Modernism

> "Islam" represents the threat of a resurgent atavism, which suggests not only the menace of a return to the Middle Ages but the destruction of what Senator Daniel Patrick Moynihan calls the democratic order in the Western world. (Said, 1998)

The sentiment that domination of the Muslim East as rationalized or moralized as being the "White man's burden" to civilize "backward" people, through cool, detached scientific impartiality, has been a tool to justify and precede military aggression for quite some time: "We can now see retrospectively that during the nineteenth century both France and England preceded their occupations of portions of the Islamic East with a period in which the various scholarly means of characterizing and understanding the Orient underwent remarkable technical modernization and development" (Said, 1998). Much of the Western sentiment of the "East as uncivilized" can still be seen in comments such as Brooks's (2006) response to the large demonstrations against the Danish Prophet Muhammad cartoons and the sophomoric (as Brooks rightfully describes it) reaction by an Iranian newspaper: "Our mind-set is progressive and rational. Your mind-set is pre-Enlightenment and mythological." Although Brooks is careful to note that he is not directing his comments toward "genuine Islamic scholars and learners," rather to "you Islamists," it is hard not to escape the continuous generalizations of the Western image of "good" Muslims and "bad" Muslims, an image that has drastically changed since Said's original printing of the article "Islam Through Western Eyes" in 1980, reprinted in 1998, with the "good" Muslims being Soviet-fighting Afghan Muslims and the oil-friendly Saudis. Said maintains that it is through these types of generalized caricatures that the "Islamic world is presented in such a way that makes it vulnerable to military aggression." One of the major and enduring caricatures of Islam is that it stands in opposition to the West's concept of modernism, postmodernism, enlightenment, positivism, and so on—as some kind of archaic, irrational, monolithic mind-set as opposed to a Muslim way of knowing that is both complex, unique, and diverse.

> From Zbigniew Brzezinski's vision of "crescent of crisis" to Bernard Lewis's "return of Islam," the picture drawn is a unanimous one. "Islam" means the end of civilization as "we" know it. Islam is antihuman, antidemocratic, anti-Semitic, antirational. (Said, 1998)

Abukhattala (2004) describes the prevalent negative imagery of Arabs or Muslims or the otherwise general Middle Easterner as the West's "new bogeyman under the bed"—given this, perhaps by demonstrating diversity in what is otherwise a monolith, may provide a better appreciation for other perspectives and interpretations. The attempt here is to demonstrate multiple responses to a Western concept of modernity in order to move away from the projection of monolithic modes of Muslim ways of knowing. However, within the diversity comes a problem: Which perspectives should be forwarded? In Euben's (1999) *Enemy in the Mirror,* in which she tackles Islamic fundamentalism and its relation to modernity, she acknowledges the problematic nature of carrying out interdisciplinary work and quotes, "Is there anyone in the room I haven't offended?" musing the hazard of becoming the Lenny Bruce of scholars. The Bruce quote also rings true for attempting to analyze Islamic or Muslim responses to being defined as antimodern or antirational, in that, Islam and those who practice it are not the simple definitions that have been provided in popular media of the West. Whose Islam, then, should be the topic of discussion? Shiite? Sunni? Sufi? Moderate? Traditional? Liberal Islam? Fundamentalist? Another perhaps? Pondering her own choices for comparative analysis, Euben writes

> These are by no means the only significant voices in modern Islamic political thought, nor is this comparison the only one worth pursuing to illuminate the diversity of Islamic responses to a modernity associated with Western colonialism and imperialism. (Euben, 1997, p. 434)

Mindful of the tendency of scholars and media to focus on constructed extremes of either fundamentalists and/or secular modernizers, Nasr (2004) cautions that "after the dust settles in this tumultuous period of both Islamic and global history, it will be the voice of traditional Islam that will have a final say in the Islamic world" (p. 112). Nasr also notes that with various schools of thought to consider, there are also the multiple followers of Islam, Muslims, and their distinct cultures, subcultures, and individuality to consider as well. Moreover, the consideration should also be made that just as there is a difference between Christianity and the wide scope of people who call themselves Christians, there is a difference between Islam and Muslims. This is not to discount the teachings of Muhammad through his life or the guidance of the Qur'an as the primary unifier between Muslims, but it would be irrational, the very thing the Islamic East is accused of, to believe that there is a single response to all things (although, when I discuss colonial and imperialist responses, there may be indeed a current significant growing collective perspective). In comparing Islamic responses to Western concepts of modernism, both Nasr and Euben, among others, note the Islamic modernist and fundamentalist perspectives, with Euben (2002) once again exorcising the notion of the monolithic by stating, "These perspectives emerge from different historical moments and sometimes disagree profoundly with each other" (p. 26) and with Nasr (2004) noting that "until the impact of European colonialism on the heart of the Islamic world, there were those who fought against Western rule in the extremities of the 'Abode of Islam,' but there were no Muslim modernists or fundamentalists" (p. 100). Nasr continues by documenting three reactions to the crisis of the increasing subjugation of Muslim people by foreign rule: The first was that it had occurred because they strayed from the original teachings of Islam, the second was that it marked the eschatological hadiths marking the end of the world, and the third was to respond as the European modernists and reform Islam to the modern context (pp. 102–103). From these perceptions grew modes of resistance to colonialism and imperialism that ranged from Jamal al-Din al-Afghani's (1839–1897) modernist Islamism to Ayatollah Khomeini's (1900–1989) Islamic fundamentalism. Once again, the reader must remember that these are simply some of many responses and are meant as a point of comparison and illustration and in no way meant to be definitive.

Whereas Ayatollah Khomeini's response to Western imperialism was for a unified recognition of the omniscience of God, an acknowledgment of the failings of Western claims to rationalist science, and rejection of "Westoxification," Islamic modernists, like Afghani, promoted resistance to colonialism through the unity of Muslims and acknowledgment that Islam was the true religion of reason and scientific discovery. The "knee-jerk" reaction may be to state that fundamentalist perspectives is a "turn-back-the-clock" response, and for some sects, this may be true (as it is with other religious groups), but I think the response is best elucidated by a comic an older (Iranian) cousin showed me of President Jimmy Carter and Ayatollah Khomeini playing chess: In the first panel, Ayatollah Khomeini moves a chess piece; in the second panel, President Carter smiles and moves his chess piece; in the third panel, the president's grin grows bigger and he says "checkmate"; in the final panel, the shocked president is looking at Ayatollah Khomeini as he is chewing and swallowing the president's chess piece while continuing to play *his* game. Although my cousin was by no means a fundamentalist or even a traditionalist, he kept this cartoon cut-out for years and, when I finished looking at it, asked me if I understood it. I responded, "Yes, it means Ayatollah Khomeini doesn't play by the rules." "No," he responded with grudging admiration, "it means he doesn't play by the West's rules." Here we see two different perspectives toward a concept such as modernism: On one hand, a student of Afghani, Muhammad Abduh (1845–1905), responded that there is no basis in the Western assumption of conflict between religion (Islam in particular) and the advancements associated with rational science; in fact, he argues that "Islam actually anticipate sciences such as modern astronomy and studies of the earth's resources, and prefigures much of the educational, economic and political institutions necessary for growth in the modern world" (Euben, 1997, p. 439). On the other hand, some Islamic fundamentalists argue that "the challenge of modernity is to recognize how rationalist epistemology erodes divine authority, expresses and accelerates Western power, and inhibits the establishment of a legitimate Islamic social system" (Euben, 2002, p. 34). Individuals such as Afghani and Ayatollah Khomeini, along with many other diverse perspectives, had visions of healing the Muslim Ummah they saw as being under attack, and both had different perspectives on how to meet this end. The common thread among the various perspectives is the response to the Western concept of modernism as it facilitates colonialism and imperialism and still affects the Muslim collective consciousness. Nasr (2004) notes that categories that exist with the West regarding the Muslim East usually contain a "vast spectrum of people into its fold" (p. 106) and then subsequently are branded with a term such as *fundamentalist* for purposes of demonizing. In the end, as Nasr reminds us, it is the majority traditionalists that will have their say and to comprehend the diversity of all the responses; "it is necessary to have a context within which to place these actions" (p. 110). For most, when we speak of contextualizing experience, "imperialism frames the Indigenous experience" (Smith, 1999, p. 19).

Collective Consciousness, Colonialism, and Imperialism

> The Western encroachment had made politics central to the Islamic experience once more. (Armstrong, 2002, p. 152)

Imperialism, in its simplest form, is defined as the practice by which powerful nations exert control and domination over nations or people of lesser strength. Throughout history and in present times, these actions have been and are justified through a number of reasons. These may be categorized roughly as economic, such as the Marxist theory that links imperialism to capitalist motives to dominate others in order to expand the economic base, such as securing oil interests in the Middle East; political, whereby a nation's needs and security interests are argued to be best served by controlling another nation or people, such as the preemptive doctrine used by the Blair and Bush governments; and ideological aims, best described through Britain's era of colonialism in which domination was rationalized or moralized as being the "White man's burden" to civilize "backward" peoples. Put succinctly, "imperialism was the system of control which secured the markets and capital investments. Colonialism facilitated this expansion by ensuring there was European control, which necessarily meant securing and subjugating the Indigenous populations"

(Smith, 1999, p. 21). If imperialism is referred to at all in our media or classrooms, it is usually referred to today in historical terms, but for those who have experienced its actions, it is still perceived to be an ongoing subjugation. John Mohawk (1992) wrote,

> Imperialism and colonialism are not something that happened decades ago or generations ago, but they are still happening now with the exploitation of people.... The kind of thing that took place long ago in which people were dispossessed from their land and forced out of subsistence economies and into market economies—those processes are still happening today.

Smith (1999) reinforces this notion by quoting "activist Bobbi Sykes, who mockingly asked at an academic conference on post-colonialism, 'What? Post-colonialism? Have they left?'" (p. 24). The effect of these principles of continued imperialism and colonialism, resulting in a feeling of helplessness and objectification, has had a profound impact on Indigenous perceptions of self, cultural identity, and knowledge. As educators and teacher researchers, we cannot ignore that these are not events that *may* have occurred in the past; rather, they continue to have current individual and global impacts. However, it is also important to comprehend the past as to its impact on the present, especially in regard to its development of both Western and Muslim collective consciousness.

Hampton (1993, 1995) writes that North American Indigenous educational issues cannot be understood without concepts of oppression, resistance, and historical analysis, and I believe that the current condition of the Muslim voice as it relates to ways of knowing cannot be understood apart from these perspectives either. In Armstrong's (2001) chapter, "Muhammad the Enemy" (referring to the West's view of Islam, not her own), she chronicles the long and bloody history of Europe's (and its colonial children's) story with the Muslim Middle East. It is a history that has not been forgotten by Muslims (the word *Crusade* rightfully has an entirely different meaning to Muslims), but it is also a past that has not left the consciousness of the West either:

> When General Allenby arrived in Jerusalem in 1917, he announced that the Crusades had been completed, and when the French arrived in Damascus their Commander marched up to Saladin's tomb in the Great Mosque and cried: "Nous revenons, Saladin!" (Armstrong, 2001, p. 40)

Current Western leaders have used the term *crusade* when discussing military conflicts/aggression against Muslim people. From the Middle Eastern perspective, the word has deep meaning, and the knowledge of history, oppression, and resistance all becomes part of the thought processes. In Hampton's (1993) analysis, the collective consciousness of the Indigenous people of North America arose through the harsh realities of colonial oppression. The comparison between the "pan-Indian" (Cornell, 1988; Nagel, 1996) identity of North American Native people and Muslim people is worth examining given the mind-set that we have heard regarding the West's vision of its relationship with the East; as politicians and soldiers imagine playing wild west, cowboys and Indians through such statements as G. W. Bush's 2001 "I want justice ... There's an old poster out West, as I recall, that said, 'Wanted: Dead or Alive'" or the manner in which Afghanistan and Iraq are thought of by political advisers (Robert D. Kaplan), U.S. officers (Brigadier General Richard Neal), or what "Marines call, in their typically politically incorrect way, 'Indian country'" (Hess, 2005). It was through a shared sense of a collective experience, past and present, of oppression that some North American Natives began to think of themselves as "pan-Indian."

The term *pan-Indian* refers to a sense of ethnic, political, cultural, or other identity among Native American groups that crosses tribal boundaries and refers to the collectiveness that encompasses all Natives, defined as the larger-than-tribal "Indian" level of American Indian ethnicity, similar to "Black," "Latino," "Asian," or "White" (Cornell, 1988; Nagel, 1996). Rhea (1997) notes that this came about as a result of a nation or a people who had to turn "to history for a sense of Identity" (p. 8) and contends that the shared beliefs that Natives began to develop about their past acknowledged a collective memory or collective consciousness that made them a people. A Native collective consciousness implies a shared sense of experience and identity among Native people despite their tribal differences. This collective consciousness is derived, in part, from the empathetic feeling that Indigenous persons have toward one another that they both perceive as belonging to the same way of life and background and, therefore, having similar histories and intertwined fate. Kincheloe and Steinberg (1997) discuss this in terms of "dominant memory" that can serve to bleach the bloodstains of historical records (p. 242) and, within the context of the West, justify current power blocs and their relationship to the rest of the world. As an example, they cite popular collective perceptions of Iran by North Americans and are shaped by what is allowed and not allowed to be said in the public forum:

> Such power is illustrated by the American public's memory of the United States' relations with Iran. Most Americans remember only angry Iranians chanting anti-American slogans in the streets of Tehran, a crazed Ayatollah preaching martyrdom and hostages torn away from their families. Not included in the dominant memory are images of CIA working to overthrow the government of Iranian Premier Mohammed Mossedegh in 1953 and replacing it with the "friendly" Pahlavi Dynasty represented by the young Shah. The structuring of such memories makes a difference. (Kincheloe & Steinberg, 1997, p. 242)

For most North Americans, the "popular discourse" of Eastern/Western relations starts with "Iran is part of an axis of evil," not "in 1998, the United States Navy ship, the USS *Vincennes,* shot down the civilian Iran Air Flight 655, killing just under 300 people, including 60 children" or "Iraq's a threat to the free world" and not "British/U.S.-led UN sanctions have killed over half a million Iraqi children." In Churchill's (2003) much criticized *On the Justice of Roosting Chickens,* there was no backlash to his statement of the collective "yawn" from the West over the onetime American Secretary of State Madeline Albright's confirmation of, at the time, the death of half a million children by their own governments. Rather, the outrage came over the lack of sensitivities Churchill demonstrated over the victims of 9/11. I have brought this tragedy to the attention of my undergraduate students on a number of occasions, and the response is often one of bewilderment. One student told me, "It's not that we don't care, it's just that the number is so big we can't imagine it." I never questioned that the half a million number is overwhelming, but I believe part of the reason why they can't "imagine it" is that it has been purposefully left out of the Western collective consciousness. The number of Iraqi children dead has increased since 2001, and unlike the victims of 9/11, whose individual stories through the media connected so closely to our own, we have no idea of any of those Iraqi children's stories and their families, friends, and neighbors who grieve for them.

In the months before Gulf War II, I wrote about how the aggressive actions, discourse, and purposively political and media-fueled paranoia of the East created an image of the Other as being "all dangerous" and asked, "Are we witnessing the creation of some sort of Pan-Arabism or Pan-Terrorist-Arabism in the West; a forced construction of the image of the dangerous Arab, which pays no respect to the rich linguistic, historic, cultural, political, geographic, religious and ethnic differences of these diverse people of the so called East?" (Stonebanks, 2004, p. 88). Islam has touched many different cultures, ethnicities, and nations. So whatever name someone comes up to describe it, perhaps some label that is already being used, such as "pan-Islamic" or a new one that has a wider scope, perhaps something to the effect of "Supra-Other," it will always fall short of reflecting everyone within the group and will never do it justice to the diversity that exists within it, but there will be something that is a unifier. Of course, no Muslim is going to glibly say, something to the effect of, "Hello, I'm a Pan-Terrorist-Arab," but there may be a response to a dominant power bloc continuously projecting and controlling the public imagery of your identity.

> The fundamentalist elements of the (Middle) East are increasingly recognizing that their common

> problems are forcing them, sooner or later, to act as one, and the West is more than primed to see even the majority moderate in one all-encompassing broad stroke. (Stonebanks, 2004, p. 96)

Whatever the name is, although it may at first be ascribed by the power blocs, it will certainly come to represent an Indigenous collective consciousness that will remember a shared history, like over half a million children dead and cavalier responses. Perhaps what has been in the mind of the West when imagining the Muslim-Other has begun to take shape in the mind of the East as well. The ensuing war against Iraq did not end on May 1, 2003, with the fall of the Baath party, and the ensuing violence between "the coalition of the willing" and the often termed "insurgence" or "foreign fighters," be they portrayed in a negative or sympathetic light, lends credence to a possible growing, albeit in this case militant, pan-Islamic identity.

> Iraq has also seen an influx of foreign "jihadi" fighters, most of whom have joined the Sunni Muslim insurgency. Their number is small—estimated at no more than 3,000—but their profile is high. Washington points to their presence as proof that neighbouring nations such as Iran and Syria are trying to destabilise Iraq. Organisations such as al-Qaeda meanwhile praise the foreign fighters as ideal recruits, the vanguard of a global, pan-Islamic uprising. (British Broadcasting Corporation [BBC], 2005)

Both the BBC (2005) and CNN (2005) take a conservative position on the number of "foreign fighters," estimating there could be upwards of 1,500 to 3,000. However, both acknowledge the ideological significance, stating that they have "little in common beyond a commitment to attack US forces or their perceived allies" (BBC, 2005). It is truly unfortunate that the bond that has been created has arisen from oppression, but it is a condition that has been played out before, for instance, with North America's 19th-century Tecumseh. It was through the collective Native knowledge of the injustices against their people that drew so many to the calling of Tecumseh and his brother Tenskwataya, the "Shawnee Prophet." Hampton (1993) describes a 1982 Minnesota Chamber of Commerce meeting in which various concerned Native North American Indian university students expressed their concerns over a proposed "pageant" depicting the 1892 mass hanging of 38 Sioux Indians. As the Native students individually spoke to the Chamber of Commerce, they prefaced each statement with an acknowledgment to their tribal roots, stating, for instance, "I am Lakota," "I am Creek," or "I am Winnebago." When the secretary of the Chamber of Commerce asked, "What is it that all Indians have in common?" Iris Drew, the Creek, answered, "The white man" (p. 288). Political writer Muna Shuqair (*The Daily Star,* November 30, 2002) draws a similar scenario when writing of a growing "supra-Arab" phenomenon:

> It is a "supra-Arab" phenomenon, in the sense that it pervades all Arab countries and peoples. Driven by a need among youth for faith, their inclination toward piety and yearning for a distinctive cultural identity, this religious phenomenon has haphazardly crossed boundaries and infiltrated entire societies. Up to the present time, it does not seem that specific political movements have tapped this religious current. It has not yet been used for political gain. It is a purely faith-driven current that might have been strengthened by the West's hostility to Islam. (Shuqair, 2002, ¶ 14)

For Shuqair, the question isn't whether "supra-Arabism" exists or is growing beyond the border of Jordan, where her story takes place; it is who will take advantage of the growing collective consciousness and "lead and politicize it." Whether the leadership that captures this growing consciousness moves it toward peaceful political change or militant resistance remains to be seen. Tragically, current news indicates spiraling sectarian violence in Iraq (with the risk of spreading within the region), and although the Western media indicate a possible—and, in some media circles, an inevitable—civil war along Shiite and Sunni lines, voices from Iraq suggest that perhaps, like the ousting of Iranian Prime Minister Mohammed Mossadegh in 1953, there may be outside influences at hand, a similar divide-and-conquer mentality. Haifa Zangana, Iraqi-born author and artist, recently said, "In Iraq we never had any civil war, not in the last 1,500 years. So this is a totally novel idea." She noted that the media are playing a decisive role in manufacturing the new confrontational labels of the Middle East, escalating the sectarian divide (Democracy Now, 2006). This creation of identity and collective consciousness, within all communities, by either significant forces or significant others, is often overlooked by teachers despite its profound impact on students' perceptions of the Middle East and Islam.

Muslim communities continue to be dehumanized (both in the West and in the East), and if the hope is for research to benefit the group of people being researched, then given the current tragedies relating to the Muslims, there has been a failing. Through the continued consequences of colonialism and imperialism, Muslim voices have been marginalized, twisted, and ignored, creating a perception of the Muslim as less than human in the Western consciousness. For Muslim narratives to begin to enter the collective consciousness of the West, we must develop methodologies that value the knowledge of Muslims, the history, perspectives, and experiences, and be respectful of the relationship to Islam for the research to be truthful, ethical, and, in the way of the Prophet Muhammad, beneficial to the Ummah. For educator-researchers, the use of the transformative classroom is an initial space to allow Muslim counternarratives and promote Muslim ways of knowing and is the primary location to begin a peaceful resistance to an unjust master narrative. If the desire of the educator is to create learning spaces that are truly transformative, then teachers must consider themselves as researchers and move beyond the usual narratives that have been fed to them and facilitate the counternarrative. In this sense, the counternarrative is used to empower and repair group and individual damaged identities that have derived from the dominant group constructs of identities of certain people through their socially shared narratives or master narratives. In this act of noncompliance, teachers seek to foster Muslim "ways of knowing" that are both complex and diverse and to actively move away from the continuous message of Muslim perspectives as an irrational monolith as opposed to intellectual contributions that should be weighed on individual merit and balanced with the Muslim collective experience that has been severely affected by years of destructive imperial and colonial efforts. The ethical questions in one's research continue when considering theory and methodology in relation to the Muslim knowledge.

Again, theory and methodology must be considered in relation to the Muslim experience and knowledge, specifically carrying out research that is ethical and beneficial to the Ummah. Concentrating on the idea of "objectivity" and "impartiality," the question asked is the following: What has Western research, the researcher himself or herself, done to improve the lives of those being researched? In considering methodology, the approach of this chapter in regard to de-Westernizing knowledge is not to denounce theories and methodologies that have been initiated or reinitiated within a Western context; rather, it is to acknowledge that knowledge, like our schools, is value laden. This chapter is an invitation to all educators, Muslim or non-Muslim, Indigenous or non-Indigenous, who are interested in the use of exploring critical research to become a part of the dialogue in creating methodologies that can reflect Muslim ways of knowing and develop humanizing voices that have been absent from the master narratives that dominate our communities and schools. It is hoped that starting this process in our classrooms that will ultimately lead to changes in our communities. The first personal step toward accomplishing this end is to identify the influences that silence Muslim perspectives and diminish their presence and ways of knowing in schools.

Within this chapter, I discussed one such element, that being the continued distortion of humanity, and questioned whether teachers are exempt from these powers of persuasion they consume, along with their students, in formal and nonformal locations of education. Once the teacher sees himself or herself as a researcher and moves beyond the passive to the active professional, then the sometimes difficult task of reflecting and accounting one's preconceptions must take place. By taking the professional responsibility of critically assessing the values being delivered through their teaching, teachers must then ask whether they consciously, unconsciously, or dysconsciously repeat or address these miseducations in their classrooms. The personal undertaking of acknowledging one's values and subjectivity within one's research must come about to position one's self within the work and give transparency and reflection to the question of "what and whose politics am I teaching in my class and to what end?" The collective experience for Muslims has been, for the most part, a witnessing of increased dehumanization—a dehumanization that is manufactured through oppression that educators can decide will either be or not be part of their classroom.

▣ Counternarrative and the Transformative Classroom

How much is the dehumanization of Islam a part of our schools? When my wife, who is of English European descent, announced to her staffroom that she was engaged to marry me, she received some congratulations but overwhelming gasps that many of them had seen the film *Not Without My Daughter* and would never let their daughters marry an Iranian. Can anyone imagine the same response to a young teacher saying she's marrying someone of Irish descent? Would they warn her of the film *Angela's Ashes?* Of course not, because this is one perspective of the rich mosaic of voices we hear from people of Irish descent—a humanizing narrative mosaic that is lost to Islam in the West.

> Often in the West Islam is depicted as a monolith, and little attention is paid to the rich diversity within both the religion and civilization of Islam. (Nasr, 2004. p. 57)

Far too few recognize the diversity of Muslims and the subtle to wide differences in which Islam is practiced or the common bond of a growing shared experience that has been created in opposition to the effects of being the Other, an experience that being half Iranian exposes you to, and it is an exposure that, *if you are open to it,* changes and/or shapes your perspective on worldviews, your relationships, your education, and even what you bring to your research. Taking artistic license from Wolcott's (1992) perspective on qualitative theory and methodology, my experience with Islam is that submission to its teaching comes in many forms, where Muslims follow this great religion on a gentle interpretive "plain" where distinguishing features are not so prominent, watersheds not so sharply divided. In the West, we are mired in perspectives that portray Islam in singular ways and singular approaches as opposed to a religion that includes ethnic/cultural diversity that is equal to or supersedes many other religions, philosophies, or beliefs. Is it possible that Islam and the cultures associated with it are the monolith extremes that are portrayed by popular pundits or the extreme fundamentalist Muslim voices that are given consistent "airtime"? Often, the answer to the question is right in front of us but somehow does not penetrate our collective imagery. For example, while in the process of contemplating this chapter, I approached a friend, a man who is my senior, is Muslim, who is quite knowledgeable of Islam and whom I respect and told him during a social event of my challenges in writing this chapter. Immediately, he happily pulled me aside and, with his hand waving a tumbler glass full of Scotch and ice precariously close to my face, lovingly told me of the beauty of the Qur'an, the majesty of the Prophet Muhammad, and its unifying power. Like the 14th-century Iranian Sufi Hafiz, he has no problem mixing "wine with God."

> Preachers who display their piety in prayer and pulpit
>
> behave differently when they're alone.
>
> It puzzles me. Ask the learned ones of the assembly:
>
> "Why do those who demand repentance do so little of it?"
>
> It's as if they don't believe in the Day of Judgment
>
> with all this fraud and counterfeit they do in His name.

I am the slave of the tavern-master, whose dervishes,

in needing nothing, make treasure seem like dust.

O lord, put these nouveaux-riches back on their asses

because they flaunt their mules and Turkic slaves.

O angel, say praises at the door of love's tavern,

for inside they ferment the essence of Adam.

(Translation of Hafiz by Gray, 1995, p. 103)

Reminiscent of Hafiz, this friend is blissfully happy with his relationship with God and also espouses that God/Allah is found within many different places. Would other Muslims agree with this perspective? Some would; some, vehemently, would not. Some, perhaps many, would say that his transgressions demonstrate he is not a true Muslim. However, the Qur'an states that each individual is answerable to God alone; therefore, it can be argued that this relationship should be left deeply personal.

> We have bound each human being's destiny to his neck. On the Day of Resurrection, We shall bring out a record for each of them, which they will find spread wide open, "Read your record. Today your own soul is enough to calculate your account." Whoever accepts guidance does so for his own good; whoever strays does so at his own peril. No soul will bear another's burden, nor do We punish until We have sent a Messenger. (17: 13–15, The Qur'an, translated by Abdul-Haleem, 2004)

During Ramadan of 2003, I asked one of my undergraduate students if she would explain to our Intercultural class at McGill University the significance of the religious observance. The young student, a very intelligent yet sometimes shy Canadian born of South Asian descent, who also chose to wear a hijab, made her way cautiously to the front of the class. As the class settled down to listen to her, she immediately composed herself and started by explaining that Ramadan was an obligation of all healthy Muslims and continued with a strict interpretation of the Holy Month that stunned most of the class with her stark description. Sensing that most of the class seemed perturbed by the lack of "holidayness" to Ramadan, I interjected that I had many friends and colleagues who described Ramadan as, yes, a time of fasting, reflection, and alms giving but also described the evening meal after fast breaking as a caring time for family and extended family to get together in a happy way. She listened politely to my description of Ramadan, nodding the whole time, and as I finished, she responded, "I know some people *celebrate* Ramadan that way" and then forcefully added with a beautiful and impish smile, "*but they are wrong.*"

Despite the collective consciousness of the Muslim community, the unifying message of the Qur'an, diversity exists within the Islamic community. For example, compare Irshad Manji's (2003) *The Trouble With Islam: A Wake-Up Call for Honesty and Change* with Asma Gull Hasan's (2005) *Why I Am a Muslim;* from the titles, we immediately read differing perspectives. Within the texts, we hear two very different narratives, two very different perspectives on Islam and its meaning to themselves and those significant others who surround them. Within their narratives, there will be experiences and positions that I, as a half-Iranian, half-European Canadian, will agree with and others I will not. Some I will be familiar with and some I will not. Both views are valid and must be heard, all the while weeding through the dialogue with an appreciation of the history and positioning that the author of the voice brings to the piece and assessing the authors' contributions to the Muslim community. Their voices are important, and it is only when we hear a great many of them can we move from the generalized stereotypes to the individual narratives that humanize. It is difficult, perhaps impossible, for someone in my position to even partially suggest what should be done by Muslims residing in the East. What I can do is provide an impetus to create an atmosphere where diverse Muslim voices in the West, a significant number, can be heard, at the very least within our Western classrooms. But with this accountability comes fear for some teacher researchers.

In a new twist, student-teachers and recently graduated teachers have expressed their reluctance to include the minority voices of their students within their classroom for fear of "singling them out." After all, one student told me, "We're told that no one is representative of their race or ethnic group." In a misunderstanding of Freire's theory of meaningful reciprocity, young teachers await passively for the children to bring their knowledge forward and, as is typical of the context of most of our elementary and high schools, receive no meaningful dialogue. So, with an "all of my students are the same" mantra, Indigenous voices are being excluded in the classroom because of their very Indigenousness. In effect, the Indigenous child becomes the "null student," and whatever is still disseminated comes from a top-down approach. Teachers, as Steinberg (2004) notes, are as much a product of receiving misinformed knowledge before entering the classroom as their students and, with the passivity of considering this Western information as "objective," repeat the same pedagogy of oppression. Said (1985) asked, "Who writes? For whom is the writing being done? In what circumstances? These it seems to me are the questions whose answers provide us with the ingredients making a politics of interpretation" (p. 7). That "'A' can represent 'B' is now a controversial statement, rather than a taken-for-granted assumption" (Cairns, 2000, p. 15). From a current perspective and wrapped in our "post-9/11" world, it is plain to anyone who comes from "the East," "the Arab world," or the "Muslim world" how experts of these people within the media are usually not *of* these people, and when they are, there is always the presupposition that they are somehow not objective due to their Indigenousness.

Teachers must begin to ask themselves, How do these experts and the research they have done to gain the title of expert benefited from the people they have studied? This by no means suggests that one has to *be* of the Indigenous group to be able to speak of it in a scholarly or exploratory way; we have too many examples of individuals who come from power blocs whose research has had a great benefit in validating the Indigenous/minority experience and educating members of the larger Western context. And they do so at a consequence:

> Those Americans—Gore Vidal, Susan Sontag, Noam Chomsky amongst many others—who assert their independence from chauvinism or refuse to conform by drawing attention to some of the flawed and grim realities of the Empire are viciously denounced by the superpatriots. (Ali, 2003, p. 281)

In the spirit of the Vidals, Sontags, Chomskys, and Ward Churchills of this world, teachers and researchers can be active educators of social justice and help promote their voices and ways of knowing. Within the school setting, some educational researchers and teacher-researchers may be thinking to themselves that given many of the new policy changes across Canada regarding the separation of schools and religion, classrooms are now "religion free." This is not the case and is a reality that is often lost on Muslim scholars who bemoan the so-called radical secularism of the West. I still see many schools that teach Christmas carols to non-Christians; read C. S. Lewis's Narnia series with no critical analysis to the Christian overtones; and have Muslim and Jewish children draw Crusade-based "coats of arms" on cardboard paper shield-shaped cut-outs. This is not to say that these things should not be within our schools; the problem arises when they are taught as norms, as pure Christian-derived knowledge without context or counterperspectives.

After 9/11, many Canadian teachers put American flags in their class, as they should have in honor of a terrible day. On the day the "coalition of the willing" began their "shock and awe" bombing of Iraq, I asked my students going off to do their student-teaching practicum to contact me and let me know if any teachers decided they would honor the victims of this horror. Student teachers contacted me, but only to say their teachers acted like it was a normal day like any other; null curriculum = null humanity. Many of the classrooms the student teachers were carrying out their field experience within had Muslim students, and yet, the teachers decided to avoid or ignore the subject. Were their choices malicious in intent? I don't believe so. Although there are teachers who make the conscious choice to omit these world events from their class and teachers who unconsciously pay no attention to the plight of things that have no personal meaning to them, I believe King's (1991) description of dysconsciousness may play a significant dynamic in the exclusion of the Other's pain:

> Dyconscious racism is a form of racism that tacitly accepts dominant White norms and privileges. It is not the *absence* of consciousness (that is, not unconsciousness) but an *impaired* consciousness or distorted way of thinking about race as compared to, for example, critical consciousness. Uncritical ways of thinking about racial inequality accept certain culturally sanctioned assumptions, myths, and beliefs that justify the social and economic advantages White people have as a result of subordinating diverse others. (p. 135)

On many occasions, I have heard from many very educated and kind people statements such as, "*They* (meaning their conception of "Middle Easterners") just don't care about life like *we* do." It is an example of the dysconsciousness that is repeated in the classroom, the kind of uncritical thinking that places value on life of the power bloc and uncritically dehumanizes the Other. This becomes the impetus for teacher as researcher. To move beyond the passive acceptance of power and analyze them critically, as Kincheloe (2003) urges, "critical teachers as researchers [should] understand the centrality of power in understanding everyday life, knowledge production, curriculum development, and teaching" (p. 17). From a Canadian perspective, critical teachers should ask themselves, "Why did we hold a remembrance ceremony for the victims of 9/11, but ignored the tens of thousand civilian deaths in Iraq? What played into this decision making?" Critical educators, from nursery to university, are accountable and realize teaching is not a haphazard process; our decision making has meaning to our students, and we are aware of it. Critical teachers realize that even in the supposed absence of diversity in their classroom, like Jane Elliot in the 1960s, they have a responsibility to a multicultural democracy to seek out other ways of knowing, other voices and promote identities outside of the power bloc in an authentic and humanizing manner.

I have read about some wonderful teachers who have developed rich Muslim counternarratives in their classrooms (Shah, 1996), and I have seen and heard of a lot of wonderful teachers and student teachers who do wonderful things in their classrooms as well. One student teacher, shortly after 9/11 and within a predominantly White, Christian school, decided she was going to have her students carry out their own study to research why people within the Middle East *may* dress differently than the students were accustomed to. Over a particularly hot period of time in early spring, she had half of the class wear different traditional clothing of the Middle East and the other half not. The students carried out research on the different types of clothing—their origins and cultural and/or religious significance, if any—and documented their comfort level wearing the Middle Eastern clothes and compared their responses with those of the students who dressed in their usual manner. The final outcome: Students realized the practical aspects of wearing the clothes in a hotter climate, as well as their cultural and religious significance (if any), and moved from viewing these clothing as exotic or strange to an appreciation for their use, possible meaning, and aesthetics. In light of the stereotypes that permeate the other aspects of their lives, this was a transformative experience. Another student teacher decided to do a unit on Nowruz (a commemoration of spring celebrated in Afghanistan, Azerbaijan, India, Iran, Pakistan, and Turkey, celebrated by a wide variety of religious beliefs); when she discovered that there was a boy of Iranian descent in her class, she asked him what he knew of the holiday. Bewildered, he responded, "Nothing." Prepared for this response, she said that before embarking on this lesson idea, she knew nothing either but would really appreciate if he could ask his family if they had anything to contribute so they could all share from their knowledge. An atmosphere of classroom dialogue was then created where information was reciprocal, and a single counternarrative of Iranian life was established within a classroom that would have otherwise never have benefited from this knowledge. Neither example is exempt from criticism, but it must be noted that they represent teachers who are taking critical curriculum risks to elicit positive change in their classrooms.

My wife Melanie is also an example I use often of the critical teacher. Within her Grade 6 social studies class, she has moved from the normative teaching of "explorers to the new world" to having her multicultural class investigate their own family's history of coming to Canada. In this model, she shares her own story and then encourages narratives from children and asks them to seek out stories from their elders on what they know about who made the journey to this country and why they did it. She has children decide who they think should be on Canadian stamps, research the individuals, and then design and present the final product. The result is a wonderful multicultural mosaic of their own Indigenous knowledge and pride. This is not to say that Melanie's personal journey to be a critical teacher has not been problematic. Coming from a power bloc background, she readily admits that the progress from being a dysconscious teacher to a critical teacher has been rough at times. Recently, in one of her projects dealing with narratives, derived from Emery, Tiseo, and Lewellyn's (2000) *Rainbow of Dreams,* she had her students find old family pictures and then seek out relatives who could tell the story behind the photo. The problem arose when her student teacher showed her a photo that a young student of Iranian descent brought to the class. The photo was of his father during his military service in the Iran/Iraq war perched on top of an antiaircraft gun. Both were unsure of the appropriateness of the image. The three of us sat down and had a pedagogical discussion of the picture, and the simple question was posed: "What would we have said if this was a picture from a Canadian of British descent who had a picture of a British uncle sitting in a bomber during World War II?" Both knew they would have unquestionably accepted it. Both then realized that they would let their student develop his family's narrative and explore the picture. In the end, what was the nature of the narrative? That his father was proud to serve his country, wear the uniform, and protect his country from a country that had declared war on it; that he had fond memories of the friends he had made; that there were many times he was scared; and, finally, that he was happy to serve with honor and then come to Canada.

Conclusion

All that has been presented thus far must seem like a daunting dilemma and task for the teacher-researcher: rethinking Islam in relation to the Western conceptualization of it, recognizing the diversity of Muslims while contextualizing experience as affecting collective consciousness, developing theory as it relates to Muslim ways of knowing, and considering the ongoing dehumanization of Islam and Muslims. In 1979, I had an elementary school teacher who I believe had every intention of moving from the dysconscious to the critical, but the tools of creating the transformative class were unlikely part of her own professional education. Home life was consumed by the Iranian Revolution, and the anxiety that came from not knowing if I would ever see Iran or my mamanjoon again was agonizing. Report cards would say that I seemed distracted, and the teacher did her best to ask me what was wrong, but I never felt that the atmosphere of the classroom was safe enough to share what I was going through. Over time, the disconnect between what we did in school and what I knew from my own background became increasingly obvious, and like the Native students who have to endure historical accounts they know are wrong, I would either half-heartedly do the same or simply not participate. Today's teacher has a choice to be a tacit agent of reproduction or a critical teacher of transformation. Islam, Muslim students, and students from the East are subjected to continuous bombardment of negative imagery and must learn to negotiate within school systems that pay little attention to their knowledge, perspectives, or humanity. Actively critical teachers have the ability to research these dilemmas and contribute solutions that will create a classroom where a young student will be as comfortable to speak of his or her Muslim mamanjoon as other students do of their respective own. This will be the test in a decade from now; have the counternarratives that humanize begun to pierce the stereotypes that have been so detrimental to the Muslim communities?

In the fall semester of 2005, I was fortunate enough to be in a student-directed undergraduate course where students reviewed a chapter I had written in Kincheloe and Steinberg's (2004) *The Miseducation of the West* regarding the dangers of the acceptance of negative stereotypes by teachers and its impact on students; on the perceived "Eastern" or Muslim students' conception of self and/or denunciation of their ways of knowing. After giving a brief account of the main parts of the chapter, they broke out into numerous groups, and I milled around the room to listen in on their conversations as they politely pretended I was not there. In one group, the discussion leader asked, "He points out the problem, so . . . *what can we do?*" Silence continued, probably in part because I was hanging overhead, and then one student looked at me and said, "What *can* we do?" We discussed the main parts of the chapter, and I encouraged them that as teachers they have the ability to be active participants in change. That I would hope they become willing participants in counteracting the negative view of Muslim people, influenced by misconceptions and misrepresentation, within the mind of the West. And finally, that as educators and teacher researchers, we have a moral obligation to provide an avenue to allow the legitimate and free narrative of Muslim ways of knowing and trust that their classroom will then create positive change in society. In effect, I told them that as critical teachers, they will have the responsibility to seek out ways of accomplishing all of this within their own classrooms. Politely they nodded, and then the question came again, "But what *can* we do?" Committed educators like examples; I like examples; so I trust this piece of writing did just that, provide first steps and clarification in the complex discussion of Muslim ways of knowing and develop methods in which the authors of this knowledge begin to be heard and humanized.

References

Abdel-Haleem, M. (2004). *The Qur'an: A new translation.* Oxford: Oxford University Press.

Abukhattala, I. (2004). The new bogeyman under the bed: Image formation of Islam in the Western school curriculum and media. In J. L. Kincheloe & S. R. Steinberg (Eds.), *The miseducation of the West: The hidden curriculum of Western-Muslim relations* (pp. 153–170). New York: Greenwood.

Al-Attas, M. A. N. (2002). *Islam and secularism.* New Delhi: Hindustan Publications.

Ali, T. (1997). *Shadows of the pomegranate tree.* New York: Verso.

Ali, T. (2003). *The clash of fundamentalisms: Crusades, jihads and modernity.* New York: Verso.

Apple, M. (1996). *Cultural politics & education.* New York: Teachers College Press.

Apple, M. (2004). *Ideology and curriculum* (3rd ed.). New York: RoutledgeFalmer.

Armstrong, K. (2001). *Muhammad: A biography of the Prophet.* London: Phoenix Press.

Armstrong, K. (2002). *Islam.* Toronto: Random House.

Barth, F. (1999). *Ethnic groups and boundaries.* Bergen: Universitetsforlaget.

Bloom, H. (2005). *Jesus and Yahweh: The names divine.* New York: Riverhead Books.

British Broadcasting Corporation (BBC). (2005). *Who are the insurgents in Iraq?* Retrieved from http://news.bbc.co.uk/1/hi/world/middle_east/4268904.stm

Brooks, D. (2006, February 9). Drafting Hitler. *New York Times,* p. A27.

Burnham, G., Lafta, R., Doocy, S., & Roberts, L. (2006). *Mortality after the 2004 invasion of Iraq: A cross-sectional cluster sample survey.* Retrieved from http://www.thelancet.com/webfiles/images/journals/lancet/s0140673606694919.pdf

Cairns, A. C. (2000). *Citizens plus: Aboriginal peoples and the Canadian state.* Vancouver: UBC Press.

Canadian Broadcasting Corporation News Online. (2005). *Casualties in the Iraq war.* Retrieved from http://www.cbc.ca/news/background/iraq/casualties.html

Canadian Islamic Congress (CIC). (2005). *Anti Islam in the media.* Retrieved from http://www.canadianislamiccongress.com/rr/rr_2003.php

Chomsky, N., & Herman, E. S. (1988). *Manufacturing consent: The political economy of the mass media.* New York: Pantheon.

Choudry, A. A. (2006). *Global justice movement? Colonial amnesia.* Paper presented at the Society for Socialist Studies session, Congress 2006, York University, Toronto, Canada.

Churchill, W. (2003). *On the justice of roosting chickens: Consequences of American conquest and carnage.* Oakland, CA: AK Press.

CNN. (2005). *Iraq insurgency 101.* Retrieved from http://www.cnn.com/2005/WORLD/meast/10/12/schuster.column/index.html

Congalton, A. A., & Daniel, A. E. (1976). *The individual in the making.* Sydney, Australia: John Wiley.

Cooley, C. H. (1964). *Human nature and the social order.* New York: Schocken.

Cornell, S. (1988). *The return of the Native: American Indian political resurgence.* New York: Oxford University Press.

DeMarrais, K. B., & LeCompte, M. D. (1999). *The way schools work: A sociological analysis of education.* White Plains, NY: Longman.

Democracy Now. (2006, March 9). *Iraqi novelist Haifa Zangana: U.S. troops must withdraw now.* Retrieved from http://www.democracynow.org/article.pl?sid=06/03/09/1428223

Denzin, N. K. (1989). *Interpretive interaction.* Newbury Park, CA: Sage.

Drury, S. B. (1999). *Leo Strauss and the American right.* New York: St. Martin's.

Eisner, E. (1990). *The enlightened eye: Qualitative inquiry and the enhancement of educational practice.* New York: Macmillan.

Emery, W., Tiseo, F., & Lewellyn, L. (2000). *Rainbow of dreams: Memories in black and white.* Calgary: Detselig Enterprises Ltd.

Euben, R. (1997). Premodern, Antimodern or Postmodern? Islamic and Western Critiques of Modernity. *The Review of Politics*, Vol. 59, No. 3, pp. 429-459.

Euben, R. (1999). *Enemy in the mirror.* Princeton, NJ: Princeton University Press.

Euben, R. (2002). Contingent borders, syncretic perspectives: Globalization, political theory, and Islamizing knowledge. *International Studies Review, 4*(1), 23–48.

Fairness & Accuracy in Reporting (FAIR). (2001). *"This isn't discrimination, this is necessary": Beware the "Arab-looking."* Retrieved from http://www.fair.org/index.php?page=1081

Fouché, G. (2006). *Danish paper rejected Jesus cartoons.* Retrieved from http://www.guardian.co.uk/cartoonprotests/story/0,,1703552,00.html#article_c

Freire, P. (2005). *Pedagogy of the oppressed: 30th anniversary.* New York: Continuum.

Gray, E. (1995). *The green sea of Heaven.* Ashland, OR: White Cloud Press.

Hampton, E. (1993). Toward a redefinition of American Indian/Alaska Native education. *Canadian Journal of Native Education, 20*(2), 261–309.

Hampton, E. (1995). Towards a redefinition of Indian education. In M. Battiste & J. Barman (Eds.), *First Nations education in Canada: The circle unfolds* (pp. 5-46). Vancouver: University of British Columbia Press.

Hasan, A. G. (2005). *Why I am a Muslim.* London: HarperCollins.

Hess, P. (2005). *Raid in Iraq's "Indian Country."* Retrieved from http://www.upi.com/inc/view.php?StoryID=20030804-022042-6813r

Kikim Media and Unity Productions Fdnt (with KQED). (2002). *Muhammad: Legacy of a prophet* [Videotape]. United States: Public Broadcasting Corporation.

Kincheloe, J. L. (2003). *Teachers as researchers: Qualitative inquiry as a path to empowerment.* New York: RoutledgeFalmer.

Kincheloe, J. L., & Steinberg, S. R. (1997). *Changing multiculturalism.* London: Open University Press.

Kincheloe, J. L., & Steinberg, S. R. (Eds.). (2004). *The miseducation of the West: The hidden curriculum of Western-Muslim relations.* New York: Greenwood.

King, J. E. (1991). Dysconscious racism: Ideology, identity, and the miseducation of teachers. *Journal of Negro Education, 60*(2), 133–146.

Lindemann Nelson, H. (2001). *Damaged identities, narrative repair.* Ithaca, NY: Cornell University Press.

MacArthur, J. R. (2004). *Second front: Censorship and propaganda in the 1991 Gulf War.* Berkeley: University of California Press.

Macedo, D. (2005). Introduction. In P. Freire, *Pedagogy of the oppressed: 30th anniversary.* New York: Continuum.

Manji, I. (2003). *The trouble with Islam: A wake-up call for honesty and change.* Toronto: Random House Canada.

Mead, G. H. (1934). *Mind, self and society.* Chicago: University of Chicago Press.

Mohawk, J. (1992). *Columbus.* Retrieved from http://www.indians.org/welker/columbu1.htm

Nagel, J. (1996). *American Indian ethnic renewal: Red power and the resurgence of identity and culture.* New York: Oxford University Press.

Nasr, S. H. (2004). *The heart of Islam: Enduring values for humanity.* New York: HarperCollins.

Norton, A. (2004). *Leo Strauss and the politics of American empire.* New Haven, CT: Yale University Press.

O'Hearn, C. C. (1998). *Half and half: Writers on growing up biracial and bicultural.* New York: Pantheon.

Program on International Policy Attitudes (PIPA). (2003). *Misperception, the media and the Iraq War.* Retrieved from http://www.pipa.org/OnlineReports/Iraq/IraqMedia_Oct03/IraqMedia_Oct03_rpt.pdf

Rahul, M. (2001). *"We think the price is worth it": Media uncurious about Iraq policy's effects—there or here.* Retrieved from http://www.fair.org/index.php?page=1084

Regan, T. (2002). *When contemplating war, beware of babies in incubators.* Retrieved from URL http://www.csmonitor.com/2002/0906/p25s02-cogn.html

Rhea, T. J. (1997). *Race pride and the American Indian.* Cambridge, MA: Harvard University Press.

Rogerson, B. (2003). *The prophet Muhammad: A biography.* London: Little, Brown.

Said, E. (1978/1994). *Orientalism.* Harmondsworth, UK: Penguin.

Said, E. (1985). Opponents, audiences, constituencies and community. In H. Foster (Ed.), *Postmodern culture* (pp. 135–139). London: Pluto Press.

Said, E. (1998). Islam through Western eyes. *The Nation.* Retrieved from http://www.thenation.com/doc/19800426/19800426said

Said, E. W. (2002, July). Impossible histories: Why the many Islams cannot be simplified. *Harper's Magazine,* pp. 69–74.

Semali, L., & Kincheloe, J. (1999). *What is indigenous knowledge? Voices from the academy.* New York: Falmer.

Shah, U. (1996). Creating space: Moving from the mandatory to the worthwhile. In L. Beyer (Ed.), *Creating democratic classrooms* (pp. 41-61). New York: Teachers College Press.

Shaheen, J. G. (1984). *The TV Arab.* Bowling Green, OH: Bowling Green State University Popular Press.

Shaheen, J. G. (1991, November–December). The comic book Arab. *The Link, 24*(5).

Shaheen, J. G. (2001). *Reel bad Arabs.* New York: Olive Branch Press.

Shor, I., & Pari, C. (1999). *Education is politics.* Portsmouth, NH: Boynton/Cook.

Shuqair, M. (2002). *Jordanian youths are part of Mideast Islamic revival.* Retrieved from http://www.lebanonwire.com/0211/02113019DS.asp

Smith, L. T. (1999). *Decolonizing methodologies.* London: Zed.

Solomon, N. (2002). *Determined journalism can challenge injustice.* Retrieved from http://www.commondreams.org/views02/0925-08.htm

Steinberg, S. (2004). Desert minstrels: Hollywood's curriculum of Arabs and Muslims. In J. L. Kincheloe & S. R. Steinberg (Eds.), *The miseducation of the West: The hidden curriculum of Western-Muslim relations* (pp. 171–180). New York: Greenwood.

Stonebanks, C. D. (2004). Consequences of perceived ethnic identities (reflection of an elementary school incident). In J. L. Kincheloe & S. R. Steinberg (Eds.), *The miseducation of the West: The hidden curriculum of Western-Muslim relations* (pp. 87–102). New York: Greenwood.

Stonebanks, C. D. (2008). *James Bay Cree students and higher education: Issues of identity and culture shock.* Rotterdam, The Netherlands: Sense Publishers.

Taylor, R., Rizvi, R., Lingard, B., & Henry, M. (1997). *Educational politics and the politics of change.* New York: Routledge.

Vakily, A. (2001). Methodological problems in the study of Islam, and Ali Shariati's proposed methodology for the study of religions. *American Journal of Islamic Social Sciences, 18*(3), 91–109.

Vickers, S. B. (1998). *Native American identities.* Albuquerque: University of New Mexico Press.

Wintonick, P., & Achbar, M. (Directors). (1992). *Manufacturing consent: Noam Chomsky and the media* [DVD]. Montreal: National Film Board of Canada.

Wolcott, H. (1992). Posturing in qualitative inquiry. In M. D. LeCompte, W. L. Millroy, & J. Preissle (Eds.), *The handbook of qualitative research in education* (pp. 3–52). New York: Academic Press.

Wright, W. (1992). *Stolen continents: The new world through Indian eyes since 1492.* Boston: Houghton Mifflin.

Zinn, H. (2003). *A people's history of the United States: 1492–present.* New York: HarperCollins.

Part III

CRITICAL AND INDIGENOUS METHODOLOGIES

The five chapters in Part III reflexively implement critical indigenous methodologies. They do this by transforming, rereading, and criticizing existing research practices, including life story, life history, ethnographic, autoethnographic, narrative, visual, and postcolonial methodologies. These are the standard interpretive methodologies.

It is necessary to elaborate our definition of indigenous methodology, which was presented in the Preface. Critical indigenous methodologies have these characteristics. They implement indigenous pedagogies. They are fitted to the needs and traditions of specific indigenous communities. This fitting process may include creating new methodologies, as well as modifying existing practices. In each instance, pragmatic and moral criteria apply. The scholar must ask if these practices or modifications will produce knowledge that will positively benefit this indigenous community. And if so, which members? Of course, this answer cannot always be given in advance. The meaning of any set of actions is only visible in the consequences that follow from the action.

Life Stories and the New Indian Story

Elizabeth Cook-Lynn surveys three decades of American Indian literatures. She offers a critical reading of recent work in this broad genre, including first-person narratives, biographies, life stories, Indian romance and mixed-blood novels, magical Indian realism, tribal parables, and ethnographies. She is especially critical of Indian stories told by non-Natives, especially those told by Hollywood filmmakers (e.g., *Dances With Wolves*).

She observes that the new Indian story rarely conveys traditional knowledge, history, or myth. Instead, contemporary writers have produced a burst of self-interpretation, celebrating their own subjectivity, while ignoring the myths of origin that are central to Native American life. She argues, for example, that a great deal of work done in the mixed-blood literary movement is "personal, invented, appropriated, and irrelevant to First Nation status in the United States." She continues, if that work "becomes too far removed from what is really going on in Indian enclaves, there will be no way to engage in responsible intellectual strategies in an era when structures of external cultural power are more oppressive than ever."

Cook-Lynn sets a high standard for Native American fiction writers. She wants them to be, in Gramsci's sense, true organic intellectuals. They should not just write about themselves. They have an obligation to write from and through the languages of culture to the experiences of Native American persons. As organic intellectuals, they should write in ways that criticize the larger culture and its colonizing ways. They should not succumb to the temptations of assimilation, Hollywood, or popular culture.

Native American writers should avoid reproducing those literary forms that arose as a result of assimilation. They should write in ways that keep the histories, stories, and origin myths of the past alive. They should embrace a critical pedagogy that helps Native Americans imagine how the world could be changed for the better.

Indigenous Ethnography

South African scholars Tomaselli, Dyll, and Francis write from their ongoing experiences doing research with some groups of San Bushman in the Kalahari Desert. Their chapter involves an unraveling of the meanings they learned to bring to auto-, reflexive, performance, and indigenous ethnography. Influenced by Stacy Holman Jones (see Chapter 18) and Ellis and Bochner (2000), they excavate the reflexive, indigenous side of autoethnography. They map a personal journey, telling a story of how they came to see that they could not *not* write themselves into their texts, that they were performers in their own ethnography.

Thus, do they work back against traditional ethnography, that writing form where the goal is to grasp the native's point of view. Tomaselli, Dyll, and Francis reverse this dictum. Their goal was to grasp not the native's point of view but to understand their reflexive place in this ethnographic project, to learn how to write themselves and their experiences into this emergent form of critical indigenous ethnography. In so doing, they wrote a decolonizing narrative. At the end, they came to understand that "10 years ago, the kind of writing discussed here was and, in many cases, continues to be dismissed as scientific aberration. Now we have textbooks on the method." And chapters like theirs!

Autoethnography Is Queer

Adams and Jones queer autoethnography as a method—that is, they redeploy the term and twist it from its prior usages, seeking an alignment between queer and autoethnographic writing. Both forms value fluidity, openness, indeterminancy, a politics of commitment. In taking up queer theory and queer projects, they move through and out of identity categories (based on sex/gender, race/class, or any combination or hierarchy of these elements) and into a queer methodological sensibility. This is a sensibility that disrupts taken-for-granted categories, understanding that a queer identity is always a contextual, interactional, political achievement. They connect their chapter to Alexander's (Chapter 6), noting how his project differs from theirs. Poetically, they map a radical poetics of change, sometimes borrowing, sometimes inventing, always working to make the personal visible and political.

Their version of autoethnography hinges on the "push and pull between and among analysis and evocation, personal experience and larger social, cultural, and political concerns" (see Chapter 18, this volume, p. 374). Their text works and dismantles the spaces where this hinge operates. Interrogating this hinge, they create new spaces where queered bodies come together, always in ideologically contested ways. Writing out of their own queered histories with sexuality, family, and identity, they trouble the poetic, the transgressive, embracing that which cannot be known in advance. In freeing themselves from epistemology, they perform a new version of the ethnographic. They dare to write in spaces where nothing is hidden any longer. They dare to transgress the personal in ways that show that nothing was ever really private anyway. In the spaces that sharing and openness embrace, they offer new queer stories, stories that move us all a little closer to empowerment and presence in our everyday lives.

Narrative Poetics and Performative Interventions

D. Soyini Madison's performance in print narrates the ways in which local human rights activists in Ghana, West Africa, are working for the rights of women and girls against the traditional cultural practice of Troxovi. She merges indigenous and critical methods with critical theory. She enacts a politics of possibility, a search for social justice that matters on the ground. In her text, each narrator poetically "narrates [his or her] own indigenous and critical methodology." This is a methodology that critically confronts the discourses of oppression that operate in these women's lives. It deconstructs these discourses from within, exposing the contradictions they rest upon.

She weaves her own commentary throughout the two oral narratives, looking for a delicate balance between her understandings and those of the narrators. Her performance text critically implicates corporate capitalism in the human rights abuses of women in the global South.

Her text is a performance of possibilities, a staging of struggles, the imagination of how injustice could be ended, a confrontation with the many faces of violence and injustice. Her analysis of the two performance narratives serves as a magnifying lens, a window into the multiple truths hidden below the surface. The subalterns do speak, and they dance and they struggle and they resist, and those resistances come alive in Madison's text.

Madison's poetic, performative intervention models new, kinder, gentler ways of being in the world, whether as fieldworkers or as academics. We should, she urges, "practice at home what we preach on paper and in the field. We work to become more generous with each other *within* the academy, as we work for a politics of global generosity." We want performances and narrative poetics that matter, interventions that serve the goals of social justice. Thus would the academy be decolonized.

▣ Reading the Visual: Postcolonial, Feminist Methodologies

Radhika Parameswaran implements a postcolonial feminist methodology, thereby extending the critical anticolonial feminist frameworks presented by Cannella and Manuelito (Chapter 3) in Part I, and Saavedra and Nymark (Chapter 13) in Part II. She understands that the global neocolonial operates through a complex set of gendered visual codes, codes that commodify and sexualize the white and brown female body. Global capitalist consumer culture requires a visual culture, a discursive public landscape that uses the sultry bodies of Third World women to promote the universal desire for modernity.

Her postcolonial feminist methodology organizes her critical reading of these media texts. She contests the empirical authority granted vision, as well as the visual field of racism in the West, showing how the histories of race and the visual are entangled in 19th-century theories of biology, skin color, intelligence, and evolution. In turn, these theories underwrote the colonial project that turned the Third World and its dark-skinned others into objects of desire, labor, and fantasy. A complex semiotics of race, gender, and nation structured these visual texts, these pedagogies of racism.

Using a combination of methods—documentary, historical, forensic, visual, semiotic—she attacks the multisited and deeply intertextual ways in which racialized visual images circulate within the spaces of the neocolonial. She illustrates the power of her method in a nuanced reading of the colorful cover photograph of the *National Geographic* magazine's 1999 millennium issue on global culture. The cover contrasts two Indian women—one older, in traditional dress with ornate red scarf, the second younger, in a tight black cat suit, unzipped to the middle of her chest. The caption tells the viewer that the older woman is biochemist, and the younger woman, her daughter, is a model and former television host. The photo maps a natural history, from colonial (past, modern) to postcolonial (present, postmodern).

These raced and gendered bodies communicate the "liberating effects of globalization in India." The use of the female body is significant, because it "harkens back to the 19th century when Indian nationalists and British colonizers deployed women's bodies . . . to wage debates over tradition and modernity." Women as consumers, women as consumed, embody and lead the way into the new capitalist culture.

This subtle postcolonial feminist reading of the pedagogies of postcoloniality contests the consumer utopias that neoliberalism promises. Analyzing the visual culture of "the powerful and privileged classes in India *and* the West, classes whose habitus may include the *National Geographic* . . . can reveal the transnational consolidation of specific ideologies of gender, nation, race, and class in multiple contexts." Multinational corporate capital requires the services of a gendered global visual media system. Parameswaran shows us how to challenge this hegemonic order.

▣ Conclusion

Each of the chapters in this section elaborates a version of indigenous methodology. Each is fitted to the needs and traditions of specific indigenous communities—Native American, South African San Bushman, queers, human rights activists in Ghana, and subaltern women. This fitting process is performative, poetic, grounded in oral discourse, reflexively critical. It is anchored both in the academy and in indigenous communities. This interpretive process engages in each pragmatic and moral concerns—that is, how can this indigenous methodology confront oppression and improve the world for indigenous persons? Thus, methodology becomes a moral concern.

Reference

Ellis, C., & Bochner, A. (2000). Autoethnography, personal narrative, reflexivity: Researcher as subject. In N. K. Denzin & Y. S. Lincoln (Eds.), *The SAGE handbook of qualitative research* (2nd ed., pp. 733–768). Thousand Oaks, CA: Sage.

16

HISTORY, MYTH, AND IDENTITY IN THE NEW INDIAN STORY

Elizabeth Cook-Lynn

There are historic and mythic journeys everywhere in Native narratives. So, when you talk of history, myth, and identity in entire tribal literary canons and even in the so-called new Indian story, you are going back to origins. When you do this, then, you recognize the importance of geography, by that I mean a specific landscape . . . (so often referred to vaguely in lit-crit studies as "a sense of place"), and you recognize the importance of language, and you recognize the holy people and you recognize all of the creature worlds and sights and sounds of the universe which surround human beings and their lives. It is an astonishing thing to ponder, especially if you are a writer.

It seems to me that in terms of the imaginative concepts, which are evident in Indian narratives, origin myths and historical migrations are probably the least accessible and least well known of the influences. Yet, they resonate in the most humble of stories and poems.

A little piece I published some years ago illustrates this point. It is taken from a 1990 collection of short stories I published with Arcade, one of my first significant publications in fiction (Cook-Lynn, 1990). This is a collection of 13 stories out of print for 10 years, being reissued by the University of Arizona Press in a few months. The collection is called *The Power of Horses and Other Stories,* but don't get the impression it's about horses. It isn't.

This collection begins with a brief story called "Mahpiyato," a kind of preface, or introduction. While you read it, try to think of "origins," try to think of geography and language and the holy people who might be known in Dakotah Sioux mythology:

> One late summer day the old woman and her grandchild walked quietly along the road toward the river, as they had done all their lives. The (k)unchi had a large soft blanket tied around her waist and shoulders, and the child swung two small pails, and, so, those who might have noticed them knew that they were going to pick wild fruit. The blanket would be thrown beneath buffalo berry bushes to catch the small red fruit as the child, climbing high, would shake the branches vigorously. The small pails would hold the larger tart, wild plums.

The (k)unchi wore a black silk kerchief over her white hair, and as she walked, she pulled it closer over her forehead to shade her eyes from the intermittent sun. She shaded her eyes, also, with a slender hand as she looked up into the sky, and the child, attentive to every movement, followed her glance.

The great expanse of the river was shining before them, but, because of a cloud moving across the watery landscape, part of the river looked blue and the other part of it appeared to be dark gray where the shadow of the cloud fell upon it.

"Look at that!" the grandmother said softly in Indian language. And she stood still for a few moments, the child at her side.

"Look, hunh-he-e-e," indicating by the sound of her voice that a sober and interesting phenomenon was taking place right before their eyes.

The child, a steadfast and modest companion of the old woman, knew from long experience about the moments when the stories came on and watched cautiously, leaning to one side so as not to catch the full glare in her eyes.

"That is what we call mahpiyato, isn't it?" said the old woman to the child.

"That is what mahpiyato really means." She stood as if entranced, her long fingers now touching the fringes of the blanket.

"To just say 'blue' or 'sky' or 'cloud' in English, you see, doesn't mean much. But mahpiyato is that Dakotah word which tells us what we are witnessing right now, at this very moment."

She pointed.

"You see, she is blue. And she is gray. Mahpiyato is, you see, one of the Creators. Look! Look! Look at Mahpiyato!"

Her voice was low and soft and very convincing.

▣ ▣ ▣

That's the story . . . and, so, what do you do with it????? How does this storytelling assist in understanding the definition of the term *indigenous* as well as the function of indigenous origins in modern thought?

▣ ▣ ▣

The Journey, you see, for Dakotahs, often originates in myth, even the little journey of the grandmother and the child going to the river to pick berries, which, on the face of it, seems a mundane and/or unremarkable event. Yet, if we accept the notion that ideas and concepts of origin are essential elements of an indigenous text, we are required as readers to look more deeply into the cultural translations such a story presents. It is important, then, to accept the idea that Creators, sometimes thought of as the Holy Persons, are everywhere, and ever present in Dakotah thought systems.

The recording of Native views while investigating philosophical formulations has always been the purpose of storytelling, especially that storytelling that tells one generation of listeners what the previous generation has come to know through the long tenancy of the tribe in a specific geography. This reality distinguishes "indigenous" storytelling from other more modern categories of storytelling. In this case, the grandmother, knowing what she knows about the universe and the river, articulates the phenomenon of sky and cloud behavior so that the symbiotic relationship between the universe and human beings is an accepted theory. The grandmother describes the sky and the cloud formulations as human behaviors, making them feminine, communicating that the ever changing sky relates those changes to the Dakotah persons standing as mere observers on the ground. The Dakota concept of sky behavior suggests a close relationship between humans and the holy persons (deities), even though the sky has existed as a holy being from near the beginnings of the Dakota universe, thus the phenomenon is deserving of the awestruck attitude of mere humans: hunh-hu-hee-e-e, she says, an expression of wonder. It is a wonder to stand on the earth and observe the behavior of what surrounds us.

▣ ▣ ▣

It is an unfortunate reality that the study of American Indian literatures today, with few exceptions, reveals that the new Indian Story being told in the mainstream is rarely believed to be the bearer of traditional knowledge, history, or myth. Perhaps we should not expect that this contemporary genre (called Native American literatures) should be all or any of that since many American

Indian writers today are not the practicing singers and chanters, tribal ritualists, medicine healers, not even committed participants in what may be called "a tribal world." Often, these writers of the new American Indian story are not even the "informants" so ubiquitous in past and present anthropological studies, and so they are by and large not well versed in the asserted knowledge available through ceremonial or ritual or tradition, or tribal language. What these writers are good at is telling stories, writing novels, practicing poetry and drama, writing memoirs and essays, making movies, and doing journalism, and they have produced in the past three decades a burst of self-interpretation that has astonished the literary world, starting with Momaday in 1968. It is the way of the present literary scene and has been an achievement of eminently readable works.

Whatever we need to say about that, origin stories (i.e., the myths of origin and historical migration stories of the tribes) remain the stuff of tradition in the new narrative and, ultimately, are what we rely on when we talk of "identity." How does one say I am Dakotah Sioux? Or Hopi? Or Diné? The other day I listened to a cultural storytelling event given by a practicing practitioner of the Navajo tribes and presenter of the Diné Hataa_ii Association. His name is Anthony Lee Sr., and he told us of the significance of the Twin Warriors of Navajo mythology and its impact on Diné society today. He told of the birth of the twins and how they grew up in a significant place (geography), to destroy what may be called in English "the Evil Monsters." You know that the "twins," sometimes referred to as the duality in Native thought, are everywhere in the stories. Mr. Lee's suggestion was that such knowledge assists modern Diné people (the Navajo) in understanding the contemporary issues that are faced today by the people, and certainly that duality shapes all intellectual and artistic activities in Native communities, even today. Duality in all things, in all presences . . . male/female . . . good/evil . . . this world . . . the upper world . . . if you are a Lakota/Dakota sundancer, you recognize that duality in the sacred tree used as the essential object in ceremony and ritual. The cottonwood tree must be carefully chosen with a fork in it about halfway up, and in its limbs it carries the perfect star signifying the beginning of time.

Native literatures are replete with these origin stories, and when the Lakota/Dakota Oyate say that "we were once the star people," they mean it literally because they understand the functions of storytelling as chronologies of the past and the future. There is probably no need to either lament or worship how these matters find their ways into contemporary literatures, though most of us react on one side or the other of it. The truth is, our literatures have suffered the oppression of colonial intrusion, much knowledge is forgotten or ignored, and we as Native people have often been confused or disillusioned as to what it all means in terms of contemporary lives. Part of what has been going on in this intrusion is what I call "the master narrative" (i.e., the White man's version of who we are as Native peoples). This master narrative is everywhere, and it is blatant and it is in my view, at least, an arrogance that is unremitting. I live 20 miles from where the White man is blowing up a mountain to sculpt the face of the great Oglala Chieftain Crazy Horse. We all know that Crazy Horse DID NOT ALLOW his photograph to be taken. Thus, we Indians don't know what he looks like. But, the White man does and carves his face on a mountain he knew as sacred. How offensive is that arrogance? How important is it to the White man in America that "the master narrative" be supreme? How absurd!!

The recent re-creation of the Lewis and Clark journal, as a literary and historical manifestation of the American epic to be honored in our collective memories, is another example of that intrusion. It is told not as a colonial event resulting in the death of thousands of Indians and the theft of a continent from peoples who had lived here for thousands of years; rather, it is told as an event of grand achievement. Much of what American Indian literary works have been doing has been to dispute that legacy of colonial intrusion, and in doing so, mythic sensibilities are rediscovered and reclaimed. The "master narrative" is coming under closer scrutiny, and the return to tradition is becoming more important in the Native American Story.

The function of mythology, then, from which all ideas about origins emerge, is an essential part of that scrutiny. Lewis and Clark are newcomers to the stage, and they say almost nothing about the indigenous life of this continent. It is left up to the Native to do that, and so concepts of indigenousness are developed, personalities are identified, events that shape eras are reviewed, and geographies become the center of cultural endeavor. What I mean by that can be thought of in this way: Tate, the wind, is thought of as the "first Dakotah" and is called sometimes Ikce. Or even Ikca Wicasta. When the earth was covered only with water, he existed. He is considered a "relative" and an "ancestor" of the Dakotahs. He is male, like the Sun, and is sometimes thought to be a "bad" relative or a "good" one. He is a determinant, sometimes, of behavior. He is one of the ancestral spirits in Native experience, one of the first characters in the stories to whom the question, "What makes people behave as they do?" must be asked. This means that ethics and morality exist in the universe, and it is up to human beings to pay attention.

When the Dakotahs and Lakotahs say, "We were once the star people," they, like the grandmother of the "Mahpiyato" story that first began this chapter, pay homage to the Creators. When the wind was the only presence, and when the earth was covered with water, the stars were made from water, and they were us, Dakotahs. Thus, Dakotas know constellations as symbols of information formed to tell us what we need to know in order to live harmoniously on this earth. There is a wonderful story about a particular constellation, for example, called by non-Dakotahs "the Big Dipper." You all know Big Dipper stories, I'm sure. Dakotas do, too. They call this star formation *wica-akiyuha(n)pi,* which can be translated as "man being carried in the sky," and it is a reference of those seven stars that make up the constellation to the seven council fires of the Sioux Nation. Reference is made, then, to what we know here on earth . . . we are seven large bands: Oglalas, Sicangu, Ihanktowan, Isanti, Minneconjou, Si Hasapa, and Hunkpati. You see, what is in the stars is on the earth and what is on the earth is in the stars. I refer to this constellation in my stories, once in *The Power of Horses* and again, I think, in my latest collection of essays, as a way to explain the Dakotah way of life.

This is how I explain it in my short story (Cook-Lynn, 1990):

> Wic'a ak'i'uhan pi is a constellation that has four stars situated at the four points of what the non-Siouan world knows as the Big Dipper, along with three stars which make up the handle, seven stars in all. These four plus three points in the constellation are thought to be "carriers," defined with sacred status. They are carriers of the seven sacred rituals of the people, and therefore are repositors of religious knowledge. Further, they are considered to be four spirit people who often assist other humans, sometimes carrying them, in the journeys across the skies during the ohunkaka (creation) period, toward humanity. (p. 49)

This myth is often re-created in the rituals of the people even today. For example, I continue to explain on page 49, "This act of assistance is often recreated in a modern Lakota/Dakota/Nakota dance ritual known in English as 'the blanket dance,' when four dancers (usually male traditional dancers, though sometimes young women dancers) hold the four corners of a blanket and make a journey around the dance arena asking that donations be placed in the blanket for the singers who, it is always said, 'have come from a far distance'" and need assistance on their homeward journey. You can see this played out at any Sioux powwow, if you are inclined to go to these summer gatherings, and some of you probably have. So, the point is myth becomes ritual and ritual eventually becomes literature (i.e., storytelling).

The miracle is that any of this has survived. But, one of the reasons to continue to tell the stories is to remind all of us that we are in danger of losing respect for all living things, including each other. We have lost some kind of communal common sense, and we really do need to talk to one another about how to bring about a new period in our concomitant histories.

▣ ▣ ▣

It is unfortunate that, despite the burgeoning body of work by Native writers, the greatest body of acceptable telling of the Indian story is still in the hands of non-Natives. The recent (1995) Disney release of *Pocahontas* is evidence of that, if there has been any doubt, and we can expect even more of the same. Much as the title to Indian land is still held by the White American government, the major Indian story is held in non-Indian enclaves though not, like the land, by overt congressional mandate. Rather, we are told, freedom of the press and the First Amendment allow any storyteller to be taken seriously. This means that the works of non-Indians invade every genre, and they can't be written fast enough, it seems.

The so-called popular Indian story is everywhere, in every paperback section of every supermarket, on every bookstand. This kind of dime-novel approach to the story is well established in American culture, though, like anything else, it can no longer be bought for a dime. These novels, though, are the precursors to the narratives of Larry McMurtry (e.g., *Lonesome Dove*) and to the stories of the White boy exemplar, Kevin Costner, who as a child "wanted to be Indian" and grew up to become successful as star, writer, and director of *Dances With Wolves,* telling the most famous modern Indian story of them all. His movie recharged the flagging paperback industry but, more significantly, geared up the television fare for such characters as Medicine Woman and Buffalo Girls. This brought hundreds of Indians to Hollywood; they hired agents and became actors and actresses, but that's a subject for another time.

Euro-American Literary Genre Influence

Despite the reality that Indian stories have had their own generic literary development within a tribal language, custom, and experience, the European influence in the newest versions or in translation is almost overwhelming. American writers have never hesitated to plunge into literary fields of exotic origin and call them their own. Thus, the borrowing and trading of literary kinds have flourished.

Anything is usable. The chant. Religious ritual. Coyote. Mother Earth. There is some feeble effort on the part of many thoughtful artists to connect indigenous literary traditions to contemporary forms such as has happened with the remarkable "trickster" figure, but for the most part, these often seem superficial or exploitative.

This means that the Indian story, as it is told outside of the tribal genres and the Indian character, has its own modern imprimatur.

In the Costner-style story told in television, movies, and paperback, the White protagonist is central. An important generic quality of the White male hero requires that he be helper to the underdog, sensitive to women, and a winner. The White heroine is strong-willed, she will not shirk her duty, and she often knows the history of Indians better than they do themselves, spouting lines about Wounded Knee, federal policy, and why a son-in-law cannot speak to his wife's mother lest he offend some tribal code. Indian characters in this genre often break into a chant at every massacre site, light the sacred pipe during the unexpected quiet moments, and sit cross-legged at gorgeously lighted campfires.

For reasons that are still obscure, Native supervisors and consultants often are employed nowadays by movie and television producers, perhaps in an effort to assert authenticity, a relatively new phenomenon perhaps brought about during the militant 1960s and 1970s when "identity politics" reached its nexus, when only Blacks could speak for Blacks, only women could speak on women's issues. This political agenda may have moved publishing houses and New York editors around to the notion that Indians could now write their own stories, but, in truth, that idea doesn't seem to have improved very much on the Indian story itself. The stereotypes still abound, and the same stories are being told only in a more sympathetic tenor.

An example of how wrong things can go was obvious in a 1995 Disney project. Russell Means, a Lakota activist turned movie actor and leader of the American Indian movement in the 1960s and 1970s, was quoted in the *Lakota Times,* a Native-owned newspaper based in Rapid City, South Dakota, as saying about the new Walt Disney picture *Pocahontas:* "It's the finest movie to ever come out of Hollywood about Indian people." Means, the voice of Chief Powhatan in the Disney blockbuster, is apparently thought by the media to be historian, literary scholar, and art critic all rolled into one. Or perhaps they are simply using his notoriety to make money. In either case, the Pocahontas story is an old story, one that is hotly debated by Native American scholars—none of whom believe the story to be truthful or that all was well in colonial America as the film implied. Because there is thought to be no Native intellectualism, no one thinks to turn to the Native American scholarship that has been done on this period. Historian Angie Debo (1970) wrote in *A History of the Indians of the United States* that the Pocahontas story was filled with errors and fantasy, and if the incidents happened at all, they were an anomaly in an otherwise barbaric history toward Native peoples. She said it need not be retold except to assuage the U.S. national conscience.

Even as we speak, though, there is the idea that to talk about something, you have to have had special experience. Everyone knows of the experience of the American Indian movement media stars of the 1970s such as Russell Means, so why not ask him to speak for Indians in any and all matters? It's sad but true that to run an alcoholism treatment center on any Indian reservation in the country (as an example of furthering this "been there, done that" notion of authenticity), your own years of alcohol abuse are your major credential. This idea is called "essentialism" in lit-crit jargon, and it is thought by critics—who paint everyone who speaks out with the same brush—to make its defenders "intellectually disreputable." A redneck comic who is making the rounds puts it, "I don't think you ought to talk about being a redneck unless you are one . . . and I are one." Very funny guy.

Whatever else may be said about experience-based intellectualism, there seems to be no real understanding of the idea as it concerns the content of art and scholarship, and some have dismissed it as a "damned if you do, damned if you don't" issue.

Fabulous Fictions and the Indian Romance Novel

Popular fiction about Indians includes the romance novel, which—developing out of the 19th-century novel that disallowed the mating of Indians and Whites—has explicit interracial love at its core. Kathleen Pierson, one of the new writers in this genre, was born in Fredricksburg, Virginia, to an Air Force family, raised in Massachusetts, and educated at Mount Holyoke, South Hadley, Massachusetts. She went to a North Dakota Indian reservation a couple of decades ago to teach and, while she was there, married a Lakota Sioux man, Clyde Eagle. She is now a successful romance novelist using Sioux themes and settings and seems to be attempting to lead the way toward harmony and assimilation between the races, with interracial love her major theme.

This is not a new idea for modern White New Englandresses. In fact, one named Elaine Goodale (1863–1953), an early Christian woman among the Sioux, educated at Sky Farm in western Massachusetts, married a Sisseton Dakota man named Charles Eastman just one year after the Wounded Knee Massacre in 1890, and they both talked openly about their collaboration as a commitment to assimilation. If you look very closely at what has been written and who is doing the writing, this model can seem almost embedded in the history of those times. Nonetheless, it hangs on as a hopeful consequence of that history.

Kathleen Pierson Eagle's *Reason to Believe,* published in 1995 by Avon, is a fictional account of the "power and magic of love." She spends her time crafting "very special stories," her publicity blurbs say. Her genre, if you look at the tips in *Writer's Market,* requires that attraction, passion, idealism, and love be the main themes; that the heroine (White woman, in this case) be self-assured and perceptive; and that the hero (Indian man, in this case) be goal oriented, upwardly mobile, and dynamic. This is known in the trade as classical romance.

I would suspect that Ms. Eagle probably wants her work considered as history because she begins with a reference to the 5-year Big Foot Memorial

Ride from Cherry Creek, South Dakota, to the Wounded Knee Site (1989–1992) in this way: "For the runners and the riders, and for all those who offered support. May the sacrifices be known, the injustices be rectified, and may the healing touch battered hearts everywhere." In the afterword, she and her husband, Clyde, thank such Lakota notables as Arvol Looking Horse, Carol Ann Heart, Ron McNeil, Isaac Dog Eagle, and Howard Eagle Shield. Ms. Eagle also wrote *This Time Forever* and *Fire and Rain* and has just finished a novel called *Sunrise Song.* The last title is a fictional story about what was called the Hiawatha Indian Insane Asylum for American Indians that opened in Canton, South Dakota, in 1902 and closed in 1934. She claims to have done considerable research into the history of the place, the only remnant of which is a cemetery now in the middle of a golf course. Her "do-gooder" approach to history and fiction seems to find enthusiastic audiences.

Book Lovers Love the Children's Story About Indians

The children's Indian story has long been a staple in the American narrative, and many of these stories are so entwined with European folk tales as to be severely corrupted. A transplanted Englishman, Paul Gobel, who lived in the Black Hills of South Dakota for a time and married a woman from Sturgis, South Dakota, with whom he has a child, has been the most intrepid explorer of this genre in recent times. He has taken Iktomi (or Unktomi) stories, the star stories, and the creation myths of the Sioux, a vast body of philosophical and spiritual knowledge about the universe, to fashion 20 or more storybooks for children ages 3 to 14 that he, himself, has illustrated in a European aesthetic and style. Now living in Minnesota, he has successfully used several people as "informants," including a popular hoop dancer, Kevin Locke, who lives on one of the South Dakota Indian reservations. It is no wonder, when Native cultural philosophy and religion are used to entertain and inform White American children, the idea of "Indian Intellectualism" in America is dismissed.

The informant-based Indian story has a long tenure in the American literary canon. Gobel—a man who says he showed artistic talent at an early age, was always fascinated by Indians, and long wanted to be considered an artiste—has taken it a step further into the popular imagination. Most of all, he simply invades the available written texts, among them Ella Deloria's (1932) *Dakota Texts,* published ethnographic work with the famed ethnographer Franz Boas in the early decades of this century.

Gobel takes his place not alongside but a step ahead of those other White writers of children's stories who, knowingly or not, have long trivialized the rather sophisticated notions the Lakotas have held about the universe for thousands of years. Children's stories about the Bible are one thing but, considering the vast ignorance the average person has concerning Native intellectualism, the non-Lakota-speaking Englishman's reinterpretation of the Native Lakota/Dakota worldview and spirituality through the lens of his own language and art is, at the very least, arrogant.

It has not occurred to anyone, least of all Gobel himself, to ask why it is that tribal writers, except in carefully managed instances, have chosen not to use these stories commercially. If one were to inquire about that, one would have to explore the moral and ethical dimensions of who owns bodies of knowledge and literature. That is a difficult exploration in a capitalistic democracy that suggests anything can be bought and sold. Many White American critics refuse to enter into this debate, believing Native American literature and knowledge cannot "belong" to any single group. A discussion of who "transmits" and who "produces" usually follows. As Americans and other world citizens enter cyberspace, increased technology will undoubtedly bring more Anglo-American interpretation and definition to these matters.

In 1995, a children's book, *The Indian in the Cupboard* (Banks, 1982), turned into a do-gooder fantasy movie about a toy Indian who becomes real in much the same way a piece of wood carved by Gippetto became Pinocchio (a real boy). This metamorphosis proves, one supposes, that there is nothing new in plot making. The media touted this movie as a marvelous step forward in movie making about Indians since it was tribally specific both in language and history, and its purpose was to teach little White moviegoers to be kind to animals, Indians, and other feathered friends. Native consultants and actors were part of the preparation of the story, and this was supposed to give it further importance.

Biography

If you want to understand the pathology of Whites and Indians in America, it is biography, the "life story," that is required reading. It is certain that the "Indian informant" model of "transmitting" and "producing" stories has had acceptance not only in the popular literary world but in the academic world as well. It probably has its origins in the rather quick rise of the discipline of anthropology in the past seven or eight decades, or in the model claimed by ethnographers who have been participants and originators of the American Indian story since the beginning and have long claimed a "scientific" methodology. It's a little like the "authorized" or "unauthorized" biography so prevalent now in American culture that has spawned not only vicious debate but, in some cases, vicious litigation.

Because of its claim to scholarship, this genre is dominated by the university presses. The University of Nebraska Press, as an example of one of the more prolific presses in this genre, has published about 40 titles in the years since its Bison Books classic, *Black Elk Speaks* (a tale of traditionalism) by John G. Neihardt (1961), invaded the imagination of the American public. *Catch Colt* by Sidner J. Larson (1995) (a tale of mixed-bloodedness) is one of the latest in the subsequent series, American Indian Lives, which gives you an idea of how diverse the genre has become. There is an editorial board for this American Indian Lives series (which now has 14 titles and offers a North American Indian Prose Award annually).

Life Story

I've become particularly interested in the "life story" as it has emerged as a genre in the literature on Indians. I've been asked by editors and agents to write my own "life story," as they send me their regretful rejections to my essays, nonfiction works, and poetry. While I may have a reasonable understanding of why a state-run university press would not want to publish my research that has little good to say about America's relationship to the tribes or art, I am at a loss to explain why anyone would be more interested in my life story (which for one thing is quite unremarkable) than they would be in my poetry, for instance, or my essays, which may generate thoughtful discussion where none had before existed.

Though I've referred to the "informant-based" Indian stories as "life story" works, I would like to suggest that they are offshoots of biography, a traditional art form in European literature. Ethnographic biography is not an Indian story at all and does not have significant ties to the interesting bodies of Native literary canons produced culturally and historically. In light of this, the question of the origins of life stories about Indians and the development of that genre seems essential to the exploration of what is called the Indian story in the American literary canon.

Biography, as I understand its literary history, has been a type of writing that was thought to merge with history but was not itself history. Distinguished personages like the Duchess of Newcastle (Margaret Cavandish) wrote biographies in the 1600s, and it was a matter of self-record. Later, anthologies of biographies were written, as in the lives of the saints, and they were among the first kinds of history that I ever read when I was a student who lived near a pitifully biased library at the Catholic Indian boarding school near Fort Thompson, South Dakota. I did not consider them history even then, though I was probably aware that biography was said to have evolved into a form that required considerable research.

Over the years, as is the case in any genre development, methods and principles evolved, although biographical methods were rather strictly adhered to in the early stages. Collecting anecdotes, for example, was thought, in early biography, to be a form of degraded "evidence," but today the anecdotal method seems primary.

Delight and entertainment, gossip and scandal have become the style of the day. All of this may account for the interest today's American readers have in the Indian story because its anecdotal nature is difficult to resist.

Indian life stories are an attempt, perhaps, to own the facts of our own lives, to keep private the most intimate facts, or to share them in the way that seems most appropriate. In the face of massive historical distortion of Indian lives over the past two hundred years, this attempt is understandable. But the truth is people do not "own" their lives at all. As Janet Malcolm (1993) suggests in her *New Yorker* essay on publishing stories about the unfortunate life and death of the White poetess, Sylvia Plath, "This ownership passes out of our hands at birth, at the moment we are first observed." Malcolm goes on to say, "Biography is the medium through which the remaining secrets of the famous dead are taken from them and dumped out in full view of the world," and "The dead cannot be libeled or slandered. They are without legal recourse." This is probably more true of Indians than of any other people on earth.

But what of the living? What of those who "inform," those who give themselves over to a White writer for collaboration and explanation?

"The biographer at work," Malcolm (1993) says, and this is what applies to the "informant-based" work, is like the professional burglar, breaking into a house, rifling through certain drawers that he has good reason to think contain the jewelry and money, and triumphantly bearing his loot away. The voyeurism and busybodyism that impels writers and readers of biography alike are obscured by an apparatus of scholarship designed to give the enterprise an appearance of banklike blandness and solidity. The biographer is portrayed almost as a kind of benefactor, seen as sacrificing years of his or her life to this task. There is no length the biographer will not go to, and the more the book reflects the industry, the more the reader believes that he or she is having an elevating literary experience, rather than simply listening to backstairs gossip and reading other people's mail. The transgressive nature of biography is rarely acknowledged, but it is the only explanation for biography's status as a popular genre.

In the case of the "informant-based" Indian story, there is no length the biographer will not go to in his or her search for the "real story." He or she spends every summer for 20 years in an Indian reservation community, attends hundreds of powwows, endures the dust and the tedium of these weekend-long or 4-day communal marathons, and puts up with the insults from those who despise his or her curiosity about their lives. The biographer makes his or her home in some faraway city available as a crash pad for traveling Indians, loans money that he or she never expects to have returned, lends a car, baby-sits, takes on the responsibilities of an "adopted" relative, and is thrilled to be given an Indian name that is said to be invested with a mysterious spirituality. Many times, this biographer takes an Indian as wife, husband, lover, or "live-in."

After 20 years, the biographer is thought to be master of this territory on Indian lives and can present a manuscript to a publisher that will satisfy any voyeur's curiosity. These manuscripts are, by and large, fantasies of Indians as nonconformists to American cultural restrictions, Indians as redeemed drunks, Indian grandmothers and grandfathers as legendary figures, quite unremarkable and decent Indians presented on pedestals, Indians as victims of racist America, Indians as mixed-blood outcasts. All in all, these manuscripts describe the significance of individual Indian lives in the tribal parable mode, those stories that exhibit "truth."

In the telling of these stories, the writer almost always takes sides with the "informant" who gives him or her specific answers to specific questions. The writer/biographer is a believer. That is the nature of the relationship between the Indian informant and writer, and that's what gives the story its authority for the reader. Unfortunately, that's also what makes these stories neither history nor art in terms of Native intellectualism. That characteristic is what will ultimately define them as anti-intellectual, and the reasons are many.

For one thing, ambiguity, the essential ingredient of art, literature, and humanity, has been sacrificed for "truth" by both the informant and the biographer. Another, more important reason is that in the process of this so-called scholarship, the essential focus is America's dilemma, not questions about who the Indian thinks he or she is in tribal America. I don't mean to say this focus is not an interesting one, nor do I mean to suggest such an inquiry should never be made. But indigenous intellectualism in art, at least, has never had as its major interest the defining of one's self as an American. That is a relatively new phenomenon, political in nature, colonialistic in perspective, and one-sided. What distinguishes Native American intellectualism from other scholarship is its interest in tribal indigenousness, and this makes the "life story," the "self"-oriented and nontribal story, seem unrecognizable or even unimportant, noncommunal, and unconnected.

What popular art and literature have to say about what it means to be an American Indian in nontribal America is not the essential function of art and literature in Native societies. If stories are to have any meaning, Indian intellectuals must ask what it means to be an Indian in tribal America. If we don't attempt to answer that question, nothing else will matter, and we won't have to ask ourselves whether there is such a thing as Native American intellectualism because there will no longer be evidence of it.

The Urban Mixed-Blood Indian and American Writing

In American Indian scholarship and art, the works of writers who call themselves mixed-bloods abound. Their main topic is the discussion of the connection between the present "I" and the past "They," as well as the present pastness of "We." Gerald Vizenor, Louis Owens, Wendy Rose, Maurice Kenny, Michael Dorris, Diane Glancy, Betty Bell, Thomas King, Joe Bruchac, and Paula Gunn Allen are the major self-described mixed-blood voices of the decade.

While there is in the writings of these intellectuals much lip service given to the condemnation of America's treatment of the First Nations, there are few useful expressions of resistance and opposition to the colonial history at the core of Indian/White relations. Instead, there is explicit and implicit accommodation to the colonialism of the "West" that has resulted in what may be observed as three intellectual characteristics in fiction, nonfiction, and poetry: an aesthetic that is pathetic or cynical, a tacit notion of the failure of tribal governments as Native institutions and of sovereignty as a concept, and an Indian identity that focuses on individualism rather than First Nation ideology. Gerald Vizenor (1993), a major voice in this mixed-blood discourse, explains it this way in "The Ruins of Representation": "The postmodern turn in literature and cultural studies is an invitation to the ruins of representation; the invitation uncovers traces of tribal survivance, trickster discourse, and the remanence of intransitive shadows." The postmodern conditions, he says, are found in aural performance, translation, trickster liberation, humor, tragic incoherence, and cross-causes in language games. Almost all of the current fiction being written by Indians is created within these aesthetics in contradistinction to the hopeful, life-affirming aesthetic of traditional stories, songs, and rituals.

The diversity of American scholarship is being developed in substantially different ways from that of the historical educational pattern of colonial coercion for captive Indians. There are new movements afoot. This means that the Indian story is included in every genre and most disciplines during this era of the rise of cultural studies, diversity, and multiculturalism. In this period, the so-called mixed-blood story, often called the "postcolonial" story, has taken center stage. The bicultural nature of Indian lives has always been a puzzle to the monoculturalists of America; thus, mixed-bloodedness becomes the paradigm of preference.

Several publishing influences are perhaps at the heart of this movement. In brief, the loneliness of *Bury My Heart at Wounded Knee,* written by a White Arkansas writer whose name is Dee Brown, was published by Holt, Rinehart, and Winston in 1970 and set the tone for much poignant and sad and angry poetry by Indian and non-Indian writers during the beginning period of modernity. In the 1980s, the Louise Erdrich saga of an inadequate Chippewa political establishment and a vanishing Anishinabe culture suggests the failure of tribal sovereignty and the survival of myth in the modern world. Erdrich's conclusion is an odd one, in light of the reality of Indian life in the substantial Native enclaves of places like South Dakota or Montana or Arizona or New Mexico.

In the subsequent decade, a plethora of stories of the individual Indian life, biographies, and autobiographies of emancipated Indians who have little or no connection to tribal national life has become the publishing fare of university presses in the name of Native scholarship. This body of work (a recent University of Nebraska Press title is *Standing in the Light: A Lakota Way of Seeing* by Severt Young Bear and R. D. Theisz [1994]) is generated by reasons of interest in the social sciences, perhaps, rather than art and literature, since its "storytelling" approach is more pedantic than dynamic. (I discuss this category separately in an essay called "Life and Death in the Mainstream of Indian Biography," which was written for a now defunct Canadian Indian journal called *Talking Stick.*)

Several new works in fiction that catalogue the deficit model of Indian reservation life, such as *Skins* by Adrian Louis (1995) and *Reservation Blues* by Sherman Alexie (1995), have been published in the past decade. These are significant because they reflect little or no defense of treaty-protected reservation land bases as homelands to the indigenes, nor do they suggest a responsibility of art as an ethical endeavor or the artist as responsible social critic, a marked departure from the early renaissance works of such luminaries as N. Scott Momaday and Leslie Marmon Silko. Reviews of these works have been published generally on the entertainment pages of newspapers rather than in scholarly journals. Atlantan Ed Hall, a book reviewer editor for *Hogan's Alley,* a magazine of the cartoon arts, says of Louis's first novel, "*Skins* starts in the outhouse and keeps returning there," a comment that is, perhaps, both literally and figuratively true. Gloria Bird (1995), a Spokane Indian professor of the arts at the Institute for American Indian Arts in Santa Fe, New Mexico, in calling Alexie the Indian Spike Lee, makes the point that Native cultures are used like props in this fiction: "*Spinkled* like bait are sage-smudging, stickgame, sweet grass enough to titillate the curiosity of non-Indian readers."

The failure of the contemporary Indian novel and literary studies in Native American studies to contribute substantially to intellectual debates in defense of First Nationhood is discouraging. The American universities that have been at the forefront of the modern study of American Indian experience in literature for the past three decades and the professors, writers, and researchers who have directed the discourse through teaching and writing have been influenced by what may be called the inevitable imperial growth of the United States. Most seem to agree that the Indian story and what is labeled "cultural studies" are the future, but their refusal or inability to use a nation-to-nation approach to Native intellectualism has prevailed.

A "tolerant" national climate with resourceful diversity curricula has forged the apparatuses through which the study of aesthetics, ideology, and identity in Native thought has flourished to the detriment of autonomous models in Native studies. In this process, there has been little defense of tribal nationhood, and the consequences of that flaw are deeply troubling. Indian Nations are dispossessed of sovereignty in much of the intellectual discourse in literary studies, and there as elsewhere, their natural and legal autonomy is described as simply another American cultural or ethnic minority. Scholarship shapes the political, intellectual, and historical nation-to-nation past as an Americanism that can be compared to any other minority past. Many successful Native writers whose major focus is "mixed-blood" liberation and individualism seem to argue their shared victimhood through America's favorite subjects about Indians (i.e., despair, rootlessness, and assimilation).

Perhaps no one should be surprised at this turn of events since, officially, American citizenship for Indians made it clear from the beginning in 1924 that Indians were not to continue toward successful and progressive roles in their own tribal nation citizenship.

As it is now heard, the American Indian literary voice seems dependent on a university setting. The university is a place where few Indians reside and where the few who are present are notable for their willingness to change tribal traditions to mainstream traditions of modernity, transcribing in English and imagining in art some principles of personal (not tribal) politics and expressing the Indian experience in assimilative and mainstream terms.

The mixed-blood literature is characterized by excesses of individualism. The "I," the "me" story, and publishing projects by university and commercial presses in the "life story" genre are the result more of the dominance and patriarchy most noted in American society than of tribalness. Mixed-blood literary instruction may be viewed as a kind of liberation phenomenon or, more specifically, a deconstruction of a tribal nation past, hardly an intellectual movement that can claim a continuation of the tribal communal story or an ongoing tribal literary tradition.

The omnipresent and evasive role of the urban mixed-blood Indian intellectual writer has not been examined in its relationship to tribal nation hopes and dreams. Yet its influence cannot be dismissed, since it may be a movement of considerable consequence whose aim seems to be to give instruction to the academic world about what the imperialistic dispossession imposed on American Indians through the development of capitalistic democracy has meant to the individual, emancipated Indian. Unfortunately, the mixed-blood literary movement is signaling that a return to tribal sovereignty on Indian homelands seems to be a lost cause, and American individualism will out. The legacy of this, realistically speaking, is sure to translate into a wider terrain of assimilation and confusion as economic questions and cultural questions and federal Indian policy questions become more a matter of power than doctrine.

Though there is little documentation in literary studies of how Indians themselves have assessed these matters, there has been the suggestion in informal discussion that the mixed-blood movement is led by those whose tribal past has never been secure. Others believe the rise of such a literary movement is simply the result of the economy and culture imposed by conquest and colonization and politics.

Non-Indian critics of the systems of American colonization and imperialism, such as the Italian intellectual Antonio Gramsci, who became the founder of the Italian Communist party, might have suggested that such a movement could be the result of not transmitting ideas and knowledge from and to those who do not belong to the so-called intellectual class. Gramsci might have theorized that American Indians who have become a part of the elite intellectualism of American universities are unable to meet the standards of the true intellectual, that they are failed intellectuals because they have not lived up to the responsibility of transmitting knowledge between certain diverse blocs of society (Gramsci, 1995). This would suggest that the mixed-blood literary movement arose as a result of the assimilation inherent in cultural studies driven by American politics and imperialism.

Gramsci (1995) has said that it is the function of intellectuals to be at the forefront of theory but, at the same time, to transmit ideas to those who are not of the so-called professional, academic, intellectual class.

Indian scholars, on the other hand, suggest that Native intellectuals are more likely to come from nonacademic enclaves. A major history/political science/theology scholar, Vine Deloria Jr. (Standing Rock Sioux), has suggested in his serious contemporary work that a turn away from academe toward tribal knowledge bases that exist at a grassroots level is the answer to the complex dilemmas of modern scholarship in Indian affairs (V. Deloria, 1988). This presents a distinct dilemma, one that has been brought up in discussions of authenticity but seldom mentioned in terms of theory. Ideas, in general, according to Native American studies disciplinary definitions, are to be generated from the inside of culture, not from the outside looking in. This fact, scholars like Russell Thornton, who has published in the UCLA journal *Culture and Research*, have suggested, has been the feature of Native studies that distinguishes it from anthropology and other social science disciplines that have claimed an "objective" (i.e., "scientific") approach. It is evident that the mixed-blood literary phenomenon is not generated from the inside of tribal culture since many of the practitioners admit they have been removed from cultural influence through urbanization and academic professionalization or even, they suggest, through biology and intermarriage. Separation of these writers from indigenous communities (reservation or urban) indicates that this is a literary movement of disengagement.

When writers and researchers and professors who claim mixed blood focus on individualism and liberation, they often do not develop ideas as part of an inner-unfolding theory of Native culture; thus, they do not contribute ideas as a political practice connected to First Nation ideology. No one will argue that Native studies has had as its central agenda the critical questions of race and politics. For Indians in America today, real empowerment lies in First Nation ideology, not in individual liberation of Americanization.

The explosion of the mixed-blood literary phenomenon is puzzling to those who believe that the essential nature of intellectual work and critical reflection for American Indians is to challenge the politics of dispossession inherent in public policy toward Indian nationhood. It is not only puzzling, but it also may be dangerous because there can be no doubt, despite recent disclaimers in the media, about the power of intellectuals at universities to direct the course of American life and thought. More worrisome is the fact that the literary people who are contributing to the Indian affairs debate in academia are in ever more increasing numbers the people who have no stake in First Nation ideology. Their desire to absolve themselves of their responsibility to speak to that ideology, their self-interest in job seeking, promotion, publishing, tenure, and economic security, dismisses the seriousness of Native intellectual work and its connection to politics.

A great deal of the work done in the mixed-blood literary movement is personal, invented, appropriated, and irrelevant to First Nation status in the United States. If that work becomes too far removed from what is really going on in Indian enclaves, there will be no way to engage in responsible intellectual strategies in an era when structures of external cultural power are more oppressive than ever.

Moreover, no important pedagogical movement will be made toward those defensive strategies that are among the vital functions of intellectualism: to change the world, to know it, and to make it better by knowing how to seek appropriate solutions to human problems. Teaching is the mode intellectuals use to reproduce, and their reproduction should be something more than mere self-service. How long, then, can mixed-blood literary figures teach a Native American curriculum in literary studies of self-interest and personal narrative before they realize (and their students catch on to it) that the nature of the structural political problems facing the First Nation in America is being marginalized and silenced by the very work they are doing?

Art for Art's Sake

Today, American Indian artists, novelists, poets, and scholars who are publishing their own works seem to take an art for art's sake approach. There are astonishingly few exceptions, like Ray Young Bear and Percy Bull Child. Publishers want to take on only what will have a reasonably wide readership, and it is thought that the purists will not be read. Few discussions about the moral issues in producing art are taken seriously.

Since Momaday published his classic novel, much bad poetry (which should be called "doggerel") and bad fiction (which should be called "pop art") has been published in the name of Native American art. I have not heard much discussion from the Modern Language Association scholars or from literary critics (mostly White) or from inner circles of Native writers who must know (if they have read John Gardner's [1978] *On Moral Fiction*) that bad art has a harmful effect on society. Native scholars often suggest that to be critical of the work of fellow Indian writers is a function of jealousy or meanness. It is my opinion that literary fiction can be distinguished from popular fiction. I think a responsible critic will challenge the generic development of what is called Native American fiction by using the idea that there are such concepts as (a) moral fiction and (b) indigenous/tribally specific literary traditions from which the imagination emerges. American Indian writers could discuss what is literary art and what is trash or fraudulent or pop in Native American literatures; there could be a dialogue about what is good or bad and why, but only a few have the stomach for it.

The truth is, Momaday's (1968) *House Made of Dawn* is considered a classic in the study of Native American literatures not simply because it adheres to the principles of the oral traditions of the tribes, though that is vital to classic indigenous literatures, nor is it a classic because it seeks out the sources of ritual and ceremony, language, and storytelling, although that, too, is essential. It is considered a classic because it is a work that explores traditional values, revealing truth and falsity about those values from a framework of tribal realism. It is diametrically opposed to fantasy, which often evades or suppresses moral issues. Momaday's work allows profound ideas to be conceptualized, allows its Indian readers to work through those ideas and move on to affirm their lives as Indian people. It adheres to the Gardner principle and the principles of the oral traditions that good stories incline the reader to an optimistic sense. In too much of what passes for Native American literature today, you couldn't find a significant idea with a 10-foot pole, let alone find one that is life affirming to the indigenes.

The art for art's sake phenomenon, more than any other in modern times, seems to thrive on the notion that art (fiction, painting, music, poetry) as a mode of thought is important as a human activity because it is a way of discovering. I can't argue with that. But it also is an idea that, if untrammeled and unexamined, lets Indian artists off the hook and leads us away from what some of us may consider a responsibility to our own tribal traditions. Though modernity suggests the inevitability of that moving away for the sake of a living art, I am not sure that art can be considered art if it ignores its own historical sense.

A major characteristic of many novels written in the 1980s and 1990s in the art for art's sake mode is the interest in the "marvelous," the expression of a magic spirit that leads to an unexpected alteration of reality. *Ceremony* by Leslie Marmon Silko (Pueblo) and *Tracks* by Louise Erdrich (Turtle Mountain Chippewa) are the major contemporary examples of this so-called magical narrative, and they have achieved enormous popularity with their American readers. South American writers such as Gabriel García Márquez and Alejo Carpentier have led this movement and are the major theorists of this North American phenomenon in storytelling, but both Silko and Erdrich have had an enormous influence on the new American Indian story.

Long before either Silko or Erdrich were out of infancy, however, this idea for a continental approach to art rose out of another colonial literature, Spanish American fiction, when Angel Florez wrote as early as 1955 in "Magic Realism in Spanish American Fiction" that "magic realism" attempts to "transform the common and everyday into the awesome and the unreal" (p. 190). Many of the writers of the work Florez spoke of were not Indians but were from Spain, one of the colonizing nations of the hemisphere, and were not Native language speakers but speakers of Spanish, as colonizing a language as any. Their interest in magical realism could be thought of, then, as another generic imposition upon the indigenous story. And the question of distortion in American Indian intellectualism or its outright dismissal again looms.

All of this may give evidence to the idea that the Native magical realism writers of our time have moved away from their own traditions and have grounded their work in a reality that is inherently fantastical. A prevailing theory about magical realism expressed by the works of South American writer Gabriel García Márquez gives these writers support. He says that the narrative dramatization of magical realism is "usually expressed through a collective voice, inverting, in a jesting manner, the values of the official culture," and by "official" culture, he means Euro-American culture. He does not ask the obvious question about how what he terms Third World (and I would term Native) cultures are distorted in the process of these fictional fantasies, but that question is as vital as his message of revolution. No one can deny the vitality of his vision when he accepted the 1982 Nobel Prize for Literature and talked about a continent stolen, bathed in blood, its Natives buried in poverty. This is, of course, also the vision of Silko (1991) in her novel, *Almanac of the Dead.*

One supposes that every age is characterized by a phrase that distinguishes it from any other. "The Age of Reason" and Thomas Paine. "The Age of Anxiety" with Freud and Margaret Mead. Do we accept the idea that the current Indian story rises out of "The Age of mixed-blood and magical fantasies"? If not, artists and critics must come to understand that popular Native American fiction is as extricably tied to specific tribal literary legacies as contemporary Jewish literature is tied to the literary legacies of the nations of Eastern Europe or contemporary Black literature is tied to the nations of tribal Africa.

The Dilemma

If it is true that writers are the intellectuals of any nation, the question of how it is that what might be called experimental work in contemporary Native American literature or "pulp fiction" narratives or fantasies will assist us with our real lives is a vital one. Does this art give thoughtful consideration to the defense of our lands, resources, languages, and children? Is anyone doing the intellectual work in and about Indian communities that will help us understand our future? While it is true that any indigenous story tells of death and blood, it also tells of indigenous rebirth and hope, not as Americans or as some new ersatz race but as the indigenes of this continent.

Perhaps much of the work produced in the past decade can be looked upon as a legitimate criticism of existing society, a realistic criticism of a system of untidy ethics written by a new generation of thinkers who are separated from a real Indian past, people who have no Native language to describe the future, young people who are tired of the whining of old people about the loss of their lives, and Indians who think they can rise to the challenge of life on the entertainment pages. But where does it all end?

Does the Indian story as it is told now end in rebirth of Native nations as it did in the past? Does it help in the development of worthy ideas, prophecies for a future in which we continue as tribal people who maintain the legacies of the past and a sense of optimism?

I can't think of questions more essential for an Indian writer today than these, which means, perhaps, that biographies, individual Indian life stories, romance novels, Ted Turner television, Costner movies, magic, children's stories, and mixed-blood visions have little or nothing to do with what may be defined as Native intellectualism.

What is Native intellectualism, then? Who are the intellectuals? Are our poets and novelists articulating the real and the marvelous in celebration of the past, or are they the doomsayers of the future? Are they presenting ideas, moving through those ideas and beyond? Are they the ones who recapture the past and preserve it? Are they thinkers who are capable of supplying principles that may be used to develop further ideas? Are they capable of the critical analysis of cause and effect? Or, are our poets and novelists just people who glibly use the English language to entertain us, to keep us amused and preoccupied so that we are no longer capable of making the distinction between the poet and the stand-up comedian? Does that distinction matter anymore? Does it matter how one uses language and for what purpose?

Who knows the answers to these questions? Who believes it is important that they be posed? In my generation, Alfonzo Ortiz, a Pueblo (Tewa) Indian, who is now deceased, published *The Tewa World* in 1969, and it became a classic. N. Scott Momaday, a Kiowa, wrote the novel *House Made of Dawn* in 1968, and it won the Pulitzer Prize for literature and became the quintessential fictional work of modern literary studies. The Lakota scholar Vine Deloria Jr. in 1967 published *Custer Died for Your Sins*, and it became the first of several essential texts he produced for use in the development of Native American studies as an academic discipline. These books were based in history and culture and politics that looked out on the White world from a communal, tribally specific indigenous past. A whole list of writers who do not situate themselves within the mixed-blood or mainstream spectrum, such as Momaday, Silko, Ortiz, Young Bear, Warrior, Medicine, Willard, Deloria, Bird, Crum, Woody, Bull Child, and dozens more for whom books matter and intellectualism has meaning, come to mind as people who will become something more than icons for American pop culture.

Since the time 30 years ago when Native American studies began to define itself as a discipline, more Indian writing has been done than ever, more Indians have had their work published, and there are more public storytellers than we ever hoped for, but it seems that little of this subsequent writing has the perspective that propelled Ortiz, Momaday, and Deloria toward a scholarship that concerned itself with indigenousness, and almost none of it can be called profound. It does not pose the unanswerable questions for our future as Indians in America.

The question of how Indians claim the story, then, is still a primary and unanswered question. If the works of non-Native storytellers haven't got it right, who says that the modern works written by American Indians, introspective and self-centered, have? Who says our modern works, which focus on the pragmatic problems of the noncommunal world of multicultural America, are worthy to be the lasting works in our legacy of artistry?

In a 1995 literary review of contemporary fiction by the preeminent Lagunan artist Leslie Marmon Silko, which appeared in *The Nation,* we are told that this "United States is this big Indian Reservation." We are told that Indian Country's poverty and violence are the defining themes in the new Indian stories and that any Indian Reservation town described in the new works, because of the nature of its poverty, could be any neighborhood in East Los Angeles or the Bronx. Except, we are told, Indian people "use car wrecks and cheap wine, not drive-by shootings and crack, to make their escape." While Silko is talking about the real lives of Indian people on Indian reservations and in America, it is possible that her reference can be taken as a major dimension of literary theory concerning the function of modern Native fiction. This literature is written and it is read for the purpose of "making an escape." The people who are writing these modern stories, Silko says, are "the best we have."

This assessment, supposedly based on a reading of the important works published in the past several decades, is probably shared by many readers and scholars of our time. This assessment makes *escape* the operative word in discussing the function of storytelling; yet any Indian artist, and surely Silko herself, has told us over and over that escapism has never been the thrust of Native storytelling. What are we to think, then? Are we to take this as a warning?

In light of the genre development of modern works illustrated here and in the context of the new novels and short stories being written, the modern Indian story (whether told by an Indian or a non-Indian) seems to have taken a very different course from its traditional path in Native societies. In doing so, it has defined the literary place where the imaginative final encounter may be staged and only time holds the answer to its continuity or rejection or obligation or interdiction. Native intellectuals, dabbling as we are in a rather shallow pool of imagination and culture, must pull ourselves together not only to examine the irrelevant stories of "other" storytellers but to critically examine the self-centered stories we presume to tell about our own people.

Indian stories, traditions, and languages must be written, and they must be written in a vocabulary that people can understand rather than the esoteric language of French and Russian literary scholars that has overrun the lit-crit scene. Scholars in Native intellectual circles must resist the flattery that comes from many corners, defend freedom, refute rejection from various power enclaves, and resist the superficiality that is so much a part of the modern/urban voice. We must work toward a new set of principles that recognizes the tribally specific literary traditions by which we have always judged the imagination. This distinguished legacy—largely untapped by critics, mainstream readers, and Native participants—is too essential to be ignored as we struggle toward the inevitable modernity of Native American intellectualism.

Now, in closing, I want you to know that the business of history and myth and identity for American Indians and for all of us is a complex matter. It deserves our attention. Yet, the sober truth is that the White man's burden of winning the West and taking over this continent, which, by the way, is the subject of much of my political writings, has dealt a crushing blow to all of this world that I have been describing here briefly. The Americans' history, in my view, what is called the "manifest destiny" colonization of this continent, is one of the crimes of human history. And, now, it would seem that America will move on from this "dark and bloody" ground, to the winning of the entire globe, to what is going on in the Middle East. The deaths of thousands of Iraqis and the destruction of their cities and their civilization seem to be inconsequential. Modern America has become the Spanish conquistadors who burned to the ground the temples of the Mayas and the Aztecs. I suppose the indigenous peoples of this continent are not surprised.

Despite the crimes of history, we write. We continue as poets, novelists, fictionists, parents, grandparents. We continue to want the stories. We have little power, but that does not mean that we have no influence. I have come to the conclusion that it is not my overriding business to create new ways of looking at the world in order to come up with smart and effective solutions in every case. It is my business to remember . . . to remember the past and recall the old ways of the people. Literature and myth and history have always been the way to shape a new world.

Finally, I want to say something about one of the first things I published after I started my professional career. It was in a little chapbook called *Then Badger Said This* (Cook-Lynn, 1983), now out of print. It is about remembering the past. It is about a tattoo (one of the important ways of writing for the Sioux in the old days). It is about the Badger and it is about storytellers, and it is about grandmothers. But mostly, it's about mythology. It really tells you something about tribal writers, I think. For me, as a writer, I see everything in the world through the prism of my tribal experiences. I see everything in the world through the prism of the theft of the sacred Black Hills . . . which tried to make us beggars, out there on the Crow Creek. I see everything through the prism of Native language and those who went ahead who did not write their names in English. So, I will end with a brief paragraph that reflects all of that. The first time I heard this story, it was told to me by an elder relative, and she told me that the Badger had said this, and so years later I wrote it down:

> Keyapi. (they say this) When the Dakotapi really lived as they wished, they thought it important to possess a significant tattoo mark. This enabled them to identify themselves for the grandmothers who stood on the ghost road entering the spirit world asking: takoja . . . where is your tattoo? If the Dakota could not show them his mark, they pushed that one down an abyss and he never reached the spirit land.

So?

That doesn't sound too much like a grandmotherly thing to do, does it?

But, what does it tell you about identity? It says you must be able to identify yourself as a Dakotah for the grandmothers who are standing on the ghost road . . . yes? The tattoo is merely the outward symbol for that otherwise profound identity.

Well, you know, the Badger said many things. He is always in Dakota stories, and he is always asked many questions even though he is not important, not like Coyote or The Trickster, or Unktomi or Ikce or any of the others. But he always has something to say . . . he always has an answer. . . . Sometimes he is right, but just as often, he is wrong. Quite wrong. But what he does, you see, is . . . he keeps the plot moving. . . . Without him, you see, the story would come to an early and unsatisfactory end.

References

Alexie, S. (1995). *Reservation blues.* New York: Atlantic Monthly Press.

Banks, L. R. (1982). *The Indian in the cupboard.* New York: Avon.

Bird, G. (1995, Fall). Telling: The changing climate in American Indian literature. *Indian Artist*, p. 65.

Brown, D. (1970). *Bury my heart at wounded knee.* New York: Holt, Rinehart, and Winston.

Cook-Lynn, E. (1983). *Then badger said this.* Fairfield, WA: Ye Galleon Press.

Cook-Lynn, E. (1990). *The power of horses and other stories.* New York: Arcade.

Debo, A. (1970). *A history of the Indians of the United States.* Norman: University of Oklahoma Press.

Deloria, E. (1932). *Dakota texts.* New York: American Ethnological Society.

Deloria, V., Jr. (1967). *Custer died for your sins: An Indian manifesto.* Norman: University of Oklahoma Press.

Eagle, K. P. (1995). *Reason to believe.* New York: Avon.

Florez, A. (1955). Magic realism in Spanish American fiction. *Hispania, 38,* 190.

Gardner, J. (1978). *On moral fiction.* New York: Basic Books.

Gramsci, A. (1995). *Further selections from the prison notebooks* (D. Boothman, Ed.). Minneapolis: University of Minnesota Press.

Larson, S. J. (1995). *Catch colt.* Lincoln: University of Nebraska Press.

Louis, A. C. (1995). *Skins: A novel.* New York: Crown.

Malcolm, J. (1993, August 23). The silent woman. *The New Yorker.*

Momaday, N. S. (1968). *House made of dawn.* New York: Harper & Row.

Neihardt, J. G. (1961). *Black Elk speaks, being the life story of a holy man for the Olgala Sioux, as told through John G. Neihardt.* Lincoln: University of Nebraska Press.

Oritz, A. (1969). *The Tewa world.* Chicago: University of Chicago Press.

Pocahontas [Motion picture]. (1995). United States: Walt Disney Studios.

Silko, L. M. (1991). *Almanac of the dead: A novel.* New York: Simon & Schuster.

Silko, L. M. (1995, June 12). Bingo big. *The Nation,* p. 857.

Vizenor, G. (1993). The ruins of representation. *American Indian Quarterly, 17,* 1–17.

Young Bear, S., & Theisz, R. D. (1994). *Standing in the light: A Lakota way of seeing.* Lincoln: University of Nebraska Press.

17

"SELF" AND "OTHER"

Auto-Reflexive and Indigenous Ethnography

Keyan G. Tomaselli, Lauren Dyll, and Michael Francis

"You will be changed," Keyan Tomaselli tells his visual anthropology and development communication graduate students when preparing for field trips and research among some groups of San Bushmen in the Kalahari Desert. "Are you ready for this experience? Your view of the world won't be the same after the visit." Apart from a very small minority who are unable to deal with the experience and who occasionally abscond en route or blame their professor and their peers for their inability to relate, most of the rest voluntarily disclose in their theses and publications how they have been changed. They enthusiastically sustain and enhance the camaraderie of the field experience after their return to the academy. Unlike student work on other topics, these students tend to dedicate their research to their host/subject communities, and they make a point of telling their professor how much they appreciated their fieldwork opportunities.

At the conclusion of writing the previous draft of this chapter, the *Handbook*'s editors referred us to Stacey Holman Jones's (2005) treatise on autoethnography (of which we were unaware). She offers similar observations, dramatically adding with regard to her chapter, "Please do not read it alone. . . . It does not act alone." This is a rather startling exhortation to potential readers of an academic text—unsettling, provocative, and totally unscientific (in the Comptean sense). Feelings, emotions, and the lived experience, largely ignored in positivist approaches, however, comprise one layer of autoethnographic accounts: "Multiple reflections" emerge from scientific, confessional, realist, and impressionist tales (Holman Jones, 2005, p. 763; Ronai, 1995). We should not be embarrassed, ashamed, or tentative about what we are doing. Neither should we allow ourselves to be intimidated by our conventional scientific peers and canonical adherents who may be unsettled by unconventional methods. We aim to develop

AUTHORS' NOTE: This article significantly develops Tomaselli and Shepperson (2003). We are indebted to Arnold Shepperson for his theoretical and philosophical insights vis-à-vis this article and the whole Kalahari project. Thanks to Vanessa McLennan-Dodd and Eduardo da Veiga for their comments. The research was funded by the Research Fund of the University of KwaZulu-Natal and the National Research Foundation (NRF), Social Sciences and Humanities. Opinions expressed and conclusions arrived at are those of the authors and not the foundation. Francis's work in the Drakensberg was funded by Wenner-Grenn.

methods in situ, from the guts of our field experiences, not only to take predigested reified textbook methods "to go." However, one should of course also work with conventional approaches as they offer complementary analysis via different, related, lenses and cast light on what we think we are doing. This chapter offers a story of one such experiment now entering its 14th year. We attempt to explain the method with illustrations from our own fieldwork, experience, and narratives.

▣ Developing Methods as We Go

Via discussion of a long-term case study, we hope to illuminate aspects of our research methods in ways that might be replicable to other contexts of study. The approach discussed here is rare in cultural studies, though less so in anthropology. It relies on basic ethnographic tropes of explication about our informants' lives. This is coupled with reflexive examination of ourselves and of our research project. We discuss a form of anthropological/ethnographic participant observation that enables our informants to have direct access to the information we have written about them in the form of an ongoing dialogue. In this chapter, we attempt to extract some principles from our extensive experience that can be applied more generally.

Ethnographic research has come a long way since Bronislaw Malinowski (1922) wrote his initial ideas on participant observation with his famous dictum, "The final goal of which the ethnographer should never lose sight . . . is . . . to grasp the Native's point of view, his relation to life, to realize his vision of his world" (p. 25). Contemporary anthropology explores

> new ways to fulfill the promises on which modern anthropology was founded: to offer worthwhile and interesting critiques of our own society; to enlighten us about other human possibilities, engendering an awareness that we are merely one pattern among many; to make accessible the normally unexamined assumptions by which we operate and through which we encounter members of other cultures. (Marcus & Fischer, 1999, p. ix)

So what does the *auto* mean for ethnography?

The reflexive nature of autoethnography seems to ask more questions than it may answer. We do not presume that autoethnography can resolve all questions that arise; the human experience is fundamentally ambiguous and far too complex for single approaches. Despite not having solid answers, many of these questions can and must be addressed. Autoethnography as a research method requires the researcher to

> gaze, first through an ethnographic wide-angle lens, focusing outward on social and cultural aspects of their personal experience; then they look inward, exposing a vulnerable self that is moved by and may move through, refract and resist cultural interpretations. (Ellis & Bochner, 2000, p. 739)

Ethnography is not simply a collection of the exotic "other"; it is reflective of our own lives and cultural practices even when discussing another culture. Autoethnography involves the use of cultural richness for self-reflection and understanding the nature of the encounter. "How much of my self do I put in and leave out?" is the way Holman Jones (2005, p. 764) frames the question. Instead of only questioning why people react as they do to the presence of researchers, we must also question social assumptions about the nature of research. "By turning the question this way we allow the anthropologist's informants the privilege of explicating and publicizing their own criticisms of the forces that are affecting their society—forces which emanate from ours" (Taussig, 1980, p. 6). Michael Taussig's work, for example, is more of a critique of colonialism and capitalism than of his own personal interaction, although there is definitely an element of personal narrative involved in coming to that understanding (cf. Taussig, 1987). The nature of this interpretation is less of a "truth" and more of a reflection and comparison filtered through our own culture.

Other authors take their personal accounts as the heart of their research, where they use cultural reflexivity to "bend back on self and look more deeply at self-other interactions" (Ellis & Bochner, 2000, p. 740). The interaction between the researcher and his or her subject(s) is highlighted through personalized narrative, written in the first person, and accompanied by personal anecdotes. It is seen as a "radical transformation in the goals of our work—from description to communication" (Ellis & Bochner, 2000, p. 748). Just as Clifford Geertz (1973) states about his approach to the interpretation of culture, "whether or not it explains everything is irrelevant; what it does explain is something" (p. 4). Identifying the "something" is a key task. The term *something* is used in this sense of inquiry throughout the chapter.

The strength of the participatory projects discussed below lies in their emergence from an empirical, real-world basis, namely, a regularized series of field trips working with three indigenous San communities in the Kalahari Desert, each respectively located in South Africa, Botswana, and Namibia. A fourth community was studied in the Drakensberg mountains in the province of KwaZulu-Natal, South Africa, where a community of Zulu speakers claiming San descendancy resides. The Kalahari project involved research visits between the periods of 1995 and 2007, ranging from between 10 and 22 days each, while the study in KwaZulu-Natal involved 2 years of close participant observation when PhD student Michael Francis (2007) lived in a rural Zulu community of San descent. The different time periods and therefore methodology applied in the two different communities illuminate similar issues when representing how experience is combined with theory.

The research process in all four communities revealed that theory and formal texts often had an endistancing effect with regard to the tangible lives of our subjects. What appeared in the text—the published grand narratives—represented but did not necessarily resemble the people and conditions we encountered in the field, with all their contradictions, flaws, hopes, ideals, expectations, and personalities. The Kalahari communities especially embodied the contradictions between text and reality, whereas the Zulu-speaking Duma clan in the Drakensberg had taken on a "secret San" identity (Prins, 2000). The "secret" related to the sublimation by the Duma clan of their San ancestry in a community where Zulus are dominant. They, however, outed themselves after apartheid in order to stake a claim in the new society. Our students constantly comment that the empirical experience of "being there" could never be substituted via reading prior research and watching videos that lack the nuanced experiential dimension of these actual encounters, how secrets are sustained, and when, why, and how they are revealed.

The San have been one of the most frequently studied, written about, and filmed peoples in the world (cf., e.g., Marshall, 1993; Tomaselli, 1999). The research process itself is obscured and often hidden under obtuse theories and research methods that say little about how one goes about actually doing research. Graduate courses on anthropological methods often reveal little about the actual messy and often incomprehensible conditions of the research process, other than the basic and often banal requirements of fieldwork. Or, they may offer idealized overviews that are lacking when applied in the field. In fieldwork, however, we are presented with a process to cultivate knowledge and a unique discipline to study humanity (Sykes, 2005). The mess of everyday life, the contradictions that befuddle the theory, and the subversion of research methodologies by informants are rarely discussed in conventional research handbooks (cf. also Conquergood, 1998; Husserl, 1969). For example:

- How does one conduct relevant research when the informants are drunk, in begging mode, or abusive?

- What happens when researchers are toyed with by their subjects (cf., e.g., Dyll, 2007)? Alternatively,

- How do researchers respond when subjects use them as their active agents in appealing through them to perhaps unresponsive authority (aid agencies, government officials, community associations) (cf., e.g., Tomaselli, 2007)?

- What are the epistemological implications when subjects commoditize research encounters (cf. Tomaselli, 2005)?

- How does one penetrate subject anthrospeak learned from decades of interaction with anthropological and other academic observers/visitors?

- Where does one begin with a project dreamed up in the university but that is unable to be implemented because existential, cosmological, political, and other influences undermine it?

- How does one deal with lies, half-truths, misrepresentations, and denial by informants (cf., e.g., Metcalf, 2002)?

- How does one process answers couched within oral storytelling conventions in response to specific, scientifically constructed questions?

- How does one deal with the politics of naming? Our peers and politicians demand the politically correct use of the pejorative *San* (a Nama word that means *bandit*), rejected by our hosts/subjects, who subversively call themselves "Bushmen." Use of the one term or the other in the wrong context can kill the usefulness and legitimacy of research for one or both constituencies (Bregin & Kruiper, 2004; Dyll, 2004; Simões, 2001).

- Convention holds that "we" (the observers) have the power to draw the line around "them" (the observed), but what if we acknowledge that "they" also have the power to draw the line around "us" (Metcalf, 2002; Von Strauss, 2000)?

- The requirements by ethics committees that even illiterate informants sign release forms bureaucratize and alienate the condition of "being there" and strip the organic nature of observation and the encounter of its spontaneity. Forms are distrusted. Signatures may imply to our subjects loss of *their* control, loss of ownership, and loss of negotiating position.

Alternatively, as far as the researchers are concerned:

- How does one deal with a situation where an individual in the research team refuses to share collectively accessed information, denies reciprocity, and then claims individual ownership of a collective process to which he or she attached himself or herself, whether by invitation or opportunism? This can have severe repercussions in terms of who is held accountable by communities when that work is published, screened, or exhibited. In other words, it is the longer term known researchers with whom deeper relationships have been established who get the "blame" (if any is to be apportioned by our subjects). This occurs when short-term visitors associated by the community with the lead project and its personnel parachute in and out, while pursuing their own individual agendas.

- The information generated should be collectively owned under the auspices of the research project and not privatized by individual writers or researchers, though of course they should be encouraged to publish where necessary under their own names while drawing on prior research and interviews (cf., e.g., McLennan-Dodd, 2003). Whole projects become mired in controversy because of tussles between individual researchers over who owns the data.

- A few individuals have appropriated our access to our research communities, exploited the trust built up over a period, and then kept the team at a distance while gathering data, which are published without adequate acknowledgment to the lead project.

Our research venture/encounter reminds us that (Western) theoretical constructs and ethical stipulations are not metaphysical ends or sets of values in their own right. They must be always laid open to reexamination and change when applied to (non-Western) empirical contexts and real-life subjects/informants. Moreover, by knowingly positioning observers and the observed within specific, polyphonic communication circuits at given points in time and space, this endeavor problematizes received models of authority in formulations of academic inquiry and writing. Orthodox research encounters generally adhere to the pecking order that separates researcher and the researched that is predetermined at the outset (cf., e.g., Worth & Adair, 1972). Relationships prefigured by autoethnography, however, suggest new terms of mutual engagement for *cultural studies researchers* at various stages of inquiry. These encompass the researchers' *host communities* and/or host *subjects*, as well as the targeted *readers* of the ensuing ethnographic accounts. The resulting inquiry of such an endeavor becomes a critique of the dominant models and often results in polyphonic texts and unusual research strategies and events woven into often surprising, but never boring, narratives.

Where Is "There"; Who Are "We"?

Moving from "here" (Durban) to "there" (Kalahari Desert or the Drakensberg), we had to rethink our research assumptions, identities, and even our understanding of cultural studies. Our respective journeys positioned us as both insiders and outsiders and as purchasers (of information, crafts, and skills). We are givers (of donated goods) and sometimes accused of being exploiters (of knowledge). We are also seen as heroes and villains, and as reporters, we evaluate the said in terms of the more usually unsaid. This is not an easy set of relations through which to negotiate. The complexity and tensions of relationships in Kalahari research are extraordinary, given the relatively small numbers of "Bushmen" subject to the intensive Western gaze and the much smaller numbers of researchers, nongovernmental organizations (NGOs), filmmakers, and other observers involved.

Our combined project encompasses a number of topics, including representation, cultural tourism, development, media, identity, marginalization, and autoethnographic methodology as a topic in its own right. All of these topics relate to the overall project as students and professors alike ponder the intricate processes of knowledge (re)construction. Contributors have generated reflexivity in forms of writing, photography, and video that are at once personalized and biographically specific, replete in descriptive detail and responsive to the bilateral relations between lived experiences and the factors that shape them. This auto-reflexive form of writing became the way in which University of KwaZulu-Natal (UKZN) students and researchers committed to a situationally ethical anthropology, in which they highlight the reciprocal relations obtained between the subjects and themselves. This often results in the authors being convincingly concerned with the campfire dissemination of, and popular access to, the written, photographic, and videoed products by aliterate and non-English-speaking communities (cf., e.g., Tomaselli, 2005; Tomaselli & McLennan-Dodd, 2003).

This chapter thus develops a reflexive argument for reverse cultural studies in discussing problems in fieldwork, globalization, academic access, and research accountability among indigenous communities. The narrative aims to forge a space for kinds of cultural studies in which detail is as important as theory, in which human agency is described and recognized, and in which voices from the field, our subjects of observation, are engaged by researchers as their equals in human dignity and thus as coproducers of valuable knowledge (cf. also Tomaselli, 2003a, 2003b). Our research project is part of the growing literature on research for and, in some ways, by indigenous peoples that "recognizes not only the knowledge accumulated in indigenous communities but also that indigenous values, beliefs and behaviors must be incorporated into the praxis of participatory research" (Fine et al., 2003, p. 176).

We excavate the reflexive indigenous side of ethnography with a discussion on the use of autoethnography in research. It is important to clarify our use of the term *native ethnography* in contrast to *indigenous ethnography.* Native ethnography

> can be distinguished from indigenous ethnography in that native ethnographers are those who have their origins in non-European or non-western cultures and who share a history of colonialism, or an economic relationship based upon subordination. (Tedlock, 2000, p. 466)

Indigenous ethnography may be conducted by anyone researching their own community. The use of the term *reflexivity* as an autoethnographic method will also be later briefly discussed in terms of how it relates to people doing an ethnographic study as an "outsider" and as an "insider" or native ethnographer.

Show and Tell

The kind of writing encouraged by our project and described in this chapter aims to "show" rather than simply "tell" a story: scene-by-scene constructions rather than large and dense chunks of narrative, extensive use of dialogue, and third-person point of view. The writing presents extensive descriptions of everyday situations and anomalies and deploys multiple narrative digressions intended to evoke critical response from readers. At the same time, it often resorts to free indirect speech rather than dialogue, frequently using autoethnographic points of view, suggesting a more personalized mode of shared ethnographic documentation (cf. Narunsky-Laden & Kohn, 2007).

Critical qualitative research has, contradictorily, become the norm since the advent of theories of poststructuralism and postmodernism. The "deconstruction" and analysis of discourses became all the rage in postcolonial texts in the late 1980s and 1990s, based as they are on antifoundationalist premises. Such analysis appeared to lead to a dead end of inactivity as deconstruction knows no end. In deconstruction, life is reduced to endless regressions of webs of discursive power that are all encompassing and pervasive but that are disconnected from material and psychospiritual conditions on the ground. A more recent trend, including not only power but countervailing discourses, inverts this trajectory and reverses the "gaze," for example, that of Orientalism. It thereby cautions assumptions about powers that reduce people to new stereotypes of victimhood (Bodley, 1999). Our use of the idea of reverse cultural studies similarly aims to invert the power relations and to emphasize Malinowski's dictum of grasping the native's perspective (Tomaselli, 2003d).

The inclusion of the research process as a topic in and of itself is to explicitly expose the contradictions of academic discourse and knowledge production. It also explicitly permits readers to see how our interactions and encounters with our informants help to shape and structure texts, argument, and explanations (scientific, media, archival, etc.).

A researcher's presence in a fieldwork situation must acknowledge the baggage his or her background brings to any research encounter; the whole impetus behind *method,* however, is the need to communicate with researchers who are both part and not part of that which they are analyzing (cf. Fabian, 1979; Ruby, 1977). This holds both for those who work within conventional science and those who choose to work against the flow. Whichever way one chooses to conduct one's work, it always involves a negotiation between the circumstances of one's choosing, the potential solidarity between researcher and subject, and the long-term communities of inquiry to which one ultimately addresses one's research findings. No single researcher disposes of the truth. If researchers are to account for the fallibility of the human condition, it is decisive that they observe two basic rules of method. They must

- communicate the facets of reality (discursive and empirical) their research has uncovered with due regard for the indefinite future community of researchers and
- account for the impact that the dissemination of their findings may have on their subject-communities.

The experience of fieldwork is somewhat romanticized in some anthropological texts. These involve tales of mis/adventure and hardship, hilarious accounts of misunderstandings or cultural blunderings, exotic locations, bureaucratic intransigence, and the like (cf., e.g., Asch, 1992; Barley, 1995; Raybeck, 1996, who nevertheless problematize these experiences). Fieldwork is often a combination of all these: humorous events, personal symbolic and significant encounters, sharing life experiences, making new friends, coming under security agency surveillance, being short of food and water, getting ill, and so forth. What is often left out of such descriptions is the complexity and frustration compounded by lack of nuanced language skills, boredom and anger at people who fail to keep appointments, misrepresentations of what is happening (community politics and social strife), and the simple longing for the comforts of home. Sometimes the field presents researchers with conditions for which their book reading has not prepared them: extreme poverty, violence, and illness, on an intensity and scale quite beyond their previous experience. Junior anthropologists and field researchers are sometimes thus reluctant to deal with the gritty details of life in the field that cannot always be a positive one for the fieldworker.

Published ethnographic studies are written as coherent wholes, and the mess and chaos of everyday life is hidden from the transcript or streamlined into often beguiling theoretical coherence. Supervisors and research committees often demand indigenous language competence from students, assuming homogeneity of the subject's tongue. In southern Botswana, the community of less than 200 with which we work variously speak Afrikaans, English, Tswana, Ndebele, Selala (!Kung-Tswana mixture), and a !Kung dialect tinged with Nama. They need intermediaries to speak even to each other; how on earth do we interact with them? Our team is usually multilingual, and we will employ interpreters from the community, which gets us by. Where does fieldwork begin and where does it end? Is it only when actually formally "doing research," discussing events in the study or when researchers are on site, clipboard and release forms at the ready, that such issues are addressed and confronted. Research is shaped by prior fieldwork experiences, but are such events that contribute to what the authors think and believe to be included? Descriptive writing that includes the journey and process is generally excluded from certain ethnographies and appears as reflective texts later in life when senior anthropologists reminisce over their careers and write texts explicitly about themselves and their fieldwork experiences (see Geertz, 1995; Raybeck, 1996).

The actual ambiguities and contradictions of lived realities make for difficult writing. Field notes are often diarized jumbles of quotes and descriptions of various encounters. Their only coherence is chronological, and that too gets twisted as books are forgotten at home or at the camp site or notes are reworked after initial understandings are proven false and events are seen anew in light of further research. Questions plague students as to how a thesis or paper will arise out of the daily mess in which they have found themselves living in the field. What is the relevance of what is recorded? What is the relevance of what will be ultimately selected for the thesis? Students constantly ask, Was something important left out? Have I missed the point entirely? Are my representations fair? Why am I feeling guilty? Who is actually in control here? Are my interpretations accurate? Have I done enough? Why am I unable to form relationships with my hosts? Why do *I* feel exploited, when they tell me that I am exploiting *them?* Students are aware that our research will only ever include selective bits and pieces, ethnographic epiphanies, and brought together, somewhat artificially, to make a coherent account of research encounters. As Geertz (1995) asks,

> What gives us the right to study them? When we speak of others in our voice do we not displace and appropriate theirs? Is a representation of others free of the play of power and domination in any way possible? Does it all come down to who writes whom? (p. 107)

These issues are echoed by our colleagues and students as they struggle through their own fieldwork experiences (Tomaselli, 2001). We work as a community of scholars and share these experiences with one another as we try to arrive at some sense of what is going on. Despite all the changes to ethnographic practices and the new issues that have been raised, "they all boil down to the same old problem of one human trying to figure out what some other humans are up to" (Agar, 1996, p. 2). The people we study and our interactions with them are part of an existing world in a state of inexorable transformation. What we are ultimately left to deal with is the constant process of change, even in the remotest of communities. What we have learned is that often global contradictions are sharpest on the peripheries. Furthermore, sometimes the change and contradictions at the periphery are far greater and more traumatic than changes at the metropolitan centers, upon which they often cast theoretically illuminating light (Tomaselli, 2005). Meaning and contexts are not fixed, and the power that gives these meanings and contexts some coherence or, in the least, some salience must be included. This results in highly fractured accounts that cannot fully explain the lives of those we research among/with, yet we can nonetheless say something salient about their situations through the experiences we relate.

Making Theoretical Sense of the Empirical Mess

The fundamental articles of faith that require critical interrogation are as follows:

> Theory is clean, logical, and coherent [as it is presented in publications].
>
> Theory is organized, categorized [but it is also sanitized].
>
> Theory is dominant, determining [and sometimes detrimental].
>
> Theory lives in texts, logic, and discourses [and also in ideology].
>
> Theory is neat, natty, and necessary [but often absent from published accounts].
>
> Theory doesn't smell, it's not dirty [though it may be confused], and it doesn't feel [hunger, thirst, illness, pain, despair, or alienation], unless written in metaphorical dramatic narrative.
>
> Theory is often beguiling, telling us what to find, even if what we do "find" does not exist.
>
> Theory is "truth" [but may also be wrong when tested in the field].

Consequently and conventionally, many researchers come to consider anything that is contrary to these qualities with some suspicion. The somewhat less-than-adequate nature of these attributes of theory—as written in books and journals by true believers—becomes immediately clear to our students when they undertake field trips (cf., e.g., Dyll, 2007; Lange, Kruiper, & Tomaselli, 2003). We ask our students to survey and personally experience the field and to tell us where, for example, development theory fits in terms of their case studies. Consternation is the initial response. After a while, patterns inhabiting the quotidian mess become clearer, and the theory sometimes becomes the mess. Students look for reassurance in theory, in the textbooks, but eventually find it in their critiques of theory from the field.

At first, in the academy, it's usually Foucault (1971), Derrida (1976), and Spivak (1988, 1990) all the way. Other gurus given to displaying the obscure idiom sometimes pepper students' writing: Bhabha (1994), Bourdieu (1991), and Baudrillard (1981). We ask, what can these postmodern scholars possibly reveal to us about the facts of poverty-stricken, hungry, illiterate, HIV-ridden premodern/modern/postmodern communities in Africa (or anywhere)? These groups negotiate (dis)organized extended family networks; they are refugees from wars or are engaged in survival strategies, where death rates are often higher than birth rates. It takes a while for the students to realize that villagers/villages in Africa operate in terms of very different social, psychological, and cultural practices and ontologies. Planting these classes of clean, sanitized explanations onto this kind of cluttered ground, they come to learn, often creates more problems—they cannot "see" the mess for the theory or methodology. The locals—our subjects, not our academic peers—do not relate to imported theory, practices, and methods very well, if at all.

Over time, there has been a significant collapsing of the positioning of theory in the discipline of teaching, on one hand, into its purpose as possible explanation in research, on the other. "Communication" consists of imparting "information," and in the university environment, this consists of placing other people's possible explanations onto an intellectual supermarket shelf from which "consumers" (that is, the fee-paying student) can choose the "brand" that best fits their proposed professional "lifestyle." (Most of our students want to study corporate communication—they want jobs, not to be ontologically changed.) The subject matter of any theory is independent of the theory one picks up off the shelf in the supermarket of ideas (the library, the Internet, the bookshop, the publishing industry).

If, we suggest to students, they are to *use* theories and theorists (some of whom have rarely themselves tested their own theories), then they must also *abuse* them. They are not gods; their work should not be quoted like born-agains quote the Bible, or fundamentalist Moslems the Qur'an, to literally justify agendas that are unholy. Hermeneutics, which originated within theology, is the study of reception, interpretation, and the role of the reader as meaning maker. Religious fundamentalists, as well as those scholars who adhere to paradigm fundamentalism, reject the possibility of interpretations that contest their own (see below). Essentialism and violence are then designed and used to eliminate contradictions and dissent and ensure ideological and behavioral compliance. Our subjects are important to the research process in constructing knowledge as they highlight these contradictions about which we then write. The construction of knowledge is therefore the result of a dialogue with our research subjects (cf., e.g., Martinez, 1992).

What can be learned in the engagement of such theories on the ground? The proof is in the empirical testing. And how the gods tremble under the proofing. Who are these gods? They sit in a pantheon that includes the modern equivalent of Hermes, the publishing houses. Athena is perhaps the goddess of journals' peer-review committees. Zeus is the head honcho, the master of the funding agencies. And so on. However, the immediate problem is the influence of the Three Fates: the one who directs university curriculum committees, the one who oversees the faculty research committees, and the one who judges the direction of university research projects.

Shake the tree sometime; assert that theory does not fit the facts or actual experience and offer a different way of making the experience intelligible. Then the Academic Pantheon's high priests and priestesses use all sorts of rhetorical strategies to marginalize and belittle quantitative, empirical, and experiential fieldwork that might disturb their power or their assumptions about science. In literature, textualization explains that fieldwork is not necessary; in some post-Birmingham cultural studies, theoreticism and antifoundationalism are linked to interpretation and subordinate argument over facts that might get in the way; post-lit-crit media theory, as opposed to media studies, is offended with political economy and studies how messages are manufactured and distributed (Windschuttle, 1997); in psychoanalysis/cinesemiology, where the theorist is alone understood to have the Rosetta Stone for narrative analysis, audiences are assumed to be semiological rejects if they (mis)read the director's assumed intentions (cf. Sless, 1986); behaviorism assumes that people on the ground, literates, illiterates, or aliterate, have nothing intelligent to say, do, or feel—that they are simply there to be told what to do and how to react. Audience studies discounts media theory, and communication science hangs gamely onto behaviorist derivations of the transmission communicator-medium-recipient (CMR) model—as do governments, corporate communications industries, and all kinds of development agencies.

One of our project's native research partners/subjects, Belinda Kruiper,[1] proves that people on the ground have much to say about their own community. They negate the old communication models imposed by CMR theorists. Belinda coauthored a book called *Kalahari RainSong* (2004) with Elana Bregin, who had been invited by the project to contribute to a San cultural tourism venture (Bregin & Kruiper, 2004). The idea for the book arose out of Tomaselli's suggestion that Belinda's local indigenous knowledge could form the basis of an MA thesis. The book facilitates a bottom-up oral narrative by Belinda, who writes, "I am not a Bushman by birth, but an Afrikaner *meisie* (girl) of Coloured descent" (Bregin & Kruiper, 2004, p. 1). Bregin highlights the ethnographic value of Belinda's insights as it is "told from the inside by someone who was not just 'passing through' but had become one of the community, experiencing first-hand the hardships and traumas of 'being Bushman' and remaining deeply committed to Kalahari life" (Bregin & Kruiper, 2004, p. xv). Belinda may therefore be located as a "complete member researcher" doing a native ethnography. Her story told to Bregin is the result of this process. The book changed the way NGO workers related to Belinda. Some had initially considered her a troublesome interloper, someone to be wary of. After publication of her book, they admitted to understanding her and the conditions about which she was reporting on much better. Previous conflictual relations were replaced by productive ones, though Tomaselli was briefly excommunicated—"our attorneys are advising us"—by an equally short-lived opportunistic self-imposed community leader who had briefly parachuted into the traditional ≠Khomani community. This attempt at exclusion occurred on the basis that "his" (Natal) University Press had published the book. Tomaselli, who has no connection with the press, was seen to be Belinda's (political) ally, who had to be deposed as the community's organic intellectual in the ensuing struggle for the patronage of the community leader. Tomaselli was targeted for "blame" by this individual, even though the book was not connected to his project. Bregin had relied on the help of some of the project's research participants well known to the community, and Tomaselli had been warmly acknowledged for introducing Bregin to the ≠Khomani a year earlier. Bregin had met Belinda and had voluntarily assisted on an exhibition the project had organized for her husband in Durban. Rupert Isaacson (2001), a journalist, similarly experienced repercussions when he facilitated initial meetings on a documentary with the traditional ≠Khomani Kruiper clan. "The filmmaker was in and out of the Kalahari so fast that people didn't remember him. They remember those who spend time among them, and hold them accountable" when things go wrong, or when payments don't filter through to the whole community, or when they fail to receive copies of the video or book (McLennan-Dodd, personal communication, August 3, 2006). All inquiry sets off impulses, both positive and negative. Writers and researchers will only be aware of how their presence, the "self," affects the "other" and those who are othered as a result (in this case, Tomaselli), if they sustain longer term relations.

Complete member researchers explore groups of which they are already members with complete identification and, in Belinda's case, relative acceptance and are therefore sometimes called indigenous researchers (Ellis & Bochner, 2000, p. 740). Belinda's story is, however, (re)told by Bregin at face value. It lacks a discussion of the nature of their discursive (observer-observed) negotiation or of their relative subjectivities and how they came to cowrite a book about Belinda's experience only. *Kalahari RainSong* (Bregin & Kruiper, 2004) arises out of the early San research project being discussed here but does not reference it. While those who assisted Bregin are acknowledged, the absence of a research context is perhaps indicative of the discipline of literature, in which Bregin is located. Textualism's infrequent referencing often differs from that of social science, which aims to support an argument with cross-referencing to prior studies and verifiable evidence.

Our own objective, however, is to offer an autoethnographic framework in which verification is possible, in which prior research is acknowledged and respected (and engaged), and in which triangulation (via the reporting of different researchers on the same observations/encounters) is encouraged (see discussion on the fire dance below). The problem with much authoethnographic writing is that the narrative of "self" is identified but that the "other" is not or not easily apprehended. In the case of *Kalahari RainSong,* the other is well described by Belinda, but Bregin never really problematizes her own role in the dialogue. She thus facilitates Belinda's native ethnography as a form of *rapportage* (see below).

How native is Belinda's native ethnography? During her days as a South African San Institute (SASI) employee, Belinda worked as a researcher among the ≠Khomani, attempting to untangle Kruiper history for the land claim that was granted on March 21, 1999. It was during this time that she met a group of ≠Khomani she called the Riverbed Kids: "The Riverbed Kids showed me everything they were and made me one of them" (Bregin & Kruiper, 2004, pp. 2, 35). She became a full member of the community when she married ≠Khomani artist Vetkat Kruiper on February 23, 2000. Another way in which Belinda embodies aspects of a complete member researcher is that a trend has developed among social scientists who have begun to view themselves as the phenomenon and to write evocative personal narratives specifically focused on their academic as well as their personal lives. "Their primary purpose is to understand a self or some aspect of a life lived in a cultural context" (Ellis & Bochner, 2000, p. 733).

Although Belinda was not born into the community within which she now lives and about which she writes, it could be said that she is doing a type of native ethnography. Being classified as a "Coloured" woman under apartheid, she is part of a group that was marginalized by that regime. She has now been integrated into a community that was and still is marginalized and exoticized by wider society and remains classified as Coloured under the democratic dispensation, though she now prefers to call herself a "Bushman." This claim to naming indicates a refusal to accept the regressive continuity of apartheid-postapartheid racial classification, on one hand, while the reclaiming of "Bushman" allows her to work the international market for her husband's art while also underlining the role and rights of an original "First Nation," which feels grievously damaged by history.

Native ethnography is a form of reflexive ethnography (Ellis & Bochner, 2000, p. 740), and through Belinda interpreting her journey into the lives of the ≠Khomani, her book may be viewed as partially reflexive. However, this is not reflexivity in Johannes Fabian's (1979) or Jay Ruby's (1977) sense of highlighting the relations of producer-process-product but a more organic application of reflexivity in which she is self-conscious of her subjectivity in her "new" community, itself part of the wider South African society. Belinda is not using reflexivity as a methodological device of which she as a writer is mindful. *Kalahari RainSong* may therefore rather be considered a "personal narrative" in Ellis and Bochner's definition (2000) as she "takes on the dual identities of academic and personal self to tell [her] autobiographical story about some aspect of [her] experience in daily life" (p. 740).

Attempting to explain Belinda's position and writing highlights the complexity of autoethnography as a researcher/writer employs different aspects of the branches of autoethnography (i.e., native ethnography, complete member research, personal narrative). The writer's position depends on his or her subjectivity, reason for research, and context in which he or she researches, writes, and videos. What is encountered in the field and what methodology is applied cannot always be "textbook" categories but fit better into these branches of autoethnography and their relevant methodologies that overlap and blur.

Foundational Matters/History

"Paradigm fundamentalism" can easily occur if a scholar remains locked into research programs or theoretical structures inherited from his or her undergraduate learning. In this kind of situation, one begins one's reading according to a canon provided a priori through the prescribed and recommended readings of various courses. What makes it specifically "fundamentalism" is when the scholar either (a) decides that anything not on the canonical list *ought not* to be read or (b) seeks to enroll with the consensus-making apparatus that establishes the "canonicity" of prescribed and recommended readings.

Despite the somewhat conspiratorial narrative inscribed in this thumbnail sketch of the academy, it is designed to illustrate one possible aspect of the shift in the intellectual vista open to South African academics, development activists, public intellectuals, and other such practitioners. Our (often retrospectively constructed) past as participants in the final resistance against apartheid frequently involved exactly this kind of struggle for canonical hegemony. Leftists of all stripes railed against the apparently monolithic bourgeois literary and theoretical canons, all the while engaging each other in (mostly) bloodless but nevertheless near-mortal theoretical combat over what should be the canon of the Left. In many respects, it is precisely this kind of experience that has sensitized our own perception that the aprioristic nature of canonical thinking is far more a feature of both postmodern and modernist thinking than their respective adherents would like to admit. As we discovered among our different subject-communities, the inherent fundamentalism of these traditions (in much the sense that Alasdair MacIntyre, 1988, deploys the term) tends to slide glibly over the pretheoretical "shit happens" kind of realism that shapes the everyday conduct of First Peoples in Southern Africa (and, most probably, elsewhere).

With reference to our postapartheid San project, we documented, over a decade, our dilemmas and dialogues with ourselves as individuals, between ourselves as a team, and with our hosts as individuals and as a community. All the participants in the dialogue and performance want to recognize themselves in this writing and imaging. Most decisively, Norman Denzin (1997) brought to our reflexive capacity a new dimension of inquiry: how to relate our present concerns to the wider social structure of theoretical debate between the various proponents of different strategies that First and displaced peoples can develop in their respective struggles to remain as viable communities in the cultural, social, and political environment of globalization. We have questions, but not always the answers:

(a) Understanding *theory* as a hypothesis abducted from a community of inquiry's experience of phenomena, how much of our informants' (or sources' or hosts') explanation informs the products of research, and how intelligibly to them?

(b) Where does a condition of liminality appear during the course of the research process, and how does this contribute to the knowledge so produced?

(c) Does our making explicit of the processes of research interaction meet possible accusations of "bias," lack of objectivity, and so on, especially from NGOs tasked with development briefs?

These questions all relate to the difficulties that sociological or humanities inquiry poses for those who are engaged in practical efforts at development. These workers—whether at community, organizational, or government level—operate within well-established discourses such as "empowerment," "development," and "democratization." The problem that we try to resolve with our questions is whether these concepts are methods or ends. If they are *methods,* then we are practically constrained to conceiving such ideas in terms of their applications in concrete situations: What empowerment, development, or democratization is for one situation will not necessarily be the same in another. If they are *ends,* on the other hand, then the research program depends not on the muscle needed to turn around an individual situation but the *hope* that all distinct but comparable situations are relevant starting points from which communities can direct their successors to a qualitatively different way of relating to the world around them and beyond the boundaries of their immediate experience. In short, we see these questions as confronting the tendency for today's researchers, academics, and activists to view concepts as situational in themselves and not as possibilities applicable to situations across a range of contexts.

Questions addressed relate to ownership of information, the relationship between the local/particular and the national/policy, and on how to ensure campfire dissemination/involvement of, and popular access to, the written product by aliterate and non-English-speaking communities. In addressing these questions, we need to be always aware of the genealogy of autoethnographic methods. The principal data unit for these methods is not a communicable representation or entity present to the minds of a community of researchers but the dialogue an individual researcher conducts with his or her own methodological and paradigm assumptions. This, in turn, determines the direction and normative basis of the subsequent dialogue between the researchers and the researched.

Autoethnography is a relatively recent form of writing that permits readers to feel the moral dilemmas confronting us as researchers, to think *with* our narratives instead of simply about them, and to join actively in the decision points that define the method (Ellis & Bochner, 2000, p. 735). This approach—in our case—also permits us to write as individuals while maintaining team and project cohesion—notwithstanding the variety of topics, approaches, and points of entry and exit. This is an important strategy given the fact that individual students of our research team are constantly changing as they enter and exit/graduate from, and occasionally reenter, our program. Our relatively geographically stable hosts were initially mystified and even perturbed about the fact that after one, two, or more visits, students with whom they had bonded and learnt to trust, in whom they had invested time, effort, and emotion, no longer visited. They feared a lack of a longer term commitment from us. The continuity, we argue, is encapsulated in the form of the research leader who accompanies the majority of research visits.

Toward a Native Autoethnography

Where initially we did not know what to do with our written narratives and interviews, narrative and self-reflexivity in written, photographic, and video forms have now become the project's prime mode of inquiry, thus redefining the relationships between authors and readers. More significantly, however, this form of inquiry and presentation is also one that is empathetically understood and creatively engaged by the project's subject-communities. These subject-communities are beginning to appreciate the symbolic value of being included in someone else's story, itself a negotiation between all concerned, whether in print, in photography, or on video. For example, when another of our project's interviewees, a Black Botswanan, who had taken on a "Bushman" identity, was asked if he would allow one of our partners to video him, he replied,

> I want to do it because we Bushmen are a people . . . they aren't well known, they are just known by name, or by their traditional . . . what a Bushmen is like. There are people who don't know what a Bushman is, or what sort of nation a Bushman is. It would be better if they had such pictures. And I who am a Bushmen, can show these pictures to people and then tell them and then I must also point out the pictures to them, myself also, yes, because I'm a Bushman. (Orileng, interview, June 1999)

It appears that Gadi Orileng considers video about the Bushmen, and with him as one of their spokespersons, to be a means through which Bushmen can express something about themselves as a people and thereby secure land rights and social resources under threat. Although this may not be the exact form of native ethnography as described by Ellis and Bochner (2000) or reflexivity in Ruby's (1977) scientific sense, it evidences a desire by our research partners/subjects to take any opportunity, however unsystematic, when and as they appear "to construct their own cultural stories" as, for example, with Gadi speaking as a Bushman, himself to "raise questions about the interpretations of others who write about them" (Ellis & Bochner, 2000, p. 741). It is therefore another example of a more organic sense of reflexivity as self-consciousness, as our research partners/subjects, with the exception of Belinda, are unaware of the theoretical constructs and methodologies applied in the field by trained researchers. But they are keenly aware of the impact that our research might have on appropriate authorities. These may range from the conveyance of their messages to authority instructing our subjects to desist from talking and cooperating with us.

Where conventional social science writing eliminates the observers and often the observed as well from its analyses, our narratives attempt to write all participants into the encounter—and their observations and often their dialogue and their subjectivities—into the various story (or stories) being told. Campfire research, disseminations, and interactions (including songs, music, mime and dance, talk and banter, open-ended interviews, anecdotes, complaints and criticism, video) between researchers and subjects on the project's prepublished work have resulted in an extraordinary process of civil, participatory collaboration that joins the researcher with the researched in an ongoing moral dialogue (Denzin & Lincoln, 2000, p. ix; Tomaselli, 2003b). Some of our sources annually join us on campus in Durban to work with our students, when they exhibit their arts and crafts at the Bergtheil Museum (Tomaselli, 2003c; www.vetkat.co.za).

▣ Autoethnography as "Therapy"

In this dialogical sense, the basic method of autoethnography is barely distinguished from the method of the therapeutic "talking cure." As such, therefore, we need to see that these questions must serve to accomplish more than self-absolution in a form of neoanalytical therapy, an unwarranted self-indulgence. In a strictly therapeutic autoethnographic process, the research topic shifts along a chain of more or less elaborated *dialogues* between a researcher and an ever increasingly abstracted hierarchy of partners in the dialectic. Holman Jones (2005) observes that autoethnography is

> a balancing act. Autoethnography and writing about autoethnography, that is. Autoethnography works to hold self and culture together, albeit not in equilibrium or stasis. Autoethnography writes a world in a state of flux and movement—between story and context, writer and reader, crisis and denouement. It creates charged moments of clarity, connection, and change. (p. 764)

The chain may well begin with a dialogue at the research site with an ethnologically authentic source, but what happens when the subject matter of the dialogue is taken to the academy? Or to the publishing industry? Or to the NGO sector that has assumed so much of the responsibility for development among the "usual suspect" communities who form the subject matter of ethnography, anthropology, and development? How does one attribute responsibility to a dialogue, in a way that raises it to the status of a communicable *record?* Who owns the copyright of that record?

A tradition of confidentiality carries over from medical therapy to autoethnography as "therapy." It is thus hard to decide where along the chain of dialogue the representations must become knowledge or be asserted as truth claims. Medical (and therapeutic) *practice* is not to be confused with medical and therapeutic *science.* It is at the point we choose to assert something about the subject matter to the general "To Whom It May Concern" of an indefinite scientific future that ethnography must re-present itself as *communication* and no longer as dialogue. We have noted the various stages through which an autoethnographic dialogue can pass; the problem is to anticipate *how* any functionary (or activist, or practitioner) at one or more of these stages can appropriate the dialogue to ends not conceived of as scientific. NGOs, publishers, and indeed the academy as an institution are driven by practical ends, whereas the claims of science (which should not be confused with the claims *scientists* make in their professional or academic capacities) are potentially directed to ends beyond the immediate accomplishment of urgent matters. Without the normative shift or, better, the *ethical commitment* to do full justice to the reality of the subject matter (or subject community) of a field of inquiry, *as it presents itself to the inquirer,* science becomes indistinguishable from engineering.

On this basis, the most urgent need in reviewing our research was to establish where the dialogues ended (or, perhaps, petered out) and the possibility for a bottom-up record begins. Where does copyright start, and where does it end? Aliterates are suspicious of formal contracts and permissions releases, which often close down dialogue, rather than protecting both parties. To address this problem, we liaise via the NGOs that represent communities, groups, and development projects. We maintain regular contact with our subject-communities, because unless they are informed about what is to be asserted about their reality, they can have no effective say in what subsequent agencies in the dialogue do with their representations. However, to do this in good faith is not enough: It is decisive that this contact generates a record, and after realizing how these questions arose from reading the texts recommended to us, we began to consider our writing as *rapportage,* the base data for developing a record that contributes to inquiry and resists its appropriation by vested interests.

Rapportage: New Interpretive Paradigms

Here is an example of rapportage.

Things happen. Belinda and Vetkat did not buy the sheep that I offered to pay for from their neighbor, because of the wind. The wind happened, so the sheep was not bought and skinned. "We can't do anything against nature" (Belinda)—the same feeling of natural agency overpowering action is what led to photographer Sian Dunn's feeling of frustration as "everything went with the weather"—and she was unable to fulfill that day's photographic brief, because the Blinkwater folk simply returned to their grass huts to escape the wind. Linje Manyozo, a master's student from Malawi, referred to Marx's concept of "commodity fetishism" and described this naturist energy-saving response by our hosts as environmental fetishism. Where industrial societies are shaped and managed by ruling elites via developing desire for, and consumption of, largely unnecessary commodities, the ≠Khomani, in contrast, understand themselves to be at the mercy of the environment, an irresistible and invisible set of forces that shape daily decisions and prior arrangements irrespective of needs. I am not sure about Linje's interpretation of the Marxist concept, but his comment sets off a semiosis. Perhaps what he is presaging is Lévi-Strauss's (1987) concept of totemism, where the signifier is semiotically collapsed into the signified and becomes the thing itself. The ensuing metonymic mystification perhaps would be better described as environmental fetishism in the semiotic sense than in terms of Marx's framework.

How does one begin to comprehend beguiling totemistic essentialism? The wind happens. The sunrise happens. The rain dance makes things happen (mainly in the rainy season). Things happen. However, often nothing happens. That is because the wind is happening. Skinning animals in the wind invests the carcass with sand and dust. So hunting does not happen. The land happens. It is not developed. Money happens—it comes in, it goes out. None of it is invested or managed. That is known as development. It comes from tourists, visitors, and charities. The misperception is that it does not come from NGOs or the government (Tomaselli & Shepperson, 2003, pp. 391–393).

Our methodological problem is how to write an analysis of a situation and a people who have come to take us seriously but who may not appreciate our analysis, our critique, and our logic. Will we also be identified for blame? It is easy and fun to be the flavor of the month; it is a much less happy situation to be excommunicated from a life's work, blamed for everything that went wrong, and to stick to one's principles through thick and thin (cf. Barnard et al., 1996; Biesele & Hitchcock, 1999; Marshall, 1996). The wind comes and goes, legitimacy waxes and wanes, and trust has to be tested over good times and bad. We are concerned with the webs of research, exploitation, and deceit that so often cloud academic and journalistic research in the Kalahari. Who is drawing the line around whom?

The problem, as far as ethnographic method goes, is that there can be no argument against a perception. If there is wind, we will perceive that wind together if we are both exposed to it, though we might disagree on its meaning. We cannot argue against either of our judgments as to the severity of the wind because perceptual judgments are "necessarily veracious" (Peirce Edition Project, 1998, p. 204). All we can do, in effect, is engage in dialogue in the hope that (in good therapeutic fashion) we can resolve any conflict of interpretation in a nonconflictual manner. However, a comparative analysis of the kinds of *inferences from perceptual judgments* made about, say, the wind on the day a sheep was scheduled for butchering already constitutes something other than a dialogue about wind and sheep. For example, the fact that wind may affect a community's will to act at all makes it possible to consider what social or communal spaces are available to people and what needs to be done to make up shortfalls in these spaces such that wind (or rain, or cold) have less impact on the capacity to act. For the present, however, our research has highlighted the need simply to set about presenting these pretheoretical dialogues or *rapportage* so that those who critically participate in them can find a common starting point from which to move on.

Supermarket-of-Ideas Theory

Every one of the approved paradigms, without exception, sees communication and development as the equivalent of the general science education in schools: African education systems drum the information into pupils' heads via means of rote learning, and when they pass the exams, they are now officially considered to be "developed" and "informed." Supermarket-of-ideas theory—no matter the paradigm—often begins with the assertion that the people on the ground do not (and ought not to) understand the structural processes that have determined their conditions, that they do not appreciate what is being done by "us" for "them," and that they do not adequately seize opportunities facilitated by externally imposed development projects, structural adjustment programs, and policy implications. Dissociation theory and participatory communication strategies may be currently the preferred paradigms taught in the academy (cf. Melkote & Steeves, 2001; Servaes, 1991), but they disappear very quickly from researchers' minds when they are faced with unmalleable confusion in the field, demands from donors, and World Bank, World Trade Organization (WTO), International Monetary Fund (IMF), and government proscriptions.

The assumptions behind modernization and behaviorist theories quickly reassert themselves when researchers are looking for explanations to explain what is seemingly unexplainable and to get projects done in terms of Western bookkeeping, accounting, and auditing methods and what is most opaque to our subjects, the notion of the "financial year." Let us stress—we are not antitheory. What has typified our approach, however, has been the inclusion of our sources' "experience" in obtaining their understanding of where they fit into, accept, shape, or resist, determining processes and structures. In other words, the mess on the ground is already a complex web of signs that is trying to tell us something.

Making theoretical sense is not easy. For example, when researching the press under apartheid, veteran left-wing journalists struggled to find explanatory frameworks within which to problematize their experiences. However, they would immediately make the necessary connections when we explained elementary gatekeeping theories of social control in newsroom production to them. These are on-the-ground things that are part of the mess. Once we see what they can reveal, already the order of the situation becomes considerably clearer. This was empowering for them at the level of professional practice at least as they now better understood the institutional conditions under which they were laboring, resisting, and shaping (cf. Tomaselli, Tomaselli, & Muller, 1987). Doing research in a community and therefore gaining from their lives is a contentious prospect in many academic circles. The image of the "other" becomes something to be created, extracted, and commodified. The San are familiar with cars, toothpaste, soda bottles, and other products because they use these items and often because they have acted in TV commercials promoting these products (see Buntman, 1996). "Culture" is sold to tourists in cultural villages attached to hotels, and various cultural artifacts are peddled on roadways and in markets as tourist trinkets. These activities do benefit individuals through employment, but there is concern about what image is being re-presented and who it is that benefits. Surrounding this whole topic are issues of domination of cultures and cultures of domination.

Similarly, our sources in the Kalahari are not unaware of the problems that development projects, aid, and investment bring: dependency, corruption, mismanagement, and personal and community debt, being a few among the many messy factors that have largely wrecked the "traditional" ≠Khomani return to the ancestral land in the Northern Cape. No communication strategy is going to arrest these kinds of outcomes:

What is required as primary strategies are skills and an understanding of bookkeeping, management, banking, investment, savings, and planning—basically, how to cope in modernity. Communication is then a means to these ends. It is not the end in itself. As Roger Carter, a previous manager of the Molopo Lodge, in the Northern Cape, observes:

> The ≠Khomani San have given more than enough evidence of their will to survive, their wish to succeed, and their hope for future generations. They have a macro vision and wish. They do not know the micro steps to achieving macro goals, however. (Letter, September 6, 2002)

Beyond communication, of course, is the ever vexing matter of power relations. Individuals and constituencies conduct themselves within these kinds of relations, often manipulating them for personal gain, while simultaneously claiming to be representing the interests of the "community." Problems then emerge over agency, goals, appropriate solutions, questions of identity, and who is included and excluded from the community, when, why, and how. Hegemony is often maintained via violence or threats of violence, intra- and interfamilial, and between opposing groups. Individuated appropriation of incoming resources meant for the "community" leads to further conflict, and usually it is not the corrupt payee who is blamed by the community but the payer, who is usually the innocent party; as Vanessa McLennan-Dodd (2004, p. 27) and Belinda Kruiper conclude, "Getting involved gets you into shit."

Much safer is to build esoteric models based on idealist assumptions about homogeneous plains, economic man, supermarket-of-ideas rationality, and established, socially functional communities. The tyranny of the "market" is unproblematically absorbed by these models that are less able to respond to another tyranny, that of the community, which restricts individual initiative and discourages financial accumulation and the means by which to affect these. As Carter observed on his often unsuccessful efforts to involve the traditional ≠Khomani in joint Molopo Lodge–community economic ventures,

> The minute [≠Khomani individuals] started achieving individual goals, they became isolated . . . they're regarded as not being part of the community . . . because they were being pro-active and doing something that benefited them, and they weren't suffering with the rest of the community. (Carter, interview, July 16, 2001)

The discourses of suffering, poverty, and victimhood thus predominate within community relations—the so-called beneficiaries of development aid. Money comes in; it goes out almost immediately. Little of it stays in the community, and if it does, it does not stay for very long. Everyone else takes a cut. Academics are often part of this endistancing and alienation: They tend to insert walls of texts between themselves and the real world, thereby protecting themselves from getting involved (Malan, 1995). No matter how much comes in, the target community is more often than not always broke. And their more assertive members always tell you so. However, researchers only learn this if they are there. Then, when chaos erupts among the communities targeted for "development," blame them, not the models, the funders, or the government. Identify "communication" as the problem, and develop yet another development support campaign based on models that have little or no capacity to understand cultures, ways of making sense, and ways of doing things (cf. Klitgaard, 1993). "DSC (Development Support Communication) is made in America," argues Stefan Sonderling (1997)—do not assume that it will automatically work elsewhere and everywhere. The material world can be measured, captured in databases, manipulated, and subjected to the potential for symbolic violence inherent in statistics. Individuals as ordinary human beings are alienated from this process. They do not exist except for planning, policy, and development purposes, using discourses that mean little or nothing to the locals. However, as a class or other aggregation, such data are signs that reveal the levels of commitment necessary to batter down the walls of poverty over which individuals and communities struggle to see in their daily subsistence. Where statistical analysis may overlook the small scale of the human condition, there is still a link between the macro- and micro-scales that proper research into what the micro-scale situation tells us as a sign. This is the reality of community succession, of how a new generation must inhabit a different world to that of their parents and grandparents, simply by virtue of the fact that the latter had to fight for the world into which the former are still to be born. If that world is bigger, richer, more mobile than the previous one, there is a vast disparity of custom and culture, tradition and science, that must be accommodated so that the new can understand their identity and the old retain their integrity.

Africans have become accustomed to seeing well-meaning development agencies, scientists, engineers, sociologists, and researchers traipsing across their fields and squatter camps. They have become equally accustomed to seeing all these efforts fail abjectly. What needs to occur is a shift in the ground of the West's common sense, which will loosen the hegemonic grip of physicalist objectivity on the activity of intercultural engagement (Shepperson & Tomaselli, 1999). This is where autoethnographic research in the form of indigenous and native ethnography can play a key role in supplementing quantitative research. When conducting ethnographic research, it is imperative that the researcher does not underestimate the subject community's perception of their lived conditions and of the research experience. A playful encounter between ≠Khomani artist Silikat Van Wyk and researchers Lauren Dyll and Charlize Tomaselli highlights this point and provides an example of how, instead of "us" (the observers) having the power to draw the line around "them" (the observed), "they" also have the power to draw the line around "us"—both literally and figuratively. Silikat, whom we met at Andriesvale in the Northern Cape, drew what he called his "middle point" in the sand and invited Charlize to stand in the center of it. He then told Lauren to stand aside, that he would only speak to her in "*die môre*" (on the morrow) on the condition that Lauren only ask four questions. He proceeded to tell Charlize that because she was standing in his "middle point," she had taken *it* away (as had the previous apartheid government). He explained that *it* was his land and because of this injustice, Charlize owed him R10. This dialogue between Silikat and the researchers reveals that he constructed the game in relation to enforced land dispossession. His discourse—the rules of the game—plays on his objectification by researchers of him as a victim. However, he turns the tables by invoking the hidden discourse of colonialism, hoping that our White liberal guilt might pay up (cf. Dyll, 2007). Silikat inverts the normal power relation where control would conventionally reside with the researcher. It is the responsibility of autoethnographers to document their research partners'/subjects' challenge to the conventional researcher-subject power relation and their understanding of their own context. This, in turn, may spur on agency accorded to voices of researched communities. This contributes to a type of reflexive indigenous ethnography where members of a community may interpret their own cultures through those who have the means to get the information "out there"—the researchers who reflexively analyze these nuances in the field, putting theory to the test.

▣ "In and Out of Texts"

Reflexive Indigenous Ethnography as Performance

Contributors to the Kalahari project, Mary Lange and Charlize Tomaselli, together with Belinda Kruiper, coauthored an article titled "Meeting Points: Symbiotic Spaces" (Lange et al., 2003). This article is defined as a "talking point, conversational essay imprinted on paper" (Lange et al., 2003, p. 72), and part of it revolves around a particular fire dance discussed below. This article evidences aspects of what Holman Jones (2005) calls "performative writing" as linked to performance ethnography. Through a series of questions and answers, she suggests that within the umbrella method of autoethnography performance ethnography and performative writing continues the "dialogue between self and world about questions of ontology, epistemology, method and praxis" (Holman Jones, 2005, p. 766). She continues,

> This dialogue asks how, in lifeworlds that are partial, fragmented, and constituted and mediated by language, we can tell or read stories as neutral, privileged or in any way complete. In answering these questions, we have looked to the personal, concrete, and mundane details of experience as a window to understanding the relationships between self and other or between individual and community. (Holman Jones, 2005, p. 766)

Charlize Tomaselli wanted to perform a traditional New Zealand Māori fire dance with poi[2] during a field trip to the Ngwatle[3] !Xoo community in 2002. The fire dance began with great confusion. She remembers,

> After a few days we asked the community if I could perform my fire dance for them. Unfortunately due to certain communication difficulties the community thought that we wanted them to do their fire dance for us to film. They then proceeded to tell us how much we had to pay to watch them. After some negotiation we were finally able to explain that I would be the one performing, not them. (Lange et al., 2003, p. 87)

Charlize, a first-year anthropology student, along with the other researchers arrived that night at the fire and began to dance. In a later entry, she explains her initial disappointment at the reaction of the community toward her:

> The medicine man of the tribe told people that I was a witch as only a witch could move fire the way I could and that they must look away or I will possess them. I must admit—I was rather offended that they refused to observe my performance. It was only later that I learned why they were afraid to look at me. After more explanations and negotiations we were finally able to get across the idea that the fire was on carbon rope-ball attached to wire and that I was not making the fire "fly." (Lange et al., 2003, p. 90)

After this realization, the community became interested, and they started to dance around their own fire. Keyan Tomaselli (2003b), who was also present, explains how this initial confusion and cultural misunderstanding resulted in *reciprocity* where everyone present became involved in the performance:

> The two fires and performances were initially in parallel, then merged as Charlize herself "became" the fire. The Bushmen did three dances: an enactment of a trance dance; the enactment of a buck and jackal, by the men, joined by a small child; and the women's dance. . . . A yin-yang relationship fused what had previously been separate, almost antagonistic, but closely adjacent, performative events. No one had ever danced for the Bushmen here. . . . What had started as an extended negotiation over commodification ended as an organic, intercultural unity. (pp. 28–29)

Holman Jones (2005) uses Laurel Richardson's (2000) criteria for creative analytical practices (CAP) ethnography, to develop a list of actions and accomplishments to look for in performance ethnography, bearing in mind that these actions are constantly in flux. The first action mentioned by Richardson is *participation as reciprocity* that should question how well "the work construct(s) participation of authors/readers and performers/audiences as a reciprocal relationship marked by mutual responsibility and obligation" (Holman Jones, 2005, p. 773). The event of the fire dance illustrates this as the previous misunderstanding becomes *participation as reciprocity* as the !Xoo join Charlize in the fire dance, becoming performers themselves. Charlize's entry explains this feeling of *reciprocity:*

> Then they got up and danced, they danced around the campfire, they danced around me and they did a re-enaction of their traditional trance dance. It certainly was one of the most exhilarating experiences of my life, to be incorporated into a tradition that I knew so little about. Later I was told by one of the other researchers that when they danced around me, I became the symbol of the fire, one of the most important elements in Bushman culture. I was transformed from a performer into a participant of something new and exciting and I felt privileged. (Lange et al., 2003, p. 90)

"Something" was understood, later explained by a number of researchers from their different subject positions, and taken further in this chapter via an application of Richardson's (2000) CAP analysis.

The second action suggested by Richardson (2000) is *partiality, reflexivity, and citationality as strategies for dialogue (and not "mastery")* where one should question how well the "work present[s] a partial and self-referential tale that connects with other stories, ideas, discourses and contexts . . . as a means of creating a dialogue among 'author's, readers and subjects written/read'" (Holman Jones, 2005, p. 773). "Meeting Points" involves three author's voices, reflexively commenting in conversation about the fire dance experience. The outcome is an analysis of the "encounter between researchers and researched, spaces, places and texts . . . with passages cited from a range of second-order publications . . . incorporated into a network of layered voices" (Lange et al., 2003, p. 72). Their conversation is supported with videos of both researchers and researched, both groups as performers within this ethnography, and drawn diagrams of various meeting points. This article takes us one step closer to performative writing than other articles written within our project. Not only does it comment on a piece of performance ethnography encountered in the field, but the personal reflections of each character/author along with photos and diagrams culminate to create a performance on the pages.

The third action of *dialogue as a space of debate and negotiation* is linked to this as the "Meeting Points" article "create(s) a space for and engage(s) in meaningful dialogue among different bodies, hearts and minds" (Holman Jones, 2005, p. 773) as each author describes her own experiences and questions different aspects of the same event (cf. also Reinhardt, 2003; Sætre, 2003). Mary Lange's entry highlights a different aspect of this fire dance: She "writes in" the frenetic Rouchian nature of the encounter and how this made her feel:

> Sharp and clear in my memory is: the cacophony of clapping, stamping, yelling, singing, laughing, whirring and swishing; the flying ash burning my eyes and the tears that wet my cheeks; the nostalgic smell of the fire and the people; the vision of Natalie full in my face mouthing impossible-to-repeat clicks, the general grasping at chaos, but most of all, the absolute exhilaration of spirit at the shared spectacle of Charlize, despite exhaustion, weaving magic lights in the air again and again and again. (Lange et al., 2003, p. 90)

Mary's entry therefore creates a "visceral life-world and charged emotional atmosphere" of the fire dance as her own "incitement to action" (Holman Jones, 2005, p. 773) in a specific way within the context of the fire dance. This speaks to a fourth action outlined by Holman Jones (2005, p. 773) for *evocation and emotion as incitement to action.* "Meeting Points" shows

> personal narrative as a situated, fluid and emotionally and intellectually charged *engagement* of self and other (performer and witness) made possible in the "involving revelatory dance between performer and spectator" (Miller, 1995:49). In such exchanges, audiences and performers (often composed of people who are classified by virtue of race, class, age, sexual preference, gender identity, and experience as "others") create and constitute a shared history and, thus, break into and diminish their marginalization. (Holman Jones, 2005, p. 773)

The last action that our project relates to is *personal narrative and storytelling as an obligation to critique* (Holman Jones, 2005, p. 773). As discussed above, the personal narrative of Lauren Dyll's encounter with Silikat and her writing up of the encounter *shows* how Silikat inverts the normal power relation where control would conventionally reside with the researcher. It also challenges the myth that Bushmen are simply premodern hunter-gatherers living in the past, unaware of the political and social influences that affect their lives, and are therefore unable to create strategies to survive in the modern world. It could therefore be said that it makes a start for the "ethical obligation to critique subject positions, acts, and received notions of expertise" (Holman Jones, 2005, p. 773) as it challenges the conventional researcher-subject power relation. It reveals that Silikat's game may be considered a type of reflexive indigenous ethnography where he interprets his own lived conditions. The encounter reveals how he had the power to persuade Charlize to perform in his game "explor(ing) bodily knowing" (Holman Jones, 2005, p. 770) based on his interpretation of the past sociocultural injustices. In the process, he infused the game with indigenous ontology to create and commodify a regulated interaction that would earn him money. It is the researcher's *obligation* to reflexively analyze these nuances in the field, putting theory and received notions of expertise to the test. Silikat's middle point game may be considered a performance ethnography as it "seeks to implicate researchers and audiences by creating an experience that brings together theory and praxis in complicated, contradictory and meaningful ways" (Holman Jones, 2005, p. 770). Although Silikat is not aware of his game as a performance ethnography, we, as researchers, can make sense of it during and after the event through our knowledge of this methodology.

Although both the encounter with Silikat in the Northern Cape, South Africa, and the fire dance in Ngwatle did not occur as performances on a stage, they can be defined as performance ethnography as they meet another of its criteria. They both evidence an audience-actor relationship, but the line between the two becomes blurred. For example, Charlize and Lauren were Silikat's audience, but at the same time, he commanded them into action/acting/moving for him in order for his middle point game/performance to make sense. The fire dance was at first a performance by Charlize for the !Xoo; then the community joined in, combining it into an intercultural performance. Both cases fulfill the criteria for performance ethnography outlined by Holman Jones (2005) as they both "explore bodily knowing, to stretch the ways in which ethnography might share knowledge of a culture, and to puzzle through the ethical and political dilemmas of fieldwork and representation" (p. 770). Both encounters negate Western philosophy of a separate subject and object or actor and spectator. Instead, the experience can be said to characterize an ontological interaction where all who were involved in the encounter performed in one way or another. This takes us closer to an understanding of performance ethnography as a potential form of reflexive indigenous ethnography. It is through this performance that indigenous people (often the subjects of research) can reflexively explore their own culture/ontology in order to explain a certain aspect of it to those who watch—and who sometimes themselves perform (i.e., the researchers). The researchers can then extend the performance and make sense of it afterwards through performative writing. For example, autoethnographies such as "Meeting Points" and "In the Sun With Silikat" explain how it is the indigenous subjects who are engaging us—the storytellers—in a dialectical way, shaping the outcome, the relationships, and finally the explanation of an encounter. Holman Jones's (2005) own story centers on the individual/the self as the subject of her observation and self-interrogation for performance ethnography. In contrast, our project shows and tells of the dialectical relationship where an organic form of reflexive indigenous ethnography by our research subject/partner affects our ways of making sense. In so doing, we are frequently required to challenge received theory.

An important question to consider when a researcher conducts a reflexive or autoethnographic study, or when someone from within a community conducts a reflexive indigenous ethnography, is this: How does one write one's self into, while staying outside of the self-same, text? Performance ethnography often takes the form of "presenting individual (auto-ethnographic) experiences as a means for pointing up the subjective and situated nature of identity, fieldwork, and cultural interpretation" (Holman Jones, 2005, p. 770). It is within the notion of the "subjective and situated of identity" in which the answer lies:

> We use the contingent and skeptical languages of poststructuralism and postmodernism (among others) to tell and understand our lives in our world, hoping to confront questions of "self, place [and] power" in ways that are more satisfying—and *yes* more subversive than in previous performances. (Holman Jones, 2005, p. 766)

Personal narratives and reflexive indigenous ethnography operating under autoethnography could be considered poststructuralist or postmodern writing, though we do try to explain the contextual conditions in which our subjects live in materialist terms also. The postmodern is characterized by its schizophrenic nature. It is argued that a person will adopt an identity that will best suit a particular context. It is this subjective and situated identity that is reflected in much reflexive writing. We are able to "write ourselves into a text" as writers (of autoethnographic texts/personal narratives), performers, and video makers (of the organic form of reflexive indigenous ethnography that we have discussed). These authors foreground that particular part of themselves that will make the intended message of the text/performance clearer, while their "other identities" are "written out."

Lauren, Mary, and Charlize's personal narratives could be considered "self-investigation of an author's . . . role in a context, a situation or a social world" (Holman Jones, 2005, p. 767) as they implicitly and respectively ask, "What am I doing here?" This self-investigation is important as it "creates a text that unfolds in the intersubjective space of individual and community and that embraces tactics for both *knowing* and *showing*" (Holman Jones, 2005, p. 767). Such self-investigation generates what Gornick (2001) terms *self-implication,* that is, seeing "one's own part in the situation"—particularly "one's own frightened or cowardly or self-deceived part" (Holman Jones, 2005, p. 767).

Writing one's self into a text depends on a certain level of honesty to *self-implicate.* One's personal feelings are a reaction to the situation one is in and with whom one is engaging. For example, Lauren admits to being "confused, and yet again embarrassed as I thought [Silikat] saw me as the typical visitor viewing him as the Other, I followed his instructions" (Dyll, 2007, p. 137). Similarly, Charlize writes about the fire dance, "I must admit—I was rather offended that they refused to observe my performance" (Lange et al., 2003, p. 90). These personal feelings not only convey the author's emotions but also comment on the nature of intercultural communication and the challenges in fieldwork.

It is impossible not to write one's self into an autoethnographic text or reflexive indigenous performance as, like all stories, one's account "is partial, fragmented, and situated in the texts and contexts of [your] own learning, interpretations and, practices" (Holman Jones, 2005, p. 776). However, one is not writing only one's self into the text as one's stories are "constructed in and through the stories of others" (Holman Jones, 2005, p. 784). For example, "In the Sun With Silikat" is Lauren's personal account but constructed through Silikat's awareness and manipulation of the discourse of land loss and Lauren's feelings of White liberal guilt.

One challenge that is key to what has been discussed in this chapter is as follows:

> When we place our lives and bodies in the texts that we create, engage and perform, they are "no longer just our own; for better or worse they have become part of the community experience" (Nudd, Schriver and Galloway, 2001:113). Write texts that insist that to be there—on location—"is to be implicated" (p. 115). (Holman Jones, 2005, p. 784)

▣ Where the Field Is Heading in the Next 10 Years

Fifty years ago, a discipline like geography seriously debated whether or not it was a science, due to its application of approaches considered non-scientific in a positivist sense. Who knows, in 10 years' time, autoethnography might itself be considered conventional, outdated, and in need of epistemological refreshment. Whatever form it is in, science should always defamiliarize the familiar. Today, we might consider autoethnography a kind of a science, in that it aims to facilitate a form of inquiry, a way of knowing, which *includes* rather than excludes the researcher(s). Malinowski's (1922) dictum that the aim of anthropology is to grasp the native's point of view remains a starting point. But now we also aim to include the researcher in addition to the researched in elaborating perspectives that are always in dialogue with each other. If nothing else, we hope to have illuminated this point.

The further development of a critical personal narrative, or autoethnography as a method in its own right, is not to retreat into another form of paradigm fundamentalism. "Like many terms used by social scientists, the meanings and applications of auto-ethnography have evolved in a manner that makes precise definition and application difficult" (Ellis & Bochner, 2000, p. 739). This, of course, is what complicates the method—and which makes it so challenging to apply. It is also uncomfortable to apply when researchers refuse or are resistant to examining their own motivations and roles.

As we hope to have illustrated in this chapter, the categories of indigenous ethnography, native ethnography, complete member research, and personal narrative should not be pigeonholed. When the *auto* is used without the *ethnographic* (method), then what results is not autoethnography but biography, unproblematized diarization, and description. These are all terms working under the umbrella of reflexive autoethnographic research. Ethnographic—and, more specifically, autoethnographic—research is characterized by its robust, messy nature, and the implications of this should be embraced and documented in the field.

The central idea to be developed must focus on further decolonizing our narratives about other people and their lives. Academic authority must not be taken for granted as our subjects are our sources and local experts in their own right. Research does not end with the article, thesis, or book but continues as a dialogue that perpetuates itself beyond the text within the subject communities. Critique is not simply the domain of trained academics. Our subjects caution us constantly through their own struggles, complaints, and performances, both shared and witnessed. They undermine the discourses that silence them, reinclude themselves in history, and engage from their legitimate position as a viable people.

Ten years ago, the kind of writing discussed here was and, in many cases, continues to be dismissed as scientific aberration. Now we have textbooks on the method.

Notes

1. Belinda Kruiper's position within the ≠Khomani community is complicated at best. She certainly is an informed source, having lived within the community and being dedicated to their plight for many years. Literate individuals like Belinda living on the periphery with the ≠Khomani are organic intellectuals (Gramsci, 1971) of a kind. She completed her second year in social science at the University of Cape Town and married ≠Khomani artist Vetkat Kruiper. Her marriage and their subsequent move to a sand dune at Blinkwater, away from the rest of the Kruiper clan, was, at times, resented by the rest of the community. The reason for their move was to escape from the communal alcohol abuse that prevents so many from living their own lives without jealousy from the community. Belinda is therefore insider/outsider, refugee/chronicler, and therapist/practitioner. She defies borders and policies, articulates what's often left unsaid, and is both ally and adversary. These are positions that she reserves for all who work with and/or against her. Embedded in her comments are both the "ego" and the collective discourse. That she previously worked for SASI and the Kgalagadi Transfontier Park (KTP) gives her good insight into how to affect issues from a variety of perspectives (Dyll, 2004, p. 88; Tomaselli, 2003b, 2006).

2. Poi comprise carbon rope balls attached to wire and then chains. The carbon rope balls are soaked in paraffin and lit so that the performer moves, swinging the ropes around himself or herself.

3. Ngwatle is situated in Kgalagadi District 1 (KD1). It is a controlled hunting area (CHA) in southwestern Botswana that lies in a proposed wildlife management area (WMA), adjacent to the Kgalagadi Transfontier Park that is jointly managed by Botswana and South Africa. The CHA is designated for community use and management by rural area dweller (RAD) communities. KD1 is approximately 13,000 square kilometers and has three settlements within its boundaries: Ukhwi, Ncaang, and Ngwatle. The total population ranges between 750 and 850 people. Ukhwi is the largest settlement with about 450, then Ngwatle with about 180, and Ncaang with about 170. The two major ethnic groups in the area are the !Xoo Bushmen and the Bakgalagadi (Flyman, 2000).

References

Primary Sources

Carter, R. (2001, July 16). Interviewed at Witdraai, Northern Cape.

Carter, R. (2002, September 6). Letter to Keyan Tomaselli.

Flyman, M. (2000). *Community mobilisation: Living for tomorrow in the Southern Kalahari.* Retrieved from http://www.cbnrm.bw/pagessubdir/Community Mobilisation.htm

Orileng, G. (1999, June). Interviewed at Ngwatle, Botswana by Gibson Mashilo Boloka.

Secondary Sources

Agar, M. H. (1996). *The professional stranger: An informal introduction to ethnography* (2nd ed.). New York: Academic Press.

Asch, T. (1992). The ethics of ethnographic film-making. In P. I. Crawford & D. Turton (Eds.) *Film as ethnography* (pp. 196–204). Manchester, UK: Manchester University Press.

Bhabha, H. (1994). *The location of culture.* London: Routledge.

Barley, N. (1995). *The innocent anthropologist: Notes from a mud hut.* Harmondsworth, UK: Penguin.

Barnard, A., et al. (1996). Visual ethics and John Marshall's *A Kalahari family. Anthropology News Letter, 37*(5), 15–16.

Baudrillard, J. (1981). *Simulacra and simulation.* Ann Arbor: University of Michigan Press.

Biesele, M., & Hitchcock, R. K. (1999). Two kinds of bioscope: Practical community concerns and ethnographic film in Namibia. *Visual Anthropology, 12*(2/3), 137–151.

Bodley, J. H. (1999). *Victims of progress* (4th ed.). London, Toronto: Mayfield.

Bourdieu, P. (1991). *Language and symbolic power.* London: Polity.

Bregin, E., & Kruiper, B. (2004). *Kalahari RainSong.* Pietermaritzburg: Natal University Press.

Buntman, B. (1996). Selling with the San: Representations of Bushmen people and artifacts in South African print advertisements. *Visual Anthropology, 8*(1), 33–54.

Conquergood, D. (1998). Beyond the text: Toward a performative cultural politics. In S. J. Dailey (Ed.), *The future of performative studies: Visions and revisions* (pp. 25–36). Indiana: Indiana State University.

Denzin, N. K. (1997). *Interpretive ethnography.* London: Sage.

Denzin, N. K., & Lincoln, Y. S. (Eds.). (2000). *The SAGE handbook of qualitative research* (2nd ed.). Thousand Oaks, CA: Sage.

Derrida, J. (1976). *Of grammatology.* Baltimore: Johns Hopkins University Press.

Dyll, L. (2004). *Close encounters with the first kind: What does development mean in the context of two Bushman communities in Ngwatle and the Northern Cape?* Unpublished MA thesis, Culture, Communication and Media Studies Department, University of KwaZulu-Natal, Durban, South Africa.

Dyll, L. (2007). In the sun with Silikat. In K. G. Tomaselli. (Ed.), *Writing in the san/d: Autoethnography among indigenous Southern Africans* (pp. 117–130). San Francisco: AltaMira Press.

Ellis, C., & Bochner A. P. (2000). Autoethnography, personal narrative, reflexivity: Researcher as subject. In N. K. Denzin & Y. S. Lincoln (Eds.), *The SAGE handbook of qualitative research* (2nd ed., pp. 733–768). Thousand Oaks, CA: Sage.

Fabian, J. (1979). Rule and process: Thoughts on ethnography as communication. *Philosophy of Social Sciences, 9*(1), 1–26.

Fine, M., Torre, M. E., Boudin, K., Bowen, I., Clark, J., & Hylton, D. (2003). Participatory action research: From within and beyond prison bars. In P. M. Camic, J. E. Rhodes, & L. Yardley (Eds.), *Qualitative research in psychology: Expanding perspectives in methodology and design* (pp. 173–198). Washington, DC: American Psychological Association.

Foucault, M. (1971). *The order of things: An archeology of the human sciences.* New York: Vintage.

Francis, M. (2007). *Ongibonabonephi—I saw where you were: Abatwa identity formation in the Drakensberg Mountains.* Unpublished PhD dissertation, University of KwaZulu-Natal, Durban.

Geertz, C. (1973). *The interpretation of cultures.* New York: Basic Books.

Geertz, C. (1995). *After the fact: Two countries, four decades, one anthropologist.* Cambridge, MA: Harvard University Press.

Gornick, V. (2001). *The situation and the story: The art of personal narrative.* New York: Farrar, Straus & Giroux.

Gramsci, A. (1971). *Prison notebooks.* London: Lawrence and Wishart.

Holman Jones, S. (2005). Autoethnography: Making the personal political. In N. K. Denzin & Y. S. Lincoln (Eds.), *The SAGE handbook of qualitative research* (3rd ed., pp. 763–791). Thousand Oaks, CA: Sage.

Husserl, E. (1969). *Ideas: General introduction to pure phenomenology.* London: Allen & Unwin.

Isaacson, R. (2001). *The healing land.* London: Fourth Estate.

Klitgaard, R. (1993). What if we knew all about cultures? *Critical Arts, 6*(2), 49–67.

Lange, M., Kruiper, B., & Tomaselli, C. (2003). Meeting points: Symbiotic spaces. *Current Writing, 15,* 72–93. Reprinted in modified form in Tomaselli (2007)

Lévi-Strauss, C. (1987). *Anthropology and myth: Lectures 1951–1982.* Oxford, UK: Blackwell.

MacIntyre, A. (1988). *Whose justice? Which rationality?* Notre Dame, IN: University of Notre Dame Press.

Malan, C. (1995). The politics of self and other in literary and cultural studies: The South African dilemma. *Journal of Literary Studies, 11*(2), 16–28.

Malinowski, B. (1922). *Argonauts of the Western Pacific.* London: Routledge.

Marcus, G. E., & Fischer, M. J. (1999). *Anthropology as cultural critique: An experimental moment in the human sciences* (2nd ed.). Chicago: University of Chicago Press.

Marshall, J. (1993). *The cinema of John Marshall* (J. Ruby, Ed.). Philadelphia: Harwood.

Marshall, J. (1996). The need to be informed: A reply to the collective letter. *Anthropology Newsletter, 37*(5), 15–16.

Martinez, M. (1992). Who constructs anthropological knowledge? Toward a theory of ethnographic film spectatorship. In P. Crawford & D. Turton (Eds.), *Film as ethnography* (pp. 131–166). Manchester, UK: Manchester University Press.

McLennan-Dodd, V. (2003). Hotel Kalahari: You can check out any time you like, but you can never leave. *Cultural Studies <=> Critical Methodologies, 3,* 448–470.

McLennan-Dodd, V. (2004). The healing land: Research methods in Kalahari communities. *Critical Arts, 18*(2), 3–30.

Melkote, S. R., & Steeves, H. L. (2001). *Communication for development in the Third World: Theory and practice for empowerment* (2nd ed.). London: Sage.

Metcalf, P. (2002). *They lie, we lie: Getting on with anthropology.* London: Routledge.

Narunsky-Laden, S., & Kohn, N. (2007). Representing representation. In K. G. Tomaselli (Ed.), *Writing in the san/d: Autoethnography among indigenous Southern Africans* (pp. 11–18). San Francisco: AltaMira.

Peirce Edition Project. (Ed.). (1998). *The essential Peirce: Selected philosophical writings* (Vol. 2B, 1893–1913). Bloomington: Indiana University Press.

Prins, F. E. (2000). Forgotten heirs: The archaeological colonisation of the southern San. In I. Lilley (Ed.), *Native title and the transformation of archaeology in the postcolonial world* (Oceania Monograph 50, pp. 138–152). Sydney, Australia: University of Sydney Press.

Raybeck, D. (1996). *Mad dogs, Englishmen and the errant anthropologist: Fieldwork in Malaysia.* Prospect Heights, IL: Waveland.

Reinhardt, T. (2003). The fire dance. *Current Writing: Text and Reception in Southern Africa, 15,* 107–117.

Richardson, L. (2000). Writing: A method of inquiry. In N. K. Denzin & Y. S. Lincoln (Eds.), *The SAGE handbook of qualitative research* (2nd ed., pp. 923–943). Thousand Oaks, CA: Sage.

Ronai, C. R. (1995). Multiple reflections of child sex abuse: An argument for a layered account. *Journal of Contemporary Ethnography, 23,* 395–426.

Ruby, J. (1977). The image mirrored: Reflexivity and the documentary film. *Journal of University Film Association, 29*(1), 3–18.

Sætre, M. (2003). The Bushmen and the others. *Current Writing, 15,* 118–134.

Servaes, J. (1991). Toward a new perspective for communication and development. In F. Casmir (Ed.), *Communication in development* (pp. 51–85). Norwood, NJ: Ablex.

Shepperson, A., & Tomaselli, K. G. (1999). African gnoses and geometries of difference: Science vs priest-craft. In R. Haines & G. Wood (Eds.), *Africa after modernity* (pp. 47–62). Port Elizabeth, South Africa: Institute for Planning and Development Research, University of Port Elizabeth.

Simões, A. (2001). *Issues of identity in relation to the Kalahari Bushmen of Southern Africa: A comparative analysis of two different Bushmen groups during the late 1990s and into 2001.* Unpublished MA thesis, Culture, Communication and Media Studies Department, University of KwaZulu-Natal, Durban, South Africa.

Sless, D. (1986). *In search of semiotics.* London: Croom Helm.

Sonderling, S. (1997). Development support communication (DSC): A change agent in support of popular participation or a double-agent of deception. *Communication, 23*(2), 34–43.

Spivak, G. C. (1988). *In other worlds: Essays in cultural politics.* London: Routledge.

Spivak, G. C. (1990). *The post-colonial critic: Interviews, strategies, dialogues.* New York: Routledge.

Sykes, K. (2005). *Arguing with anthropology: An introduction to critical theories of the gift.* New York: Routledge.

Taussig, M. (1980). *The Devil and commodity fetishism.* Chapel Hill: University of North Carolina Press.

Taussig, M. (1987). *Shamanism, colonialism, and the wild man: A study in terror and healing.* Chicago: University of Chicago Press.

Tedlock, B. (2000). Ethnography and ethnographic representation. In N. K. Denzin & Y. S. Lincoln (Eds.), *The SAGE handbook of qualitative research* (2nd ed., pp. 455–486). Thousand Oaks, CA: Sage.

Tomaselli, K. G. (Ed.). (1999). Encounters in the Kalahari [Theme issue]. *Visual Anthropology, 12*(2–3).

Tomaselli, K. G. (2001). Blue is hot, red is cold: Doing reverse cultural studies in Africa. *Cultural Studies <=> Critical Methodologies, 1*(3), 283–318.

Tomaselli, K. G. (2003a). "*Dit is die Here se asem*": The wind, its messages, and issues of auto-ethnographic methodology in the Kalahari. *Cultural Studies <=> Critical Methodologies, 3,* 397–428.

Tomaselli, K. G. (2003b). "Op die Grond": Writing in the san/d, surviving crime. *Current Writing, 15,* 20–42.

Tomaselli, K. G. (2003c). San (Bushmen), art and tourism. *Median Journal, 2,* 61–65.

Tomaselli, K. G. (2003d). Stories to tell, stories to sell: Resisting textualization. *Cultural Studies, 17*(6).

Tomaselli, K. G. (2005). *Where global contradictions are sharpest: Research stories from the Kalahari.* Amsterdam: Rozenberg.

Tomaselli, K. G. (2006). Negotiating research with communities of practice. In N. K. Denzin & M. Giardina (Eds.), *Contesting empire/globalizing dissent: Cultural studies after 9/11.* Boulder, CO: Paradigm.

Tomaselli, K. G. (Ed.). (2007). *Writing in the san/d: Autoethnography among indigenous Southern Africans.* San Francisco: AltaMira.

Tomaselli, K. G., & McLennan-Dodd, V. (2003). Introduction: Writing in the san/d, video and photography. *Current Writing, 15,* 7–19.

Tomaselli, K. G., & Shepperson, A. (2003). Introduction: From one to an-Other: Autoethnographic explorations in southern Africa. *Cultural Studies <=> Critical Methodologies, 3*(4), 383–396.

Tomaselli, R. E., Tomaselli, K. G., & Muller, J. (Eds.). (1987). *Currents of power: State broadcasting in South Africa.* Colorado Springs, CO: International Academic Publishers.

Von Strauss, A. (2000). *Intercultural encounters at the Rob Roy Cultural Village (Kwa-Zulu Natal) and the Kalahari (Northern Cape).* Retrieved from www.nu.ac.za/ccms/anthropology/visualanthropology.asp?ID=21

Windschuttle, K. (1997). The poverty of media theory. *Ecquid Novi, 18*(1), 3–20.

Worth, S., & Adair, J. (1972). *Through Navajo eyes: Explorations in film communication and anthropology.* Bloomington: Indiana University Press.

18

AUTOETHNOGRAPHY IS QUEER

Tony E. Adams and Stacy Holman Jones

Knowing Artistry

The drive-thru line at the new Starbucks—the latest corporate fixture to take up residence in my increasingly gentrified neighborhood—is 10 cars deep. I am in my pajamas, returning from driving my girlfriend to work. The now impossible anonymity of participating in the capitalist caffeinated takeover of the neighborhood is not enough to overcome my need for a $3.49 iced coffee. Not even close. So I go in and order my coffee and wait, reading over the tastefully displayed propaganda proclaiming Starbuck's environmental sensitivity and staring too long at the cover of a Sheryl Crow CD until I hear the barista call my name.

When I reach for my drink, she says, "Hey, you go to Blockbuster."

"Um, yeah."

She lifts the bill of her Starbucks cap so that I can see her eyes. "I used to work there." I steal a glace at her nametag. Sarah. Still, nothing.

"Yeah," I say, unsure. I'm not sure *why* we're having this conversation, either, but it fills the space between her calling my name and me claiming my coffee, so I don't linger on questions of relevance.

"My wife works there."

"Oh, *yeah*. She always has to call me because I forget to put the movies back in the cases before I return them."

"You know her?" She smiles. "You know who she is?"

"Yeah. Sure."

She hands me a straw. "Enjoy your coffee."

"I will. Nice to see you again."

Now, this exchange was brief, unremarkable. And that, of course, is what was so remarkable about it. In a matter of moments, in a matter of sentences, I understood that I—that we—*recognized* each other. I understood that Sarah—and her wife—knew about me. And that I knew about them. I suppose that's pretty easy when you work at Blockbuster. After all, it's not hard to remember which customers rent entire seasons of *The L Word*. And it isn't hard for me to notice which Blockbuster employees comment on what happens in Season 2 between Dana and Alice. Still, what was remarkable about this encounter was the unremarkable ease with which we slipped into another conversation—the conversation about who we were, there in the Starbucks and everywhere else. Known and unknown, hidden and present, all at once.

It was a conversation about Michel Foucault's (1980) subjugated knowledge, about what Craig Gingrich-Philbrook (2005) calls "lost arts, hidden experiences" (p. 311). Such knowledges—now multiple—are present but disguised in theory and method, criticism and scholarship, experience and disciplinary (and disciplining) conversations. Gingrich-Philbrook contrasts *subjugated knowledges* with *knowledge of subjugation*—stories of struggle, oppression, humiliation. The importance of telling these stories notwithstanding, he wonders if our hunger for and valuing of stories of loss, failure, and resistance don't often work as "advertisements for power" (p. 312). He wonders if such stories ask us to hew to an overly formalist view of what not only constitutes autoethnography but what makes for successful, viable, and remarkable personal storytelling in the *name* of autoethnography or any other academic pursuit. He wonders if our interest in realism, in evocation, in proving—once and for all—that what autoethnographers and experimental writers are doing *is scholarship*—trades in and betrays literary ambiguity, writerly vulnerability, institutional bravery, difference, and artistry. He suggests that telling stories of subjugated knowledges—stories of pleasure, gratification, and intimacy—offers one possibility for writing against and out of the bind of sacrificing a multitudinous *artistry* for clear, unequivocal *knowledge*.

As I leave the Starbucks, this is what is remarkable to me: the ease with which and the pleasure in how Sarah and I acknowledged each other. The way in which we became present and accountable to one another in this very public space. Of course, no one else noticed, no one else knew. So maybe it doesn't count.

I wonder if this moment deserves my words, warrants the hour or more I spend writing it. Perhaps I'm just procrastinating, putting off more important, more rigorous, more consequential work. It is most definitely my experience—particular to *me*. I'm not sure it has any cultural significance or insight, even though I want to believe, as I write it, that something larger than me and Sarah, that something socially and culturally and politically significant—something *queer*—happened at Starbucks. I'll never know that. Sure, I could return and ask her. Though even if Sarah shared my interpretation, even if she confirmed my telling of our story, I'm not sure that makes my efforts to write it into significance any more or less successful, any more or less significant in the big scheme of things. But then, what is the big scheme of things? What are the possibilities of particular, ambiguous, mundane, queer stories of encounter? Of intimacy? What are the promises and possibilities of this artistry (a word I substituted, just now, for *work*) for qualitative research and critical methodologies? Will such stories help us generate some type of agreement about the value, seriousness, and commitment of autoethnographic work, our approach in engaging such work, and our recognition of those who are doing it and doing it well? Will such stories provide a counterpoint to the balancing act of telling of loss and pleasure, despair and hope? Will such stories help us decide who gets invited to speak, who gets an audience, who gets tenure, who gets acknowledged? Will such stories help us build communities, maintain borders, live somewhere in between? I'm not sure they will, and I'm not sure I want them to.

▣ HINGE

Autoethnography, whether a practice, a writing form, or a particular perspective on knowledge and scholarship, hinges on the push and pull between and among analysis and evocation, personal experience and larger social, cultural, and political concerns. Our attempts to locate, to tie up, to *define* autoethnography are as diverse as our perspectives on what autoethnography is and what we want it to do. Attempts at such pinning down and hemming in—the stuff of methods textbooks, special issues, and, yes, handbooks—delineate the relationship of a self or selves (informant, narrator, I) and others/communities/cultures (they, we, society, nation, state). And so, autoethnography looks to "extract meaning from experience rather than to depict experience exactly as it was lived" (Bochner, 2000, p. 270). It puts the "autobiographical and personal" in conversation with the "cultural and social" (Ellis, 2004, p. xix). Autoethnography locates "the particular experiences of individuals in tension with dominant expressions of discursive power" (Neumann, 1996, p. 189; see also Denzin, 1997; Ellis & Bochner, 2000; Reed-Danahay, 1997). Autoethnography is analytically reflexive; it presents a "visible narrative presence" while "engaging in dialogue with informants beyond the self" in order to improve our "theoretical understandings of broader social phenomena" (Anderson, 2006, p. 375).

Autoethnography is also painted as an evocatively rendered, aesthetically compelling, and revelatory encounter. In this view, autoethnography is "the kind [of art] that takes you deeper inside yourself and ultimately out again" (Friedwald, 1996, p. 126). It exhibits aesthetic merit, reflexivity, emotional and intellectual force, and a *clear* sense of a cultural, social, individual, or communal reality (Richardson & St. Pierre, 2005, p. 964, emphasis added). It is an effort to set a scene, tell a story, and create a text that demands attention and participation; makes witnessing and testifying possible; and puts pleasure, difference, and movement into productive conversation (Holman Jones, 2005a, p. 765).

Another way of looking at things, of approaching autoethnography, is to open up definitional boundaries. Here, autoethography is a "broad orientation toward scholarship" and not a method, a specific set of procedures, or a mode of representation (Gingrich-Philbrook, 2005, p. 298). Such opening up does not abandon intersections or interests but instead makes the politics of knowledge and experience central to what autoethnography is and does, as well as what it wants to be and become. And, with particular attention to performance and embodiment, autoethnography enacts "a way of seeing and being [that] challenges, contests, or endorses the official, hegemonic ways of seeing and representing the other" (Denzin, 2006, p. 422). Autoethnographers believe that the "point of creating autoethnographic texts is to change the world" (Holman Jones, 2005a, p. 765).

The actions and meanings that we invoke and engage when we utter and inscribe the word "autoethnography" conjure a variety of methodological approaches and techniques, writing practices, and scholarly and disciplinary traditions. Those interested in autoethnography have eschewed and, in some cases, warned against settling on a single definition or set of practices (Charmaz, 2006, pp. 396–399; Ellis & Bochner, 2000, p. 739; Richardson & St. Pierre, 2005, p. 962). In this view, an abstract, open, and flexible space of movement is necessary to let the doing of autoethnography begin, happen, and grow. However, this considered, differential positioning has also caused worry about whose or what traditions we're working in, which methods of analysis and aesthetic practice we're using (or ignoring), and whether we can coexist peacefully while at the same time generating positive movement (and change) in our multiplicity. Within and beyond the crises of legitimation, representation, and praxis (see Denzin, 1997, p. 203; Holman Jones, 2005a, p. 766), questions persist about the relationship between analysis and evocation, personal experience and larger concerns, and the reason we do this work at all. Is it to advance theory and scholarship? To engage in an artistic and necessarily circuitous practice? To render clean lines of inquiry and mark sure meanings and thus knowledge? To change the world? Are we talking, as Denzin (2006) wonders, about different things, apples and oranges (p. 420)? If so, we can agree, "reluctantly and respectfully," to part ways by acknowledging our differences and claiming versions of autoethnography as our own (Denzin, 2006, p. 422). To each his, her, their, *own.* We could also return to the oppositions and to the *hinge,* to the elemental movement—metal on metal, bone on bone—that work these oppositions. And, returning there, we could ask what the hinge holds and pieces together, here solidly, there weakening, in many places coming undone: analysis and evocation, experience and world, apples and oranges. The need to do the work we love and need to do and the need for approval of that work, approval of our needs (Gingrich-Philbrook, 2005, p. 310).

We could also ask what our hinges *do,* what versions of lives, embodiments, and power these hinges put in motion, what histories they make *go* (Pollock, 1998a). These questions go beyond contextualization, historicization, and reflexivity to intervene in the very construction of such constructions (Scott, 1991, p. 779). They ask questions about "discourse, difference, and subjectivity, as well as about what counts as experience [as analysis, as authoethnography] and who gets to make that determination" (Scott, 1991, p. 790). They ask questions about what *counts*—as experience, as knowledge, as scholarship, as opening up possibilities for doing things and being in the world differently. More, they ask questions about who is *recognized*—as visible, worthy, right, and, ultimately, human (Butler, 2004, pp. 4–5). Asking these questions suggests that we *dismantle* the hinge—that we become "unhinged"—from "linear narrative deployment," creating work and texts that turn "language and bodies in upon themselves reflecting and redirecting subaltern knowledges," and in which "fragments of lived experience collide and realign with one another, breaking and remaking histories" (Spry, 2006, p. 342). These questions also remind us of the *necessity* of the hinge, of the link that it makes, however tenuously, to others even in the release of their hold on us. This necessity speaks to the threat of "becoming undone altogether," creating selves, texts, and worlds that no longer incorporate the "norm" (of sociality, of discourses, of knowledges, of intelligibility) in ways that make these selves, texts, and worlds *recognizable* as such (Butler, 2004, p. 4). Of the movements of hinges, of their doings and undoings, Butler (2004) writes,

> There is a certain departure from the human that takes place in order to start the process of remaking the human. I may feel that without some recognizibility I cannot live. But I may also feel that the terms by which I am recognized make life unlivable. This is the juncture from which critique emerges, where critique is understood as an interrogation of the terms by which life is constrained in order to open up the possibility of different modes of living. (pp. 3–4)

The juncture, the critique, the hinge. The *claiming* of experience, of a personal story, of humanity in the struggle over self-representation, interpretation, and recognition (L. T. Smith, 1999, pp. 26–28, 37). The *accounting* for oneself as constituted relationally, socially, in terms not entirely (or in any way) our *own* (Butler, 2005, pp. 21, 64). The *movement* between two "traps, the purely experiential and the theoretical oversight of personal and collective histories" (Mohanty, 2003, p. 104). The performative space both within and outside of subjects, structures, and differences where the activist (the writer, the performer, the scholar) *becomes* in the moment of acting (the moment of writing, performing, doing scholarship). Where we are *made* in the same way the judge, promiser, oath taker is made in the act of judging, promising, or swearing an oath (Sandoval, 2000, pp. 155–156). The hinge is an instrument of *transitivity,* a moral movement that is inspired and linked, acting and acted upon (p. 156). The hinge asks us to align what may seem divided perspectives—without forgetting their differences or their purposeful movements—in order to "puncture through the everyday narratives that tie us to social time and space, to the descriptions, recitals, and plots that dull and order our senses" (pp. 140–141). Rather than agree to disagree or to decide the form, subject, purpose, and value of autoethnography once and for all, this chapter takes up Sandoval's call for a "differential" methodology that aims at tactically, and we might add tectonically, shifting ways of being, knowing, and acting in the world (p. 184). As one point, or tactic for departure, we explore the hinge that links autoethnography and queer theory. We wonder if, in the binding and alliance of autoethnography and queer theory—if in recognizing their tensions and troubles, as well as the ways these "broad orientations" complement and fail each other—we might emerge with something else, something new. We are not after a homogenizing blend *or* a nihilistic prioritizing of concerns, as such attempts leave us, as they do Alexander (Chapter 6, this volume), marking and marked, "yearning for more." Instead, we want a transformation of the identities and categories, commitments and possibilities that autoethnography conjures and writes, as well as the identities and categories, commitments and possibilities of autoethnography itself. We wonder what happens when we think, say, do, and write: *autoethnography is queer.*

◘ UNDONE

I arrive early. I don't want be late for the plenary session for which I am an invited speaker. Plenary: plentiful, absolute, and unqualified. A session for all members of the collective. I arrive early and discover that I am not ready, that I am unprepared. Before the conference, I had begun by writing a paper, then stopped when I learned the session was to be devoted to discussion of truth and evidence, knowledge and spirit. I turned my attention to a response rather than a call, a conversation rather than a representation. When I arrive for the session, I am asked to present—to make evident, to provide, full and absolute—my paper. I am asked for my prose, my discourse, my words inscribed in unequivocable terms. I do not have words to give. I have, instead, fragments, lists, and a poetic reading of poetry prepared for yet another panel.

We begin, and when I am called upon to do something—to *say* something—I decide on the poetry, on the poetics. I decide that poetry is the most "economical" of arts, the one that requires the "least physical labor, the least material, and the one which can be done between" other paper presentations, right there in the conference room "on scraps of surplus paper" (Lorde, 1984, p. 116). I decide, with Lorde (1984), it is no mistake that poetry is made into a "less 'rigorous' or 'serious' art form" by the command of economic, gender, sexual, racial, and ethnic—not to mention academic, institutional, and sociocultural—*superiority* (p. 116, emphasis added). And yet, poetry is a place for voicing experience, for recognizing and challenging difference and indifference, for doing the "political work of witnessing" (Alexander, Chapter 6, this volume; Hartnett & Engles, 2005, p. 1045; Lorde, 1984). And so I begin.

I begin with Minne Bruce Pratt's (1990) poem, "All the Women Caught in Flaring Light," part of her poetry collection *Crime Against Nature.* The back cover of the collection declares Pratt a "lesbian poet, essayist, and teacher." The inside cover—the scrap of paper folded over and holding in Pratt's words—tells me that her poems take their title from the "statute under which the author would have been prosecuted as a lesbian if she had sought legal custody of her children" after she came out. After she became queer. Was queered. After that, there are poems, a place to "write what happened" (p. 17). In "All the Women," Pratt writes,

> I often think of a poem as a door that opens
> into a room where I want to go. But to go in
>
> here is to enter where my own suffering exists
> as an almost unheard low note in the music,
> amplified, almost unbearable, by the presence
> of us all, reverberant pain, circular, endless,
>
> which we speak of hardly at all, unless a woman
> in the dim privacy tells me a story. . . . (p. 31)

I write,

> All the women caught
> in the flaring light, incandescent
> movement of loss, separation, and denial
> banishment from the ranks of the entitled
> still offering hope. Poetry for
> something else, something other
> for pleasure and for *freedom.*
>
> "A few words, some gesture of our hands, some bit of story
> cryptic as the mark gleaming on our hands, the ink
> tattoo, the sign that admits us to this room, iridescent
> in certain kinds of light, then vanishing, invisible" (Pratt, 1990, p. 32)
>
> Shimmering reflection of not only what *was* possible
> but what *is* possible

Saying this, I begin. I begin with poetry, with words of my own and words I make my own. I look up, and I am signaled to continue. I say that I am reading and writing Pratt's poetry and my own (in her voice, in my voice, in ours) because the stories these poems tell are *queer*—they invoke and defy alliances, categories, and desires. I say,

This story is a "door that opens
into a room where I want to go" (Pratt, 1990, p. 31)
I want to go. To go in and to go on

I enter this room, not pausing at the threshold,
but moving over the gap into the texts
where I recognize my own experience
Not *my* experience, evidential,
foundation for an argument

My experience as always
inseparable from language
from self-subject, from others, from discourse
from difference

This is what and all I know in the world
the starting and ending points of a life (Fryer, 2003, pp. 153, 154)

I pause, then begin, again. I want to say that this poetry does not stop or end with queer. That our poetry does not stop or end with radical historization, with questioning categories or normalization, with turning cutting language inside out or making manifest violent and colonizing hierarchies, though these are things that must be done. I want to say that such poetry, such a poetics, is *also* a chance for movement, a means to transform the static of a noun—*queer*—into the action of a verb—*queering.* I want to speak about moving theory play into methodological activism. I want to say, *autoethnography is queer.* I want to make autoethnography into performative speech that creates a freedom from having to be "careful about what we say" (Pratt, 1990, p. 30).

A queering talk
a "commotion of voices" (Pratt, 1990, p. 33)
that doesn't undo the things
that have been done to us
the things we have done
the ways we have become
things and beings unbecoming
becoming undone

I want to say this, but I do not. I cannot. Before I can get the word out, I am stopped. I am asked, then told, that I am finished. Thank you. Next.

I leave the podium, the place of plenty and absolute attendance, and reclaim my seat. The words, full and ripe in my mouth, will wait. Unfinished, but not undone.

▣ Queering

What is the act of queer, of queering? Who or what does queer become in the transitive moment of queering? Who or what becomes "redeployed" and "twisted" from a "prior usage" (derogatory, accusatory, violent) in the "direction of urgent and expanding political purposes" (Butler, 1993, p. 228)? How does *queering* make manifest normalizing, subjugated knowledges?

Intentional reappropriation and an outlining of normalcy remain *perpetual endeavors* for both queer projects and queer theory itself because, as Foucault (1981) remarks, when "a program is presented, it becomes law and stops people from being inventive" (p. 6; see Butler, 1996; Sontag, 1964). Queer theory refuses to close down inventiveness, refuses static legitimacy. One could argue that queer theory has discursively achieved this legitimation and sanctioning, a form of normalcy, but it can attempt to work against this normalcy, never becoming comfortable with itself as a sensibility or its cultural acceptance. But as Perez (2005) suggests, many queer theorists unfortunately have a difficult time queering themselves.

Why hinge autoethnography to queer theory? What can we learn if we consider autoethnography a queering methodology? What might autoethnography-as-queer do to, for, and in research and scholarship? Similar to Ahmed's (2006) melding of phenomenology and queer theory, what can happen if we queer autoethnography?

Both autoethnography and queer theory share conceptual and purposeful affinities: Both refuse received notions of orthodox methodologies and focus instead on fluidity, intersubjectivity, and responsiveness to particularities (Plummer, 2005; Ronai, 1995; Slattery, 2001; Spry, 2001). Both autoethnography and queer theory embrace an opportunistic stance toward existing and normalizing techniques in qualitative inquiry, choosing to "borrow," "refashion," and "retell" methods and theory differently (Hilfrich, 2006, pp. 218–219; Koro-Ljungberg, 2004, p. 604; Plummer, 2005, p. 369). Both autoethnography and queer theory take up selves, beings, "I"s, even as they work against a stable sense of such self-subjects or experience and instead work to map how self-subjects are accomplished in interaction and act in and upon the world (Berry, 2007; Butler, 1990, 1993; Gingrich-Philbrook, 2005; Jackson, 2004; Spry, 2006). And, given their commitments to refiguring and refashioning, questioning normative discourses and acts, and undermining and refiguring how lives and lives worth living come into being, both autoethnography and queer theory are thoroughly *political* projects (Alexander, Chapter 6, this volume; Denzin, 2006; Yep, Lovaas, & Elia, 2003).

Autoethnography and queer theory are also criticized for being too much and too little—too much personal mess, too much theoretical jargon, too elitist, too sentimental, too removed, too difficult, too easy, too White, too Western, too colonialist, too indigenous. Too little artistry, too little theorizing, too little connection of the personal and political, too impractical, too little fieldwork, too few real-world applications (e.g., Alexander, 2003; Anderson, 2006; Atkinson, 1997, 2006; Barnard, 2004; Buzard, 2003; Gans, 1999; Gingrich-Philbrook, 2005; Halberstam, 2005; Johnson, 2001; Kong, Mahoney, & Plummer, 2002; Lee, 2003; Madison, 2006; Owen, 2003; Perez, 2005; Watson, 2005; Yep & Elia, 2007). Queering autoethnography both answers and exacerbates these critiques in that they are critiques of abundance and excess. Queering autoethnography takes up a broad orientation to research and representation that exists between and outside the tensions of experience and analysis. It hinges distance and closeness, equality and prioritizing oppression, conversation/dialogue and irony/rebellious debate, and accessibility and academic activism (Plummer, 2005, p. 370). Our goal is to be "inclusive without delimiting," to "remap the terrain" of autoethnography and queer theory "without removing the fences that make good neighbors" (Alexander, 2003, p. 352; see Gingrich-Philbrook, 2003). With these ideas in mind, we hinge a brief portrait of queer theory and queer projects to the purposes and practices of autoethnography.

Navigating (In)Visibility

I own a hat, a shirt, and a box of checks, all of which possess the Human Rights Campaign (HRC) logo, a logo that consists of a yellow equal sign housed within a blue square, a logo that belongs to one of the largest, U.S.-based organizations that deals with lesbian, gay, bisexual, transgender, and queer (LGBTQ) affairs. I use my hat, shirt, and checks to mark my everyday, mundane body, to show others that I am, at the very least, LGBTQ friendly, to potentially get recognized by others as possessing an LGBT and/or Q identity, to breed connection and make meaningful relationship building possible. But not everyone knows the HRC logo; its LGBTQ connotations are only known by those who seek to align with, who are aware of, or who advocate against LGBTQ rights.

A trip to Starbucks. I'm wearing my shirt with the HRC logo.

"Tall half-caf Americano, please," I say to the barista. "And a bottle of water."

"$1.82," he responds. Based on mathematical estimation, my bill should be about $4.00.

"Did you charge me for my water?" I ask.

"Yeah, but I didn't charge you for the Americano. I like your shirt."

"Thanks," I say, happy to achieve recognition and a free drink, ambivalent about my special treatment I receive for marking myself in a particular way, pleased that I have an experience based on my making nonheterosexuality visible or at least an experience with what can happen when nonheterosexual support becomes marked.

▣ ▣ ▣

My boyfriend and I take a round trip from Tampa, Florida, to Chicago, Illinois. We arrive to the Chicago airport to return to Tampa. I'm wearing my hat with the HRC logo.

"All four of your bags weigh more than 60 pounds," the male attendant says. "The weight limit is 50 pounds for each bag."

I'm upset that I/we bought so many used books. I/we forgot that the books would add a significant amount of weight to our baggage. We'll now have to pay extra money to board the plane, money that will counteract the savings we received by buying used books.

"But I like your hat," the attendant says, disrupting my used-book, additional-weight thought processing. "Don't worry about compensating for the extra weight."

Making a nonvisible sexuality visible: the benefits, experiences, recognition.

▣ ▣ ▣

A trip to Chipotle, a restaurant. I'm wearing my HRC shirt. I place my order, a vegetarian burrito, and arrive at the register. "What is that logo?" the employee asks, pointing toward my shirt. I know he knows what the logo is and thus I know that he wants to make conversation.

"It's the logo for the Human Rights Campaign, an organization that advocates for lesbian, gay, bisexual, transgender, and queer issues," I say.

"Oh," he replies and says nothing else. When I arrive to my table, I see that he's written his name and phone number on the back of my receipt: "714–874–9824. Kevin. Call me."

▣ ▣ ▣

A checkout line at Publix, a grocery store. The male customer ahead of me pays, grabs his bags, and walks away from the grocery bagger and the cashier. Upon his departure but out of his hearing range, I hear the cashier tell the bagger that he, the former customer, "was a flaming faggot." Both begin to laugh as I move forward in the line.

The cashier begins to scan my groceries while the bagger bags. Both still laugh about the cashier's flaming faggot remark, and both are not paying much attention to me.

The casher soon says what I owe. While I usually pay for my groceries with a credit card, I decide, this time, to use a check, a check that sports the HRC logo and a check that has "Working for Lesbian, Gay, Bisexual and Transgender Equal Rights" printed above the signature line. My move to pay by check will hopefully force the cashier to ask for my ID in order to verify the check's signature and to thus see the printed political text. As planned, he asks.

"May I see your ID?" he says.

"Sure," I respond as I retrieve it from my wallet. I give him the ID. He looks at the ID's signature and then compares it to the check. It is here where he pauses. I now know that he's read the print above the signature line, and I now know that he knows that I know he laughed at the flaming faggot that passed through the checkout line before me.

"Uh . . . thank you," he says, followed by, "I'm sorry for what I said about that man."

"No problem," I respond. "Thanks for your help."

Recognition: It can subvert. Violent, colloquial philosophy: Kill them with kindness. And even if I may have been cast as a second flaming faggot after I left the checkout line, I know that I received an apology from a person who called someone else a flaming faggot. I hope that the cashier also knows that he apologized to a faggot who likes to make flames as well.

▣ QUEER THEORY

Queer theory is best conceived of as a shifting sensibility rather than a static theoretical paradigm. Queer theory developed in response to a normalizing of (hetero)sexuality as well as from a desire to disrupt insidious social conventions. Fluidity and dynamism characterize queer thought, motivating queer researchers to work against disciplinary legitimation and rigid categorization. In this section, we provide an overview of queer theory, identify queer assumptions, and discern characteristics of queer projects. We then suggest how and why autoethnography functions as a queer research method.

Queer theory primarily developed from the work of three scholars: Judith Butler (1990, 1993, 1997a, 1997b, 1999, 2004, 2005), Teresa de Lauretis (1991), and Eve Sedgwick (1985, 1990, 1993, 2000, 2003). Queer theory has roots in feminism (e.g., Frye, 1983; Lorde, 1984; Moraga & Anzuldúa, 1984), lesbian and gay studies (e.g., Chesebro, 1981; Katz, 1978; McIntosh, 1968), and identity politics (e.g., Alcoff, 1991; Foucault, 1978; Keller, 1985/1995; Phelan, 1993). "Queer" can function as an identity category that avoids the medical baggage of "homosexual," disrupts the masculine bias and domination of "gay," and avoids the "ideological liabilities" of the "lesbian" and "gay" binary (de Lauretis, 1991, p. v; see Anzaldúa, 1991). As Sedgwick (1993) argues, queer can refer to "the open mesh of possibilities, gaps, overlaps, dissonances and resonances, lapses and excesses of meaning when the constituent elements of anyone's gender, of anyone's sexuality aren't made (or *can't be* made) to signify monolithically" (p. 8; see Corey & Nakayama, 1997; Khayatt, 2002; Nakayama & Corey, 2003). Queer can also serve as a temporary and contingent linguistic home for individuals living outside norms of sex and gender (e.g., intersex, transsexual) and, as such, must not just involve transgressions of sexuality (Berlant & Warner, 1995; Gamson, 2000; Henderson, 2001); a person can claim a queer signifier if she or he works against oppressive, normalizing discourses of identity (Butler, 1993; Sedgwick, 2000; Thomas, 2000). As a critical sensibility, queer theory tries to steer clear of categorical hang-ups and linguistic baggage, removes identity from essentialist and constructionist debates, and commits itself to a politics of change.

Categorical Hang-Ups and Linguistic Baggage

First, queer theory values "definitional indeterminacy" and "conceptual elasticity" (Yep et al., 2003, p. 9; see Haraway, 2003; Henderson, 2001; Thomas, 2000; Wilchins, 2004). Many queer theorists simultaneously reject "labeling philosophies" and reclaim marginal linguistic identifiers (Butler, 1993; Muscio, 1998; Nicholas, 2006, p. 317; Watson, 2005), work to disrupt binaries of personhood, and remain inclusive of identities not subsumed under canonical descriptors (Bornstein, 1994; Gamson, 2000; Hird, 2004; Khayatt, 2002; Sedgwick, 1990; C. Smith, 2000). Queer theory revels in language's failure, assuming that words can never definitively represent phenomena or stand in for things themselves.

For instance, how might we definitively define *woman* (Butler, 1996, 1999; Fryer, 2003)? Do essential qualities exist for this category? We might say, "All women can have babies," but this would position persons unable to have babies as nonwomen or unable to claim women status. We might say, "All women are terrible at math and science" but would thus position persons who excel at these subjects as nonwomen or unable to claim women status. We might say, "All women have vaginas," but this would position persons lacking vaginas as nonwomen or unable to claim women status (e.g., a male-to-female transgender who does not desire sex reassignment surgery). The more we interrogate identity categories, the more we fall into linguistic illusion, the more we recognize language's fallibility. Such an illusory, fallible condition, however, creates a "greater openness in the way we think through our categories," a goal of queer research (Plummer, 2005, p. 365). With identity, this linguistic failure becomes important: While we interact with others via socially established categories, these labels crumble upon interrogation, thus making a perpetual journey of self-understanding possible. Autoethnography, as method, allows a person to document perpetual journeys of self-understanding, allows her or him to produce queer texts. A queer autoethnography also encourages us to think through and out of our categories for interaction and to take advantage of language's failure to capture or contain selves, ways of relating, and subjugated knowledges (see Berry, 2007; Carver, 2007; Corey, 2006; Holman Jones, 2005b; Jago, 2002; Jones, 2002; Meyer, 2005; Pelias, 2006; Pineau, 2000; Spry, 2006).

Identity-as-Achievement

Second, we argue that queer theory conceives of identity as a relational "achievement" (Garfinkel, 1967). An achievement metaphor situates identities *in* interaction, in processes where we are held accountable for being persons of particular kinds, kinds that we sometimes know or try to present ourselves *as*, but also kinds about which we have no definitive control (Hacking, 1990, 1999). A queer, identity-as-achievement logic implies that we are held accountable for identities that often take the form of linguistic categories but implies we can never know what categories others may demand of us or what kinds of people others will consider us as; we can try to pass as kinds of persons, but we may not succeed or know if we succeed (see Adams, 2005). A queer, identity-as-achievement logic implies that selves emerge from and remain contingent upon situated embodied practices, acts that rely on compulsory, citational, stereotypical performances about being kinds of people (Butler, 1990, 1993, 1999, 2004; Sedgwick, 1993; West & Fenstermaker, 1995; West & Zimmerman, 1987). A queer, identity-as-achievement logic implies that identities fluctuate across time and space, thus requiring constant attention and negotiation; identities may come across as "singular, fixed, or normal" in *an* interaction but may not be singular, fixed, or normal across *all* interactions (Watson, 2005, p. 74; see also Butler, 1990; Freeman, 2001; Gamson, 2000).

Viewing identity as an achievement also distances identity from essentialist *and* constructionist debates of selfhood. Essentialists view identity as something innate, biological, and fixed. Constructionists view identities as socially established and maintained through interaction. A queer, identity-as-achievement logic, however, works outside of essentialist and constructionist perspectives: It embraces the contextual achievement of and passing as certain *kinds* of people. In one context, an individual may be perceived as heterosexual whereas in another context, the individual may be perceived as bisexual or homosexual. In one context, an individual may pass as White, and in another context, this individual may pass as Black, and in another context, this individual may pass as multiracial (Greenberg, 2002). In one context, an individual may pass as Catholic, and in another context she or he may pass as Baptist, and in another context, she or he may pass as Jewish. An identity-as-achievement perspective does not imply that biology has nothing to do with interaction, nor does it foreground environmental influences on selfhood; the essence of selves and the processes through which selves are made are not the foci of queer theory. Queer theory simultaneously embraces both "identity-constituting, identity-fracturing discourses" (Sedwick, 1993, p. 9).

However, the permanency of print, the representational livelihood upon which many autoethnographers rely, can make a queer sensibility come across as "singular, fixed, or normal" for both writers and readers (Watson, 2005, p. 74; see Sontag, 1964). With the exception of a virtual text like blogging, a written text can function as a permanent representation, a lifeless, uncompromising snapshot of culture. Finished texts solidify human trajectories in time and space, making it possible for life to imitate immobile art. Such permanency fixes identity regardless of an autoethnographer's intentions, qualifiers, and desires to present a "partial, partisan, and problematic" account (Goodall, 2001, p. 55). When we turn autoethnographic research into print—when we present it at a conference, publish it, turn it into a handbook chapter—we solidify an identity into text, and we harden a community, never allowing us or it to change unless we produce a second, solidifying account to accompany the first. We could provide two textual stories rather than just one, two accounts of a self to try to emphasize, display, the trajectories of a self-in-process, but we now have fixed two immobile versions of a self and suggest, by way of the print medium, a lack of movement. But by considering autoethnography queer, we recognize that identities may not be singular, fixed, or normal across *all* interactions (see Ellis, 1986, 1995, 2007; Johnson, 2001; Pelias, 2000, 2004; Rambo, 2005; Ronai, 1995; Wyatt, 2005, 2006). Identities constructed through a queering of autoethnography are relational; they shift and change. We are held accountable for being particular kinds of people by numerous seen and unseen forces, but our/these kinds of identities are in constant need of attention, negotiation, and care.

A Politics of Change

Third, queer theory values "political commitment" (Yep et al., 2003, p. 9; see also Alexander, Chapter 6, this volume), deconstructs what may pass as "natural" and "normal" (Garfinkel, 1967; see Berlant & Warner, 1995; Dilley, 1999; Kong et al., 2002; R. R. Smith, 2003), focuses on how bodies both constitute and are constituted by systems of power as well as how bodies might serve as sites of social change (Althusser, 1971; Berlant, 1997; Bornstein, 1994; Butler, 1990, 1993, 1999, 2004; Foucault, 1978; Yep & Elia, 2007), and embraces a "politics of transgression" (Watson, 2005, p. 68; see Hird, 2004). Queer theorists revel in "symbolic disorder" (Baudrillard, 2001, p. 125), pollute established social conventions (Haraway, 2003), and diffuse hegemonic categories and classifications. As Henderson (2001) suggests, normalcy "needs perversion to know itself" (Henderson, 2001, p. 475; see Bell, 1999). Queer projects function as this denormalizing perversion often by re/appropriating marginal discourse. While it could be argued that all re/appropriations are political, queer projects intentionally re/appropriate phenomena to pollute canonical discourse, to question what mundanely passes as normal. Queer re/appropriation tries to "twist" social order (Betsky, 1997, p. 18), counter canonical stories, and make discursive "trouble" (Butler, 1999).

The use of "queer" in "queer theory" is an example of a queer act, a queer politics. As Butler (1993) writes, something becomes "queered" when it is "redeployed" and "twisted" from a "prior usage" in "the direction of urgent and expanding political purposes" (p. 228; see Kong et al., 2002). Watson (2005) suggests that "reclaiming the word, 'queer' empties the category of its effects" (p. 73). Queer theory re/appropriates the once-taboo word and tries to reclaim abject power. Prior to this re/appropriation, *queer* possessed negative connotations, negatively deeming phenomena as out of the norm and "slightly off kilter" (Walker, cited in Johnson, 2001). By using *queer* in an affirmative sense—by incorporating it into mainstream discourse and associating the term with the academically valued *theory*—queer endeavors can emerge as desirable and esteemed. A queer re/appropriation is similar to how individuals try to reclaim other words for political purposes (e.g., *nigger* [Kennedy, 2003], *cunt* [Muscio, 1998], and *vagina* [Ensler, 2001]).

Queer projects work to disrupt insidious, normalizing ideologies by way of re/appropriating parts of discursive systems and explicitly advocate for change. For instance, Cvetkovich (2003) shows how Dorothy Allison's work disrupts common storylines of abuse in that Allison shows how she both was a victim and pleasurable recipient of abusive behaviors, expanding notions of how an abused identity functions. Alexander (Chapter 6, this volume) demonstrates how the film *Brokeback Mountain* can function as a conservative story that perpetuates heteronormativity and subordinates raced "Others" (e.g., Mexican male prostitutes) to White desire; Alexander's read disrupts the text's assumed liberal status. And another intentional queering of canonical discourse involves the television program *Noah's Arc,* a scripted show that features experiences of five, assumed-gay Black men, individuals whose sexuality is implicitly perceived to rub against canonical religious doctrine and the rampant homophobia found in predominantly Black communities (see Yep & Elia, 2007). Naming the show *Noah's Arc* is also a queer act in that it mixes the religious baggage of Noah and the Ark with nonheterosexual storylines, thus potentially disrupting and reframing common understandings of religion *and* sexuality. A politics of change, as deployed in queer projects, constitutes much of current autoethnographic work as many autoethnographers intentionally, politically try to make ideological and discursive *trouble* (Butler, 1999; see Corey & Nakayama, 1997; Foster, in press; Jeffries, 2002; Johnson, 2001; Lee, 2003; Nakayama & Corey, 2003; Owen, 2003; Pelias, 1999, 2006; Rambo, 2007; Taylor, 2000).

Maneuvering

I have a female friend who had two male friends, both of whom called me a "homo-phoney." According to her friends, a homo-phoney described a man who identified as gay but did not have any "gay qualities" and a man who would be identified as gay solely to establish intimate, sexual relations with women. According to her friends, I was straight. I, not she, had other motives in our relationship since her friends commented on and criticized my, not her, behavior. My gendered performances conflicted with a sexuality I claimed.

A colleague once asked why I was attending the National Communication Association convention. I told him I was participating on a gay-themed research panel. "Are you gay enough to be on that panel?" he asked. Gender and sexuality conflict, again.

In graduate school, a professor frequently informed me that there was a "woman out there for me" since I did not "act gay," even though she knew of my intimate relationships with men. I regularly asked her why she thought this, but because of her authoritative role of "professor" and mine of "student," I felt I could press the fake-gay issue only so far.

Each of these situations makes conditions for queering possible, conditions that I now embrace and intentionally challenge in my everyday, embodied affairs. For instance, after disclosing my sexuality to a class I taught, a student told me that he thought I was a "geek" rather than gay. "You wear black-rimmed glasses," he said. "But you're masculine. It wasn't until you said you couldn't operate a laptop computer where I began to think you might be gay." At the end of the semester when students completed course feedback, absent my physical presence, one student later told me about two debates that occurred during the feedback process: Some students believed that I was lying about my gayness; others felt that I was transgendered, a man with a vagina who wanted to undergo sex reassignment surgery. Even though I still may perpetuate scripts of masculinity by intentionally working against an effeminate gay male stereotype, such comments also suggest that my intentional queering of the categories and normative conceptualizations of sex, gender, and sexuality do generate confusion, blur categories, and make questioning possible.

Queering Autoethnography

Queering autoethnography embraces fluidity, resists definitional and conceptual fixity, looks to self and structures as relational accomplishments, and takes seriously the need to create more livable, equitable, and just ways of living. The hinge that links queer theory and autoethnography is, like Sandoval's (2000) resistive semiology, a differential and oppositional form of consciousness (p. 184). It is performative in the transitive sense of a hinge, a middle position, a form "that intervenes in social reality through deploying an action that re-creates the agent even as the agent is creating the action . . . the only predictable final outcome is transformation itself" (p. 157).

A differential, oppositional, performative, and above all transformative approach to autoethnography is one in which bodies are immersed in texts and as such lives, contexts, and cultures. The subject–selves of autoethnography are doing, speaking, and understanding beings, yes, but they are forthrightly incomplete, unknown, fragmented, and conflictual. Failing to recognize these contingencies, ellipses, and contradictions, autoethnographers paint themselves into a corner where boundaries are policed, disciplinary and scholarly turf is defined and fought over, and systems for what and who "counts" and doesn't count undermine the very liberatory impulses we imagine for our work. In the place of relationality, performativity, and transitivity, we create singularity, clarity, and certainty. In short, we create *good stories:* stories that report on recognizable experiences, that translate simply and specifically to an "actionable result"—an emotional response, a change in thinking or behavior, a shift in policy or perception, publication, tenure (Eisenberg et al., 2005, p. 394). As scholars have responded to a perceived need for good autoethnographic stories, we have:

- Favored *clarity and transparency* of knowledge via criteria or "rules of art" over *ambiguity*—room for interpretation, misunderstanding, not knowing, leaving things unfinished, unanswered (Gingrich-Philbrook, 2005; Madison, 2006; Pollock, 2006)
- Foregrounded *knowledge* claims and publication in sanctioned or legitimate outlets (journals, academic books) and glossing over *aesthetic* (literary) concerns (Gingrich-Philbrook, 2005; Richardson & St. Pierre, 2005)
- Sought proof of *worth* and *legitimacy* by creating typologies for good stories to enact (Bochner, 2000; Clough, 2000; Ellis, 2000; Holman Jones, 2005a; Pollock, 1998b), even as we resisted doing so
- Engaged in recursive debates about how to define autoethnography, about what constitutes authentic or legitimate autoethnographic research, and about what the purposes and meanings of autoethnographic work are for research, for academic careers, for ourselves, for the world (Alcoff, 1991; Anderson, 2006; Atkinson, 2006; Bochner, 2000; Buzard, 2003; Corey, 2006; Denzin 2006; Gans, 1999; Madison, 2006; Rambo, 2007; Ronai, 1995; Spry 2006)

The necessity and helpfulness of methodological primers and criteria for the evaluation of our work notwithstanding, a queering of autoethnography asks us to find ways of living together, "without agreement, without confirmation, without clarity" (Gingrich-Philbrook, 2005, p. 298). Gingrich-Philbrook (2005) recommends writing, as we noted earlier, subjugated knowledges, stories that are present but disguised (pp. 311–312; see Conquergood, 2002). These are stories of pleasure, of gratification, of the mundane, as they intersect, crisscrossing rhizomatically with stories of subjugation, abuse, and oppression. One of the most ready forms for such tellings is found in narrative accounts of our lives. And so, autoethnography is queer. Saying so means taking a stand on a poetics of change. Saying so treats identities and communities as a performative, relational accomplishment. Butler (2005) reminds us that whatever stories we choose to tell, and however provisionally *or* transparently we work to tell them, we are always doing so in order to make ourselves "recognizable and understandable" (p. 37). This is recognition of a need to unfasten the hinge that separates experience and analysis and the personal and the political, even as we need it to create an intelligible humanity, a life both livable and worth living. It is a recognition of humanity that doesn't end or stop in the move from the space of illegitimacy, all breath and speech, dark and hollow, to the place of legitimacy, resplendent and lucid in word and text (see Delany, 1988/2004). In the next breath, in the next book, however, Butler (2005) ends with the pleasure and ethics of being *undone* in a radical relationality:

> We must recognize that ethics requires us to risk ourselves precisely at moments of unknowingness, when what forms us diverges from what lies before us, when our willingness to become undone in relation to others constitutes our chance of becoming human. To be undone by another is a primary necessity, an anguish, to be sure, but also a chance—to be addressed, claimed, bound to what is not me, but also to be moved, to be prompted to act, to address myself elsewhere, and so to vacate the self-sufficient "I" as a kind of possession. (p. 136)

We wonder if the ethics of undoing that Butler describes enacts both the pleasures and the oppressions of autoethnography and, furthermore, if it anticipates the juncture, the stitching together—the hinging—of autoethnography and queer theory. Consider, for example,

- Making work that *becomes,* like a perpetual horizon, rather than an artifact of experience; making work that acts *as if,* rather than says *it is.* Such work understands the importance of being tentative, playful, and incomplete in equal measure with radical historicization, persistent questioning, and perpetual revision.

- Making work that simultaneously imagines fluid, temporary, and radically connected identities *and* that creates and occupies *recognizable* identities. Such work views identities as relational accomplishments: manifestations of selves that shift and change, that must be negotiated and cared for, and for which we are held personally, institutionally, and ethically responsible.

- Making work that advocates for trouble, that takes a stand in and on the otherwise. Such work disrupts taken-for-granted, normalizing stories and posits more open, more free, and more just ways of being in the world.

Making autography a queer method offers a way to trade in the debates around legitimacy, value, and worth and for conversations about practicality, necessity, and movement. It is a move autoethnographers are ready to take, are taking. We encourage you to claim and reclaim the word *queer* in the name of autoethnography, in the name of challenging categories and achieving identities and communities that are fluid yet complex, multiple yet cognizant of the attention, negotiation, and care that impinge on any scholarly project. We encourage you to twist *autoethnography* from its prior usages, whether diminishing or valorizing, and put it to use for altogether new and other political purposes.

▣ Recognition

Making coffee at home—a home I share with my girlfriend and my son—I thought about a conversation I had with my mother a few months after I left my other home, my other life. For months, I could not summon the courage to tell my mother the details of the split, of my reversal, my betrayal. And then, in an unremarkable moment, I told that story in sentence. When my mother asked if I was interested in having another relationship some day, if I would date someone and maybe be married again, I simply said, "No."

> "Oh. . . . Why?"
>
> "Mom, I'm not interested in dating."
>
> "What if you meet someone nice? A good man?"
>
> "Mom, I'm not interested in dating men."
>
> "Oh. . . . *Oh.* Okay. As long as you're happy."

And that was it. Unremarkable except for the remarkable way she moved without hesitation into my new narrative. Unremarkable except for the remarkable way she chose to accept and, yes, *believe* my story—a queer story with no immediate recognition, no diagnosis or translation, no ready or apparent ending—as true. Or at least good enough. Later, we would talk about this story in more detail, and still, my mother did not waver in her acknowledgment of what she could not know. She did not read or tell this story as extraordinary or rare, mournful or wasted. She did, however, share one concern: She was worried I'd be alone. That I wouldn't have someone to share my life with, to grow old with. All I could say was, "There's no guarantee of that—of having someone—for anyone. I don't think it's any different for women. Maybe we just don't see women growing old together. Or maybe we do, but we don't recognize it." I don't know whether this satisfied her or put her or my worries about what is surely the inevitability of loneliness in life at bay, but that was the end of our conversation, at least for now.

Making coffee at home, I thought about my mother's gift to me: an unblinking, unmoving acceptance of the "lost arts" and "hidden experiences" that had become my life. In her recognition of me, in her acknowledgment and claiming of my story, she taught me what I could not teach myself in those long months: the importance of risking ourselves in moments of unknowingness, the necessity of resisting offers of certainty or stability, and the flattery of legitimacy. The importance of taking a chance motivated not out of a misplaced or, worse, righteous self-sufficiency, but a willingness to become undone *and* moved to act. Why not write over, on, and through the boundaries of what constitutes and contributes to autoethnography—to qualitative and critical research—by creating a few queer stories, a few queer autoethnographies? Why not embrace a critical stance that values opacity, particularity, indeterminateness for what they bring and allow us to know and forget, rather than dismissing these qualities as slick deconstructive tricks, as frustrating, as unmoving and unrecognizable? Why *not* write (Gingrich-Philbrook, 2005, p. 311)? *Why not?*

References

Adams, T. E. (2005). Speaking for others: Finding the 'whos' of discourse. *Soundings, 88*(3–4), 331–345.

Ahmed, S. (2006). *Queer phenomenology: Orientations, objects, others.* Durham, NC: Duke University Press.

Alcoff, L. (1991). The problem of speaking for others. *Cultural Critique, 20,* 5–32.

Alexander, B. K. (2003). Querying queer theory *again* (or queer theory as drag performance). *Journal of Homosexuality, 45*(2–4), 349–352.

Althusser, L. (1971). Ideology and ideological state apparatuses (B. Brewster, Trans.). In *Lenin and philosophy and other essays* (pp. 121–173). London: NLB.

Anderson, L. (2006). Analytic autoethnography. *Journal of Contemporary Ethnography, 35*(4), 373–395.

Anzaldúa, G. (1991). To(o) queer the writer—Loca, escritora y chicana. In B. Warland (Ed.), *InVersions: Writings by dykes, queers, and lesbians* (pp. 249–263). Vancouver: Press Gang.

Atkinson, P. (1997). Narrative turn or blind alley? *Qualitative Health Research, 7*(3), 325–344.

Atkinson, P. (2006). Rescuing autoethnography. *Journal of Contemporary Ethnography, 35*(4), 400–404.

Barnard, I. (2004). *Queer race: Cultural interventions in the racial politics of queer theory.* New York: Peter Lang.

Baudrillard, J. (2001). *Jean Baudrillard: Selected writings.* Stanford, CA: Stanford University Press.

Bell, E. (1999). Weddings and pornography: The cultural performance of sex. *Text and Performance Quarterly, 19*(3), 173–195.

Berlant, L. (1997). *The queen of America goes to Washington City.* Durham, NC: Duke University Press.

Berlant, L., & Warner, M. (1995). What does queer theory teach us about X? *PMLA, 110*(3), 343–349.

Berry, K. (2007). Embracing the catastrophe: Gay body seeks acceptance. *Qualitative Inquiry, 13*(2), 259–281.

Betsky, A. (1997). *Queer space: Architecture and same-sex desire.* New York: Morrow.

Bochner, A. P. (2000). Criteria against ourselves. *Qualitative Inquiry, 6*(2), 266–272.

Bornstein, K. (1994). *Gender outlaw.* New York: Routledge.

Butler, J. (1990). Performative acts and gender constitution: An essay in phenomenology and feminist theory. In S. E. Case (Ed.), *Performing feminisms: Feminist critical theory and theatre* (pp. 270–282). Baltimore: Johns Hopkins University Press.

Butler, J. (1993). *Bodies that matter: On the discursive limits of "sex."* New York: Routledge.

Butler, J. (1996). Gender as performance. In P. Osborne (Ed.), *A critical sense: Interviews with intellectuals* (pp. 109–125). New York: Routledge.

Butler, J. (1997a). *Excitable speech: A politics of the performative.* New York: Routledge.

Butler, J. (1997b). *The psychic life of power: Theories in subjection.* Stanford, CA: Stanford University Press.

Butler, J. (1999). *Gender trouble: Feminism and the subversion of identity* (2nd ed.). New York: Routledge.

Butler, J. (2004). *Undoing gender.* New York: Routledge.

Butler, J. (2005). *Giving an account of oneself.* New York: Fordham University Press.

Buzard, J. (2003). On auto-ethnographic authority. *The Yale Journal of Criticism, 16*(1), 61–91.

Carver, M. H. (2007). Methodology of the heart: A performative writing response. *Liminalitics: A Journal of Performance Studies, 3*(1), 1–14. Retrieved May 12, 2007, from http://liminalities.net/3-1/heart.htm

Charmaz, K. (2006). The power of names. *Journal of Contemporary Ethnography, 35*(4), 396–399.

Chesebro, J. W. (Ed.). (1981). *Gayspeak: Gay male and lesbian communication.* New York: The Pilgrim Press.

Clough, P. T. (2000). Comments on setting criteria for experimental writing. *Qualitative Inquiry, 6*(2), 278–291.

Conquergood, D. (2002). Performance studies: Interventions and radical research. *The Drama Review, 46*(2), 145–156.

Corey, F. C. (2006). On possibility. *Text and Performance Quarterly, 26*(4), 330–332.

Corey, F. C., & Nakayama, T. K. (1997). Sextext. *Text and Performance Quarterly, 17*(1), 58–68.

Cvetkovich, A. (2003). *An archive of feelings: Trauma, sexuality, and lesbian public culture.* Durham, NC: Duke University Press.

Delany, S. (2004). *The motion of light in water.* Minneapolis: University of Minnesota Press. (Original work published 1988)

de Lauretis, T. (1991). Queer theory: Lesbian and gay sexualities. *differences: A Journal of Feminist Cultural Studies, 3*(2), iii–xvii.

Denzin, N. K. (1997). *Interpretive ethnography: Ethnographic practices for the 21st century.* Thousand Oaks, CA: Sage.

Denzin, N. K. (2006). Analytic autoethnography, or déjá vu all over again. *Journal of Contemporary Ethnography, 35*(4), 419–428.

Dilley, P. (1999). Queer theory: Under construction. *International Journal of Qualitative Studies in Education, 12*(5), 457–472.

Eisenberg, E., Murphy, A., Sutcliffe, K., Wears, R., Schenkel, S., Perry, S., et al. (2005). Communication in emergency medicine: Implications for patient safety. *Communication Monographs, 72*(4), 390–413.

Ellis, C. (1986). *Fisher folk: Two communities on Chesapeake Bay.* Lexington: University Press of Kentucky.

Ellis, C. (1995). Emotional and ethical quagmires in returning to the field. *Journal of Contemporary Ethnography, 24*(1), 68–98.

Ellis, C. (2000). Creating criteria: An ethnographic short story. *Qualitative Inquiry, 6*(2), 273–277.

Ellis, C. (2004). *The ethnographic I: A methodological novel about autoethnography.* Walnut Creek, CA: AltaMira Press.

Ellis, C. (2007). Telling secrets, revealing lives: Relational ethics in research with intimate others. *Qualitative Inquiry, 13*(1), 3–29.

Ellis, C., & Bochner, A. P. (2000). Autoethnography, personal narrative, reflexivity. In N. K. Denzin & Y. S. Lincoln (Eds.), *The SAGE handbook of qualitative research* (2nd ed., pp. 733–768). Thousand Oaks, CA: Sage.

Ensler, E. (2001). *The vagina monologues.* London: Virago.

Foster, E. (in press). Commitment, communication, and contending with heteronormativity: An invitation to greater reflexivity in interpersonal research. *Southern Communication Journal.*

Foucault, M. (1978). *The history of sexuality* (Vol. 1). New York: Vintage.

Foucault, M. (1980). *Power/knowledge: Selected interviews and other writings 1972–1977* (C. Gordon, Ed.). New York: Pantheon.

Foucault, M. (1981). Friendship as a lifestyle: An interview with Michel Foucault. *Gay Information, 7,* 4–6.

Freeman, M. (2001). From substance to story: Narrative, identity, and the reconstruction of self. In J. Brockmeier & D. Carbaugh (Eds.), *Narrative and identity: Studies in autobiography, self and culture* (pp. 283–298). Philadelphia: John Benjamins.

Friedwald, W. (1996). *Jazz singing: America's great voices from Bessie Smith to bebop and beyond.* New York: Da Capo.

Frye, M. (1983). *The politics of reality: Essays in feminist theory.* Trumansburg, NY: Crossing Press.

Fryer, D. R. (2003). Toward a phenomenology of gender: On Butler, positivism, and the question of experience. *Listening: Journal of Religion and Culture, 37*(2), 136–162.

Gamson, J. (2000). Sexualities, queer theory, and qualitative research. In N. K. Denzin & Y. S. Lincoln (Eds.), *The SAGE handbook of qualitative research* (2nd ed., pp. 347–365). Thousand Oaks, CA: Sage.

Gans, H. J. (1999). Participant observation: In the era of "ethnography." *Journal of Contemporary Ethnography, 28*(5), 540–548.

Garfinkel, H. (1967). *Studies in ethnomethodology.* Englewood Cliffs, NJ: Prentice Hall.

Gingrich-Philbrook, C. (2003). Queer theory and performance. *Journal of Homosexuality, 45*(2–4), 353–356.

Gingrich-Philbrook, C. (2005). Autoethnography's family values: Easy access to compulsory experiences. *Text and Performance Quarterly, 25*(4), 297–314.

Goodall, H. L. (2001). *Writing the new ethnography.* Walnut Creek, CA: AltaMira.

Greenberg, J. A. (2002). Definitional dilemmas: Male or female? Black or white? The law's failure to recognize intersexuals and multiracials In T. Lester (Ed.), *Gender nonconformity, race, and sexuality* (pp. 102–124). Madison: University of Wisconsin Press.

Hacking, I. (1990). Making up people. In E. Stein (Ed.), *Forms of desire: Sexual orientation and the social constructionist controversy* (pp. 69–88). New York: Garland.

Hacking, I. (1999). *The social construction of what?* Cambridge, MA: Harvard University Press.

Halberstam, J. (2005). Shame and white gay masculinity. *Social Text, 23*(3–4), 219–233.

Haraway, D. (2003). *The Haraway reader.* New York: Routledge.

Hartnett, S. J., & Engels, J. D. (2005). "Aria in Time of War": Investigative poetry and the politics of witnessing. In N. K. Denzin & Y. S. Lincoln (Eds.), *The SAGE handbook of qualitative research* (3rd ed., pp. 1043–1067). Thousand Oaks, CA: Sage.

Henderson, L. (2001). Queer communication studies. In W. B. Gudykundst (Ed.), *Communication yearbook 24* (pp. 465–484). Thousand Oaks, CA: Sage.

Hilfrich, C. (2006). "The Self is a People": Autoethnographic poetics in Hélène Cixous's fictions. *New Literary History, 37,* 217–235.

Hird, M. J. (2004). Naturally queer. *Feminist Theory, 5*(1), 85–89.

Holman Jones, S. (2005a). Autoethnography: Making the personal political. In N. K. Denzin & Y. S. Lincoln (Eds.), *The SAGE handbook of qualitative research* (3rd ed., pp. 763–791). Thousand Oaks, CA: Sage.

Holman Jones, S. (2005b). (M)othering loss: Telling adoption stories, telling performativity. *Text and Performance Quarterly, 25*(2), 113–135.

Jackson, A. Y. (2004). Performativity identified. *Qualitative Inquiry, 5,* 673–690.

Jago, B. J. (2002). Chronicling an academic depression. *Journal of Contemporary Ethnography, 31*(6), 729–757.

Jeffries, T. (2002). An autoethnographical exploration of racial 'I'dentity. *Journal of Intergroup Relations, 29*(2), 39–56.

Johnson, E. P. (2001). "Quare" studies, or (almost) everything I know about queer studies I learned from my grandmother. *Text and Performance Quarterly, 21*(1), 1–25.

Jones, J. L. (2002). Performance ethnography: The role of embodiment in cultural authenticity. *Theatre Topics, 12*(1), 1–15.

Katz, J. (1978). *Gay American history: Lesbians and gay men in the USA.* New York: Avon.

Keller, E. F. (1995). *Reflections on gender and science.* New Haven, CT: Yale University Press. (Original work published 1985)

Kennedy, R. (2003). *Nigger: The strange career of a troublesome word.* New York: Vintage.

Khayatt, D. (2002). Toward a queer identity. *Sexualities, 5*(4), 487–501.

Kong, T. S. K., Mahoney, D., & Plummer, K. (2002). Queering the interview. In J. F. Gubrium & J. A. Holstein (Eds.), *Handbook of interview research* (pp. 239–258). Thousand Oaks, CA: Sage.

Koro-Ljungberg, M. (2004). Impossibilities of reconciliation: Validity in mixed theory projects. *Qualitative Inquiry, 4,* 601–621.

Lee, W. (2003). Kuaering queer theory: My autocritography and a race-conscious, womanist, transnational turn. *Journal of Homosexuality, 45*(2–4), 147–170.

Lorde, A. (1984). *Sister outsider.* Berkeley, CA: The Crossing Press.

Madison, D. S. (2006). The dialogic performative in critical ethnography. *Text and Performance Quarterly, 26*(4), 320–324.

McIntosh, M. (1968). The homosexual role. *Social Problems, 16*(2), 182–192.

Meyer, M. D. E. (2005). Drawing the sexuality card: Teaching, researching, and living bisexuality. *Sexuality & Culture, 9*(1), 3–13.

Mohanty, C. T. (2003). *Feminism without borders: Decolonizing theory, practicing solidarity.* Durham, NC: Duke University Press.

Moraga, C., & Anzaldúa, G. (Eds.). (1984). *This bridge called my back: Writings by radical women of color.* Boston: Kitchen Table.

Muscio, I. (1998). *Cunt: A declaration of independence.* Seattle, WA: Seal Press.

Nakayama, T. K., & Corey, F. C. (2003). Nextext. *Journal of Homosexuality, 45*(2–4), 319–334.

Neumann, M. (1996). Collecting ourselves at the end of the century. In C. Ellis & A. P. Bochner (Eds.), *Composing ethnography: Alternative forms of qualitative writing* (pp. 172–198). Walnut Creek, CA: AltaMira.

Nicholas, C. L. (2006). Disciplinary-interdisciplinary GLBTQ (identity) studies and Hecht's layering perspective. *Communication Quarterly, 54*(3), 305–330.

Owen, A. S. (2003). Disciplining "Sextext": Queers, fears, and communication studies. *Journal of Homosexuality, 45*(2–4), 297–317.

Pelias, R. J. (1999). *Writing performance: Poeticizing the researcher's body.* Carbondale: Southern Illinois University Press.

Pelias, R. J. (2000). The critical life. *Communication Education, 49*(3), 220–228.

Pelias, R. J. (2004). *A methodology of the heart: Evoking academic and daily life.* Walnut Creek, CA: AltaMira.

Pelias, R. J. (2006, May). *Jarheads, girly men, and the pleasures of violence.* Paper presented at Second International Congress of Qualitative Inquiry, Urbana-Champaign, IL.

Perez, H. (2005). You can have my brown body and eat it, too! *Social Text, 23*(3–4), 171–191.

Phelan, P. (1993). *Unmarked: The politics of performance.* New York: Routledge.

Pineau, E. (2000). *Nursing mother* and articulating absence. *Text and Performance Quarterly, 20*(1), 1–19.

Plummer, K. (2005). Critical humanism and queer theory: Living with the tensions. In N. K. Denzin & Y. S. Lincoln (Eds.), *The SAGE handbook of qualitative research* (3rd ed., pp. 357–373). Thousand Oaks, CA: Sage.

Pollock, D. (1998a). Introduction: Making history go. In *Exceptional spaces: Essays in performance and history* (pp. 1–45). Chapel Hill: University of North Carolina Press.

Pollock, D. (1998b). Performing writing. In P. Phelan & J. Lane (Eds.), *The ends of performance* (pp. 73–103). New York: NYU Press.

Pollock, D. (2006). Marking new directions in performance ethnography. *Text and Performance Quarterly, 26*(4), 325–329.

Pratt, M. B. (1990). *Crime against nature.* Ithaca, NY: Firebrand.

Rambo, C. (2005). Impressions of grandmother: An autoethnographic portrait. *Journal of Contemporary Ethnography, 34*(5), 560–585.

Rambo, C. (2007). Handing IRB an unloaded gun. *Qualitative Inquiry, 13*(3), 353–367.

Reed-Danahay, D. E. (1997). *Auto/ethnography: Rewriting the self and the social.* Oxford, UK: Berg.

Richardson, L., & St. Pierre, E. A. (2005). Writing: A method of inquiry. In N. K. Denzin & Y. S. Lincoln (Eds.), *The SAGE handbook of qualitative research* (3rd ed., pp. 959–978). Thousand Oaks, CA: Sage.

Ronai, C. R. (1995). Multiple reflections of child sex abuse. *Journal of Contemporary Ethnography, 23*(4), 395–426.

Sandoval, C. (2000). *Methodology of the oppressed.* Minneapolis: University of Minnesota Press.

Scott, J. W. (1991). The evidence of experience. *Critical Inquiry, 17*(4), 773–797.

Sedgwick, E. K. (1985). *Between men: English literature and male homosocial desire.* New York: Columbia University Press.

Sedgwick, E. K. (1990). *Epistemology of the closet.* Berkeley: University of California Press.

Sedgwick, E. K. (1993). *Tendencies.* Durham, NC: Duke University Press.

Sedgwick, E. K. (2000). *A dialogue on love.* Boston: Beacon.

Sedgwick, E. K. (2003). *Touching feeling: Affect, pedagogy, performativity.* Durham, NC: Duke University Press.

Slattery, P. (2001). The educational researcher as artist working within. *Qualitative Inquiry, 7*(3), 370–398.

Smith, L. T. (1999). *Decolonizing methodologies: Research and indigenous species.* New York: Zed.

Smith, C. (2000). How I became a queer heterosexual. In C. Thomas (Ed.), *Straight with a twist: Queer theory and the subject of heterosexuality* (pp. 60–67). Urbana: University of Illinois Press.

Smith, R. R. (2003). Queer theory, gay movements, and political communication. *Journal of Homosexuality, 45*(2–4), 345–348.

Sontag, S. (1964). Notes on "camp." *Partisan Review, 31*(4), 515–530.

Spry, T. (2001). Performing autoethnography: An embodied methodological praxis. *Qualitative Inquiry, 7*(6), 706–732.

Spry, T. (2006). A "performative-I" copresence: Embodying the ethnographic turn in performance and the performative turn in ethnography. *Text and Performance Quarterly, 26*(4), 339–346.

Taylor, J. (2000). On being an exemplary lesbian: My life as a role model. *Text and Performance Quarterly, 20*(1), 58–73.

Thomas, C. (2000). Introduction: Identification, appropriation, proliferation. In C. Thomas (Ed.), *Straight with a twist: Queer theory and the subject of heterosexuality* (pp. 1–7). Urbana: University of Illinois Press.

Watson, K. (2005). Queer theory. *Group Analysis, 38*(1), 67–81.

West, C., & Fenstermaker, S. (1995). Doing difference. *Gender & Society, 9*(1), 8–37.

West, C., & Zimmerman, D. H. (1987). Doing gender. *Gender & Society, 1*(2), 125–151.

Wilchins, R. (2004). *Queer theory, gender theory.* Los Angeles: Alyson.

Wyatt, J. (2005). A gentle going? An autoethnographic short story. *Qualitative Inquiry, 11*(5), 724–732.

Wyatt, J. (2006). Psychic distance, consent, and other ethical issues. *Qualitative Inquiry, 12*(4), 813–818.

Yep, G. A., & Elia, J. P. (2007). Queering/quaring blackness in *Noah's Arc.* In T. Peele (Ed.), *Queer popular culture: Literature, media, film, and television* (pp. 27-40). New York: Palgrave Macmillan.

Yep, G. A., Lovaas, K. E., & Elia, J. P. (2003). Introduction: Queering communication: Starting the conversation. *Journal of Homosexuality, 45*(2–4), 1–10.

19

NARRATIVE POETICS AND PERFORMATIVE INTERVENTIONS

D. Soyini Madison

Practice without thought is blind; thought without practice is empty.

—Kwame Nkrumah (1998)

One day in my performance ethnography graduate seminar, a student who was frequently absent and not keeping up with the course readings was becoming more and more frustrated with the critical and theoretical aspects of the course. He did not approve of my approach to include critical and political theory in a course he felt should focus exclusively on performance "methods." Toward the end of one session, he looked around at all of us sitting in the seminar circle and said, "With all this emphasis on theory and politics, you are not really interested in what people are actually doing in your fieldwork; but, instead, you are telling people what to do!" My blood was boiling at the accusation that all that was said, read, done, and discussed in the seminar up to this point was so blatantly diminished to "telling people what to do!" Although the young man was often absent and not keeping up with the rest of the class, I had to take his complaint seriously. Perhaps he was not doing well in the class because there was some truth to his accusation, and I was overemphasizing theory and politics at the expense of sound methodological practice. The student's comment was also difficult to understand, because it has always been impossible for me to separate theory from method. How can there be such a thing as *critical methods* without critical theory or politics and political theory? Can't we embrace theory and politics in the field and work for social justice—out of which our methods are generated—without being accused of "telling people what to do"?

A few weeks before the unhappy student's remark, I was attending a presentation on campus by two Afro-Peruvian women who were human rights activists in Peru. Their talk was inspiring and informative. One of the points they made that will always stay with me concerned the motives of fieldwork research. They said it is a problem and waste of time when academics come to Peru to engage in what they called "folklore" encounters. They went on to explain that rights violations and structures of racial oppression and poverty have affected their communities for generations, but academics will come and want to know about "beads, songs, myths, and weaving without associating them to the material conditions of our lives." According to these activists, some of us seem to care more about "crafts and customs while ignoring the injustices that pervade the day to day." The women were concerned that the "apolitical" approach that extricates the dirty details of political life for "weaving and myths" was another form of "romanticizing the native" while whitewashing the urgent realities of oppressive forces. I left the presentation of the Peruvian activists even more determined to teach and write in ways that recognize the importance of theories that inform a critical approach to methodology—a critical approach that is guided by political theory that matters on the ground, but at the same time believing in the power and beauty of cultural expression.

After the student made the comment in class, I thought about the Peruvian activists. The student equated a critical theory approach to methodology as "telling people what to do"; the Peruvian activists equated a lack of political and critical consciousness in the field as "folklore encounters" that ignored material suffering. What critical, performance ethnography hopes to bridge is the frustration and feelings of lack in both these positions: the poetics of a space AND its politics as well as its politics and its poetics. Haven't we learned by now that expressive and cultural traditions always occur within the machinations of power that encompass them?

▣ ▣ ▣

Critical performance ethnography is animated by the dynamics interacting between power, politics, and poetics (Alexander, 2006; Conquergood, 2002; Denzin, 2003; Hamera, 2007; Pollock, 2005). This chapter examines these dynamics within the oral narrative performances of local human rights activists in Ghana, West Africa, who are working for the rights of women and girls against traditional cultural practices that impede their freedom and well-being. For several years now, I have been conducting field research with Ghanaian activists working in rural areas who are involved in remarkable and courageous initiatives for the defense of human rights, particularly as it relates to women and girls. The activists in this chapter are concerned with a specific cultural practice known as Trokosi by most rights activists and Troxovi by most adherents of traditional African religion. The Troxovi/Trokosi practice involves a young girl, usually between ages 6 and 12, depending on the location, which is assigned to a village shrine. This can be for a certain period of years or for the duration of her life; again, this depends on the area where the shrine is located. In some areas, the Fiashidi/Trokosi are sent to the shrine in atonement for a crime or transgression that is said to be against God and the community. The crime is committed by a family relation, usually a male, and can range from a variety of transgressions such as an insult, stealing, or an act of violence. To appease the wrath and punishment of God against the family or village for the moral transgression, the virgin girl of the family is sent as reparation for the "crime." In certain shrines, the abuse involves "slave labor" and often becoming "concubines" for the shrine's priests. However, these shrines, according to many traditionalists, are not genuine Trokosi shrines. It is said that these shrines are actually violating the principles of the religion and are considered "breakaway or outlaw" shrines. In the other areas that traditionalists regard as genuine Troxovi/Trokosi shrines, the women and girls attend the shrines for "moral and cultural training," serving as "protection" or "proper moral teaching" from a family that has violated the moral codes of the community and religion. In these shrines, the traditionalists state that the girls have freedom of movement and may live at home; moreover, it is against the laws of the religion for the priests to sexually abuse them. Instead, they must to be treated respectfully.

Since I began my research, the Troxovi/Trokosi institution[1] has undergone many changes and transformations. Some traditionalists and rights activists have joined together in a campaign to reform the institution and eradicate those shrines and shrine priests in areas that were committing human rights violations. Some of these shrines remain for religious worship, but in several cases, the girls and women are no longer being sequestered or abused. However, there are some areas where Trokosi girls and women are still being violated and "breakaway" shrines are practicing "underground."

This chapter presents the oral narratives of rights activists who are working against these "breakaway" or "outlaw" shrines. I hope the chapter will serve as a bridge and opportunity for readers to listen to "indigenous" activists telling us (and each other) what *they do.* The chapter operates from a polemic of social justice relative to human rights, but the intention is to use this chapter as a platform and a means to forefront the polemic of those Ghanaians *themselves* who are fighting for the future of their own country, critiquing their own traditions, defending human rights from their own tactics and strategies, and desiring that others hear what they say and be exposed to what they do. I am claiming the "native point of view," but I would be committing the same crime of false objectivity as those researchers who do not take responsibility for their biases, who refuse to recognize their inherent subjectivity and their ingrained power over the data (a power that always trails the ethnographic project), if I did not state in the beginning my admiration, support, and bias toward these rights activists and their work.

These narratives serve as examples of critical performance ethnography because the narrators poetically narrate their own indigenous and critical methodologies based on the politics of their performative interventions in defending the human rights of Others. As a critical performance ethnographer, I am "being there" within the time and space of others who guide, advise, and inspire me to further embrace performance (in different and contextually specific ways) as a means to interpret, illuminate, and advocate a politics of change. I interpret the in-depth interview with each rights activist through a performance lens to capture the complexity and multilayered dimensions reflected in the expressiveness of the human voice and body in the act of telling as well as the immediate environment or scene—ripe with influence and meaning—of the telling. In this sense, poetic transcription aims to capture the signification of what Richard Bauman (1977) calls the narrative event and the narrated event or what Della Pollock (1999) calls the telling and the told. Poetic transcription aims to capture the content of *what* is said and the form of *how* it is said in gesture, movement, vocal affect, and the symbolic surrounding reported and expressed.

The chapter will present two oral narratives by members of International Need Network, Ghana. International Needs Ghana (ING)[2] is a human rights organization that has been at the forefront of reforming the Troxovi/Trokosi institution and releasing or "liberating" girls and women from certain shrines. The first narrative by Patience Vormawor describes the tactics employed by ING in the liberation of Fiashidi/Trokosi from the religious shrines that inhibit their freedom. The second narrative by Agnes Okudzeto describes the ING school for liberated Toxovi/Trokosi that is prompted by a response to a charge made by a particular traditionalist who opposes the work of ING.

Throughout the narratives, I weave my own commentary and observations to illuminate the *implications* of their words and experience. There has been general and legitimate criticism far and wide of this "weaving" approach of "researcher" and "Other" by numerous observers and practitioners of qualitative research (including myself on occasion). In summary, the criticisms argue the following:

- The researcher's analysis is an intrusion where the subject's narrative is often *silenced.* The authoritative voice and heavy hand of the researcher overshadow the voice and presence of the narrator. The researcher's analysis "upstages" the narrative, leaving the narrator's actual words almost forgotten and their meanings but whispers in the booming volume of the researcher's interpretation.

- The researcher's analysis is his or her own idiosyncratic interpretation and *distorts* the interpretative report and expressions of the narrator. The researcher does not necessarily silence the narrative but rather imposes a reversal or counterdirectional meaning to the directions and implications of meanings that constitute the narrative. Keep in mind, the researcher's interpretation does not deepen narrative analysis here or open possibilities of meanings but actually closes them by "twisting" and "distorting" the paths of truths that define the narrative and bring it into existence. The "falseness" of the researcher's interpretation betrays the promise of illumination and self-reflexive engagement.

- The researcher's analysis promotes theoretical jargon that renders the narrative analysis itself *ineffectual* at best and silly at worst. The researcher becomes so enamored with "theoretical speak" and impressing colleagues that honoring the narrative becomes less important than acrobatics of abstraction and theoretical word play. The researcher's analysis does not necessarily silence or distort the narrative; it just becomes undesirable to it. It becomes an alien indecipherable object alongside the vitality of a narrative still open for honest interpretation.

- The researcher's analysis is descriptive analysis that is only a simple restatement, a *redundant* summary that becomes an obtuse repetition of what is already apparent and more powerfully articulated in the words of the narrator. Here, the narrative is narrated again, but only second hand, by the researcher in the absence of new insights and possibilities of meaning. Analysis becomes useless repetition.

Although I often agree with these criticisms, I also believe a delicate balance of analysis can open deeper engagement with the narrative text and unravel contexts and connections within the undercurrents of the narrative universe, without the researcher acting as a psychoanalyst, clairvoyant, or prophet. What I hope to accomplish by including commentary is to attend to the narration—as one is compelled to attend to or interpret the significance of any object or text rich with meanings, history, value, and possibility—by entering selected moments of subtext and implicit moments of signification so that we may engage the depth of inferences, the overreaching consequences, and the politically valuable import in order that we as readers may be offered an *additional realization of the narrative and the narrator.* In summary, the aim is as follows:

- The researcher's analysis serves as a *magnifying lens* to enlarge and amplify the small details and the taken-for-granted. Too often hidden in plain sight of words spoken and written are meanings and implications below the surface that need to be excavated, contemplated, and engaged. We may listen to a story or point of view, and on first impression, it may come across as nothing special or uneventful. The researcher points to those moments or small details that we might take for granted as "ordinary talk" or prosaic and opens us to layers of complexity and associations that we may otherwise not come to realize.

- The researcher's analysis serves to *clarify and honor the significance* of the "telling and the told" (Pollock, 1990).

- This point is particularly important for performance ethnography. The interview is more than just questions and answers that simply happen to occur in an innocuous location. It is a substantive event—a surrounding scene of signification and its objects—a gestalt where the immediate telling becomes a richly descriptive environment of symbolic worth. And where the immediacy of the telling environment frames and relates to its content or is told. Now, the interview becomes an eventful enactment of witnessing, testimony, and dialogue constituted by a form (i.e., engaged, meaningful bodies and a scenic space that are no longer ignored by *what* is said as content or a priori information).

- The researcher's analysis serves to employ theory in order to *unlock the multiple truths* embedded below the surface. Theory serves as a bright light out of which we can now see with fullness and precision what has always been present and in our midst but before was obscure and more difficult to name and reach. Theory must be quintessentially revelatory. It should not block our access to the narrative but lead us deeper into its paths or truths. Instead of theory becoming its own narrative (in interpreting the narratives of Others), theory reveals how we may encounter, describe, and name the narrative's essential insights. Without theoretical analysis, the power, complexity, and expanse of narrative knowledge become unengaged.

- The researcher's analysis serves to emphasize, reiterate, and *make apparent the beauty and poignancy* of description. As narrators describe certain persons, places, things, and ideas, the researcher may feel compelled to then describe the description. Instead of relying entirely on theory or more cognitive analysis, the researcher now embraces the emotions and sensuality of *what* is being described and *how* it is being described—the telling and the told—to illuminate the textures, smells, sounds, tastes, and sights being rendered within the content of the told and within the form of the telling. Performance ethnography demands a felt-sensing experience—emotions and sensuality—that employs lyrical, poetic, or performative language to wisely embellish the existential gestalt of the interview event, making it more present before us, with heart and beauty.

I bullet point what I believe to be the labor of analysis, not to claim a kind of authority for the researcher but to acknowledge the great importance of narrators and their narratives in our fieldwork.

The subaltern does speak, always, and we must listen with more radical intent. These subaltern knowledges are sometimes hidden away in locations that are at times hard for us to reach as they speak the philosophies, logics, and approaches of their life worlds and in their own languages. How indigenous people in this global/local dance and struggle often make a way out of no way—creating tactics for survival and victories out of the vestiges of an extremely unjust state of affairs—is why we call upon our local advisers in the field to help us try to comprehend. We listen so we can be of use to them—a messenger and an interpreter to make what they say and do known to other Others.

Juliana Makuchi Nfah-Abbenyi (1997) states that within the narratives of African women writers, "theory is embedded in the polysemous and polymorphous" nature of the narration. I contend that this is also true of the oral narratives that inform and enrich our fieldwork. She goes on to state that narratives "re-inscribe and foreground teleological, ontological, and epistemological insights and praxis relevant to the specific histories and politics that preceded" them (p. 20). For Nfah-Abbenyi, these narratives as theory (or theories as narratives) are not only "preceded" by history and politics but show us that "indigenous theory is autonomous, self-defining, and exists in unconventional places . . . such theory can qualify as a kind of performance in print" (p. 20).

I: "We Are Not Outsiders"

Local Narrations of Rights and Critical Methodologies

It is a September morning in 1999, during the early stages of my fieldwork, and I am at the office of the ING, the nongovernmental organization (NGO) that has taken the lead in reforming the Troxovi/Trokosi institution. ING is located in The Scripture Union office building in Accra. As I come to the second floor of the building, I meet the director, Reverend Walter Pimpong. He greets me with a big smile; he has a calming and warm presence. I tell Walter I have come to interview Patience. He is pleased and suggests we conduct the interview in his private office where we will have more privacy. I am looking forward to this time with Patience, because when we are together in the field, she has no time to talk about herself or discuss personal reflections of her work. She is too busy focusing her attention on the people who need her help—listening, talking, and doing what needs to be done. I have watched her time and again in various villages of the Volta region interact with people with respect and affectionate attention, as if nothing in the world was more important to her than them and what they say to her. Patience has been one of the activists working very closely with the community as well as the shrine owners and priests in liberating several Trokosi women and girls from the shrines.

The room is air-conditioned and a nice relief from the suffocating December heat in Ghana. There is a large desk in the front of the room. On the wall is a poster with the picture of a young Trokosi girl wearing brightly colored African fabric; both her hands are placed on the top of her head to signify mourning or suffering. Written across the poster in red and white letters are "Stop Trokosi Now!" and beneath it ". . . respect the rights of girls and women." Patience takes a seat on the couch across from the desk, and I am sitting in the chair next to her. Patience is soft-spoken with a gentle manner. She is a striking woman, tall with a round face and high cheekbones. She sits with both hands resting in her lap. I ask about the campaign ING has waged to liberate the Trokosi against a religious tradition that is ancient and where the belief is so strongly held and defended. I ask her to talk about the strategy of persuading the priests and shrine owners to free the women and girls. Patience sits up on the couch and confidently speaks into the tape recorder sitting on the table next to the couch:

> Before a release, we go to visit the shrine priest.
> We find out from him how he feels about the Trokosi system.
> We find out why he feels he can or cannot release the women and girls.
> We try to find out what he can do to help them.
> We counsel him in adjusting to things he does not understand
> [she moves closer toward me—her voice softens].
> Those who don't know our work fear that we are coming to break the whole shrine.
> But we come to help make the shrine more progressive, more humane.
> After we come to an understanding [pause], we ask the priest to release the women and girls.
> If he understands and we come to an agreement [speaking tenderly], he will let us speak to the Trokosi.
> We meet the girls and we counsel them one by one.
> We help them psychologically about being separated from their parents,
> about being sent into the shrine,
> about going back into the village,
> about what kind of work they will do,
> about who they will live with?
> [she clasps her hands and places them gently on her lap, tilting her head toward me],
> about how they will take care of their children.

The "power of persuasion" is given profound force and meaning because persuasion here is dependent not only on human lives and freedom but the disruption of a sacred worldview. How do you persuade one human being not to deny the humanity of another? How do you make them listen to you? How do you make them stop believing in what they believe is God's will when God's will means devaluing the lives of others? The urgency of the kind of "persuasion" being crafted here begins with empathy and respect that is explicitly concerned with how the other "feels" and "understands." This is a magnanimous gesture because it is ultimately a confrontation with "wrongness." To sit across from someone you know is not only wrong but also acting wrongfully and to *genuinely listen* to that person is not only a good tactic of persuasion but also an act of compassionate engagement. The structures of feeling that encompass the Troxovi/Trokosi practice must be replaced by another discursive practice and another structure of feeling that must begin with trust. Feelings of wrongness are eclipsed by the importance of being trusted. Trust is the foundation on which persuasion begins—compassionate engagement and empathetic listening becomes its method. In *The Teachings of Ptahhotep* (ca. 2400 BCE), one of the earliest ancient Kemetian (Egyptian) "books of instruction" (Hord & Lee, 1995, p. 17), the mayor of the city, Vizier Ptahhotep, presents an elaborate list (approximately 37) of codes of conduct. These codes are "life instructions" that ensure each individual a place in the eternal network of the universe after his or her death. This is one of the codes in the ancient writing that speaks to the notion of trust:

> If you are among the people, then gain your supporters by building trust. The trusted man is one

> who does not speak the first thing that comes to mind; and he will become a leader. A man of means has a good name, and his face is benign. People will praise him even without his knowledge. On the other hand, he whose heart obeys his belly asks for contempt of himself in the place of love. His heart is naked. His body is unanointed. The great-hearted is a gift of God. He who is ruled by his appetite belongs to the enemy. (Hord & Lee, 1995, p. 26)

In accordance with this passage, Patience is trusted because she listens, she is humble among them, and the people have spoken among themselves of her "good name." They believe she is not motivated by greed or self-interest—her heart does not "obey her belly"—but the interests of Others, their interests. I witnessed the affection and "trust" among the people she worked with from village to village. The question now becomes this: Once trust is gained and a new discourse is possible, what are the alternative actions offered by these rights activists that lead to sustained change? First, we understand that when the girls and women are released from the shrine, they are not left alone. Patience continues,

> We help them go to school for professional training if that is what they want to do
> [looks intently into my eyes].
> All this is not a one-day affair.
> When they are released, we go with them to their homes.
> And we continue to go back to see how they are adjusting
> [she holds her hand up and counts with her fingers].
> We counsel the family/the household/and the community who fear the girls are still Trokosi and should remain as outcasts
> [raises her voice].
> We must counsel the Trokosi and the non-Trokosi because the fear is very powerful
> [counting with her finger again, she almost sings the list].
> We follow them for about 2 years to be sure they are socially integrated, economically independent, psychologically adjusted, and healthy.
> We encourage them to think on their own and for themselves
> [softly but with determination].
> The priest does not need to think for them anymore.
> We even study all aspects of their body movements and facial expressions to observe
> [raises her head and smiles].
> They are happy.
> During this time of tracking we keep profiles of the women.
> We check in on all the factors [pause]—health, finances, social adjustments, and so forth.
> We want them to realize they can be independent
> [hands together in a fist and voice raised].
> When they have a problem [pause] they don't have to wait for someone to come.
> They can take care of it themselves.

▣ ▣ ▣

Once the priests were able to have trust, the conversation began, and then the possibility of an alternative logic became possible and, finally, plausible. What evolves from the meeting between priest and rights activist is more than compromise and negotiation; it is to create something not done before, to create a generative cultural formation, that is, an alternative practice and belief now valued and shared anew. It is a different way of being. The religion remains, but reformed and consciously changed from a reevaluation of the past in order to save its future and preserve the core of its meaning. They must change a practice within the discourse of rights and freedom in order to save the religion. But to remake cultural practice means that the point between what was and what the activists hope the religion will become requires creating the connection between past and future, the connection that constitutes what is to be done *now*. As Patience says, "All this is not a one-day affair"; it is a long-term commitment. Kwame Nkrumah (1998), the intellectual, socialist philosopher, and the first president of Ghana after Independence, stated, "Indeed, for the African, everything that exists, exists as a complex of forces in tension.... It is out of tension that being is born. Becoming is tension, and being is the child of that tension of opposed forces and tendencies" (pp. 90–92). This "being" that is "born" is based on the relentless labor—the indigenous, critical methodology—of local human rights activism that was in opposition to the practices of the Trokosi shrine. Nkrumah reminds us that we begin with these tensions, these opposing forces, in order for change and for rebirth to occur. Here, tension is not simply the differing ideological beliefs between the priests and the activists on first contact, but it is how these tensions were manifest and enacted through persistent and continued visitations by the activists to the shrines. Each encounter that was constituted by tension was a move closer to Nkrumah's rebirth.

I observed the dedication of Patience and the other activists at ING through their comings and goings and coming back again and again with the commitment to give the Troxovi/Trokosi the knowledge that they possessed a *self.* I witnessed ING activists do the work of gifting these women and girls with the tools toward independent living while helping them to reenter their communities against the forces of a long-held stigma. I witnessed the infinitely human right of selfhood come slowly and methodically into being.

> Some believe that we do not know the Trokosi system because we have not lived there and that we are outsiders
> [shakes her head].
> This is not true.
> We have lived there.
> We are not outsiders.
> We have Trokosi relatives
> [hands raised and speaking in an empathic tone].
> The village people should not think we are just city people trying to go in and change the system
> [moves in to make sure I am listening to this point].
> We have people who are victims of the system on our team [with emphasis].
> So we know what we are doing.
> We have been there talking to people one-on-one.

The position of being both an "insider" and "outsider" suggests that one possesses a certain kind of knowledge or authority regarding the relational dynamics of two contrasting or competing worlds. It also implies that the insider/outsider has the ability to move between these worlds with difficulty or ease, translating and often enacting his or her divergent codes, costumes, laws, and so on. Therefore, the assumption of a certain authority of knowledge is also based on the experience and history of what it means to be *affected* corporally and emotionally by what happens or has happened in those contrasting worlds and, moreover, to have survived them. It is important for the activists to make it known to the Troxovi/Trokosi as well as the priests that they are not just outsiders but are "from where they are from" not only in knowledge but have experienced through body and feelings what it is to be of a place—to know the people, to eat the food, to speak the language, to walk the same paths for water, to share the same memories of the place. This being *from* the same place conjoined with being *of* a different place is an interesting paradox. Being from the same place provided an authority of knowledge of what goes on in the same place and the unique feelings about it, that is, "I care and know about what goes on here." But being of a different place provides an authority of knowledge of what the alternatives or other possibilities of what the same place could be: "I care and know about another way to be." I do not mean to privilege a one-way direction of change; that is, the outsider domain always wants to change the insider domain or vice versa. The point is that the insider/outsider position does garner hybrid knowledge or specialized knowledge that creates the space of different and new realities (Anzaldúa, 1987; Collins, 1990; hooks, 1989; Madison, 2005). Ghanaians in exile most penetratingly experience the insider/outsider phenomenon from a slightly different perspective than these rights activists, but it is nonetheless relevant to this discussion. The Ghanaian poet, Abena P. A. Busia (1993), states,

> In every instance, my various identifications—as scholar, as poet, as Black, as female, as African, an exile, as an Afro-Saxon living in Afro-America—are always present. Even in my identification as Ghanaian, which I stated so boldly at the start, I am the child of a woman whose people are patrilineal who married a man whose people are matrilineal. Am I thus doubly claimed, or doubly disposed? None of these categories is mutually exclusive. They coexist and are the boundaries within which I must exist or which I have come to cross every waking moment. (p. 209)

Many of the rights activists who work with ING choose not to leave the country. They stay in Ghana to do the work of human rights. However, when they leave the city to go to the villages—taking with them their new ideas about an ancient religion and a revered cultural practice—they are often regarded as foreigners, as outsiders. I have witnessed the "various identifications" that Busia (1993) describes: Patience and her colleagues move in and out between English in the city and Ewe and Twi in the villages; between the faster body rhythms of the city and the slower, deliberate strength demanded of village life; and between their philosophical interchanges on human rights at meetings and conferences and their flesh-to-flesh embodied interchanges of food, story, and companionship in the village. It is in these "waking moments" that I have witnessed the multiple identities of Ghanaian people in Ghana doing the work for themselves on their land.

The final section of the narrative is a poetic treatise on *difference* and how to embrace what is innately human about difference for the sake of making a radical and revolutionary *difference* for the life of another. It reflects the value of both the antihumanist and humanist philosophy. In the antihumanist tradition, this section of the narrative further shows us that humankind is *produced by* discourse, events, and history. And, in the humanist tradition, the narrative shows us that humankind are *producers of* discourse, events, and history, especially when one human being communicates a yearning to another and thereby creates a dialogical alchemy that, in turn, sets forth alternative ways of being.

The interview was about to end as I said thank you and slowly reached over to turn off the tape recorder when Patience raised her hand very gently to indicate that there was one more thing she wanted to say:

> One thing about human beings [pause], they are not like machines.
> In this work you learn a lot about human beings.
> And one thing you learn is that they all behave differently.
> You learn how the environment changes them
> and then you begin to develop relationships with them [pause] even if you believe in different things.
> You get to know them very well and you learn all about them.
> And you respect them even if you have different ideas from them/you respect them
> [sitting up in her seat and moving closer to the edge].
> We see ourselves really helping them.
> When I play a part in this person's life to make it better
> [smiling, she rests her hands together on her lap]
> I am happy.
> Thank you, Patience.
> You are welcome, Soyini.

As I am about to leave the room, my friend Wisdom Mensah, who is program director of ING, enters. Wisdom is an invaluable resource for me in understanding all sides of the issues and what it meant to witness human rights in action as I watched him go into the field negotiating with stakeholders on all sides, counseling rights activists, and working with Reverend Pimpong in setting the record straight against the attacks by certain traditionalists against ING so they may keep up the struggle to liberate more women and girls from the shrines. Wisdom informs me that Mrs. Okudzeto, the headmaster of the ING Trokosi Vocational Training School, is outside and wants to come in and say hello. I met Mrs. Okudzeto several months before when I went to visit the school where they teach the newly freed Troxovi/Trokosi how to read and write, as well as vocational training in dressmaking, cosmetology, catering, batik, weaving,[3] and making soap. Mrs. Okudzeto carries herself with unwavering confidence; she is outspoken and cheerful with a witty sense of humor. Before I met her, Wisdom mentioned how much she "loved the girls" at the school and how she was such a "very efficient" headmaster. I am pleased to know Mrs. Okudzeto has arrived because I wanted to speak with her about a gentleman who had come by my flat about 2 weeks ago to tell me that any Ghanaian who was against the Trokosi practice was against their ancestors and their heritage. He said the activists were spreading lies about the abuses in the shrines because "the fact is the girls are treated honorably, like queens." He went on to say, "The people that want to stop the practice are spreading lies in order to get European and American money." He then stated emphatically, "Trokosi will never come to an end and if any one tries to stop it, they will stop it over my dead body!"

When I told Mrs. Okudzeto about the visitor, her response was a mixture of exasperation and irritation:

> We should eradicate all outmoded customs
> [turns toward me with a very serious, intense look].
> That man says these women are carriers of the society?
> He says they are queens?
> He says we honor them?
> He says they are special women?
> That is what he tells you?! [with a small ironic, resentful laugh]
> Hmm, hmm but they are not!
> The girls themselves will tell you they have been treated like slaves.
> He says those of us who want to stop the Trokosi practice will only stop it over his dead body? [laughing ironically]
> Well, he is going to die soon!
> He says the women that go through the shrines are only going there as an education for training to teach them purity and to prepare them to have children for the gods?
> [Raised her hands up in astonished disbelief]
> They don't teach them anything in the shrines except you wake up in the morning and go to the bush to farm,
> you gather firewood. They don't learn anything!
> Do they teach them how to read, to write? No!
> They don't teach them anything!
> [Irritation is building]
> They would rather sexually abuse them!
> These are the people who are trying to suppress women in this country?
> [shaking her head in disdain]
> I am with these girls and they have been sexually abused a lot!

The African symbol of *Sankofa* is a majestic bird whose commanding body is positioned forward while the bird's long, elegant neck dramatically circles backward gazing into the past. Sankofa symbolizes the significance of the past and tradition in order to move toward the present and future. The man who came to see me referred to the Sankofa symbol and then explained that his mission was to "uphold and defend African culture and religion against those who want to denigrate and destroy our traditions." He did not make a distinction between the shrines that were abusive and those that were not. His defense of tradition was in many ways contrary to the organization Afrikania or Afrikan Renaissance Mission, a well-known traditional organization in Ghana that openly exposes and condemns the abusive "break-away shrines" while also identifying itself explicitly as being of "Sankofa faith" in its mission as a defender, teacher, and celebrant of African tradition. My visitor was more concerned about defending the Troxovi/Trokosi institution from its critics, without exception, than he was about women and girls being maltreated in certain shrines. This was also the case for several other defenders of the Troxovi/Trokosi institution. For the visitor to say "over my dead body" was not an uncommon charge for those who believe that criticizing African tradition (particularly African religious tradition) was an abomination.

In Ghana, I came to understand more than ever (for better and for worse) that tradition is the life breath of the past and the very ground upon which the present stands and the future is even possible. Traditional religion is evidence of the past but, more, it is also the hope, creation, and embodiment of a *generation of people.* Tradition is evidence. It is the sacred materialization of what those who came before believed, valued, and yearned. I learned that to defy cultural and religious tradition is to defy the sacred debt we owe to the ancestor. It is to defy the sacred being of our kinship. But I also had to ask, What happens when tradition does harm? What of those who did defy tradition and dare to oppose it and want to change it? How did Mrs. Okudzeto and other rights activists begin to believe differently and work for change? In Kwame Gyekye's (1997) important and classic book *Tradition and Modernity,* he eloquently addresses this question:

> To say that a belief or practice is handed down to a generation is to say that it is bequeathed to the generation, passed on to it. But what this really means is that the belief or practice is placed at the disposal of the new generation in the expectation that the generation would preserve it. But the preservation of it, in part or in whole, would depend very much on the attitude the new generation adopts toward it and would not necessarily be automatic, as the word "transmit" would suggest. If we look back across the line, we find that some of the cultural values created . . . are dropped by subsequent generations, or they simply sink into oblivion—winnowed away by time. Those values were, for one reason or another, not accepted, maintained, or preserved by subsequent generations. This means that the continuity and survival of a pristine cultural product depends on the normative considerations that will be brought to bear on it by a subsequent generation. The forebears—the previous generation—do not "transmit" their cultural creation as such; what they do, rather is to place them at the disposal of subsequent generations of people. But the subsequent generations may on normative or other rational grounds, either accept, refine, or preserve them or spurn, depreciate them, abandon them. The desire or intention of a subsequent generation to preserve or abandon inherited cultural products often results from some kind of *evaluation* [emphasis added] of those cultural products and the tradition they lead to. *Such critical evaluations are essential for the growth and revitalization of cultural tradition.* (p. 221)

I experienced in Ghana that "evaluation" of the kind that invokes *alternatives* within one's own culture and society is primarily an admixture of (1) serious reflection. I am compelled, often by my circumstances or a particular situation, to contemplate and evaluate where and how I live and, in turn, the workings of my life and my environment. What is guiding and determining the world of my being? I begin to dream of possible alternatives. (2) Mobility. I move from the micro-space of my own world to witness another world and way of being. My world is not all there is. I discover how Others live. I experience their movements, ways of speaking, productions, and their futures as different from my own. I witness alternative experiences. (3) Disturbance. I feel the weight of a lingering and substantial discontent. I am not at ease or at peace within my environment. I begin to resent the workings of my world and feel disconnected to it. (4) Language. I embrace a new language. I begin to formulate the words out of which I can now name and describe my discontent and the doomed future of my own world. I now speak about alternative ways of being within my own world and alternative futures. Language orders, generates, and materializes my lingering discontent as well as new reflections and hopes for a different world and way of being. (5) Comrades. I am emboldened by like minds and comrades. I can now speak, act, and feel with others who substantiate and inspire my hope for alternatives. Together, we act for change.

So what does it mean when the evaluation must now move to change? Mrs. Okudzeto has evaluated the tradition as an "outmoded practice," and she, like Reverend Pimpong, Wisdom, Patience, and so many others, takes "evaluation" a step further. She is an activist, and her evaluation generates praxis.

> The school is helping the girls to feel free inside themselves
> [joyfully with pride and confidence].
> We teach them to use the potential within themselves.
> When they come to the school they cannot read,
> they cannot write
> [softly], they don't know about the things around them.
> We try to make them feel free and to go out and see things for themselves—how life is.
> We teach them they can work with their own hands.
> They can create with their own hands.
> They can live with dignity and love.
> They must feel free and they have the right to feel happy
> [almost pleading with her hands to her chest].
> Last week we took them out into the city.
> They went to the airport, to the harbor, to the zoo in the city!
> For many of them that was the first time they'd been to the city
> [small laughter].
> They saw a two-story building.
> It is good exposure to them.
> Some of them, even when they finish the course [pause], they don't want to go back home.

They want to stay with me
[smiling, raising her hands and placing them near her heart].
The school is changing their lives.
They feel safe and worthy.
Some of them are now on their own
[nodding her head, her eyes widen, and her voice raises].
They are making their own life.

II: The Location of Poverty

I have been traveling back and forth across the Atlantic to Ghana, West Africa, since 1998. I remain struck by the abiding harm some religious traditions around the world have upon the life and freedom of others, particularly women and girls. I am also struck by how often these same traditions are revered and glorified by some members of the culture in the face of the blatant abuse the traditions impose upon the female body. But I am more struck by something else that I believe is equally, if not more, unjust and life threatening, but certainly more convoluted and disguised, and that is how the history and present of global politics and power operate in affecting people across the world, particularly in the global South. I am referring specifically to the injustice of the location of poverty.[4]

It is at this point where the politics of poverty must enter the conversation. My work with Ghanaian human rights activism and my experiences with the Troxovi/Trokosi institution were complicated even further when I came into contact with what seemed to be an ingrained ideology of phallocentrism[5] and male domination that was inseparable from the stark reality of wretched poverty. It is often difficult to summarize the Troxovi/Trokosi institution because how it is practiced, even what it is called, is contingent on the *economy of its location.* I include here an excerpt from my field journal of March 1999:

Dear Journal,

This is becoming yet another classic case of human rights and its relationship to poverty. As I travel through the areas where Troxovi/Trokosi is practiced, I am struck by how the maltreatment of women and girls is in direct correlation with the economic and material conditions of the area. What has "Development" over the past decades accomplished here? Sometimes one can only feel rage. Arturo Escabar's work on Development speaks to the question. I paste his words here on this page.

> Whatever these traditional ways might have been, and without idealizing them, it is true that massive poverty in the modern sense appeared only when the spread of the market economy broke down community ties and deprived millions of people from access to land, water and other resources. With the consolidation of Capitalism, systematic pauperization became inevitable (Escabar, 1992, p. 22).

In the poorest areas, the areas that are more remote and distanced from the city and where piped water, electricity, education are scarce or inaccessible, the treatment of women and girls is more severe and their labor more demanding. It is clear to me that the Trokosi/Troxovi Institution is not one monolithic or unified cultural practice. What it is and how it is performed across the various shrines is very different and, again, contingent on the level of the economy in the area. There is a tension here between oppression from male dominance and oppression from poverty—the colonial past complicates each within discretely differing force fields.

March 22, 1999

Regrettably, in some conversations, poverty is becoming wearisome, and sexism is too easily separated from the political economy. The point here is that traditional patriarchy and phallocentrism alone do not account for the consequences of poverty or "determine relations of production and reproduction" that exploit the lives and labor of African women:

> Patriarchal relations do not determine the material basis of the relations of production and reproduction. What is revealed here is that an examination of only the patriarchal relations of both precapitalist and colonial capitalist societies will not explain

> how women's exploitation and oppression were shaped by the historical limits, changes and differences of these societies. The cultural, familial and political reality of African women was restructured with the introduction of commodity production based on monopoly of the means of production, racist ideology, and a policy of separate political and economic development. Under colonial capitalism African women experienced three forms of exploitation based on African Women's position in production, African women's position in the family and African Women's racial position in colonial society. (Courville, 1993, p. 42)

Courville (1993) echoes the position of postcolonial writers in asserting that with the onset of the colonial epoch, African women were now exploited by the "coexistence of dual political systems, dual patriarchal systems and dual modes of production," yet they were not identical dualities (p. 41). The existence of a colonial capitalist mode of production was of a different kind and degree of production than it was under the traditional, African patriarchal mode of production. Although African women lived under the oppressive and exploitive forces of male control, despite these constraints, they still had a certain amount of power within the familial household. The family was "the source of their social standing and their limited protection within the society, and the site and foundation for collective action to express their dissatisfaction and bring about change" (Courville, 1993, p. 36). Therefore, from a more *local commodity production* to foreign *monopoly colonial capitalism,* "Colonialism was the process of the forced and violent integration of the African continent into the world capitalist system" (Courville, 1993, p. 36).

Major factors that combined to bring forth colonial domination were (a) military intervention, (b) the transformation of African economies into monetary economies, (c) the intrusion and exploitation of imperialist colonial trade, and (d) foreign investment in the development of infrastructure and metropolitanism (Ake, 1981, p. 32). Compounding these forces was the colonial policies of indirect rule where "the colonial state controlled and supervised the separate political and economic development of the colonizer" and, as a result, sealed the "underdevelopment of the colonized" (Ake, 1981).

The oppressive constraints upon African women from antiquity to Independence were a factor of both traditional African society and colonial capitalism. Indeed, African women were constrained under traditional African patriarchy, yet under the very nature of these laws (by which the patriarchal society existed), they were still able to carve out for themselves precarious elements of independence, and yet this troubled and fragile independence was, in many circumstances, diminished with the intrusion of colonial capitalism. Therefore, the idea that colonialism brought "progress" to a "backward" continent by introducing technology, culture, and infrastructural development becomes an assertion riddled with falsehoods, contradictions, and contingencies, as does the idea by some Afrocentrists of a traditional African culture based on egalitarian bliss and a spiritual utopia. How does this history of traditional patriarchy and colonial capitalism speak to present-day poverty and human rights? How does it "seal the 'underdevelopment of the continent'"? Drawing from the work of Claude Ake, Courville (1993) summarizes the contemporary economic and social effects of colonial capitalism and patriarchy:

> The economic relations were characterized by an aggregation of disparate modes of production, dependence on external trade and technology, disarticulation of resources, development of export commodities, market imperfections, and limited indigenous capital to mobilize for investment and development. The social relations of the colonial society were based on disparate aggregations of African and European patriarchies accompanied by racially structured domination and subordination. (p. 40)

Ake (1981) lists the very foundations upon which present-day poverty rests: trade, technology, natural resources, indigenous capital, the market, and modes of production. Each of these domains combines to form a political economy that breeds poverty and that sets a climate for human rights offenses. In the face of global capitalism and poverty, indigenous human rights activists carry the legacy of a colonial past that makes their work even harder.

III: Conclusion: My Wish List

In this chapter, indigenous methods of human rights defense are narrated as a "performance in print" (Nfah-Abbenyi, 1997) and as a subaltern praxis in the determination to make a change in the troubled time and space and on the contested land where these Ghanaian activists live and choose to remain. Against the representations and effects of popular discourse, African people are more than victims and abusers of human rights who are enlightened and/or saved by Western ideology and benevolence.

I enter the day-to-day labor "on the ground" with those in their own country working for human rights and who choose to face the added struggle of going against the forces of tradition and economic forces. The questions that now begin to surface are the following: What does it mean for our scholarly projects to seek out and present the theoretical offerings and scholarly arguments from those not popularly known but profoundly worthy? What does it mean to seek out and present the "doings" and the work "done" of indigenous activism in locations that are some of the most contested in the world? These are the guiding questions that constitute my work as a critical performance ethnographer and that undergird this chapter. These questions also enliven my ever growing *wish list.* This "wish list" not only enumerates the direction I tried to follow in this chapter but the direction in which I continue to work toward in the future.

Wish List

First. We do not become senselessly enthralled with critical theory, nor do we become dour theory bashers. Instead, we learn critical theory thoughtfully, rigorously, and purposefully for the politically charged objective of clarifying unproductive confusion and precisely naming what could be otherwise dangerously imprecise.

Second. We resist theoretical feudalism by not assigning the power of interpretation *exclusively* to a few lords of knowledge in privileged, expected, and anticipated Towers of Ivory or Babel. The form of this kind of theorizing that is taking place in certain circles is undemocratic, and the contents have become repetitive clichés. We seek theory from near and far, the expected and the unexpected, from the tower and from the ground, so theory remains relevant, useful, interesting, and generative. Knowing all these different theories demands hard, rigorous work, but these troubled times demand it even more.

Third. We do not speak for Others when we can *listen* while Others speak.

Fourth. We do not, not speak while *only* humbly listening to the Other speak. Listening does not mean NOT speaking; it means paying attention to when it is the right time to speak. At that time, speak to and from the tower AND the ground, even if *your voice shakes.*[6]

Fifth. We practice at home what we preach on paper and in the field. We work to become more generous with each other *within* the academy as we work for a politics of global generosity. I wish that we are generous with each other at every opportunity, and when there are no opportunities, we create them. I wish that academic generosity (of information, influence, resources, and praise) becomes as important to us as academic freedom.

Patience's deep and simple clarity is the point:

> When I play a part in this person's life to make it better, I am happy.

Notes

1. Many traditionalists will refer to Troxovi/Trokosi as an institution while others regard it as a practice; I use *practice* and *institution* interchangeably throughout the chapter.

2. International Needs Ghana is now International Needs Network–Ghana.

3. Sleeping mats are very common in many parts of the developing world. They are used for sleeping (in the house or outside) as floor coverings and sometimes as prayer mats. They range in appearance from plain straw mats to colorful designs of varying sorts.

4. What I am calling "the location of poverty" is a supplement to the notion of a "location of culture." In the Ghana context relative to Trokosi, an understanding of culture is impossible without an understanding of the systems of poverty that affect and in many ways determine it.

5. I am consciously using the term *phallocentrism* here to echo bell hooks's (1989) notion of the phallic as sexually centered male domination over the female body without necessarily having structural or material power or membership within the national or dominant political system.

6. I am referring here to one of my favorite bumper stickers: "Speak the truth, even if your voice shakes."

References

Ake, C. (1981). *A political economy of Africa.* New York: Longman.

Alexander, B. K. (2006). *Performing Black masculinity: Race, culture, and queer identity.* New York: AltaMira Press.

Anzaldúa, G. (1987). *Borderlands/la frontera: The new mestiza.* San Francisco: Spinsters/Aunt Lute.

Bauman, R. (1977). *Verbal art as performance.* Rowley, MA: Newbury House.

Busia, P. A. (1993). Performance, transcription and the languages of the self: Interrogating identity as a "post-colonial" poet. In S. M. James & A. B. Busua (Eds.), *Theorizing Black feminisms: The visionary pragmatism of Black women* (pp. 203–213). New York: Routledge.

Collins, P. H. (1990). *Black feminist thought: Knowledge, consciousness, and the politics of empowerment.* New York: Routledge.

Conquergood, D. (2002). Performance studies: Interventions and radical research. *The Drama Review, 46,* 145–156.

Courville, C. (1993). Re-examining patriarchy as a mode of production: The case of Zimbabwe. In S. M. James & A. B. Busua (Eds.), *Theorizing Black feminisms: The visionary pragmatism of Black women* (pp. 31–43). New York: Routledge.

Denzin, N. K. (2003). *Performance ethnography: Critical pedagogy and the politics of culture.* Thousand Oaks, CA: Sage.

Escabar, A. (1992). *Encountering development: The making and unmaking of the Third World.* Princeton, NJ: Princeton University Press.

Gyekye, K. (1997). *Tradition and modernity: Philosophical reflections on the African experience.* Oxford, UK: Oxford University Press.

Hamera, J. (2007). *Dancing communities: Performance, difference and connection in the global city.* New York: Palgrave.

hooks, b. (1989). *Talking back: Thinking feminist, thinking black.* New York: South End.

Hord, L. F., & Lee, J. S. (Eds.). (1995). *The teachings of Ptahhoptep: I am because we are: Reading in Black philosophy.* Amherst: University of Massachusetts Press.

Madison, D. S. (2005). *Critical ethnography: Method, ethics, and performance.* Thousand Oaks, CA: Sage.

Nfah-Abbenyi, J. M. (1997). *Gender in African women's writing: Identity, sexuality, and difference.* Bloomington: Indiana University Press.

Nkrumah, K. (1998). *African philosophy.* Oxford, UK: Blackwell.

Pollock, D. (1990). Telling the told: Performing like a family. *The Oral History Review, 18*(2), 1–35.

Pollock, D. (1999). *Telling bodies performing birth: Everyday narratives of childbirth.* New York: Columbia University Press.

Pollock, D. (2005). *Remembering: Oral history performance.* New York: Palgrave.

20

READING THE VISUAL, TRACKING THE GLOBAL

Postcolonial Feminist Methodology and the Chameleon Codes of Resistance

Radhika Parameswaran

It is late evening in the bustling global city of Hyderabad, India, in July 2004—a large billboard with a single human figure looms out of the horizon alongside a new highway bridge that adjoins high-rise office buildings, apartments, and shopping complexes. A young Indian woman dressed in low-rise blue jeans and a tight tank top with her thumb inserted suggestively into the waistband of her jeans looks down on commuters from her elevated position on the white space of the billboard. Anchoring her inviting sexual gaze to the titillating promise of the investigative scoop, the local newspaper *Deccan Chronicle*'s bold copy on the billboard declares, "We dare to bare. Investigative reporting at its best." Standing tall in the midst of the city's traffic, the visual spectacle of the modern Indian woman, packaged within the commodity aesthetics of erotic White femininity, signals the softening of semiotic boundaries between the pure nationalist self (modest woman in Indian clothing) and the impure Western other (promiscuous woman in Western clothing) in a globalizing India—these gendered boundaries of insider/outsider structured the discursive landscape of public culture in earlier eras of colonial and postcolonial nation building (Chatterjee, 1989). The *Deccan Chronicle*'s deployment of a sexualized image of a young woman to court readers, a promotional strategy that would have been declared crude and sensational merely two decades ago, follows in the wake of recent dramatic changes in the Indian economic and cultural landscape: aggressive economic liberalization, truncation of socialist state policies, spread of capitalist consumer culture, and the rapid penetration of visual media in urban and rural India.

Although consumer culture's alluring canvases in postliberalized India tempt us to believe that

AUTHORS' NOTE: I am grateful to Norman Denzin, Carol Polsgrove, and an anonymous reviewer for their insightful comments on an early draft of this chapter. I thank Sara Friedman for her support and Spring Duvall, PhD candidate at Indiana University, for her outstanding research assistance.

they represent universal desire for modernity, Derne's (2005) recent work on the distinctions among the middle classes in India reminds us that media representations can gloss over divergent and competing social interests. The billboard's cosmopolitan and rebellious (yet patriarchal) mode of address—slim, sexy young woman in jeans—may not resonate closely with the strata of lower-middle-class Indians, who do not possess the economic or cultural capital to participate in transnational consumerism. Voicing their preferences for simple, domestic, and modest Indian wives, feminine subjects who (unlike the figure on the billboard) have the will to resist the "immoral" lures of modernity, the upwardly mobile young men Derne interviewed in north India rejected the destabilization of traditional gender arrangements that has accompanied affluent Indians' embrace of new, Westernized lifestyle choices and material practices.

Discarding her jeans and tank top for even more skimpy clothing, the sexy young woman of the global consumer cosmos in India has already appeared across the border in China, although in her previous incarnation there in the early nineties, her racial marking resembled that of a White woman, and thus her persona radiated a different matrix of significations. Anthropologist Schein (1994) describes the hectic preparations for a wedding that was under way in 1993 in the Miao Mountains of Ghuizou, China. Schein's narration of the wedding foregrounds the arrival of special guests from the city, who come bearing a strange gift—an inappropriate visual artifact—that she methodically unwraps to focus attention on the complex ways in which signifiers of the West intervene in the cultural production of class, ethnic, and gender difference in China's reform period:

> Then, the piece-de-resistance—the gift borne on shoulder poles. It is an ostentatious yard-long framed wall hanging behind glass, a photographic decoration slated for the walls of the nuptial chamber. The picture, in a bizarre juxtaposition with the bride, even upstaging her, is of a blonde model in a hot-pink G-string bikini supine atop a snazzy racing car. Lovingly, the hanging is given center placement among the other gifts—heaps of quilts and household goods—on display in the nuptial chamber for guests to review. Upon completion of her ethnic adornment, the bride poses with the thing. (p. 141)

Observing the wild circulation of such mediated signs in a China that was courting global capitalism, Schein (1994) writes that the slippery surface of the White female body "virtually prickles with polysemy" (p. 142). Any facile reading of the White woman as evidence of China's submission to consumer modernity, she points out, is incomplete because the White woman's body has been written over by a palimpsest of densely intertextual meanings that also reference freedom, individualism, democracy, and progress. For example, in contrast to her sultry and cosmopolitan sexiness in the modern wedding gift in Ghizou, the White woman, in her wholesome embodiment as the "Goddess of Democracy" (referential to the Statue of Liberty) during the 1989 Tiananmen Square demonstrations in China, symbolized young Chinese citizens' organized opposition to the totalitarian state (pp. 144–145). Suspended within the semiotic spaces of global and local culture, both the picture of the nude blond model and the Goddess of Democracy inhabited a China that was beginning to experience a frenzied fever of modernization whose most visible symptom was an "almost obsessive consumption" of the Occident ranging from "dishwashers to divorce" and "such disparate elements as the Bible and Picasso" (Schein, 2000, p. 22).

How do we read and make sense of the shifting social valences of an immensely agile visual culture that moves swiftly across and within national boundaries? Acknowledging the crucial role of modern visual media in shaping "culture" in those parts of the world that were historically aligned with tropes of primitivism, exoticism, and tradition, anthropologists, who had hitherto avoided mass media as a "taboo topic that was too redolent of Western modernity," have had to confront the fact that "media were penetrating societies once seen as beyond their reach" (Ginsburg, Abu-Lughod, & Larkin, 2002, p. 3). The images and ideologies of a rapidly spreading visual culture that has accompanied the arrival of globalization in Asia, Africa, and

Latin America in the past two decades are thoroughly entangled with emerging discourses of cosmopolitanism, nationalism, and hybrid global-local cultural formations. As the two examples of visual artifacts in Asia (billboard in India and photographic poster art in China) indicate, the mobile meanings of media texts are inseparable from their local and global economic, political, and historical contexts. This chapter models the contours of a postcolonial feminist methodology to unpack the fertile, historic symbolism of visual images, particularly the still photograph, in order to advance our skills in decoding the representational politics of resistance and hegemony in the contemporary moment of globalization.

Postcolonial feminism originated in the humanities, primarily in literary theory and criticism; however, its more recent migrations to cultural studies and the social sciences have expanded the field's scope of inquiry to include global and national consumer and popular culture, newspaper and advertising texts, Internet communities, media audiences, and global marketing and corporate practices (Fernandes, 2000; Grewal, 1999; Mallapragada, 2005; Mankekar, 1999; Munshi, 1998; Oza, 2001; Parameswaran, 2002; Shome & Hegde, 2002; Zacharias, 2003). Postcolonial feminism's methodology, although hard to pin down in its varied interdisciplinary formations, has a foundational mission to historicize the normative—taken-for-granted and axiomatic—assumptions we make about our contemporary conditions of modernity and postmodernity. Building on Black feminists' intersectional and multiplicative model of oppression (race and class matter as much as gender) that sought to challenge White feminism's singular focus on patriarchy, postcolonial feminists have argued that the geometries of global and national power slide between and among the vectors of gender *and* sexuality, nation, religion, class, caste, and ethnicity. Finally, in stretching its intellectual muscles to critique the flexible and mobile flows of global media and capital, postcolonial feminism's antiessentialist methodology grapples with the complexities of gender in relation to the ever changing "chameleon world" of institutional power: "We need to articulate the relationship of gender to scattered hegemonies such as global economic structures, patriarchal nationalisms, 'authentic' forms of tradition, local structures of domination, and legal-juridical oppression on multiple levels . . . we need new analyses of how gender works in the dynamic of globalization and the counter-measures of new nationalisms and ethnic and racial fundamentalisms" (Grewal & Kaplan, 1994, pp. 17, 19). Thus, postcolonial feminism's methodology refuses the comfort of erecting the familiar binary opposition of powerful global (West)/marginal local (non-West) to instead contest the uneven ways in which transnational collaborations among nation-states, religious fundamentalisms, and global and domestic capital police the formations of gender in diverse locations. Calling for historical, creative, and intertextual analyses of globalization's visual significations of gender, race, nation, and class, this chapter will demonstrate that postcolonial feminist interpretations of visual culture can unravel the multiple and intersecting strands of power and resistance that surround cultural representations.

Despite the exponential geographic expansion of visual media in recent years, an analysis of the visual that focuses merely on its contemporary global manifestations would only perpetuate a neocolonial and technologically determinist understanding of global modernity. How is the supremacy of the visual as a symbolic vehicle of globalization linked to the repressive historical discourses of Western science and colonial conquest and trade? A recent essay assessing the current state of visual communication research makes a strong concluding plea for robust doses of history in order to enrich the interdisciplinary contributions of the field (Barnhurst, Vari, & Rodriguez, 2004). Hence, this chapter begins by tracing the emergence of an imperialist epistemology of vision whose problematic equation of visibility to "reality" and "neutral information" continues to haunt our contemporary practices of seeing and processing codes of race and gender in visual culture. This first section situates the compelling authority of the contemporary visual and its relation to unequal hierarchies of global power within the historical trajectories of Euro-American colonialism and postcolonial nationalism. Using globalization's recent transplant to India as a case study, the second section takes up the challenge of outlining and modeling a postcolonial feminist methodology that can dissect the anatomies of race, gender, and nation in the visual traffic of global media. This section takes into account historical trajectories and contemporary socioeconomic forces to probe the shifting meanings of a single iconic image, the cover photograph of the August 1999 *National Geographic* magazine—my critical exercise here illustrates the process of an "itinerant" mode of analysis that confronts squarely the flexible travels of our objects of study (Schein, 2000, p. 28). Such a methodological approach to uncovering visual media's oscillation between the nodes of resistance and hegemony locates images along the axes of representation, audience, and political economy *and* juggles alterations in the signifying potential of images when we insert them into different geographies and multiple representational genealogies of gender, race, and class. As globalization's visual masks of gender traverse the globe, how can postcolonial feminism contribute to the mission of interrupting hegemonic versions of modernity? How can educators use the model of visual literacy outlined in this chapter to mobilize our students to embrace the responsibilities of global citizenship? The final and concluding section of the chapter will address these questions to dwell on the progressive pedagogic potential of an antiessentialist, postcolonial feminist critique of visual culture.

Historical and Foundational Matters: Imperial Legacies and Nationalist Fantasies

"Seeing is Believing." These were the bald words of a teaching consultant, who was helping me understand that my future success as a college teacher depended on my willingness to build an archive of visual images that would stimulate young, television-savvy students to pay attention to the less appealing oral lecture. The teaching consultant insisted that visual displays of concepts and data were powerful and indispensable aids to authenticate the spoken words of instructors' traditional lectures. But, is seeing really believing? And, how has history taught us that we must see if we want to believe? How do the immensely mobile and kaleidoscopic representations of the global visual domain train audiences to "see" and "believe" in particular discourses of gender, nation, race, or class?

Visions of Difference: Science and the Sensation of Race

A *critical* postcolonial feminist inquiry into the global terrain of the visual must acknowledge at the outset that the primacy accorded to the pedagogy of the "seeing eye"—the empirical authority we invest in its capacity to harness truth—emerged out of the bowels of imperial history. As proponents of the reflexive agenda of critical globalization studies have argued, the term *critical* implies a commitment to interrogating the historical specificity of our current material and political conditions and hence a rigorous correction to the hypothesis that globalization is an inevitable and timeless force without a beginning and an end (Mittelman, 2005; Robinson, 2005). The technologies of visual culture that have spread across geographic borders in the wake of globalization's extending economic tentacles are faithful to colonial modernity's realist *and* empiricist ideology of vision, that is, the notion that audiences everywhere want to "see" in order to "believe." Tunneling backwards from the ascendancy of the visual in contemporary global culture to historical configurations of the visible and vision, and finally to the practice of "seeing" itself, Wiegman (1995) argues that the epistemology of our modern economies of visibility was inaugurated, legitimized, and refined in the midst of imperial projects that sought to discover and fix racial and gender difference. Wiegman defines the visual as both an economic system and a representational economy that was inextricable from the politics of racial oppression and inequality:

> In Western racial discourse, for instance, the production of the African subject as non- or sub-human, as

> an object or property, arises not simply through the economic necessities of the slave trade, but according to the epistemologies attending vision and their logics of corporeal signification: making the African "black" reduces the racial meanings attached to flesh to a binary structure of vision, and it is this structure that precedes the disciplinary emergence of the humanities and its methodological pursuits of knowledge and truth. (p. 4)

Wiegman's (1995) elegant genealogy of the evolving symbiotic relations between the development of visual economies and the scientific refinement of racial difference locates the biology of the eye's optical abilities within the history of the visual: "For what the eye sees, and how we understand that seeing in relation to physical embodiment and philosophical and linguistic assumptions, necessitates a broader inquiry into the articulation of race, one that takes the visual moment itself as a historically contingent production" (p. 24).

How is the history of the growing dominance of the visual tethered tightly to the production of knowledge on race and gender? To address this question, I draw extensively below on Wiegman's (1995) pioneering work *American Anatomies,* which takes up the task of examining the changing trajectory of the status of vision, visibility, and the body in the nascent science of race and gender—from natural history to the human sciences or biology—to reveal the reciprocal ties that bound the emergence of visual modernity with disturbing paradigms of race and racism. Compensating for the weakening of religious authority's mystical logic in the late 17th century, natural history embraced the task of producing a comprehensive inventory and classification of nature. Most important, natural history departed from the earlier classical method of locating resemblances among creatures and phenomena to demonstrate harmonious unity between God and nature. Propelled by an increasing faith in empiricism, natural historians began to subject these coincidental resemblances to "proof by comparison," a methodology that relied fundamentally on "the apparent simplicity of a description of the visible," and it is this dependence on accurate and detailed descriptions of the visible that gave birth to "rationalized vision" (Wiegman, 1995, pp. 26–27).

In the framework of rationalized vision, visibility was detached from its holistic relationship to the other senses because the eye, the superior organ, was reappointed to become the primary means to produce disengaged observation and hence to "see and only to see" without any distraction whatsoever (Foucault, 1973, pp. 136–137, quoted in Wiegman, 1995, p. 25). Rationalized vision put its faith in scientific observation, the peephole model of the singular and isolated eye that "purportedly took its place in visual space suspended from the body, observing but not interpreting" (Wiegman, 1995, p. 26). Gradually, the representational relations underlying the metaphor of the peephole became operational in various instruments that shared the same name, *camera obscura,* instruments whose power of disembodied vision was harnessed to study natural diversity and the racial order of its most important species, man (Crary, 1988, pp. 30–33, quoted in Wiegman, 1995, p. 27). As Wiegman (1995, p. 28) notes, the crucial figures of early natural history—Francois Bernier, Carolus Linnaeus, George Louis Leclerc Buffon, and Johann Friedrich Blumenbach—may not have set out to establish proof of a hierarchical order of White supremacy, yet their reliance on the powers of observation and comparisons of identity and difference reified the visual terrain of the body—especially skin color—as the origin of racial distinction. Optical vision, venerated for its ability to harvest visible forms of knowable "data," thus became the sensory pillar for the articulation of the racial order, that is, first, for the European's claim to a universal, normative position and, second, for the specificity of race being reduced to the "Black" and consequently non-White body.

The intricate entanglement between the histories of race and that of vision and the visible takes a different turn in the 19th century when biology began to replace natural history. Moving beyond the visible surface of the body—skin color—as the primary source of raw material for racial classification, practitioners of the science of "man" began to open up the body and delve into the interior space of subterranean corporeality, those bodily elements that are invisible, and hence offered up the challenge of discovery and domestication to the requirements of visibility (Wiegman, 1995, p. 31). Penetrating the skin to study the skull and the brain, comparative anatomy's quest to master the calibration of race involved the mapping of relations and connections between the visible and the yet to be rendered visible. Whereas the primacy of the visible—the potential for information inherent in surfaces of humans and material objects—receded, the empirical authority of vision and the seeing eye only deepened further. Drawing from Stepan's (1990) work on the 19th-century project of race science, Wiegman (1995) argues that "calipers, cephalometers, craniometers, and parietal goniometers," prosthetic apparatuses of vision, were inventions that sought to transcend the limitations of the eye (Stepan, 1990, p. 43, quoted in Wiegman, 1995, p. 32). Furthermore, comparative anatomists' studies of brain weights, brain structures, and skull formations heralded the power of scientific vision to gain access to invisible layers of data on race and gender, data that generated new analogies to explain similarities between the African male and the Anglo-American woman: "In short, lower races represented the 'female' type of the human species, and females the 'lower race' of gender" (Stepan, 1990, pp. 39–40, quoted in Wiegman, 1995, p. 33).

In related historical developments of visual power outlined by Foucault and scholars who have analyzed the visual field of racism in the West, the disciplinary practices of control that emerged from cross-cutting regimes of specular (production of spectacle) and panoptic (practices of surveillance that emulate the eye's seeing/judging/penetrating gaze) vision were crucial to the maintenance of the racial order's economic and social hierarchies. The Ku Klux Klan's ceremonial public displays of mutilated bodies that were then reproduced in posters and newspaper photographs may appear to conform solely to the dynamics of spectacle on the surface, but the Klan's white hoods and capes with perforations for the eyes that concealed individuals also had a panoptic effect (Wiegman, 1995, pp. 39–41). These costumes of torture stood for known yet unknowable and diffuse institutional power, and the whiteness of the robes multiplied the symbolism of white skin as the omniscient source of power. The Klan's racist rituals, according to Wiegman (1995), were only the most extreme enactments of a panoptic regime of control that radiated through more mundane everyday forms of visual popular culture (trade cards, cartoons, and children's books) and practices of segregation in housing, medical care, education, and prisons. Similarly, the convergence in the specular and panoptic regimes of racism and sexism directed at Black women gave birth to the visual aesthetics of a commodified pornographic gaze that today pervades the globe, not merely in the pornography industry per se, but in the intimate address of our wider visual culture of global consumption. In her refutation of the myth that Black women were added to pornographic content as an afterthought, Hill Collins (1995) argues that the treatment of Black women's bodies in conditions of slavery—objectification, sexual violence, demands of passivity, and exploitation for profit—serves as the foundation for the commercial and visual economy of pornography. The pornographic exhibition of Sarah Bartmann, the Hottentot Venus, at fashionable parties in early 19th-century Europe points to the overlapping visual modalities of popular pornographic imagination and science; as an entertaining icon of deviant Black female sexuality, Bartmann provoked amused horror among the European elite, and upon her death, scientists dissected her body to study her genitalia. The microscopic appetite for the intimate, the real, and the bizarre, for the obscene excess of relentlessly "truthful" representations that promise greater gratification than the object being represented, feeds the visual hunger of a range of global media, from food and fashion photography to the slew of reality shows that serve up graphic surgeries, failed relationships, and dangerous displays of physical endurance.

Colonialism and Nationalism: The Envisioning and Revisioning of Power

Shifting gears from the epistemology of vision to questions of visual technologies and imperial conquest, the pioneering work of postcolonial scholars—inspired by Edward Said (1978)—on colonial discourse has shown that the abundant visual images of the 18th and 19th centuries serviced the expansion of Europe's colonial economies. The invention of colorful technologies of visual media—photography and cinema—that entertain millions of global audiences today "coincided with the giddy heights of the imperial project, with an epoch where Europe held sway over vast tracts of alien territory and hosts of subjugated peoples" (Shohat & Stam, 2002, p. 117). It is beyond the scope of this chapter to map the nuances of different colonial regimes or provide a detailed overview of postcolonial studies, but the insights of a few key critiques of colonialism's visual scaffolding uncover the fluctuating and ambivalent construction of the non-White "native" body as the Other. Contrary to the concept of "stereotype," which proposes that visual media cage their subjects in isolated and fixed cells of representation, significations of Otherness in colonial discourse blended to produce interwoven motifs of barbarism, eroticism, tradition, and exoticism. Working in tandem with the economic relations of colonization, such motifs of Othering the colonized were deployed unevenly and non-equivalently in scattered cultural and historical sites. Modifying Said's exclusive focus on colonizers' imperial construction of the Orient as the Other, Stoler and Cooper (1997) have argued that students of postcolonial studies must strive to bring the dynamic (not Manichean) relations between and among nation and empire, colonizer and colonized, and metropole and colony into one analytic field. Although my brief discussion below concentrates on visual representations of the *colonized,* it is important to remember that tropes of the otherness of Africans, Asians, or Native Americans entered into equally complex relations with the hierarchies of gender and class that positioned Euro-American women and working-class citizens on the margins of empire.

Libidinal sign systems of the native Other in the global commerce of colonial culture sustained the burgeoning spheres of industrialization and consumption in the empire—the visual incarnations of gender and race that purvey the riches of global commodity culture in Asia continue this trajectory of linking consumer desire to corporeal signification. As Lears (1989) notes in his analysis of the aesthetics of display, "the nineteenth century market was a liminal space linking East with West in a profusion of exotic images that surrounded consumer goods in an aura of sensuous mystery and possibility" (p. 77). Orientalism's visual field of high and low culture in Europe—paintings, public exhibitions, mall displays, trade cards, and picture postcards—offered an alternative to the mechanical rhythms of an industrializing society by transforming "consumption into a process charged with fantasy and escape" (Lalvani, 1995, p. 275). The exaggerated performances of belly dancers at international expositions, reproductions of Oriental palaces and harems in department stores, and illustrations of singing, dancing, and reclining women on advertisements displaced the threat of the Other within the fetishized pleasures of consumption (Leach, 1989; Williams, 1982). Alloula's (1986) oft-cited analysis of the touristic gaze in colonial picture postcards of Algerian women under French rule deconstructs colonizers' obsessive preoccupation with the bodies of veiled Muslim women in order to expose the "perfect expression of the violence of the gaze" (p. 131). In different iterations of Othering in the United States where colonialism was predicated on the permanent occupation of the colony, systematic genocide, and the forced importation of slave labor, the visual vocabulary of popular print culture regurgitated the imperial impulses of control and domestication. The fantasy drawings on advertising trade cards for food and medicines, for example, featured Native

Americans sprouting out of corn and other flowering plants—such images not only aligned Native Americans with nature and tradition but also represented them as consumable (and hence extinguishable) products (Steele, 1996).

Turning the colonies into entertainment for the voyeuristic pleasures of the metropole's masses, cinematic fictions of the lives of "natives" in distant lands created a visceral, spatial sense of imperial conquest, thus consolidating nationalist imaginaries and sentiments of pan-European racial solidarity. Although cinema prolonged the colonizing gaze of photography, the ritualized gathering of audiences meant that celluloid spectacles could be mobilized more efficiently to extend the visualist inclinations of Western scientific discourse into the realm of popular fantasy, and such fantasy in turn was conducive to the forging of collective identities. Shohat and Stam (2002) survey the multiple cinematic tracks of a predatory Euro-American colonial gaze that penetrated foreign lands to gather raw visual material to be reworked in the motherland. These critics argue that colonial cinema achieved the twin goals of proving the existence of Others *and of* exhibiting their indisputable Otherness:

> Operating on a continuum with zoology, anthropology, botany, entomology, biology, and medicine, the camera, like the microscope anatomized the other. The new visual apparatuses demonstrated the power of science to display and even decipher otherized cultures. Technological inventions in other words mapped the globe as a disciplinary space of knowledge. Topographies were documented for purposes of economic and military control, often on the literal backs of the natives who carried the cinematographers and their equipment. (p. 122)

Analyzing the scopophilic display of alien native bodies in a vast corpus of films ranging from *Tarzan* to *The Dance of Fatima,* Shohat and Stam (2002) write, "The cinematic exposure of the dark body nourished spectatorial desire, while marking off imaginary boundaries between 'self' and 'other,' thus mapping homologous spheres, both macroscopic (the globe) and microcosmic (the sphere of carnal knowledge)" (p. 124). The invention of and experimentation with color cinema in the United States coincided with the early fashioning of the art deco aesthetic, an eclectic and extravagant visual palette that "borrowed and combined elements from the mechanical, the avant-garde, the primitive, the exotic, and the Oriental, especially Chinese and Japanese culture" (Wang, 2005, p. 167). The art deco–style coloring of the cinematic canvas spilled into the hyperbolic narrative coloring of racial identity, namely, the spurt in White actors' yellowface performances: "Contrary to conventional racial passing, which hinges on erasing all traces of performance and disguise, screen passing in the form of yellowface or blackface masquerade highlights the white actor or actress behind the racially marked screen persona" (p. 168). Spiraling outward to deliver distant lands, objects, and peoples to audiences in the metropole and the colony, the visual apparatus of early photography and cinema—not merely its equipment or images, but also museums, living rooms, laboratories, world fairs, and theaters—thus generated the semiotic environment where constellations of power between nations, races, and classes were made visible (Berger, 2002; Faris, 2002; Lutz & Collins, 2002; Shohat & Stam, 2002). The enduring purchase of the colonial gaze, distilled through the discursive trope of visual conquest, resurfaces in Peter Jackson's 2005 version of *King Kong,* a cinematic story replete with well-rehearsed historic idioms of gender, color, race, nation, and sexuality: Intrepid White male filmmaker discovers a dark and mysterious island; savage "Black" tribes capture White victims and offer them up for ritual sacrifice; the seductive spell of White femininity captivates and civilizes Black bestiality; and finally, the strategic power of Western warfare extinguishes the aggressive threat of the Other, a defeated creature that clings to the phallic architecture of urban civilization before it crashes toward death.

While the dominant images of visual culture in the 19th century helped cement an imperial sense of belonging among Euro-American citizens, the public visual culture of 20th-century postcolonial nationalism in the former colonies also drew on codes of race, gender, and nation (and caste, religion, and ethnicity) to forge independent political and cultural identities. Analyzing the ideological complexities of 19th-century debates over modernity and tradition in India, for example, a number of postcolonial critics have focused their scrutiny on the gendered vocabulary of anticolonial resistance (Chatterjee, 1989; Grewal, 1996; Kandiyoti, 1991; Mani, 1991; Mankekar, 1999; Moghadam, 1994). In order to counter British colonizers' charges of "horrific" patriarchal traditions that oppressed passive "native" Indian women (objects of the White man's salvation), elite Indian male social reformers began to fashion a nationalist discourse of superior morality that was based in the glorification of the devoted and chaste Indian wife, mother, and citizen. As Chatterjee (1989) notes, the discursive desexualization of the upper-caste bourgeois Indian (Hindu) woman, a mascot of the nation's uncorrupted purity, was achieved through the displacement of sexual promiscuity onto the White/foreign European woman, a racialized symbol of the ills of colonial modernity.

The discursive inheritances of 19th-century anticolonial ideologies continued to inflect and structure the visual landscape of 20th-century popular culture in postcolonial India. Such iconic films as *Mother India* (1957), whose chief female protagonist defends her virtue and respectability in the midst of personal crises and natural calamities, encapsulated the nation's traditional yet modernizing spirit in the immediate aftermath of independence. Representing the strength and purity of an India that could embrace scientific modernity without sacrificing the authentic moral essence of national identity, the heroine of the film is shown gazing upon the nation's future prosperity, which unfolds through spectacular images of large-scale dams, steel and power plants, and factories (Khilnani, 1997). Nayar (2004) writes that the visual semiotics of *Mother India*'s culturally familiar narrative of women's fidelity, postcolonial modernization, and resilient family values resonated with audiences in other non-Western nations: "Indeed, a film as indigenous and nationalistic as *Mother India* (1957) continues to be embraced by audiences of other nations and races and languages and histories, as if it were in fact recounting the story of Mother Nigeria, or Mother Egypt, or of Romany Gypsies in Eastern Europe or Swahili speaking girls in Zanzibar" (p. 14). The early nationalist practice of grafting patriotic subjectivity onto the emotive apparatus of visual technology has only gained disturbing momentum in the past two decades as state and commercial institutions in postcolonial nations have rushed to mine cultural nationalism's persuasive rhetoric to usher in new modes of governance (Abu-Lughod, 2005; Kumar, 2004; Rajagopal, 1998; Zacharias, 2003).

Global Culture and Its Visual Nomenclature

Cut to the present, the past two decades, a time capsule of visual modernity's triumphant spread to new locales, and an era that has witnessed an intensified cross-cultural traffic in currencies, consumer commodities, capitalist ideologies, tourists and migrants, and media technologies (Appadurai, 1996). The saturation of contemporary human experience from Asia to North America and multiple locations in between with the optical sensation of visual modernity is both a consequence of and a contributor to the global economic changes that have dominated the world in the past two decades. The economic process of globalization that has entailed rapid reforms to accommodate free trade—the relaxing of state controls and licensing, opening of markets for foreign trade and tourism, and dispersed multinational investment—swept through a number of developing nations during the late eighties and nineties. While Harvey (2000) notes that the business practices of globalization per se are not new because international trade dates back to the 15th century, the increased mobility of capital, as well as the rapid and flexible circulation of goods, services, and images across geographic borders, marks the "complex, overlapping, and disjunctive order" of the global economy (Appadurai, 1996, p. 32).

Appearing frequently in the pages of the *Wall Street Journal* since the mid-nineties, India is a prime example of an "emerging market," a developing nation that has been renegotiating actively its marginal position in the global economic order. Responding to International Monetary Fund (IMF) demands in exchange for a bailout, the Indian government launched an economic liberalization package in the late eighties that resulted in a shift in national political culture from socialist modernity—development of infrastructure, reduction of poverty, and a rhetoric of social justice—to capitalist modernity—promotion of the urban middle classes as a workforce for outsourced labor and as a lucrative market for the sale of consumer commodities. The media explosion that has taken place in India in the past 10 years, an explosion that has aided the transformation of a protected economy into a lucrative site for global production and consumption, encompasses older print and cinematic forms, newer vernacular and English-language magazines and newspapers, television and the Internet, and billboards and electronic displays. State, capitalist, and activist forces, which jostle each other for space in India's emergent public culture of journalism, advertising, and entertainment, harness discourses of gender, ethnic pride, religion, and nationalism to capture the imagination of new global consumers and workers (Appadurai & Breckenridge, 1995; Fernandes, 2000; Grewal, 1999; Mankekar, 1999; Munshi, 1998; Parameswaran, 2004b).

Animating Globalization's Textual Archive: Multisited Meanings, Intertextual Imaginaries

Guided by an awareness of the contingencies of history and the priorities of our global economic order, how can we develop a framework for reading and contesting the semiotics of race, gender, and nation in *visual texts* that make sense of globalization for dispersed audiences? A good starting point for a postcolonial feminist exploration into the archeology of globalization's visual texts would involve a more active, ethnographic definition of what we mean by the term *text* itself (a reformulation of *text* has become even more urgent in light of the turf wars between textual media critics and audience ethnographers). Although we use *text* in the routine parlance of media studies to refer to visual artifacts, we need to formulate a methodological approach that does not approximate the term *text* to imply the passivity of an inert object or the transparency of a mimetic surface for the reproduction of reality. Taking their cue from ongoing debates over "textuality" in anthropology and performance studies, media scholars can begin to *problematize* texts as performative practices of "iteration," mediated utterances that react to and coalesce with a host of other typologies of "iterations" to produce modernity as a structure of feeling.

Anthropologist Schein (2000) marshals the insights of performance theory to resuscitate popular texts as "cultural productions" that circulate within the arteries of social networks rather than mute "cultural objects" that invite the postmortem gaze of dissection, a dynamic reorientation to texts that "obviates notions of culture as straightforwardly inertial" (p. 17). Schein's approach brings simultaneously to the foreground social actors, who deploy their expert skills to assemble coherent texts out of fragments of culture, *and* those far-flung collectives of actors, who are called upon to decode the contextual meanings of textual scripts and images. Strine's (1998) essay in the book *The Future of Performance Studies* challenges the usefulness of the "functional separation and distancing" between everyday social relations and cultural forms of representation: "For even the casual observer it would be difficult to deny that the increasingly sophisticated mass media 'culture industry' with its ever-expanding range of influence has a decisive formative impact on virtually all aspects of contemporary social life" (p. 4). Strine draws from the work of social theorist Chaney (1993), who has argued that changing forms of representation are "generative, not merely imitative" of social conventions and structures, to define textual genres of culture as performative practices because these mediated representations display "production characteristics, product characteristics, and reception characteristics" (p. 4). Even as we attempt to inject theoretical life into the textual artifact in media studies, it is important to remember, as Conquergood (1998) warns us in his analysis of African slaves' improvisational musical performances, that it is difficult to extricate the textual imagination of social relations from histories of exclusion and domination: "Instead of holding texts that properly belonged to them, slaves were themselves objects of 'intextuation,' held in subordinate place by an array of legal statutes, commercial auction posters, bills of sale, broadside advertisements for runaways, and so forth" (p. 28). Posing a series of questions that probe the "consequences of thinking about performance and textuality as fluid, exchangeable, and assimilable terms," Conquergood advocates for a complementary and conversational performance-text paradigm of cultural critique (p. 25): "Although I very much appreciate contributions made by the world-as-text paradigm, particularly the way it has functioned as a counter-project to positivism, its limits need to be acknowledged and pre-suppositions critiqued.... Performance as both an object and method of research will be most useful if it interrogates and decenters, without discarding the text" (pp. 32–33).

At the forefront of forging interdisciplinary approaches to texts in cultural studies, Hartley (1996) pleads for more animated, finely textured, and taxonomic analyses of the images and words of journalism. Texts, as Hartley notes, are the traceable sediments of "dialogue, relationship, meaning and communication between text-makers (publishers, photographers, writers, etc.), the medium in which texts appear (journalism, cinema, cultural studies, pornography, etc.), and a readership (public construed as citizen, audience, voyeur, expert, policymaker, moralist, etc.)" (p. 5). When collated, these diverse texts originating from different sources and varied generic conventions constitute a "gigantic archive of textuality, a huge store of human sense-making" that offers critics the opportunity to explore the dynamic "social production of meaning in the historical circumstances of modernity" (Hartley, 1996, pp. 3–4). Echoing Hartley's sentiments, Hall (1996) urges critics to recognize the intimate relations between texts and their social contexts: "How things are represented and the machineries and regimes of representation do play a constitutive, not merely a reflexive, after-the-event role" (p. 443). Arising in the midst of myriad personal, social, and economic interactions, media texts should thus be reconceptualized as recoverable material evidence and as performative practices that contain clues to active and diverse sociohistorical practices of representation.

A postcolonial feminist reading and contestation of textual practices, particularly the *mapping* of semiotic registers of resistance and accommodation, requires a combination of methods—forensic, documentary, historical, and metaphorical—that can unravel the *multisited* and densely intertextual ways in which visual images circulate within fields of social relations. Strine's (1998) definition of "mapping" captures the spirit in which I use the term here: "Mapping as a critical trope implies a process of exploration and organization, of charting relationships and marking possibilities not readily observable across dense and diversified terrain" (p. 8). Multisited ethnography, a methodological innovation that responds to "empirical changes in the world"—namely, the disintegration of "culture" as a discrete, bounded, and holistic object of study—tracks the mobile and shape-shifting formations of culture that arise as images, ideas, artifacts, economies, and people move across and within national boundaries (Marcus, 1995). Suited well to analyze the dislocated ways in which global media images are conceived and reproduced in numerous spaces, multisited ethnography moves out of "single sites and conventional research designs" in an open-ended and speculative manner to trace the comparative emergence of meaning as things (images, commodities, works of art, etc.) circulate in different contexts (p. 97). Similarly, the methodology of critical globalization studies, a field that seeks to build bridges between varied constituencies of academics, activists, policy makers, and private industry, is one that is open-ended, dialectical, and sensitive to the "interplay of market dynamics, power relations and social forces that slice across borders" (Mittleman, 2005, p. 21). Commitment to the dialectical logic of critical globalization studies would call for focusing "not on things themselves but on the interrelations among them"; that is, cultural analyses of the *social life* of objects and human experiences must address "how distinct elements of social reality may be analytically distinct, yet are mutually constitutive of each other as internal elements of a more encompassing process" (Robinson, 2005, p. 17). A postcolonial feminist critique of the visual architecture of globalization can weave together the methodological sensibilities of multisited ethnography and critical globalization to "map" the nuances of hegemony and resistance in visual texts that are embedded in larger systems of representations.

Continuous Stories, Discontinuous Histories: Visual Imprints of Resistance and Hegemony

This section treats the colorful cover photograph of the *National Geographic* magazine's 1999 millennium issue on global culture, an emblematic visual citation of India's recent experiments with globalization, as a vivid palimpsest whose multisited and intertextual meanings illustrate the chameleon (fluctuating) codes of resistance *and* compliance (see Figure 20.1). The polychromatic portraiture of this playful and dramatic cover, a departure from the magazine's routine repertoire of images of India that speak to knowledge of natural science, ritual, or religion, deploys Indian women's bodies and subjectivities as blueprints that busy readers can scan quickly to trace a non-Western nation's passage from tradition to modernity. Invoking the cultural politics of age, class, motherhood, and feminine fitness, a plump older Indian woman (mother, positioned on the left) dressed in an ornate red silk sari and elaborate gold jewelry signifies the inertness of tradition while a thin young Indian woman (daughter, positioned on the right) dressed in a tight black cat suit, unzipped to the middle of her chest, and sharply pointed black boots purveys the vitality of modernity. The two women are shown sitting slightly apart on a raised platform that is flanked by wrought iron frames, and the quiet and colorless background, the lower face of a grayish white marble building, accentuates the contrastive colors of tradition and modernity. The caption to the reproduced image of the cover inside the magazine's pages points to the privileged caste and class position of the two Indian women; readers are told that the older woman, Nakshatra Reddy, is a biochemist, and the younger woman, her daughter, Meghana Reddy, is a model and former television host.

This photograph's most visible colonial/modernist—natural history's linear, binary, and sharply polarized logic—rendering of the "new and hip" as radically different from the "old and outmoded" is just the most banal of its hegemonic interpretations of globalization, a contrived moment that was preserved for the public gaze when light from the mother-daughter dyad fell onto a photographic surface. The tangible (tactile and optical) narrative of the cover is significant for what it reveals about negotiations among an authoritative institution (*National Geographic*), renowned for its interpretations of the non-Western world; an individual photographer; posed subjects; and an elite transnational readership. But, it is the intangible and ambiguous multiplicity of such iconic visual stimuli, the different meanings that travel through time and space when we get beyond the camera's documentation of an instant, that will guide us toward the analysis of an image's affiliations with codes of resistance and hegemony. Berger (2002) explains that the ambiguity of the photograph arises out of the abyss, the rupture of discontinuity, which lies between the moment recorded and the moment of looking: "All photographs are ambiguous. All photographs have been taken out of a stream of continuity. If the event is a public event, this continuity is history; if it is personal, the continuity, which has been broken, is a life story. . . . Discontinuity always produces ambiguity" (p. 50). The meaning of a photograph, Berger asserts, arises out of the amorphous abyss of ambiguity that lies between the recorded past and the interpreted future: "An instant photographed can only acquire meaning insofar as the viewer can read into it a duration extending beyond itself. When we find a photograph meaningful, we are lending it a past and a future" (p. 49).

Figure 20.1

SOURCE: Reprinted with permission of Joe McNally Photography.

What are some of the stories of the past and future that shroud the female figures on the 1999 *Geographic* magazine's cover with meanings of resistance? Drawing from the insights of multi-sited ethnography and critical globalization studies, how does a particular sign system's potential alliance with resistance fluctuate when we travel to alternate geographic sites and consider the dialectics of varied stories of continuity? Walking into an upscale restaurant in Mumbai in 2004, I spotted an enlarged and framed copy of the very same magazine cover occupying a position of prominence on the center of the back wall. This long-awaited pictorial testimony to modern/urban/civilized India from the United States, the excited restaurant manager in Mumbai insisted, "says everything about India's future reputation in America because it shows that we are not seen as the backward country of death and disease, the same as Africa." This manager's worship of the cover image in Mumbai mirrored the enthusiastic notes and e-mail messages I received from the Indian immigrant community in the United States soon after the August 1999 *Geographic* magazine appeared in bookstores.

The subtext of resistance in the story of the picture's enshrined social rebirth in a Mumbai restaurant, 5 years after its publication, becomes legible only when we listen to a rather long tale of the picture's past. When measured against the historical fabric of the West's essentialized popular iconography of a rural "Third World" India, a nation beset with problems of poverty, famines, riots, natural disasters, and primal violence against women, the image of cosmopolitan India, labeled as "Global Culture," gains the undertones of resistance. Media critics have pointed out that the First World tradition of recycling the Third World through the ahistoric lenses of disorder serves to consolidate a collective self of industrialized Western nations as belonging to a higher order of civilization, one that is typified by order and stability (Dahlgren & Chakrapani, 1982; Parameswaran, 1996). Another dominant story of the past that propels the picture's representational momentum toward the semiotics of resistance originates within the Western academy. When we situate the *Geographic*'s picture within the large body of academic narratives on the "development" and modernization of Asia, narratives that have fetishized the backwardness of rural

India, it becomes a representation that challenges the conformity of an earlier authoritative discourse. In staking out her intellectual terrain, feminist anthropologist Mankekar (1993) writes about anthropology's fascination with village India: "As an Indian student of anthropology in the United States, I have been startled by how frequently typical anthropological discourse on South Asia, craving authenticity, had obsessively attempted to represent 'village India' as the true India and has stubbornly resisted acknowledging the presence of dynamic cosmopolitan cultural formations in postcolonial India" (p. 58). Our historical consciousness about the limits of Western *popular* and *academic* representations of India thus lends the portrait of urban, upper-class Indians the oppositional possibilities of a progressive postcolonial critique that questions the othering of India in the First World.

On a more cautionary note, however, despite the picture's inclination to inaugurate a new representational space for India, celebrations of America's recognition of cosmopolitan India at the expense of "Third World" India can also feed into the exclusionary impulses of religious and elite Indian nationalism. Sanitizing India of its embarrassing problems of poverty and disease, the majority Hindu fundamentalist tale of loyalty to the nation would position the clean, orderly image of affluent urban Hindu women within the continuity of India's glorious history of Hinduism, a past of wealth and widespread prosperity that unseemly foreign (Muslim and Western) "invaders" had interrupted. Such recent hegemonic discourses of fundamentalist nationalism have attributed problems of disorder and violence to India's poor minorities, particularly Muslims. Another overlapping strand of "secular" nationalism (a silent endorser of religious fundamentalism) that circulates among the urban, educated managerial classes, a socioeconomic bloc that is fast shedding its allegiance to the socialist vocabulary of poverty reduction, looks ahead to India's future as a technocratic consumer utopia. Emulating the confidence of the *Geographic*'s youthful, urban mascot of global modernity, the hybrid global-national imagery of the glossy popular print media of postliberalization India caters to the growing consumer ebullience of the Indian middle and upper classes who "aspire to be members of a globalizing first world elite which crosses national borders" (Scott, 1996, pp. 17–18). Postcolonial feminists have argued that the visual project of configuring global consumption for the elite classes has two goals: to convince the urban middle classes that they, members of a deserving meritocracy, have earned the right to transnational consumerism and to persuade them that they can preserve their authentic national identities even as they pursue lifestyles associated with the West.

Although it appears unrelated to the *Geographic*'s gendered visual performance of a bifurcated tradition and modernity, a playful cover photograph of a 1998 issue of an Indian magazine—*Business World*—reads like a fraternal slide in an ongoing storyboard of India's march into the global economy. The picture fuses gender, ethnicity, tradition, and modernity together while deploying masculinity rather than femininity as a semiotic resource. A nerdy, upper-caste South Indian man, an archetype parodied frequently in Bollywood films for his resistance to Western modernity, sports simultaneously the sartorial signifiers of the traditional and the modern. Tradition, the lavishly dressed Hindu mother of the *Geographic* cover, surfaces in the ash markings on the man's forehead, the thread across his torso, and his white dhoti wrapped around his legs, whereas modernity, the daughter in the tight black outfit, manifests here in the man's designer cowboy boots, dark glasses, Pepsi can, and Burberry umbrella. If the aesthetics of the *National Geographic* cover signals India's assimilation into global culture, *Business India* declares that the schizophrenia of its cover's hybrid South Indian man embodies the new "Sexy South," a region of India that, contrary to stereotypes of being populated with "take-it-easy plodders," was turning into a major attraction—a thriving production and consumption hub—for multinational investment (Mukurjea, Shekar, Radhakrishna, Sen, & Dhawan, 1998, p. 19). Together, the playful and intertextual binaries of the two visual artifacts, *National Geographic* and *Business World*, emerging from capitalist technologies of vision in different cultural sites pay homage to a market nationalism that seeks to minimize the "Gandhian hangover" of guilt associated with wasteful lifestyle consumption (Fernandes, 2000). The disappearance of signs of Third World poverty in such collaborative journalistic representations, as critics of recent media images in India have argued, works to repress knowledge that provokes ideas of social justice and responsibility toward India's poor, a key constituent of the nation's flickering socialist past. P. Sainath (2001), a leading journalist and antipoverty activist, might argue that the *Geographic*'s modern woman, signaling the arrival of MTV in India, and *Business World*'s trendy global South Indian consumer point to the disturbing class politics of media: "Journalists are more interested in telling the world that India's burgeoning new middle class finally has access to McDonald's burgers and international designer labels . . . topics that generate advertising revenue, not unpleasant stories about starvation deaths and the lack of clean drinking water, even in the heart of large cities" (p. 44).

Significantly, the two figures on the *Geographic* magazine, who communicate the liberating effects of globalization in India, are *women,* raced and gendered subjects, and hence we can now turn to stories of non-Western femininity and postcolonial feminism to excavate other semiotic layers of resistance and hegemony. Postcolonial feminist Mohanty's (1991a) influential work criticizes Western feminism's ethnocentric narratives for deifying the homogeneous and frozen category of "Third World woman," a *passive* subject of racial and ethnic difference whose life in the social sciences is "operationalized" through the "objective" and well-intentioned but lifeless indicators of well-being: sex ratio, nutrition, infant mortality, life expectancy, and death rate (pp. 5–6). Arguing that these measures "by no means exhaust the meaning of women's day today lives," Mohanty urges knowledge producers in the West to foreground discursively non-Western women's agency as active subjects, that is, to represent the subtle and overt ways in which these women resist their subordination to create a social space for themselves (p. 6). The *National Geographic*'s cover responds affirmatively to Mohanty's advice to produce knowledge that destabilizes the "authorizing signature of Western humanist discourse," a project that requires Third World difference (victimology) to project the West as free, democratic, and egalitarian (Mohanty, 1991b, p. 53). Although the cover's modest Indian mother, with hands folded demurely and feet close together, encodes a rather passive subject position, the young daughter Meghana Reddy's bold act of claiming her personal space—her upright physical pose and assertive demeanor—captures visually the intellectual spirit of Mohanty's recommendation to dislodge the Third World woman from her consignment to the "debilitating generality" of the category of oppressed woman (Mohanty, 1991b, p. 71). Meghana's legs are splayed wide apart, her left arm is poised akimbo style, and her left palm grips her hips in a strong masculine gesture. She disdains her mother's soft smile and tender gaze to stare defiantly into the camera.

Furthermore, the young daughter's unsmiling and almost hostile face (whether staged or spontaneous) carries historical traces of anticolonial and gendered resistance to the camera's routinized appetite for obedient, smiling feminine subjects. The "threatening potential" of non-Western women's unsmiling, defiant faces, as Eileraas (2003) asserts in her reading of French army photographer Garanger's identity portraits of Algerian women, can radically unsettle the boundaries between self and other and the asymmetric positions of photographer and subject. The Algerian women in Garanger's identity portraits, who had to be clearly recognizable to colonial authorities, were unveiled forcibly and commanded to confront the camera's eye in full frontal view. Eileraas probes the internal ambivalence of these visual representations of Algerian women: "But exactly where and how do they look, and how do these women's looks gesture towards resistance?"

> The women photographed by Garanger most strikingly communicate resistance with their eyes and facial expressions. As one might expect, none of

> these women opt to smile for the camera. This is important to note in a cross-cultural encounter in which the smile would typically serve a "mitigating" function to mute the potentially disruptive or confrontational role of the "other's" return gaze. Instead of smiling to efface or palliate the asymmetrical power relations between colonizer and colonized that might emerge from these photographs, Algerian women confront Garanger's camera with lips tightly pursed, their mouths conveying resolve and the desire to be recognized on their own terms. (p. 817)

When we move forward in time to plug the *Geographic*'s young Indian woman into the stories of commercial media images that stitch warm, feminine "happiness" into the tapestry of consumer prosperity, her strong, chilly facial expression deviates markedly from that of her young, feminine peers whose smiling faces animate cosmetics, clothing, and cars in multiple national sites that traverse the globe. Kotchemidova's historical genealogy of American women's ubiquitous smile in photographic portraits unearths Kodak Corporation's careful orchestration of the camera as an indispensable instrument of happiness—the act of shooting, the smile of the posed subject, and the perusing of archived images were represented as events that incited happy narratives of family and community (Kotchimedova, 2005). She observes astutely that the gestalt communication of visual technology generated the epidemic of the contagious smile: "I suggest that the model of the smile was readily absorbed in popular photography partly because it was imparted visually . . . the smile just sits in the visuals, taken for granted. It is assumed" (p. 14). In India, photographs of young, smiling women on billboards and covers of newsmagazines distill the pleasures of shopping, competing in beauty contests, and dieting; these hypervisible tropes of feminine happiness signal the nation's openness to the seductions of First World material abundance. On one of the Discovery channel's television programs, an exuberant Thomas Friedman, populist cheerleader of globalization, accompanies young, smiling Indian women who have adopted American names and accents—night-shift workers in the sweatshops of multinationals' callcenters—on "happy" shopping trips in the daytime. Thus, on embedding the *Geographic* magazine's young woman, a recalcitrant non-Western photographic subject, within feminist stories of the past and global corporate consumerism's scripts of modernity, we can begin to detect ripples of resistance.

Again, these subterranean shades of resistance in the *Geographic*'s palette on Indian femininity and global culture take on the hues of hegemony if we process the cover through the lens of colonial history outlined in the previous section. The magazine's representational strategy of using Indian women to illuminate the transformation wrought by the arrival of Western-style consumer culture harkens back to the 19th century, when Indian nationalists and British colonizers deployed Indian women's bodies, subjectivities, and behaviors (without actually engaging women) to wage debates over tradition and modernity. Colonial discourses harnessed the burdens of "native" womanhood to claim that a benevolently interventionist colonial state could liberate Indian women—victims of a "barbaric" patriarchy—from their oppression. If such historical discourses of salvation (white men saving brown women from brown men) supported the modernizing mission of colonialism, the young Indian woman who gains confidence and assertiveness when she consents to wearing a tight-fitting costume from the West, not the Indian sari or traditional jewelry like her placid mother, recuperates the hegemonic story of Western/capitalist modernity as the harbinger of women's liberation in South Asia. The thin, empowered model/media personality in the black cat suit is also conjoined to the visual terrain of commodity feminism's recent excursions in India; the currency of appearance as symbolic capital has accelerated in these contemporary discourses of patriarchal quasi-feminism. Grewal (1999) describes the expanding reach of pop feminism's brand of empowered Indian femininity that creates a constant demand for women's thin and sexy bodies encased in the latest fashion:

> This Indian pop feminism, denoting a participation in a globalized economy not only as consumers but

> also as professionals (models, advertising executives, marketing experts, and small business owners, especially in garment manufacturing) is influencing the career goals of more Indian urban women of the middle and upper classes, just as the role of working-class and poor women as factory workers is also increasing. (pp. 815–816)

Such a newly minted "racy" symbol of Indian pop feminism cajoles the *Wall Street Journal*'s elite transnational reading public to visit modern India (Sesser, 2006). A vivid front-page picture in the newspaper's lifestyle section portrays a glittering street scene in the shopping district of the city of Bangalore in South India. An illuminated billboard of a thin young Indian woman with flowing hair, bikini bra, and tight jeans towers above the scene—the spectacle of the female body symbolizes the seduction of the nation's resistance to local tradition and capitulation to global modernity. The glowing image of the racy woman and the juxtaposed title of the article "A Passage to India's Future" (echoing E. M. Forster's novel *A Passage to India*) chart femininity's entanglement in colonial history, urban development, global consumerism, and the aesthetics of visual production. Returning to the opening passage of this chapter, the sexy young woman on the billboard in Hyderabad, the *Wall Street Journal*'s female icon of a future India, and the *Geographic*'s slim young woman can be located on a continuum of pop feminism's global paradigm of feminine transgression. Such visual embodiments of "hip" Indian women wrapped in the rebellious nomadic codes of Western femininity preclude the possibility that there are alternative and more complex, indigenous models of women's empowerment. Elderly Indian mothers in saris, as the *National Geographic* might suggest, are not always obedient students of patriarchy, and feminists who wear traditional clothing can also be vocal advocates of Indian women's right to sexual pleasure and lifestyle choices; however, these feminists may not endorse cultural practices that conflate Indian women's strength, fearlessness, and independence with jeans and skirts or cleavage, curves, and slim bodies.

Where Do We Go From Here? Visual Culture and Pedagogies of Postcolonial Feminism

My reading of globalization's visual modalities modeled in this chapter began with an overview of the historical particularity of global media technologies whose extended radars of vision have swept through most of the world today. After detailing the companionate role of the visual in expanding globalization's horizons, I undertook the task of reviving the comatose text of media studies as cultural production, a performative practice that marks a nodal point in the ongoing process of representation. My postcolonial feminist—multisited, contextual, and dialectical—analysis of the 1999 *Geographic*'s cover image of globalization in India unpacks the gendered performances of resistance and accommodation that unfold as we travel inward into history and outward into contemporary cultural politics. As postcolonial feminist studies moves from its originary terrain of literary criticism to intervene in the newer arenas of global modernity and its competing social forces, it can uncover the interlocked ways in which gender, race, class, and nation are deployed as semiotic resources to push forward the agendas of scattered constituencies of global and local power. Postcolonial feminism, as Sangari (1991) proposes, must expose the colonial, national, and capitalist structures of power that filter the symbolic imagination of womanhood: "Femaleness is not an essential quality. It is constantly made, and redistributed. One has to be able to see the formation of femaleness in each and every form at a given point . . . see what it is composed of, what its social correlates are, what its ideological potentials are, what its freedoms may be" (p. 57). Postcolonial feminism's mapping of the chameleon codes of resistance and hegemony in relation to visual representations of gender and globalization documents the transnational operations of power that cannot be easily demarcated into divisions of First World/Third World, White/non-White, or Man/Woman. The oscillating pendulum of resistance and accommodation in the *National*

Geographic's gendered canvas of global culture reveals the crucial need to forge political and intellectual agendas that are vigilant of the collusions among global/local market and media imperatives, state policies, elite nationalism, and historical developments, despite the practical urgencies that call upon us to embrace singular visions of change.

As globalization creates First Worlds in the Third World and Third Worlds in the First World, postcolonial feminism, in the words of Shome and Hegde (2002), must remain committed to the task of contesting the diffused configurations of power that service particular versions of modernity: "The issue is not that difference, marginality, disempowerment, etcetra, do not matter; rather, the issue is *how* they matter, *how* they are evoked . . . and *how* they are reconstituted through the differential logics in globalization" (p. 176). When we push the fast-forward button on the spool of time to 2006, we arrive at a moment when India consolidates its position as a global economic powerhouse (along with China) in the United States. The cover photo of *Newsweek*'s March 6, 2006, issue bolsters the *Geographic*'s 1999 mission to translate India's economic engagement with the West into the familiar metaphoric language of the feminine. Served up as appetizing visual bait, *Newsweek*'s sumptuous cover, bathed in the tropical colors of golden yellow and deep red, tempts readers to proceed to the magazine's cover story on President Bush's impending visit to India. Rearticulating elements from the *Geographic*'s visual composition of tradition and modernity, the cover features a touristic portrait of the slim and light-skinned actress, Padma Lakshmi, standing below the optimistic title "The New India," with her hands folded in front of her torso as swathes of rich red fabric float in a dream-like fashion above her shoulder. Like the *Geographic*'s modern young daughter, Padma Lakshmi's direct stare, erect body, and loose wavy hair signal youth and confidence; however, the red sequined fabric wrapped around her body and her traditional hand gesture (namaste) signifying "welcome" invoke the feminized new age India of Hinduism, spirituality, and yoga, and thus link her to the Orientalized realm of the *Geographic*'s traditional mother.

On one hand, the magazine's choice of Padma Lakshmi—a resident of Manhattan and London and daughter of an Indian father and European mother—challenges the limits of the nation as taking up residence within specific geographical and racial boundaries. On the other hand, *Newsweek*'s linguistic silence on the cover image, aside from the editor's short reference to Padma Lakshmi as novelist Salman Rushdie's wife, reduces her exotic visual splendor to mute feminine ornamentation (readers learn nothing about Lakshmi's own modeling or acting careers). Moreover, this light-skinned, hybrid female figure's embodiment of global India aligns her with the sorority of women whose postcolonial whiteness in India's media and advertising discourse of the nineties "opened up new spaces of desire and commodification, forming a culturally seductive logic for market liberalization" (Zacharias, 2003, p. 396). Zacharias (2003) argues that these signifiers of feminine shades of whiteness in the postliberalized nation's public sphere formed "intertextual links with existing social hierarchies of caste and community in India, where propertied classes and more privileged communities could aspire for social mobility through consumption" (p. 396). What remains invisible in *Newsweek*'s staged visual production of a glamorous and whitened new India—a nation that has developed hundreds of luxurious gated communities in the past decade—is the story of the other old village India that continues to be home to "a third of the world's poor and where some 300 million people live on less than $1 a day" (Ramesh, 2006). Just a few hundred miles from the upscale residential settlement of Aamby Valley (new India) in the state of Maharashtra, a private settlement that boasts of golf courses, year-round cool temperatures, water parks, hiking trails, five-star restaurants, a hospital, and an airport, is the village of Vidarbha (old India) where an alarming number of poor farmers, unable to compete with growers from the United States and the European Union after the "last vestiges of Indian government support were withdrawn," have committed suicide, thus adding to the toll of thousands of Indian farmers who have taken their own lives in the past decade (Ramesh, 2006).

The postcolonial feminist methodological approach to analyzing the antiessentialist politics of resistance and hegemony outlined here can also be useful to debate the democratic possibilities of more participatory forms of visual production. In February 2005, British-born and Cambridge-educated photojournalist Dana Briski's documentary *Born Into Brothels,* a poignant visual odyssey of her sojourn among the children of impoverished prostitutes in Calcutta, won the Best Documentary Feature Oscar at a televised ceremony whose costs alone may have helped fund several of the very same children's education. Among other things, Briski gave several children cameras and taught them how to take pictures. The children's snapshots of their families, friends, and surrounding streets have earned them admiring audiences and sympathetic donors and supporters in the West. Such projects highlight the creative and progressive potential of an intertextual visual genre—a filmic narrative about a photographic production—to interrupt and resist the most ostentatious display of wealth and glamour in the West. Yet at the same time, it is important to ground visual productions of activism within the hegemonic fabric of history not to dismiss entirely the worth of such projects, but to push forward the momentum of social action toward realities that we may not have imagined today. Faris's (2002) thoughts about converting the subaltern subject into a producer are useful here: "Within the traditional, limited conceptions of representation, one obvious solution was to put cameras in the hands of the mis-represented subaltern . . . but cross-cultural photography is very problematic, for unless it can manage to enforce a boundary cross-culturally, it normally drags the framing practices of the dominant photographer along" (p. 81). Can films like *Born Into Brothels* produce long-term help for poor children in the non-West? How do the specular and panoptic regimes of the Academy Awards' ceremony where the documentary film won acclaim amid a broader audience fortify the boundaries of Self/Other in the West? Crossing over to India, the question becomes this: Was the film viewed positively by the Indian political and educated elite, who might be provoked to set aside their amnesia and offer arguably as much assistance to these poor children as Western audiences?

Finally, a postcolonial feminist critique of global modernity's compelling visual artifacts can serve as an effective pedagogical tool to challenge our students to debate the representations and implications of globalization for marginalized constituencies. How do the visual images of globalization immunize us from questioning its democratic promises of consumer utopia for the world? Applebaum and Robinson (2005) chart the future agenda for a critical globalization studies that is centrally concerned with the uneven path of neocolonial capital, an agenda that challenges the proposition that an inevitable liability of progress is the creation of abjection and poverty for some and not for others. One key recommendation in their endeavor to promote dialogue between academic discourse and movements of social justice involves the rigorous interrogation of the fundamental meanings of globalization: "Debate over the meaning of essentially contested concepts such as globalization goes beyond mere semantics. The contending battleground of such concepts is a leading edge of political conflict. Their meanings are closely related to the problems they seek to discuss and what kind of social action people will engage in" (p. xiv). George (2005), a leader in the global justice movement, calls on academics to turn their classrooms into an arena for the transnational educated elite to engage precisely in such debates over globalization and the responsibilities of global citizenship; she thus asks, "What should be the role and the responsibilities of academia and intellectuals in the global justice movement?" Progressive academics, she writes, must resist the temptation "to transmit the received wisdom" and "acquire a vested interest in mainstream interpretations of a given reality" (George, 2005, p. 5). They must "make explicit these [mainstream] presuppositions and visible this ideological framework, particularly for their students" (George, 2005, p. 6).

Encouraging students to think in multidimensional ways about historical contexts and the formation of global audiences, academics can deploy the very visual artifacts that students are immersed in, not merely to authenticate or liven up lectures, but as pedagogical material that can provoke thoughtful interrogation of the power relations among nations, classes, races, and men and women. Studying global visual media in a sense is always already a study of the nexus among powerful forces of multinational corporate capital and elite transnational producers and marketers, although the audiences interpellated by the fantasies of these media may belong to a wide range of socioeconomic strata. Thus, despite some media ethnographers' dismissal of visual-textual studies as removed from "real" audiences, creative and ethnographic analyses of the performative lives of visual images can aid the postcolonial feminist project of contesting the masculinist, colonial, and capitalist edifices of a multitude of representations. Analyzing the visual culture of the powerful and privileged classes in India *and* the West, classes whose shared habitus may include the *National Geographic, Newsweek,* and the *Wall Street Journal,* can reveal the transnational consolidation of specific ideologies of gender, nation, race, and class in multiple contexts (Parameswaran, 2001, 2004a).

REFERENCES

Abu-Lughod, L. (2005). *Dramas of nationhood: The politics of television in Egypt.* Chicago: University of Chicago Press.

Alloula, M. (1986). *The colonial harem* (M. Godzich & W. Godzich, Trans.). Minneapolis: University of Minnesota Press.

Appadurai, A. (1996). *Modernity at large: Cultural dimensions of globalization.* Minneapolis: University of Minnesota Press.

Appadurai, A., & Breckenridge, C. (1995). Public modernity in India. In C. Breckenridge (Ed.), *Consuming modernity: Public culture in a South Asian world* (pp. 1–20). Minneapolis: University of Minnesota Press.

Applebaum, R., & Robinson, W. (2005). Introduction: Toward a critical globalization studies. In R. Applebaum & W. Robinson (Eds.), *Critical globalization studies* (pp. xi–xxxiii). New York: Taylor & Francis.

Barnhurst, K., Vari, M., & Rodriguez, I. (2004). Mapping visual studies in communication. *Journal of Communication, 54,* 616–644.

Berger, J. (2002). The ambiguity of the photograph. In K. Askew & R. Wilk (Eds.), *The anthropology of media: A reader* (pp. 47–55). Oxford, UK: Blackwell.

Chaney, D. (1993). *Fictions of collective life: Public drama in late modern culture.* New York: Routledge.

Chatterjee, P. (1989). Colonialism, nationalism, and the colonialized women: The contest in India. *American Ethnologist, 16,* 622–633.

Conquergood, D. (1998). Beyond the text: Toward a performative cultural politics. In S. Dailey (Ed.), *The future of performance studies* (pp. 25–36). Annandale, VA: National Communication Association.

Crary, J. (1988). Modernizing vision. In H. Foster (Ed.), *Vision and visuality* (pp. 29–44). Seattle, WA: Bay Press Inc.

Dahlgren, P., & Chakrapani, S. (1982). The Third World on TV news. In W. C. Adams (Ed.), *Television coverage of international affairs* (pp. 48–60). Norwood, NJ: Ablex.

Derne, S. (2005). Globalization and the making of a transnational class: Implications for class analysis. In R. Applebaum & W. Robinson (Eds.), *Critical globalization studies* (pp. 177–186). New York: Taylor & Francis.

Eileraas, K. (2003). Reframing the colonial gaze: Photography, ownership, and feminist resistance. *MLN, 118,* 807–840.

Faris, J. (2002). The gaze of Western humanism. In K. Askew & R. Wilk (Eds.), *The anthropology of media: A reader* (pp. 77–91). Oxford, UK: Blackwell.

Fernandes, L. (2000). Nationalizing the global: Media images, cultural politics, and the middle class in India. *Media, Culture, and Society, 22,* 611–628.

Foucault, M. (1973). *The order of things: An archaeology of the human sciences.* New York: Vintage.

George, S. (2005). If you want to be relevant: Advice to the academic from a scholar-activist. In R. Applebaum & W. Robinson (Eds.), *Critical globalization studies* (pp. 3–10). New York: Taylor & Francis.

Ginsburg, A., Abu-Lughod, L., & Larkin, B. (Eds.). (2002). *Media worlds: Anthropology on new terrain.* Berkeley: University of California Press.

Grewal, I. (1996). *Home and harem: Nation, gender, empire, and the cultures of travel.* Durham, NC: Duke University Press.

Grewal, I. (1999). Traveling Barbie: Indian transnationality and new consumer subjects. *Positions, 7,* 799–824.

Grewal, I., & Kaplan, C. (1994). *Scattered hegemonies: Postmodernity and transnational feminist practices.* Minneapolis: University of Minnesota Press.

Hall, S. (1996). New ethnicities. In D. Morley & K. Chen (Eds.), *Stuart Hall: Critical dialogues in cultural studies* (pp. 441–449). London: Routledge.

Hartley, J. (1996). *Popular reality: Journalism, modernity, popular culture.* New York: St. Martin's.

Harvey, D. (2000). *Spaces of hope.* Berkeley: University of California Press.

Hill Collins, P. (1995). Pornography and Black women's bodies. In G. Dines & J. Humez (Eds.), *Gender, race, and class in media* (pp. 279–286). Thousand Oaks, CA: Sage.

Kandiyoti, D. (1991). Identity and its discontents: Women and the nation. *Millennium: Journal of International Studies, 20,* 429–443.

Khilnani, S. (1997). *The idea of India.* New York: Farrar, Straus & Giroux.

Kotchimedova, C. (2005). When we say "cheese": Producing the smile in snapshot photography. *Critical Studies in Media Communication, 22*(1), 2–25.

Kumar, S. (2004). Inside the home theatre: The hyperreal world of television in India. *South Asian Popular Culture, 2*(2), 127–144.

Lalvani, S. (1995). Consuming the exotic other. *Critical Studies in Mass Communication, 12*(3), 263–286.

Leach, W. (1989). Strategies of display and the production of desire. In S. J. Bonner (Ed.), *Consuming visions: Accumulation and display of goods in America, 1890–1980* (pp. 99–132). New York: Norton.

Lears, J. (1989). Beyond Veblen: Rethinking consumer culture in America. In S. J. Bronner (Ed.), *Consuming visions: Accumulation and display of goods in America, 1880–1920* (pp. 73–97). New York: Norton.

Lutz, C., & Collins, J. (2002). The color of sex: Postwar photographic histories of race and gender. In K. Askew & R. Wilk (Eds.), *The anthropology of media: A reader* (pp. 92–116). Oxford, UK: Blackwell.

Mallapragada, M. (2005). Home, homeland, homepage: Belonging and the Indian-American web. *New Media & Society, 8*(2), 207–227.

Mani, L. (1991). Cultural theory and colonial texts. In L. Grossberg, C. Nelson, & P. Treichler (Eds.), *Cultural studies* (pp. 392–408). New York: Routledge.

Mankekar, P. (1993). *Reconstituting Indian womanhood: An ethnography of television viewers in a North Indian city.* Unpublished doctoral dissertation, University of Washington, Seattle.

Mankekar, P. (1999). *Screening culture, viewing politics: An ethnography of television, womanhood, and nation.* Durham, NC: Duke University Press.

Marcus, G. (1995). Ethnography in/of the world system: The emergence of multi-sited ethnography. *Annual Review of Anthropology, 24,* 95–117.

Mittelman, J. (2005). What is a critical globalization studies? In R. Applebaum & W. Robinson (Eds.), *Critical globalization studies* (pp. 19–32). New York: Taylor & Francis.

Moghadam, V. M. (Ed.). (1994). *Identity politics and women: Cultural reassertions and feminisms in international perspective.* Boulder, CO: Westview.

Mohanty, C. (1991a). Introduction: Cartographies of struggle. In C. T. Mohanty, A. Russo, & L. Torres (Eds.), *Third World women and the politics of feminism* (pp.1–47). Bloomington: Indiana University Press.

Mohanty, C. (1991b). Under Western eyes: Feminist scholarship and Western discourses. In C. T. Mohanty, A. Russo, & L. Torres (Eds.), *Third World women and the politics of feminism* (pp. 51–80). Bloomington: Indiana University Press.

Mukurjea, D. N., Shekar, M., Radhakrishna, G. S., Sen, S., & Dhawan, R. (1998, July 22). Seductive South. *Business World,* pp. 18–25.

Munshi, S. (1998). Wife/mother/daughter-in-law: Multiple avatars of homemaker in 1990s Indian advertising. *Media, Culture & Society, 20,* 573–591.

Nayar, S. (2004). Invisible representation. *Film Quarterly, 57*(3), 13–23.

Oza, R. (2001). Showcasing India: Gender, geography, and globalization. *Signs, 26,* 1067–1096.

Parameswaran, R. (1996). Coverage of bride burning in the *Dallas Observer:* A cultural analysis of the other. *Frontiers: A Journal of Women's Studies, 16*(2/3), 69–100.

Parameswaran, R. (2001). Global media events in India: Contests over beauty, gender, and nation. *Journalism & Communication Monographs, 3*(2), 51–105.

Parameswaran, R. (2002). Reading fictions of romance: Gender, sexuality, and nationalism in postcolonial India. *Journal of Communication, 52,* 832–851.

Parameswaran, R. (2004a). Global queens, national celebrities: Tales of feminine empowerment in post-liberalization India. *Critical Studies in Media Communication, 21,* 346–370.

Parameswaran, R. (2004b). Spectacles of gender and globalization in India: Mapping Miss World's media event space in India. *Communication Review, 7,* 371–406.

Rajagopal, A. (1998). Advertising, politics, and the sentimental education of the Indian consumer. *Visual Anthropology Review, 14*(2), 14–31.

Ramesh, R. (2006, April 5). *A tale of two Indias.* Retrieved April 14, 2006, from htttp://www.guardian.co.uk

Robinson, W. (2005). What is a critical globalization studies? Intellectual labor and global society. In R. Applebaum & W. Robinson (Eds.), *Critical globalization studies* (pp. 11–18). New York: Taylor & Francis.

Said, E. (1978). *Orientalism.* New York: Vintage.

Sainath, P. (2001, June). None so blind as those who will not see. *Unesco Courier,* pp. 44–46.

Sangari, K. (1991). Response to Susie Tharu, 'Women writing in India.' *Journal of Arts and Ideas, 20*(1), 56–59.

Schein, L. (1994). The consumption of color and the politics of white skin in post-Mao China. *Social Text, 41,* 141–164.

Schein, L. (2000). *Minority rules: The Miao and the feminine in China's cultural politics.* Durham, NC: Duke University Press.

Scott, C. (1996). Sushmita and Aishwarya: Symbols of national pride? *Voices: A Journal on Communication for Development, 4*(3), 16–18.

Sesser, S. (2006, February 4–5). A passage to India's future. *Wall Street Journal,* pp. 1, 4.

Shohat, E., & Stam, R. (2002). The imperial imaginary. In K. Askew & R. Wilk (Eds.), *The anthropology of media: A reader* (pp. 117–147). Oxford, UK: Blackwell.

Shome, R., & Hegde, R. (2002). Culture, communication, and the challenge of globalization. *Critical Studies in Media Communication, 26,* 172–189.

Steele, J. (1996). Reduced to images: American Indians in nineteenth century advertising. In E. Bird (Ed.), *Dressed in feathers: The construction of the Indian in American popular culture* (pp. 17–42). Boulder, CO: Westview.

Stepan, N. (1990). Race and gender: The role of analogy in science. In D. T. Goldberg (Ed.), *The anatomy of racism* (pp. 38–57). Minneapolis: University of Minnesota Press.

Stoler, A. L., & Cooper, F. (1997). Between metropole and colony. In A. L. Stoler & F. Cooper (Eds.), *Tensions of empire: Colonial cultures in a bourgeois world* (pp. 1–56). Berkeley: University of California Press.

Strine, M. (1998). Mapping the 'cultural turn' in performance studies. In S. Dailey (Ed.), *The future of performance studies* (pp. 3–9). Annandale, VA: National Communication Association.

Sunder Rajan, R. (1993). *Real and imagined women.* London: Routledge.

Wang, Y. (2005). The art of screen passing: Anna May Wong's yellow yellowface performance in the art deco era. *Camera Obscura, 20*(60), 159–191.

Wiegman, R. (1995). *American anatomies: Theorizing race and gender.* Durham, NC: Duke University Press.

Williams, R. (1982). *Dream worlds: Mass consumption in late nineteenth century France.* Berkeley: University of California Press.

Zacharias, U. (2003). The smile of Mona Lisa: Postcolonial desires, nationalist families, and the birth of television in India. *Critical Studies in Media Communication, 20,* 388–406.

Part IV

POWER, TRUTH, ETHICS, AND SOCIAL JUSTICE

With the eight chapters in Part IV, the handbook comes full circle. Each chapter in this section connects indigenous theories, pedagogies, and modes of inquiry with emancipatory discourses. Each works through and around, even if indirectly, critical theory and critical pedagogy. (The ghost of Paulo Freire is on every page.) Each chapter is a call to work through a progressive, indigenous politics of critical inquiry, and each works against the backdrop of global capitalism and neoliberal political, economic, and educational ideologies. Each charts a path into this new decade, the Decade of Critical Indigenous Inquiry. In this decade, there will be a thorough-going transition from discourses about and on method, to discourses centering on power, ethics, and social justice. This discourse will bring new meanings to these terms. It will also involve a rethinking of terms such as *democracy, science,* and *education.*

Kaupapa Māri as Theory

According to Russell Bishop, kaupapa Māori is a discourse of proactive theory and practice aimed at giving Māori increased self-determination and autonomy in their own lives. Kaupapa Māori is an indigenous theory. It asks that individuals be free to determine their own goals and make sense of their world in terms of culturally meaningful terms. This call for autonomy is not a call for separatism, but rather is an invitation for a dialogue between Māori and non-Māori. It asks that work done with Māori be initiated by Māori, benefit them, represent them without prejudice, be legitimated in terms of key Māori values, and be done by researchers who are accountable for the consequences of their work.

These understandings translate into a culturally responsive pedagogy. This pedagogy, which is implemented in the classroom, also extends into family, community, Māori culture, and language. It rests on how caring, dialogic, mutually responsible relations are established. Within this framework, a culturally responsive pedagogy of relations is put into practice.

Bishop demonstrates, with case materials including the Effective Teaching Profile, how this pedagogy works. Its implementation rests on the production of trusting, caring, dialogic relationships between teachers and students. This implementation involves collaborative storytelling, the construction of counternarratives, and the creation of classrooms as discursive, sacred spaces where Māori values were experienced. Out of these practices emerged students who were able to exercise self-determination in their own education, students able to achieve their own sense of cultural autonomy and healthy well-being.

Indigenous Models of Governance

Tim Begaye reads the violent history of modern democracy in the United States through Native American eyes. Based on his reading of Native American models of democracy, he outlines the essential features of democracy. It involves an emphasis on inclusion and the free and full participation of all members of a society in civic discourse, regardless of social or political status, gender, ethnicity, or race. He elaborates this model with examples drawn from the models of democracy that were employed by the Iroquois Confederacy, the Cherokees, Mississippi Choctaw, the White Mountain Apaches, and the Navajo Nation. The architects of American democracy subverted this full-inclusion model when they wrote the U.S. Constitution. They denied citizenship rights to Native Americans, African Americans, and women as well as to slaves.

The American model of democracy did not give freedom and justice to all. Begaye reviews the history of the treatment of Native Americans from 1778 to the present, noting how the sovereign rights of tribal groups were continually violated and eroded under U.S. law. In 1830, the U.S. Supreme court ruled that all tribal groups would be considered domestic dependent nations. In 1887, the Dawes Act authorized the president of the United States to survey Native American tribal lands and divide the areas into allotments for individual Native American families, not tribal communities. Over the 47 years of the act's life, about 90 million acres of treaty land—about two thirds of the 1887 land base—were lost to Native Americans, and about 90,000 Indians were made landless. In 1934, Congress passed the Indian Reorganization Act, giving the government the right to approve or disapprove all activities of tribal governments.

This depressing history underscores the need for the return of full sovereignty to all Native Americans. Their indigenous models of democracy should be allowed to flourish under full federal financial sponsorship. Begaye closes with this note: "In a truly legitimate democratic society, the discussion of democracy and education would be irrelevant because everyone would be free to participate and express themselves regarding the welfare of the community or society." Sadly, this has not been the case for Native Americans in the United States.

▣ Rethinking Collaboration

Jones and Jenkins (writing as a single voice) criticize the desire for collaborative inquiry between indigenous and settler colleagues. They trouble this desire and this relationship, noting that this binary does not represent two fixed, radically different, homogeneous groups. (Few indigenous persons have escaped even partial assimilation into the White culture.) Furthermore, the desire for collaboration between the two groups may, in fact, represent an unwitting imperialist demand and "thereby [be] in danger of strengthening the very impulses it seeks to combat."

Jones and Jenkins work both sides of the indigene-colonizer hyphen, asking who speaks for whom. Jones writes as a Pakeha, a White woman, a member of settler society. Jenkins writes as a Māori. Their interconnected discourse exposes the "inevitable tangle of caution, passion, ignorance, ambivalence, desire, and power that attends" the indigene-colonizer collaborating relationship. This tangle is exposed in the differing interpretations they offer of the first sermon in New Zealand by Samuel Mardsen of the Church Missionary Society, on Christmas Day 1814. Each tells the story differently, such that it no longer appears to be the same event.

The hyphen that connects Māori and non- Māori defines a colonial relationship; that is, each term forces the other into being. The hyphen can never be erased. There may be, however, an impulse for indigenous (and nonindigenous) persons to write from both sides of the hyphen—the outsider-within. This is an impossibility. Nonetheless, collaborative inquiry can be guided by a set of ethical principles that include respect, care, equity, empathy, a commitment to fairness, and a commitment to honoring indigenous culture and its histories. Indigene-colonizer collaboration can then become a site of "learning *from* difference rather than learning *about* the Other." Such a commitment respects and upholds difference, understanding that the Other is fundamentally unknowable, visible only in their cultural performances.

In unraveling this complex hyphen, they cut to the core of critical indigenous inquiry, exposing the boundaries and limits of the collaborative model. We all stand exposed in these spaces that connect us to one another.

▣ Indigenous Science Education

Gregory Cajete moves the conversation into the educational arena, outlining principles and orientations for the development of indigenous science education. These orientations embody a culturally based approach to indigenous education. They represent new developments in a long and tenuous history of Native American schooling. As such, they reflect a commitment to "self-determination, community education, and a renaissance of American Indian identity."

Cajete briefly reviews the history of the attempts by Euro-Americans to educate American Indians under missionary and governmental models. Early missionary and government teachers assumed that Native Americans had no education at all and that their mission was to remedy this "great ignorance." In reality, every Native American tribe had its "own system of enculturation that involved a wide variety of learning strategies." Traditional American Indian systems of educating "were characterized by observation, participation, assimilation, and experiential learning." Native education was interactive, based on tutor-student relationships, and relied on intrapersonal, interpersonal, kinesthetic, and spatial learning "as expressed in oral language and active involvement within tribal culture."

Cajete outlines standards for a Native American curriculum, emphasizing the importance of storytelling, tutoring, dreaming, ritual, and ceremony in this process. Indigenous knowledge (and science) is experiential, holistic, contextual, empirical, communal, spiritual, inclusive, and cooperative. He argues that "most American Indian groups recognize seven orientations: the four cardinal directions, north, south, east, and west; the center; . . . [and] the Above and the Below, the below representing the earth and the above, the celestial." This cosmology, with the four sacred and symbolic cardinal directions, has traditionally oriented Native American life. Effective indigenous education is fitted to this cosmology.

▣ Indigenous Research Ethics

Marie Battiste offers a set of research ethics for protecting indigenous knowledge and heritage. These ethical principles specify institutional and researcher responsibilities. These principles are based on the guidelines developed by the Mi'kmaq Nation and the Mi'kmaw Ethics Watch (*Ethics Eskinuapimk*). Battiste helped write these guidelines, as she is a member of this tribal community. She writes that they represent significant steps "toward ensuring Mi'kmaw people's self-determination and the protection of our cultural and intellectual property." The Mi'kmaq community has a responsibility to educate aboriginal and nonaboriginal people about these principles.

Battiste, like Russell Bishop (Chapter 21), insists that indigenous people have control over their own knowledge. They must have mechanisms that will inform them when research is being done on, among, or with them. They must train people in protocols for doing research, and this must be research that will benefit, strengthen, and revitalize the community.

She is blunt: "Eurocentric research methods and ethics are issues of intellectual and cultural property rights." The challenge, as the previous chapters in this section argue, is how to create ethical mandates and ethical behavior in a "knowledge system contaminated by colonials and racism. Nowhere is this work more needed than in the universities that pride themselves on their discipline-specific research."

Mi'kmaw Ethics Watch oversees research proposals on behalf of the larger community, applying the following guidelines and principles that are taken from their Web site (http://mrc.uccb.ns.ca/prinpro.html):

1. Mi'kmaw people are the guardians and interpreters of their culture.

2. Mi'kmaw knowledge, culture, and arts are inextricably connected with their traditional lands, districts, and territories.

3. Mi'kmaw people have the right and obligation to exercise control to protect their cultural and intellectual properties and knowledge.

4. Mi'kmaw knowledge is collectively owned, discovered, used, and taught and so also must be collectively guarded by appropriate delegated or appointed collective(s) who will oversee these guidelines and process research proposals.

5. Each community shall have knowledge and control over their own community knowledge and shall negotiate locally respecting levels of authority.

Any research done in the community must be reviewed by the Ethics Watch. All research, study, or inquiry into Mi'kmaw knowledge, culture, and traditions involving any research partners belongs to the community and must be returned to that community.

All research on the Mi'kmaq should be as follows:

1. Research is to be approached as a negotiated partnership, taking into account all the interests of those who live in the community (or communities).

2. Participants shall be recognized and treated as equals in the research done instead of as "informants" or "subjects."

3. All research partners must show respect for language, traditions, and standards of the communities and uphold the highest standards of scholarly research.

4. All research scholars shall assume responsibility to learn the protocols and traditions of the local people with whom they do research and to be knowledgeable and sensitive to cultural practices and issues that ensure respect and accommodation to local norms.

5. All research partners shall provide descriptions of research processes in the participant's own language (written and oral), which shall include detailed explanations of the usefulness of study, potential benefits, and possible harmful effects on individuals, groups, and the environment. Researchers must clearly identify sponsors, purposes of the research, sources of financial support and investigators for the research (scholarly and corporate), tasks to be performed, information requested from Mi'kmaw people, participatory research processes, the publication plans for the results, and anticipated royalties for the research.

6. All consent disclosures shall be written in both Mi'kmaq and English, depending on the community norms. No coercion, constraint, or undue inducements shall be used to obtain consent. All individuals and communities have the right to decline or withdraw from participating at any time without penalties.

7. All research involving children (younger than age 14) or information obtained about personal histories of children will involve informed consent of parents or guardians.

8. All research partners shall inform participants in their own language about the use of data-gathering devices—tape, video recordings, photos, and physiological measurements—and how data will be used. They shall also provide information on the

anonymity or confidentiality of their participation and, if not possible, to inform the participant that anonymity is not possible. Participants shall be informed of possible consequences of their choice to remain in the research and their rights to withdraw consent or participation in the research at any time.

9. All research partners shall provide each person or partner involved in the research with information regarding the anticipated risks involved in their participation and any anticipated benefits.

10. All research partners must be duly informed of each research step along the way and be provided with information about the research process and the distribution of results and information.

11. All research partners should attempt to impart new skills into the community.

12. All research scholars shall invite Mi'kmaw participation in the interpretation and/or review of any conclusions drawn from the research to ensure accuracy and sensitivity of interpretation.

13. All research scholars should consider a variety of research processes, including qualitative and participatory research methods, and move beyond the dominant quantitative methods to empower indigenous voice and skills.

14. The Mi'kmaw Ethics Watch shall operate on the basis of self-determination of each community and consider the risks and benefits of research and the rights of individuals and collectives to be recognized and protected.

15. The Mi'kmaw Ethics Watch shall consider the credentials and intentions of each research project, its sensitivity to Mi'kmaw culture and heritage, and how the research can benefit the community.

16. The Mi'kmaw Ethics Watch shall consider problems surrounding the purchase or publication of private materials and removal of artifacts. Private papers, photographs, or artistic productions are protected under copyright. One cannot legally cite, reproduce, publish, refer to, or distribute documents without permission from the authors, heirs, or institutions that hold copyright. Any research involving collection of human genes or Mi'kmaw genetic material or involving the Human Genome Diversity Project shall be rejected or considered only as to its benefits to the Mi'kmaq people.

17. The Mi'kmaw Ethics Watch shall increase efforts to educate each community and its individuals to the issues, concerns, benefits, and risks of research involving Mi'kmaq people, heritage, and environment and promote ethical conduct and conformity concerning protocols and guidelines for doing research in and about indigenous peoples with some kind of disciplinary action against those who do not comply.

18. The Mi'kmaw Ethics Watch shall consider the context of the research being requested and the issues of power and control that influence research topics, questions, and results.

19. The Mi'kmaw Ethics Watch shall encourage researchers to consult with and interpret the research from the tribal perspective and to make research and results available to Mi'kmaw people in their own language(s) and/or orthographies.

These ethical guidelines are typical of the kinds of procedures that now regulate inquiry in indigenous communities. They represent ways of bringing control back into the local community. They also represent ways of decolonizing inquiry.

Justice as Healing

Wanda McCaslin, a Metis from northern Saskatchewan, and Denise Breton, a White American of Celtic ancestry, present an indigenous, decolonizing view of justice as healing. Seeking to get outside the colonizer's cage, they criticize the Eurocentric criminal justice system, which treats the law within a coercive "might makes right" framework. Implementing a version of critical legal theory, they assert that Western law implements the perspective of those who hold economic and political power in a society. They show how this legal model (legal positivism) has oppressed indigenous persons. It has caused great harm and destruction in Native communities while undermining indigenous concepts of natural law.

They advocate a restorative view of justice that is based on indigenous ways of healing, not scapegoating and punishing "offenders."[1] Restorative justice represents a paradigm shift; violations to persons and their properties are regarded as violations of relationship and only secondarily of the law. Punishment of offenders, as in the traditional legal system, is not practiced. The key features include speaking the truth, healing, respect, provision of equal voice, and prevention of future harm. Restorative justice can be achieved through various practices, "including mediation, sentencing circles, healing circles, and community conferencing" (Groh, 2005, p. 182).

Restorative justice is a spiritual process that celebrates balance, harmony, and making persons whole again. It honors the intrinsic worth and good of each person. Healing is not about fixing persons but about transforming relationships, about being good relatives and good neighbors. Healing is spiritual, involving "sincere and genuine efforts by all those involved to practice values such as fairness, honesty, compassion, harmony, inclusiveness, trust, humility, openness, and, most important, respect."

They show how this view of justice and healing was taken up by First Nation communities in Canada. A 2002 report, "Mapping the Healing Journey," draws on in-depth consultations with six First Nation communities. Community members emphasized how personal healing, national building, and decolonization go hand-in-hand. Decolonization is "the therapy most needed . . . it forms the critical 'fourth stage' of a four-stage process of community transformation." This four-stage process moves through the four seasons of healing: winter, springtime, summer, and fall. In winter, members are moved to begin the healing journey. In spring, hope runs high, but in the long, hot summer, paradoxes, resistances, and disillusionment set in. Fall pares back all the essential structures, leaving only those structures that support regeneration. These seasons of healing offer a framework for restorative justice work.

Healing and restorative justice, in contrast to colonial justice, works to restore dignity. It refuses to engage in negative labeling, including applying harmful labels to disempowered youth. This is the core challenge, to confront the colonizing cage that traps both indigenous and nonindigenous people in genocide, fraud, theft, institutional racism, and abuse. But restorative justice should not become yet another tool of colonizing institutions where the goal is not to heal the root harm of colonization but to find "new . . . ways for one people to dominate another." The goal is to remove the cage altogether, and to rebuild our "long houses, hogans, iglus, pueblos, wikiups, earth lodges, wigwams, plank houses, grass houses, or chickees."

The truth tribunals and truth commissions that confront "the immense harms of colonial oppression, as such as were held in South Africa, offer dramatic images of honoring Indigenous expressions, overturning colonial structures, and challenging their legitimacy." These tribunals are the topic of the next chapter.

South African Truth and Reconciliation Commissions

Antjie Krog, Nosisi Mpolweni-Zantsi, and Kopano Ratele offer a detailed interpretation, based on multiple readings, of the testimony given to the South African Truth and Reconciliation Commission by a South African mother, Mrs. Konile, who bore witness to her son's death. The Truth and Reconciliation Commission (TRC) was a court-like body assembled in South Africa after the end of apartheid. Anybody who felt they had been a victim of violence could come forward and be heard at the TRC. Perpetrators of violence could also give testimony and request amnesty from prosecution. The TRC was seen by many as a crucial component of the transition to full and free democracy in South Africa and, despite some flaws, is generally—though not universally—regarded as successful.

Mrs. Konile's narrative, which included a dream episode and an incident with a goat, was hard to understand. Mrs. Konile testified in her mother tongue. Difficulties arose when it was translated and an official transcript was produced. Her testimony seemed ill-fitting, strange, and incoherent. A deeper interpretation (and more accurate translation) suggested that her narrative was coherent and that she was resisting other frameworks that were imposed on her.

Within "a postcolonial context, a woman may appear either incoherent because of severe suffering or unintelligible because of oppression—while in fact she is neither. Within her indigenous framework she is logical and resilient in her knowledge or her loss and its devastating consequences in her life." Their collaborative method of interpretation allowed them to show how the dominant discourse was unable to hear the testimony of Mrs. Konile.

Hearing her voice in this way allows us to better understand how the TRC operated for indigenous South African persons. Indigenous methods allow this to happen, and at this level, they serve as vehicles for facilitating social justice initiatives.

The Transnational Indigenous Racial Subject

Luis Mirón notes that the large literature on globalization has spawned a counternarrative—namely, the critical examination of indigenous peoples. However, this discourse is at times held suspect because it at times lacks an honest engagement with race. Matters are complicated by work on transnationals, who occupy multiple spaces, possess hybrid identities and dual loyalties, and are not indigenous. Mirón suggests they are fluid, "nonnative" subjects.

He debunks the notion of a passive human subject trapped in the iron cage of globalization. Transnational, national, and indigenous subjects do have agency and use it to resist the global oppression of transnational forces. Advancing a model of performance ethnography and drawing on case study and life story materials, he charts a path that can bring marginalized racial subjects into new borderlands in dialogue and solidarity with one another. This entails a critique of the new nativism. At the same time, Mirón connects his model of performative ethnography with a grounded critical pedagogy ala McLaren and Henry Giroux and Susan Giroux (in this volume). For example, "Katrina victims and other racial subjects" can benefit from a ground-level critical pedagogy that is framed around the tenets of restorative justice.

Mirón advances the argument by asking, Where locally are the new spaces in which democratic practices such as dialogue, coalition building, negotiation, and consensus building can occur? Furthermore, in the context of globalization, where can transnational, national, and indigenous racial subjects meet? He suggests that critical pedagogy and performative ethnography are two sites where these processes can come together.

Conclusion

In the next decade, there will be renewed efforts to embed critical and indigenous methodologies in decolonizing discourses. These discourses will interrogate the ways in which power, ethics, and social justice intersect. Multiple models of justice will be explored. Feminist, communitarian ethics will be informed by the empowerment ethics of specific indigenous peoples. Indigenous and nonindigenous scholars will refine models of restorative justice that heal the wounds of globalization. They will develop new indigenous methodologies that better address the social and economic concerns of oppressed persons.

It is our hope that in the next decade, utopian dreams of universal social justice will be better realized. It is our belief that this handbook will help advance those causes.

Note

1. Elliot and Gordon (2005) offer a historical overview of the restorative justice movement, noting its connections to prior formations, including victim-offender mediation, the victims' rights movement, family group conferences, reintegrative shaming combined with the Wagga Wagga approach (New Zealand), and community justice forums (British Columbia).

References

Elliot, E., & Gordon, R. M. (2005). Introduction: Restorative justice and best practices. In E. Elliott & R. M. Gordon (Eds.), *New directions in restorative justice* (pp. xiii–xxiv). Cullompton, Devin, UK: Willan Publishing.

Groh, A. (2005). Restorative justice: A healing approach to elder abuse. In E. Elliott & R. M. Gordon (Eds.), *New directions in restorative justice* (pp. 175–192) Cullompton, Devin, UK: Willan Publishing.

21

TE KOTAHITANGA

Kaupapa Māori in Mainstream Classrooms

Russell Bishop

> *This then is the great humanistic and historical task of the oppressed: to liberate themselves and their oppressors as well. The oppressors, who oppress, exploit and rape by virtue of their power, cannot find in this power the strength to liberate either the oppressed or themselves. Only power that springs from the weakness of the oppressed will be sufficiently strong to free both.*
>
> —Paolo Freire (1972, p. 21)

Kaupapa Māori as Theory

Kaupapa Māori is a discourse of proactive theory and practice that emerged from within the wider revitalization of Māori communities that developed in New Zealand following the rapid Māori urbanization in the 1950s and 1960s. This movement grew further in the 1970s and, by the late 1980s, had developed as a political consciousness among Māori people that promoted the revitalization of Māori cultural aspirations, preferences, and practices as a philosophical and productive educational stance and resistance to the hegemony of the dominant discourse. As G. H. Smith (1997) explains,

> Māori communities armed with the new critical understandings of the shortcomings of the state and structural analyses began to assert transformative actions to deal with the twin crises of language demise and educational underachievement for themselves. (p. 171)

G. H. Smith (1997) explains that it is especially since the advent of Te Kohanga Reo (language nests: Māori medium preschools) in 1982 that kaupapa Māori has become "an influential and coherent philosophy and practice for Māori conscientisation, resistance and transformative praxis to advance Māori cultural capital and learning outcomes within education and schooling" (p. 423). The kaupapa Māori approach developed among Māori groups across a wide range of educational sectors, such as Te Kohanga Reo, Kura Kaupapa Māori (Māori medium schools), Wharekura (Māori medium secondary schools), and Waananga Māori (Māori tertiary institutions), and also included other groups such as the

NZ Māori Council, The Māori Congress, Māori Health and Welfare bodies, Iwi (tribal) Authorities, and, most recently, a Māori political party. For Māori, the specific intention was to achieve "increased autonomy over their own lives and cultural welfare" (G. H. Smith, 1992, p. 12). In education, this call for autonomy grew in response to the lack of programs and processes within existing educational institutions that were designed to "reinforce, support or proactively co-opt Māori cultural aspirations in ways which are desired by Māori themselves" (G. H. Smith, 1992, p. 12). G. H. Smith (1992) further suggests that the wish for autonomy also challenged the "increasing abdication by the State of its 1840 contractual obligation [The Treaty of Waitangi] to protect Māori cultural interests" (p. 10). In other words, if the government granted the right to govern in Article 1 of the Treaty of Waitangi (Durie, 1998) but was unable or unwilling to facilitate Māori protection of cultural treasures that were guaranteed in Article 2 of the treaty, then Māori groups would need to take on this task themselves.

This call for autonomy is operationalized in a kaupapa Māori approach as self-determination (*tino rangatiratanga*) by and for Māori people (Bishop, 1996; Durie, 1995, 1998; Pihama, Cram, & Walker, 2002; G. H. Smith, 1997; L. T. Smith, 1999). Self-determination, in Durie's (1995) terms, "captures a sense of Māori ownership and active control over the future" (p. 45). Such a position is consistent with the Treaty of Waitangi where Māori people are able "to determine their own policies, to actively participate in the development and interpretation of the law, to assume responsibility for their own affairs and to plan for the needs of future generations" (Durie, 1995, p. 45).

Nevertheless, despite self-determination meaning the right to determine one's own destiny, to define what that destiny will be, and to define and pursue means of attaining that destiny, there is a clear understanding among Māori people that such autonomy is relative, not absolute, that it is self-determination in *relation to others.* As such, Māori calls for self-determination are often misunderstood by non-Māori people. It is not a call for separatism or noninterference, nor is it a call for non-Māori people to stand back and leave Māori alone, in effect to relinquish all responsibility for the ongoing relationship between the peoples of New Zealand. Rather, it is a call for all those involved in education in New Zealand to reposition themselves in relation to these emerging aspirations of Māori people for an autonomous voice (Bishop, 1994; Durie, 1998; G. H. Smith, 1997). In other words, kaupapa Māori seeks to operationalize Māori people's aspirations to restructure power relationships to the point where partners can be autonomous and interact from this position rather than from one of subordination or dominance.

Young (2004), in considering the development of the notion of self-determination among Western nation-states, explains how this misunderstanding is caused because the dominant discourse on self-determination (which stands in contrast to indigenous people's understandings) speaks of self-determination in absolute terms. This dominant discourse on self-determination was informed by the development of sovereign nation-states, particularly following the two world wars of the 20th century, and posits that self-determination means sovereignty over a space and all the constituent activities within a designated boundary—a boundary that broaches no interference from outside. In other words, self-determination is related to territoriality. On the other hand, indigenous people's aspirations for self-determination are relational, acknowledge interdependence, and "are better understood as a quest for an institutional context of non-domination" (Young, 2004, p. 187). That is, being self-determining is possible if the relations in which peoples and individuals stand to each other are nondominating. To ensure nondomination, "their relations must be regulated both by institutions in which they all participate and by ongoing negotiations among them" (Young, 2004, p. 177).

The indigenous position on self-determination therefore in practice means that individuals should be free to determine their own goals and make sense of the world in their own culturally generated manner. However, as Young (2004), emphasizes, self-determining individuals cannot ignore their interdependence with others and the claims that others may have to their own self-determination. Therefore, the implications for educational institutions are that they should be structured and conducted in such a way, by the participants in these institutions, as to mediate these potential tensions by actively minimizing domination, coordinating actions, resolving conflicts, and negotiating relationships.

Māori attempts to promote this indigenous people's understanding of self-determination has been limited to date, and the most successful Māori education initiatives have been those that, on the surface at least, have most closely approximated the majority culture's notion of self-determination. Perhaps they have been successful because of this perceived approximation. Māori medium preschools, schools, and tertiary education institutions have been developed in recent years by Māori people themselves and have become a major success story among indigenous people's efforts to address the impact of colonization on their lives. However, these efforts have messages for the mainstream (where most Māori children are enrolled), for as G. H. Smith (1992, 1997) has suggested, these projects share some common elements that have formed out of the cycle of conscientization, resistance, and transformative praxis that typifies the struggle of Māori people. Although these elements arise from the Māori education sector, particularly Kura Kaupapa Māori, they may also speak to the "general crisis in schooling" for Māori.

This chapter sets out to examine what might constitute this "speaking to" the wider crisis in Māori education, particularly disparities in achievement in mainstream educational settings from Māori experiences of successful Māori innovations in education. This examination is further informed by a range of studies into effective innovation in Māori medium schooling (Alton-Lee, 2003; Bishop, Berryman, & Richardson, 2001; G. H. Smith, 1997) and focuses on, in particular, Māori metaphor that might provide solutions to the Māori educational crisis in mainstream settings. The metaphors used in this part of this chapter are those that G. H. Smith (1997) identifies as fundamental to Māori medium schooling (*rangatiratanga, taonga tuku iho, ako, kia pike ake, whanau,* and *kaupapa*) and are expanded here to provide a picture of what might constitute an appropriate pedagogy for Māori students in mainstream schools.

Rangatiratanga: Relative Autonomy/Self-Determination

Fundamental to Māori educational institutions is the concept of rangatiratanga. Literally, rangatiratanga means chiefly control, but increasingly, it has taken on its figurative meaning of self-determination, which, as described above, means the right to determine one's own destiny, to define what that destiny will be, and to define and pursue a means of attaining that destiny in *relation to others,* with this notion of relations being fundamental to Māori epistemologies. For example, Māori cultural practices for formally establishing relationships (*powhiri*), the complex set of interactions undertaken by people when meeting and greeting each other at the commencement of ceremonial and decision-making interactions (*hui*), illustrates the centrality of Māori understandings of self-determination to such events. These interactions contain metaphoric meaning in terms of both recognizing the *mana* (power/status) and *tapu* (the potentiality for power) of each participant while also acknowledging and ritualizing the necessary relatedness of the participants. In this way, a kaupapa Māori analysis of the metaphor fundamental to this discourse is both a means of proactively promoting a Māori worldview as legitimate, authoritative, and valid in relationship to other cultures in New Zealand and also is suggested here as a means of addressing educational disparities in New Zealand. In other words, it is suggested that educational relationships and interactions, predicated on a Māori understanding of self-determination that includes nondominating relations of interdependence, could well be a means of addressing the seemingly immutable problems of disparate achievement levels within mainstream educational institutions. In this way, issues of power relations, such as initiation, benefits, representation, legitimation, and accountability (see, e.g., Bishop, 2005, Table 5.1), will be addressed in totally different ways than they have been in the past, and as Bruner (1996) suggests, participation on one's own terms brings commitment, and commitment brings about learning (Applebee, 1996).

One way of implementing such an approach in classroom contexts is, as Beane (1997) suggests, to have children participate in the process of decision making about curriculum planning to the extent of participating in a pedagogy of sharing power over decisions about curriculum content and the directions that learning will take. In Applebee's (1996) terms, this is the process of developing and participating in knowledge-in-action and is far closer to what happens in real life. Scientists, for example, do not make discoveries by solely being recipients of the thinking processes of others. They use their own in a kaleidoscope of ways to investigate the natural world. Artists and writers also use a similar process.

Central to this concern is that the attempt to reduce disparities does not just focus on bringing low-achieving students up to the current levels of their peers by traditional means; rather, all students' achievement levels need to be raised so that educators can create learning contexts that will provide students with those tools that are vital for future citizens in a democracy—the tools of planning, relationships, creativity, critical reflection, and communication. In order to do so, we need to immerse students in power-sharing relationships with their peers and their teachers from an early age. In short, the principle of self-determination within nondominating relations of interdependence should be relevant to all involved in classroom interactions (including teachers, of course) and should raise educational achievement of all involved while reducing disparities.

Taonga Tuku Iho (Cultural Aspirations)

Literally meaning the treasures from the ancestors, this phrase nowadays is almost always used in its metaphoric sense as meaning the cultural aspirations that Māori people hold for their children and include those messages that guide our relationships and interaction patterns such as *manaakitanga* (caring), *kaitiakitanga* (oversight), and *mana motuhake* (respect for specialness). Above all, this message means that Māori language, knowledge, culture, and values are normal, valid, and legitimate and indeed are valid guides to classroom interactions. The implication of this principle for educational contexts is that educators need to create contexts where to be Māori is to be normal, where Māori cultural identities are valued, valid, and legitimate. In other words, where Māori children can be themselves.

Stereotyping of Māori children, however, needs to be avoided by classroom teachers; rather, it is important that learning relationships allow for the many realities within which Māori children might live and grow up: urban/rural, tribal/nontribal, rich/poor, and single-parent/dual-parent/extended families (Durie, 1998). A further dimension that needs consideration is the realization that individual identities are multifaceted and multigenerative. Students are no longer, if they ever were, monocultural. Indeed, some will have experiences of many cultural settings. As Kalantzis and Cope (1999) identify, "Just as there are multiple layers and facets to everyone's identity, so too there are multiple discourses of identity and multiple discourses of recognition to be negotiated" (p. 270). In short, a pedagogy is needed that is holistic, flexible, and complex, that will allow children to present their multiplicities and complexities and their individual and collective diversities, rather than a pedagogy that perpetuates teacher images.

Taonga tuku iho therefore teaches us to respect the tapu (potentiality for power) of each individual child and to acknowledge his or her mana (power) rather than ascribe cultural meanings to the child. Just as *manuhiri* (visitors) at a hui (meeting) must have their mana and tapu respected in the process of bringing them onto a *marae* (meeting place), so this image can guide us in our relationships with young people. In Kalantzis and Cope's (1999) terms, in order to recognize the diversity of lifestyles and their discursive practices, "learning processes need to recruit, rather than attempt to ignore and erase, the different subjectivities students bring to learning" (p. 270). This is because "individuals have at their disposal a complex range of representational resources, never of one culture, but of many cultures in their lived experience, the many layers of their identity and the many dimensions of their being" (p. 271). Taonga tuku iho, far from being a prescriptive set of knowledges to be transmitted for regurgitation, suggests a set of principles by which to live and interact with one another.

Ako (Reciprocal Learning)

Literally meaning to teach and to learn, this term metaphorically emphasizes reciprocal learning, which means that the teacher does not have to be the fountain of all knowledge but rather should be able to create contexts for learning where the students can enter the learning conversation. Teachers and students can take turns as in the metaphor of the conversation when storying and restorying their realities, either as individual learners or within a group context. Reciprocal learning also promotes, in Applebee's (1996) terms, learning as knowledge-in-action—that is, learning through participation in the discursive practices that creates knowledge in contrast to knowledge-out-of-context, which promotes learning *about,* often through transmission education practices. One implication of this principle is that active learning approaches are preferred because in this way, the processes of knowledge-in-action are able to be brought to the interaction—indeed, for the interaction. This means that students can participate using sense-making processes they bring to the relationship and share these with others, as a right, and this has clear implications for the type of classroom interactions and pedagogies that will be useful in promoting this vision.

Kia piki ake i nga raruraru o te kainga (Mediation of Socioeconomic and Home Difficulties)

Participation in Kura Kaupapa Māori reaches into Māori homes and brings parents and families into the activities of the school because it is understood that when parents are incorporated into the education of their children on terms they can understand and approve of, then children do better at school. This contention is well supported by research data (e.g., Durie, 1995; Glynn, Berryman, & Glynn, 2000; Glynn & Glynn, 1986). This feature also has implications for better and less problematic home-to-school transitions. These studies show that the closer that classroom and home experiences are for students, the more likely that students will be able to participate in the educational experiences designed at the school. This addresses the preference Māori people have for their problems to be dealt with in culturally familiar ways that intervene in the educational crisis in a way quite different from a socioeconomic status (SES) intervention, for example, because they deal with a collective entity through the promotion of culturally acceptable alternatives. As G. H. Smith (1992) explains, difficulties, such as those that are created by economic poverty, child relationships, and health and social issues, are resolved by a collective action that in turn involves individual responses and commitments.

Whanau (Extended Family)

Whanau is a primary concept (a cultural preference) that contains both values (cultural aspirations) and social processes (cultural practices) that has multiple meanings for mainstream education. The root word of *whanau* literally means family in its broad, "extended" sense. This generic concept of whanau subsumes other related concepts: *whanaunga* (relatives), *whanaungatanga* (relationships), *whakawhanaungatanga* (the process of establishing relationships), and *whakapapa* (literally, the means of establishing relationships). The term *whanau* is, as Metge (1990) explains, a term that Māori people can and do apply to a variety of categories and groups usually linked by blood ties. However, above all, the most rapid growth in the application of the term *whanau* has been in the metaphorical use of the term to refer to collectives of people working for a common end who are not connected by kinship, let alone descent, but act as if they were.

These metaphoric whanau attempt to develop relationships, organizations, and operational practices based on similar principles to those that order a traditional whanau. Metge (1990) explains that to use the term is to identify a series of rights and responsibilities, commitments and obligations, and supports that are fundamental to the collectivity. These are the *tikanga* (customs) of the whanau—warm interpersonal interactions, group solidarity, shared responsibility for one another, cheerful cooperation for group ends, corporate responsibility for group property, and material or nonmaterial (e.g., knowledge) items and issues. These attributes can be summed up in the words *aroha* (love in the broadest sense), *awhi* (helpfulness), *manaaki* (hospitality), and *tiaki* (guidance).

When imaging or theorizing classroom interactions in terms of, for example, metaphoric whanau relationships, classroom interactions will be fundamentally different from those created when teachers talk of method and process using machine or transmission metaphors to explain their theorizing/images. For example, in Bishop (1996, 2005), the centrality of whanau and the process of establishing extended family-like relationships was used metaphorically as a research strategy to address concerns about research initiation, benefits, representation, legitimation, and accountability created by the imposition of the researcher's agenda, concerns, and interests in the research process. This approach gave voice to a culturally positioned means of collaboratively constructing research stories in a culturally conscious and connected manner by focusing on the researcher's connectedness, engagement, and involvement with others in order to promote self-determination, agency, and voice of those involved in the interaction. Indeed, establishing and maintaining whanau-type relationships is a fundamental, often extensive and ongoing part of the research process. This involves the establishment of whanau of interest through a process of spiral discourse. This means establishing a whanau-like relationship among the research group and using collaborative storying and restorying (spiral discourse) as a means of creating a collective response.

Similarly, in classrooms where whanau-type relationships are established, commitment and connectedness would be paramount, and responsibility for the learning of others would be fostered. Furthermore, the classroom would be seen as an active location for all learners, and this includes the teachers, to participate in the decision-making processes through the medium of spiral discourse—a major means of addressing current power imbalances. Whanau processes may also be used, literally or metaphorically, to give substance to a culturally positioned and understood means of collaboratively constructing learning objectives and "texts" to promote culturally positioned self-determination, agency, and voice, as opposed to predetermined learning objectives and developing a commitment in learners and teachers to these objectives in a culturally conscious and connected manner.

Establishing whanau relationships in mainstream classrooms also addresses the power and control issues in a manner of, to use Heshusius's (1994) term, *participatory consciousness,* which facilitates the sharing of power and control. In classroom interactions, such an approach seeks to create a consciousness among educators where the metaphors of engagement are inclusive, dialogic, interactive, and participatory. The clear implication for classroom relationships is that where the establishment of whanau-type relationships in the classroom is primary, a pattern of interactions would develop where commitment and connectedness are paramount, where responsibility for the learning of others is fostered, and where the classroom becomes an active location for all learners to participate in decision-making processes through the process termed *spiral discourse.*

Kaupapa (Collective Vision, Philosophy)

Just as Kura Kaupapa Māori have a collective vision, a kaupapa provides guidelines for what constitutes excellence in Māori education that connects with "Māori aspirations, politically, socially, economically and spiritually" (G. H. Smith, 1992, p. 23). To do so, mainstream institutions need such a philosophy or agenda for achieving excellence in both languages and cultures that make up the world of Māori children. Such a kaupapa is essential for the development of education relations and interactions that will promote educational achievement and reduce disparities.

Implications of These Metaphors

This series of metaphors, drawn from the experiences of kaupapa Māori educational theorizing and practice and expanded here to address Māori students in mainstream settings, does provide us with a picture of the sort of alternative educational relations and interactions that are possible when educators draw upon an alternative culture than that previously dominant. This picture consists of a collective vision, focusing on the need to address Māori students' achievement that identifies the need for power over reciprocal decision making to be constituted within relationships and interactions constructed within a collective whanau context. Whanau relationships would enact reciprocal and collaborative pedagogies in order to promote educational relationships between students, between pupils and teachers (also between whanau members in decision making about the school), and between the home and the school as a means of promoting excellence in education. One wider indicator of this pattern is the development of inextricable two-way connections between the home and the school.

Such a pattern of metaphor also creates an image of classroom relations and interactions where students are able to participate on their own terms—terms that are determined by the student because the very pedagogic process holds this as a central value. Furthermore, the terms are to be culturally determined, through the incorporation and reference to the sense-making processes of the student. Learning is to be reciprocal and interactive, home and school learning is to be interrelated, and learners are to be connected to each other and learn with and from each other. In addition, a common set of goals and principles guides the process. Furthermore, just as using Māori metaphors for research repositions researchers within Māori sense-making contexts (Bishop, 1996, 2005), so too does using new metaphors for pedagogy reposition teachers within different contexts where students' sense-making processes offer new opportunities for them to engage with learning. In these contexts, learners' experiences, representations of these experiences, and sense-making processes are legitimated.

In detail, therefore, such a pattern of metaphor suggests that educators can create learning contexts that will address the learning engagement and improve the achievement of Māori students by developing learning-teaching relationships where the following notions are paramount:

- *Where power is shared:* Learners can initiate interactions, their right to self-determination over learning styles and sense-making processes are regarded as fundamental to power-sharing relationships, and collaborative critical reflection is part of an ongoing critique of power relationships.

- *Where culture counts:* Classrooms are places where learners can bring "who they are" to the learning interactions in complete safety, and their knowledges are "acceptable" and "legitimate."

- *Where learning is interactive and dialogic:* Learners are able to be co-inquirers (i.e., raising questions and evaluating questions and answers); learning is active, problem based, integrated, and holistic; learning positionings are reciprocal (ako) and knowledge is co-created; and classrooms are places where young people's sense-making processes and knowledges are validated and developed in collaboration with others.

- *Where connectedness is fundamental to relations:* Teachers are committed and inextricably connected to their students and the community and vice versa; school and home/parental aspirations are complementary.

- *Where there is a common vision:* There is a common agenda for what constitutes excellence for Māori in education.

In short, this is an education where power is shared between self-determining individuals within nondominating relations of interdependence, where culture counts, and where learning is interactive, dialogic, and spirals and participants are connected and committed to one another through the establishment of a common vision for what constitutes educational excellence. Drawing on Gay (2000) and Villegas and Lucas (2002), who identify the importance of a culturally responsive pedagogy, and Sidorkin (2002) and Cummins (1996), who propose that relations ontologically precede all other concerns in education, such a pattern might well be termed a *culturally responsive pedagogy of relations.*

A Culturally Responsive Pedagogy of Relations

With this framework in mind, this chapter now seeks to examine what a culturally responsive pedagogy of relations might look like in practice. To do this, a large-scale research project is examined. This project, called Te Kotahitanga, is one where Māori metaphors inform educational theorizing and practice in ways that seeks to mediate the ongoing educational crisis facing Māori people in mainstream education from within a kaupapa Māori framework.

Te Kotahitanga: Improving the Educational Achievement of Māori Students in Mainstream Schools (Bishop, Berryman, Tiakiwai, & Richardson, 2003) is a kaupapa Māori research/professional development project that aims to improve the educational achievement of Māori students through operationalizing Māori people's cultural aspirations for self-determination within nondominating relations of interdependence by developing classroom relations and interactions and in-school institutions for this purpose.

The project commenced in 2001, seeking to address the self-determination of Māori secondary school students by talking with them and other participants in their education about just what is involved in limiting and/or improving their educational achievement through an examination of the main influences on Māori students' educational achievement. The project sought to examine how a number of groups might address this issue and commenced with the gathering of narratives of students' classroom experiences and meanings by the process of collaborative storying (Bishop, 1996) from a range of engaged and nonengaged Māori students (as defined by their schools), in five nonstructurally modified mainstream secondary schools. These stories were also complemented by gathering stories of experience and meaning from those parenting these students, as well the students' principals and their teachers.

Cook-Sather (2002, p. 3) suggests that an approach that authorizes student perspectives is essential to reform education because of the various ways that it can improve educational practice, reinform existing conversations about educational reform, and point to the discussions and reform effects yet to be undertaken. From a detailed analysis of the literature, she identified that such authorizing of students' experiences and understandings can directly improve educational practice in that when teachers listen to and learn from students, they can begin to see the world from the perspective of those students. This, in turn, can help teachers make what they teach more accessible to students. These actions can also contribute to the conceptualization of teaching, learning, and the ways we study as being more collaborative processes. Furthermore, students can feel empowered when they are taken seriously and attended to as knowledgeable participants in learning conversations, and they can be motivated to participate constructively in their education. In addition, she further identifies that authorizing students' perspectives is a major way of addressing power imbalances in classrooms in order for students' voices to have legitimacy in the learning setting.

Such understandings inform this project for it is a kaupapa Māori position that when teachers share their power with students, they will better understand the world of the "others" and those "othered" by power differentials, and students will be better able to successfully participate and engage in educational systems on their own culturally constituted terms. In turn, teachers will create culturally appropriate and responsive contexts for learning (Bishop et al., 2003; Gay, 2000) through drawing on a different pattern of metaphor such as described earlier. In this way, Māori students will be able to interact with teachers and others in ways that legitimate who they are and how they make sense of the world. It is suggested that such positive, inclusive interactions will lead to improved student engagement in learning. Numerous studies (Applebee, 1996; Bruner, 1996; Fisher et al., 1981; Widdowson, Dixon, & Moore, 1996) identify that improving student engagement is a necessary condition for improving educational achievement. Furthermore, improved student on-task engagement has been identified as a moderate to good predictor of long-term student achievement (Fisher et al., 1981; Gage & Berliner, 1992; Widdowson et al., 1996; Ysseldyke & Christianson, 1998).

Fundamental to kaupapa Māori theorizing is an analysis of that which might limit Māori advancement in education. Therefore, as part of this project, in addition to the narratives of the students, those parenting the students, the students' principals (as the agenda setters of the schools), and a representation of the students' teachers (approximately 23% of the teachers in the five schools) were also asked to narrate their experiences in order to develop narratives of the experiences and involvement of these groups in the education of Māori students. In this way, the students' experiences could be understood within the wider context of their education and their lives in general. The analysis of these narratives provided some very illuminating information about the positions taken by people in relation to one another, the consequent pattern of interdependence, and the potential of a variety of discursive positionings for perpetuating or offering solutions to the problem of educational disparities.

The Students

While there were differences between the experiences of the engaged and nonengaged students, most students reported that being Māori in a mainstream secondary school was a negative experience for them. Few reported that being Māori in their classrooms, currently or in the past, was a positive experience. Furthermore, most of the students identified that the relationships they have with their teachers were the most influential factor in their ability to achieve in the classroom. In particular, the students emphasized that the ways in which teachers taught—that is, how they interacted with Māori students—influenced them into either becoming engaged in their learning or not. To a lesser extent, students identified how issues related to their home experiences and to structural issues within the school affected their learning and contributed to their educational experience being less productive. Overall, the majority of the students interviewed wanted to be able to attend school, to have positive educational experiences, and to achieve. Most of all, however, they wanted to be able to do this as Māori.

In so doing, they alerted us of the need for education to be responsive to them as culturally located people and, in this way, to the emerging literature on the creation of learning contexts and how these contexts might be constituted as appropriate and responsive to the culturally generated sense-making processes of the students. This notion of cultural responsiveness (after Gay, 2000; Nieto, 2000) offers a means whereby teachers can acknowledge and address Māori students' self-determination within their classrooms by creating learning contexts wherein the learning relationships and interactions are such that Māori students can bring themselves into what Grumet (1995) terms the "conversation that makes sense of the world."

Those Parenting (Whanau)

Those parenting Māori students (their whanau) identified that the major influence on Māori students' educational achievement was the quality of their children's relationship with their teachers. These whanau members acknowledged that they had to take some responsibility for ensuring their child did well in the educational setting and that the relationship they had with their children contributed to their success at school. However, there remained a strong expectation that schools should take some responsibility for providing their children with good experiences. If this was to be achieved, according to the whanau members, the schools and the teachers needed to have a greater understanding of things Māori, including the reality that Māori people have their own cultural values, aspirations, and ways of knowing. This realization was seen as vital so as to allow the culture of the child to be present, recognized, and respected within the school and the classroom. This expectation was also raised by both student groups.

The Principals

Like the students and those parenting, the principals also drew primarily upon the discourse of relationships to identify the main influences on Māori students' educational achievement. In particular, the principals identified that the attitude of the teacher was crucial to the development of positive learning relationships between the teacher and their Māori students. Teachers' low expectations of Māori students and the need for teachers to adjust to the individual learning requirements of their students were also identified as critical factors.

The principals identified that one way teachers might facilitate a more responsive relationship was by recognizing Māori students' culture and taking cognizance of Māori cultural aspirations and notions of belonging. They identified that developing more culturally responsive relationships required schools to build Māori pedagogies that went beyond the limited inclusion of Māori cultural iconography into their curriculum and programs. This type of initiative was seen by principals as a means of enhancing the relationships between Māori students and staff, as well as a means of gaining positive support from parents of Māori students. Pivotal to this was the building and maintaining of relationships with their Māori communities.

The Teachers

Contrary to the narratives of experience provided by the students, those parenting, and the principals, most teachers identified factors from within the discourse of the child and the home as having the greatest influence on Māori students' educational achievement. In particular, teachers perceived deficits within the home or problems that Māori students brought with them to school from home as having the major influence on Māori students' educational achievement.

In terms of influences outside of the school, teachers identified problems of home background and socioeconomic problems, leading to greater mobility and transience of Māori students, as being problematic. Deficit influences were further elaborated by teachers' perceptions of Māori students' lack of access to resources, inadequate nutrition, condoned absenteeism, access to drugs and alcohol, other antisocial behaviors in the community, participation in work outside of school, and inadequate parental support or positive role models.

In addition, teachers identified the problems that Māori students cause when they are at school. Teachers argued that Māori student underachievement was the result of the low-level aspirations of Māori students and their lack of motivation and poor behavior. Teachers also spoke of the negative influence of peers (Māori) and the wasted talent of Māori students being unwilling to stand out from the crowd (a perceived cultural issue). Teachers identified that Māori students were disorganized, not prepared for their classes or for learning, and difficult to discipline. Many teachers expressed a great deal of disillusionment about their ability to effect change in the face of these constant pressures.

Although teachers as a group were less convinced that in-class relationships were of importance to Māori students' educational achievement, a small group of teachers did identify that positive relationships were built in their classrooms through their respecting the cultural knowledge and aspirations of Māori students. They further suggested that these actions resulted in improved student behavior, engagement, and involvement in learning.

The teachers identified that structural and systemic issues had the least influence on Māori students' educational achievement. These included curriculum demands being placed on teachers and high student and staff turnover.

Overall, however, the teachers argued strongly about the perceived deficits of the child/home as having the most significant impact on Māori students' educational achievement.

Interpretation of the Narratives of Experience: Development of the Analytical Model

A critical reading of the narratives of experience identified that there were three main discourses within which the participant groups positioned themselves when identifying and explaining both positive and negative influences on Māori students' educational achievement. First, there was the discourse of the child and his or her home, which included those influences that were to be found outside of the school and the classroom. Second, there was the discourse of structure and systems or those influences outside of the classroom but pertaining to the school itself and/or the wider education system. Third, there was the discourse of relationships and classroom interaction patterns, which included all those influences that were identified as being within the classroom.

This schema was used in the analysis of all the narratives as a means of comparing the relative weightings that the various groups of interview participants gave to each set of influences within the major discourses. This was undertaken by compiling frequency tables of unit ideas (see Bishop et al., 2003; Figure 21.1). In this way, researchers sought to identify which influence each group gave primacy to and which discourse each group drew upon most frequently.

The analysis of the narratives was coded according to idea units and the number of times those units were repeated across the schools, rather than within each school. In this way, we were attempting to develop a picture from across all the schools, as opposed to letting the experiences of one school dominate even one articulate student or teacher. Therefore, the frequency count shown in Figure 21.1 is a tally of idea units. These idea units were then listed according to the discourse they illustrated and ranked according to the number of times such idea units were mentioned in the narratives.

This analysis of the narratives was conducted within the same kaupapa Māori approach that had been used in the process of interviewing. Primacy in the interviewing approach was given to acknowledging the self-determination of the interview participants to be able to explain their own experiences in their own culturally constituted terms. The interviews were undertaken as in-depth, semistructured interviews as conversations (Bishop & Glynn, 1999) and sought to minimize the imposition of the researchers' own sense making and theorizing on the experiences and explanations of the interview participants. As a result, in the construction of the narratives, emphasis was given to the meanings that interview participants had ascribed to their experiences and in this way produced a representation that the participants would legitimate.

Similarly, when coding the narratives, the research team was particular to refer to the meaning that the various participants ascribed to their experiences; that is, coding was based on what the experiences meant to the speaker rather than what it meant to us as researchers. For example, some of the students' references to peer influences may have been coded to relationships, whereas for parents and teachers, these idea units may have been coded as part of the discourse of the child and home. Another example is coding references to the curriculum. For many of the students, this was coded as part of the discourse of relationships, but for many of the teachers, it was coded as part of the discourse of structures. On the surface, this may appear to be inconsistent, but all of those who were coding were fully conversant with the process of constructing narratives of experience through the process of spiral discourse/collaborative storying (Bishop, 1996) and therefore, when coding, were reading the narratives widely so as to identify the meaning that the interview participants had attributed to that particular issue.

For purposes of consistency, the coding was undertaken by a small number of members of the research team who were both familiar with the process of collaborative storying and who had developed a common agreement as to what constituted idea units, themes, subthemes, and, more important, how participants positioned themselves in relation to the various discourses. However, as this analysis of the interviews came from only a small number of schools, it is suggested that rather than this graph representing firm generalizations, it provides a means of ascribing a rough weighting to each discourse that might be indicative of patterns and trends that one may well find in other, similar settings.

Therefore, the picture presented here is more one that others can reflect upon, so that they can critically evaluate where they position themselves when constructing their own images, principles, and practices in relation to Māori students from their own settings, than a truly summative picture of classroom relations in New Zealand. Indeed, when we share these stories with teachers in professional development and other workshops, many people voice their own familiarity with these experiences and also express that reading these narratives of experience enables them to reflect on their own discursive positioning and its potential impact on their students' learning. We present these stories not so others can generalize, but rather so that educators can particularize as to their own experiences.

The interpretative process, which drew on both qualitative and quantitative means of measurement, provided frequency bars for all four interviewee groups. When viewed together as in Figure 21.1, they provide a clear picture of the conflict in theorizing that is to be found about the lived experiences of Māori students, a picture that, from anecdotal evidence, is to be found time and again in New Zealand schools. In addition, while it may be tempting to attribute significance to some minor differences in numbers or percentages, it is the overall pattern of differences that is of importance to this argument. It is also important to note that the frequency figures refer to the number of narratives where such a factor was found; these are frequencies from groups of students (and later of groups of parents and of teachers) rather than of individual responses.

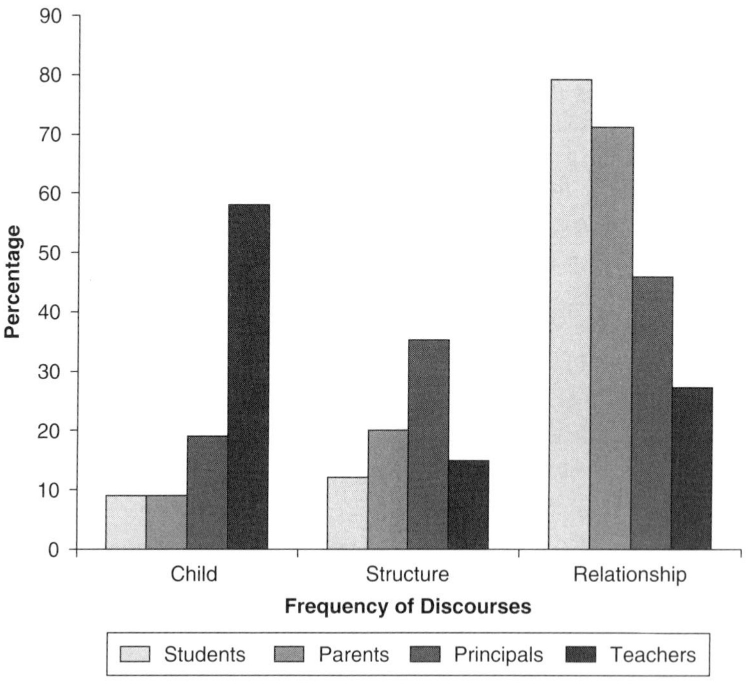

Figure 21.1 Frequency of Discourses

SOURCE: Bishop et al. (2003).

Only in the principals' narratives are there individual responses.

Discursive Positioning

It is clear from the pattern shown in Figure 21.1 that the main influences on Māori students' educational achievement that people identify vary according to where they position themselves within the three discourses. Those who identify that from their experiences, in-class relationships between teachers and students (and others involved in the educational community) have the greatest influence on Māori students' educational achievement, stand in contrast to those who identify the main influences as being Māori students themselves, their homes, and/or the structure of the schools (i.e., influences from outside of the classroom). What is problematic for education is that it is mainly teachers who position themselves in significant numbers within this latter group. In so doing, a large proportion of the teachers were pathologizing Māori students' lived experiences by explaining their lack of educational achievement in deficit terms, either as being within the child or their home, or within the structure of the school.

Positioning within this latter group also means that the speakers tended to blame someone or something else outside of their area of influence; as a result, they suggested that they had very little responsibility for the outcomes of these influences. The main consequence of such deficit theorizing for the quality of teachers' relationships with Māori students and for classroom interactions is that teachers tend to have low expectations of Māori students' ability or a fatalistic attitude in the face of systemic imponderables. This, in turn, creates a downward spiraling, self-fulfilling prophecy of Māori student achievement and failure.

Furthermore, those who position themselves here see very few solutions to solve the problems. This is a very nonagentic position in that there is not much individuals can do from this position other than change the child's family situation or the education "system," solutions often well outside of their own agency. Therefore, along with others (Gay, 2000; Kincheloe & Steinberg, 1997; Nieto, 2000; Wagstaff & Fusarelli, 1995), it is suggested that this deficit theorizing by teachers is the major impediment to Māori students' educational achievement; as Bruner (1996) identifies, unless these positionings and theorizings by teachers are addressed and overcome, they will not be able to realize their agency, and little substantial change will occur.

Indeed, in Shields, Bishop, and Mazawi (2005), we found three case studies of the impact of pathologizing theories and practices on Navaho, Māori, and Bedouin peoples: Pathologizing the lived experiences of these peoples was all pervasive and deeply rooted in psychological, epistemological, social, and historical discourses. Indeed, we found that

> pathologising is manifested in education and schooling in knowledge, power, agency, structures and relationships including both the pedagogical and home-schooling relationships. In fact pathologising in the form of deficit theorizing is the major impediment to the achievement of minoritised students; an understanding that is only too well known by indigenous peoples such as Māori and which forms the basis of Māori resistance to such theorizing. (p. 196)

In contrast, speakers who position themselves within the discourse of relationships and interactions understand that in this space, explanations that seek to address the power differentials and imbalances between the various participants in the relationships can be developed and implemented. In addition, these speakers tend to accept responsibility for their part in the relationships and are clear that they have agency, in that they are an active participant in educational relationships. That is, speakers who position themselves here have a personal understanding that they can bring about change and indeed are responsible for bringing about changes in the educational achievement of Maori students.

Uses of the Narratives

The narratives of experience and the collaborative storying approach were therefore useful in a variety of ways in the project.

First, the analysis of the narratives identifies the usefulness of the concept of discourse as a means of identifying the thoughts, words, and actions shaped by power relations—those complex networks of images and metaphors that the various people in the stories drew upon to create meaning for themselves about their experiences with the education of Māori students. A critical reading of the narratives illustrates the impact of discursive positioning where some discourses offer solutions and others merely perpetuate the status quo. For example, despite most teachers wishing to make a difference for Māori students' educational achievement, they are not able to do so because of their discursive positioning, whereas others, discursively positioned differently, are able to offer numerous solutions to seemingly immutable changes. However, despite discursive positionings making available to teachers different concepts, metaphors, images, and language that "derive from our occupation of subject positions within discourses" (Burr, 1995, p. 146), it is possible for teachers to positively and vehemently reject deficit theorizing as a means of explaining Māori students' educational achievement levels through discursive (re)positioning because it is not just a matter of our being subject to, or a product of, discourse; we have agency that allows us to (re)story our lives. As Burr (1995) argues, this narrative notion "allows us the possibility of personal and social change through our capacity to identify, understand and resist the discourse we are also subject to" (p. 153).

Second, the interviews for the narratives were conducted in a kaupapa Māori manner (Bishop, 1997, 2005) so that the participants were able to explain the meanings they constructed about their educational experiences either as or with Māori students in ways that acknowledged their self-determination. The students, for example, clearly identified the main influences on their educational achievement by articulating the impact and consequences of their living in a marginalized space. That is, they explained how they were perceived in pathological terms by their teachers and how this has had a negative effect on their lives. The whanau members and the principals were also able to identify the main influences on Māori students' education from their own experiences. Similarly, their teachers were able to explain the vast range of experiences and meanings they ascribed to these experiences so that they were able to speak in ways that legitimated their representations.

Third, the detailed narratives of experience are used at the commencement of the professional development part of this project in response to Bruner's (1996) understanding that "our interactions with others are deeply affected by our everyday intuitive theorizing about how other minds work" (p. 45). In other words, it is necessary to acknowledge that teachers are not simply vessels to be "filled" by the expert outsider and that they do have strongly held theories of practice that affect and direct their practice, and maybe some of these positions offer hope and maybe some do not. Indeed, it is clear from Figure 21.1 that many of these theories that teachers hold could well do with being challenged through the creation of a situation of cognitive, cultural, and/or emotional dissonance by providing evidence that is outside of the usual experiences of the teachers; this evidence is used to critically reflect on one's discursive positioning and the implications of this positioning for student outcomes. However, in line with the principles outlined earlier, it is clear that this challenging needs to be undertaken in a nonconfrontational manner, one that acknowledges the mana (power) of the teachers where manaakitanga (caring for others) overrides aspirations to argue with, to chastise, or to correct the ideas of one's guests. Therefore, the focus of the professional development is to create a culturally appropriate and responsive context for learning wherein teachers can reflect on the evidence of the experiences of others in similar circumstances, including, perhaps for the first time, the students. In this manner, teachers can critically evaluate where they position themselves when constructing their own images, principles, and practices in relation to Māori students in their own classrooms. Sharing these vicarious experiences of schooling enables teachers to reflect on their own understandings of Māori children's experiences and consequently on their own theorizing/explanations about these experiences and their consequent practice. And in this way, teachers are afforded the opportunity to reflect critically on their own discursive positioning and the implication of this positioning for their own agency and for Māori students' learning.

Fourth, the students were clear about how teachers, in changing how they related and interacted with Māori students in their classrooms, could create a context for learning wherein Māori students' educational achievement could improve, again by placing the self-determination of Māori students at the center of classroom relationships and interactions. In addition, those others who positioned themselves within the relationship discourse were able to add numerous practical solutions to the problems of educational disparities facing Māori students. These stood in contrast to the very limited solutions and mainly impractical (especially for classroom teachers) solutions offered by those who discursively positioned themselves within the other two discourses, that of the child and their home and the structural discourse. It was from the ideas of those who were positioned with the agentic relationships discourse that an Effective Teaching Profile was developed (see Figure 21.2).

This profile represents an operationalization of Māori people's aspirations for education identified earlier in this chapter and attempts to illustrate just what a culturally responsive pedagogy of relations might look like in practice. Fundamental to this profile is the creation of a culturally responsive context for learning where teachers understand the need explicitly to reject deficit theorizing as a means of explaining Māori students' educational achievement levels and where they take an agentic position in their theorizing about their practice—that is, taking a position where they see themselves as being able to express their professional commitment and responsibility to bringing about change in Māori students' educational achievement and accept professional responsibility for the learning of their students. This notion of agentic positioning addresses what Covey (2004) terms *response ability*—that is, teachers understanding the power they have to respond to who the students are and to what they bring to the classroom, often the invisible elements of culture. In short, this is the realization that learning comes about through changing the learning relations and interactions in classrooms, not just changing one of the parties involved, be they the students or the teachers. These two central understandings are observable in these teachers' classrooms on a daily basis and are expressed again here and understood in terms of Māori metaphors such as manaakitanga, mana motuhake, *whakapiringatanga, wānanga*, ako, and kotahitanga. In practice, these mean that teachers care for and acknowledge the mana of the students as culturally located individuals, have high expectations of the learning for students, are able to manage their classrooms so as to promote learning (which includes subject expertise), reduce their reliance on transmission modes of education so as to engage in a range of discursive learning interactions with students or enable students to engage with others in these ways, know a range of strategies that can facilitate learning interactively, and promote, monitor, and reflect on learning outcomes that in turn lead to improvements in Māori student achievement and sharing this knowledge with the students so that they are let in on the secret of what constitutes learning.

This profile, constructed from Māori students' suggestions (and reinforced by significant others involved in their education) as to how to improve education for themselves and their peers, matches the principles identified as metaphor earlier in this chapter. At center stage is the necessity for a common kaupapa or philosophy that rejects deficit thinking and pathologizing practices as a means of explaining Māori students' educational achievement. In concert is the underlying aspiration for rangatiratanga that promotes the agency of teachers to voice their professional commitment, willingness to engage in whānau relations and interactions, and reciprocal practices that are fundamental to addressing and promoting educational achievement for Māori students. The ways suggested for attaining success draw on Māori cultural aspirations in the way that the interview participants identified the need for caring as

Effective teachers of Māori students create a culturally appropriate and responsive context for learning in their classroom. In doing so they demonstrate the following understandings:

a) they positively and vehemently reject deficit theorising as a means of explaining Māori students' educational achievement levels (and professional development projects need to ensure that this happens); and

b) teachers know and understand how to bring about change in Māori students' educational achievement and are professionally committed to doing so (and professional development projects need to ensure that this happens);

In the following observable ways:

1) Manaakitanga: They care for the students as culturally-located human beings above all else.
(Mana refers to authority and āaki, the task of urging some one to act. It refers to the task of building and nurturing a supportive and loving environment.)

2) Mana motuhake: They care for the performance of their students.
(In modern times mana has taken on various meanings such as legitimation and authority and can also relate to an individual's or a group's ability to participate at the local and global level. Mana motuhake involves the development of personal or group identity and independence.)

3) Whakapiringatanga: They are able to create a secure, well-managed learning environment by incorporating routine pedagogical knowledge with pedagogical imagination.
(Ngā tūranga takitahi me ngā mana whakahaere: involves specific individual roles and responsibilities that are required in order to achieve individual and group outcomes.)

4) Wānanga: They are able to engage in effective teaching interactions with Māori students as Māori.
(As well as being known as Māori centres of learning wānanga as a learning forum involves a rich and dynamic sharing of knowledge. With this exchange of views ideas are given life and spirit through dialogue, debate and careful consideration in order to reshape and accommodate new knowledge.)

5) Ako: They can use strategies that promote effective teaching interactions and relationships with their learners.
(Ako means to learn as well as to teach. It is both the acquisition of knowledge and the processing and imparting of knowledge. More importantly ako is a teaching-learning practice that is culturally specific and appropriate to Māori pedagogy.)

6) Kotahitanga: They promote, monitor and reflect on outcomes that in turn lead to improvements in educational achievement for Māori students.
(Kotahitanga is a collaborative response towards a commonly held vision, goal or other such purpose or outcome.)

Figure 21.2 The Te Kotahitanga Effective Teaching Profile

SOURCE: Bishop et al. (2003).

manaakitanga, for teachers demonstrating their high expectations, and for the creation of secure, well-managed learning settings again in terms of the mana of the students. The preferred discursive teaching interactions, strategies, and focus on formative assessment processes that are identified in the narratives also resonate with Māori cultural aspirations, above all the creation of whanau-type relations and interactions within classrooms and between teachers, students, and their homes. Reciprocal approaches to learning—through cooperative learning strategies, for example, in concert with the underlying aspiration for relative autonomy—underlie that desire to improve the educational achievement of Māori students in New Zealand through operationalizing Māori people's cultural aspirations for self-determination within nondominating relations of interdependence.

▣ Conclusions

In this chapter, an indigenous model of classroom relations and interactions has been presented both theoretically and in practice. Methodologically, this model was developed from a theoretical examination of Māori people's resistance to neocolonial hegemonies and also from their aspirations for and actualization of a proactive, culturally constituted educational intervention in the educational crisis facing Māori people in Aotearoa/New Zealand today. This analysis took the form of an examination of what the metaphor fundamental to kaupapa Māori-generated educational institutions and kaupapa Māori research might mean for mainstream educational institutions. These latter institutions, which attempt to provide an education for the vast majority of Māori students, are dominated by metaphors based in the dominant culture such as hierarchical notions of self-determination and are sites of struggle for Māori people, culture, and language. The model suggests that mainstream classrooms that are constituted as places where power is shared between self-determining individuals within nondominating relations of interdependence, where culture counts, where learning is interactive and dialogic and spirals, where participants are connected and committed to one another, and where there is a common vision of excellence will offer Māori students educational opportunities currently being denied to them.

Methodologically, putting this model into practice involved a variety of approaches. The first involved the use of collaborative storying (Bishop, 1996, 2005) as a means of developing a series of narratives of experience. This approach seeks to address Māori people's concerns about researcher imposition by focusing on the collaborative co-construction of the meaning that the participants ascribe to their reported experiences. As a result, the authorizing of student experiences and the meanings they constructed from these experiences are conducted in ways that address the power of determination over issues such as who initiates research interactions, who determines what benefits there will be, who will benefit, whose reality or experiences (voice) are present in the narratives, with what authority research participants speak, and to whom researchers are accountable (Bishop, 1996, 2005).

The narratives were then used in the project in four main ways. First, they were used to identify a variety of discursive positions pertaining to Māori student achievement and the potential impact of these positions on Māori student learning. Second, the narratives were used to give voice to the participants (students, parents, principals, and teachers) in a manner that addressed issues of power relations pertaining to issues of initiation, benefits, representation, legitimation, and accountability. Third, the narratives were used in the professional development phase of the project to provide teachers with a vicarious means of understanding how students experienced schooling in ways that they might not otherwise have access to. This experience provided teachers with a means of critically reflecting on their own discursive positioning and the impact this might have on their own students' learning. Fourth, the narratives provided us with a practical representation of the theoretical model that was identified in the first part of this chapter.

Operationalizing a culturally effective pedagogy of relations means implementing the Effective Teaching Profile. Such a profile creates a learning context that is responsive to the culture of the child and means that learners can bring who they are to the classroom in complete safety and where their knowledges are acceptable and legitimate. Such a context for learning stands in contrast to the traditional classroom, where the culture of the teacher is given central focus and has the power to define what constitutes appropriate and acceptable knowledges, approaches to learning and understandings, and sense-making processes. This model suggests that when the learners' own culture is central to their learning activities, they are able to make meaning of new information and ideas by building on their own prior cultural experiences and understandings. The visible culture of the child need not necessarily be present but may well become present as a result of co-constructing learning experiences with his or her teachers, in this way addressing the potential imposition of the teacher displaying cultural iconography. Such contexts for learning also teach learners how to reflect critically on their own learning, how they might learn better and more effectively and ensure greater balance in the power relationship of learning by modeling this approach in class. In effect, therefore, raising expectations of students' own learning and how they might enhance and achieve these expectations engages students actively, holistically, and in an integrated fashion in real-life (or as close to) problem sharing and questioning, and students can use these questions as catalysts for ongoing study; this engagement can be monitored as an indicator of potential long-term achievement. This shift from traditional classrooms is important because traditional classroom interaction patterns do not allow teachers to create learning contexts where the culture of the child can be present but rather assume cultural homogeneity (Villegas & Lucas, 2002), which in reality is cultural hegemony (Gay, 2000). Discursive classrooms have the potential to respond to Māori students' and parents' desires to "be Māori," desires that were made very clear in their narratives of experience. However, it must be stressed that fundamental to the development of discursive classrooms that include Māori students is the understanding that the deficit theorizing by teachers must be challenged. Deficit theorizing will not be addressed unless there are more effective partnerships between Māori students and their teachers within the classrooms of mainstream schools. This understanding applies equally to those parenting Māori students. Once these aspects are addressed, the culture of the child can be brought to the learning context with all the power that has been hidden for so long.

The metaphors that Te Kotahitanga draws on are holistic and flexible and able to be determined by or understood within the cultural contexts that have meaning to the lives of the many young people of diverse backgrounds who attend modern schools today. Teaching and learning strategies that flow from these metaphors are flexible and allow the diverse voices of young people primacy and promote dialogue, communication, and learning with others. In such a pedagogy, the participants in the learning interaction become involved in the process of collaboration, in the process of mutual storytelling and restorying, so that a relationship can emerge in which both stories are heard, or indeed a process where a new story is created by all the participants. Such a pedagogy addresses Māori people's concerns about current pedagogic practices being fundamentally monocultural and epistemologically racist. This new pedagogy recognizes that all people who are involved in the learning and teaching process are participants who have meaningful experiences, valid concerns, and legitimate questions.

This model constitutes the classroom as a place where young peoples' sense-making processes are incorporated and enhanced, where the existing knowledges of young people are seen as "acceptable" and "official," in such a way that their stories provide the learning base from whence they can branch out into new fields of knowledge through structured interactions with significant others. In this process, the teacher interacts with students in such a way (storying and restorying) that new knowledge is co-created. Such a classroom will generate totally different interaction patterns and educational outcomes from a classroom where knowledge is seen as something that the teacher makes sense of and then passes onto students and will be conducted within and through a culturally responsive pedagogy of relations, wherein self-determining individuals interact with one another within non-dominating relations of interdependence.

Te Kotahitanga began in 2001 in a small way, and now in 2008, as we move into our fifth year in 12 large secondary schools, we are beginning to see significant improvements in Māori student engagement with learning and achievement along with major improvements in their enjoyment of the learning experience. Such an approach to creating learning contexts of course is not without its detractors, coming as it does from a once dominated and marginalized culture. Nevertheless, one of the main messages and challenges here for mainstream educators is, as Freire (1972) identified above, that the answers to Māori educational achievement and disparities do not lie in the mainstream, for given the experiences of the past 150 years, mainstream practices and theories have kept Māori in a subordinate position while creating a discourse that pathologized and marginalized Māori people's lived experiences.

The counternarrative that is kaupapa Māori demonstrates that the means of addressing the seemingly immutable educational disparities that plague Māori students in mainstream schools actually lie elsewhere than in mainstream education. The answers lie in the sense-making and knowledge-generating processes of the culture that the dominant system has sought to marginalize for so long.

The power of counternarratives such as kaupapa Māori, which has grown out of Māori resistance to the dominance of majority culture aspirations on our lives (Bishop, 1996; G. H. Smith, 1997; L. T. Smith, 1999), is such that alternative pedagogies that are both appropriate and responsive can be developed out of the cultural sense-making processes of peoples previously marginalized by the dominance of colonial and neocolonial educational relations of power. Such pedagogies can create learning contexts for previously pathologized and marginalized students in ways that allow them to participate in education on their terms, to be themselves, and to achieve on their own terms as Māori, as well as becoming, in Durie's (2002) terms, "citizens of the world."

References

Alton-Lee, A. (2003). *Quality teaching for diverse students in schooling: Best evidence synthesis.* Wellington, New Zealand: Ministry of Education.

Applebee, A. (1996). *Curriculum, as conversation.* Chicago: University of Chicago Press.

Beane, J. (1997). *Curriculum integration: Designing the core of democratic education.* New York: Teachers College Press.

Bishop, R. (1994). Initiating empowering research. *New Zealand Journal of Educational Studies, 29*(1), 1–14.

Bishop, R. (1996). *Collaborative research stories: Whakawhanaungatanga.* Palmerston North, New Zealand: Dunmore Press.

Bishop, R. (1997). Interviewing as collaborative storying. *Education Research and Perspectives, 24*(1), 28–47.

Bishop, R. (2005). Freeing ourselves from neocolonial domination in research: A Kaupapa Māori approach to creating knowledge. In N. K. Denzin & Y. S. Lincoln (Eds.), *The SAGE handbook of qualitative research* (3rd ed., pp. 109–138). Thousand Oaks, CA: Sage.

Bishop, R., Berryman, M., & Richardson, C. (2001). *Te Toi Huarewa.* Report to the Ministry of Education, Wellington, New Zealand.

Bishop, R., Berryman, M., Tiakiwai, S., & Richardson, C. (2003). *Te Kotahitanga: The experiences of Year 9 and 10 Māori students in mainstream classrooms.* Report to the Ministry of Education, Wellington, New Zealand.

Bishop, R., & Glynn, T. (1999). *Culture counts: Changing power relations in education.* Palmerston North, New Zealand: Dunmore Press.

Bruner, J. (1996). *The culture of education.* Cambridge, MA: Harvard University Press.

Burr, V. (1995). *An introduction to social constructionism.* London: Routledge.

Cook-Sather, A. (2002). Authorizing students' perspectives: Towards trust, dialogue, and change in education. *Education Researcher, 31*(4), 3–14.

Covey, D. (2004). Becoming a literacy leader. *Leadership, 33*(4), 34–35.

Cummins, J. (1996). *Negotiating identities: Education for empowerment in a diverse society.* Los Angeles: California Association for Bilingual Education.

Durie, M. (1995). Tino Rangatiratanga: Self determination. *He Pukenga Korero, 1*(1), 44–53.

Durie, M. (1998). *Te Mana, Te Kawanatonga: The politics of Māori self-determination.* Auckland, New Zealand: Oxford University Press.

Durie, M. (2002). Universal provision, indigeneity and the Treaty of Waitangi—Victoria. *University of Wellington Law Review, 33*(3–4). Retrieved from http://www.austlii.edu.au/nz/journals/VUWLRev/2002/24.html

Fisher, C., Berliner, D., Filby, N., Marliave, R., Cahen, L., & Dishaw, M. (1981). Teaching behaviours, academic learning time, and student achievement: An overview. *Journal of Classroom Interactions, 17*(1), 2–15.

Freire, P. (1972). *Pedagogy of the oppressed.* New York: Continuum.

Gage, N., & Berliner, D. (1992). *Educational psychology.* Boston: Houghton Mifflin.

Gay, G. (2000). *Culturally responsive teaching: Theory, research and practice.* New York: Teachers College Press.

Glynn, T., Berryman, M., & Glynn, V. (2000). *The Rotorua Home and Literacy Project.* A report to Rotorua Energy Charitable Trust and Ministry of Education, Rotorua, New Zealand.

Glynn, T., & Glynn, V. (1986). Shared reading by Cambodian mothers and children learning English as a second language. *The Exceptional Child, 33*(3), 159–172.

Grumet, M. R. (1995). The curriculum: What are the basics and are we teaching them? In J. L. Kincheloe & S. R. Steinberg (Eds.), *Thirteen questions* (2nd ed., pp. 15–21). New York: Lang.

Heshusius, L. (1994). Freeing ourselves from objectivity: Managing subjectivity or turning toward a participatory mode of consciousness? *Educational Researcher, 23*(3), 15–22.

Kalantzis, M., & Cope, B. (1999). Multicultural education: Transforming the mainstream. In S. May (Ed.), *Critical multiculturalism: Rethinking multicultural and antiracist education* (pp. 245–276). London: Falmer.

Kincheloe, J., & Steinberg, S. (1997). *Changing multiculturalism.* Buckingham, UK: Open University Press.

Metge, J. (1990). Te rito o te harakeke: Conceptions of the whanau. *Journal of the Polynesian Society, 99*(1), 55–91.

Nieto, S. (2000). *Affirming diversity: The sociopolitical context of multicultural education* (3rd ed.). New York: Longman.

Pihama, L., Cram, F., & Walker, S. (2002). Creating methodological space: A literature review of Kaupapa Māori research. *Canadian Journal of Native Education, 26,* 30–43.

Shields, C., Bishop, R., & Mazawi, A. E. (2005). *Pathologizing practices: The impact of deficit thinking on education.* New York: Lang.

Sidorkin, A. M. (2002). *Learning relations.* New York: Lang.

Smith, G. H. (1992, December). *Tane-nu i-a-rangi's legacy . . . propping up the sky: Kaupapa Māori as resistance and intervention.* Paper presented at the New Zealand Association for Research in Education/Australia Association for Research in Education, Melbourne.

Smith, G. H. (1997). *Kaupapa Māori as transformative praxis.* Unpublished doctoral dissertation, University of Auckland, New Zealand.

Smith, L. T. (1999). *Decolonising methodologies: Research and indigenous people.* Dunedin, New Zealand: Zed Books/University of Otago Press.

Villegas, A. M., & Lucas, T. (2002). *Educating culturally responsive teachers: A coherent approach.* Albany, NY: SUNY Press.

Wagstaff, L., & Fusarelli, L. (1995). Establishing collaborative governance and leadership. In P. Reyes., J. Scribner, & A. Scribner (Eds.), *Lessons from high-performing Hispanic schools: Creating learning communities* (pp. 19–35). New York: Teachers College Press.

Widdowson, D., Dixon, R., & Moore, D. (1996). The effects of teacher modelling of silent reading on students' engagement during Sustained Silent Reading. *Educational Psychology, 16,* 171–180.

Young, I. M. (2004). Two concepts of self determination. In S. May, T. Mahood, & J. Squires (Eds.), *Ethnicity, nationalism and minority rights* (pp. 176–198). Cambridge, UK: Cambridge University Press.

Ysseldyke, J., & Christenson, S. (1998). *TIES-II, the instructional environment system II: A system to identify a student's instructional needs.* Longmont, CO: Sopris West.

22

MODERN DEMOCRACY

The Complexities Behind Appropriating Indigenous Models of Governance and Implementation

Tim Begaye

Trying to understand democracy and its evolution in the United States is difficult because there is a multitude of interpretations regarding its true meaning. Over time, various models of democracy have been explored, theorized, and tried, but each new evolution somehow misses its attempt at inclusion, and thus it struggles to evolve because it meanders, fluctuates, and is subject to interpretation. Real democracy, it seems, is elusive, ambiguous, and ultimately subjective. However, a key feature of a democratic society, a free and nonpartisan participation by its entire people, has actually left many in the margins and others doubting whether there can be equal participation by all. The early architects of a democratic state such as the Iroquois and Wabanki Confederacies and numerous Native groups along the current western United States practiced a kind of unwavering democracy that afforded equal and inclusive participation, a model of governance that the early colonists would borrow from to help develop their understandings of freedom and democracy in the new world.

A democratic society is described by the early Native confederacies and the early colonists as having qualities of a government that is run by the people. As it turned out, the colonists appropriated a new interpretation and established a new social and political system that gave further definition of participation in governance, but the colonists had a different understanding of inclusion, equal participation, and freedom of expression because of their history with oppression and religious persecution in England.

Today, the colonial descendants are still evolving an interpretation that is not inclusive; participation and access by citizens is minimal. Native people were once the exemplars of democracy, but that model has been forced to change, and now an assimilative mind-set serves as a mechanism in making them socially, culturally, and politically dependent using the new definition of democracy. What, then, does democracy mean if the "founders" theoretically espouse certain values but its practice is limited to a few? Are equality, participation, and freedom of expression values of a democracy, or are they merely metaphors of theory from the past and not achievable practices as it is often espoused in the mainstream? What lessons can be learned from such models of democracies, and could past (colonial) or current (postcolonial) indigenous[1] communities serve as new models? What qualities and consideration are features that would promote a good model of democracy in Native communities?

Native Models of Democracy

The Native example of a democratic society shows how people exercise their right of participation by contributing to and affecting the rules for social and political interaction. The Iroquois Confederacy had established notions of representation by selecting individuals to speak on behalf of each of the six Nations when making decisions relative to external issues. Each of the six Nations had a leader called "Clanmother," who had a cabinet consisting of additional leaders selected and voted into position by the community. Their system also had mechanisms for disposing of a leader should this person fail to perform as expected. Initiating a removal process belonged to the head of the cabinet, the Clanmother, who would confer with the failed leader and properly "impeach" the person with the consent of the community. Representation and participation were extended to all members of the community who were willing and capable. The Great Law of the Iroquois gave basic rights to people, resolved disputes by giving all a fair and equal hearing, and emphasized honor, duty to the clan, and community (Grinde & Johansen, 1991). In addition, the Iroquois emphasized education through the way they "prized competence as a protector/provider more than material wealth. Their children were trained to think for themselves as well as provide for others" (Grinde & Johansen, 1991, p. 28). As more and more Europeans began to settle the East Coast, many aspects of the Great Law of the Iroquois would eventually appear in the Articles of Confederation and the U.S. Constitution.

Similarly, the Cherokees had a developed system for social and political order through elected individuals who represented the voices of six communities. Up to the 18th century, each Cherokee village consisted of approximately several hundred people and each village could control its own internal affairs. Villages could also send delegates to a larger national council when there was a national emergency (Grinde & Johansen, 1991, p. 33). Participation was held in such high value that if a village became so large that certain adults could not express their views, the village was usually split in two. "The clan system cemented the Confederacy, giving it enough strength and endurance to prevent such a high degree of autonomy from degenerating into anarchy" (Grinde & Johansen, 1991, p. 34). Using common bonds of clanship, participation was open to all willing adults in the community, and expression was offered to everyone even though it was mainly deferred to select matriarchs based on skill and ability (Andrew, 1992).

Early example of Native precedence for participation, citizenship, and exercising responsibility in a democratic government is evident in a number of groups besides the Iroquois and Cherokees. The Penacook federation of New England, the Wabanaki Confederacy, and the Powhatan Confederacy formed a community of groups with democratic qualities similar to their neighbors, the Iroquois. Anthony Wallace, an early scholar, observed that long before the 17th century, "Ethnic confederacies were common among all the Indian tribes of the Northeast." In some places, villages and tribes spoke similar languages and shared many traditions and formed unions to minimize internal conflicts, as well as to serve as strength against others (Anthony F. C. Wallace, as cited in Grinde & Johansen, 1991, p. 19). Among each and in communities, participation and representation was a valuable attribute of Native approaches to democracy.

Similar examples are evident today among the Mississippi Choctaw, the White Mountain Apaches, and the Navajo Nation (Cornell & Kalt, 1998). These tribal nations and others have unique structures of governance. They combine cultural traditions, norms, and rules with Western concepts to their hybrid government. Even though it was originally forced upon them, the Navajo people refused to accept a Constitution that included elements of Western ideas and intent. Instead, they opted for their own version, "a government by resolution" that includes a more Navajo-centric rules of order referred to as Navajo Common Law (Wilkins, 2007). Many other tribal nations have retained their traditional democratic approaches to formation and execution of governance. More important, they have integrated certain facets into part of the governments to accommodate changes that have occurred over time. Rather than have choices and options, many tribes were forced to use foreign models of governance that are often taken on under subtle threats on sovereignty and other freedoms (Wilkins, 2007).

American Model of Democracy

To more recent architects of American democracy such as John Adams, Thomas Jefferson, and Benjamin Franklin, the channels for expression became inherently controlled by the checks and balances of a three-branch government intent on limiting roles and powers. Representation evolved through states and local authority structures. Whether the society is Native groups looking for freedom from colonists or Western colonists seeking social control and freedom from European monarchy, the common interpretation is the value of individual participation in the functioning of the government. However, achieving freedom and participation has been dependent on the way people themselves voice their hopes and vision.

The apparent limited value of inclusion and participation as a democratic quality was noticeable in the founding of the University of Virginia, established by one of the founding fathers of the United States, Thomas Jefferson. The university of Virginia remained all White and male only for the first 145 years of its existence.[2] The architect of early colonial democracy did not realize the full scope of a democratic society by excluding women, African Americans, and Native people as part of its citizenry. Linda Darling-Hammond (1995a), a modern African American scholar, points to the obvious inequality in social status and limited definition of democracy in her statement, "The resources devoted to the education of poor children and children of color in the U.S. continues to be significantly less than those devoted to other American children on virtually every measure" (p. 4). She notes the unequal treatment of the children and families clearly noticeable along racial lines as certainly not a democratic value. John Dewey, who lived at the end of the American Industrial Revolution when an adolescent United States was becoming divided, noted, "A democracy is more than a form of government; it is primarily a mode of associated living, of conjoint communicated experience" (Dewey, 1969–1991, vol. 9, p. 93). Dewey understood democracy as an inclusive connected experience that is central to all citizens that extends beyond mere organizational structure and mechanics of governance established for social control. He believed a democratic society existed where everyone experienced the freedom to participate without recognizing barriers limited by race, class, religion, and so on. Early definitions of democracy can be viewed as having the value of exclusion, which continues to be accepted today. This exclusion is evident in the marginalization of the poor and in the treatment of "the other," which frequently turns out to be separated along racial lines.

The evolving definition of American democracy has been deeply influenced by recent trends powerful enough to force another definition of democracy. This trend has narrowly defined the political pendulum into a new binary paradigm of majority and minority, left and right, conservative and liberal, Republican and Democrat, and so on. If the inherent quality of expressing differences is a legitimate attribute of a democratic state, then the two-dimension effect has become a new characteristic of democracy created by the dominant political forces, whether it has the effect of diminishing any hope for equal participation of the already marginalized minority. Without the democratic tools of avenues for dissension and activism, historically divided groups become further victims in a society that espouses equality, freedom, and justice for all.

Yet, it seems the founders of modern democracy didn't anticipate, acknowledge, or account for the ensuing diversity of people through change and immigration. It took the U.S. government nearly 250 years to reluctantly offer African Americans, originally brought to the United States as slaves, basic human rights equal to other Americans (J. D. Anderson, 1988). Even after the ruling by the U.S. Supreme Court that citizens have equal rights, the social cultural element of human beings struggles to view one another as equals. Native people didn't fare much better at equality than African Americans or other so-called minorities. They were considered "savages and heathens" and, at different periods of the growing United States, less than all other humans (Adams, 1995). Through revolutions and radical changes from slavery to gaining citizenship, African Americans were eventually elevated but continue to be subjects of broad discrimination. Natives became worthy citizens of the United States but only to become target of a massive attempt at Christianization (Adams, 1995).

While the U.S. population, industrialization, and wealth flourished tremendously in the White mainstream, little has changed over time in other ethnic/racial or cultural groups who are as much participants and citizens with access in a democratic society. Today, some of the poorest, economically deprived places in the United States continue to be on Native land (Cornell & Kalt, 1998). The urban poor and Native reservations in the isolated and remote corners of the United States are missing out on the social and economic benefits of a democratic society because of their status and position within the broader social economic hierarchy.

The colonists' arrival in the present-day eastern United States would ultimately be challenged in their own search for freedom and they would be forced to define the attributes of a democratic society. In developing a new country, they knew of their paternalistic intentions and were well aware that participation and expression was a limited attribute evident in the work of the "founding fathers" (Adams, 1995). The first constitutional convention in 1776 was attended largely by English men who desired a government with limited authority over the people and certainly not like their previous one, which they escaped in England. Yet the outline of a government they produced had limited participation and representation, leaving out others; the women who "belong elsewhere" remained at home, and the nearby Native people were subhuman and not invited. Those whose beliefs and values were not consistent with the majority, such as the self-proclaimed pacifist William Penn, were exiled. Finally, the nearby Iroquois Confederacy, from whom the concept of representation, participation, and membership was retrieved, was not included (Grinde & Johansen, 1991). The colonial attempt at forming a democratic government had only focused on a future that limited who would be the participants in the new government.

In attempting to form a representative government while guarding against tyranny, the early settlers excluded its citizenry of people. In efforts to build a democratic society, the nearby Natives—because they didn't speak the English language, didn't practice the same religion, and did not believe in practices of the Anglican Church—were not allowed to be participants in the formation of a new government. In fact, for the same reasons, once a government was established, the first order of business was finding ways to remove the Indians as barriers to the westward progress, and efforts to save those heathens began by converting them to Christianity. While the line between marginalization and ostracism was finely evident in its treatment of people, the early formers of a democratic society also used divisiveness and exclusion as a necessary tool for addressing factions that may have existed.

▣ (MIS)APPLICATIONS OF DEMOCRACY: "EQUALITY AND JUSTICE FOR ALL"

The white man says there is freedom and justice for all. We have had "freedom and justice," and that is why we have been almost exterminated.

—1927 Grand Council of American Indians

As the fledgling United States grew in population and states flourished, the Natives continued to be a challenge to the ideals of democracy. In the post-Revolution years, from approximately 1778 to 1830, a series of policies clearly attempted to treat the Native tribes as equals or as sovereign nations. There were nearly 380 treaties signed between Natives tribes and the federal government that showed examples of recognition and desire to establish democratic relations. Most notable was language stating, "The utmost good faith shall always be observed towards Indians: their land and property shall never be taken from them without their consent" (Thorpe, 1909, p. 957). Additional well-intentioned paternalistic policies surrounding commerce were legislated that allowed organizations, businesses, and countries to trade with Indian tribes but only with a bureaucratic approval by Congress (Clinton, Newton, & Price, 1991). While the policies of this era had signs of building good relations with all Native tribes, business deals with them were byproducts of regulations more focused on developing a stronger federal government and economy.

The era of good relations didn't last in the following years as a new array of federal policies were passed that sought to remove Native people from their homelands so that European settlers could farm their land. Along with a litany of treaties and policies aimed at solving the Indian problem, the policy trend reversed its earlier positions of good relations with Indians and respecting each other as sovereigns. The increasing immigration of Europeans made land and resources scarce as fluctuating federal government policies became the catalyst for refining its previous liberal approach of making treaties to merely making policy. In 1830, the U.S. Supreme Court under Chief Justice John Marshall ruled that the Cherokee tribe and therefore all tribal groups would be considered "domestic dependent nations" (Wilkins & Lomawaima, 2001; see also Andrew, 1992; George, 2000; Norgren, 2004). With this interpretation, Congress again changed its position to limit its view of Native people as sovereign nations while carefully including definition of a dependent status. By renouncing its earlier position of treating tribes as nations, the federal government gave itself a new formula to address the continuous Indian problem. With the assistance of the U.S. Supreme Court, President Andrew Jackson ordered many tribal groups, including the Cherokee Nation, to relocate west of the Mississippi River or risk losing their good relations with the federal government and tribal sovereignty. Those tribes who chose not to comply were eventually forced to move, a trek across several southeastern states often referred to as the "Trail of Tears" (W. L. Anderson, 1991). What were once two governments treating each other as equals deteriorated to one of dependency. On one hand, a democratic society flourished, but on the other hand, another part of its citizens was made dependent and their population decimated.

In refining its approach to dealing with Native people, the United States designated a branch of the government to deal directly with the Indians. The new department eventually came to be known as the Bureau of Indian Affairs, and it became the focal point from where future negotiations with Indian tribes would take place. This department had the authority to call on the military if diplomacy didn't work. In fact, in 1886, a zealous Army general named William Pratt was lauded for his heroics for raiding Indian tribes and taking the children from their homes to be civilized in the ways of the colonizers. Families were displaced and children were removed from their homes and taken across the country in railroad boxcars to military schools in Pennsylvania, Virginia, and Florida (Adams, 1995).

In the waning year, a new string of policies surfaced shifting federal efforts to assimilation rather than removal. The federal government enlisted the support of Christian groups in a national attempt to "civilize" and assimilate the Native people (Adams, 1995). In 1887, Congress passed the Dawes Act (also known as the General Allotment Act) where nearly half of all remaining Native lands were lost to settlers through government-allowed allotments and homesteading. The justification for Indian lands becoming a target for the land grab by settlers was that Indians were not exploiting it through agricultural means. While the new policy was another reversal, the "assimilation" period offered Native families financial incentives to leave reservations and by suggestions of economic opportunity in the growing American society (Adams, 1995). Urban areas such as Chicago, Phoenix, Denver, and Los Angeles became places where Native families could live and become part of the mainstream society regardless of whether they were culturally able or spoke the language (Deloria, 1990). What was left of vacated reservation land would be parceled out to non-Indian families with additional small tracts of land designated especially for agricultural use, giving non-Indians ownership of Native land and reservations for the first time.

Even as the attempts at making the Native people in the likeness of White people was failing, and without serious consideration of past disastrous federal policies, another reversal occurred. In 1934, Congress passed the Indian Reorganization Act (IRA), which had the intentions to "rehabilitate the Indian's economic life and to give him a chance to develop the initiative destroyed by a century of oppression and paternalism." The passage of this legislation had two rather ironic impacts: It helped to affirm one of the rights exercised by the Native people in a democratic society to govern themselves, despite always having to get approval by the U.S. government. It also reversed a previous policy that failed at urbanizing and assimilating Native families by moving them to major cities and away from their traditional homelands.

The Indian Reorganization Act was a double-edged sword in that it gave some tribes the means to control their destinies, but it also paved the way for further paternalism paths by setting up a mechanism where the U.S. government had the power to approve or disapprove all activities of tribal governments. This, in essence, gave the government complete authority to set new precedents by offering tribes a template to form a Western-type of government while wiping out all previously established traditional governance. Despite the changing policies, tribal nations were not without previous established forms of traditional governance. Some tribes had managed to maintain some parts of their traditional systems of governance, some in the likeness of a theocracy, some parliamentary, and some constitutional governments (Grinde & Johansen, 1991). However, with the new policy, many were forced to adopt many new Western models. The introduction of a new template for governance as another federal government solution further forced tribes to adopt another foreign approach to social order. This era of "reorganization" brought another shift of policy by introducing a new template of governance that supposedly exemplified a democratic system. It was one similar in structure to the federal government.

In the late 1940s and the early 1950s, the federal government again shifted its position. The previous policy of allowing tribes to exercise local governance, form constitutional governments, and practice self-determination was eliminated along with the special legal and political relationship between tribal governments and the federal government. In effect, the new policy eliminated federal benefits and support for services to tribes as nearly 109 tribes across the United States were "terminated" ("Termination" policy, with House Concurrent Resolution 108: U.S. House of Representatives Resolution 108, 83rd Congress, 1953. [U.S. Statutes at Large, 67: B132]). The termination ceased formal relations and recognition of tribes as sovereign, as legal entities, and virtually violated all past treaty obligations and authority. In addition, the U.S. government ceased to recognize 50 newly formed tribal governments that they had enticed many tribes to form in the previous progressive period of reorganization. The most prominent policy with long-term effects during this period would be the enactment of "Public Law 280," which took away tribal government jurisdiction of criminal activity on Indian lands, transferring jurisdiction to state courts (Public Law 83-280, the 280th Public Law enacted by the 83rd Congress in 1953 (2), 2 Act of August 15, 1953, ch. 505, 67 Stat. 588-590 [now codified as 18 U.S.C. 1162, 28 U.S.C. 1360 and other scattered sections in 18 and 28 U.S.C.]).

In 1975, the U.S. government once again softened its stance on dealing with Native people when Congress passed the Indian Self-Determination Act (Clarkin, 2001; see also Indian Self-Determination and Education Assistance Act of 1975). This policy loosened the reins of federal government control by allowing Native tribes to handle many of their own political and government affairs. President Richard Nixon laid the foundation for a new policy by reintroducing and reaffirming the special legal and political relationship with Indian tribes. He declared how an era of termination had ended and called for ceasing the excessive dependence on the federal government by giving tribal governments the authority to administer their own federal programs and services for its members. In the years following Nixon's historic affirmation of the principles of self-determination and economic self-reliance, successive presidents have reaffirmed the federal commitment as a means to building stronger tribal economies and responsive tribal governments.

The fluctuating pattern of federal government policy as it struggled to form a new viable democratic society was evidenced by its lack of understanding of its citizenry. The policy failed to recognize the contributions and existence of the Native people who were crucial to their survival. While the lack of acknowledgment didn't affect the government or its relationship with the Native people, many tribal groups were no longer acknowledged because of their "termination" status and remained ill-treated participants in developing a democratic government. As unwanted neighbors who were often considered a problem to "progress," there were still interactions, exchanges, and exercise of diplomatic relations as numerous democracy concepts and ideas were borrowed, integrated, and translated into the U.S. Constitution. The growth of immigrating Europeans to the new world ultimately increased the need for more land, and the pressure to establish a form of government brought with it challenges, strained relations, and ultimately marginalization. While the colonists managed to survive their new harsh reality with the assistance of Native people, they also sought democratic ideals in the form of sovereignty and religious freedom but soon abandoned these ideals for selfish reasons. They knew their future was bleak unless they developed methods for creating relations with the Native people, who were important allies and whose trust they had to earn and maintain. While the need to build good relations and understanding with its entire people was going to be evident if democracy was going to be practiced, there was clearly a different colonial mind-set displayed in attitude and treatment of Native peoples.

Rethinking Democracy: Can There Be "Justice for All"?

Democracy as practiced by Native people has been an important model for the early settlers. Such a government meant contribution by all people and that everyone had equal voice in community affairs. While the ancient Greeks, Romans, and the early English settlers of New England were able to reach a certain practice of democracy that worked for them, there were still in communities that marginalized and they remained in fear of monopolized power. Plato suggested that such a democratic government would ultimately encounter problems of tyranny. He raised concerns that such narrow access to power or rule by a member of a particular group was dangerous and not consistent with the principle of rule by the people. He was also concerned that rule by a common people would happen at the likely expense of the poor, who would be prevented from participation. Yet, there is potential for respectable people with access to power to still participate and contribute to a democratic society.

Since the arrival of the colonists and right up to the 18th century, Native leaders repeatedly voiced a perspective based on freedom and participation: "We don't want any part of the establishment. . . ." They were hesitant to be included in a practice of democracy that ostracized their way of life and antagonized their beliefs. Even though they were doubtful of what they were seeing as Western ways, they also expressed another sentiment: "We want to be free to raise our children in our religion, in our ways, to be able to hunt and fish and to live in peace." Native groups practiced a way of life that they knew was different from the colonists and desired to continue it. In addition, they explicitly stated their observation in how democracy was practiced: "We don't want power, we don't want to be congressmen, bankers, we want to be ourselves" (Yunkaporta, n.d.). Even though Native people observed differences in how democracy was defined, they displayed their examples by forming confederacies and attempting to share their perspectives of democracy. The example most often referred to are the Iroquois, who managed to form a union of six different nations, each with different ideas and philosophy, which were willing to share their understanding behind their model of governance, which appeared to be a government that worked. They observed the common traits to be recognized and valued within clans and community. From the children to the elders, they were effective in giving voice to each one. Dissension and participation were open avenues for all members of the community where they could assert their ideas. Community and villages had a mechanism for factions within the government, and as long as individuals wished to remain in the community, they had responsibilities. If they for some reason decided against the union, they were also free to leave. While there are differences in how practices of democracy evolved, our society today could learn and share the values that have emerged. In order to allow further evolution of ideas around models of democracy, people need to recognize and take on the difficult task of changing old values and learning new ones.

At its original conception, beliefs about democracy had Western philosophers such as Thomas Hobbes and Jean Rousseau argue that government is subjected to the good will of the people, presuming that people are basically good and rulers would only want what is good for the people. Aside from the basic belief about the natural surrounding, Native people also saw the basic good. "Iroquois political philosophy was rooted in the concept that all life was spiritually unified with the natural environment and other forces surrounding people" (Grinde & Johansen, 1991, p. 27).

While there may have been agreement in certain respects and disagreement in others regarding the essence of democracy, the fundamentally accepted ideology of allowing direct participation by people in government activities remained central to Native people's approach to organization and governance. The warnings and concerns behind establishing measures to prevent tyranny may have been actualized on occasion in the past, but the difficult challenge of fulfilling the principles of an ideal democratic society is real and remains a struggle that continues to plague mainstream America. As Plato and others have suggested, historically, the marginalized, poor, and unrecognized "others" will not be given the opportunity to contribute in such a society. Not only was this scenario the situation in ancient times, but it has remained as a thorn to this day. The means and the reasons are readily available this day and age, but we lack the will and impetus to address such an issue.

The path to acknowledgment and recognition or to healing is embedded in the sense of community that was formed when tribes and groups were held together with a common bond of clan and strong community values. Clans meant community, friendship, and respect for every thing considered alive among humans and nature. The path to being inclusive means resurrecting the original deep understanding in each person, rather than relying on the aesthetics of modernism that prevails and is reinforced by materialistic and superficial ways.

The Next Step: Toward a Truer Democracy?

The long history of the U.S. government's schizophrenic relations with Native people illustrates that democracy is truly an essential value and a practice in need of refinement and revision. In trying to make sense of the term through fluctuating policies along with distracting ideas about definition, one conclusion is clear: Scholars and educators all agree that the elements of democracy are inclusion and access and that education is an essential antecedent. John Powell, a modern-day historian, suggests that education is a key ingredient that gave the poor colonists an understanding of what it means to have equal access and participation (Powell, 2006).

From Plato to the early colonial settlers, the value of education played itself out in the need for skill development, which ultimately instilled knowledge and understanding in people about daily labor practices, governance, and social order among citizens. Over time, both democracy and education converged as important qualities, but rather than expanding on the definition, it remained stuck in its narrow interpretation, and so did society. Education is a democratic quality that should not be limited to skill development in a society that values knowledge and understanding. In the 21st century, it is an inclusive value that can be extended to all because it gives people an opportunity to learn from one another and provides deeper insight into understanding issues such as poverty, equality, sovereignty, values, and race. Knowledge and learning have become important components of a democratic society that affords everyone an opportunity.

There are many approaches to opening the human mind and improving the human capacity to learn so that society can understand particular tendencies in group epistemology. While the potential of education was not recognized by the early colonists, David Wallace Adams (1995) argues that the Indians were considered less than human because of their "different" definition of education and knowledge and therefore were not acknowledged as worthy of an Anglo education among the colonies. Yet, what was not considered but rather excluded was that Native people too had an education system. The community and children were educated by elders, families, and experiences and observation of the natural environment. Knowledge was an important value passed from generation to generation through stories. This was democracy and thus a community where strong spiritual, cultural, and social values were practiced and where learning these values took a lifetime. Rather than take an educative approach, the early colonists and the leaders of today have sought to control and change groups in an undemocratic fashion.

The Native people also desired a free and open-minded person but different from the one envisioned by the colonists. The colonists practiced a form of democracy limited to a few—those willing to be ruled rule under the guise of "this is what the people want." Even though education in the colonial times excluded many groups of people, there was much to learn from the practices of Native confederacies that, to this day, could still have meaningful and practical utility. A willing society has the potential to learn from its past as well as learn from the early Native groups. Learning from both will produce better informed citizens.

Where democracy promoted a sense of individualism, it also had an inherent mechanism that did not exclude collective voices and expression that could potentially divide people and societies. There are lessons to be learned from centuries of practicing democracy without inclusion. One can observe from recent social and political clashes and revolutions where the poor, the marginalized, and minorities have been able to gain a respectable role in the activity of the government. While there may be groups who do not wish to be part of the mainstream because of historical frustrations, the irony is that they remain on the outside of a society that espouses democratic practices. One of the attributes of democracy is that groups and organizations are given an opportunity to disagree and express their dissatisfaction, a quality that was evident among the Iroquois. Today, this quality is not explicit in the discourse about resolving differences because one could be labeled unpatriotic or un-American. If democracy means the equal participation of all those citizens who live within its domain, then its breadth and depth of participation has been ignored at the cost of alternative minority views, marginalization, and dissenting expressions. In order to reach a level of understanding and consensus, we must have discourse on finding ways to minimize this void.

A democratic society must have a reflective process that learns from its past and have the ability to see the historical path of inclusion that is really a form of exclusion. Since the early days of Native confederacies, forming alliances and establishing formal relations included considerations of equality and fairness as an important aspect of a democracy. The early Romans and Greeks gave it a twist that established a new foundation to how it would be practiced; that same foundation has, in recent times, evolved with modern political trends due to the diversity of people. Born of the type of revolutionary thinking that left the controlling policies founded in the Church of England, the early English settlers leaned toward practices they deemed as inviting participation of its citizens. However, as the colonists began to establish a comfortable foothold on current-day New England, their view of self narrowed and focused only on personal opportunity and preservation. The new definition now serves as the precursor to current practice of democracy. As Western society developed, the Native infrastructure of community and governance deteriorated as it was swallowed up by Western notions of democracy. In many places, complete tribes were terminated, and their governments vanished only to be replaced by a foreign and oppressive model of governance that today prevents equal participation. The long history of ill treatment of "others" and putting the rest outside of the margins is an experience from which our current society can learn many valuable lessons.

A new form of democracy could contain the essential element of a democracy that still includes the original Native conception of inclusion and participation. Leaders would begin to assume responsibility and be accountable to the people, and they would also take it upon themselves to transform and practice a new value system that includes all groups regardless of past histories. Eliminating the voice of the "minorities" by getting rid of participation would be unthinkable because such a move means relinquishing the very source of power that is perceived to stabilize society. Preparing communities to accept differing points of view would enhance the moral obligation of the dominant society to truly practice legitimacy democracy. Decision making among tribal groups would no longer be influenced and co-opted by dominant outside forces and selfish ideals. There would be a convergence of the minority and dominant forces that would allow all groups to integrate value systems from their own and develop more effective definition of democracy where participation and expression are open to everyone.

CONCLUSION

In a truly legitimate democratic state, the discussion of democracy and education would be irrelevant because everyone would be free to participate and express themselves regarding the welfare of the community or society. Freedom of expression was a value held in high regard by Native groups. They took days and even weeks to make a decision that was agreed upon by all members of the community. With their approach, participation and expression would mean taking the time to dismantle the foundation of democracy, giving up power, and giving access to all. While the Western conception of democracy left out women, in many Native societies, women made prominent decisions as participants in a democratic society. In other cultures, men made decisions on behalf of the community and often based on the consensus of the larger tribe. Arriving at a decision was a process, and only when there was consensus did the group move forward. This approach to a democracy minimized the element of time as a factor in decision making while enhancing contribution and participation as an important value.

The question, then, is this: What are the necessary ingredients, and what should be the prevailing political values in a legitimate democratic state? One thing is clear; all citizens must be participating members of the society. Inclusion should be just that—inclusive regardless of race, color, creed, beliefs, and so on. Native tribal groups should have the freedom to participate in civil discourse regardless of social and political status, and societal structures of governance would need to be realigned with the larger social and cultural ethics of the mainstream population. Membership should be redefined to allow everyone to have access to the political process. People of color have not always had complete access or been recognized as members of society. A democratic society cannot achieve effectiveness as long as groups are marginalized because of the political reasons used as justification for denying them membership and participation.

Notes

1. I use the terms *indigenous, Native, American Indians, tribes, groups,* and *communities* interchangeably knowing that there may be disagreement over which term is more acceptable, appropriate, or correct. While I have my preferences over which term to use, I believe its usage depends on context, audience, and intentions. Please view my decision to use certain terms as "exercising my sovereignty" based on my preference.

2. The University of Virginia was founded in 1819 by Thomas Jefferson. When the university opened for classes in 1825, there were 68 students and 8 faculty members. The design of Mr. Jefferson's original "academical village" remains widely acclaimed for its architectural achievement.

References

Adams, D. W. (1995). *Education for extinction: American Indians and the boarding school experience 1875–1928.* Lawrence: University Press of Kansas.

Anderson, J. D. (1988). *The education of Blacks in the South, 1860–1935.* Raleigh: University of North Carolina Press.

Anderson, W. L. (Ed.). (1991). *Cherokee removal: Before and after.* Athens: University of Georgia Press.

Andrew, J. A. (1992). *From revivals to removal: Jeremiah Evarts, the Cherokee Nation, and the search for the soul of America.* Athens: University of Georgia Press.

Clarkin, T. (2001). *Federal Indian policy in the Kennedy and Johnson administrations, 1961–1969.* Albuquerque: University of New Mexico Press.

Clinton, R. N., Newton, N. J., & Price, M. B. (1991). *American Indian law cases and material* (3rd ed.). Charlottesville, VA: The Michie Company Law Publishers.

Cornell, S., & Kalt, J. P. (1998). Sovereignty and nation-building: The development challenge in Indian country today. *American Indian Culture and Research Journal, 22,* 187–214.

Darling-Hammond, L. (1995a). Cracks in *The bell curve:* How education matters. *Journal of Negro Education, 64,* 211–385.

Deloria, V., Jr. (1990). *Behind the trail of broken treaties: An Indian declaration of independence* (3rd ed.). Austin: University of Texas Press.

Dewey, J. (1969–1991). *The collected works of John Dewey* (J. A. Boydston, Ed.). Carbondale: Southern Illinois University Press.

George, R. P. (2000). *Great cases in constitutional law.* Princeton, NJ: Princeton University Press.

Grinde, D. A., Jr., & Johansen, B. E. (1991). *Exemplar of liberty: Native Americans and the evolution of democracy.* Los Angeles: University of California, American Indian Studies Center.

Indian Reorganization Act, 25 U.S.C. 478 (1934).

Indian Self-Determination and Education Assistance Act, Pub. L. No. 93–638 (1975).

Norgren, J. (2004). *Cherokee cases: Two landmark federal decisions in the fight for sovereignty.* Norman: University of Oklahoma Press.

Powell, J. A. (2006). *The ethical imperative of democracy in education.* Retrieved September 20, 2006, from http://www.kirwaninstitute.org

Thorpe, F. N. (Ed.). (1909). *Federal and state constitutions: Volume 2.* Retrieved May 1, 2007, from http://usinfo.state.gov/usa/infousa/facts/democrac/5.htm

Wilkins, D. E. (2007). *American Indian sovereignty and the U.S. Supreme Court: The masking of justice.* Austin: University of Texas Press.

Wilkins, D. E., & Lomawaima, K. T. (2001). *Uneven ground: American Indian sovereignty and federal law.* Norman: University of Oklahoma Press.

Yunkaporta, T. (n.d.). *Statement from the 1927 Grand Council of American Indians.* Retrieved November 9, 2006, from http://aboriginalrights.suite101.com/blog.cfm/grand_council_of_american_indians

23

RETHINKING COLLABORATION

Working the Indigene-Colonizer Hyphen

Alison Jones, with Kuni Jenkins

To rethink collaboration between indigene and colonizer is both to desire it and to ask troubling questions about it. This chapter critiques desire for collaborative inquiry understood as face-to-face, ongoing dialogue between indigenous and settler colleagues or students. Interrogating the logic of (my own) White/settler enthusiasm for dialogic collaboration, I consider how this desire might be an unwitting imperialist demand—and thereby in danger of strengthening the very impulses it seeks to combat. I do not argue for a *rejection* of collaboration. Rather, I unpack its difficulties to suggest a less dialogical and more uneasy, unsettled relationship, based on learning (about difference) *from* the Other, rather than learning *about* the Other.

WORKING

In Aotearoa/New Zealand, Kuni Jenkins and I sit down together to write. She is Māori, from the *iwi* (tribal group) Ngati Porou; I am Pakeha, White, born locally. Her Māori ancestors are the indigenous people of Aotearoa/New Zealand; my English ancestors are among those who colonized this country about 150 years ago. She is older than me. I was her teacher at university and supervised her doctoral research on Māori education. We now teach together. We have become friends and research collaborators and have decided to extend for publication a section of Kuni's doctoral research about the origins of schooling in New Zealand. No one has yet done this work, and we are both convinced there is a fascinating story to be told.

We read books by the popular historians. "Hah!" says Kuni. "That didn't happen." "What didn't?" I ask. She talks about a well-known event: the delivery of the first sermon in New Zealand, by Samuel Marsden of the Church Missionary Society, on Christmas Day 1814 (Cloher, 2003, p. 86; King, 2003, p. 141; Nicholas, 1817, p. 205; Salmond, 1997, p. 465). "How could he have 'given a sermon'?" she asks.

I hesitate. Here is the first Western formal mass pedagogical event in New Zealand. About four hundred Māori men, women, and children are gathered on the slopes above the beach to hear a chiefly visitor, Marsden, a few days after his arrival in New Zealand, from Australia. But he cannot speak the Māori language, and they certainly cannot understand English. Ruatara, a young chief who has invited both Marsden and a teacher to Aotearoa/New Zealand to start a school, is the interpreter of Marsden's sermon.

There is no record of what Ruatara said. Kuni is unconvinced that Ruatara would have attempted any direct translation. Instead, she says, he would have spoken with passionate eloquence about the benefits and status of the new settlers; he would have enjoined the people to be good to the visitors and to protect them, in anticipation of the technological, agricultural, and knowledge advantages they would bring to the iwi.

The people heard Ruatara; Marsden's words were indistinct to them—merely foreign sounds. So it was *Māori* desires, words, and authority to which the people responded. In an important sense, it was Ruatara who gave that first "sermon," which might more properly be called Ruatara's political meeting.

Kuni and I talk about the arrival of Marsden's ship, with its small cargo of the first settlers, a few days before the sermon. The historians refer to a sham fight on the beach, staged for the entertainment of the new arrivals (Cloher, 2003, p. 85; Nicholas, 1817, p. 193; Salmond, 1997, p. 462). "That was no sham fight," says Kuni, "that looks like a massive *pôwhiri* or *waka taki.*"[1] Suddenly, a bit of thrilling but trivial entertainment on the beach becomes a very significant mass ritual of encounter, by which the local people indicate their willingness to engage and negotiate with the new arrivals, as well as signal to them that they now have some obligatory connections to the tribes of the area.

Almost at once, two historical events are turned upside down.

Focusing on how the stories might be framed, I take notes as Kuni speaks. In each retelling of these familiar scenes from our shared past, their power relations shift and become dramatically more complex. The standard account implies that power lies largely with the settlers: It is Marsden who talks to the people and thereby introduces Christianity to a new land; his important arrival is marked by a vigorous bit of entertainment by excited natives. But Kuni reads these stories through a different lens: Ruatara decided on and gave a major address to the people about Pakeha settlement, which he sought to control; the Māori leaders choreographed a major welcome so that the local people would understand the significance of the settlers and their proper place within the protection of the tribe. The play of power, knowledge, and reality—there is our potential article, right there, and a direction for more research and consultation. I write, weaving Kuni's interpretations and my analysis into a joint account (Jones & Jenkins, 2001, 2004).

Several things happen through this collaboration. The stories of the relationships leading to the establishment of the first Western school in New Zealand become layered, richer, more complex. We know the different historical experiences cannot be homogenized into one single account (even though our joint academic publication is genuinely shared work, and neither could do it without the other). At the same time, our new, rich account is not produced through mutual dialogue; neither of us attempts fully to understand the other. What we do understand is that the careful, tense interplay of our histories provides an interesting account of the complexity of contemporary as well as past indigenous-colonizer relations.

Another dynamic is played out in the micropractice of this collaboration: the negotiation of voice. Who speaks? Does joint authorship denote harmonized voices? Is it possible to hear my Māori colleague if I am the one who writes the text, using her insights? There is never anything simple or settled about indigenous-colonizer writing collaboration. All collaborative arrangements differ depending on the personalities, the partnership, the relative power, and academic desires of the participants. Kuni and I sometimes coauthor our collaborative work; sometimes we do not. This negotiated flexibility reflects a self-consciously conditional and open approach to our joint work on Māori-Pakeha relationships in education. We agree that coauthorship, when it implies speaking with one voice, is impossible. We know that we cannot and do not have a homogeneous viewpoint; I speak out of my social position as a critical Pakeha academic, and she takes a Māori/Ngati Porou cultural and political perspective shaped by her academic training. Though this means we often find enough shared ground to speak together as coauthors, it also means that sometimes we speak separately—depending on the audience, the standpoint, or the politics of the writing.

This particular chapter, authored by Alison, addresses colonizer interests in cross-cultural engagement. It reflects my experience as a White settler/colonizer researcher and addresses similarly positioned others about desires for collaboration with indigenous colleagues. Many of my insights have developed over years of engagement with Kuni, as well as with other Māori colleagues and students, including Linda Tuhiwai Smith. Those voices echo strongly here.

Working the Hyphen

In our collaboration about our respective people's shared histories, Kuni and I *work the hyphen.* Using this phrase as a qualitative researcher working across cultures, Michelle Fine (1994) calls attention to the complex gap at the Self-Other border. For those of us engaged in postcolonial cross-cultural collaborative inquiry, this hyphen, mapped onto the indigene-colonizer relationship, straddles a space of intense interest.

The colonizer-indigene hyphen always reaches back into a shared past. Each of our names—indigene and colonizer—discursively produces the other. In New Zealand, the local names Māori and Pakeha form identities created in response to the other. Linda Tuhiwai Smith (1999) notes, "Maori is an indigenous term . . . a label which defines a colonial relationship between 'Maori' and 'Pakeha,' the non-indigenous settler population" (p. 6). Each term forced the other into being, to distinguish "us," the ordinary (the word *māori* means ordinary in Māori language) people, from the others, the white-skinned strangers. The shared indigene-colonizer/Māori-Pakeha hyphen not only holds ethnic and historical difference and interchange; it also marks a relationship of power and inequality that continues to shape differential patterns of cultural dominance and social privilege. Therefore, in a research setting, the politics of the indigene-colonizer hyphen becomes a struggle, as Linda Tuhiwai Smith puts it, between "the interests and ways of knowing of the West and the interests and ways of resisting of the Other" (p. 2). As collaborators across these interests, Kuni and I attempt to create a research and writing relationship based on the tension of difference, not on its erasure. In that the indigene-colonizer hyphen marks the indelible relationship that has shaped both sides in different ways, the hyphen as a character in the research relationship becomes an object of necessary attention.

The indigene-colonizer hyphen has attracted a range of discursive postures in collaborative inquiry. A marker of the relationship between two generalized groups, the hyphen has been erased, softened, denied, consumed, expanded, homogenized, and romanticized. The discursive hyphen has stood in for an unbridgeable chasm between the civilized and the uncivilized; it has marked a romantic difference between the innocent noble savage and corrupt Western man; it has held the gap between the indigenous subjects of study and their objective White observers.

Modern anxieties about this gap, as well as the paradoxical desire both for difference *and* for its dissolution via communicative relationships, have led to calls for dialogue and mutual engagement across difference. The current (colonizer) researcher ideal of the *mutuality* of the indigene-colonizer hyphen was perhaps first asserted by anthropologist Margaret Mead (1969): "Anthropological research does not have subjects," she said. "We work with [indigenous] informants in an atmosphere of trust and mutual respect" (p. 361). This fantasy/model of respectful sharing often shapes the hyphen in contemporary liberal cross-cultural research and teaching. Especially in education research which reaches across cultural boundaries, calls for—or assertions of—dialogue, understanding, and empathy between cultures are common.

When mutual understanding is fundamental to cross-cultural engagement, the hyphen becomes a barrier to close empathetic collaboration. Therefore, the hyphen is softened, or reduced, in the interests of mutuality. Shared understandings reduce distance and enable progress toward the social ideal of equality. Structural power differences, as well as other differences in perspective and history, are downplayed as collaborators attempt to come to some shared perspective. In education, research that focuses on such shared social goods as teacher effectiveness, children's learning needs, and multiculturalism requires a softened hyphen to allow the foregrounding of mutually shared values and outcomes. The hyphen becomes submerged in researchers' enthusiastic, all-encompassing visions of humanity, quality, and diversity.[2] Social theorists such as Brian Barry (2001), Martha Nussbaum (1997), and Todd Gitlin (1995) express eloquently the powerful desires for universal moral norms that reduce any ruptures suggested by the hyphen.

An extreme form of this approach to cultural difference is articulated by those who seek actively to *erase* the hyphen as they look "toward the ultimate unity of human experience" (Hansen, 2002, p. 2; Hollinger, 1995). On this sort of view, diversities are "not something to be celebrated, but a problem to be solved . . . as avenues to unified understanding" (Hansen, 2002, p. 338; see also Harrison & Huntington, 2000). To ensure unity, the hyphen, as a marker of difference, is best dissolved altogether.

The denial/erasure of the hyphen is also expressed in the language of hybridity, a codeword for sameness. We are all hybrid mixes of one shared sort or another—we are all settlers (we all came to this land at some point); we are all indigenous (most of us were born here); we are all "mixed breeds" (intermarriage is widespread, and most indigenous peoples are assimilated into Western lifestyles). Or, we are all citizens; we are all students; we are all equal under the law, in the eyes of God, or in terms of needs and opportunities. On this logic, the hyphen becomes a marker of social division and a barrier to communication and democracy, something to be (dis)*solved.* Disavowing the hyphen in the name of sameness becomes literally a productive political act *for* "us all."

The almost universal indigenous and Other response to the ideal of what I am calling the erased, denied, dissolved, or softened hyphen has been a firm reinstatement of the gap. Critics refer to the "ethnocentric universality" (Mohanty, 1997, p. 272), which enables Western researchers to ignore the indigenous-colonizer hyphen as they write across it, recolonizing as they go. Taking this critique seriously, some colonizer researchers who work with indigenous peoples emphasize the gap of difference. They position themselves as outsiders, coming "to the Native culture as a privileged guest" (Haig-Brown, 1988, p. 155), seeking to "present Native perspectives" (p. 25; see also, e.g., Martin, 1999). Such collaboration often elicits a posture of self-effacement in White researchers who feel that the powerful and moving colonization stories of indigenous people must speak for themselves. The hyphen becomes a bridge, a moment of translation (and sometimes romanticization) for the colonizer researcher who gives voice to the oppressed indigenous person enabling a direct and sympathetic hearing from others.

While I have focused here on research relationships between indigenous and colonizer collaborators, struggles at the hyphen also characterize some collaborations between indigenous researchers and their own people. These collaborations become a rather different exercise in translation as indigenous researchers find themselves outsiders in their own communities. Their educational status and colonizer knowledge (and sometimes their lack of indigenous language) may create what Black feminist scholar Patricia Hill Collins (1986, 1998) called the outsider-within, as indigenous researchers attempt to write from both sides of the hyphen. Such an uncomfortable, though insightful, position requires a constant struggle with tensions and contradictions (Islam, 2000, and Twine, 2000, provide good examples of these).

Pragmatic Collaboration Across the Hyphen

To those colonizer researchers who would dissolve/consume/soften/erase the indigene-colonizer hyphen into a sharing collaborative engagement between "us," there is one, harshly pragmatic, response: *It does not work.* Indigenous peoples and others who resist their disappearance into Western stories about us either remain focused elsewhere (i.e., silent, outside the hearing of their colonizer colleagues) or echo the words of Tonto, the Lone Ranger's "faithful Indian companion": "What do you mean, 'we,' white man?" However hurtful, perplexing, frustrating, and disappointing this response might be, colonizers interested in joint work with indigenous subjects *as indigenous subjects* have little choice but to work *with* that sharp, shocking difference named by Tonto, and many others such as Mohanty, rather than deny, ignore, or condemn it or wish it away.

In other words, however much the Lone Ranger and other colonizer peoples assert the us in a shared modern life, indigenous peoples—as a matter of political, practical, and identity survival *as indigenous peoples*—insist on a profound difference at the Self-Other border. The hyphen is nonnegotiable. Indeed, in indigene-colonizer research and teaching work, the hyphen is to be protected and asserted and is a positive site of productive methodological *work.* Settler/colonizer researcher Michelle Fine (1994) puts it this way: "'Working the hyphen' in cross-cultural inquiry means creating occasions for researchers and informants to discuss what is, and is not, 'happening between,' within the negotiated relations of whose story is being told . . . and whose story is being shadowed" (p. 72). Fine addresses the Self-Other hyphen as a moment of methodological self-consciousness about the "between"; in other words, she understands the hyphen as marking a difficult but always necessary *relationship.* This is not only a relationship between collaborating people but also their respective relationship to *difference.* The relationship is also—from the indigenous side of difference—significantly one of struggle, resistance, and caution, as Smith (1999) reminds us.

Before I go on to discuss the inevitable difficulties with working the hyphen, I need to address some of the drawbacks of my apparent criticism of "us" in collaborative inquiry. Mine is *not* a rejection of possibilities for joint work. In fact, I believe that collaborative research relationships are essential to insight, and there are far too few good colonizer-indigene collaborations; the hyphen, after all, joins as well as separates. In addition, a united front in indigenous-colonizer research collaborations is at times pragmatically important, and "us" may name that collaboration. My point is that "us" cannot *stand in place* of the hyphen; it can only name an always conditional relationship-between.

Another obvious problem with the discussion so far is the apparently uncritical use of an indigenous-colonizer binary, marking two fixed, radically different, apparently homogeneous groups. After all, significant divisions and differences exist *within* both groups named by these terms. Differences among indigenous peoples are significant on the basis of language and education, tribal histories, and cultures. In fact, while it may be a basis for internal collaboration and a politics of strength, the term *indigenous* may itself be a homogenizing term, produced within colonization and continuing its colonizing work by brushing over national or tribal differences. Another problem with the assertion of a clear indigenous-colonizer binary is that few indigenous peoples have avoided substantial assimilation into Western cultures and languages (Semali & Kincheloe, 1999). It is the case (especially in New Zealand) that intermarriage has always been very common and also that indigenous values and language have affected colonizer peoples, as well as vice versa. In addition, colonizer and indigenous peoples often do not understand themselves in these terms. The boundaries between "us" and "them" on the street, in workplaces, and in classrooms have diminished substantially since our first encounters. Such mutual assimilation, in that it marks pockets of equality, has been and should be a cause for celebration. My argument is not about such interrelationships in the social and personal world. It is important to recognize that arguments about collaborative inquiry across the indigene-colonizer hyphen entail the assertion, at some crucial points, of an indigenous political and social id/entity distinct from that of a colonizer subject. For indigenous subjects, this is a *necessary* distinction and disjuncture; for collaborators, a *necessary* "between."

▣ Anger and Learning About the Other

Collaboration between indigenous and colonizer researchers, where invitations and relationships are established over time, differs from the more short-lived cross-cultural relationships in classrooms, although desires for democratic communication tend to underlie both. As educators, Kuni and I struggle to assist our students toward a productive relationship with difference; our joint teaching experiences in classrooms where indigenous and colonizer students sit alongside each other formed the basis for some of our collaborative research work. Teaching together, Kuni and I have attempted to model the difficulties and rewards of collaborative inquiry, emphasizing that mutual understanding or "learning *about* the Other" is not the aim—or even possible—for dominant group students. Learning *from* the Other, that is, *from* difference, *from* the hyphen, becomes the possibility we seek—as I explain below.

Learning *about* the Other is the most popular form of teaching about difference for colonizer or dominant groups. "Walking in other's shoes" allows the dominant group to empathize with, and therefore supposedly to understand, the point of view of the Other. Ideally, this results in shared aspirations, democratic tolerance, and social harmony. But it is rarely recognized that learning about the Other may *not* be required for *indigenous* groups in classrooms. They have achieved this learning simply as members of a colonized society. They are already deeply familiar with the language, experiences, and views of the dominant group—indeed, some indigenous activists call for *unlearning* about the dominant Other, through what they call decolonizing the mind (see Smith, 1999, p. 23). The difference between the needs and knowledges of each side means that collaborative inquiry becomes problematic.

This major skew in learning needs at the indigene-colonizer hyphen has meant that, in some cases, the indigene has refused face-to-face collaboration. It was at one of these moments of refusal that Kuni's and my sense of collaborative inquiry was forced to become explicit. Some of our Māori students stated that they preferred to study their histories, knowledges, and experiences separately from their Pakeha (White) peers. They found the development of their own cultural memories was disrupted by Pakeha classmates who, although positively keen to engage with them on the subject of education, generally had a very different view of it. Māori students, often disheartened and weary, had become unwilling constantly to explain themselves, to listen to cultural ignorance, even hostility, and to encounter again and again what they experienced as a disappointing lack of knowledge in many of their Pakeha classmates.

So, in a spirit of pedagogical experimentation and guided by the ideal of social justice, Kuni and I divided the class on the basis of ethnicity for a large portion of the following year's program. Māori—along with Pacific Islands[3]—students were invited to form one group; Pakeha and others formed another.

Although some teachers in the United States would like to try such an experiment, they believe it is dangerous even to attempt because it transgresses too deeply the mainstream cultural abhorrence of separatism (Srivastava, 1997). In New Zealand, protected perhaps by our good relationships with our students and each other, Kuni and I took turns to teach both groups. The Māori students enjoyed the program and did well in their assessments. They reported that the separation from White peers enabled them to engage more freely and deeply in the debates about Māori education as well as colonization. They enjoyed the opportunity to talk directly with each other, and teach each other, about their experiences (Pihama & Jenkins, 2001).

Many of the White students, on the other hand, were furious. They saw the segregation from their Māori peers as denying them something they very much wanted. They wanted to *learn,* they said, and to *share.* They asked, How can we learn about each other if we are separated? Surely it is better to be together so we can share our experiences? Isn't separation reinforcing difference, rather than reducing it (see Jones, 1999)?

While their White peers sought to reduce difference, this was not a priority for the indigenous students. Indeed, for the indigenous students, difference was both a fact (as their White peers did not share their knowledges and experiences *as* Māori) and something actively *desired* as significant to their identity and political location as indigenous people (rather than as, say, brown-skinned diverse citizens). In addition, the indigenous students did not feel the need to be the recipients of sharing—their Pakeha peers *as* Pakeha had no information about themselves Māori needed or wanted. To the indigenous students, the White students seemed to be the sole beneficiaries of sharing.

Interestingly, many of the White students were no happier in the joint classes, which formed parts of the course. These classes were taught by Māori, Pakeha, and a guest Tongan teacher. Some White students were uneasy when teachers used brief phrases in languages they did not understand; they reported these teachers expected them to know "cultural things" that they did not know. These White/settler students were "marginalized," feeling they "did not belong." In their journals, they recorded the following:

> I felt marginalised in this class . . . it made me feel personally that I wasn't part of the lecture . . . it served to emphasise rather than diminish my status as an "outsider." . . . I had been told in a subtle way I did not belong. (see Jones, 2001, pp. 281–282)

In both sorts of classes—the separated lessons and those taught by non-Pakeha teachers—many of the White students experienced a keen sense of *exclusion.*

The feelings of these White students are not unique. There are many anecdotal and published examples of White anxiety at other ethnic groups' attempts to caucus separately or to debate issues that they believe White people do not readily share or understand. We heard of White people who felt left out when their non-White peers formed groups. Some schools were wary of organizing meetings for particular ethnic groups, fearing the angry response of the White mainstream. For instance, when Virginia Chalmers (1997) organized a highly successful and lively evening at her New York school for parents of color (a group that normally did not come to school meetings), angry White parents expressed their disappointment in terms of exclusion and loss.

How, then, is indigene-colonizer collaboration possible when learning about the Other seems so problematic for both groups? As teachers and researchers interested in forms of collaborative inquiry, how might we think through the colonizer/dominant group request for sharing and possible indigenous resistance to it? To consider possibilities for cross-cultural collaborative work, I return to the logic of colonizer desire for collaboration.

Who Is Outside?

> . . . I had been told in a subtle way I did not belong.

When the indigenous person fails to address the needs or wishes of the well-meaning, would-be collaborator-colonizer, the latter experiences a shock. Any withdrawal of the indigene from accessible engagement is felt as an unbearable exclusion. But the resulting anxiety for the new outsider is not from loss of social power so much as *loss of ability to define the conditions* or the social-political space within which, they believe, getting to know each other becomes possible. The terms of engagement are no longer controlled by the dominant group.

The *progressive* terms of engagement have been spelled out by educators seeking collaboration in the name of justice. They argue that Western social history, including its institutions such as education, has operated as a series of exclusions—of people of color, indigenous people, women—where "the voice of the other is consigned to the margins" (Aronowitz & Giroux, 1991, p. 115). A logically progressive response to exclusion is for marginalized groups to be *included.* Inclusion means they—the Others—must be brought in to the center by us—the powerful. According to this logic, the decolonizing researcher or teacher seeks to "make room for those groups generally defined as the excluded others" (Aronowitz & Giroux, 1991, p. 122). Making room entails "redrawing the map of modernism so as to effect a shift of power from the privileged . . . to those groups struggling" through "establishing new boundaries with respect to knowledge most often associated with the margins" (Aronowitz & Giroux, 1991, pp. 115, 120). Or, as Sandra Harding (1998) puts it, we must develop "borderlands epistemologies" that value various knowledges from diverse cultures (see also Semali & Kincheloe, 1999).

The vehicle for this movement over the terrain of power, out from the margins and into the centers—the mechanism for shifting the boundary pegs and redrawing the maps of power—is *voice.* Speaking, the colonized subject is able to name the world and thus rename it in the interests of social change. This speaking is not simply to enable verbal sparring with the colonizers, nor is it an expression of a simple liberal pluralism (Shor & Freire, 1987, p. 13). And nor is it necessarily authentic; critical theorists recognize that notions of authentic voice are utopian and misunderstand the complexities of power and identity (Aronowitz & Giroux, 1991, p. 117; McLaren, 1995). Such complexities notwithstanding, researchers and educators interested in liberation wish to "hear the voices" of the colonized/oppressed/other (Aronowitz & Giroux, 1991, p. 129), as these Others "become the mediators of their own narratives" (McLaren, 1995, p. 115) and therefore actors in their own emancipation. What we might "become together" in such renegotiation, suggests McLaren (1995, p. 109) takes precedence over "who we are"—in other words, whether we are indigene or colonizer, our *shared talk* is most important.

It is these terms of engagement that are problematic.

▣ Hearing Voices?

Here is the problem with the call for shared speaking. The desire for shared talk is, at its core, a desire for the dominant/colonizer group to engage in some benevolent action—for them/us to *grant a hearing to* the usually suppressed voice and "realms of meaning" of the indigene. After all, as already mentioned, *indigenous* access into the realms of meaning of the dominant Other is hardly required; members of marginalized/colonized groups are immersed in it daily. It is the colonizer, wishing to hear, who calls for dialogue.[4]

If we take seriously Barthes's (1994) arguments about the power of the reader to make the text and that understanding "lies not in [a text's] origin but in its destination" (p. 148), it is obvious that the indigene's *audience* in the site of inquiry becomes the key player in meaning. Therefore, when dominant group members are unable to understand the speaker, the indigene's ability to speak is reduced dramatically. Even good intentions by the dominant group are not always sufficient to enable their ears to hear and *therefore* for the other to speak. Uma Narayan (1988) has argued that members of disadvantaged groups "cannot fail to be aware of the fact that presence of goodwill on the part of members of advantaged groups is not enough to overcome assumptions and attitudes born out of centuries of power and privilege" (p. 35)—assumptions and attitudes that produce at least a partly and necessarily nonshared language and meaning system for naming the world. Deafness of the colonizers to indigenous speakers is one of the necessary conditions of a colonized society. While usually unintentional, such dis-ability enables imposition on others in the name of development and engagement.

Even progressive settler educators who seek collaboration with indigenous others necessarily remain only partially able to hear and see. What determines this ability is not merely indigeneity. It is not *simply* that Kuni is Māori that gives her the privileged ability to see what I cannot as we work together; it is an issue of *access to knowledge.* One's experience, knowledge, and recognition by one's own people provide an indigenous person with the authority and insight to contribute *as Māori* to research on Māori things. With enough immersion in Māori language and culture, it may be logically *possible* for me as a Pakeha/settler to interpret past and current events "from a Māori point of view." But in practical terms, outside such complete immersion, it is unlikely as a Pakeha that I will see, hear, and feel from that viewpoint or get emphatically inside, say, the story of Ruatara.

The reasons are as simple as they are powerful. Compared with Kuni, I have been less exposed to the speeches of *rangatira* (leaders) and other knowledgeable Maori people, and I am less familiar with their forms of address; my aunties and grandpas have not taught me subtle forms of engagement that mark me as polite, knowledgeable, and relaxed in Māori company; I have less chance of getting my interpretations checked and validated by expert indigenous people, or access to formal and informal indigenous knowledges through conversations and meetings conducted in *te reo Māori* (Māori language) or in English. I am unlikely to have had forms of Māori spiritual experience. And I am unlikely to be accepted (politically or personally) as providing a Māori perspective when I am not of Māori descent and cannot trace my ancestral links to Māori leaders of the past. As a Pakeha subject engaging in cross-cultural work, then, I am limited—in both senses (see also McConaghy, 2000, p. xiii). It becomes necessary for me to abandon the hope that collaborative inquiry—and progressive education—can be a product of my enabling the indigenous voice and promoting shared engagement.

Even as an accepted collaborator, I know that, from a Māori perspective, if the settler collaborator is not of some use, she or he is politely abandoned. Kuni is often called on by indigenous colleagues to justify her working with me. She is asked to consider the extent of nonindigenous influence. We both value these sometimes bitter critiques because they remind us—as if we could forget—that this is always already contested and risky territory on which we work.

The Logic of Learning From the Other

The limits to understanding between indigene and colonizer are not only rooted in our different histories, experiences, and cultures—and therefore what we can hear and what we are told. Limited understanding can also be seen as epistemologically inevitable. Working with a view of the Other as absolute difference, Sharon Todd (2003), following Levinas, argues that in order to know the Other, I am forced to make the Other in my own image: "When I think I know, when I think I understand the Other, I am exercising my knowledge over the Other, shrouding the Other in my own totality. The Other becomes an object of *my* comprehension, *my* world, *my* narrative, reducing the Other to me" (p. 15). This means that the alterity of the Other is "reabsorbed into my own identity, as a . . . possessor" (Levinas, 1969/2000, p. 33). For Todd, as well as Levinas, the "it does not work" pragmatics of knowing the Other is a matter of the *logic* of knowing.

Todd (2003) points out that, as one who is absolutely different from me, the Other cannot be totally learned about, known, or understood by me. The relationship is necessarily much more oblique. Todd explains, "If I am exposed to the Other, I can listen, attend and be surprised; the Other can affect me, she 'brings me more than I contain'" (p. 15). What she brings me is the experience of difference. This experience confronts me with limits to my knowledge and learning, when I had no idea of their limits before.

Like many other (White) writers who address difference, Todd (2003) seems to assume that the Self-Other hyphen always maps onto colonizer-indigene *in that order;* that is, the Self refers to the positive subject colonizer, the Other to the abject indigene. In philosophical terms, this may be a necessary hierarchy. But what about the inversion, which has to be a characteristic of reciprocal collaborative inquiry (see Oliver, 2001, p. 6)? When the indigene-Self speaks, what does it mean to say, "If I attend to the Other I can be surprised"? Why would the indigene be surprised when attending to the colonizer who is so familiar as to be part of one's Self? Isn't surprise the prerogative only of the attentive dominant subject who, having been deaf to the Other, finds her or him suddenly speaking?

Nevertheless, Todd (2003) makes very useful observations about ethical principles of collaborative inquiry. Social justice education and collaborative research work, in which the Self–Other relationship makes a central appearance, she suggests, often get routed down a particular pedagogical path. Participants have to learn and apply certain ethical principles about how to get along (such as respect, fairness, equity, empathy). This runs the risk that social justice education and collaborative inquiry become a form of moral training rather than a quest for knowledge and engagement. Furthermore, as a mode of relating across difference, she says, respect and empathy can miss the target completely in terms of recognizing that difference.[5] Empathy's impulse, as I mentioned above, is to *overcome* difference, to break down the hyphen between Self and Other. Engaging across differences through empathy may provide us with useful raw material for *self*-reflection, Todd insists, but "it cannot offer the ethical attentiveness to difference qua difference so necessary to projects of social justice" (p. 63).

Todd (2003) brings us to the nub of the argument: The indigene-colonizer collaboration—if we are open and susceptible—is a site of learning *from* difference rather than learning *about* the Other. The Self-Other hyphen as a positive marker of irreducible difference is a pedagogical site. The hyphen ideally demands a posture of alert vulnerability to or recognition of difference, rather than a pose of empathetic understanding that tends to reduce difference to the same. This is not a moral injunction, but one in the interests of knowledge. It is openness to difference that can provoke meanings beyond our own culture's prescriptions—and lead to new thought (Garrison, 2004, p. 94).

A desire to learn from otherness is in tension with the more common desire to make room for the voices of the Other. The liberal injunction to listen to the Other can turn out to be *access for dominant groups* to the thoughts, cultures, and lives of others (see also Boler, 1997; Roman, 1997, 1993). So while marginalized groups may be invited—with the help of the teacher or researcher—to make their own social conditions visible to themselves, the crucial aspect of this liberating process is making themselves visible to the powerful. To extend the metaphor: In attempting, in the name of justice and dialogue, to move the boundary pegs of power into the terrain of the margin-dwellers, the powerful require those on the margins not to be silent, or to talk alone, but to open up their territory and share what they know. The imperialist resonances are uncomfortably apt.

Some White researchers have been careful to reject the notion that their demands for dialogical engagement might simply become a form of surveillance and neocolonization. Radical educators emphasize that they seek merely to respect and uphold difference, as well as have it influence the world, through having it spoken and politically shared, where once it was suppressed. Homi Bhabha (1994) suggests that such pure motives may be more problematic than they seem. Using Derrida's phrase, he talks of the colonizer's demand for narrative, "the narcissistic, colonialist demand it should be addressed directly, that the Other should authorise the Self, recognise its priority, fulfil its outlines" (p. 98). Addressing the Other involves answering the colonizer's benign, maybe even apologetic, request: "Tell us exactly what happened. I care," "What is it like for you? I want to learn about you." Bhabha suggests that such demands are a significant "strategy of surveillance and exploitation" (p. 99) and reensure the authority of the colonizer. Other postcolonial writers such as Spivak (1988) also argue that desire for accessibility to the Other can be simply another colonizing gesture. Both Spivak and Bhabha make calls to Western intellectuals and researchers to abandon the myths of representational clarity and total accessibility to the Other.

After Bhabha and Spivak (let alone some of their own disappointing experiences!), it is unsurprising that indigenous scholars or researchers might be cautious about collaboration and dialogue with members of colonizer groups. If shared talk becomes an exercise only in making themselves more understandable or accessible to colonizer groups, with no commensurate shifts in real political power, then it becomes better to engage in strengthening the internal communication and knowledge, as well as self-reliance, of the people.

Out of Grasp

Nor should it be surprising that the colonizer/settler feels anxious about any refusal of indigenous collaboration. Sharon Todd (2003) reminds us that learning is a psychical rather than merely an epistemological event. Learning from the Other—including learning about difference from the Other's otherness—leads to all kinds of "connections, disjunctions, and ruptures" (Todd, 2003, p. 10). There is thus a kind of trauma in encountering what is outside the subject, she argues, because "that outside threatens the stability of the ego. . . . Precisely because the Other is seen to be that which disrupts its coherency, the subject tumbles into uncertainty, its past strategies for living challenged by the very strangeness of difference itself" (Todd, 2003, p. 11). It is the strangeness of difference—the unfamiliar space of not knowing—that is so hard to tolerate for the colonizer whose benevolent imperialism assumes both herself or himself as the center of knowing and that everything can be known.

For the colonizer/settler engaged in critical inquiry, there is an inevitable and disturbing moment when the indigenous teacher or informant speaks. It is a moment of recognition—perhaps unconscious—that some things may be out of one's grasp. It is a fleeting, slippery glimpse of (the possibility of) something inaccessible and unknowable. In the Western academy, the unknowable holds a paradoxical position (Readings, 1996). Critical traditions in Western thought would concur that, as the ultimate expression of intellectual curiosity, Western science and scholarship is a major source of uncertainty; what is *not* known is the product of, and the machine driving, intellectual work. Nevertheless, it remains the case that the traditional Hegelian basis of education and pedagogy is not radical uncertainty but the ultimate *accessibility* and *knowability* of things. Indeed, the not-known is understood in terms of the still-to-be-known, or the potentially-knowable—a notion that has radically underpinned the impetus for exploration and colonization. Western knowledge and colonization are both premised on the ideal of discovering, making visible, and understanding the entire natural and social world (Haraway, 1997).

In contrast, for some indigenous cultures, as Linda Tuhiwai Smith (1991, 1999) points out, free access to all knowledge is not a pedagogical or social ideal. Because knowledge contributes to a person's power and status, it is not given out to just anyone: "Some knowledge can be gained only by its being given" (Smith, 1991, p. 50) and therefore is not made available to those who simply want to know. Therefore, indigenous researchers tend to look extremely carefully at potential collaborators. In working with Māori-speaking Pakeha anthropologist Anne Salmond, in order to pass on his knowledge to future generations, Māori elder Eruera Stirling "looked to see if I had the 'right spirit,' and he wove a metaphor of kinship and apprenticeship between us that made our work together peaceful and unworried" (Salmond, 2005, p. 247). Right spirit, kinship, and apprenticeship are interesting choices of terms to describe this collaborative work. Lasting loyalty as well as humility and trust were the key elements in their shared inquiry; there is no suggestion of a liberal equality, sharing, or dialogue in working this hyphen.

Ignoring a right spirit, the Western university encourages researchers, students, and teachers to assume the happy position as potential knowers on an open epistemological territory awaiting anyone with the desire to explore. Pedagogy and research, especially at university, becomes predicated on the *possibility of* and *entitlement to* an accessible and shared terrain of knowledge. When this fantasy of entitlement is disrupted—for instance, when access to indigenous knowledge and experience is denied, such as when indigenous students remain separate or when indigenous concepts are not adequately explained—settler inquiry experiences a threat. The threat has particular emotional force for those who feel it, I think, because it threatens the dominant group at the very point of our/their power—our ability to know.

▣ Necessary Fantasy

The modernist project of mapping the world, rendering it visible and understood, that is, accessible, is an expression of a Western Enlightenment desire for coherence, authorization, and control. It can also be seen as central to liberal White desire for racial harmony, collaboration, and understanding. The assumption held by dominant cultures and our pedagogies and research programs—that everything is in principle knowable—forms not only the epistemological basis for our being and knowing but also our fantasies and desires for a better, less fragmented world. Such progressive desires are important, but they must also be seen as based in *fantasy*—a redemptive fantasy of unity that attempts to overcome history and ongoing effects of colonization. Such fantasy is a necessary but always troubled ingredient in cross-cultural work.

These troubles at the indigene-colonizer hyphen invite both sides to avoid the relationship as too difficult. Indeed, those whose teaching practice has led them, like me, to question progressive notions of dialogue (particularly Ellsworth, 1989) have been criticized as courting "a crippling form of political disengagement . . . [which] reduces one to paralysis in the face of . . . differences" (Aronowitz & Giroux, 1991, p. 132).[6] But a critical position is not as negative, or impotent, as it might appear. Rather than paralysis, it suggests hard work—not the work of face-to-face conversation in the name of liberatory practice but the work of coming to know our own location in the Self-Other binary and accepting the difference marked by the hyphen. The desire for engagement must lead colonizer scholars to a deeper understanding of our own settler culture, society, and history as deeply embedded in a relationship with the culture, society, and history of the indigenous people. Such an orientation to the hyphen invites colonizer peoples to seek to know ourselves in the relationship with Others, to locate ourselves in the "between"—to develop a stronger sense of how our Selves are and have been formed in the troubled engagement with indigenous peoples and their lands and spaces. Such cross-cultural work necessarily involves thinking about and engaging with the indigenous peoples and/or their texts. This orientation *to a relationship*—to the hyphen—rather than to the Other, is the most feasible posture for a colonizer collaborator.

Levinasian philosophers such as Sharon Todd (2003) make the point more emphatically. The Other is *necessarily* not knowable, being what "we" are not. Rather than learning *about* the Other on our terms and therefore failing because we are obliterating the Other, what we can do, says Todd, is attempt to learn more obliquely *from* the Other as "one who is absolutely different from myself" (p. 15). What I learn is not about you, but I learn from you about *difference*. This, of course, returns us to the hyphen, that stroke that both enforces difference and makes the link between. The hyphen's space does not demand destructive good understanding; indeed, it is a space that *insists* on ignorance and therefore a perpetual lack of clarity and certainty.[7]

Uncertainty is no longer a stranger to scholars; the ongoing crisis of representation in Western thought means many of us have abandoned already the unalloyed right to know (Lincoln & Denzin, 1994). As a result, addressing White/colonizer researchers, some assert that "disappointment—of certainty, clarity, illumination, generality—is both a choice and an inevitability; something to be both resigned and committed to," not (or not just) as a state of resignation about the impossibility of fully coming to know the Other, but "as a strategic act of interruption of the methodological will to certainty and clarity of vision" and the colonizing impulses that attend it (Stronach & MacLure, 1997, pp. 4–5). Jim Garrison (2004) suggests that those of us interested in this sort of work adopt a "passionate ambivalence" (p. 89). As well as taking on a politics of disappointment and ambivalence, we might also add a practical politics of hope and of sharp, unromantic pragmatic engagement.

Failure and the Teacher

The inevitable tangle of caution, passion, ignorance, ambivalence, desire, and power that attends the indigene-colonizer hyphen provides rich, though uncertain, pickings for research collaborators. It is within this interesting space, and with a determination to proceed, that Kuni and I continue to invite each other to work the hyphen. We experiment with genres for writing through and against the hyphen. We turn to Māori language. Kuni develops a notion of *aitanga* (turning toward the other to have sex) as a metaphor for the potential of the Māori-Pakeha relationship. She collects data from elders on the term's potential, and then she returns both to her Māori advisers and colleagues, and to me, with the data so we can discuss how it might be written. She writes it up for a Māori audience; I consider working the data into a joint piece for academic publication, writing carefully under Kuni's guidance. We turn to the archives; we both read them, and Kuni again leads the analysis, with me as the writer. Through me, her voice (but not the bones of her analysis) must be compromised; we just have to live with that when we coauthor.

And we keep on with our reading and writing about how the first school in New Zealand came to be. The historians called the school a failure because it stayed open for less than 2 years, and the children did not attend regularly (Binney, 1968). "That school was a success," Kuni declares. Two years was enough time for the Pakeha teacher to become educated—to learn to speak the Māori language and to understand something about the beliefs of the people. As an educated man, the teacher became useful to the local Ngāpuhi chief and the iwi and worked within the local rules (much to the horror of the Church Missionary Society, as well as other tribes, because he enabled Ngāpuhi to get access to guns). The school had thus served as an effective site of Māori teaching and Pakeha learning.

Kuni and I know that these two accounts and the earlier ones are not merely parallel stories about the past and its colonizer-indigene relationships. They undo each other at a deep level, providing radically different memories of power and "what went on" between Pakeha and Māori. If we remember Marsden as *the* speaker at the first big meeting between Māori and Pakeha, if we recall the sham fight on the beach and the failed school, whether we are Māori or Pakeha, the colonizer's power, and the story of colonization, is normalized. Its normalization seeps into the present, into the accepted, commonsense status quo. To remember Ruatara as the speaking subject, to recall the pôwhiri, and to see the first Pakeha teacher as mere learner is to have quite a different memory, where Māori power is centered and normalized, and where struggle more than colonization is foregrounded. The juxtaposition of these stories does not simply enable multiple voices to speak; rather, it allows the indigene-colonizer relationship to be interrogated in uneasy ways that insist on examining power and common sense, as well as the place of histories in the present. In this tension is the fecundity of collaboration.

Notes

1. A *pôwhiri* is usually a very large welcome ceremony put on by the host group to their visitors who come by land. In the ceremony, a *taki* (a challenge) might be made (where warrior lays down a dart that has to be picked up by the leader of the visitors). Once the challenge is received, it is followed by calls from the women. The calls can range from wailing cries to high-pitched chanting with actions beckoning the visitors to come. The men may also perform very vigorous *haka* in raised voices that reach screaming point accompanied by energetic actions and ritual movements of their bodies that, to the onlooker, could look very fearsome and violent as to be described as a "sham fight." A *waka taki* (meaning a canoe challenge) is a pôwhiri that sees visitors arriving from the sea and on to the land to complete the welcoming ceremonial formalities.

2. Martha Nussbaum's (1997) book *Cultivating Humanity* is an interesting example of the disavowal of the hyphen. While Nussbaum purports to address all of us in her argument for multicultural engagement in a shared liberal education, she unwittingly tends to address only middle-class White students in such statements as, "This requires a great deal of knowledge that American college students rarely got . . . knowledge of non-Western cultures, of minorities" (p. 10).

3. This grouping of Māori (Polynesian indigenous people of New Zealand) and Pacific Islands people (Polynesian immigrants) was an attempt to have a roughly evenly divided class. We recognize, however, that this combination is problematic, given the very different histories in the group. Similar remarks might be made about the eclectic ethnic-cultural mix in the other "Pakeha" group.

4. A somewhat similar argument has been made by those critical of empowerment education as a form of critical pedagogy; as Gore (2003) puts it, such critics consider the problems in "the exercise of power . . . to help others exercise power" (p. 346).

5. See also Nancy Fraser and Axel Honneth's (2003) arguments about recognition and social justice that extend the arguments about recognition and their significance.

6. The passion of the opposition to critical arguments such as Ellsworth's and my own, as well as the desire for "a vision of community" (Aronowitz & Giroux, 1991, p. 132), resonates with that of our White students dismayed by the withdrawal of their indigenous peers.

7. It perhaps needs to be noted, to be taken up further elsewhere, that we might want to equivocate about the *absolute* difference of the Other when the Self is the indigenous self and the Other represents the colonizer. It might be argued that, as a result of colonization, the indigene is never absolutely different, and it is precisely this annihilation of difference that the indigene, necessarily, resists. The indigene *as indigene* is absolutely different; in speaking *as* Māori within collaborative inquiry, Māori assert an absolute and necessary difference from Pakeha partners.

▣ References

Aronowitz, S., & Giroux, H. (1991). *Postmodern education: Politics, culture and social criticism.* Minneapolis: University of Minnesota Press.

Barry, B. (2001). *Culture and equality: An egalitarian critique of multiculturalism.* Cambridge, MA: Harvard University Press.

Barthes, R. (1994). *Image-music-text.* New York: Hill & Wang.

Bhabha, H. (1994). *The location of culture.* New York: Routledge.

Binney, J. (1968). *The legacy of guilt: A life of Thomas Kendall.* Christchurch: Oxford University Press.

Boler, M. (1997). The risks of empathy: Interrogating multiculturalism's gaze. *Cultural Studies, 11*(2), 253–273.

Chalmers, V. (1997). White out: Multicultural performances in a progressive school. In M. Fine, L. Weis, L. C. Powell, & L. M. Wong (Eds.), *Off white: Readings on race, power and society* (pp. 66–78). New York: Routledge.

Cloher, D. E. (2003). *Hongi Hika: Warrior chief.* Auckland, New Zealand: Viking.

Collins, P. H. (1986). Learning from the outsider within: The sociological significance of Black feminist thought. *Social Problems, 33*(6), S14–S32.

Collins, P. H. (1998). *Fighting words: Black women and the search for justice.* Minneapolis: University of Minnesota Press.

Ellsworth, E. (1989). Why doesn't this feel empowering? Working through the repressive myths of critical pedagogy. *Harvard Educational Review, 59,* 297–324.

Fine, M. (1994). Working the hyphens: Reinventing the self and other in qualitative research. In N. K. Denzin & Y. S. Lincoln (Eds.), *Handbook of qualitative research* (pp. 70–82). Thousand Oaks, CA: Sage.

Fraser, N., & Honneth, A. (2003). *Redistribution or recognition? A political-philosophical exchange.* New York: Verso.

Garrison, J. (2004). Ameliorating violence in dialogues across differences. In M. Boler (Ed.), *Democratic dialogue in education: Troubling speech, disturbing silence* (pp. 89–103). New York: Peter Lang.

Gitlin, T. (1995). *The twilight of common dreams: Why America is wracked by culture wars.* New York: Metropolitan Books.

Gore, J. (2003). What we can do for you! What can "we" do for "you"? Struggling over empowerment in critical and feminist pedagogy. In A. Darder, M. Baltodano, & R. D. Torres (Eds.), *The critical pedagogy reader* (pp. 331–348). New York: Falmer.

Haig-Brown, C. (1988). *Resistance and renewal: Surviving the Indian residential school.* Vancouver: Arsenal Pulp Press.

Hansen, E. (2002). *The culture of strangers: Globalisation, localisation and the phenomenon of exchange.* Lanham, MD: University Press of America.

Haraway, D. (1997). *Modest-witness @ second-millennium: FemaleMan-meets-oncomouse: Feminist and technoscience.* New York: Routledge.

Harding, S. (1998). *Is science multicultural? Postcolonialisms, feminisms, and epistemologies.* Bloomington: Indiana University Press.

Harrison, L. E., & Huntington, S. P. (Eds.). (2000). *Culture matters: How values shape human progress.* New York: Basic Books.

Hollinger, D. A. (1995). *Postethnic America: Beyond multiculturalism.* New York: Basic Books.

Islam, N. (2000). Research as an act of betrayal: Researching race in an Asian community in Los Angeles. In F. W. Twine & J. W. Warren (Eds.), *Racing research, researching race: Methodological dilemmas in critical race studies* (pp. 35–66). New York: New York University Press.

Jones, A. (1999). Desire at the pedagogical borders: Absolution and difference in the university classroom. *Educational Theory, 49,* 299–315.

Jones, A. (2001). Cross-cultural pedagogy and the passion for ignorance. *Feminism and Psychology, 11,* 279–292.

Jones, A., & Jenkins, K. (2001). Disciplining the native body: Handwriting and its civilising practices. *History of Education Review, 29*(2), 34–46.

Jones, A., & Jenkins, K. (2004). Pedagogical events: Rereading shared moments in educational history. *Journal of Intercultural Studies, 25*(2), 143–160.

King, M. (2003) *The Penguin history of New Zealand.* Auckland, New Zealand: Penguin.

Levinas, E. (2000). *Totality and infinity: An essay on exteriority* (A. Lingis, Trans.). Pittsburgh, PA: Duquesne University Press. (Original work published 1969)

Lincoln, Y. S., & Denzin, N. K. (1994). The fifth moment. In N. K. Denzin & Y. S. Lincoln (Eds.), *Handbook of qualitative research* (pp. 575–586). Thousand Oaks, CA: Sage.

Martin, C. L. (1999). *The way of the human being.* New Haven, CT: Yale University Press.

McConaghy, C. (2000). *Rethinking indigenous education: Culturalism, colonialism and the politics of knowing.* Queensland, Australia: Post Pressed.

McLaren, P. (1995). *Critical pedagogy and predatory culture.* London: Routledge.

Mead, M. (1969). Research with human beings: A model derived from anthropological field practice. *Daedalus, 98,* 361–386.

Mohanty, C. T. (1997). Under Western eyes: Feminist scholarship and colonial discourses. In A. McClintock, A. Mufti, & E. Shohat (Eds.), *Dangerous liaisons: Gender nation and postcolonial perspectives* (pp. 255–277). Minneapolis: University of Minnesota Press.

Narayan, U. (1988). Working together across difference: Some considerations on emotions and political practice. *Hypatia: A Journal of Feminist Philosophy, 3*(2), 35.

Nicholas, J. L. (1817). *Narrative of a voyage to New Zealand* (Vol. 1). Auckland, New Zealand: Wilson and Horton.

Nussbaum, M. C. (1997). *Cultivating humanity: A classical defense of reform in liberal education.* Cambridge, MA: Harvard University Press.

Oliver, K. (2001). *Witnessing: Beyond recognition.* Minneapolis: University of Minnesota Press.

Pihama, L., & Jenkins, K. (2001). Matauranga Wahine: Teaching Māori women's knowledge alongside feminism. *Feminism and Psychology, 11,* 293–303.

Readings, B. (1996). *The university in ruins.* Cambridge, MA: Harvard University Press.

Roman, L. (1993). White is a color! White defensiveness, postmodernism, and antiracist pedagogy. In C. McCarthy & W. Crichlow (Eds.), *Race, identity, and representation in education* (pp. 71–88). New York: Routledge.

Roman, L. (1997). Denying (White) racial privilege: Redemption discourses and the uses of fantasy. In M. Fine, L. Weis, L. C. Powell, & L. M. Wong (Eds.), *Off white: Readings on race, power and society* (pp. 270–282). New York: Routledge.

Salmond, A. (1997). *Between worlds: Early exchanges between Māori and Europeans 1773–1815.* Auckland, New Zealand: Viking.

Salmond, A. (2005). Eruera: The teachings of a Māori elder. Auckland, New Zealand: Penguin.

Semali, L. M., & Kincheloe, J. L. (Eds.). (1999). *What is indigenous knowledge? Voices from the academy.* New York: Falmer.

Shor, I., & Freire, P. (1987). What is this "dialogical method" of teaching? *Journal of Education, 169*(3), 11–31.

Smith, L. T. (1991). Te Rapunga I te Ao Marama (a search for the world of light): Māori perspectives on research in education. In J. Morss & T. Linzey (Eds.), *Growing up: The politics of human learning* (pp. 46–55). Auckland, New Zealand: Longman Paul.

Smith, L. T. (1999). *Decolonising methodologies: Research and indigenous peoples.* London: Zed.

Spivak, G. (1988). Can the subaltern speak? In C. Nelson & L. Grossberg (Eds.), *Marxism and the interpretation of culture* (pp. 271–313). Bassingstoke, UK: Macmillan.

Srivastava, A. (1997). Anti-racism inside and outside the classroom. In L. Roman & L. Eyre (Eds.), *Dangerous territories: Struggles for difference and equality in education* (pp. 113–126). New York: Routledge.

Stronach, I., & MacLure, M. (1997). *Educational research undone: The postmodern embrace.* Buckingham, UK: Open University Press.

Todd, S. (2003). *Learning from the other: Levinas, psychoanalysis and ethical possibilities in education.* Albany, NY: SUNY Press.

Twine, F. W. (2000). Racial ideologies and racial methodologies. In F. W. Twine & J. W. Warren (Eds.), *Racing research, researching race: Methodological dilemmas in critical race studies* (pp. 1–34). New York: New York University Press.

24

SEVEN ORIENTATIONS FOR THE DEVELOPMENT OF INDIGENOUS SCIENCE EDUCATION

Gregory Cajete

Introduction: Culturally-Based Science Curriculum in American Indian Education

The idea of a culturally-based approach to science education for American Indians is a new development in a long and tenuous history of American Indian education and reflects an evolution of thought related to self-determination, community education, and a renaissance of American Indian identity.

Over the course of contact between European and American Indian cultures, the sustained effort to "educate" and assimilate American Indians as a way of dealing with the "Indian problem" inevitably played a key role in how American Indians have historically responded to American "schooling." As is true with many "colonized" cultural groups throughout the world, the first attempts were met with resistance. This resistance to schooling continues today in more psychologically submerged forms.

Historically, the first attempts at introducing Euro-American schooling to American Indians were met with suspicion, apathy, and indignation. However, once education became viewed as an essential aspect of adapting to modern society, it rapidly evolved into an indispensable key to personal and tribal success in direct proportion to the assimilation or adaptation of "core" American cultural values. This general scenario was replayed for each American Indian tribal culture.

American Indian cultures first encountered Euro-American educational forms through contact with missionaries. Missionaries consistently focused on changing the religion of American Indians, which in most instances entailed a drastic change in the tribal culture as a whole. Such schooling directly conflicted with traditional forms of American Indian education. Early missionary and government teachers naïvely assumed that American Indians had no education at all and that their mission was to remedy this "great ignorance." The notion that the learning process is adapted to the environment and cultural configurations of that society did not occur to educators until the late 1920s.

In reality, every American Indian tribe had its own system of enculturation that involved a wide variety of learning strategies. The available research concerning the educative processes in many "primal cultures" suggests that a child was educated and educated himself or herself through various formal and informal interactions from birth to old age involving both simple and highly complex forms of education.

Traditional American Indian systems of educating were characterized by observation, participation, assimilation, and experiential learning rather than by the low-context, formal instruction characteristic of Euro-American schooling. For example, among the high cultures of Mexico and Central and South America, education was highly interactive and formalized by tutor-student relationships, and elite "academies" creatively integrated formal with informal learning and teaching. Education was highly dependent on intrapersonal, interpersonal, kinesthetic, and spatial learning as expressed in oral language and active involvement within the tribal culture.

What follows are seven guiding orientations that may guide the development of a contemporary expression of Indigenous education. These orientations also provide a framework for engaging Indigenous wisdom in the science education and addressing some of the issues raised by Greene (1981).

Orientation 1: Redefining Science Education for Native Americans

As Native communities take control of more of their own education, the integration of traditional and contemporary values in quality education becomes a greater possibility.

Presently, little improvement in science education has been realized. Few schools that serve Native students have integrated cultural content in any serious or systematic form. This lack of progress is reflected in the continued underachievement of Native students in science and math.

The need for expertise among Native people in the area of science has never been greater because of the scientific and technical literacy and skill needed to effect self-determination in tribal resource management, health, and economic development.

Encouragement and support are crucial in the development of a foundation in science literacy. However, given the prior history of Western education of Native students, there is a need for a radically different approach.

Such an approach necessarily requires the development of a new view of Native education in which the new teaching and learning may be contexted. What would a modern Indigenous philosophy of education consist of? Curricular change in Native education must stem from "cultural standards" firmly grounded in Native thought and orientation.

Eber Hampton (1995) outlines 12 standards for a Native American curriculum.

1. Spirituality: Respect for spiritual relationships
2. Service: To serve the community given its needs
3. Diversity: Respect and honoring of difference
4. Culture: Culturally responsive education process
5. Tradition: A continuance and revitalization of tradition
6. Respect: Personal respect and respect for others
7. History: A well-developed and researched sense for history
8. Relentlessness: Honing a sense of tenacity and patience
9. Vitality: Instilling vitality in both process and product
10. Conflict: Being able to deal constructively with conflict
11. Place: A well-developed researched sense for place
12. Transformation: The transformation of Native education

The reality is that Indigenous people's worldviews are about integration of spiritual, natural, and human domains of existence and human interaction. Characteristic of this reality include:

1. a culturally constructed and responsive technology mediated by nature;

2. a culturally based education process constructed around myth, history, and observation of nature, animals, plants, and their ways of survival;

3. use of natural materials to make tools and art, as well as the development of appropriate technology for surviving in one's "place"; and

4. the use of thoughtful stories and illustrative examples as a foundation for learning to "live" in a particular environment.

Various overt and covert disruptions of these traditional educational systems have led to the personal, psychosocial, and spiritual dysfunction we now see in Indigenous societies. Benefits of "modernity" are offset by inefficient housing, disruptions in parent-child relationships, domestic violence, suicides, alcohol/drug abuse, and other forms of dysfunctional behavior. With these has come a general sense of powerlessness and loss of control experienced by many Indigenous people.

Orientation 2: Traditional Native American Education

Holistic learning and education has been an integral part of traditional Native American education and socialization until relatively recent times. Teaching and learning were natural outcomes of living in close communion with the natural world. It is only within the past three or four generations that Native Americans are experiencing "holism" as if it were new.

A major purpose of this science curriculum is to reintroduce the idea of holism and integrated learning in an interactive social environment such as the school or community. The intent is to make education for Native American students related to other learning situations and interdisciplinary activities and more culturally interactive process than it has been in the school environment.

Experiential learning is the most basic and the most holistic type of human learning and is a part, in one form or another, of every Native American context and mechanism of learning. This learning requires the simultaneous "internalization" of concepts, methods, and classifications that are predominately nonverbal and unconscious. The old maxim that "experience teaches" was extensively exploited in traditional Native American education. Such things as learning a traditional art form, learning to build a shelter, learning to farm or hunt, or surviving in a given environment were predominately experiential in nature. Children experienced basic education through everyday work and play.

Storytelling was both an enjoyable and very effective means of teaching and learning in Native American traditional life. Through the mechanism of storytelling, every individual was introduced to various levels of meanings, practices, concepts, ethics, and codes of conduct that were meant to partially answer the "why" of the "way of the people." That is, such storytelling related the ever evolving group life processes and introductory understanding of its members as part of a unique tribal people. Accomplished storytellers exploited the rich symbolism inherent in mythology and used it to its fullest potential to illuminate many aspects of human psychology and the resulting behavior therein. The hidden symbolism and use of metaphoric communication in myths of ancient peoples are only now being explored. The sophisticated nature of the storyteller's art, which employs creative use of language, evocation of imagery, and theatrical ability, is becoming appreciated and accepted in modern education. The ability to tell and listen to stories develops a whole range of verbal and nonverbal skills, as well as what we today call right and left brain functions, in both the storyteller and listener. This is an especially significant characteristic for teaching and learning by children. Telling or listening to stories is an almost universal activity of younger children, but it is a capacity that is rarely capitalized on, guided, or developed toward positive learning. It is one of those subtle human activities that needs only to be exercised and valued.

The *tutor* and the master-apprentice relationship was a widely used form of teaching and learning in Native American society. In general, this type of education took two forms. Relationships between father and son, or grandfather and grandson, or aunt and niece, or any combination therein, constituted informal tutor-student relationships within the extended family or clan. Indeed, it was within the context of these relationships that much formal and informal learning and teaching took place. Many important aspects of practical knowledge, such as care for oneself, the daily work of a household, finding food, making shelter, protection, and social education, took place in this situation. The techniques used to teach and learn varied widely from formal lectures and demonstrations to stories and show-and-tell.

The *dream* was widely respected as a way to access knowledge of life and events. Patricia Garfield (1974), in her book *Creative Dreaming*, wrote,

> Any child who receives recognition and praise for dreaming will certainly learn to recall and use more dreams as he is rewarded for doing so. . . . We in the West are told that dreams are nonsense, or amusing, or psychologically revealing; accordingly we never hear the suggestion that dreams can be actively used; we do not deliberately engage ourselves in our dreams to help ourselves. (p. 92)

Almost without exception, American Indian societies valued dreams, dreaming, and imagination as very unique and powerful ways of learning, understanding, teaching, and creating. The ways in which Native American cultures used dreams varied tremendously. Dreams were often an important part of religious systems because they were viewed as one of the primary means for contacting spirits to gain power and knowledge from them. Likewise, dreams were often viewed as important entities within the value structure of the social system, and because of this, the dream interpreter and dream interpretation were assigned special roles and status.

Ritual and ceremony infused every aspect of traditional Native American life. The spirit and the spiritual were at the center of each human being and all that made up the universe. Through ritual and ceremony, teaching and cultivation of the spirit and the spiritual were engendered, from very simple symbolic acts recognizing one's relationship to the spiritual to highly organized, high-contextual events that involved all the people of a particular tribe for several days.

A ritual's main purposes were to provide a focus of reflection on the great mystery in one or more of its manifestations and to help revitalize the individual and the group connection to themselves and the world.

Through the symbolic use of prayer, song, dance, and communal activity, Native Americans developed highly creative techniques for guiding social behavior and ethics. The social psychology inherent in ritual and ceremony provided powerful group empathy and cohesion, which reinforced the social self-image of each individual participant.

Orientation 3: An Epistemology of Indigenous Science: A Personal Perspective

"Indigenous science" is a category of traditional environmental knowledge (TEK) that includes everything from metaphysics to philosophy to various practical technologies practiced by Indigenous peoples both past and present. At its most inclusive definition, Indigenous science may also be said to include practically all of human invention before the advent of Cartesian-mechanistic science. These include areas such as astronomy, healing agriculture, study of plants, animals, and natural phenomena. Yet, Indigenous science extends beyond these areas to also include a focus on spirituality, community, creativity, appropriate technology that sustains environments, and other essential aspects of human life.

Indigenous science can include exploration of basic questions such as the nature of language, thought and perception, the movement of time, the nature of human feeling, the nature of human knowing, the nature of proper human relationship to the cosmos, and a host of other questions about natural reality. Indigenous science is essentially a tremendous inheritance of human experience with the natural world. It is a map of reality drawn from the experiences of thousands of human generations that gave rise to a diversity of technologies for hunting, fishing, gathering, making art, building, communicating, visioning, healing, and being.

There are those who would argue that there is no such thing as Indigenous science. They would argue that "science" is an invention of modern Western society and that Indigenous peoples have a body of cultural folklore, living practices, and thought that cannot be considered a rational and ordered system of theory and investigation comparable to anything found in Western science. Whether there exists an Indigenous science in Western terms is largely an incestuous argument of semantic definition. Using Western orientations to measure the credence of non-Western ways of knowing and being in the world has been applied historically to deny the reality of Indigenous peoples. The fact is that Indigenous people *are;* they exist and do not need an external measure to validate their existence in the world. Attempts to define Indigenous science, which is by its nature alive, dynamic, and ever changing through generations, fall short, as this science is a high-context inclusive system of knowledge.

Indigenous science offers both challenges and opportunities for Western science education. Its insights and processing of knowledge parallel what many of the most innovative and reflective thinkers in education are advocating we do to extend our use of science to address the ever more pressing and complex problems we will face in the 21st century.

The development of a simultaneous exploration and comparison of Indigenous science and Western science can provide the foundation for the flexibility and creative orientation to thinking and application in science that is essential for the future of human societies. Scientists of "color," though few in number, have the opportunity to become leading advocates for such a necessary rethinking and transformation.

Western science is founded upon the premises of objectivity, abstraction, weighing, and measuring. "If it cannot be tested, it does not exist!" is an often voiced credo of the mainstream scientist. Yet the focus on objectivity can block deeper insight into the metaphysics of the reality and process of the natural world. Western science does not consider the affective, intuitive, and soulful nature of the world.

In comparison, the Indigenous perspective is more inclusive and moves far beyond the boundaries of objective measurement. Indigenous science honors the essential importance of direct experience, interconnectedness, relationship, holism, quality, and value.

In the structure of the tribal universe, no body of knowledge exists for its own sake outside of a moral framework of understanding. Humans are co-creators with the higher powers of nature so that everything that we do has importance for the rest of the world. Also, everything that we experience has importance. All of our experience is a circle of learning, living, and relationship. Education from this standpoint is totally inclusive of information from every source needed to make a decision in a moral and ethical relationship. All relationships have a history. People have a history of relationship with each other and with plants, animals, a land, and the forces of Nature.

Orientation 4: Border Crossings

Indigenous knowledge of nature tends to be thematic, survival oriented, holistic, empirical, rational, contextualized, specific, communal, ideological, spiritual, inclusive, cooperative, coexistent, personal, and peaceful.

This essential orientation difference challenges Native American students as they attempt to cross the borders into the subculture of Western science as represented in schools. If the teaching and learning of science are supportive of the student's culture orientation, "enculturation" is the result.

If the teaching and learning of science are at odds with the student's cultural orientation, the result is "assimilation," forcing students to abandon or marginalize their way of knowing to reconstruct a new (generally dysfunctional) way of knowing. Unfortunately, the latter is more often the case.

The essential question is, How can students from Indigenous cultures learn non-Native subjects such as science without being assimilated harmfully by the underlying value structure? "First nations students should develop the facility to cross from everyday sub-cultures of peers, family, community and tribe into the sub-cultures of school science, science and technology . . . students and teachers should become cultural border crossers" (Pomeroy, 1994, p. 50). Yet, "Crossing over from one domain of meaning to another is exceeding hard" (Hennessy, 1993, p. 9).

Students generally get very little help doing this kind of border crossing. Few teachers are inclined to assist students, and if they are, they have few resources for being trained in this kind of cross-cultural negotiation.

Four worlds for student transitions have been identified. These include a congruent world that supports smooth transitions, a different world that requires transitions to be managed, diverse worlds that lead to hazardous transitions, and highly discordant worlds that cause students to resist transitions and in which they become virtually impossible.

Determining what kinds of skills and knowledge are appropriate for "First Nations students" to learn with reference to economic development, environmental responsibility, and cultural survival is the next step of developing such a comprehensive process.

Sound, integrated education that helps students be flexible and adaptable and enhances their ability to train on the job is the most strategic form of science education. Restructuring scientific knowledge into new forms for Native contexts requires knowledge of both a different cultural orientation and a different approach to teaching and learning science. Essentially, Native knowledge comes already contexted and ready for use; Western scientific knowledge does not. As this is the way Western science is taught in school, it is no wonder that many students cope by developing a view of science as apart from their real lives.

An approach that integrates scientific, technological, and Indigenous knowledge into real-life situations and issues has the best chance of being effective. Participatory research is one way of accomplishing this.

An integration of selected science and technology content in an Indigenous worldview requires coordination with relevant economic, social, and resource needs. One might apply a cross-cultural science-technology-society (STS) model that has been used by science educators in Third World countries. STS is a dedicated student-oriented, critical, and environmentally responsible approach to science, and it de-contextualizes Western science in the social and technological settings relevant to students.

Applying an anthropological approach from an Indigenous perspective to the teaching and learning of Western science is another possibility since this promotes autonomous acculturation, or the intercultural borrowing or adaptation of attractive content or aspects. This would be a more constructive and culturally affirming alternative for Native students than assimilating or enculturating themselves to Western science. Students may act as anthropologists learning about another culture. Like cultural anthropologists, they would not need to accept the cultural ways of their "subjects" in order to understand or engage in some of those ways (Aikenhead, 1997).

Combining the STS approach with that of "the student as anthropologist" in the context of an Indigenous perspective and community reality can form an ideal foundation for Indigenous students learning science. The teacher's role is to learn to act as kind of cultural broker who assists students in handling cultural negotiation and conflict between views. Essentially, students act as "cultural tourists" in a constructive way, and teachers take on the role of "tour guides" and "travel agents" as they help students cross the cultural knowledge borders between science and their own worlds.

Orientation 5: A Strategy for Curriculum Modeling

The strategy of the curriculum model is to provide the presentation of the basic principles of general science by first introducing students to the ways in which these principles are communicated, used, or otherwise exemplified in Native American culture. Students are then presented with a comparison of these cultural examples with similar elements in Western science. The idea is to illustrate that these principles are the result of the creative thought process and to establish this as a point of commonality between both cultural perspectives. Finally, the students are provided with a variety of opportunities to review and apply the basic principles. It is not the purpose of this model to supplant the teaching of basic science principles through more conventional science curricula but rather to facilitate their transfer through culturally meaningful communication.

The overall process is meant to closely parallel real-life creative problem solving. First, a situation is perceived; it is analyzed in order to understand it and discover the problem; what is learned is then synthesized, and new ideas are formed. These ideas are evaluated in search of the best ideas or solution; the best idea is applied and then reacted to.

This cyclic process of looking at a problem creatively in reference to one's cultural mind-set is the most important aspect of the approach. It not only allows for a greater perspective and understanding of science, but it is transferable to all other areas of the educative process.

Orientation 6: Indigenous Students

In 1974, when this writer began teaching general biology at the Institute of American Indian Arts High School (IAIA) in Santa Fe, New Mexico, it became immediately apparent that the introduction of Native American cultural content into the presentation of the natural sciences was not only appropriate but essential given the characteristics of the students attending the institute.

The institute began in 1962 as a culturally responsive innovation engaged in a unique educational experiment. The school has served well over 8,000 students through its various programs, including Native Americans from over 100 recognized tribes in North America. Art education that relied heavily on cultural content was an integral part of its mission, philosophy, and approach to education. Therefore, the introduction of cultural content in the presentation of science was a natural step.

During the evolution and implementation of the program from 1974 to 1984, students (a) more successfully retained those science concepts that were integrated with Native American cultural examples, as measured by teacher-prepared tests; (b) were more highly motivated to learn about Native American cultural sciences in relationship to modern sciences, as measured by student responses and level of class participation and activity; (c) became more positive about science and other academic areas, as measured by student evaluations; (d) retained more through the use of relevant art activities and actual science experiences; and (e) improved their learning and retention with the incorporation of combinations of familiar concrete and symbolic modalities with activities involving kinesthetic, spatial, tactile, visual, or musical perceptions.

I found that students who can be called "rural traditional" are the least assimilated and have a strong orientation to traditional Native American cultural patterns and personality configurations. They usually live in their tribal communities. The preservation of a Native American tribal identity is a visible focus in such groups. For example, many Pueblo and Navajo male students within this group wear their hair tied in a bun with a traditional woven hair tie called a *cango* (a Spanish slang word).

Other students can be called "transitional" and are characterized by movement toward the assimilation of many American sociocultural, economic, and personality norms in preference to traditional Native American cultural patterns. Members are from both rural and urban areas. Students from this group express the desire to gain the best from both their traditional Indian groups and mainstream American society.

The third group of students can be called the "urban assimilated." This group is characterized by an almost complete assimilation of American cultural norms. Many members of this group are second- or third-generation "urban Indians" and have only a nominal relationship to their ancestral tribal community. The syncretization of

Native American and non-Native cultural patterns is slanted toward American urban cultural norms.

Orientation 7: A Model for Creative Native Science

From the Native American perspective, science is an abstract, symbolic, and metaphoric way of perceiving and understanding the world. From the Western cultural perspective, science is essentially practiced as a rational way to solve problems.

These two approaches can complement one another. Like the sacred twins in Native American mythology, they are by nature intimately interrelated. Each derives its meaning from the other. Science as a whole is based on both the intuitive and rational minds. This curriculum represents one way of enhancing and flowing with this natural relationship, which Einstein expressed well in the maxim, "The intuitive mind is a sacred gift, the rational mind is a faithful servant."

The creative process is the most essential universal that centers people and learning and understanding. It is the elemental process in the natural world as well as the world of thought. How to go about conditioning oneself for creative thought is what I try to establish as the first foundation in this science curriculum. The students I taught at IAIA were immersed in a variety of experiences and encounters that enlivened their ability to think creatively and to think in multidimensional ways using not only the five senses but all their faculties. Most American Indian groups recognize seven basic orientations: the four cardinal directions, North, South, East, and West; the center, usually the community itself or village, or the center of the territory; and then the Above and the Below, the below representing the earth and the above, the celestial or universe.

First is the "centering place," the womb, which contains the essence of all that emanates from it. In Native American mythological terms, it is the primal source of everything, symbolized by balance and by all the colors of the rainbow, the dwelling place of the spirit and the essence of creation. In this curriculum, it is the domain of the creative thought process and holistic thinking.

The first direction, East, the domain of the rising sun, is the source of "First Light," dawn, purification, and insight. Its characteristic process and product is symbolized by Wisdom and by the color white. In this curriculum, it is associated with philosophy through rational/intuitive thought.

The West is the domain of the setting sun, the source of sustenance and social well-being and relationship within community. In this curriculum, it is associated with the domain of social psychology and self-knowledge. It is the dwelling place of the self and the group mind.

The South harbors plants, good fortune, spiritual richness, and the fertility of the earth. It is the place of daylight, the full sun, and the warm, feminine fruit bearing spirit. Its characteristic process and product is symbolized by the health of the whole. In this curriculum, it is connotated with the domain of medicine and the quest for health and wholeness.

The North, the domain of animals, is the night, the unconscious and the unknown. In mythological terms, it is the place of the cold dark wind, origins, and internal space. Its characteristic process and product is symbolized by the primal instinct, myth, and dreaming. In this curriculum, it is associated with animals, mythology, and the quest for understanding "the animal within" and the archetypal unconscious.

Below (Nadir) is the domain of the earth mother and the archetypal elements of earth, fire, water, air, and ether. This is the place of earth woman, mother of the winds, the waters, the earth mounds (mountains), the fire inside the earth, and the breath of life and thought. Its characteristic process and product is the dynamic interplay of the archetypal elements in geophysical processes such as weather, volcanic activity, erosion, plate tectonics, and bioregional ecology.

The "Above" (Zenith) is the place of the Celestial Father, the Great Mystery, and the ultimate expansive spirit symbolized by explicate order in the cosmos and man's quest for an understanding of the Universe and the Universal.

This basic idea has ramifications that go deep into the cosmology of each tribal group. A cosmology is a culture's guiding story, and that story reflects on ways of relating and understanding themselves in natural community. I began to evolve models and build conceptual orientations that I felt were true to the universals I had come to understand with regard to Indigenous people.

Native American cultures have traditionally oriented aspects of their lives with the four sacred and symbolic cardinal directions. The East is associated with the first rays of the sun on the new day, the metaphoric symbol of first insights and first understandings. I associate this orientation with a course that I call Native Philosophy. In that course, we explore different kinds of Indigenous philosophies related to how the world was created and how things came into being in the natural world, not only Native American philosophies but also those of other Indigenous peoples around the world, compared with Western philosophies. Students must understand that there are differences in orientation that relate to the philosophies people hold about the way they learn and the way that they define themselves. Philosophy is tied to something even more primal, the guiding story that not only is spiritual and religious but also forms the frame of reference for a people and how they understand themselves. Ceremonies and rituals and other ways of a people's worldview are a direct result of that cosmology.

In Native cultures, the West is the orientation of community. We are communal beings, and as such, we cannot exist outside of community. No person is an island. I call this course "Native Social Psychology," and it is about people in community. Students find out how community can teach and how it conditions people. We explore social structures and social organizations and tie those to cosmology. We explore differences between Western social organization and Indigenous social organization, give examples, and reflect on those things. We then examine some difficult issues—conflicts between social psychology and sense of community that lead to abuses, such as alcoholism. We explore what happens to a community when you take away the sources of its identity and why certain communities (like Indian communities) suffer so grievously because part of their way of being is obstructed or degraded or dismantled. We explore social psychology, community action, and politics, and we come to understand our communal selves more deeply.

As students complete their exploration of these seven orientations, they feel the wonder and the awe of being alive in a natural place. They see how Indigenous people reflected a very sophisticated understanding of the natural process and established their relationship in the natural world. They experience nature in some very direct and specific ways.

Final Thoughts

The approach to science education described within this chapter presents a significant departure from more conventional approaches. This is because the underlying assumptions are very different when compared to those that have guided curriculum development in the past.

The model, thesis, and underlying assumptions have been presented to stimulate the development of new insights for science educators and address the needs of previously uninspired students in the area of science. Many Native American students openly express their negative feelings based on their previous encounters with conventional science curricula. Some even view science as one of the tools Western societies have used to exploit endogenous populations and natural environments. A student's association of science with exploitation is often a result of poor understanding of science within Native American cultures.

Science is a form of communication and involves a kind of literacy. This literacy in turn involves the development of basic skills as tools for understanding and solving problems in reference to nature. Such literacy entails an understanding of concepts and natural processes from the perspective of a particular cultural system of thought. It follows from this assumption that science must be approached as a type of dynamic literacy that must be internalized.

How an encounter with natural phenomena affects students and the meaning that it has for them encompasses personal, cultural, and creative dimensions of perception. Meaning is the key to relevance. If science is to have meaning for students, that meaning must be inherent in both the content and presentation.

Learning is a natural activity for all human beings. The first step in motivating and enhancing learning of any sort is by encouraging involvement in the learning process. Learning is lifelong and holistic. Modern science education must widen its parameters and open up its paradigm to allow a more holistic and integrated perception of itself to take hold and grow in the minds of students.

The nature of the world today and the projection of the needs of the future require science education that can enable students to develop cognitive abilities more completely. It has been said that the problems that will face the next few generations of mankind will be of a nature and magnitude never before faced in the entire history of man on earth. Science and education will play pivotal roles in terms of how, or even if, these future monumental problems will be solved.

This work is one small step toward a brighter future for Native Americans.

▣ References

Aikenhead, G. S. (1997). Toward a First Nations cross-cultural science and technology curriculum. *Science Education, 81,* 217–238.

Garfield, P. (1974). *Creative dreaming.* New York: Simon & Schuster.

Greene, R. (1981). *Culturally-based science: The potential for traditional people; science and folklore.* London: Proceedings of the Centennial Observation of the Folklore Society.

Hampton, E. (1995). Towards a redefinition of Indian education. In M. Battiste & J. Barman (Eds.), *First Nations education in Canada: The circle unfolds* (pp. 5–46). Vancouver: University of British Columbia Press.

Hennessy, S. (1993). Situated cognition and cognitive apprenticeship: Implications for classroom learning. *Studies in Science Education, 22,* 1–41.

Pomeroy, D. (1994). Science education and cultural diversity: Mapping the field. *Studies in Science Education, 24,* 49–73.

25

RESEARCH ETHICS FOR PROTECTING INDIGENOUS KNOWLEDGE AND HERITAGE

Institutional and Researcher Responsibilities

Marie Battiste

> *The term "research" is inextricably linked to European imperialism and colonialism. The word itself, "research," is probably one of the dirtiest words in the indigenous world's vocabulary.*
>
> —Linda Smith (1999, p. 1)

Indigenous peoples around the world have lived in their natural contexts, acquiring and developing sustaining relationships with their environments and passing this knowledge and experience to succeeding generations through their language, culture, and heritage. Their acquired knowledge embodies a great wealth of science, philosophy, oral literature, art, and applied skills that have helped sustain Indigenous peoples and their land for millennia. From their elders and within their spiritual connections, Indigenous peoples have learned to heal themselves with the medicines of the earth that have been naturally part of their environment. They have observed the patterns in nature and learned how to live and flourish within them. This knowledge has been embedded in the collective community's oral and literacy traditions;[1] transmitted in the values, customs, and traditions; and passed on to each generation through their Indigenous language as instructed by the Creator and their elders.

Eurocentric education and political systems and their assimilation processes have severely eroded and damaged Indigenous knowledge, however. Unraveling the effects of generations of exploitation, violence, marginalization, powerlessness, and enforced cultural imperialism on Aboriginal knowledge and peoples has been a significant and often painful undertaking in the past century. Today, Indigenous peoples throughout the world are feeling the tensions created by a modern conventional education system that has taught them not only to mistrust their own Indigenous knowledge and elders' wisdom but also their own instincts, creativity, and inspirations. Aware of the growing eroding environmental land base, Indigenous elders have been urging new ways of thinking and interacting with the earth and with each other. The growing awareness of the limitations of technological knowledge, as well as its capacity to provide solutions to their health, environment, and biodiversity, has increasingly moved science to consider Indigenous people's potential capacity for addressing the need of urgent reform and action.

Mainstream educational institutions are also feeling the tensions and the pressures to make education accessible and relevant to Aboriginal people. With the rise in Aboriginal populations, especially in the northern territories and prairie provinces, where it is expected that the future economy will depend on a smaller number of employed people, the pressure is on conventional educational institutions to make Aboriginal populations more economically self-sufficient. In addition, educators are aware of the need to increase the diversity of the population they train as they seek to address the diversity that will exist in the population at large. As integration is pursued and diversity is recognized, so also are questions about the processes for engendering inclusiveness, tolerance, and respect.

Of late, the challenge is not so much about finding receptivity to inclusion but the challenge of ensuring that receptivity to inclusive diverse education is appropriately and ethically achieved and that the educators become aware of the systemic challenges for overcoming Eurocentrism, racism, and intolerance. The add-and-stir model of bringing Aboriginal education into the Canadian postsecondary curricula, environment, and teaching practices has not achieved the needed change but rather sustains difference and superiority of Eurocentric knowledge and processes. The challenge thus continues for educators to be able to reflect critically on the current educational system in terms of whose knowledge is offered, who decides what is offered, what outcomes are rewarded and who benefits, and, more important, how those processes are achieved in an ethically appropriate manner in higher educational institutions.

While finding a receptive climate for Indigenous knowledge is one challenge, finding educational institutions and educators to be inclusive within culturally appropriate and ethical standards is the next challenge. This chapter offers some background to the importance of Indigenous knowledge for all peoples and its vitality and dynamic capacity to help solve contemporary problems and address Eurocentric biases, the cultural misappropriations that are endangering Indigenous peoples and the benefits they may receive, an overview of the current regimes of ethics that impinge on Indigenous knowledge, and, finally, a critique of institutional ethics processes that continue to hold on to individual and institutional protections and not collective Indigenous interests. In concluding, I offer a process for Aboriginal communities to address protection of their knowledge, culture, and heritage, through a protocol entry process, calling to mind the protective actions taken internationally and regionally among Indigenous communities to stop the erosion of our Indigenous knowledge and heritage. An example of an Indigenous nation that has considered these ethical issues and provided their one, albeit partial, solution is offered.

The Mi'kmaq Grand Council of Mi'kma'ki (also known as Sante Mawio'mi within the seven districts of the Mi'kmaq Nation) has assigned the Mi'kmaw Ethics Watch (*Ethics Eskinuapimk*) to oversee research processes that involve Mi'kmaw knowledge sought among Mi'kmaw people, ensuring that researchers conduct research ethically and appropriately within Mi'kma'ki (Mi'kmaq Nation territories). As a member of that working group who participated in the process of arriving at principles and guidelines for ensuring the protection of Mi'kmaq knowledge and now am involved in enforcing these principles and guidelines, I offer, with permission from the Mi'kmaw Ethics Watch, a discussion of some the principles and measures taken and the processes articulated in the protocols, together with an appendix of these principles and guidelines. This is a significant process toward ensuring Mi'kmaw people's self-determination and the protection of our cultural and intellectual property. The responsibility for educating both Aboriginal and non-Aboriginal people about these principles and guidelines is both a community and personal responsibility of every Indigenous person and among those using or taking up Indigenous knowledge. Hence, in so understanding, I take on this task to continue to educate both Aboriginal and non-Aboriginal people about these minimum standards in approaching research in our communities in respectful inquiry and relations.

Indigenous Peoples and Knowledge

Indigenous knowledge is derived from Indigenous peoples. More than 5,000 Indigenous peoples live in 70 countries with a world population of over 300 million peoples. In each province in Canada, Aboriginal people represent a tremendous diversity of peoples, languages, cultures, traditions, beliefs, and values. Such diversity at the world level has been difficult to capture within a working definition. The International Labour Organization (ILO) has defined Indigenous peoples as

> tribal peoples in independent countries whose social, cultural and economic conditions distinguish them from other sections of the national community, and whose status is regarded wholly or partially by their own customs or traditions or by special laws or regulations. (ILO, 1989)

Indigenous people's epistemology is derived from the immediate ecology; from peoples' experiences, perceptions, thoughts, and memory, including experiences shared with others; and from the spiritual world discovered in dreams, visions, inspirations, and signs interpreted with the guidance of healers or elders. Most Indigenous peoples hold various forms of literacies in holistic ideographic systems, which act as partial knowledge meant to interact with the oral traditions. They are interactive, invoking the memory, creativity, and logic of the people. The most significant meanings quickly pass from family to family and to succeeding generations through dialogue, storytelling, and appropriate rituals and legendary archetypes. Through analogies and personal style, each person in tribal society modeled the harmony among humans and the environment in their stories, through art and design on their crafts, and on their personal objects and clothing. The personal and tribal experience with their immediate environment and with their personal and intense interaction with the spiritual world provided the core foundations for knowledge. Many cultural manifestations of those diverse experiences are available today, although many also have been lost to environmental conditions, colonization, and neglect. Ideographs on petroglyphs, pictographs, birch bark, hides, trees, and other natural materials thus catalogued the deep structure of the knowledge of the two worlds in holistic, meaningful ideas or visions. Finally, through the oral tradition and appropriate rituals, traditions, ceremonies, and socialization, each generation transmitted the collective knowledge and heritage to the next.

All of the products derived from the human Indigenous mind represent a wealth of diverse knowledge, which is in a constant flux and dependent on the social and cultural flexibility and sustainability of each nation. Indigenous knowledge represents a complex and dynamic capacity of knowing, a knowledge that results from knowing one's ecological environment, the skills and knowledge derived from that place, knowledge of the animals and plants and their patterns within that space, and the vital skills and talents necessary to survive and sustain themselves within that environment. It is a knowledge that required constant vigor to observe carefully, to offer those in story and interactions, and to maintain appropriate relationships with all things and peoples in it. The relationships are preserved not just in the story and daily dialogue of the people but also in language structures. Algonkian languages preserve those relationships in multiple dialects with the language family that acknowledges the animate and inanimate, in their acknowledged experiential knowledge of others, and in the diverse prefixes and suffixes that allow creativity in language and thought to be transmitted orally so that others may understand the deep complexity of the dynamic experience (Inglis, 2002).

Indigenous knowledge, then, is a dynamic knowledge constantly in use as well as in flux or change. It derives from the same source: the relationship within the global flux that needs to be renewed, kinship with the other living creatures and life energies embodied in their land, and kinship with the spirit world. The natural context is itself a changing ecosystem that manifests itself in many Indigenous sociocultural forms: stories, ceremonies, and traditions that can be explained in any number of disciplinary knowledge such as science, art, humanities, mathematics, physics, linguistics, and so forth. Within a functional system of family and community dynamics, Indigenous knowledge is constantly shared, making all things interrelated and collectively developed and constituted. There is no singular author of Indigenous knowledge and no singular method for understanding its totality.

Erica Irene Daes (1993), former special rapporteur and chairperson of the Working Group on Indigenous Populations, reported that the heritage of Indigenous people is not merely a collection of objects, stories, and ceremonies but a complete knowledge system with its own languages, with its own concepts of epistemology, philosophy, and scientific and logical validity. She underscored the central role of Indigenous people's own language, through which each people's heritage has traditionally been recorded and transmitted from generation to generation, and urged legal reforms to recognize the unique and continuing links to the ecosystem, language, and heritage of the Indigenous peoples. Reporting to the United Nations (UN) Sub-Commission on Prevention of Discrimination and Protection of Minorities, Daes emphasized that

> such legal reforms are vital to a fair legal order because Indigenous peoples cannot survive or exercise their fundamental human rights as distinct nations, societies, and peoples without the ability to conserve, revive, develop, and teach the wisdom they have inherited from their ancestors. (p. 13)

From a sociological perspective, despite the fact that all peoples have knowledge, the transformation of knowledge into a political power base has been built on controlling the meanings and diffusion of knowledge. Different groups in society use knowledge and control of knowledge and its meanings in order to exercise power over other groups (Apple, 1993, 1996; Corson, 1997). Such has been the controlling agents of education that have linked these diffused meanings with economics, ensuring that some knowledge is diffused with rewards and others not. It ensures a cognitive imperialism around knowledge that positions some groups in power and others to be exploited and marginalized (Battiste, 1986).

The realization of the losses to Indigenous people's cultures, languages, histories, and knowledge is not without repercussions for those seeking to redefine or restore Indigenous cultures and societies. Most academics are not lost to the fact that Indigenous peoples have been colonized and marginalized and suffer from the effects of them. Poverty has been the overarching common experience of Indigenous peoples, and to be able to use their resources and talents in order to develop their economic potential has been recognized by many academics and countries. This need not and should not, however, open the door for individual Indigenous people to have rights that ignore their responsibilities to the group for protecting the collective aspects of their knowledge. Nor do culturally sensitive protocols and ethics provide an open door or a "superhighway" for those, however well intentioned, to take what appears necessary for their own purposes. Corporations or universities seeking to include Indigenous people in their research for their purposes, even when some benefits accrue to some of those individuals, are insufficient. Furthermore, vetting research on Indigenous knowledge or among Indigenous peoples through a university ethics committee that does not consider protection issues for the collective may contribute to the appropriation and continuing pillage of Indigenous culture, heritage, and knowledge.

How Indigenous peoples achieve economic and educational self-determination is an important issue today, and education has much to offer. However, research and education must examine not only the Eurocentric foundations of that inquiry but also the partnerships of trust that will achieve equity. How can ethics processes and responsibilities in them ensure protection for the heritage and benefits that accrue to Indigenous peoples for their knowledge and not only to the researchers and/or their institution?

Indigenous knowledge and issues of principles and responsibility of the researcher dealing with sensitive knowledge and protection are fraught with both ambiguity and certainty for Indigenous peoples. They are ambiguous when dealing with areas such as how communities can recover their languages where they have been lost or how schooling should be used to recover or teach Aboriginal heritage. Clearly, elders and community members must be part of those decisions. The role of Indigenous knowledge and languages in any sphere must arise from the first principle that Indigenous peoples must be the custodians of that knowledge. Schools cannot and should not be responsible for teaching Aboriginal knowledge in all its complexity and diversity, nor should they be solely responsible for reviving Aboriginal languages, even if they could. Indigenous knowledge is diverse and must be learned in the similar diverse and meaningful ways that the people have learned it for it to have continuing vitality and meaning. Educators must also respect the fact that Indigenous knowledge can only be fully known from within the community contexts and only through prolonged discussions with each of these groups. This process must also acknowledge and respect the limitations placed on Indigenous knowledge by the community or people of what knowledge can be shared and in what contexts can or should they be shared.

The issues regarding what principles will guide the protection of Indigenous communities and issues of cultural and intellectual property governing those decisions are at the cornerstone of a recent book titled *Protecting Indigenous Knowledge and Heritage: A Global Challenge* (Battiste & Henderson, 2000). The universal losses among Indigenous peoples and the current resource rush on Indigenous knowledge require that a uniform and fair policy or set of practices be established and used by nation-states and multinationals. This will then guide research practices that seek to engage Indigenous knowledge or protect communities' current resources, knowledge, ideas, expressions, trade secrets, and teachings from tourism and other forms of commodification. In addition, such guidelines must be part of every university or research institution. Indigenous peoples have a responsibility to be sensitive and inclusive while also pressuring and ensuring universities protect the collective interests in Indigenous knowledge. The need for protective practices intensifies within these institutions, and it is the following section that addresses some of the issues surrounding their research ethics and the vulnerabilities that are identified. Battiste and Henderson (2000) have asserted that the main principles for research policy and practice must be that Indigenous people should control their own knowledge, that they do their own research, and that if others should choose to enter any collaborative relationship with Indigenous peoples, the research should empower and benefit Indigenous communities and cultures, not just researchers, their educational institutions, or Canadian society.

Indigenous knowledge thus embodies a web of relationships within a specific ecological context; contains linguistic categories, rules, and relationships unique to each knowledge system; has localized content and meaning; has customs with respect to acquiring and sharing knowledge; and implies responsibilities for possessing various kinds of knowledge. No uniform or universal Indigenous perspective on Indigenous knowledge exists—many do. Its unifying concept lies in its diversity. Each group holds a diversity that is not like another, although as Tewa educator Gregory Cajete (1995) has offered, there are unifying strands among Indigenous nations that lie beyond the colonizing features of each group.

These strands are related again to ecology, to place, and to the relationships embedded with that place. To acquire Indigenous knowledge, one cannot merely read printed material, such as books or literature, or do field visits to local sites. Rather, one comes to know through extended conversations and experiences with elders, peoples, and places of Canada.

While many social scientists continue to explore the exotic aspects of Aboriginal cultures, only recently have private corporations and multinationals begun to see how these once-thought "primitive and exotic" cultures could become instrumental to their economic and social political growth. In particular, Indigenous people's knowledge of plant and animal behavior, as well as of their self-management of natural resources, has inspired a new burgeoning field of involvement and interest among researchers and academicians worldwide. Much of this is still embedded in the hegemonic relations in society and is largely exploitative. Pharmaceuticals are bypassing the multiple and expensive trials on plants by going directly to Indigenous experts to ascertain how each plant is used, doing its tests on these derivatives, and then patenting the knowledge and products for mass consumption and financial gain. Delivering back a journal essay on the knowledge is not delivering benefit back to the communities that have held that knowledge. Their interest, as well as those of others seeking Indigenous knowledge, has been the thrust of a new hot-button issue dealing with Indigenous knowledge and intellectual and cultural property that has fueled a political confrontation of Indigenous and non-Indigenous peoples. The national and international community is again faced with a new form of global racism that threatens many Indigenous peoples, a racism in which cultural capital is used as a form of superiority over colonized peoples.

Using international and national funds, nation-states and multinational corporations have commodified the very productions of Indigenous knowledge without Indigenous people's collective consent and knowledge or without adequate compensation or consideration of the impact on the collective who have developed this knowledge. This seemingly accepted practice of globalized commodification of knowledge is evident in books, marketing, and institutions and is very much an ongoing enterprise in modern capital systems, including education. However, the commodification of Indigenous knowledge without consent, consideration, or compensation is another form of exploitation and marginalization of Indigenous peoples. The benefits of this commodification do not accrue to Indigenous peoples per se; rather, they remain the profits of corporations and institutions or the academic and personal gain of individuals. Often, the knowledge is acquired by less than ethical means and used in a manner that distorts or marginalizes it. While there is some literature that counts medicinal knowledge or botanical knowledge as belonging to traditional ecological knowledge, and acknowledged as being threatened and exploited, the same value has not been put to the breadth of knowledge in Indigenous language, songs, stories, and kinship relationships. These elements of culture are internally threatened for loss of use, although not externally exploited. The tension around protecting Indigenous knowledge ultimately surrounds the boundaries of what counts as knowledge in educational institutions and what does not, as the all-encompassing macro terms of "knowledge" make it difficult to legislate protection for it.

As discussions develop regarding the principles and ethics governing Indigenous research, the issue of control or decision making reverberates the singular most important principle—Indigenous peoples must control their own knowledge, a custodial ownership that prescribes from the customs, rules, and practices of each group. This can only be achieved through the involvement of those groups holding the custodial relationships with the knowledge. More often, this will not be the elected leader of that community (for example, the chief) but others whose responsibilities are directly related to the knowledge and teachings of the clan, family, or nation. Thus, a problem is raised about how can any research in the community be vetted or controlled by the rightful owners. While seemingly problematic, the inclusion of local community voice seems necessary for arriving at the issue of control. First, inclusion necessarily requires that local Indigenous peoples and nations become informed and aware of the research being done on, among, or with them. Second, they must train local people in the holistic understanding of issues, practices, and protocols for doing research. In so doing, they will build capacity to do their own research and consequently use research for their own use and benefit, strengthening and revitalizing their communities, territories, and people while warding off the threats to their culture from those who seek to take their knowledge for benefits defined outside their community. Third, they must decide on processes that will ensure that principles of protection and use are developed, disseminated, and used as normative procedures in their territory.

Ethical Issues in Conducting Research in and With Indigenous Communities

Ethical research systems and practices should enable Indigenous nations, peoples, and communities to exercise control over information relating to their knowledge and heritage and to themselves. These projects should be managed jointly with Indigenous peoples, and the communities being studied should benefit from training and employment opportunities generated by the research. Above all, it is vital that Indigenous peoples have direct input into developing and defining research practices and projects related to them. To act otherwise is to repeat that familiar pattern of decisions being made for Indigenous people by those who presume to know what is best for them.

Some Indigenous communities want to share what they know, and many have created their own protocols and procedures for doing so. In so doing, they may limit what can be shared and the conditions for sharing. But all communities want their knowledge and heritage to be respected and accorded the same rights, in their own terms and cultural contexts, that are accorded others in the area of intellectual and cultural property. They want a relationship that is beneficial to them and to those who collectively own that knowledge. Therefore, Indigenous peoples should be supported in developing their knowledge for commercial purposes when they think it is appropriate and when they choose to do so. When this knowledge creates benefits for others, policy and legislation should ensure that Indigenous people share those benefits.

The commoditization of knowledge has been in practice for 500 years. At their core, Eurocentric research methods and ethics are issues of intellectual and cultural property rights. The issues vary from whether life forms and their DNA should be patented to make them private property, to whether knowledge that is freely given in one culture should be commoditized for private profit in another, to confidentiality and trade secrets. Indigenous knowledge can become protected intellectual property in modern society, thus raising new ethical issues.

Most existing research on Indigenous peoples is contaminated by Eurocentric biases. Ethical research must begin by replacing Eurocentric prejudice with new premises that value diversity over universality. Researchers must seek methodologies that build synthesis without relying on negative exclusions based on a strategy of differences. At the core of this quest is the issue of how to create ethical behavior in a knowledge system contaminated by colonialism and racism. Nowhere is this work more needed than in the universities that pride themselves in their discipline-specific research. These academic disciplines have been drawn from a Eurocentric canon, an ultra theory that supports production-driven research while exploiting Indigenous peoples, their languages, and their heritage.

Few academic contexts exist within which to talk about Indigenous knowledge and heritage in an unprejudiced way. Most researchers do not reflect on the difference between Eurocentric knowledge and Indigenous knowledge. Most literature dealing with Indigenous knowledge is written and developed in English or in other European languages. Very few studies have been done in Indigenous languages. This creates a huge problem of translatability.

Linguistic competence is a requisite for research in Indigenous issues. Researchers cannot rely on colonial languages to define Indigenous reality. If Indigenous people continue to define their reality in terms and constructs drawn from Eurocentric diffusionism, they continue the pillage of their own selves. The reconstruction of knowledge builds from within the spirit of the lands and within Indigenous languages. Indigenous languages offer not just a communication tool for unlocking knowledge; they also offer a theory for understanding that knowledge and an unfolding paradigmatic process for restoration and healing. Indigenous languages reflect a reality of transformation in their holistic representations of processes that stress interaction, reciprocity, respect, and noninterference. For Indigenous researchers, there is much to be gained by seeking the soul of their peoples in their languages. Non-Indigenous researchers must learn Indigenous languages to understand Indigenous worldviews. As outsiders, non-Indigenous researchers may be useful in helping Indigenous peoples articulate their concerns, but to speak for them is to deny them the self-determination so essential to human justice and progress.

Indigenous peoples who have lost their languages due to government genocidal and assimilation policies are presented with a great challenge. Second-language research, however, has confirmed that language is more than just sound. Language includes ways of knowing, ways of socializing, and nonverbal communication. The spirits of the consciousness that created those languages are remarkably persistent and are still embedded in many Indigenous communities. Indigenous languages have spirits that can be known through the people who understand them, and renewing and rebuilding from within the peoples is itself the process of coming to know. The Indigenous peoples of Australia have found that essence of spirit in their dreamtime paintings; for others, it is in their creativity or in their hunting skills.

Universality is another ethical research issue. Eurocentric thought would like to categorize Indigenous knowledge and heritage as being peculiarly local, merely a subset of Eurocentric universal categories. These negative innuendoes are the result of European ethnocentrism. The search for universality is really just another aspect of diffusionism, and claiming universality often means aspiring to domination. *Mainstreaming* is another term that raises concerns. It suggests one "main" stream and diversity as a mere tributary. The goal is to try to achieve some normalcy (Minnick, 1990). Together, mainstreaming and universality create cognitive imperialism, which establishes a dominant group's knowledge, experience, culture, and language as the universal norm (Battiste, 1986). Colonizers reinforce their culture by making the colonized conform to their expectations. Because Eurocentric colonizers consider themselves to be the ideal model for humanity and carriers of a superior culture, they believe they can assess the competencies of others. They do this using intelligence and normative educational achievement tests and psychological assessments. They define deviancies from the norm as sins, offenses, and mental illness. Eurocentric thinkers also believe they have the authority to impose their tutelage over Indigenous peoples and to remove from those peoples the right to speak for themselves.

In his analysis of colonial racism, writer Albert Memmi (1965, p. 186) identifies four related strategies used to maintain colonial power over Indigenous peoples: (1) stressing real or imaginary differences between the racist and the victim; (2) assigning values to these differences, to the advantage of the racist and to the detriment of the victim; (3) trying to make these values absolutes by generalizing from them and claiming that they are final; and (4) using these values to justify any present or possible aggression or privileges. All these strategies have been the staple of Eurocentric research, which has created and maintained the physical and cultural inferiority of Indigenous peoples.

In assessing the current state of research on Indigenous knowledge, researchers must understand both Eurocentric and Indigenous contexts. A body of knowledge differs when it is viewed from different perspectives. Interpretations of Indigenous knowledge depend on researchers' attitudes, capabilities, and experiences, as well as on their understanding of Indigenous consciousness, language, and order. Indigenous knowledge may be utilitarian or nonutilitarian or both; it may be segmented or partial depending on Eurocentric reductionistic analysis. Indigenous knowledge needs to be learned and understood and interpreted based on form and manifestation as understood by Indigenous peoples. Indigenous knowledge must be understood from an Indigenous perspective using Indigenous language; it cannot be understood from the perspective of Eurocentric knowledge and discourse.

Knowledge in the Indigenous contexts has its own filters and accessibility criteria. Access to sacred knowledge is ordinarily restricted to particular individuals and organizations within Indigenous communities, such as initiated men or women, or to the members of special spiritual societies. This can pose two kinds of problems for researchers. No single individual can ever be aware of all the cultural concerns that may exist in the community; a broad process of consultation with different groups and elders may be needed before determining whether a site, object, or design is important. In addition, the necessary information may be confidential, such that it cannot be revealed completely to outsiders or even to the rest of the community. Many Indigenous nations have their own medicine or spiritual societies that manage by customs and ceremonies their own initiates who receive knowledge and how and when this specialized knowledge is used. These societies or groups would ensure that all appropriate elders are contacted before a decision is made. Unfortunately, elders or societies are not always consulted, particularly as government or research projects have no information of these societies' responsibilities and knowledge.

Because of the pervasiveness of Eurocentric knowledge, Indigenous peoples today have at their disposal few, if any, valid or balanced methods to search for truth. Every academic discipline has a political and institutional stake in Eurocentric knowledge. Every university has been contrived to interpret the world in a manner that reinforces the Eurocentric interpretation of the world and is thus opposed to Indigenous knowledge. The faculties of contemporary universities remain the gatekeepers of Eurocentric knowledge in the name of universal truth; they represent little more than the philosophy of Western Europe to serve a particular interest. Most academic research is methodologically flawed with multiple forms of cognitive imperialism when it approaches Indigenous issues. The rise of Indigenous centers of learning offers some hope as well as the Indigenous renaissance of Indigenous humanities. The persistent current quest for Indigenous knowledge has inspired many Indigenous writers, scholars, and researchers to pursue institutional protection for Indigenous knowledge. At least one university, the University of Alaska Fairbanks, has developed a cross-cultural master's-level program that centers Indigenous knowledge and develops students' awareness of Indigenous people's cultural and intellectual property rights and the distinctive protocols and practices for investigating Indigenous knowledge.

The Royal Commission of Aboriginal Peoples in Canada (1996) and some institutions of higher learning, particularly in Australia and New Zealand, have established policies and programs to protect Indigenous peoples and their knowledge. Some of these programs involve committees, such as university ethics committees or the newly organized Indigenous ethics committees at the University of Auckland and University of South Australia, which vet all research activity dealing solely with Indigenous communities. The universities must respect the committees' identification of what comprises Indigenous cultural and intellectual property and must respect the gatekeepers of knowledge within Indigenous communities. This respect includes drawing up appropriate protocols for entering into reciprocal relationships following traditional laws and rights of ownership. The reciprocal relationships embody both recognition of the custodians of knowledge and awareness of the associated responsibilities of the custodians and the receivers of knowledge. Furthermore, the universities must also accept that Indigenous peoples are living entities and that their heritage includes objects, knowledge, literacy, and artistic works that may be created in the future (Janke, 1998).

As discussions develop regarding the ethics governing Indigenous research, issues of control and decision making reverberate as the most important principle. Indigenous peoples must control their own knowledge and retain a custodial ownership that prescribes from the customs, rules, and practices of each group. This control can only be realized if the groups that hold these custodial relationships are involved in the research. Often these groups are not elected community leaders, but others whose responsibilities are directly related to the knowledge and the teachings of the clan, family, or nation.

This raises the problem of how a group that vets any research in the community can be controlled by the right owners. Local groups must be informed of threats to their cultures, communities, and knowledge by virtue of the research being done on them. Local people must also be trained in the holistic understanding of the issues, practices, and protocols of doing research. This will enable Indigenous peoples to use research for their benefit, using it to strengthen and revitalize their communities, places, and people while warding off threats to their cultures from those who seek to take their knowledge from them for benefits defined outside their communities.

▣ Procedural Duty to Inform and Seek Consent: The Singular or Double Door Approach

Indigenous peoples throughout the world are concerned about the global onslaught of their knowledge and culture. They seek protection at all levels and increasingly are becoming attuned to the political issues and questions facing them today. The issues associated with protecting Indigenous knowledge are deeply concerned with the structural inability of the law to give Indigenous peoples control of their humanity, heritage, and communities. The absence of protection of the humanity of Indigenous peoples in local and international law is particularly disturbing (Battiste & Henderson, 2000). In the absence of clear guidelines at the national and international levels, each community then must work to effect its own process. This takes me finally to the work of the Mi'kmaw Ethics Watch among the Mi'kmaw Nation in Nova Scotia. Under the treaty authority of the Grand Council of Mi'kma'kik, the official treaty holders and residual beneficiaries of the Constitution of Canada Section 35 (1), the Mi'kmaw Eskinuapimk (Mi'kmaw Ethics Watch) oversee the research protocol and ethical research processes among the Mi'kmaw communities throughout the seven traditional districts of the Grand Council, which includes the Maritime provinces of Newfoundland, New Brunswick, Nova Scotia, and Prince Edward Island as well as Quebec. The Mi'kmaw Ethics Watch is to ensure that Mi'kmaw people and knowledge are protected within Mi'kma'ki territory to the degree that research processes can ensure this capacity.

In the summer of 1999, discussions among elders and families about the issues of protecting Mi'kmaw heritage at the annual customary gathering of the Grand Council of Mi'kmaq at Chapel Island, Nova Scotia, led to a discussion within the Grand Council about protection issues facing the Mi'kmaw people. During the St. Ann Mission speeches, the Grand Captain of the Mi'kmaq announced the appointment of a group of Mi'kmaw community elders, leaders, and researchers to the task of considering the issues of protecting Mi'kmaw knowledge and heritage. They were to return the following year with an update and recommendations from their deliberations.

The group convened over the following year through various means, including telephone, e-mail, and local community meetings, to arrive at the identification of the central issues affecting their Mi'kmaw knowledge. Through further collaboration and consultation with elders, including more research and drafting sessions, a set of draft principles and guidelines was developed, largely drawn from the UN Principles and Guidelines for the Protection of Indigenous Heritage (Daes, 1993). At the conclusion of the St. Ann Mission in the year 2000, delegates of the assigned research and drafting committee presented their findings and recommendations in a drafted document at the traditional meeting of the Grand Council. In turn, the Grand Council announced the creation of an ongoing committee to oversee the principles, guidelines, and protocols for the Grand Council. The name given to this group was the Ethics Eskinuapimk.

The name of the Mi'kmaw Ethics Watch (Ethics Eskinuapimk) derives from an ancient traditional role among Mi'kmaw people. At each major gathering involving the Grand Council, a person (or persons) was assigned responsibility for ensuring the safety of the Grand Council by watching the door of the wigwam. The person would ensure that those who entered had their wampum or protocols in place, had a reason and purpose for being there, and were told where they should seat themselves and how they should behave. This role was both normative and prohibitive. It maintained relations among the group and ensured the safety of the group inside as well as providing guidance for those outside seeking counsel among the elders and leaders. Each wigwam had its own person as well who acted in this capacity such that normative relations were engendered and safety was ensured for everyone. In so adopting this term, the Grand Council seeks to provide researchers the manner and relationships necessary for a harmonious relationship as well as to protect Mi'kmaw people and their knowledge and heritage from exploitation.

The Mi'kmaw Ethics Watch[2] oversees the research protocols, on behalf of the Grand Council of Mi'kmaq, by receiving and assessing research proposals for the Grand Council, applying the principles and guidelines to the proposals, and making comments on the omissions found or on the needed clarity of the proposals for addressing the protocols. They then return these comments and their assessments to the chairperson of the Mi'kmaw Ethics Watch, currently the director of the Mi'kmaq Research Institute at the University College of Cape Breton (now called Cape Breton University), who communicates this information among all the relevant parties.[3] The cycle of communication is then reenacted after the researchers respond to the comments, with final consensus made on the approval of the research or for the need to revise the proposal. When approval has been granted, a final letter of approval is then sent to the researchers for their use in finalizing their research protocols within their own institutions.

The Mi'kmaw guidelines are divided into three sections: The first addresses the principles underlying Mi'kmaw authority and holds that the responsibility for Mi'kmaw knowledge, heritage, and language, including their rights and obligations to exercise control to protect their cultural and intellectual properties and knowledge, rests with Mi'kmaw people. The second section identifies the obligations and protocols and responsibilities for researchers seeking to conduct research among Mi'kmaw people, and such research involves collecting information from any Mi'kmaw person, regardless of topic. The final section deals with the obligations and responsibilities of the Mi'kmaw Ethics Watch (Ethics Eskinuapimk) and processes for dealing with these obligations through the Grand Council and Mi'kmaw communities. The Mi'kmaw Ethics Watch (2000) principles and guidelines offer prospective researchers help in how to derive their respectful inquiry. These, however, also may be useful to researchers as they begin the process of preparing for the ethics review process in the Mi'kmaw community and that may require Mi'kmaw Ethics Watch approval.

Conclusion

Indigenous knowledge represents the protection and preservation of Indigenous humanity. Such protection is not about preserving a dead or dying culture. It is about the commercial exploitation and appropriation of a living consciousness and cultural order. It is an issue of privacy and commerce. The use of Indigenous knowledge for private or public profit by others under existing laws is a central issue. As each of the local communities becomes informed of the actual and potential threats to their communities, due to the destruction of their languages and cultures, the increased interest in renewal and restoration of Indigenous cultures increases the need for protection from continued exploitation and expropriation.

Indigenous peoples are in a precarious position, and their continued existence is threatened. We fear the loss of our languages, identity, cultural integrity, and spiritual teachings. We also fear the loss of commercial gain to help relieve us of our existing poverty. While communities are developing these priorities for themselves, institutions of higher learning should not impose standards that are not inclusive to Indigenous communities who want and should control their own knowledge. In addition, any research conducted among Indigenous peoples should be framed within basic principles of collaborative participatory research, a research process that seeks as a final outcome the empowerment of these communities through their own knowledge.

Indigenous knowledge offers Canadian and other nation-states a chance to comprehend another view of humanity as they never have before. It should understand Indigenous humanity and its manifestations without paternalism and without condescension. In practical terms, this means that Indigenous peoples must be involved at all stages and in all phases of research and planning, as articulated in the UN Working Group's Guidelines and Principles in Protection of Indigenous Populations. These principles and protocols can offer each nation-state an opportunity to rededicate itself to protecting humanity; redressing the damage and losses of Indigenous peoples to their language, culture, and properties; and enabling Indigenous communities to sustain their knowledge for their future.

What is becoming clear to educators is that any attempt to decolonize education and actively resist colonial paradigms is a complex and daunting task. We cannot continue to allow Indigenous students to be given a fragmented existence in a curriculum that offers them only a distorted or shattered mirror; nor should they be denied an understanding of the historical context that has created that fragmentation. A postcolonial framework cannot be constructed without Indigenous people renewing and reconstructing the principles underlying their own worldview, environment, languages, communication forms, and how these construct their humanity. In addition, the fragmenting tendencies and universalizing pretensions of current technologies need to be effectively countered by renewed investment in holistic and sustainable ways of thinking, communicating, and acting together.

▣ Notes

1. For a comprehensive examination of literacy traditions among the Mi'kmaq, see Battiste (1984).
2. The Mi'kmaw Ethics Watch comprises several persons appointed by the Grand Council of Mi'kmaq in cooperation with the local, educational, and political institutions.
3. The Mi'kmaq College Institute address is P.O. Box 5300, Sydney, NS, B1P 6L2 (902-563-1827). The Mi'kmaw Ethics Watch is available at the following on line location: http://www.cbu.ca/ cbu/pdfs/Ethics%20Watch%20Guidelines.pdf

▣ References

Apple, M. W. (1993). *Official knowledge.* New York: Routledge.

Apple, M. W. (1996). *Cultural politics and education.* New York: Teachers College Press.

Battiste, M. (1984). *An historical investigation of the social and cultural consequences of Micmac literacy.* Unpublished EdD dissertation, Department of Curriculum and Teacher Education, Stanford University, Stanford, CA.

Battiste, M. (1986). Micmac literacy and cognitive assimilation. In J. Barman, Y. Hébert, & D. McCaskill (Eds.), *Indian education in Canada: The legacy.* Vancouver: University of British Columbia Press.

Battiste, M., & Henderson, J. (Sa'ke'j) Youngblood. (2000). *Protecting Indigenous knowledge and heritage: A global challenge.* Saskatoon, SK: Purich Press.

Cajete, G. (1995). *Look to the mountain: An ecology of Indigenous education.* Durango, CO: Kivaki Press.

Corson, D. (1997). Linking social justice and power. Clevedon, England: Multilingual Matters Ltd.

Daes, E. (1993). *Study on the protection of the cultural and intellectual property rights of Indigenous peoples* (E/CN.4/Sub. 2/1993/28). Geneva, Switzerland: Sub-Commission on Prevention of Discrimination and Protection of Minorities, Commission on Human Rights, United Nations Economic and Social Watch.

Inglis, S. (2002). *Speakers experience: A study of Mi'kmaq modality.* Unpublished doctoral dissertation, Department of Linguistics, Memorial University, Newfoundland, Canada.

International Labour Organization. (1989). *Convention on Indigenous and tribal peoples in independent countries* (No. 169, 28 I.L.M. 1382). Geneva, Switzerland: Author.

Janke, T. (1998). *Our culture, our future: Report on Australian Indigenous cultural and intellectual property rights.* Surrey Hills, UK: Michael Frankel and Company Solicitors.

Memmi, A. (1965). *The colonizer and the colonized* (H. Greenfield, Trans.). New York: Orion Press.

Minnick, E. (1990). *Transforming knowledge.* Philadelphia: Temple University Press.

Mi'kmaw Ethics Watch. (2000). *Mi'kmaw ethics: Principles, guidelines and protocols.* Sydney, NS: Mi'kmaq College Institute, University College of Cape Breton. Available at http://mrc.uccb.ns.ca/prinpro.html

Royal Commision of Aboriginal Peoples in Canada. (1996). *Report of the Royal Commission on Aboriginal Peoples: Volume 2.* Ottawa, ON: Canada Communication Group.

Smith, L. (1999). *Decolonizing methodologies: Research and Indigenous peoples.* London: Zed.

26

JUSTICE AS HEALING

Going Outside the Colonizers' Cage

Wanda D. McCaslin and Denise C. Breton

Colonization refers to both the formal and informal methods (behaviors, ideologies, institutions, policies, and economies) that maintain the subjugation or exploitation of Indigenous Peoples, lands, and resources.

Decolonization is the intelligent, calculated, and active resistance to the forces of colonialism that perpetuate the subjugation and/or exploitation of our minds, bodies, and lands, and it is engaged for the ultimate purpose of overturning the colonial structure and realizing Indigenous liberation. . . . It is not about tweaking the existing colonial system to make it more Indigenous-friendly or a little less oppressive.

—Waziyatawin Angela Wilson and
Michael Yellow Bird (2005, pp. 2, 5, 4)

Koucheehiwayhk[1] (challenge) describes what many Indigenous peoples face today as we seek to move in healing directions. Healing our communities from the onslaught of imperialism and colonization in every form—economic, political, social, educational, emotional, religious, cultural, cognitive—is a complex, sometimes confusing, and often overwhelming process. Every effort has been made to throw us off our original balance and to get us to conform to "norms" that were never ours and do not fit us. Our journey is filled with obstacles, resistance, pressure, force, and, at times, appropriation of our cultures.

Nowhere is koucheehiwayhk more intense than in matters of what the Eurocentric society calls "justice." Even by Euro-definitions, justice is not what Indigenous peoples on this continent have experienced from the invaders-turned-colonizers—not historically, not now. At best, colonial reformers have attempted to make the criminal justice system "more Indigenous-friendly or a little less oppressive," but their efforts fall far short. Not only do they leave the existing colonial power-over structures in place and unchallenged, but they also leave unchallenged the entire history of genocide, theft, betrayal, oppression, and every manner of cruelty and injustice that had become the painful legacy that every Indigenous person, community, and nation now inherit.

Even if the criminal justice system were the only problem, though, a shackle lined with cotton is still a shackle. Yes, it may not hurt quite as much, but the structure of the relationship—and the structure framing relationships is what counts—remains oppressive. Granted, any movement toward greater compassion, humanity, and respect in how we treat one another is to be welcomed, especially in places of raw brute force, which prisons and the criminal justice system are. But these steps toward what should be common humanity in no way diminish the realities of colonial oppression and hence the need to address colonialism as the root harm.

The very essence of colonialism and its criminal justice system is rule by force, which leads us back to what the colonial project against Indigenous peoples has always been. The colonial concept of "law"—referred to for perhaps public relations reasons as "*positive* law"—is fundamentally inconsistent with and indeed opposed to the virtually universal Indigenous understanding of law. For Indigenous peoples, law is not about coercion but about learning how to move "in a good way" with the order of things. It is not imposed but organic.

By contrast, legal positivism downplays its reliance on force and "might makes right" and instead defends law on the claim that it is being "fair and equitable" to all people by imposing and then protecting what it views as universal interests or values. In practice, laws hold insofar as those in economic and political power say they do and enforce them, yet positivist law is rigidly and vigorously applied under the "fair and equitable" banner. Moreover, Western legal theory argues that once a practice becomes law, it must be followed regardless of whether it is still "good" or "fair." Although it is obviously in the best interests of Western legal theory to maintain an image of its law as "good law," few Indigenous people or peoples experience it as such.

Clearly, how we approach law and talk about it are very much influenced by the colonial views of universality, its underlying concepts of what is "fair and equitable," and its "big stick" underpinnings of force, military might, and coercion. Consistent with this coercive framework, positivism exalts the principles of punishment and has an exotic passion to imprison lawbreakers. Instead of peeling away the layers to understand the root causes of harmful actions, positivist law locks up harm-doers.

Therefore, to discuss issues around "justice" as many Indigenous people experience them, we need both a critique of colonialism and a deeper understanding of Aboriginal culture, practices, traditions, and historical experiences.

Because the existing criminal justice system is not only alien and damaging to us but also the ultimate enforcer of colonial oppression, rethinking justice from the ground up is what Indigenous peoples—and arguably all peoples—must do. However, rethinking justice is precisely what strikes fear in the hearts of many status quo proponents, be they Indigenous or non-Indigenous. Even those who mean well and may attempt to assist in rethinking justice have nonetheless internalized any number of colonial habits. In the face of entrenched institutions, these internalized colonial habits ultimately surface and create new forms of resistance to decolonizing the justice system in the fundamental ways that are long overdue. Yet despite resistance, rethinking justice is precisely how Aboriginal justice dialogues gather strength because it points directly toward the root harm: colonial domination.

Our purpose in this chapter is to participate in this dialogue not by offering administrative or other blueprint-type solutions but rather by considering the frameworks within which we seek solutions. Most specifically, we seek to reclaim frameworks that create space for deep healing by transforming the roots of harm and to critique those frameworks that sabotage healing efforts by reinforcing colonial power. Over the past few decades, these have been crucial yet unaddressed questions for the restorative justice movement.

Who We Are

To begin, we want to introduce ourselves and our perspectives: One of us is Indigenous, the other non-Indigenous. That is, one is of the colonized, and the other is of the colonizers. We come together to write about rethinking justice because we are both committed to decolonization and for at least three reasons.

First, decolonization is critical for both Indigenous and non-Indigenous peoples. Indigenous peoples need to know our own decolonizing pathways, and to do this, we must reclaim our ways of knowing how to be in good relationships. This is not easy, simple, or quick since many of us have become too comfortable with the colonizers' methodologies. Instead, we need to decolonize the positivistic regimes and remember our traditional healing ways of remedying conflicts. In decolonizing approaches, we must always ask ourselves whether our cultural integrity is being promoted, respected, and honored. Anything less will not be decolonizing.

In addition, colonizers need to learn the ways of decolonization that teach respect and the honoring of all relationships. What is destructive and catastrophic to the well-being of one cannot be good for the other. To dehumanize others can only dehumanize the dehumanizers, the controllers, the ones who treat others as objects and benefit materially from doing so. Not only that, but colonizers almost immediately start treating themselves as objects as well—objects that are judged successful or not, objects that command high or low salaries, objects that hold high or low positions in hierarchical societies. We who are White, who are colonizers, desperately need decolonization too.

Second, it is clear to both of us—as it is to all colonized people—that rule by force is inherently oppressive and cannot somehow turn benign or benevolent. Indeed, the foremost tool of punishment—prison—deprives a person of choice, consent, and self-determination. Colonization denies entire peoples of these inherent human rights and the empowering responsibilities that go with them. Colonialism feels bad and punishing because that is what it is. If, as is often said, we cannot get to a good place in a bad way, then we cannot get to a good society or a good relationship between peoples as long as colonialism is the dominant model. Rule by force, colonization, is an intrinsically bad way. It is the core of disrespect because it punishes people and peoples just for who we are. And we know this: Our "punishment" is not for a particular action alone but for who we are as members of a people. Report after report has confirmed this as an undisputable fact. Until we address and rectify this root of harm, we are kidding ourselves if we believe lesser remedies will "fix things," whether it be patterns in the criminal justice system or in the relations between peoples.

Again, we need remedies for human suffering on all levels. But the piecemeal doctoring of symptoms will not heal a disease if the cause is not also addressed. More to the point, constructing a profit-making industry, as the prison industry has become, that depends for its existence on the continuation of those "symptoms" of human suffering gives further evidence of the brutal nature of colonialism.

Third, given the dynamics of colonization and human history, the programming that turns little babies into colonizers is very deep, very entrenched, and certainly very reinforced by rewarding colonizers with every privilege and advantage. Even so, there are those who argue that somewhere in our origins, we (as colonizers) were not this way. At one time, we as peoples (as precolonizers) knew other ways of being in relationship. Our decolonization is about getting our ancestral wisdom back, so that respecting ourselves and others can once again be our way of life.

Certainly, we as Indigenous people are told by our elders time and again that Eurocentric colonial ways are not our ancestral ways of being. We must, therefore, not only recognize the colonizer in others but also recognize it when we are wearing the colonizer's coat. The steps toward decolonization and the recognition of colonialism can be challenging because it is disheartening when we hear our own people espouse colonizer rhetoric.

In this chapter, then, the words *our* and *we* will sometimes refer to Indigenous peoples, while other times they will refer to non-Indigenous peoples, the colonizers, Euro-whoevers, to Whites. And what we're describing can apply to one group or the other or often both. We have chosen to leave this ambiguity or fluidity of referents because the alternative is to use an impersonal, distanced, objectified voice, and that feels contrary to the decolonizing movement away from objectification and toward owning our perspectives as conscious human beings.

The Currents We Face

No matter who we are, rethinking justice down to the root harm of colonization is no easy task. Embarking on this journey means entering rough waters. For Indigenous peoples who have endured despite generations of colonial assault, many currents now flow in us and in our communities. Some of the currents are clearly not ours, and yet they are in us—alienating concepts and attitudes that we have internalized from the colonizing process. These cause trouble and divisions among us. Not many of us, if any, have escaped these currents, and when they surge, we each see in the other the colonizer's shadow lurking in ourselves.

For example, because the root harm of colonization comes from power-over hierarchies and the abuse of power that follows, our internalized colonizer tends to rear its ugly head most whenever that same pattern of power imbalance is perceived among us. When people in power and nonpower positions attempt to communicate, even though we are all Indigenous, we feel the impact of colonization because colonizer-colonized dynamics start affecting how we interact. We do not want this to happen—none of us do—and yet it does. It is the unaddressed programming and unhealed trauma of colonization surfacing.

Another scenario where our internalized colonizers tend to surface is when we take positive steps to decolonize. No matter what type of steps we take, the more decolonizing they are, the more they are resisted at micro and macro levels—and not only from our dominant-society colonizers. Our decolonization methodologies must therefore be prepared to handle resistance from both the dominant society and, at times, our own community members.

For example, after centuries of colonizer programming to which we have all been subjected, some people are now firmly entrenched in a criminal justice mind-set and believe that the best way to reduce crime and ensure safe communities is to "lock 'em up," "break 'em down," or "forget about 'em." We pass laws that exclude our fellow community members from participating in our governments because they now bear the colonizer label of "felon." Yet besides being our relatives, these are the very people who could most effectively help our Indigenous youth avoid the destructive paths that many are on.

In our communities, many of us have also been negatively affected by the Western family law system. Our children have been taken away from our families, placed in residential schools, stripped of dignity as human beings, and molested at every level—physical, mental, emotional, and spiritual. The colonizer assaults the very core of our family strength, our language, our customs, and our ways of being. Our children were stripped of their ability to know how to be good parents and were taught in unrelenting and unforgiving ways how NOT to love. While we are now slowly on our way to recovery by reclaiming our traditions, practices, and customs, the harms continue to torture us at many levels. Toxic colonizer currents have swept away our most sacred gifts: our children.

These are some of the internalized colonizer currents that make the waters of decolonizing rough. The remedy is to peel away the layers of colonization within us, so that we can feel the lifeblood of healing justice and plant ourselves within Mother Earth by affirming who we are as peoples. As we stay connected to our homelands and communities, we can support each other in what it means to "be good relatives" and can hold open the space for our own Indigenous thoughts and perspectives to gather strength and thrive.

Our internalized colonizers are not, however, the only forces causing the waters to churn and heave as we chart a decolonizing route. Other currents are powered by our own responses to all that has happened and still happens. These currents can be rough as well, filled as they are with trauma, pain, grief, anger, rage, and disorientation.

Although these currents are a direct response to what has been imposed on us, they are nonetheless ours, because they flow straight from who we are. In a thousand different ways, they represent our authentic Indigenous voices saying no to racism, colonization, oppression, degradation, and injustice. Our reactions may be intense and passionate, conflicted, or sometimes even unhealthy, misdirected, or hurtful, but if we respect them for what they are and for their role in the healing, decolonizing process, they can bring us together and provide opportunities for rebalancing ourselves.

Precisely because these currents express our Indigenous responses to colonization, they are often used to dismiss our decolonizing work: "She's just another angry Indian"; "Why don't you stop being angry and do something constructive [i.e., colonizer conforming]?" Our wisdom keepers are called "too theoretical and not connected to practical matters." Far too often, those who point the way to decolonization are dismissed, abused, and discounted. Our nations are filled with horrific stories and experiences of dismissal by those entrenched in hierarchical structures. Even those places that are said to be "safe places" to share, teach, and discuss the arduous decolonizing journey can fall under the colonizers' shadow.

The ugly head of colonization rising to squash our resistance can indeed take many forms. Some of us have been told, "To succeed here, you just have to be a good Indian: keep your head down, and don't make waves." When we tell the colonizer that something is offensive to our traditions, we are told, "There is no reason to be upset. We meant to honor you. We checked with a couple of other Indians, and it doesn't bother them." When we pursue the issue, we can be disciplined or—at times—fired. Others become targets of racial reprisals.

These are some of the rough waters we face as we struggle against colonial oppression. Who that is Indigenous does not face on a daily basis systemic discrimination and oppressive legal structures and policies? And who has not faced attacks from our own community members as we challenge colonization within and without?

We could dream of walking away from the colonial system altogether, and yet for many if not most of us, this is not a viable option. Who has not faced the very real dilemma of striving to be true to who we are as a person and as a people, yet also needing to carry out some form of bill-paying work that involves interacting with colonizing institutions and their one-sided exercise of power?

If we adapt to what these structures demand, we carry a load of frustration and fury at what we experience ourselves and see done to others, and we also risk losing connection to who we are in the process. We become disconnected and get a "split head." One side of our brain says no to the colonizer, while the other side says yes to keep our job. When we try to change the structures, we are in for a long and often lonely fight. Those in power seem to hold all the cards and are not afraid to play them when we "act up."

Those who do fight are labeled as "too harsh" in our criticism; our words are deemed "not saleable" for Eurocentrics. We are told that, while "they agree" with our points, they won't be acceptable to others; we risk losing "credibility." Our strong Indigenous voices are not intending to make Eurocentrics comfortable or to court their approval but rather to defend our people and to celebrate our own cultures, practices, and traditions. Even so, when we make waves and stand our ground in opposing colonialism, we risk being marginalized by being excluded altogether. These waves represent "another day in the life of colonial oppression," and they are some of the roughest, the ones that can wear us down the most.

But we are not without help. Most fundamentally, as Indigenous peoples, we can call on the deep, abiding currents of our traditions, cultures, and communities. Some Indigenous peoples feel these currents more strongly than others, depending on the access we have to elders, traditional family structures, and culturally rooted communities. These currents align us to who we are as Indigenous peoples and help us respond in good, sustainable ways to the colonial onslaughts. Our culture, traditions, and communities give us energy, hope, and direction as we do our best to negotiate rough waters.

Indeed, this is our challenge as we rethink justice—namely, to respond in an Indigenous way to whatever arises, including harms. If we are disconnected from who we are as Indigenous peoples, we will be out of balance in our lives and communities. Instead of turning to our Indigenous ways when troubles arise, we will resort to remedies that were designed by and for our colonizers.

Yet because these are not *our* remedies, they will not address the underlying causes of harm. The "solutions" they bring will be superficial and symptom oriented at best and will extend the damage of colonization, residential schools, and assimilation at worst. The more we resort to them and use them, even to fight colonization, the more we depend on them instead of on our own ways. In the name of fighting colonization, we risk finding ourselves being gradually molded in the colonizers' image since using colonizer methods has a way of leaving its mark on us.

To reclaim an experience of justice that is healing, we need to rely on ways that build on the millennia-old foundations of our cultural wisdom and learning as Indigenous peoples. Indigenous ways can restore us by helping us understand how to be in good relationship—how to "be a good relative"—whether it is with ourselves, our families, our communities, other Indigenous peoples and nations, or with the peoples of the natural world. Engaging Indigenous ways of being in relationship, especially when hurts and conflicts arise, is how we must rethink justice, yet it is not easy, simple, or clear-cut.

Restorative Justice and Its Aborted Season

Restorative justice started in many communities, especially Indigenous ones, as a way to do just that. Putting the criminal justice system out of business by relying on community-based Indigenous ways of healing relationships and communities was a common dream—a goal to work toward. Healing harms was not about scapegoating individuals who have been caught in destructive patterns but about healing. This means that people would come together to create a balance and harmony in how a community was relating, so that everyone could be "made whole." The vision is a fundamentally spiritual process because it is about being connected in a good way—a way that honors the intrinsic worth and good of each person. Indigenous knowledge is based on a profound and thorough awareness of our relatedness in all directions, so it was natural to apply this knowledge to healing harms. In this context, healing was not about "fixing" individuals but about transforming relationships. It was always about "being good relatives" to each other—something that we as Indigenous people are taught to do from the moment we're born.

This depth of healing can't be forced or managed from without; it is something that those involved must seek to hold a space for in themselves, so that they can respond in a good way to others. Again, it is spiritual. Healing broken relationships must involve the sincere and genuine efforts by all of those involved to practice values such as fairness, honesty, compassion, harmony, inclusiveness, trust, humility, openness, and, most important, respect. It is about engaging our best selves to respond to harms, so that instead of causing divisions among us, harms can be used to bring us together and to make our families and communities stronger.

Restorative justice began, therefore, with community efforts to create spaces where commitments to such values and to expressing them in relationships and communities became not only possible but also natural—simply the way to be. Justice was not, therefore, about courts or punishment but about "being a good relative," especially when harms occurred. Instead of resorting to coercion or force, restorative justice meant responding to harms in ways that engaged everyone's powers of transformation. Victims, offenders, and the communities of each came together not for blame or revenge but to work things out in a good way. Restorative justice was not therefore something that was "done to" a particular person; it was a way of being together that was by nature healing and transformative for all those involved.

Encouraged by the dominant society's initial receptivity to a more healing approach and faced with the unrelenting oppressiveness of the criminal justice system, Indigenous communities over the past few decades have led the way in engaging a wide range of healing, restorative, community-building practices. Through determined efforts to increase community connectedness with the wisdom of elders, for example, Indigenous communities have often held talking or peacemaking circles to address harms. Globally, the practices that Indigenous peoples use and have used are as diverse as the peoples themselves, but they generally have entailed bringing together those harmed with those who did the harm within the context of the communities of each, so that amends and rectification could be achieved that are satisfying to all. As communities have done this work, not only individuals but also the communities themselves have experienced healing and transformation. Moreover, the transformation they have experienced has occurred in a pattern that some describe as "the seasons of healing."

To document some of the healing work going on in First Nation communities, the First Nations Research Project on Healing in Canadian Aboriginal Communities issued a 2002 report titled "Mapping the Healing Journey" (see Lane, Bopp, Bopp, & Norris, 2005), which draws on in-depth consultations with six First Nations communities. After describing how multigenerational trauma and abuse are manifested in Indigenous communities, the report shares the many insights and experiences of community members engaged in healing work. Community members consistently emphasized that personal healing and nation building go hand in hand. Decolonization, they reported, is the therapy most needed as the framework for personal and community transformation. Indeed, it forms the critical "fourth stage" of a four-stage process of community transformation.

As with individuals, the community members explained, communities also heal through stages, which some First Nation community members compared to the four seasons—"the seasons of healing." The healing journey of communities begins with *winter,* when community members confront how bad things really are and realize that it is not okay to let things slide unchanged. Harsh necessities spur community members to embark on the healing journey.

The *springtime* of community healing feels like a thaw, as energies for positive change gather momentum. Hopes run high, and community members rally by volunteering time and energies.

Yet as the healing work progresses, communities come to a stage that feels like hitting the wall. This is the long, hot *summer;* the honeymoon stage is over, as people realize that the scope of change needed takes more than good will and good intentions. Rough, entrenched patterns, both within and without, surface and threaten to overwhelm those on the healing path. All sorts of paradoxes also surface, and disillusionment can set in. It can feel like everything is becoming undone.

The only way to continue is to make a deep shift from healing to transformation. This critical next step is *fall,* which pares away all but the most essential structures. It is a time of asking the following: Which structures support our regeneration, and which extend our oppression? Fixing "problems" yields to the more fundamental task of changing systems and structures. It is the time when communities realize that healing will not occur without the deeper transformation that involves decolonization and nation building. To put it differently, we cannot "heal" ourselves of the sense of suffocating entrapment as long as we remain locked inside a cage. Nothing less than getting out of the cage will do. The seasons of the healing journey describe a path by which communities grow to this realization, and as they do, they gain the strength, unity, resolve, and wherewithal to embark on the larger task of decolonization.

These seasons of healing offer a framework for considering what has happened—and what has not yet happened—in restorative justice work. In the decades since restorative justice started as a movement within the mainstream Western legal system, the original vision of community-based healing and transformation has somehow gotten lost—really lost. Restorative justice no longer inspires such a vision. Instead, it seems as if the seasons of the healing path got aborted, frozen, or blocked. As it is now conceived, restorative justice represents one more tool for colonizers to maintain power, hierarchy, mistrust, and imbalance. What happened?

Some say lack of funding for community justice programs derailed the best of intentions and efforts, and certainly this played a part. Community justice programs have saved the criminal justice system and taxpayers uncounted millions of dollars, given the many lives saved from the revolving doors of courts and prisons. Yet these huge savings have not been passed on to the communities who did the work—or even offered to other communities to start similar programs—but have been absorbed by the criminal justice system and used to further its model of punishment. Working on a volunteer basis with little or no resources to address the human costs of centuries of racism and oppression, many community members simply burned out.

Yet as significant as funding issues are, especially in how they reflect the priorities and values of a society, what has gone wrong with restorative justice goes much deeper. The central and critical understanding of justice as a way of life—justice as practicing the responsibilities of being good relatives to each other—fell by the way, and for a definite reason. The profound shift from summer to fall was aborted. Justice cannot be a way of life for Indigenous peoples—or anyone else, for that matter—as long as colonization remains the ruling framework. Colonization is coercive and exploitative at its core. It is about oppressing certain groups, classes, or peoples in order to benefit others. This framework is antithetical to the authentic practice of justice.

The fourth season of community transformation demands that we confront these realities. The challenge of the fourth stage is to address the deeper structures that give rise to harm, so that healing and transformation can continue down to the roots of what is causing imbalance and disharmony. Colonialism cannot continue unnamed, as if it were an invisible backdrop or neutral bystander to harms. It must be brought front and center and named as the root cause. Healing without this level of decolonizing transformation may temporarily fix immediate breakdowns, but it will not address the structures that led to them. Similar harms will recur. If the fourth stage is prohibited or shut down, the crises of summer become crushing for communities, and the energizing spirit for doing the work will be overwhelmed. The despair that follows can be paralyzing for both colonizers and the colonized. Decolonization is the only hope, but as yet, it is not on the restorative justice radar.

As conceived from its Indigenous origins, healing justice calls for a profound paradigm shift from the dominant society's ways of responding to harms. Instead of handing our conflicts over to "experts" or "professionals," everyone feels equally called to be humble, self-critical, open, self-disclosing, willing to change, and prepared to own some role in the dynamics that led to harm. These are difficult demands, and they entail responsibilities that the criminal justice system enables us to ignore and pass off to colonial institutions. Justice as a way of life is demanding on persons and communities.

Moreover, these responsibilities challenge colonizer thinking. Colonizer programming makes us view some people as inherently inferior to others. Its language is rampant with "them" as "the problem" and colonizers or colonizer surrogates as "the solutions." The "social norm" is that "those others" don't fit and don't belong, and "their problem" is that "they" need to learn to be just like "us," namely, the colonizers.

How the criminal justice system responds to the problem of Aboriginal youth gangs provides a clear example of why colonizer "solutions" inevitably fail. It is true that we have lost some of our youth to the gang culture, which has often been introduced through the criminal justice system. Far too often, our youths' negative behaviors have caused them to be hastily and inappropriately labeled as gang "members" or "associates." Thus labeled, our youth are then sent to jails or, for those lucky ones, placed in the community, but now rival gangs know them. The youths' very survival requires them to become even more closely associated to their gang for their own protection, whether on the streets or in jails. Instead of understanding that such behaviors are merely symptoms of hidden feelings and emotions, the colonial system responds by imposing a negative label.

As the Federation of Saskatchewan Indian Nations (2005) pointed out, these prepackaged labels are subjective and carry severe consequences for the youth. Labeling Indigenous youth negatively builds not on objective reasoning but on stereotypes of Aboriginal youth. Instead of resorting to snap-decision labeling, the Federation of Saskatchewan Indian Nations advocates understanding the underlying causes that put youth at risk and reevaluating the language and approach that is being used on our children.

We know that as we restore the dignity of our communities, we give our youth an experiential road map to follow. But instead of supporting Aboriginal efforts to restore dignity and address the root harms of colonialism, the criminal justice system encourages the practice of labeling our children negatively. It is easier to assign a harmful label to a disempowered youth—though this may have lifelong consequences—than it is to look at the systemic roots of harm. Indeed, it is antithetical to colonial programming to think that the deeply entrenched colonizer paradigm—the control-oriented worldview with all the institutions, practices, and habits that go with it—is *itself* the problem or in any way responsible for harms.

This, then, is the core challenge: We cannot practice justice as a way of life and remain colonizers. We cannot avoid confronting the colonizing cage—a cage that traps both Indigenous and non-Indigenous people. If there is a genuine effort to practice justice as our way of life—a way informed by values of respect, humility, inclusivity, and all the other values essential to healing justice—then we will invariably come to a point where it is apparent to all of us that Eurocentric thought, with its inherently colonizing assumptions, expectations, behaviors, norms, and institutions, must go. After centuries of horrific experiences, even many colonizers are realizing that colonialism cannot work as justice. This realization and a commitment to decolonizing is the fourth season of healing justice, and this is the season that has been shut down.

Given the extent to which colonizer categories have been internalized, it is no surprise that this happened. Writing as a colonizer committed to decolonization, I (Denise) know how hard it is to confront the many roles I now bear as a colonizer. I know that decolonization necessarily challenges my privileged treatment, and I also know that I and my fellow colonizers have vested material interests in keeping things "as is." But more than that, I know that my social conditioning and the socially constructed sense of who I am—all the mental, emotional, and material habits that I have been raised to accept—support oppression in a thousand subtle and blatant ways. These dynamics of oppression have been rendered invisible to me, however painfully visible they are to others. The decolonizing work begins here with naming these dynamics, so that I can engage the lifelong work of breaking their hold.

Without this persistent work, I lapse into the default mode of supporting the colonizer paradigm without realizing that this is what I am doing. My efforts toward decolonization and justice—which is the potential of restorative justice—will be sabotaged by my lack of awareness of how I have been programmed to serve and perpetuate the colonial model.

This seems to have been the dilemma for many well-meaning colonizers who have come into restorative justice. For those of us who were exposed to the paradigm of justice as a way of life, we were brought face-to-face with our programming as colonizers and faced a clear call to abandon that way of life—to reject and undo the power-over paradigm into which we were born. Doing this is our koucheehiwayhk.

As challenges go, though, it's a big one. If we embark on decolonization, we know the Eurocentric worldview will lose its privileged status. Claims to racial superiority will have to go, and White supremacist programming in all its forms will have to be confronted. We as a people will also have to confront horrific wrongs in how we got to where we are as a society—the centuries of costs paid by others for White privilege and for the inheritances now being passed to White children and not to Indigenous children. Suddenly, those of us who have been the privileged people in the racially organized hierarchy are placed in the role of wrongdoers, offenders, and perpetrators of harms. It is no longer the "degraded other" who is on the hot seat.

If given a choice between confronting all these realities and running back to the colonizer model that allows denial, privilege, and marginalizing the "other," what are Eurocentric people likely to choose? Given lifetimes of programming, given the stakes, given the hard road ahead of working to make things right with peoples who know what has been done and the history of Whites getting away with horrific colonizer actions through all sorts of rationalizations, self-justifications, and academic and sociological variations of "blaming the victim," which road is a born-and-bred colonizer likely to choose? It's not rocket science. It is also not a surprise, then, that the restorative justice movement came to this inevitable crossroads and chose as it did.

When justice as a way of life—hence the fourth season of decolonization—dropped out and thereby failed to take hold in the restorative justice work, everything unraveled. The sense of community disappeared, replaced by a group who conceived of their role as working to "fix" the person who was designated as having "the problem." The dynamics of force instantly reentered since now groups exerted their force and combined power on a single person, the one cast as the "lone wrongdoer." The community became the power enforcer placed at the top of a hierarchical order. These dynamics did not give the now-isolated wrongdoer any genuine sense of connectedness that would inspire authentic change. A process that has the emotional effect of being "ganged up on" by people in power who believe they are superior and who treat us as inferior is not pleasant, and the natural reaction is to resist it or to have nothing to do with it.

The word then got around that restorative justice doesn't work, and those who tried to revive it did so with "new and improved" techniques for making offenders change. These, of course, don't work because techniques miss the point entirely of what went wrong. What is needed is not another technique of colonizing control but a paradigm shift that takes us out of the colonizers' cage altogether. People notice when they are being coerced—that control by force is what is happening. Not for a moment were the colonized fooled when restorative justice came to the crossroads and chose against decolonization.

In spades, we're back to the same old criminal justice model.

On this analysis, what really has caused the downfall of restorative justice is colonialism. Colonizers simply refused to give up the role, yet decolonization is precisely what restorative justice requires—if, that is, it is to "work" as a healing, transformative process in more than superficial, Band-Aid, scapegoating ways. Either we embrace the fall season and turn our focus on the deeper structures generating harm, or we admit that we are using "healing" to protect privilege and power—to keep our lives unaffected by "those others" whom we conceive of as "the problem." Every time those working in restorative justice have chosen colonizer status over justice, restorative justice has lost credibility with us, the colonized, who, as we all know, are the target populations of the prison industries.

Some Aboriginal people now want nothing to do with restorative justice, and precisely on these grounds. The core vision of "going to the roots of harm" and "doing what it takes to make things right" has been exposed as empty rhetoric, invoked only when colonial power structures deem it advantageous to do so. Instead of working toward wholeness for peoples—which means addressing genocide, fraud, theft, systematic and institutional racism and abuse, and the culture-wide cover-up or defense of these crimes—restorative justice has bailed out. Insofar as it focuses exclusively on individual crimes within the criminal justice framework, restorative justice as a movement has failed to address the "elephant in the living room" of how we got to where we are as peoples, and the colonizers' cage continues to be reinforced.

Because of these choices, restorative justice now functions as another tool of colonizing institutions and hence of oppression. The goal is not to heal the root harm of colonization but to find "new and improved" or "nicer" ways for one people to dominate another. Restorative justice is used to make the violence of the criminal justice system—the colonizers' control-by-fear-and-force fist—seem more humane. Instead of remedying the wider contexts that generate harms, the focus stays on trying to fix person-to-person conflicts. Individuals, families, or communities are viewed as "the problem," while the larger reasons that individuals, families, or communities have problems remain invisible.

What are these larger reasons? They are the everyday realities for the colonized that colonizers contend are "things of the past." They include the systemic and institutional racism that costs people education, housing, health care, banking services, and jobs; the massive land theft that continues to leave Indigenous peoples economically, socially, politically, and multigenerationally ravaged; and the genocide, diasporas, and assimilate-or-die boarding school experiences and traumas that are passed down from generation to generation.

As long as these actions against Indigenous peoples are kept off the ledger of restorative accountability, restorative justice cannot be credible; neither can it work as a genuinely healing, transformative force. Too many of the realities related to the total picture of harms are excluded from the dialogue. The transformation of people, communities, and nations is aborted by the refusal to acknowledge colonialism as the root harm.

In short, until colonialism is named, challenged, and overturned, no talk about justice will be convincing to the colonized or authentic and genuinely transformative for anyone else. After a honeymoon of colonizers stating, "Wow, isn't it great that we're talking to people we would never otherwise dream of talking to, and don't we feel good about ourselves and rather enlightened or even righteous for doing this otherwise unimaginable thing?" the whole process falls flat because it's obvious to everyone that nothing is going to change. The structure of the relationship, firmly established by the colonizer-colonized roles, is not on the table, and so it's not budging. At best, we spend a couple hours talking and acting as if we're all equal, but then we go home to our dramatically and systemically unequal realities, and we don't connect the dots. What most needs to be discussed is off-limits for discussion, and so what most needs to be changed remains "as is." If we want to give restorative justice a fighting chance, then we have to call colonialism out from its pervasive invisibility as "the norm," name it for what it does to peoples and people, name why it cannot work as justice, and commit ourselves to undoing it. The fourth season of healing calls.

Life Outside the Cage: From Positive Law to Reclaiming Indigenous Law

Can we really decolonize, though? Is it possible to get outside the colonizer's cage? What does that look like? It's not just possible; it's mandatory and for many reasons—certainly for justice to be a way of life. As for what life outside the cage looks like, we'll have to discover that as we decolonize, and each people will shape the contours of their own decolonized society.

To start, the truth tribunals and truth commissions that confront the immense harms of colonial oppression, such as were held in South Africa and currently being proposed in Canada to address the horrors of residential schools, seek to offer dramatic images of honoring Indigenous experiences, overturning colonial structures, and challenging their legitimacy. The past must be rectified not from revenge but as an essential means of transformation. This is a core understanding of restorative justice and healing. Harms are not to be ignored, denied, minimized, forgotten, or in any way glossed over, because they are the doorway exactly fitted to bringing about the change that's needed, that is, if we respond appropriately. How can we respond appropriately as a people and as a society, though, if we fail to officially acknowledge what has happened? Truth telling is the first essential step of breaking down the walls of silence about life inside the cage.

As we undergo this first rite of leaving the colonizer's cage, we naturally start rethinking law and justice: How do we as Indigenous peoples choose to preserve harmony among us? How do we understand law, and how do we keep it? These are critical questions for life outside the cage, because the colonial concept of law and the general Indigenous concept are very different. At the root of the incompatibility between the original idea of restorative justice and what colonialism calls justice are two fundamentally different concepts of law, which in turn stem from two completely different worldviews. We want to take a look at these two concepts because their stark incompatibility clears the cobwebs of thinking that we can somehow graft one onto the other—that Indigenous ways can be used to save the existing colonial system.

As we mentioned, the prevailing Eurocentric concept of law is grounded in *legal positivism.* It defines law as a set of rules and norms that become binding insofar as some authority has the power to strictly enforce them as such. In democracies, this authority is made up of the majority of people, who in turn vest their power in those whom they elect to represent them and those whom the elected appoint to public offices.

The rules and norms—the body of law—that this authority establishes and calls *objective rules* have no relation to moral values, natural law, or inherent order. They can be arbitrary, inequitable, and unjust, or they can be idealistic, equitable, and high-minded. Whichever those who have the power to enforce "the law" decide which rules and norms will be treated as binding and will enforce them accordingly. Their binding character derives not from any intrinsic quality of connectedness to the nature of things but simply from the fact that some person or group has the external power to impose a particular set of rules as binding on everyone else.

In other words, inherent in this concept of law is force: "might makes right." It's the notion that a group that holds a power advantage can impose its laws on others—that the power to enforce one's will makes it legitimate and "right" to do so. This is precisely how law is made, established, and legitimized according to legal positivism. It is also intrinsic to a democracy: The majority, having a power advantage, can impose its collective will on any minority. Even when the majority says it adheres to the ideals of democracy, which assert that the aspirations of minorities be respected, the reality is much different, particularly for Aboriginal peoples.

Because law is established within the colonial context, the law-created "norm" is designed to protect the colonial status quo. One way to do this is to obscure its oppressive nature—to make colonialism seem not so oppressive. Aboriginal peoples do not *always* lose their cases. The colonizer-serving function of the law is more subtle and covert in operation. Sometimes the law is clearly oppressive; other times it appears to be "neutral and fair." But that is just the point: It is the colonizers' privilege to be fair or oppressive at will, namely, as it serves colonizing interests to do so. It is not in the colonizers' interests to be consistently oppressive. Effective colonization must maintain the image of fairness, or the whole edifice would collapse. Too much energy would have to go into enforcing consistent, unrelenting oppression.

Yet an image of fairness is not the same as actual fairness, nor does it make a system based on force and might truly fair. Once we start peeling away the layers of colonization (rule by force), we soon see how positive law is not by nature fair or unbiased. Behind the impression of fair and unbiased legal "norms," the law carries out its mandate to enforce a colonial framework, which is by nature oppressive. Exerting force on those who lack the sufficient power to resist and compelling them to obey "the norm," as those in power so decide it, follow from the essential meaning of law as legal positivism defines it. In this calculus, power is all that matters—not values, not justice, not respect. What matters is the power to force others to abide by whatever serves the interests of those who hold a preponderance of power. All the inequities and injustices that follow are not therefore unfortunate side effects or occasional deviations from an otherwise just and equitable concept of law. They are the tentacles of colonial power, which reveal the true character of law when it is defined as rule by force.

Given that using power imbalances to benefit some at the expense of others is inherent in the legal positivist concept of law, can this model "do justice" for more people than those who are the self-designated beneficiaries? Though proponents of positive law construct defenses, the historical and global track record suggests otherwise. The model clearly fails to do justice for the billions of people globally who do not find themselves at the top of the power hierarchy. Moreover, who in this scheme of law represents all the peoples of the natural world? In other words, can this model of law produce "fair and equitable treatment"—"due process"—for all the beings affected, or is injustice built into this paradigm of law at its core? The latter is arguably the case, given not only the number of patches that the system requires to achieve some semblance of justice but also the alarming mess our world is in.

In contrast to legal positivism, the Indigenous concept of law is generally described as *natural law.* This term, though, can be misleading. Before we go further, we must note that the Eurocentric definition of "natural law" is very different from the understanding of law that Indigenous peoples generally have. The Eurocentric concept of "natural law" revolves around humans and is based on a certain notion of human nature and rationality; it is concerned only with human beings in human societies. By contrast, Indigenous views of law generally describe a lawfulness inherent in the nature of things—humans, the natural world, and the unseen worlds all woven together. This concept is very different from the Eurocentric notion of natural law, and for that reason, it seems clearer to use the term *Indigenous law.*

The difference between both Eurocentric concepts of law (positive and natural) and Indigenous law is profound. Whereas both European notions of law begin and end with human beings, to an Indigenous way of thinking, Indigenous law encompasses far more. It is inherent in the natural and cosmic order of which we are all a part and on which we depend for our existence. For this reason, the lawfulness that surrounds us on every level is binding. Because we are part of the natural order, it is wise and good to understand the natural way of things, so that we can interact with our worlds in good ways—ways that are sustainable and that support ongoing good relationships. So, too, it is unwise not to know these ways and harmful, even self-destructive, to go against them. If we try, our actions will not blend or be fruitfully aligned with the wider contexts in which we exist.

Understanding the lawfulness of things begins with the core concept of respect. Treating others disrespectfully, for example, will not build good relations, and coercion will not be experienced as respectful treatment. Good relations require a foundation of respect, which involves finding ways to work things out not by coercion but rather by honoring the needs, views, interests, competence, and autonomy of others. These "laws" that govern how to be in a good relationship inhere in the very nature of things; they do not need to be enforced; they just are, given how things are. And they hold whether our relationships are with people, communities, other nations, or those of the natural world (water, air, earth, plants, and animals).

This understanding of law simply makes sense, that is, if our priority is to be in a good relationship with the people, nations, and world around us. Naturally, it's a different story if our priority is to gain power or to assert dominance over others; then law as "might makes right" makes more sense. But if being in a good way with others is what matters to us, then we cannot escape the considerations that our Indigenous view of law raises. We cannot, for example, pass a law stating that disrespectful treatment will build good relationships and make it stick, no matter how much force we may have at our disposal. Neither can we pass a law declaring that toxic waste is good nutrition for life forms.

The most fundamental reality factor that Indigenous law acknowledges (and Eurocentric law does not) is the reality that we are all related. Understanding the lawfulness of things helps to align us with our world by making us mindful of *how* we are all related. What we call moral and spiritual values are guidelines for how we can be in relationships in a good way—how we can acknowledge our relatedness and be good relatives—as we go through life. Moral and spiritual values arc fundamental to the cosmic and natural order precisely because they speak to our intrinsic relatedness to all that is. This is why adhering to these values is so important. From the perspective of many Indigenous peoples, we cannot successfully have or do justice without adherence to such values.

Eurocentric anthropologists and sociologists have interpreted Indigenous law and "justice" systems through the lens of positive law since this is the only concept of law and social order that they view as binding. As a result, they have read their own power-organized, hierarchical, positive-law categories into their analyses of how our Indigenous societies work. They are unrelenting in their desire to recast our Indigenous ways into "consistent" approaches, rather than respecting our diversity and the strengths of our different ways. As a result, their characterizations of how we maintain balance, harmony, and good relations in our families, communities, and nations do not fit our experiences, nor do they reflect how we understand what we are doing.

We adhere to lawful, hence respectful, ways of being, not because we are compelled to do so by groups or authorities through fear of punishment but because this is a sustainable way to live, and we understand that. Our ways of understanding law hold us in a good relationship with each other and the natural world. To go against a lawful way of being would be to embark on a path that is inherently destructive. It would lead us to act disrespectfully and hurtfully to our relationships, yet these are what sustain us. If we violate lawfulness by acting disrespectfully, we are the ones hurt, if not now then in the generations to come. We strive to show respect for others in all our relations, therefore, because our millennia of experiences as peoples have proven to us that to do otherwise is damaging not only to others but to ourselves as well.

The difference in these fundamental concepts of law underscores why colonialism has been so destructive for Indigenous peoples and will remain so. Indigenous ways are based on values of respect, talking things out, patience, compassion, shared responsibilities, deep family and community bonds, and healing. They are not about giving orders or commands, coercion, or telling people what they must or must not do. Indigenous ways are not prescriptive in nature but permissive. They provide broad guidance on what we should do, and then they trust everyone's innate learning processes to guide each person in a good way, a way that maximizes their learning as human beings.

By contrast, colonial law is all about control. It supports hierarchies of power, and it uses judgment and punishment to enforce compliance with win-lose, individualistic, adversarial, and divisive norms. The colonial system of laws was not designed with Indigenous values in mind or to favor Indigenous interests, nor does it inspire respect for how we human beings are related. Because colonial law has been forcibly imposed on Indigenous peoples to benefit others, and because the values behind these laws are antithetical to Indigenous ways, the "might makes right" system of legal positivism can only damage Indigenous people and communities; it cannot work for us as Indigenous peoples, and no amount of tinkering will change that.

Contrary to appearances, the colonial model of law does not actually benefit colonizers either. Yes, it bestows every outward advantage on those whom it privileges, but is it good for someone who has a power advantage to hurt others for personal benefit and to get away with it? In schoolyard terms, is it good for a child to get away with bullying? Moral, soul, and culture issues aside—and these are huge—being conditioned over generations to think that we can do whatever we want to whomever we want as long as we have the power to do it and to get away with it has generated a mind-set that has not developed respect for the real-world consequences of actions.

Indeed, it would seem that no measure of human suffering is sufficient to challenge the model. We have to wonder about a mind-set that is so entrenched in the rule of force that even the extreme crises in our Indigenous communities—not to mention in the natural world—fail to warrant a paradigm shift. A basic sensitivity to humanity seems missing or to have been lost. We, both the colonized and the colonizers, are confronted with a baffling unwillingness to consider the lawfulness inherent in good relationships and an arguably pathological commitment to wielding power no matter what the consequences.

So, to return to the original question about justice, can the practice of legal positivism be improved? Considering the criminal justice system, can we tweak it or reform it, so that it works better? Can, for example, the criminal justice system adopt more Indigenous values without having to change the overall framework? Can restorative justice provide the needed "fix"? In other words, can we renovate this cage?

To be genuine, changes would have to honor Indigenous self-determination since this is what the value of respect requires. The criminal justice system, entrenched within the colonial framework, could no longer dominate. Once again, colonialism would have to be front and center as the problem on the table since virtually every ill that Indigenous peoples suffer can be traced to it. Any meaningful change would have to be achieved with Indigenous people leading and working at the forefront. Short of this, "improvements" are suspect—the same controlling, oppressive system hiding under "Indigenous" clothing.

To approach the issue another way, can the dominant system simply be made less force centered and coercive, hence less disrespectful and oppressive, without changing its core paradigm? Again, it would seem not. If the core model is not changed, then the practice of force continues, though under the guise of being somehow mitigated or more benign. Once again, for those on whom force is exerted, guises do not hide what is actually happening: Force will be experienced as force. The message will be one of disrespect. Accordingly, transformation and healing will not occur, and so patterns of harm will continue.

Abandoning the colonial system of law now imposed on Indigenous peoples seems the most reasonable route if we are interested in achieving a practice of justice that feels just, respectful, and healing to all those involved, and yet the realities of power make this unlikely, at least in the near future. That being so, and given the further realities of huge numbers of Indigenous people being incarcerated daily, our challenge—koucheehiwayhk—is to find paths from where we are to where we want to be.

The Fall Season: What Decolonizes and What Doesn't?

Again, truth commissions and other forums for Indigenous peoples to tell what has happened to us during invasion and colonization are an essential starting point, and these forums can be organized not only nationally but also locally. Hearing the stories is where healing begins. We start moving out of the cage by refusing to stay silent about its ugly realities.

A second step is clarifying our values and goals: What is it that we want to do, and how do we want to do it? Which values do we want to bring to the process? Is our goal to "fix" some isolated person or set of circumstances, or is it to think and work more holistically, which means addressing the larger contexts of harm? Of course we want to help people in crisis, and of course we want the existing system to function in less oppressive and racist ways. But these goals quickly become demoralizing and pursuing them losing battles unless we follow the trail to the origins of harm.

The fall season of healing brings the realization that merely reforming how the criminal justice system operates is not what we seek. Instead, we seek thorough transformation, a total system change that involves new ways of doing things. Reform takes the current structure and tinkers with it to make things better. The limits of change are fixed by a particular context and framework—in this case, by the colonizers' cage. Transformation, by contrast, expands the scope of what must be changed; the cage itself must go.

For transforming how we do justice, then, decolonization serves as the measuring stick: Which methods move us in a decolonizing direction, and which reinforce colonial power? Behind the question of method, therefore, is the deeper question of framework: Which frameworks support the magnitude of change that we as Indigenous peoples seek and that healing justice requires? Which frameworks promote decolonization?

We return to what we discussed at the beginning of this chapter, namely, to the abiding, life-giving currents of our traditions, identities, and cultures as Indigenous peoples. Who we are as Indigenous peoples provides the framework we need for the thorough transformation that is required. Our traditions, based as they are on respect and understanding, lead the way to decolonizing methods. For example, restoring our languages connects us immediately with who we are as peoples. Our languages express the framework for our methods as peoples by shaping our thoughts, concepts, and ways of interacting. They embody millennia of wisdom gained through experiences, and as a result, our languages reveal ways of responding to harms that are quite different from the colonizers' force-based responses.

So, too, our Indigenous ways of honoring our relatives through our extensive kinship systems are another core expression of who we are as peoples, and this too provides a powerful framework for transformation. How to "be a good relative" is foundational to our continued existence as peoples. If we embrace these ways as our framework for responding to harms, we will experience a profound transformation that will ultimately leave the colonizers' cage behind us.

For First Nations of Canada and many other Indigenous peoples, treaties are another manifestation of who we are as peoples and so provide a legal framework for the transformation we seek. Treaty relationships are built on an understanding that relationships must be undertaken in a respectful, meaningful way. True, our colonizers have not upheld their own promises with our nations and have often had to be forced to do so through court actions, which we occasionally win. Yet even though the colonizers have not upheld the treaty agreements, their failure does not mean that the treaty milieu is gone. Treaty relationships still exist and are transformative by their very nature. Engaging our treaties as a framework for legal transformation not only transforms how we respond to harms (currently the domain of the criminal justice system) but also engages us in decolonization as peoples. Why?

Fraudulent and shamelessly exploitative as the implementation of many treaties was, they nonetheless provide a foundation for decolonization because, as sociopolitical, geographical documents and nation-to-nation agreements, treaties affirm that we are and always have been sovereign nations. They locate us in our precolonized culture and so serve as a beacon from our past for our present and future decolonization work. They assert our continuity as peoples, despite colonization. And because many treaties spell out the boundaries of jurisdiction between Indigenous peoples and modern states, they spell out who has jurisdiction over whom and under which circumstances. To comply with the colonizers' modus operandi of ignoring these documents as a means of further extending colonial power is to be complicit in the dismantling of our self-determination. This is why treaties speak to the core issue for restorative justice: Who has the power and authority to decide how to respond to harms in Native communities? Treaties defend our existence as sovereign nations and therefore clearly state: We do.

Given these frameworks, how do we push past the colonizers' entrapping mazes and get to the cage's door? Can we, for example, bring those in the criminal justice system around to recognizing the colonizing framework as such and its devastating effects on us?

One step in this direction that held promise for many was the 1999 watershed *R. v. Gladue* ruling of the Supreme Court of Canada (SCC). The Court clarified the duty of judges to take into account the unique circumstances and systemic discrimination that Aboriginal people suffer when they sentence Aboriginal offenders. According to this ruling, restorative justice principles and reparative values are remedial in nature, and as such, the Court endorsed "healing" as a normative value. The actual sentence should support the healing ways of Indigenous communities and, wherever possible, engage communities in helping offenders rectify their harms.

It has been many years now since this ruling, and we see once again how the colonial model operates to reassert its power and neutralize movements such as this one in a restorative justice direction. On a daily basis, the principles articulated by the SCC are overridden by methods that reinforce the colonial status quo. In any number of ways and instances and for any number of reasons and justifications, the directions laid down by the Court are co-opted, until they are now functionally close to meaningless. Defense council, prosecutors, and judges are overwhelmed by the Court's directive to integrate restorative justice principles in sentencing, and so they use any number of tactics to deal with—or more accurately avoid—the responsibilities of acknowledging systemic discrimination.

For example, when reports are prepared, cursory information can be provided, which then allows lawmakers to "check off" that the discriminatory factors have been taken into consideration. Resistance to healing values are voiced all the time by statements such as, "Well, we did provide this information before, but now we are just having to put it under a different heading," "I don't see what the fuss is all about," or "Why should Aboriginal people have 'special' consideration?" Other times, the justice system will ignore the legacy of systemic injustices altogether and blithely reduce the issue at hand to nothing more than, say, two little girls in a dispute fighting over clothes.

For example, when I (Wanda) started talking about the factors in *Gladue* at the sentencing of a young girl charged with robbery, this is precisely what a judge said to me. The Crown and other bureaucratic justice personnel in attendance were no more sympathetic than the judge was to my submissions. My young client was, in effect, told that her unique circumstances and the history of colonization were meaningless and had no bearing on her actions. Instead of examining the impact of systemic discrimination and the unique circumstances of the young Aboriginal girl, the Crown and court found it much easier to reduce her and the situation to a "dispute" over clothes.

The situation was clearly much more serious than a schoolyard "dispute" between friends, since the *Criminal Code* with all of its mechanisms of force had been engaged. By its very nature and application, the *Criminal Code* is a blunt and brutish colonizers' tool used to enforce compliance with and acceptance of its rules. Having first "whitewashed" our history, the dominant justice paradigm then dismisses the devastating impact of colonization on us and holds us solely and exclusively responsible for the harms leveled against us.

In the colonizers' mind, the core understanding that what we have experienced as peoples affects what we experience now as people is missing, and one ruling by the Supreme Court of Canada is not sufficient to change that. As encouraged as we all were by the *Gladue* ruling, we are also not surprised that its impact has been neutralized, because connecting these dots means that we must confront head-on and then work to rectify centuries of colonial oppression and the ongoing consequences of that history today.

It is no reach to say that judges in the current colonial system are totally unprepared to redress this. How could they be otherwise? They are trained to be *the* representatives of colonial power—the ones who determine what will be done to us if we fail to obey colonial law. Every detail of the standard courtroom's physical layout and every nuance of legal procedure exude colonial supremacy, authority, and might. The colonial power has had devastating effects on Aboriginal peoples, yet reform initiatives and Supreme Court rulings fall far short of remedying the injustices. Again, how could there be success? The judges in the criminal justice system—even the ones who are Indigenous and well versed within Indigenous worldviews with a personal commitment to incorporate peacemaking principles into the process and court structures—cannot by themselves overturn the harm done by centuries of colonial might. This requires a commitment by the government as whole—which also implies a commitment by the society as whole—to confront the realities of colonialism, to acknowledge the massive harms done, and to work with Aboriginal peoples to put things right.

Another step toward changing the criminal justice system has been to try to "indigenize" the criminal justice system. Whether this practice is to be welcomed depends on how it is used. If it represents an authentic step toward dismantling colonial power and empowering Aboriginal communities in their inherent self-determination and reclamation of language, then it is surely to be welcomed.

However, this has not often been the case. Instead, in the name of using culturally appropriate processes, colonial governments appropriate Indigenous culture by using Indigenous images, representations, and traditions to further impose colonial rule. The practice leaves a severely bitter taste because it adds insult to injury. Its goal is to lessen the oppressive feel of colonial rule without challenging colonialism itself as the root harm. Even with the best of intentions, it is offensive.

It is not wrong to use Indigenous images, representations, and processes, especially among Indigenous people; what is wrong is that these ways are employed by colonizer authorities as devices for perpetuating colonialism, not for promoting the authentic self-determination of Indigenous peoples. How could it not be offensive to have our own cultures used to further our subjugation? If the power does not shift to Indigenous peoples, no one is fooled as to who is controlling the processes and their outcomes. Indigenizing the criminal justice system fails because it is another attempt to make something that is oppressive by nature seem less so in order to keep the oppressive structure in place and unchallenged. Indigenous cultures are being manipulated to meet policy and administrative ends, enabling law as force—a system that is obviously failing Indigenous peoples—to prevail.

Efforts to *reform* but not to *transform* the colonial system further support the view of many Indigenous people that our energies are wasted in trying to make our shackles hurt a little less. Transformation begins with naming colonialism as the root harm. The shackles must come off, and the cage must go; this is the goal for justice that is truly healing—the end to which our means must be aligned. This is no news to Indigenous people. Our children know this from birth, and our leaders have sacrificed their lives for this cause. Perhaps the day is drawing closer, though, when colonizers can embrace this truth as well and begin to recognize the lethal and self-destructive nature of colonization.

Restorative justice could still serve a vision of decolonization because it is not tied to the existing fact-based, positivistic legal protocol or to the body of case-based colonial law. Restorative justice operates from different premises and toward different goals. It does not start by trying to prove a person's guilt or innocence. Its premise is that a harm has occurred, and people come together with a commitment to hearing the stories on all sides and working together to put things right to everyone's mutual satisfaction. Those involved share some responsibility for what has happened or at least for doing what they can to work things out in a good way. Some people engage from a spirit of healing and transformation, while others simply strive to bring their best values to resolving the conflict. Each person participates on a voluntary basis, and if the perpetrators of harm participate, they do so because they wish to take responsibility for having done something that hurt others. If court personnel and law enforcement participate, they do so in personal, community-oriented capacities rather than professional ones.

The apparatus of colonial law and courts is not therefore the framework for restorative justice or its modus operandi. Whereas courts hand down judgments, rulings, verdicts, and sentences, restorative practices seek consensus about how to achieve peacemaking in any given situation. Because the participants themselves work out which steps need to be taken for the harm to be repaired, mechanisms of coercion are not helpful. The community members participating do, however, support each other in following through on the decisions made. Only when restorative processes break down do the courts take over.

Other critiques of colonial law—as well as the dialogues that stem from these critiques—can also contribute to decolonization. American-based critical legal theory acknowledges that positive law is not neutral but serves to maintain the status quo. The fact that the existing criminal justice system in no way meets the needs of victims, offenders, or communities suggests that the focus of law should shift from defending rights to meeting needs. Black legal theorists reject this suggestion, however, arguing that this move would open the floodgates of paternalism. Moreover, critical race theory observes that focusing on rights has enabled colonized and oppressed peoples to have a voice and that this gain should not be lost or minimized in its importance. We do not need to lessen our focus on rights, according to this view, but to increase it since what is missing is a lack of implementation of those rights.

Suffice it to say, for the purposes of this chapter, we cannot map a step-by-step administrative, legal, theoretical, or any other specific path of decolonization. This is not a job for two people but for entire nations and peoples, and many paths are needed. What we do suggest—and it is by no means news for the colonized—is that any step of change, however well intentioned, will fall prey to the default framework of perpetuating colonial oppression if those involved do not consciously and intentionally make a paradigm shift and claim a framework of decolonization. If we are serious about justice, healing, transformation, and systemic change, then we must doggedly use decolonization as the standard for evaluating whatever is being proposed or implemented: Does it move us closer or farther from our decolonization? Put positively, does it flow from the framework of who we are as peoples and hence engage us in transformation?

Certainly this shift begins with naming colonialism as the root harm that needs to be healed. We must assert the reality—shocking and ungrateful as it may seem to many colonizers—that the colonial system is not the savior of Indigenous people but our oppressor, the systemic cause of our suffering.

Certainly the shift of framework empowers Indigenous peoples to use our own Indigenous means to respond to harms among our people. Indigenous perspectives must be listened to and heard outside the assumption of colonial rule, and Indigenous autonomy and competence in handling our own affairs through our own ways must be unconditionally respected.

And certainly the shift of framework involves the serious, genuine, and difficult nation-to-nation work of rectifying the immense crimes against humanity that we have suffered and that have brought us to where we are now as peoples. We do not need more studies or well-meaning programs to "solve our problems" by colonizer governments. We call for nation-to-nation relationships, land return, reparations, restitution, return of resources or payment for their exploitation with interest, adherence to treaties, and hence the return of our sovereign jurisdiction over our homelands and ancestral land bases. *Decolonizing* is not just a big word; it is the core of healing justice for Indigenous peoples. It signifies a scope of transformation the likes of which we have not yet seen. And, like the fall season, it must come, because the costs of avoiding it are too great for everyone.

In short, the vision of the future is not to leave the colonizer's house for a better colonizer's house or to construct a better, more Indigenous-friendly cage for our oppression. The aim is remove the cage altogether and instead to rebuild our tipis—or long houses, hogans, iglus, pueblos, wikiups, earth lodges, wigwams, plank houses, grass houses, or chickees. As we move in a decolonizing direction, we will move closer to practicing justice as a way of life—a way that holds the promise of being transformative for all those involved and hence profoundly healing for both the colonized and the colonizers. May the vision of this koucheehiwayhk inspire and sustain us through the rough waters we inevitably face as we move in this turbulent but fundamentally healing direction.

▣ Note

1. From the Michif language, *koucheehiwayhk* is loosely translated to the English word *challenge.*

▣ References

Federation of Saskatchewan Indian Nations. (2005). Alter-Natives to non-violence report: Aboriginal youth gangs exploration: A community development process. In W. D. McCaslin (Ed.), *Justice as healing: Indigenous ways* (pp. 302–307). St. Paul, MN: Living Justice Press.

Lane, P., Jr., Bopp, M., Bopp, J., & Norris, J. (2005). Mapping the healing journey: First Nations research project on healing in Canadian aboriginal communities. In W. D. McCaslin (Ed.), *Justice as healing: Indigenous ways* (pp. 369–407). St. Paul, MN: Living Justice Press.

R. v. Gladue, [1999] 1 S.C.R. 688, [1999] 2 C.N.L.R. 252.

Waziyatawin, A. W., & Yellow Bird, M. (Eds.). (2005). *For indigenous eyes only: A decolonization handbook.* Santa Fe, NM: School of American Research Press.

27

THE SOUTH AFRICAN TRUTH AND RECONCILIATION COMMISSION (TRC)

Ways of Knowing Mrs. Konile

Antjie Krog, Nosisi Mpolweni-Zantsi, and Kopano Ratele

He laughs when he tells how he braaied my son.

—Charity Kondile about Security Operative Dirk Coetzee

It happened fifteen years ago, now they fucking cry for the first time.

—(During the PEBCO 3 amnesty hearing [1998] in Port Elizabeth, lawyer Francois van der Merwe whispered this to his legal team and amnesty applicants, but it was audible on radio journalist Darren Taylor's headphones.)

How do we read one another? How do we "hear" one another in a country where the past often still bleeds among us? How much of what we hear translates into finding ways of living together? How do we overcome a divided past in such a way that "the Other" becomes "us"?

To form an idea of some of the many stumbling blocks toward understanding one another in a society with a divisive history, we want to look at a single incident in a single testimony delivered to the South African Truth and Reconciliation Commission (TRC), 1996–1998. We hope that our efforts to understand only one small part of a testimony will reveal both the barriers, as well as the extent of the trouble, one has to go to arrive at some comprehension of one's fellow human beings. We hope to underline the necessity of making use of indigenous languages and knowledge systems to access greater understanding and respect for one another. We also want to emphasize the personal enrichment and understanding our working method has brought us.

Aims

As the South African TRC is often discussed as a possible "model" of how societies can deal with their pasts, one needs to remember that some testimonies do not fit the general framework. We want to point out that it may be important to reread these "nonfitting" testimonies in particular ways, in order to arrive at a fuller knowledge of who we are, as we begin to say this: We know one another.

In the South African context, it has become crucial to look critically at the way in which research into TRC testimonies has been done. The vast majority of research done on the South African TRC had been done from what we will call in this chapter a "Western education and viewpoint."

With the risk of oversimplifying, we briefly define the difference between Eurocentric and Afrocentric cultures as follows: Eurocentric culture is based on 25 centuries of Greek culture (philosophy), Roman culture (jurisprudence), and Judeo-Christian cultures (religion). It places high priority on individuality and reason and is inclined to presuppose that European values could be applied universally. The tension between the particular and the universal is assumed to be dissolved since the particular is supposed to be universal.

Afrocentric culture, on the other hand, reflects the cultural values, symbolic forms, and achievements of Africa that claim recognition and respect for being the cradle of mankind—both physically and spiritually. With its rich source of oral and other literature, indigenous artworks, and plurality of religions and languages, it places the emphasis on communality and a view of a human being that presupposes interpersonal relationships as expressed in *umuntu ngumuntu ngabantu,* which means a person is a person through other persons (see http://www.unisa.ac.za/default.asp?Cmd=ViewContent&ContentID=11500).

First, then, we hope that our contribution will caution against any conclusion that does not take into account translation aspects as well as transcultural and philosophical knowledge and contexts.

Second, we want to reconstitute the sensibility of one witness, Mrs. Konile. It is easy to misrepresent her and other people's testimonies in a way that perpetuates cultural and racial stereotypes of Black rural women in South Africa.

Third, we hope to show how using indigenous knowledge can sometimes bring one to a completely different or sometimes even opposite conclusion to one arrived at via more usual channels.

Fourth, we want to underscore the importance of the original version of testimonies. We are pleading that all the original versions of the South African TRC should be transcribed. Currently, researchers can only rely on the official English translation on the TRC Web site. By having the original version available, testimonies could contribute to intercultural knowledge that will help people to live together with empathy and understanding.

In this chapter, we provide a capsule history of apartheid, a short description of the TRC, and a background to Mrs. Konile's testimony. Then our ways will split. Antjie Krog will do what we have come to term a "Western reading" of the testimony, followed by Nosisi Mpolweni-Zantsi's exploration into the original Xhosa version, to see how translation problems have obscured some of the cultural codes. Kopano Ratele will conclude the separate readings by exploring how the African psyche manifests in Mrs. Konile's "incoherent" testimony.

Apartheid

South Africa gave the world the word *apartheid*—declared by the United Nations as a crime against humanity. Although different kinds of discrimination and exploitation existed since the first Westerners set foot in southern Africa, the National Party that came to power in 1948 turned it into a vicious legal system where an individual's civil and political rights were determined by skin color.

The list of some of the early legislation passed by the newly elected National Party in 1948 demonstrates how the state took complete control of people's lives. Every aspect of political, economic, cultural, sporting, and social life was segregated, using what had become the bedrock of the apartheid state, namely, the Population Registration Act of 1950. This law provided for the classification of every South African into one of the four racial categories. The Group Areas Act of 1950 demarcated urban areas into zones for exclusive occupation by designated racial groups. The Prohibition of Mixed Marriages Act of 1949 and the 1950 Immorality Amendment Act prescribed who one could marry and who one could have sexual relations with, while the Separate Amenities Act of 1953 determined where the activities of the different groups should take place. The Suppression of Communism Act of 1950 effectively outlawed opposition, while the Bantu Education Act of 1953 laid the basis for a separate and inferior education system for African pupils and so forth.

Apartheid, in the words of the *TRC Final Report* (1998), brought about a

> social engineering project of awesome dimensions through which the inherited rural and urban social fabric of South Africa was torn asunder and recreated in the image of a series of racist utopias. In the process millions of black people and a hand full of poor whites were shunted around like pawns on a chessboard. Forced to relocate to places that often existed only on the drawing boards, . . . entire communities were simply wiped out. These included rural villages, traditional communities and homelands, schools, churches and, above all, people. Sometimes the demolition was total. These deeds may not have been "gross," as defined by the TRC Act, but were nonetheless, an assault on the rights and dignities of millions of South Africans. . . . Amongst apartheid's many crimes, perhaps its greatest was the power to humiliate, to denigrate and to remove the self-confidence, self-esteem and dignity of its millions of victims. (pp. 30–34)

In the year after South Africa's first democratic elections in 1994, Parliament's Justice Portfolio Committee drafted legislation to establish a Truth and Reconciliation Commission. The 17-member commission was given the task of establishing as complete a picture as possible of the causes, nature, and extent of the gross human rights violations committed in the period between March 1, 1960, and the cutoff date (May 10, 1994) by conducting investigations and holding hearings. It also had to facilitate the granting of amnesty to persons who made full disclosure of all the facts relating to acts associated with a political objective. In addition, the commission was required to restore the human and civil dignity of victims and recommend reparation measures. The commission had to compile a report of its findings and activities and recommend measures to prevent future violations of human rights (see *TRC Final Report,* 1998, vols. 1–5).

The Truth and Reconciliation Commission consisted of three committees. The first of these was the Human Rights Violation Committee, which had to look into the accounts of victims (such as Mrs. Konile) through hearings and investigations. The second was the Amnesty Committee, which had to evaluate amnesty applications. The third committee was the Reparation and Rehabilitation Committee, which had to formulate a reparation policy. The first hearings were held in April 1996 in the Eastern Cape where most of the harshest human rights abuses took place over the years. The second hearing took place in Cape Town, and that was the hearing in which Mrs. Konile testified.

Mrs. Konile

During the mid-1980s, seven young men were lured by an *askari* (a "turned" former liberation movement cadre) to receive military training inside the country in order to become soldiers of *Umkhonto weSizwe,* the military wing of the ANC. As they were about to embark on their "first mission" early in the morning of March 3, 1986, they were killed in an ambush by the security forces. Witnesses from a nearby hostel, however, saw how some of them were shot point-blank after emerging from the bushes with their hands in the air. It was also said that Russian hand grenades and guns were planted on their bodies before the National television broadcaster was summoned to capture the "extermination of terrorists." The incident became known as the Gugulethu 7 (see *TRC Final Report,* 1998).

One of the seven young men was Zabonke Konile. His mother came to testify with three other mothers: Cynthia Ngewu, Irene Mtsingwa, and Mia Eunice Thembiso. (Apart from misspelling Miya, it seems that the transcript also mistakenly changes Mrs. Miya's surname to Thembiso, despite the fact that the latter introduced herself as Eunice Tembisa Mia, or Miya.) The families of Zola Swelani, Themba Mlifi, and Zenneth Mjobo had never been traced. Of the mothers of the Gugulethu 7, Mrs. Konile testified last and is the only one mentioned by her surname alone. It too was misspelled: Khonele instead of Konile.

Working Method

We think our method of working has been as important as our findings. We first discussed the official version on the Web site, and all three of us found it largely incoherent and incomprehensible. Among the possible explanations were bad translation and an unintelligible witness, which in turn opened up another set of questions: Was the witness apparently unintelligible because she was traumatized or because she simply did not understand what had happened and what was happening around her? Antjie Krog presented a reading to the group of how she could not "hear" Mrs. Konile and indicated some of the problems she encountered when analyzing the testimony.

We then ordered the tape with the original Xhosa version from the South African National Archives and used our different disciplines, backgrounds, cultures, and languages to gradually devise a way to "hear" Mrs. Konile. Nosisi Mpolweni-Zantsi transcribed Mrs. Konile's testimony, making it one of the first Xhosa testimonies to be transcribed in full. (Testimonies had also been transcribed by students of Zannie Bock from the University of the Western Cape.) Then she and Kopano Ratele retranslated it into English, and it soon became evident that there were translation mistakes as well as transcription mistakes.

As Mpolweni-Zantsi was exploring the cultural content and Ratele the psychological undercurrents, it became clear that incomprehension had been created at different stages of the process toward an official version. In other words, there were

> ordinary interpretation mistakes (*from the victim to the interpreter*);
>
> an inability, at times, to incorporate cultural codes into the interpretation, which led to additional misreadings (*victim to interpreter*);
>
> transcription mistakes from the spoken English (*interpreter to transcriber*);
>
> a kind of TRC framework in place that could not render the inner monologue of Mrs. Konile comprehensible (*TRC to victim*).

The process we engaged in was rather like an archaeological excavation—every weekly session unearthed a new reality closer and closer to a multifaceted and complex original. We also took seriously Vivien Burr's warning (cited in Ratazzi, 2005, p. 23) that an individual's understanding of the world is temporally and spatially contextualized and not a static entity with a stable core.

However, Mrs. Konile's testimony was so ill-fitting, strange, and incoherent that we initially assumed that it was perhaps more of an intuitive and spontaneous expression of her inner self than a deliberate and conscious construction of a narrative identity. Deeper analysis showed, however, that Mrs. Konile was not only narrating coherently within particular frameworks but also resisting other frameworks imposed on her. Many of the discoveries were only uncovered by our study of the original version. This strengthened the notion that the meta-codes that could have transmitted her shared reality with many other South Africans were greatly hamstrung by language and an absence of cultural and psychological context.

Reading of Official TRC Transcript (Antjie Krog)

During the 2 years of weekly hearings that followed Mrs. Konile's testimony, her narrative stayed with me as the most incoherent female testimony I had to report on as a journalist. Everything in it was confusing and pandering to the racist stereotype of Black women that the TRC testimonies were trying to undermine.

I remember thinking that if I did a normal reporting job of Mrs. Konile's narrative on radio, it would only strengthen old racist views. At the same time, I suspected that her testimony was important, precisely because it was different from the others and that, perhaps, one needed other tools to make sense of it.

Close Reading of the Goat Incident

> Bearing witness is . . . not just a linguistic, but an existential stance.
>
> —Terrence Des Pres (1977, p. 32)

With her appearance before the TRC, Mrs. Konile bore witness to her son's death. While she was testifying, those around her bore witness how she was busy constituting an identity for herself at that moment within that particular context. Fiona Ross (2004, p. 62) suggests that the TRC testimonies were co-creations at best in which commissioners, audience, and the TRC framework of truth and reconciliation all played a role.

But that was not the only process happening. Everybody listening to Mrs. Konile was interpreting her narrative: literally by an interpreter and figuratively by an audience. Listeners could reformulate their own identities in response to the testimonies because the stories they were listening to, related to them in a first-person way, could become their own private story. A story, made and told by somebody else, can become deeply one's own. Plus one could locate oneself within other larger public narratives (e.g., the suffering-under-apartheid narrative) or perhaps a smaller personal one. Mrs. Konile's story, however, placed barriers in the way of empathetic interpretation. On the footage of the testimony, one could see how restless and uncomfortable the other mothers became when she testified. It was as if they were perhaps also trying not to draw conclusions about her or "those like her."

The goat incident early in Mrs. Konile's narrative is key to her whole story. In the preceding paragraph, she says,

> During that process Peza arrived, we were on our way to get pensions, if I am not mistaken it was on a Thursday, I was on my way out. Peza said to me no here he is, quickly I was scarred.

Without any introduction, Peza enters Mrs. Konile's narrative. In the testimony of one of the other mothers, we have learned that Peza was an African National Congress (ANC) activist on the Cape Flats. He says to Mrs. Konile, "Here he is." Who is this *he?* Why was she *scarred?* By whom, how?

> But I never thought that because Peza was usually coming to Cape Town I am not—I don't even know Cape Town and now we went on to the pensions. We went and came back from getting our pensions. I said oh! I had a very—a very scary period, there was this—this was this goat looking up, this one next to me said oh! having a dream like that with a goat looking up is a very bad dream.

For the first time in the testimony, Mrs. Konile locates herself: Cape Town. But she says she doesn't know Cape Town. People living on the Cape Flats (the sprawling townships around Cape Town) often feel cut off from Cape Town proper and would only refer to the name of the township where they live. Mrs. Konile keeps mentioning Cape Town. Peza is coming *to* Cape Town. She "doesn't even *know*" Cape Town. In the next paragraph, she suggests that the ANC is *living* in Cape Town.

There is a perception among some White people that Black people have difficulty thinking in three dimensions. This is given as the reason why they step in front of cars, or crash into driveways, or domestic workers put bedcovers and tablecloths upside down: They cannot distinguish a pattern from a messy design. (When this statement about White people's view on Black people's ability to perceive three dimensions was vehemently denied by one of our White colleagues, I phoned a member of my family. The conversation went something like this:

Antjie: Can Black people think three-dimensionally?

Family member: No, definitely not.

Antjie: Can you give me an example?

Long pause.

Family member: I can't immediately give you one, but we all know they can't.)

Mrs. Konile's inability to pinpoint herself in a township on the Cape Flats as part of a city stretching out around her seems to confirm problems with space perception.

When one reads the word *scary,* one wonders whether the word *scarred* in the first paragraph should not have been *scared.* In other words, is this a transcription mistake instead of an incoherent remark? (The video of the hearing confirmed that we were indeed dealing with a transcription mistake. This made us aware of another factor: Mistakes not only happened in interpretation but also in transcription.)

Who went with Mrs. Konile to get her pension? Peza? A friend? Could we assume that she was addressing Peza when she described a goat looking up at her? Who or what was this goat? Was it a real goat she saw that day that she simply made part of her TRC narrative? Was she using it as a psychological image to enable her to bring the unconscious to the conscious?

Was she living in a world where goats and people alternate? Why would "this one" suggest it was a dream? Was Mrs. Konile known for day-dreaming or "seeing" things?

Was *superstition* a word to be used in this context? Did Mrs. Konile see a goat and superstitiously read all kinds of messages in it? Or should the goat be regarded in terms of universal symbolism? According to a book of symbols (Cooper, 1995, p. 74), the goat signifies abundant virility, creative energy, and superiority. In Christian symbolism, the goat signifies the devil, the sinner, the scape-goat. The goat was therefore spelling evil and disaster to Mrs. Konile as well as creative energy.

If the goat formed part of a dream, then maybe one had to go into the realm of dream language with Sigmund Freud and recognize that "free associations . . . raise to a conscious level material that has been repressed and kept at bay by resistance" (Meier, 1987, p. 13). Mrs. Konile linked the goat to bad news, but I found it hard to assume that she was concerned about the safety of her son when her testimony spent hardly two paragraphs on him.

She mentioned that the goat was "looking up"—to where? To her? To the sky? Why was "looking up" bad? Was the goat pointing toward Peza as the harbinger of death?

> When we saw on TV—I am sorry Peza came in, I was very scared when I saw Peza and I said Peza what is it that you have to tell me. Say to me now—say it—say it now, Peza said he asked me where is Zabonke, I said he is in Cape Town. Then he said I am here I am sent by the comrade in Cape Town the ANC.

This paragraph broadened the confusion of Mrs. Konile about Cape Town: *She* is in Cape Town, Zabonke is in Cape Town, and Peza is in Cape Town, sent by the *ANC* in Cape Town. The spatial incoherency in this paragraph gets joined by a political confusion when Mrs. Konile said "the comrade in Cape Town the ANC." To Mrs. Konile, the ANC was one single comrade living in Cape Town. Does one accept that it was possible to live in one of the most highly politicized areas on the Cape Flats during the mid-eighties with one's child recruited for military action for the ANC's military wing while at the same time not having a clue what the ANC was? Later in her testimony, Mrs. Konile seemed to confirm this by asking, "What is ANC? What is ANC?"

Her testimony also posed problems for a possible counternarrative reading. The testimonies before the TRC were putting forward a counternarrative to the main racist narrative of the apartheid government. The three other mothers testifying with Mrs. Konile provided prime models of this counternarrative. They presented acute, yet harrowing, detail of their last interactions with their sons on the mornings of their deaths. All three articulated the unforgettable moment they saw on television: how the police pulled their sons' bodies so that they lay face up for the television camera. All three could formulate precisely how they regarded these gross violations and what they wanted from the TRC. All three had a very clear perception of the moral questions at stake.

In contrast, Mrs. Konile's testimony seemed to drift from one surrealist scenario to the next; most of her testimony had nothing to do with her son but was describing her own personal suffering in a highly confused way—leaving the impression that her son's main value for her was monetary and that she was in any case not really aware what was happening around her. She also seemed to have no idea what to ask of the perpetrators or the commission.

If she was presenting a counternarrative, what did that mean? Was she diverting back to and therefore confirming the main racist narrative of stupid, uncaring Black woman? Was she exposing the TRC's counternarrative as a new master narrative (and if so, what exactly does she propose?), or was she deepening the counternarrative? Or was she merely an exception—a per chance narrative that did not work out for a variety of reasons?

Testimony as Firsthand Knowledge

In their work on testimony, Shosana Felman and Dori Laub (1992) say that the task of testimony is to impart knowledge: a firsthand, carnal knowledge of victimization, of what it means to be "'from here' . . . a firsthand knowledge of a historical passage through death and the way in which life will forever be inhabited by that passage and by that death; knowledge of the way in which 'this history concerns us all'" (p. 111).

Mrs. Konile's testimony was clearly a firsthand knowledge of something, but was it firsthand knowledge of the death of a son, or was it perhaps more a kind of firsthand knowledge of poverty? On the other hand, little of what she said dealt directly with poverty or the death of her son.

In comparison with the other mothers, who formed a close-knit and articulated unit, her testimony had no resonance of communality. Although she was clearly urgently trying to tell the audience something, there was no sense that what she was telling came from a community. Her story did not carry any mark of shared experiences. The other mothers mentioned children, neighbors, and bosses, but Mrs. Konile simply said "I." She would in fact say, "I didn't even see my son on TV" as if she felt deprived from even the collective horror of seeing her dead child on television. She became the testifier of a solitary figure thrown around in an incoherent and cruel landscape.

To use the formulation of Felman and Laub (1992), Mrs. Konile's testimony did not seem to carry the historical weight, the self-evident significance of a group experience, but rather "embodied the in-significance of a missed encounter with reality" (p. 171).

Effect of Pain on Language

In her seminal work on the effect of torture on language, Elaine Scarry (1985) says that "physical pain . . . is language destroying" (p. 19). One can describe many things, but the moment one describes pain, language begins to falter. It is always hard to listen to a narrative of pain as the narrative is also often unconvincing. Possibly the inability of Mrs. Konile to contain and lift her pain out of herself and show it to the TRC was because that pain had destroyed her language. Scarry observes that before destroying language, pain usually monopolizes language and eventually deepens it so much that coherence is displaced by the sounds interior to learned language (p. 54). In other words, pain first takes control of the language, then turns it incoherent (because the pain is everywhere) and then changes the language from incoherency into nonverbal sounds—moans, sighs, shouts, groans.

Pain first resists expression and then destroys the capacity for speech. It "annihilates not only the objects of complex thought and emotion but also the objects of the most elemental acts of perception" (Scarry, 1985, p. 54).

Looking at the official transcript, however, there is no sign of any nonverbal sounds. Only *listening* to the original version or watching the video confirmed how much pain did manifest in Mrs. Konile's language, suggesting that she had indeed lost her grip on the complexity around her son's death. (The absence of nonverbal sounds in the transcribed version provides a further obstacle to adequately interpreting TRC texts.)

Effect of Pain on Memory

Research has been done into the different ways memory deals with trauma in order to survive. In their piece "Intergenerational Memory of the Holocaust," Nanette Auerhan and Dori Laub (Danieli, 1998, p. 23) identified nine different forms of remembering trauma. One of them is called fragmentation, which means that the memory retains parts of a lived experience in such a way that they are decontextualized and no longer meaningful.

The individual has an image, sensation, or isolated thought but does not know to what it is connected, what it means, or what to do with it. The observer sees not the memory but a derivative, a symptom that infuses the individual's life. The individual may know that the symptom is irrational yet be unable to discount it. Although these intrusive incoherent fragments may allow a person to continue day-to-day living, it can also block a person from pursuing his or her life to the fullest (Danieli, 1998, p. 29).

Should one accept that Mrs. Konile's life became the fragments that she was able to live with? The fact that it was incoherent to an outsider was of lesser importance than the fact that it was precisely the decontextualized and isolated fragmentation that made it possible for her to survive the death of her son. She mentioned the goat because she could live with the memory of the goat "looking up." But between the goat and the news that her son was killed lies the real tragedy of her life, the real suffering that she could not articulate, because living with it was not possible.

But that day in April 1996, she had an opportunity before the TRC to have her story and her son acknowledged and her self restored. Yet she did not use it to glorify her son or to lay claim on the right to be compensated. She preferred to put the fragments of her life on the table, and in the brokenness of it, one could see the chaos and pain, and only guess at the suffering.

Reading of Original Transcribed Version in IsiXhosa (Nosisi Mpolweni-Zantsi)

After I had listened to Mrs. Konile from the tape and later read the official document, I keenly felt some gaps. Some of the reasons for the gaps could be attributed to the difficulty or challenges of simultaneous interpreting, but others seemed to be more problematic. The interpreter listened to the speaker, internalized what the speaker was saying, and then tried to attach meaning to what the speaker had said and only then gave an interpretation. The role of an interpreter should not be underestimated because he or she had to restructure what the speaker said in a way that brought meaning to the audience.

In highlighting the importance of an interpreter, Angelelli (2004) has this to say: "The concept of visible interpreters goes beyond the fact that they are active participants in the linguistic interaction. It takes into consideration the power that interpreters possess" (p. 9). Since it is never possible to recall everything that the speaker says, loss of information during interpreting is always inevitable. A similar scenario might have happened during Mrs. Konile's testimony. The interpreters were working under pressure, trying to keep up with the relentless pace of TRC hearings. It was possible that a further loss of information occurred during the transcription and translation of the testimonies.

My aim was first to investigate whether there was information lost in the interpretation and translation of Mrs. Konile's testimony. Second, I wanted to determine how this lost information influenced intercultural communication between Mrs. Konile, on one side, and the TRC officials, audience, and other possible readers, on the other side. Third, I wanted to determine whether knowledge of an indigenous context would lead to a fuller interpretation that would do justice to the person who testified.

My analysis of these aspects was based on the following extracts:

(Official version)

> We went and came back from getting our pensions. I said oh! I had a very—a very scary period, there was this—this was this goat looking up, this one next to me said oh! having a dream like that with a goat looking up is a very bad dream.

Transcribed original words of Mrs. Konile (which we refer to as IsiXhosa version):

> Sihambe sibuy' epeyini. Ndithi kulo ndihamba naye, ndithi, "Heyi! Yhaz' umbilini wam, undiphethe kakubi. Phezolo ndiphuphe kakubi. Ndiphuphe apha ngasemnyango, kukho ibhokhwe emileyo, eyenjenje, ehh . . . , emileyo, ethe," ahleke athi lo, athi "Eyi! Uphuphe kakubi nyhani." Ngasemthini.

Retranslated, the text reads as follows. (Note the use of active voice by Mrs. Konile of her words and those of her friend.)

> We [she is referring to herself and an unnamed accompanying woman] went and came back from the grant's office. I said to the one I was going with, I said, "Heyi! You know what, my heart is palpitating with a strange feeling, and it persists. Last night I had a terrible dream. I dreamt that here at the door, there was a goat that was standing, like this, ehh . . . , standing, like this" [gesturing with her hands], and my friend laughed and said, "Eyi! You really had a bad dream." Next to the tree.

Slippages in Translation

Mrs. Konile made use of exclamations to express her feelings about the terrible dream, for example, "Heyi! Yhaz' umbilini wam undiphethe kakubi. Phezolo ndiphuphe kakubi." As she related her story, she seemed to have a vivid picture of the events because she even demonstrated how the goat was standing. For example, she said, "emileyo, eyenjenje, ehh . . ., ethe" ("that was standing, like this, ehh . . ., like this"). The way in which the goat was standing *seemed* to be very strange as we saw how Mrs. Konile demonstrated with her hands on the videotape to show that it was standing on its hind legs. In other words, the goat was not looking up but was standing up. She used repetition in the form of three consecutive synonyms to emphasize the strangeness in the way it was standing—namely, *emileyo, eyenjenje, ethe.* Her friend further highlighted the strangeness in the appearance of this goat when she said, "Eyi! Uphuphe kakubi nyhani" ("Eyi! You really had a bad dream").

In the official version, there was no indication of the direct words of Mrs. Konile and her friend. She did not mention the word *dream* but talked about "a very scary period" and then continued, "There was this—this was this goat looking up." There *seemed* to be no clear connection between the scary period and the goat. The remark of Mrs. Konile's friend—"Having a dream like that . . . is a very bad thing"—confused things even further: Was it now a scary period or a bad dream, or was the scary period *like* a bad dream?

Bringing in the lost information via the original text allows a conclusive reading: First, she dreamt about the goat. Then, she went with a friend to get a grant. She saw Peza there and regarded his presence as ominous. As the story unfolded, her foreboding plus the dream seemed to take on greater significance in terms of cultural habits.

The word *umbilili* in the original Xhosa testimony meant a very strange feeling, which could be read as a kind of foreboding—implying that the goat dream was picking up crucial cultural implications. By omitting these cultural allusions, the interpreter removed important information that could be seen as pointers to the tragic death of Mrs. Konile's son, Zabonke. She was not only talking about her own personal forebodings but was trying to express her own pain. Schaffner and Kelly-Holmes (1995) warned that "translators (and interpreters) have to be aware of the fact that cultures not only express ideas differently, but they also *shape* concepts and text differently" (p. 6, emphasis added). If we were to refer to Mrs. Konile's testimony, it meant that an interpreter who was familiar with her culture would have understood that the sighs, repetition, and exclamations in her speech conveyed important information about her emotional state. But how were these indicators to be transferred into English and afterwards into written text?

Cross-Cultural Communication

The crucial role of culture in the testimony of Mrs. Konile became clear the moment the very first omission was picked up. Mrs. Konile did not come from Cape Town, but right at the very beginning of her testimony, she said that she came from Indwe—a village situated near Queenstown in the Eastern Cape.

The word *Indwe* was either not picked up by the interpreter or unrecognizable for the (non-Xhosa) transcriber. Initially, I also missed the word but immediately picked up other rural accents that indicated to me that Mrs. Konile was living in or near the Transkei and could not possibly live in Cape Town (for example, her pronunciation of the word *mortuary*). This and other clues made me return to the beginning, and then I distinguished the word *Indwe.*

To take care of the three-dimensional perception raised earlier, Mrs. Konile's testimony was *not* framed by Cape Town but by a small rural village in the Eastern Cape. As a person who came from the rural areas, she could never be as politically conscious as her fellow testifiers from Gugulethu but would be more closely connected to traditional habits instead. This was evident right through her testimony, not only through her symbols and gestures but also through particular pronunciation and expressions.

Earlier on in the reading, before Mrs. Konile shared her dream story, she was with her friend on their way to the grants office. She told her friend that immediately after she saw Peza she had this foreboding. She knew Peza and that he frequently traveled between Cape Town and Indwe. Her own son was also in Cape Town. She connected the strange feeling with the appearance of Peza, and it seemed to haunt her as she remarked, "Xa ndizawuphuma, ndibon' ukuthi, ath' uPeza, 'Hayi nguye lo'. Ndi—kuthi dwe ngumbilini." ("Just when I was on my way out, I saw Peza and he looked at us and said, 'No, it's this one.' I—my heart just throbbed.")

On their way back from the grants office, they met Peza for the second time, and the strange foreboding persisted. She became increasingly impatient about this: "Xa sithi thu, Tyhini! Nank' uPeza kwakhona. Hee! Yhaz' uba yintoni na lent' izawuthethwa nguPeza kum." ("Just when we were approaching the houses, would you believe it! Here was Peza again. Hee! I wonder what is it that Peza is going to say to me?") In the end, she anxiously burst out, "Yintoni lent' uzayithetha kum? Yithethe, yithethe ngoku" ("What is it that you are going to say to me? Say it, say it now!"). Immediately after her remarks, Peza related the news about the death of her son.

The sequence of forebodings every time Mrs. Konile saw Peza, plus the story of the goat dream, indicate that, culturally, these incidents were connected for her. She obviously read them as warning signs from the ancestors that she should expect bad news. In other words, by relating these incidents, Mrs. Konile was communicating a message to the TRC audience that effectively said, "Long before I heard of my child's death, I was already in pain through the premonitions and the bad dream." But the interpreter seemed to have either missed the cultural codes or was unable to effectively find a way to transfer them into English.

Under normal circumstances, a goat in Xhosa culture is associated with ancestral rituals. These rituals are a way of maintaining a bond between people and their ancestors. Some families slaughter a goat when a child is introduced to the ancestors, while other families use a sheep. The persistent strange feeling and the strange stance of the goat could be seen as techniques of the ancestors to prepare Mrs. Konile emotionally to receive the bad news about her son. Similarly, her concern about the strange feeling would also prepare other Xhosa listeners at the TRC hearings that the goat was foreshadowing her son's death.

I have to mention Mrs. Konile's unhappiness about the fact that her son was not buried in Indwe as she had requested but with the other seven comrades in Cape Town. Her request that her son be buried at Indwe has important cultural implications. According to Xhosa culture, it is important for one to be buried next to one's ancestors. This is seen as a way of maintaining a chain of communication between the deceased and the ancestors. In this way, a person remains protected by the ancestors. If her son had been buried in Indwe, the bond between him and herself could be kept, for she could visit the grave. His burial in Cape Town must have left her with a deep wound because not only had she been deprived from any connection with her own child, but his burial in a far-away place cut her, as well as him, off from the ancestral chain.

After she told about her skirmish with the police to get the body of her child, she said, "And I gave up." These words illustrated her deepening sense of helplessness and powerlessness. Her only son, who was her main source of support, had been cut off from her. Symbolically, she was describing a huge loss, not only monetary, but an unbridgeable rupture had taken place.

My Concluding Remarks

The above discussion highlights that the process of interpreting and translating should also be seen as cross-cultural communication. As there were slippages in the interpretation and translation of Mrs. Konile's testimony, the valuable information with regard to her feelings and aspirations could not reach the TRC officials and the audience. Instead, her testimony seemed incoherent. Slippages in translation can lead to misinterpretation and misrepresentation of a testifier, while, on the other hand, intimate cultural knowledge can lead to a fuller and more just interpretation of a mother tongue testimony that could restore the dignity of the testifier.

An African Psychological Reading (Kopano Ratele)

A Forewarning

On the eve of the day the news of the death of Zabonke Konile was brought to her, Mrs. Konile had a dream. In the dream she saw a goat. The animal was in a strange pose and stood under a tree next to her door. A goat in a strange pose next to a door is construable as an untoward sign. In her testimony, Mrs. Konile said that on the day after the night of the dream, she felt out of sorts, and it was the dream with which she associates her funny feeling.

At the level of deep affect or unconscious, it is *not* strange when Mrs. Konile says an animal was the sign of what she would learn about the next day. But the dream also functions at a much simpler level. The word *dream* is the vital missing link that could have made Mrs. Konile intelligible. What she told the commission turned from incoherent to coherent through a single line missing from the official English text. In isiXhosa, this line ("Phezolo ndiphuphe kakubi"; seven words in English: "Last night I had a terrible dream") brings Mrs. Konile back from the psychopathological wilderness—into which a reader of the English text might have put her—to a cultural embeddedness. Even if the sentence fails to make her wholly imaginable as an adult psychological subject, these words render her into somebody whose story is "followable." She had a dream: a bad, or strange, dream.

A Resistant Psyche

In identifying and calling the mothers and other family members of the Gugulethu 7 to give testimony, the TRC was looking for a certain kind of story: that of a brutal regime, stoic struggle, resilient mothers and families, and an eventual triumph over evil. To a large extent, the commission already got parts of this grand narrative from the other women. But it did not get this from Mrs. Konile.

Mrs. Konile began her testimony by sighing heavily six times within five rather short sentences as if she was saying, "I am so tired—I'm tired even before this process, of which I already despair, begins." While the TRC hearings were meant to deal precisely with "telling," its cathartic effect, and thus forgiveness, the commissioners appeared unprepared for and uneasy about Mrs. Konile—they addressed very few questions to her. It was as if her story was *resisting* the imposed framework of the hearings; as if her mind resisted easy readings. She seemed to say, "Mine is not part of what you want to hear. I will tell you of my dreams, my miserable life. I want to do my own kind of accounting."

In the Realm of Dreams

Many African people use dreams to help interpret wakeful life in contrast to the West, where the significance of dreams became somewhat less unacceptable and more legitimate in enlightened Vienna and elsewhere in the Old and New Worlds, after Freud's first major work, *The Interpretation of Dreams,* was published. Even without knowledge of psychoanalytic discoveries, dreams seem to have been an acceptable part of the existential methods many African people used and continue to employ to make sense of their lives. In this light, it is a terribly ordinary thing for Mrs. Konile to come to the hearings and talk of a dream. It makes so much sense that it would be easy for some readers to miss this part of her psychological makeup: how things are related to one another in the world for her regarding cause-effect.

When we recognize the dream, the goat, and its place in the story, much of Mrs. Konile's testimony becomes clear. The dream is a central part of the story, for it is an essential element of Mrs. Konile's psyche, because it is a key to her world. All of these elements, it is important to underline, are connected to language in critical ways, unable to be routed to others by any other mean expect through stories and other discursive practices. In accessing Mrs. Konile's testimony in the language in which she told her story, it becomes clear that underestimating this fact is likely to contribute to misunderstanding her and her world.

Having mentioned psychoanalysis, even the work of someone like Carl Jung or Sigmund Freud would be of little help here. What is demanded by the language of Mrs. Konile, given what Africans such as she believe about dreams, is to seek to understand what the goat dream means for her and her mainly African audience. Unanalyzed for Africa, Jung, Freud, and other dream analysts are likely to fail us principally because Mrs. Konile's culture and worldview accommodate and carry the dream of the goat.

A Connection Between Worlds

What, then, does the dream say? First, I interpret the dream of the goat as, in Mrs. Konile's telling, a connection to the ancestral worlds. The goat and the dream are messengers from the other world. Dreaming of a goat, Mrs. Konile is suggesting, was like receiving a letter from the ancestors that something is amiss.

The dream of the goat also means, in the second place, the living, just as the dead, are not too far; they are not far from her unconscious awareness or from her everyday life. Any contact with the ancestors in dreams or at the grave side is not only cultural but also spiritual and, given the history of South Africa, social and political too. The dream of the goat connects Mrs. Konile to her culture, her people, her Gods, and wider society and its politics. Culturally, socially, and spiritually, that is, the dream means that her ancestors are communicating to her that they are still around, and others are around, irrespective of the nature of the news they are about to bring to her door. What is important is that she is reminded that she is interconnected to a wider world of her people and with other worlds.

In order to underscore it, the third meaning of the dream is in how it appears to connect her to what is happening elsewhere in the world, the world of politics and wider South African society. That is to say, the dream brought into her life politics, which she exists far from, yet her son was murdered in the struggle to liberate his and her country.

Last, from a discursive African psychological perspective, the dream reconnects Mrs. Konile to herself. Mrs. Konile is in the midst of (re)constituting her self and her world as an individual person of African heritage.

In sum, the dream of the goat is a guide, a connecting cable, a warning, and a psychological tool. It leads her at once to her people, her son, those in the other world, and herself. The dream is part of an individual's psychic structure, of a cultural world, and of unspoken politics. It developed out of its very specific system of cultural symbols into a psychological meaningfulness, as well as from the culturally decontextulized meaninglessness of the translated version into a psychic coherency of the original text, where it makes perfect sense that the dream is there and told in that way.

An Individual Within Africa: A Psychology of Relations

There is no way of understanding Mrs. Konile without understanding how dominating modes of knowing rupture indigenous modes of knowing—in this case, how neoliberal capitalist Western psychology violently interrupts African indigenous psyches.

A simple and dominant definition of what psychologists do is to say they study individual behavior. A vital point grows out of this definition—namely, that the discipline of psychology presumes a lot of things about what an individual is, what the individual can do, and what his or her relation is to the world.

Let me present an example. Most African students, from rural areas or townships, who come into contact with the discipline of psychology at South African universities (which is no different from other English-speaking European and especially North American universities) at first appear terribly confused. What confuses them? Well, we teach students to get rid of everything they were taught about the nature of social relations and persons. If they do not quickly shed their notions about what a person is and how people relate to each other, they are bound to struggle. Students learn in the first week that they cannot regard their teachers as their "fathers" or "mothers." They have to get rid of what they were taught: that any older person is your *mme* or *nkgono* (mother or grandmother), *ntate* or *ntate moholo* (father or grandpa), *abuti* or *ausi* (brother or sister); they must turn away from the lesson they received at home that any person of similar age to you is your sibling (*ngwaneso* or *kgaitsedi*).

This has far-reaching implications in how they learn and whether or not they pass or fail. Not only do they have to treat their teachers as unrelated to them, not deserving respect for living to a certain age, but they also have to learn to be critical about what their teachers tell them and do critique in a way defined by White Western thought. If they do not get all of this into their African heads, they will fail their assignments.

Given all of this, then, if one talks about African psychology, one always feels a bit exotic, as if African psychology is not psychology proper. It is a flavor, something "other" cultures have. Psychology defines its task as studying the individual mind—not the North American or the African individual mind. Here, then, is the problem: How do you study Mrs. Konile's so-called incoherence if you assume that there is no difference between her and the average North American mind?

The phrase *motho ke motho ka batho* (a person is made into being a person by other persons) is seldom fully apprehended—even African intellectuals do not fully apprehend what is carried in that value. Nhlanhla Mkhize (2004a, 2004b) is one of the few psychologists who have tried to show that it is precisely because of a lack of understanding about the *self-in-community* and the *unity-of-the-world* that makes Mrs. Konile sound incoherent. Indeed, what racism, apartheid, and colonialism did and do is to destroy those specific values, because it is incomprehensible that *one lives for others.* It is very difficult for the Western mind or psyche to accept that *others make one.* In Western psychology, the individual comes first and is foremost, the family is constituted by individuals, and the world is made up by individual minds.

But what Mrs. Konile brings to our attention is that, for some people, this does not hold. In fact, it is the other way round. If she wants to do the ritual with a goat, she cannot simply get up one morning and say, "I had a dream and I am going to buy a goat and offer it as a sacrifice to my ancestors and invite people." No, she must first tell people about the dream. They will help her to decipher it. If she wants a ritual, they will have to agree and find a date suitable for all. One cannot simply slaughter a goat and say now I have my ritual. People would stay away for they would ask themselves, "Who is this person?"

On the deeper philosophical level, I interpret the dream as telling Mrs. Konile about a wholeness being threatened because she is *not an individual,* not in the way it is defined in the dominant frameworks of psychology. Rather, the dream reveals that she is still whole in that she is part of a world where she is in contact with the living and the dead.

There is little existential loneliness here. It is only later, on learning of the death of her son, that her wholeness is ruptured, that she feels she is becoming an individual in a terrible way.

Her son's death introduces her to a deep loneliness. She experiences it as being cut off from the community. She is sighing because she has become an individual through the death of her son—selected as it were to become an individual. She is saying, I am suffering, because I had been forced to become an individual. All the other mothers are together here in Gugulethu, they talk and support each other, but I am outside of it all.

The word *I* is actually not talking about her real psychological individuality. Mrs. Konile is using *I* as a form of complaint. She is saying, I don't want to be I. I want to be us, but the killing of my son, made me into an I. This deed has removed me and I can't get back to where I belong. The last time I was whole was when the goat spoke to me; since then I have been simply removed, cut off.

So to understand Mrs. Konile, to get to a psychological comprehensibility, our approach needs to be founded on her reality; her notion of her position in a universe of people, animals, and things; and her thoughts and feeling of how she relates to others and the environment. In other words, meaning systems undergird the possibility of being understood by others.

Our Conclusion

One of the specific tasks of the South African Truth and Reconciliation Commission was to begin restoring the personal dignity of victims. A step toward this was to allow people to testify in their mother tongues, accessing dignity and wisdom. These testimonies were simultaneously interpreted, which meant that people's mother tongues were no longer treated as cul-de-sacs but were specifically used to open up hitherto unknown and silent spaces.

Restoration could only begin when the testimonies were "heard" and "understood"—also and especially those who fell outside the norm. By critical qualitative research into Mrs. Konile's psychological and cultural framework, we have come to the opposite conclusion of the "Western reading" earlier in this chapter. Where the constant harping on the word *I* initially carried selfish and obsessive undertones, in Mrs. Konile's own context, it became a desperate plea to get rid of the sudden individualism forced upon her.

By analyzing her testimony through the notion of African individuality within community, we have taken a radical step. We are saying that within a postcolonial context, a woman may appear either incoherent because of severe suffering or unintelligible because of oppression—while in fact she is neither. Within her indigenous framework, she is logical and resilient in her knowledge of her loss and its devastating consequences in her life. She is not too devastated to make sense; she is devastated because she intimately understands the devastation that has happened to her. However, the forum she finds herself in and the way narratives are being read make it very hard for her to bring the depth of this devastation across.

We have to reemphasize the importance of our working method because we think it has radical and new implications regarding the study of TRC testimonies. In a country emerging from a divisive past, some narratives, such as that of Mrs. Konile, are likely to reproduce old cultural, racial, and geographical divisions. To overcome that, as well as inevitable interpretation and transcription mistakes, we suggest that there is almost no other way to proceed than by collaboratively working within a communally orientated, human-centered methodology.

By this, we mean that every narrative is rooted. In order to really "hear" the story, one has to take the rootedness into account—especially in light of a divisive past. Understanding the "ground" from which narratives sprout is sometimes only possible through the input of those who have deep knowledge of this "ground." By ignoring the "ground" of her narrative, one is cutting

Mrs. Konile from her roots as well as a larger humanity. In other words, one is trying to interpret her without *all* that makes her herself.

Our collaborative method allowed us to

> realize that the dominant discourse has no way of "hearing" Mrs. Konile because her narrative defies all the elements that render narratives "audible" within the dominant tone;
>
> make use of the fact that at least two of us are able to traverse culture and language in order to enter both the dominant and indigenous discourse or "ground";
>
> recode Mrs. Konile from the "incomprehensible" into a new discourse that values her resistance to the master narrative;
>
> challenge, among other things, cultural and racial stereotypes;
>
> come to a radically different interpretation from what she was saying than some of us initially had; and
>
> be deeply influenced in our own "listening" to one another as cultural psychological work was happening in the researchers themselves.

In this way, knowledge of Mrs. Konile opens up ways for people emerging from a context of conflict and estrangement to access understanding and respect for one another. Mrs. Konile has made us hear her and, through her, one another.

References

Angelelli, C. (2004). *Medical interpreting and cross-cultural communication.* Cambridge, UK: Cambridge University Press.

Cooper, J. C. (1995). *An illustrated encyclopedia of traditional symbols.* London: Thames and Hudson Ltd.

Danieli, Y. (Ed.). (1998). *International handbook of multigenerational legacies of trauma.* New York: Kluwer.

Des Pres, T. (1977). *The survivor: An anatomy of life in the death camps.* New York: Pocket Books.

Felman, S., & Laub, D. (1992). *Testimony: Crises of witnessing in literature, psychoanalysis, and history.* New York: Routledge.

Meier, C. A. (1987). *The psychology of C. G. Jung: The meaning and significance of dreams.* Boston: Sigo Press.

Mkhize, N. (2004a). Psychology: An African perspective. In D. Hook, N. Mkhize, P. Kiguwa, & A. Collins (Eds.), *Critical psychology* (pp. 24–52). Landsdowne, South Africa: UCT Press.

Mkhize, N. (2004b). Sociocultural approaches to psychology: Dialogism and African conceptions of the self. In D. Hook, N. Mkhize, P. Kiguwa, & A. Collins (Eds.), *Critical psychology* (pp. 53–83). Landsdowne, South Africa: UCT Press.

Ratazzi, E. A. (2005). *Narrating rape at the Truth and Reconciliation Commission in South Africa.* Unpublished MA thesis, Department Political Studies, UCT.

Ross, F. (2004). Testimony. In C. Villa-Vicencio & E. Doxater (Eds.), *Pieces of the puzzle: Keywords on reconciliation and transitional justice* (pp. 58–64). Cape Town, South Africa: IJR.

Scarry, E. (1985). *The body in pain: The making and unmaking of the world.* New York: Oxford University Press.

Schaffner, C., & Kelly-Holmes, H. (1995). *Cultural functions of translation.* Cleveland, UK: Multilingual Matters.

TRC final report (Vol. 1). (1998). Cape Town, South Africa: CTP Book.

28

TRANSNATIONAL, NATIONAL, AND INDIGENOUS RACIAL SUBJECTS

Moving From Critical Discourse to Praxis

Luis Mirón

The vast literature on globalization and related theoretical discourses such as neoliberalism has apparently spawned a counternarrative: the critical examination of indigenous people and culture. In the United States, however, the latter conversation is at times held suspect in part because of the perception that, like the macro discussions of globalization, scholarship on indigenous everyday lived experience lacks an honest intellectual engagement of "race."

Complicating these issues further is the substantial scholarly and ethnographic work on transnationalism (see below). By definition, transnationals—for example, Mexicans who occupy multiple spaces in the United States and Mexico and potentially assume hybrid identities and dual loyalties (Smith & Favell, 2006)—are *not* indigenous. They are fluid, "nonnative" subjects. Likewise, U.S.-born African Americans and Latinos are not considered "native" Americans.

In this chapter, I propose to accomplish a number of tasks in a relatively short space. First, I seek to debunk the widespread idea that the processes of globalization are so totalizing that resistance is nearly unfathomable. Capital is totalizing in its denial of political and human agency, or so the ideological argument goes. Second, I try to show that despite clear racial differences that transnational, national, and indigenous subjects embody and culturally experience daily in the exercise of citizenship (see below), these subjects are difficult to categorize. Potentially, they have more in common than previously theoretically imagined, and the possibilities for coalition building remain strong. Third, I advance a conception of *performative ethnography,* building on discourse theory and semiotics, in hopes of pointing a path by which the racial subjects named above, who historically have occupied the periphery, or the margins, may now enter new borderlands in dialogue and solidarity with one another. Social action and social change may ensue. Finally, I conclude with the possibilities for democracy in multiple social and political spaces, including education (broadly conceptualized) embodied in the rapidly growing eco-green consciousness.

This chapter intends to dialogically challenge "globalization," that is, to show how the processes of globalization are interactive—they both constrain and render possible new forms and spaces of democratic practice. Moreover, I draw from one specific site of these practices—the emerging struggle against global warming—in hopes of facilitating dialogue and coalition building among multiple racial subjects. I begin with an analysis of multifarious racial subjects, the first of whom are transnationals.

▣ Transnational Subjects

I argue in this chapter that these categories of subjectivity and identity are just that—abstract categorizations. In reality—that is, on the ground of everyday lived experience and social practice—people, whether conceptualized as individuals or as inhabiting collective, social identities, partly defy fixed categorization. They exhibit fluid lives. This chapter will examine in both ethnographic and broad analytical strokes the dimensions of this argument, focusing on transnational flows of people, culture, capital, and knowledge, typical of the spaces all of these racial subjects occupy in the age of information and the shift in capital from production to the mode of information (Castells, 1991; Poster, 1990). The first section begins with a critically grounded look at transnational migrants, cultural citizens who defy legal designations.

In 1982, there was a drought in most of Mexico that destroyed crops and made water scarce. With no water and the crops dying or dead, many people started coming to the United States in hopes of finding work. One of these men was Antonio Mejia from Boquerón, Pueblo, in Mexico. He came to Newburgh, New York, to find work and send money back to his family in Mexico. Mejia was able to work in the United States for a while but was then deported back to Mexico. Once in Mexico, he realized how bad it was in his hometown. After making it back to the United States, he helped to form the Grupo Unión and served as their president.[1]

What follows is a synthesis of ethnographic case studies drawn from Smith and Bakker (2005) and my own work (Mirón, Darder, & Inda, 2005). These studies empirically illustrate the actual processes by which actors exercise their human and political agency on the ground of everyday lived cultural experience: a lived experience that embraces the political terrain of cultural citizenship. However, these narratives move beyond the multiple terrains of citizenship toward an admittedly more abstract sphere of subjectivity, especially the formation of racial subjectivity. It is precisely at this meta-level of lived cultural experience, however, that the potential for racial subjects to occupy new social spaces of democracy within the constraints of neoliberal ideologies is most acute.

The avant-garde video, *The Sixth Section,* is a startling example of what Smith (2001) has aptly characterized as "transnational urbanism." Here filmmaker and cyberartist Alex Rivera vividly documents the formation and successes of Grupo Unión, a Mexican community development organization in Newburgh, New York. Grupo Unión represents one of more than 3,000 such organizations in the United States, groups that have in one fashion or another apparently exploited the inexpensive labor market, as well as the abundance of service and other relatively low-paying jobs, to establish new economic residence while maintaining close family ties with their home in Mexico.

The Grupo Unión is a collection of migrant workers all from the same hometown of Boquerón, Mexico, who got together to help improve their hometown by combining their money and putting it toward a townwide project or need. The first civic improvement the group decided to focus on was a baseball stadium. After building the stadium, they also paid for players to play in the stadium because all of the young men from the area had gone to the United States. The group also bought an ambulance for the local clinic, band instruments, a kitchen for the kindergarten, and necessities for the church.

The more the collective did for the town, the more powerful it became to the Mexican politicians. For example, the governor of Puebla came to New York to talk to some of the migrants, and after pressure from the Grupo Unión, the government started helping with paving the roads. The group says that the state of Puebla (where the members of El Grupo Unión are from) is broken apart into five sections. The Grupo Unión considers Newburgh, New York, in the United States the *6th Section.*

What makes this group both unique and representative of a larger social movement is the political effect it has created on economic development and on politicians in its hometown, as well as its collective solidarity with similar organizations in the United States. Filmmaker Rivera calls the group's political capacity "transnational organizing." These political-economic impacts, moreover, are genuinely transnational in process in that the effects of its community organizing are felt both in the United States, the northern empire, and Mexico, its putative southern periphery neighbor. Such transnational urbanism, I argue and demonstrate below, flies in the theoretical face of structurally oriented social theorists who almost universally state that poor immigrant citizens lack the capacity to effectively resist the deleterious forces of global capital (Harvey, 1989). Global capitalism is totalizing in its denial of agency. I counter below that such a unidimensional view of the processes of globalization rests on empirically questionable as well as conceptually flawed models of citizenship.

With respect to everyday cultural practices, the question of language is crucial because the transnational migrant workers depicted above emphasize the importance of becoming polyglot cultural citizens, allowing them to move in spaces that transcend the nation and potentially but not as readily the state as well (see Mirón et al., 2005). What I am working with here, then, is a notion of cultural citizenship (see below) that goes beyond legalistic definitions to encompass the more informal aspects of how people integrate into their environments, so that legal citizenship is not the end, or even the beginning, of numerous, active local mediations over the terms of the local-transnational integration of people (Mitchell, 1997).

The members of El Grupo Unión exercise their newly negotiated civic entitlements by establishing hybrid cultural identities in upstate New York. When in possession of legal documents permitting them to work as low-wage earners in the United States, these immigrants exploit the state apparatus (see below) by holding a form of dual-culture citizenship as citizens of Mexico and legal residents of the United States. Although structurally oriented globalization theorists may reasonably argue that performing menial jobs such as waiting on tables and driving taxis help to reproduce the totalizing effects of capital, such a view is theoretically unsophisticated. This is so because from the perspective of the members of these organizations, their economic status as U.S. workers pushes the Mexican state to be more responsive—and potentially less corrupt—to communities, and their extra earnings support their families rather than U.S. corporations. In short, we need a new theoretical paradigm to highlight the complexities of transnationalism, a theory that is more sensitive to cultural forces and politics on the ground. I summarize the theoretical work of Michael P. Smith (below). However, first I will expand on the notion of *cultural citizenship.*

Cultural Citizenship

One of the major problems with the new nativism (Delgado, 1999), as well as its corresponding politics of citizenship, is that it operates under the assumption that we still live in a world in which the nation-state can properly be bounded and, by extension, in which the only meaningful form of community is one localized within those boundaries. But this world simply does not exist (which is not to say that the nation-state has become irrelevant). As we have seen, global restructuring since the mid-1970s has involved such a transformation of the economy that capital is able to flow across national boundaries with relative ease. This same restructuring has been responsible for the major demographic transformation not only of the United States but of other nations of the West. Thus, the world has witnessed what has variously been called the peripheralization of the core or the implosion of the Third World into the First (Rosaldo, 1988; Sassen, 2000a, 2000b).

In other words, the nations of the West, of which the United States is one example, have been "invaded," to use a popular metaphor, by peoples from non-Western or Third World countries, so that you now have Algerians in France, Moroccans and Dominicans in Spain, Senegalese in Italy, and folks from just about everywhere in the United States. But the crucial thing about these migrants is that, quite unlike what the traditional literature on immigration suggests, transnational immigrants have not uprooted themselves, leaving behind their homeland and facing the often-painful process of incorporation into a new national culture. Instead, in part because of the facilitation of two-way traffic, both physical and metaphorical, made possible by modern technologies of transport and communication (the Internet, telephone, television, airplanes, fax machines, etc.), they have been able to forge multistranded ties that link together their society of settlement and origin.

These immigrants, then, as Glick Schiller, Basch, and Szanton Blanc (1995) suggest, are best understood as transmigrants: "Transmigrants are immigrants whose daily lives depend on multiple and constant interconnections across international borders and whose public identities are configured in relationship to more than one nation-state" (p. 48). What we are witnessing, then, through these transmigrants, is a world in which significant social ties are no longer simply confined within the boundaries of a single territorial national space. This means that we have to think of citizenship in slightly different terms when it comes to (many) contemporary immigrants. Citizenship must be thought of in terms of the strategies migrants use to navigate transnational spaces.

In the minds of Mexican officials, migrant workers in the United States should have a sense of "double gratitude" and "dual loyalty" to Mexico and the United States. Migrants should blindly send money to Mexico to be used for various civil and social works, as well as support the government without question. In terms of the United States, migrants should provide a solid skilled workforce and their sense of culture (which should help to enhance the United States). These supposed roles for migrant workers in the United States have not turned out exactly as expected.

Smith (2005) illustrates the processes of citizenship formation—in particular, cultural citizenship—by following Angel Calderon, a U.S. citizen living in California who came from El Timbinal, Mexico.

Angel

Angel and his migrant cohorts living in and around Napa Valley, California, have managed to become a vital political force in both Mexico and the United States through their connections with both of these countries. This group originally started out by sending money back home to their families and contributing to townwide needs such as a potable water supply and a renovated town plaza (Smith, 2005, p. 18).

The government attempted to take over these projects and convinced the group to become investors of a factory in their hometown. The group put up the seed money and then took out a loan from the government for the rest. This placed a certain level of stress on the group because they wanted to be doing things more specifically for the town and not necessarily for the money. This factory also caused controversy because in order to make money from the factory, sometimes things had to be done that were not in the best interests of the community, but as owners, the group had to make such decisions. One example of this is that Angel had to fire his nephew from the position of manager of the factory because he was not treating the workers well. While this helped the factory, it did not help the relationship between Angel and his brother (the nephew's father).

Yet even though the group has cooperated with Mexican government officials, they do not blindly support the government. The group pressed for things that they feel the government should be providing. Thus, there is no blind support or giving of money, but a pushing and pulling to get the

Mexican government to do things to help the community with the group helping to back this support.

In terms of the United States, Angel helped to bring artists, musicians, and some of the Mexican politicians to Napa, California, for the enjoyment of the Americans as well as some political meetings with the U.S. and Mexican officials. This helped to legitimize Angel and his group to the Napa politicians, who then started to include him in their campaigning and socializing. Angel has campaigned for and won a rezoning of land that enabled better migrant housing to be built. Consequently, when looking at the transnational context of the situation, it is clear that Angel and his group are actively participating in both the Mexican home as well as their new American home and are doing things to help both communities.

The Tomato King

Andres Bermudez, a migrant from Jerez, Mexico, who has become the "Tomato King" at his place of business and residence in Northern California, decided to campaign for mayor of Jerez. In his campaign, he focused on wanting to "Americanize" Mexican political life (Smith, 2005, p. 25). By this, Bermudez made sure to illustrate how he was able to go from being a migrant worker to owning his own business and being the "Tomato King." Therefore, he understood about the corrupt political system of Mexico and showed how he was one of them (the townspeople), and by electing him, they were "not just empowering Andres Bermudez. They will empower themselves" (Smith, 2005, p. 26).

Using this reasoning during his campaign worked, and Bermudez initially won the election, but it was invalidated because of an issue regarding Bermudez's actual place of residence. With help from several grassroots organizations in the United States, manned by organized migrants, Bermudez was able to campaign again and be permanently elected as mayor. Smith (2005) notes that the political campaign of Andres Bermudez can be used to better understand the place of "El Migrante" (migrants) both in Mexico and in the United States. Bermudez was supported not only by the townspeople of Jerez, Mexico, but also by migrant hometown clubs in the United States, "who supported the Tomato King in part because they themselves were largely entrepreneurial small business owners who might gain new opportunities for investments in Mexico as a longer term result of the Bermudez victory" (Smith, 2005, p. 31).

Transnationalism and Globalization on the Ground

In numerous writings, Smith (among other works, see 1992, 2001) has theorized the processes of globalization and transnationalism. Smith is particularly interested in the vast networks of social movements, networks, kin groups, and pan-ethnic identities to recover the sense of human and political agency. This he conceptualizes as ""transnational urbanism," or social networks in migration from below. His principal aim in doing so is to strike a conceptual balance with what he sees as the totalizing discourses of the global economy (Castells, 1998, 2000; Harvey, 1989), one that he aptly characterizes as global economism, or "transnational capital from above" (Guarnizo & Smith, 1998, p. 3). Smith (2001) views the theoretical and practical results of this conceptualization as producing a cultural reductionism, which (dis-) "connects macro-economic and geopolitical transformations [from] the micro networks of social action that people create, move in, and act upon in their daily lives" (p. 6).

Smith's innovative theoretical alternative is anchored in an agency-oriented social theory, which encapsulates the following conceptual and practical dimensions. These dimensions of agency, moreover, are embedded in a metatheoretical framework of social construction; that is, the structures and processes of capitalism (globalization) are invented, challenged, and potentially transformed by actors.

First, social theorists describe and interpret the world largely in terms of how they perceive social reality. Smith believes that social scientists view the world as they perceive themselves. Second, the social structures that shape the actions of human agents and the actors themselves are both "socially constructed understandings of how the world works" (Smith, 2001, p. 8). Third, direct observation of social and cultural practices, including the texts of urban theorists, is needed to arrive at a deeper understanding of social reality. Finally, deconstruction is not an end in itself. It is a tool of praxis that ultimately leads to "a new discursive space for social inquiry" (Smith, 2001, p. 8). In short, Smith seeks to plow conceptual ground to give new meaning to the everyday practices of social actors, most especially those transnational migrants and citizens exercising human agency from below. In a nutshell, these processes Smith conceives as transnational urbanism—in effect, processes that point to how migrant-citizens negotiate hybridity in transnational urban spaces (McCarthy & Crichlow, 1993, esp. p. 45).

Smith, I want to emphasize, is not without his critics, some of whom such as Gordon Mathews (2000) have relied on his theoretical writings as well as his innovative use of extended case studies throughout their careers. I briefly review alternate, yet potentially compatible, perspectives next.

▣ The Missing Link

One major point of contention between Mathews and Smith is Smith's lack of attention to consciousness. Because Smith does not usually theoretically foreground the individual, a complete understanding of social life is not possible. Mathews further notes that although Smith interviews people from all lifestyles, he only specifically discusses people of importance or who have political or economic power, that is, elites. Thus, Mathews concludes that, empirically and methodologically, there is a problem with Smith's ethnography, the subjects he selects for interviews, and the presupposed lack of subjectivity (in Mathews's [2000] parlance, "consciousness of the individual") of those Smith excludes from his sampling procedures.

According to Mathews (2000), this is a major shortcoming when attempting to gain a full understanding of how social researchers understand social life. Smith's methodology—or, more precisely, his theory of methodology—would be better served if there had been specific discussion of a wider range of people "representing multiple levels of social, economic, and political life. . . . if Smith's [work generally] emphasizes larger social, political, and economic forces at the expense of individual consciousness, my own work [Mathews], based as it is in phenomenology, has stressed individual consciousness at the expense of social, political, and economic forces" (p. 39). Current research by Mathews focuses on national identity, and he goes on to suggest that a combined methodology of his own focus on consciousness with Smith's focus on social lives and how they are affected by transnationality could "serve as a powerful analytical tool indeed" (p. 35). Below I present a macro theory of a methodology of ethnography as a heuristic tool to accomplish the twin tasks of researching social life and individual consciousness.

On Loving One's Countries

Mathews (2000) critiques Smith's "explicit premise of loyalty to two countries" and states that "the idea of loving two countries seems rare indeed" (p. 40). Data Mathews has collected from focus groups about national identity, as well as other examples, illustrate that it does seem rare for an individual to "love more than one mother" (p. 40). Mathews illustrates how Smith uses many examples in his work about how "Smith is excellent at setting forth the institutionalized expectations of state versus migrants, with the former seeking the latter's money and unquestioning obedience, and the latter seeking to bring change to the former by making Mexico more like the United States" (p. 41). Yet in this analysis, as Mathews points out, there is no discussion about the consciousness of the individual in terms of where his or her loyalties are—with Mexico, the United States, or with both?

In this regard, what is needed is a theoretical framework of transnational urbanism "to better account for how subjective consciousness of national belonging is both created by and creating of the institutional processes of state maintenance" (Mathews, 2000, p. 41). A possible way to look at this questions comes from Appadurai (1996), who has written of habitus, which Mathews (2000) sees as "becoming a less powerful force today, in that many of us are increasingly aware of multiple possibilities in our lives, and thus no longer take a single habitus fully for granted" (p. 41). The implications for social theory of *not* having a single habitus are at least partially examined by Smith, but Mathews feels that by looking more in depth to the consciousness of the individuals and their national identity, we would better understand not only the "mystery of belonging to two countries" but also "the even greater mystery of belonging to a single country" (p. 42).

State, Market, and the Trojan Horse of Neoliberalism

Mathews (2000) points out that Smith criticizes binary thinking; however, Mathews argues that there are in fact normally two different contrasting ways of thinking or looking at a situation, specifically in the interplay between the state and market. Mathews sees the discourse of the state as, "you must cherish and defend your country and its way of life," and that of the market as, "you can buy, do, and be anything in the world that you want" (p. 42). A few examples given for when these two forces have been in opposition are eating "French" fries for Americans (i.e., freedom fries) and "eating McDonald's hamburgers" for Koreans. In both cases, Mathews states that the consumption of a particular item is seen as going against national identity (or by not consuming the item, it is seen as protecting national identity).

Thus, there is direct conflict between the market and the state, yet more often than not, this is subtly ignored. Mathews (2000) gives examples of the French still wearing blue jeans and Americans still having Persian rugs in their homes. The point in bringing up all of these issues revolves around Mathew's main focus that the "understanding of the nature of individuals' sense of commitment or lack of commitment to the nation and the state is as essential as understanding larger institutional and historical forces in comprehending the interrelation of nation and state in the world today" (p. 45).

This brief review of the methodological criticisms serves the understanding of transnationalism and the formation of multiple racial subjects in particular. I return to the theoretical and methodological gains of these criticisms to briefly offer a theory on "performative ethnography" (below). My hope is that this approach may capture the full range of hybrid subjectivities described in this chapter—transnational, national, and indigenous. It is a practical way to conduct critical theory from the ground up.[2]

Extending Critical Methodologies: A Conception of Performative Ethnography

According to Fabian (1990), "Ethnography is essentially, not incidentally, communicative or dialogical; conversation, not observation, should be the key to conceptualizing ethnographic knowledge production" (p. 17). I want to argue that an alternate paradigm of ethnography—grounded in a theory of performativity (Parker & Sedgwick, 1995; also see Rumbaut, 1999)—renders possible the everyday representation and understanding of racial subjectivities and identities. In particular, within the self-understanding of Latinos and African Americans, Native Americans (North, Central, and South America), and Aborigines, both synchronistic difference and commonality are made possible. These deeper understandings, coupled with representation in ethnography, may inform the politics of knowledge, coalition building across racial groups, and social change (see below). In brief, this alternate paradigm allows for the possibility of constructing a new racial self. A conception of performative ethnography briefly outlined here allows for a more radical *style* (Sontag, 1966), a style that is embodied in the practice of silence (deep listening to the racial Other), the normative goal of which is the achievement of the racial subjects' own will to power. Anticipating historical moments, as well as possibly the use of video and other new ethnographic tools, Susan Sontag (1977) observes,

> Though an event has come to mean, precisely something worth photographing, it is still ideology (in the broadest sense) that determines what constitutes an event. There can be no evidence, photographic or otherwise, of an event *until the event itself has been named and characterized.* And it is never photographic evidence which can construct—more properly, identify—events; the contribution of photography always follows the naming of the event. What determines the possibility of being affected morally by photographs is the existence of a relevant consciousness. Without a politics, photographs of the slaughter-bench of history will most likely be experienced as, simply, unreal or as a demoralizing emotional blow. (p. 19)

Furthermore, Sontag (1977) appears to presciently anticipate the performative/performance turn in ethnography and critical ethnography in particular (Carspecken, 1996; Madison, 2005). Recently, Lovett (2007) has pushed the methodological boundaries of social research and, implicitly, the performative turn in the social sciences and humanities. Her syncopated blend of video, narrative, and critical pedagogy in studying the Lower Ninth Ward in New Orleans post-Katrina renders possible not only her singular representation of Herbert Gettridge, her subject, a heroic 83-year-old whose single-minded determination was to rebuild his devastated home—and thus bring his wife of more than 50 years back home. More important, perhaps, it moves representation to the sphere of social action and the politics of rebuilding. Lovett, therefore, appears to bring to life in the 21st century Sontag's notions 30 years earlier as the United States struggles with the question of saving the soul of its nation while much of the available federal and state labor (military) implement democracy through occupation.

Lovett (2007) theorizes that the production of the visual image replaces the (historical) moment. This replacement, or substitution, for reality (Baudrillard, 2002) fixes social and material reality and "locks" it in space and time. This practice—similar to observational social research—subsequently isolates the real people affected, the victims, be they the Katrina diaspora, the more than 3,000 murdered on 9/11 and in Iraq, the children of Darfur, or, of late, the students, faculty, or families affected by the shooting at Virginia Tech. Clearly, if social researchers are to remain at all relevant during these dark times, something has to give. My intellectual inclination, or bias, is to turn outside of the social sciences toward the humanities and the arts.

I turn, therefore, to what literary theory may suggest in this discussion of "performance" and "performativity." My goal is to build on current theory and scholarship in the social sciences by delving into the humanities, especially literary theory and semiotics. In so doing, the purpose is to make complementary these apparent disparate disciplines in the intellectual "borderlands" where they may intersect.

Writing of the poetry of Sir Philip Sidney, Clark (2000) theorizes that "Sidney's 'soldier-poet' represents the political use of literature to challenge the status quo and effect positive social change. . . . the intent of this [performative] kind of poetry is well-doing and not merely well knowing" (p. 5). On a metatheoretical level, Clark interprets the poststructuralist work of Roland Barthes (1979) and notes a distinction within literary theory between the artistic *work* and the *text.* Clark uses semiotics to develop this distinction, and its political-ethical dimensions in particular, further. I analogically build on this distinction to argue that performance and performativity are analytically distinct constructs as well.

The literary creation, the "work," is treated within formal literary criticism as an inherently, that is fixed, material object that is independent of the artist's intentions and contexts in which the literary artists create, for example, novels.[3] For my purposes, I view the act of considering the work as a *performance.* This performance, I argue, conventionally ignores, or usually suppresses, performativity[4] (see distinction below). In other words, the reader's consideration of the material work—the performance of the work—"reduces its social or political effect to an aesthetic judgment of taste rather than action" (Clark, 2000, p. 10). Qualitatively, artistic creation (the "work") may be represented in research (Barone, 2000; Denzin; 1997; Eisner; 1997; Fabian, 1990). The goal of this type of representation of research is simply to render a different aesthetic form so as to evoke emotions to the artistry embedded, for example, in teaching. As such, this alternate representation is purportedly value neutral, a social epistemological axiom I reject. The performance necessitates either a "live" or a cyber-audience who is somewhat engaged with the work. In part, the function of the work is to provide aesthetic feedback to the speaking poet or actor, the performer.

Theoretically complementary to literary, artistic works as performance, yet I wish to argue distinguished from them, is the "text." "The text is held only in language, it exists only as discourse" (Barthes, 1979, p. 75). For this reason, discourse specifically carries forever with the possibility of repetition the naming and renaming of racial subjectivity and identity, for example (Butler, 2004; Sontag, 1977). Central to purposes here, Clark (2000) interprets poststructural literary theory to argue that beyond the artistic sense of "play" that the literary, dramatic text engenders, "textuality is inextricably embedded in action and so exists beyond the boundaries of formal closure that constitute the 'work' as such" (p. 5). Furthermore, Clark argues that the opening of the text socially to a collaborative reader (see the quote by Fabian, 1990, above) theoretically establishes the text as a social space and, by implication of collaboration with the reader, its political efficacy as well. By extension, performative research texts such as ethnographies facilitate or creatively establish the social space for subject formation, subjectivity, and identity.

My theoretical and methodological interests lie in the formation of racial subjectivity through the use of visual text (video, film, and animation). Like performance, these discourses interact with audiences. Their substantive difference, I assert, however, is that these audiences are not engaged in subject formation but rather, as Barthes (1979) conceives, in engagement with the creative "play" of the artistic work. Aesthetically, this is an important, desire-full engagement. I argue, however, that the space for politics and ethics is for the most part lacking, owing to the emphasis on the literary artist's creative or improvisational effect on the audience. Conceived thusly, ethnographies constitute creative expression and productive uses of power. I want to extend this analysis of the political uses of literary text to ethnography and qualitative research more generally to argue that ethnography constitutes a performative text of science[5] that is also embedded in politics, morality, and ethics.

This conception of the performative (Mirón & Inda, 2000), particularly its relation to social research, stands ideologically on the ground of a vision of social action and, ultimately, social change. Owing to an apparent lack of language, this ideological perspective represents a "progressive" view of social change. By this, I mean a vision that is located in politics and praxis around which the fragmented left can hopefully coalesce. Moral–ethical values that come to mind, however abstract, are restorative justice (see Braithwaite, 2002), racial equity, and the public interest, especially in the context of public schools and other political institutions where poor citizens of color seem to suffer chronically from a seeming perpetual lack of financial and policy resources.

These values, it is hoped, become self-evident when pursued within the performance of ethnography. But why the emphasis on the space of critical pedagogy or "revolutionary" education (McLaren, 2000)? It is within the political and social space of education—as distinct from learning (Biesta, 2006; Segarra & Dobles, 1999)—where there remains the practical possibility, however powerfully constrained as by the processes of globalization, McLaren (McLaren & Jaramillo, Chapter 10, this volume) and others have pointed out of achieving democratic social and cultural practices. Freire (in Segarra & Dobles, 1999) observes that "an educational act has a political nature and a political act has an educational nature. If this is generally so, it would be incorrect to say that Latin American education (or education for indigenous subjects) alone has a political nature. Education worldwide has a political nature" for all racial subjects, whether visibly or invisibly oppressed.

Although public schools are one site where this dream lingers, the world has changed. Globally, we have moved into what Goldfarb (2002) has called "visual pedagogy." This is what makes Lovett's (2007) methodological work compelling and the need to integrate pedagogy, methodology, and action apparently urgent. Moreover, it is in the broad space of education where the indigenous racial subject can shake metaphoric hands with the domestically indigenous (African American, Latino, and Asian American, among others) and the transnational subject.

Next I describe theoretically the dynamics of racial subject formation. This is significant, I assert, because as Sontag (1966) points out and Butler (1993) theorizes, "events"—including the formation of racial subjectivity—assume the capacity for representation, or investigation, after they take on names. Naming, in turn, renders possible renaming or what I call reconstituting. This process is itself pedagogical in nature.

Reproducing and Reconstituting the Racial Subject

According to Judith Butler (1993), performative discourses succeed "only because that action echoes prior actions, and *accumulates the force of authority through the repetition or citation of a prior, authoritative set of practices*" (pp. 226–227). Extending Butler's writing on gender performativity to issues of racialization and racial identity (see Mirón, Torres, & Inda, 1999), I suggest that the act of racial subject formation should not be conceptualized as a singular action but rather as a series of reiterative practices through which discourse produces the effect that it names.[6] Latino transurban agents' apparent exploitation of and political gains derived from globalization described above are cases in point. This performative discourse, however, does not so much bring into being what it names as it produces through its reiterative power the very "thing" that it regulates and controls, if not dominates. An example from a research tradition would help make these rather abstract statements from discourse theory more palpable. I draw from anthropology, a discipline that has been heavily invested in scientific approaches to ethnography.

> Though not immune to the white man's burden, anthropology was drawn through the course of the nineteenth century, even more towards causal connections between race and culture. As the position and status of the 'inferior' races became increasingly to be regarded as fixed, so socio-cultural differences came to be regarded as dependent upon hereditary characteristics. Since these were inaccessible to direct observation, they had to be inferred from physical and behavioral traits, which in turn they were intended to explain. Socio-cultural differences among human populations became subsumed within the identity of the individual human body. (Green, 1985, pp. 31–32, qtd. in Hall, 1997, p. 244)

The constitution of the racial subject through performative ethnography is another example.[7] In other words, a discursive practice appears to gain the scientific "authority to bring about what it names through citing the conventions of authority," such that a norm "takes hold to the extent that it is 'cited' as such a norm, but it also derives its power through the citations that it compels" (Butler, 1993).[8]

I suggest that the subject is constituted not to imply that the subject is left without agency. Such a discursive constitution through the uses of language creates the very possibility for agency. Therefore, human and political agency is a somewhat paradoxical and ironic by-product of the knowledge-power relation mentioned above. It is a political outcome, if you will, of *productive* power relations. In this precise manner, the racialized subject can be reconstituted.[9]

In summary, I have laid this theoretical path to develop the methodological ground for an alternate paradigm of ethnography. A performative ethnography grounded in everyday cultural practice produces material consequences for the racial subject (Smith, 2005). Using Austin's (1975) language, ethnography "performs" the words it describes or the subjects it names. Performative research enacts. As Stone (1999) correctly argues, this action is inextricably ethical in outcomes in that it concerns the ever elusive issues of social justice. I extend Stone's argument here to focus on the formation of the racial subject. Understood thusly, performative ethnography embeds not only the uses of the imagination, including the postcolonial imagination and that of the indigenous (McCarthy, 2003), but social action as well. I will demonstrate below that as a performative discourse, ethnographic research practices may ultimately generate the racial subjects' own will to power (Nietzsche, 1967).

Paul Willis (2000) offers intellectual hope and a possible revolutionary imaginary when he states that economic forces do not directly change the cultural sphere of the social formation. His notion of agen*cy* has substantially evolved since publication of *Learning to Labour* (Willis, 1977). Then, Willis's concept of agency was primarily based on the work of Anthony Giddens (1984). Now, Willis's conceptualization has traveled from notions of reflexivity to creative agency (see Mirón, 2002, pp. 368–369). Willis (2000) observes, "The role of the 'creative self activity,' ethnographically registerable, of agents continues to be crucial to the indeterminacy and variety of how these technological and political-economic changes pass into (or read into) cultural and social change" (p. xvii). Social change, therefore, may emanate from a grounded aesthetics that locates creative self-expression in the realm of everyday cultural practice. Social justice advocates, including ethnographers, need not necessarily mount campaigns to overthrow the capitalist economic system. Instead, a creative alternative might be to transform lived cultural experience through the relentless new labor of self-expression, a "work that is never done," a notion with which Butler (1993, 2004) would resonate.

On a broader social scale, the politics of a culturally grounded performativity makes possible the conditions for rewriting history. What seems to be missing from even the most rigorous class analysis is the fundamental Marxist recognition that capitalism is a historical—and relational—process. Therefore, *social* class, like the idea of "race," is a historical and social construction as well. A practical application derived from performative ethnographic techniques is that scientific knowledge of the racial subject may compel classroom teachers of poor, working-class minority students across the globe to join teachers and parents of White, middle-class students to revolt against economically overdetermined high-stakes testing. Self-transformation (Fromm, 1955) through the labor of continuous cultural reproduction potentially transforms into societal transformation. The politics of place then weaves into a more critical justice pedagogy (see below), a pedagogy I propose that may begin with an alternate model of ethnographic research.

Willis's (2000) idea of a culturally grounded aesthetics is relevant to my purposes here on two fronts. The first and perhaps most important dimension is the creative expressions of knowledge or, in Willis's words, "expressive struggle" (p. xv). At the risk of repetition, his observations are worth noting at some length:

> Human beings are driven not only to struggle to survive by making and remaking their material conditions of existence, but also to survive by making sense of the world and their place in it. This is a cultural production, as making sense of themselves as actors in their own cultural worlds. Cultural practices of meaning making {performative subject constitution} are intrinsically self-motivated as aspects of identity-making and self construction: in making our cultural worlds we make ourselves. At least for those who have moved out of economic subsistence, perhaps the balance has tipped from instrumental to expressive struggle, so that humans are concerned more with the making of their cultural world than with the material world. Even in their material struggles for survival, they grapple with choices in "how to go on," so as to deal with the maintenance of a viable cultural identity and its distinction and acknowledgement from others. (p. xiv)

One type of self-knowledge, following Willis (2000), is "expressive knowledge" or creative discourse. Knowledge of their social class location as classroom teachers provides a contemporary example (note the relevance of this location in the aftermath of Katrina, below). The second form of knowledge, one crucial to the normative goals of this chapter, is awareness of the social plight of the racial subject. Willis's call for artistically forged relations of expression provides theoretical opportunities and radical methodologies to represent multiple racial subjects (see Mirón, 2002, p. 372; Sontag, 2001).

A culturally grounded creativity, in summary, permits ethnographic researchers to reflexively articulate what the racial subject instinctively "knows"—self-knowledge and knowledge of his or her racial identity. It is a creative expression of power or, as Nietzsche (1967) puts it, a "will to power." This will to power, I assert, is hastened by the ethnographer's attention to the *form* of ethnographic research.

In summary, the mooring of knowledge, creativity, and power embedded in the formation and everyday lived cultural experiences of the racial subject has profound implications for a new paradigm of ethnography. I say this because racial subjects—as creative collaborators in social action on behalf of restorative justice—are potentially transformed into political agents. An emphasis on the racial subject's own will to power casts serious doubt on the utility, if not validity, of traditional ethnographic research and perhaps even critical ethnography. Traditionally, they become disembodied from lived, culturally grounded creative experience. These subjects cannot speak and, therefore, may lose their agency or become relegated to acts of resistance as passing moments in time. Moreover, knowledge of the racialized other, following Nietzsche, is suspect, if not impossible to produce, without the embodied presence and will of subaltern subjects. In this chapter, I have drawn on a form of action research (Lovett, 2007), critical ethnography, and extended case studies as examples. These modes of qualitative inquiry on and for collective social actions are inevitably, or so it may appear, undertaken in an uneven distribution of power. My hope is that the conception of performative ethnography advanced above may begin to turn this paradigm on its head.

▣ Observations for Praxis

There seems little doubt today that we live in an enduring moment of national and international uncertainty. It is an uncertainty fueled by an alarmist rhetoric that poses the possibility of invasion as a clear and present danger—whether that danger is inspired by the Islamaphobia that points to Muslim fundamentalist terrorists or the xenophobia launched against undocumented immigrants. The threat to our national uncertainty is presently more vividly imprinted on our psyches than ever before. Meanwhile, war acts are perpetuated by the United States against Iraqi citizens and other citizens in the Middle East, and "military insurgents," despite the absence of weapons of mass destruction, an absence of any initiating aggression by the Iraqis toward the United States, and inequality of economic, political, and military power, are rendered invisible by an evangelizing patriotism. It is this patriotic nationalism that not only supported the passage of the Patriot Act but also condoned the invasion of Afghanistan and then Iraq, orchestrated to protect economic interests and political influence in the Middle East, in the name of freedom and democracy. It is also this patriotic nationalism that has turned a blind eye to the genocide in Darfur—where the United States clearly claims no political or economic interests in the region to defend.

The Bush administration's metaphor of the war against terror upholds its "New World Order," justifying the use of military force, occupation of territory, and regime change and rule by an imperial power. Whether at home or in the international arena, U.S. cultural citizens are systematically warned to be afraid of the poor and the different (in other words, fear themselves and each other)—both major sectors of the population that are rapidly expanding, given the impact of deepening and hardening structures of economic inequality in this country and abroad.

It is my vision and political-ethical dream that a performative ethnography described above can serve an educational purpose, a kind of grounded critical pedagogy. Such pedagogical uses of ethnography may, in fact, net practical political gains. For example, Katrina victims and other racial subjects may benefit from social action toward a restorative justice that would emanate from a performative ethnography (Mirón, 2007).

As I have asserted, education conceptualized as pedagogy (Friere, 1971) is one major social, political, and cultural space. Education is a sphere that clearly extends beyond schooling and, as some scholars argue, beyond learning, where learning means technical processes leading to measurable, standardized student outcomes. There exists such a broad educational space, I believe, at the dawn of the 21st century. The color of this space is "green," or eco-green to be precise. In this space, we may find the strongest, most creative opportunities for the deep practice of cultural citizenship across the globe, where multiple racial subjects may meet and coalesce around the need to save the planet from unimaginable natural and social destruction owing to intense global warming.

I situate this space—expressed locally in eco-friendly charter schools in New Orleans, rooftop gardens in high-rises in New York, and the reforestation of the Amazon region in Brazil—within global environmentalism and ecology.

Friedman (2007, p. 42) has recently put forth arguments concerning the loss and the potential recapture of the U.S. role in the world:[10]

> Green really has gone Main Street—thanks to the perfect storm created by 9/11, Hurricane Katrina, and the Internet revolution. The first flattened the twin towers, the second flattened New Orleans and the third flattened the global economic playing field. The convergence of all three has turned many of our previous assumptions about "green" upside down in a very short period of time. (p. 42)

Given the theoretical and methodological discussion above, the central questions appear to move from ones of conception to ones of place: (a) Where—locally—are the new spaces in which democratic practices such as dialogue, coalition building, negotiation, and consensus possible? (b) In the context of neoliberalism and globalization, where can transnational, national, and indigenous racial subjects "meet" as they move ontologically from the periphery to the borders? In hopes of spurring further exploration, I offer that these multiple racial subjects can meet in two specific social spaces: critical pedagogy (or, education broadly conceived) and critical ethnography, or what I have called in this discussion performative ethnography.

▣ Notes

1. I thank Kona Taylor for her research assistance with this section.

2. Conversation with Norman K. Denzin, November 15, 2006.

3. The same case can be made, obviously, for paintings and the visual arts in general.

4. Michael Clark, personal correspondence, September 20, 2005.

5. Space does not permit elaboration of this complex idea.

6. For an application of this theory to race and racial identity, see Mirón and Inda (2000, pp. 95–103).

7. I provide these examples upon the advice of Jennifer Greene, Walter Feinberg, and Thomas Schwandt, who in their careful reading of earlier drafts suggested the use of examples in the probability that readers may not be all that acquainted with speech act theory and the manner in which this article interprets that philosophical linguistic tradition.

8. Discourse and everyday cultural practices in institutions thus are related dialectically. What appears to happen is that through the force of such reiterations, the subject that these multiple acts (cultural practices) discursively name acquires a rather naturalized effect. It becomes sedimented. In order to maintain this naturalized effect, the subject must be continuously interpellated (the process through which one is hailed as a subject) in various times and places. As such, there is no reference to a "pure subject," which does not itself contribute to the further formation of that subject. From this perspective, the utterance "It's a girl," Butler (2004) notes, which traditionally welcomes a baby into the world, is not so much a constative utterance, an empirical statement of fact. Rather, it is one in a long series of performative speech acts that reproductively constitutes the subject, whose arrival they announce and through which the girl is continuously gendered through her lifetime.

9. This chapter will be expanded into a book-length project. Suffice to say for now that although it is certainly the case that a performative subject acquires a naturalized effect through the reiterative practices through which discourse as an effect of

power produces the effects that it names, the fact that this reiteration is necessary to begin with suggests that the constitution of a subject is never fully complete. It is the very same necessity of reiteration, of citing previous norms in the constitution of the subject, which makes it possible for this process of normalization to be subverted—that is, culturally if not politically resisted. Indeed, the necessity of reiteration offers the possibility of reiterating the identity of the subject otherwise, with a difference (hybridity) (see McCarthy, 2003). The iterability—that is, the capacity of being cited—is what makes it possible for any subject to acquire a naturalized effect and, paradoxically, makes it impossible to ever truly succeed in doing so. The upshot is that the reiterative process, the process of infinite repeatability through which a subject is produced, opens up that subject to redeployment to being constituted differently through, for example, counternarratives. Therefore, to approach the constitution of the subject through performativity calls our sustained attention to those constitutive instabilities that contest the naturalizing effects of discourse and, more generally, of power itself. My interest in this regard is the creative expression of the subject's own will to power.

10. I fully acknowledge that the eco-green social movement, as well as Friedman's (2007) articulation of it, is controversial. The movement, as well as the social space that I theorize envelops it, may in itself constitute a form of neoliberal ideology.

References

Appadurai, A. (1996). *Modernity at large: Cultural dimensions of globalization.* Minneapolis: University of Minnesota Press.

Austin, J. L. (1975). *How to do things with words* (2nd ed.). Cambridge, MA: Harvard University Press.

Barone, T. (2000). *Aesthetics, politics and educational inquiry.* New York: Peter Lang.

Barthes, R. (1979). From work to text. In J. V. Harari (Ed.), *Textual strategies: Perspectives in post-structuralist criticism.* Ithaca, NY: Cornell University Press.

Baudrillard, J. (2002). *The spirit of terrorism and requiem for the Twin Towers.* London: Verso.

Biesta, G. (2006). *Beyond learning: Democratic education for a human future.* Herndon, VA: Paradigm.

Braithwaite, J. (2002). *Restorative justice & responsive regulation.* Oxford, UK: Oxford University Press.

Butler, J. (1993). *Bodies that matter: On the discursive limits of "sex."* New York: Routledge.

Butler, J. (2004). *Undoing gender.* New York: Routledge.

Carspecken, P. F. (1996). *Critical ethnography in educational research.* New York: Routledge.

Castells, M. (1991). *The informational city.* New York: Blackwell.

Castells, M. (1998). *End of millennium.* Oxford, UK: Blackwell.

Castells, M. (2000). *The rise of the network society* (2nd ed.). Oxford, UK: Blackwell.

Clark, M. P. (Ed.). (2000). *The revenge of the aesthetic: The place of literature in theory today.* Berkeley: University of California Press.

Delgado, R. (1999). Citizenship. In R. D. Torres, L. F. Milton, & J. X. Inda (Eds.), *Race, identity, and citizenship: A reader.* Oxford, UK: Blackwell.

Denzin, N. (1997). *Interpretive ethnography: Ethnographic practices for the 21st century.* Thousand Oaks, CA: Sage.

Eisner, E. (1997). The promise and perils of alternative forms of data representation. *Educational Researcher, 26*(6), 4–10.

Fabian, J. (1990). *Power and performance: Ethnographic explorations through proverbial wisdom and theater in Shaba, Zaire.* Madison: University of Wisconsin Press.

Freire, P. (1971). *Pedagogy of the oppressed.* New York: Herder & Herder.

Friedman, T. (2007, April 15). Green power. *New York Times Magazine.*

Fromm, E. (1955). *The sane society.* New York: Rinehart.

Giddens, A. (1984). *The constitution of society: Outline of the theory of structuration.* Berkeley: University of California Press.

Glick Schiller, N., Basch, L., & Szanton Blanc, C. (1995). From immigrant to transmigrant: Theorizing transnational migration. *Anthropological Quarterly, 68,* 48–63.

Goldfarb, B. (2002). *Visual pedagogy: Media cultures in and beyond the classroom.* Durham, NC: Duke University Press.

Guarnizo, L., & Smith, M. P. (1998). *Transnationalism from below.* New Brunswick, NJ: Transaction Publishers.

Hall, S. (1997). The spectacle of the other. In S. Hall (Ed.), *Representation: Cultural representations and signifying practices* (pp. 223–291). London: Sage.

Harvey, D. (1989). *The condition of postmodernity.* Oxford, UK: Blackwell.

Lovett, M. (2007). *Creative intervention through video action research and pedagogy.* Unpublished dissertation, University of Illinois, Urbana-Champaign.

Madison, D. S. (2005). *Critical ethnography: Method, ethics, and performance.* Thousand Oaks, CA: Sage.

Mathews, G. (2000). *Global culture/individual identity: Searching for home in the cultural supermarket.* New York: Routledge.

McCarthy, C. (2003, April). *Art and the postcolonial imagination: Rethinking the center periphery thesis.* Paper presented at the Colloquium of the Program for Criticism and Interpretive Theory, University of Illinois, Urbana.

McCarthy, C., & Crichlow, W. (Eds.). (1993). *Race, identity, and representation in education.* New York: Routledge.

McLaren, P. (2000). *Che Guevara, Paulo Freire and the pedagogy of revolution.* New York: Rowman & Littlefield.

McLaren, P. (2002). *Life in schools: An introduction to critical pedagogy in the foundations of education* (4th ed.). Boston: Allyn & Bacon.

Mirón, L. (2002). The Zen of revolutionary pedagogy: Is there a middle path? *Educational Theory, 52,* 359–373.

Mirón, L. (2007). *A conception of performative ethnography.* New York: Peter Lang.

Mirón, L., Darder, A., & Inda, J. X. (2005). Transnationalism, transcitizenship, and the implications for the "new world order." In C. McCarthy, W. Crichlow, G. Dimitriadis, & N. Dolby (Eds.), *Race, identity, and representation in education* (2nd ed., pp. 289–305). New York: Routledge.

Mirón, L., & Inda, J. (2000). Race as a kind of speech act. *Cultural Studies: A Research Annual, 5,* 85–107.

Mirón, L., Torres, R. D., & Inda, J. X. (Eds.). (1999). *Race, identity, and citizenship: A reader.* Oxford, UK: Blackwell.

Mitchell, K. (1997). Transnational subjects: Constituting the cultural citizen in the era of Pacific Rim capital. In A. Ong & D. M. Nonini (Eds.), *Ungrounded empires: The cultural politics of modern Chinese transnationalism* (pp. 228–256). New York: Routledge.

Nietzsche, F. (1967). *The will to power* (W. Kaufman & R. J. Hollingdalc, Trans.). New York: Random House.

Parker, A., & Sedgwick, E. K. (Eds.). (1995). *Performativity and performance.* Durham, NC: Duke University Press.

Poster, M. (1990). *The mode of information.* Chicago: University of Chicago Press.

Rosaldo, R. (1988). Ideology, place, and people without culture. *Cultural Anthropology, 3,* 77–87.

Rumbaut, R. G. (1999). Assimilation and its discontents: Ironies and paradoxes. In C. Hirschman, P. Kasinitz, & J. DeWind (Eds.), *The handbook of international migration: The American experience* (pp. 172–195). New York: Russell Sage Foundation.

Sassen, S. (2000a). *Cities in a world economy.* Thousand Oaks, CA: Pine Forge Press.

Sassen, S. (2000b). Forward. In V. M. Valle & R. D. Torres (Eds.), *Latino metropolis* (pp. ix–xiii). Minneapolis: University of Minnesota Press.

Segarra, J., & Dobles, R. (1999). Educational politics from below. *Harvard Educational Review, 33,* 357–379.

Smith, M. P. (1992). Postmodernism, urban ethnography, and the new social space of ethnic identity. *Theory and Society, 21,* 493–531.

Smith, M. P. (2001). *Transnational urbanism: Locating globalism.* Malden, MA: Blackwell.

Smith, M. P., & Bakker, M. (2005). The transnational politics of the tomato king: Meaning and impact. *Global Networks, 5*(2), 129–146.

Smith, M. P., & Favell, A. (2006). *The human face of global mobility: International highly skilled migration in Europe, North America and the Asia-Pacific.* New Brunswick, NJ: Transaction Publishers.

Sontag, S. (1966). *Against interpretation and other essays.* New York: Picador USA.

Sontag, S. (1977). *On photography.* New York: Straus & Giroux.

Sontag, S. (2001). *Illness as metaphor; and, AIDS and its metaphors.* New York: 1st Picador.

Stone, L. (1999). Educational reform through an ethic of performativity. *Studies in Philosophy and Education, 18,* 299–307.

Willis, P. (1977). *Learning to labour: How working class kids get working class jobs.* Farnborough, England: Saxon House.

Willis, P. (2000). *The ethnographic imagination.* Cambridge, UK: Polity.

29

EPILOGUE

The Lions Speak

Yvonna S. Lincoln and Norman K. Denzin

Until the lion can tell his own stories, tales of the hunt will be told by the hunter.

—Old African Proverb

On most occasions, an epilogue serves to render the ultimate or penultimate word on the matters under consideration. In this instance, however, as in most of the epilogues we have prepared, the epilogue serves different purposes. Here, as in other places, the epilogue serves primarily as a punctuation mark, a semi-colon to a thought or thoughts unfinished, or a coda for themes and a series of motifs that are incomplete, partial, sometimes fragmentary. As we have tried to make clear, we hope that the chapters herein initiate a dialogue, a dialogue that seeks to find common ground between critical theoretical positions, which advance discriminating and often unflattering analyses of colonial, postcolonial, and geopolitical social economies, as well as indigenous methodologies, which simultaneously seek to "reenchant" social inquiry with its sacred and spiritual connections to social life and also to propose research design strategies that honor native lifeways and wrest social science away from a dominant and domineering Western model of use and commodification. There is much common ground here, as indigenous methodologies have embedded within them specific critiques of Western modes of research and a profound rejection of Western appropriation of indigenous knowledge for the marketized usages of the West.

As a consequence, there is no final punctuation, no ending stress on the statements from our authors here. There are only proposals, some of which are backed up by the force of laws protecting the rights of First Nations peoples, for creating a more just and kind social world. The clearest elements of these proposals lie not in their final statements but rather in their potential for furthering a dialogue around the world both between indigenous and First Nations peoples, as well as between critical theorists and researchers who stand ready to help in any way that can serve.

We believe there are three precarious but urgent issues that await both more theorizing and more praxis. The first such issue is whether or not the lions, having spoken, will exert a powerful voice over more than just their own "territory." The lions, as the aphorism suggests, are now speaking. While it is true that the lions will police their own boundaries and place serious restraints on Western scientists who wish to do work among them, it is not clear what effect the lions speaking will have on Western science in a broader sense. A second issue, and very much a legal as well as a social justice and equity issue, is the question of who owns the past. Claims by First Nations peoples on art, artifacts, and remains of indigenous peoples will not go unchallenged by the taxonomists, bone collectors, and cataloguers of the Western world, bones and skeletal remains returned notwithstanding. The third issue, unfinished in both the West and among First Nations peoples, is the issue of ethics. What constitutes ethical behavior within and among First Nations research enterprises? Although there are proposals advanced (see Denzin and Lincoln, Chapter 1, this volume, and interstitial material), it is not clear where there might be a set of overriding principles emerging (Christians & Traber, 1997). Each of these three issues will likely foreground indigenous methodologies for the foreseeable future. Thus, they are the genuine epilogue to the essays between these covers.

The Lions Speak

The lions have found, and are finding, their voices amid the clamor of the West and in the spaces between globalizing, capitalized conquests of the rest of the world. And the lions have much to tell in their stories of the hunt. The lions tell tales of exploitation, of slavery, of domination, of being hunted (Benmalek, 2000), being displaced from the land, having the collected knowledge of whole peoples, whole tribes, appropriated and stolen. Out of this lament and pain, however, a new saga is arising, a new tale of the hunt. In this new tale of the hunt, it is the hunter who finds himself or herself in a cage. This cage is a set of regulations that govern strictly how the Western hunter will conduct himself or herself and who will be both the arbiter of that behavior and the protector, conservator, and dispenser of any knowledge that is co-created with First Nations research participants. In this way, the lions—the indigenous peoples of the world—regain some control over their lives.

This is not to say that the lions now rule. The stories of the hunters are strong, and they have many listeners and believers. Increasingly, however, Western researchers will find themselves locked out of research with indigenous peoples unless they are willing to bend themselves to the rule of law that indigenous peoples have crafted for themselves and their own protection (Battiste, this volume; Grande, 2004, this volume; Sandoval, 2000; L. T. Smith, 1999).

It is unfortunate that not all native and/or indigenous peoples have availed themselves of protections that they might seek by crafting legislation for themselves. Some tribes and First Nations, however, do not have the status to do so. In light of that situation, it is even more unfortunate that the United States, New Zealand, Canada, and Australia refused to sign the United Nations (UN) resolution, "Declaration on Rights of Indigenous Peoples" (United Nations, 2007a). In the formal minutes of the Plenary Session, the record states that "countries voting against the Declaration said they could not support it because of concerns over provisions on self-determination, land and resources rights, and among others, language giving indigenous peoples a right of veto over national legislation and State management of resources" (United Nations, 2007a, pp. 1–2).

Canada's representative to the UN declared that "the provisions in the Declaration on lands, territories and resources were overly broad, unclear, and capable of a wide variety of interpretations, discounting the need to recognize a range of rights over land" (United Nations, 2007a, p. 2). Australia, while "support[ing] and encourage[ing] the full engagement of indigenous peoples in the democratic decision-making process," nevertheless would not entertain "a concept that could be construed as encouraging action that would impair . . . the territorial and political integrity of a State" (United Nations, 2007a, p. 2).

The United States took a somewhat different stance. The Declaration is not entirely a consensus document but rather is described as a statement on which most of the working group could agree was consonant with international law on human rights. The chairperson of the Global Indigenous Caucus characterized the text as "not represent[ing] the sole viewpoint of the United Nations, nor did it represent the viewpoint of all the world's indigenous people. It was based on mutual respect. It contained no new provisions of human rights. It was based on rights that had been approved by the United Nations system but which had somehow, over the years, been denied to indigenous peoples" (United Nations, 2007a, p. 2). The United States used the first portion to vote against the Declaration, declaring that

> it was disappointing that the Human Rights Council had not responded to his country's [the U.S.'s] calls, in partnership with Council members, for States to undertake further work to generate a consensus text. The Declaration had been adopted by the Council in a splintered vote ". . . and risked endless conflicting interpretations and debate about its application, as already evidenced by the numerous complex interpretive statements issued by States at its adoption at the Human Rights Council, and the United States could not lend its support to such a text." (United Nations, 2007a, p. 2)

New Zealand is not reported to have had any comment on its negative vote.

A careful deconstruction of the statements recorded in the minutes of the 61st plenary reported above evinces a sad spectacle indeed: Much of the more developed world—the United States, Canada, Australia, New Zealand, and the abstaining Russian Federation—excluding Europe, closed ranks to defend their nations against any and all claims to self-determination, rights over land and resources usage, or rights to preserve distinct cultural heritages from indigenous peoples. The chair of the Indigenous People's Caucus of the UN, Les Malezer, in commenting on the African Group's "'political decision' to oppose the Declaration as a bloc" as well as on the opposition of the Western bloc, sadly observes that

> it is an offence to all peoples of the world, a brutal reminder that discrimination against indigenous peoples is entrenched in modern geopolitics, and a cover-up of the extreme predicaments that demanded the gestation of an indigenous declaration 25 years ago and a renewed commitment every year since then. (United Nations, 2007b)

Malezer is very clear about what was going to happen—and did happen—on September 13, as the vote was taken. Vast nation-states reasserted their rights to the "territorial and political integrity of the State" over the rights of the First Nations peoples whom primarily (but not exclusively) Westerners have displaced. In calling for the adoption of this Declaration, the American Anthropological Association's spokesperson, current President Alan H. Goodman, and Chair of the AAA Committee for Human Rights Robert Albro observed that, over the 24 years this Declaration has been in the process of creation, "indigenous representatives have patiently worked with UN member states to create a balanced and equitable statement recognizing indigenous peoples as distinct, articulating their right to self-determination, to their lands and other resources, and to the exercise of a free, prior and informed consent in matters affecting their welfare, but while not also dismissing their responsibilities to the states in which they live" (American Anthropological Association, 2007, p. 2). It is not a long stretch to imagine that the sticking points in this statement, made all too clear in the objection and negative vote from Australia, are the phrases "their right . . . to their lands and other resources" and "their right . . . to the exercise of a free, prior and informed consent in matters affecting their welfare." While Australia makes it clear that it invites democratic participation in all matters pertaining to indigenous peoples, it is difficult to conceive how one might participate democratically in a polity when one possesses no rights to self-determination.

The Declaration, in any event, was a nonbinding resolution. Therefore, a vote for the adoption of the Declaration carried with it no responsibilities other than moral obligations and respect for international human rights laws to which the United States, Canada, Australia, and New

Zealand were already signatories. An affirmative vote would have signaled that some of the richest and most populous countries of the West were in agreement at least in principle with the document, without it having committed the four to any binding resolution.

The critical point is that the lion is speaking. It has taken centuries, and an especially difficult time the past quarter century, while the Declaration itself was being hammered out, but the sleeping lion has awakened and found its voice. There is, however, another issue waiting in the wings, and that is the issue of intellectual and artistic property, signs, symbols, artifacts, bones, and other forms of material and intellectual culture.

Who Owns the Past?

It is only in the past several decades that the question of who owns the past has become important enough to be debated and litigated. Indeed, prior to the advent of the new critical historicism, literary historicism, and the press from professional associations, who owned the past, in practice, was virtually whomever could dig it up and get it out of the country. Now, we read of the Italian Ministry of Culture arguing with the Getty Museum over which pieces in the Getty collection should be returned to Italy (the piece in highest contention being one that was not found in Italy at all but rather in the Mediterranean Ocean, outside of Italy's claimed boundaries). The government of Greece has been in sore contention for decades over the marbles taken by Lord Elgin from the Acropolis, which now reside in the British Museum. A museum in the United States recently purchased at auction an extremely old and rare English quilt, a one-of-a-kind example, for its collection. As the papers for export were being prepared, the museum having paid for the work, the British determined that the quilt was a piece of important British history and critical to the textile and needlework annals of the period, and so resolved that the quilt should not leave England, but rather remain there in the possession of a museum. It is not merely indigenous peoples who are conscious of reclaiming legacies and exemplars of cultural heritage.

It is, however, indigenous peoples who have the most to lose in the cultural heritage wars. From sanctioned archaeological expeditions, permitted and approved by governments and tribal authorities, to "low-end looting" (Zimmerman, Vitelli, & Hollowell-Zimmer, 2003) by nonprofessionals who want pots and potsherds for their own private collections, to systematic looting for the antiquities trade (Brodie, Kersel, Luke, & Tubb, 2006), to warfare in remote regions of the world (e.g., Afghanistan, Iraq), to the destruction of historic and cultural heritage sites for development projects and purposes, the cultural heritage of indigenous peoples is under attack. And indigenous peoples are fighting back.

In some instances, the Hague Convention for the Protection of Cultural Property in the Event of Armed Conflict of 1954 is one valuable legal tool for avoiding or minimizing damage to cultural artifacts and sites, and it offers some modest protections from the kinds of cultural heritage theft and destruction perpetrated, for instance, in the destruction of the Bamiyan Buddhas (by the Taliban, in Afghanistan) or the looting of the Baghdad Museum, which destroyed a priceless collection of materials and artifacts recording the dawn of civilization in the Mesopotamian valley and the earliest creation of genuine urban centers (Brodie et al., 2006). The United States and Australia, however, are not signatories to the Hague Convention, although the United States has cooperated with Interpol to recover some of the artifacts from Baghdad.

In other instances, First Nations peoples themselves have moved in concert to reclaim artifacts, bones, and materials that they consider remains belonging to descendent communities. The Native American Graves Protection and Repatriation Act of 1990 (at the outset of the Decade of the Indigenous Person), for which Native Americans had lobbied for several years, rebalanced the archaeological equation somewhat by guaranteeing that "archaeologists now must share control of the archaeological record with Native Americans, and Native Americans have the right to request the return of their ancestors' bodies and religious artifacts" (McGuire, 2003, p. ix). Sharing, however, is not the same as granting control of native artifacts, archaeological digs on Native American lands, or uses of bones and artifacts to First Nations peoples. Even in the instance of this remarkable legislation, Native Americans must negotiate with archaeologists, including federally directed employees (e.g., archaeologists hired or funded by the Smithsonian), for final disposition.

The "mining" of these treasures has a rationale. Hollowell (2005) suggests the deeply rooted origins of the looting, mining, and archaeological fervor that created these digs in the first place, observing that "wall text in the galleries [of the Art Institute of Chicago's 2005 exhibit, "*Hero, Hawk and Open Hand*"] discusses the damage done to so many ancient earthworks and sites by the growth of cities and agriculture, yet there is no reference to the antiquarianism that fueled avid digging (in fact, mining) by curiosity seekers and commercial interests for over 300 years. *Early U.S. beliefs that Moundbuilders were a "lost tribe" or separate race from the more "primitive" extant peoples "justified the right of Euro-Americans to collect relics, destroy sites and develop the land" [Fowler, 1986, p. 137]*" (Hollowell, 2005, pp. 494–495, emphasis added). Thus, claiming that there were no living "heirs" to the Moundbuilders provided a key logic vindicating and legitimating both the systematic excavation and unofficial looting of these sites, even though the objects and artifacts "still have great meaning for those with ancestral roots in the region" (Hollowell, 2005, p. 489).

The foregoing arguments are primarily about the *material world*—the world of burial objects, sites, potsherds, ancient cities, and villages uncovered from the sandstorms, landslides, earthquakes, and wars of long past aeons. There is, however, yet another quarrel regarding who owns the past, who is empowered to collect it—or leave it be—and for whom and under what circumstances it has meaning, spiritual power, identity, and agency. That quarrel revolves around so-called intellectual property. In academic circles, we have come to understand intellectual property only recently in historical terms. We work with fair use copyright laws; attempt to protect films, movies, and music from pirating; and attempt, in many countries, to give credit for works of art or the intellect that are the products of one person's mind, genius, creativity, and/or performance. In general, intellectual property is defined as "intangible personal property in creations of the mind" (Dratler, 1994, pp. 1–2, cited in Nicholas & Bannister, 2004a), but in the world of indigenous peoples, intellectual property may also be ethnobotanical, ceremonial, imagistic/photographic, or symbolic (McBryde, 1986; Nicholas & Bannister, 2004a, 2004b; Riley, 2004; C. Smith, 2004). To complicate the matter, and to take it into the realm of First Nations peoples and away from the realm of technological innovation, intellectual property rights reference "the protection of the cultural knowledge and property of Indigenous societies," where cultural property is defined as "movable objects that have sacred, ceremonial, historical, traditional or other purposes integral to the culture of a First Nations community and [which] may be viewed as collective property of Aboriginal people" (Bell & Patterson, 1999, p. 206, cited in Nicholas & Bannister, 2004a). Indigenous *knowledge* is likely to be even stickier since

> indigenous knowledge as a concept concerns information, understanding, and knowledge that reflects symbiotic relationships between individuals, communities, generations, the physical environment and other living creatures, and the spiritual relationships of a people. (Mann, 1997, p. 1, cited in Nicholas & Bannister, 2004a, p. 328)

What is clear from these definitions (of indigenous knowledge and indigenous property) is that Western concepts such as intellectual property, copyright, patents, and other legal tools may not be the most useful ways to think about the role of research with First Nations peoples. Intellectual property, for example, may be cultural property and a somewhat slipperier construct than a musical performance, film, or book. Indigenous knowledge may extend to ethnobotanical elements (plants, native medical treatments, ceremonies to healing, e.g., with the *griots* of Central America), geographic features (where secret sources of water might be in a desert, for example), or symbols of various sorts (think about the mysterious and—to Westerners—unreadable paintings of Australian Aboriginals, where each figure, each dot has a meaning, but the meaning can only be read by an Aboriginal who understands the sign system, when the symbols themselves remain a closely guarded secret).

There is an argument going on regarding who owns the past and, therefore, who "owns the future" (Nicholas & Bannister, 2004a). Both sides, of course, have much merit. On one side are conservationists whose interests lie in ensuring that artifacts recovered from the near and far past are preserved in the best (most technologically sound) way, both to further study of the past and its material and spiritual practices and also to inform ordinary nonscientists of the deep humanity that connects all human life on earth through the ages. On the other side of the argument are those for whom cultural connection and preservation are paramount, and who thus see First Nations rights as virtually superseding those of all others, including Western scientists. In the middle are those who point out that far removed artifacts—far removed in time—cannot necessarily be connected to living descendent peoples and might therefore belong to the larger civilizations extant now. This is not an argument that is likely to be resolved any time soon, although the "knowledge corporatization" (Ouzman, 2004, p. 344) of colonial and neocolonial efforts at preservation will need to be firmly rejected. Both Battiste (Chapter 25, this volume) and Grande (Chapter 12, this volume) speak to this issue, but it is far from decided. Nicholas and Bannister (2004a) have observed that "archaeology [and other forms of research such as those discussed in this volume] will not move beyond being a colonialist enterprise unless it actively seeks to understand the underlying issues of ownership and control of material and intellectual property as related to cultural knowledge and heritage" (p. 329).

Ethics

Both of the foregoing issues—who speaks for whom and who owns the past—are, in their purest form, ethical issues. Many of our authors have spoken passionately regarding the need to reformulate a research ethics that enables us to participate morally and authentically with indigenous and First Nations collaborators and that permits knowledge to be cogenerated, which can then be shared with interested communities, while at the same time seeking a way for the indigenous communities to share in the benefits and the "profits" of our research.

It is not that the authors between these covers have not detailed extensive guidelines for ethical relationships between researchers and researched. Many have. Rather, the issue is that there may be no universal prescribed, orthodox, or agreed upon ethical standards, only universal values (on human rights), general guidelines, and "a set of negotiated practices" that shift from site to site and from cultural group to cultural group. The cultural knowledge of one community may demand some kinds of culturally appropriate behaviors, while another community may be more comfortable with another set more appropriate to their cultural system. So while it is clear that the U.S. federal regulations on the protection of human subjects have worked well for some years with some kinds of studies, it is equally clear that fundamentally reconfigured forms of research—what Richardson and St. Pierre (2005) term "a radically interpretive form of representation" (p. 480)—demand not only vastly different relationships with our research participants but also extreme revisioning of our ethical stances and practices. In more utilitarian terms, the work on ethics is not done, and even when "done" is likely to be a provisional "work in progress," open for reinterpretation, renegotiation, or revision as new circumstances emerge. For the moment, however, there is a sense of partiality, a nagging sense of underdevelopment, about the ethics under which we work. However clear and direct our professional association statements, there are always situations arising that never quite "fit" the circumstances envisioned by the many authors of those statements of ethics.

One hopeful sign is the congruence in conclusions between Western researchers (primarily if not exclusively qualitative, alternative paradigm, and/or critical) and First Nations peoples around the world, both groups of whom have recognized that Western principles embodied in Protections of Human Subjects legislation regarding ethical behavior are insufficient either to protect research participants—especially indigenous peoples—or to provide appropriate cultural sensitivity to non-Western lifeways, customs, and cosmologies. When Linda T. Smith (1999) refers to the indigenous description of Western research as a "dirty word," she references not only the practices that Reinharz (1979) describes as the "rape model" of research—researchers take what they want and need and leave research participants feeling very much like victims—but she is also referring to the inadequacy of various federal models of ethics statements as wholly deficient and unsatisfactory for work with indigenous peoples. Indigenous peoples see the legislated human subjects protection ethics as serving the Western model of research that has so ill-served their own interests and needs.

One response to this perceived inadequacy has been the formulation of a number of local, tribal-centered, or culture-centered sets of ethical principles. Frequently administered by special councils that represent a group, community, tribe, or people, the community may deny access to researchers who refuse to abide by the community's formal guidelines or may be ejected for violation of rules after entry is achieved. Local indigenous protocols grow both more plentiful and more sophisticated by the hour, and newer versions have begun to cover "all images, text, ceremonies, music, songs, stories, symbols, beliefs, customs, ideas and other physical and spiritual objects and concepts" (Indian-Apache Summit on Repatriation, 1995, p. 3, cited in Nicholas & Bannister, 2004a, p. 340), as well as "cultural property mark[s]" (Nicholas & Bannister, 2004a), the range of which clearly begins to move from what Westerners (with their focus on the binary of human subject protection and corporate patent law) might term *ethics* to copyright, patent, and trademark law. *Thus, ethics and cultural property are clearly intertwined in ways that make sense to indigenous peoples but that are legally precarious to Westerners.*[1]

The important thing to note regarding ethics in this framework is one that we have been making throughout this volume: Both Western social scientists (who practice alternative interpretive research) and indigenous communities alike have been moving toward the same goals. They seek a set of ethical principles that are feminist, caring, communitarian (rather than individual), holistic, respectful, mutual (rather than power imbalanced), sacred, and ecologically sound. To the extent that Western researchers cannot or will not bend themselves to the needs of indigenous peoples to have research with and about them serve the community first, they will increasingly be denied access. And rightly so.

◼ What Is Missing?

While every handbook strives to be complete, there is no "perfect handbook" just as there is no "perfect record player" (Hofstadter, 1980). Such books, of course, are planned at the outset (insofar as the editors can "plan" such books) to be complete and comprehensive, to have representatives from all corners have space to make their arguments. It rarely ever works out that way, and this handbook is no exception.

The editors may consult and nominate the names of those whom we would like to have write statements for us, but those potential authors have "works and lives" of their own. As a consequence, they frequently turn us down, begging unfinished projects of their own, incipient sabbaticals, personal or familial emergencies or illnesses, or other reasonable and indeed, compelling, reasons for refusing to undertake a chapter. We understand. But it means that sometimes, there are intellectual gaps, and we are painfully aware of them.

Substantively, we might have heard from more poststructuralists, although we have critical poststructuralists represented here (see Chapter 3 by Cannella and Manuelito). We would like to have had a critical ecologist speak. Geographically, we are missing voices from Asia: China, Japan, and the vast Indian subcontinent, where much interesting postcolonial and culture recovery work is ongoing. We could have used an Aboriginal voice from

Australia. We needed to hear from Latin and South America, where important work is being done from a critical and ecological perspective. It would have been equally useful to hear from European scholars who are doing important critical work with workers' cooperatives, both in Europe and also in India, South America, and Africa (although we have strong African voices). We have simply not been able to convince some of these scholars to withdraw from the work they are doing to work for the handbook. Perhaps a subsequent set of scholars, or a second edition, will be able to address these gaps and elicit a different kind of coverage.

We are, however, justifiably proud of the scholars who did agree to work with us. They are committed; deeply involved as researchers, scholars, and activists; experienced; and, frequently, living the "border" lives between the West and their own First Nations communities themselves. Many of them are the avatars of their communities: deeply connected to the past and its many meanings, living in the present moment, leading their communities into the future. Both individually and together, they represent a different set of research practices and an emerging globalized sensibility that undercuts the commodified, marketized, neoliberal forces of globalization sweeping the developed, developing, and underdeveloped regions of the world today. It is to them, and to their peoples, that we dedicate this book.

Note

1. While the elision of the line between ethical treatment of human research participants and the protection, conservation, and repatriation of cultural property may be dicey—or a legal quagmire—for federal officials who govern territories in which indigenous peoples have residence, it is well worth noting that these categories pose far less difficulty for many of those who work with indigenous peoples as anthropologists, archaeologists, and other social scientists. Social scientists negotiate access and entry, as well as cordial and respectful working relationships on a daily basis with First Nations groups. While ethical relationships "on the ground" are not always easy, they are nevertheless far less fraught with the kinds of tense legal concerns that frequently confront legislative and governmental personnel. Anthropologists and other social scientists have long recognized that indigenous peoples pose issues that are culturally specific and have responded with statements that draw broadly a set of principles governing work with such groups.

References

American Anthropological Association. (2007, May 29). *AAA letter on UN Declaration.* Arlington, VA: Author.

Benmalek, A. (2000). *The child of an ancient people.* Sydney: Random House Australia.

Brodie, N., Kersel, M. M., Luke, C., & Tubb, K.W. (Eds.). (2006). *Archaeology, cultural heritage, and the antiquities trade.* Gainesville: University Press of Florida.

Christians, C., & Traber, M. (Eds.). (1997). *Communication ethics and universal values.* Thousand Oaks, CA: Sage.

Dratler, J. (1994). *Licensing of intellectual property.* New York: Law Journal Seminars-Press.

Fowler, D. (1986). Conserving American anthropological sources. In D. Meltzer, D. Fowler, & J. Sabloff (Eds.), *American archaeology, past and future* (pp. 135–172). Washington, DC: Smithsonian Institution Press.

Grande, S. (2004). *Red pedagogy: Native American social and political thought.* Lanham, MD: Rowman & Littlefield.

Hofstadter, D. R. (1980). *Gödel, Escher, Bach: An eternal Golden Braid.* New York: Vintage.

Hollowell, J. (2005). Ancient North American art surfaces in the art world: A review of *Hero, hawk and open hand. American Anthropologist, 107,* 489–497.

McBryde, I. (Ed.). (1986). *Who owns the past?* Melbourne, Australia: Oxford University Press.

McGuire, R. H. (2003). Foreword. In L. J. Zimmerman, K. D. Vitelli, & J. Hollowell-Zimmer (Eds.), *Ethical issues in archaeology* (pp. vii–ix). Walnut Creek, CA: AltaMira Press.

Nicholas, G. P., & Bannister, K. P. (2004a). Copyrighting the past? Emerging intellectual property rights issues in archaeology. *Current Anthropology, 45,* 327–350, erratum.

Nicholas, G. P., & Bannister, K. P. (2004b). Reply [to Claire Smith]. *Current Anthropology, 45,* 528–529.

Ouzman, S. (2004). Comment on Nicholas & Bannister. *Current Anthropology, 45,* 444–445.

Reinharz, S. (1979). *On becoming a social scientist.* San Francisco: Jossey-Bass.

Richardson, L., & St. Pierre, E. A. (2005). Qualitative writing. In N. K. Denzin & Y. S. Lincoln (Eds.), *The SAGE handbook of qualitative research* (3rd ed., pp. 474–499). Thousand Oaks, CA: Sage.

Riley, M. (2004). *Indigenous intellectual property rights: Legal obstacles and innovative solutions.* Walnut Creek, CA: AltaMira Press.

Sandoval, C. (2000). *Methodology of the oppressed.* Minneapolis: University of Minnesota Press.

Smith, C. (2004). On intellectual property rights and archaeology. *Current Anthropology, 45,* 527.

Smith, L. T. (1999). *Decolonizing methodology.* London: Zed.

United Nations. (2007a, September 13). *Plenary session, sixty-first general assembly, minutes of meeting.* New York: United Nations, Department of Public Information, News and Media Division. Retrieved September 28, 2007, from http://www.un.org/News/Press/docs/2007/gal0612.doc.htm

United Nations. (2007b, July 18). Press conference by Indigenous Peoples' Caucus. New York: United Nations, Department of Public Information, News and Media Division. Retrieved October 1, 2007, from http://www.un.org/News/briefings/doc/2007/070718_Indigenous.doc.htm

Zimmerman, L. J., Vitelli, K. D., & Hollowell-Zimmer, J. (Eds.). (2003). *Ethical issues in archaeology.* Walnut Creek, CA: AltaMira Press.

AUTHOR INDEX

SUBJECT INDEX

ABOUT THE EDITORS

Norman K. Denzin is Distinguished Professor of Communications, College of Communications Scholar, and Research Professor of Communications, Sociology, and Humanities at the University of Illinois, Urbana-Champaign. He is the author, editor, or coeditor of numerous books, including *Flags in the Window: Dispatches From the American War Zone; Searching for Yellowstone: Identity, Politics and Democracy in the New West; Performance Ethnography: Critical Pedagogy and the Politics of Culture; Screening Race: Hollywood and a Cinema of Racial Violence; Performing Ethnography;* and *9/11 in American Culture.* He is past editor of the *Sociological Quarterly,* coeditor of *The SAGE Handbook of Qualitative Research* (3rd ed.), coeditor of *Qualitative Inquiry,* editor of *Cultural Studies <=> Cultural Methodologies,* editor of *Studies in Symbolic Interaction,* and founding President of the International Association of Qualitative Inquiry.

Yvonna S. Lincoln is Ruth Harrington Chair of Educational Leadership and Distinguished Professor of Higher Education at Texas A&M University. In addition to this volume, she is coeditor of the first and second editions of the *The SAGE Handbook of Qualitative Research,* the journal *Qualitative Inquiry* (with Norman K. Denzin), and the Teaching and Learning section of the *American Educational Research Journal* (with Bruce Thompson and Stephanie Knight). She is the coauthor, with Egon Guba, of *Naturalistic Inquiry, Effective Evaluation, and Fourth Generation Evaluation;* the editor of *Organizational Theory and Inquiry;* and the coeditor of several other books with William G. Tierney and with Norman Denzin. She is the recipient of numerous awards for research and has published journal articles, chapters, and conference papers on higher education, research university libraries, and alternative paradigm inquiry.

Linda Tuhiwai Smith is Professor of Education at the University of Auckland. She is Joint Director of Nga Pae o te Maramatanga, The National Institute for Research Excellence in Māori Development and Advancement, a center of research excellence hosted by the University of Auckland. She is a leading Māori and indigenous educationist and is well sought after as a speaker and commentator. Her work is recognized internationally through her book *Decolonising Methodologies: Research and Indigenous Peoples.* She has also published research on the history of Māori schools, Māori women and education, and other social justice themes.

ABOUT THE CONTRIBUTORS

Tony E. Adams is an Assistant Professor in the Department of Communication, Media, and Theatre at Northeastern Illinois University. He is the author of several articles on identity, sexuality, qualitative research, and nature (re)presentation.

Bryant Keith Alexander is Professor in the Department of Communication Studies at California State University, Los Angeles. His published essays have appeared in a wide variety of scholarly journals and books, including the *Handbook of Performance Studies* and the *Handbook of Qualitative Inquiry.*

Marie Battiste is Mi'kmaq, full Professor at the University of Saskatchewan in the Department of Educational Foundations, and Academic Director of the Aboriginal Education Research Centre in the College of Education. She has published widely and remains involved in research on Aboriginal education, languages, and decolonizing teacher education.

Tim Begaye is Diné from Tse' Dildooh'ii' (Hardrock), Navajo Nation, Arizona. He is an Assistant Professor in the College of Education in the Division of Educational Leadership and Policy Studies at Arizona State University. He teaches courses on research methodologies and adaptive leadership. His research interest is the intersection of culture, change, adaptation, and leadership. A former high school math and social science teacher, he has a doctoral degree in education from Harvard University.

Russell Bishop is foundation Professor for Māori Education in the School of Education at the University of Waikato, Hamilton, New Zealand. He is also a qualified and experienced secondary school teacher. Prior to his present appointment, he was a senior lecturer in Māori Education in the Education Department at the University of Otago and Interim Director for Otago University's Teacher Education program. His research experience is in the area of collaborative storying as Kaupapa Māori research, having written *Collaborative Research Stories: Whakawhanaungatanga* and published nationally and internationally on the topic. His other research interests include institutional change, critical multicultural education, and collaborative storying as pedagogy. The subject of *Culture Counts: Changing Power Relationships in Classrooms,* coauthored with Professor Ted Glynn (1999), demonstrates how the experiences developed from within kaupapa Māori settings, schooling, research, and policy development can be applied to mainstream educational settings. Other books include *Pathologising Practices: The Impact of Deficit Thinking on Education,* coauthored with Carolyn Shields and Andre Mazawi, and *Culture Speaks,* coauthored with Mere Berryman.

Denise C. Breton, a White American of Celtic ancestry, is coauthor of *The Paradigm Conspiracy* (1996) and *The Mystic Heart of Justice* (2002), as well as founder and executive director of Living Justice Press in St. Paul, Minnesota.

Gregory Cajete, a Tewa from Santa Clara Pueblo, New Mexico, is an educator, artist, and educational consultant. He was the founding Director of the Institute of American Indian Arts in Santa Fe and is currently an Associate Professor in the College of Education at the University of New Mexico. He is the author of several books, including *Look to the Mountain* (1994), *Native Science* (2000), and *A People's Ecology* (1999).

Gaile S. Cannella is Research Professor at Tulane University, New Orleans, Louisiana. She has written four books, including *Deconstructing Early Childhood Education: Social Justice and Revolution* (1997), as well as published in such journals as *Qualitative Inquiry* and *Critical Studies <=> Critical Methodologies.*

Elizabeth Cook-Lynn is Professor Emerita of Indian Studies/English, Eastern Washington University, Cheney, Washington, and a Visiting Professor of Indian Studies, Arizona State University, Tempe. She is an enrolled member of the Crow Creek Sioux Tribe, Ft. Thompson, South Dakota, and lives in the Black Hills of South Dakota. She is one of the founding scholars of Native American studies, and her latest book, *New Indians, Old Wars* (2007), argues that Native American studies must be considered and pursued as an autonomous discipline rather than as a subset of history or anthropology.

Cynthia B. Dillard is Professor of Multicultural Teacher Education in the School of Teaching and Learning at Ohio State University. Her major research interests include critical multicultural education, spirituality in teaching and learning, and African/African American feminist studies. She has published numerous book chapters and articles in journals, including the *Journal of Teacher Education, International Journal of Qualitative Studies in Education,* and *Urban Education.* Her first book, *On Spiritual Strivings: Transforming an African American Woman's Academic Life,* was published in 2006. Her current research and service are focused in Ghana, West Africa, where she has established a preschool and a new elementary school and is enstooled as Nana Mansa II, Queen Mother of Development, in the village of Mpeasem, Ghana. She can be reached at dillard.17@osu.edu.

Jamel K. Donnor is an Assistant Professor in the Department of Afro-Ethnic Studies at California State University, Fullerton.

Christopher Dunbar Jr. is an Associate Professor of Educational Administration at Michigan State University. His research focuses on issues of equity and school reform with a particular interest in children most vulnerable to academic and social failure.

Lauren Dyll is a PhD student and is on staff at Culture, Communication, and Media Studies at the University of KwaZulu-Natal. She lectures on African cinema and film appreciation. She has published an autoethnography in Current Writing. She has an MA on the topic of development communication and is a communication, media, and drama graduate.

Michelle Fine, Distinguished Professor of Social Psychology, Women's Studies and Urban Education at the Graduate Center, CUNY, has taught at CUNY since 1990. Her research focuses on youth in schools, communities, and prisons, developed through critical feminist theory and method. For information about her research or the work of the Graduate Center Participatory Action Research Collective, visit http://web.gc.cuny.edu/psychology or http://web.gc.cuny.edu/che/start.htm. Recent awards include the 2007 Willystine Goodsell Award from the American Educational Research Association, the 2005 First Annual Morton Deutsch Award, an Honorary Doctoral Degree for Education and Social Justice from Bank Street College in 2002, and the Carolyn Sherif Award from the American Psychological Association in 2001.

Michael Francis, is a research fellow at the University of KwaZulu-Natal, Durban in the department of Culture, Communication and Media Studies. Also a graduate of the program, his MA was on alternate understandings of development among remote rural communities, while his dissertation examined issues of identity among remote communities in Southern Africa. He has also worked in tourism.

Henry A. Giroux currently holds the Global TV Network Chair Professorship at McMaster University in the English and Cultural Studies Department. His most recent books include *Take Back Higher Education* (coauthored with Susan Giroux, 2006), *Beyond the Spectacle of Terrorism* (2006), *The Giroux Reader* (2006), *Stormy Weather: Katrina and the Politics of Disposability* (2006), and *The University in Chains: Confronting the Military-Industrial-Academic Complex* (2007).

Susan Searls Giroux is Associate Professor of English and Cultural Studies at McMaster University in Ontario. She is the author, with Henry A. Giroux, of *Take Back Higher Education: Race, Youth and the Crisis of Democracy in the Post–Civil Rights Era* (2006) and, with Jeffrey T. Nealon, *The Theory Toolbox: Critical Concepts for the Humanities, Arts and Social Sciences* (2003). She is also managing editor of the *Review of Education, Pedagogy, and Cultural Studies.*

Sandy Grande is an Associate Professor in the Education Department at Connecticut College and also works as a research consultant for the Ford Foundation. Her research and teaching are profoundly inter- and cross-disciplinary and interfaces critical, feminist, Indigenous, and Marxist theories of education with the concerns of Indigenous education. Her book, *Red Pedagogy: Native American Social and Political Thought* (2004), has been met with critical acclaim. She has also published several articles, including "Critical Theory and American Indian Identity and Intellectualism," in the *International Journal of Qualitative Studies in Education,* and "American Indian Geographies of Identity and Power: At the Crossroads of Indigena and Mestizaje," in *Harvard Educational Review.*

Stacy Holman Jones is an Associate Professor at the University of South Florida. She is the author of *Torch Singing: Performing Resistance and Desire From Billie Holiday to Edith Piaf* (2007) and several articles on the intersections of performance and women's subjectivities.

Nathalia Jaramillo is Assistant Professor of Cultural Foundations at the College of Education, Purdue University. She is author and co-author of numerous publications on the topic of critical pedagogy and socio-political critique. Her writing and research are inter-disciplinary and draw from feminist theory and post-colonial studies.

Dr Kuni Jenkins is Director of Research at Te Whare Wānanga ō Awanuiārangi, a "tribal university" in Whakatane, Bay of Plenty, New Zealand. She is of Ngati Porou descent. Her main current research interest is the Māori story of schooling.

Alison Jones is Professor of Education in the Faculty of Education at the University of Auckland, New Zealand. She has published widely in post-structuralist theory in education, feminist theory, and the educational relationships between the indigenous people of New Zealand (Māori) and the first colonizer people (Pakeha).

Joe L. Kincheloe is the Canada Research Chair in Critical Pedagogy in the Faculty of Education and founder of the Freire project at McGill University in Montreal. He has written more than 40 books and numerous articles on issues of race, class, gender, culture, power, and indigeneity in education.

Antjie Krog reported on the South African Truth and Reconciliation Commission as a journalist and later wrote *Country of My Skull* (2000) about her experiences. She is currently Extraordinary Professor at the Faculty of Arts, University of Western Cape, Bellville, South Africa.

Gloria Ladson-Billings is the Kellner Family Chair in Urban Education at the University of Wisconsin–Madison.

D. Soyini Madison is a full Professor at Northwestern University in the Department of Performance Studies. She is an affiliate faculty member in the Program of African Studies, and she holds appointments in the Department of African American Studies and the Department of Anthropology. She is the author of *Critical Ethnography: Methods, Ethics, and Performance* (2005); coeditor of *The SAGE Handbook of Performance Studies* (2006); and editor of *The Woman That I Am: The Literature and Culture of Contemporary Women of Color* (1997). She has lived and worked in Ghana, West Africa, as a Senior Fulbright Scholar conducting field research on the interconnections between traditional religion, political economy, and indigenous performance tactics. In 2003, she received a Rockefeller Foundation Fellowship in Bellagio, Italy, for her current book project, *Acts of Activism: Human Rights and Radical Performance,* based on fieldwork in Ghana. She also adapts and directs her ethnographic work for the public stage in such performances as *I Have My Story to Tell; Mandela, the Land, and the People; Is It a Human Being or a Girl?;* and *Water Rites.* Professor Madison has won numerous teaching awards, including the Tanner University Award at Chapel Hill for "Outstanding and Inspirational Teaching."

Kathryn D. Manuelito is from the Diné (Navajo) Nation and is Naakai Diné'é and born into the Kinlichiinii clan. She has worked in Indian Education for more than 25 years at the local, regional, and national levels. Her research focus includes language and literacy, teacher education, self-determination in indigenous communities, decolonizing methodologies, and indigenous womanism. She recently joined the faculty at the University of New Mexico as an associate professor.

Wanda D. McCaslin, a Métis from northern Saskatchewan, obtained her BA and LLB, and she is an LLM (Candidate) at the University of Saskatchewan. She is the Law Foundation of Saskatchewan Research Officer with the Native Law Centre of Canada. Her portfolio includes editing *Justice as Healing: Indigenous Ways* (2005); editing a newsletter on Aboriginal concepts of justice; coordinating the Young Professionals International Project; and lecturing on the academic support program at the College of Law.

Peter McLaren is Professor of Urban Education, Graduate School of Education and Information Studies, University of California, Los Angeles. His most recent books include *Pedagogy and Praxis in the Age of Empire* (with Nathalia Jaramillo, 2007), *Teaching Against Global Capitalism and the New Imperialism* (with Ramin Farahmandpur, 2005), and *Capitalists and Conquerors: Critical Pedagogy Against Empire* (2005). His writings have been translated into 20 languages. He serves in the capacity of Cooperantes Internacionales for Centro Internacional Miranda, Venezuela. He is a member of the Industrial Workers of the World.

Manulani Aluli Meyer is an Indigenous epistemologist teaching at the University of Hawaii in Hilo. She is from a large family working on these issues in the fields of law, medicine, education, community, and business. She loves to carve stones and swim in secluded waterways along the Hilo Pali Ku coastline.

Luis Mirón is Dean of the College of Education at Florida International University (FIU). He is the author of *The Social Construction of Urban Schooling: Situating the Crisis* (1996) and coauthor of *Urban Schools: The New Social Spaces of Resistance* (2005).

Kagendo Mutua is Associate Professor of Special Education at the University of Alabama. She has been a secondary school teacher in Kenya, where she taught language and literature in Kiswahili and English. Currently, her work with adolescents and youth with severe disabilities in the United States connects their marginalized identities with other marginalized groups cross-culturally in terms of limited access in research to the position of narrator of own desires/aspirations, lack of agency, and limited access to desired adult outcomes. Her work also looks at how marginality constitutes itself around issues of race, class, and gender using semiotics as well as postcolonial and disability studies to connect disability as marginality with other marginalized groups.

Nosisi Mpolweni-Zantsi teaches in the Department of isiXhosa, University of the Western Cape, Bellville, South Africa. She completed a master's degree in Translation Studies and forms part of a group, under the guidance of Zannie Bock, who has transcribed and retranslated original Xhosa TRC texts for the first time.

Ellen D. Nymark is a doctoral candidate at Texas A&M University and works as a program coordinator and part-time faculty member at Northern Arizona University. Her teaching and research interests include foundations of education, childhood studies, critical feminist and post-structural theories, and critical qualitative research methodology.

Radhika Parameswaran is Associate Professor in the School of Journalism, Indiana University, Bloomington. She is an affiliate faculty member in the Cultural Studies and India Studies programs. Her areas of research include feminist cultural studies, gender and media globalization, South Asia, and postcolonial studies. Her recent publications have appeared in *Critical Studies in Media Communication, Communication Theory, Qualitative Inquiry, Communication Review,* and *Journalism & Communication Monographs.*

Kopano Ratele was formerly Professor in the Department of Psychology and Women and Gender Studies, University of the Western Cape, Bellville, South Africa. He has contributed several articles and books, among them *Intergroup Relations: A South African Perspective.* He is currently at the University of South Africa.

Cinthya M. Saavedra was born in Managua, Nicaragua, and moved to Texas with her family in 1981. She worked as a bilingual third-grade and pre-K teacher for 4 years. During that time, she embarked on doctoral studies at Texas A&M University and received her PhD in curriculum and instruction with a cultural studies emphasis in May 2006. She works as a Visiting Assistant Professor at University of North Carolina, Greensboro (UNCG), in Human Development and Family Studies. At UNCG, she teaches courses in the birth through kindergarten program. Throughout her courses, she always incorporates critical multicultural perspectives to move her students beyond monocultural and ethnocentric views of working with diverse families and children. Her scholarship revolves around issues of language and culture, and she is also particularly interested in explorations of research methodologies and marginalized populations. Her explorations and interests have compelled her to find refuge in Chicana feminist epistemology as a way to decolonize research and practice and to critically bridge understanding between and among marginalized and dominant perspectives.

Shirley R. Steinberg is Associate Professor at McGill University. She is the Director of the Paulo and Nita Freire International Project for Critical Pedagogy. The author and editor of numerous books and articles, she is the founder and editor of *Taboo: The Journal of Culture and Education.* She is also the editor of *Much Ado About Borat, Teen Life in Europe, Multi/intercultural Conversations: A Reader,* and, with Joe Kincheloe, *Kinderculture: The Corporate Construction of Childhood* and *The Miseducation of the West: How Schools and the Media Distort Our Understanding of the Islamic World.* With Joe Kincheloe, she is the author of *Changing Multiculturalism: New Times, New Curriculum, and Contextualizing Teaching.* Her expertise and research areas are in critical media literacy, social drama, youth studies, and critical pedagogy.

Christopher Darius Stonebanks is Associate Professor in Education at Bishop's University, Canada, and is a member of the Founding Scholars Advisory Board for the Paulo and Nita Freire International Project for Critical Pedagogy (McGill University). Recent publications include *James Bay Cree and Higher Education* (2007) and the forthcoming *Teaching Against Islamophobia* (2009), coauthored with Ozlem Sensoy.

Beth Blue Swadener is Professor of Early Childhood Education and Policy Studies at Arizona State University. Her research links global discourses to local education and childrearing issues, particularly in Africa. She has published eight books, including *Decolonizing Research in Cross-Cultural Contexts* and *Power and Voice in Research With Children,* as well as numerous articles and chapters. Her current research focuses on cross-national studies of children's rights and voices in issues affecting them.

Keyan G. Tomaselli is Senior Professor in Culture, Communication, and Media Studies, University of KwaZulu-Natal, Durban. He is author of *Where Global Contradictions Are Sharpest* (2005),

Encountering Modernity (2006), *Writing in the San/d* (2007), and *Appropriating Images: The Semiotics of Visual Representation* (1999).

Eve Tuck (Aleut) is a doctoral candidate in Urban Education at the Graduate Center of the City University of New York. Her research interests include disparities of quality and access in urban education, urban student and Indigenous student school noncompletion, possibilities and consequences of education policy, and participatory policy analysis.

Sarah Zeller-Berkman is a doctoral candidate in the Social-Personality Psychology program at the CUNY Graduate Center. She has worked as a facilitator of youth participatory action research projects focused on issues ranging from parental incarceration to sexual harassment in schools. Her current research interests include exploring the conditions of possibility for productive intergenerational partnerships for social change.